Handbook of Massachu...

2017 Edition

by Mark S. Brodin and Michael Avery

The *Handbook of Massachusetts Evidence* is a comprehensive and practical guide to the law of evidence in Massachusetts. Providing clear explanations of the settled law and expert advice on more complicated evidentiary problems, this one-volume compendium provides in-depth coverage of everything attorneys need for analyzing and weighing evidence, planning litigation strategy, and justifying objections. It is an invaluable aid in determining the admissibility of evidence in Massachusetts courts.

Highlights of the 2017 Edition

The 2017 Edition brings you up to date on the latest new cases, statutes, and developments, including these:

- New procedures for individual voir dire of potential jurors by attorneys. (See chapter 1)
- New limitations on consciousness of guilt instructions where the only issue is the identity of the fleeing offender. (See chapter 4)
- New statutory provisions regarding defraying the costs of a jury view in a civil action. (See chapter 4)
- New procedures for post-verdict attorney-initiated communications with jurors, superseding *Com. v. Fidler*. (See chapter 5)
- New cases re: fallout from Annie Dookhan misconduct at state lab. (See chapter 7)
- Limitation on the reference on direct examination to material not in evidence relied upon by the expert is a common-law evidentiary rule that operates in both civil and criminal cases and applies to both sides. (See chapter 7)
- New DNA cases. (See chapter 7)
- Distinction between computer generated data and computer stored data for hearsay analysis. (See chapter 8)

- Where witness was not present at hospital, testimony based on rape kit inventory list violated Confrontation Clause because defendant could not cross-examine nurse who collected swabs. (See chapter 8)
- While declining to adopt a residual hearsay exception, Supreme Judicial Court recognized a constitutionally based hearsay exception in *Com. v. Drayton*. (See chapter 8)
- New voice identification cases. (See chapter 11)
- New admonition from the Supreme Judicial Court regarding honoring the rights of suspects being interrogated. (See chapter 12)

The Tables and the Index have been updated to reflect all the changes to the text.

11/16

For questions concerning this shipment, billing, or other customer service matters, call our Customer Service Department at 1-800-234-1660.

For toll-free ordering, please call 1-800-638-8437.

HANDBOOK
of
MASSACHUSETTS
EVIDENCE

2017 Edition

MARK S. BRODIN
Professor of Law and Michael and Helen Lee Distinguished Scholar
Boston College Law School

MICHAEL AVERY
Emeritus Professor
Suffolk University Law School

Published by Wolters Kluwer in New York.

Wolters Kluwer Legal & Regulatory US serves customers worldwide with CCH, Aspen Publishers and Kluwer Law International products.

Printed in the United States of America

ISBN 978-1-4548-7227-6

1 2 3 4 5 6 7 8 9 0

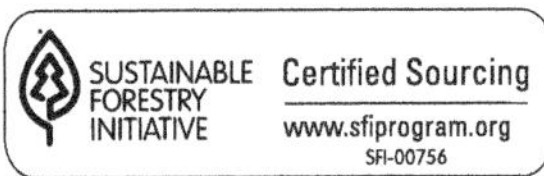

About Wolters Kluwer Legal & Regulatory US

Wolters Kluwer Legal & Regulatory US delivers expert content and solutions in the areas of law, corporate compliance, health compliance, reimbursement, and legal education. Its practical solutions help customers successfully navigate the demands of a changing environment to drive their daily activities, enhance decision quality and inspire confident outcomes.

Serving customers worldwide, its legal and regulatory portfolio includes products under the Aspen Publishers, CCH Incorporated, Kluwer Law International, ftwilliam.com and MediRegs names. They are regarded as exceptional and trusted resources for general legal and practice-specific knowledge, compliance and risk management, dynamic workflow solutions, and expert commentary.

WOLTERS KLUWER SUPPLEMENT NOTICE

This product is updated on a periodic basis with supplements and/or new editions to reflect important changes in the subject matter.

If you would like information about enrolling this product in the update service, or wish to receive updates billed separately with a 30-day examination review, please contact our Customer Service Department at 1-800-234-1660 or email us at: *customer.service@wolterskluwer.com*. You can also contact us at:

Wolters Kluwer
Distribution Center
7201 McKinney Circle
Frederick, MD 21704

Important Contact Information

- To order any title, go to *www.wklawbusiness.com* or call 1-800-638-8437.
- To reinstate your manual update service, call 1-800-638-8437.
- To contact Customer Service, e-mail *customer.service@wolterskluwer.com*, call 1-800-234-1660, fax 1-800-901-9075, or mail correspondence to: Order Department—Wolters Kluwer, PO Box 990, Frederick, MD 21705.
- To review your account history or pay an invoice online, visit *www.WKLawBusiness.com/payinvoices.*

In 2006, we dedicated the Eighth Edition to the lawyers who were fighting to secure for the prisoners then held by the United States Government in Guantanamo and secret rendition centers around the globe and the due process they were denied in violation of international and domestic law and constitutional principles. We hoped we would have to come up with a new dedication for the next edition, but unfortunately Guantanamo has not been closed. In fact, as we have all learned, thanks to Mr. Snowden and others, the threats to freedom and privacy created by the "War on Terror" have multiplied. So again we dedicate our work on the rules of evidence to all those opposing trial by secret evidence and detention without any trial.

Mark S. Brodin
Michael Avery

Summary of Contents

Table of Contents

CHAPTER 2
JUDICIAL ADMISSIONS, JUDICIAL NOTICE, and BINDING TESTIMONY 41

CHAPTER 3
BURDEN of PROOF, PRESUMPTIONS and INFERENCES 65

CHAPTER 6 WITNESSES 333

CHAPTER 7
OPINION and EXPERT EVIDENCE 461

CHAPTER 8
HEARSAY 565

CHAPTER 9 AUTHENTICATION 689

CHAPTER 10
THE BEST EVIDENCE RULE 713

CHAPTER 11
EYEWITNESS IDENTIFICATION EVIDENCE 727

CHAPTER 12 CONFESSIONS and INCRIMINATING STATEMENTS 769

CHAPTER 13 OPENING STATEMENTS and CLOSING ARGUMENT 861

CHAPTER 14
EVIDENCE in ADMINISTRATIVE PROCEEDINGS 891

Preface

We are happy to welcome our readers to the 2017 Edition of the *Handbook of Massachusetts Evidence*. The changes we have made in this edition will, we hope, make the Handbook even more helpful to trial lawyers and judges.

The biggest change is that it will no longer be necessary for the reader to have both a hardback volume and the current paperback supplement in order to remain up to date. With this edition and in the future, the book will be published in a paperback format and each year the reader will receive a new book rather than merely a supplement. We hope our readers approve and find this format less cumbersome.

While the overall organization of the volume remains the same, we have endeavored to present the material in a more accessible style. We have eliminated repetitive discussion wherever feasible, and deleted many of the older and unnecessary footnotes.

Now that the Supreme Judicial Court has promulgated the Massachusetts Guide to Evidence (a project in which we both participated), it is clearer to us what the mission of our book is. Evidence, like most areas of the law, is more complicated than a mere presentation of black letter concepts. The difficulty typically lies in the application of general principles to new and unique factual settings. This treatise supplies enough detail to follow the trail of general principles through the weeds, so to speak, of the cases. A good example is Chapter 7, where we first discuss the rules that govern expert testimony and scientific evidence, and then show how they have been applied to the physical sciences, biological sciences, behavioral sciences, and law enforcement.

The problem of how rules are changed and shaped by the facts of individual cases has informed our decisions about which footnotes to retain and which to eliminate. In each instance, the role of the footnotes is to provide the relevant authority for the general rule, and then to illustrate its application in as many varying factual situations as possible. We believe this will assist the reader both in gaining an understanding of the rules, and in researching their application to their cases.

Our mission includes going beyond presentation of the jurisprudence of the Massachusetts courts to providing critical commentary where appropriate, as well as offering suggestions about how evidence law in Massachusetts might be improved.

As in the past, we are truly grateful to our readers, colleagues, and students for the suggestions they have made to us. We hope our book will continue to be a valuable resource for the busy trial lawyer and the judiciary.

Mark S. Brodin
Michael Avery

November 2016

Special Notice

This volume covers cases reported in West's Massachusetts Decisions through May 25, 2016 (West's Massachusetts Decisions Issue 21, 49 NE3d No. 1).

CHAPTER

1

GENERAL PROVISIONS

The rules of evidence stand guard to ensure that only relevant, reliable, noninflammatory considerations may shape fact finding. Without these rules, there would be nothing to prevent trials from being resolved on whim, personal affections, or prejudice.[*]

A. INTRODUCTION

§ 1.1 Sources

Massachusetts evidence law derives from various sources including common law, statutes, procedural rules, and the federal and state constitutions. Unlike the federal system and that of most states, Massachusetts evidence law remains uncodified. An effort to adopt a code in the form of the Proposed Massachusetts Rules of Evidence was rejected by the Supreme Judicial Court on December 30, 1982. In its announcement, the court explained:

> The Justices recognize that if the Proposed Rules were to be adopted, (1) there would have to be careful coordination with the legislature to repeal, revise, or modify many statutes which deal with the admissibility and effect of evidence; (2) many of the Proposed Rules involve departures from the principles set forth in the Federal Rules of Evidence; (3) some of the Proposed Rules are subject to significant and arguably valid criticisms.
>
> A majority of the Justices conclude that promulgation of rules of evidence would tend to restrict the development of common law principles pertaining to the admissibility of evidence. The valid objective of uniformity of practice in federal and State courts would not necessarily be advanced because the Proposed Rules, in their present form, depart significantly from the Federal Rules of Evidence. Additionally, in the view of some of the justices, the Federal Rules of Evidence have not led to uniform practice in the various Federal courts and are, in some instances, less well adapted to the needs of modern trial practice than current Massachusetts law. Accordingly, a majority of the Justices have concluded that it would not be advisable to adopt the Proposed Massachusetts Rules of Evidence at the present time. The Proposed Rules have substantial value as a comparative standard in the continued and historic role of the courts in developing principles of law relating to

---

* *Adoption of Sherry*, 435 Mass 331, 338, 757 NE2d 1097, 1103 (2001).

evidence. Parties are invited to cite the Proposed Rules, wherever appropriate, in briefs and memoranda submitted.[1]

Consistent with its announcement, the Supreme Judicial Court has continued to make reference to the Proposed Rules in its decisions and has, on a case-by-case basis, adopted some in Massachusetts practice.[2] Reference is made to the Proposed Rules below when they reflect current practice.

In 2008, the Supreme Judicial Court published a *Massachusetts Guide to Evidence* (updated annually) summarizing the Commonwealth's evidentiary law and organized along the lines of the Federal Rules of Evidence.

§ 1.2 Applicability

Massachusetts evidence law is generally applicable to all proceedings, civil and criminal, in the courts of the Commonwealth. Proposed Mass R Evid 1101, which reflects current practice, provides that, except with respect to privileges, the rules of evidence (including the hearsay prohibition) do *not* apply in the following situations:

(1) **Preliminary questions of fact**. The determination of questions of fact preliminary to admissibility of evidence when the issue is to be determined by the court.

(2) **Grand jury**. Proceedings before grand juries.[1]

---

§ 1.1 [1] See generally (Jeramiah) Healy, Ten Years After: A Reconsideration of the Codification of Evidence Law in Massachusetts, 15 Western New England L Rev 1 (1993).

[2] See, e.g., *Com. v. Daye*, 393 Mass 55, 65-75, 469 NE2d 483, 490-496 (1984) (admissibility of certain prior inconsistent statements for substantive purposes) discussed in § 6.13.2.(g), and *Flood v. Southland Corp.*, 416 Mass 62, 616 NE2d 1068 (1993) (extending a hearsay exception to judgments in criminal cases) discussed in § 8.16.

§ 1.2 [1] See Mass R Crim P 4(c). Hearsay alone may support an indictment, *Com. v. Dilone*, 385 Mass 281, 284, 431 NE2d 576, 578 (1982), but the preference is for direct testimony. *Com. v. St. Pierre*, 377 Mass 650, 654-657, 387 NE2d 1135, 1139-1140 (1979). See also *Com. v. Washington W.*, 462 Mass 204, 210, 967 NE2d 615, 621 (2012); *Com. v. Fleury*, 417 Mass 810, 816-817, 632 NE2d 1230, 1233-1234 (1994) (integrity of grand jury not impaired by introduction of videotape of interview of victim); *Com. v. Pina*, 406 Mass 540, 549, 549 NE2d 106, 112 (1990); *Com. v. Riley*, 73 Mass App 721, 727, 901 NE2d 151, 158 (2009). Compare *Com. v. Salman*, 387 Mass 160, 439 NE2d 245 (1982) (judge acted properly in dismissing indictments where defendant made substantial showing that false hearsay testimony was knowingly presented to grand jury).

(3) **Miscellaneous proceedings**. Proceedings for small claims; sentencing,[2] or granting or revoking probation;[3] issuance of

---

For the presentation of knowingly false evidence to the grand jury, see *Com. v. Hunt*, 84 Mass App 643, 999 NE2d 1104 (2013).

[2] A sentencing judge may consider hearsay information about defendant's character, behavior, and background. *Com. v. Goodwin*, 414 Mass 88, 92, 605 NE2d 827, 831 (1993).

[3] Hearsay is admissible at probation violation hearings, but the legal sufficiency of the hearsay requires that the court find in writing that it is "substantially reliable." See Rule 7, District/ Municipal Courts Rules for Probation Violation Proceedings (effective September 8, 2015). The Supreme Judicial Court has clarified that due process no longer requires, where the hearsay is substantially reliable, separate proof as to good cause for the absence of a live witness. See *Com. v. Bukin*, 467 Mass 516, 522, 6 NE3d 515, 520 (2014) (no abuse of discretion in the judge's determination that a probation violation had occurred, where officer testified that assault victim volunteered all of the information regarding the incident, did not struggle to answer questions, and understood that his allegations could result in criminal charges against defendant). See generally *Com. v. Durling*, 407 Mass 108, 118, 551 NE2d 1193, 1199 (1990) (police reports were sufficiently reliable); *Com. v. Bukin*, supra, 467 Mass at 516, 6 NE2d at 515; *Com. v. Ivers*, 56 Mass App 444, 445, 778 NE2d 942, 943 (2002); *Com. v. Foster*, 77 Mass App 444, 449-451, 932 NE2d 287, 292-294 (2010). The Supreme Judicial Court has rejected the contention that admission of hearsay from victims violates defendant's confrontation rights under *Crawford v. Washington*, 541 US 36 (2004). See *Com. v. Wilcox*, 446 Mass 61, 841 NE2d 1240 (2006) and *Com. v. Nunez*, 446 Mass 54, 841 NE2d 1250 (2006).

Reliability can be inferred where the evidence falls within a firmly rooted hearsay exception. *Com. v. Durling*, supra, 407 Mass at 118, 551 NE2d 1193, 1198. Compare *Com. v. Negron*, 441 Mass 685, 808 NE2d 294 (2004) (wife's statements to police appeared reliable), *Com. v. Henderson*, 82 Mass App 674, 9787 NE2d 95 (2012) (verified domestic abuse prevention complaint and police incident report were sufficient), and *Com. v. Hill*, 52 Mass App 147, 751 NE2d 446 (2001) (young victim's grand jury testimony was sufficiently reliable) with *Com. v. King*, 71 Mass App 737, 886 NE2d 727 (2008) (victim's hearsay statements in police report were insufficiently reliable), *Com. v. Delaney*, 36 Mass App 930, 629 NE2d 1007 (1994) (hearsay testimony of defendant's ex-wife improperly admitted at probation revocation hearing where declarant was available to be called and statement did not bear indicia of reliability), *Com. v. Ortiz*, 58 Mass App 904, 788 NE2d 599 (2003) (police officer's testimony relating complainant's hearsay version of events lacked reliability), *Com. v. Emmanuel E*, 52 Mass App 451, 754 NE2d 1067 (2001) (unsubstantiated and unreliable hearsay testimony of police officer insufficient as sole basis for revocation), *Com. v. Wilson*, 47 Mass App 924, 716 NE2d 649 (1999) (police report lacked indicia of reliability—no observations, no corroboration, no investigation), and *Com. v. Podoprigora*, 48 Mass App 136, 717 NE2d 1046 (1999) (hearsay testimony of police officer regarding interview of defendant's daughter lacked sufficient indicia of reliability). For a list of factors informing the reliability decision, see Rule 7, District/ Municipal Courts Rules for Probation Violation Proceedings, supra.

For videotaped statements and interviews, see *Com. v. Patton*, 458 Mass 119, 131-134, 934 NE2d 236, 248-250 (2010) (videotaped interview of child sexual assault victim was substantially trustworthy and reliable); *Com. v. Cates*, 57 Mass App 759, 786

warrants for arrest, criminal summonses, and search warrants; and proceedings with respect to release on bail or otherwise.[4]

(4) **Contempt proceedings**. Contempt proceedings in which the court may act summarily.

Additionally, the rules of evidence do not apply strictly in the following proceedings:

- Prison disciplinary hearings.[5]
- Domestic abuse prevention order proceedings (GL 209A).[6]
- Disbarment proceedings.[7]
- Trials under the "sexually dangerous person" statute, GL 123A.[8]

NE2d 411 (2003) (videotaped statement by sexual assault victim substantially reliable for admission). For GPS records monitoring defendant's movements, see *Com. v. Thissell*, 457 Mass 191, 928 NE2d 932 (2010).

For the similar rules regarding parole revocation proceedings, see *Doucette v. Massachusetts Parole Board*, 86 Mass App 531, 536, 18 NE2d 1096, 1101-1102 (2014) (police reports are admissible as long as they bear indicia of reliability)..

[4] See *Mendonza v. Com.*, 423 Mass 771, 785-786, 673 NE2d 22, 31-32 (1996) (pretrial detention hearing at which rules of evidence would not apply and hearsay evidence could be admitted did not violate state constitutional due process and confrontation rights); *Abbott A. v. Com.*, 458 Mass 24, 33-35, 933 NE2d 936, 945-946 (2010) (Commonwealth may satisfy burden of proof at § 58A hearing by relying solely on hearsay evidence, such as police reports and videotapes of police interrogations of co-defendants and witnesses, as long as it bears substantial indicia of reliability).

[5] See *Murphy v. Superintendent, Massachusetts Correctional Institution*, 396 Mass 830, 489 NE2d 661 (1986) (hearsay may be admitted).

[6] See *Frizado v. Frizado*, 420 Mass 592, 597-598, 651 NE2d 1206, 1211 (1995). But despite the informality in abuse prevention proceedings, certain minimum standards of fairness must be observed. See *S.T. v. E.M.*, 80 Mass App 423, 429-430, 953 NE2d 269, 275-276 (2011). For harassment prevention orders pursuant to GL c. 258E, see *F.A.P. v. J.E.S.*, 87 Mass App 595, 602-603, 33 NE3d 1245, 1252 (2015) (remanding for consideration of whether plaintiff child's statements carried sufficient indicia of reliability, in which case they should be admitted).

[7] See Board of Bar Overseers Rule 3.39 (admissibility of evidence governed by GL 30A, State Administrative Procedure Act, discussed below in Chapter 14). See also *Matter of Tobin*, 417 Mass 92, 102, 628 NE2d 1273, 1279 (1994); *Matter of Abbott*, 437 Mass 384, 393, 772 NE2d 543, 550 (2002) (admission of videotaped deposition proper). At hearings before the Commission on Judicial Conduct, however, "all testimony shall be under oath" and "the rules of evidence applicable to civil proceedings shall apply." GL 211C, § 7(3). See also *In Re Enforcement of Subpoena*, 436 Mass 784, 791 n.6, 767 NE2d 566, 573 n.6 (2002).

[8] See GL 123A, § 14(c), making admissible various court and psychiatric records, police and incident reports, and victim statements. The statute "provides a 'very radical departure' from ordinary evidentiary rules, particularly in regard to the

- Restitution hearings.[9]
- Civil commitment pursuant to GL 123 § 35 (alcoholism or substance abuse).[10]
- Hearings to terminate Section 8 housing assistance.[11]

In contrast, hearsay is not admissible at either the adjudicatory or dispositional phase of a care and protection proceeding.[12] The rules of evidence are fully applicable at probable cause hearings (GL 276, § 38)[13] and similarly at hearings on workers' compensation

---

qualified examiners." *In re Gammell*, 86 Mass App 8, 11, 12 NE3d 409, 411 (2014). See also *Com. v. Given*, 441 Mass 741, 808 NE2d 788 (2004) (police report referring to uncharged conduct admissible without redaction; reliable hearsay may be admitted in civil commitment hearing without violating due process). But see *Com. v. Markvart*, 437 Mass 331, 335-336, 771 NE2d 778, 781-782 (2002) (police reports and witness statements from nolle prossed case not admissible, although they may be used as basis for qualified examiner's opinion).

The Sex Offender Registry Board is not bound by the rules of evidence, and its hearing officer could consider as substantive evidence the victim's statements contained in a police report and Department of Corrections Records. See *Doe v. Sex Offender Registry Board*, 459 Mass 603, 638-639, 947 NE2d 9, 37-38 (2011); *Doe v. Sex Offender Registry Board*, 70 Mass App 309, 312, 873 NE2d 1194, 1196 (2007). Even multiple level hearsay may be admissible at classification hearings. *Doe v. Sex Offender Registry Board*, 88 Mass App 73, 76-80, 35 NE3d 788, 791-794 (2015) (history of sexual misconduct documented in prison disciplinary records, and police report recounting allegations of sexual abuse of which Doe was acquitted of).

The Board has determined, however, that while the rules of evidence do not apply to classification hearings, "evidence may be admitted and given probative effect only if it is the kind of evidence on which reasonable persons are accustomed to rely in the conduct of serious affairs." *Doe v. Sex Offender Registry Board*, supra, 459 Mass at 638, 947 NE2d at 37; *Poe v. Sex Offender Registry Board*, 456 Mass 801, 809-810, 926 NE2d 187, 194 (2010) (Board could properly exclude sex offender's documentation from expert that could not be tested by cross-examination).

[9] "Although a restitution hearing need not be overly formal, it must afford certain guarantees, including an opportunity for the defendant to cross-examine witnesses and present rebuttal evidence." *Com. v. Denehy*, 466 Mass 723, 740, 2 NE3d 161, 176 (2014). See also *Com. v. Amaral*, 78 Mass App 557, 560-561, 940 NE2d 1242, 1244-1246 (2011); *Com. v. Morris M.*, 70 Mass App 688, 697, 876 NE2d 462, 469 (2007).

[10] *In re GP*, 473 Mass 112, 120-122, 40 NE3d 989, 996-997 (2015) (substantially reliable hearsay admissible).

[11] *Seales v. Boston Housing Authority*, 88 Mass App 643, 650-651, 40 NE3d 1046, 1052 (2015) (hearsay may form the basis of the decision as long as it contains substantial indicia of reliability).

[12] See *Custody of Two Minors*, 19 Mass App 552, 476 NE2d 235 (1985) (& citations).

[13] *Eagle-Tribune Publishing Co. v. Clerk Magistrate*, 448 Mass 647, 653-654, 863 NE2d 517, 524-525 (2007) (contrasting show cause hearings pursuant to GL 218, § 35A, at which neither the rules of evidence nor the hearsay prohibition apply); *Myers v. Com.*, 363 Mass 843, 850 n.6, 298 NE2d 819, 824 n.6 (1973).

claims.[14] Evidence in proceedings seeking equitable relief is taken in the same manner as actions seeking legal remedies, except that more liberal use of affidavits is permitted. GL 233, § 67.

While the rules of evidence apply equally in bench trials as in jury trials, assessment of the impact of admission of improper evidence differs, as it is assumed the trial judge will not be influenced by extraneous matters.[15] Pro se litigants are bound by the same rules as attorneys.[16]

Evidence in administrative proceedings is discussed in Chapter 14.

B. EXCLUDING EVIDENCE

§ 1.3 Objection/Motion to Strike/Offer of Proof

§ 1.3.1 Necessity for Objection or Motion to Strike

Counsel are obligated to object to evidence in "a precise and timely fashion, as soon as the claimed error is apparent, so as to afford the trial judge an opportunity to act promptly to remove from the jury's consideration evidence [or whatever else is claimed to have been improperly presented] . . . which has no place in the trial."[1] Failure to so object operates to waive any objections,[2] and the evidence, even though it would have been excluded upon objection, retains its full probative force.[3] The obligation to object applies equally in

---

[14] See 452 CMR § 1.11(S).

[15] See *Com. v. Montanez*, 439 Mass 441, 449-450, 788 NE2d 954, 962 (2003).

[16] *Com. v. Forte*, 469 Mass 469, 489,14 NE3d 900, 917 (2014).

§ 1.3 [1] *Com. v. Perryman*, 55 Mass App 187, 192-193, 770 NE2d 1, 5 (2002). See also Mass R Civ P 46; § 1.3.2 and 1.3.3, infra.

[2] *Com. v. Haley*, 363 Mass 513, 517, 296 NE2d 207, 210 (1973); *Diaz v. Gomez*, 82 Mass App 55, 63-63, 970 NE2d 355, 361 (2012). See also Mass R Civ P 46; Mass R Crim P 22.

[3] See *Nancy P. v. D'Amato*, 401 Mass 516, 524-525, 517 NE2d 824, 829 (1988); *Com. v. Keevan*, 400 Mass 557, 562, 511 NE2d 534, 538 (1987) (hearsay); *Com. v. Luce*, 399 Mass 479, 482, 505 NE2d 178, 180 (1987) (prior inconsistent statement); *Abraham v. Woburn*, 383 Mass 724, 726 n.1, 421 NE2d 1206, 1209 n.1 (1981) (hearsay); *Com. v. Salyer*, 84 Mass App 346, 354-355, 996 NE22d 488, 495 (2013) (private conversation between spouses). But see *Com. v. Reynolds*, 338 Mass 130, 136, 154 NE2d 130, 135(1958) (reserving question "whether circumstances could ever exist in which the requirements of due process of law and substantial justice would make it necessary to consider the extent to which highly prejudicial but palpably incompetent evidence improvidently admitted without objection or proper limitation should be used as the basis of a conviction").

jury-waived as well as jury trials, and to judicial conduct as well as that of opposing counsel.[4]

A motion to strike is the proper means of eliminating an answer that is objectionable either on evidentiary grounds[5] or because it is non-responsive.[6] Where evidence is admitted conditionally, it is incumbent upon the objecting party to move to strike it if the condition has not been satisfied. See § 1.6, infra. The filing of a motion in limine to prevent the introduction of evidence does not, by itself, preserve appellate rights.[7]

A timely objection or motion to strike is necessary to preserve an issue for appeal.[8] "This rule of procedure stems from the necessity of placing an affirmative obligation on trial counsel to inform both the

---

[4] *Com. v. Watkins*, 63 Mass App 69, 73-74, 823 NE2d 404, 406-407 (2005).

[5] See *Com. v. Rosado*, 59 Mass App 913, 914, 795 NE2d 596, 599 (2003) (citing Text). Failure to move to strike an improper answer allows its admission as evidence, which may defeat a motion for required finding of not guilty. *Com. v. Sepheus*, 468 Mass 160, 169, 9 NE3d 800, 809 (2014).

[6] *Com. v. Bishop*, 5 Mass App 738, 740, 370 NE2d 452, 454 (1977).

[7] See *Com. v. Jones*, 464 Mass 16, 18, 979 NE2d 1088, 1090-1091 (2012). There is no need to object at trial when the pretrial motion is based on constitutional grounds. See *Com. v. Whelton*, 428 Mass 24, 25-26, 696 NE2d 540, 543-544 (1998); *Com. v. Brown*, 83 Mass App 772, 774, 989 NE2d 915, 917 (2013). See also *Com. v. Canty*, 466 Mass 535, 539, 998 NE2d 322, 327 (2013) (error preserved where judge, in deciding motion in limine, noted defendant's objection was preserved); *Com. v. Aviles*, 461 Mass 60, 66-67, 958 NE2d 37, 44-45 (2011) (where defendant objected to denial of motion in limine and judge stated "Your objection noted, and your rights saved," defendant was relieved of necessity to object at trial).

The Appeals Court discourages the practice of judges "preserving" rights after ruling on a motion in limine, and thus purportedly excusing the need for an objection at trial, "A motion in limine is not an adequate substitute for a properly placed objection .. [as] the proponent of evidence challenged on appeal is deprived of an opportunity during trial to rephrase the question in light of an objection [and] the judge [is deprived of] an opportunity to reconsider his earlier ruling to determine its continued correctness in the context of a question actually posed and the answer given." *Com. v. Almele*, 87 Mass App 218, 224-225, 27 NE2d 832,838-839 (2015).

A party claiming an abuse of discretion regarding evidentiary rulings on a motion in limine assumes a heavy burden. See *Com. v. Spencer*, 465 Mass 32, 48, 987 NE2d 205, 218 (2013).

[8] See Proposed Mass R Evid 103:

> (a) Effect of erroneous rulings. Error may not be predicated upon a ruling which admits or excludes evidence unless a substantial right of the party is affected, and
> (1) Objection. In case the ruling is one admitting evidence, a timely objection or motion to strike appears of record, stating the specific ground of objection, if the specific ground was not apparent from the context; or
> (2) Offer of proof. In case the ruling is one excluding evidence, the substance of the evidence was made known to the court by offer or was apparent from the context within which questions were asked.

trial court and subsequent courts of review of alleged error in the admission of evidence at the earliest possible time and in the most direct manner. Furthermore, since it is not uncommon for a lawyer to forego the exercise of such a right as part of the trial tactics or strategy being employed for his client, this court cannot be put in a position of giving defense counsel the benefit of hindsight and in effect allowing the opportunity to compensate for erroneous, but conscious strategic, decisions."[9] "A lawyer cannot try a case on one theory and then, having lost on that theory, argue before an appellate court about alleged issues which might have been, but were not, raised at the trial. That is true whether or not the trial lawyer and the appellate lawyer are the same person, and whether or not they are in any way associated. The appeal must be based on what took place at the trial, not on anything which is presented for the first time before an appellate court."[10] "Appellate review should not be the occasion to convert the consequences of unsuccessful trial tactics and strategy into alleged errors by the judge."[11]

Thus, for example, a defendant who objects at trial to a telescope demonstration on the sole ground that the lighting conditions in court were different from those on the evening of the drug transaction cannot mount a holistic appellate challenge to the demonstration *per se*.[12] Similarly, where defense counsel sought to cross-examine a witness about pending drug charges to show bias, defendant could not argue on appeal that the cross-examination should have been allowed to show impairment of testimonial faculties.[13]

(b) Record of offer and ruling. The court may add any other of further statement which shows the character of the evidence, the form in which it was offered, the objection made, and the ruling thereon. It may direct the making of an offer in question and answer form.
(c) Hearing of jury. In jury cases, proceedings shall be conducted, to the extent practicable, so as to prevent inadmissible evidence from being suggested to the jury by any means, such as statements or offers of proof or asking questions in the hearing of the jury.
(d) Plain error. Nothing in this rule precludes taking notice of plain errors affecting substantial rights although they were not brought to the attention of the court.

See also *Nancy P. v. D'Amato*, 401 Mass 516, 524, 517 NE2d 824, 829 (1988).

[9] *Com. v. Harris*, 371 Mass 462, 471, 358 NE2d 982, 987-988 (1976).

[10] *Com. v. Olson*, 24 Mass App 539, 544, 510 NE2d 787, 790 (1987). See also *Com. v. Bly*, 444 Mass 640, 648-651, 830 NE2d 1048, 1055-1057 (2005) (abrogating power of resurrection); *Cooper v. Keto*, 83 Mass App 798, 803, 990 NE2d 76, 81 (2013); *Adoption of Astrid*, 45 Mass App 538, 542, 700 NE2d 275, 278 (1998).

[11] *Com. v. Shruhan*, 89 Mass App 320, 324, 48 NE3d 487, 491 (2016) (citation omitted).

[12] *Com. v. Perryman*, 55 Mass App 187, 193, 770 NE2d 1, 5-6 (2002).

[13] *Com. v. Hrabak*, 57 Mass App 648, 652-653, 785 NE2d 410, 413-414 (2003). *Com. v. Huertas*, 34 Mass App 939, 940-941, 613 NE2d 113, 115 (1993).

Notwithstanding the general requirement for a timely objection, unobjected errors are reviewed in a criminal case for substantial risk of miscarriage of justice.[14] Such power is "rarely used," and it is exercised only when a "decisive matter has not been raised at trial."[15] A verdict based upon legally insufficient evidence is inherently serious enough to create a substantial risk of a miscarriage of justice, and thus such claims may be reviewed without regard to defendant's procedural shortcomings.[16]

In civil cases, the "established principle" is that issues not properly raised in the trial court will not be considered on appeal.[17]

An objection is generally necessary to preserve an issue regarding the giving or failure to give an instruction to the jury; the objection must be made before the jury retires.[18] The objection must adequately inform the judge of specific language objected to and of the

---

[14] *Com. v. Comtois*, 399 Mass 668, 674, 506 NE2d 503, 507 (1987); *Com. v. Dragotta*, 89 Mass App 119, 127-128, 46 NE3d 563, 570-571 (2016). For discussion of the standard of review applicable to unpreserved trial errors, see *Com. v. McCoy*, 456 Mass 838, 850, 926 NE2d 1143, 1157 (2010); *Com. v. Alphas*, 430 Mass 8, 13, 712 NE2d 575, 580 (1999).

Where inadmissible evidence is admitted because of a defendant's reasonable tactical decision, there is no substantial likelihood of a miscarriage of justice. *Com. v. Pytou Heang*, 458 Mass 827, 852, 942 NE2d 927, 948 (2011). For discussion of the concept of invited error, see *Com. v. Roderiques*, 78 Mass App 515, 940 NE2d 1234 (2011), *aff'd on other grounds*, 462 Mass 415, 968 NE2d 908 (2012) (no substantial risk of miscarriage of justice where defendant requested the instruction she now challenges on appeal). See also GL 278, § 33E (mandatory review by Supreme Judicial Court of first-degree murder convictions); *Com. v. Keo*, 467 Mass 25, 34, 3 NE3d 55, 63 (2014) (standard of review in ineffective assistance of counsel claim).

[15] *Com. v. Young*, 35 Mass App 427, 442, 621 NE2d 1180, 1189 (1993) (citations omitted). For illustrative cases reversing convictions on this standard, see *Com. v. Thomas*, 401 Mass 109, 118-119, 514 NE2d 1309, 1315 (1987) (jury instructions); *Com. v. Cobb*, 397 Mass 105, 109, 489 NE2d 1246, 1247-1248 (1986) (missing witness instruction).

[16] See *Com. v. Williams*, 63 Mass App 615, 616-617, 827 NE2d 1281, 1283 (2005) (no indication in record that defendant made motion for required finding of not guilty).

[17] *Vassallo v. Baxter Healthcare Corp.*, 428 Mass 1, 11, 696 NE2d 909, 917 (1998). See also Advisory Committee Note to Proposed Mass R Evid 103 ("Massachusetts law contains no statutory or rules counterpart to the plain error provision of (d). In criminal matters, however, case law has recognized error, although not brought to the attention of the trial judge, if it constitutes a substantial risk of miscarriage of justice."); Reporter's Notes to Mass R Civ P 46 ("Massachusetts does not follow the 'fundamental error' doctrine.").

[18] See Mass R Civ P 51(b) and Mass R Crim P 24(b). See also *In re McHoul*, 445 Mass 143, 157, 833 NE2d 1146, 1157 (2005) (where petitioner failed to request jury instruction on matter and did not object to particular aspect of charge, issue is waived); *Harlow v. Chin*, 405 Mass 697, 703 n.5, 545 NE2d 602, 606 n.5 (1989) ("We

grounds.[19] Counsel are advised to renew any earlier objection with specificity following the charge.[20] In a criminal case, even in the absence of an objection, review is available to determine whether the instructions created substantial risk of miscarriage of justice.[21]

Even with a proper objection, an error below is not ground for overturning a judgment on appeal unless it is determined that the error affected the substantial rights of the party, i.e., that the error could have made a material difference.[22] Under the harmless error standard, the court considers the importance of the evidence in the prosecution's case, the relationship between the evidence and the premise

---

ordinarily insist on exceptions with respect to any inadequacies in curative instructions."); *Com. v. Eberle*, 81 Mass App 235, 238-239, 961 NE2d 604, 608-609 (2012) (defendant did not preserve claim of error regarding trial court's failure to give self-defense instruction, where counsel merely made oral request, but did not submit proposed instructions or renew his request); *Com. v. Doyle*, 67 Mass App 846, 858 NE2d 1098 (2006) (defendant failed to preserve objection for appellate review where, without objecting to any part thereof, he merely requested further instruction on entrapment and responded "thank you" when the judge declined).

[19] *Com. v. Chapman*, 433 Mass 481, 489, 744 NE2d 14, 19-20 (2001). See also *Composto v. MBTA*, 48 Mass App 477, 480-481, 722 NE2d 984, 987 (2000) (mere conversation with judge does not constitute specific objection). See § 1.3.3, infra.

[20] See *Rotkiewicz v. Sadowsky*, supra, 431 Mass at 751, 730 NE2d at 287; *Fein v. Kahan*, 36 Mass App 967, 968 n.4, 635 NE2d 1, 2 n.4 (1994). But compare *Rotkiewicz v. Sadowsky*, 431 Mass 748, 750-752, 730 NE2d 282, 286-287 (2000) (defendant's oral request for jury instruction on actual malice standard in defamation action, made at close of plaintiff's evidence, was sufficient to preserve objection to failure to give instruction where noted by trial judge before closing arguments began, even though objection not renewed at end of jury charge); *Com. v. Biancardi*, 421 Mass 251, 253-254, 656 NE2d 1234, 1235-1236 (1995) (no need for postcharge objection where defendant's request for instruction, judge's rejection of request, and giving of instruction inconsistent with request was sufficient to preserve appellate rights); *Com. v. Grenier*, 415 Mass 680, 686 n.8, 615 NE2d 922, 925 n.8 (1993) (defendant saved appellate rights where he submitted written request for instruction that judge denied at charging conference stating defendant's exception was saved); *In re Miller*, 71 Mass App 625, 627 n.3, 885 NE2d 148, 152 n.3 (2008) (error preserved even though counsel failed to object at conclusion of charge where objection and extensive argument was made during precharge conference).

[21] *Com. v. Pares-Ramirez*, 400 Mass 604, 610, 511 NE2d 344, 348 (1987); *Com. v. Barbosa*, 399 Mass 841, 844, 507 NE2d 694, 696 (1987); *Com.v Gorman*, 84 Mass App 482, 491-492, 998 NE2d 344, 352 (2013).

[22] GL 231, §§ 119, 132. See *Com. v. Kelly*, 470 Mass 682, 688, 25 NE3d 288, 296 (2015) ("An error is not prejudicial if it did not influence the jury, or had but very slight effect."); *DeJesus v. Yogel*, 404 Mass 44, 47-48, 533 NE2d 1318, 1321 (1989); *Com. v. Haggett*, 79 Mass App 167, 171, 944 NE2d 601, 605 (2011). For analysis of harmless error in the context of *Melendez-Diaz* error, see *Com. v. Ramsey*, 466 Mass 489, 995 NE2d 1110); *Com. v. Mendes*, 463 Mass 353, 358-365, 974 NE2d 606, 611-615 (2012); *Com. v. Marte*, 84 Mass App 136, 993 NE2d 1201 (2013).

of the defense, who introduced the issue at trial, the frequency of reference, whether the erroneously admitted evidence was merely cumulative, the effect of curative instructions, and the weight of evidence of guilt.[23] If it cannot be determined "with fair assurance, after pondering all that happened without stripping the erroneous action from the whole, that the judgment was not substantially swayed by the error," then it is prejudicial.[24]

The so-called clairvoyance exception permits an appellate court to entertain an error of constitutional dimension where the principle was not sufficiently developed at the time of the trial to afford a meaningful opportunity to raise it.[25] Similarly, even in the absence of an objection, where the trial judge does not clearly instruct the jury that they must find that the defendant committed separate and distinct criminal acts to convict on multiple charges, the resulting convictions must be vacated as duplicative if there is *any significant possibility* that the jury may have based the convictions on the same acts or series of acts.[26]

---

[23] *Com. v. Monroe*, 472 Mass 461, 472-473, 35 NE3d 677, 687 (2015) (declining to decide if harmless error standard applies to erroneous admission of defendant's incriminating statement); *Com. v. Dyette*, 87 Mass App 548, 559-560, 32 NE3d 906, 917-918 (2015) (a constitutional violation gives rise to presumptive prejudice that can be overcome only where the Commonwealth makes an affirmative showing of harmlessness beyond a reasonable doubt."

[24] *Com. v. Asher*, 471 Mass 580, 590, 31 NE3d 1055, 1063 (2015) (erroneous jury instructions).

[25] See *Com. v. Hinckley*, 422 Mass 261, 264-267, 661 NE2d 1317, 1319-1321 (1996). See also *Com. v. Verde*, 444 Mass 279, 282 n.2, 827 NE2d 701, 704 n.2 (2005) (failure to object was excusable because U.S. Supreme Court's *Crawford* decision changing Confrontation Clause analysis was decided after defendant's trial and notice of appeal); *Com. v. D'Agostino*, 421 Mass 281, 284-286, 657 NE2d 217, 219-220 (1995). Compare *Mains v. Com.*, 433 Mass 30, 739 NE2d 1125 (2000) (defendant waived claim challenging reasonable doubt instructions by not taking appeal from denial of fourth motion for new trial at time when case law was fully developed). The clairvoyance exception applies only to errors of a constitutional dimension and not to new common law rules of evidence. See *Com. v. Peppicelli*, 70 Mass App 87, 100, 872 NE2d 1142, 1152 (2007) (*Adjutant* rule permitting evidence of specific acts of violence by victim).

For an extensive discussion of this and other recognized exceptions to the rule requiring contemporaneous objection at trial to preserve appellate review, see *Com. v. Randolph*, 438 Mass 290, 294-296, 780 NE2d 58, 64-66 (2002) and *Com. v. Miranda*, 22 Mass App 10, 14-19, 490 NE2d 1195, 1198-1201 (1986). For other "exceptional circumstances" permitting review, see *White v. White*, 40 Mass App 132, 133, 662 NE2d 230, 232 (1996) (judge's decisions on custody and visitation were based on testimony received in private session) and *Atlas Tack Corp. v. DiMasi*, 37 Mass App 66, 70-71, 637 NE2d 230, 233 (1994) (defendants would not have had the opportunity to present the issue below).

[26] *Com. v. Traylor*, 472 Mass 260, 274-276, 34 NE3d 276, 287-289 (2015).

The rules requiring proper objections apply equally to *pro se* litigants.[27]

In appropriate circumstances, the judge may exclude or limit evidence on her own, even in the absence of an objection.[28] Where prejudicial excesses in a prosecutor's closing are clear, preferable practice is for the judge to intervene.[29]

§ 1.3.2 Timeliness

An objection to evidence must be made as soon as the error is apparent.[30] Thus, an objection to a question that calls for inadmissible testimony or is improper in form must usually be made before the answer is given.[31] Objection to an item of real evidence must usually be made before the item is admitted in evidence.[32] With regard to objections to argument, counsel need not immediately interrupt opposing counsel on each occasion when he believes the argument is improper; it is usually sufficient if the matter is called to the attention of the judge at the end of the argument.[33]

If grounds for the objection are not apparent until after the evidence is admitted or because the answer came too quickly for the objection to be made, such fact should be called to the attention of the court and a motion to strike the evidence should immediately be made.[34] Mass R Civ P 46 and Mass R Crim P 22 provide that "if a party

---

[27] See *Mains v. Com.*, supra, 433 Mass at 35-36, 739 NE2d at 1129-1130.

[28] See *Com. v. Haley*, 363 Mass 513, 516-519, 296 NE2d 207, 210-211 (1973).

[29] See *Com. v. Smith*, 387 Mass 900, 911 n.7, 444 NE2d 374, 382 n.7 (1983).

[30] *Com. v. Baptiste*, 372 Mass 700, 706, 363 NE2d 1303, 1307 (1977).

[31] See *Com. v. Senior*, 454 Mass 12, 16-17, 906 NE2d 981, 986 (2009). See also *Com. v. Miskel*, 364 Mass 783, 792-793, 308 NE2d 547, 553 (1974) (objection to earlier question does not carry over to later one); *Com. v. Silvia*, 343 Mass 130, 135-136, 177 NE2d 571, 576 (1961) (objection based upon motion to strike answer that is responsive to a question to which no objection was made is of no avail); *Com. v. Navarro*, 86 Mass App 780, 21 NE3d 982, 988 n.7 (2014) (defense counsel's belated objections during direct examination of prosecution witness did not preserve the issue).

[32] *Com. v. Silvia*, supra, 343 Mass at 135-136, 177 NE2d at 575.

[33] *Com. v. Cancel*, 394 Mass 567, 574, 476 NE2d 610, 616 (1985). Objection after the jury retires is insufficient to preserve error. *Com. v. Boyajian*, 68 Mass App 866, 867-868, 865 NE2d 1153, 1155 (2007).

[34] See *Com. v. Cancel*, supra, 394 Mass at 571, 476 NE2d at 614; *Com. v. Wood*, 17 Mass App 304, 307, 457 NE2d 1131, 1133 (1983) (failure of defendant to make motion to strike after it became apparent that adequate factual basis for expert testimony was lacking constituted waiver of the objection).

has no opportunity to object to a ruling or order at the time it is made, the absence of an objection does not thereafter prejudice him."

A motion to strike erroneously admitted evidence must be made prior to the close of the evidence.[35]

§ 1.3.3 Form of the Objection/Specificity

When objecting, counsel should state the specific ground of the objection unless it is apparent from the context.[36] Specificity serves to call the attention of the judge and the opposing party to the particular problem asserted at a time when it can still be corrected, thus avoiding the necessity of a new trial.[37] "Trial counsel need not achieve perfection in identifying every impropriety . . . so long as the objection alerts the judge to the grounds."[38] The adequacy of an objection must be assessed in the context of the trial as a whole.[39]

A general objection must be overruled if the evidence is admissible for any purpose.[40] The ruling of a lower court on a general objection will be upheld if it is supportable on any ground. It is assumed that the ruling was based on the proper ground.[41] If the objection is

---

[35] See *Jarry v. Corsaro*, 40 Mass App 601, 609, 666 NE2d 1012, 1017 (1996).

[36] See Mass R Civ P 46, Mass R Crim P 22; Proposed Mass R Evid 103(a)(1), see generally *Com. v. Lenane*, 80 Mass App 14, 19, 951 NE2d 361, 365 (2011) (citing Text).

[37] See *Com. v. Keevan*, 400 Mass 557, 563-564, 511 NE2d 534, 538-539 (1987); *Com. v. Costa*, 88 Mass App 750, 753-754, 42 NE3d 1162, 1165-1166 (2015); *Com. v. Saulnier*, 84 Mass App 603, 606, 999 NE2d 148, 151 (2013) (defense counsel failed to explain basis for objection, and trial judge apparently misunderstood it as to form of the question); *Hobbs v. TLT Construction Corp.*, 78 Mass App 178, 179 n.8, 935 NE2d 1290, 1292 n.8 (2010). Compare *Com. v. De La Cruz*, 405 Mass 269, 271, 540 NE2d 168, 169-170 (1989) and *Com. v. Susi*, 394 Mass 784, 788 n.3, 477 NE2d 995, 998 n.3 (1985) (defendants' requests, although not precisely on point, made judge aware of the juror selection issue); *Com. v. Cancel*, 394 Mass 567, 573, 476 NE2d 610, 615 (1985) (ground for exclusion should have been obvious to judge and opposing counsel).

[38] *Com. v. Olmande*, 84 Mass App 231, 235, 995 NE2d 797, 801 (2013).

[39] See *Com. v. Koney*, 421 Mass 295, 299-300, 657 NE2d 210, 213-214 (1995) (defendant's objection, although not specifically mentioning art. 12, was nonetheless sufficient); *Com. v. Tanner*, 66 Mass App 432, 440 n.5, 848 NE2d 430, 437 n.5 (2006) (defendant's general objection was sufficient to alert judge to the hearsay issue in light of previous discussions).

[40] *Com. v. Errington*, 390 Mass 875, 882, 460 NE2d 598, 603 (1984).

[41] See *G.E.B. v. S.R.W.*, 422 Mass 158, 168, 661 NE2d 646, 654 (1996).

too broad, including unobjectionable matter within its scope, the overruling of the objection is not error.[42] Similarly, a motion to strike that is directed to both admissible as well as inadmissible evidence may properly be denied.[43]

A party who has made an objection at trial specifically stating the grounds therefor is not entitled to urge different grounds upon appeal of the court's overruling of the objection.[44] Thus, the overruling of an incorrect specific objection is not error even if a correct ground for exclusion appears to exist. When an incorrect specific objection is sustained, generally no error will be found if some other proper ground for exclusion exists, since a retrial would probably only result in the exclusion of the evidence on the correct ground.[45]

The proponent of evidence which is objected to is obliged "to bring to the judge's attention with sufficient clarity the grounds upon which the admission of the evidence was sought, so that, upon its exclusion, the points of law actually presented for the judge's consideration would be apparent and provide a basis for correction of the ruling if there was error."[46] If the proponent urges its admissibility on an incorrect ground at trial, he cannot press on appeal that it should have been admitted on a different ground, even if it appears that the evidence was admissible on the other ground.[47]

---

[42] *Bruyer v. P. S. Thorsen Co.*, 327 Mass 684, 686-687, 100 NE2d 684, 686 (1951).

[43] *Griffin v. General Motors Corp.*, 380 Mass 362, 365, 403 NE2d 402, 404-405 (1980); *Com. v. Sandler*, 368 Mass 729, 738-739, 335 NE2d 903, 909-910 (1975) (motion to strike "entire testimony" of witness was properly denied).

[44] See *Com. v. Bonds*, 445 Mass 821, 828-829, 840 NE2d 939, 946 (2006); *Com. v. Tyree*, 387 Mass 191, 213, 439 NE2d 263, 276 (1982). See, e.g., *Com. v. Sok*, 439 Mass 428, 435, 788 NE2d 941, 948 (2003) (having been asked to state his reasons for cross-examining witness on particular subject, defendant may not raise for first time on appeal an argument not presented to trial judge); *Com. v. Emeny*, 463 Mass 138, 145 n.8, 972 NE2d 1003, 1010 n.8 (2012) (defendant's "overall objection" to autopsy photographs did not preserve issue where the basis was prejudicial nature, and on appeal he asserts lack of proper authentication); *Com. v. Caraballo*, 81 Mass App 536, 539 n.2, 965 NE2d 194, 198 n.2 (2012) (defendant waived issue when he initially objected to the foundation of officer's testimony, but did not object again, and now contends on appeal that the testimony was impermissible profiling evidence).

[45] *Com. v. Mandeville*, 386 Mass 393, 397-398, 436 NE2d 912, 916 (1982).

[46] *H. H. Hawkins & Sons v. Robie*, 338 Mass 61, 66, 153 NE2d 768, 770 (1958).

[47] *Com. v. White*, 353 Mass 409, 420-421, 232 NE2d 335, 343 (Mass 1967).

§ 1.3.4 Offer of Proof

Where evidence is excluded the proponent must, in order to preserve the issue for appeal, make an offer of proof stating the substance of the evidence—for example, what the witness would have answered to an excluded question.[48] "The offer of proof requirement serves several purposes. An offer of proof may assist the trial judge in making the correct ruling. And the presence of an offer of proof in a record on appeal enables an appellate court to determine whether an error was made and, if so, how harmful it was to the [proponent]."[49]

Ordinarily no formal offer of proof is required when the evidence is excluded on cross-examination since an offer must point to evidence "actually available, and the cross-examiner will often be unable to state what the answer would have been if the question had been allowed."[50] In cases where the purpose or significance of the question is obscure or the prejudice to the cross-examiner is not clear, an offer may be required.[51] The cross-examiner should certainly be permitted to make an offer of proof if he wishes to do so to show the pertinency of the question excluded where it is not otherwise apparent.[52]

No offer of proof has been required on direct examination where the trial judge has in effect treated the witness as not qualified to testify at all on a particular issue or has otherwise excluded all evidence on that issue.[53]

---

[48] Mass R Civ P 43(c) (examining counsel "may" make offer); Proposed Mass R Evid 103(a)(2). See also *Mazzaro v. Paull*, 372 Mass 645, 652-653, 363 NE2d 509, 514 (1977); *Palmer v. Palmer*, 27 Mass App 141, 149, 535 NE2d 611, 616 (1989).

[49] *Com. v. Chase*, 26 Mass App 578, 581-582, 530 NE2d 185, 188 (1988) (citing Text). See also *Com. v. Dyer*, 460 Mass 728, 743-744, 955 NE2d 271, 286 (2011) (in absence of offer of proof at trial as to contents of claimed conversations, "we can discern neither the substance of what the testimony would have indicated, nor the state of mind that it was being proffered to show"); *Com. v. Clemente*, 452 Mass 295, 316, 893 NE2d 19, 39 (2008) ("No offer of proof was made regarding the excluded testimony. Because we do not know the content of the conversations, the record is insufficient for us to measure whether the exclusion was error or, if so, what impact the error may have had.").

[50] *Com. v. Barnett*, 371 Mass 87, 95, 354 NE2d 879, 884-885 (1976).

[51] See *Com. v. Ahearn*, 370 Mass 283, 286, 346 NE2d 907, 909 (1976); *Breault v. Ford Motor Co.*, 364 Mass 352, 357-358, 305 NE2d 824, 828 (1973).

[52] *Com. v. Barnett*, supra, 371 Mass at 95, 354 NE2d at 884-885.

[53] *First National Bank of Mount Dora v. Shawmut Bank of Boston, N.A.*, 378 Mass 137, 141, 389 NE2d 1002, 1005 (1979). See also *Ratner v. Canadian Universal Ins. Co.*, 359 Mass 375, 385, 269 NE2d 227, 232 (1971) (but it is "better practice" to make offer); *Ford v. Worcester*, 339 Mass 657, 659, 162 NE2d 264, 266 (1959); *Charles River Mortgage Co., Inc. v. Baptist Home of Massachusetts*, 36 Mass App 277, 280, 630 NE2d 304, 306 (1994).

Where the general nature and purpose of the expected testimony are sufficiently clear to enable the judge to make an informed decision, an offer of proof may not be necessary.[54] An offer of proof must of course be responsive to the question excluded.[55]

§ 1.4 The Ruling

§ 1.4.1 Preliminary Questions of Fact

It frequently happens that a ruling on evidence requires the determination of a preliminary question of fact—e.g., the "good faith" of a declaration under GL 233, § 65 or § 78 (see § 8.20, infra) or the unavailability of the original document under the best evidence rule (§ 10.3.1, infra). Although questions of fact are ordinarily for the jury, it is the province of the judge to determine these preliminary questions and she may hear evidence on them in the absence of the jury.[1] As a general principle, foundational facts conditioning the application of technical exclusionary rules like hearsay are reserved for the judge, while facts conditioning the logical relevance of evidence are submitted to the jury where there is sufficient evidence to support a jury determination that the condition has been fulfilled. See § 1.6.

The rules of evidence are not binding on the judge in the determination of such preliminary questions, except those rules concerning

---

[54] See *Com. v. Caldron*, 383 Mass 86, 89 n.2, 417 NE2d 958 (1981) (offer of proof may be dispensed with where there is no doubt what testimony would be given); *Urban Investment & Development Co. v. Turner Construction Co.*, 35 Mass App 100, 102-103, 616 NE2d 829, 832 (1993).

[55] *Com. v. Hubbard*, 371 Mass 160, 174, 355 NE2d 469, 478 (1976).

§ 1.4 [1] See Proposed Mass R Evid 104 (a), (c):

> (a) **Questions of admissibility generally**. Preliminary questions concerning the qualification or competency of a person to be a witness, the existence of a privilege, or the admissibility of evidence shall be determined by the court, subject to the provisions of subdivisions (b) and (f). In making its determination it is not bound by the rules of evidence except those with respect to privilege, the existence of a conspiracy, and on questions arising in hearing on motions to suppress evidence.
> (c) **Hearing of jury**. Hearings on the admissibility of confessions shall in all cases be conducted out of the hearing of the jury. Hearings on other preliminary matters shall be so conducted, when the interests of justice require or, when an accused is a witness, if he so requests.

See also *Nally v. Volkswagen of America, Inc.*, 405 Mass 191, 198, 539 NE2d 1017, 1012-1022 (1989); *Fauci v. Mulready*, 337 Mass 532, 540, 150 NE2d 286, 291 (1958).

privileges and except on preliminary questions concerning the existence of a conspiracy or arising in hearings on motions to suppress.[2] The determination of the trial judge on preliminary questions concerning admissibility of evidence is conclusive upon appeal as long as there is evidence to support it.[3]

With respect to certain preliminary facts in criminal cases, it is the practice for the judge, after finding the facts and admitting the evidence over objection, to nonetheless instruct the jurors to disregard the evidence if they do not believe that the preliminary facts exist. Where the voluntariness of a confession is in issue, for example, the accused is entitled under the so-called humane practice (see § 12.1, infra) to both a voir dire examination in the absence of the jury and, in the event the judge admits the confession, to an instruction that the jury disregard the confession if upon their reconsideration of the issue they conclude that it was involuntary.[4] Similarly, the jury must be advised that they must make an independent determination (based on admissible evidence other than the statement themselves) that a conspiracy existed before they may consider the co-conspirators'" out-of-court statements.[5]

Other situations in which the determination of a preliminary question is shared between the judge and the jury include:

---

[2] Proposed Mass R Evid 104 (a). Compare Fed R Evid 104(a) (only exception is for rules concerning privileges). For conspiracy findings, see *Com. v. Bright*, 463 Mass 421, 426-427, 974 NE2d 1092, 1100 (2012) ("A trial judge may allow the admission of such statements, but only after a preliminary determination, based on a preponderance of admissible evidence other than the out-of-court statements themselves, that a criminal joint venture existed between the declarant and the defendant, and that the statement was made in furtherance of the venture."); *Com. v. Navarro*, 39 Mass App 161, 166-167, 654 NE2d 71, 75 (1995). Compare FRE 801(d)(2) ("The statement must be considered but does not by itself establish the existence of the conspiracy or participation in it"). For motions to suppress hearings, see the Advisory Committee Note to Proposed Mass R Evid 104 (a): "Because a motion to suppress is likely to involve a serious factual dispute on an issue which may be decisive in the case, the Committee believes that the witness should be present and subject to cross-examination under the rules of evidence."

[3] *Fauci v. Mulready*, supra, 337 Mass at 540, 150 NE2d at 291; *Torre v. Harris-Seybold Co.*, 9 Mass App 660, 672-673, 404 NE2d 96, 106 (1980).

[4] See Proposed Mass R 104(f): "In a criminal case tried to a jury, if the court admits evidence of a confession, or a statement under Rule 804(b)(2) [dying declaration], it shall submit for determination by the jury the respective questions of the voluntariness of the confession and the belief that death was imminent."

[5] *Com. v. Bright*, supra, 463 Mass at 426-427, 974 NE2d at1100.

- The question of whether the requirements for a dying declaration have been established.[6]
- The question of whether in a criminal case the foundational requirements for admission of a document as a business record have been met.[7]
- The question of whether a document is in the handwriting of a particular person.[8]

While the "reasonable doubt" standard of proof applies to the admission of a confession (see § 12.1, infra), a "preponderance of the evidence" is sufficient to warrant admission in all other situations.[9] The jury, of course, has no role to play unless the judge has made an affirmative finding that the evidence is admissible.[10]

In the absence of an express finding of preliminary facts, the appellate court will make the following inferences:

- If the evidence is admitted, it will be inferred from the admission that the necessary preliminary findings were made and that there was evidence to support them unless the record shows that no such finding was or could have been made.[11] A preliminary finding by the judge that a confession

---

[6] Proposed Mass R Evid 104(f), supra. See also *Com. v. Key*, 381 Mass 19, 22, 407 NE2d 327, 330-331 (1980).

[7] See GL 233, § 78: "[W]hen such [business record] entry, writing or record is admitted in a criminal proceeding all questions of fact which must be determined by the court as the basis for the admissibility of the evidence involved shall be submitted to the jury, if a jury trial is had for its final determination."

[8] See *Com. v. Tucker*, 189 Mass 457, 471, 76 NE 127, 133-134 (1905).

[9] *Com. v. Polian*, 288 Mass 494, 498-499, 193 NE2d 68, 70 (1934) (explicitly rejecting the "reasonable doubt" standard); *Com. v. Key*, supra, 381 Mass at 25.

[10] See *Com. v. Reagan*, 175 Mass 335, 56 NE 577 (1900) (judge erred in permitting witness to testify and leaving question of competency to the jury after he determined as a preliminary matter that she was not competent).

[11] See *Com. v. Bjorkman*, 364 Mass 297, 302, 303 NE2d 715, 718 (1973) ("It was not necessary for the trial judge explicitly to state his conclusion as to relevancy as a preliminary finding, since that conclusion was implicit in his ruling that the evidence was admissible."); *Greenberg v. Weisman*, 345 Mass 700, 703, 189 NE2d 531, 534 (1963) ("The admission of the [business] records imports the necessary findings."); *Mitchell v. Hastings & Koch Enterprises, Inc.*, 38 Mass App 271, 275, 647 NE2d 78, 81 (1995) (failure to articulate preliminary findings for admission of declaration of deceased person). Compare *Middlesex Supply, Inc. v. Martin & Sons, Inc.*, 354 Mass 373, 237 NE2d 692 (1968) (rule permitting inference of foundational facts does not apply where facts concerning admission are not in dispute and declaration itself shows that it is not within statute). See also *Ricciutti v. Sylvania Electric Products Inc.*, 343 Mass 347, 351, 178 NE2d 857, 860 (1961) (admission of document implies finding of prerequisite

of a criminal defendant was voluntary beyond a reasonable doubt must, however, appear from the record with "unmistakable clarity." See § 12.1.

- If the evidence is excluded, it will be presumed that the trial judge did not find the necessary preliminary facts to exist.[12]

§ 1.4.2 Correction of Erroneous Ruling

It sometimes happens that the court, having admitted evidence, becomes convinced that it should have been excluded. Ordinarily this can be corrected by an instruction to the jury to disregard the evidence.[13] The practice, however, is disfavored because it is "always desirable that the person who determines the facts, whether he be judge or juror, should hear only what the law says he may hear" and it is "hard to be sure of one's self after the evidence is introduced, even if one tries to disregard it."[14] There are cases, of course, in which the evidence is so damaging that nothing but a new trial will remedy the error.[15]

---

facts, but latter may be reviewed and error found where necessary findings could not be made); *Old Colony Trust Co. v. Shaw*, 348 Mass 212, 216, 202 NE2d 785, 789 (1964) (same).

[12] See *Day Trust Co. v. Malden Savings Bank*, 328 Mass 576, 580, 105 NE2d 363, 365 (1952). See also *H. E. Fletcher Co. v. Com.*, 350 Mass 316, 321, 214 NE2d 721, 724-725 (1966) and *H. H. Hawkins & Sons v. Robie*, 338 Mass 61, 66, 153 NE2d 768, 770 (1958) (judge not required to state grounds for excluding testimony).

[13] See, e.g., *Com. v. Gordon*, 356 Mass 598, 604, 254 NE2d 901, 904 (1970) ("While we recognize that there are certain circumstances under which error is not alleviated by instructions to the jury, we shall not assume that jurors will slight strong and precise instructions of the trial judge to disregard the matters which have been withdrawn from their consideration"). See also *Com. v. Amirault*, 404 Mass 221, 231-232, 535 NE2d 193, 200-201 (1989); *Bouley v. Reisman*, 38 Mass App 118, 128, 645 NE2d 708, 714 (1995).

[14] *Holcombe v. Hopkins*, 314 Mass 113, 118, 49 NE2d 722, 724 (1943).

[15] See, e.g., *Bruton v. United States*, 391 US 123, (1968) (admission of codefendant confession implicating defendant); *Com. v. Perkins*, 39 Mass App 577, 584, 658 NE2d 975, 980 (1995) (expert testimony concerning child abuse victims); *Com. v. Adamides*, 37 Mass App 339, 341-344, 639 NE2d 1092, 1094-1095 (1994) (hearsay regarding uncharged sexual misconduct). Compare *Com. v. Charles*, 397 Mass 1, 12, 489 NE2d 679, 687 (1986) ("It is well within the discretion of the trial judge to deny a mistrial and rely on appropriate curative instructions to erase error even in a case of intentional misstatement.").

For curative instructions regarding improper closing arguments, see Chapter 13.

C. GENERAL CONSIDERATIONS CONCERNING ADMISSIBILITY

§ 1.5 Limited Admissibility/Limiting Instructions

Certain evidence may be admissible only on one issue, or for one purpose, or (in a multiparty trial) against one party. Thus, for example, a prior statement of a witness may be admissible to impeach his credibility, but not to prove the truth of the matters asserted. Proposed Mass R 105, which reflects Massachusetts practice and tracks the Federal Rule, provides:

> **Limited Admissibility**
>
> When evidence which is admissible as to one party or for one purpose but not admissible as to another party or for another purpose is admitted, the court, upon request, shall restrict the evidence to its proper scope and instruct the jury accordingly.[1]

A party desiring to restrict the scope of the evidence must, at the time the evidence is offered or admitted, specifically call the attention of the judge to any limitations by moving to have the jury so instructed.[2] The judge may refuse to limit the scope of the evidence where the objecting party fails to request limiting instructions until a later point in the trial.[3] If the nature of the evidence is such that a jury could not reasonably be expected to adhere to a limiting instruction, exclusion of the evidence may be required to protect the rights of the objecting party.[4]

---

§ 1.5 [1] See also *Com. v. Carrion*, 407 Mass 263, 275, 552 NE2d 558 (1990).

[2] See *Com. v. Errington*, 390 Mass 875, 882, 460 NE2d 598, 603-604 (1984) (where evidence was admissible for one purpose, admission over a general objection was not error, and since no request was made for a limiting instruction, judge's failure to give one was not error); *Com. v. Pinnick*, 354 Mass 13, 16-17, 234 NE2d 756, 758 (1968) (general objection is insufficient to raise issue of limited admissibility at trial or preserve it for appeal). See also *Com. v. De La Cruz*, 405 Mass 269, 275-276, 540 NE2d 168, 172-173 (1989) (failure of counsel to object to adequacy of limiting instruction deprived judge of opportunity to correct error and thus appellate review is limited to whether there was substantial risk of miscarriage of justice).

[3] *Com. v. Roberts*, 433 Mass 45, 48, 740 NE2d 176, 179 (2000).

[4] See, e.g., *Bruton v. United States*, 391 US 123, 88 S Ct 1620, 20 L Ed 2d 476 (1968) (limiting charge could not effectively protect defendant where co-defendant confession was admitted), discussed in § 8.6.7.

§ 1.6 Conditional Admissibility

Proposed Mass R Evid 611(a) provides, consistent with long-standing practice, that the "court has discretion to admit evidence conditionally upon the representation that its relevancy will be established by evidence subsequently offered."[1] Thus, for example, evidence concerning sales of four parcels may be admitted in a takings case before evidence of comparability has been offered.[2] If the promised evidence is not produced, the evidence provisionally admitted may be stricken; but it is the obligation of opposing counsel to move to strike, and if counsel fails to make such a motion, the evidence is available to the fact-finder for its full probative value, and no error is committed by the failure of the court to strike it out.[3]

A court may choose instead to exclude the evidence with the proviso that it may be reoffered after other evidence establishing its relevancy has been adduced.[4] If the other evidence is admitted, it is the proponent's obligation to offer the original evidence again.[5]

---

§ 1.6 [1] See Proposed Mass R 104(b), which tracks the federal rule:

> **Relevancy conditioned on fact**
> When the relevancy of evidence depends upon the fulfillment of a condition of fact, the court shall admit it upon, or subject to, the introduction of evidence sufficient to support a finding that the condition has been fulfilled.

See also *Com. v. Irene*, 462 Mass 600, 606 n.13, 970 NE2d 291, 297 n.13 (2012) (relevance of statement offered by prosecution was conditional on finding that defendant in fact made the statement, and judge must instruct jury accordingly); *Com. v. Bright*, 463 Mass 421, 426 n.9, 974 NE2d 1092, 1100 n.9 (2012) (conditional findings of conspiracy).

[2] See *Boyd v. Lawrence Redevelopment Authority*, 348 Mass 83, 84, 202 NE2d 297, 298 (1964).

[3] See *Com. v. Salyer*, 84 Mass App 346, 355-356, 996 NE2d 488, 496 (2013); *Harris-Lewis v. Mudge*, 60 Mass App 480, 485 n.4, 803 NE2d 735, 740 n.4 (2004) (Text cited); *Foreign Car Center, Inc. v. Salem Suede, Inc.*, 40 Mass App 15, 23, 660 NE2d 687, 694 (1996); *Com. v. Navarro*, 39 Mass App 161, 166, 654 NE2d 71, 75 (1995). But see *Roddy v. Fleishman Distilling Sales Corp.*, 360 Mass 623, 625-626, 277 NE2d 284, 287 (1971) (failure to make motion to strike did not foreclose defendant from challenging *de bene* evidence on appeal because of subsequent evidentiary developments).

[4] See Proposed Mass R Evid 104(b).

[5] See *Thalin v. Friden Calculating Machine Co., Inc.*, 338 Mass 67, 69, 153 NE2d 658, 660 (1958).

§ 1.7 Rule of Verbal Completeness

Whenever a portion of an oral or written statement of a person is introduced into evidence, the opponent may require that the remainder of the statement, insofar as it relates to the same subjects, be admitted as well. The rule of completeness permits the opponent to put before the trier of fact the context of the fragmentary statement admitted, as well as any contradictions, modifications, or explanations made at the same time (but which would not otherwise be admissible). It does not render automatically admissible portions of the statement that do not explain or qualify the portion admitted, or that relate to other subject matters. The doctrine permits an opposing party to add what has been omitted to give a full picture; it does not open the gate for admission of everything in a document or statement.[1]

---

§ 1.7 [1] See generally *Com. v. Watson*, 377 Mass 814, 824-834, 388 NE2d 680, 686-691 (1979) (quoting Text) (extensive discussion). See, e.g., *Com. v. Aviles*, 461 Mass 60, 73-76, 958 NE2d 37, 50-51 (2011) (where defense counsel introduced only the portion of victim's grand jury testimony that helped defendant's case, he opened up for admission the limited portion that clarified where defendant had touched her); *Com. v. Tennison*, 440 Mass 553, 563-564, 800 NE2d 285, 295 (2003) (defendants elicited on cross only portions of witness's statement to police officer, thereby opening door to admission of remainder of statement to put testimony in context); *McAllister v. Boston Housing Authority*, 429 Mass 300, 302-303, 708 NE2d 95, 97-98 (1999) (portion of deposition excluded by the judge did not explain further the picture painted by defense counsel); *Com. v. Carmona*, 428 Mass 268, 271-272, 700 NE2d 823, 827 (1998) (once defendant presented portion of teletype showing he had turned himself in, he opened door for admission of portion explaining why he had done so); *Com. v. Hamilton*, 411 Mass 313, 321-322, 582 NE2d 929, 934-935 (1991) (when defendant introduced portions of his tape-recorded interrogation, that rendered entire recording admissible); *Com. v. Owens*, 402 Mass 639, 641 n.2, 524 NE2d 387, 388 n.2 (1988) (where one party puts part of conversation in evidence, other party is entitled to put in evidence balance of what was said); *Com. v. Mitchell*, 89 Mass App 13, 25, 45 NE3d 111, 122 (2016) (the implication of the redaction of the exculpatory portion of co-defendant's statement left the impression that defendant may have been one of the persons identified as the perpetrator); *Com. v. Doyle*, 83 Mass App 384, 391, 984 NE2d 297, 303 (2013) (defendant, by asking police officer if he had obtained the name and telephone number of eyewitness, did not open door to hearsay testimony); *Com. v. Slonka*, 42 Mass App 760, 771-772, 680 NE2d 103, 110-111 (1997) (rule requires that if entry of one page of victim's medical record is admitted by prosecution, another page offered by defendant should be admitted notwithstanding its privileged status); *Kobayashi v. Orion Ventures, Inc.*, 42 Mass App 492, 497-498, 678 NE2d 180, 185 (1997) (excluded parts of memo should have been admitted to give full picture); *Com. v. Thatch*, 39 Mass App 904, 653 NE2d 1121 (1995) (once defense counsel introduced portion of rape victim's statement to police officer, prosecutor was entitled to put into evidence complete version); *Com. v. Graves*, 35 Mass App 76, 87-88, 616 NE2d 817, 824 (1993) (rape victim, who had been referred to a portion of her written statement given to police, was properly allowed to read entire statement).

A defendant cannot compel the admission of his entire statement simply because the Commonwealth offers part of it. The defendant must show that the portion of the statement he seeks to admit qualifies, explains, contradicts, or puts in context the portion introduced by the Commonwealth.[2] To hold otherwise would "permit a defendant to make a statement containing an admission and then load it with any amount of self-serving statements admissible at his option."[3]

Compare *Com. v. Sharpe*, 454 Mass 135, 145, 908 NE2d 376, 385 (2009) (Commonwealth's admission of four abuse orders obtained against defendant by victim did not render admissible for the defense the separate affidavits in support); *Com. v. Gaynor*, 443 Mass 245, 270-271, 820 NE2d 233, 254 (2005) ("The portion of the statement that was admitted on redirect examination did not serve to clarify the context of the portion that was admitted during cross-examination or serve to correct any distortion that might have been caused by a fragmented version of events. It involved a different subject, and as such, was not admissible under the rule of completeness."); *Com. v. Martinez*, 431 Mass 168, 175-176, 726 NE2d 913, 922 (2000) (for purpose of testimony of extrajudicial identifications, the doctrine extends only to testimony as to the identifying witness's identification of the defendant, not a complete description of the event); *Com. v. Eason*, 427 Mass 595, 597-598, 694 NE2d 1264, 1266 (1998) (fact that declarant made two statements in course of same conversation did not make second admissible, where it did not concern same subject as first statement which was admitted); *Com. v. Foster F*, 86 Mass 734, 739, 20 NE2d 967, 972s (2014) (defense cross-examination of victim on limited issue of whether she agreed to go with him based on sexual abuse intervention interview did not open door to admission of the entire transcript under verbal completeness doctrine where very little of it explained or clarified the victim's response); *Com. v. McBrown*, 72 Mass App 60, 63, 888 NE2d 976, 979 (2008) (doctrine inapplicable to agent's report prepared several days after his notes of the interrogation which had been referred to on cross examination, and was thus a different statement); *Com. v. Bruce*, 61 Mass App 474, 481-482, 811 NE2d 1003, 1008-1009 (2004) (citing Text) (judge erroneously relied on rule of verbal completeness where grand jury statements were entirely separable); *Com. v. Richardson*, 59 Mass App 94, 99, 793 NE2d 1278, 1282 (2003) (second page of victim's statement to police should not have been admitted under doctrine as it neither qualified nor explained admitted portion).

The doctrine is one of inclusion, not exclusion, and thus does not require exclusion of testimony concerning defendant's statements on the grounds that the witness was unable to recall entire conversation See *Com. v. Santiago*, 30 Mass App 207, 221, 567 NE2d 943, 952 (1991).

[2] See *Com. v. Smith*, 460 Mass 385, 397-398, 951 NE2d 674, 685-686 (2011); *Com. v. Eugene*, 438 Mass 343, 350-351, 780 NE2d 893, 899-900 (2003). Thus where the prosecution introduced defendant's admission to the detective that he had used the library computer, the judge should not have excluded the portion of the interview in which defendant denied viewing child pornography on it, because otherwise the jury was left with a false impression. *Com. v. Crayton*, 470 Mass 228, 246-247, 21 NE3d 157, 173-174 (2014).

[3] *Com. v. Leftwich*, 430 Mass 865, 872, 724 NE2d 691, 698 (2000). See also *Com. v. Thompson*, 431 Mass 108, 114-115, 725 NE2d 556, 563-564 (2000) (excluded portion of defendant's statement concerned only his alibi); *Com. v. Garrey*, 436 Mass 422, 432-434, 765 NE2d 725, 736-737 (2002) (judge properly balanced conflicting interests in

The doctrine of verbal completeness does not permit the Commonwealth, or any party, to ask a witness selective questions concerning a prior statement that itself would be inadmissible, and then admit the entire statement by claiming that the opposing party on cross-examination asked equally selective questions about the same statement.[4]

When a third-party witness testifies to an extrajudicial identification (see § 11.1.1), the verbal completeness doctrine extends only to testimony as to the identification of the defendant, and not to matters such as a description of the crime or subsequent events.[5]

Case law regarding the doctrine envisions the subsequent admission of the completing material by the opposing party. It has been suggested, however, that in order to give the jury the full picture at the outset, the better practice is to require an objection from the opposing party and permit contemporaneous introduction of the complete statements when the original is offered.[6]

§ 1.8 Curative Admissibility/Opening the Door

Where evidence otherwise inadmissible is admitted without objection, it may be rebutted by the opponent as a matter of right under the doctrine of curative admissibility. Thus a judge who erroneously, but without objection, admitted hearsay evidence of a face-to-face accusation of defendant by the victim,[1] committed reversible error in refusing to allow defendant to counter with otherwise inadmissible

---

refusing to admit portion of defendant's statement where he asserted self-defense after admitting stabbing victim); *Com. v. Bianchi*, 435 Mass 316, 327-328, 757 NE2d 1087, 1095-1096 (2001) (purported suicide note offered by defendant not admissible because, although taken from same pad of paper as statement admitted by prosecution, it was not part of that statement).

[4] See *Com. v. Avila*, 454 Mass 744, 758, 912 NE2d 1014, 1026 (2009).

[5] See *Com. v. Martinez*, 431 Mass 168, 175-176, 726 NE2d 913, 922 (2000) (citing Text).

[6] *McAllister v. Boston Housing Authority*, supra, 429 Mass at 303, 708 NE2d at 98. This is the approach adopted in Proposed Mass R Evid 106:

> **Remainder of or Related Writings or Recorded Statements**
> When a writing or recorded statement or part thereof is introduced by a party, an adverse party may require him at that time to introduce any other part or any other writing or recorded statement which ought in fairness to be considered contemporaneously with it.

§ 1.8 [1] Accusatory statements followed by the defendant's denial are not admissible. See § 12.6.8, infra.

evidence that he had denied the accusations at the time.[2] In order for the doctrine to apply, the opponent's evidence must at least be relevant, and offered to counter relevant (although otherwise inadmissible) evidence that has prejudiced his case.[3]

The doctrine of curative admissibility allows a party harmed by incompetent evidence to rebut it only where:

- the original evidence being rebutted was improperly admitted;[4] and
- the evidence created significant prejudice.[5]

A party may thus open to door to the admission of otherwise inadmissible evidence by raising the matter on direct examination or otherwise.[6] On a related matter, there has been "modest recognition" in the Commonwealth of the notion that a party in closing argument should be permitted some latitude to "fight fire with fire,"—i.e., to rebut improper argument with improper argument.[7]

---

[2] See *Com. v. Reed*, 444 Mass 803, 809-810, 831 NE2d 901, 907 (2005) and *Com. v. Ruffen*, 399 Mass 811, 813-814, 507 NE2d 684, 686-687 (1987). See also *Com. v. Wakelin*, 230 Mass 567, 576, 120 NE 209, 213 (1918) (evidence of third party's confession, inadmissible but admitted without objection, could be rebutted by Commonwealth as of right); *Burke v. Memorial Hospital*, 29 Mass App 948, 950, 558 NE2d 1146, 1149-1150 (1990) (performance evaluations of patient's work by supervisor were admissible to rebut supervisor's memo, portions of which were improperly admitted).

[3] *Goodyear Park Co. v. Holyoke*, 298 Mass 510, 511-512, 11 NE2d 439, 441 (1937).

[4] See *Vassallo v. Baxter Healthcare Corp.*, 428 Mass 1, 17, 696 NE2d 909, 920 (1998); *Com. v. Martin*, 73 Mass App 526, 537, 899 NE2d 869, 877 (2009), *rev'd on other grounds*, 457 Mass 14, 927 NE2d 432 (2010).

[5] See *Judge Rotenberg Educational Center, Inc. v. Commissioner of Dep't of Mental Retardation*, 424 Mass 430, 462, 677 NE2d 127, 148-149 (1997).

[6] *Com. v. Quinn*, 469 Mass 641, 648, 15 NE3d 726, 733 (2014); *Com. v. Magraw*, 426 Mass 589, 594, 690 NE2d 400 (1998); *Com. v. Navarro*, 86 Mass App 780, 21 NE3d 982, 987-988 (2014) (prosecutor's question to accomplice about guns he had seen in defendant's barbershop was proper, as defense counsel opened the line of inquiry in the opening statement); *Com. v. Torres*, 86 Mass App 272, 277-278, 15 NE3d 778, 784 (2014) ("It was defense counsel who alleged that the victims fabricated their accusations and first brought out statements that exceeded permissible first complaint testimony, which opened the door to further testimony beyond the scope of the first complaint doctrine. . . . Once the defendant 'opened the door' to these statements, the Commonwealth was appropriately permitted to explore the contents and the context of the statements in more detail.").

[7] See *Com. v. Amirault*, 404 Mass 221, 236-237, 535 NE2d 193, 203 (1989) (but the better course is to seek redress from the judge). See, e.g., *Com. v. Mello*, 420 Mass 375, 380-381, 649 NE2d 1106, 1111 (1995); *Com. v. Smith*, 342 Mass 180, 186, 172 NE2d 597, 601-602 (1961). Compare *Com. v. Smith*, 387 Mass 900, 908, 444 NE2d 374, 380-381 (1983) (concept is limited to correcting error by opponent). See also § 13.2, supra.

D. JUROR SELECTION

§ 1.9 Individual Juror Voir Dire for Bias or Prejudice

Because the jury is the centerpiece of the American litigation system, a brief focus on jury selection is in order.

Juror voir dire was revised (effective May 10, 2016 by repeal of GL 234 §§ 26B, 28, and 34, and adoption of GL 234A, § 67A):

> Upon motion of either party, the court shall, or the parties or their attorneys may under the direction of the court, examine on oath a person who is called as a juror, to learn whether the juror related to either party or has any interest in the case, or has expressed or formed an opinion, or is sensible of any bias or prejudice. The objecting party may introduce other competent evidence in support of the objection. If the court finds that the juror does not stand indifferent in the case, another juror shall be called in. In a criminal case such examination shall include questions designed to learn whether such juror understands that a defendant is presumed innocent until proven guilty, that the commonwealth has the burden of proving guilt beyond a reasonable doubt, and that the defendant need not present evidence on the defendant's behalf. If the court finds that such juror does not so understand, another juror shall be called in.
>
> To determine whether a juror stands indifferent in the case, if it appears that, as a result of the impact of considerations which may cause a decision to be made in whole or in part upon issues extraneous to the case, including, but not limited to, community attitudes, possible exposure to potentially prejudicial material or possible preconceived opinions toward the credibility of certain classes of persons, the juror may not stand indifferent, the court shall, or the parties or their attorneys may, with the permission and under the direction of the court, examine the juror specifically with respect to such considerations, attitudes, exposure, opinions or any other matters which may cause a decision to be made in whole or in part upon issues extraneous to the issues in the case. Such examination may include a brief statement of the facts of the case, to the extent the facts are appropriate and relevant to the issue of such examination and shall be conducted individually and outside the presence of other persons about to be called as jurors or already called.[1]

---

§ 1.9 [1] See also Mass R Crim P 20(b); Mass R Civ P 47(a). For application of former GL 234, § 28 in a civil case, see *Blank v. Hubbuch*, 36 Mass App 955, 633 NE2d

GL 234A, § 67D further provides for all criminal and civil superior court jury trials:

(1) In addition to whatever jury voir dire of the jury venire is conducted by the court, the court shall permit, upon the request of any party's attorney or a self-represented party, the party's attorney or self-represented party to conduct an oral examination of the prospective jurors at the discretion of the court.
(2) The court may impose reasonable limitations upon the questions and the time allowed during such examination, including, but not limited to, requiring pre-approval of the questions.
(3) In criminal cases involving multiple defendants, the commonwealth shall be entitled to the same amount of time as that to which all defendants together are entitled.
(4) The court may promulgate rules to implement this section, including, but not limited to, providing consistent policies, practices and procedures relating to the process of jury voir dire.

"A defendant is not entitled to a jury that knows nothing about the crime, so long as jurors are able fairly to weigh the evidence in the case, set aside any information they learned outside the court room, follow the judge's instructions, and render an impartial verdict."[2] The responses to the judge's queries need not be unequivocal.[3] A judge may generally rely on a juror's representation of impartiality.[4]

---

439 (1994) (trial judge in medical malpractice case did not abuse discretion in refusing to conduct more extensive voir dire of physician selected to sit on jury).

[2] *Com. v. Entwistle*, 463 Mass 205, 221-222, 973 NE2d 115, 128 (2012) (extensive media coverage of murder of defendant's wife and daughter in their Hopkinton home). See, e.g., *Com. v. Leahy*, 445 Mass 481, 494-495, 838 NE2d 1220, 1232 (2005) (extensive media coverage of murder of Alexandra Zapp in highway rest-area bathroom).

[3] See *Com. v. Prunty*, 462 Mass 295, 311-312, 968 NE2d 361, 375-376 (2012) (possible race-based bias); *Com. v. Bryant*, 447 Mass 494, 500-501, 852 NE2d 1072, 1077-1078 (2006) ("I think I could [be impartial]" and "I hope I would [be impartial]" may be sufficient); *Com. v. Melo*, 67 Mass App 71, 78, 851 NE2d 1124, 1131 (2006) (juror "not certain" that he could be impartial).

[4] See *Com. v. Phim*, 462 Mass 470, 480, 969 NE2d 663, 671-672 (2012) (judge properly accepted juror's assurance of disinterest notwithstanding his vague recollection that he had taught trooper witness many years before and may have been his basketball coach); *Com. v. Dyer*, 460 Mass 728, 740-741, 955 NE2d 271, 284-285 (2011)

The judge has broad discretion as to the questions to be asked[5] as well as to whether the circumstances present a substantial risk that an extraneous influence might affect the jurors, and the defendant must show beyond speculation that such risk exists.[6] Although the U.S. Supreme Court has recognized that in extreme cases, a venire may be deemed presumptively prejudiced by virtue of extensive pretrial publicity, see *Skilling v. United States,* 130 S Ct 2896 (2010), no Massachusetts case has so found.[7]

The trial judge is ordinarily expected to ask prospective jurors in a criminal case individually whether they or any member of their family had ever been victim of a crime, had ever worked for law enforcement, or whether they would find the testimony of a police officer more credible than a civilian witness.[8]

(defendant's proffer was insufficient to require an evidentiary hearing into undisclosed bias of juror whose live-in boyfriend was a guard at the jail where defendant was being held, where juror assured judge she could be impartial); *Com. v. McCoy*, 456 Mass 838, 843, 926 NE2d 1143, 1152 (2010) (judge entitled to rely on juror's assurance she could be impartial despite having been a victim of sexual assault). But compare *Com. v. Clark*, 446 Mass 620, 628-630, 846 NE2d 765, 773-774 (2006) (reversing conviction where judge accepted juror's ambiguous representation that even though she believed African Americans were more likely to commit crime, her ability to be impartial "would depend on the person's circumstances").

[5] *Com. v. Keohane*, 444 Mass 563, 572, 829 NE2d 1125, 1133 (2005); *Com. v. Carvalho*, 88 Mass App 840, 844-845, 43 NE3d 340, 346 (2016) (trial judge not required to question jurors about their experience with domestic violence orders); *Com. v. Stack*, 49 Mass App 227, 240-241, 728 NE2d 956, 966-967 (2000). Judges have been permitted to pose questions concerning the absence of scientific evidence in the Commonwealth's case, see *Com. v. Gray*, 465 Mass 330, 339, 990 NE2d 528, 537 (2012), and the absence of eyewitness testimony. See *Com. v. Andrade*, 468 Mass 543, 546-549, 11 NE3d 597, 601-603 (2014).

[6] *Com. v. Pena*, 455 Mass 1, 10-11, 913 NE2d 815, 824 (2009).

[7] See *Com. v. Entwistle*, 463 Mass 205, 219-222, 973 NE2d 115, 127-128 (2012); *Com. v. Hoose,* 467 Mass 395, 406-409, 5 NE2d 843, 854-856 (2014). For additional cases involving pretrial publicity, compare *Com. v. Toolan*, 460 Mass 452, 951 NE2d 903 (2011) (trial court's voir dire procedure was inadequate to assure impartial jury in light of extensive pretrial publicity in small island community, requiring reversal of conviction) with *Com. v. Druce*, 453 Mass 686, 697, 905 NE2d 70, 80 (2009) (proper remedy for possible exposure to newspaper article regarding defendant's reenactment of killing on videotape was voir dire of prospective jurors); *Com. v. Morales*, 440 Mass 536, 800 NE2d 683 (2003) (voir dire questioning regarding pretrial publicity); *Com. v. Gerhartsreiter*, 82 Mass App 500, 507-508, 975 NE2d 890, 898 (2012) (pervasive pretrial publicity did not deprive defendant of fair trial where judge through careful voir dire process was able to empanel jurors who appeared impartial).

[8] *Com. v. Silva*, 455 Mass 503, 512-513, 918 NE2d 65, 77-78 (2009) (but failure to do so is not reversible error); *Com. v. Lopes*, 440 Mass 731, 735-738, 802 NE2d 97, 101-103 (2004) (although not required, common practice is for trial court to ask venire collectively whether they or a family member had ever been victim of violent

Individual voir dire has been mandated in the following categories of cases:

- Interracial rape or other sexual offense, with respect to racial prejudice.[9]
- Interracial murder, with respect to racial prejudice.[10]
- Cases of child sexual abuse, with respect to each prospective juror's own experience with such abuse.[11]

---

crime). See also *Com. v. Thomas*, 448 Mass 180, 186-187, 859 NE2d 813, 818 (2007) (no abuse of discretion in refusing to ask questions pertaining to violence against women).

[9] See *Com. v. Sanders*, 383 Mass 637, 640-641, 421 NE2d 436, 438 (1981); *Com. v. Hobbs*, 383 Mass 863, 873, 434 NE2d 633, 641 (1982) (interracial sexual abuse); *Com. v. Hooper*, 42 Mass App 730, 679 NE2d 602 (1997) (any case involving interracial sex and violence). But compare *Com. v. De La Cruz*, 405 Mass 269, 540 NE2d 168 (1989) (Hispanic defendant and white sexual assault victim was not "interracial").

[10] *Com. v. Benoit*, 452 Mass 212, 214, 892 NE2d 314, 318 (2008); *Com. v. Young*, 401 Mass 390, 398, 517 NE2d 130, 135 (1987). But compare *Com. v. Robinson*, 78 Mass App 714, 719-720, 942 NE2d 980, 986 (2011) (that defendant is black and the jury pool predominately white did not establish requisite foundation for individual voir in murder case with no overtly racial issues).

The mandate has not been extended to cases where defendant and victim are of different ethnic backgrounds. See *Com. v. Hunter*, 427 Mass 651, 654-655, 695 NE2d 653, 656-657 (1998); *Com. v. Pina*, 430 Mass 66, 72-74, 713 NE2d 944, 950-951 (1999) (Cape Verdian defendant failed to establish that he was of different race from white Portuguese victim; fact that some members of community might consider Cape Verdians "black" did not suggest substantial risk of bias). See also *Com. v. Companonio*, 445 Mass 39, 52-53, 833 NE2d 136, 146-147 (2005) (defendant, victim, and witnesses were Cuban immigrants and there was no suggestion that ethnicity played any part in the killing).

The Supreme Judicial Court has also declined to extend the mandatory voir dire rule to other interracial crimes such as armed robbery or assault and battery by means of a dangerous weapon. See *Com. v. LaFaille*, 430 Mass 44, 49-53, 712 NE2d 590, 594-597 (1999).

[11] *Com. v. Flebotte*, 417 Mass 348, 353-356, 630 NE2d 265, 268-270 (1994). See also *Com. v. Holloway*, 44 Mass App 469, 691 NE2d 985 (1998) (reversible error to refuse rape defendant's request to interview jurors individually as to whether they or a member of their families had been victims of sexual assault). But see *Com. v. Sanchez*, 423 Mass 591, 594-595, 670 NE2d 377, 379-380 (1996) (*Flebotte* not retroactive); *Com. v. DiRusso*, 60 Mass App 235, 236, 800 NE2d 1067, 1069 (2003) (trial judge not required in indecent assault on child case to inquire individually whether any juror had been victim of sexual abuse in absence of request from counsel); *Com. v. Whiting*, 59 Mass App 104, 106, 794 NE2d 642, 644 (2003) (trial judge not required in indecent assault on child case to inquire individually whether friends or family members had been victims of sexual abuse); *Com. v. Place*, 81 Mass App 229, 233-234, 961 NE2d 597, 601 (2012) (no abuse of discretion where trial judge refused in child rape case to excuse juror who disclosed that his son had been sexually assaulted 20 years before, but was assured by juror he could be impartial). Broad discretion is permitted in determining what questions to ask on this sensitive issue. *Com. v. Vickery*, 82 Mass App 234,

- Cases involving the insanity defense, with respect to any opinion that would prevent the juror from returning a verdict of not guilty by reason of insanity.[12]

The courts have declined to extend the categories of cases for which individual voir dire is mandatory to domestic violence crimes,[13] although it has suggested that "in many instances, individual voir dire on the issue of domestic violence may well be the more appropriate procedure."[14]

In cases where the victim is a homosexual or bisexual, the subject of juror attitudes toward those groups "requires careful attention," but individual voir dire is not mandated.[15] A trial court is not required to conduct individual voir dire regarding prospective jurors' ability to remain impartial after hearing prior bad act evidence (see § 4.4.6, infra).[16] And, in any event, the party seeking the inquiry must show

---

972 NE2d 29 (2012) (trial judge's questioning was adequate even though two prospective jurors were not specifically asked about whether they themselves had been victims).

[12] *Com. v. Bishop*, 461 Mass 586, 591-593, 963 NE2d 88, 93-95 (2012); *Com. v. Seguin*, 421 Mass 243, 249, 656 NE2d 1229, 1233 (1995) The rule applies only to cases in which defendant seeks a verdict of not guilty by reason of insanity; the court has declined to expand it to cases where evidence of mental illness or impairment is presented in an effort to obtain a verdict of murder in the second degree. See *Com. v. Ashman*, 430 Mass 736, 740, 723 NE2d 510, 514 (2000); *Com. v. Morales*, 440 Mass 536, 549, 800 NE2d 683, 694 (2003).

[13] See *Com. v. Reavis*, 465 Mass 875, 885-890, 992 NE2d 304, 313-316 (2013) (defendant was not entitled to question each member of panel about their experience with domestic violence in murder prosecution charging defendant with stabbing wife during altercation); *Com. v. Lao*, 443 Mass 770, 778, 824 NE2d 821, 828 (2005) (same); *Com. v. Carvalho*, 88 Mass App 840, 844-845, 43 NE3d 340, 346 (2016) (trial judge not required to question jurors about their experience with domestic violence orders).

[14] *Com. v. Reavis*, supra, 465 Mass at 890 n.10, 992 NE2d at 316 n.10.

[15] *Com. v. Plunkett*, 422 Mass 634, 641, 664 NE2d 833, 838 (1996). See also *Toney v. Zarynoff's, Inc.*, 52 Mass App 554, 557-561, 755 NE2d 301, 306-309 (2001) (where there is a possibility of prejudice against homosexual litigants in civil case, the better practice is to question prospective jurors).

[16] *Com. v. Kater (Kater VII)*, 432 Mass 404, 412-414, 734 NE2d 1164, 1174-1175 (2000), *habeas petition denied in Kater v. Maloney*, 459 F3d 56, 65-67 (1st Cir 2006).

For juror screening regarding anticipated evidence of gang activity, see *Com. v. Akara*, 465 Mass 245, 268-269, 988 NE2d 430, 449 (2013); *Com. v. Phim*, 462 Mass 470, 477-478, 969 NE2d 663, 670 (2012) (judge limited any prejudicial effect of gang affiliation evidence by asking jurors at voir dire if it would affect their impartiality); *Com. v. Wallace*, 460 Mass 118, 124, 949 NE2d 908, 913-914 (2011) (specific screening not required where there was no indication before trial that gang affiliation would become an issue); *Com. v. Rosario*, 460 Mass 181, 194-195, 950 NE2d 407, 419 (2011), *habeas*

more than mere speculation concerning a possible improper influence.[17]

Individual voir dire should be conducted in open court (pursuant to the Sixth Amendment to the United States Constitution) and in the presence of defendant and counsel;[18] spectators may be barred only in

---

denied, Rosario v. Roden, 2014 WL 7409584 (D Mass 2014) (judge appropriately questioned juror regarding her fear of being followed in murder trial involving gang activity); *Com. v. Pytou Heang*, 458 Mass 827, 856, 942 NE2d 927, 950-951 (2011) (trial judge's questioning of prospective jurors regarding whether evidence of gang activity would prejudice them did not taint the jury, even though such evidence was ultimately barred at trial); *Com. v. Weeks*, 77 Mass App 1, 927 NE2d 10213 (2010) (judge's decision not to question prospective jurors about gang membership did not create substantial risk of miscarriage of justice even though evidence of defendant's gang affiliation was admitted).

For screening regarding the so-called "CSI effect," i.e., jurors' expectation that scientific evidence will be presented to prove guilt, see *Com. v. Gray*, 465 Mass 330, 337-341, 990 NE2d 528, 536-538 (2013) (rejecting defendant's claim that voir dire questions concerning lack of DNA or fingerprint evidence tainted the jury; but expressing skepticism about the need for such questions); *Com. v. Perez*, 460 Mass 683, 688-691, 954 NE2d 1, 8-11 (2011) (no abuse of discretion in questioning prospective jurors about whether they believed Commonwealth was required to present scientific evidence).

[17] *Com. v. Mitchell*, 89 Mass App 13, 30-31, 45 NE3d 111, 126 (2016).

[18] See *Com. v. Dyer*, 460 Mass 728, 734-736, 955 NE2d 271, 280-282 (2011) (but defendant waived any argument that his right to public trial was violated where judge conducted voir dire in chambers, as defendant and counsel were present and judge moved to air-conditioned chambers to avoid heat in courtroom); *Com. v. Greineder*, 458 Mass 207, 219-234, 936 NE2d 372, 383-393 (2010) (finding that voir dire was not closed to the public or media by action of the court); *Com. v. Horton*, 434 Mass 823, 831, 753 NE2d 119, 127 (2001); *Com. v. Dosanjos*, 52 Mass App 531, 535, 754 NE2d 746, 749 (2001) (exclusion of defendant was harmless). Compare *Com. v. Cohen*, 456 Mass 94, 117, 921 NE2d 906, 925-926 (2010) (courtroom was improperly partially closed during jury selection); *Com. v. White*, 85 Mass App 491, 11 NE3d 628 (2014) (closure of courtroom during general questioning of potential jurors was no de minimis and thus violated defendant's Sixth amendment right).

Defense counsel may waive, with or without defendant's express consent, the right to public trial during jury selection where it is a reasonable trial strategy. *Com. v. Lang*, 473 Mass 1, 8-9, 38 NE3d 262, 268-269 (2015) (defendant waived his right to public trial where his experienced trial counsel was aware that the courtroom was routinely closed during empanelment and did not object); *Com. v. Fritz*, 472 Mass 341, 345-347, 34 NE3d 705, 709-711 (2015) (noting prior practice in Suffolk Superior Court of excluding public and media during empanelment); *Com. v. Alebord*, 467 Mass 106, 113, 4 NE2d 248, 255 (2014) (defense counsel was aware of court practice of closing courtroom during empanelment, and did not object); *Com. v. Morganti*, 467 Mass 96, 4 NE3d 241 (2014) (defendant waived error in trial court's closure of courtroom during jury selection, where defense counsel was aware of closure and did not object); *Com. v. Lavoie*, 464 Mass 83, 88-89, 981 NE2d 192, 197-198 (2013).

The defendant after conviction may claim that his attorney provided ineffective assistance of counsel for failing to object to the closure of the courtroom. In order to obtain relief, however, defendant must show the substantial likelihood of a miscarriage

limited circumstances and with specific determinations to justify it.[19] A defendant asserting a claim of violation of the right to public trial during empanelment bears the burden of showing that the courtroom was closed.[20]

The judge enjoys considerable discretion in the scope and nature of individual voir dire questions put to the prospective jurors, and need not ask specific questions framed by defense counsel or ask all prospective jurors the same questions.[21] It has been recognized that when requesting individual voir dire based on possible racial or other prejudice, a defendant runs the risk that the questions themselves "may activate latent racial bias in certain prospective jurors or may insult others without uncovering evidence of bias in hard-core bigots who refuse to acknowledge their prejudice."[22]

When a judge determines that the jury may have been exposed during the course of trial to material beyond the record or other influences that raise a serious risk of prejudice, the judge should conduct a voir dire to determine the nature and extent of the exposure and potential prejudicial effect.[23] Because the determination of a juror's impartiality is essentially one of the credibility and demeanor, the trial

---

of justice. *Com. v. Penn*, 472 Mass 610, 622-623, 36 NE3d 552, 563-564 (2015). Compare *Com. v. Celester*, 473 Mass 553, 578, 45 NE3d 539, 560 (2016) (defense counsel's ignorance of public trial right did not constitute ineffective assistance of counsel).

The exclusion of persons identified as witnesses is generally not considered to be partial closure of the courtroom; but such exclusion would ordinarily not include jury empanelment proceedings. See *Com. v. Buckman*, 461 Mass 24, 29 n.2, 957 NE2d 1089, 1096 n.2 (2011).

A judge may properly decide that prospective jurors should not be asked answer certain questions in open court where the answers may embarrass them (such as racial bias questions) or reveal private information, but such answers should be preserved in the record. *Com. v. Shea*, 460 Mass 163, 169, 950 NE2d 393, 399-400 (2011).

For further discussion of the requirement for public trial, see § 6.6, infra.

[19] *Com. v. Alebord*, supra, 467 Mass at 111 n.12, 4 NE2d at 254 n.12.

[20] *Com. v. Cadet*, 473 Mass 173, 179, 40 NE3d 1015, 1021 (2015).

[21] See *Com. v. Entwistle*, 463 Mass 205, 223-225, 973 NE2d 115, 129-130 (2012).

[22] *Com. v. Prunty*, 462 Mass 295, 314, 968 NE2d 361, 377 (2012).

[23] See *Com. v. Roman*, 470 Mass 85, 95-97, 18 NE3d 1069, 1077-1079 (2014) (trial judge's determination after individual voir dire that jurors during murder trial were unaffected by troublesome behavior by defendant's family was not abuse of discretion); *Com. v. Meas*, 467 Mass 434, 451-452, 5 NE2d 864, 879(2014) (rock thrown through window of juror's car, with possible connection to defendant's gang); *Com. v. Womack*, 457 Mass 268, 278-281, 929 NE2d 943, 952-954 (2010) (reports of juror intimidation); *Com. v. Blanchard*, 88 Mass App 637, 638-640, 41 NE3d 746, 748-750 (2015) (trial judge acted within her discretion when, after determining the jurors had

judge's determination is given great deference on appeal.[24] On the matter of proving extraneous influences upon jurors, see § 5.7, infra.[25]

Challenges for cause must be raised in a timely fashion after voir dire and before the jurors are seated.[26] For an extensive discussion of challenges for cause, see *Com. v. Long*, 419 Mass 798, 647 NE2d 1162 (1995).[27] For the process of removal of a deliberating juror for cause,

---

been exposed to a binder containing motions in limine with documents and photographs excluded at trial as well as transcripts of jail telephone calls, the judge conducted individual voir dires and instructed the jury to resume deliberations disregarding the binder and with new verdict slips).

[24] *Com. v. Cassino*, 474 Mass 85, 97, 48 NE3d 27, 38 (2016).

[25] See also *Com. v. Federici*, 427 Mass 740, 746-747, 696 NE2d 111, 116 (1998); *Com. v. Caldwell*, 45 Mass App 42, 694 NE2d 1309 (1998).

[26] *Com. v. Bryant*, 447 Mass 494, 498-499, 852 NE2d 1072, 1075-1076 (2006). A defect in jury empanelment, including voir dire, does not warrant reversal unless defendant objects to it "as soon as possible after its discovery or after it should have been discovered and unless [he] has been specially injured or prejudiced thereby." GL 234A, § 74. See also *Com. v. Seng*, 456 Mass 490, 495, 924 NE2d 285, 291 (2010); *Com. v. Mora*, 82 Mass App 575, 578-579, 976 NE2d 196, 200-201 (2012) (dismissal of six prospective jurors who expressed suspicion of testimony from informant witnesses). Compare *Com. v. Hinds*, 457 Mass 83, 92, 927 NE2d 1009, 1016-1017 (2010) (no objection). Where a defendant fails to challenge a juror for cause, the questions of impartiality of that juror and the adequacy of voir dire are waived. *Com. v. McCoy*, 456 Mass 838, 842, 926 NE2d 1143, 1151 (2010).

[27] See also *Com. v. Hunt*, 462 Mass 807, 820-821, 971 NE2d 768, 779-780 (2012) (prospective juror's statements that he believed the SDP law was too lenient and that the medical community could not predict future dangerousness warranted his excusal for cause); *Com. v. Shea*, 460 Mass 163, 168 n.4, 950 NE2d 393, 399 n.4 (2011) (no abuse of discretion where judge denied defendant's motion to excuse juror who disclosed during trial that he and state ballistics expert used to live in same town and were friends but had not spoken in eight years); *Com. v. Ruell*, 459 Mass 126, 136-138, 943 NE2d 447, 455-456 (2011) (mere fact that prospective juror sympathized with the elderly and had a family member who had been a victim of violence did not constitute sufficient cause for exclusion in trial for murder of elderly woman; nor did fact that another was a firefighter and murder charge was accompanied by arson charge); *Com. v. Gambora*, 457 Mass 715, 731-732, 933 NE2d 50, 62-63 (2010) (dismissal of seated Hispanic juror before she was sworn was proper where she was observed speaking with woman who then spoke to defendant's family, and was not forthcoming when questioned about the incident); *Com. v. Auguste*, 414 Mass 51, 605 NE2d 819 (1992) (discussing obligation of judge to adequately question venirepersons who expressed concerns about impartiality); *Com. v. Dupont*, 75 Mass App 605, 606-611, 915 NE2d 1078, 1079-1082 (2009) (trial judge had ample cause to dismiss prospective juror on ground of bias where he had supported district attorney's opponent in recent election); *Com. v. Young*, 73 Mass App 479, 487, 899 NE2d 838, 845-846 (2009), *habeas denied*, 2012 WL 3638824 (D Mass 2012) (judge acted properly in dismissing unsworn juror on ground her strong body odor would interfere in other jurors' ability to concentrate); *Com. v. Seabrooks*, 433 Mass 439, 442-445, 743 NE2d 831, 835-837 (2001) (exposure to pretrial publicity); *Com. v. Clark*, 432 Mass 1, 17-19, 730 NE2d 872, 887-888 (2000) (rejecting claim that jurors who visited roadside memorial for state trooper homicide victim should have been excused); *Com. v. John*, 442 Mass 329, 339-340, 812

see GL 234A, § 39.[28] For the problem of the sleeping juror, see *Com. v. Beneche*, 458 Mass 61, 77-79, 933 NE2d 951, 966 (2010).[29] For the problem of jurors who fail to disclose their criminal records, see *Com. v. Hampton*, 457 Mass 152, 165-171, 928 NE2d 917, 927-931 (2010).[30]

GL 234A, § 3 prohibits exclusion of jurors on the basis of race, color, religion, sex, national origin, economic status, or

---

NE2d 1218, 1226-1227 (2004), *habeas denied*, 561 F3d 88 (1st Cir 2009) (judge reasonably determined after questioning juror who raised concern about her safety that there was no serious question about possible prejudice and no need for further voir dire); *Com. v. Chongarlides*, 62 Mass App 709, 819 NE2d 971 (2004) (no abuse of discretion in failing to excuse juror who stated she knew victim casually by virtue of living in same town and attending same high school); *Com. v. Fredette*, 56 Mass App 253, 255-260, 776 NE2d 464, 467-470 (2002) (reversal required where trial judge failed to respond effectively to juror's exposure to news program).

In questioning a juror about his ability to be fair, the judge must not inquire into the juror's assessment of a witness's credibility based on what the juror observed in court. *Com. v. Arana*, 453 Mass 214, 229-230, 901 NE2d 99, 111 (2009) (juror's observation of what he took to be coaching of witness by a spectator was not an extraneous influence).

[28] GL 234, § 26B was repealed as of May 2016. See also *Com. v. Freeman*, 442 Mass 779, 787-789, 817 NE2d 727, 735-736 (2004); *Com. v. Garcia*, 84 Mass App 760, 3 NE2d 1105 (2014) (trial court should not have discharged juror without determining that his emotional distress was unrelated to the deliberations).

[29] When a judge observes that a juror is asleep, or is provided reliable information to that effect, the judge is required to intervene to protect both the rights of the defendant as well as those of the Commonwealth. *Com. v. McGhee*, 470 Mass 638, 642-64625 NE3d 251, 255-258 (2015) (reversing conviction because the judge declined to conduct a voir dire of the juror identified as sleeping through testimony, or take any other steps to determine if the juror was fit) (extensive discussion); *Com. v. Lawton*, 82 Mass App 528, 542-544, 976 NE2d 160, 172-173 (2012). The judge has an obligation to conduct a sensitive voir dire to determine the extent to which the juror remains capable of fulfilling his or her obligation to render a verdict based on all of the evidence. *Com. v. Dancy*, 75 Mass App 175, 179-182, 912 NE2d 525, 531-532 (2009). For cases reversing convictions where the trial judge failed to conduct a voir dire of a juror identified as sleeping during trial see *Com. v. Braun*, 74 Mass App 904, 905 NE2d 124 (2009); *Com. v. Dyous*, 79 Mass App 508, 512-514, 947 NE2d 576, 580-581d (2011); *Com. v. Gonzalez*, 86 Mass App 253,15 NE3d 774 (2014). Compare *Com. v. Wood*, 469 Mass 266, 281, 14 NE3d 140, 155 (2014) (judge conducted thorough voir dire and determined juror was alert) and *Com. v. The Ngoc Tran*, 471 Mass 179, 27 NE3d 1261, 1271 (2015) (trial judge's designating sleeping juror as an alternate did not amount to substantial likelihood of miscarriage of justice).

[30] A defendant has no constitutional right to obtain the CORI records of potential jurors, even though the prosecutor has obtained such records. See *Com. v. Hampton*, supra, 457 Mass at 165, 928 NE2d at 927-928. See also *Com. v. Vasquez*, 462 Mass 827, 838-839, 971 NE2d 783, 794-795 (2012) (Commonwealth permitted to exercise peremptory challenge against juror who had not accurately disclosed his criminal record on juror questionnaire).

occupation.[31] "Physically handicapped persons shall serve except where the court finds such service is not feasible."

§ 1.10 Discriminatory Use of Peremptory Challenges

Peremptory challenges, which require no statement of reason, cannot be used by either the prosecution or defense to exclude prospective jurors solely by virtue of their race, ethnicity, or gender.[1] The prohibition apples in civil cases as well.[2] Neither age[3] nor "persons of color" (combining African Americans and Hispanics)[4] constitute suspect categories for purposes of this doctrine. The Supreme Judicial Court has not reached the question whether sexual orientation or transgender status are forbidden categories for this purpose.[5]

The party raising the issue must demonstrate a prima facie case by showing: (1) a pattern of conduct whereby prospective jurors who have been challenged peremptorily are members of a discrete protected group, and (2) a likelihood that they are being excluded solely on the basis of their group membership.[6] Factors in this assessment include the numbers and percentage of group members excluded, as well as the common group membership of the defendant and the

---

[31] Thus students are not to be excused simply on that basis. *Com. v. Brown*, 449 Mass 747, 772, 872 NE2d 711 (2007). But compare *Com. v. Oppenheim*, 86 Mass App 359, 372-373, 16 NE3d 502, 513 (2014) (trial court did not violate statute by identifying full-time student status as an available, but automatic, ground of hardship).

§ 1.10 [1] *Batson v. Kentucky*, 476 US 79 (1986); *Gray v. Brady*, 592 F3d 296 (1st Cir 2010) (extensive analysis of prosecutor's challenges to multiple-minority group members); *Com v. Long*, 419 Mass 798, 806, 647 NE2d 1162, 1167-1168 (1995) (Hispanic origin); *Com. v. LeClair*, 429 Mass 313, 319, 708 NE2d 107, 112 (1999) (gender); *Com. v. Soares*, 377 Mass 461, 486, 387 NE2d 499, 515 (1979) (race).

[2] *Gates v. Flood*, 57 Mass App 739, 743, 785 NE2d 1289, 1292-1293 (2003).

[3] *Gates v. Flood*, supra.

[4] *Com. v. Sanchez*, 79 Mass App 189, 193, 944 NE2d 625, 628-629 (2011), *habeas denied*, 2013 WL 593960 (D Mass 2013), *vacated and remanded*, *Sanchez v. Roden*, 753 F3d 279 (1st Cir 2014).

[5] See *Com. v. Smith*, 450 Mass 395, 405, 879 NE2d 87, 96 (2008).

[6] See, e.g., *Com. v. Benoit*, 452 Mass 212, 218-219, 892 NE2d 314, 321 (2008); *Com. v. Maldonado*, 439 Mass 460, 462-467, 788 NE2d 968, 971-975 (2003); *Com. v. Rodriguez*, 431 Mass 804, 811, 731 NE2d 71, 77-78 (2000) (defendant's use of ninth straight peremptory to strike a female juror established prima facie case even though jury venire contained disproportionate number of women and defendant did not challenge five women). Compare *Com. v. Suarez*, 59 Mass App 111, 114, 794 NE2d 647, 650 (2003) (no pattern of exclusion of Hispanic jurors); *Com. v. Smith*, 58 Mass App 166, 174, 788 NE2d 977, 985 (2003), *rev'd on other grounds*, 543 US 462 (2005) (no pattern of gender-based strikes).

jurors excluded and of the victim and the remaining jurors,[7] and the seating of similarly situated jurors from outside the allegedly targeted group.[8] The fact that *some* members of the targeted group are seated does not defeat a prima facie case.[9] A cross-racial trial setting is not required in order to establish a prima facie case.[10]

In appropriate circumstances, such as the paucity of African Americans in the venire, a prima facie case can be established based even on a single peremptory challenge.[11]

If the judge determines that a sufficient showing has been made that it is likely a prospective juror has been excluded because of membership in a discrete group, the burden shifts to the allegedly offending party to provide a group-neutral reason for challenging the prospective juror, such as his or her occupation.[12] The reason must be "clear and reasonably specific" and must be "personal to the juror and

---

[7] See *Com. v. Issa*, 466 Mass 1, 8-10, 992 NE2d 336, 344-345 (2013) (trial judge did not abuse discretion by not requiring prosecutor to explain challenge to only African-American male juror, because judge had learned during voir dire that juror had been arrested 13 years before; but urging trial judges to require prosecutor to put explanation for challenge on record, and make appropriate findings of fact); *Com. v. Garrey*, 436 Mass 422, 428, 765 NE2d 725, 733 (2002); *Com. v. Mason*, 85 Mass App 114, 5 NE3d 1262 (2014) (information elicited during voir dire supported trial court's determination that Commonwealth's strike of two of three African-American prospective jurors was not based on race, but because of their experiences with criminal justice system).

[8] *Sanchez v. Roden*, supra, 753 F3d at 302.

[9] *Id.* at 289, 299.

[10] *Com. v. Carvalho*, 88 Mass App 840, 843, 43 NE3d 340, 345 (2016).

[11] *Com. v. Garrey.*, supra, 436 Mass at 428-429, 765 NE2d at 733-734.; *Com. v. Carvalho*, 88 Mass App 840, 842, 43 NE3d 340, 344 (2016) (defense counsel's challenge to sole minority juror). See, e.g., *Com. v. Rodriguez*, 457 Mass 461, 931 NE2d 20 (2010) (challenge to only Hispanic juror on venire); *Com. v. Benoit*, 452 Mass 212, 218, 214, 892 NE2d 314, 321 (2008) (challenge to the only African-American juror in case involving black defendant and white murder victim); *Com. v. Van Winkle*, 443 Mass 230, 236, 820 NE2d 220, 227 (2005) (judge could properly require defendant to provide explanation for challenge of sole African American in venire); *Com. v. Curtiss*, 424 Mass 78, 79, 676 NE2d 431, 432 (1997) (disallowed white defendant's challenge to only black potential juror); *Com. v. Fryar*, 414 Mass 732, 737, 610 NE2d 903, 907 (1993) (prosecutor's use of peremptory challenge against only eligible black venireperson). But compare *Com. v. Roche*, 44 Mass App 372, 378, 691 NE2d 946, 951 (1998) (challenge to single prospective juror within class does not, by itself, constitute prima facie showing of impropriety in all circumstances).

[12] *Com. v. Garrey*, supra, 436 Mass at 429-430, 765 NE2d at 734; *Com. v. Walker*, 69 Mass App 137, 142-144, 866 NE2d 958, 963-964 (2007) (prosecutor's proffered reason for strikes, that prospective jurors had family members who had been arrested but did not disclose that in questionnaires, was group-neutral). Compare *Com. v. Burnett*, 418 Mass 769, 642 NE2d 294 (1994) (prosecutor's explanation that "people who work with young people have certain feelings about youth and crime" should not have been accepted).

not based on the juror's group affiliation."[13] The party challenging the use of the peremptory strikes must then be given the chance to rebut the proffered explanation as a mere pretext.[14] The judge is required to make an independent evaluation of the reasons and determine whether they are bona fide or pretextual.[15]

The courts have stressed the importance of the judge making a clear finding on the record as to whether a prima facie case has been made out, and, if so, whether the reason given for removal is adequate and genuine.[16] Mere assumptions based on a group characteristic such as race will not suffice as a neutral reason for the strike.[17]

---

[13] *Com. v. Garrey*, supra, 436 Mass at 428, 765 NE2d at 733. See also *Com. v. LeClair*, 429 Mass 313, 319-320, 708 NE2d 107, 112-113 (1999); *Com. v. Long*, 419 Mass 798, 806, 647 NE2d 1162, 1167-1168 (1995); *Com. v. Pasteur*, 66 Mass App 812, 825, 850 NE2d 1118, 1131 (2006).

[14] See *Com. v. LeClair*, supra, 429 Mass at 323, 708 NE2d at 114; *Com. v. Burnett*, 418 Mass 769, 642 NE2d 294 (1994); *Com. v. Futch*, 38 Mass App 174, 178, 647 NE2d 59, 62 (1995). See generally *Aspen v. Bissonnette*, 480 F3d 571 (1st Cir 2007) (extensive discussion).

[15] *Com. v. Prunty*, 462 Mass 295, 968 NE2d 361 (2012) (trial court could determine that white defendant's proffered reason for peremptory strike of only African-American potential juror was a sham, where murder victim was African American and reason offered was that juror was a teacher who might not be impartial regarding young men involved with drugs); *Com. v. Rodriguez*, 457 Mass 461, 473, 931 NE2d 20, 33(2010) (prosecutor's reason for challenging only Hispanic juror was based on her experience with the court system, and failure to reveal them); *Thaler v. Haynes*, 130 S. Ct. 1171 (2010) (where explanation for challenge is based on prospective juror's demeanor, judge should take into account his own observations of juror, but is not required to reject explanation if he did not observe or cannot recall juror's demeanor); *Com. v. Benoit*, 452 Mass 212, 221-226, 214, 892 NE2d 314, 321-326 (2008) (judge's findings regarding the adequacy of the prosecutor's stated reasons were simply conclusions, and entitled to no deference, and since the Commonwealth did not meet its burden of countering the prima facie finding of improper use of the peremptory challenge, defendant's conviction is reversed); *Com. v. Douglas*, 75 Mass App 643, 649-650, 915 NE2d 1111, 1117-1118 (2009) (reversal required where trial judge failed to make specific findings on adequacy of prosecutor's race-neutral explanation for challenging African-American prospective juror).

[16] *Com. v. Rodriguez*, 457 Mass 461, 471, 931 NE2d 20, 32 (2010); *Com. v. Povez*, 94 Mass App 660, 666, 1 NE3d 774, 779 (2013) (record must reflect judge's consideration of both the adequacy and genuineness of the proffered explanation; reversing conviction because of judge's contradictory statements on record regarding adequacy of prosecutor's explanation for strike of prospective Hispanic juror)). Compare *Com. v. Scott*, 463 Mass 561, 571, 977 NE2d 490, 499 (2012) (judge implicitly agreed with prosecutor that there was no pattern of discrimination, as minority jurors had been seated without challenge the previous day, and thus did not require prosecutor to state reason for challenge).

[17] See *Com. v. Prunty*, supra, 462 Mass at 311-314, 968 NE2d at 375-377.

When a defendant uses a peremptory challenge to excuse a juror that the judge improperly refused to excuse for cause, and defendant is then forced to accept a juror he would have challenged peremptorily, the defendant is entitled to a new trial without a showing of prejudice.[18]

[18] See *Com. v. Clark*, 446 Mass 620, 629, 846 NE2d 765, 773 (2006); *Com. v. Berardi*, 88 Mass App 466, 473-474, 38 NE3d 765, 771-772 (2015). The erroneous denial of a peremptory challenge requires automatic reversal, without a showing of prejudice. See *Com. v. Hampton*, 457 Mass 152, 164, 928 NE2d 917, 927 (2010). But see *Com. v. Berardi*, supra. Where the challenged juror does not actually participate in the deliberations, there is no reversible error. See *Com. v. Bockman*, 442 Mass 757, 762, 817 NE2d 717, 722 (2004) (juror excused on first day of testimony); *Com. v. Smith*, 461 Mass 438, 442-443, 961 NE2d 566, 569-570 (2012) (potential juror was designated an alternate).

CHAPTER

2

JUDICIAL ADMISSIONS, JUDICIAL NOTICE, and BINDING TESTIMONY

§ 2.1 Introduction

This chapter discusses two ways of establishing facts without presenting evidence: (1) propositions of fact that the opponent has conclusively admitted are true (judicial admissions[1]) and (2) propositions of law and of fact that are unquestionably true and are either well known or easily confirmed (judicial notice). This chapter also discusses the subject of binding testimony.

A. JUDICIAL ADMISSIONS

§ 2.2 Effect of Judicial Admissions

Judicial admissions are acts (including failures to act) and statements of a party or his attorney, made in connection with court proceedings that conclusively determine an issue. They relieve the proponent who offers them of the necessity of presenting other evidence on the issue. Moreover, they preclude the party who made the admission from offering contrary evidence unless the court allows the party to withdraw the admission.

§ 2.3 Admissions Under the Massachusetts Rules of Civil Procedure

§ 2.3.1 Rule 36

Mass R Civ P 36 (a) provides that a party may serve upon any other party a written request for the admission of the truth of any facts, the application of law to fact, and the genuineness of any document. The matter must be relevant to the pending action, and the admission is made only for the purpose of the pending action. The opposing party has 30 days to respond. A request under Rule 36 need not be served by registered mail. A party may not give lack of information or of knowledge as a reason for failing to admit or deny unless he states

---

§ 2.1 [1] For a discussion of the admissibility of statements by a party opponent ("admissions") generally, see § 8.6.

that he has made a reasonable inquiry and that the information known or readily obtainable by him is not sufficient to enable him to admit or deny.

The rule allows the requesting party to move to determine the sufficiency of the answer or objection. If the court determines that the objection is not justified, it can order that an answer be made; if it determines that an answer is deficient, it can order that the matter be admitted. Sanctions for noncompliance are prescribed in Mass R Civ P 37(c).

The rule provides that any matter admitted is "conclusively established" for the purpose of the pending action. The admission binds the party making it, as well as the one requesting it. Rule 36 (b), however, authorizes the court, under certain prescribed conditions, to permit withdrawal or amendment of the admission. Rule 36 governs district, municipal, superior courts, and the Housing Court, suits of a civil nature in the Land Court, and proceedings seeking equitable relief in the Probate and Family Court.

Facts established by use of Rule 36 may be the basis, in whole or in part, of summary judgment proceedings under Mass R Civ P 56.

Responses to requests for admissions must be distinguished from answers to interrogatories in that admissions contained in answers to interrogatories are not binding upon the admitting party. At most, the answers of a party to interrogatories may be read by the other party into evidence at trial. See GL 231, § 89; Mass R Civ P 33(b).[1]

§ 2.3.2 *Rule 16*

Mass R Civ P 16 provides for a pretrial proceeding at which the parties may make admissions of fact and stipulate to the authenticity of documents, to avoid unnecessary proof. The court enters an order, which recites the action taken at the conference including, among other matters, any agreements made by the parties, and which limits the issues for trial to those not disposed of by admissions or agreements of counsel. The order controls the subsequent course of the action, unless modified at the trial to prevent manifest injustice.

---

§ 2.3 [1] *Federico v. Ford Motor Co.*, 67 Mass App 454, 461, n.8, 854 NE2d 448, 454 (2006) (Text cited).

Agreements and stipulations by the parties are binding, unless they are later vacated for good cause shown.[2]

See Mass R Crim P 11 for pretrial procedures in criminal cases in district and superior courts.[3]

§ 2.3.3 Rules 8(b) and 9(a)

Mass R Civ P 8(b) provides, in part: "The signature to an instrument set forth in any pleading shall be taken as admitted unless a party specifically denies its genuineness." The rule is consistent with GL 106, § 3-307 (Uniform Commercial Code), which requires a specific denial of genuineness.

Mass R Civ P 8(b) also provides, in part: "An allegation in any pleading that a place is a public way shall be taken as admitted unless a party specifically denies such allegation."

As to matters pertaining to fiduciary capacity or corporate existence, Mass R Civ P 9(a) provides that it is not necessary to aver the capacity of a party to sue or be sued, individually or in a representative capacity, or the legal existence of an organization that is made a party. The opposing party is required to raise the issue by a specific negative averment. It would appear that a judicial admission will come about when the issue is not so raised.

§ 2.4 Statutory Admissions

§ 2.4.1 Demand for Admission of Fact or Execution of Paper

GL 231, § 69, provides for admissions in district court actions not governed by the District-Municipal Courts Rules of Civil Procedure. Admissions made in response to a notice to admit are, unless the court

---

[2] See *Com. v. Buswell*, 468 Mass 92, 105, 9 NE3d 276, 286 (2014) (Commonwealth relieved from stipulation not to introduce nude photos that constituted prior bad act evidence when defendant made defense of entrapment); *Slade v. Slade*, 43 Mass App 376, 682 NE2d 1385 (1997) and cases cited therein; *Norton v. Vaughan*, 13 Mass App 1075, 435 NE2d 634 (1982) (plaintiff bound by counsel's admission that there was no evidence of medical malpractice, case dismissed).

[3] See *Com. v. Walorz*, 79 Mass App 132, 134, 944 NE2d 1061, 1063 (2011) (defendant was bound by written and signed stipulation made just before trial began).

otherwise directs, conclusive on the admitting party.[1] Strict compliance with the terms of § 69 is required for the statute to have effect.[2] The trial judge has power to relieve a party of binding admissions improvidently made due to lack of diligence of his counsel.[3] Facts admitted under § 69 do not preclude a finding of other facts by a judge.[4]

§ 2.4.2 *Pleadings as Admissions*

GL 231, § 87, provides: "In any civil action pleadings shall not be evidence on the trial, but the allegations therein shall bind the party making them." Matters admitted in the pleadings are not open to dispute.[5]

The word *pleadings* under § 87 includes matter filed in response to a motion for a more definite statement under Mass R Civ P 12(e), documents or articles attached to the pleadings and incorporated by reference,[6] but not formal allegations as to unliquidated damages made by the attorney without special instructions from his client.[7] Pleadings amended or withdrawn are not binding and may not be used as evidence in the same case.[8]

However, such pleadings from another case may come in as evidence if otherwise competent. Pleadings from another case are admissible against the party who made them, see § 8.6.3, including from a case that has been discontinued.[9] Pleadings from another case

---

§ 2.4 [1] *Gishen v. Dura Corp.*, 362 Mass 177, 285 NE2d 117 (1972); *Snowden v. Cheltenham*, 337 Mass 295, 149 NE2d 606 (1958). Cf. Mass R Civ P 36 (discussed supra at § 2.3.1).

[2] *Plante v. Louro*, 345 Mass 456, 463, 187 NE2d 866, 871 (1963) (extensive discussion of the nature of this statute; affidavit of counsel rather than party was not compliance with the statute); *Deutsch v. Ormsby*, 354 Mass 485, 238 NE2d 339 (1968); *McElaney v. Hubby*, 3 Mass App 717, 323 NE2d 770 (1975).

[3] *Plante v. Louro*, supra.

[4] *Manoogian v. Manoogian*, 1 Mass App 825, 296 NE2d 516 (1973). For other cases discussing GL 231, § 69, see *Loew v. Minasian*, 361 Mass 390, 280 NE2d 688 (1972); *Merchants National Bank v. New York Life Ins. Co.*, 346 Mass 745, 196 NE2d 201 (1964); *Town Bank & Trust Co. v. Sheraton Investment Corp.*, 2 Mass App 852, 312 NE2d 592 (1974).

[5] *Willett v. Webster*, 337 Mass 98, 101, 105, 148 NE2d 267, 270, 272 (1958) (order for judgment given on the pleadings); *Provincetown Chamber of Commerce, Inc. v. Grace*, 14 Mass App 903, 436 NE2d 177 (1982).

[6] *H. P. Hood & Sons v. Whiting Milk Co.*, 345 Mass 287, 186 NE2d 904(1963); Mass R Civ P 10(c).

[7] *Maney v. Maney*, 340 Mass 350, 164 NE2d 146 (1960).

[8] *Harrington v. MTA*, 345 Mass 371, 187 NE2d 818 (1963).

[9] *Clarke v. Taylor*, 269 Mass 335, 168 NE 806 (1929).

introduced as statements by a party opponent are not judicial admissions and thus do not conclusively determine an issue.[10]

In *Com. v. Zuluaga*,[11] the court questioned whether the Commonwealth's statements made in opposition to a motion to suppress were judicial admissions. The court ruled that, in any event, it was not error for the trial court to relieve the Commonwealth of the consequences of having made them.[12]

While a party may be bound by allegations of fact he makes or admits, *Zaleski v. Zaleski*,[13] admissions as to allegations of law or jurisdictional facts are not binding, although admissions of allegations of mixed fact and law may conclude the issue.[14]

The prior practice under GL 231, §§ 87 and 90 (limited to the district courts by amendment in 1973 and repealed in 1975) was not changed by the enactment of the Massachusetts Rules of Civil Procedure (Mass R Civ P 8(e)).[15] The cases construing these statutes held that parties could plead on separate issues without being bound thereby on other issues and that such pleas could not be used as evidence with regard to other issues. One may plead inconsistent or alternative defenses without fear of making binding judicial admissions. An admission by one party does not bind a co-party, even if the coparty is his insurer.[16]

Although pleadings are binding on the party making them and findings to the contrary cannot be made,[17] the court may allow the party to amend where the contrary fact is established.[18]

Mass R Civ P 15 provides a liberal opportunity for a party to amend pleadings. Rule 15(a) allows amendment as a matter of right before a responsive pleading is served. Rules 15(b) through (d) deal with amendments to conform pleadings to the evidence and provide for supplemental pleadings. While amendments other than those specified in Rule 15(a) require leave of court or written consent, the rule states that leave to amend "shall be freely given when justice so

---

[10] *Hibernia Savings Bank v. Bomba*, 35 Mass App 378, 620 NE2d 787 (1993).

[11] *Com. v. Zuluaga*, 43 Mass App 629, 686 NE2d 463 (1997).

[12] *Id.*, 43 Mass App at 638.

[13] *Zaleski v. Zaleski*, 330 Mass 132, 111 NE2d 451 (1953).

[14] *Wasserman v. Tonelli*, 343 Mass 253, 178 NE2d 477 (1961).

[15] *Linthicum v. Archambault*, 379 Mass 381, 398 NE2d 482 (1979).

[16] *Kneeland v. Bernardi*, 317 Mass 517, 520, 58 NE2d 823, 824 (1945).

[17] *DeNunzio v. City Manager of Cambridge*, 341 Mass 420, 169 NE2d 877 (1960).

[18] *Wasserman v. Tonelli*, supra, 343 Mass at 253, 178 NE2d at 477; *Carson v. Brady*, 329 Mass 36, 40-41, 106 NE2d 1, 3-4 (1952).

requires."[19] Unexcused delay and prejudice to the opposing party may, however, justify the denial of a motion to amend.[20]

§ 2.5 Common-Law Admissions

The attorney for a party may make a judicial admission binding upon his client.[1] Such admissions may be made (a) by stipulations during the trial or before it, (b) by the opening statement of counsel at the trial, (c) by remarks or statements made by counsel during the trial, or (d) by conduct of counsel during the trial.

Otherwise, controvertible facts may be agreed to and eliminated as issues by stipulation.[2] A fact may be admitted prior to the trial under the authority of a court rule such as Mass R Civ P 16 or Mass R Crim P 11.[3] Ordinarily, stipulations made prior to trial or other than in open court must be in writing in order to be valid and binding. Neither the rules nor the statutes apply to agreements made in open court and acted on by the court. In a criminal trial a "stipulation concerning the existence of an element of the crime charged or of any material fact related to proof of the crime" must be "presented in some manner to the jury as part of the evidence of the case."[4]

Stipulations may have binding effect in subsequent parts of the same proceeding.[5] Compare *Com. v. Arsenault*[6] distinguishing stipulations from a retrial on a different theory of the case.

Either the trial court or the appellate court has power, in its discretion, to relieve a party from a stipulation improvidently made or one not conducive to justice.[7] The courts may discharge a stipulation

---

[19] See, e.g., *Sullivan v. Lantosca*, 409 Mass 796, 569 NE2d 822 (1991) and cases cited therein.

[20] See, e.g., *Mathis v. Massachusetts Electric Co.*, 409 Mass 256, 565 NE2d 1180 (1991) and cases cited therein.

§ 2.5 [1] *Lucia v. Water & Sewer Commissioners of Medford*, 332 Mass 468, 125 NE2d 776 (1955); *Lewis v. Sumner*, 54 Mass (13 Met.) 269 (1847).

[2] *Mirashefski v. White City Apartments, Inc.*, 343 Mass 774, 178 NE2d 30 (1961).

[3] GL 231, §§ 71 and 72, govern civil proceedings that are not "governed by the Massachusetts Rules of Civil Procedure or by the District-Municipal Courts Rules of Civil Procedure." These statutes provide for pretrial orders and written agreements of counsel in a manner similar to Mass R Civ P 16 and Mass R Crim P 11.

[4] *Com. v. Ortiz*, 466 Mass 475, 476, 995 NE2d 1100 (2013).

[5] *Household Fuel Corp. v. Hamacher*, 331 Mass 653, 121 NE2d 846 (1954); Wigmore § 2593 (Chad rev 1981).

[6] *Com. v. Arsenault*, 361 Mass 287, 298, 280 NE2d 129, 136 (1972).

[7] See *Pastene Wine & Spirits Co. v. Alcoholic Beverages Control Comm'n*, 401 Mass 612, 615, 518 NE2d 841, 843 (1988) (party claiming to have been misled by opposing

where fuller development of the facts is desired by the court.[8] In interpreting a stipulation that is unclear, a court should attempt to effectuate the parties' manifested intentions.[9]

Stipulations as to facts are to be distinguished from stipulations as to law. Stipulations as to questions of law are of no effect.[10] However, parties are bound by a stipulation that an item of evidence is admissible unless the court vacates it as improvident or not conducive to justice.[11]

An agreed statement of facts may be entered into by the parties and may serve as the basis of determination of their rights and obligations under, for example, the provisions of Mass R Civ P 56 (motions for summary judgment). Thus, an "agreed statement of facts" or a "case stated" involves an agreement as to all material ultimate facts upon which the rights of the parties depend; a stipulation as to facts involves an agreement as to certain facts with the remaining facts to be found from evidence submitted.

Distinguishable from a "case stated" and a stipulation of facts is a stipulation or agreement as to testimony or evidence. In the latter case, there is an agreement not as to the facts but as to the evidence of them. This leaves to the trier of fact the determination of those facts based on the agreed evidence and to the appellate court only the question of whether the evidence as stated warrants the finding of the trier of fact.[12]

Opening statements by counsel that fail to indicate that the party will establish a cause of action or defense have been construed as binding judicial admissions.[13] Mass R Civ P 50, which explicitly provides

---

counsel not relieved from stipulation where material information was readily discoverable); *Com. v. Walker*, 392 Mass 152, 466 NE2d 71 (1984) (stipulation that result of polygraph test would be admissible will not be enforced even if all parties have agreed in writing to admissibility); *Com. v. Lopes*, 85 Mass App 341, 10 NE3d 146 (trial court could decline to allow defendant to stipulate to all but one element of OUI while OAS); Gore *v. Daniel O'Connell's Sons, Inc.*, 17 Mass App 645, 649, 461 NE2d 256, 260 (1984) (Appeals Court vacated stipulation as "improvident and not conducive to justice").

[8] *Francesconi v. Planning Board of Wakefield*, 345 Mass 390, 187 NE2d 807 (1963).

[9] *Granby Heights Ass'n, Inc. v. Dean*, 38 Mass App 266, 647 NE2d 75 (1995).

[10] *Swift & Co. v. Hocking Valley Railway*, 243 US 281, 289, 37 S Ct 287, 290, 61 L Ed 722, 725-726 (1917); *Kolda v. National Ben Franklin Fire Ins. Co.*, 290 Mass 182, 195 NE 331 (1935); cf. *Marotta v. Board of Appeals*, 336 Mass 199, 143 NE2d 270 (1957).

[11] *Com. v. Sanchez*, 405 Mass 369, 377, 540 NE2d 1316, 1322 (1989).

[12] *Benmosche v. Board of Reg. in Medicine*, 412 Mass 82, 588 NE2d 621 (1992).

[13] *Cohen v. Suburban Sidney-Hill, Inc.*, 343 Mass 217, 178 NE2d 19 (1961) (judge properly granted directed verdict for defendant after hearing plaintiff's opening

for a motion for a directed verdict following the close of the opponent's evidence, does not by its terms preclude a motion for directed verdict at the close of an opening statement.

Remarks, statements, or admissions by counsel during the course of the trial will also be binding judicial admissions.[14] But it must appear with reasonable certainty that such an admission was made.[15] So, too, conduct by counsel during the course of the trial may constitute an admission.[16] An admission made by a party while testifying at the trial is distinguishable from the judicial admissions discussed above. A testimonial admission is not binding on the party making the admission in the sense that further evidence on the matter is irrelevant.[17]

Testimony by an expert witness does not bind the party who called him, and is not a judicial admission.[18]

§ 2.5.1 *Judicial Estoppel*

The Supreme Judicial Court has not yet thoroughly developed how it will treat the doctrine of judicial estoppel. The court has, however, indicated that the doctrine does preclude a party from asserting a position in one proceeding that is contrary to a position that the party previously asserted successfully in another proceeding.[19] Settlement

---

statement); cf. *Com. v. Sandler*, 368 Mass 729, 335 NE2d 903 (1975); *Mallard v. Waldman*, 340 Mass 288, 163 NE2d 658 (1960) (trial judge may refuse to grant a motion for a directed verdict).

[14] *Brocklesby v. Newton*, 294 Mass 41, 42-43, 200 NE 351, 352 (1936); *Labovitz v. Feinberg*, 47 Mass App 306, 713 NE2d 379 (1999) (subsequent counsel's statement in criminal case—that there was no allegation that plaintiff's former attorneys had coerced him to plead guilty—was a judicial admission binding against plaintiff in later malpractice action against former attorneys).

[15] *Marotta v. Board of Appeals*, 336 Mass 199, 201, 143 NE2d 270, 272 (1957).

[16] *Drinkwater v. D. Guschov Co.*, 347 Mass 136, 140, 196 NE2d 863, 865 (1964); *Owens v. Dinkins*, 345 Mass 106, 185 NE2d 645 (1962) (acquiescence by silence of counsel); *Dalton v. Post Publishing Co.*, 328 Mass 595, 105 NE2d 385 (1952) (choice of one theory of defense held waiver as to another). Cf. *Bouley v. Reisman*, 38 Mass App 118, 129, 645 NE2d 708, 715 (1995) (questions asked during cross-examination by party's attorney did not constitute a judicial admission).

[17] Cf. *Quinn v. Mar-Lees Seafood, LLC*, 69 Mass App 688, 871 NE2d 511 (2007) (court confuses concepts of judicial admissions and binding testimony, but correctly holds that party is not bound by his testimony regarding conclusions of law).

[18] *Turners Falls Ltd. v. Board of Assessors*, 54 Mass App 732, 738, 767 NE2d 629, 634 (2002) (Text cited).

[19] See *Bay State Gas Co. v. Dep't of Public Utilities*, 459 Mass 807, 818, 947 NE2d 1077, 1088 (2011); *Fay v. Federal National Mortgage Ass'n*, 419 Mass 782, 647 NE2d 422 (1995); *Com. v. McGilvery*, 74 Mass App 508, 908 NE2d 783 (2009) (Commonwealth

of a former action would not be defined as representing success for the purpose of invoking the doctrine of judicial estoppel.[20]

In *Otis v. Arbella Mutual Insurance Co.*,[21] the Court again explained that the doctrine cannot be defined with precision, but it should be employed whenever a "party is seeking to use the judicial process in an inconsistent way that courts should not tolerate."[22] Its application is a matter of discretion. The Court identified two fundamental elements for judicial estoppel to bar a claim or defense. First, the position asserted in the second litigation must be directly inconsistent, that is, mutually exclusive with the position taken originally.[23] Second, the

could not argue that amendment to complaint was one of form, when it had previously argued to Single Justice that it was one of substance); *Com. v. Gardner*, 67 Mass App 744, 856 NE2d 896 (2006) (Commonwealth could not charge defendant with unarmed robbery after prosecuting him for receiving the same stolen goods and he had pleaded guilty—convictions for stealing and receiving the same property would be inconsistent); *Tinkham v. Jenny Craig, Inc.*, 45 Mass App 567, 574, 699 NE2d 1255, 1259 (1998) (plaintiffs who sought remand to state court from federal court based on representation that claims were not greater than monetary threshold for diversity actions could not demand greater damages in state court). Cf. *Com. v. Boe*, 456 Mass 337, 341, n.7, 924 NE2d 239, 242 (2010) (commissioner of probation could challenge expungement of defendant's record, although district attorney's office had agreed to it, because they were different parties, the former in the judicial branch and the latter in the executive branch).

[20] *East Cambridge Savings Bank v. Wheeler*, 422 Mass 621, 664 NE2d 446 (1996); *Paixao v. Paixao*, 429 Mass 307, 708 NE2d 91 (1999) (judicial estoppel applies to oral separation agreements, but parties must acknowledge their assent to agreement in open court); *Basis Technology Corp. v. Amazon.com, Inc.*, 71 Mass App 29, 878 NE2d 952 (2008), the court noted that principles of judicial estoppel supported enforcement of a mid-trial settlement reported to the court in a commercial dispute.

[21] *Otis v. Arbella Mutual Ins. Co.*, 443 Mass 634, 824 NE2d 23 (2005).

[22] *Id.*, 443 Mass at 640, 824 NE2d at 29 (2005).

[23] See *Com. v. Middlemiss*, 465 Mass 627, 637, 989 NE2d 871, 879 (2013) (Commonwealth was not barred by judicial estoppel from arguing that victim's identification of one shooter at second trial was reliable because it had argued in earlier trial that victim's identification of second shooter was mistaken due to victim's blood alcohol level and blood loss, because these positions were not mutually exclusive); *Com. v. DiBenedetto*, 458 Mass 657, 672, 941 NE2d 580, 592 (2011) (Commonwealth not barred by judicial estoppel from arguing that evidence that defendant's sneakers contained DNA, which excluded victim as source, had little probative value on motion for new trial, when it had argued in closing argument at trial that substance on defendant's sneakers was victim's blood—closing argument was merely that this evidence offered a small bit of corroboration and was not "be-all and end-all," which was not "directly inconsistent" with its later position); *Choy v. Com.*, 456 Mass 146, 154, n.12, 927 NE2d 970, 978 (2010) (in dictum Court notes that pursuing joint venture theory at retrial after mistrial when original theory was principal liability would not be prohibited by judicial estoppel, "joint venture liability is not 'directly contrary' to principal liability"); *Com. v. Semedo*, 456 Mass 1, 18, 921 NE2d 57, 72 (2010) (confession by co-defendant that Commonwealth introduced before grand jury was not factually inconsistent with its position at trial with respect to defendant's role in joint venture, and

party must have succeeded in the first litigation in getting the court to adopt its position. The Court noted that this would almost always inevitably result in the party obtaining an unfair advantage in the second litigation. The Court noted that there may be exceptions, for example where the original position was taken in good faith and then new information surfaced, but it declined to catalogue possible exceptions.[24] It is not necessary for the party to have testified under oath to its position for judicial estoppel to apply.[25] The doctrine of judicial estoppel, however, may not be employed to support an argument that a court had subject matter jurisdiction when such jurisdiction was lacking.[26] Other decisions of the court have recognized the principle that "[a] party who has successfully maintained a certain position at a trial cannot in a subsequent trial between the same parties be permitted to assume a position relative to the same subject that is directly contrary to that taken at the first trial."[27]

Commonwealth did not prevail before grand jury on an inconsistent position); *Blanchette v. School Committee of Westwood*, 427 Mass 176, 692 NE2d 21 (1998) (no inconsistency in party's position); *Labonte v. Hutchins & Wheeler*, 424 Mass 813, 820, 678 NE2d 853 (1997) (if evidence creates a disputed issue of fact whether handicapped person can perform essential functions of job, then estoppel based on disability application is not appropriate in discrimination case); *Sandman v. McGrath*, 78 Mass App 800, 943 NE2d 945 (2011) (motorcyclist recovered large verdict from motorist for negligence, then took assignment of motorist's claims against lawyer and insurer; claim that defendants failed to prepare adequately for trial was judicially estopped because motorcyclist was real party in interest and had taken position at underlying trial that motorist was liable; claim that defendants had failed to explore settlement opportunities and convey them to motorist was not barred because not inconsistent with position motorcyclist had taken at trial).

[24] *Id.*, 443 Mass at 642, 824 NE 2d at 30. In *A.H. v. M.P.*, 447 Mass 828, 857 NE2d 1061 (2006), a former same-sex partner sought recognition of parental rights for custody and visitation. She claimed that the defendant mother was barred from contesting the petition by judicial estoppel because earlier in the litigation the defendant had sought child support from the plaintiff and her attorney had acknowledged that the plaintiff had "de facto parent status." The Court declined to impose judicial estoppel, noting that it "is not a principle that automatically prohibits a party from the rather unexceptional practice of assuming inconsistent positions in the same litigation as the facts and the state of the law evolve or as a party changes counsel." 447 Mass at 845, 857 NE2d at 1075. The Court also concluded, "general estoppel principles, while appropriate for commercial transactions," are "an unwieldy and inappropriate tool by which a judge may probe into the intimate, private realm of family life." 447 Mass at 846, 857 NE2d at 1076.

[25] *Id.*, 443 Mass at 646, 824 NE2d at 33.

[26] *Lee v. Mt. Ivy Press, L.P.*, 63 Mass App 538, 827 NE2d 727 (2005).

[27] *Gordon v. Lewitsky*, 333 Mass 379, 381, 131 NE2d 174 (1955) and see cases cited therein; *Spilios v. Cohen*, 38 Mass App 338, 340 n.2, 647 NE2d 1218, 1220 n.2

B. JUDICIAL NOTICE

§ 2.6 Proposed Massachusetts Rule of Evidence and Federal Rule of Evidence 201

Proposed Mass R Evid 201 provides:

> (a) *Scope of rule.* This rule governs only judicial notice of adjudicative facts.
>
> (b) *Kinds of facts.* A judicially noticed fact must be one not subject to reasonable dispute in that it is either
>
> (1) generally known within the territorial jurisdiction of the trial court or
>
> (2) capable of accurate and ready determination by resort to resources whose accuracy cannot reasonably be questioned.
>
> (c) *When discretionary.* A court may take judicial notice, whether requested or not.
>
> (d) *When mandatory.* A court shall take judicial notice if requested by a party and supplied with the necessary information.
>
> (e) *Opportunity to be heard.* A party is entitled upon timely request to an opportunity to be heard as to the propriety of taking judicial notice and the tenor of the matter noticed. In the absence of prior notification, the request may be made after judicial notice has been taken.
>
> (f) *Time of taking notice.* Judicial notice may be taken at any stage of the proceeding.
>
> (g) *Instructing jury.* In a civil action or proceeding, the court shall instruct the jury to accept as conclusive any fact judicially noticed. In a criminal case, the court shall instruct the jury that it may, but is not required to, accept as conclusive any fact judicially noticed.

Proposed Mass R Evid 201 is identical with Fed R Evid 201.[1] It is the only rule of evidence dealing with the subject of judicial notice. The rule provides for judicial notice of "adjudicative" facts, that is facts in issue in the dispute before the court. Matters that are material to the interpretation, determination, nature, and application of the law,

---

(1995) (collecting recent decisions supporting proposition that a party's affidavit, submitted to avoid summary judgment, may be disregarded where it directly contradicts that party's earlier statements made under oath, by deposition or otherwise).

§ 2.6 [1] See GL 30A, § 11(5), with respect to judicial notice in agency adjudications. With reference to judicial notice in the federal courts, in addition to Fed R Evid 201, see Fed R Civ P 44.1, Fed R Crim P 26.1.

whether it be constitutional, statutory, or judicial in nature, are not included; nor are matters necessary to judicial reasoning. The practice and power of the courts to consider matters legislative, political, or legal in nature as part of the process of dispute resolution and the determination of valid principles of law is unaffected by the limited scope of Rule 201.

§ 2.7 Meaning and Purpose of Judicial Notice

The purpose of a trial is to settle disputes according to law. To do this rationally, the court must be able to determine the relevant law and the relevant facts. The relevant law may range from well-known local statutes to remote foreign law and obscure municipal ordinances. The relevant facts may range from specific facts directly bearing on the case to propositions of generalized knowledge useful only to put the particular facts in a meaningful context. Much of this information is most efficiently obtained by way of evidence adduced at the trial. When information is permitted to influence the outcome of the case without its having been introduced in evidence—that is, when the information is already a part of the court's knowledge or when the court gets the information from an authoritative source not in evidence—the matter is said to have been judicially noticed. Matters are judicially noticed only when they are indisputably true.[1] Such matters are generally categorized as either being matters that the judge knows because of his judicial function, matters of common knowledge within the community, or subjects of generalized knowledge that are readily ascertainable from authoritative sources.

---

§ 2.7 [1] *Dimino v. Secretary of the Commonwealth*, 427 Mass 704, 707, 695 NE2d 659, 662 (1998). In considering a motion for judgment on the pleadings a court may consider facts of which judicial notice can be taken. It may take judicial notice of docket entries and papers filed in separate cases, but not of facts or evidence brought out in those separate actions. *Home Depot v. Kardas*, 81 Mass App 27, 958 NE2d 531 (2011).

§ 2.8 Matters Subject to Judicial Notice

§ 2.8.1 Law

a. Domestic Law

General or public law of the Commonwealth is judicially noticed without request.[1] But whether a public statute has been accepted in a particular locality will not be judicially noticed.[2]

It should be noticed that under GL 233, § 74, legislative acts of incorporation are "public acts" and therefore subject to judicial notice without request.[3]

Similarly, county and town limits are prescribed by public statutes. Thus, it is noticed that Suffolk is a Massachusetts county,[4] that the town of Springfield is in Hampshire County,[5] and that Milton is very close to Boston.[6] The identity of government officers of any considerable importance (including the medical examiner of a county, clerk of the state senate, and federal deputy controller of the currency) is judicially noticed.[7]

---

§ 2.8 [1] *DiMaggio v. Mystic Building Wrecking Co.*, 340 Mass 686, 689, 166 NE2d 213, 216 (1960). See also *Chopelas v. City Clerk of Malden*, 1 Mass App 241, 295 NE2d 395 (1973) (city charter and amendments thereto will be judicially noticed when charter found in statute).

[2] *City of Worcester v. Hoffman*, 345 Mass 647, 189 NE2d 226 (1963) (court refused to judicially notice whether statute was accepted by city); *Nayor v. Rent Board of Brookline*, 334 Mass 132, 135, 134 NE2d 419, 421 (1956) (same with regard to acceptance by town); *Bouchard v. City of Haverhill*, 342 Mass 1, 171 NE2d 848 (1961) (particular form of charter adopted by city would not be judicially noticed). Compare *American Mutual Liability Ins. Co. v. Com.*, 379 Mass 398, 403 n.11, 398 NE2d 491, 495 n.11 (1980) (court took judicial notice of unsuccessful legislative attempts to amend statute to require local approval of state agency decision).

[3] *Salisbury Water Supply Co. v. Town of Salisbury*, 341 Mass 42, 167 NE2d 320 (1960) (statute incorporating public water supply company and subsequent amendments thereto); *Grant v. Aldermen of Northampton*, 316 Mass 432, 435, 55 NE2d 705, 706 (1944) (city charter); *Mariani v. Trustees of Tufts College*, 1 Mass App 869, 306 NE2d 833 (1974) (charter of Tufts College); *Baizen v. Board of Public Works of Everett*, 1 Mass App 602, 304 NE2d 586 (1973) (statute authorizing establishment and operation of water system and city charter).

[4] *Com. v. Desmond*, 103 Mass 445, 447 (1869).

[5] *Id.*

[6] *Brush Hill Development, Inc. v. Com.*, 338 Mass 359, 366, 155 NE2d 170, 175 (1959).

[7] *Gahn v. Leary*, 318 Mass 425, 426, 61 NE2d 844, 846 (1945). Compare *Com. v. Ficksman*, 340 Mass 744, 166 NE2d 726 (1960) (whether investigators employed by state Alcoholic Beverages Control Commission were public officers of the Commonwealth could not be determined without evidence).

Matters pertaining to the organization, structure, and jurisdiction of the courts of the Commonwealth are judicially noticed.[8]

Records and files of the court as to the case in issue, including proceedings ancillary thereto, will be judicially noticed.[9]

As to such related proceedings, a court may also take judicial notice of the records of other courts.[10]

Court records of other proceedings in the same or another court need not be judicially noticed.[11] A judge may not take judicial notice of the undisclosed basis of his decree in an earlier case.[12] Nor may a judge reviewing an administrative agency's decision go beyond the administrative record to judicially notice the defense of collateral estoppel, where such defense was neither pleaded nor proved.[13]

---

[8] *Cohen v. Assessors of Boston*, 344 Mass 268, 182 NE2d 138 (1962) (rules of Appellate Tax Board judicially noticed); *Com. v. Desmond*, supra, 343 Mass 253, 178 NE2d 477. Judicial notice extends to the identity of judicial officers, *Assessors of Lawrence v. Arlington Mills*, 320 Mass 272, 69 NE2d 2 (1946); *Broitman v. Silver*, 278 Mass 510, 180 NE 311 (1932); and to their duties and function, *Martin v. Wyzanski*, 191 F Supp 931 (D Mass 1961).

[9] *Adoption of Simone*, 427 Mass 34, 691 NE2d 538 (1998) (in proceeding to dispense with biological parents' consent to adoption, permissible to judicially notice earlier findings in care and protection proceeding, although such findings could not be given dispositive effect in later proceeding); *In re Andrews*, 368 Mass 468, 476, 334 NE2d 15, 20 (1975); *Dwight v. Dwight*, 371 Mass 424, 357 NE2d 772 (1972). Cf. *Board of Assessors v. Ogden Suffolk Downs*, 398 Mass 604, 605, 499 NE2d 1200, 1201 (1986) (Board of Assessors may notice its previous determination of value of subject premises). But see *Com. v. Berry*, 463 Mass 800, 804, n.6, 979 NE2d 218, 221 (2012) (Supreme Judicial Court declined to take judicial notice of police report filed with papers in Boston Municipal Court, where the report was not part of record on appeal and was not introduced in evidence at motion hearing).

[10] *Jarosz v. Palmer*, 436 Mass 526, 766 NE2d 482 (2002) (Text cited); *Cannonball Fund, Ltd. v. Dutchess Capital Management, LLC*, 84 Mass App 75, 993 NE2d 350 (2013) (court could not take judicial notice of plaintiffs' reasons for dismissing prior complaint, essentially questions of motivation and state of mind; court may take judicial notice of docket entries and papers filed from separate cases, but not facts or evidence brought out in separate actions); *Nantucket Conservation Foundation v. Russell*, 2 Mass App 868, 316 NE2d 625 (1974); *Flynn v. Brassard*, 1 Mass App 678, 306 NE2d 446 (1974) (Appeals Court, in both cases, took judicial notice of the records of the Supreme Judicial Court); *Brookline v. Goldstein*, 388 Mass 443, 447 n.5, 447 NE2d 641, 644 n.5 (1983) (court examined certified copies of pleadings in related cases to discover nature of the claims asserted).

[11] *Grenda v. Kitchen*, 270 Mass 559, 170 NE 619 (1930); *Great Northern Indemnity v. Hartford Acc.*, 40 Mass App 686, 666 NE2d 1320, 1323 (1996) (impermissible to take judicial notice of facts purportedly established in a separate case between different parties) (Text cited).

[12] *Morrison v. Krauss*, 353 Mass 761, 233 NE2d 301 (1968); *Ferriter v. Borthwick*, 346 Mass 391, 193 NE2d 335 (1963).

[13] *Methuen Retirement Board v. Contributory Retirement Appeal Board*, 384 Mass 797, 424 NE2d 242 (1981).

Private acts of the legislature are not judicially noticed.[14] Nor are municipal ordinances or town bylaws properly the subject of judicial notice.[15]

Generally, it had been stated that a court would not take judicial notice of the rules and regulations of administrative bodies.[16] However, judicial notice of administrative regulations was taken in cases where the regulations were readily accessible in a state publication.[17] The question of administrative regulations appears to have been resolved in large part by legislative enactment. St 1976, c459, rewrote GL 30A, § 6, to provide for the publication by the Secretary of State of a "Massachusetts Register" and designated its contents to include, inter alia, certain executive orders and regulations filed under GL 30A, § 5. It is also provided by § 6 that the contents of the Massachusetts Register "shall be judicially noticed."[18]

GL 233, § 75, simplifies proof of private acts, regulations, municipal ordinances and the like, but it does not dispense with such proof. (See § 9.3.3)

---

[14] *Brodsky v. Fine*, 263 Mass 51, 160 NE 335 (1928). Burnham v. Webster, supra.

[15] *Easthampton Savings Bank v. City of Springfield*, 470 Mass 284, 296, n.8, 21 NE3d 922 (2014); *Warren v. Board of Appeals of Amherst*, 383 Mass 1, 8, 416 NE2d 1382, 1386 (1981); *Boulter Brothers Construction Co., Inc. v. Zoning Board of Appeals of Norfolk*, 45 Mass App 283, 697 NE2d 997 (1998) (zoning bylaws are not judicial noticed); *Shwachman v. Khoroshansky*, 15 Mass App 1002, 448 NE2d 409 (1983) (trial judge not required to take judicial notice of Boston rent control ordinance). Cf. *Camara v. Board of Appeals of Tewksbury*, 40 Mass App 209, 662 NE2d 719 (1996) (although judge could not take judicial notice of municipal bylaw not in evidence, court could rely on findings in earlier Supreme Judicial Court opinion based on evidence introduced in that case). Regulations of executive departments are not judicially noticed. *York v. Sullivan*, 369 Mass 157, 160, 338 NE2d 341, 344 (1975) (regulations of the state attorney general); *Building Comm'r of Boston v. Santilli*, 358 Mass 816, 266 NE2d 634 (1971) (zoning code of the city of Boston); *Com. v. Berney*, 353 Mass 571, 233 NE2d 739 (1968) (traffic rules and regulations promulgated by traffic commission of town). A ruling by an officer of the executive department is not judicially noticed. *White v. Universal Underwriters Ins. Co.*, 347 Mass 367, 373, 197 NE2d 868, 872 (1964).

[16] *Baxter v. Com.*, 359 Mass 175, 177, 268 NE2d 670, 671 (1971).

[17] See, e.g., *Ferreira v. Arrow Mutual Liability Ins. Co.*, 15 Mass App 633, 447 NE2d 1258 (1983); *Bagge's Case*, 5 Mass App 839, 363 NE2d 1321 (1977). Cf. *Paananen v. Rhodes*, 1 Mass App 12, 294 NE2d 434 (1972) (court declined to take judicial notice of administrative regulations where defendant had not had an opportunity to litigate the applicability of the regulation).

[18] But see *Shafnacker v. Raymond James & Associates, Inc.*, 425 Mass 724, 683 NE2d 662 (1997) (not error to decline to judicially notice regulations of National Association of Securities Dealers); *Saxon Coffee Shop, Inc. v. Boston Licensing Board*, 380 Mass 919, 407 NE2d 311 (1980) (regulations not published in the Massachusetts Register will not be judicially noticed and must be made part of the appellate record); *Tartarini v. Department of Mental Retardation*, 82 Mass App 217, 223, n.6, 972 NE2d 33, 38 (2012) (court not permitted to take judicial notice of unpublished state regulatory history).

b. Law of Other Jurisdictions

Taking judicial notice of the law of other jurisdictions is regulated by statute and court rules. In the absence of statute, the law of other jurisdictions, except well-known admiralty law, is generally not judicially noticed.[19]

GL 233, § 70, provides: "The courts shall take judicial notice of the law of the United States or of any state, territory or dependency thereof or of a foreign country whenever the same shall be material." Section 70 applies to criminal as well as civil proceedings.[20] The word *law* in GL 233, § 70, includes "decisions,"[21] but does not include judgments of foreign courts. GL 233, § 69, and the applicable rules provide the manner in which records and judicial proceedings (including judgments) of the courts of another state or of the United States are admissible in evidence. (See § 9.3.3). Mass R Civ P 44.1 provides that a party raising an issue of law from other jurisdictions must give notice of the intent to do so, that the court may consider any relevant material or source in determining the law, and that the determination is treated as a ruling on a question of law.

Rule 44.1 did not materially alter pre-rule practice under GL 233, § 70. Under both the statute and the rule, a court is not required to take judicial notice of foreign law unless it is brought to its attention. Rule 44.1 permits the court to consider "any relevant material or source," which is in accord with practice under the statute.[22] The trial court's determination of foreign law is reversible if the appellate court is in disagreement.

Mass R Crim P 39, which is applicable in district and superior courts, provides that records of courts of other states or the United States are admissible in evidence if properly authenticated, and that trial courts may upon request take judicial notice of the law of other jurisdictions. With respect to court records, Rule 39 follows GL 233, § 69. A complete record is not required under § 69 as long as the essential facts are set forth on the portion produced.[23] It can be assumed

---

[19] *Hellenic Lines Ltd. v. Rhoditis*, 412 F2d 919, 922 (5th Cir 1969), *aff'd*, 398 US 306, 90 S Ct 1731 (1970).

[20] *Com. v. White*, 358 Mass 488, 265 NE2d 473 (1970).

[21] *Lenn v. Riche*, 331 Mass 104, 117 NE2d 129 (1954).

[22] See *Berman v. Alexander*, 57 Mass App 181, 782 NE2d 14 (2003) (whether to admit testimony with respect to foreign law is within court's discretion; trend of modern authority is to treat it as question of law for judge to consider and explicate in his instructions and rulings).

[23] *Com. v. Rondoni*, 333 Mass 384, 131 NE2d 187 (1955).

that this is so under Rule 39(a). With respect to the law of other jurisdictions, Rule 39(b) is taken, with no material difference, from GL 233, § 70. The Rule does not limit a court's authority under § 70 to notice foreign law on its own initiative.

As to foreign law in a foreign language, it is not sufficient to call the court's attention to authorities without providing authentic translations.[24] Expert testimony as to the status of such law has been received.[25]

Federal Administrative Regulations. Public acts of Congress and presidential proclamations and reports to Congress are noticed.[26] However, even though § 70 provides that the courts shall take judicial notice of the "law" of the United States and 44 USC § 1507 provides that the contents of the Federal Register shall be judicially noticed, it is not clear that a Massachusetts court must notice regulations of federal offices and boards. It is clear that a Massachusetts court need not notice a federal regulation if the regulation is not brought to its attention.[27] The appellate court may or may not take judicial notice of such a regulation where the attention of the trial court has not been called to it.[28] It is also clear that a federal court sitting in Massachusetts may notice a federal regulation without having had the regulation called to the attention of the trial court.[29]

§ 2.8.2 Fact

Dates, the chief facts of history, and a broad and indefinite group of indisputable and either generally known or easily ascertainable facts are judicially noticed. There is a plethora of such cases in history,[30]

---

[24] See *Rodrigues v. Rodrigues*, 286 Mass 77, 83, 190 NE 20, 22 (1934).

[25] *Vergnani v. Guidetti*, 308 Mass 450, 454, 32 NE2d 272, 275 (1941); compare *Eastern Offices, Inc. v. P. F. O'Keefe Advertising Agency*, 289 Mass 23, 26, 193 NE 837, 838 (1935).

[26] *Stankus v. New York Life Ins. Co.*, 312 Mass 366, 369, 44 NE2d 687, 689 (1942).

[27] *Mastrullo v. Ryan*, 328 Mass 621, 105 NE2d 469 (1952).

[28] *Gilbert v. Merrimack Development Corp.*, 333 Mass 758, 759, 133 NE2d 491, 492 (1956) (notice refused); *Ralston v. Comm'r of Agriculture*, 334 Mass 51, 133 NE2d 589 (1956) (notice taken).

[29] *Green v. United States*, 176 F2d 541 (1st Cir 1949) (notice by district court); *Batista v. Nicolls*, 213 F2d 20 (1st Cir 1954) (notice by circuit court).

[30] *Nickols v. Commissioners of Middlesex County*, 341 Mass 13, 22, 166 NE2d 911, 918 (1960) (the reputation of Walden Pond that grew out of Thoreau's book *Walden*); *DeSautels, Petitioner*, 1 Mass App 787, 307 NE2d 576 (1974) (notice of the conquest of

government,[31] geography,[32] traffic and transportation,[33] and science.[34] It should be noted that questions involving scientific or technological facts are constantly moving from the realm of the unknown

---

Lithuania in 1940 by Soviet Russia and of the fact that the United States did not recognize the forced incorporation of Lithuania into the Soviet Union).

[31] *Michaud v. Sheriff of Essex County*, 390 Mass 523, 535, 458 NE2d 702, 709 (1983) (prison facilities of the Commonwealth are filled beyond capacity); *Com. v. Harris*, 383 Mass 655, 421 NE2d 447 (1981) (threats of violent acts directed at courthouses give rise to urgent need for protective measures); *Karchmar v. Worcester*, 364 Mass 124, 301 NE2d 570 (1973) (many collective bargaining agreements governing public employees are for a short period of time); *Sheridan v. Gardner*, 347 Mass 8, 196 NE2d 303 (1964) (legislation frequently is proposed by governor and other executive officers); *Allston Finance Co., Inc. v. Hanover Ins. Co.*, 18 Mass App 96, 463 NE2d 562 (1984) (1977 policy year was one of unusual regulatory turbulence).

[32] *Crowe v. Ward*, 363 Mass 85, 292 NE2d 716 (1973) (distance between weather station and locus of accident); *Chin Kee v. Com.*, 354 Mass 156, 164, 235 NE2d 787, 793 (1968) (save for a few family-owned business operations there were few persons of Oriental heritage in Middlesex County in 1932); *May v. Boston & M.R.R.*, 340 Mass 609, 165 NE2d 910 (1960) (Porter Square in North Cambridge is thickly settled with industrial plants and businesses); *Opinion of the Justices*, 333 Mass 773, 780, 128 NE2d 557, 562 (1955) (historic nature and character of Nantucket); *Com. v. King*, 150 Mass 221, 22 NE 905 (1889) (location of a river).

[33] *Berger v. MBTA*, 355 Mass 695, 246 NE2d 665 (1969) (occasional jolts and jerks are a normal incident to riding streetcars); *Medford v. Marnucci Brothers & Co.*, 344 Mass 50, 57, 181 NE2d 584, 588 (1962) (Commonwealth must often act through others to construct roads and bridges of a modern highway system); *Wilmington v. Department of Public Utilities*, 340 Mass 432, 438, 165 NE2d 99, 103 (1960) (matters of public transportation are of great importance to persons living in the communities surrounding Boston); *Green v. Wilmington*, 339 Mass 142, 158 NE2d 143 (1959) (many streets in suburbs and rural communities have no sidewalks); *American Oil Co. v. Alexanderian*, 338 Mass 112, 154 NE2d 127 (1958) (a way eight feet in width is required for passage of motor vehicles); *Mann v. Parkway Motor Sales*, 324 Mass 151, 85 NE2d 210 (1949) (existence of parkways in metropolitan Boston).

[34] *Com. v. Greco*, 76 Mass App 296, 300, 921 NE2d 1001, 1005 (2010) (trial judge properly took judicial notice that pills labeled Seroquel had same composition as quetiapine, a class E controlled substance, based on Physicians' Desk Reference); *Com. v. Wilborne*, 382 Mass 241, 250, 415 NE2d 192, 199 (1981) (dosage and effect of Demerol as set forth in Physician's Desk Reference book); *Com. v. Johnson*, 59 Mass App 164, 794 NE2d 1214 (2003) (not proper to take judicial notice of contents of CVS Pharmacy "pill book" concerning side effects of drugs); *Richards v. McKeown*, 9 Mass App 838, 399 NE2d 877 (1980) (reliability of standard mortality tables); *Com. v. Whynaught*, 377 Mass 14, 384 NE2d 1212 (1979) (radar speed meter is an accurate and reliable means of measuring velocity); *Com. v. LePage*, 352 Mass 403, 226 NE2d 200 (1967) (capacity of trained dogs to follow a human's trail); *Com. v. D'Avella*, 339 Mass 642, 162 NE2d 19 (1959) (conclusive reliability of properly administered blood tests showing nonpaternity); *Vincent v. Nicholas E. Tsiknas Co.*, 337 Mass 726, 151 NE2d 263 (1958) (propensity of glass to break under pressure); *Brookline v. Barnes*, 327 Mass 201, 97 NE2d 651 (1951) (recent emphasis on preventive medicine); *Deerfoot Farms, Inc. v. New York, N.H. & H.R. Co.*, 327 Mass 51, 96 NE2d 872 (1951) (wind tends to communicate fire from one property to another); *Silke v. Silke*, 325 Mass 487, 91 NE2d 200 (1950) (normal period of human gestation is approximately 280 days); *Maguire v. Director of Office*

or debatable to the realm of the accepted and established, but in some instances the reverse occurs. What facts of generalized knowledge are judicially noticeable thus depends on the state of knowledge more than it does on questions of stare decisis or precedent.[35] The appropriateness of judicial notice of scientific facts frequently arises in making the determination of whether evidence of scientific tests or procedures is admissible.

A wide variety of facts have been held to be appropriate for judicial notice on the theory that they are generally known and cannot reasonably be subject to dispute.[36] The courts found that judicial notice of the proposed facts was not appropriate in a number of cases.[37]

---

of Medicaid, 82 Mass App 549, 551, n.5, 976 NE2d 205, 207 (2012) (dementia is a group of symptoms caused by disorders that affect the brain, not a specific disease).

[35] Wigmore § 2580 (Chad rev 1981).

[36] *Com. v. Milo M.*, 433 Mass 149, 156, 740 NE2d 967, 973 (2001) (recent school shootings as evidence of actual and potential violence in public schools); *In re McInerney*, 389 Mass 528, 536, 451 NE2d 401, 406 (1983) (fact that attorney continued to list himself as an attorney in telephone directory after suspension from practice); *Com. v. Stowell*, 389 Mass 171, 175, 449 NE2d 357, 360 (1983) (adultery frequently has a destructive impact on a marital relationship and is a factor in many divorces); *Smith v. Ariens Co.*, 375 Mass 620, 377 NE2d 954 (1978) (reliance of public on trademarks and trade names as proof of identity of manufacturer of product); *Sorensen v. Sorensen*, 369 Mass 350, 339 NE2d 907 (1975) (widespread existence of automobile liability insurance); *Benavides v. Stop & Shop, Inc.*, 346 Mass 154, 190 NE2d 894 (1963) (bland, pure, neutral soap sometimes causes slight, temporary burning sensation when introduced into the eye); *Mudge v. Stop & Shop, Inc.*, 339 Mass 763, 162 NE2d 670 (1959) (grocery carts and stock trucks are frequently used in aisles of supermarkets); *Samuel v. White Fuel Corp.*, 332 Mass 264, 124 NE2d 270 (1955) (fuel oil is customarily pumped into basement tank through hose to opening on outside of building); *Shaw v. Boston American League Baseball Co.*, 325 Mass 419, 90 NE2d 840 (1947) (spectators at baseball games are subjected to possibility of being hit by ball); *Katz v. Gow*, 321 Mass 666, 75 NE2d 438 (1947) (golf ball hit by unskilled person does not always fly straight toward intended mark); *McMillen v. McMillen*, 57 Mass App 568, 574, n.8, 784 NE2d 1130, 1135 (2003) (dictionary may be consulted for ordinary meaning of term used in a will, unless word has acquired a different meaning under statutory or common law).

[37] *Stasiukevich v. Nicolls*, 168 F2d 474 (1st Cir 1948) (the Communist Party advocates the violent overthrow of United States government); *Com. v. Hartman*, 404 Mass 306, 313 n.9, 534 NE2d 1170 n.9 (1990) (symptoms of insulin shock); *Mendel Kern, Inc. v. Workshop, Inc.*, 400 Mass 277, 282, 508 NE2d 853, 856 (1987) (location of redevelopment project where location was not subject of general knowledge); *Weinberg v. MBTA*, 348 Mass 669, 205 NE2d 5 (1965) (whether fracture of ankle can give rise to varicose veins and shortness of breath); *Faulkner v. J. H. Corcoran & Co.*, 342 Mass 94, 172 NE2d 94 (1961) (that a terrazzo floor becomes dangerously slippery when wet); *Jensen v. McEldowney*, 341 Mass 485, 170 NE2d 472 (1960) (Registry of Motor Vehicles table showing distance car will travel at given speeds after brakes are applied); *Foss v. Mutual Life Ins. Co.*, 247 Mass 10, 15, 141 NE 498, 499 (1923) (that angina pectoris tends to shorten life); *Com. v. Kirk*, 39 Mass App 225, 654 NE2d 938 (1995) (not

Judicial notice is limited to subjects of general knowledge and is not extended to personal observations of the judge or juror.[38]

§ 2.9 Conclusiveness of Judicial Notice

Historically, judicial notice was conclusive. The court might hear argument of counsel and consider submissions by the parties before taking notice of a fact, but once the court had resolved to take judicial notice it would not receive evidence offered to contradict a matter judicially noticed.[1]

Fed R Evid 201 (g) specifically provides that with respect to criminal matters, the jury is to be instructed "that it may, but is not required to, accept as conclusive any fact judicially noticed." Proposed Mass R Evid 201(g) contains the same language. In a criminal trial, the judge must expressly submit all factual issues to the jury, including matters of which the court has taken judicial notice.[2] Proof of an essential element of a crime may not be supplied by judicial notice taken at the appellate level, and where the trial court has failed to take judicial notice

---

proper to take judicial notice of earlier 209A order to establish identity of victim's assailant; judicial notice cannot be taken of material factual issues that can only be decided by fact finder on competent evidence); *Com. v. Gonzales*, 33 Mass App 728, 604 NE2d 1317 (1992) (whether a particular school was an elementary, vocational, or secondary school not subject to judicial notice); *Rice v. James Hanrahan & Sons*, 20 Mass App 701, 707, 482 NE2d 833, 838 (1985) (judicial notice of administrative regulations not appropriate to prove insulation governed by them was hazardous).

[38] *Nantucket v. Beinecke*, 379 Mass 345, 398 NE2d 458 (1979); *Com. v. Byfield*, 32 Mass App 912, 585 NE2d 746 (1992) (peculiar experience and knowledge of magistrate may not support issuance of search warrant); *DeSautels, Petitioner*, 1 Mass App 787, 307 NE2d 576 (1974). Cf. *Com. v. Howard*, 42 Mass App 322, 326, 677 NE2d 233, 236 (1997) (error for sentencing judge to attempt to send a message to residents of town based on his perception of the extent of child abuse in the area). This rule does not preclude the finder of fact from considering the evidence in the light of general human knowledge and experience. *Com. v. Kingsbury*, 378 Mass 751, 393 NE2d 391 (1979); *Crowe v. Ward*, 363 Mass 85, 292 NE2d 716 (1973); *Richmond v. Richmond*, 340 Mass 367, 164 NE2d 155 (1960); *Com. v. Peckham*, 68 Mass (2 Gray) 514 (1854). Compare *Casey's Case*, 348 Mass 572, 204 NE2d 710 (1965), with *Lovely's Case*, 336 Mass 512,2 146 NE2d 488 (1957), as to the extent that lay members of an administrative body can rely on such knowledge with regard to medical questions.

§ 2.9 [1] *Com. v. Marzynski*, 149 Mass 68, 72, 21 NE 228, 229 (1889) (refusal to hear evidence that cigars were drugs or medicine). Cf. *Stasiukevich v. Nicolls*, 168 F2d 474 (1st Cir 1948) (authenticity of report of legislative committee noticed; evidence admissible to dispute truth of assertions in report).

[2] *Com. v. Kingsbury*, 378 Mass 751, 755, 393 NE2d 391, 393-394 (1979); *Com. v. Finegan*, 45 Mass App 921, 699 NE2d 1228 (1998) (judge may not implicitly take judicial notice of an element of the crime).

of an essential element of a crime, even though it could have done so, the defendant is entitled to a required finding of not guilty.[3]

§ 2.10 Miscellaneous Statutes

There are a number of special statutory provisions relating to judicial notice: GL 21, § 24(8) (seal of supervisors of conservation districts); GL 25, § 1 (seal of Department of Telecommunications and Energy); GL 58A, § 1 (seal of Appellate Tax Board); GL 138, § 36 (signature and office of alcoholic beverage analyst); and GL 271, § 27 (general methods and character of lotteries). See also GL 30A, § 6 (added by St 1976, c459) (providing that the contents of the Massachusetts Register shall be judicially noticed); GL 30A, § 11(5) (administrative agencies may, in addition to judicial notice, "take notice of general, technical or scientific facts within their specialized knowledge"); and GL 277, § 33 (matters that may be judicially noticed need not be alleged in criminal indictments).

C. BINDING TESTIMONY

§ 2.11 Definition and Application of Doctrine

Generally speaking, it is the jury's function to pass on the credibility of testimony.[1] There are, however, certain limitations to this prerogative. A party may be "bound" by his own testimony. He is bound not in the judicial admission sense that his testimony renders other evidence on the point immaterial, but rather in the sense that his testimony may be disbelieved only to his disadvantage. A party is bound by his testimony if:

---

[3] *Com. v. Green*, 408 Mass 48, 50, 556 NE2d 387, 389 (1990); *Com. v. Kingsbury*, supra. See also *Com. v. Barrett*, 1 Mass App 332, 296 NE2d 712 (1973) (appellate court will not take judicial notice that defendant was represented by counsel in prior criminal proceeding). But see *Com. v. Milo M.*, 433 Mass 149, 156, 740 NE2d 967, 973 (2001) (in a delinquency proceeding tried to the court, SJC took judicial notice of recent school shootings as evidence of actual and potential violence in public schools in order to establish objective basis for teacher's fear that student could carry out threat against her).

§ 2.11 [1] *Com. v. Fitzgerald*, 376 Mass 402, 412, 381 NE2d 123, 131 (1978).

(1) the testimony was given in the pending trial[2] and
(2) where (a) there is no evidence more favorable to him than his own testimony[3] or (b) there has been an election by a witness between conflicting statements and any evidence more favorable to the party has been repudiated[4] or (c) the testimony concerns the witness-party's subjective emotions, feelings, motives, intentions or knowledge, whether or not there is more favorable evidence from other witnesses.[5]

Subject to similar limitations, a party who introduces in evidence his opponent's answers to interrogatories is in the same sense bound by them.[6]

Testimonial admissions relating to questions of law, and not of fact, are not binding within the meaning of these rules.[7]

The jury is not required to believe the uncontradicted testimony of a witness unless it comes within the special rules described above.[8]

---

[2] *291 Washington Street v. School Street Liquors*, 331 Mass 150, 117 NE2d 809 (1954); *Brown v. MTA*, 345 Mass 636, 189 NE2d 214 (1963) (party's testimony at auditor's hearing admissible at trial but not binding).

[3] *Jacquot v. William Filene's Sons Co.*, 337 Mass 312, 316, 149 NE2d 635, 639 (1958); *Gaynor v. Laverdure*, 362 Mass 828, 841, 291 NE2d 617, 625 (1973) (but where the party gives evidence leading to inconsistent conclusions, the jury may decide which version it will accept as true); *McClean v. University Club*, 327 Mass 68, 73, 97 NE2d 174, 178-179 (1951); *Gow v. Buckminster Hotel, Inc.*, 336 Mass 606, 608, 146 NE2d 924, 926 (1958).

[4] *Harlow v. Chin*, 405 Mass 697, 706 n.11, 545 NE2d 602, 608 n.11 (1989); *Siira v. Shields*, 360 Mass 874, 277 NE2d 825 (1972) (see § 6.13.3); *Ravosa v. Zais*, 40 Mass App 47, 661 NE2d 111 (1996).

[5] *Carey v. Lynn Ladder and Scaffolding Co., Inc.*, 427 Mass 1003, 691 NE2d 223 (1998) (plaintiff bound by his testimony as to his knowledge of ladder's instability); *Davidonis v. Levielle*, 356 Mass 716, 248 NE2d 645 (1969); *Hultberg v. Truex*, 344 Mass 414, 182 NE2d 483 (1962); *Fraser v. Fraser*, 334 Mass 4, 133 NE2d 236 (1956); *Motta v. Mello*, 338 Mass 170, 154 NE2d 364 (1958). Cf. *Charles Dowd Box Co. v. Fireman's Fund Ins. Co.*, 351 Mass 113, 121, 218 NE2d 64, 69 (1966) (knowledge of objective or physical facts not included within this doctrine); *Reynolds v. Sullivan*, 330 Mass 549, 116 NE2d 128 (1953).

[6] *Tanguay v. Wood Conversion Co.*, 347 Mass 530, 533, 199 NE2d 181, 183 (1964) (introducing party bound by opponent's uncontradicted answers); *Hoban v. Trustees of New York, N.H. & H.R.R. Co.*, 326 Mass 566, 569-570, 95 NE2d 651, 654 (1950) (introducing party not bound by opponent's contradicted answers); *Gannon v. Summerfield Co.*, 323 Mass 25, 80 NE2d 51 (1948) (answers introduced by answering party; interrogating party not bound).

[7] *Adams v. Adams*, 338 Mass 776, 780, 157 NE2d 405, 408 (1959). See also *Wasserman v. Tonelli*, 343 Mass 253, 178 NE2d 477 (1961). Compare *Shamrock Liquors, Inc. v. Alcoholic Beverages Control Comm'n*, 7 Mass App 333, 387 NE2d 204 (1979).

[8] *Manias v. Director of Division of Employment Security*, 388 Mass 201, 205 n.7, 445 NE2d 1068, 1070 n.7 (1983) (Text cited); *Lenn v. Riche*, 331 Mass 104, 111, 117 NE2d

Specifically, a party is not bound by the testimony of a witness called by him, even if the testimony is uncontradicted.[9]

The jury may believe part and disbelieve part of a witness's testimony, provided it does not distort an integral portion of the witness's statements.[10]

129, 133 (1954). Cf. *Shipp v. Boston & M.R.R. Co.*, 283 Mass 266, 186 NE 653 (1933) (court invoked federal rule in Federal Employees Liability Act case that testimony of witness cannot be disregarded when not open to doubt from any reasonable point of view).

[9] *Com. v. Britt*, 358 Mass 767, 770, 267 NE2d 223, 225 (1971); *Salvato v. DiSilva Transportation Co.*, 329 Mass 305, 108 NE2d 51 (1952) (witness is not a party); *Gordon v. Bedard*, 265 Mass 408, 164 NE 374 (1929) (witness is party opponent).

[10] *Donovan v. DiPaolo*, 4 Mass App 576, 355 NE2d 484 (1976). See also *Com. v. Cinelli*, 389 Mass 197, 204, 449 NE2d 1207, 1211 (1983); *Com. v. Hill*, 387 Mass 619, 624, 442 NE2d 24, 28 (1982); *Com. v. Fitzgerald*, 376 Mass 402, 411, 381 NE2d 123, 131 (1978); *Lydon v. Boston Elevated Railway Co.*, 309 Mass 205, 34 NE2d 642 (1941).

CHAPTER

3

BURDEN of PROOF, PRESUMPTIONS and INFERENCES

§ 3.1 Burden of Proof Defined

The phrase "burden of proof" refers to two distinct concepts: burden of persuasion and burden of production. The burden of persuasion is the burden to ultimately convince the jury on the matter. The burden of production is the burden to produce sufficient evidence to "get to the jury"—i.e., enough evidence so that a reasonable jury could find that way.[1]

The burden of persuasion instructs the fact finder concerning the "degree of confidence our society thinks [it] should have in the correctness of factual conclusions for a particular type of adjudication."[2] If at the close of the evidence the fact finder determines that a fact has not been proven to the required level of certainty, it must decide the issue against the burdened party. As a general rule, the burden of persuasion does not shift between the parties during the course of the trial because it does not come into play until the fact finder deliberates on its decision.[3]

The burden of production requires the party who bears it to come forward with some evidence on the matter. If the party does not satisfy this burden, the court will decide the issue against it (by directing a verdict) without submitting it to the jury. Unlike the burden of persuasion, the burden of production may shift between the parties during

---

§ 3.1 [1] See *Com. v. Porter*, 462 Mass 724, 730-731, 971 NE2d 291, 296 (2012); *Com. v. Walker*, 370 Mass 548, 578 n.21, 350 NE2d 678, 698 n.21 (1976); *Horvitz v. Commissioner of Revenue*, 51 Mass App 386, 395, 747 NE2d 177, 184 (2001).

[2] *C.C. v. A.B.*, 406 Mass 679, 686-687, 550 NE2d 365, 370-371 (1990) (quoting *In re Winship*, 397 US 358, 370 (1970) (Harlan, J, concurring)). See also *Conroy v. Conservation Commission of Lexington*, 73 Mass App 552, 559, 899 NE2d 879, 884 (2009). For discussion of the policy implications surrounding burden of proof and its allocation, see *In re* Angela, 445 Mass 55, 64-66, 833 NE2d 575, 582-584 (2005) (CHINS proceeding); Care and Protection of Robert, 408 Mass 52, 556 NE2d 993 (1990); *Spence v. Gormley*, 387 Mass 258, 274-277, 439 NE2d 741, 750-751 (1982) (eviction from public housing); *Hampton Associates v. Board of Assessors of Northampton*, 52 Mass App 110, 119 n.19, 751 NE2d 437, 445 n.19 (2001); *Eliot Discount Corp. v. Dame*, 19 Mass App 280, 284-285, 473 NE2d 711, 714-715 (1985) (citing Text).

[3] See Proposed Mass R Evid 301 (b) and Fed R Evid 301 ("the burden of proof in the sense of the risk of nonpersuasion remains throughout the trial upon the party on whom it was originally cast.").

the course of the trial.[4] Adequate proof in both civil and criminal cases may come from either direct or circumstantial evidence.[5]

§ 3.2 Burden of Production/Civil and Criminal Cases

§ 3.2.1 *Amount of Evidence Required/Motions to Challenge*

A party has sustained its burden of production when it has adduced evidence sufficient to form a reasonable basis for a verdict in that party's favor.[1] The opponent may test this with a motion for a directed verdict in a civil case[2] and a motion for required finding of not guilty in criminal cases.[3] Where the judge, considering the evidence in the light most favorable to the party against whom the motion is directed and without weighing the credibility of the witnesses, determines that the jury could not reasonably find for that party, the motion must be allowed.[4]

In criminal cases, a motion for a required finding of not guilty must be allowed if the evidence and the inferences permitted to be drawn, in the light most favorable to the Commonwealth, cannot

---

[4] See § 3.5, infra.

[5] *Abraham v. Woburn*, 383 Mass 724, 729, 421 NE2d 1206, 1210 (1981). See § 4.2, infra.

§ 3.2 [1] See *Hampton Associates v. Board of Assessors of Northampton*, 52 Mass App 110, 118 n.18, 751 NE2d 437, 445 n.18 (2001) (Text cited).

[2] Mass R Civ P 50(a). The judge may defer ruling on the motion until after the jury renders a verdict and then entertain a motion for a judgment notwithstanding the verdict (n.o.v.). Mass R Civ P 50(b).

[3] Mass R Crim P 25. Mass R Crim P 25(a) authorizes the judge to enter a finding of not guilty on his own motion. Although Mass R Civ P 50(a) does not similarly authorize such action in a civil case, older precedent does. See *Field v. Hamm*, 254 Mass 268, 150 NE 3 (1926). Mass R Crim P 25(c) provides the Commonwealth with a right of appeal where the judge sets aside a verdict of guilty.

[4] *O'Brien v. Pearson*, 449 Mass 377, 383, 868 NE2d 118, 124 (2007); *Bonin v. Chestnut Hill Towers Realty Corp.*, 392 Mass 58, 59, 466 NE2d 90, 91 (1984). The same standard applies for a judgment notwithstanding the verdict. See *Cahaly v. Benistar Property Exchange Trust Co., Inc.*, 451 Mass 343, 350, 885 NE2d 800, 809 (2008); *Zaniboni v. Massachusetts Trial Court*, 81 Mass App 216, 217, 961 NE2d 155, 158 (2012), *remanded on other grounds*, 465 Mass 1013 (in reviewing a denial of a motion for judgment notwithstanding the verdict, the question is whether anywhere in the evidence, from whatever source, any combination of circumstances could be found from which a reasonable inference could be drawn in favor of the party moved against).

reasonably support a finding of guilt beyond a reasonable doubt on each element of the crime charged.[5] Defendant's contrary evidence does not undercut the sufficiency unless it is so overwhelming that no rational jury could find him guilty. Deterioration of the Commonwealth's case occurs only where its evidence is shown to be incredible or conclusively incorrect; and where the evidence turns on the credibility of the defendant's witnesses, the Commonwealth's case cannot deteriorate.[6]

Where the question of guilt is left to conjecture or surmise, or the evidence tends equally to sustain guilt or innocence, proof is obviously insufficient.[7] But that the evidence is conflicting does not demand a required finding of not guilty, as the jury is free to believe or disbelieve any or all of the evidence they hear.[8]

Directed verdicts are rarely given in favor of the party having the burden of proof (usually the civil plaintiff) because such a ruling would mean that as a matter of law, it had sustained its burden of persuasion

---

[5] *Com. v. Penn*, 472 Mass 610, 618-619, 36 NE3d 552, 560-561 (2015) (comparing "any rational trier of fact" perspective to "a reasonable jury" perspective); *Com. v. Arce*, 467 Mass 329, 333, 4 NE2d 1259, 1263 (2014); *Com. v. Mejia*, 461 Mass 384, 391-392, 961 NE2d 72, 80 (2012); *Com. v. Linton*, 456 Mass 534, 544, 924 NE2d 722, 733 (2010); *Com. v. Renaud*, 81 Mass App 261, 262, 961 NE2d 1102, 1104 (2012) (in order to sustain the denial of a motion for required finding of not guilty, it is not enough for appellate court to find that there was some evidence, however slight, to support each essential element of the offense, rather, the appellate court reviews the evidence introduced up to the time the Commonwealth rested to determine whether the evidence, viewed in the light most favorable to the Commonwealth, was sufficient for a reasonable jury to infer the existence of each essential element of the crime charged, beyond a reasonable doubt); *Com. v. Kappler*, 416 Mass 574, 578-579, 625 NE2d 513 (1993); *Com. v. Pratt*, 407 Mass 647, 651, 555 NE2d 559, 562 (1990). See also *O'Laughlin v. O'Brien*, 568 F2d 287 (1st Cir 2009) (circumstantial identification evidence was insufficient to establish defendant as perpetrator beyond reasonable doubt).

[6] *Com. v. Martin*, 467 Mass 291, 312-313, 4 NE2d 1236, 1254 (2014); *Com. v. Patton*, 458 Mass 119, 130-131, 934 NE2d 236, 248 (2010) ("Deterioration would occur not because [the probationer] contradicted the Commonwealth's evidence, but because evidence for the Commonwealth necessary to warrant submission of the case to the jury is later shown to be incredible or conclusively incorrect."); *Com. v. Merry*, 453 Mass 653, 664, 904 NE2d 413, 422 (2009); *Com. v. Nhut Huynh*, 452 Mass 481, 485, 895 NE2d 471, 475 (2008); *Com. v. Gomez*, 450 Mass 704, 710-711, 881 NE2d 745, 750-751 (2008). *Com. v. Ferreira*, 77 Mass App 675, 679, 933 NE2d 685, 689 (2010), *rev'd on other grounds*, 460 Mass 781, 955 NE2d 898 (2011).

[7] *O'Laughlin v. O'Brien*, supra, 568 F2d at 301; *Com. v. Prentice P.*, 57 Mass App 766, 768, 786 NE2d 415, 417-418 (2003).

[8] *Com. v. Charlton*, 81 Mass App 294, 302, 962 NE2d 203, 210 (2012).

as well as its burden of production of evidence.[9] A verdict may not be directed against a defendant in a criminal case.[10]

§ 3.2.2 Allocation of Burden of Production

The party with the burden of persuasion (plaintiff in a civil case, the Commonwealth in a criminal case) has the burden of production at the outset of the trial. In a civil case, when the plaintiff has presented a prima face case, the burden of production shifts to the opponent, and if the opponent does not carry that burden, a finding against the opponent is required.[11]

In a criminal case, the Commonwealth has both the burden of production and the burden of persuasion as to each element of the offense charged.[12] Defendant has burden of production on affirmative defenses,[13] which when met places the burden on the Commonwealth to disprove.[14] When the defendant enters a stipulation with the Commonwealth as to the existence of an element of the crime charged that relieves the Commonwealth of the burden of introducing evidence other than the stipulation to prove that element.[15]

---

[9] See *Goldstein v. Gontarz*, 364 Mass 800, 804, 309 NE2d 196, 199 (1974); *Workmen's Circle Education Center v. Board of Assessors of City of Springfield*, 314 Mass 616, 621, 51 NE2d 313, 317 (1943); *Spence v. Gillis*, 16 Mass App 905, 449 NE2d 391 (1983) (citing Text).

[10] See § 3.4, infra.

[11] See *Com. v. Taylor*, 383 Mass 272, 281-282 n.10, 418 NE2d 1226, 1232 n.10 (1981).

[12] See § 3.4.1, infra; *Com. v. Burke*, 390 Mass 480, 483-484, 457 NE2d 622, 624-625 (1983).

[13] "An affirmative defense is defined as a matter which, assuming the charge against the accused to be true, constitutes a defense to it; an 'affirmative defense' does not directly challenge any element of the offense. Further, an affirmative defense 'involves a matter of . . . justification peculiarly within the knowledge of the defendant on which he can fairly be required to adduce supporting evidence.'" *Com. v. Farley*, 64 Mass App 854, 860, 835 NE2d 1159, 1166-1167 (1985), [citing Model Penal Code § 1.12(3)(c)] (justification for lack of license in unlawful possession of firearm case). For the affirmative defense to larceny charge of mistake of fact concerning ownership or abandonment of the property, see *Com. v. Liebenow*, 84 Mass App 387, 391-396, 997 NE2d 109, 113-116 (2013).

[14] *Com. v. Farley*, supra, 64 Mass App at 860-862, 835 NE2d at 1166-1167. For a discussion of the burden of production on a criminal defendant seeking to raise an insanity defense, see *Com. v. Mills*, 400 Mass 626, 511 NE2d 572 (1987) (& citations).

[15] *Com. v. Ortiz*, 466 Mass 475, 481-485, 995 NE2d 1100, 1105-1107 (2013) (such stipulation should be placed before the jury before the close of evidence). See also

§ 3.2.3 Discrimination Cases

Discrimination cases present a vivid illustration of the use of shifting burdens of production to sharpen the factual issues in dispute. Although the plaintiff bears the ultimate burden of proving intentional discrimination, establishment of a "prima facie case" shifts the burden of production to the employer to articulate a lawful explanation for the challenged adverse treatment.[16] Plaintiff's prima facie case is generally made out with evidence that: (1) plaintiff is a member of a protected class; (2) plaintiff was qualified for the position in question; (3) the plaintiff was rejected, terminated, or otherwise adversely treated; and (4) the employer sought to fill the position with individuals of similar qualifications to plaintiff's.[17] In an age case, plaintiff must demonstrate that she was replaced by someone "substantially younger" (defined as five years or more), or otherwise present some evidence supporting a reasonable inference that age was a determinative factor.[18]

The burden of production then shifts to the defendant employer, who must rebut by articulating a legitimate, non-discriminatory reason(s) for its decision. If the employer fails to meet its burden, the

---

Com. v. Ramsey, 466 Mass 489, 496, 995 NE2d 1110, 1115 (2013) (defendant unequivocally admitted on the stand to possession, and jury was told with defendant's consent that the parties agreed the substance was cocaine and that the jury need not consider the issue).

[16] See generally *Bulwer v. Mount Auburn Hospital*, 473 Mass 672, 46 NE3d 24 (2016). The prima facie case eliminates the most common nondiscriminatory reasons for rejection—lack of competence and lack of job availability. See *Lipchitz v. Raytheon Co.*, 434 Mass 493, 502, 751 NE2d 360, 368 (2001); *Lynn Teachers Union, Local 1037 v. Massachusetts Commission Against Discrimination*, 406 Mass 515, 526-527, 549 NE2d 97, 103-104 (1990); *Pryor v. Holiday Inns, Inc.*, 401 Mass 506, 508-510, 517 NE2d 472, 474-475 (1988).

[17] See *Godfrey v. Globe Newspaper Co., Inc.*, 457 Mass 113, 120, 928 NE2d 327, 334 (2010) (disability-based discrimination); *Chi-Sang Poon v. Massachusetts Inst. of Tech.*, 74 Mass App 185, 195-196, 905 NE2d 137, 145-146 (2009) (race and retaliation); *Romero v. UHS of Westwood Pembroke, Inc.*, 72 Mass App 539, 893 NE2d 355 (2008) (medical provider whistleblower statute and pregnancy); *Everett v. 357 Corp.*, 453 Mass 585, 610, 904 NE2d 733, 753 (2009) (disability); *Dartt v. Browning-Ferris Industries, Inc.*, 427 Mass 1, 691 NE2d 526 (1998) (handicap); *Blare v. Husky Injection Molding Systems Boston, Inc.*, 419 Mass 437, 441, 646 NE2d 111, 115 (1995) (age); *McLaughlin v. City of Lowell*, 84 Mass App 45, 992 NE2d 1036 (2013) (handicap).

[18] *Zaniboni v. Massachusetts Trial Court*, 81 Mass App 216, 218-219, 961 NE2d 155, 158-159 (2012), *remanded on other grounds*, 465 Mass 1013 (2013); *Somers v. Converged Access, Inc.*, 454 Mass 582, 595, 911 NE2d 739, 751-752 (2009); *Knight v. Avon Products, Inc.*, 438 Mass 413, 422-426,780 NE2d 1255, 1263-1265 (2003).

plaintiff is entitled to judgment.[19] If the defendant meets the burden, the proceedings move on to a third stage where the plaintiff has the opportunity to prove that the stated reasons are pretextual.[20] As Massachusetts is a "pretext only" jurisdiction, plaintiff need not further prove that the pretext was a cover for discriminatory animus.[21] The employer may counter by showing that even if the articulated reason is found untrue there was no discriminatory intent, or that the adverse action was based on a different, non-discriminatory reason.[22]

Trial judges have been cautioned against burdening the jury with the rules regarding shifting burdens, or terms like "pretext" and "mixed-motive." Rather, instructions should focus on the ultimate issues of discriminatory animus and causation.[23]

§ 3.3 Burden of Persuasion in Civil Cases

§ 3.3.1 Allocation of Burden of Persuasion in Civil Cases

a. General Principles

In civil cases the burden of persuasion is on the plaintiff as to some issues and on the defendant as to others. It is variously stated that the burden of persuasion should fall on the party who:

- Must plead that fact.
- Initiated the suit.

---

[19] *Blare v. Husky Injection Molding Systems Boston, Inc.*, supra, 419 Mass 441-442, 646 NE2d at 115.

[20] A finding that at least one of the proffered reasons is a pretext would constitute sufficient evidence of discriminatory intent. See *Haddad v. Wal-Mart Stores, Inc.*, 455 Mass 91, 98, 914 NE2d 59, 66 (2009).

[21] *Bulwer v. Mount Auburn Hospital*, 473 Mass 672, 681-682, 46 NE3d 24, 33 (2016).

[22] See *Abramian v. President & Fellows of Harvard College*, 432 Mass 107, 117-118, 731 NE2d 1075, 1085-1086 (2000), modifying *Blare v. Husky Injection Molding Systems Boston, Inc.*, supra, 419 Mass 441-442, 646 NE2d at 115. See also *Lipchitz v. Raytheon Co.*, 434 Mass 493, 751 NE2d 360 (2001) (extensive discussion of burdens in indirect and direct evidence cases); *Dragonas v. School Committee of Melrose*, 64 Mass App 429, 440-443, 833 NE2d 679, 689-690 (2005); *Ventresco v. Liberty Mutual Ins. Co.*, 55 Mass App 201, 205-209, 770 NE2d 23, 26-29 (2002) (jury instructions in age case). For discussion of the analysis in mixed-motive cases, see *Brownlie v. Kanzaki Speciality Papers, Inc.*, 44 Mass App 408, 416-419, 691 NE2d 953, 96 0-961 (1998).

[23] *Lipchitz v. Raytheon Co.*, supra, 434 Mass at 507-508, 751 NE2d at 372-373. For the operation of this analytical framework in the context of a jury-waived trial. See *Weber v. Community Teamwork, Inc.*, 434 Mass 761, 752 NE2d 700 (2001).

- Would change the status quo.
- Asserts the affirmative proposition.
- Asserts the unlikely proposition.
- Has freer access to the evidence.[1]

In accordance with these considerations, the burden of persuasion has been allocated to the plaintiff as to most classes of disputed facts.[2]

b. Actions Alleging Statutory Liability

In actions alleging statutory liability, the burden of persuasion is on the plaintiff as to all facts that by statute are necessary to create the liability.[3] Similarly, one who seeks relief under a statute has the burden of proving himself within its terms.[4] The party seeking to come within a statutory exception has the burden of persuasion on that matter.[5]

---

§ 3.3 [1] See *Cantres v. Director of the Division of Employment Security*, 396 Mass 226, 231, 484 NE2d 1336, 1339 (1985) (citing Text); *Kasper v. Registrar of Motor Vehicles*, 82 Mass App 901, 903, 970 NE2d 808, 812 (2012) (burden is on motorist to explain why breathalyzer test showed no reading for several samples) (citing Text). For examples of allocation analysis, see *Cleary v. Cleary*, 427 Mass 286, 692 NE2d 955 (1998) (party challenging will or other document on ground it was procured through fraud or undue influence bears burden of proving allegation); *Cantres v. Director of the Division of Employment Security*, supra n.2, 396 Mass at 230-233, 484 NE2d at 1338-1340 (employer bears burden on willful misconduct exception); *Eliot Discount Corp. v. Dame*, 19 Mass App 280, 284-285, 473 NE2d 711, 715 (1985) (burden of proof on creditor to establish that debtor was rendered insolvent as to creditors by transfers of real property without payment for fair monetary value of property) (citing Text). For an extensive discussion of the burdens of proof in tax cases, see *Horvitz v. Commissioner of Revenue*, 51 Mass App 386, 391-395, 747 NE2d 177, 181-184 (2001) (Commissioner, not taxpayer, has burden of persuasion on issue of change in domicile in abatement proceeding).

[2] See, e.g., *Jernigan v. Giard*, 398 Mass 721, 500 NE2d 806 (1986) (burden on plaintiff in legal malpractice action to prove that judgment would have been collectible). For will contests, see *Estate of Sharis*, 83 Mass App 839, 842990 NE2d 98, 102 (2013) (while the burden of proof ordinarily rests with the party contesting the will, a fiduciary who benefits in a transaction with the decedent bears the burden of establishing the transaction did not violate his obligations).

[3] *Tileston v. Inhabitants of Brookline*, 134 Mass 438 (1883).

[4] *William Rodman & Sons v. State Tax Comm'n*, 373 Mass 606, 610-611, 368 NE2d 1382, 1384-1385 (1977); *Treasurer & Receiver General v. Cunniff*, 357 Mass 206, 257 NE2d 459 (1970).

[5] *Somers v. Converged Access, Inc.*, 454 Mass 582, 591 n.12, 911 NE2d 739, 749 n.12 (2009); *Cantres v. Director of the Division of Employment Security*, supra, 396 Mass at 231, 484 NE2d at 1340.

The legislature may by statute designate the party with the burden of persuasion.[6]

c. *Affirmative Defenses*

The burden of persuasion is on the defendant as to affirmative defenses. An affirmative defense is one that, rather than meeting or negating the allegations of the proponent, sets up new and distinct propositions that avoid the effect of the proponent's allegations even if they are established.[7] Examples of affirmative defenses include statute of limitations, comparative negligence,[8] payment,[9] illegality,[10] and res judicata.[11]

---

[6] See, e.g., GL 231, § 85 (comparative negligence). The Uniform Commercial Code (GL 106) has various provisions pertaining to burdens of persuasion. See, e.g., § 1-201(8) (definition of burden of persuasion); § 1-309 (burden of establishing lack of good faith is on the party against which the power has been exercised); § 2-607(4) (burden on buyer to establish breach after goods accepted); § 3-115 (burden of establishing unauthorized completion of paper on party so asserting); § 3-308 (burden of establishing genuineness of signature on party claiming under signature; burden of proving party is holder in due course is on party claiming those rights); § 4-202(b) (collecting bank has burden of establishing it took proper action within reasonable time when that time was longer than that expressly stipulated by § 4-202); § 4-403 (customer has burden of establishing fact and amount of loss from payment contrary to binding stop order). See also *Universal CIT Credit Corp. v. Ingel*, 347 Mass 119, 125, 196 NE2d 847, 851 (1964) (burden on defendants to rebut plaintiff's prima facie case of holder in due course).

[7] *Perky v. Perley*, 144 Mass 104, 10 NE 726 (1887).

[8] GL 231, § 85, eliminated the defenses of contributory negligence and assumption of risk in negligence cases, substituting comparative negligence, which may diminish the amount of recovery. The burden of alleging and proving comparative negligence is upon the party who seeks to establish such negligence.

[9] *McCarthy v. Simon*, 247 Mass 514, 521, 142 NE 806, 807 (1924).

[10] Although illegality is an affirmative defense to be pleaded by the defendant, the court will not act to enforce an illegal contract contrary to public policy even though neither party raises the issue. See *Cadillac Automobile Co. of Boston v. Engeian*, 339 Mass 26, 29-30, 157 NE2d 657, 659-660 (1959); *O'Donnell v. Bane*, 385 Mass 114, 117, 431 NE2d 190, 192 (1982) (extensive review of authorities) (contingent fee agreement for attorney's representation in criminal matter).

[11] See Mass R Civ P 8(c). For a sampling of the variety of affirmative defenses, see *Highlands Ins. Co. v. Aerovox, Inc.*, 424 Mass 226, 231, 676 NE2d 801, 805 (1997) (insured has burden of proving "sudden and accidental" release exception to pollution exclusion); *McGinnis v. Aetna Life & Casualty Co.*, 398 Mass 37, 494 NE2d 1322 (1986) (burden of proof on insurer to prove plaintiff intentionally procured loss); *Three Sons, Inc. v. Phoenix Ins. Co.*, 357 Mass 271, 257 NE2d 774 (1970) (laches); *Benoit v. Fisher*, 341 Mass 386, 169 NE2d 905 (1960) (cancellation of insurance coverage prior to accident); *Wellesley v. Brossi*, 340 Mass 456, 164 NE2d 883 (1960) (nonconforming use). For discussion of affirmative defenses in criminal cases, see § 3.4.1, infra.

§ 3.3.2 Degree of Persuasion in Civil Cases

a. Preponderance of the Evidence

Generally in civil cases the party who bears the burden of persuasion must persuade the fact finder that its contention is more probably true than not—proof "by a preponderance of the evidence."[12] The jury must find for the opponent if it believes either that the burdened party's contention is more probably false than true, *or* is as probably false as true.[13] Where the private interests of the litigants are not "fundamental" and there is no unusual risk of error, higher degrees of proof (as described in the following sections) have not been required.[14] Even allegations in a civil proceeding as to acts that may be penal in nature require no more proof than a preponderance of the evidence.[15]

The standard of proof in a probation revocation proceeding is the civil standard of preponderance of the evidence rather than the criminal standard of beyond a reasonable doubt.[16] When seeking restitution in connection with the commission of a crime, the Commonwealth bears the burden of proving the amount of the loss by a

---

[12] See *Goffredo v. Mercedes-Benz Truck Co.*, 402 Mass 97, 102-103, 520 NE2d 1315, 1318 (1988); *Corsetti v. The Stone Co.*, 396 Mass 1, 23-24, 483 NE2d 793, 805 (1985); *School Committee of Brookline v. Bureau of Special Education Appeals*, 389 Mass 705, 716, 452 NE2d 476, 482 (1983). See also Uniform Commercial Code, GL 106, § 1-201(8) (" 'Burden of establishing a fact' means the burden of persuading the triers of fact that the existence of the fact is more probable than its non-existence.").

[13] See *Corsetti v. The Stone Co.*, supra, 396 Mass at 24, 483 NE2d at 805; *Sargent v. Massachusetts Accident Co.*, 307 Mass 246, 251, 29 NE2d 825, 827-828 (1940) (where evidence tends to equally support two inconsistent propositions, neither can be found to be true).

[14] See, e.g., *Spence v. Gormley*, 387 Mass 258, 274-277, 439 NE2d 741, 750-751 (1982) (in proceedings to evict public housing tenant on basis of violent acts of member of tenant's household, ordinary civil standard of proof by preponderance of evidence is sufficient); *Phipps v. Barbera*, 23 Mass App 1, 4-6, 498 NE2d 411, 413-414 (1986) (with regard to latent ambiguity in will, claimant is required to show only by preponderance of evidence that it was intended beneficiary).

[15] See, e.g., *Frizado v. Frizado*, 420 Mass 592, 597, 651 NE2d 1206, 1210 (1995) (domestic abuse prevention proceeding pursuant to GL 209A); *Com. v. Guilfoyle*, 402 Mass 130, 136, 521 NE2d 984, 987 (1988) (issuance of injunction for civil rights violations); *Vaspourakan Ltd. v. Alcoholic Beverages Control Commission*, 401 Mass 347, 352, 516 NE2d 1153, 1157 (1987) (violation of criminal antidiscrimination statute); *Craven v. State Ethics Commission*, 390 Mass 191, 199-201, 454 NE2d 471, 476-477 (1983) (civil action alleging conduct for which criminal sanctions could have been imposed).

[16] See *Com. v. Hill*, 52 Mass App 147, 154, 751 NE2d 446, 451 (2001).

preponderance of the evidence.[17] Under the Massachusetts drug forfeiture statute, GL 94C, § 47(d), the Commonwealth need only prove the existence of probable cause to institute the action, shifting to the claimant the burden of proving the property is not forfeitable.[18]

While the phrase "preponderance of the evidence" has sometimes been defined in terms of probabilities,[19] statistical definition is disfavored.[20] It is "not enough that mathematically the chances somewhat favor a proposition to be proved; for example, the fact that colored automobiles made in the current year outnumber black ones would not warrant a finding that an undescribed automobile of the current year is colored and not black, nor would the fact that only a minority of men die of cancer warrant a finding that a particular man did not die of cancer."[21] The preponderance, which determines the verdict must be a preponderance of credible testimony, not a "balance of probabilities."[22]

b. Clear and Convincing Evidence

As to certain issues in civil cases where particularly important individual interests or rights are at stake, an intermediate standard of proof, "clear and convincing" evidence, applies. It is greater than "a preponderance" but less than "beyond a reasonable doubt."[23] "Clear

---

[17] *Com. v. McIntyre*, 436 Mass 829, 834, 767 NE2d 578, 583 (2002); *Com. v. Palmer P.*, 61 Mass App 230, 233, 808 NE2d 848, 850 (2004).

[18] See *Com. v. Brown*, 426 Mass 475, 688 NE2d 1356 (1998); *Com. v. One 2004 Audi Sedan Automobile*, 456 Mass 34, 38-39, 921 NE2d 85, 89-90 (2010).

[19] See, e.g., *Evangelio v. Metropolitan Bottling Co., Inc.*, 339 Mass 177, 182, 158 NE2d 342, 346 (1959).

[20] *Stepakoff v. Kantar*, 393 Mass 836, 842-843, 473 NE2d 1131, 1136 (1985).

[21] *Sargent v. Massachusetts Accident Co.*, supra, 307 Mass at 250, 29 NE2d at 827. See also *King's Case*, 352 Mass 488, 491-492, 225 NE2d 900, 902 (1967).

[22] *Callahan v. Fleischman Co.*, 262 Mass 437, 437-438, 160 NE 249, 250 (1928). For cases dealing with the wording of jury instructions on the preponderance standard, see *Sullivan v. Hamacher*, 339 Mass 190, 158 NE2d 301 (1959); *Knox v. Lamoureaux*, 338 Mass 167, 154 NE2d 342 (1958); *Tucker v. Pearlstein*, 334 Mass 33, 133 NE2d 489 (1956); *Footit v. Monsees*, 26 Mass App 173, 178-180, 525 NE2d 423, 427-428 (1988); *Grassis v. Retik*, 25 Mass App 595, 601-602, 521 NE2d 411, 415 (1988); *Fire Commissioner of Boston v. Joseph*, 23 Mass App 76, 82, 498 NE2d 1368, 1372 (1986). Instructions using "firm and abiding conviction" language to explain the preponderance of the evidence standard are disfavored. See *Shafnacker v. Raymond James & Associates*, 425 Mass 724, 736-737, 683 NE2d 662, 670-671 (1997).

[23] See generally *MacDonald v. Caruso*, 467 Mass 382, 5 NE2d 831 (2014); *Medical Malpractice Joint Underwriting Association of Massachusetts v. Commissioner of Ins.*, 395 Mass 43, 46-47, 478 NE2d 936, 939 (1985), *Stone v. Essex County Newspapers, Inc.*, 367 Mass 849, 871, 330 NE2d 161, 175 (1975).

and convincing" proof requires that the evidence must be sufficient to convey a "high degree of probability" that the proposition is true.[24] The proof must be "strong, positive and free from doubt;" it has also been described as "full, clear and decisive."[25]

The "clear and convincing" standard is applicable in the following contexts:

- Termination of parental rights.[26]

---

[24] *Tosti v. Ayik*, 394 Mass 482, 493 n.9, 476 NE2d 928, 936 n.9 (1985).

[25] *Doe v. Sex Offender Registry Board*, 473 Mass 297, 309, 41 NE3d 1058, 1068 (2015); *Callahan v. Westinghouse Broadcasting Co., Inc.*, 372 Mass 582, 584, 363 NE2d 240, 241 (1977).

[26] As a matter of federal constitutional law, termination of parental rights requires proof by "clear and convincing" evidence. *Santosky v. Kramer*, 455 US 74 (1982). For Massachusetts cases, see *Adoption of Carla*, 416 Mass 510, 517-518, 623 NE2d 1118, 1122 (1993) (GL 210, § 3); *Adoption of Carlos*, 413 Mass 339, 348, 596 NE2d 1383, 1388 (1992); *Care and Protection of Martha*, 407 Mass 319, 327, 553 NE2d 902, 906-907 (1990) (GL 119, § 24); *Care & Protection of Yetta*, 84 Mass App 691, 695-696, 2 NE2d 910, 914-915 (2014). Where the proceeding can deprive the parent of custody only temporarily, the lesser standard of "fair preponderance of the evidence" governs. See *Care and Protection of Manuel*, 428 Mass 527, 534, 703 NE2d 211, 216 (1998) and *Care and Protection of Robert*, 408 Mass 52, 556 NE2d 993 (1990) (72 hour hearings pursuant to GL 119, §§ 24 and 25).

The burden of proof in care and protection cases and proceedings to dispense with consent to adoption remains on the petitioner, and never shifts to the parents. *Adoption of Larry*, 434 Mass 456, 470, 750 NE2d 475, 487 (2001). Similarly, in a petition for review and redetermination of an initial finding that a child was in need of care and protection, the Department of Social Services bears the ultimate burden to prove by clear and convincing evidence that the child is still in need; the party filing the petition has the initial burden to produce some credible evidence that circumstances have changed. *Care & Protection of Erin*, 443 Mass 567, 823 NE2d 356 (2005). See also *Petitions of the Department of Social Services to Dispense with Consent to Adoption*, 389 Mass 793, 802-803, 452 NE2d 497, 503 (1983) (declaring invalid GL 210, § 3(c), establishing presumption against parental rights for child in the care of the DSS or licensed child care agency for more than one year). But see *Opinion of the Justices*, 427 Mass 1201, 691 NE2d 911 (1998) (finding constitutional a proposed burden-shifting bill that would provide that in custody dispute, if one parent proves by preponderance of evidence that other parent engaged in abuse of child, rebuttable presumption arises that it is not in child's best interest to be in custody of challenged parent). Circumstantial evidence is sufficient to meet the "clear and convincing" standard in child custody cases. See *Adoption of Keefe*, 49 Mass App 818, 824-825, 733 NE2d 1075, 1080 (2000).

In the parental rights area, careful factual inspection and specific, detailed findings by the trial court are mandated. *Adoption of Hugo*, 428 Mass 219, 224, 700 NE2d 516, 520 (1998); *Care and Protection of Three Minors*, 392 Mass 704, 467 NE2d 851 (1984). See, e.g., *Adoption of Ramona*, 61 Mass App 260, 809 NE2d 547 (2004) (judge failed to make specific and current findings regarding mother's fitness); *Adoption of Nancy*, 61 Mass App 252, 258, 809 NE2d 554, 560 (2004) (judge failed to make specific findings on best interests of children); *Adoption of Stuart*, 39 Mass App 380, 656 NE2d

- Sex Offender Registry Board classification hearings.[27]
- Temporary civil commitment proceedings for treatment of alcohol or drug abuse pursuant to GL 123, § 35.[28]
- Action by putative father to establish paternity of child born out of wedlock to married woman.[29]
- Issue of malice in a public figure defamation case.[30]
- Claim for reformation of contract for mutual mistake.[31]
- Contents of a lost will.[32]
- Gift causa mortis.[33]
- Pretrial detention on grounds of dangerousness pursuant to GL 276, § 58A.[34]
- Claims under the Massachusetts Erroneous Convictions Law, GL 258D.[35]

---

916 (1995) (reversing trial court's termination of parental rights); *Petition of the Department of Social Services to Dispense with Consent to Adoption*, 391 Mass 113, 461 NE2d 186 (1984) (judge's findings inadequate to sustain conclusion of unfitness of putative biological father); *Adoption of Inez*, 45 Mass App 171, 696 NE2d 164 (1998) (clear and convincing evidence did not support finding of unfitness). Subsidiary evidentiary findings, however, need only be proved by a fair preponderance of the evidence. *Adoption of Hugo*, supra; *In re Care and Protection of Rebecca*, 419 Mass 67, 81, 643 NE2d 26, 34 (1994).

[27] *Doe v. Sex Offender Registry Board*, 473 Mass 297, 41 NE3d 1058 (2015) (substituting clear and convincing standard for prior standard of preponderance of the evidence).

[28] *In re G.P.*, 473 Mass 112, 118-120, 40 NE3d 989, 994-996 (2015).

[29] *C.C v. A.B.*, 406 Mass 679, 686-687, 550 NE2d 365, 370-371 (1990).

[30] *New York Times Co. v. Sullivan*, 376 US 254 (1964); *Tosti v. Ayik*, 394 Mass 482, 491, 476 NE2d 928, 935 (1985); *Callahan v. Westinghouse Broadcasting Co., Inc.*, 372 Mass 582, 363 NE2d 240 (1977). See also *Bose Corp. v. Consumers Union of the United States*, 466 US 485 (1984) (issue of malice in defamation action for product disparagement).

[31] *Kidder v. Greenman*, 283 Mass 601, 613-614, 187 NE 42, 47-48 (1933) (distinguishing reformation for mutual mistake, to which higher standard applies, from reformation for unauthorized completion of instrument, to which higher standard does not apply); *Covich v. Chambers*, 8 Mass App 740, 397 NE2d 1115 (1979).

[32] *Coghlin v. White*, 273 Mass 53, 55, 172 NE 786 (1930). But compare *Rubenstein v. Royal Ins. Company of America*, 44 Mass App 842, 846, 694 NE2d 381, 384 (1998) (mere preponderance of evidence required to prove existence and contents of lost insurance policy).

[33] *Foley v. Coan*, 272 Mass 207, 172 NE 74 (1930).

[34] See *Mendonza v. Com.*, 423 Mass 771, 782-784, 673 NE2d 22, 30-31 (1996) (failure to require proof beyond reasonable doubt does not violate constitutional protections).

[35] *Guzman v. Com.*, 458 Mass 354, 357, 937 NE2d 441, 444 (2010).

- Motions to terminate abuse prevention orders issued under GL 209A.[36]

The Supreme Judicial Court has suggested the following form of jury instruction with regard to the clear and convincing evidence standard:

> The burden of persuasion, therefore, in those cases requiring a showing of clear and convincing proof is sustained if evidence induces in the mind of the trier a reasonable belief that the facts asserted are highly probably true, that the probability that they are true or exist is substantially greater than the probability that they are false or do not exist.[37]

The instruction should be preceded by an instruction that the jury should examine the evidence and weigh the probabilities with particular care.[38]

The courts have been reluctant to extend the clear and convincing evidence standard beyond the instances set out above, suggesting that it too often serves as the "functional equivalent" for the reasonable doubt standard.[39]

On a petition brought by a guardian of a mentally incompetent person seeking an order to permit involuntary sterilization of the ward, the court has rejected both the "proof beyond a reasonable doubt" and the "clear and convincing evidence" standards. The preponderance of the evidence standard, augmented by the requirement of "utmost care" and "detailed written findings" by the judge, was found sufficient to protect the incompetent ward's rights.[40]

---

[36] *MacDonald v. Caruso*, 467 Mass 382, 5 NE2d 831 (2014) (defendant who seeks to terminate order must show by clear and convincing evidence that, as result of a significant change in circumstances, the order is no longer necessary).

[37] *Callahan v. Westinghouse Broadcasting Co., Inc.*, supra, 372 Mass at 588, 363 NE2d at 244.

[38] *Id.*

[39] See *Medical Malpractice Joint Underwriting Association of Massachusetts v. Commissioner of Ins.*, 395 Mass 43, 47, 478 NE2d 936, 939 (1985).

[40] *In re Moe*, 385 Mass 555, 570-572, 432 NE2d 712, 723-724 (1982) (but suggesting that such petition brought by the Commonwealth might require a higher standard of proof). See also *In re Moe*, 31 Mass App 473, 479, 579 NE2d 682, 686-687 (1991) (judge erred in requiring "a higher standard of proof" on petition seeking authorization for abortion and sterilization of ward).

c. Beyond a Reasonable Doubt

Certain types of proceedings designated "civil" have been deemed to involve such fundamental interests that a requirement of proof beyond a reasonable doubt is warranted:[41]

- Commitment or transfer to treatment center for sexually dangerous persons.[42]
- Involuntary commitment to or retention in mental health facility.[43]
- Need for involuntary administration of antipsychotic drugs.[44]

---

[41] For an extensive discussion of the use of the reasonable doubt standard in civil cases, see *In re Andrews*, 449 Mass 587, 870 NE2d 610 (2007).

[42] *In re Wyatt*, 428 Mass 347, 360, 701 NE2d 337, 346 (1998). The Commonwealth bears the burden (in either an original commitment or petition to discharge) of proving beyond a reasonable doubt that the individual is currently a sexually dangerous person, meaning a present mental condition that results in uncontrolled sexual impulses and creates a likelihood of sexually dangerous conduct in the future. See *In Re Dutil*, 437 Mass 9, 15-17, 768 NE2d 1055, 1062-1063 (2002). See also *Kansas v. Hendricks*, 521 US 346 (1997) and *Kansas v. Crane*, 534 US 407 (2002). The Commonwealth is not required to prove likelihood of danger to any particular mathematical quantum; rather, "likely" means it is reasonably to be expected in the context of the particular facts and circumstances at hand. *Com. v. Boucher*, 438 Mass 274, 780 NE2d 48 (2002).

The standard of proof for temporary commitment under the SDP statute, GL 123A, § 12(e), is the probable cause to arrest standard. *Com. v. Bruno*, 432 Mass 489, 507-508, 735 NE2d 1222, 1235-1236 (2000). The standard to have an offender civilly committed under § 12(c) for further examination is the bind-over directed verdict standard, i.e., whether there is enough credible evidence to send the case to the jury. *Com. v. Reese*, 438 Mass 519, 781 NE2d 1225 (2003).

In contrast, the preponderance of the evidence standard controls at sex offender classification hearings. See *Soe v. Sex Offender Registry Board*, 466 Mass 381, 396, 995 NE2d 73, 85-86 (2013) (acquittal at criminal trial does not foreclose finding to the contrary); *Doe v. Sex Offender Registry Board*, 428 Mass 90, 100-104, 697 NE2d 512, 518-520 (1998) (Board must show risk of reoffense by preponderance of evidence for purpose of classification).

[43] *Kirk v. Com.*, 459 Mass 67, 72, 944 NE2d 135, 139 (2011); *D. L. v. Commissioner of Social Services*, 412 Mass 558, 564 n.11, 591 NE2d 173, 176 n.11 (1992). But compare *Addington v. Texas*, 441 US 418 (1979) (federal due process requires only "clear and convincing" proof); *Jones v. United States*, 463 US 354, 368 (1983) (preponderance of evidence standard satisfies due process for commitment of insanity acquittees). A patient applying for transfer or discharge from a secure mental health facility bears the burden of proving by a fair preponderance of the evidence that his situation has significantly changed. See *In re Andrews*, 449 Mass 587, 870 NE2d 610 (2007) (extensive discussion).

[44] *In re Guardianship of Roe*, 383 Mass 415, 422-426, 421 NE2d 40, 45-47 (1981).

- Petition to retain custody of juvenile under GL 120, § 17.[45]
- Adjudication of delinquency. See GL 119, § 58.

The standard of proof under GL 123, § 17(b), allowing an incompetent defendant an opportunity to have the charges dismissed, is lack of substantial evidence.[46]

d. Standards of Proof Under Administrative Procedure Act

See § 14.2, infra.

§ 3.4 Burden of Persuasion in Criminal Cases

§ 3.4.1 Allocation of Burden of Persuasion in Criminal Cases

In criminal cases, the burden of persuasion (as well as production) as to all elements of the crime is on the Commonwealth.[1] Where the issue is raised by defendant,[2] the Commonwealth must prove the following beyond a reasonable doubt:

- The sanity of the defendant.[3]

---

[45] *Department of Youth Services v. A Juvenile*, 384 Mass 784, 791-793, 429 NE2d 709, 713-714 (1981). See also *Kenniston v. Department of Youth Services*, 453 Mass 179, 190, 900 NE2d 852, 862 (2009) (DYS proposed "probable cause" standard was constitutionally deficient).

[46] *Com. v. Hatch*, 438 Mass 618, 783 NE2d 393 (2003).

§ 3.4 [1] *Sandstrom v. Montana*, 442 US 510 (1979); *Mullaney v. Wilbur*, 421 US 684 (1975); *In re Winship*, 397 US 358 (1970). See also *Com. v. Amirault*, 404 Mass 221, 240, 535 NE2d 193, 205 (1989); *Com. v. Pickles*, 393 Mass 775, 778, 473 NE2d 694, 696-697 (1985); *Com. v. Teixera*, 396 Mass 746, 748, 488 NE2d 775, 777-778 (1986); *Com. v. Burke*, 390 Mass 480, 483-484, 457 NE2d 622, 624-625 (1983). *See also Com. v. Cruz*, 456 Mass 741, 751-753, 926 NE2d 142, 150- 151 (2010) (any confusion engendered by defense counsel's opening statement was corrected by judge's admonitions that Commonwealth bore the burden of proof).

[2] The question of whether a defendant has sufficiently "raised" an issue of insanity or other defense "relates not to the burden of persuasion but to the burden of producing evidence." *Com. v. Mills*, 400 Mass 626, 632, 511 NE2d 572, 576 (1987) (O'Connor, J, dissenting). See § 3.2.1, supra. See also *Simopoulos v. Virginia*, 462 US 506 (1983) (defense of medical necessity must be disproved by state only where defendant's evidence raises issue); *Com. v. Johnston*, 63 Mass App 680, 685, 828 NE2d 568, 573 (2005) (an instruction on malice is not required until defendant offers evidence of justification, excuse, or mitigation).

[3] See *Com. v. Keita*, 429 Mass 843, 849, 712 NE2d 65, 70 (1999) (declining to change burden of proof on criminal responsibility from prosecution to defendant);

- The absence of mental disease or defect or diminished capacity.[4]
- The absence of self-defense or use of excessive force.[5]
- The absence of accident.[6]
- The lack of consent.[7]
- The presence of malice or intent, or the absence of reasonable provocation or heat of passion.[8]

Com. v. Kappler, 416 Mass 574, 578-579, 625 NE2d 513, 516 (1993); *Com. v. Mills*, 400 Mass 626, 630, 511 NE2d 572, 575 (1987); *Com. v. Berry*, 457 Mass 602, 612, 931 NE2d 972, 980 (once defendant raises issue of criminal responsibility, Commonwealth has burden to prove, beyond a reasonable doubt, that defendant did not lack responsibility). In contrast, the Commonwealth's burden of proving the defendant is competent to stand trial is preponderance of the evidence. *Com. v. Hilton*, 450 Mass 173, 179-180, 877 NE2d 545, 551-552 (2007).

[4] See *Com. v. Goudreau*, 422 Mass 731, 735-736, 666 NE2d 112, 115 (1996); *Com. v. Angelone*, 413 Mass 82, 84, 594 NE2d 866, 867 (1992).

[5] See *Com. v. Walker*, 443 Mass 213, 219, 820 NE2d 195, 201-202 (2005), *habeas petition denied in Walker v. Russo*, 483 F Supp 2d 128 (D Mass 2007); *Com. v. Whitman*, 430 Mass 746, 755-757, 722 NE2d 1284, 1292-1293 (2000); *Com. v. Rodriguez*, 370 Mass 684, 352 NE2d 203 (1976); *Com. v. Graham*, 62 Mass App 642, 652-653, 818 NE2d 1069, 1077-1078 (2004) (where evidence supports a claim of excessive or unnecessary force by police and concomitant right to self-defense, judge must instruct that Commonwealth must prove beyond a reasonable doubt that police did not engage in excessive force as well as that defendant did not act in self-defense); *Com. v. Haddock*, 46 Mass App 246, 248, 704 NE2d 537, 540 (1999). See also *Com. v. Baseler*, 419 Mass 500, 502-503, 645 NE2d 1179, 1181 (1995) (conviction reversed because jury instructions lowered state's burden of proof on self-defense); *Com. v. Koonce*, 418 Mass 367, 370-375, 636 NE2d 1305, 1307-1309 (1994) (patently erroneous instruction on excessive force did not shift burden to defendant).

[6] See *Com. v. Podkowka*, 445 Mass 692, 699, 840 NE2d 476, 482 (2006); *Com. v. Jewett*, 442 Mass 356, 370, 813 NE2d 452, 463-464 (2004), *habeas denied, Jewett v. Brady*, 634 F3d 67 (1st Cir 2011); *Com. v. Lowe*, 391 Mass 97, 108-112, 461 NE2d 192, 199-200 (1984).

[7] See *Com. v. Shore*, 65 Mass App 430, 431, 840 NE2d 1010, 1011 (2006) (indecent assault).

[8] See *Francis v. Franklin*, 471 US 307 (1985); *Sandstrom v. Montana*, supra; *Mullaney v. Wilbur*, supra; *Com. v. Randolph*, 438 Mass 290, 298, 780 NE2d 58, 67 (2002) (instruction impermissibly shifted burden of proving absence of provocation to defendant); *Com. v. Laoage*, 435 Mass 480, 483-484, 759 NE2d 300, 304 (2001) (reversing conviction because of erroneous instruction shifting burden to defendant to prove provocation); *Com. v. Little*, 431 Mass 782, 787-791, 730 NE2d 304, 308-311 (2000) (trial judge's misstatements on Commonwealth's burden of proving provocation, as factor negating malice, outweighed correct instructions and required reversal); *Com. v. Carlino*, 429 Mass 692, 710 NE2d 967 (1999) (instructions concerning provocation, self-defense, and defense of another were either erroneous or misleading); *Com. v. Acevedo*, 427 Mass 714, 695 NE2d 1065 (1998) (absence of provocation); *Com. v. Giguere*, 420 Mass 226, 230, 648 NE2d 1279, 1282 (1995) (use of phrase "reduce murder to manslaughter" did not shift burden of proof to defendant); *Com. v. Eagles*, 419 Mass 825, 834-837, 648 NE2d 410, 416-418 (1995); *Com. v. A Juvenile (No. 1)*, 396 Mass 108, 115, 483 NE2d 822, 826-827 (1985); *Com. v. Nieves*, 394 Mass 355, 359-360, 476 NE2d

- Predisposition of defendant where entrapment defense is presented.[9]
- In willful non-support case, the defendant's financial ability to support the child.[10]
- When age is an element of offense charged, the Commonwealth must prove that fact.[11]
- Absence of lawful authority of a bail bondsman.[12]
- The Commonwealth must disprove any affirmative defense.[13]

179, 182 (1985); *Com. v. McLeod*, 394 Mass 727, 738-740, 477 NE2d 972, 982 (1985); *Com. v. Rodriguez*, 58 Mass App 610, 611-618, 792 NE2d 131, 133-138 (2003) (erroneous instruction on provocation created substantial risk of miscarriage of justice); *Com. v. Dempsey*, 49 Mass App 247, 729 NE2d 293 (2000) (confusion in instructions on provocation and malice required reversal); *Com. v. Grant*, 49 Mass App 169, 727 NE2d 1207 (2000) (incorrect burden-shifting language on provocation required reversal even though central issue was self-defense). *DeJoinville v. Com.*, 381 Mass 246, 408 NE2d 1353 (1980). Compare *Com. v. Fickling*, 434 Mass 9, 18-20, 746 NE2d 475, 483-484 (2001) (no reversal required where two correct instructions were sandwiched between two incorrect instructions); *Com. v. Mandeville*, 386 Mass 393, 406-408, 436 NE2d 912, 921-922 (1982) (court would not consider argument that judge's instructions on malice improperly shifted burden of proof in absence of objection and where only seriously contested issue was identity). See also *Com. v. Vick*, 454 Mass 418, 430, 910 NE2d 339, 351 (2009) (where there is no credible evidence of provocation, Commonwealth had no burden to prove absence of mitigation beyond a reasonable doubt).

Where it is raised to negate the element of malice in a homicide case, the Commonwealth need not disprove defendant's intoxication beyond a reasonable doubt. *Com. v. Purcell*, 423 Mass 880, 882, 673 NE2d 53, 54 (1996).

[9] See *Com. v. Monteagudo*, 427 Mass 484, 487, 693 NE2d 1381, 1384 (1998).

[10] See *Com. v. Teixera*, 396 Mass 746, 488 NE2d 775 (1986).

[11] See *Com. v. Pittman*, 25 Mass App 25, 514 NE2d 857 (1987).

[12] *Com. v. Cabral*, 443 Mass 171, 819 NE2d 951 (2005) (defendant claiming to have lawful authority as a bail bondsman to apprehend a principal bears only the burden of production to raise the defense; once that burden is met, the Commonwealth must prove beyond a reasonable doubt that defendant lacked the lawful authority or exceeded its bounds).

[13] See *Com. v. Cabral*, supra, 443 Mass at 178-182, 819 NE2d at 957-960; *Com. v. Vives*, 447 Mass 537, 540-541, 854 NE2d 1241, 1243-1244 (2006) (armed robbery defendant's claim that he honestly and reasonably believed he was collecting a debt from the victim is an affirmative defense; as such, once defendant has met his burden of production, it is incumbent upon the Commonwealth to disprove it). Where in a larceny case the defendant meets his burden of production on the defense that he honestly but mistakenly believed he had legal right to the property, the Commonwealth must disprove that beyond a reasonable doubt. *Com. v. St. Hilaire*, 470 Mass 338, 348, 21 NE3d 968, 977-978 (2015); *Com. v. Liebenow*, 470 Mass 151, 152-153, 20 NE3d 242, 244 (2014).

In a firearm possession prosecution, defendant has the burden to produce evidence of the affirmative defense that he possessed a license; if such evidence is presented, the Commonwealth has the burden to disprove the defense. See *Com. v. Allen*, 474 Mass 162, 174, 48 NE3d 427, 438 (2016); *Com. v. Tavares*, 471 Mass 430, 444, 30

Instructions or argument suggesting to the jury that has the defendant has the burden of proof on any of these matters are improper.[14] Instructions using "finding" language—"if you find that defendant acted in self-defense"—may erroneously lead the jury to believe the defendant has the burden of proof and are thus disfavored.[15] Argument suggesting that defendant has the burden of producing exculpatory evidence,[16] or suggesting that defendant has the burden to

---

NE3d 91, 105 (2015); *Com. v. Gouse*, 461 Mass 787, 802-804, 965 NE2d 774, 786-789 (2011); *Com. v. Eberhart*, 461 Mass 809, 813-814, 965 NE2d 791, 795 (2012); *Com. v. Powell*, 459 Mass 572, 582, 946 NE2d 114, 124 (2011), *habeas denied, Powell v. Tompkins*, 783 F3d 332 (1st Cir 2015); *Com. v. Smith*, 75 Mass App 196, 201, 912 NE2d 542, 547-548 (2009), *aff'd on other grounds*, 458 Mass 1012, 935 NE2d 770 (2010) (burden is on the defendant in an unlawful possession prosecution to come forward with evidence that he possesses a license); *Com. v. Farley*, 64 Mass App 854, 860-862, 835 NE2d 1159, 1166-1167 (2005) (it is an affirmative defense under GL 269, § 10, unlawful possession of firearm without license, that defendant's license expired; defendant has burden of production, which when met places burden on Commonwealth to disprove). See also *Com. v. Jefferson*, 461 Mass 821, 833-834, 965 NE2d 800 (2012) (defendant has burden of production on exemption for antique firearms; if such evidence is presented, the Commonwealth has the burden to disprove it); *Com. v. Indrisano*, 87 Mass App 709, 713-714, 35 NE3d 722, 727 (2015) (burden is on defendant asserting affirmative defense of licensure to present sufficient evidence to contest the presumed fact that he had no justification for his lack of license).

The prosecution has the burden to prove that a firearm is operable and capable of firing a bullet, but the burden is to produce "competent evidence" from which the jury reasonably can draw inferences that the weapon will fire. *Com. v. Drapaniotis*, 89 Mass 267, 270, 48 NE3d 45, 47-48 (2016).

Where the parental privilege defense is raised in an assault and battery case involving the child, the Commonwealth bears the burden of disproving it beyond a reasonable doubt. *Com. v. Dorvil*, 472 Mass 1, 13, 32 NE3d 861, 871 (2015).

[14] See *Com. v. Palacios*, 66 Mass App 13, 15, 845 NE2d 382, 385 (2006).

[15] See *Com. v. Beauchamp*, 424 Mass 682, 689-8-690, 677 NE2d 1135, 1139 (1997). Compare *Com. v. Petetabella*, 459 Mass 177, 191-193, 944 NE2d 582, 594-595 (2011) (instruction "it becomes incumbent upon the Court to discuss with you what would be the effect of drunkenness or what would be the effect of intoxication, if you should *find* that any or either or all these defendants were intoxicated or drunk," was not error in its context, but finding language is disfavored); *Com. v. Williams*, 450 Mass 879, 884, 883 NE2d 249, 254 (2008) (rejecting attempt to equate "must have" and "must be" language in self-defense instruction with impermissible "finding" language); *Com. v. Kirker*, 441 Mass 226, 229-230, 804 NE2d 922, 925-926 (2004) (disfavored "finding" language does not automatically require reversal and may be corrected by appropriate instructions); *Com. v. Whitman*, 430 Mass 746, 756, 722 NE2d 1284, 1292-1293 (2000) (although "finding" language in connection with self-defense instructions could have given jury impression that burden was on defendant, instructions prevented prejudice); *Com. v. Shea*, 401 Mass 731, 742-743, 519 NE2d 1283, 1289-1290 (1988) (judge's use of "finding language" did not require reversal).

[16] *Com. v. Martinez*, 431 Mass 168, 178-179, 726 NE2d 913, 924 (2000).

counter expert evidence,[17] are improper. Instructions concerning alibi which appear to shift the burden of proof to the defendant must be avoided.[18]

Presumptions that relieve the government of its burden of persuasion are impermissible. See § 3.5.6, infra.

§ 3.4.2 Degree of Persuasion in Criminal Cases

a. Proof Beyond a Reasonable Doubt

In criminal cases, proof of guilt beyond a reasonable doubt is required by the Due Process Clause of the Fourteenth Amendment to the United States Constitution.[19] The requirement applies to every element of the offense charged and also extends to non-existence of facts or circumstances that would mitigate the degree of the defendant's culpability (as discussed in § 3.4.1, supra).[20]

"The reasonable-doubt standard plays a vital role in the American scheme of criminal procedure. It is a prime instrument for reducing

---

[17] *Com. v. Conkey*, 430 Mass 139, 147, 714 NE2d 343, 350-351 (1999). But compare *Com. v. Walker*, 443 Mass 213, 223, 820 NE2d 195, 204 (2005) *habeas petition denied in Walker v. Russo*, 483 F Supp 2d 128 (D Mass 2007) (instruction on credibility that "when you disbelieve a witness it means that you have to look elsewhere for credible evidence about the issue. It does not mean that something did not happen," did not shift burden of proof to defendant); *Com. v. Farley*, 443 Mass 740, 744-747, 824 NE2d 797, 802-804 (2005), *habeas denied*, *Farley v. Bissonnette*, 544 F3d 344 (1st Cir 2009) (instruction that Commonwealth did not have burden of proving that no one else had committed the murder did not impermissibly shift burden of proof to defendant, even though defendant presented third-party culprit theory).

[18] See *Com. v. Gonzalez*, 473 Mass 415, 427-428, 42 NE3d 1078, 1089 (2015) (prosecutor was entitled to question defendant about missing alibi witness to establish the predicate for the instruction, which did not shift burden to defendant to corroborate his alibi); *Com. v. Murphy*, 442 Mass 485, 497-498, 813 NE2d 820, 831-832 (2004) (instruction stating "if you believe the defendant's alibi" did not shift burden of proof; recommended instruction set out); *Com. v. Berth*, 385 Mass 784, 434 NE2d 192 (1982); *Com. v. Bowden*, 379 Mass 472, 480-482, 399 NE2d 482, 488-489 (1980); *Com. v. Williams*, 378 Mass 242, 390 NE2d 1114 (1979).

[19] *In re Winship*, 397 US 358 (1970).

[20] Although every necessary element of the crime must be proved beyond a reasonable doubt, it does not follow that every piece of evidence must be admissible beyond a reasonable doubt or that any inference drawn be proved beyond a reasonable doubt. *Com. v. Azar*, 32 Mass App 290, 309-310, 588 NE2d 1352, 1364-1365 (1992). Nor is defendant entitled to an instruction that in order to draw inferences or conclusions from facts, those subsidiary facts must be proven beyond a reasonable doubt. See *Com. v. Walker*, 443 Mass 213, 222-223, 820 NE2d 195, 204 (2005), *habeas petition denied in Walker v. Russo*, 483 F Supp 2d 128 (D Mass 2007).

the risk of convictions resting on factual error. The standard provides concrete substance for the presumption of innocence—that bedrock axiomatic and elementary principle whose enforcement lies at the foundation of the administration of our criminal law."[21]

b. "Reasonable Doubt" Defined/Jury Instructions

For more than 150 years, the gold standard definition of reasonable doubt in Massachusetts was the *Webster* charge:

> [Reasonable doubt] is a term often used, probably pretty well understood, but not easily defined. It is not mere possible doubt; because everything relating to human affairs, and depending on moral evidence, is open to some possible or imaginary doubt. It is that state of the case, which, after the entire comparison and consideration of all the evidence, leaves the minds of jurors in that condition that they cannot say they feel an abiding conviction, to a moral certainty, of the truth of the charge.[22]

The Supreme Judicial Court consistently reaffirmed its confidence in the *Webster* formulation,[23] and repeatedly encouraged trial judges to use it substantially verbatim.[24] But mindful of the criticism of the charge over the years, particularly the practice of defining reasonable doubt in terms of "moral certainty,"[25] the Supreme Judicial Court

---

[21] *In re Winship*, supra, 397 US at 363. See also *Com. v. Blanchette*, 409 Mass 99, 105, 564 NE2d 992, 995-996 (1991); *Com. v. Figueroa*, 451 Mass 566, 571-572, 887 NE2d 1040, 1045 (2008) (presumption of innocence is closely tied to State's burden of proof beyond reasonable doubt).

[22] *Com. v. Webster*, 59 Mass (5 Cush) 295, 320 (1850).

[23] See *Com. v. Ortiz*, 435 Mass 569, 579-580, 760 NE2d 282, 290-291 (2002) (& citations). "Because the *Webster* charge, apart from the term 'moral certainty,' defines reasonable doubt in a manner that conveys to a jury the need to determine guilt based solely on all evidence and to a state of near certitude, and avoids language that would permit conviction by a lesser standard of guilt or on factors other than courtroom proof, the charge has always been, and remains today, the preferred and adequate charge on the Commonwealth's burden of proof." *Com. v. Watkins*, 433 Mass 539, 546-547, 744 NE2d 645, 650 (2001).

[24] See *Com. v. Holman*, 51 Mass App 786, 790, 748 NE2d 509, 512-513 (2001) (& citations).

[25] See, e.g, *Victor v. Nebraska*, 511 US 1, 14-15 (1994); *Cage v. Louisiana*, 498 US 39 (1990) (invalidating "moral certainty" instruction, which reasonable juror could have interpreted to lower constitutionally required proof). *Gilday v. Callahan*, 59 F3d 257, 262-263 (1st Cir 1995); *Lanigan v. Maloney*, 853 F2d 40, 47 n.4 (1st Cir 1988).

in 2015 exercised its supervisory power to require a uniform instruction employing more modern language, and further defining "moral certainty":

> The burden is on the Commonwealth to prove beyond a reasonable doubt that the defendant is guilty of the charge(s) made against him (her).
>
> What is proof beyond a reasonable doubt? The term is often used and probably pretty well understood, though it is not easily defined. Proof beyond a reasonable doubt does not mean proof beyond all possible doubt, for everything in the lives of human beings is open to some possible or imaginary doubt. A charge is proved beyond a reasonable doubt if, after you have compared and considered all of the evidence, you have in your minds an abiding conviction, to a moral certainty, that the charge is true. When we refer to moral certainty, we mean the highest degree of certainty possible in matters relating to human affairs—based solely on the evidence that has been put before you in this case.
>
> I have told you that every person is presumed to be innocent until he or she is proved guilty, and that the burden of proof is on the prosecutor. If you evaluate all the evidence and you still have a reasonable doubt remaining, the defendant is entitled to the benefit of that doubt and must be acquitted.
>
> It is not enough for the Commonwealth to establish a probability, even a strong probability, that the defendant is more likely to be guilty than not guilty. That is not enough. Instead, the evidence must convince you of the defendant's guilt to a reasonable and moral certainty; a certainty that convinces your understanding and satisfies your reason and judgment as jurors who are sworn to act conscientiously on the evidence.
>
> This is what we mean by proof beyond a reasonable doubt.[26]

While there is no constitutional requirement to specifically charge the jury to presume the defendant innocent, the instructions on the Commonwealth's burden of proof must amply fulfill this core purpose.[27] The *Russell* charge is designed with this in mind.

Pre-*Russell* decisions had warned against:

---

[26] *Com. v. Russell*, 470 Mass 464, 23 NE3d 867 (2015) (Cordy, J.).

[27] See *Com. v. Viera*, 42 Mass App 916, 917-918, 676 NE2d 66, 67 (1997) (& citations).

- Language implying that the presumption of innocence disappears as the Commonwealth begins to introduce evidence of guilt.[28]
- Reference to specific examples of important personal decisions in the jurors' own lives, which risks trivializing the matter.[29]
- Attempts to quantify proof beyond a reasonable doubt or to give numeric examples.[30]
- Use of the phrase "doubt based upon a reason," because of its potential to shift the burden of proof to the defendant (but the phrase "doubt based *on reason*" is permissible).[31]

Instructions that incorporated negative definitions of reasonable doubt—what reasonable doubt is *not*—had been upheld where the negative definitions were counterbalanced by instructions following *Com. v. Webster*.[32] Judges were permitted to contrast reasonable doubt with absolute certainty,[33] or the doubt that might exist in the mind of

---

[28] *Com. v. Rodriguez*, 437 Mass 554, 560, 773 NE2d 946, 952 (2002); *Com. v. O'Brien*, 56 Mass App 170, 174, 775 NE2d 798, 801 (2002); *Pagano v. Allard*, 218 F Supp 2d 26, 32-33 (D Mass 2002). The presumption disappears only after the Commonwealth has presented evidence that convinces the jury of defendant's guilt beyond a reasonable doubt. *Com. v. O'Brien*, 56 Mass App at 174 n.5, 775 NE2d at 801-802 n.5. Nor may it be implied that the defendant is required to produce evidence or witnesses to halt the downward slide of the presumption. *Id.*

[29] See *Com. v. McGrath*, 437 Mass 46, 48, 768 NE2d 1075, 1076 (2002); *Com. v. Bonds*, 424 Mass 698, 677 NE2d 1131 (1997) (instructions that equate proof beyond reasonable doubt with moral certainty, and then compare that with certainty required to make important personal decisions, are unconstitutional). See also *Com. v. Rupp*, 57 Mass App 377, 385, 783 NE2d 475, 481 (2003) (prosecutor's comments that jurors use circumstantial evidence in their everyday lives to draw conclusions beyond a reasonable doubt improperly trivialized the concept).

[30] See *Com. v. Rosa*, 422 Mass 18, 27-29, 661 NE2d 56, 62-63 (1996) (& citations). "The idea of reasonable doubt is not susceptible to quantification; it is inherently qualitative." *Com. v. Ferreira*, 77 Mass App 675, 680-682, 933 NE2d 685, 689-691 (2010), *rev'd on other grounds*, 460 Mass 781, 955 NE2d 898 (2011) (prosecutor's probability-based argument regarding identifications of defendant was improper). See also Com. v. Hunt, 462 Mass 807, 971 NE2d 768 (2012) (references to "an even balance in the evidence" should be avoided).

[31] See *Com. v. Anderson*, 425 Mass 685, 690, 682 NE2d 859, 863 (1997). See also *Com. v. Slonka*, 42 Mass App 760, 762, 680 NE2d 103, 105-106 (1997) (use of phrase "fair doubt" could lower Commonwealth's burden of proof, and constituted reversible error); *Com. v. Burke*, 44 Mass App 76, 80-81, 687 NE2d 1279, 1283 (1997) (term "reservoir of doubt" should be avoided).

[32] See *Com. v. Scanlon*, *Com. v. Scanlon*, 412 Mass 664, 677-678, 592 NE2d 1279, 1287 (1992) (& citations).

[33] See *Com. v. Gonzalez*, 426 Mass 313, 318, 688 NE2d 455, 458 (1997).

someone searching for doubt;[34] but contrasts with proof beyond a shadow of doubt were to be avoided,[35] as well comparisons with the civil preponderance of evidence standard.[36] It has been proper to instruct that the Commonwealth need not exclude every other hypothesis to the effect that a person other than the defendant could have committed the offense.[37]

The determination of whether the definition of reasonable doubt has been conveyed accurately to the jury requires consideration of the charge as a whole, and not an isolated portion or "bits and pieces" that misstate the burden.[38] In assessing the possible impact of an alleged error, the Massachusetts courts have asked whether a reasonable juror *could have* used the instruction incorrectly, in contrast to the more strict federal standard which requires reversal only where there is a "reasonable likelihood" that the jury used an inappropriate standard.[39]

Failure to instruct the jury properly on reasonable doubt can never be deemed harmless error.[40] A trial judge's failure to give any instruction on the meaning of reasonable doubt constitutes reversible error.[41] There are suggestions in the cases that written instructions

---

[34] See *Com. v. Walkins*, 425 Mass 830, 839, 683 NE2d 653, 659 (1997).

[35] *Com. v. Richardson*, 425 Mass 765, 768, 682 NE2d 1354, 1356 (1997).

[36] *Com. v. Mercado*, 466 Mass 141, 153-154, 993 NE2d 661, 671 (2013). For other pre-*Russell* cases dealing with the proper articulation of the reasonable doubt standard, compare *Com. v. Awad*, 47 Mass App 139, 144-146, 712 NE2d 601, 605-606 (1999) (prosecutor's statement that all government need do to establish defendant's guilt is offer evidence that "sounds right" impermissibly shifted burden of proof) with *Com. v. Cook*, 419 Mass 192, 203, 644 NE2d 203, 210 (1994) (prosecutor's statement that jury should "not be intimidated by phrase 'reasonable doubt'" not improper when viewed in context). See also *Com. v. Thomas*, 439 Mass 362, 369, 787 NE2d 1047, 1055 (2003) (defendant not entitled to supplemental instruction that "in essence, you need to reach a subjective state of near certitude of the guilt of the accused.").

[37] *Com. v. Mejia*, 463 Mass 243, 255-257, 973 NE2d 657, 666-667 (2012) (but better practice is to include such instruction as part of the *Bowden* instruction, see § 3.6.1, infra).

[38] See *Com. v. Limone*, 410 Mass 364, 367, 573 NE2d 1, 3 (1991); *Com. v. Morse*, 402 Mass 735, 737, 525 NE2d 364, 365-366 (1988). See also *Smith v. Butler*, 696 F Supp 748, 754 n.9 (D Mass 1988) (& cases collected).

[39] See *Com. v. Rosa*, 422 Mass 18, 27 n.10, 661 NE2d 56, 62 n.10 (1996); *Com. v. Torres*, 420 Mass 479, 490-491 n.10, 651 NE2d 360, 367 n.10 (1995).

[40] See *Sullivan v. Louisiana*, 508 US 275, 280-282 (1993). Older precedent in Massachusetts had applied harmless error analysis. See *Com. v. Kelleher*, 482 NE2d 804, 808 (Mass 1985) and *Com. v. Garcia*, 379 Mass 422, 441-442, 399 NE2d 460, 472-473 (1980).

[41] See *Com. v. James*, 54 Mass App 908, 763 NE2d 1127 (2002); *Com. v. Stellberger*, 25 Mass App 148, 149, 515 NE2d 1207, 1207-1208 (1987).

should not be provided the jury absent consent of the parties.[42] The instructions must not suggest that the defendant has the burden to create reasonable doubt.[43]

§ 3.5 Presumptions/Prima Facie Evidence/Inferences

Generalization with respect to "presumptions" is difficult at best, mainly because the word is used to describe a number of quite different concepts.[1] Four such concepts are described and illustrated below:

---

[42] See *Com. v. Lavalley*, 410 Mass 641, 652 n.15, 574 NE2d 1000, 1007 (1991); *Com. v. Walker*, 68 Mass App 194, 206, 861 NE2d 457, 467 (2007) (procedure employed by judge of distributing copies of a preliminary and incomplete reasonable doubt instruction to jury in the midst of the trial should not be employed). But see *Com. v. Walker*, 68 Mass App 194, 204, 861 NE2d 457, 465-466 (2007) (declining to read *Lavalley* to establish any such proscription).

[43] *Com. v. Gonzalez*, 473 Mass 415, 426, 42 NE3d 1078, 1088 (2015).

§ 3.5 [1] The Advisory Committee Note to Proposed Mass R Evid 301 observed that the law regarding presumptions "has been a nightmare of confusion to lawyers and has not been consistently applied by judges." The confusion in terminology is evident when looking at older cases dealing with the "presumption" that a plaintiff had normal skin. Compare *Payne v. R. H. White Co.*, 314 Mass 63, 49 NE2d 425 (1943) (may be an inference, a presumption, or the sum of the two—prima facie evidence—that plaintiff had normal skin), *Graham v. Jordan Marsh Co.*, 319 Mass 690, 67 NE2d 404 (1946) (jury could draw an inference that plaintiff's skin was normal), *Jacquot v. William Filene's Sons Co.*, 337 Mass 312, 316, 149 NE2d 635, 638 (1958) (there might be a presumption or permissible inference that plaintiff's skin was normal), and *Casagrande v. F. W. Woolworth Co.*, 340 Mass 552, 555-557, 165 NE2d 109, 112 (1960) (presumption, as distinguished from inference, that skin is normal).

Proposed Mass R Evid 301 would apply a uniform rule for all presumptions in civil cases, and another rule for the concept of "prima facie evidence" as created by various statutes. Rule 301(a) provides that a presumption shifts the burden of persuasion to the party against whom it is directed, in sharp contrast to Fed R Evid 301 ("a presumption imposes on the party against whom it is directed the burden of going forward with evidence to rebut or meet the presumption, but does not shift to such party the burden of proof in the sense of the risk of nonpersuasion."). The operation of "prima facie evidence" as set out in Proposed Mass R Evid 301(b) is consistent with the federal version of a presumption.

Proposed Mass R Evid 301 provides:

Presumptions in Civil Actions and Proceedings

(a) Scope. In all civil actions and proceedings, except as otherwise provided by statute or by these rules, a presumption imposes on the party against whom it is directed the burden of proving that the non-existence of the presumed fact is more probable than its existence.

(b) Prima facie evidence. In all civil actions and proceedings, a statute by providing that a fact or group of facts is prima facie evidence of another fact imposes upon the party

1. Conclusive or irrebutable presumptions.
2. Presumptions as shorthand references.
3. Prima facie evidence.
4. Inferences.

§ 3.5.1 *Conclusive or Irrebuttable Presumptions*

"Conclusive" or "irrebutable" presumptions may be statutory or common-law in nature. In truth they are not presumptions at all, but rules of substantive law removing the issue from the area of evidence and proof.[2] The following are illustrative:

- Conclusive presumption of dependency of spouses under worker's compensation law. GL 152, § 32.
- Child victim is incapable of consent in prosecution for rape and abuse under GL 265, § 23.[3]
- Wrongful acts of the landlord upon the premises that render them permanently unsafe and unfit for occupancy, so that the tenant loses the enjoyment of them, carry with them the presumption of the intent to deprive the tenant of that enjoyment.[4]
- A written agreement unambiguous in its terms is conclusively presumed to express the whole intent of the parties, and cannot be modified by extrinsic evidence.[5]

---

against whom it is directed the burden of producing contrary evidence. If evidence is introduced sufficient to warrant a finding contrary to the presumed fact, the factfinder is permitted to infer the existence of the presumed fact from the prima facie evidence, but the burden of proof in the sense of the risk of nonpersuasion remains throughout the trial upon the party on whom it was originally cast.

(c) Inconsistent presumptions. If two presumptions arise which are conflicting with each other, the court shall apply the presumption which is founded on the weightier considerations of policy and logic. If there is no such preponderance, both presumptions shall be disregarded.

Proposed Mass R Evid 302 would control presumptions in criminal cases. See § 3.5.6, infra.

[2] An example is the old English common law presumption that a child under 14 years of age was incapable of committing rape, which was repudiated in *Com. v. Walter R.*, 414 Mass 714, 610 NE2d 323 (1993).

[3] *Com. v. Gallant*, 373 Mass 577, 585-586, 369 NE2d 707, 713 (1977).

[4] *Westland Housing Corp. v. Scott*, 312 Mass 375, 382-383, 44 NE2d 959, 963 (1942). See also *Lowery v. Robinson*, 13 Mass App 982, 432 NE2d 543 (1982).

[5] *Nelson v. Hamlin*, 258 Mass 331, 340, 155 NE 18, 21 (1926). For cases refusing to create a conclusive presumption, see *Com. v. Burke*, 390 Mass 480, 484-487, 457 NE2d 622, 625-626 (1983) (declining to establish "age of consent" below which child

- A conclusive presumption recently created in response to the investigation of the state crime laboratory provides that a defendant seeking to vacate a guilty plea as a result of chemist Annie Dookhan's misconduct, who proffers a drug certificate from his case signed by Dookhan, is entitled to the conclusive presumption that egregious government misconduct occurred in his case.[6]

§ 3.5.2 *Presumptions as Shorthand References*

Some "presumptions" serve merely as an allusion to the allocation of the burden of persuasion to one party from the outset of the case. By way of example, the "presumption of innocence" in criminal cases is not a presumption in the usual sense but a "shorthand reference to the premises from which a criminal trial proceeds" with the burden of persuasion falling upon the government at all times.[7] The "presumption" of validity of assessments is similarly a recognition that the taxpayer bears the burden to prove the property has been overvalued,[8] as the presumption of prospective application of statutes puts the burden on the party asserting retroactive application,[9] the presumption that the judge as a trier of fact applied correct legal principles and puts the burden on the party asserting the contrary[10] and the presumption that a statute is constitutional puts the burden on the party claiming otherwise.[11]

---

is to be considered incapable of consent as a matter of law in prosecution for indecent assault and battery on child under GL 265, § 13B); *Commissioner of Corporations & Taxation v. Bullard*, 313 Mass 72, 79, 46 NE2d 557, 561 (1943) (no general irrebuttable presumption applicable to all classes of cases that a woman is capable of bearing children throughout her life). The common-law presumption of legitimacy, see *Taylor v. Whittier*, 240 Mass 514, 138 NE 6 (1922), has been effectively eliminated by legislative and judicial action. See *C. C. v. A. B.*, 406 Mass 679, 688-691, 550 NE2d 365, 371-373 (1990). See also *P. B. C. v. D. H.*, 396 Mass 68, 483 NE2d 1094 (1985). See also § 5.2.4, infra.

[6] *Com. v. Scott*, 467 Mass 336, 352-354, 5 NE3d 530, 545-546 (2014).

[7] *Com. v. Petetabella*, 459 Mass 177, 184, 944 NE2d 582, 589 (2011).

[8] *Analogic Corp. v. Board of Assessors of Peabody*, 45 Mass App 605, 607, 700 NE2d 548, 550 (1998).

[9] *Watts v. Com.*, 468 Mass 49, 55, 8 NE3d 717, 722 (2014) (statute prohibiting initiation of criminal proceedings against an under-18 person did not apply retroactively).

[10] *Com. v. Dragotta*, 89 Mass App 119, 128, 46 NE3d 563, 571 (2016).

[11] *St. Germaine v. Pendergast*, 416 Mass 698, 703, 626 NE2d 857, 860 (1993) (& citations).

Other "presumptions" serve as recognition of common realities, such as the "presumption of sanity" as a shorthand expression for fact that the majority of people are sane,[12] or the presumption of regularity of proceedings.[13]

§ 3.5.3 Prima Facie Evidence & Traditional Presumptions

The Massachusetts concept of "prima facie evidence" is described as "evidence which, standing alone and unexplained, maintains the proposition and warrants the conclusion to support which it is introduced. If such evidence is not in any way met or controlled, and relates

---

[12] See *Com. v. Robinson*, 14 Mass App 591, 594, 441 NE2d 553, 556 (1982). See also *Moroni v. Brawders*, 317 Mass 48, 55-56, 57 NE2d 14, 18 (1944) ("presumption" that the conduct of a person is lawful, regular, proper, innocent, honest and in good faith, because most human conduct is of that sort); *Goodman v. New York, N.H. & H. R.R.*, 295 Mass 330, 3 NE2d 777 (1936) ("presumption" that damage to goods happened while in possession of last of a series of common carriers). But see *Connolly v. John Hancock Mutual Life Ins. Co.*, 322 Mass 678, 79 NE2d 189 (1948) (whatever "presumption" there is that a person is in sound health, it could not itself satisfy plaintiff's burden of proving that he was in sound health at time policy was issued.

[13] See *Com. v. Cartagena*, 466 Mass 1021 (2013) (where a record of the plea proceedings no longer exists, and cannot be reconstructed, the defendant must present some articulable reason why the presumptively proper proceedings were defective); *Com. v. Gautreaux*, 458 Mass 741, 753-754, 941 NE2d 616, 627 (2011) (burden is on defendant to present evidence to rebut the presumption that plea proceeding was conducted correctly); *Com. v. Wilson*, 443 Mass 122, 129, 819 NE2d 919, 927 (2004) (presumption of regularity of earlier proceedings where transcript is unavailable); *Com. v. Saunders*, 435 Mass 691, 695, 761 NE2d 490, 493-494 (2002) (presumption of regularity that a defendant was represented by counsel in prior conviction); *Com. v. Carson*, 349 Mass 430, 208 NE2d 792 (1965) (regularity of corporate proceedings is "presumed"); *Com. v. Haskell*, 76 Mass App 284, 921 NE2d 988 (2010) (regularity of plea proceedings); *Com. v. Backus*, 78 Mass App 625, 941 NE2d 663 (2011) (presumption of regularity of proceeding in which defendant waived jury trial); *Com. v. Hoyle*, 67 Mass App 10, 14-15, 851 NE2d 469, 473 (2006) ("presumption of regularity, afforded collateral review of proceedings in which the record has been lost or destroyed, stands, unless and until a defendant advances countervailing credible and persuasive evidence sufficient to rebut that presumption. It is only when the presumption of regularity is so rebutted that the burden of proof shifts to the Commonwealth to prove the proceedings were conducted in accordance with applicable standards."). The Commonwealth may not rely on the presumption as a substitute for evidence proving an element of its case. See *Com. v. Oyewole*, 470 Mass 1015, 1016, 21 NE3d 179, 181 (2014); *Com. v. Norman*, 87 Mass App 344, 346, 30 NE3d 121, 123 (2015) (regular practice of RMV of automatically generating a suspension notice on conviction of OUI and placing notice in mail is insufficient to prove defendant received notice).

The presumption of regularity does not apply to challenges based on failure to provide immigration warnings). *Com. v. Grannum*, 457 Mass 128, 133, 928 NE2d 339, 344 (2010).

to the decisive issue in the case, a verdict or finding is required in accordance with its effect."[14] In the absence of contradictory evidence, prima facie evidence "requires a finding that the evidence is true; the prima facie evidence may be met and overcome by evidence sufficient to warrant a contrary conclusion; even in the presence of contradictory evidence, however, the prima facie evidence is sufficient to sustain the proposition to which it is applicable."[15] Prima facie evidence, in sum, imposes upon the party against whom it is directed the burden of producing contrary evidence.[16] It does not shift the burden of persuasion.

The Massachusetts decisions distinguish prima facie evidence from traditional presumptions (of the type described in Fed R Evid 301) by emphasizing the different consequences that ensue with regard to the rebuttal of the evidence. Like these presumptions, prima facie evidence retains its artificial legal force only until evidence appears that warrants a finding to the contrary. Unlike these presumptions, however, the effect of prima facie evidence does not "disappear" upon being rebutted, but rather remains as evidence sufficient to get the case to the jury. And the jury may consider such evidence like any other evidence upon any question of fact to which it is relevant.[17]

Thus, those rules of law that make proof of Fact A "prima facie evidence" of Fact B operate as follows: Proof of A by Proponent places upon Opponent the burden of production of evidence as to the nonexistence of B. The additional effect of such a presumption, while it is still operative, is to assist Proponent in carrying its burden of persuasion on that issue and, in the absence of countervailing evidence as to the presumed Fact B, to require a finding of B as a matter of law. As the Supreme Judicial Court has summarized:

> According to the Massachusetts view, when, by statute or common law, one fact probative of another is denominated prima facie evidence of that second fact, proof of the first or basic fact requires a finding that the second, the inferred or presumed fact, is also true. The finding is mandatory. To avert this result, the opponent must assume the burden

---

[14] *Thomes v. Meyer Store, Inc.*, 268 Mass 587, 588, 168 NE 178, 179 (1929).

[15] *Scheffler's Case*, 419 Mass 251, 258-259, 643 NE2d 1023, 1027 (1994).

[16] See *Ford Motor Co. v. Barrett*, 403 Mass 240, 242-243, 526 NE2d 1284, 1286 (1988) (citing Text); Proposed Mass R Evid 301(b).

[17] See generally *Burns v. Com.*, 430 Mass 444, 449-451, 720 NE2d 798, 803-804 (1999); *Tuttle v. McGeeney*, 344 Mass 200, 206, 181 NE2d 655, 659 (1962); *Malloy v. Coldwater Seafood Corp.*, 338 Mass 554, 564-565, 156 NE2d 61, 67 (1959). See also *Anderson's Case*, 373 Mass 813, 370 NE2d 692 (1977) (same principles apply to administrative proceedings in workers' compensation cases).

of production (the burden of persuasion remains with the proponent). It is only when the opponent has introduced sufficient evidence, which, cast against the natural inferential value of the basic fact, creates an issue of fact for the trier, that the opponent has satisfied his burden and the mandatory effect disappears. In a case tried by jury where the opponent does not assume his burden, the judge should charge that if the jury find the basic fact, they are required to find the inferred fact; if the basic fact is admitted or otherwise undisputed, the judge should charge that the jury must find the inferred fact, and if the inferred fact encompasses the substance of the case, the judge should direct a verdict.[18]

In criminal cases, the prima facie device creates only a permissive, not mandatory, presumption—in the absence of contradictory evidence, the jury is permitted, but not required, to find that the presumed fact is true beyond a reasonable doubt.[19]

The Supreme Judicial Court has emphasized that a "presumption does not shift the burden of proof; it is a rule of evidence that aids the party bearing the burden of proof in sustaining that burden by throw[ing] upon his adversary the burden of going forward with evidence."[20]

The following are examples of (mostly statutory) formulations of prima facie evidence and presumptions:

- In a motor vehicle accident case, proof of registration in the name of the defendant creates "prima facie evidence" that the vehicle was operated by and under the control of a person for whom the defendant was legally responsible. GL 231, § 85A.[21]

---

[18] *Com. v. Pauley*, 368 Mass 286, 290-291, 331 NE2d 901, 904 (1975) (citing Text).

[19] *Com. v. Parenteau*, 460 Mass 1, 6 n. 8, 948 NE2d 883, 888 n.8 (2011) (notice of license suspension mailed by Registry of Motor Vehicles is prima facie evidence of receipt GL 90, § 22(d)). See also § 3.5.6, infra.

[20] *Standerwick v. Zoning Board of Appeals*, 447 Mass 20, 34, 849 NE2d 197, 209 (2006) (presumption that abutting landowners have standing to challenge issuance of comprehensive permit).

[21] See *Cheek v. Econo-Car Rental System of Boston, Inc.*, 393 Mass 660, 662, 473 NE2d 659, 660 (1985); *Mitchell v. Hastings & Koch Enterprises, Inc.*, 38 Mass App 271, 276, 647 NE2d 78, 82 (1995). But see *Gallo v. Veliskakis*, 357 Mass 602, 259 NE2d 568 (1970) (statute does not make registration prima facie evidence that operator was empowered by owner to invite others to ride with him). Where there is evidence to contradict the prima facie evidence created by the statute, the agency issue is a question of fact for the jury—or in the case of a bench trial, the judge. *Cheek v. Econo-Car Rental System of Boston, Inc.*, supra, 393 Mass at 662, 473 NE2d at 661 (in view of evidence

- Presumption that accident vehicle was operated with the consent of the owner. GL 231, § 85C.[22]
- Presumption that plaintiff exercised due care for purposes of comparative negligence defense. GL 231, § 85.[23]
- Presumption that a vehicle was parked by its registered owner. GL 266, § 120A.
- Rebuttable administrative presumption of fault in excess of 50 percent when the vehicle's doors are opened or opening resulting in a collision with another vehicle.[24]
- In a worker's compensation case where the employee is physically or mentally unable to testify, certain facts "shall be prima facie evidence that the employee was performing his regular duties on the day of the injury" and that the claim is compensable. GL 152, § 7A.[25]
- The impartial physician's report is prima facie evidence of the medical issues in a worker's compensation case. GL 152, § 11A(2).[26]

---

contradicting agency relationship, judge's ruling that finding of agency was compelled was erroneous); *Feltch v. General Rental Co.*, 383 Mass 603, 421 NE2d 67 (1981). Compare *Nugent v. Classic Car Corp.*, 379 Mass 913, 393 NE2d 934 (1979) (error to direct verdict on issue of control where GL 231, § 85A applies) with *Bergdoll v. Suprynowicz*, 359 Mass 173, 268 NE2d 362 (1971) (GL 231, § 85A does not preclude judge from ordering new trial on ground that verdict against owner-defendant was against weight of evidence on issue of control). The validity of § 85A has been called into question in *Deikan v. Blackwelder*, 2011 Mass App Div 66 (2011), suggesting it has been preempted by 49 USC § 30106, the so-called Graves Amendment,

[22] See *Scaltreto v. Shea*, 352 Mass 62, 223 NE2d 525 (1967).The statutory presumption that the vehicle was being operated with the insured's consent does not apply in an excess policy case. See *United National Ins. Co. v. Kohlmeyer*, 81 Mass App 32, 958 NE2d 848 (2011).

GL 231, § 85A, § 85B, § 85C go on to provide that absence of responsibility or consent "shall be an affirmative defense to be set up in the answer and proved by the defendant." This shifts the burden of proof to defendant on these matters. See *Covell v. Olsen*, 65 Mass App 359, 363-364, 840 NE2d 555, 559 (2006).

[23] See *Coyne v. John S. Tilley Co.*, 368 Mass 230, 331 NE2d 541 (1975); *Duarte v. Kavanaugh*, 340 Mass 640, 642, 165 NE2d 746, 747 (1960).

[24] *DiLoreto v. Fireman's Fund Ins. Co.*, 383 Mass 243, 248, 418 NE2d 612, 615-616 (1981).

[25] See *Anderson's Case*, 373 Mass 813, 370 NE2d 692 (1977); *Collin's Case*, 21 Mass App 557, 559, 488 NE2d 46, 48 (1986). The establishment of prima facie evidence under § 7A does not carry over to other entitlements such as double compensation under GL 151. *Moss's Case*, 451 Mass 704, 889 NE2d 43 (2008).

[26] See *O'Brien's Case*, 424 Mass 16, 673 NE2d 567 (1996) (rejecting due process challenge to statute); *Scheffler's Case*, 419 Mass 251, 259, 643 NE2d 1023, 1028 (1994); *May's Case*, 67 Mass App 209, 214, 852 NE2d 1120, 1124 (2006) ("in the absence of contradictory medical evidence, the impartial physician's determination whether an employee's disability has as its predominant contributing cause an injury arising out

- Docket entries are prima facie evidence of the facts recorded therein.[27]
- Proper mailing of a letter is prima facie evidence in civil and criminal cases of its receipt by the addressee.[28]
- Bill of lading is prima facie evidence that, as to all circumstances which were open to inspection and visible, goods were in good order.[29]
- Birth, marriage, and death certificates are prima facie evidence of the facts therein recorded. GL 46, § 19.
- A death certificate is prima facie evidence of the time and cause of death, but "nothing which has reference to the question of liability for causing the death shall be admissible in evidence." GL 46, § 19.[30]

---

of the course of the employee's employment must be accepted as true.") But see *Brommage's Case*, 75 Mass App 825, 827-828, 917 NE2d 256, 259 (2009) (ALJ was not required to adopt conclusions of IME report where there are deficiencies in its reasoning or findings). See also *Tobin's Case*, 424 Mass 250, 255, 675 NE2d 781, 785 (1997) (rejecting due process challenge to presumption of non-entitlement to compensation benefits at age 65, GL 152, § 35E).

[27] See *Com. v. Jewett*, 471 Mass 624, 636, 31 NE3d 1079, 1091 (2015) (sufficiency of docket sheets as evidence of prior convictions); *Com. v. Mattos*, 404 Mass 672, 677, 536 NE2d 1072, 1076 (1989); *Com. v. Sigman*, 41 Mass App 574, 575 n.2, 671 NE2d 1008, 1010 n.2 (1996); *Com. v. Oyewole*, 84 Mass App 669, 672, 2 NE2d 189, 193 (2014). There may, however, be other evidence that rebuts the prima facie effect of the docket. See *Com. v. Denehy*, 466 Mass 723, 727, 2 NE2d 161, 167 (2014); *Com. v. MacDonald*, 435 Mass 1005, 1007, 757 NE2d 725, 727 (2001); *Com. v. Rodgers*, 448 Mass 538, 542, 862 NE2d 727, 731-732 (2007).

[28] *Com. v. Koney*, 421 Mass 295, 303-304, 657 NE2d 210, 215 (1995); *Com. v. Royal*, 89 Mass App 168, 175, 46 NE3d 583, 590 (2016) (mailing confirmation records permit, but do not require, the trier of fact to find defendant received notice). Consistent with the so-called bursting bubble theory of presumptions, the courts have explained: "As soon as evidence is introduced that warrants a finding that the letter failed to reach its destination, the artificial compelling force of the prima facie evidence disappears, and the evidence of nondelivery has to be weighed against the likelihood that the mail service was efficient in the particular instance, with no artificial weight on either side of the balance." *Hobart-Farrell Plumbing & Heating Co. v. Klayman*, 302 Mass 508, 510, 19 NE2d 805, 807 (1939). See also *Bouley v. Reisman*, 38 Mass App 118, 125-126, 645 NE2d 708, 713 (1995) (refusing to apply presumption in face of evidence of nondelivery of radiologist's report).

[29] See *Joseph Freedman Co. v. North Penn Transfer, Inc.*, 388 Mass 551, 555, 447 NE2d 657, 659 (1983).

[30] See *Com. v. Lykus*, 406 Mass 135, 143-144, 546 NE2d 159, 164-165 (1989) (time of death); *Pahigian v. Manufacturer's Life Ins. Co.*, 349 Mass 78, 85, 206 NE2d 660, 665 (1965) (cause of death). For interpretation of the proviso excluding matters of liability as applied in criminal and civil cases, see *Com. v. Lannon*, 364 Mass 480, 306 NE2d 248 (1974). The preferred practice is to redact the means and manner of death before admitting the death certificate. See *Com. v. Almonte*, 465 Mass 224, 242, 988 NE2d 415, 428-429 (2013).

- An affidavit of the tax collector sending a tax bill or notice as to the time of sending shall be prima facie evidence that the same was sent at such time. GL 60, § 3.[31]
- Presumption that where a taxpayer seeks to assign loans to a location not a regular place of business, the loans should be assigned to its commercial domicile. GL 63, § 2A(e)(6)(B).[32]
- Town clerk's certificate attesting parcel is used as a public way.[33]
- The "presumption" of death from an unexplained absence for more than seven years has the effect of shifting to the party denying death the burden of production on this issue; it does not shift the ultimate burden of persuasion, which remains on the party alleging death.[34]
- Presumption that the testator had the requisite testamentary capacity.[35]
- Presumption that one who signs a will knows its contents.[36]
- Presumption of proper execution of a will upon proof of all signatures required by statute.[37]
- Presumption that when original copy of will cannot be located, the testator destroyed it with the intention to revoke.[38]
- Presumption that testamentary term "child" includes adopted child.[39]

See also *Blake v. Pellegrino*, 329 F3d 43 (1st Cir 2003) (trial judge had no authority to redact cause of death from patient's death certificate on ground it lacked persuasive force).

[31] See *Roda Realty Trust v. Board of Assessors of Belmont*, 385 Mass 493, 495, 432 NE2d 522, 524 (1983) (affidavit submitted under GL 60, § 3, is prima facie evidence of date real estate notices were sent).

[32] *First Marblehead Corp. v. Commissioner of Revenue*, 470 Mass 497, 505, 23 NE3d 892, 900-901 (2015).

[33] *Matulewicz v. Planning Board of Norfolk*, 438 Mass 37, 43-44, 777 NE2d 153, 159-160 (2002).

[34] *Jacobs v. Town Clerk of Arlington*, 402 Mass 824, 827, 525 NE2d 658, 660 (1988).

[35] *Duchesneau v. Jaskoviak*, 360 Mass 730, 732, 277 NE2d 507, 509 (1972); *In re Estate of Galatis*, 88 Mass App 273, 278, 36 NE3d 1247, 1252 (2015) (once contestants produce some evidence of lack of capacity, the presumption loses effect); *Estate of Rosen*, 86 Mass App 793, 798, 23 NE2d 116, 121 (2014); *Paine v. Sullivan*, 79 Mass App 811, 817-818, 950 NE2d 874, 881 (2011) (daughter rebutted presumption of testamentary capacity with evidence that testator exhibited signs of dementia).

[36] *Barounis v. Barounis*, 87 Mass App 667, 672, 34 NE3d 756, 761 (2015).

[37] *Farrell v. McDonnell*, 81 Mass App 725, 728, 967 NE2d 637, 639-640 (2012).

[38] *Estate of Beauregard*, 456 Mass 161, 921 NE2d 954 (2010).

[39] *Bird Anderson v. BNY Mellon, NA*, 463 Mass 299, 974 NE2d 21 (2012).

- Presumption that children born into a legal spousal relationship are presumed to be children of both spouses, GL 209C, § 6, including children of same sex partners conceived by artificial insemination.[40]
- Presumption of resulting trust arises where purchaser takes title in name of another.[41]
- Common law presumption regarding original intent of developer to retain fee in the way.[42]
- Corporate charter is prima facie evidence of charitable character and purpose.[43]
- Certified copies of court records constitute prima facie evidence of prior OUI convictions. GL 90, § 24(4).[44]
- Affidavit of sale attesting to statutory mortgage-foreclosure sale form is prima facie evidence of purchaser's compliance with the power of sale for establishing right of possession against mortgagor.[45]
- Presumption that the owner of property nearby to the subject of an application for a variance or permit, who receives notice of that application, is a person aggrieved.[46]
- "The decision, and the amount of damages assessed, if any, by a district court shall be prima facie evidence upon such matters as are put in issue by the pleadings [in the superior court]." GL 231, § 102C.[47]
- "A finding for the plaintiff [in a small claims case] in the district court department shall be prima facie evidence for the plaintiff in the trial by jury of six. At such trial the plaintiff may, but need not, introduce evidence." GL 218, § 23.[48]

---

[40] *Hunter v. Rose*, 463 Mass 488, 975 NE2d 857 (2012).

[41] *Cavidi v. DeYeso*, 458 Mass 615, 631, 941 NE2d 23, 36 (2011).

[42] *Hickey v. Pathways Ass'n Inc.*, 472 Mass 735, 743, 37 NE3d 1003, 1010 (2015).

[43] *Boxer v. Boston Symphony Orchestra, Inc.*, 342 Mass 537, 538, 174 NE2d 363, 364 (1961).

[44] See *Com. v. Dussault*, 71 Mass App 542, 546, 883 NE2d 1243, 1248 (2008).

[45] *Federal National Mortgage Ass'n v. Hendricks*, 463 Mass 635, 977 NE2d 552 (2012).

[46] *Standerwick v. Zoning Board of Appeals*, 447 Mass 20, 32-35, 849 NE2d 197, 208-209 (2006); *Redstone v. Board of Appeals of Chelmsford*, 11 Mass App 383, 384-385, 416 NE2d 543, 544 (1981).

[47] See also *Lubell v. First National Stores, Inc.*, 342 Mass 161, 172 NE2d 689 (1961), *Cole v. New England Mutual Life Ins. Co.*, 49 Mass App 296, 297, 729 NE2d 319, 321 (2000), *Dwyer v. Piccicuto*, 25 Mass App 910, 515 NE2d 596 (1987), *Forrey v. Dedham Taxi, Inc.*, 19 Mass App 955, 473 NE2d 726 (1985).

[48] See *Todino v. Arbella Mutual Ins. Co.*, 415 Mass 298, 612 NE2d 1181 (1993); *Boat Maintenance & Repair Co. v. Lawson*, 50 Mass App 329, 332-333, 737 NE2d 494,

- Mass R Civ P 53(i)(l) ("the master's findings upon all issues submitted to him are admissible as prima facie evidence of the matters found and may be read to the jury and, in the discretion of the court, may be submitted to the jury as an exhibit, subject, however, to the rulings of the court upon any objections properly preserved."[49]
- Presumption of validity is afforded to parents' judgments as to the best interests of their children with respect to grandparent visitation. GL 119, § 32D.[50]
- Presumption that money or other property delivered by one spouse to another is intended as a gift.[51]
- State laboratory lead detection report is prima facie evidence of facts stated. GL 111, § 195.[52]

The suggestion to adopt a general presumption that stepparents act in loco parentis to their spouse's children has been declined.[53]

In a series of landmark cases beginning with *Crawford v. Washington*,[54] through *Melendez-Diaz v. Massachusetts*,[55] the United States Supreme Court invalidated on Confrontation Clause grounds the use of "testimonial" certificates as proof in criminal trials. See §§ 8.4.2 and 8.12.2. This development forbids in criminal cases what previously had been the routine use of forensic reports under several provisions of Massachusetts law, such as a:

---

497 (2000) (defendant must be given every opportunity to test sufficiency of evidence in support of district court finding if it is to be given prima facie effect at subsequent jury trial).

[49] See *Delano Growers' Cooperative Winery v. Supreme Wine Co., Inc.*, 393 Mass 666, 671-672, 473 NE2d 1066, 1070 (1985).

For a case refusing to create a presumption on policy grounds, see *Totman v. Malloy*, 431 Mass 143, 725 NE2d 1045 (2000) (declining to create presumption or inference of permissive use among close family members for purposes of establishing adverse possession requirements).

[50] *Care & Protection of Jamison*, 467 Mass 269, 281, 4 NE3d 889 (2014); *Blixt v. Blixt*, 437 Mass 649, 657-658, 774 NE2d 1052 (2002). Compare *Custody of Zia*, 50 Mass App 237, 242, 736 NE2d 449, 453 (2000) (refusing to create presumption that custody should be awarded to primary caretaking parent) with *Smith v. McDonald*, 458 Mass 540, 550-551, 41 NE2d 1, 11 (2010) (presumption that when one parent has sole physical custody of child, other parent is ordinarily entitled to reasonable visitation, applies to parents of nonmarital children).

[51] *Bakwin v. Mardirosian*, 467 Mass 631, 642, 6 NE3d 1078, 1088 (2014).

[52] *Smola v. Higgins*, 42 Mass App 724, 728, 679 NE2d 593, 596 (1997) (rebuttal evidence is permitted).

[53] *Com. v. Packer*, 88 Mass App 585, 590, 39 NE3d 753, 758 (2015).

[54] 541 US 36 (2004).

[55] 557 US 305 (2009).

- Certificate signed and sworn to by a state police chemist is prima facie evidence of the percentage of alcohol in motorist's blood. GL 90, § 24(1)(e).
- Certificate by ballistics expert of Department of Public safety is prima facie evidence that item is a "firearm." GL 140, § 12A.[56]
- Certificate by state police chemist is prima facie evidence of presence of sperm cells or seminal fluid, GL 22C, § 41, and of the composition, quality, and weight of the particular drug, GL 22C, § 39.[57]

The following statutory and judicial presumptions explicitly shift the burden of persuasion as well as production:

- Where the plaintiff in a dog bite case is a child under seven, "it shall be presumed that such minor was not committing a trespass or other tort, or teasing, tormenting or abusing such dog, and the burden of proof thereof shall be upon the defendant in such action." GL 140, § 155.
- Where not otherwise provided in a judgment of divorce or in an agreement between the parties, the recipient spouse's remarriage does not of itself automatically terminate alimony, but makes a prima facie case that requires the court to end alimony absent proof of some extraordinary circumstances, established by the recipient spouse, warranting continuation.[58]
- A regulation setting forth operational situations in which fault is presumed to be in excess of 50 percent for purpose of adjusting automobile insurance rates and premiums creates a presumption that requires a "showing" contrary to the

---

[56] See *Com. v. Rhodes*, 389 Mass 641, 644 n.4, 451 NE2d 1151, 1153 n.4 (1983)). See also *Com. v. Furr*, 58 Mass App 155, 162, 788 NE2d 592, 597-598 (2003) (proper to instruct jury that they were permitted, but not required, to accept ballistics certificate as proof).

[57] See *Com. v. Paine*, 86 Mass App 432, 436, 16 NE3d 1139, 1143 (2014) (but it was clear from the face of the certificate that the chemist did no more than a visual inspection).

[58] See *Keller v. O'Brien*, 420 Mass 820, 826-827, 652 NE2d 589, 593 (1995).

presumption to be demonstrated in order to rebut the presumption, rather than merely introduction of some contradictory evidence.[59]

§ 3.5.4 Inferences

Sometimes confused with the evidentiary devices discussed above is the concept of "inference." An inference simply describes the situation where proof of Fact A *logically permits* (but certainly does not require) a finding that Fact B exists because of the relationship of the two facts in light of common experience. By way of example, discriminatory intent may be inferred from the fact of differences in treatment between groups of employees,[60] and intent to distribute may be inferred from the large quantity of cocaine possessed.[61] As a mere generalization based on the logical connection between facts, an inference does not carry any artificial evidentiary weight.[62] Nonetheless, "an inference is an important means by which a party may satisfy his burden

---

[59] *Yazbek v. Board of Appeal on Motor Vehicle Liability Policies*, 41 Mass App 915, 916, 670 NE2d 200, 201 (1996).

[60] *Lynn Teachers Union, Local 1037 v. Massachusetts Commission Against Discrimination*, 406 Mass 515, 526-527, 549 NE2d 97, 103-104 (1990).

[61] *Com. v. Humberto H.*, 466 Mass 562, 568, 998 NE2d 1003, 1009 (2013) (discussing factors such as weight, amount, packaging, and street value); *Com. v. Ridge*, 37 Mass App 943, 945, 641 NE2d 1059, 1061 (1994). For other examples, see *Com. v. Pratt*, 407 Mass 647, 652-653, 555 NE2d 559, 562 (1990) (inference of possession of contraband from proximity to defendant's personal effects; inference of intent to distribute from possession of large quantity of contraband); *Com. v. Lawrence*, 404 Mass 378, 392, 536 NE2d 571, 580 (1989) (fact that an empty condom package was found in pocket of jacket next to nude body of victim supports inference that sexual activity occurred); *Com. v. Seven Thousand Two Hundred Forty-Six Dollars*, 404 Mass 763, 537 NE2d 144 (1989) (insufficient evidence to support inference that monies seized were proceeds of marijuana sales); *Com. v. Watson*, 36 Mass App 252, 260, 629 NE2d 1341, 1346 (1994) (inference of possession from defendant's possession of similar drugs in similar packages); *Com. v. Reilly*, 23 Mass App 53, 55, 498 NE2d 1366, 1368 (1986) (inference that defendant had "carried" pistol drawn from proximity of gun to other items in van defendant admittedly owned); *Com. v. Rarick*, 23 Mass App 912, 499 NE2d 1233 (1986) (inference that defendant was in possession of contraband drawn from proximity of contraband to personal effects of defendant in dwelling). Compare *Com. v. True*, 16 Mass App 709, 711-712, 455 NE2d 453, 454 (1983) (intent to defraud may not be inferred from mere nonperformance of a promise) with *Com. v. Wilson*, 16 Mass App 369, 451 NE2d 727 (1983) (citing Text) (construing GL 140, § 12, to permit inference of intent to defraud from refusal to pay hotel bill upon demand).

[62] Sometimes what is referred to as an inference seems more properly identified as a presumption. See, e.g., *Evans v. Lorillard Tobacco Co.*, 465 Mass 411, 442, 990 NE2d 997, 1023 (2013) (under Massachusetts law, there is an inference that a warning,

of persuasion sufficiently to transfer the burden of going forward to the other party, who may be in a better position to know certain facts essential to the case."[63]

Inferences must be based on probabilities rather than possibilities, and cannot be the result of mere speculation.[64] Whether an inference is warranted is determined "not by hard and fast rules of law, but by experience and common sense."[65] Where conflicting inferences arise from the evidence, it is for the fact finder to determine where the truth lies.[66]

An inference may be based on another inference as long as the inference is not speculative.[67] For a discussion of inferences in the context of circumstantial proof and relevance, see §§ 4.1 and 4.2, infra.

§ 3.5.5 Conflicting Presumptions

In the case of conflict between presumptions or prima facie evidence, both lose their artificial compelling force and neither prevails as a matter of law over the other. The issue is then thrown open to be decided as a fact upon all the evidence.[68]

---

once given, would have been followed; once a plaintiff establishes that a warning should have been given, the burden is on the defendant to come forward with evidence rebutting it).

[63] *Rolanti v. Boston Edison Corp.*, 33 Mass App 516, 522, 603 NE2d 211, 216-217 (1992).

[64] See *Com. v. Dinkins*, 440 Mass 715, 720, 802 NE2d 76, 81 (2004).

[65] *Com. v. Joyner*, 467 Mass 176, 180, 4 NE2d 282, 288 (2014); *Com. v. Oyewole*, 84 Mass App 669, 675, 2 NE2d 189, 194 (2014).

[66] *Com. v. Oyewole*, supra.

[67] *Continental Assurance Co. v. Diorio-Volungis*, 51 Mass App 403, 409, 746 NE2d 550, 555 (2001) (& citations) (inference that wife had motive to have husband killed, and took actions that contributed to killing).

[68] See *Krantz v. John Hancock Mutual Life Ins. Co.*, 335 Mass 703, 141 NE2d 719 (1957) (conflict between prima facie evidence of suicide and presumption against suicide); *Boyas v. Raymond*, 302 Mass 519, 20 NE2d 411 (1939). Proposed Mass R Evid 301(c) would alter Massachusetts practice in this regard by providing:

> If two presumptions arise which are conflicting with each other, the court shall apply the presumption which is founded on the weightier considerations of policy and logic. If there is no such preponderance, both presumptions shall be disregarded.

§ 3.5.6 Presumptions in Criminal Cases

Presumptions pose special problems in criminal cases, where care must be taken to avoid giving the jury the impression that the burden of persuasion shifts to the defendant on any element of the crime.[69] Further, because of the long-established principles that a verdict may not be directed against a criminal defendant and that the jury cannot be compelled to find against the defendant as to any element of the crime, neither a presumption nor prima facie evidence, even if unrebutted, can have the effect it does in a civil case.[70]

---

[69] See § 3.4.1, supra; *Francis v. Franklin*, 471 US 307 (1985) (jury instruction in murder trial that acts of a person of sound mind are presumed to be product of person's will and that a person is presumed to intend the natural and probable consequences of his acts created mandatory presumption which unconstitutionally shifted to defendant the burden of persuasion); *Connecticut v. Johnson*, 460 US 73 (1983) (error to instruct jury that intent may be inferred from conduct and that every person is conclusively presumed to intend natural and necessary consequences of his act); *Com. v. Petetabella*, 459 Mass 177, 188-190, 944 NE2d 582, 591-593 (2011) (error for judge to charge that "the law justly says that [defendant] must be taken to intend all consequences which naturally flow from his act"); *Com. v. Nolin*, 448 Mass 207, 217-218, 859 NE2d 843, 852-853 (2007) (instruction that "a person is presumed to intend the natural and probable consequences of his acts" impermissibly shifted burden to defendant of proving lack of intent); *Com. v. Teixera*, 396 Mass 746, 750, 488 NE2d 775, 778-779 (1986) (jury instruction which stated that proof of failure to make reasonable provisions for support was prima facie evidence that neglect was willful and without cause in criminal nonsupport action was inconsistent with Commonwealth's burden of proving element of neglect or willful refusal reasonably to support); *Com. v. Nieves*, 394 Mass 355, 360, 476 NE2d 179, 182-183 (1985) (reasonable jury could interpret instructions as establishing a mandatory presumption of malice or as placing on defendant burden of proving heat of passion); *Dejoinville v. Com.*, 381 Mass 246, 253-254, 408 NE2d 1353, 1358 (1980) (charge in murder prosecution which instructed jury that every man is presumed to have intended the natural or probable consequences of his voluntary acts and that in absence of evidence to the contrary that he intended such consequences created a mandatory presumption and was unconstitutional). Compare *Com. v. Lykus*, 406 Mass 135, 143, 546 NE2d 159, 165 (1989) (judge did not create a presumption in favor of the time of death noted on the death certificate); *Com. v. Gonsalves*, 56 Mass App 506, 512, 778 NE2d 997, 1002 (2002) (although judge told jury that evidence of an altered VIN, if unexplained or uncontradicted, had prima facie effect establishing element of scienter in prosecution for receiving stolen motor vehicle, judge also emphasized presumed fact must be proven beyond reasonable doubt).

The presumption that a defendant prosecuted for unlawful possession was not authorized to carry the firearm has been held constitutional. See *Com. v. Smith*, 75 Mass App 196, 201-202, 912 NE2d 542, 548 (2009).

[70] See *Com. v. Pauley*, 368 Mass 286, 291, 331 NE2d 901, 904-905 (1975) ("prima facie" evidence in criminal case means only that in the absence of competing evidence, the jury were permitted, but not required, to find that the inferred or presumed fact was true beyond a reasonable doubt); *Com. v. McDuffee*, 379 Mass 353, 363, 398 NE2d 463, 469 (1979).

Interpreting "Melanie's Law" (GL 90, § 24(4))) governing the prosecution of OUI offenses, the Supreme Judicial Court has explained regarding prima facie evidence in criminal cases:

> Such provisions [providing that a court record of a prior conviction or other specified criminal justice documentation would be prima facie evidence that a defendant had been convicted previously] serve to identify evidence that the Commonwealth may introduce to meet its burden and which, while just as probative as other evidence, is less burdensome to produce [as with the use of narcotics analysis certificates which reduce court delays and the inconvenience of having the analyst called as a witness]. They do not, however, alter the Commonwealth's substantive burden of proof, render admissible any evidence that previously was inadmissible, or render sufficient any evidence that necessarily was insufficient beforehand. Rather, when properly employed by the Legislature, such provisions are merely a matter of administrative convenience that eliminate uncertainty as to what will constitute sufficient proof. Accordingly, we have held that the Legislature's decision that "A" is prima facie evidence of "B" does not impermissibly lower the Commonwealth's burden of proof, at least where "A" is enough to establish "B" beyond a reasonable doubt.[71]

Instructions to the jury in criminal cases must be phrased in permissive, not mandatory, terms. The use of the word "presumed" should be avoided.[72] The essential factfinding process must be left to

---

[71] *Com. v. Maloney*, 447 Mass 577, 581-582, 855 NE2d 765, 769-770 (2006). See also *Com. v. Bowden*, 447 Mass 593, 599-600, 855 NE2d 758, 763-764 (2006) (comparing "Melanie's Law" to prior version of statute); *Com. v. Dussault*, 71 Mass App 542, 546, 883 NE2d 1243, 1248 (2008) (providing that certified copies of court papers shall be prima facie evidence of prior conviction pursuant to GL 90, § 24(4)). But see §§ 8.4.2 and 8.12.2 (*Melendez-Diaz v. Massachusetts*, 129 S Ct 2527 (2009), invalidated on Confrontation Clause grounds the use of "testimonial" certificates as proof in criminal trials).

[72] By way of example, GL 90, § 24(1)(e) was amended after *Com. v. Moreira*, 385 Mass 792, 434 NE2d 196 (1982), invalidating the "presumption" of being under the influence arising from breathalyzer results. It now provides for a "permissible inference," which the jury are free to ignore even in the absence of other evidence. *Com. v. Rollins*, 65 Mass App 694, 701, 843 NE2d 118, 124 (2006). See also (use of "presumption" language regarding certificates of chemical analysis was improper).

For pre- *Melendez-Diaz v. Massachusetts* cases on jury instructions regarding forensic certificates, compare *Com. v. Claudio*, 405 Mass 481, 484, 541 NE2d 993, 995 (1989) (jury instruction concerning significance of certificates of chemical analysis, which required jury to accept information in certificates as true or to accept it as true unless defendant proved otherwise, unconstitutionally deprived defendant of her due process rights) and *Com. v. Johnson*, 405 Mass 488, 542 NE2d 248 (1989) (reasonable juror could have understood that jury was required to accept as true the report in certificate

the jury, which may perform that function by drawing reasonable inferences from the evidence provided that there is a rational connection between the underlying fact and the presumed fact, and that the burden remains on the prosecution to establish every element of the crime beyond a reasonable doubt.[73] Instructions in the form of permissive inferences (e.g., "it is reasonable to infer that a person ordinarily intends the natural and probable consequences of any acts that he does intentionally") have been upheld.[74] The jury is permitted, for example, to make inferences regarding malice and intent from particular circumstances, but instructions containing presumption language is forbidden.[75]

---

of analysis that confiscated substance was cocaine or that defendant had burden of proving that substance was not cocaine) with *Com. v. Berrio*, 43 Mass App 836, 837-838, 687 NE2d 644, 644-646 (1997) ("judge's charge adequately emphasized the fact that the certificate of analysis was like any other piece of evidence in the case, to be accepted or rejected according to the judgment of the jury.").

[73] See *McInerney v. Berman*, 621 F2d 20, 23 (1st Cir 1980); *Com. v. Lykus*, supra, 406 Mass at 143-144, 546 NE2d at 164-165; *Com. v. Pauley*, supra, 368 Mass at 292-298, 331 NE2d at 905-908; *Com. v. Callahan*, 401 Mass 627, 633, 519 NE2d 245, 249-250 (1988) (*Callahan III*).

[74] See *Com. v. Soares*, 51 Mass App 273, 279, 745 NE2d 362, 367 (2001); *Com. v. Rivera*, 50 Mass App 532, 538-539, 739 NE2d 278, 283-284 (2000); *Com. v. Sibinich*, 33 Mass App 246, 598 NE2d 673 (1992) (instruction that "everybody is presumed to intend what he or she did in fact do" did not impermissibly shift burden of proof to armed robbery defendant).

[75] Compare *Com. v. Medina*, 430 Mass 800, 802-805, 723 NE2d 986, 989-992 (2000) (instruction to presume malice from unlawful killing impermissibly shifted burden of proof), *Com. v. Sires*, 405 Mass 598, 542 NE2d 580 (1989) (instructions on intent referring to "the natural presumption of malice" impermissibly shifted burden of proof to defendant), and *Com. v. Repoza*, 400 Mass 516, 510 NE2d 755 (1987) (*Repoza II*) (instruction that intentional use of a deadly weapon created presumption of malice was error) with *Com. v. Akara*, 465 Mass 245, 9254, 88 NE2d 430, 439 (2013) (judge properly instructed jury that intent to kill may be inferred from use of firearm), *Com. v. Guy*, 441 Mass 96, 107, 803 NE2d 707, 718 (2004) (jury are permitted to infer malice from use of dangerous weapon), *Com. v. Pierce*, 419 Mass 28, 37-38, 642 NE2d 579, 585 (1994) (judge properly instructed jury that they might, but were not required to, draw inference of malice from use of deadly weapon), *Com. v. Blake*, 409 Mass 146, 149-154, 564 NE2d 1006, 1009-1012 (1991) (instructions permitting jury to infer malice from deliberate or cruel act did not shift burden of proof). See also *Com. v. Simpson*, 434 Mass 570, 588-589, 750 NE2d 977, 995 (2001) (no mandatory presumption in language "Any intentional killing of a human being without legal justification or excuse, with no extenuating circumstances sufficient in law to reduce a crime to manslaughter, is malicious within the meaning of malice aforethought."); *Com. v. Wallace*, 417 Mass 126, 132, 627 NE2d 935, 939 (1994) (prosecutor's statement during closing argument that human beings intend natural consequences of their acts did not, in context, require reversal). For instructions on the malice element of arson, see *Com. v. McLaughlin*, 431 Mass 506, 512-514, 729 NE2d 252, 258-259 (2000).

Proposed Mass R Evid 302(c) takes cognizance of these principles by providing that in criminal cases

> Whenever the existence of a presumed fact against the accused is submitted to the jury, the court shall instruct the jury that it may regard the basic facts as sufficient evidence of the presumed fact but is not required to do so. In addition, if the presumed fact establishes guilt or is an element of the offense or negatives a defense, the court shall instruct the jury that its existence, on all the evidence, must be proved beyond a reasonable doubt.

The Supreme Judicial Court has rejected the argument that an instruction allowing a permissive inference of sanity based on the fact "that a great majority of men are sane" violates art. 12 of the Massachusetts Declaration of Rights.[76] The jury may be advised of the reasonable inference of sanity and may rely on it together with other evidence.[77] The court has never held that the presumption of sanity is alone insufficient to meet the Commonwealth's burden.[78]

Because it would impermissibly shift the burden of persuasion and impose a burden of rebuttal on the defendant, Massachusetts does not impute any conclusive presumption of sexual innocence regarding the knowledge of child victims.[79]

For discussion of the role of an appellate court in assessing the impact of constitutionally erroneous burden-shifting language in jury instructions and the question of harmless error, see *Com. v. Medina*, supra, 430 Mass at 802-806, 723 NE2d at 990-992 (2000); *Com. v. Doherty*, supra, 411 Mass at 102-105 (& citations); *Com. v. Repoza II*, supra, 400 Mass at 521-522, 510 NE2d at 758-759.

[76] *Com. v. Keita*, 429 Mass 843, 846, 712 NE2d 65, 68 (1999); *Com. v. Kappler*, 416 Mass 574, 585-587, 625 NE2d 513 (1993).

[77] *Com. v. Amoral*, 389 Mass 184, 190-193, 450 NE2d 142, 146-147 (1983); *Com. v. Brown*, 387 Mass 220, 439 NE2d 296 (1982); *Com. v. Robinson*, 14 Mass App 591, 594, 441 NE2d 553, 556 (1982) (jury may consider "presumption of sanity" as "shorthand expression for fact that the majority of people are sane").

[78] See *Com. v. Keita*, supra, 429 Mass at 847, 712 NE2d at 69. "To the contrary, . . . the fact that a great majority of men are sane, and the probability that any particular man is sane, may be deemed by a jury to outweigh, in evidential value, testimony that he is insane." *Id.* See also *Com. v. Rasmusen*, 444 Mass 657, 664, 830 NE2d 1040, 1045-1046 (2005).

[79] See *Com. v. Beaudry*, 63 Mass App 488, 495, 826 NE2d 782, 789 (2005) (jury is merely entitled to consider evidence of precocious sexual knowledge as one factor supporting an inference of abuse).

§ 3.6 Adverse Inferences

*§ 3.6.1 In General/***Bowden** *Defense*

In certain situations, an adverse inference may be drawn from the failure of a party to produce evidence or take other action that might reasonably be expected of it. Thus, for example, the failure to conduct certain forensic tests may be used to rebut the Commonwealth's case by suggesting that such tests, if properly conducted, would have resulted in evidence favorable to the defendant—the so-called *Bowden* defense.[1] Defendants also have the right to base their defense on the failure of police to adequately investigate and to pursue other potential suspects.[2]

The decision to give a *Bowden* instruction allowing the jury to draw such an inference against the Commonwealth is within the trial

---

§ 3.6 [1] See *Com. v. Bowden*, 379 Mass 472, 485-486, 399 NE2d 482, 491 (1980); *Com. v. Alcantara*, 471 Mass 550, 561-563, 31 NE3d 561, 572-573 (2015). The *Bowden* instruction advises the jury that reasonable doubt may arise from their conclusion that law enforcement failed to adequately investigate the crime. See also *Com. v. Seng*, 456 Mass 490, 501-504, 924 NE2d 285, 295-297 (2010); *Com. v. Sanders*, 451 Mass 290, 300, 885 NE2d 105, 115 (2008); *Com. v. Mathews*, 450 Mass 858, 866-867, 882 NE2d 833, 841 (2008); *Com. v. Cordle*, 412 Mass 172, 176-178, 587 NE2d 1372, 1375-1376 (1992); *Com. v. Benoit*, 382 Mass 210, 221, 415 NE2d 818, 825 (1981); *Com. v. Remedor*, 52 Mass App 694, 699-701, 756 NE2d 606, 611-612 (2001). In appropriate circumstances, the prosecutor may make the same argument regarding a defense expert. *Com. v. Viriyahiranpaiboon*, 412 Mass 224, 231-232, 588 NE2d 643, 649 (1992).

Where defendant calls into question the integrity of the police investigation, the fact of, but not the details of, an inconclusive test result may be admitted to show the extent of the police investigation. *Com. v. Buckman*, 461 Mass 24, 34-35, 957 NE2d 1089, 1099 (2011); *Com. v. Mathews*, 450 Mass 858, 872, 882 NE2d 833 (2008).

[2] *Com. v. Fitzpatrick*, 463 Mass 581, 597, 977 NE2d 505, 519 (2012). Unlike third-party culprit evidence, see § 4.1.2, infra, the *Bowden* defense requires a showing that the police learned of other suspects during the investigation and failed to pursue the leads. *Id.* For extensive discussion of comparison between third-party culprit evidence and *Bowden* defense of failure to pursue other suspects, see *Com. v. Silva-Santiago*, 453 Mass 782, 801-805, 906 NE2d 299, 315-317 (2009). See also *Com. v. Wood*, 469 Mass 266, 278, 14 NE3d 140, 153 (2014) (exclusion of evidence of police failure to investigate murder victim's boyfriend was proper where there was no evidence he was involved in her death); *Com. v. Mattei*, 455 Mass 840, 857-860, 920 NE2d 845, 859-862 (2010) (refusal to allow defendant to cross-examine police officers about failure to pursue other possible suspects was improper); *Com. v. Ridge*, 455 Mass 307, 314-318, 916 NE2d 348, 357-360 (2009) (judge allowed defendant to challenge the adequacy of the police investigation, regarding others with whom murder victims were involved in the drug trade); *Com. v. Reynolds*, 429 Mass 388, 390-392, 708 NE2d 658, 661-662 (1999) (failure to pursue leads concerning other suspects).

judge's discretion and not a matter of right.[3] Unlike the situation regarding the missing witness inference, see § 3.6.2, counsel may be permitted to argue that the failure to conduct tests or pursue investigatory steps creates reasonable doubt even where the judge decides not to give a corresponding instruction.[4]

If defendant raises a *Bowden* defense, the Commonwealth has the right to rebut it, and explain why investigators chose the particular path they did.[5] To prevent the jury from reaching unwarranted inferences concerning a failure to test, the prosecution should be allowed to elicit on direct or redirect examination the reason for the omission of a test.[6] The broader the defendant's attack on the police investigation, the broader the Commonwealth's response may be, including the admission of evidence concerning information conveyed to the police that would not otherwise be admitted on hearsay or relevance grounds.[7]

As with other evidence (see § 4.3, infra), the trial judge must determine whether, in the particular circumstances of the case, the probative value of the *Bowden* evidence exceeds the risk of unfair prejudice to the Commonwealth by diverting the jury's attention to collateral matters.[8]

---

[3] *Com. v. Kaeppeler*, 473 Mass 396, 406, 42 NE3d 1090, 1099-1100 (2015); *Com. v. Fitzpatrick*, supra, 463 Mass at 598, 977 NE2d at 520; *Com. v. Perez*, 460 Mass 683, 692, 954 NE2d 1, 11 (2011); *Com. v. Semedo*, 456 Mass 1, 16, 921 NE2d 57, 71 (2010) (trial court not required to instruct jury on police failure to preserve notes, investigate fully, and conduct certain tests, since defendant was permitted to argue the points); *Com. v. Williams*, 439 Mass 678, 687, 790 NE2d 662, 670 (2003) (murder defendant who challenged reliability of gathering and storing blood evidence not entitled to instruction that if jury found procedures defective, such finding may raise reasonable doubt); *Com. v. Thomas*, 439 Mass 362, 370, 787 NE2d 1047, 1055 (2003); *Com. v. Boateng*, 438 Mass 498, 506-507, 781 NE2d 1207, 1215 (2003); *Com. v. Martinez*, 437 Mass 84, 91-92, 769 NE2d 273, 281 (2002) (judge need not give particular instruction requested by defendant nor use particular term, such as investigation).

[4] *Com. v. Komnenus*, 87 Mass App 587, 593, 32 NE3d 1286, 1293 (2015); *Com. v. Saletino*, 449 Mass 657, 671 n.21, 871 NE2d 455, 467 n.21 (2007).

[5] *See Com. v. Avila*, 454 Mass 744, 754-757, 912 NE2d 1014, 1023-1025 (2009) (extensive discussion).

[6] *Com. v. Flanagan*, 20 Mass App 472, 476 n.2, 481 NE2d 205, 208 n.2 (1985). The *Bowden* instruction is not intended to permit jurors to speculate about the results of investigative steps not taken; there must be actual evidence of such omissions. *Com. v. Tolan*, 453 Mass 634, 652, 904 NE2d 397, 412-413 (2009).

[7] *Com. v. Avila*, supra, 454 Mass at 754-757, 912 NE2d at 1024-1026.

[8] *Com. v. Alcantara*, 471 Mass 550, 561-563, 31 NE3d 561, 572-573 (2015); *Com. v. Cassidy*, 470 Mass 201, 210, 21 NE3d 127, 137 (2014) (no prejudice to defendant in exclusion of wide variety of evidence suggesting police failure to investigate other suspects where evidence was cumulative or lacking in probative value); *Com. v. Scott*, 470 Mass 320, 331-332, 21 NE3d 954, 964-965 (2014) (unlikely that the

Because *Bowden* evidence is usually offered not to show the truth of the matter asserted, but simply that the information was provided to the police, it is not subject to the limitations applicable to hearsay third-party culprit evidence (see § 4.2.2, infra).[9]

In appropriate circumstances, the defendant's failure to produce evidence may be a proper subject for argument, as for example, the failure to secure available records like employment time cards that would have confirmed his alibi.[10] Care must be taken, however, not to suggest that defendant has any burden to prove his innocence. See § 3.4.1, supra.

Refusal of a plaintiff claiming personal injuries to submit to a physical examination has long been held a proper cause for comment.[11] Similarly, by statute, in an action to establish paternity, the "fact that any party refuses to submit to a genetic marker test shall be admissible and the court may draw an adverse inference from such refusal."[12] An adverse inference may be drawn from a party's destruction of evidence,[13] and against the Commonwealth based on lost or missing evidence.[14]

---

shortfalls in the police investigation suggested by the excluded evidence could raise a reasonable doubt about defendant's guilt); *Com. v. Bright*, 463 Mass 421, 439, 974 NE2d 1092, 1109 (2012) (court properly rejected defendant's offer to prove that police failed to investigate gang affiliations of victim).

[9] *Com. v. Scott*, supra, 470 Mass at 330, 21 NE3d at 963.

[10] *Com. v. Ramey*, 368 Mass 109, 111-112, 330 NE2d 193, 195 (1975); *Com. v. Matthews*, 45 Mass App 444, 450, 699 NE2d 347, 352 (1998). See also *Automobile Insurers Bureau v. Comm'r of Ins.*, 430 Mass 285, 291, 718 NE2d 830, 836 (1999) (commissioner could draw adverse inference, in rate-setting proceeding, from AIB's failure to produce complete information on subject peculiarly within its knowledge). Similarly the jury may consider the absence of adequate medical records to justify drug prescriptions and draw an adverse inference against the defendant. *Com. v. Wood*, 17 Mass App 304, 306-307, 457 NE2d 1131, 1133 (1983) (citing Text).

[11] *Slack v. New York, N. H. & H. R.R. Co.*, 177 Mass 155, 157, 58 NE 686, 686 (1900).

[12] GL 209C, § 17.

[13] See *Gath v. M/A-Com, Inc.*, 440 Mass 482, 489-491, 802 NE2d 521, 528-529 (2003) (jury could infer from removal and destruction of gate on landowner's property that it would have provided evidence adverse to landowner in negligence action for injuries sustained by bicyclist).

[14] See *Com. v. Kee*, 449 Mass 550, 553-559, 870 NE2d 57, 62-66 (2007) (extensive discussion). See also § 9.5.2, infra.

§ 3.6.2 Failure to Call Witnesses

Perhaps the most common example of an adverse inference of this type involves the failure to call a witness who would normally be expected to be called. "Where a party has knowledge of a person who can be located and brought forward, who is friendly to, or at least not hostilely disposed toward, the party, and who can be expected to give testimony of distinct importance to the case, the party would naturally offer that person as a witness. If, then, without explanation, he does not do so, the jury may, if they think reasonable in the circumstances, infer that person, had he been called, would have given testimony unfavorable to the party."[15] Failure to call available witnesses to support an alibi is a typical example.[16] The inference is of course permissive, not mandatory.[17]

The courts have advised that "[b]ecause the inference, when it is made, can have a seriously adverse effect on the noncalling party—suggesting, as it does, that the party has willfully attempted to withhold or conceal significant evidence—it should be invited only in clear cases, and with caution."[18] Circumspection in this regard is especially called for where the inference would run against a criminal defendant, because that comes "uncomfortably close to invading constitutional rights."[19]

---

[15] *Com. v. Figueroa*, 413 Mass 193, 199, 595 NE2d 779, 783 (1992). See also *Com. v. Saletino*, 449 Mass 657, 667-673, 871 NE2d 455, 464-468 (2007); *Com. v. Zagranski*, 408 Mass 278, 287, 558 NE2d 933, 939 (1990); *Graves v. R.M. Packer, Inc.*, 45 Mass App 760, 770, 702 NE2d 21, 28 (1998) (failure of defendant to call its president and controlling stockholder, the person presumably most knowledgeable of facts in question and present during entire trial).

[16] See, e.g., *Com. v. Daye*, 435 Mass 463, 477, 759 NE2d 313, 326 (2001); *Com. v. Thomas*, 429 Mass 146, 706 NE2d 669 (1999); *Com. v. MacKenzie*, 413 Mass 498, 515-516, 597 NE2d 1037, 1048 (1992); *Com. v. Lee*, 394 Mass 209, 219, 475 NE2d 363, 369-370 (1985); *Com. v. Luna*, 46 Mass App 90, 94-96, 703 NE2d 740, 743-744 (1998) (defendant was properly cross-examined about his failure to search for alibi witnesses). But compare *Com. v. Johnson*, 46 Mass App 398, 407-408, 706 NE2d 716, 723-724 (1999) (no foundation for inference where defendant never mentioned being with anyone).

[17] *Com. v. Armstrong*, 54 Mass App 594, 598, 766 NE2d 894, 897 (2002) (& citations).

[18] *Com. v. Figueroa*, supra, 413 Mass at 199, 595 NE2d at 783. See also *Com. v. Rollins*, 441 Mass 114, 120, 803 NE2d 1256, 1261 (2004); *Com. v. Lo*, 428 Mass 45, 50-51, 696 NE2d 935, 939-940 (1998); *Com. v. Zagranski*, supra; *Com. v. Groce*, 25 Mass App 327, 329-331, 517 NE2d 1297, 1298-1299 (1988) (judge failed to exercise caution in instructing jury that it could draw adverse inference from defendant's failure to call mother and girlfriend).

[19] *Com. v. Ortiz*, 61 Mass App 468, 471, 811 NE2d 518, 522 (2004). But see *Com. v. Niziolek*, 380 Mass 513, 404 NE2d 643 (1980) (rejecting argument that inference erodes presumption of innocence).

Whether an inference can be drawn from the failure to call witnesses necessarily depends upon the posture of the particular case and the state of the evidence. "When it appears that the witness may be as favorable to one party as the other, no inference is warranted. Further, if the circumstances, considered by ordinary logic and experience, suggest a plausible reason for nonproduction of the witness, the jury should not be advised of the inference."[20] There is no basis for the inference when it appears that the testimony would be "unimportant—merely corroborative of, or merely cumulative upon, the testimony of one or more witnesses who have been called."[21] A decision not to call a witness for tactical reasons does not necessarily suggest the inference that the witness's testimony would have been unfavorable.[22]

Assuring an adequate foundation for comment or instruction on a missing witness usually requires, at minimum, a colloquy with counsel and a finding on the record.[23] A showing of availability is a

---

[20] *Com. v. Anderson*, 411 Mass 279, 282-283, 581 NE2d 1296, 1298 (1991) (citing Text). See also *Com. v. Dwyer*, 448 Mass 122, 134-135, 859 NE2d 400, 411 (2006) (had defense counsel explained to judge that he did not call witness because latter did not remember events of seven years earlier, judge likely would not have given missing witness instruction); *Com. v. Figueroa*, 79 Mass App 389, 400-401, 946 NE2d 142, 152 (2011) (Commonwealth had legitimate reason for not calling 88-year-old nursing home resident victim as witness); *Com. v. Melton*, 77 Mass App 552, 559, 933 NE2d 125, 131 (2010) (no error where judge declined to give missing witness instruction regarding detective who would have invoked privilege against self-incrimination if called).

[21] *Com. v. Schatvet*, 23 Mass App 130, 134, 499 NE2d 1208, 1211 (1986). See, e.g, *Com. v. Morales*, 453 Mass 40, 51-52, 899 NE2d 96, 105 (2009) (witness would have added nothing of significance to Commonwealth's case); *Com. v. Niels N.*, 73 Mass App 689, 703, 901 NE2d 166, 178 (2009) (juvenile has not shown what testimony of "distinct importance" the missing officers could have been expected to provide); *Com. v. Thomas*, 439 Mass 362, 370-371, 787 NE2d 1047, 1055-1056 (2003) (missing witnesses would have merely repeated prosecution witnesses corroborative prior consistent statements); *Com. v. Lo*, 428 Mass 45, 51, 696 NE2d 935, 940 (1998) (missing witness's testimony would probably have been cumulative); *Com. v. Wilson*, 38 Mass App 680, 685-688, 651 NE2d 854, 857-858 (1995) (no error in warning jury not to draw adverse inference where missing informant and officers were not present during transaction in question).

[22] *Com. v. Saletino*, 449 Mass 657, 668, 871 NE2d 455, 465 (2007) (Commonwealth had logical tactical reasons for not calling informant, i.e., defense counsel planned to impeach him with prior convictions); *Com. v. Santos*, 440 Mass 281, 294, 797 NE2d 1191, 1201 (2003); *Hoffman v. Houghton Chemical Corp.*, 434 Mass 624, 640-641, 751 NE2d 848, 861-862 (2001).

[23] See *Com. v. Giberti*, 51 Mass App 907, 908-909, 748 NE2d 982, 985-986 (2001); *Com. v. O'Brien*, 56 Mass App 170, 173, 775 NE2d 798, 801 (2002).

foundational prerequisite for the inference.[24] Availability does not necessarily mean proof of actual whereabouts. Rather, it refers to the likelihood that the party against whom the inference is to be drawn would be able to procure the missing witness' physical presence in court.[25] Comment may be impermissible if the witness cannot easily be called, or if the negative inference would otherwise be unfair.[26] Where it is determined that the missing witness cannot be located and brought forward,[27] or is equally available to both sides,[28] no inference should be drawn for failing to call the witness.

---

[24] See *Com. v. Gagnon*, 408 Mass 185, 198 n.8, 557 NE2d 728, 737 n.8 (1990) (no inference permitted where missing witness has successfully invoked testimonial privilege); *Com. v. Cobb*, 397 Mass 105, 108, 489 NE2d 1246, 1247-1248 (1986) (substantial risk of miscarriage of justice where jury was permitted to draw adverse inference from defendant's failure to produce store employees where nothing to suggest that missing witnesses were available or within his control); *Com. v. Fredette*, 396 Mass 455, 465-466, 486 NE2d 1112, 1119-1120 (1986); *Com. v. Franklin*, 366 Mass 284, 318 NE2d 469 (1974) (extensive discussion); *Com. v. Crawford*, 46 Mass App 423, 428-429, 706 NE2d 1141, 1145-1146 (1999) (where evidence was that missing witness was arrested at same time as defendant, and is silent as to outcome of arrest, inference and instruction were improper because witness might still be in custody); *Com. v. Vasquez*, 27 Mass App 655, 659, 542 NE2d 296, 298-299 (1989) (insufficient foundation for inference where no evidence of physical availability of missing witness).

[25] *Com. v. Happnie*, 3 Mass App 193, 197, 326 NE2d 25, 29 (1975).

[26] See *Com. v. Melendez*, 12 Mass App 980, 981, 428 NE2d 824, 826 (1981); *Com. v. Ivy*, 55 Mass App 851, 861, 774 NE2d 1100, 1107 (2002) (Commonwealth had plausible reasons for not calling homeless victim).

[27] *Com. v. Williams*, 450 Mass 894, 900-901, 882 NE2d 850, 856-857 (2008) (no showing that Commonwealth knew of or was deliberately concealing whereabouts of witness); *Com. v. Garcia*, 82 Mass App 239, 253, 972 NE2d 40, 52 (2012) (judge properly determined that victim could not be located, and thus no instruction required); *Com. v. Joyner*, 55 Mass App 412, 417-418, 771 NE2d 193, 199 (2002) (Commonwealth had issued subpoenas for victim and his girlfriend, made phone calls, spoken to members of their households, and sent cruisers to locate them); *Com. v. Ortiz*, 61 Mass App 468, 811 NE2d 518 (2004) (reversible error to give missing witness instruction regarding alibi witness where defense counsel had believed, erroneously, that witness had been served with subpoena). A judge is not required, in the absence of corroborative evidence, to accept counsel's excuse for nonproduction. *Com. v. Rollins*, 441 Mass 114, 120, 803 NE2d 1256, 1260 (2004).

[28] *Com. v. Hoilett*, 430 Mass 369, 375-376, 719 NE2d 488, 493-494 (1999); *Com. v. Crawford*, 417 Mass 358, 366-367, 629 NE2d 1332, 1337 (1994); *Com. v. Figueroa*, 413 Mass 193, 199, 595 NE2d 779, 783-784 (1992). But compare *Com. v. Saletino*, 449 Mass 657, 668 n.17, 871 NE2d 455, 465 n.17 (2007) (fact that the informant was present in the courtroom does nor render the adverse inference impermissible where the other party, the Commonwealth, was more closely acquainted with him and would naturally be expected to call him); *Com. v. Rollins*, supra, 441 Mass at 119-120, 803 NE2d at 1260 (fact that Commonwealth could have called missing witness does not preclude adverse inference because defendant was more closely acquainted with her and would naturally be expected to call her); *Com. v. Johnson*, 39 Mass App 410, 412, 656 NE2d

The most significant factors considered by courts in determining whether to give a "missing witness" instruction against a party have been summarized as follows: (1) the case against the party is strong, so that the party would naturally be expected to call favorable witnesses; (2) the purported evidence of the missing witnesses is not unimportant, collateral, or cumulative; (3) the party has superior knowledge of the identity and whereabouts of the witness; and (4) the party has not furnished a plausible reason, in the light of ordinary logic and experience, for nonproduction of the witness (stated otherwise, the evidence did not establish the missing witness' unavailability to the party).[29] At the least, a jury should not be permitted to draw inferences from the failure of a criminal defendant to call witnesses unless it appears to be within his power to do so and unless the evidence against him is so strong that, if innocent, he would be expected to call them.[30] "A party need not call everyone who might have information on a given subject, on pain, if he omits any, of suffering a jury inference that he is wrongly withholding damaging evidence."[31]

929, 931 (1995) (mere fact that witness appears equally available to both parties does not preclude missing witness instruction if it appears that defendant would be naturally expected to call friend).

[29] *Com. v. Ortiz*, 67 Mass App 349, 357, 853 NE2d 1079, 1086 (2006); *Com. v. Graves*, 35 Mass App 76, 81-87, 616 NE2d 817, 821-824 (1993). See also *Com. v. Olszewski*, 416 Mass 707, 723-724, 625 NE2d 529, 540 (1993), *habeas petition denied in Olszewski v. Spencer*, 466 F3d 47 (1st Cir 2006); *Com. v. Alves*, 50 Mass App 796, 800-805, 741 NE2d 473, 478-482 (2001) (discussing the factors in situation where witness is called but fails to resume stand after recess); *Com. v. McQuade*, 46 Mass App 827, 830-833, 710 NE2d 996, 999-1000 (1999) (discussing factor regarding importance of missing witness to case).

[30] *Com. v. Fredette*, 396 Mass 455, 466, 486 NE2d 1112, 1119-1120 (1986) (& citations).

[31] *Com. v. Schatvet*, 23 Mass App 130, 136, 499 NE2d 1208, 1212 (1986). Compare *Bencosme v. Kokoras*, 400 Mass 40, 44, 507 NE2d 748, 751 (1987) (no indication that missing witness knew anything bearing on issues at trial, and thus not clear that defendants naturally would be expected to call her), *Com. v. Tripolone*, 57 Mass App 901, 780 NE2d 966 (2003) (trial judge was right to refuse instruction and deny defense counsel permission to comment where missing detective was not easily available and likely to be very peripheral witness), *Com. v. Spencer*, 49 Mass App 383, 729 NE2d 662 (2000) (prejudicial error to give missing witness instruction where witness's testimony would have been merely cumulative and not of distinct importance to case), *Com. v. Matthews*, 45 Mass App 444, 447-450, 699 NE2d 347, 349-352 (1998) (improper for prosecutor to argue inference where defendant claimed he did not have opportunity to produce witnesses and unlikely that they would have offered important and helpful testimony), *Com. v. Resendes*, 30 Mass App 430, 569 NE2d 413 (1991) (cross-examination, prosecutor's comment, and instruction on missing witness constituted reversible error where evidence strongly suggested that defendant and missing

The decision to give a missing witness instruction to the jury is within the discretion of the judge, and a party who seeks the instruction cannot require it of right.[32] It has been suggested, however, that once a judge authorizes counsel at the charge conference to make a "missing witness" comment to the jury, the judge must also give a missing witness instruction to the jury; otherwise the effect is to undercut counsel's closing argument.[33]

---

witness were unfriendly), *Com. v. LeBlanc*, 30 Mass App 1, 7-8, 565 NE2d 797, 801 (1991) (in view of facts that defendant's testimony inculpated missing witness in drug activity and person does not appear to have any personal knowledge of the transactions in question, caution is advised regarding missing witness inference upon retrial), *Com. v. Vasquez*, 27 Mass App 655, 659, 542 NE2d 296, 298-299 (1989) (insufficient foundation for inference where testimony from missing witness would not have been crucial to Commonwealth's case), and *Com. v. Fulgham*, 23 Mass App 422, 423-427, 502 NE2d 960, 961-963 (1987) (judge did not err in refusing to give missing witness instruction against Commonwealth for failure to call two witnesses to testify as to fresh complaint where their testimony would have been cumulative of police officer's testimony and where prosecutor provided satisfactory explanation for not calling them) with *Com. v. Olszewski*, 416 Mass 707, 724-725, 625 NE2d 529, 541 (1993), *habeas petition denied in Olszewski v. Spencer*, 466 F3d 47 (1st Cir 2006) (where defendant offered no convincing reason why he failed to call father and sister to challenge confession, proper foundation for inference was laid), *Com. v. Bryer*, 398 Mass 9, 12-13, 494 NE2d 1335, 1337-1338 (1986) (fact that defendant's roommate could not have fully corroborated defendant's testimony did not bar prosecutorial comment since defendant would be expected to call him for even partial corroboration), *Com. v. Perryman*, 55 Mass App 187, 197-200, 770 NE2d 1, 9-10 (2002) (judge properly gave instruction where defendant's former girlfriend would have been central to alibi defense), and *Grassis v. Retik*, 25 Mass App 595, 600-601, 521 NE2d 411, 414-415 (1988) ("It is reasonable in the usual case to expect a plaintiff to call an available physician who first attended her after her injury.").

[32] *Com. v. Figueroa*, 413 Mass 193, 199, 595 NE2d 779, 784 (1992); *Com. v. Anderson*, supra, 411 Mass at 283, 581 NE2d at 1298. But see *Com. v. Smith*, 49 Mass App 827, 831-832, 733 NE2d 159, 162-163 (2000) (while rejecting argument that defendant was entitled to missing witness instruction where requirements were met, Appeals Court indicated that degree of court's discretion is lessened when it is defendant rather than Commonwealth seeking instruction, since inference would run against Commonwealth and would not erode presumption of innocence). See also *Rolanti v. Boston Edison Corp.*, 33 Mass App 516, 526-527, 603 NE2d 211, 219 (1992) (no error in judge's refusal to give missing witness instruction where he allowed defense counsel extensive questioning and closing comment regarding missing doctor's assessment).

[33] *Com. v. Sena*, 29 Mass App 463, 468 n.7, 561 NE2d 528, 531 n.7 (1990). See also *Com. v. Pratt*, 407 Mass 647, 654-658, 555 NE2d 559, 565-566 (1990) (judge's instructions admonishing jury to refrain from speculation regarding credibility of informants not called by Commonwealth did not impermissibly frustrate defendant's missing witness inference argument). Cf. *Com. v. DelValle*, 443 Mass 782, 794-795, 824 NE2d 830, 841 (2005) (testimony of prosecution expert that he had met with defense experts to discuss his findings may have raised impermissible inference in jurors' minds that defendant elected not to call his experts because their testimony would be damaging).

A missing witness instruction need not identify the missing witness by name.[34]

With regard to a criminal defendant, the judge should instruct that the jury should not draw an inference from defendant's failure to call a witness unless it is persuaded of the truth of the inference beyond a reasonable doubt.[35]

Failure to call a witness who would normally be expected to be called is a proper subject for comment in argument in both civil and criminal cases. Before commenting on the absence of a witness, the better practice is to notify the court and opposing counsel.[36] The argument is "a powerful accusation—that a party is withholding evidence that would be unfavorable—and that is why we regulate it closely and require judges to assess very carefully whether to give the instruction and to permit the argument in a given case."[37]

The trial judge should rule that there is sufficient foundation for such inference in the record before comment is made.[38] The judge may permit comment on defendant's failure to produce exculpatory

[34] See *Com. v. Johnson*, 39 Mass App 410, 412-413, 656 NE2d 929, 931 (1995) (identity of witness was clear from arguments).

[35] See *Com. v. Olszewski*, supra, 416 Mass at 724 n.18, 625 NE2d at 540; *Com. v. Niziolek*, 380 Mass 513, 522, 404 NE2d 643, 648 (1980); *Com. v. Johnson*, supra, 39 Mass App at 412-413, 656 NE2d at 931. But compare *Com. v. Lawrence*, 404 Mass 378, 394, 536 NE2d 571, 581 (1989) (defendant not entitled to instruction that in order to draw inferences, Commonwealth must prove subsidiary facts beyond reasonable doubt); *Com. v. Matthews*, 49 Mass App 365, 729 NE2d 1133 (2000) (failure to instruct against drawing adverse inference unless jurors were convinced of truth of inference beyond a reasonable doubt did not require reversal); *Com. v. Ruggerio*, 32 Mass App 964, 966, 592 NE2d 753, 753 (1992) (no requirement that each inference from facts made must be proved beyond reasonable doubt).

[36] See *Com. v. Fredette*, 396 Mass 455, 466, 486 NE2d 1112, 1120 (1986); *Com. v. Matthews*, supra, 45 Mass App at 448, 699 NE2d at 351; *Com. v. Calcagno*, 31 Mass App 25, 29, 574 NE2d 420, 423 (1991).

[37] *Com. v. Beltrandi*, 89 Mass App 196, 203, 46 NE3d 1029, 1035-1036 (2016) (prosecutor's improper comment required reversal of conviction.)

[38] *Com. v. Vasquez, Vasquez*, 27 Mass App 655, 658, 542 NE2d 296, 298 (1989); *Com. v. Broomhead*, 67 Mass App 547, 550-552, 855 NE2d 413, 417-418 (2006) (prosecutor's failure to obtain permission to comment on missing witness, coupled with judge's failure to take corrective action, constituted substantial risk of miscarriage of justice). But see *Com. v. Caldwell*, supra, 36 Mass App at 582, 634 NE2d at 131 (failure of prosecutor to obtain favorable ruling from judge before commenting on missing witness does not of itself ordinarily create basis for reversal; it merely creates risk that attorney will be interrupted by judge who may then give an unfavorable instruction to the jury). See also *Com. v. Rodriguez*, 49 Mass App 370, 729 NE2d 669 (2000) (prosecutor's comment on failure to call witness, after judge ruled such comment improper, required reversal).

witnesses only if the evidence against defendant is so strong that, if innocent, defendant would be expected to call them.[39]

The Supreme Judicial Court has advised regarding the connection between instruction and argument regarding a missing witness:

> A missing witness instruction from a judge and a missing witness argument by counsel go hand in hand. If a judge determines that the foundational requirements for the instruction are met, and that the adverse inference is warranted on the facts of the case, the instruction informs the jury that they may infer from a party's failure to call a witness that the witness would have testified unfavorably to that party. Counsel may then urge the jury in closing argument affirmatively to draw that inference. But before giving the instruction, and before permitting counsel to argue the point, the judge must be satisfied that the foundational requirements for the instruction and argument are in fact met and that the adverse inference is warranted in the circumstances. The same considerations apply in determining whether to permit the argument as apply in determining whether to give the instruction. If the judge determines that a missing witness adverse inference is not appropriate in a given case, the jury should not, regardless whether by argument or by an instruction, be given the option of drawing that inference; in such circumstances the jury should not be instructed on the adverse inference, nor should counsel be given permission to argue it. Put another way, counsel should not be permitted to encourage the jury to draw the adverse inference after the judge has determined that the inference is not appropriate and he will not instruct on it.[40]

The failure of a party to take the stand in his own behalf is a proper subject for comment in a civil case,[41] but not in the case of a

---

[39] See *Com. v. O'Brien*, 56 Mass App 170, 173 n.4, 775 NE2d 798, 801 n.4 (2002).

[40] *Com. v. Saletino*, 449 Mass 657, 670-671, 871 NE2d 455, 466-467 (2007). See also *Com. v. Pena*, 455 Mass 1, 15-17, 913 NE2d 815, 827-828 (2009) (trial judge properly instructed jury sua sponte to disregard defense counsel's comment on prosecution's failure to call an expert witness to rebut defense testimony on mental impairment, where counsel failed to request or secure permission, and failed to request a missing witness instruction).

[41] See *McGinnis v. Aetna Life & Casualty Co.*, 398 Mass 37, 39, 494 NE2d 1322, 1323 (1986). See also *Frizado v. Frizado*, 420 Mass 592, 596, 651 NE2d 1206, 1210 (1995) (adverse inference is permissible in domestic abuse case even where criminal proceedings are pending against defendant); *Custody of Two Minors*, 396 Mass 610, 617, 487 NE2d 1358, 1363-1364 (1986) (privilege against self-incrimination applicable in criminal proceedings, which prevents drawing negative inference from a defendant's failure to testify, is not applicable in child custody case); *Adoption of Nadia*, 42 Mass 304, 306-308, 676 NE2d 1165, 1167 (1997) (negative inference of unfitness permissible from father's failure to testify at adoption hearing).

criminal defendant, who enjoys the privilege against self-incrimination.[42] The adverse inference drawn from the failure of a party to testify is not sufficient, by itself, to meet an opponent's burden of proof.[43]

A judge may draw the adverse inference in a bench trial as long as there is a case presented adversely affecting the party's interests. See *Millennium Equity Holdings, LLC. v. Mahlowitz*, 456 Mass 627, 643-644, 925 NE2d 513, 527 (2010).

[42] See § 5.14.8, infra.

[43] *Frizado v. Frizado*, supra, 420 Mass at 596, 651 NE2d at 1210; *McGinnis v. Aetna Life & Casualty Co.*, supra; *Custody of Two Minors*, supra, 396 Mass at 616, 487 NE2d at 1363.

CHAPTER

4

RELEVANCE and CIRCUMSTANTIAL PROOF

§ 4.1 Relevance

§ 4.1.1 Defined

Both Proposed Mass R Evid and Fed R Evid 401 reflect Massachusetts practice in providing a liberal definition:

> "Relevant evidence" means evidence having any tendency to make the existence of any fact that is of consequence to the determination of the action more probable or less probable than it would be without the evidence.

The cases speak variously of evidence that has a "rational tendency to prove an issue in the case,"[1] or sheds light on an issue.[2]

The concept of relevancy has two components:

1. the evidence must have some tendency to prove or disprove a particular fact (probative value); and
2. that particular fact must be material to an issue in the case.

Probative value is as much a real-world as a legal concept. Where evidence is offered to establish Fact A, it must be shown that from the viewpoint of logic, experience, or common sense, the evidence tends to make Fact A more likely as compared to its probability without the evidence. "Inquiries into relevancy should relate to the way people

---

§ 4.1 [1] *Com. v. Fayerweather*, 406 Mass 78, 83, 546 NE2d 345, 347 (1989); *Com. v. Mandeville*, 386 Mass 393, 398, 436 NE2d 912, 917 (1982) (evidence "must render the desired inference more probable than it would be without the evidence").

[2] See *Adoption of Carla*, 416 Mass 510, 513, 623 NE2d 1118, 1120 (1993); *Com. v. Woods*, 414 Mass 343, 355, 607 NE2d 1024, 1033 (1993).

learn and should permit jurors to draw inferences, whatever they may be, necessary to reach a correct verdict."[3]

Materiality is dictated by the particular substantive law that controls the case. Evidence of a worker's carelessness would not, for example, be material in a worker's compensation action because GL 152 eliminates the defense of contributory negligence. If an issue is material to the case, the fact that the issue is conceded by the opponent, or there is an offer to stipulate, does not render the evidence inadmissible (although such concession is a factor to be weighed in assessing possible discretionary exclusion, discussed in § 4.3, infra).[4]

§ 4.1.2 Relevancy and Admissibility

Evidence that is relevant is admissible unless barred by some statute, rule, or policy of exclusion. Evidence that is not relevant is not admissible.[5] Gratuitous appeals to the jury's sympathy by manipulative portrayals of the victim are, for example, not pertinent to the issues to

---

[3] *Com. v. Dorsica*, 86 Mass App 776, 787 n.20, 42 NE3d 1184, 1193 n.20 (2015) (citation omitted).

[4] See, e.g., *Com. v. McCoy*, 456 Mass 838, 850, 926 NE2d 1143, 1157 (2010) (defendant's willingness to stipulate he was the person who had intercourse with victim at time and place in question did not preclude Commonwealth from proving it); *Gath v. M/A-Com, Inc.*, 440 Mass 482, 490, 802 NE2d 521, 528 (2003) (citing Text); *Com. v. Sleeper*, 435 Mass 581, 599, 760 NE2d 693, 708 (2002); *Com. v. Roderick*, 411 Mass 817, 819-820, 586 NE2d 967, 968-969 (1992); *Com. v. Nadworny*, 396 Mass 342, 367, 486 NE2d 675, 690 (1985); *Com. v. Worcester*, 44 Mass App 258, 262, 690 NE2d 451, 454 (1998). But compare *Old Chief v. United States*, 519 US 172 (1997) (defendant's offer to stipulate to prior felony element of firearm possession charge precludes introduction of full record of offense); *Com. v. Santos*, 463 Mass 273, 295-296, 974 NE2d 1, 19-20 (2012) (on retrial, defendant's offer to stipulate that he and witness were in prison together should suffice to establish how witness identified defendant, without allowing prosecution to again prove defendant's prior convictions and drug dealing). See also *Com. v. Lopes*, 85 Mass App 341, 10 NE3d 146 (2014) (trial court's decision to vacate partial stipulation that prior suspension of defendant's license was for Operating Under the Influence (OUI) in trial for OUI was not abuse of discretion).

[5] Proposed Mass R Evid 402, which essentially tracks the federal rule, provides:

> **Relevant Evidence Generally Admissible; Irrelevant Evidence Inadmissible.** All relevant evidence is admissible, except as limited by constitutional requirements, or as otherwise provided by statute or by these rules, or by other rules applicable in the courts of this Commonwealth. Evidence which is not relevant is not admissible.

See also *Com. v. Vitello*, 376 Mass 426, 440, 381 NE2d 582, 590 (1978).

be tried and should be excluded.[6] It is not a basis for excluding relevant evidence that it is "self-serving."[7]

The trial judge is accorded substantial discretion in deciding whether evidence is relevant.[8] An error by the trial judge in excluding relevant evidence must be shown to have been prejudicial in order to constitute grounds for a new trial.[9] The proponent must make a plausible showing that the trier of fact might have reached a different result had the evidence been admitted.[10] So too with the erroneous admission of irrelevant evidence.[11]

Once admitted, the weight to be accorded the evidence is a question for the jury.[12]

To be admissible, it is not necessary that the evidence be conclusive of the issue.[13] It is sufficient if it constitutes a link in the chain of

---

[6] Compare *Com. v. Santiago*, 425 Mass 491, 497 n.4, 681 NE2d 1205, 1211 n.4 (1997) (where victim's sister was permitted to testify in substantial detail about her life, it was "abundantly clear" she offered no evidence relevant to the crime charged) with *Com. v. Flint*, 81 Mass App 794, 806-807, 968 NE2d 928, 939 (2012) (references to victim's troubled family life were relevant to explain what might have drawn victim and defendant together).

[7] See *Com. v. Caldron*, 383 Mass 86, 90, 417 NE2d 958 (1981) (error to exclude testimony by defendant as to his intent at time of alleged crime).

[8] See *Com. v. Rogers*, 459 Mass 249, 267, 945 NE2d 295, 311 (2011); In re *Wyatt*, 428 Mass 347, 355, 701 NE2d 337, 343 (1998) ("The issue of relevancy is a matter on which the opinion of the trial judge will be accepted on review except for palpable error.").

[9] See *DeJesus v. Yogel*, 404 Mass 44, 47-49, 533 NE2d 1318, 1321-1322 (1989).

[10] See *Com. v. Santos*, 460 Mass 128, 137-138, 950 NE2d 60, 67 (2011) (exclusion of testimony regarding conduct of police that allegedly caused disturbance defendants were charged with was prejudicial); *Foreign Car Center, Inc. v. Salem Suede, Inc.*, 40 Mass App 15, 17, 660 NE2d 687, 691 (1996) ("[T]he erroneous exclusion of relevant evidence is reversible error unless, on the record, the appellate court can say with substantial confidence that the error would not have made a material difference.").

[11] See *Com. v. Cavitt*, 460 Mass 617, 635, 953 NE2d 216, 230-231 (2011) (erroneous admission of testimony regarding inconclusive DNA evidence was not prejudicial); *Com. v. Silva*, 455 Mass 503, 519-522, 918 NE2d 65, 82-85 (2009) (erroneous admission of preparation manuals for police officer examination was not prejudicial).

For the standard in assessing harmless error in the constitutional context, see *Com. v. Loadholt*, 456 Mass 411, 432-433, 923 NE2d 1037, 1055-1056 (2010) (erroneous admission of ballistics certificate); *Com. v. Muniz*, 456 Mass 166, 169, 921 NE2d 981, 984 (2010) (same); *Com. v. Marte*, 84 Mass App 136, 993 NE2d 1201 (2013) (drug analysis certificate).

See also § 1.3.1, supra.

[12] *Com. v. Weichell*, 390 Mass 62, 74, 453 NE2d 1038, 1045 (1983).

[13] *Com. v. Ashley*, 427 Mass 620, 624-625, 694 NE2d 862, 867 (1998) (no requirement that evidence of motive be conclusive).

proof.[14] "Evidence must go in piecemeal, and evidence having a tendency to prove a proposition is not inadmissible simply because it does not wholly prove the proposition. It is enough if in connection with other evidence it helps a little."[15] Expressions of uncertainty in a witness's testimony go to the weight, not admissibility, of the evidence.[16]

Illustrative of the breadth of the relevancy concept is *Com. v. Yesilciman*,[17] admitting evidence that bloodstains were found inside defendant's automobile and on his clothes, even though it could not be scientifically determined that the blood came from the murder victim: "The evidence was relevant to the issue whether the defendant was the perpetrator. Other evidence introduced at trial made it clear that whoever committed the crime would have gotten blood on himself or on his clothing. Therefore, evidence that there was blood in the

---

[14] See, e.g., *Com. v. Arroyo*, 442 Mass 135, 144, 810 NE2d 1201, 1210 (2004); *Com. v. Sicari*, 434 Mass 732, 750-751, 752 NE2d 684, 698 (2001); *Liarikos v. Mello*, 418 Mass 669, 672, 639 NE2d 716, 718 (1994); *Com. v. Gordon*, 407 Mass 340, 351, 553 NE2d 915, 921 (1990).

[15] *Com. v. Tucker*, 189 Mass 457, 467, 76 NE 127, 130 (1905). See, e.g., *Com. v. Guy*, 454 Mass 440, 443-444, 910 NE2d 358, 361 (2009) (evidence of defendant's fascination with serial killings was relevant to issue of intent and motive); *Com. v. Barnoski*, 418 Mass 523, 538, 638 NE2d 9, 17 (1994) (testimony that defendant repeatedly rubbed hand through his hair was admissible to show why gunshot residue test might have been negative); *Com. v. Gordon*, supra, 407 Mass at 351, 553 NE2d at 921 (evidence of prior confrontation between victim and defendant was relevant to issue of victim's reasonable fear of defendant); *Com. v. Fayerweather*, 406 Mass 78, 83, 546 NE2d 345, 350 (1989) ("Evidence that the complainant claimed to hear the voice of the defendant telling her to do things could have made it more likely, in the jury's view, that the complainant did not perceive the event accurately. The evidence could have been helpful for the jury to determine whether the complainant was telling the truth or whether she imagined the entire incident. The evidence, then, met the threshold test of relevancy."); *Com. v. Borodine*, 371 Mass 1, 7-9, 353 NE2d 649, 653 (1976) (evidence that homicide victim had abandoned plans to marry defendant and planned to terminate their relationship was relevant to motive, even in absence of direct evidence that this was communicated to defendant); *Sydney Binder, Inc. v. Jewelers Mutual Ins. Co.*, 28 Mass App 459, 461-463, 552 NE2d 568, 569-570 (1990) (evidence that principal officer of corporate plaintiff was in financial straits was admissible as tending to establish motive for burglary of his own store); *Com. v. Phong Thu Ly*, 19 Mass App 901, 471 NE2d 383 (1984) (rubber dishwashing gloves found on defendant was probative of intent to conceal fingerprints). But compare *Com. v. Talbot*, 444 Mass 586, 589, 830 NE2d 177, 180 (2005) (expert testimony on effects of defendant's diabetic condition was irrelevant to issue of her mental state at time of offenses).

[16] See *Com. v. Scesny*, 472 Mass 185, 199, 34 NE3d 17, 28 (2015) (testimony that witness was "pretty certain" defendant had been a patron at bar where victim was last seen was relevant, as it made his connection to victim more probable than without the evidence); *Com. v. Dumas*, 83 Mass App 536, 538, 986 NE2d 878, 880 (2012).

[17] 406 Mass 736, 744, 550 NE2d 378, 383 (1990).

defendant's car and on an item of his clothing was a link in the chain of proof of his identity as the perpetrator of the crime."[18]

Similarly, evidence that two knives were found in the vicinity of the defendant at the time of his arrest two months after the stabbing was held properly admitted to show that he possessed instruments that could have been used in the commission of the crime, despite the lack of any demonstrable connection between the knives and the murder weapon.[19] Although similar weapon evidence is frequently admitted to prove defendant had the means to commit the crime,[20] even when

---

[18] See also *Com. v. Voisine*, 414 Mass 772, 781-782, 610 NE2d 926, 931 (1993) (expert testimony that stains on defendant's hat were human blood was admissible despite unknown source); *Com. v. Durand*, 457 Mass 574, 598, 931 NE2d 950, 970 (2010) (no error in allowing forensic chemist to testify defendant's hands tested positive for blood even though test did not reveal origin, age, or identity of the blood). For use of evidence connecting defendant to a particular location to link him to the crime, see *Com. v. Gambora*, 457 Mass 715, 730, 933 NE2d 50, 62 (2010) (sneaker found in closet at defendant's mother's home matched type that left print at crime scene).

[19] *Com. v. Marangiello*, 410 Mass 452, 456-457, 573 NE2d 500, 503-504 (1991).

[20] See, e.g., *Com. v. Carney*, 472 Mass 252, 256, 33 NE3d 1234, 1238 (2015) (although unrelated to the killing, BB gun and ammunition recovered from defendant's closet showed his knowledge of firearms and was particularly relevant to his accident defense); *Com. v. Rosa*, 468 Mass 231, 236-237, 9 NE3d 832, 837 (2014) (shell casings, bullets, and ammunition found in defendant's bedroom hours after the shooting were relevant to existence of a joint venture); *Com. v. McGee*, 467 Mass 141, 156, 4 NE2d 256, 268 (2014) (defendant previously possessed same caliber revolver as murder weapon); *Com. v. Perez*, 460 Mass 683, 695-696, 954 NE2d 1, 13-14 (2011) (defendant seen in possession of a silver handgun of the type used in the murder); *Com. v. Williams*, 456 Mass 857, 871, 926 NE2d 1162, 1174 (2010) (firearm found on defendant's cousin five days after murder properly admitted to show defendant had means to commit the crime); *Com. v. Ashman*, 430 Mass 736, 743-744, 723 NE2d 510, 516 (2000) (knives similar to murder weapon); *Com. v. Hamilton*, 411 Mass 313, 322, 582 NE2d 929, 934-935 (1991) (gun taken from defendant at arrest four months after crimes could have been used in murder); *Com. v. Mitchell*, 89 Mass App 13, 45 NE3d 111 (2016) (two knives that could have been used in the murder). Even where the proffered evidence could not have been used in the crime, it may be admissible to prove defendant's "access to" and "familiarity with" such items. See *Com. v. Mejia*, 88 Mass App 227, 234, 36 NE3d 612, 618 (2015).

But compare *Com. v. Hernandez*, 471 Mass 1005, 27 NE3d 380 (2015) (prejudicial effect of witness testimony that while in California defendant had referred to possessing a gun outweighed its probative value as there was no showing the gun had been transported to Massachusetts at time of the murder); *Com. v. Hoose*, 467 Mass 395, 409-410, 5 NE2d 843, 857 (2014) (knife seen in days following murders one-half mile away from scene, offered by defendant as third-party culprit evidence, was insufficiently connected to murder to be admitted); *Com. v. Barbosa*, 463 Mass 116, 121-124, 972 NE2d 987, 992-994 (2012) (extensive discussion of weapons-related evidence unconnected to the commission of the crime) (nine millimeter ammunition and magazine found in defendant's apartment should not have been admitted, as they could not have been used in commission of the crime charged); *Com. v. Graham*, 431 Mass 282,

distant in time from the crime,[21] the Supreme Judicial Court has warned that "the introduction of evidence that a defendant possessed a weapon on a prior occasion creates a risk that the jury will use the evidence impermissibly to infer that the defendant has a bad character or a propensity to commit the crime charged."[22] Where the weapon could not have been used in the crime, it should not be admitted.[23] Similarly, evidence showing only a person's general acquaintance with weapons should not be admitted.[24]

Where the links in the chain are too attenuated, evidence will be excluded as "remote" or "speculative."[25] In *Com. v. Burke*,[26] for example, evidence showing that the defendant and a woman had occupied an apartment together for a short time seven months before his wife's death was held, in the absence of any proof that the relationship had continued, too remote on the issues of hostility toward the victim or motive to kill her.[27]

287-288, 727 NE2d 51, 56-57 (2000) (unnecessary to introduce four crossbows owned by defendant but not used in murder, because there was sufficient evidence to demonstrate his familiarity with the weapon); *Com. v. Mejia*, supra, 88 Mass App at 234-235, 36 NE3d at 619-620 (connection between the handgun and defendant was too attenuated). See also *Com. v. Anderson*, 448 Mass 548, 559-560, 862 NE2d 749, 759-760 (2007) (testimony from three inmates regarding defendant's skill with knife tended to prove he possessed the means and ability to commit the murder); *Com. v. Evans*, 438 Mass 142, 151-152, 778 NE2d 885, 894-895 (2002) (absence of evidence that crimes were committed with mask seized from defendant at arrest did not preclude admission into evidence, where mask was relevant to intent and means).

[21] See, e.g., *Com. v. Corliss*, 470 Mass 443, 449-451, 23 NE3d 92, 98-100 (2014) (witness's testimony that he saw defendant with a firearm 16 months before the store robbery and shooting was admissible); *Com. v. Daye*, 435 Mass 463, 474-475, 759 NE2d 313, 324 (2001) (.38 caliber bullets found in defendant's possession when captured ten months after shooting, where victim was killed by a .38 caliber bullet).

[22] *Com. v. McGee*, supra, 467 Mass at 157-158, 4 NE2d at 269-270.

[23] *Id.*, 467 Mass at 156, 4 NE2d at 268.

[24] *Com. v. Bonnett*, 472 Mass 827, 841, 37 NE3d 1064, 1077 (2015).

[25] See *DeJesus v. Vogel*, 404 Mass 44, 47 n.3, 533 NE2d 1318, 1320 n.3 (1989).

[26] 339 Mass 521, 533-534, 159 NE2d 856, 864 (1959).

[27] See also *Com. v. Crouse*, 447 Mass 558, 567-568, 855 NE2d 391, 400 (2006) (bathing suit found in function room on morning of fire was too tentatively linked to crime to be relevant; but adult magazine found there bearing defendant's thumb print tended to prove he had access to the room); *Com. v. Martinez*, 437 Mass 84, 88-89, 769 NE2d 273, 278 (2002) (evidence of defendant's sexual frustration day before murder was too remote to be relevant to his state of mind when he killed victim); *Com. v. Stote*, 433 Mass 19, 27, 739 NE2d 261, 267 (2000) (evidence of homicide victim's arrest eight years before killing too remote); *Com. v. Gilbert*, 423 Mass 863, 870-871, 673 NE2d 46, 51 (1996) (evidence that victim turned down long-term job too attenuated to show she was contemplating suicide); *Com. v. Kirkpatrick*, 423 Mass 436, 447-448, 668 NE2d 790, 797 (1996) (in absence of medical testimony explaining records, jury

Relevant and necessary background evidence is admissible as long as its probative value outweighs its prejudicial effect (see § 4.3, infra). Thus, where relevant, the judge may permit background testimony from a representative of a regulatory agency about how the agency interprets and carries out its mandates.[28] Evidence which corroborates a defendant's or another witness's testimony may also be admitted.[29]

The issue of admissibility must of course be distinguished from the question of the sufficiency of the evidence. The fact that defendant's fingerprint was found on a mask left at crime scene may be admissible, but is not sufficient to warrant a finding beyond a reasonable doubt that the print was placed on mask during the crime.[30]

For evidence the relevancy of which is conditioned on the finding of a preliminary fact, see § 1.4, 1.6, supra.

§ 4.2 Direct and Circumstantial Evidence

Probative evidence takes two forms. Direct proof is evidence that actually asserts or demonstrates the fact proposition for which it is offered, and which if believed by the trier of fact will prove the particular fact in question without reliance upon inference or presumption.[1] Testimony

---

could only have speculated on the importance of sexually transmitted disease in defendant and absence of it in alleged victim of sexual assault); *Com. v. Woods*, 414 Mass 343, 355, 607 NE2d 1024, 1032-1033 (1993) (chain of inference from evidence that front seat passenger possessed marijuana at time of accident to conclusion that he, not vehicular homicide defendant, was driving was too tenuous); *Maillet v. ATF-Davidson Co.*, 407 Mass 185, 186-189, 552 NE2d 95, 96-98 (1990) (evidence that beer was available on premises of industrial accident and that plaintiff was seen handling a beer can was irrelevant to prove that plaintiff had consumed a beer prior to the accident). Compare *Com. v. Taylor*, 426 Mass 189, 687 NE2d 631 (1997) (notebook and tape-recorded conversation disclosing discordant relationship between defendant and murder victim's parents was relevant to possible motive, even though they predated trial by three years); *DeJesus v. Yogel*, supra, 404 Mass at 46-47, 533 NE2d at 1320-1321 (evidence that porch railing was loose two months before accident and no repairs were made during intervening period was not too remote).

[28] See *Com. v. Springfield Terminal Railway Co.*, 80 Mass App 22, 42-43, 951 NE2d 696, 713 (2011).

[29] *Com. v. Strickland*, 87 Mass App 46, 54, 23 NE3d 135, 143 (2015) (medical testimony would have corroborated defendant's inferences about victim's injuries being self-inflicted).

[30] See *Com. v. Morris*, 422 Mass 254, 257, 662 NE2d 683, 685 (1996).

§ 4.2 [1] *Com. v. Doste*, 425 Mass 372, 375, 681 NE2d 282, 284 (1997) (citing Text); *Rolanti v. Boston Edison Corp.*, 33 Mass App 516, 521, 603 NE2d 211, 216 (1992).

of an eyewitness describing the murder, or the murder weapon itself,[2] are examples of direct proof.

Circumstantial proof, on the other hand, requires the trier of fact to make inferences to reach the fact proposition.[3] Testimony of a witness who observed the defendant standing over the body with the proverbial smoking gun shortly after the murder is an example of circumstantial proof.

It is not necessary that the inference proposed to be drawn from the circumstantial evidence be the *only* one possible; it is sufficient if the inference is a reasonable one.[4] Nor is it required that every inference be premised on an independently proven fact; in certain circumstances, a jury is permitted to make an inference based on an inference as long as it is not speculative.[5]

The scope of circumstantial evidence is as broad as human experience[6] and, although "indirect," can carry persuasive value equal to or even greater than that of direct proof.[7] It is well-settled that circumstantial evidence may be sufficient to establish guilt beyond a reasonable doubt in a criminal case.[8] Where, however, the evidence tends

---

[2] Real evidence may also be used circumstantially. See, e.g., *Com. v. Merola*, 405 Mass 529, 542 NE2d 249 (1989) (photos of bruises on child's body not linked to defendant or to child's death were admissible to show consciousness of guilt, as defendant denied seeing any bruises); *Com. v. Drayton*, 386 Mass 39, 48, 434 NE2d 997, 1005 (1982) (defendant's fingerprints on box found at murder scene were circumstantial evidence of his identity); *Com. v. Stroud*, 375 Mass 265, 272, 376 NE2d 849, 853 (1978) (bloodstained shirt was relevant to manner in which victim died).

[3] *Abraham v. Woburn*, 383 Mass 724, 730, 421 NE2d 1206, 1210 (1981).

[4] *Com. v. Merry*, 453 Mass 653, 661, 904 NE2d 413, 421 (2009); *Com. v. Angelo Todesca Corp.*, 446 Mass 128, 132-133, 842 NE2d 930, 936 (2006); *Com. v. Marquetty*, 416 Mass 445, 452, 622 NE2d 632, 638 (1993).

[5] *Com. v. Doste*, supra, 425 Mass at 375-376, 681 NE2d at 284 (1997). Compare *Com. v. Montalvo*, 76 Mass App 319, 339, 922 NE2d 155, 164 (2010) (conviction for intent to distribute reversed because it rested upon the speculative piling of inference upon inference).

[6] In appropriate cases, for example, "dream testimony" (i.e., that defendant recounted his dream of killing the victim) may be admitted. See *Com. v. McIntyre*, 430 Mass 529, 538-539, 721 NE2d 911, 919-920 (1999) (& cases cited). But compare *Com. v. Almeida*, 433 Mass 717, 720, 746 NE2d 139, 142 (2001) (admitting out-of-court statements made by child complainant while sleeping was reversible error).

[7] *Abraham v. Woburn*, supra, 383 Mass at 729, 421 NE2d at 1210 (1981) (citing Text). See, e.g., *Com. v. Palmer*, 59 Mass App 415, 421-422, 796 NE2d 423, 428 (2003) (records of electronics store showing someone using defendant's name, address, and phone number purchased walkie-talkies identical to those used in armed robbery were circumstantial evidence linking defendant to crime).

[8] See *Com. v. Woods*, 466 Mass 707, 713, 1 NE2d 762, 767-768 (2014) (intent to kill and joint venture); *Com. v. Doste*, supra, 425 Mass at 375, 681 NE2d at 284. See,

equally to support inconsistent conclusions as to the defendant's guilt, the evidence is insufficient to support a conviction.[9]

---

e.g., *Com. v. Deane*, 458 Mass 43, 50-52, 934 NE2d 794, 800-802 (2010) (jury could reasonably have inferred that defendant was present at killings, and aided in the murders); *Com. v. Linton*, 456 Mass 534, 545, 924 NE2d 722, 733-734 (2010) (jury could reasonably have concluded that victim could have been strangled only by someone who had the keys to her apartment, and that defendant had ample opportunity and motive to commit the crime); *Com. v. Aponte*, 71 Mass App 758, 761-762, 887 NE2d 266, 270-271 (2008) (sufficient circumstantial proof to prove defendant knew vehicle was stolen where his possession was "in a context fraught with suspicion"); *Com. v. Reynolds*, 67 Mass App 215, 217-220, 852 NE2d 1124, 1127-1129 (2006) (even in the absence of scientific evidence of the actual presence of drugs in defendant's system, circumstantial evidence including defendant's erratic driving, her appearance, and her access to prescription narcotics met standard of proof for intoxication). But compare *Com. v. Jansen*, 459 Mass 21, 27-28, 942 NE2d 959, 964-965 (2011) (evidence was insufficient to establish defendant acted as part of a joint enterprise in committing rape, as inferences urged by Commonwealth were based on conjecture); *O'Laughlin v. O'Brien*, 568 F3d 287 (1st Cir 2009) (circumstantial identification evidence was insufficient to establish defendant as perpetrator beyond reasonable doubt). The presence of a fingerprint at the crime scene is not by itself sufficient to support a guilty verdict. *Com. v. French*, 88 Mass App 477, 478, 38 NE3d 774, 776 (2015).

For proof solely by circumstantial evidence that: defendant was operator of motor vehicle, see *Com. v. Beltrandi*, 89 Mass App 196, 199-202, 46 NE3d 1029, 1032-1035 (2016); *Com. v. Cabral*, 77 Mass App 909, 931 NE2d 44 (2010); that patron was exhibiting outward signs of intoxication, see *Rivera v. Club Caravan, Inc.*, 77 Mass App 17, 20-21, 928 NE2d 348, 351-352 (2010). For circumstantial proof of fraud and undue influence, see *Estate of Sharis*, 83 Mass App 839, 845-846, 990 NE2d 98, 104 (2013). For the inference of intent to distribute from the large amount of the drug, see *Com. v. Sepheus*, 468 Mass 160, 164-165, 9 NE3d 800, 806 (2014) (but quantity here was too small). For circumstantial proof of knowledge, see *Com. v. Lovering*, 89 Mass App 76, 78 n.5, 46 NE3d 69, 72 n.5 (2016) (evidence that firearm was found underneath defendant's belongings, that was of Nazi vintage, and that defendant collected Nazi memorabilia was sufficient basis to infer that defendant had knowledge of firearm); *Com. v. Tavares*, 87 Mass App 471, 475, 31 NE3d 1167, 1170 (2015) (jury could reasonably infer that defendant knew bills were counterfeit).

[9] See *Com. v. McCauliff*, 461 Mass 635, 642, 963 NE2d 719, 725 (2012); *Com. v. Lombard*, 419 Mass 585, 589, 646 NE2d 400, 404 (1995). The concept applies only if the circumstances require a leap of conjecture with respect to the essential elements of the crime. *Com. v. Merry*, 453 Mass 653, 663, 904 NE2d 413, 422 (2009); *Com. v. Chongarlides*, 62 Mass App 709, 712, 819 NE2d 971, 975 (2004). Compare *Com. v. Morgan*, 449 Mass 343, 349-351, 868 NE2d 99, 106-108 (2007), *habeas denied, Morgan v. Dickhaut*, 677 F3d 39 (1st Cir 2012) (evidence pointed more strongly in direction of defendant); *Com. v. Winfield*, 76 Mass App 716, 721-723, 926 NE2d 550, 554-556 (2010), *habeas denied, Winfield v. O'Brien*, 775 F3d 1 (1st Cir 2014) (since defendant was the only adult with access to victim during time span of attack, and had motive, line of cases involving evidence equally sustaining inconsistent propositions was in apposite); *Com. v. Torres*, 442 Mass 554, 563-566, 813 NE2d 1261, 1270-1271 (2004) (evidence was not in equipoise but pointed more strongly to defendant than to victim's mother), and *Com. v. Doyle*, 12 Mass App 786, 429 NE2d 346 (evidence was sufficient to support conclusion that defendant had been operator of vehicle involved in accident) with *Corson v. Com.*, 428 Mass 193, 699 NE2d 814 (1998) (evidence was insufficient to permit

In order to convict on circumstantial evidence, it is not necessary to show that no person other than the defendant could have committed the crime.[10] The question of guilt must not, however, be left to conjecture or surmise.[11] Nor may a conviction rest upon piling inference upon inference.[12]

In instructing the jury on the use of circumstantial proof, as with reasonable doubt (see § 3.4.2, supra), numeric or quantifiable examples should be avoided.[13]

§ 4.2.1 *Consciousness of Guilt/Innocence; Consciousness of Liability Evidence*

A classic illustration of circumstantial proof is "consciousness of guilt" evidence, frequently encountered in criminal cases. Evidence of flight, escape, false statements,[14] or concealment after the crime is admissible under appropriate circumstances as probative of the defendant's guilty state of mind.[15] Inconsistent statements of denial by a

---

inference that defendant had requisite criminal intent), *Com. v. Mullen*, 3 Mass App 25, 322 NE2d 195 (1975) (evidence was insufficient to permit inference that defendant had been driving vehicle), and *Com. v. Prentice P.*, 57 Mass App 766, 786 NE2d 415 (2003) (insufficient evidence that juvenile stole vehicle). The concept regarding evidence, which equally supports conflicting conclusions, is used to evaluate the sufficiency of the evidence and is not favored as a jury instruction. *Com. v. Saladin*, 73 Mass App 416, 419, 898 NE2d 514, 518 (2008).

[10] *Com. v. Lao*, 443 Mass 770, 780, 824 NE2d 821, 830 (2005); *Cramer v. Com.*, 419 Mass 106, 111-112, 642 NE2d 1039, 1043-1044 (1994).

[11] *Com. v. Kelly*, 470 Mass 682, 693-694, 25 NE3d 288, 300-301 (2014); *Com. v. Jansen*, supra, 459 Mass at 27-28, 942 NE2d at 964-965.

[12] *Com. v. Kately*, 461 Mass 575, 582, 962 NE2d 747, 753 (2012); *Com. v. White*, 452 Mass 133, 136, 891 NE2d 675, 679 (2008) (but every inference need not be premised on an independently proven fact); *Com. v. Darnell D.*, 445 Mass 670, 672, 840 NE2d 33, 36 (2005); *Com. v. Montalvo*, 76 Mass App 319, 339, 922 NE2d 155, 164 (2010) (conviction for intent to distribute reversed because it rested upon the speculative piling of inference upon inference).

[13] See *Com. v. Rosa*, 422 Mass 18, 26-29, 661 NE2d 56, 61-63 (1996); *Com. v. Brooks*, 422 Mass 574, 578-579, 664 NE2d 801, 806 (1996) (same); *Com. v. Rosado*, 434 Mass 197, 208, 747 NE2d 156, 166-167 (2001) (use of examples is permissible, but not required). For instructions based on the "footprints in the snow" analogy, see *Com. v. Gil*, 393 Mass 204, 221-222, 471 NE2d 30 (1984).

[14] False statements are not ensnared by the rule against hearsay because they are not offered for their truth. *Com. v. Alcantara*, 471 Mass 550, 555, 31 NE3d 561, 567 (2015) (defendant's attempt to lie to police about his role in the killing, as well as other inconsistent statements.)

[15] For the myriad varieties of such evidence, see *Com. v. Penn*, 472 Mass 610, 620-621, 36 NE3d 552, 562 (2015) (flight); *Com. v. Bruneau*, 472 Mass 510, 519, 36

defendant in response to police accusations, however, are not admissible, because that would eviscerate the rule forbidding introduction of defendant's unequivocal denials.[16]

Standing alone, evidence of consciousness of guilt is insufficient to warrant submission of the case to a jury;[17] but "when coupled with other probable inferences, it may be sufficient to amass the quantum of proof necessary to prove guilt."[18]

NE3d 3, 11 (2015) (refusal to answer door in response to repeated knocking by police, and inconsistent statements to police); *Com. v. Evans*, 469 Mass 834, 847, 17 NE3d 1084, 1096 (2014) (defendant's statements to police were attempt to conceal his whereabouts); *Com. v. Woods*, 466 Mass 707, 715, 1 NE2d 762, 769 (2014) (false and inconsistent statements to police); *Com. v. Roy*, 464 Mass 818, 827-828, 985 NE2d 1164, 1172-1173 (2013) (recording of defendant's jailhouse call in which he speculated about how he might explain away results of DNA testing); *Com. v. Vick*, 454 Mass 418, 423-425, 910 NE2d 339, 347 (2009) (false statement to police, flight from scene); *Com. v. Nhut Huynh*, 452 Mass 481, 489, 895 NE2d 471, 477 (2008) (defendant fled, nearly causing an accident, and left his friends stranded); *Com. v. Perez*, 444 Mass 143, 147, 825 NE2d 1040, 1045 (2005) (assault on prosecution witness); *Com. v. Jackson*, 419 Mass 716, 730-731, 647 NE2d 401, 409 (1995) (giving false name to police officer); *Cramer v. Com.*, 419 Mass 106, 111, 642 NE2d 1039, 1043 (1994) (conflicting explanations about how child was burned); *Com. v. Paradise*, 405 Mass 141, 157, 539 NE2d 1006, 1016-1017 (1989) (hiding clothing, change of appearance); *Com. v. Tyree*, 387 Mass 191, 439 NE2d 263 (1982) (defendant authored anonymous statement that exculpated him in attempt to mislead police); *Com. v. Basch*, 386 Mass 620, 624-625, 437 NE2d 200, 203 (1982) (defendant faked break-in to divert suspicion from himself); *Com. v. Pereira*, 82 Mass App 344, 348-349, 973 NE2d 679, 684 (2012) (alteration of license plate); *Com. v. Manzelli*, 68 Mass App 691, 694, 864 NE2d 566, 570 (2007) (defendant's efforts to elude arrest and to avoid having his recording equipment seized by throwing it into crowd).

But compare *Com. v. Stuckich*, 450 Mass 449, 452-454, 879 NE2d 105, 110-111 (2008) (conviction reversed where consciousness of guilt instruction was not supported by evidence); *Com. v. Renaud*, 81 Mass App 261, 264-265, 961 NE21d 1102, 1105-1106 (2012) (where detective did not order defendant to do anything, but merely informed him that he could pick up his EBT card if he wanted to, defendant's failure to do so was not evidence of consciousness of guilt); *Com. v. Barnoski*, 418 Mass 523, 537-538, 638 NE2d 9, 17 (1994) (testimony that defendant repeatedly rubbed his hand through his hair was admissible only if it is shown he knew this might affect gunshot residue test); *Com. v. Brown*, 414 Mass 123, 126-127, 605 NE2d 837, 839 (1993) (judge erred in instructing jury concerning flight as evidence of consciousness of guilt where defendant's peculiar behavior at crime scene was not "flight"); *Com. v. Hightower*, 400 Mass 267, 269, 508 NE2d 850, 852 (1987) (where there was no evidence to show that defendant's failure to appear was motivated by desire to avoid trial, reversible error to admit evidence of the default and instruct the jury as to consciousness of guilt).

[16] *Com. v. Spencer*, 465 Mass 32, 50, 987 NE2d 205, 220 (2013).

[17] *Com. v. Darnell D.*, 445 Mass 670, 674, 840 NE2d 33, 36 (2005); *Com. v. Sespedes*, 442 Mass 95, 102, 810 NE2d 790, 794 (2004).

[18] *Com. v. Vick*, 454 Mass 418, 424, 910 NE2d 339, 347 (2009); *Com. v. Porter*, 384 Mass 647, 653, 429 NE2d 14, 15 (1981).

"There are two assumptions that underlie the inference of guilt that may be drawn from evidence of flight, concealment, or similar acts. The first assumption is that a person who flees or hides after a criminal act has been committed does so because he feels guilt concerning the act. The second is that one who feels guilt concerning an act has committed that act."[19] Both assumptions have been the subject of some judicial criticism.[20]

Consciousness of guilt evidence may be admitted even though the defendant presents plausible alternative explanations for the conduct that are consistent with innocence of the crime charged. In *Com. v. Booker*,[21] for example, evidence that the defendant attempted to hide from the police was held properly admitted despite the fact that there was an outstanding default warrant for him on an unrelated crime that he had knowledge of at the time police arrived. "That there may have been other reasons for the flight presents a question for the jury in considering the probability that the defendant fled because of a consciousness of guilt of the crime charged in the indictments for which he was on trial."[22]

Defendant has an unqualified right to rebut the consciousness of guilt evidence and to negate the inference of consciousness of guilt by explaining to the jury why he took the action in question;[23] and they

---

[19] *Com. v. Toney*, 385 Mass 575, 585-586, 433 NE2d 425, 432 (1982). The Commonwealth does not have to prove that the defendant knew, in fact, that the police were looking for him. *Com. v. Siny Van Tran*, 460 Mass 535, 553, 953 NE2d 139, 157 (2011); *Com. v. Figueroa*, 451 Mass 566, 579, 887 NE2d 1040, 1050 (2008).

[20] *Com. v. Toney*, supra, 385 Mass at 585-586, 433 NE2d at 432.

[21] 386 Mass 466, 436 NE2d 160 (1982).

[22] *Id.*, 386 Mass at 469-471, 436 NE2d at 163-164. See also *Com. v. Hardy*, 431 Mass 387, 394, 727 NE2d 836, 842 (2000) (defendant's assertion that he lied to police about whereabouts on night of murder to hide drug transaction, not murder, went to weight, not admissibility); *Com. v. Sheriff*, 425 Mass 186, 199-200, 680 NE2d 75, 83 (1997) (evidence of defendant's attempt at suicide was admissible despite argument that paranoid schizophrenics are ten times more likely to kill themselves); *Com. v. Burke*, 414 Mass 252, 260-261, 607 NE2d 991, 997 (1993) (evidence of defendant's flight from police was properly submitted to jury despite his contention it resulted from housebreak just committed, and not murder charged; rejecting federal authority excluding consciousness of guilt evidence where defendant stands trial for an offense that occurred before the offense that allegedly prompted defendant to flee).

[23] *Com. v. Chase*, 26 Mass App 578, 580-581, 530 NE2d 185, 187-188 (1988) (& citations). But compare *Com. v. Camacho*, 472 Mass 587, 596, 36 NE3d 533, 542 (2015) (excluding defense witness's hearsay testimony about why defendant fled); *Com. v. Daye*, 435 Mass 463, 473-474, 759 NE2d 313, 323-324 (2001) (no error in excluding defense witness's hearsay testimony that she met with defendant one month after shooting and he told her that he planned to leave state because he feared being framed for murder). See also *Com. v. Banville*, 457 Mass 530, 542, 931 NE2d 457, 467

should be instructed that it is for them to weigh the alternative explanations.[24]

Evidence tending to show consciousness of guilt is not rendered inadmissible simply because it may reveal to the jury that the defendant has committed another offense.[25] Acts of a joint venturer amounting to evidence of consciousness of guilt may be attributed to another joint venturer if the acts occurred during the course of the joint venture and in the furtherance of it.[26]

Because a suspect has the right to remain silent and is under no obligation to say anything to police (see § 12.6, infra), it is improper for the Commonwealth to invite the jury to infer consciousness of guilt from a defendant's failure to deny his guilt during interrogation, or to come forward to police prior to arrest.[27]

While consciousness of guilt evidence is admissible on the question of whether a homicide was committed, it cannot be used to prove

---

(2010) (where defendant on direct examination disclosed his prior convictions to explain why he fled homicide scene, prosecutor's use of those convictions to argue defendant was not credible was proper).

[24] *Com. v. Burgos*, 462 Mass 53, 67-68, 965 NE2d 854, 867-869 (2012); *Com. v. Toney*, supra, 385 Mass at 584-585, 433 NE2d at 431.

[25] *Com. v. Fernandes*, 427 Mass 90, 94, 692 NE2d 3, 6 (1998); *Com. v. Jackson*, 419 Mass 716, 731, 647 NE2d 401, 410 (1995); *Com. v. Burke*, supra, 414 Mass at 260.

[26] *Com. v. Mahoney*, 405 Mass 326, 330-331, 540 NE2d 179, 182 (1989) (& citations); *Com. v. McQuade*, 46 Mass App 827, 828-829, 710 NE2d 996, 998 (1999). But compare *Com. v. Pringle*, 22 Mass App 746, 751-752, 498 NE2d 131, 134-135 (1986) (error to instruct jury that companion's use of false name could be considered evidence of defendant's own consciousness of guilt where defendant gave his correct name). Evidence of consciousness of guilt is only relevant where it permits an inference of *a defendant's guilt* of the crime charged—purportedly false statements by victims are not encompassed in the doctrine. See *Com. v. Medina*, 81 Mass App 525, 533-534, 965 NE2d 201, 208 (2012).

[27] See *Com. v. Haas*, 373 Mass 545, 558-562, 369 NE2d 692, 702-703 (1977); *Com. v. Harris*, 371 Mass 462, 358 NE2d 982 (1976) (defendant's "hanging his head" and "biting his lips" in response to police interrogation could not be viewed as evidence of consciousness of guilt in light of defendant's right to remain silent while in custody); *Com. v. Irwin*, 72 Mass App 643, 650-651, 893 NE2d 414, 421 (2008) (prosecutor's use of defendant's pattern of avoiding detective seeking to interview him required reversal); *Com. v. Martinez*, 34 Mass App 131, 608 NE2d 740 (1993) (reversal required where prosecutor suggested in cross-examination of rape defendant that inference of guilt could be drawn from defendant's pretrial failure to voluntarily offer to furnish physical evidence to district attorney's office). Compare *Com. v. Mejia*, 461 Mass 384, 390-391, 961 NE2d 72, 78-79 (2012) (observations of defendant's behavior at hospital after murder victims were discovered was admissible as consciousness of guilt where defendant was not subject to custodial interrogation at the time); *Com. v. Lavalley*, 410 Mass 641, 649, 574 NE2d 1000, 1005-1006 (1991) (prosecutor did not refer to defendant's failure to deny the crime, but only his failure to mention in his first statement to police that victim had made sexual advances).

that a homicide was murder rather than manslaughter.[28] Evidence of consciousness of guilt is "rarely relevant to the issue of premeditation," although there are exceptions (as for example where plans for flight were made before the killing),[29] and there is "no blanket prohibition" on the use of consciousness of guilt to infer premeditation.[30] Trial judges have not been required to give an explicit instruction preventing the jury from considering such evidence in connection with issues of deliberate premeditation or malice aforethought.[31] The jury may consider consciousness of guilt when determining whether defendant had the mental capacity to establish criminal responsibility.[32] And lying as evidence of consciousness of guilt has supported conviction for murder by extreme atrocity and cruelty.[33]

An escape or attempted escape need not be contemporaneous with the crime or arrest to be probative of consciousness of guilt.[34] A temporal connection between the crime and evidence suggesting that defendant abandoned his usual environs justifies a consciousness of guilt instruction to the jury.[35]

Like all evidence, consciousness of guilt evidence is subject to exclusion where its probative value is outweighed by its likely prejudicial impact.[36]

Evidence of consciousness of guilt may be sufficient, together with other evidence, to establish guilt.[37] When consciousness of guilt evidence is admitted, the jury should be instructed that they are not to convict on the basis of that evidence alone, that they may, but need not, consider the evidence as one factor tending to prove the guilt of the defendant, and they should be cautioned about the dangers of

---

[28] See *Com. v. Niland*, 45 Mass App 526, 529, 699 NE2d 1236, 1239 (1998) (& citations).

[29] See *Com. v. Dagenais*, 437 Mass 832, 843-844, 776 NE2d 1010, 1019 (2002).

[30] *Com. v. Auclair*, 444 Mass 348, 360-361, 828 NE2d 471, 481 (2005).

[31] *Com. v. Clemente*, 452 Mass 295, 333-334, 893 NE2d 19, 51-52 (2008); *Com. v. Auclair*, supra; *Com. v. Dagenais*, supra.

[32] *Com. v. Boateng*, 438 Mass 498, 508, 781 NE2d 1207, 1216 (2003).

[33] See *Com. v. Auclair*, supra, 444 Mass at 361, 828 NE2d at 481.

[34] See *Com. v. Lam*, 420 Mass 615, 617-618, 650 NE2d 796, 798 (1995) (evidence of attempted escape shortly before defendant's trial was scheduled was admissible even though several years after offense).

[35] *Com. v. Burgos*, 462 Mass 53, 67, 965 NE2d 854 (2012) (several weeks); *Com. v. Siny Van Tran*, 460 Mass 535, 553, 953 NE2d 139, 157 (2011) (three weeks); *Com. v. Tu Trinh*, 458 Mass 776, 779-782, 940 NE2d 871 876-878 (2011).

[36] *Com. v. Roberts*, 407 Mass 731, 735-736, 555 NE2d 588 (1990) (but refusing to exclude the evidence).

[37] *Com. v. Martin*, 467 Mass 291, 315, 4 NE3d 1236, 1255 (2014).

inferring guilt from flight.[38] In the absence of a request, however, the judge is not required to instruct the jury *sua sponte* on their evaluation of such evidence.[39] It is preferable for the judge to explicitly limit the consciousness of guilt instruction to only those defendants whose conduct is in question.[40] Where appropriate it is not error to instruct the jury on consciousness of guilt over defendant's objection.[41]

A consciousness of guilt instruction regarding flight is generally inappropriate where there is no dispute that the crime was committed by the person fleeing the scene, and the only contested issue is the

---

[38] *Com. v. Toney*, 385 Mass 575, 585-586, 433 NE2d 425, 432 (1982) (required cautionary instruction set out); *Com. v. Hardy*, 464 Mass 660, 671, 984 NE2d 727, 736 (2012). The Supreme Judicial Court has recently reaffirmed its confidence in the *Toney* principles as embodied in the Criminal Model Jury Instructions. See *Com. v. Morris*, 465 Mass 733, 991 NE2d 1081 (2013). For cases reversing convictions because of the failure to give proper instructions on this point, see *Com. v. Matos*, 394 Mass 563, 476 NE2d 608 (1985); *Com. v. Estrada*, 25 Mass App 907, 908, 514 NE2d 1099, 1100 (1987); *Com. v. Rivera*, 23 Mass App 605, 608-610, 504 NE2d 371, 372-374 (1987). Compare *Com. v. Avellar*, 416 Mass 409, 421, 622 NE2d 625, 631-632 (1993) (failure to instruct unlikely to have affected verdict); *Com. v. Lavalley*, supra, 410 Mass at 650-652, 574 NE2d at 1006-1007 (no reversal required where judge omitted supplemental instruction in his written instructions but included it in oral charge); *Com. v. Nadworny*, 396 Mass 342, 371 n.14, 486 NE2d 675, 692 n.14 (1985) (while instruction was "not a model of clarity regarding the fact that a defendant may not be convicted on consciousness of guilt evidence alone, it contained the substance of what we required in *Toney*").

For cases reviewing instructions that erroneously referred to acts of concealment in the absence of any evidence of the act, see *Com. v. Serino*, 436 Mass 408, 419-420, 765 NE2d 237, 246 (2002); *Com. v. Birks*, 435 Mass 782, 789-790, 762 NE2d 267, 274 (2002). See also *Com. v. Burgos*, 462 Mass 53, 68, 965 NE2d 854 (2012) (judge's erroneous instruction that defendant may have fled after he discovered he was about to be charged with murder was immediately addressed by subsequent instruction). For a discussion of the propriety of consciousness of guilt evidence and corresponding instructions in a case where the principal issue in contention is identification, see *Com. v. Horsman*, 47 Mass App 262, 712 NE2d 1152 (1999) (& cases cited).

[39] See *Com. v. Brousseau*, 421 Mass 647, 652, 659 NE2d 724, 727 (1996); *Com. v. Simmons*, 419 Mass 426, 434-436, 646 NE2d 97, 102-103 (1995).

[40] See *Com. v. Gordon*, 422 Mass 816, 852-853, 666 NE2d 122, 144 (1996).

[41] *Com. v. Cole*, 473 Mass 317, 325-326, 41 NE3d 1073, 1082-1083 (2015); *Com. v. Chappell*, 473 Mass 191, 206-207, 40 NE3d 1031, 1044 (2015) (although defendant did not contest that he killed the victim, and his defense was mental state, the Commonwealth was still required to prove the killing and the evidence of defendant's actions following the killing constituted consciousness of guilt); *Com. v. Morris*, supra, 465 Mass 733, 991 NE2d 1081; *Com. v. Robles*, 423 Mass 62, 70-72, 666 NE2d 497, 503-504 (1996).

identification of the defendant as the fleeing offender.[42] Where a defendant fails to reappear during a trial, the judge should give a neutral instruction to the jury to the effect that they should not speculate as to reasons for his absence and should not draw adverse inferences, because there are many reasons why a defendant may not be present for full trial.[43]

Evidence suggesting consciousness of innocence has been treated with considerable skepticism in the Commonwealth, given the perception that there are many reasons why a person does not flee or refuses to accept a plea offer or engages in similar conduct from which innocence might be inferred.[44] A judge is not required to draw the jury's attention to the defendant's own innocent explanation for the act alleged to imply consciousness of guilt;[45] nor to instruct on defendant's evidence of consciousness of innocence, such as failure to flee.[46] Such matters are more appropriately left to the defendant's closing argument.[47]

"Consciousness of liability" evidence has been admitted in civil cases in the following circumstances:

---

[42] *Com. v. Bastaldo*, 472 Mass 16, 33-34, 32 NE3d 873, 888 (2015). See also *Com. v. Lopez*, 87 Mass App 642, 646-647, 34 NE3d 750, 754 (2015) (since there was no witness to the fatal punch, the jury could have found defendant fled from the scene without already having determined he was the perpetrator).

[43] *Com. v. Muckle*, 59 Mass App 631, 639-640, 797 NE2d 456, 463-464 (2003) (outlining protocol to be followed). Compare *Com. v. Baro*, 73 Mass App 218, 221-222, 897 NE2d 102-103 (2008) (protocol need not be followed where defendant absents himself during jury deliberations).

[44] *Com. v. Espada*, 450 Mass 687, 698, 880 NE2d 795, 806 (2008). See, e.g., *Com. v. Cassidy*, 470 Mass 201, 218-220, 21 NE3d 127, 143-145 (2014) (sincerity of defendant's evidence was unreliable, and some was based on multiple hearsay); *Com. v. Jones*, 464 Mass 16, 19-21, 979 NE2d 1088, 1092-1093 (2012) (a suspect's recantation of an initial refusal to take a breathalyzer test is arguably as consistent with desire to avoid license suspension as with consciousness of innocence); *Com. v. Fitzpatrick*, 463 Mass 581, 602-603, 977 NE2d 505, 523 (2012) (judge properly excluded statements defendant made in secretly recorded phone conversation urging murder victim's wife to be honest with police about their romantic relationship, as not probative of consciousness of innocence); *Com. v. Martinez*, 437 Mass 84, 88, 769 NE2d 273, 278 (2002) (a defendant's offer to submit to a polygraph is not admissible to show innocent state of mind); *Com. v. DoVole*, 57 Mass App 657, 662, 785 NE2d 416, 420 (2003) (defendant's refusal of time-served offer not admissible).

[45] *Com. v. Knap*, 412 Mass 712, 716-717, 592 NE2d 747, 749-750 (1992); *Com. v. Sowell*, 22 Mass App 959, 961, 494 NE2d 1359, 1362-1363 (1986).

[46] *Com. v. Lam*, supra, 420 Mass at 619-620, 650 NE2d at 799.

[47] *Com. v. Lam*, supra, 420 Mass at 619, 650 NE2d at 799.

- Leaving the scene of an accident without identifying oneself.[48]
- Evasive conduct and false statements to police.[49]
- Giving a false name.[50]
- Testimony by a litigant that the jury could have found to be intentionally false and inconsistent with statements made out of court.[51]
- Conveying one's property away immediately before action was begun.[52]
- Suborning a witness to testify falsely, bribing a juror, or sup pressing evidence.[53]
- Destruction of potential evidence.[54]

As in criminal cases, however, such evidence will not warrant submitting a case to the jury where there is no other evidence of liability.[55]

§ 4.2.2 *Third-Party Culprit Evidence*

A defendant is constitutionally entitled (both under the federal and state constitutions) to present third-party culprit evidence—that another person committed the crime—as long as it is not too remote or speculative.[56] See also § 4.4.7, infra. Where the evidence is of

---

[48] *Olofson v. Kilgallon*, 362 Mass 803, 806, 291 NE2d 600, 602-603 (1973). But see *Kelliher v. General Transportation Services*, 29 F3d 750, 754 (1st Cir 1995) (there must be evidence that defendant knew he had been involved in an accident before leaving scene in order to entitle plaintiff to instruction).

[49] *Parsons v. Ryan*, 340 Mass 245, 248, 163 NE2d 293, 295 (1960).

[50] *Rich v. Finley*, 325 Mass 99, 105, 89 NE2d 213, 216 (1949).

[51] *Sheehan v. Goriansky*, 317 Mass 10, 16-17, 56 NE2d 883, 886 (1944).

[52] *Credit Service Corp. v. Barker*, 308 Mass 476, 481, 33 NE2d 293, 295 (1941). But compare *Matteo v. Livingston*, 40 Mass App 658, 663-664, 666 NE2d 1309, 1313 (1996) (defendant's conveyance of property five years after accident and two years after lawsuit was filed was temporally too remote).

[53] *Bennett v. Susser*, 191 Mass 329, 331, 77 NE 884, 885 (1906) (& citations).

[54] *Gath v. M/A-Com, Inc.*, 440 Mass 482, 489-491, 802 NE2d 521, 528-529 (2003) (landowner's removal and destruction of gate that swung into passing bicyclist).

[55] *Miles v. Caples*, 362 Mass 107, 114, 284 NE2d 231, 236 (1972); *Parsons v. Ryan*, supra, 340 Mass at 249, 163 NE2d at 296.

[56] See *Holmes v. South Carolina*, 547 US 319 (2006); *Com. v. Scesny*, 472 Mass 185, 202-203, 34 NE3d 17, 32 (2015) (prosecutor improperly discredited the third-party defense); *Com. v. Scott*, 470 Mass 320, 332-333, 21 NE3d 954, 965 (2014); *Com. v. Santos*, 463 Mass 273, 974 NE2d 1 (2012) (defendant had constitutional right to make third-party culprit argument where two witnesses identified a third-party friend of a co-defendant as being at co-defendant's house shortly before the shooting with a

substantial probative value and will not tend to confuse, "all doubt should be resolved in favor of admissibility."[57]

---

gun); *Com. v. Silva-Santiago*, 453 Mass 782, 800-801, 906 NE2d 299, 314 (2009) (such evidence is given wide latitude, but not unbounded). See also *Com. v. Rosario*, 444 Mass 550, 556-559, 829 NE2d 1135, 1140-1141 (2005) (judge improperly prevented defendant from displaying third party to jury to support defense of misidentification); *Com. v. Conkey*, 443 Mass 60, 66-70, 819 NE2d 176, 183-185 (2004) (evidence of third party's sexual assault against his former girlfriend was relevant as part of pattern of sexual aggressiveness toward women who resisted him). But compare *Com. v. Cassidy*, 470 Mass 201, 215, 21 NE3d 127, 141 (2014) (third-party culprit evidence was properly excluded where it did not establish a "substantial connecting link" between third party and the murder); *Com. v. Hoose*, 467 Mass 395, 409-410, 5 NE2d 843, 857 (2014) (knife seen in days following murders one-half mile away from scene, offered by defendant as third-party culprit evidence, was insufficiently connected to murder to be admitted); *Com. v. Fitzpatrick*, 463 Mass 581, 595-596, 977 NE2d 505, 517-518 (2012) (defendant's proffered evidence about hostility between third party and victim's family was too remote and speculative); *Com. v. Smith*, 461 Mass 438, 443-448, 961 NE2d 566, 570-573 (2012) (extensive discussion) (testimony of witnesses that in days prior to murder, victim had expressed fears about being harmed as a result of problems with an unknown woman was speculative, of minimal probative value, and thus properly excluded); *Com. v. Buckman*, 461 Mass 24, 29-32, 957 NE2d 1089, 1096-1098 (2011) (evidence that a serial killer had been released from prison two weeks before murder was not admissible, as too speculative); *Com. v. Ruell*, 459 Mass 126, 130-135, 943 NE2d 447, 451-454 (2011) (judge properly excluded third-party culprit evidence regarding four individuals who could have committed the crimes by concluding its probative value, which was speculative and remote, was outweighed by the risk of unfair prejudice to the Commonwealth; extensive discussion); *Com. v. Mosher*, 455 Mass 811, 828, 920 NE2d 285, 300 (2010) (judge properly excluded prosecution witness' alleged offer to commit murder as prior bad act evidence and too remote to be relevant); *Com. v. Mattei*, 455 Mass 840, 858-860, 920 NE2d 845, 860-862 (2010) (convictions of other possible suspects were too remote in time and weak in probative value to show that another person committed the assault); *Com. v. Pimental*, 454 Mass 475, 478-479, 910 NE2d 366, 371 (2009) (defendant failed to show that prior bad acts of alleged third-party culprit shared singular features with the charged crime); *Com. v. Phinney*, 446 Mass 155, 163, 843 NE2d 1024, 1032 (2006) (evidence of potential third-party culprits with ties to the victim); *Com. v. Podkowka*, 445 Mass 692, 697-698, 840 NE2d 476, 481 (2006) (defendant was not deprived of right to present defense that mother of infant victim killed her); *Com. v. Keohane*, 444 Mass 563, 570-572, 829 NE2d 1125, 1132 (2005) (trial court properly excluded racial animus component of defendant's third-party culprit evidence because it was purely speculative).

For the proper instructions regarding third-party culprit evidence, see *Com. v. Hoose*, supra, 467 Mass at 411-413, 5 NE2d at 858 and *Com. v. Gomes*, 459 Mass 194, 207-208, 944 NE2d 1007, 1018 (2011) (not error to instruct jury that Commonwealth does not have burden to prove no one else may have committed the crime); *Com. v. Scesny*, supra, 472 Mass at 206-207, 34 NE3d at 35 (same).

[57] *Com. v. Scott*, supra, 470 Mass at 326-327, 21 NE3d at 960-961. For a case concluding that defense counsel's failure to present available third-party culprit evidence (inter alia) constituted ineffective assistance of counsel, see *Com. v. Alcide*, 472 Mass 150, 33 NE3d 424 (2015).

Such evidence is often hearsay, and hearsay evidence pointing to a third party may be admitted, even if it does not fall within an exception, but only if, in the judge's discretion, the evidence is otherwise relevant, will not tend to prejudice or confuse the jury, and there are other substantial connecting links to the crime.[58] A defendant's opinion concerning a third party's role in the crime, based on speculation and not personal knowledge, is inadmissible.[59] Evidence of a third party's ill will or possible motive is insufficient alone to support a third-party culprit defense.[60] Where a defendant seeks to admit prior bad acts of an alleged third-party culprit, he must show that the acts are so closely connected in time and method as to cast doubt on the defendant's guilt.[61]

Because weak third-party culprit evidence poses a real risk of prejudice to the Commonwealth, especially of confusing and distracting jurors' attention to collateral matters, the trial judge must determine whether the matters are so remote and speculative that the evidence should be excluded.[62]

---

[58] See *Com. v. Alcantara*, 471 Mass 550, 559, 31 NE3d 561, 570-571 (2015) (witness's testimony merely repeated an unsubstantiated rumor); *Com. v. Scott*, supra, 470 Mass at 327, 21 NE3d at 961 (defendant's evidence was too remote and speculative); *Com. v. Wood*, 469 Mass 266, 275-276, 14 NE3d 140, 151 (2014) (defendant's proffered third-party testimony was inadmissible hearsay, and inference that boyfriend was the culprit was entirely speculative); *Com. v. Morgan*, 460 Mass 277, 291, 951 NE2d 14, 25 (2011) (defendant did not establish that third-party's armed robberies bore "substantial connecting links" to the offenses against the victim). See also *Com. v. Cassidy*, 470 Mass 201, 216-217, 21 NE3d 127, 142 (2014) (judge properly excluded evidence based on multiple hearsay); *Com. v. Walker*, 460 Mass 590, 611-612, 953 NE2d 195, 213-214 (2011) (it was not known whether the declarant personally observed the crime, and there was no corroborating evidence); *Com. v. Bizanowicz*, 459 Mass 400, 417-418, 945 NE2d 356, 369-370 (2011) (third-party culprit evidence involving possible romantic relationship between victim and landlord was properly excluded as hearsay and highly speculative); *Com. v. Jenkins*, 458 Mass 791, 810, 941 NE2d 56, 74 (2011) (third-party culprit evidence purportedly implicating a drug supplier to victim was inadmissible in murder prosecution where defense counsel was unable to identify any person or present anything other than hearsay).

[59] *Com. v. Cassidy*, supra, 470 Mass at 217, 21 NE3d at 142.

[60] *Com. v. Watkins*, 473 Mass 222, 41 NE3d 10 (2015) (no error in excluding evidence that the victim had been convicted of killing a person whose brother therefore had a motive to kill the victim); *Com. v. Alcantara*, supra, 471 Mass at 560, 31 NE3d at 570 (only evidence of motive was that third party and victim had recently ended their relationship); *Com. v. Wright*, 469 Mass 447, 466, 14 NE3d 294, 312 (2014).

[61] *Com. v. Wood*, supra, 469 Mass at 276-277, 14 NE3d at 152.

[62] *Com. v. Scott*, supra, 470 Mass 327-329, 21 NE3d at 961-962 (defendant identified no "connecting links" between third parties and the crime); *Com. v. Bright*, 463 Mass 421, 438-440, 974 NE2d 1092, 1108-1109 (2012) (defendant's offer of evidence

§ 4.2.3 Statistical and Probabilistic Evidence

Although it has been said that "the admission of evidence of statistical probability is disfavored in this Commonwealth,"[63] such evidence may be admitted where the probabilities upon which the evidence depends are based on established empirical data rather than on speculation, and where the evidence is more probative than prejudicial.[64] The statistical evidence must cross a threshold of reliability to be probative.[65]

Extrapolated calculation and random sampling is permitted regarding the weight of contraband.[66] Statistical evidence to explain the import of DNA results has been required of the Commonwealth, as we will "not permit the admission of test results showing a DNA match (a positive result) without telling the jury anything about the likelihood of that match occurring."[67] See also § 7.6.3(e), infra.

Statistical data concerning the racial or gender composition of a workforce may be (and routinely is) admitted by either party in employment discrimination cases as probative on the issue of

---

of gang affiliations of victim and others connected to case was of minimal relevance because it did not point to any particular third party who might have committed the crime).

[63] *Com. v. Beausoleil*, 397 Mass 206, 217 n.15, 490 NE2d 788, 795 n.15 (1986) (& citations) (but admitting HLA tests in paternity actions).

[64] See, e.g., *Com. v. Sylvia*, 456 Mass 182, 191-194, 921 NE2d 968, 977-978 (2010) (chemist's testimony regarding frequency of detecting gunshot residue); *Com. v. Gomes*, 403 Mass 258, 273-275, 526 NE2d 1270, 1279-1280 (1988) (genetic markers in bloodstain); *Com. v. Rocha*, 57 Mass App 550, 555-558, 784 NE2d 651, 655-658 (2003) (probability of paternity based on DNA tests); *Com. v. Colon*, 49 Mass App 289, 293 n.4, 729 NE2d 315, 318 n.4 (2000) (testimony on percentages abused children with physical signs). Compare *Santos v. Chrysler Corp.*, 430 Mass 198, 205-206, 715 NE2d 47, 54-55 (1999) (rejecting statistician's testimony of expected frequency of fatal accidents); *Com. v. Grinkley*, 75 Mass App 798, 803-804, 917 NE2d 236, 240-241 (2009) (DNA statistical testimony was irrelevant and misleading). For statistical likelihood of survival evidence in "loss of chance" malpractice cases, see *Matsuyama v. Birnbaum*, 452 Mass 1, 17-19, 890 NE2d 819, 832-834 (2008).

[65] *Kiely v. Teredyne, Inc.*, 85 Mass App 431, 442, 13 NE3d 615, 624 (2014).

[66] *Com. v. Crapps*, 84 Mass App 442, 446-449, 997 NE2d 444, 448-450 (2013) (discussing requirement that defense counsel raise any challenges pretrial).

[67] *Com. v. Cole*, 473 Mass 317, 327, 41 NE3d 1073, 1083-1084 (2015). See also *Com. v. Mattei*, 455 Mass 840, 850-855, 920 NE2d 845, 854-858 (2010). For discussion of the different approaches to the admissibility of "nonexclusion" and "inconclusive" DNA testimony, see *Com. v. Cameron*, 473 Mass 100, 106, 39 NE3d 723, 728 (2015). See also *Com. v. Lally*, 473 Mass 693, 703, 46 NE3d 41, 51-52 (2016) (trial counsel performed unreasonably in failing to challenge state's use of DNA evidence "without accompanying statistical references.")

discriminatory intent.[68] Racial profiling may be proven by statistics.[69] Similarly epidemiological evidence is admissible in toxic tort, pharmaceutical, and other cases as long as it is scientifically reliable.[70]

Where the Commonwealth seeks to provide the jury with mathematical probability analysis, it must do so through expert testimony (subject to reliability challenges), not closing argument.[71] Such evidence has great potential for prejudice, as it carries the aura of infallibility to the layperson.[72]

Judges and litigants are advised not to quantify the concept of proof beyond a reasonable doubt, or the accuracy of eyewitness identification, in probabilistic terms.[73]

On the matter of the sufficiency of probabilistic evidence,

> it is not enough that mathematically the chances somewhat favor a proposition to be proved; for example, the fact that colored automobiles made in the current year outnumber black ones would not warrant a finding that an undescribed automobile of the current year is colored and not black, nor would the fact that only a minority of men die of cancer warrant a finding that a particular man did not die of cancer. The most that can be said of the evidence in the instant case is that perhaps the mathematical chances somewhat favor the proposition that a bus of the defendant caused the accident. This was not enough. A proposition is proved by a preponderance of the evidence if it is made to appear more likely or probable in the sense that actual belief in its truth, derived from the evidence, exists in the mind or minds of the tribunal notwithstanding any doubts that may still linger there.[74]

---

[68] See, e.g., *Lipchitz v. Raytheon Co.*, 434 Mass 493, 508-509, 751 NE2d 360, 373 (2001) (& citations); *Brackett v. Civil Service Comm'n*, 447 Mass 233, 850 NE2d 533 (2006). Statistical data of disparate impact is required as later stages of the proceedings, but not at the pleading stage. See *Lopez v. Com.*, 463 Mass 696, 712 n.20, 978 NE2d 67, 81 n.20 (2012).

[69] *Com. v. Lora*, 451 Mass 425, 442, 886 NE2d 688, 701 (2008) (racial composition of traffic stops).

[70] See, e.g., *Linnen v. A.H. Robins Co.*, Inc., 11 Mass L Rptr 205 (Super. Ct. 2000) (2000 WL 145758). But see *Vassallo v. Baxter Healthcare Corp.*, 428 Mass 1, 12-15, 696 NE2d 909, 917-919 (1998) (causation opinions of expert witnesses regarding effects of silicone breast implants were scientifically valid and admissible in products liability action, notwithstanding lack of classical epidemiological studies). See also § 7.5.1, infra.

[71] See *Com. v. Ferreira*, 460 Mass 781, 786-787, 955 NE2d 898, 903 (2011).

[72] See generally *People v. Collins*, 68 Cal. 2d 319, 438 P.2d 33 (1968); L. Tribe, Trial By Mathematics: Precision and Ritual in the Legal Process, 84 Harv L Rev 1329 (1971).

[73] *Com. v. Ferreira*, supra, 460 Mass at 787-788, 955 NE2d 898, 904.

[74] *Smith v. Rapid Transit*, 317 Mass 469, 470, 58 NE2d 754, 755 (1945), quoting *Sargent v. Massachusetts Accident Co.*, 307 Mass 246, 250, 29 NE2d 825, 827 (1940). See

§ 4.2.4 Negative Evidence

Testimony that something did *not* happen may be of probative value in certain instances. Such negative testimony, however, is usually less reliable than positive testimony. A witness's failure to recall perceiving an event, for example, can often be explained by many hypotheses other than that the event did not occur—e.g., the witness may not have been in a position to perceive the event or may not have been paying attention.

As the Supreme Judicial Court explained in *Schwartz v. Feinberg*,[75] such evidence is admissible on a proper foundation:

> There was no direct evidence to show . . . the condition or appearance of the stairway in question on any exact date. At best, the evidence relative to conditions or appearances goes no further than that the witnesses did not notice or see any [protruding] nail. . . . The probative value of testimony of witnesses as to sensory reactions depends upon the attendant circumstances. If it appears that there was no particular reason why their senses should, or should not, react, such testimony is merely negative and of no value as evidence. But, if the circumstances are such, and the witnesses are in a position where such reactions would have been likely to occur, then their failure to hear a signal that should have been given, or to see an object, is evidence from which it is permissible to draw the inference that the signal was not given or that the object was not there to be seen.[76]

Evidence of the absence of a record may in certain circumstances be admitted to establish that a particular event or transaction did not occur.[77] It is well established that disbelief of

---

generally Charles Nesson, The Evidence or the Event? On Judicial Proof and the Acceptability of Verdicts, 98 Harv L Rev 1357 (1985).

[75] 306 Mass 331, 334-335, 28 NE2d 249, 250-251 (1940).

[76] For examples of negative evidence, see *Nickerson v. Boston & M.R.R.*, 342 Mass 306, 313, 173 NE2d 248, 253 (1961); *Byrne v. Dunn*, 296 Mass 184, 186-187, 5 NE2d 10, 11 (1936) (no warning horn blown); *Sodekson v. Lynch*, 314 Mass 161, 49 NE2d 901 (1943) (no will executed).

[77] See, e.g., *Cohen v. Boston Edison Co.*, 322 Mass 239, 76 NE2d 766 (1948) (no bank ledger card); *Com. v. Scanlan*, 9 Mass App 173, 181-182, 400 NE2d 1265, 1271 (1980) (citing Text) (witness may testify that he has examined records and did not find particular entry); *Johnson v. Wilmington Sales, Inc.*, 5 Mass App 858, 364 NE2d 1291 (1977) (lack of entry in cash journal admissible to show absence of cash payment). Compare *Bouley v. Reisman*, 38 Mass App 118, 123, 645 NE2d 708, 712 (1995) (evidence that there was no notation of telephone call from defendant doctor did not necessarily warrant jury's drawing inference that doctor did not make call). Proposed Mass R Evid 803(7), like its federal counterpart, would allow evidence of the absence

testimony does not of itself warrant a finding that the contrary fact is true.[78]

§ 4.2.5 Demonstrative Evidence

Demonstrative evidence, as its name suggests, refers to items employed for illustrative purposes such as drawings, sketches, diagrams, chalks, or models. They are not evidence in the ordinary sense of the word, but the trial judge has considerable discretion as to their use by counsel.[79]

Charts summarizing voluminous records or other documents may be used as chalks when helpful to the factfinder.[80] DNA "notebooks" summarizing profile comparisons have, for example, been provided to jurors during the testimony of the forensic expert to permit them to

---

of recorded entry to be admitted to prove nonoccurrence of an event. See § 8.11, infra. For cases admitting evidence of lack of complaints, see § 8.2.7, infra. For the absence of evidence because of a party's spoliation (alteration or destruction), see *Gath v. M/A-Com, Inc.*, 440 Mass 482, 489-491, 802 NE2d 521, 528-529 (2003), discussed supra at § 4.2.1.

[78] See *Cahaly v. Benistar Property Exchange Trust Co., Inc.*, 451 Mass 343, 357, 885 NE2d 800, 814 (2008); *Com. v. Michaud*, 389 Mass 491, 498, 451 NE2d 396, 400 (1983); *Com. v. DiRusso*, 60 Mass App 235, 241, 800 NE2d 1067, 1072 (2003); *Com. v. Dube*, 59 Mass App 476, 487, 796 NE2d 859, 868 (2003).

[79] See, e.g., *Com. v. Girouard*, 436 Mass 657, 667, 766 NE2d 873, 881 (2002) (mannequin used to demonstrate how knife wound had been inflicted); *Com. v. Trowbridge*, 419 Mass 750, 757, 647 NE2d 413, 419 (1995) (child sexual abuse victim's use of anatomically correct doll during her testimony) (citing Text); *Goldstein v. Gontarz*, 364 Mass 800, 309 NE2d 196 (1974) (plaintiff's counsel used blackboard to tabulate elements of damages); *Alholm v. Wareham*, 371 Mass 621, 631, 358 NE2d 788, 794 (1974) (police officer's diagram of accident scene); *LeBlanc v. Ford Motor Co.*, 346 Mass 225, 191 NE2d 301 (1963) (expert witness used models to illustrate testimony); *Com. v. Shea*, 38 Mass App 7, 11-12, 644 NE2d 244, 247 (1995) (use of videotapes as chalks to illustrate victims' testimony concerning condition of ocean when defendant threw them into water); *Teller v. Schepens*, 25 Mass App 346, 518 NE2d 868 (1988) (use of slides as chalks); *Com. v. Walter*, 10 Mass App 255, 406 NE2d 1304 (1980) (not error to permit jury to use chalk during deliberations).

[80] Proposed Mass R Evid 1006, which reflects Massachusetts practice, provides: "The contents of voluminous writings, recordings, or photographs which cannot conveniently be examined in court may be presented in the form of a chart, summary, or calculation." See, e.g., *Com. v. Carnes*, 457 Mass 812, 825, 933 NE2d 598, 609-610 (2010) (charts summarizing telephone records); *Com. v. Mimless*, 53 Mass App 534, 760 NE2d 762 (2002) (charts summarizing Medicaid payments received by defendant); *Welch v. Keene Corp.*, 31 Mass App 157, 165, 575 NE2d 766, 771 (1991) (chart containing redacted versions of articles on asbestos).

more readily follow the testimony.[81] Where a chart contains summaries, "care must be taken to insure that summaries accurately reflect the contents of the underlying documents and do not function as pedagogical devices that unfairly emphasize part of the proponent's proof."[82]

§ 4.2.6 *Views*

GL 234A, § 69A (effective May 10, 2016) provides:

> The court may, upon motion, allow the jury in a civil case to view the premises or place in question or any property, matter or thing relative to the case if the party making the motion advances an amount sufficient to defray the expenses of the jury and the officers who attend them in taking the view, which shall be taxed as costs, if the party who advanced them prevails. The court may order a view by a jury impanelled to try a criminal case.

This section essentially confirms the inherent common-law power of the court, sitting with or without jury, to take a view either upon request of a party or upon its own motion.[83] Whether a view will be taken rests in the sound discretion of the court; a view should be allowed whenever the judge determines it would be of assistance to understand better the testimony that has been or may be presented.[84] In certain cases, by statute, a view may be a matter of right upon the request of a party.[85]

---

[81] *Com. v. Guy*, 454 Mass 440, 445-446, 910 NE2d 358, 362-363 (2009).

[82] *Welch v. Keene Corp.*, supra, 31 Mass App at 165-166, 575 NE2d at 771.

[83] *Madden v. Boston Elevated Railway Co.*, 284 Mass 490, 493-494, 188 NE 234, 236 (1933).

[84] *Com. v. Clark*, 432 Mass 1, 17, 730 NE2d 872, 887 (2000) (taking view was within court's discretion, despite fact that road construction had altered the site and a memorial to the slain victim state trooper had been erected); *Com. v. Cataldo*, 423 Mass 318, 327 n.8, 668 NE2d 762, 767 n.8 (1996) (within court's discretion to refuse view where it would not likely have helped jurors because events at issue were not amenable to replication before jury); *Com. v. King*, 391 Mass 691, 694, 463 NE2d 1168, 1070-1071 (1984) (within court's discretion to refuse of prison); *Terrio v. McDonough*, 16 Mass App 163, 173, 450 NE2d 190, 196 (1983). See also *Frade v. Costa*, 342 Mass 5, 171 NE2d 863 (1961) (master took a view).

[85] GL 79, § 22 (eminent domain cases); GL 80, § 9 (betterment assessments); GL 253, § 7 (mill flowage cases). Cf. *Jarvinen v. Com.*, 353 Mass 339, 231 NE2d 366 (1967) (trial judge is not required to attend a view taken under GL 79, § 22).

The information acquired at a view is not evidence in a strict and narrow sense, but the jury may use it in reaching a verdict.[86] The proper procedure for taking a view is described in *Com. v. Dascalakis*.[87] No evidence should be taken or testimonial comments made during the taking of a view.

In a trial without a jury, a view ought not be taken without notice to the parties or counsel, in order that they can be present.[88] In a jury trial, an unauthorized view by one or more jurors may constitute sufficient grounds for a new trial. The court may receive testimony from jurors to show that an unauthorized view occurred, but not with respect to the role the improper influence played in the jury's decisions. The judge "must focus on the probable effect of the extraneous facts on a hypothetical average jury."[89] See § 5.7, infra.

Since no evidence is taken, it is not error to refuse a criminal defendant the right to be present during a view, so long as he is represented by counsel.[90]

---

[86] *Com. v. Gomes*, 459 Mass 194, 199, 944 NE2d 1007, 1012 (2011) (citing Text); *Com. v. Semedo*, 456 Mass 1, 10-11, 921 NE2d 57, 67 (2010) (jury could consider their experience in taking bus ride to view location where defendant had been stopped by police to determine time it would have taken to drive there from murder scene); *Com. v. Curry*, 368 Mass 195, 330 NE2d 819 (1975). Cf. *Rivers v. Town of Warwick*, 37 Mass App 593, 641 NE2d 1062 (1994) (view of dirt roads running through woods could not assist jury in determining whether roads were public or private, thus fact that jury took a view could not be given dispositive effect on appeal); *Com. v. Jefferson*, 36 Mass App 684, 635 NE2d 2 (1994) (trial court's instruction to jury that it could use the view as evidence was technically incorrect, but not error that created a substantial risk of a miscarriage of justice requiring reversal in the absence of objection).

[87] 246 Mass 12, 29-30, 140 NE 470, 477 (1923).

[88] *Sargeant v. Traverse Building Trust*, 267 Mass 490, 495, 167 NE 233, 235 (1929). Cf. *Berlandi v. Com.*, 314 Mass 424, 449-453, 50 NE2d 210, 225-226 (1943) (taking of view without parties was nonprejudicial error in light of judge's statement that view did not affect his decision).

[89] *Com. v. Cuffie*, 414 Mass 632, 637, 609 NE2d 437 (1993) (new trial required where juror made independent visit to scene of crime). See also *Markee v. Biasetti*, 410 Mass 785, 789, 575 NE2d 1083, 1085 (1991) (new trial required where several jurors visited scene and made measurements); *Com. v. Coles*, 44 Mass App Ct 463, 691 NE2d 969 (1998) (new trial affirmed where jurors visited scene and came back with "totally different information than the lawyers presented"). Compare *Com. v. Jones*, 15 Mass App 692, 695, 448 NE2d 400, 402 (1983) (unauthorized view of much used public facility was improper, but not prejudicial under circumstances of case).

[90] *Com. v. Corliss*, 470 Mass 443, 448, 23 NE3d 92, 97-98 (2014) (given the security risk posed, it was not improper to confine defendant to a police vehicle during the jury view); *Com. v. Morganti*, 455 Mass 388, 402-403, 917 NE2d 191, 204 (2009) (rejecting defendant's argument that the view of an automobile of the same make, model, and year of the one in which victim was killed was a demonstrative aid, thus requiring his presence); *Com. v. Thomas*, 448 Mass 180, 187, 859 NE2d 813, 818-819 (2007); *Com. v. Evans*, 438 Mass 142, 778 NE2d 885 (2002); *Com. v. Mack*, 423 Mass 288, 667 NE2d 867 (1996);

A judge is not required to allow a view to be taken at the same time of day the crime occurred or under the same weather conditions that prevailed when the crime occurred.[91] During the taking of a view, counsel may point out objects or features to be noted by the jury but may not otherwise comment; but an impropriety occurring on a view generally can be cured by cautionary instruction and will not require a mistrial.[92] The trial judge is required to attend the view.[93]

§ 4.3 Discretion to Exclude Relevant Evidence

§ 4.3.1 Discussion

Proposed Mass R Evid 403, which basically tracks its federal counterpart and reflects Massachusetts practice, provides:

> Although relevant, evidence may be excluded if its probative value is substantially outweighed by the danger of unfair prejudice, confusion of the issues, or misleading the jury, or by considerations of undue delay, waste of time, or needless presentation of cumulative evidence.[1]

Admissibility of evidence is thus a function of relevancy—probative value and materiality (see § 4.1, supra)—as well as the discretionary balancing of the counterweights: prejudicial unfairness, confusion, and undue consumption of time.

Certain evidence, particularly in the category of real evidence, tends to be powerful, even sensational. The victim's blood-stained clothes, for example, may excite the passions of jurors and present the risk that the verdict may not be based on reason and logic, but on emotions. Such evidence should not be admitted if unduly prejudicial.[2]

Com. v. Gordon, 422 Mass 816, 849, 666 NE2d 122, 142 (1996). Cf. *Com. v. Curry*, supra (not error to refuse to allow defendant to consult with counsel during view).

[91] *Com. v. Curry*, supra; *Com. v. Gabbidon*, 17 Mass App 525, 535, 459 NE2d 1263, 1270 (1984).

[92] *Com. v. Hardy*, 431 Mass 387, 727 NE2d 836 (2000); *Com. v. Cresta*, 3 Mass App 560, 336 NE2d 910 (1975); *Com. v. Gomes*, 459 Mass 194, 200-201, 944 NE2d 1007, 1013-1014 (2011) *Com. v. Martinez*, 458 Mass 684, 700-701, 940 NE2d 422, 436-437 (2011).

[93] *Com. v. Gomes*, 459 Mass 194, 201-202, 944 NE2d 1007, 1014 (2011).

§ 4.3 [1] See also *Com. v. Lewin (No. 2)*, 407 Mass 629, 631, 555 NE2d 557, 558 (1990); *Green v. Richmond*, 369 Mass 47, 59-60, 337 NE2d 691, 699 (1975).

[2] See, e.g., *Com. v. Berry*, 420 Mass 95, 109, 648 NE2d 732, 741 (1995); *Com. v. Zagranski*, 408 Mass 278, 558 NE2d 933 (1990). For cases involving exhibition of scars

"[T]rial judges must take care to avoid exposing the jury unnecessarily to inflammatory material that might inflame the jurors' emotions and possibly deprive the defendant of an impartial jury."[3] In balancing probative value against risk of prejudice, the fact that the evidence goes to a central issue in the case weighs in favor of admission.[4] Thus, evidence probative of extreme atrocity or cruelty will often be gruesome, but that alone is not sufficient to render it inadmissible in a murder trial.[5]

The question in these cases is not whether the evidence is prejudicial, but rather whether it is unfairly and unduly prejudicial.[6]

Whether the probative value of evidence is outweighed by its prejudicial effect is within the sound discretion of the trial judge, whose determination will be upheld on appeal unless there is palpable error.[7] In reviewing such determinations, the effectiveness of limiting instructions in minimizing the risk of prejudice will be considered. In

---

or wounds, compare *Tuttle v. McGeeney*, 344 Mass 200, 205, 181 NE2d 655, 658 (1962) (exhibition of scars refused) with *Com. v. MacDonald*, 368 Mass 395, 400, 333 NE2d 189, 192-193 (1975) (exhibition of scar allowed), *Com. v. Bertuzzi*, 6 Mass App 937, 381 NE2d 1312 (1978) (victim allowed to display wound caused by surgical intervention, not by defendant's attack), *Com. v. Beaulieu*, 3 Mass App 786, 337 NE2d 710 (1975) (gruesome and hideous scars inflicted by defendant exhibited), and *Com. v. Perry*, 3 Mass App 308, 329 NE2d 150 (1975) (victim allowed to display scar caused by stab wound inflicted by defendant even though other scars were caused by subsequent surgery).

[3] *Com. v. Berry*, supra, 420 Mass at 109, 648 NE2d at 741. Before a judge admits evidence that defendant used an offensive racial epithet, for example, the judge must be convinced that the probative weight justifies the risk. See *Com. v. Bishop*, 461 Mass 586, 595-597, 963 NE2d 88, 96-97 (2012).

[4] See *Gath v. M/A-Com, Inc.*, 440 Mass 482, 490-491, 802 NE2d 521, 529 (2003) (Text cited). See also *Com. v. Jaime*, 433 Mass 575, 579-580, 745 NE2d 320, 323-324 (2001); *Com. v. Medeiros*, 395 Mass 336, 352, 479 NE2d 1371, 1381 (1985).

[5] *Com. v. Bresilla*, 470 Mass 422, 437, 23 NE3d 75, 88 (2015).

[6] *Com. v. Rosa*, 468 Mass 231, 241, 9 NE3d 832, 840 (2014) (defendant's recorded jail telephone call ripe with offensive and profane language was nonetheless highly probative, and the judge took pains to redact the most offensive portions). See also *Com. v. Wall*, 469 Mass 652, 660-663, 15 NE3d 708, 716-718 (2014) (evidence of defendant's four recorded phone calls with his girlfriend on day of murder were relevant to his mental state, and even though they painted defendant in a negative light, prejudice was cured by judge's extensive instructions). Compare *Com. v. Hunt*, 462 Mass 807, 819, 971 NE3d 768, 778 (2012) and *Com. v. Cahoon*, 86 Mass App 266, 270, 15 NE3d 787, 790 (2014) (evidence that a sexually dangerous person (SDP) defendant refused treatment conditioned on a waiver of confidentiality is inherently more prejudicial than probative).

[7] See *Com. v. Pike*, 430 Mass 317, 325, 718 NE2d 855, 862 (1999); *Com. v. Woods*, 414 Mass 343, 355, 607 NE2d 1024, 1033 (1993); *Com. v. Roderick*, 411 Mass 817, 819, 586 NE2d 967, 968-969 (1992).

Com. v. Dunn,[8] for example, defendant argued that the trial judge erred in admitting evidence that the murder victim, his wife, was pregnant at the time of her death and carrying a 22-week-old fetus. Given other evidence indicating that the defendant believed someone other than himself was the father, the evidence was held to be highly relevant in proving motive. Observing that "the chance of prejudice was minimized by a specific limiting instruction cautioning the jury to consider the testimony only on the issue of the defendant's state of mind at the time of the crime," the court concluded that the probative value outweighed the potential prejudicial effect.[9]

In contrast, unfair prejudice was demonstrated in *Com. v. LaSota*,[10] where defendant's conviction for rape and abuse of his daughter was reversed because a pamphlet found among his papers had been admitted into evidence with underlined passages speaking favorably about incest. In holding that its admission constituted palpable error, the court observed:

> Even if we were to ascribe some probative value to the pamphlet, its prejudicial potential and probable impact were considerable. The ideas expressed in the pamphlet were likely to offend the jury. The prosecutor's use of the pamphlet, and particularly her numerous references to it as "that Penthouse publication," sought to make the most of probable juror revulsion so as to depict the defendant as a lewd man and to lead the jury to believe that a man of his character would be likely to commit the crimes charged.[11]

---

[8] 407 Mass 798, 556 NE2d 30 (1990).

[9] 407 Mass at 807, 556 NE2d at 35-36. See also *Carrel v. National Cord & Braid Corp.*, 447 Mass 431, 445-447, 852 NE2d 100, 112-113 (2006); *Com. v. Martinez*, supra, 431 Mass at 174, 726 NE2d at 921; *Com. v. Ashley*, 427 Mass 620, 625-626 n.5, 694 NE2d 862, 867 n.5 (1998); *Com. v. Harvey*, 397 Mass 351, 358-359, 491 NE2d 607, 612 (1986); *Com. v. Cruz*, 373 Mass 676, 692, 369 NE2d 996, 1006 (1977); *Com. v. Azar*, 32 Mass App 290, 300, 588 NE2d 1352, 1359-1360 (1992). For a discussion of the different standard for measuring prejudicial harm in bench trials, see *Com. v. Darby*, 37 Mass App 650, 655-656, 642 NE2d 303, 306 (1994).

[10] 29 Mass App 15, 557 NE2d 34 (1990).

[11] 29 Mass App at 26-27, 557 NE2d at 40-42. See also *Com. v. Rollins*, 470 Mass 66, 80-81, 18 NE3d 870, 682-683 (2014) (improper to admit several "representative photographs" that were not child pornography but which depicted young children in provocative poses, as there was risk that jury would use them as evidence of defendant's bad character); *Com. v. Crayton*, 470 Mass 228, 248-252, 21 NE3d 157, 175-177 (2014) (risk of prejudice from sexually explicit drawings of young girls found in child pornography defendant's jail cell outweighed their probative value); *Com. v. Jaundoo*, 64 Mass App 56, 61-64, 831 NE2d 365, 370-371 (2005) (reversal required where trial court admitted in child sex offenses trial substantial quantity of unrelated pornographic materials seized from defendant). Compare *Com. v. Tassinari*, 466 Mass 340,

Similarly in *Com. v. Lewin (No. 2)*[12] the Court affirmed an order excluding from evidence a homicide defendant's statement made while detained in a holding cell that he would be agreeable to pleading guilty to manslaughter. Noting that the statement was of ambiguous probative value but nonetheless might be weighed heavily by the jury as an admission of guilt, the court concluded: "The judge could draw on his knowledge and particular experiences with the case in balancing the factors of probative value and prejudicial effect and in deciding whether exclusion of the evidence was necessary in the interests of a fair trial."[13]

350-352, 995 NE2d 42, 51-52 (2013) (evidence referencing defendant's viewing of pornographic websites was relevant to his state of mind in weeks prior to murder); *Com. v. Carey*, 463 Mass 378, 386-391, 974 NE2d 624, 632-635 (2012) (photographs, Internet article, and computer search records from defendant's home computer, depicting images of strangulation, was not abuse of discretion in prosecution for attempted murder by strangulation, as it showed defendant's interest in asphyxiation of a partner; but trial court abused its discretion by relying on Commonwealth's description of video found on defendant's computer, rather than viewing it, in determining admissibility, given its highly inflammatory nature); *Com. v. Wallace*, 70 Mass App 757, 764-770, 877 NE2d 260, 267-271 (2007) (probative value of pornographic photographs and magazines taken from defendant's car as evidence of his voyeuristic interest in young females was not outweighed by potential for prejudice in indecent assault prosecution), and *Com. v. O'Brien*, 432 Mass 578, 589-590, 736 NE2d 841, 852 (2000) (no error in admitting in murder prosecution newspaper article concerning motion picture Natural Born Killers found in defendant's bedroom).

[12] Supra n.1, 407 Mass 629, 555 NE2d 557.

[13] 407 Mass at 632, 555 NE2d at 559. See also *Com. v. Gray*, 463 Mass 731, 752-753, 978 NE2d 543, 559-560 (2012) (witness's testimony concerning her introduction to the defendant months after shooting was far more prejudicial than probative; rap video, in which defendant appeared and pledged his allegiance to gang, was only minimally probative and highly prejudicial); *Com. v. Stuckich*, 450 Mass 449, 457-458, 879 NE2d 105, 113-114 (2008) (description of the investigative process leading to charges of indecent assault on minor daughter was irrelevant and extremely prejudicial); *Com. v. Martinez*, supra, 431 Mass at 173-174, 726 NE2d at 920-921 (testimony by defendant's girlfriend that his niece had threatened to kill her if she testified against defendant was improperly admitted, as probative value was minimal and risk of prejudice significant); *Com. v. Bior*, 88 Mass App 150, 155-156, 37 NE3d 31, 35-36 (2015) (admission of evidence regarding the clerk-magistrate's rulings on cross-complaints created substantial risk of miscarriage of justice); *Com. v. Prashaw*, 57 Mass App 19, 22-26, 781 NE2d 19, 22-25 (2003) (prejudicial error to admit sexually provocative nude photographs of defendant in prosecution for drug and firearms charges); *Com. v. Petrillo*, 50 Mass App 104, 109, 735 NE2d 395, 399 (2000) (graphic display on pornographic video added little to victim's direct testimony of her sexual relations with defendant and could only inflame the jury against the defendant; *Com. v. Demars*, 38 Mass App 596, 650 NE2d 368 (1995) (prejudicial impact of testimony suggesting defendant had previously engaged in sexual misconduct far outweighed its relevance). But compare *Com. v. Faust*, 81 Mass App 498, 504, 964 NE2d 987, 992 (2012) (police officer's testimony that he was responding to a report of a stolen vehicle, admitted to explain why defendant was pulled over, should have been redacted in defendant's receiving stolen property trial, but was

Evidence that may evoke sympathy for the victim, while not *per se* inadmissible, must be received with caution, and the risk of prejudice to defendant tested carefully against probative value.[14] So too regarding evidence concerning the effect of the crime on the victim,[15] and the effect of the crime on the victim's family.[16] "Some limited biographical detail may be given to humanize a victim," and the judge's

---

not prejudicial); *Com. v. Doyle*, 73 Mass App 304, 897 NE2d 1025 (2008) (evidence of locations and conditions of child victims of fatal automobile crash was probative in trial of involuntary manslaughter and motor vehicle homicide charges, and not outweighed by risk of undue prejudice); *Harris-Lewis v. Mudge*, 60 Mass App 480, 485-487, 803 NE2d 735, 740-741 (2004) (evidence of patient's use of cocaine was more probative than prejudicial).

[14] See *Com. v. Santiago*, 425 Mass 491, 497 n.4, 681 NE2d 1205, 1211 n.4 (1997) (victim's sister's testimony about victim's difficult life had no relevance to crime charged and should have been excluded); *Com. v. Bonds*, 445 Mass 821, 834, 840 NE2d 939, 950 (2006); *Com. v. Shippee*, 83 Mass App 659, 662-663, 998 NE2d 859, 862-863 (2013) (testimony of victim's sister that she was a good person was not relevant at trial for indecent assault; but photograph of victim was relevant to put human face on her since she was not alive at time of trial). Compare *Com. v. Holliday*, 450 Mass 794, 816, 882 NE2d 309, 327 (2008) (testimony from victims' mothers identifying their photographs and providing biographical details was properly admitted); *Com. v. Marshall*, 434 Mass 358, 367-368, 749 NE2d 147, 156 (2001) (in murder cases, member of victim's family may testify as to relevant issue even where likely to elicit sympathy); *Com. v. Tarjick*, 87 Mass 374, 379, 30 NE3d 125, 130 (2015) (poster-sized versions of school portraits of defendant's stepdaughter, who he was charged with abusing, were relevant in depicting her at relevant times, and not unduly prejudicial); *Com. v. Dale*, 86 Mass App 187, 194-195, 15 NE3d 232, 239 (2014) (testimony about and photographs of abuse victim's physical injuries was particularly probative given defendant's attacks on her credibility); *Com. v. Flint*, 81 Mass App 794, 806-807, 968 NE2d 928, 939 (2012) (references to victim's troubled family life were relevant to explain what might have drawn victim and defendant together); *Com. v. Place*, 81 Mass App 229, 961 NE2d 597 (2012) (photograph of rape victim from time of crime several years before trial, at age 13, was admissible as relevant on element of constructive force used, as it showed her size and immaturity). For the parameters of closing argument regarding sympathy for the victim, see § 13.2.

[15] See *Com. v. Sanchez*, 405 Mass 369, 540 NE2d 1316 (1989) (evidence that child rape victim frequently awoke at night trembling and screaming tended to show he did not fabricate his story and was not unduly prejudicial) *Com. v. Smith*, 58 Mass App 166, 177-178, 788 NE2d 977, 987 (2003), *rev'd on other grounds*, 543 US 462 (testimony regarding location and extent of victim's gunshot wounds was probative of intent to kill; testimony concerning post-assault medical treatment was relevant to victim's ability to identify defendant; but testimony concerning necessity for liver transplant was substantially outweighed by danger of unfair prejudice); *Com. v. Gill*, 37 Mass App 457, 640 NE2d 798 (1994) (medical testimony concerning victim's extensive brain injuries relevant to establish that assault was intentional and to demonstrate reason for victim's lack of memory of incident).

[16] See *Com. v. Lorette*, 37 Mass App 736, 643 NE2d 67 (1994) (defendant was unfairly prejudiced by testimony of rape victim's father that "this whole thing has ruined my life"). Compare *Com. v. Murphy*, 426 Mass 395, 402, 688 NE2d 966, 972 (1998) (evidence that victim's two-year-old son was in room and possibly witnessed death of

immediate limiting instruction could minimize the risk of engendering sympathy or an emotional response.[17]

Relevant evidence may also be excluded on the grounds that it would constitute undue consumption of time,[18] or risk confusion or distraction of the jury.[19] A party's offer to stipulate to the matter may be weighed in the balance of probative value versus the counterweights.[20]

Where a party opens the subject, an opposing party may be permitted to respond with evidence that would otherwise be inadmissible.[21] Evidence that poses a risk of unfair prejudice need not always, however, be admitted solely because a defendant has opened the door; the judge must still weigh its probative value against the risk of prejudice.[22]

Against this backdrop of ad hoc weighing of probative value and its counterweights, several special rules operate to exclude certain recurring categories of circumstantial evidence in which probative value is generally outweighed by the risk of undue prejudice. Sections 4.4 through 4.7, infra, will focus on these categorical rules.

---

victim was relevant in prosecution for murder by extreme atrocity or cruelty); *Com. v. Shruhan*, 89 Mass App 320, 323-324, 48 NE3d 487, 491 (2016) (testimony of victim's family members as to their shock at victim's injuries supported the evidentiary basis for "serious bodily injury" and was not unduly prejudicial).

[17] *Com. v. Mazariego*, 474 Mass 42, 55-56, 47 NE3d 420, 432 (2016).

[18] See, e.g., *Com. v. Avalos*, 454 Mass 1, 9, 906 NE2d 987, 993 (2009) (weighing marginal relevance against undue exploration of collateral issues).

[19] See *Com. v. Lyons*, 444 Mass 289, 299-300, 828 NE2d 1, 10 (2005), *habeas denied, Lyons v. Brady*, 666 F3d 51 (1st Cir 2012); *Com. v. Urrea*, 443 Mass 530, 544, 822 NE2d 1192, 1204 (2005).

[20] See *Com. v. Harris*, 464 Mass 425, 430-431, 983 NE2d 695, 701 (2013). See also § 4.1.1, supra.

[21] See, e.g., *Com. v. Dyer*, 460 Mass 728, 955 NE2d 271 (2011) (evidence that murder victim and his family feared the defendant was admissible on issue of who was the first aggressor, since defendant claimed he acted in self-defense); *Com. v. Sylvia*, 456 Mass 182, 191-194, 921 NE2d 968, 978 (2010) (in view of fact that defense raised issue of possible contamination of gunshot residue during cross-examination of prosecution expert, it was reasonable for prosecutor to anticipate it in direct examination of another witness); *Com. v. Stone*, 70 Mass App 800, 807, 877 NE2d 620, 626 (2007) (evidence that defendant had previously received *Miranda* warnings in a prior investigation). see also § 1.8 supra.

[22] *Com. v. Gray*, 463 Mass 731, 753, 978 NE2d 543, 560 (2012).

§ 4.3.2 Photographs of the Victim and Crime Scene

A common scenario requiring the balancing of probative value and prejudicial harm concerns the admissibility of photographs (including autopsy) of the victim or crime scene. Where such photographs have probative value, they are not rendered inadmissible merely because they are gruesome or may be considered inflammatory, as the Commonwealth "is entitled to a full presentation of its case."[23] The admissibility of such evidence is a matter left to the sound discretion of the judge, and a defendant bears a heavy burden of demonstrating an abuse of that discretion.[24] Indeed, the courts have rarely reversed a conviction because of the admission of photographs of a victim.[25]

Photographs will generally not be excluded merely because an expert or other witness has already provided a detailed description of the

---

[23] *Com. v. Bell*, 473 Mass 131, 142-145, 39 NE3d 1190, 1199-1202 (2015) ("horrific" photos of arson victim while being treated in hospital ER, including some showing medical intervention, while disturbing, were relevant on the question of her pain and not unduly prejudicial). See, e.g., *Com. v. Amran*, 471 Mass 354, 357-358, 29 NE3d 188, 192-193 (2015) (postmortem photographs of victim's body in advanced state of decomposition showing how it was found bound and wrapped in plastic in a suitcase was evidence of malice and consciousness of guilt); *Com. v. Tassinari*, 466 Mass 340, 349, 995 NE2d 42, 51 (2013) (autopsy photographs of victim's fractured and open skull); *Com. v. Haith*, 452 Mass 409, 414, 894 NE2d 1122, 1127 (2008) (autopsy photograph showing part of victim's shaved skull with bent screwdriver inserted); *Com. v. Olsen*, 452 Mass 284, 293-294, 892 NE2d 739, 746 (2008) (photographs of victim's massive injuries to face and head); *Com. v. Liptak*, 80 Mass App 76, 82-84, 951 NE2d 731, 738-739 (2011) (photographs depicting damage to victim's car and extensive injuries to victim in motor vehicle homicide trial). Compare *Com. v. Obershaw*, 435 Mass 794, 803-804, 762 NE2d 276, 286 (2002), *habeas petition denied in Obershaw v. Lanman*, 453 F3d 56 (1st Cir 2006) (admission of over 80 photographs was not error given the circumstances of the case, but ordinarily this quantity should not be admitted "as it is likely to be cumulative and may have unanticipated effects on the jury").

[24] *Com. v. Anderson*, 445 Mass 195, 209, 834 NE2d 1159, 1171 (2005) ("In order to find an abuse of discretion, it is necessary to decide that no conscientious judge, acting intelligently, could honestly have taken the view."); *Com. v. Vizcarrondo*, 431 Mass 360, 727 NE2d 821 (2000) (not error to admit eight hospital photos of ten-month-old murder victim, depicting external bruises and bite marks); *Com. v. Stockwell*, 426 Mass 17, 20, 686 NE2d 426, 429 (1997) (not error to admit gruesome photo of victim discovered nine days after death, even though picture was of debatable relevance).

[25] *Com. v. DeSouzas*, 428 Mass 667, 670, 704 NE2d 190, 193 (1999); *Com. v. Nadworny*, 396 Mass 342, 366, 486 NE2d 675, 689-690 (1985). But see *Com. v. Hrycenko*, 31 Mass App 425, 578 NE2d 809 (1991) (error to send inflammatory photos to deliberating jury in response to question).

crime scene or victim's wounds;[26] or because the photograph is cumulative of other evidence.[27] Nor will a party's offer to stipulate as to the matters depicted by the photographs preclude their admissibility.[28]

In determining the probative value of such evidence, it may be useful for the trial court to voir dire an appropriate witness outside the presence of the jury to learn if photographs will be of assistance in understanding the testimony.[29]

The judge should caution the jurors to curb their emotional reactions to such photographs, in order to alleviate any prejudicial impact they may have. An admonition to the jury is one factor to be weighed in determining whether the risk of prejudice has been avoided.[30]

Numerous cases have held photographs of the victim admissible on the issue of extreme atrocity and cruelty, or deliberate premeditation, in murder prosecutions.[31] Photographs have been held admissible, although arguably inflammatory, when they identify or describe the defendant in a material way,[32] or have other

---

[26] *Com. v. Bell*, supra, 473 Mass at 144, 39 NE3d at 1201; *Com. v. DeSouza*, supra; *Com. v. Paradise*, 405 Mass 141, 156, 539 NE2d 1006, 1016 (1989); *Com. v. Benoit*, 389 Mass 411, 429, 451 NE2d 101, 112 (1983).

[27] *Com. v. Gouse*, 461 Mass 787, 797, 965 NE2d 774, 783 (2012).

[28] *Com. v. Pena*, 455 Mass 1, 12, 913 NE2d 815, 825 (2009); *Com. v. Winfield*, 76 Mass App 716, 725, 926 NE2d 550, 557-558 (2010), *habeas denied*, *Winfield v. O'Brien*, 775 F3d 1 (1st Cir 2014) (eight color photos of child victim showing burns and bruises were probative of penetration and force, even though identify of perpetrator, not nature of injuries, was only contested issue at trial); *Com. v. Nadworny*, supra, 396 Mass at 367, 486 NE2d at 690.

[29] See *Com. v. Medeiros*, 395 Mass 336, 479 NE2d 1371 (1985).

[30] See *Com. v. Allison*, 434 Mass 670, 751 NE2d 868 (2001) (photographs of victim demonstrating 79 stab wounds) (Text cited); *Com. v. Cardarelli*, 433 Mass 427, 743 NE2d 823 (2001) (autopsy photographs of victim's partially decomposed head); *Com. v. Jackson*, supra; *Com. v. Richenburg*, 401 Mass 663, 673, 518 NE2d 1143, 1148 (1988) (judge instructed jurors to be "cold, calculating and professional in dealing with this type of evidence" and not to "get fired up").

[31] *Com. v. McNulty*, 458 Mass 305, 329, 37 NE2d 16, 35 (2010); *Com. v. Pena*, 455 Mass 1, 12-13, 913 NE2d 815, 824-825 (2009); *Com. v. Olsen*, supra, 452 Mass at 293-294, 892 NE2d at 746; *Com. v. Meinholz*, 420 Mass 633, 651 NE2d 385 (1995) (photos depicted differences between discoloration caused by blunt object and discolorations resulting from decomposition); *Com. v. Berry*, 420 Mass 95, 648 NE2d 732 (1995) (photograph of victim's naked body); *Com. v. Gallagher*, 408 Mass 510, 562 NE2d 80 (1990) (autopsy photo showing interior of the skull); *Com. v. Lawrence*, 404 Mass 378, 536 NE2d 571 (1989) (autopsy photo of fetus to show that victim's pregnancy would have been obvious to third parties).

[32] See *Com. v. Lamoureux*, 348 Mass 390, 392-393, 204 NE2d 115, 117 (1965) (photos of open scalp wounds demonstrated probability that blood would flow onto clothing of one assaulting victim); *Com. v. Appleby*, 389 Mass 359, 374-375, 377, 450 NE2d 1070, 1080-1081 (1983) (photographs of defendant's residence); *Com. v. Izzo*,

relevance.[33] Photographs of the defendant that are inflammatory and of marginal relevance may be held to be unduly prejudicial.[34]

Photographs showing the victim's body in an altered state (as in the course of an autopsy) present special problems.[35] The Supreme Judicial Court has provided the following guidance:

---

359 Mass 39, 267 NE2d 631 (1971) (photos of rape defendant wearing swastikas and German helmet admissible as a fair representation of his appearance at time of alleged crime).

[33] See, e.g., *Com. v. Degro*, 432 Mass 319, 322, 733 NE2d 1024, 1032 (2000) (photograph of victim prior to death introduced to tell jury something of person whose life has been lost); *Com. v. Andrade*, 422 Mass 236, 661 NE2d 1308 (1996) (two videotapes of crime scene, depicting blood, multiple photos of victim, and autopsy photos were admissible); *Com. v. Benson*, 419 Mass 114, 642 NE2d 1035 (1994) (color photos of victim's facial injuries were relevant to dispute self-defense claim); *Com. v. Robertson*, 408 Mass 747, 563 NE2d 223 (1990) (photo of homicide victim taken after earlier beating by defendant was relevant to show hostility); *Com. v. Merola*, 405 Mass 529, 544-545, 542 NE2d 249, 258-259 (1989) (photos of child victim's bruises helped jury understand medical testimony and assess defendant's credibility inasmuch as he had denied seeing any bruises); *Com. v. Nadworny*, 396 Mass 342, 366-367, 486 NE2d 675, 689-690 (1985) (photo of body showing advanced state of decomposition relevant to pathologist's testimony that he was unable to determine precise cause and time of death; photo of victim while she was alive showing "youthful and smiling face" was relevant as tending to show that death due to ill health or suicide was unlikely); *Com. v. Todd*, 394 Mass 791, 796, 477 NE2d 999, 1003-1004 (1985) (photos probative of degree of guilt, tended to refute defendant's claim of intoxication, and showed direction from which shot came); *Com. v. Perry*, 385 Mass 639, 644, 433 NE2d 446, 450 (1982) (photos of room where fire occurred and of victim's body relevant to refute claim of accidental smoking death) (Text cited); *Com. v. Zhan Tang Huang*, 87 Mass App 65, 77-78, 25 NE3d 315, 325-326 (2015) (photographs of victims' bodies were probative on the manner of their death in manslaughter and reckless violation of fire code prosecution).

[34] See, e.g., *Com. v. Prashaw*, 57 Mass App 19, 25, 781 NE2d 19, 25 (2003) (error to admit photographs depicting defendant naked in sexually provocative positions where she was charged with non-sex-related offenses) (Text cited); *Com. v. Darby*, 37 Mass App 650, 642 NE2d 303 (1994) (error to admit grossly offensive and inflammatory photo of defendant alone, sitting fully dressed, with penis exposed in turgid state, where defendant did not claim impotence or sexual dysfunction).

[35] See, e.g., *Com. v. Bastarache*, 382 Mass 86, 105-106, 414 NE2d 984, 997 (1980) (autopsy photographs of the victim's brain and interior of his skull were inflammatory, graphic, and grisly); *Com. v. Richmond*, 371 Mass 563, 358 NE2d 999 (1976) (face of corpse severely mutilated by dog prior to retrieval of body by police); *Com. v. St. Peter*, 48 Mass App 517, 722 NE2d 1002 (2000) (autopsy photos depicting victim's open skull and brain).

While reversing the defendant's conviction in *Richmond*, the Court cautioned: "[W]e have never, so far as we know, upset a verdict on this type of error, and this opinion is not to be taken to indicate that we are likely to do so again, but there are limits to the employment of judicial discretion and those limits were exceeded in this instance." 371 Mass at 566, 358 NE2d at 1001. See also *Com. v. Carney*, 472 Mass 252, 255-256,

> [T]he judge should carefully assess the photographs. If they are apt to be inflammatory or otherwise prejudicial, he should admit them, in his discretion, only if they are important to the resolution of any contested fact in the case. In some instances, an expert may testify and be cross-examined concerning autopsy photographs without any need to show them to the jury. Unless the viewing of an autopsy photograph would aid the jury, as lay people, in making a finding of fact on a contested point, the actual viewing of a photograph showing the body as altered in the course of an autopsy would serve no proper purpose. It may often be difficult to determine the admissibility of such photographs before any expert testifies, and a decision to exclude such photographs might properly be changed during or after the testimony of one or more experts. The exercise of discretion to admit such photographs should be based in part on an assessment of the contested issues of fact.[36]

Photographs showing a body in a state of decomposition have been admitted where relevant to the manner of death.[37] Disturbing photographs of other subject matters have also been held admissible.[38]

---

33 NE3d 1234, 1237-1238 (2015) (autopsy photo of victim's gunshot wound was relevant to issue of deliberate premeditation); *Com. v. Lyons*, 444 Mass 289, 828 NE2d 1 (2005), *habeas denied*, *Lyons v. Brady*, 666 F3d 51 (1st Cir 2012) (not error to admit autopsy photographs of infant, including one showing skull after skin had been peeled back and top of skull removed and another of back after skin had been pulled back to expose muscle); *Com. v. Urrea*, 443 Mass 530, 822 NE2d 1192 (2005) (not error to admit autopsy photograph showing suturing from surgical scar across victim's breast); *Com. v. Dagenais*, 437 Mass 832, 841, n.15, 776 NE2d 1010, 1017 (2002) (not error to admit photograph in which medical examiner held back piece of scalp to show portion of fracture beneath); *Com. v. Vazquez*, 419 Mass 350, 644 NE2d 978 (1995) (photo of murder victim's broken hyoid bone after removal from body was admissible on issue of whether victim had been strangled).

For a case restricting defense use of autopsy photographs, see *Com. v. Mercado*, 456 Mass 198, 202-204, 922 NE2d 140, 145-147 (2010) (excluded photographs had minimal probative value and were particularly disturbing).

[36] *Com. v. Bastarche*, supra, 382 Mass at 106, 414 NE2d at 997.

[37] See *Com. v. Nadworny*, supra, 396 Mass at 366-367, 486 NE2d at 689-690. But compare *Com. v. Allen*, 377 Mass 674, 387 NE2d 553 (1979) (photographs and slides of victim's body in state of "moderately advanced decomposition" were questionably admitted).

[38] See *Com. v. Simmons*, 419 Mass 426, 646 NE2d 97 (1995) (photographs and videotape of blood-stained apartment); *Com. v. Perry*, 385 Mass 639, 644, 433 NE2d 446, 450 (1982) (photo of room where fire occurred).

§ 4.4 Character Evidence

§ 4.4.1 General Inadmissibility of Character Evidence to Prove Conduct

As a general rule, evidence of a person's character (i.e., a generalized description of his disposition or traits)[1] is not admissible to prove that he acted in conformity with that character on a particular occasion.[2] Thus, for example, plaintiff is not permitted to offer evidence that defendant is a "careless person" or "accident prone" in order to prove that he drove negligently at the time of the litigated collision.[3] The prosecution is similarly barred from offering in its case-in-chief evidence that the accused is a violent or dishonest person in order to demonstrate that he has a propensity to commit the crime charged (although, as we shall see in § 4.4.2, infra, such evidence may be offered in rebuttal once the defendant "opens the door" by offering favorable character evidence).[4]

Moreover, it generally is not permissible for purposes of proving that A did a particular act to show that he did a similar act on another occasion.[5] Thus it may not be shown that the defendant had been

---

§ 4.4 [1] Compare *Com. v. Bonds*, 445 Mass 821, 829-831, 840 NE2d 939, 946-948 (2006) (testimony of mother of rape victim with mental disorder that victim was "too trusting" was not a generalized description of character, but a specific manifestation of her disorder relevant to the central issue of consent).

[2] Proposed Mass R Evid 404(a), which tracks the federal rule and reflects Massachusetts practice, provides:

> (a) **Character evidence generally**. Evidence of a person's character or a trait of his character is not admissible for the purpose of proving that he acted in conformity therewith on a particular occasion [with certain enumerated exceptions discussed below].

See also *Com. v. Doherty*, 23 Mass App 633, 636-637, 504 NE2d 681, 683-684 (1987) (& citations).

[3] See *Figueiredo v. Hamill*, 385 Mass 1003, 431 NE2d 231 (1982); *Com. v. Mandell*, 29 Mass App 504, 507, 562 NE2d 111, 113 (1990).

[4] See, e.g., *Com. v. Martin*, 63 Mass App 587, 597, 527 NE2d 1263, 1272 (2005) (admission of a defendant's mug shot is "laden with potential for characterizing the defendant as a careerist in crime.").

[5] Proposed Mass R Evid 404(b), which tracks the federal rule (except for a notice provision in Fed R Evid 404(b)) and reflects Massachusetts practice, provides:

> (b) **Other crimes, wrongs, or acts**. Evidence of other crimes, wrongs, or acts is not admissible to prove the character of a person in order to show that he acted in conformity therewith. It may, however, be admissible for other purposes, such as proof of motive, opportunity, intent, preparation, plan, knowledge, identity, or absence of mistake or accident.

See also *Maillet v. ATF-Davidson Co.*, 407 Mass 185, 188, 552 NE2d 95, 97 (1990).

negligent at another time in order to create an inference that he was negligent at the time of the litigated event.[6] Nor may it be shown that a criminal defendant has committed a crime on a prior occasion to raise an inference of guilt on the charges in issue.[7] "This rule stems from the belief that such evidence forces the defendant to answer accusations not set forth in the indictment, confuses his defense, diverts the attention of the jury, and may create undue prejudice against him."[8]

In sum, "evidence of character in any form, whether reputation, opinion from observation, or specific acts will not generally be received to prove that the person whose character is sought to be shown, engaged in certain conduct, or did so with a given intent, on a particular occasion."[9]

The exclusion of "character evidence" in both its general and specific act form is referred to as the "propensity doctrine" because the purpose of such circumstantial evidence is to suggest a propensity to act in a particular manner. Rejection of this evidence is based not solely on relevance grounds, as it may in certain situations make it somewhat more likely that the subject acted in conformity with an established trait or pattern of conduct. Rather, the doctrine is premised on concern that such evidence will have a prejudicial and distorting impact on the jurors (who may overvalue its significance) and distract them from the particular facts of the incident before the court. As the Supreme Judicial Court has explained:

> Our principal concern in admitting character evidence is that a person might not necessarily act in conformity with his or her character on a particular occasion. As such, evidence of a person's character might erroneously lead a jury to conclude a person acted in a particular way simply because his character suggests that he would. [E]vidence of a person's character may also lead a jury to return a verdict improperly based on their dislike of a party rather than one based on the particular facts before them.[10]

---

[6] See *Com. v. Mandell*, 29 Mass App 504, 507, 562 NE2d 111, 113 (1990) (exclusion of testimony that defendant had previously caused minor accidents).

[7] *Com. v. Bassett*, 21 Mass App 713, 717, 490 NE2d 459, 461 (1986).

[8] *Com. v. Clifford*, 374 Mass 293, 298, 372 NE2d 1267, 1271 (1978).

[9] *Com. v. Doherty*, supra, 23 Mass App at 636-637, 504 NE2d at 683.

[10] *Com. v. Bonds*, supra, 445 Mass at 829-830, 840 NE2d at 946-947 (citing Text).

Despite the general exclusion, character evidence is admissible in several contexts:

- Evidence of his own good character when offered by the criminal defendant (and subject to rebuttal by the prosecution). See § 4.4.2, infra.
- Evidence of the violent character of the victim in self-defense cases. See § 4.4.3, infra.
- In civil actions where the character of a party is directly in issue, such as defamation cases raising a truth defense. See § 4.4.5, infra.
- Evidence of specific crimes, wrongs, or acts where there is relevance beyond mere propensity logic. See § 4.4.6, infra.
- Evidence of bad character for truthfulness and veracity when used to impeach the testimony of a witness at trial. See § 6.16, infra.

§ 4.4.2 Character of the Criminal Defendant

The prosecution may not offer evidence of the defendant's bad character as part of its case-in-chief.[11] As Justice Cardozo famously put it, "the law has set its face against the endeavor to fasten guilt upon him by proof of character or experience predisposing to an act of crime."[12] Nor may the prosecution introduce evidence that a defendant "previously has misbehaved, indictably or not, for the purposes of showing his bad character, or propensity to commit the crime charged."[13] Evidence of prior incarceration may, however, be admitted

[11] Proposed Mass R Evid 404(a), note 2, supra.

[12] *People v. Zackowitz*, 254 N.Y. 192, 197, 172 NE 466 (1930). See, e.g., *Com. v. Reddy*, 85 Mass App 104, 5 NE3d 1243 (2014) (error to admit unredacted abuse prevention order stating in bold capitals that there was a substantial likelihood defendant was an immediate danger as improper propensity evidence).

[13] *Com. v. Helfant*, 398 Mass 214, 224, 496 NE2d 433, 440-441 (1986). See, e.g., *Com. v. Caldwell*, 459 Mass 271, 277-278, 945 NE2d 313, 321-322 (2011) (judge should have struck witness' reference to defendant selling drugs in murder case); *Com. v. Foster F*, 86 Mass App 734, 739-740, 20 NE3d 967, 973 (2014) (error to admit evidence of interview where victim stated that her friends told her juvenile was "a perv.") (citing Text); *Com. v. McCollum*, 79 Mass App 239, 258-259, 945 NE2d 937, 954-955 (2011) (prosecutor should not have questioned defendant about unspecified "problems with the law"); *Com. v. McClendon*, 39 Mass App 122, 126-128, 653 NE2d 1138, 1141-1142 (1995) (error to admit evidence regarding murder defendant's bad temper when drinking and alleged prior attempt to strangulate stepmother). Compare *Com. v.*

where relevant to a purpose other than to show criminal propensity or bad character.[14]

This prohibition broadly includes evidence from which bad character may be inferred.[15] Thus, for example, evidence that the defendant possessed weapons not connected to the crime charged may be excluded because of the unfavorable impact it might have on the

---

Evans, 415 Mass 422, 424-426, 614 NE2d 653, 656 (1993) (no error allowing Commonwealth to rehabilitate witness on redirect even though testimony permitted inference that defendant had prior criminal record); *Com. v. Ryan*, 79 Mass App 179, 188, 944 NE2d 617, 624 (2011) (defendant's status as a work-release inmate was inextricably intertwined with the facts of the credit card fraud case, including defendant's ability to gain the victim's sympathy).

[14] *Com. v. Tarjick*, 87 Mass App 374, 380, 30 NE3d 125, 130-131 (2015) (recordings of jailhouse phone calls were relevant to defendant's relationship with uncooperative witness and his knowledge of nude photos of his sons). See also *Com. v. Foxworth*, 473 Mass 149, 160-161, 40 NE3d 1003 (2015) (evidence of defendant's prior incarceration was relevant to defendant's relationship with the murder conspiracy).

[15] For examples of the wide variety of "bad character" evidence, see *Com. v. Mosher*, 455 Mass 811, 829-830, 920 NE2d 285, 301 (2010) (testimony that murder defendant was in jail at time of trial should have been avoided); *Com. v. Simpson*, 434 Mass 570, 582-583, 750 NE2d 977, 991 (2001) (evidence that defendant possessed police scanner and assault weapon case label, not tied to crimes charged, improperly suggested bad character); *Com. v. McIntyre*, 430 Mass 529, 539-540, 721 NE2d 911, 920-921 (1999) (witness's testimony concerning fear of defendant served improper purpose of suggesting defendant's bad character); *Com. v. Mendes*, 75 Mass App 390, 395, 914 NE2d 348, 352-353 (2009) (reference to defendant's fingerprints being on file was error); *Com. v. McCoy*, 59 Mass App 284, 289, 795 NE2d 1183, 1188 (2003) (prosecutor improperly impugned defendant's character with guilt by association with drug dealer); *Com. v. Snow*, 58 Mass App 917, 792 NE2d 1005 (2003) (evidence that defendant was heroin addict inadmissible in prosecution for breaking and entering as it painted defendant as an outlaw likely to commit property crimes); *Com. v. Siano*, 52 Mass App 912, 913-914, 755 NE2d 324, 326-327 (2001) (blank social security cards and other documents found in defendant's home improperly suggested criminal propensities).

Compare *Com. v. Borgos*, 464 Mass 23, 35-36, 979 NE2d 1095, 1105-1106 (2012) (evidence that prosecution witnesses feared for their lives, which murder defendant argued painted him in a threatening light, was properly admitted in response to defendant's suggestion that witnesses had been put up in a hotel in exchange for their testimony); *Com. v. Brown*, 462 Mass 620, 627-628, 970 NE2d 306, 313-314 (2012) (evidence of defendant's prior incarceration was admissible to show accuracy of witness's identification of defendant); *Com. v. Hour*, 446 Mass 35, 41, 841 NE2d 709, 714 (2006) (testimony that defendant was arrested by a team of officers did not unfairly portray him as a dangerous fugitive).

For cases involving defendant's viewing of pornographic websites, see § 4.3.1, n.9.

For a discussion of the unique issues raised by evidence that the defendant has AIDS or has tested positive for HIV, see *Com. v. Martin*, 424 Mass 301, 304-306, 676 NE2d 451, 453-455 (1997) (rape victim's testimony that she was informed by defendant that he had tested positive for HIV was relevant on issue of consent).

jury.[16] Use of an alias can be suggestive of bad character and prior criminality, and thus present a clear risk of unfair prejudice,[17] as does evidence of gang membership.[18]

Similarly, identification evidence such as "mugshot" photographs which might reveal to the jury that the defendant had been previously arrested or convicted must either be excluded or purged of any characteristics from which a prior record may be inferred.[19]

---

[16] See *People v. Zackowitz*, supra; *Com. v. Toro*, 395 Mass 354, 480 NE2d 19 (1985) (& cases cited). Compare *Com. v. Otsuki*, 411 Mass 218, 235-237, 581 NE2d 999, 1009-1010 (1991) (no error in admission of evidence that defendant was seen with handgun months before murder because relevant to his possession of means to commit the crime); *Com. v. Sims*, 41 Mass App 902, 667 NE2d 1165 (1996) (no error in admitting evidence that defendant possessed handgun after shooting, where he testified he "never had a gun"). For additional cases admitting evidence of weapons unconnected to the crime, see § 4.1.2, supra.

[17] See *Com. v. Martin*, 442 Mass 1002, 809 NE2d 536 (2004) (prosecution's repeated use of defendant's alias required reversal); *Com. v. Carter*, 423 Mass 505, 514-515, 669 NE2d 203, 208 (1996). But compare *Com. v. Dyer*, 460 Mass 728, 754-755, 955 NE2d 271, 293 (2011) (defendant's use of aliases and false ID cards were relevant to premeditation and intent to flee); *Com. v. Martinez*, 458 Mass 684, 697-698, 940 NE2d 422, 434-435 (2011) (defendant's nickname was relevant to his identity and not exploited by prosecution); *Com. v. Reeder*, 73 Mass App 750, 752-754, 901 NE2d 701, 704-705 (2009) (prosecution did not exploit references to defendant's alias in certificates of drug analysis); *Com. v. Navarro*, 86 Mass App 780, 21 NE3d 982, 987 (2014) (defendant's nickname was material to his identification); *Com. v. Manning*, 44 Mass App 695, 705, 693 NE2d 704, 712 (1998) (testimony that defendant had used aliases was properly admitted as relevant to issue of identity of shooter).

[18] See *Com. v. Akara*, 465 Mass 245, 266-268, 988 NE2d 430, 447-449 (2013). Gang affiliation may, however, be proven to establish motive or joint venture. See *Com. v. Akara*, supra; *Com. v. Keo*, 467 Mass 25, 31-34, 3 NE3d 55, 61-62 (2014); *Com. v. Leng*, 463 Mass 779, 781-783, 979 NE2d 199, 203-205 (2012); *Com. v. Phim*, 462 Mass 470, 476-477, 969 NE2d 663, 669-670 (2012); *Com. v. Rosario*, 460 Mass 181, 193, 950 NE2d 407, 418 (2011), *habeas denied, Rosario v. Roden*, 2014 WL 7409584 (D Mass 2014); *Com. v. Smith*, 459 Mass 538, 545-547, 946 NE2d 95, 103-104 (2011); *Com. v. Smith*, 450 Mass 395, 398-399, 879 NE2d 87, 91-92 (2008); *Com. v. Sok*, 439 Mass 428, 432, 788 NE2d 941, 946 (2003). See also *Com. v. Bright*, 463 Mass 421, 437-440, 974 NE2d 1092, 1108-1109 (2012) (defendant's offer of evidence of gang affiliation of victim and others involved in murder was inadmissible, where it merely raised speculation that another gang member had motive to kill victim).

Where evidence such as gang affiliation is deemed admissible, trial judges should take steps to minimize the prejudicial impact, including screening potential jurors and providing limiting instructions. See *Com. v. Rosario*, supra, 460 Mass at 193, 950 NE2d at 418; *Com. v. Wallace*, 460 Mass 118, 123, 949 NE2d 908, 913 (2011); *Com. v. Smith*, supra, 450 Mass 400, 879 NE2d at 92-93 (& citations).

[19] See *Com. v. Blaney*, 387 Mass 628, 634-640, 442 NE2d 389, 394-396 (1982). But compare *Com. v. Hour*, 446 Mass 35, 40, 841 NE2d 709, 713 (2006) (no notations on photo array suggested they were mugshots or that defendant had prior criminal record); *Com. v. Picher*, 46 Mass App 409, 415-416, 706 NE2d 710, 715 (1999) (where defense claims misidentification and alibi, Commonwealth may admit mug shots to explain how defendant became suspect). *Blaney* includes an extensive discussion of the

The door that is closed to the prosecution may, however, be opened by the defendant. According to long-standing practice, the accused may introduce evidence of his own good character to show that he is not the type of person to commit the crime charged.[20] When such evidence is offered by the accused and there is a proper foundation, it has been held that there is no discretion to exclude it.[21]

Defendant's evidence must be limited to character traits that are pertinent to the crime charged, such as peacefulness for assault crimes and honesty for crimes of fraud. Evidence of a character trait not pertinent to the crime charged is not admissible.[22] Evidence offered for this purpose must be in the form of reputation testimony, and not personal opinion.[23] See § 4.4.4, infra.

When admitted, the prosecution may rebut through testimony of its own reputation witnesses.[24] The Commonwealth also has the right

---

procedures to be followed to sanitize such evidence, including the testimony of witnesses who have previously viewed mug shots. See also *Com. v. Valentin*, 420 Mass 263, 270-272, 649 NE2d 1079, 1083-1084 (1995); *Com. v. Perez*, 405 Mass 339, 344, 540 NE2d 681, 684 (1989); § 11.1.4, infra.

Mugshots may be admitted where (1) the prosecution shows some particular need for them (as where the jury needs to see the photo to understand why the victim failed to select it); (2) they are offered in a form that does not imply a criminal record; and (3) the manner of their introduction does not call attention to their source. *Com. v. Martin*, 447 Mass 274, 285-286, 850 NE2d 555, 564-565 (2006).

Unlike mugshots, evidence of the defendant being identified in a lineup does not signal that he has a history of involvement with the criminal justice system and thus may not carry a risk of prejudicial effect. See *Com. v. Kachoul*, 69 Mass App 352, 357-358, 868 NE2d 153, 157-158 (2007). But along with police testimony about how they were compiled, photographs from an array shown to eyewitnesses may impermissibly reveal defendant's past criminal involvement. See *Com. v. DeJesus*, 71 Mass App 799, 801-804, 887 NE2d 283, 287-288 (2008). See also *Com. v. Reeder*, 73 Mass App 750, 754-756, 901 NE2d 701, 705-706 (2009) (references to defendant's prior incarceration should have been avoided, but were not prejudicial).

For the inadmissibility of profile evidence regarding the purported characteristics of perpetrators, see *Com. v. Johnson*, 461 Mass 1012, 965 NE2d 176 (2012); § 7.6.5(b), infra.

[20] Proposed Mass R Evid 404(a)(1), which tracks the operative language of the federal rule and reflects Massachusetts practice, provides:

> **Character of accused.** Evidence of a pertinent trait of his character offered by an accused, or by the prosecution to rebut the same [is admissible].

See *Com. v. Belton*, 352 Mass 263, 267-268, 225 NE2d 53, 55-56 (1967).

[21] See *Com. v. Schmukler*, 22 Mass App 432, 437-438, 494 NE2d 48, 52 (1986).

[22] See *Com. v. DeVico*, 207 Mass 251, 253, 93 NE 570 (1911) (evidence offered by defendant charged with assault that he was of an excitable disposition would have no tendency to show that he acted in self defense).

[23] See *Com. v. Chambers*, 465 Mass 520, 536, 989 NE2d 483, 495-496 (2013).

[24] Proposed Mass R Evid 404(a)(1), supra.

to cross-examine the defendant's character witnesses on matters he is aware of that are inconsistent with the character trait to which the witness has testified, including reports (or even rumors) of misconduct or criminal activity.[25] "The credibility of the [reputation] witness is tested in the following manner—if the witness states that he has not heard of the report of prior misconduct, his professed knowledge of the defendant's reputation in the community may be doubted by the jury or, if he states that he has heard of the report but still testifies that the defendant's reputation is good in the community, the jury may consider whether the witness is fabricating or whether the community standards in regard to character are too low."[26] The prosecutor must have a good faith basis for the question, and defendant is entitled to a limiting instruction to protect against undue prejudice.[27]

When character evidence is admitted, its weight is left to the jury; and if a reasonable doubt of guilt is generated from such evidence in the mind of the jury, it is its duty to acquit. Under Massachusetts law, however, the defendant has no right to a specific instruction that favorable character evidence itself may create a reasonable doubt; it is sufficient if the judge adequately charges the jury on the burden of proof and how to evaluate the evidence generally.[28] The federal circuit courts are split on whether the defendant is entitled to the "standing alone" instruction, and the Supreme Court has not resolved the conflict.[29]

---

[25] Proposed Mass R Evid 405(a), which tracks the federal rule and reflects Massachusetts practice, provides in pertinent part:

> On cross examination [of a character witness], inquiry is allowable into relevant specific instances of conduct.

See also *Michelson v. United States*, 335 US 469 (1948); *Com. v. Aspen*, 85 Mass App 278, 281, 8 NE3d 782, 786 (2014); *Com. v. Piedra*, 20 Mass App 155, 160-161, 478 NE2d 1284, 1288-1289 (1985) (& cases cited).

[26] *Com. v. Montanino*, 27 Mass App 130, 136-137, 535 NE2d 617, 621 (1989). See also *Com. v. Brown*, 411 Mass 115, 118, 579 NE2d 153, 155 (1991) (witness who testifies to defendant's reputation for truthfulness may be cross-examined as to allegedly false statements defendant made as to his military record).

[27] *Com. v. Piedra*, supra, 20 Mass App at 161, 478 NE2d at 1286-1287.

[28] See *Com. v. Dilone*, 385 Mass 281, 288-289, 431 NE2d 576, 581 (1982); *Com. v. Simmons*, 383 Mass 40, 42-44, 417 NE2d 430, 431-432 (1981).

[29] See *Spangler v. United States*, 487 US 1224 (1988) (& citations) (White, J., dissenting from denial of certiorari).

§ 4.4.3 Character of the Victim in a Criminal Case

a. Self-Defense

In certain criminal cases, the character of the alleged victim may be relevant to the issue of the defendant's guilt, and an exception to the general rule against propensity evidence is recognized. Most notably, the accused in a prosecution for homicide or assault and battery may in most jurisdictions offer evidence of the victim's character for violence when he asserts a claim of self-defense and the identity of the first aggressor is in dispute.[30] Massachusetts law traditionally permitted such evidence only if defendant could show that the violent character of the victim (by way of reputation) *was known to him prior to* the incident in question, as it was deemed relevant "solely on the issue of reasonable apprehension, and, accordingly, admissible only if the defendant has knowledge of the reputation."[31]

Defendant has also been permitted to offer evidence of specific violent acts directed at him by the victim (if not too remote in time) as relevant to his state of mind at the time of the incident,[32] as well as

---

[30] Fed R Evid 404(a)(2), for example, provides for admission of:

> Evidence of a pertinent trait of character of the alleged victim of the crime offered by an accused, or by the prosecution to rebut the same, or evidence of a character trait of peacefulness of the alleged victim offered by the prosecution in a homicide case to rebut evidence that the alleged victim was the first aggressor.

[31] Advisory Committee Note to Proposed Mass R Evid 404. See *Com. v. Dilone*, 385 Mass 281, 285, 431 NE2d 576, 579 (1982).

Fed R Evid 404(a)(2), supra, does not impose a requirement of knowledge on the part of the defendant and thus permits evidence respecting the victim's reputation for violence to be used for a purely propensity purpose—i.e., to suggest that because the victim had been violent in the past he may have been the aggressor on the occasion in question. The federal rule was deliberately omitted from Proposed Mass R Evid 404(a).

[32] See *Com. v. Rodriquez*, 418 Mass 1, 4-7, 633 NE2d 1039, 1041-1042 (1994) (exclusion of evidence of prior abuse required new trial). See also GL 233, § 23F, which provides:

> In the trial of criminal cases charging the use of force against another where the issue of defense of self or another, defense of duress or coercion, or accidental harm is asserted, a defendant shall be permitted to introduce either or both of the following in establishing the reasonableness of the defendant's apprehension that death or serious bodily injury was imminent, the reasonableness of the defendant's belief that he had availed himself of all available means to avoid physical combat or the reasonableness of a defendant's perception of the amount of force necessary to deal with the perceived threat
>
> (a) evidence that the defendant is or has been the victim of acts of physical, sexual or psychological harm or abuse

evidence of the victim's threats of violence against the defendant, even if unknown to him, as tending to show that the victim was attempting to carry out the threat.[33]

The doctrine in this area has been significantly expanded in recent years, first to permit evidence of a victim's specific acts of violence toward third persons *if known to the homicide defendant*,[34] and finally to include evidence of specific incidents of violence allegedly initiated by the victim *even if unknown to the defendant at the time of the incident*.[35] In

---

(b) evidence by expert testimony regarding the common pattern in abusive relationships; the nature and effects of physical, sexual or psychological abuse and typical responses thereto, including how those effects relate to the perception of the imminent nature of the threat of death or serious bodily harm; the relevant facts and circumstances which form the basis for such opinion; and evidence whether the defendant displayed characteristics common to victims of abuse. Nothing in this section shall be interpreted to preclude the introduction of evidence or expert testimony as described in clause (a) or (b) in any civil or criminal action where such evidence or expert testimony is otherwise now admissible.

[33] See *Com. v. Rubin*, 318 Mass 587, 588-589, 63 NE2d 344, 345-346 (1945). But see *Com. v. Young*, 35 Mass App 427, 442-443, 621 NE2d 1180, 1189 (1993) (suggesting threats must be known to defendant).

[34] See *Com. v. Fontes*, 396 Mass 733, 488 NE2d 760 (1986). See also *Com. v. Pidge*, 400 Mass 350, 509 NE2d 281 (1987) (evidence that defendant was told on night of killing of previous assaults committed by victim was admissible on his claim of self-defense). The incidents must be close in time to the killing and not remote. *Com. v. Fontes*, supra, 396 Mass at 736, 488 NE2d at 762-763; *Com. v. Kartell*, 58 Mass App 428, 431-432, 790 NE2d 739, 743 (2003) (excluding incident seventeen years earlier and other incidents closer in time but not involving physical violence); *Com. v. Phachansiri*, 38 Mass App 100, 105-106, 645 NE2d 60, 63-64 (1995) (victim's violent acts nine years before homicide were too remote).

Recognizing the potential risks of admitting such evidence—i.e., the intrusion of collateral matters and the propensity inference created by the negative information about the victim—*Fontes* nonetheless concluded that a "jury assessing the reasonableness of the defendant's reaction to the events leading to the homicide should in fairness have that information." 396 Mass at 737, 488 NE2d at 763. Compare *Com. v. Kosilek*, 423 Mass 449, 458-459, 668 NE2d 808, 815 (1996) (excluding evidence that victim had used physical force to discipline her son); *Com. v. Doherty*, 23 Mass App 633, 636-637, 504 NE2d 681, 683-684 (1987) (excluding evidence of victim's aggressive behavior toward third parties where defendant had already been permitted to inquire concerning victim's reputation for violence and acts of violent behavior directed against, or committed in presence of, defendant).

When so admitted, the trial judge is advised to point out to the jury the limited purpose for which the evidence was admitted—i.e., it was to be considered solely on the question of the defendant's reasonable apprehension of danger, and not to show that the victim was more likely to have been the aggressor. *Com. v. Fontes*, supra, 396 Mass at 736 n.1, 488 NE2d at 763 n.1. But see *Com. v. Simmons*, 383 Mass 40, 42-43, 417 NE2d 430, 432 (1981) (no requirement that judge specifically instruct jury as to relevance of defendant's knowledge of the victim's character for violence).

[35] *Com. v. Adjutant*, 443 Mass 649, 824 NE2d 1 (2005) (citing Text). Compare *Com. v. Sommer*, 77 Mass App 907, 929 NE2d 973 (2010) (Commonwealth conceded

the latter instance, the Court observed in *Com. v. Adjutant* that the defendant's proffered evidence of the victim's violent acts "would have supported the inference that [the victim], with a history of violent and aggressive behavior while intoxicated, probably acted in conformity with that history by attacking [defendant], and that the defendant's story of self-defense was truthful."[36] While thus allowing evidence of the victim's propensity to violence, the Court added this cautionary note:

> It is for the trial judge to evaluate the proffered evidence's probative value and admit so much of that evidence as is noncumulative and relevant to the defendant's self-defense claim. In addition, through their instructions, trial judges should mitigate the dangers of prejudice and confusion inherent in introducing evidence of the victim's specific acts of violence by delineating the precise purpose for which the evidence is offered.[37]

Adjutant has recently been extended to include cases where the dispute is not about who was the first aggressor, but who initiated the use of deadly force:

> Where a victim's prior act acts of violence demonstrate a propensity for violence, we conclude that *Adjutant* evidence is as relevant to the issue of who initiated the use or threat of deadly force as it is to the issue of who initiated an earlier nondeadly assault, and such evidence may be admitted to assist the jury where *either* issue is in dispute, because the resolution of both issues may assist the jury in deciding whether the prosecution has met its burden of proving that the defendant did not act in self-defense. Here, the critical question in determining whether the

---

judge erred in understanding *Adjutant* to apply only when defendant had knowledge of the victim's earlier aggressive behavior).

[36] *Com. v. Adjutant*, 443 Mass at 658, 824 NE2d at 9. Compare *Com. v. Amaral*, 78 Mass App 557, 558-559, 940 NE2d 1242, 1244 (2011) (evidence of victim's experience as a boxer, trained fighter, or martial artist was inadmissible to prove he was first aggressor).

[37] *Com. v. Adjutant*, 443 Mass at 663-664, 824 NE2d at 13.

The court has declined to apply *Adjutant* retroactively. See *Com. v. Clemente*, 452 Mass 295, 304-305, 893 NE2d 19, 31 (2008); *Com. v. Peppicelli*, 70 Mass App 87, 97-99, 972 NE2d 1142, 1151-1152 (2007). Although *Adjutant* stated the new rule would apply only prospectively, the court refused to find an abuse of discretion where a trial judge granted a defendant in the same shoes as Adjutant a new trial to permit evidence of the prior acts of violence of the victim and his companion to be offered. See *Com. v. Pring-Wilson*, 448 Mass 718, 735-737, 863 NE2d 936, 949-950 (2007).

> Commonwealth proved that the defendant did not act in self-defense when he killed the victim was who first grabbed the kitchen knife that ultimately was the instrument of death, not who shouted first or who struck the first punch, because the grabbing of the knife was the act that transformed a relatively harmless fight among roommates into a deadly altercation. Therefore, in cases like this one, *Adjutant* evidence cannot serve its intended purpose if it is admissible only to help the fact finder determine who initially provoked the altercation rather than who unreasonably escalated it by initiating the use or threat of deadly force. While *Adjutant* evidence is clearly admissible in many cases to help determine who initiated or provoked a nondeadly assault, particularly in cases where no deadly force was ever threatened or used, it is equally admissible in homicide cases where, even if the initiator of the nondeadly assault is known, it is disputed whether the victim or the defendant was the first to use or threaten deadly force.[38]

Evidence of the victim's general reputation for violence, the form of evidence favored in federal and many state courts, remains inadmissible in Massachusetts unless known to defendant at the time.[39]

Where there are multiple aggressors, *Adjutant* may permit the admission of a third party's violent acts if he acted in concert with or to assist the victim.[40]

A defendant who intends to introduce evidence of the victim's specific acts of violence must provide timely notice to the court and the Commonwealth.[41] It is not necessary for the defendant himself to take the stand to offer either reputation or specific acts evidence regarding the victim. Other witnesses may testify to the victim's reputation and to the defendant's knowledge of that reputation,[42] or to the victim's prior acts of violence.[43]

---

[38] See *Com. v. Chambers*, 465 Mass 520, 529-530, 989 NE2d 483, 490-491 (2013).

[39] *Com. v. Adjutant*, 443 Mass at 664, 824 NE2d at 13.

[40] *Com. v. Camacho*, 472 Mass 587, 595-596, 36 NE3d 533, 542 (2015); *Com. v. Pring-Wilson*, supra, 448 Mass at 737, 863 NE2d at 950.

[41] *Com. v. Adjutant*, 443 Mass at 665-666, 824 NE2d at 14.

[42] See *Com. v. Edmonds*, 365 Mass 496, 501-502, 313 NE2d 429, 432-433 (1974).

[43] See *Com. v. Adjutant*, supra, 443 Mass at 652-653, 824 NE2d at 5 (testimony of neighbors).

The Supreme Judicial Court has refused to expand admission of evidence of the victim's violent character beyond self-defense cases.[44] *Adjutant* is also inapplicable where it is uncontroverted that the victim was the first aggressor and the only contested issues are whether the defendant had the right to use deadly force and the opportunity to retreat.[45]

Once the defense has opened the door on the issue of the victim's violent character, the prosecution can rebut with evidence of the victim's "peaceful propensities."[46] Such evidence may not, however, be admitted unless and until the defense presents some evidence of the victim's violent character.[47] An opening statement by the defense attorney is not evidence and thus does not constitute opening the door on the issue of the victim's character.[48]

Where defendant raising a claim of self-defense offers evidence of prior violent acts by the alleged victim on the issue of who was the first aggressor, the Commonwealth may respond with evidence of prior violent acts of the defendant. But the Commonwealth may do so only if it had provided defendant with sufficient advance notice of its intent (to permit defendant to make an informed decision whether to go forward with the *Adjutant* evidence), and the trial judge determines the evidence is more probative than prejudicial. If such evidence is

---

[44] See *Com. v. Benoit*, 452 Mass 212, 227-228, 892 NE2d 314, 327-328 (2008) (declining to extend *Adjutant* to defense of provocation or sudden passion); *Com. v. Benjamin*, 430 Mass 673, 679, 722 NE2d 953, 958 (2000) (mental impairment defense). But see *Com. v. Sok*, 439 Mass 428, 434, 788 NE2d 941, 947 (2003) (assuming without deciding that same principles apply where defense theory is that killing occurred in heat of passion).

[45] *Com. v. Camacho*, supra, 472 Mass at 591-596, 36 NE3d at 538-542 (*Adjutant* was not applicable because there was no dispute at trial, given surveillance footage, as to who started the chain of events leading to the victim's death, or who escalated the encounter to deadly force, but only whether defendant was legally entitled to use the force he did in defense of his fellow gang member; and since the victim played no part during the melee, evidence of his past violent acts were properly excluded); *Com. v. Gaynor*, 73 Mass App 71, 73-76, 895 NE2d 758, 761-763 (2008).

[46] *Com. v. Adjutant*, supra, 443 Mass at 666 n.19, 824 NE2d at 14 n.19. See also *Com. v. Lapointe*, 402 Mass 321, 325, 522 NE2d 937, 939-940 (1988) (reputation for peacefulness admissible to rebut defense showing of victim's violent character).

Adjutant left open the question of whether the Commonwealth may also rebut with evidence of prior violent acts initiated by the defendant, observing that Fed R Evid 404(a) has been amended to provide for the admission of evidence of defendant's violent character once he attacks the character of the victim. 443 Mass at 666 n.19, 824 NE2d at 14 n.19.

[47] *Com. v. Williams*, 450 Mass 879, 887, 883 NE2d 249, 256 (2008).

[48] *Com. v. Lapointe*, supra, 402 Mass at 325, 522 NE2d at 939-940.

admitted, the trial judge must instruct the jury specifically on the limited use of the evidence, both contemporaneously with the introduction of the evidence and at the end of the trial.[49]

b. "Rape Shield" Statute

A second situation where the character of the victim was once deemed relevant to the accused's guilt is in rape and sexual assault cases in which the defense is consent. Massachusetts (like most jurisdictions) permitted the defendant to offer evidence of the unchaste character of the victim to support such a defense.[50]

Since 1977, however, the matter has been controlled by a "rape shield" law. Aimed at eliminating a common defense strategy of trying the complaining witness rather than the defendant, which resulted in "further humiliation of the victim as well as discouraging victims of rape from reporting the crimes to law enforcement authorities,"[51] GL 233, § 21B provides:

> Evidence of the reputation of a victim's sexual conduct shall not be admissible in any investigation or proceeding before a grand jury or any court of the Commonwealth for a violation of sections thirteen B, thirteen F, thirteen H, twenty-two, twenty-two A, twenty-three, twenty-four and twenty-four B of chapter two hundred and sixty-five or section five of chapter two hundred and seventy-two [indecent assault and battery on child under fourteen; indecent assault and battery on mentally retarded person; indecent assault and battery on person fourteen or older; rape; rape of a child; assault with intent to commit rape; assault of a child with intent to commit rape]. Evidence of specific instances of a victim's sexual conduct in such an investigation or proceeding shall not be admissible except evidence of the victim's sexual conduct with the defendant or evidence of recent conduct of the victim alleged to be the cause of any physical feature, characteristic, or condition of the victim; provided, however, that such evidence shall be admissible only after an in camera hearing on a written motion for admission of same and an offer of proof. If, after said hearing, the court finds that the weight and relevancy of said evidence is sufficient to outweigh its prejudicial effect

[49] See generally *Com. v. Morales*, 464 Mass 302, 982 NE2d 1105 (2013).
[50] See *Com. v. Gouveia*, 371 Mass 566, 569, 358 NE2d 1001, 1003-1004 (1976).
[51] *Com. v. Joyce*, 382 Mass 222, 228, 415 NE2d 181, 186 (1981).

to the victim, the evidence shall be admitted; otherwise not. If the proceeding is a trial with jury, said hearing shall be held in the absence of the jury. The finding of the court shall be in writing and filed but shall not be made available to the jury.[52]

Evidence of the victim's reputation for promiscuity, as well as specific acts of "sexual conduct,"[53] are excluded because such evidence "tends to put the witness on trial, it can be highly prejudicial to the prosecution, it tends to encourage litigation of collateral matters, and it has little probative value on the issue of consent."[54] The victim's consent to intercourse with one man is clearly of no relevance as to the issue of consent with another.[55] Moreover, Massachusetts does not recognize a reasonable good faith belief in the victim's consent as a defense to rape.[56]

---

[52] Apart from the rape shield statute, a defendant would have the right to introduce evidence concerning his state of mind tending to disprove the criminal act, including evidence of victim's past sexual conduct. *Com. v. Thevenin*, 33 Mass App 588, 591, 603 NE2d 222, 225 (1992). Fed R Evid 412 similarly excludes evidence of the victim's "sexual predisposition" as well as instances of "other sexual behavior," and permits evidence of specific acts of sexual conduct with the accused offered to prove consent and with others when offered to prove that someone "other than the accused was the source of semen, injury, or other physical evidence." For an extensive discussion of the Massachusetts statute, see *Com. v. Harris*, 443 Mass 714, 825 NE2d 58 (2005).

[53] The term is not defined in § 21B, and the Court has not addressed whether an offer of sex constitutes "sexual conduct" under the statute. *Com. v. Parent*, 465 Mass 395, 404-405, 989 NE2d 426, 434-435 (2013) (victim's offer, over cell phone, to perform oral sex, overheard on night of alleged assault).

[54] *Com. v. Simcock*, 31 Mass App 184, 197-198, 575 NE2d 1137, 1144-1145 (1991). See, e.g., *Com. v. Mendez*, 77 Mass App 253, 929 NE2d 975 (2010) (testimony that victim was "flirtatious with a lot of people" and "made advances" to bartender on several occasions was in contravention of the statute and should have been excluded); *Com. v. McGregor*, 39 Mass App 919, 655 NE2d 1278 (1995) (evidence that male rape victim had previously engaged in homosexual activities and that defendant, based on what he had been told concerning victim's sexuality, had good faith belief that victim consented to intercourse, was not admissible).

[55] *Com. v. Gentile*, 437 Mass 569, 583, 773 NE2d 428, 440 (2002) (& citations). See also *Com. v. Harris*, supra, 443 Mass at 722, 825 NE2d at 65. The same logic was applied to deny sex trafficking defendants the opportunity to question a victim about her past history of prostitution designed to show she consented to their malfeasance. *Com. v. McGhee*, 472 Mass 405, 426-427, 35 NE3d 329, 347-348 (2015). For further discussion of GL 233, § 21B, see Burnim, Massachusetts Rape Shield Law—An Overstep in the Right Direction, 64 Mass L Rev 61 (1979).

[56] *Com. v. Simcock*, supra, 31 Mass App at 192, 575 NE2d 1142. Compare *Doe v. United States*, 666 F2d 43 (4th Cir 1981) (defendant may support defense of reasonable mistake by offering evidence of what he had had previously heard about victim's specific sex acts and reputation for promiscuity).

The statutory exceptions authorize admission of evidence of specific acts of sexual conduct by the victim in two contexts:

- Where the prior acts were with the defendant.
- Where the acts are offered to explain the victim's physical condition subsequent to the alleged crime, such as the presence of semen or bruises in the vaginal area.

The victim's prior acts of intercourse with the defendant may be relevant to the issue of consent, particularly if there is a pattern of recent consensual activity.[57] Prior acts with another person may be relevant to establishing an alternative cause for the victim's physical condition.[58] Lack of virginity is not generally deemed a "condition" under the latter exception. "Normally, lack of virginity cannot be linked to the time of the rape, nor can the identity of the sexual partner be determined from this physical characteristic. Evidence of lack of virginity is unlike evidence of the presence of sperm, bruises in the vaginal area, and other data that are more relevant to the proof of rape. Since lack of virginity has such a tenuous connection to most rape cases, it ordinarily should not be admitted."[59] Similarly, evidence of the victim's pregnancy is generally inadmissible.[60]

Specific act evidence is admissible under the exceptions in GL 233, § 21B only after a written motion for admission, an offer of proof, and an in camera hearing[61] in which the judge determines (and makes

---

[57] See, e.g., *Com. v. Grieco*, 386 Mass 484, 436 NE2d 167 (1982). Compare *Com. v. Fionda*, 33 Mass App 316, 321-322, 599 NE2d 635, 638-639 (1992) (provocative conversation and kissing on prior occasion was not probative of consent to intercourse on later occasion).

[58] See, e.g., *Com. v. Fitzgerald*, 412 Mass 516, 590 NE2d 1151 (1992) (citing Text) (presence of sperm, where defendant had had vasectomy); *Com. v. Cardoza*, 29 Mass App 645, 647-648, 563 NE2d 1384, 1386-1387 (1990) (presence of foreign pubic hair not belonging to defendant). Compare *Com. v. Martin*, 424 Mass 301, 312-313, 676 NE2d 451, 458-459 (1997) (testimony that victim was with another man on night of rape was properly excluded where no particularity as to time-frame or identity of man).

[59] *Com. v. Elder*, 389 Mass 743, 753, 452 NE2d 1104, 1111 (1983).

[60] *Com. v. Quinn*, 469 Mass 641, 650-651, 15 NE3d 726, 734 (2014) (& citations).

[61] The Supreme Judicial Court has recently held that the public trial right attaches to rape shield hearings, but explaining that a major change in practice is not contemplated because the overriding interest in protecting the privacy of the victim will usually mean that the majority of these proceedings are properly closed. The ruling "simply means that, in view of the importance of the public trial right, before the court room properly may be closed during a rape shield procedure, the trial judge must conduct an individualized analysis consistent with" constitutional requirements. *Com. v. Jones*, 472 Mass 707, 729, 37 NE3d 589, 607 (2015).

a finding in writing) that the prejudicial effect to the victim is outweighed by the probative value of the evidence.[62] Failure to comply with these requirements is "no trifling procedural omission; the sharply limited exception to the rape shield statute is not to be made available on the basis of surprise and snap reaction by a trial judge."[63]

When a defendant seeks to admit evidence under one of the statutory exceptions, he must have a demonstrable good faith basis for asking any question even remotely connected with complainant's sexual conduct;[64] and he must make a preliminary showing that the theory under which he proceeds is based on more than mere hope or speculation.[65]

Where the proponent of evidence of prior sexual conduct is not seeking to use it for a purpose forbidden by the statute—i.e., to attack the victim's credibility by depicting her as promiscuous—the offer may fall outside the scope of the statute. Thus, for example, GL 233, § 21B did not require exclusion of evidence that complainant had previously been raped when offered to show that resulting psychiatric problems and similarities to the present incident rendered her unable to distinguish between the two situations.[66]

The case law has further recognized the following situations where such specific act evidence may be used to impeach a complainant:

- Where the evidence suggests bias or motive to fabricate.
- Where the evidence explains a child victim's age-inappropriate knowledge of sexual matters.

---

[62] See *Com. v. Grieco*, supra, 386 Mass at 488-489, 436 NE2d at 170-171; *Com. v. Cortez*, 438 Mass 123, 129, 777 NE2d 1254, 1259 (2002).

[63] *Com. v. Gauthier*, 32 Mass App 130, 133, 586 NE2d 34 (1992).

[64] *Com. v. Mosby*, 11 Mass App 1, 413 NE2d 754 (1980).

[65] See *Com. v. Chretien*, 383 Mass 123, 138, 417 NE2d 1203, 1210 (1981) (judge properly refused to permit defendant to question victim in front of jury regarding her sexual activities with other men, for purpose of explaining the presence of semen when victim categorically denied she had had any contacts with other men for one week prior to event); *Com. v. Hynes*, 40 Mass App 927, 929, 664 NE2d 864, 867 (1996) (no evidence to support defendant's contention that victim confused incidents of abuse by third party). See also *Com. v. Cameron*, 69 Mass App 741, 746-747, 871 NE2d 1096, 1101 (2007) (defendant was not entitled to cross-examine victim regarding her prior sexual acts where he made no attempt to pursue the questioning at voir dire of victim).

[66] *Com. v. Baxter*, 36 Mass App 45, 51, 627 NE2d 487, 491 (1994). But compare *Com. v. Syrafos*, 38 Mass App 211, 217-219, 646 NE2d 429, 433 (1994) (*Baxter* distinguishable because the two prior rapes here were not similar to one being tried and there was no evidence of psychological connections).

- Where the evidence demonstrates that the victim has made prior false allegations of rape or abuse.
- Where the evidence is necessary to defendant's constitutional right to present a defense.

Bias or Motive to Fabricate. Specific instances of a complainant's sexual conduct may be admissible to demonstrate her bias or motive to fabricate.[67] In *Com. v. Joyce*,[68] for example, defendant unsuccessfully sought to introduce evidence that the rape complainant had been charged with prostitution on two prior occasions; his purpose was to show that her allegation against him may have been motivated by a desire to avoid further prosecution. Emphasizing that it was not departing from the statute's general rule that evidence of prostitution or lack of chastity is inadmissible, the court held: "Where, however, such facts are relevant to a showing of bias or motive to lie, the general evidentiary rule of exclusion must give way to the constitutionally based right of effective cross-examination."[69] The Court has confirmed the trial judge's discretion to permit impeachment of a sexual assault complainant by showing a prior conviction for prostitution.[70]

Another permissible form this impeachment may take is demonstrating that the victim's sexual relationship with a third party suggests a motive to fabricate a rape accusation. Defense counsel in *Com. v. Stockhammer*[71] was held entitled to question the complainant about her intimate relationship with her boyfriend to demonstrate reasons for falsely accusing defendant (whose defense was consent), i.e., to avoid alienating her boyfriend and to prevent her parents from learning she was sexually active.[72]

---

[67] For a general discussion of these modes of impeachment, see § 6.5, infra.

[68] 382 Mass 222, 415 NE2d 181 (1981).

[69] 382 Mass at 231, 415 NE2d at 187.

[70] See *Com. v. Harris*, 443 Mass 714, 726, 825 NE2d 58, 68 (2005). The judge must determine that the probative value of the conviction for purposes of impeaching the complainant outweighs the prejudice to the Commonwealth and the complainant. *Id. Harris* thus holds that the rape shield statute does not override GL 233, § 21 (see § 6.16.2, infra), permitting impeachment by way of prior convictions, resolving the issue left open in *Com. v. Houston*, 430 Mass 616, 625-626, 722 NE2d 942, 948 (2000) (where no showing that evidence was relevant to bias or motive to lie, victim's prior conviction for prostitution-related offenses was properly excluded). See also *Com. v. Noj*, 76 Mass App 194, 198-199, 920 NE2d 894, 897-898 (2010) (victim's prior convictions for prostitution were not admissible to show motive to lie because their marginal relevance was outweighed by prejudicial effect).

[71] 409 Mass 867, 873-880, 570 NE2d 992, 996-1001 (1991).

[72] See generally *Com. v. Shaw*, 29 Mass App 39, 43, 556 NE2d 1058, 1060 (1990). See also *Com. v. McGregor*, supra, 39 Mass App 919, 655 NE2d 1278 (exclusion of prior

Given the clear potential prejudicial effect on the victim as well as the Commonwealth's case, judges must assure that there is a plausible showing of bias or motive to fabricate, and that the probative value of the evidence of the victim's sexual conduct outweighs the risk.[73]

Child Victim's Age-Inappropriate Knowledge. In prosecutions for rape or indecent assault on a child, prior sexual abuse of the victim may be admissible (with proper instructions to the jury) to show knowledge about sexual acts and terminology apart from any experience with the defendant.[74] The defendant must have a good faith basis for the inquiry, upon which showing the judge should permit voir dire to determine whether the child has been a victim of prior sexual abuse that is factually similar to the abuse in the case on trial.[75]

---

statements by victim of homosexual prison rape that could have shown motive to lie created substantial risk of miscarriage of justice). Compare *Com. v. Mountry*, 463 Mass 80, 86-88, 972 NE2d 438, 444-445 (2012) (evidence of 16-year-old victim's prior sexual conduct with her boyfriend was not admissible on issue of her motive to fabricate, where she had not made any effort to conceal her relationship with him); *Com. v. Pearce*, 427 Mass 642, 647-648, 695 NE2d 1059, 1063-1064 (1998) (relevance of evidence that victim had been previously molested and raped, offered to demonstrate bias, was outweighed by prejudicial effect to victim); *Com. v. Elder*, 389 Mass 743, 749-751, 452 NE2d 1104, 1109-1110 (1983) (evidence of complainant's prior sexual conduct was inadmissible where defendant was able to elicit evidence of hostility and bias without the proffered evidence); *Com. v. Sa*, 58 Mass App 420, 423-427, 790 NE2d 733, 736-738 (2003) (evidence that victim had sexual intercourse with boyfriend soon after rape not admissible, as defendant's theory that a woman traumatized by rape would not have done that was speculative); *Com. v. Gagnon*, 45 Mass App 584, 587-589, 699 NE2d 1260, 1263-1264 (1998) (same); *Com. v. Herrick*, 39 Mass App 291, 294-295, 655 NE2d 637, 639-640 (1995) (by merely offering at voir dire that victim was romantically involved with third party, defendant failed to make plausible showing of motive to lie).

[73] *Com. v. Parent*, 465 Mass 395, 405-406, 989 NE2d 426, 435-436 (2013). See also *Com. v. Sealy*, 467 Mass 617, 622-625, 6 NE3d 1052, 1057-1058 (2014) (judge properly excluded evidence of prior sexual assault on victim proffered by defendant as evidence of motive to lie regarding her immigration status); *Com. v. Quinn*, 83 Mass App 759, 706-707, 989 NE2d 901, 906 (2013) (judge properly excluded evidence that rape victim was pregnant when she first disclosed sexual abuse).

[74] See *Com. v. Ruffen*, 399 Mass 811, 814-816, 507 NE2d 684, 686-688 (1987). See also *Com. v. Owen*, 57 Mass 538, 784 NE2d 660 (2003) (trial counsel's failure to pursue motion in limine to admit child victim's prior exposure to sexual abuse constituted ineffective assistance of counsel). But compare *Com. v. Pyne*, supra, 35 Mass App at 37-38 (no abuse of discretion in excluding evidence of prior sexual experiences of alleged statutory rape victim to show alternative source of knowledge of sexual matters where victim's testimony did not display knowledge extraordinary for teenage boy); *Com. v. Rathburn*, 26 Mass App 699, 706-708, 532 NE2d 691, 695-697 (1988) (trial judge found that the sexual acts involved in the prior case were not similar).

[75] See *Com. v. Walker*, 426 Mass 301, 306, 687 NE2d 1246, 1250 (1997) (& citations) (insufficient foundation to require voir dire); *Com. v. Scheffer*, 43 Mass App 398, 683 NE2d 1043 (1997).

Where the prosecution offers evidence of a victim's age-inappropriate sexual knowledge for the purpose of supporting an inference of sexual abuse, the defendant is entitled (provided there is an appropriate foundation) to demonstrate the existence of alternative sources of such knowledge, including prior instances of abuse. But in order to avoid the effective shifting of the burden of persuasion onto the defendant, Massachusetts does not impute any conclusive presumption of sexual innocence to child victims that would impose on defendant a burden of rebuttal. Nor may a prosecutor rely on any such presumption in closing argument. The prosecutor may suggest that an *inference* of abuse by defendant may be raised from age-inappropriate sexual knowledge, but only with a firm evidentiary basis to support the inference, i.e., "there must be some record evidence indicating that a child victim's knowledge of sexual matters was, in fact, derived from the abuse charged, and not from some other source."[76]

Prior False Allegations of Rape or Abuse. Evidence of prior false allegations of rape is another matter that falls outside the coverage of GL 233, § 21B, and thus may be used to impeach a complainant.[77] Where there is evidence the complainant at another time has made false accusations of sexual assault, suggesting a motive to lie, defendant is entitled under the Sixth Amendment Confrontation Clause to explore the accusations on cross-examination.[78]

Such allegations may be admitted only if there is evidence of falsity.[79] This cannot be shown by incompetent hearsay

---

[76] *Com. v. Beaudry*, 63 Mass App 488, 495-496, 826 NE2d 782, 788-789 (2005). See also § 3.5.6, supra.

[77] See *Com. v. Bohannon*, 376 Mass 90, 378 NE2d 987 (1978) (*Bohannon I*) (trial judge erred in excluding evidence of prior false accusations of rape made by complainant where her credibility as to consent was the critical issue in the case, her testimony was inconsistent and confused, and defendant made offer of proof indicating an independent factual basis for concluding the prior allegations were false).

[78] See *White v. Coplan*, 399 F3d 18 (1st Cir 2005).

[79] See *Com. v. Scanlon*, 412 Mass 664, 675-676, 592 NE2d 1279, 1285-1286 (1992) ("No evidence was proffered which would create a basis to conclude that any prior accusation was made falsely. A mere hope of recantation is not a justification for a fishing expedition under the guise of the *Bohannon* rule."); *Com. v. Vieira*, 401 Mass 828, 838-839, 519 NE2d 1320, 1326-1327 (1988); *Com. v. McDonough*, 400 Mass 639, 650, 511 NE2d 551, 558 (1987). See also *Com. v. Pyne*, supra, 35 Mass App at 38-41 (trial court abused discretion by denying defense counsel's request for brief continuance or leave to conduct voir dire to determine whether alleged statutory rape victim had falsely accused another woman of sexual abuse). Cf. *Com. v. Clayton*, 52 Mass App 198, 200-203, 752 NE2d 788, 790-791 (2001) (exclusion of evidence that victim had been previously abused by her father, complained about it to her mother, and that her

evidence.[80] There must be a basis in "independent third-party records" for concluding that the prior accusations were made and were false.[81] Evidence that the victim failed to pursue the prior accusation is not evidence that it was falsely made.[82] Nor is the circumstance that authorities did not pursue the case sufficient basis for inferring falsity.[83]

The *Bohannon* exception has been held to apply even though the false allegations were made *after* the complaint against defendant.[84]

The Court has consistently emphasized that *Bohannon* is a narrow exception applicable in "special circumstances."[85] The Commonwealth is under no obligation to seek information on behalf of the defendant concerning previously reported sexual assaults.[86] Nor is defendant entitled to discovery of information pertaining to possible false allegations merely upon an unsupported assertion that they had been made.[87]

Necessary to Defendant's Constitutional Right to Present a Defense. In certain instances, exclusion of evidence falling within the prohibitions of GL 233, § 21B has been found to conflict impermissibly with the defendant's constitutional right to present a full defense.[88] In

---

mother took action, offered by defense to rebut victim's explanation for delay in reporting defendant's offense, constituted prejudicial error).

[80] *Com. v. Bohannon*, 385 Mass 733, 749-752, 434 NE2d 163, 172-174 (1982) (*Bohannon II*); *Com. v. Savage*, 51 Mass App 500, 503-504, 746 NE2d 1029, 1033 (2001).

[81] *Com. v. Fruchtman*, 418 Mass 8, 17-18, 633 NE2d 369, 374 (1994); *Com. v. Hrycenko*, 417 Mass 309, 319, 630 NE2d 258, 264 (1994).

[82] *Com. v. Hrycenko*, supra.

[83] *Com. v. Wise*, 39 Mass App 922, 923, 655 NE2d 643, 645 (1995) ("To open the gate to cross-examination, the evidence of falsity of an accusation must be solid, as when the accusing witness has recanted the other allegation."); *Com. v. Costa*, 69 Mass App 823, 831, 872 NE2d 750, 756 (2007) (neither victim's failure to prosecute nor Commonwealth's decision not to move forward with criminal charges are sufficient to establish falsity).

[84] *Com. v. Wise*, supra, 39 Mass App at 922, 655 NE2d at 645.

[85] *Com. v. Talbot*, 444 Mass 586, 590-591, 830 NE2d 177, 181 (2005); *Com. v. Sperrazza*, 379 Mass 166, 169, 396 NE2d 449, 451 (1979). See also *Com. v. Haynes*, 45 Mass App 192, 199-201, 696 NE2d 555, 560-561 (1998) (prior accusation was not part of pattern; complainant's testimony was neither inconsistent nor confused); *Com. v. LaVelle*, 414 Mass 146, 151-152, 605 NE2d 852, 855-856 (1993) (exception not applicable to informer's false accusation of threats); *Com. v. Rathburn*, supra, 26 Mass App 699, 532 NE2d 691.

[86] See *Com. v. Beal*, 429 Mass 530, 533 n.2, 709 NE2d 413, 416 n.2 (1999).

[87] *Com. v. Brescia*, 61 Mass App 908, 810 NE2d 842 (2004).

[88] The federal rape shield rule explicitly excepts from its prohibitions "evidence the exclusion of which would violate the constitutional rights of the defendant." FRE 412(b)(1)(C).

Com. v. Thevenin, evidence that defendant had been told by friend that he had had intercourse with the victim and developed pubic lice as result was deemed highly relevant to the defense, although the court rejected "an open-ended exception for state-of-mind evidence concerning a defendant's fear of contacting a disease."[89] "Where the rape shield statute is in conflict with a defendant's constitutional right to present evidence that might lead the jury to find that a Commonwealth witness is lying or otherwise unreliable, the statutory prohibition must give way to the constitutional right."[90]

Although GL 233, § 21B does not by its terms apply to criminal proceedings for all sexual offenses, evidence relating to the complainant's prior sexual activity has been held excludable under common-law principles. "At common law, evidence of the prior sexual conduct of the victim with persons other than the defendant is inadmissible for the purpose of impeaching the victim's credibility. Prior unrelated instances of sexual conduct also are inadmissible for the purpose of proving consent to intercourse with the defendant. These evidentiary principles have been applied not only to charges of rape, but also to charges of assault and battery, sodomy, and unnatural and lascivious acts. They reflect a judicial determination that prior sexual acts are simply not relevant to the victim's trustworthiness, or to consent to sexual activity on a particular occasion."[91]

Finally, it should be noted that GL 233, § 21B does not come into play if the evidence offered fails to meet the threshold standard of relevance. Evidence that the victim was taking birth control pills, for example, was properly excluded as irrelevant without regard to the applicability of the rape shield statute.[92]

For the use by defendant of evidence regarding the victim's provocative clothing, speech, or conduct in a civil action alleging sexual harassment and hostile work environment, see *Dahms v. Cognex Corp.*, 455 Mass 190, 199-202, 914 NE2d 872, 880-882 (2009).

---

[89] 33 Mass App 588, 591, 603 NE2d 222, 225 (1992).

[90] *Com. v. Polk*, 462 Mass 23, 37-39, 965 NE2d 815 (2012) (defendant should have been permitted to admit evidence of victim's sexual abuse by her uncles to demonstrate the significant possibility that she suffered from dissociative memory and confabulated her memory of defendant's alleged assaults).

[91] See *Com. v. Domaingue*, 397 Mass 693, 698-699, 493 NE2d 841, 845 (1986) (incest).

[92] *Com. v. Chretien*, 383 Mass 123, 136, 417 NE2d 1203, 1211 (1981).

§ 4.4.4 Form of Character Evidence/Reputation

Where character evidence is admissible, it generally must be offered in the form of reputation. Thus, the only permissible form of evidence that may be offered by the criminal defendant regarding his own character, or the prosecution in rebuttal (see § 4.4.2, supra), is testimony about his reputation.[93] The character witness must testify as to the composite opinion of the defendant held by those likely to have observed a representative sample of his conduct. Evidence in the form of either private opinions or specific acts is not admissible for this purpose:[94]

> The principal reason for precluding proof of character by evidence of specific acts is that a multiplicity of issues would be raised if specific acts, covering perhaps a lifetime, could be shown. It might be necessary to go into the circumstances attending each act before it could be determined what its nature was, and what effect should be given to it. It would be impossible for the opposing party to be prepared to meet evidence upon matters in regard to which he had no notice, and great injustice might be done by hearing biased and false testimony to which no answer could be made.[95]

The case law rejection of character evidence in opinion form contrasts with Proposed Mass R Evid 405(a) and Fed R Evid 405(a), which provide: "In all cases in which evidence of character or a trait of character of a person is admissible, proof may be made by testimony as to reputation *or by testimony in the form of an opinion* (emphasis added)." The Supreme Judicial Court has explicitly refused to adopt Proposed Mass R Evid 405(a), observing that "[i]t is difficult to see how testimony from a multitude of witnesses, each expressing his or her personal opinion of the defendant's character, would assist a jury. Personal opinions, without more, simply cannot substantiate a defendant's good character."[96]

The reputation may be either in one's community or among his business associates. GL 233, § 21A provides:

---

[93] *Com. v. Roberts*, 378 Mass 116, 129, 389 NE2d 989, 997 (1979).

[94] *Com. v. Roberts*, supra, 378 Mass at 129, 389 NE2d at 997; *Com. v. Belton*, 352 Mass 263, 269, 225 NE2d 53, 57 (1967) (recognizing, however, that the "distinction between general reputation and individual opinions often is difficult to determine.").

[95] *Miller v. Curtis*, 158 Mass 127, 131, 32 NE 1039, 1040 (1893).

[96] *Com. v. Walker*, 442 Mass 185, 197-199, 812 NE2d 262, 273-274 (2004).

> Evidence of the reputation of a person in a group with the members of which he has habitually associated in his work or business shall be admissible to the same extent and subject to the same limitations as is evidence of such reputation in a community in which he has resided.[97]

A trial judge may exclude reputation evidence if a proper foundation is lacking for the testimony.[98] A character witness may be cross-examined as to the witness's knowledge of a specific instance of conduct inconsistent with the reputation vouched for. See § 4.4.2, supra.

For discussion of the use of reputation evidence to impeach or rehabilitate a witness, see § 6.16.1, infra.

§ 4.4.5 Character Evidence in Civil Cases

As noted in § 4.4.1, evidence of the character of either party to a civil action is generally inadmissible. "The fact that a person's habits or character are such that he would be apt to do an act is not competent evidence that he did the act."[99] The right of a criminal defendant to offer character testimony (see § 4.4.2) does not apply in civil actions, even if the civil action is one for which a criminal prosecution might have been brought (in which case character evidence would be admissible when offered by the accused) or where the offense set up in justification involves a crime.[100]

---

[97] See also *United States v. Mandel*, 591 F2d 1347, 1370 (4th Cir 1979) ("the realities of our modern, mobile, impersonal society should also recognize that a witness may have a reputation for truth and veracity in the community in which he works and may have impressed on others in that community his character for truthfulness or untruthfulness.").

On the reputation of a business, see GL 108A, § 35(2) (b) and *Warner v. Modano*, 340 Mass 439, 444, 164 NE2d 904, 907 (1960) (business reputation of a partnership is its standing in the business community).

[98] See, e.g., *Com. v. Gomes*, 11 Mass App 933, 416 NE2d 551 (1981) (character witness who had known subject for just two years and spoken of her with just five other persons did not have a sufficient basis to offer reputation evidence).

[99] *Cucchiara v. Settino*, 328 Mass 116, 117-118, 102 NE2d 430 (1951). See also *Brennan v. Bongiorno*, 304 Mass 476, 477, 23 NE2d 1007 (1939) (evidence that defendant's employee, alleged to have committed assault, had reputation as prize fighter, was improperly admitted); *Whitney v. Lynch*, 222 Mass 112, 109 NE 826 (1915) (in action for deceit, evidence of reputation of defendant for honesty and fair dealing was inadmissible).

[100] See *Davidson v. Massachusetts Casualty Ins. Co.*, 325 Mass 115, 122, 89 NE2d 201, 205 (1949) (evidence of plaintiff's good character is not admissible to rebut defense that he made false misrepresentations in application for insurance); *Stearns v.*

Character evidence (including proof of specific instances[101]) may be admissible where the character of a party is directly in issue, as in actions for:

- Malicious prosecution.[102]
- Libel or slander.[103]
- Child custody and adoption cases, on the issue of parental fitness.[104]

Certain statutes explicitly provide for the admission of character type evidence in civil proceedings. GL 139, § 9, for example, provides that "[f]or the purpose of proving the existence of [a] nuisance the general reputation of a place shall be admissible in evidence." Thus the general reputation of a lounge as a place where acts of prostitution occur is admissible on the issue of whether a nuisance exists.[105]

Long, 215 Mass 152, 155, 102 NE 326, 327 (1926). Fed R Evid 404(a) explicitly bars in civil actions character evidence of the type admissible in criminal cases.

[101] Proposed Mass R Evid 405(b), which tracks the federal rule, provides:

> **Specific instances of conduct**. In cases in which character or a trait of a [sic] character of a person is an essential element of a charge, claim, or defense, proof may also be made by specific instances of conduct.

[102] See *Clark v. Eastern Massachusetts Street Railway Co.*, 254 Mass 441, 442-443, 150 NE 184, 185 (1926) ("The ordinary rule, that the reputation of a party in a civil action is inadmissible, does not apply in actions for malicious prosecution of a criminal charge if it is known to the person responsible for the complaint."); *Lewis v. Goldman*, 241 Mass 577, 578, 136 NE 67, 67-68 (1922) (evidence of the plaintiff's good reputation, if known to the defendant, is relevant in proving absence of probable cause because "the same facts, which would raise a strong suspicion in the mind of a cautious and reasonable man, against a person of notoriously bad character for honesty and integrity, would make a slighter impression if they tended to throw a charge of guilty upon a man of good reputation.").

[103] Evidence of the plaintiff's good character is admissible on the issue of damages. It may also be admissible on the liability issue where the defamation involves an allegation of the commission of a crime by the plaintiff. See *Stearns v. Long*, supra, 215 Mass at 155, 102 NE at 327. The defendant may offer evidence of the plaintiff's poor reputation in those respects assailed by the alleged slander in mitigation of damages. *Clark v. Brown*, 116 Mass 504 (1875). The defendant may show that "the plaintiff's general reputation for integrity and moral worth was so bad that any damage done by the slander uttered by the defendant would be but nominal." *Hastings v. Stetson*, 130 Mass 76, 78 (1881).

[104] See *Care and Protection of Martha*, 407 Mass 319, 326 n.6, 553 NE2d 902, 906 n.6 (1990); *Adoption of Anton*, 72 Mass App 667, 673, 893 NE2d 436, 441 (2008).

[105] See *Com. v. United Food Corp.*, 374 Mass 765, 767-770, 374 NE2d 1331, 1336 (1978).

For the unique questions of admissibility of character evidence in proceedings under the "sexually dangerous person" statute, GL 123A, see *Com. v. Bladsa*, 362 Mass 539, 288 NE2d 813 (1972) and *In re Wyatt*, 428 Mass 347, 701 NE2d 337 (1998).

§ 4.4.6 *Specific Act Evidence for Non-Propensity Purposes*

Although inadmissible to prove conduct in conformity with a particular character trait (see § 4.4.1), evidence of specific acts may be admissible if probative for another purpose.[106] Where evidence of other crimes, wrongs, or acts is relevant in establishing motive, opportunity, intent, preparation, plan, knowledge, identity, absence of mistake or accident, or a particular way of doing an act or a particular skill, the evidence may be admitted if its probative value is not substantially outweighed by the risk of prejudice.[107]

Admission is justified on the theory that the evidence relates not to a general disposition to commit the crime or act in a particular way, but rather tends to prove other facts relevant to the issues in the case.[108] If, for example, the modus operandi of defendant's prior

---

[106] A sentencing judge may properly consider information concerning uncharged misconduct. See *Com. v. Goodwin*, 414 Mass 88, 605 NE2d 827 (1993) (& citations). While a defendant may not be punished for conduct other than that for which he stands convicted, Massachusetts decisions have recognized the relevance at sentencing of reliable evidence of defendant's prior misconduct. *Com. v. Junta*, 62 Mass App 120, 128-129, 815 NE2d 254, 261-262 (2004). Where the trial judge considers uncharged conduct, it must be demonstrated she did so only for a proper purpose, such as its bearing on defendant's amenability to rehabilitation. *Com. v. Wallace*, 76 Mass App 411, 419, 922 NE2d 834, 840-841 (2010). *Blakely v. Washington*, 542 US 296 (2004), holding that any fact that increases the penalty for a crime beyond the prescribed statutory maximum must be submitted to a jury and proved beyond a reasonable doubt, does not apply to the Massachusetts scheme of indeterminate sentences. *Com. v. Junta*, supra, 62 Mass App at 129, 815 NE2d at 262.

[107] Proposed Mass R Evid 404(b), which essentially tracks the federal rule and reflects Massachusetts practice, provides:

> (b) **Other crimes, wrongs, or acts**. Evidence of other crimes, wrongs, or acts is not admissible to prove the character of a person in order to show that he acted in conformity therewith. It may, however, be admissible for other purposes, such as proof of motive, opportunity, intent, preparation, plan, knowledge, identity, or absence of mistake or accident.

See also *Com. v. Fordham*, 417 Mass 10, 22, 627 NE2d 901, 908 (1994); *Com. v. Martino*, 412 Mass 267, 280, 588 NE2d 651, 659 (1992); *Com. v. Otsuki*, 411 Mass 218, 236, 581 NE2d 999, 1009-1010 (1991); *Com. v. Helfant*, 398 Mass 214, 224, 496 NE2d 433, 440-441 (1986).

[108] *Com. v. Trapp*, 396 Mass 202, 206, 485 NE2d 162, 165 (1985).

bank robbery functions as an identifying feature because it is so distinctive, it may be admitted to connect defendant to the charged bank robbery which shares the same M.O.[109] Similarly, evidence of defendant's uncharged drug dealing may be admissible to prove a motive to murder the victim, who stole defendant's drugs.[110]

A two-staged analysis is employed in determining the admissibility of prior bad act evidence in both state and federal court. The judge must initially determine whether the evidence is probative of a matter other than mere propensity to commit the crime or engage in the act, such as demonstrating knowledge, intent, motive, common scheme, or identity (distinctive modus operandi). If so, the judge must weigh its probative value against the danger of unfair prejudice.[111]

It has been observed that the Supreme Judicial Court "may have been more willing recently than in prior years to allow evidence of bad acts to be admitted to prove an element of a crime."[112] Indeed, "other bad act" evidence appears to be almost routinely admitted in both state and federal courts, notwithstanding the general prohibition, as proponents are able to make plausible arguments for relevance on a purpose other than propensity.

Given the distinct risk of undue prejudice, great caution must nonetheless be exercised in the admission of such evidence. As the Appeals Court has observed, "all cases where prior bad acts are offered invite consideration of the potency of this type of evidence, the risk that it may be misused, and the importance, in jury trials, of delivering careful limiting instructions."[113] The Supreme Judicial Court has similarly warned that the line between considering other crimes evidence for a legitimate purpose and using it impermissibly as propensity evidence "is indeed a thin one; the need for a judge to weigh the probative value of the evidence against its prejudicial potential is great."[114]

---

[109] See *Com. v. Jackson*, 428 Mass 455, 459-460, 702 NE2d 1158, 1162 (1998); *Com. v. Cordle*, 404 Mass 733, 537 NE2d 130 (1989); *Com. v. Kater (Kater VII)*, 432 Mass 404, 415-416, 734 NE2d 1164, 1176 (2000), *habeas petition denied in Kater v. Maloney*, 459 F3d 56 (1st Cir 2006) ("the abduction of Jacalyn Bussiere and the abduction of Mary Lou Arruda are strikingly similar. This is as close as a crime gets to being a signature crime.").

[110] See *Com. v. Gunter*, 427 Mass 259, 262-263, 692 NE2d 515, 519-520 (1997).

[111] See generally *Com. v. White*, 60 Mass App 193, 198-200, 800 NE2d 712, 716-718 (2003) (extensive discussion).

[112] *Com. v. Brusgulis*, 406 Mass 501, 505, 548 NE2d 1234, 1237 (1990).

[113] *Com. v. Gollman*, 51 Mass App 839, 845, 748 NE2d 1039, 1044 (2001), *rev'd on other grounds*, 436 Mass 111, 762 NE2d 847 (2002) (extensive discussion).

[114] *Com. v. Hamilton*, 459 Mass 422, 438, 945 NE2d 877, 889 (2011).

These considerations weigh equally in jury-waived as well as jury trials.[115]

If the probative value of the specific acts evidence is substantially outweighed by the danger of uncorrectable prejudice, the evidence should be excluded.[116] This determination is for the trial judge and will be overturned on appeal only upon a showing of abuse of discretion.[117] Because of the substantial risk of prejudice, "other crimes" evidence should be admitted only where it has substantial probative value.[118] The Commonwealth is not required to show the "need" for the evidence to establish admissibility.[119]

To be admissible, evidence of uncharged conduct must be related in time, place, and/or form to the charges being tried. There must be a sufficient nexus to render the conduct relevant and probative.[120]

---

[115] *Com. v. Jacobs*, 52 Mass App 38, 47, 750 NE2d 1028, 1035 (2001).

[116] *Com. v. Chalifoux*, 362 Mass 811, 816, 291 NE2d 635, 638-639 (1973). See, e.g., *Com. v. Dwyer*, 448 Mass 122, 127-129, 859 NE2d 400, 406-408 (2006) (probative value of testimony regarding seven uncharged acts of sexual abuse against victim was overwhelmed by unfair prejudice in rape prosecution); *Com. v. Montanino*, 409 Mass 500, 505-507, 567 NE2d 1212, 1215-1216 (1991) (reference to defendant's other sexual misconduct was not relevant and highly prejudicial); *Com. v. Emence*, 47 Mass App 299, 304-305, 713 NE2d 374, 378 (1999) (reversible error to admit testimony that assault and battery defendant committed similar offense while awaiting trial).

[117] *Com. v. Bly*, 448 Mass 473, 497-498, 862 NE2d 341, 361-362 (2007) (evidence concerning carjacking incident and intimidation of a witness was highly probative of why defendant wanted to kill assistant attorney general); *Com. v. Fordham*, 417 Mass 10, 22-23, 627 NE2d 901, 908 (1994); *Com. v. Robertson*, 408 Mass 747, 750, 563 NE2d 223, 225 (1990).

[118] *Com. v. Burke*, 339 Mass 521, 533-534, 159 NE2d 856, 864 (1959).

[119] *Com. v. Copney*, 468 Mass 405, 413, 11 NE3d 77, 84 (2014) (distinguishing *Old Chief v. United States*, 519 US 172, 182-183 (1997).

[120] *Com. v. Barrett*, 418 Mass 788, 794, 641 NE2d 1302, 1307 (1994). Compare *Com. v. Anderson*, 439 Mass 1007, 788 NE2d 951 (2003) (prior assaults too remote in time and form to be admitted), *Com. v. Yetz*, 37 Mass App 970, 643 NE2d 1062 (1995) (evidence of defendant's sexual abuse of another child improperly admitted where it occurred two years before alleged abuse of complainant and type of conduct was dissimilar), and *Com. v. Johnson*, 35 Mass App 211, 617 NE2d 1040 (1993) (alleged sexual touching occurring 40 months after alleged sexual offense was improperly admitted) with *Com. v. Jackson*, 417 Mass 830, 841-842, 633 NE2d 1031, 1037-1038 (1994) (two years between incidents, although near limit, not too great considering distinctiveness of incidents), *Com. v. Hanlon*, 44 Mass App 810, 819-820, 694 NE2d 358, 366-367 (1998) (abuse of altar boys over decade was admissible despite fact that last incident occurred nine years after last charged act), *Com. v. Scullin*, 44 Mass App 9, 15-16, 687 NE2d 1258, 1263 (1997) (gap of two and one-half years did not prevent admission of prior assault, given the two incidents were nearly identical), and *Com. v. Calcagno*, 31 Mass App 25, 27-28, 574 NE2d 420, 422 (1991) (defendant's abuse of victim going back eight years was probative to put single instance charged into context).

Evidence of bad acts close in time to the crime may render admissible earlier acts.[121] Such evidence may be admitted even if the acts occurred outside the Commonwealth.[122]

"There is no bright-line test for determining temporal remoteness of evidence of prior misconduct. Where the prior misconduct is merely one instance in a continuing course of related events, the allowable time period is greater. Where the logical relationship between the charged and the uncharged offenses is more attenuated, a time span of fifteen minutes may be too much."[123] The fact that the "bad acts" occurred after the event that is the subject of the pending charges is not in itself a bar to admission.[124]

Specific act evidence relevant for non-propensity purposes is not rendered inadmissible merely because it tends to prove the commission of other crimes.[125] As with any other evidence, there is no requirement that the prior bad acts be proved beyond a reasonable doubt.[126]

Incidents which resulted in an acquittal may not, under Article 12 of the Massachusetts Declaration of Rights, be admitted as other crimes evidence.[127]

Where evidence of prior bad acts is offered, it must of course be in the form of otherwise admissible evidence.[128] Before the evidence can

---

[121] See, e.g., *Com. v. Rosenthal*, 432 Mass 124, 127-129, 732 NE2d 278, 282 (2000), *habeas denied, Rosenthal v. O'Brien*, 814 F Supp 2d 39 (D Mass 2011) (evidence of defendant's hostility toward victim spouse made testimony concerning past violent acts admissible). See also *Com. v. Fickling*, 434 Mass 9, 15-16, 746 NE2d 475, 481 (2001) (prior incidents of violent conduct toward victim within fifteen months of murder).

[122] See *Com. v. Frank*, 51 Mass App 19, 23-24, 742 NE2d 586, 590 (2001) (& citations).

[123] *Com. v. Helfant*, 398 Mass 214, 228 n.13, 496 NE2d 433, 443 n.13 (1986). See also *Com. v. Kater (Kater VII)*, 432 Mass 404, 412-414, 734 NE2d 1164, 1174-1175 (2000), *habeas petition denied in Kater v. Maloney*, 459 F3d 56 (1st Cir 2006) ("Although the abduction of Jacalyn Bussiere occurred ten years before the abduction of Mary Lou Arruda, we agree with the judge that the length of time between the two crimes is not so temporally remote as to preclude admission of the earlier offense because Kater spent most of that ten-year period in prison.").

[124] *Com. v. Myer*, 38 Mass App 140, 143 n.2, 646 NE2d 155, 157 n.2 (1995).

[125] See *Com. v. Jackson*, 384 Mass 572, 577, 428 NE2d 289, 292 (1981); *Com. v. Titus*, 32 Mass App 216, 225, 587 NE2d 800, 805-806 (1992).

[126] *Com. v. Azar*, 32 Mass App 290, 309, 588 NE2d 1352, 1364 (1992).

[127] *Com. v. Dorazio*, 472 Mass 535, 540-548, 37 NE3d 566, 571-577 (2015) (declining to follow *Dowling v. United States*, 493 US 342, 348-349 (1990) and overturning *Com. v. Barboza*, 76 Mass App 241, 243, 921 NE2d 117, 119-120 (2010).

[128] See, e.g., *Com. v. Hubbard*, 45 Mass App 277, 697 NE2d 551 (1998) (prosecutor's references to prior assault incident required reversal because based on hearsay).

be admitted, the Commonwealth (or other proponent) must satisfy the judge that the jury could reasonably conclude that the act occurred and that the defendant was the actor; the proponent need only show these facts by a preponderance of the evidence.[129]

Prompt cautionary instructions to the jury are critical to protecting a defendant against prejudice where bad act evidence is admitted. The instructions should "offset any improper prejudicial effect of evidence that might be thought to show the defendant's bad character or propensity for violent acts" and should "focus the jury's attention on the proper application of the evidence."[130] The judge should carefully instruct the jury as to the limited admissibility of "other crimes" evidence as well as the need to connect up the other event with the defendant before the jury can consider it at all.[131]

The courts have recognized that bad act evidence, even when offered for a legitimate purpose, becomes "dangerously confusing to the triers of fact when piled on and unduly exaggerated."[132] Further caution is warranted when the charge is that the defendant aided in the commission of the crime or acted as an accessory before the fact; in such cases, the triers "may find it hard to distinguish between the uncharged acts and the real thing."[133]

---

[129] *Com. v. Leonard*, 428 Mass 782, 785-786, 705 NE2d 247, 250 (1999) (& citations). Compare *Com. v. LeClair*, 68 Mass App 482, 485-487, 862 NE2d 774, 778-779 (2007) (offer of proof was insufficient to support finding that coventurer committed robbery and that defendant was an actor in it).

[130] *Com. v. Morgan*, 460 Mass 277, 290, 951 NE2d 14, 24 (2011); *Com. v. Walker*, 442 Mass 185, 202-203, 812 NE2d 262, 277 (2004) (citing Text); *Com. v. McGeoghean*, 412 Mass 839, 842, 593 NE2d 229, 231 (1992). Compare *Com. v. Kent K.*, 427 Mass 754, 756-757, 696 NE2d 511, 514-515 (1998) (curative instruction adequately instructed jury to ignore testimony concerning mugshot of defendant) with *Com. v. Mills*, 47 Mass App 500, 506, 713 NE2d 1028, 1032 (1999) (reversal required when judge failed to give limiting instruction and suggested in response to jury question that they could give prior-act evidence whatever weight they deemed appropriate).

[131] *Com. v. Barbosa*, 457 Mass 773, 794-797, 933 NE2d 93, 113-114 (2010); *Com. v. Collins*, 26 Mass App 1021, 1022-1023, 533 NE2d 214, 215-216 (1989). Defendant must request the instruction, as there is no requirement that the judge give it sua sponte. *Com. v. Leonardi*, 413 Mass 757, 764, 604 NE2d 23, 28 (1992). *Com. v. Sullivan*, 436 Mass 799, 809, 768 NE2d 529, 537 (2002); *Com. v. Myer*, 38 Mass App 140, 145 n.3, 646 NE2d 155, 158 n.3 (1995).

[132] *Com. v. Mills*, supra, 47 Mass App at 505, 713 NE2d at 1031-1032 (& citations).

[133] *Id.* at 504, 713 NE2d at 1031.

The appropriateness of joinder of offenses for trial often turns on whether evidence of the other crimes would be admissible in a separate trial on each indictment.[134]

Evidence of other acts, crimes, or wrongs was held admissible as relevant to a non-propensity purpose in the following categories of cases:

Intent. *Com. v. Carlson*, 448 Mass 501, 508, 862 NE2d 363, 369 (2007) ("Although evidence of a prior bad act offered to show a defendant's intent at the time of a killing often involves an expression of an intent to kill, there is no requirement that the prior hostility be homicidal in any respect."); *Com. v. Sullivan*, 436 Mass 799, 809, 768 NE2d 529, 537 (2002) (defendant's statement "I like to rob jewelry stores; that's what I do" admissible as evidence of intent); *Com. v. Gollman*, 436 Mass 111, 113-115, 762 NE2d 847, 850-851 (2002) (evidence of defendant's prior drug sales relevant to his intent to distribute and to rebut inference that cocaine was for personal use); *Com. v. Donlan*, 436 Mass 329, 338-339, 764 NE2d 800, 807-808 (2002) (prior assault week before forcible rape relevant to intent and motive); *Com. v. Stroyny*, 435 Mass 635, 641-642, 760 NE2d 1202, 1208-1209 (2002) (previous acts of abuse toward murder victim); *Com. v. Marshall*, 434 Mass 358, 365-367, 749 NE2d 147, 154-155 (2001) (defendant's threats against victim); *Com. v. Ashman*, 430 Mass 736, 740-742, 723 NE2d 510, 514-515 (2000) (prior altercation between defendant and victim); *Com. v. Fallon*, 423 Mass 92, 668 NE2d 296 (1996) (evidence of defendant's incarceration for civil contempt for refusal to disclose location of victim's money relevant on issue of fraudulent intent); *Com. v. Helfant*, 398 Mass 214, 496 NE2d 433 (1986) (evidence that defendant doctor charged with rape had the year before sexually assaulted two women after injecting them with valium probative of defendant's illegal intent).

Knowledge. *Com. v. Ridge*, 455 Mass 307, 322, 916 NE2d 348, 362-363 (2009) (evidence of defendant's access to, and knowledge of, guns and bullets); *Com. v. Pearson*, 77 Mass App 95, 104, 928 NE2d 961, 968-969 (2010) (evidence linking credit card fraud defendant to theft of other cards in same building, to show knowledge that credit cards were stolen); *Com. v. Sullivan*, 76 Mass App 864, 869-870, 927 NE2d 519, 524-526 (2010) (informant's testimony regarding prior

---

[134] See *Com. v. Pillai*, 445 Mass 175, 180-181, 833 NE2d 1160, 1166-1168 (2005) (common pattern of sexual assaults); *Com. v. Gaynor*, 443 Mass 245, 260-263, 820 NE2d 233, 247-249 (2005).

purchases of cocaine from defendant relevant to establish nature of relationship between the two); *Com. v. Terminal Railway Co.*, 80 Mass App 22, 43-44, 951 NE2d 696, 713-714 (2011) (testimony that environmental consultant had had difficulty collecting payment from corporate defendants admissible to show knowledge of the proper procedure for reporting fuel release); *Com. v. Mullane*, 445 Mass 702, 708-709, 840 NE2d 484, 492-494 (2006) (testimony of police officer concerning prior investigation of defendant's massage business admissible to show his knowledge that prostitution was occurring); *Com. v. Stewart*, 411 Mass 345, 354, 582 NE2d 514, 520 (1991) (evidence that co-defendant shot cat prior to shooting of victim relevant to defendant's knowledge that co-defendant was armed); *Com. v. Cordle*, 404 Mass 733, 744, 537 NE2d 130, 137 (1989) (evidence of defendant's prior break-in into murder victim's home relevant to show knowledge of how to break into home). But compare *Com. v. Sapoznik*, 28 Mass App 236, 239-245, 549 NE2d 116, 118-123 (1990) (evidence of defendant's prior arrest on drug-related charge only minimally relevant to issue of knowledge and highly prejudicial).

Motive/State of Mind/Intent. *Com. v. Mazariego*, 474 Mass 42, 56, 47 NE3d 420, 432-433 (2016) (defendant's past history of bringing prostitutes to the crime area was relevant to show intent and absence of mistake); *Com. v. Hernandez*, 473 Mass 379, 393-394, 42 NE3d 1064, 1077 (2015) (evidence of armed robbery in which defendant unsuccessfully tried to use victim's debit card was relevant to show intent and motive when participating in a later home invasion); *Com. v. DaSilva*, 471 Mass 71, 79, 27 NE3d 383, 391 (2015) (evidence of prior shooting incident was relevant to defendant's motive of revenge); *Com. v. Forte*, 469 Mass 469, 480, 14 NE3d 900, 910 (2014) (prior instances of aggressive conduct by defendant within 16 hours preceding the murder were relevant to his state of mind); *Com. v. Howard*, 469 Mass 721, 739-740, 16 NE3d 1054, 1070-1071 (2014) (confrontation between defendant and victim three months prior to workplace shooting, and between defendant and another employee, were relevant to defendant's motive and state of mind); *Com. v. Gonzalez*, 469 Mass 410, 420-421, 14 NE3d 282, 291-292 (2014) evidence of victim's prior dissatisfaction with defendant's drinking suggested a motive for the killing); *Com. v. Riley*, 467 Mass 799, 825, 7 NE3d 1060, 1081 (2014) (murder defendant's prior abusive behavior toward his children bore on his state of mind regarding death of his four-year-old daughter); *Com. v. Tassinari*, 466 Mass 340, 346-349, 995 NE2d 42, 49-50 (2013) (testimony about violent incident regarding victim relevant to hostile relationship and motive for killing); *Com. v. Dung Van Tran,* 463 Mass 8, 14-15, 972 NE2d 1, 7-8 (2012) (testimony of defendant's estranged wife about defendant's physical and verbal abuse admissible to show his intent, motive, and rationale in setting fire); *Com. v. Cheremond*, 461 Mass 397, 406-410, 961 NE2d 97, 105-107 (2012) (evidence of defendant's prior abuse of murder victim, contained in her application for an abuse prevention order, admissible to show her state of mind negating consent to sexual intercourse with defendant); *Com. v. Walker*, 460 Mass 590, 612-613, 953 NE2d 195, 214 (2011) (evidence that defendant was involved in his gang's drug dealing provided the motive for his involvement in murder); *Com. v. Morgan*, 460 Mass 277, 288-290, 951 NE2d 14, 23-24 (2011) (defendant's prior bad acts of breaking into motor vehicles relevant to motive as it tended to show he needed money and went to extremes to get it); *Com. v. Hamilton*, 459 Mass 422, 437-438, 945 NE2d 877, 889 (2011) (evidence of defendant's prior convictions admissible in extortion prosecution on issue of whether the victim probation officers reasonably believed he would carry out the threats); *Com. v. Greindeder*, 458 Mass 207, 239-242, 936 NE2d 372, 397-398 (2010) (evidence of defendant's extramarital sexual activity relevant to motive to kill wife); *Com. v. Barbosa*, 457 Mass 773, 793-794, 933 NE2d 93, 112-113 (2010) (evidence that shooting victims had witnessed defendant shoot someone else two weeks before was relevant to motive); *Com. v. Sharpe*, 454 Mass 135, 143-145, 908 NE2d 376, 383-385 (2009) (evidence of defendant's physical abuse of former girlfriend seven years before murder of victim relevant to pattern of conduct, motive, intent, and to negate defendant's claim of sudden rage); *Com. v. LeBeau*, 451 Mass 244, 260-261, 884 NE2d 956, 969-970 (2008), *habeas denied, LeBeau v. Roden*, 806 F Supp 2d 384 (D Mass 2011) (evidence that defendant had been rejected by female bartender on night of the murder and owed a substantial amount in child support relevant to his state of mind); *Com. v. Thomas*, 448 Mass 180, 188, 859 NE2d 813, 819 (2007) (testimony about defendant's controlling nature and hostile relationship with victim probative to show pattern of conduct and that he acted intentionally when he killed victim); *Com. v. Swafford*, 441 Mass 329, 332, 805 NE2d 931, 934 (2004) (evidence of defendant's gang affiliation relevant to motive for murder); *Com. v. Bradshaw*, 86 Mass App 74, 78-79, 13 NE3d 638, 642-643 (2014) (defendant's statement to friend that he was attracted to young boys was relevant to his motive in prosecution for indecent assault and battery of child) (citing Text); *Com. v. Riley*, 84 Mass App 272, 284-285, 995

NE2d 823, 833 (2013) (evidence of defendant's scheme to secure psychiatric medication for her children was probative of her motive for giving them unnecessary medication); *Com. v. Berendson*, 73 Mass App 395, 398-399, 897 NE2d 1276, 1280 (2008) (evidence of prior rape the same day relevant to defendant's intent to rape second victim).

Compare *Com. v. Carriere*, 470 Mass 1, 18 NE3d 326 92014) (testimony concerning prior theft should not have been admitted as it was too remote in time to be probative of motive for the murder); *Com. v. Freeman*, 430 Mass 111, 115-117, 712 NE2d 1135, 1141 (1999) (general rule permitting evidence of motive does not apply when defendant seeks to support diminished-capacity claim);

Plan, Common Scheme, or Course of Conduct. *Com. v. Roby*, 462 Mass 398, 413-414, 969 NE2d 141, 155 (2012) (evidence regarding number of times defendant sexually touched each victim admissible to show common scheme and pattern); *Com. v. Walker*, 442 Mass 185, 201-203, 812 NE2d 262, 276-277 (2004) (evidence of uncharged incident involving another female acquaintance of defendant admissible to show common scheme); *Com. v. Source One Associates, Inc.*, 436 Mass 118, 128-130, 763 NE2d 42, 51-52 (2002) (evidence of telephone calls made outside of state and subsequent to period in issue admissible to show plan and modus operandi in civil enforcement action); *Com. v. Feijoo*, 419 Mass 486, 494-495, 646 NE2d 118, 124-125 (1995) (karate instructor's use of relationship to students relevant as modus operandi to induce submission to homosexual activity); *Com. v. Daggett*, 416 Mass 347, 349-352, 622 NE2d 272, 274 (1993) (evidence that defendant had been previously arrested for soliciting a prostitute at time when his log records indicated he was working at plant admissible in prosecution for murder of another prostitute when records again indicated defendant was at work, to show plan or scheme and opportunity to commit crime); *Com. v. Scott*, 408 Mass 811, 817-820, 564 NE2d 370, 375-377 (1990) (evidence of defendant's harassment of three women days before alleged murder probative of plan to procure a sexual encounter at the time of murder); *Com. v. King*, 387 Mass 464, 469-473, 441 NE2d 248, 251-253 (1982) (evidence that defendant had had similar sexual relations with sibling of victim probative of pattern of conduct) (citing Text); *Com. v. Torres*, 86 Mass App 272, 278, 15 NE3d 778, 784-785 (2014) (evidence that defendant had sexually abused his stepdaughter was relevant to show pattern or common scheme where stepdaughter and victim were of similar age, acts occurred in similar places, and there were other similarities) (citing Text); *Com. v. Clayton*, 63 Mass App 608, 614, 827 NE2d 1273, 1278

(2005) (pattern of sexual conduct with victim); *Com. v. Ramos*, 63 Mass App 379, 826 NE2d 245 (2005) (testimony of five noncomplainant witnesses describing similar inappropriate touching by doctor was admissible to show plan or pattern as well as absence of mistake); *Com. v. Boyer*, 52 Mass App 590, 596-597, 755 NE2d 767, 772 (2001) (prior attempt by attorney's assistant to bribe witness admissible against attorney in prosecution for bribery arising from two other cases);. *Com. v. Fleury-Ehrhart*, 20 Mass App 429, 430-432, 480 NE2d 661, 663 (1985) (at trial on indictment charging indecent assault and battery upon a patient, evidence that defendant doctor committed similar misconduct against two other female patients probative of common scheme, pattern of conduct, and absence of accident or mistake).

***Identity* /Modus Operandi.** *Com. v. Montez*, 450 Mass 736, 743-746, 881 NE2d 753, 761-762 (2008) (distinctiveness of prior housebreaks was probative of defendant's identity); *Com. v. Holliday*, 450 Mass 794, 815, 882 NE2d 309, 326-327 (2008) (evidence of subsequent shooting of gang members connected defendants to the murder weapon); *Com v. Leonard*, 428 Mass 782, 787-788, 705 NE2d 250, 251 (1999) (prior and current fires had meaningfully distinctive similarities); *Com. v. Jackson*, 428 Mass 455, 459-460, 702 NE2d 1158, 1162 (1998) (similar *modus operandi* to identify defendant); *Com. v. Jackson*, 417 Mass 830, 633 NE2d 1031 (1994) (prior incident involving "hog-tied" victim admissible in murder trial alleging similar means); *Com. v. Zagranski*, 408 Mass 278, 281, 558 NE2d 933, 935-936 (1990) (proposed scheme to purchase parcel of land and kill owner properly admitted to identify defendant as person who killed victim); *Com. v. Blackmer*, 77 Mass App 474, 480-482, 932 NE2d 301, 307-308 (2010) (evidence of defendant's other act of public masturbation only five days earlier and on same all-female college campus admissible to prove identity); *Com. v. Iguabita*, 69 Mass App 295, 299-301, 867 NE2d 783, 787-789 (2007) (defendant priest's sexual conduct with two other women at rectory showed modus operandi); *Com. v. Delong*, 60 Mass App 122, 129-130, 799 NE2d 1267, 1275-1276 (2003) (evidence of prior and subsequent robberies severed for trial admissible as showing distinctive pattern tending to identify perpetrator); *Com. v. Whiting*, 59 Mass App 104, 108-109, 794 NE2d 642, 645-646 (2003) (testimony by child complainants on severed sexual assault cases admissible to show modus operandi and absence of mistake).

Care must be taken to avoid treating the commonalties of certain crimes as sufficiently distinctive to constitute a signature. See *Com. v. Brusgulis*, 406 Mass 501, 507, 548 NE2d 1234, 1238 (1990) ("The fact is that the circumstances of each [sexual assault] incident were characteristic of numerous assaults on women walking or jogging in unpopulated portions of public parks or in similar areas. If we were to uphold the admission of the evidence of prior bad acts in this case, we would be endorsing a rule that evidence of prior assaults by a person is admissible in the trial of every future assault charge against that person, provided that there is a general, although less than unique or distinct, similarity between the incidents. Such a rule would be unfair to defendants and inconsistent with our well-established law on the use of evidence of prior bad acts to prove identity."). See also *Com. v. Iago I.*, 77 Mass App 327, 331-333, 931 NE2d 47, 51-53 (2010) (evidence connecting juvenile accused of arson to other fires in Holyoke was improper where only connection was defendant's nickname spray painted near three of six prior incidents, but no such mark was left at current scene); *Com. v. McClendon*, 39 Mass App 122, 129-130, 653 NE2d 1138, 1143 (1995) (evidence that defendant became violent when drunk and attempted to strangle someone was not distinguishing pattern of conduct to constitute signature or absence of accident).

Sexual Misconduct Cases.[135] "When a defendant is charged with any form of illicit sexual intercourse, evidence of the commission of similar crimes by the same parties though committed in another place, if not too remote in time, is competent to prove an inclination to commit the [acts] charged in the indictment . . . and is relevant to show the probable existence of the same passion or emotion at the time in issue."[136] Evidence of similar misconduct may also be used to show the relationship between the defendant and the victim.[137]

---

[135] Fed R Evid 413, 414, and 415 render admissible in federal criminal and civil cases charging sexual assault or child molestation evidence of the defendant's commission of similar offenses, which may be considered by the fact-finder "for its bearing on any matter to which it is relevant."

[136] *Com. v. Barrett*, 418 Mass 788, 794, 641 NE2d 1302, 1307 (1994). See also *Com. v. Robertson*, 88 Mass App 52, 35 NE3d 771 (2015) (prior bad acts testimony was properly admitted, as the incidents were sufficiently similar in that defendant was a father figure to both victims, threatened both in a similar fashion, both victims were the same age when the abuse began, and the sort of abuse was almost identical, notwithstanding the time span of eight years between the incidents); *Com. v. Hanlon*, 44 Mass App 810, 817-819, 694 NE2d 358, 365-366 (1998) (evidence of sexual assaults of four other altar boys by defendant priest). For the admissibility of evidence of Internet searches for pornography, see *Com. v. Vera*, 88 Mass App 313, 36 NE3d 1272 (2015) (Internet searches for pornography involving young girls were highly probative of charges of open lewdness and rape of a child).

[137] *Com. v. Roby*, 462 Mass 398, 413-414, 969 NE2d 142,155; *Com. v. Morris*, 82 Mass App 427, 440-441, 974 NE2d 1152, 1164-1165 (2012); *Com. v. Newcomb*, 80 Mass App 519, 954 NE2d 67 (2011).

Entrapment. Where an entrapment defense is raised, evidence of past similar crimes may be offered by the Commonwealth to prove that defendant was predisposed to commit the crime.[138]

Other Purposes. *Com. v. Rousseau*, 465 Mass 372, 388-389, 990 NE2d 543, 557-558 (2013) (other incidents were part of single criminal enterprise); *Com. v. Emeny*, 463 Mass 138, 146-147, 972 NE2d 1003, 1012 (2012) (references in defendant's police interview to his traffic citation and probation record relevant to explain how police discovered his whereabouts and came to search his vehicle); *Com. v. Dyer*, 460 Mass 728, 744-745, 55 NE2d 271, 287 (2011) (witness's testimony that murder defendant had previously set up her rape admissible to explain why she had not reported it); *Com. v. Colleran*, 452 Mass 417, 425-426, 895 NE2d 425, 432-433 (2008) (defendant's prior drug history offered to discredit her experts by showing she was not truthful with them); *Com. v. Pires*, 453 Mass 66, 74, 899 NE2d 787, 793 (2009) (evidence of a rifle found in vicinity of defendant admissible for purpose of eliminating other possible sources of the handgun); *Com. v. Moure*, 428 Mass 313, 318-320, 701 NE2d 319, 323-324 (1998) (prior bad acts of gang members relevant to establish motivation of prosecution witness to testify); *Com. v. Marrero*, 427 Mass 65, 67-69, 691 NE2d 918, 920-921 (1998) (context for the killing); *Com. v. Richardson*, 423 Mass 180, 187, 677 NE2d 257, 263 (1996) (evidence that victim's friend told her she was also raped by defendant admissible to explain delay in reporting); *Com. v. Robles*, 423 Mass 62, 68-69, 666 NE2d 497, 501-502 (1996) (evidence of defendant's drug activities connected him to homicide victim); *Com. v. Brousseau*, 421 Mass 647, 650-651, 659 NE2d 724, 726-727 (1996) (evidence of defendant's prior use of

---

For the use of "other offense" evidence in sexually dangerous person (SDP) proceedings, see *Com. v. Given*, 441 Mass 741, 808 NE2d 788 (2004) (portion of police report referring to uncharged sexual assault admissible in SDP commitment proceeding); *Com. v. Mazzarino*, 81 Mass App 358, 368-369, 963 NE2d 112, 120-121 (2012); *Com. v. Hunt*, 462 Mass 807, 972 NE2d 768 (2012) (unsubstantiated rumors that SDP defendant had raped another prisoner inadmissible in commitment proceeding).

[138] See *Com. v. Vargas*, 417 Mass 792, 632 NE2d 1223 (1994) (& cases cited); *Com. v. Penta*, 32 Mass App 36, 47-49, 586 NE2d 996, 1002-1003 (1992); *Com. v. Buswell*, 83 Mass App 1, 14-16, 979 NE2d 768, 778-780 (2012) (evidence of defendant's sexually explicit Internet conversations with young girls and nude images admissible to negate his entrapment defense). But compare *Com. v. Dingle*, 73 Mass App 274, 283-285, 898 NE2d 1, 9-10 (2008) (prior bad act evidence too remote in time). Where appropriate, defendant may offer evidence of the informant's background and past criminality as a foundation to present evidence of what, if anything, the government agent promised the informant. See *Com. v. Podgukski*, 81 Mass App 175, 183-185, 961 NE2d 113, 120-122 (2012).

murder weapon relevant to show control over it); *Com. v. Austin*, 421 Mass 357, 364-365, 657 NE2d 458, 462-463 (1995) (videotape depicting another bank robbery relevant for limited purpose of assisting jury in assessing reliability of identification evidence); *Com. v. Elam*, 412 Mass 583, 585-586, 591 NE2d 186, 188-189 (1992) (evidence that weapon carried by co-defendant had been fired into house in unrelated incident relevant to rebut defendants' evidence that others were responsible for crimes charged); *Com. v. Hyde*, 88 Mass App 761, 774-775, 42 NE3d 1171, 1183 (2015) (checks written to defendant involving uncharged accidents were highly probative of insurance defendant's referral relationship in insurance fraud prosecution); *Com. v. Beaulieu*, 79 Mass App 100, 102-103, 944 NE2d 1057, 1059-1060 (2011) (admission of redacted certified copy of defendant's prior conviction for OUI was proper to show that at time of arrest, his license had been suspended); *Com. v. Serrano*, 74 Mass App 1, 6, 903 NE2d 247, 251 (2009) (evidence of defendant's prior incarceration was relevant to his unavailability when his girlfriend broke up with him and began dating the murder victim).

Cases Rejecting Specific Act Evidence. *Com. v. Anestal*, 463 Mass 655, 978 NE2d 37 (2012) (evidence that defendant had twice struck her son and that DSS had removed her children as result of abuse not relevant to murder charge); *Com. v. Santos*, 463 Mass 273, 974 NE2d 1 (2012) (evidence that defendant went to home of former boyfriend of co-defendant's girlfriend and punched him not relevant to events of the shooting); *Com. v. Rebello*, 450 Mass 118, 127-129, 876 NE2d 851, 859-860 (2007) (testimony that defendant planned to and did use the gun to shoot third person and testimony that he sold heroin that supposedly killed some people did not bear on his connection to the drug ring); *Com. v. Triplett*, 398 Mass 561, 562-564, 500 NE2d 262, 263-264 (1986) (evidence that murder defendant had assaulted his mother, lost his job because he could not control his temper, and received a dishonorable discharge from the Army merely portrayed defendant as a violent and dangerous person).

Where the defendant takes the stand and opens the subject on direct examination, questions relating to other crimes and bad acts (otherwise inadmissible) may be permissible within the proper scope of cross-examination.[139]

---

[139] *Com. v. Key*, 381 Mass 19, 28-29, 407 NE2d 327, 334 (1980); *Com. v. Quinn*, 83 Mass App 759, 765-766, 989 NE2d 901, 905-906 (2013); *Com. v. Graham*, 62 Mass App 642, 647-648, 818 NE2d 1069, 1074 (2004) (citing Text); *Com. v. Wilson*, 52 Mass App 411, 417-418, 754 NE2d 113, 119 (2001).

The use of prior convictions to impeach a witness (see § 6.16.2, infra) must be distinguished from the substantive use of other crimes to prove such matters as knowledge, scheme or identity, as discussed above. The former bears solely on the credibility of the defendant and may not be used as evidence of guilt. Further, use of prior convictions for impeachment is possible only if the defendant chooses to testify in his own behalf. In contrast, when admissible for substantive purposes, "specific acts" evidence may be offered whether the defendant testifies or not. Second, when prior crimes are used for impeachment purposes, they may be proven only by record of conviction. See § 6.16.2. No such requirement exists for specific act evidence, where it need only be shown by a preponderance of the evidence or by such evidence as warrants submission to the jury that the act occurred and that the defendant was the actor.[140]

§ 4.4.7 *Specific Act Evidence Offered by Defendant*

Evidence of other similar crimes or acts may be introduced by the defendant as well as the prosecution. "It is well established that a defendant should be allowed to introduce evidence that another person recently committed a similar crime by similar methods, since such evidence tends to show that someone other than the accused committed the particular crime."[141]

---

[140] See *Com. v. Leonard*, supra, 428 Mass 782, 785-786, 705 NE2d 247, 250 (citing *Huddleston v. United States*, 485 US 681 (1988)). See, e.g., *Com. v. Hamilton*, 459 Mass 422, 439, 945 NE2d 877, 889 (2011) (defendant's prior convictions admitted on issue of whether victim was reasonable in her fear that he would carry out his threats); *Com. v. Kater*, 432 Mass 404, 414-416, 734 NE2d 1164, 1175-1176 (2000) (*Kater VII*) (defendant's commission of strikingly similar abduction of young girl ten years before charged crime); *Com. v. Truong*, 78 Mass App 28, 30-31, 934 NE2d 1274, 1276-1277 (2010) (defendant's juvenile probation record admitted to rebut his contention that he did not know what a shell casing was). See also *Dowling v. United States*, 493 US 342 (1990) (evidence of prior crime admissible on issue of identity under Fed R Evid 404(b) even though defendant had been tried and acquitted of prior offense).

[141] *Com. v. Scott*, 408 Mass 811, 815-816, 564 NE2d 370, 374-375 (1990). See, e.g., *Com. v. Conkey*, 443 Mass 60, 819 NE2d 176 (2004) (defendant denied due process by exclusion of evidence that victim's landlord engaged in several acts of sexual aggression toward women over span of years prior to the murder) (extensive discussion of third-party culprit evidence); *Com. v. Signorine*, 404 Mass 400, 407-408, 535 NE2d 601, 605-606 (1989); *Com. v. Jewett*, 392 Mass 558, 562, 467 NE2d 155, 158 (1984) (similar rapes). See also *Holmes v. South Carolina*, 547 US 319 (2006) (defendant's federal constitutional right to introduce evidence of third-party guilt).

The acts must be "so closely connected in point of time and method of operation as to cast doubt upon the identification of defendant as the person who committed the crime."[142] The judge has considerable discretion in determining whether the proffered evidence meets these conditions.[143]

"Moreover, there must be reasonable assurance that the defendant at bar did not commit the 'similar' offense, that it was in fact committed by someone else; thus the cases admitting evidence of similar crimes customarily establish that the particular defendant was in custody or in jail or in some predicament at the time."[144] Given such a showing, it is error to bar defendant's evidence of a prior misidentification of him by another victim of a similar crime based on the same police photograph used to identify him in the case on trial.[145]

---

[142] *Com. v. Holliday*, 450 Mass 794, 811, 882 NE2d 309, 324 (2008) (evidence of another person's motive, intent, and opportunity to commit the crime is admissible only if it has a rational tendency to cast doubt upon defendant's guilt); *Com. v. Perkins*, 450 Mass 834, 843, 883 NE2d 230, 240 (2008); *Com. v. Keizer*, 377 Mass 264, 267, 385 NE2d 1001, 1003 (1979). See, e.g., *Com. v. Podkowka*, 445 Mass 692,696-697, 840 NE2d 476, 480-481 (2006) (evidence that victim's mother abused drugs and was neglectful parent did not cast doubt on defendant's guilt); *Com. v. Bregoli*, 431 Mass 265, 274-275, 727 NE2d 59, 68-69 (2000) (evidence that five months after murder victim's boyfriend was arrested for pushing current girlfriend out of vehicle properly excluded because not sufficiently similar to features of murder); *Com. v. Pina*, 430 Mass 66, 77-78, 713 NE2d 944, 952-953 (1999) (trial court properly excluded evidence that murder victim had been abused by her boyfriend as too remote in time and nature). *Com. v. Rosa*, 422 Mass 18, 22-25, 661 NE2d 56, 59-61 (1996) (look-alike evidence properly excluded because insufficient similarities between crimes); *Com. v. Perito*, 417 Mass 674, 684-686, 632 NE2d 1190 (1994) (other robberies committed after defendant's arrest not significantly comparable to require admission; robbery committed before defendant's arrest properly excluded where defendant failed to show he was not the perpetrator of that crime); *Com. v. Hunter*, 426 Mass 715, 690 NE2d 815 (1998) (no error in excluding evidence that neighbor may have strangled victim because prior incident too dissimilar); *Com. v. Brown*, 27 Mass App 72, 76, 534 NE2d 806, 808 (1989) (evidence of other crime properly excluded because the two crimes were "commonplace" and "there was nothing in them so striking or salient as to connect them to a single putative offender"). But compare *Com. v. Conkey*, supra, 443 Mass at 68-70, 819 NE2d at 184-186 (although at first trial defendant's proffered evidence of sexual abuse by third-party seven years before murder was deemed too remote, at second trial defendant also offered more recent incidents establishing a pattern of sexual aggression continuing to several months prior to the murder).

[143] *Com. v. Lawrence*, 404 Mass 378, 387, 536 NE2d 571, 577 (1989); *Com. v. Carver*, 33 Mass App 378, 381-383, 600 NE2d 588, 592-593 (1992).

[144] *Com. v. Brown*, supra, 27 Mass App at 76, 534 NE2d at 808-809. See also *Com. v. Dew*, 443 Mass 620, 627, 823 NE2d 771, 777 (2005).

[145] *Com. v. Jewett*, supra, 392 Mass at 562-563, 467 NE2d at 158-159.

The admission of evidence offered by the defendant to show others had a motive to commit the crime has been viewed with caution because of its potential to divert the jurors' attention to collateral matters.[146] For third-party culprit evidence, see § 4.1.2, supra.

§ 4.4.8 Habit and Custom

While "character" encompasses a broad aggregate of attributes and qualities, "habit" refers to a narrowly specific and routine response to a particular set of circumstances. Habit is thus deemed more probative of how an actor conducted himself on the particular occasion in question. Evidence of the habit of a person and the routine practice of an organization is admissible in the federal courts to prove conduct in conformity with it, Fed R Evid 406, and Proposed Mass R Evid 406 takes the same position, although with a caveat limiting the use of such evidence in negligence trials and with a requirement not explicit in the federal rule that habit be proven by specific instances of conduct, not reputation or opinion evidence.[147]

---

[146] See *Com. v. Rise*, 50 Mass App 836, 844, 744 NE2d 66, 73 (2001). See also *Com. v. Carroll*, 439 Mass 547, 551-553, 789 NE2d 1062, 1066-1067 (2003) (exclusion of evidence of third person's motive to beat victim was proper where defense was not misidentification and there was direct evidence that third person committed the crime).

[147] Proposed Mass R Evid 406 provides:

> (a) **Admissibility**. Evidence of the habit of a person or of the routine practice of an organization, whether corroborated or not and regardless of the presence of eyewitnesses, is relevant to prove that the conduct of the person or organization on a particular occasion was in conformity with the habit or routine practice, but such evidence is not admissible for the purpose of proving that a person or organization did or did not conform on a particular occasion to the prescribed standard of care.
>
> (b) **Method of Proof**. Habit or routine practice may be proved by specific instances of conduct sufficient in number to warrant a finding that the habit existed or that the practice was routine.

With regard to the caveat for negligence cases, the Advisory Committee Notes explain:

> A majority of the Committee believes that habit evidence would have a disruptive effect on the trial of negligence cases and therefore favored the express prohibition in subdivision (a). Negligence, they urge, is a deviation from the norm and proof of a habit of care does not warrant the inference of conformity with the habit on the occasion giving rise to the lawsuit. The minority thinks that adoption of the rule without this exclusion would not significantly change Massachusetts law and that the exclusion reflects undue rigidity. In any event the judge has discretion to exclude habit evidence pursuant to Rule 403 if he finds its probative value to be substantially outweighed by the danger of unfair prejudice.

Notwithstanding the caveat in Rule 406(a) and the Committee's Note, it has been held that:

Massachusetts case law, however, has traditionally rejected the use of habit evidence to prove the conduct of an individual. "For the purpose of proving that one has or has not done a particular act, it is not competent to show that he has or has not been in the habit of doing similar acts."[148] It should be noted, however, that the evidence proffered in many of the cases in any event falls short of demonstrating "habit," defined as "the regular practice of a person to meet a particular kind of situation with a specific type of conduct."[149]

Habit evidence regarding individuals has been admitted in certain circumstances. The habit of intoxication of defendant's watchman, for example, was deemed relevant to establish that he was not a suitable person to be employed in that capacity and that the defendant "by reasonable diligence might have [so] discovered."[150] And evidence of the decedent's "acts and habits of dealing tending to disprove or to show the improbability of the making of" a disputed oral promise or statement is admissible by statute in an action on the promise.[151]

> [E]vidence of a custom or practice, even when not embodied in a written policy, also may be considered in determining whether conduct was negligent: it may be evidence of a defendant's negligence, also, that he failed to follow his usual practice or habit in operating his vehicle, that the plaintiff knew of such custom, relied upon it, and suffered injury as a result.

Com. v. Angelo Todesca Corp., 446 Mass 128, 138, 842 NE2d 930, 940 (2006).

[148] *Davidson v. Massachusetts Casualty Ins. Co.*, 325 Mass 115, 122, 89 NE2d 201, 205 (1949). See, e.g., *Com. v. Williams*, 450 Mass 879, 886, 883 NE2d 249, 256 (2008) (testimony that witness never saw victim with a gun); *Com. v. Wilson*, 443 Mass 122, 138, 819 NE2d 919, 933 (2004) (owner's personal, not business, habit of locking door would be inadmissible); *Figueiredo v. Hamill*, 385 Mass 1003, 431 NE2d 231, 232-233 (1982) (evidence that pedestrian accident victim habitually acted in reckless manner properly excluded); *Com. v. Hodge (No.2)*, 380 Mass 858, 862, 406 NE2d 1015, 1018 (1980) (evidence that defendant frequently used phrase "he'll leave in a hearse" in a joking, non-threatening manner properly excluded); *Brownhill v. Kivlin*, 317 Mass 168, 171, 57 NE2d 539, 540 (1944) (evidence that deceased had caused three prior fires by falling asleep with cigarette in mouth inadmissible); *Com. v. Mandell*, 29 Mass App 504, 507-508, 562 NE2d 111, 113 (1990) (evidence that victim was habitually accident-prone properly excluded).

[149] See Advisory Committee Notes to Proposed Mass R Evid 406.

[150] See *Cox v. Vermont Central Railroad Co.*, 170 Mass 129, 139-140, 49 NE 97, 102 (1898). But compare *Com. v. Shine*, 25 Mass App 613, 614-615, 521 NE2d 749, 750 (1988) (references to possibility that deceased accident victim was an alcoholic were properly excluded because not relevant to whether he was intoxicated at time of accident). See also *Com. v. Kartell*, 58 Mass App 428, 434, 790 NE2d 739, 744-745 (2003) (evidence that defendant normally carried gun in leg holster but placed it in his pocket at time of shooting was not inadmissible habit evidence in homicide prosecution because offered not to show conformity with habit but rather defendant's intent).

[151] See GL 233, § 66.

In recognition of the reality that with regard to large organizations such evidence is often the only practical means of proof, evidence of the custom or routine practice of a business or institution is generally admitted to prove that a particular act was performed.[152] The line between a personal habit (presumptively inadmissible) and a business habit (presumptively admissible) is often not easy to draw, and a trial judge has broad discretion in making this determination.[153] The proponent's burden is to demonstrate both that the routine in question constitutes a habit, and that it is a *business* habit.[154]

Evidence of the habits of animals is generally admissible. "It is a familiar fact that animals are more likely to act in a certain way at a particular time, if the action is in accordance with their established habit or usual conduct, than if it is not. There is a probability that an animal will act as he is accustomed to act under like circumstances. For this reason, when disputes have arisen in regard to the conduct of an animal, evidence of his habits in that particular has often been received."[155]

---

[152] See *Com. v. Martin*, 467 Mass 291, 316-317, 4 NE3d 1236, 1256-1257 (2014) (taxi driver victim's business habit of carrying bag containing cash); *Com. v. Ashmon*, 434 Mass 1005, 746 NE2d 1018 (2001) (judge's customary practice in taking guilty pleas); *Com. v. Robles*, 423 Mass 62, 73-74, 666 NE2d 497, 504-505 (1996) (usual practice of court clerk regarding transcript); *Palinkas v. Bennett*, 416 Mass 273, 620 NE2d 775 (1993) (pediatrician's routine practice when discharging premature infants); *Com. v. Carroll*, 360 Mass 580, 276 NE2d 705 (1971) (routine police department practice in case of fugitives returned to state); *Singer Sewing Machine Co. v. Assessors of Boston*, 341 Mass 513, 519, 170 NE2d 687, 691 (1960) (customary practice of mail clerk competent to prove that bills in dispute were mailed); *Com. v. Cortez*, 86 Mass App 789, 22 NE3d 928 (2014) (customary practice of judge at plea hearings); *O'Connor v. Smithkline Bio-Science Laboratories, Inc.*, 36 Mass App 360, 631 NE2d 1018 (1994) (citing Text) (usual practice of lab technician); *Elias v. Suran*, 35 Mass App 7, 11-13, 616 NE2d 134, 136-137 (1993) (practice at hospital of administering morphine in particular doses to angiogram patients). But compare *Com. v. Levin*, 11 Mass App 482, 503, 417 NE2d 440, 451 (1981) (insufficient foundation to establish insurance broker's practice of signing names of customers to insurance applications).

[153] *Palinkas v. Bennett*, supra, 416 Mass at 277, 620 NE2d 778.

[154] *Com. v. Martin*, supra, 467 Mass at 317, 4 NE3d at 1256.

[155] *Broderick v. Higginson*, 169 Mass 482, 485, 48 NE 269, 270 (1897) (proof that dog had habit of attacking passing teams). See also *Palmer v. Coyle*, 187 Mass 136, 72 NE 844 (1905).

§ 4.4.9 *Similar Circumstances Offered for Various Purposes*

a. Similar Occurrences

The occurrence of an event or transaction similar to the one in issue may arguably have some relevance in the lawsuit. To prove that a particular defect in the road caused the accident, for example, plaintiff may offer evidence that similar accidents have occurred at the same location. Such evidence (sometimes referred to as *res inter alios acta*, or a thing done between others[156]) is generally viewed with disfavor because it raises collateral issues that may distract from the central questions in the case. As the Supreme Judicial Court has cautioned:

> The admissibility of evidence of injury to others at other times by reason of the same thing that caused the plaintiff's injury, for the purpose of showing that thing to be dangerous, has often come before this court. Such evidence is open to grave objections. Its persuasive force depends upon the similarity in the circumstances of different injuries, of which it is hard to be certain. Substantial identity in the alleged defective condition is only the first essential. The person who was injured at the time to which the offered evidence related may have been defective in eyesight, feeble, or careless. The fact that he was injured may have little or no bearing upon the danger to the normal traveller. Moreover, though the same defective condition may have been present at both times, the actual causes of the two injuries may have been different. Unless a comparison of the circumstances and causes of the two injuries is made, the injury to another is without significance. But if such comparison is undertaken, the minds of the jurors must be diverted from the injury on trial into a detailed and possibly protracted inquiry as to injuries received by others at various times. Those injuries have only a collateral and often minor bearing upon the case. As to them the opposing party will often be ill prepared to present evidence. There is danger that a jury may disregard the real differences in the circumstances of the two incidents, and find upon mere superficial similarity that a dangerous condition existed. Similar considerations apply where evidence that other people, confronted at other times with the same alleged danger, suffered no injury, is offered to prove the want of a dangerous condition.[157]

---

[156] See *Denton v. Park Hotel, Inc.*, 343 Mass 524, 527, 180 NE2d 70, 72 (1962).

[157] *Robitaille v. Netoco Community Theatre*, 305 Mass 265, 266-267, 25 NE2d 749, 750-751 (1940) (in action for personal injuries sustained in fall on stairway, evidence that other persons had fallen at same spot two weeks before was not admissible to prove carpet was loose). See also *Crivello v. All-Pak Machinery Systems, Inc.*, 446 Mass 729, 737-738, 847 NE2d 307, 314 (2006) (judge properly excluded evidence of prior accidents on same bagging machine as not sufficiently similar); *Kromhout v. Com.*, 398

Where, however, there is substantial identity in the circumstances and the danger of unfairness, confusion, or undue expenditure of time in the trial of collateral issues appears minimal, such evidence may be admitted.[158] Evidence of the similar behavior of machinery or animals has been admitted given these conditions.[159] Similarly, the noxious character of food and other substances may be shown by their effect upon other persons similarly exposed.[160] Conversely the lack of similar occurrences has been held admissible to prove absence of a dangerous condition.[161] Evidence of a similar occurrence may also be admissible for the limited purpose of proving knowledge, notice, or state of mind.[162]

Mass 687, 692-694, 500 NE2d 789, 792-794 (1986) (in action to recover for motorist's death allegedly caused by defect in highway, reversible error to admit plaintiff's evidence that 21 other accidents occurred at the intersection during past five years in absence of showing that circumstances were substantially similar); *Reil v. Lowell Gas Co.*, 353 Mass 120, 135-136, 228 NE2d 707, 719 (1967) (in action for personal injuries sustained in plant explosion, judge properly excluded evidence of other fires in plant and in another plant of same proprietor because it would be of little help in determining cause of explosion); *Com. v. Guinan*, 86 Mass App 445, 456, 17 NE3d 439, 448 (2014) (defendant's offer of proof regarding witness's accident in vehicle of same make, model, and year, was properly excluded in motor vehicle homicide trial because there was a marked difference in the steering systems of the two cars).

Com. v. Levin, 11 Mass App 482, 503, 417 NE2d 440, 451 (1981) (testimony of other customers that they authorized defendant insurance broker to sign their applications not admissible to prove that insured had authorized defendant to sign his application).

[158] *Robitaille v. Netoco Community Theatre*, supra, 305 Mass at 266, 25 NE2d at 750 (& cases cited). See, e.g., *Santos v. Chrysler Corp.*, 430 Mass 198, 202-205, 715 NE2d 47, 52-53 (1999) (although they did not replicate exact circumstances of plaintiff's accident, trial court properly admitted testimony of six Chrysler minivan owners regarding other braking incidents).

[159] See *Edward Rose Co. v. Globe & Rutgers Fire Ins. Co.*, 262 Mass 469, 160 NE2d 306 (1928) (evidence of other cotton fires under substantially same conditions near time of fire admissible to prove cause was spark from milling machine).

[160] See *Brek's Case*, 335 Mass 144, 149, 138 NE2d 748, 751 (1948) (testimony of physician that all asbestosis patients he had ever treated had worked at insurer's plant admissible to refute evidence of absence of asbestos dust in plant); *Carter v. Yardley & Co.*, 319 Mass 92, 94, 64 NE2d 693, 694 (1946) (evidence that other users of defendant's perfume suffered skin irritation after applying product properly admitted to show causation); *Johnson v. Kanavos*, 296 Mass 373, 375, 6 NE2d 434, 436 (1937) ("When, under the same conditions, several persons who have eaten the same food become similarly ill an inference may be warranted that the food which all had eaten was unwholesome and was the cause of their illness.").

[161] See, e.g., *Haskell v. Boat Clinton-Serafina, Inc.*, 412 F2d 896 (1st Cir 1969) (& citations) (evidence that no prior accident had occurred on ship's deck properly admitted to contradict plaintiff's testimony that there was large patch of slime there).

[162] See, e.g., *Santos v. Chrysler Corp.*, supra, 430 Mass at 202-205, 715 NE2d at 52-53 (evidence of other braking incidents involving minivans admitted to establish

b. Similar Transactions/Sale Price of Similar Land

Evidence of similar transactions has been held admissible in a variety of commercial law settings, such as evidence of other sales of similar stock for the purpose of showing what might have been a reasonable time in which stock in question could have been sold[163] Perhaps the most common is proof of the value of a parcel of land by evidence of the sale price of other similar land.[164] Such evidence must relate to similar property sold at a time not too remote from the time relevant in the disputed case and sold at a noncompulsory sale between a willing seller and a willing buyer.[165] Admissibility of evidence of comparable sales is within the broad discretion of the trial judge, and the judge's decision will be reversed only if manifestly erroneous.[166]

---

notice); *Burnham v. Mark IV Homes, Inc.*, 387 Mass 575, 584-585, 441 NE2d 1027, 1033 (1982) (testimony that dealer informed sales manager of leakage problems in roofs of other units admissible to prove notice of defect). But compare *Read v. Mt. Tom Ski Area, Inc.*, 37 Mass App 901, 902, 639 NE2d 391, 393 (1994) (evidence of other accidents not admissible to prove knowledge of dangerous condition because no showing other accidents were substantially identical). The absence of complaints of similar incidents may be relevant to show lack of notice, or the reason a product was not tested in a certain way. See *Carrel v. National Cord & Braid Corp.*, 447 Mass 431, 447-448, 852 NE2d 100, 113 (2006).

[163] See *Steranko v. Inforex*, 8 Mass App 523, 530-531, 395 NE2d 1303, 1307 (1979).

[164] See *Nonni v. Com.*, 356 Mass 264, 268-269, 249 NE2d 644, 646 (1969); *H. E. Fletcher Co. v. Com.*, 350 Mass 316, 324-326, 214 NE2d 721, 725-727 (1966); *Boyd v. Lawrence Redevelopment Authority*, 348 Mass 83, 202 NE2d 297 (1964); *Consolini v. Com.*, 346 Mass 501, 194 NE2d 407 (1963). Compare *Massachusetts-American Water Co. v. Grafton Water District*, 36 Mass App 944, 946, 631 NE2d 59, 61 (1994) (significant dissimilarities between sales); *Brush Hill Development, Inc. v. Com.*, 338 Mass 359, 366-367, 155 NE2d 170, 175 (1959) (comparable property four miles away); *Wright v. Com.*, 286 Mass 371, 190 NE2d 593 (1934) (differences in parcels and a question about the voluntary nature of the comparable sale). See also *North American Philips Lighting Corp. v. Board of Assessors of Lynn*, 392 Mass 296, 465 NE2d 782 (1984) (board did not err in assigning little weight to taxpayer's evidence of other sales where there were differences in size, location, and market conditions).

[165] See *United-Carr, Inc. v. Cambridge Redevelopment Authority*, 362 Mass 597, 599-601, 289 NE2d 833, 834-835 (1972); *Massachusetts-American Water Co. v. Grafton Water District*, 36 Mass App 944, 946, 631 NE2d 59, 61 (1994) (significant dissimilarities between sales),

[166] See *Anthony's Pier Four, Inc. v. HBC Associates*, 411 Mass 451, 479, 583 NE2d 806, 824 (1991); *Analogic Corp. v. Board of Assessors of Peabody*, 45 Mass App 605, 609-610, 700 NE2d 548, 552-553 (1998).

The sale price of land to a party possessing the power of eminent domain may be admissible if found to be voluntary.[167] The courts have given a narrow definition to the "compulsion" that requires exclusion of evidence of a comparable sale, and the burden is on the party opposing the evidence to show that the sale price should be disregarded because it was not the product of free bargaining.[168]

Zoning differences may properly preclude evidence of the sale price of otherwise similar land.[169] There is, however, "no hard and fast rule that a difference in zones in and of itself renders such evidence inadmissible."[170] Nor would the absence of water rights necessarily bar evidence of otherwise comparable sales.[171] The sale price of land whose value has been enhanced by a nearby taking for turnpike purposes is clearly inadmissible.[172]

For discussion of expert testimony concerning the value of property, see § 7.6.7, infra.

c. Similar and Altered Objects

The relevance of certain real evidence may be brought into question if the object is similar to but not identical with the object in question. Evidence that a commonplace article similar to one involved in a crime was found in a place connected to a criminal defendant may well

---

[167] *Amory v. Com.*, 321 Mass 240, 256, 72 NE2d 549, 559 (1947).

[168] See *Westwood Group, Inc. v. Board of Assessors of Revere*, 391 Mass 1012, 462 NE2d 115 (1984); *Ramacorti v. Boston Redevelopment Authority*, 341 Mass 377, 170 NE2d 323 (1960) (plaintiff unsuccessfully sought to refute low sale price of land by offering evidence of "compelled" sale due to age of sellers); *Pankauski v. Greater Lawrence Sanitary District Com.*, 13 Mass App 929, 430 NE2d 1228 (1982) (even though evidence of sale price of comparable land may have been excluded as "under duress" because of pending eminent domain taking, not error to admit evidence in view of owner's failure to develop involuntary nature of sale).

[169] See *Congregation of Mission of St. Vincent de Paul v. Com.*, 336 Mass 357, 145 NE2d 681 (1957) (no abuse of discretion in exclusion of evidence of sale price of nearby land located entirely in residential zone).

[170] *Gregori v. City of Springfield*, 348 Mass 395, 397, 204 NE2d 113, 114 (1965).

[171] *Valley Paper Co. v. Holyoke Housing Authority*, 346 Mass 561, 569, 194 NE2d 700, 705-706 (1963).

[172] See *Alden v. Com.*, 351 Mass 83, 87, 217 NE2d 743, 746-747 (1966). Compare *Burchell v. Com.*, 350 Mass 488, 490, 215 NE2d 649, 651 (1966) and *Zambarano v. Massachusetts Turnpike Authority*, 350 Mass 485, 215 NE2d 652 (1966) (nothing in record to indicate enhancement in value because of taking).

be more prejudicial than probative. Where the item is less common, evidence that the defendant possesses that type of item may be admissible.[173]

An object similar to the article in issue, but unconnected with any party to the case, may be offered as merely illustrative of the object.[174] Any differences between the item offered and the one in issue must be such that the jury can perceive and take account of them.[175]

If an article is identified as the identical article in issue but has changed in its condition, similar requirements are appropriate. The fact that the article has changed does not bar its admissibility but only affects the weight to be given the evidence.[176] However, the nature of the change must be shown to be such as not to affect its evidentiary value and to allow the jury to perceive and take account of it.[177]

d. *Experimental Evidence*

If certain natural forces produce a particular effect on one occasion, it is likely that they will do so on another similar occasion. When such a cause-effect relationship is in dispute in a case, the outcome of an experiment duplicating the alleged causes may be probative. The

---

[173] See, e.g., *Com. v. Paszko*, 391 Mass at 195, 461 NE2d at 241 (1984) (drugs found in defendant's car corresponded to those missing from pharmacy where druggist was killed); *Com. v. Johnson*, 46 Mass App 398, 706 NE2d 716 (1999) (knife recovered from defendant's residence admissible as one similar to knife used by robber); *Com. v. McDonald*, 11 Mass App 944, 416 NE2d 992 (1981) (safety pin found at scene, similar to one used by defendant; jackknife on defendant's person when arrested consistent with wounds of victim); *Com. v. Kinney*, 12 Mass App 915, 423 NE2d 1017 (1981) (hats found in apartment similar to those defendant had been seen wearing relevant to show his control of apartment); *Com. v. McJunkin*, 11 Mass App 609, 620-621, 418 NE2d 1259, 1266-1267 (1981) (knife surrendered by defendant on arrest properly allowed to be described by victim as "similar" to one used in assault). Compare *Com. v. Chasson*, 383 Mass 183, 423 NE2d 306 (1981) (knives offered by defendant allegedly discovered at crime scene after fruitless intensive search for same by police were properly excluded in discretion of judge). See also § 4.1.2, supra, text accompanying note 18.

[174] See, e.g., *Com. v. Kalhauser*, 52 Mass App 339, 754 NE2d 76 (2001) (gun); *Com. v. Luna*, 46 Mass App 90, 703 NE2d 740 (1998) (gun).

[175] *Flynn v. First National Stores*, 296 Mass 521, 6 NE2d 814 (1937).

[176] *Poirier v. Plymouth*, 374 Mass 206, 210, 372 NE2d 212, 213 (1978) (construction plans).

[177] See *Com. v. Sheeran*, 370 Mass 82, 345 NE2d 362 (1976) (witness's verification of photograph as representing earlier condition sufficient to indicate no change had taken place).

evidentiary problem in these cases usually relates to the similarity of the conditions between the experiment and the disputed event.

The general rule is that evidence of an experiment is admissible provided that the conditions are sufficiently similar to make it of value in aiding the jury. This judgment rests in the discretion of the judge, who must determine whether the differences in conditions raise so many collateral issues that the jury will be confused or misled. Admission of such evidence requires that the trial judge weigh its probative value against the possibility that it will prejudice the jury.[178]

The standard for admissibility does not require precise replication.[179] "Evidence of tests or experiments, which do not exactly replicate the conditions giving rise to the alleged injury, are admissible upon a showing of adequate test controls where there is a substantial similarity between experimental conditions and the conditions that gave rise to the litigation."[180] Lesser dissimilarities go to the weight of such evidence, not its admissibility.[181] But where, for example, the defense at the fabled Brink's robbery trial offered testimony of a chauffeur who replicated the route allegedly traveled by the defendants and

---

[178] See *Com. v. Corliss*, 470 Mass 443, 456-457, 23 NE3d 92, 103-104 (2014) (insufficient showing that floor level and surveillance camera positioning at store were same during expert witness's videotaping); *Griffin v. General Motors Corp.*, 380 Mass 362, 365-366, 403 NE2d 402, 405 (1980) (in negligence action by plaintiff burned when car burst into flames as she was lighting cigarette, judge did not abuse discretion by admitting evidence of test conducted on similar vehicle, but using ammonia rather than gasoline); *Lally v. Volkswagen Aktiengesellschaft*, 45 Mass App 317, 332-334, 698 NE2d 28, 40-41 (1998) (no abuse of discretion in admitting evidence of sled test performed by defendant which sought to recreate accident).

[179] *Ducharme v. Hyundai Motor America*, 45 Mass App 401, 408, 698 NE2d 412, 417 (1998) (crash tests).

[180] *Welch v. Keene Corp.*, 31 Mass App 157, 166, 575 NE2d 766, 772 (1991). See also *Lally v. Volkswagen Aktiengesellschaft*, supra, 45 Mass App at 333, 698 NE2d at 41 (standard is whether test is similar enough to allow jury to infer "something material").

[181] *Ducharme v. Hyundai Motor America*, supra, 45 Mass App 401 at 408-409, 698 NE2d at 417. See also *Com. v. Ellis*, 373 Mass 1, 4-6, 364 NE2d 808, 811-812 (1977) (no error in admission of expert ballistics evidence even though some dissimilarities between experiment and actual shooting); *Sarkesian v. Cedric Chase Photographic Laboratories, Inc.*, 324 Mass 620, 621-622, 87 NE2d 745, 746 (1949) (on issue of whether roll of photographic film lost by defendant contained pictures, testimony that plaintiff had obtained satisfactory pictures using the same camera and film type sufficient to warrant finding that pictures had been recorded). See also *Crivello v. All-Pak Machinery Systems, Inc.*, 446 Mass 729, 736, 847 NE2d 307, 313 (2006) (plaintiff was free to explore the differences between the bagging machine defense counsel demonstrated and the one plaintiff was injured on).

Compare *Aleo v. SLB Toys USA, Inc.* 466 Mass 398, 406, 995 NE2d 740, 749 (2013) (substantial differences between conditions of expert witness's experiments

determined they could not have arrived in time to commit robbery, the evidence was excluded because there was no showing that traffic, weather, and light conditions were sufficiently similar to the actual trip.[182]

Experimental evidence is useful and commonly offered to prove that an undisputed effect may have resulted from a cause other than the one alleged.[183] Experimental evidence may also be used to prove that a particular feat is at least possible.[184]

The use of the factfinder as a participant in an experiment or demonstration is problematic and has been discouraged.[185] Allowing the jury to take exhibits to the jury room during deliberations provides

---

with mannequin on inflatable pool slide); *Com. v. Weichell*, 390 Mass 62, 78, 453 NE2d 1038, 1047 (1983) (photographic experiment offered by defendant on issue of witness's ability to perceive and identify a human figure at scene of murder properly excluded because conditions of experiment not sufficiently similar); *Read v. Mt. Tom Ski Area, Inc.*, 37 Mass App 901, 903-904, 639 NE2d 391, 393-394 (1994) (judge properly excluded experimental evidence where expert testified he had no information about actual conditions at time of plaintiff's accident); *Sacks v. Roux Laboratories*, Inc., 25 Mass App 672, 674-676, 521 NE2d 1050, 1051-1052 (1988) (judge acted within discretion in excluding results of product test conducted under control of manufacturer because test lacked probative value); *Terrio v. McDonough*, 16 Mass App 163, 173, 450 NE2d 190, 196 (1983) (reenactment of plaintiff's fall down staircase did not sufficiently represent actual event).

[182] See *Com. v. Geagan*, 339 Mass 487, 511, 159 NE2d 870, 887 (1959).

[183] See, e.g., *Calvanese v. W. W Babcock Co.*, 10 Mass App 726, 729-731, 412 NE2d 895, 901 (1980) (in action for personal injuries sustained when plaintiff fell from ladder, results of tests conducted by defendant's expert to show that ladder could not have failed under normal use described by plaintiff, but that substantially similar damage could be reproduced in an identical ladder by improper loading); *Szeliga v. General Motors Corp.*, 728 F2d 566 (1st Cir 1984) (films depicting experiment conducted by defendant's expert to demonstrate that impact of car, and not loss of lug nuts, was cause of wheel leaving axle).

[184] See, e.g., *Griffin v. General Motors Corp.*, supra, 380 Mass at 365-366, 403 NE2d at 405; *Com. v. Makarewicz*, 333 Mass 575, 592-593, 132 NE2d 294, 303-304 (1956) (evidence of experiment conducted by police officer four months after crime to prove that person of defendant's size could climb through particular window at scene of murder).

[185] *Com. v. DeDomenicis*, 42 Mass App 76, 674 NE2d 1099 (1997) (error for motion judge to "frisk" defendant to determine whether wad of bills would have felt like a weapon to officer during a pat-down, court noting that courtroom circumstances were different than those facing officer on the street). But see *Com. v. Perryman*, 55 Mass App 187, 770 NE2d 1 (2002) (not error to allow jurors in courtroom to look through telescope through which officer perceived drug transaction, where judge explained to jurors the differences in conditions and cautioned them that the viewing was not evidence).

a potential opportunity for the jurors to conduct their own experiments with the exhibits. Nonetheless, whether to send exhibits to the jury room is within the judge's discretion.[186]

Videotapes of experiments conducted outside of court are admissible within the discretion of the trial judge by the same criteria that govern experiments performed in court.[187]

e. Demonstrations

Sworn witnesses may, within the discretion of the judge, demonstrate the manner in which an event occurred.[188] A plaintiff was thus allowed to demonstrate the working of the machine upon which he was injured to show how the accident in question happened; he was not, however, allowed to use the demonstration as evidence that he lacked the strength to operate the machine properly, because of the danger of undiscoverable fraud inherent in such subjective demonstrations.[189] A young son was permitted to use a couch to demonstrate how his mother, the murder victim, was positioned as the defendant killed her.[190]

---

[186] *Com. v. Pixley*, 42 Mass App 927, 928, 677 NE2d 273, 275 (1997) (allowing binoculars into jury room without limiting instruction). For the problem of experimentation by jurors during deliberations, see *Com. v. Greineder*, 458 Mass 207, 247-248, 936 NE2d 372, 402 (2010) (jurors' experiment with banana to observe whether glove was capable of making blood pattern similar to stain on defendant's glasses and jacket was proper, as within the scope of the evidence presented at trial and cumulative of expert testimony).

[187] Compare *Szeliga v. General Motors Corp.*, 728 F2d 566 (1st Cir 1984) (films of experimental auto crashes admissible to illustrate expert's theory of cause of accident), *Com. v. Chipman*, 418 Mass 262, 635 NE2d 1204 (1994) (videotaped simulation of the view from the fatal shooting site through the defendant's telescopic site was admissible), and *Welch v. Keene Corp.*, 31 Mass App 157, 166, 575 NE2d 766, 772 (1991) (videotaped experiment showing visibility of dust concentrations was admissible) with *Com. v. Nadworny*, 30 Mass App 912, 566 NE2d 625 (1991) (excluding videotaped re-creation of accident) and *Terrio v. McDonough*, 16 Mass App 163, 173, 450 NE2d 190, 196 (1983) (excluding videotape of re-enacted fall down stairs).

[188] *Whalen v. Shivek*, 326 Mass 142, 147-148, 93 NE2d 393, 397 (1950). Such demonstrations, even if inconsistent with the witness's oral description of the event, may be relied upon by the fact-finder.

[189] *Probert v. Phipps*, 149 Mass 258, 21 NE 370 (1889). Compare *Com. v. Shea*, 401 Mass 731, 737, 519 NE2d 1283, 1287 (1988) (tapping of defendant's shoes against rail by prosecutor in closing argument to illustrate sound they made was permissible where shoes were in evidence and witness had testified to "clicking sound" of shoes of perpetrator).

[190] *Com. v. McGee*, 469 Mass 1, 9-12, 11 NE3d 1043, 1049-1051 (2014) (position of body was probative of whether defendant acted with deliberate premeditation).

It is in the judge's discretion to grant permission for the in-court demonstration, and to determine whether the conditions are sufficiently similar to render the demonstration of value to the jury.[191] Where a measuring device is used in court, the party proffering the evidence must make a threshold showing that the device is accurate.[192]

§ 4.5 Subsequent Repairs

The fact that an alleged defect was repaired or other safety measures were taken after an accident may appear to the fact-finder as a tacit admission of liability. Yet the act may simply reflect risk-avoidance and tell us nothing meaningful about legal responsibility for the earlier event. Moreover, admission of such evidence could very well discourage actors from making repairs to dangerous conditions.

Given its dubious probative value and potential to undercut the public policy favoring safety measures, a nearly universal rule excludes evidence of post-accident repairs as proof of negligence or the existence of a defect. Proposed Mass R Evid 407 reflects Massachusetts practice:

> **Subsequent Remedial Measures**
> When, after an event, measures are taken which, if taken previously, would have made the event less likely to occur, evidence of the subsequent measures is not admissible to prove negligence or culpable conduct in connection with the event. This rule does not require the exclusion of evidence of subsequent measures when offered for another purpose, such as proving ownership, control, or feasibility of precautionary measures, if controverted, or impeachment.[1]

---

[191] *Crivello v. All-Pak Machinery Systems, Inc.*, 446 Mass 729, 736, 847 NE2d 307, 313 (2006) (demonstration of bagging machine plaintiff was injured by); *Com. v. Perryman*, supra, 55 Mass App at 194-195, 770 NE2d 1 (demonstration for juror viewing of telescope used by police); *Com. v. Hartnett*, 72 Mass App 467, 473-474, 892 NE2d 805, 812 (2008) (judge had discretion to permit prosecutor to dim lights in courtroom to demonstrate lighting conditions at time witness observed assault).

[192] See *Com. v. Podgukski*, 81 Mass App 175, 186, 961 NE2d 113, 123 (2012) (in-court weighing of drugs on police department scale).

§ 4.5 [1] See also *Martel v. MBTA*, 403 Mass 1, 4, 525 NE2d 662, 664 (1988) (& citations).

Although modeled on the federal rule, Fed R Evid 407 has since been amended to clarify that:

The following post-accident measures have been held inadmissible to prove liability:

- Sanding stairs or the street.[2]
- Repairing steps.[3]
- Installation of a flashing light signal at a railroad crossing.[4]
- Precautions taken to avoid another collapse of a trench.[5]
- Repositioning a barrier across sidewalk.[6]
- Sweeping the sidewalk.[7]
- Nailing down a board.[8]

The exclusionary rule has been extended to the results of a defendant's investigation into the causes of the accident. In *Martel v. MBTA*, the Supreme Judicial Court reasoned:

> Although not itself a "repair" of a dangerous condition, the investigation is the prerequisite to any remedial safety measure. . . . The investigation is inextricably bound up with the subsequent remedial measures to which it may lead, and questions of admissibility of evidence as to each should be analyzed in conjunction and answered consistently. If, as a result of the investigation, the defendant had discharged the bus driver, or required him to undergo additional safety

---

- It applies only to changes made after the accident: "Evidence of measures taken by the defendant prior to the 'event' do not fall within the exclusionary scope of Rule 407 even if they occurred after the manufacture or design of the product."
- It applies in product liability as well as negligence cases. It thus excludes evidence of subsequent remedial measures when offered to prove "a defect in a product, a defect in a product's design, or a need for warning or instruction."

See Advisory Committee Note to 1997 Amendment. Massachusetts case law has yet to explicitly address these matters.

[2] *Barnett v. City of Lynn*, 433 Mass 662, 666 n.5, 745 NE2d 344, 347 n.5 (2001).

[3] *Hubley v. Lilley*, 28 Mass App 468, 474, 552 NE2d 573, 576-577 (1990).

[4] *Ladd v. New York, N.H. & H.R.R.*, 335 Mass 117, 120, 138 NE2d 346, 347-348 (1956).

[5] *Shinners v. Proprietors of Locks & Canals on Merrimack River*, 154 Mass 168, 28 NE 10 (1891).

[6] *Manchester v. Attleboro*, 288 Mass 492, 193 NE 4 (1934).

[7] *Nelson v. Economy Grocery Stores Corp.*, 305 Mass 383, 389, 25 NE2d 986, 990 (1940).

[8] *Goodell v. Sviokcla*, 262 Mass 317, 159 NE 728 (1928).

training, evidence of these steps would fall squarely within the rule excluding evidence of subsequent remedial measures. The investigation cannot sensibly be treated differently. To do so would discourage potential defendants from conducting such investigations, and so preclude safety improvements, and frustrate the salutary public policy underlying the rule.[9]

Because it is deemed more probative on these narrower matters than the broader issue of negligence, evidence of a subsequent remedial measure is admissible (with limiting instructions) to prove, where genuinely controverted:

- Ownership or control over the premises.[10]
- The feasibility of giving adequate warnings.[11]
- The feasibility of safety improvements.[12]
- Knowledge of the danger at time of accident.[13]

---

[9] 403 Mass at 5, 525 NE2d at 664.

[10] See, e.g., *Finn v. Peters*, 340 Mass 622, 625, 165 NE2d 896, 898 (1960) (where oral tenancy was ambiguous as to retention of control by landlord over porch where plaintiff fell, evidence that landlord had subsequently repaired the railing was admissible); *Perkins v. Rice*, 187 Mass 28, 30, 72 NE 323, 324 (1904) ("When repairs are made on premises by those whom it is sought to charge with liability for their defective condition, evidence of this fact has been deemed competent whether they were made before or after the accident, as being inconsistent with a denial of ownership, although such evidence is not competent as an admission of liability for the accident itself."). But see *Dias v. Woodrow*, 342 Mass 218, 172 NE2d 705 (1961) (evidence that building owner had entranceway cleaned and step repaired after accident was admissible on, but not sufficient in itself to establish, issue of control).

[11] See, e.g., *Schaeffer v. General Motors Corp.*, 372 Mass 171, 175-177, 360 NE2d 1062, 1066 (1977) (text from defendant's owners' manuals was admissible to prove practical possibility of giving cautionary warnings); *Fiorentino v. A. E. Staley Manufacturing Co.*, 11 Mass App 428, 437-438, 416 NE2d 998, 1005 (1981) (evidence of pre-accident and post-accident changes in warnings admissible to prove feasibility of providing adequate warnings).

[12] See, e.g., *doCanto v. Ametek*, Inc., 367 Mass 776, 779-782, 328 NE2d 873, 876-877 (1975) (evidence of safety features developed by manufacturer of ironing machinery after sale to plaintiff's employer, but before accident, admissible for limited purposes of showing feasibility of redesign of safety features, defendant's knowledge of defects, and duty to warn of safety deficiencies); *Torre v. Harris-Seybold Co.*, 9 Mass App 660, 677, 404 NE2d 96, 108 (1980) (evidence concerning subsequent technological advances or safety improvements utilized by same manufacturer before or after accident admissible in discretion of judge on issues of feasibility and knowledge of risk).

[13] See, e.g., *Reardon v. Country Club at Coonamessett, Inc.*, 353 Mass 702, 704-705, 234 NE2d 881, 883 (1968) (testimony of manager that protective screen was in place at time of accident together with rebuttal evidence that screen was not erected until after accident was relevant to prove defendant's knowledge of danger that golfer could be hit with ball).

Insistence that the issue of ownership, control, feasibility, or knowledge must be controverted (by the pleadings or evidence) before subsequent repair evidence can be admitted for this limited purpose assures that the exception does not swallow the rule, and also allows the defendant considerable control over the admission of such evidence. A defendant who has taken subsequent remedial measures is well advised to avoid controverting any of these matters. A general concession may not, however, be sufficient to foreclose admission.[14]

Evidence of a manufacturer's recall has been admitted to show the manufacturer was on notice of the product defect.[15] If the defect that was the subject of a recall was present in the plaintiff's vehicle at the time of the accident, evidence of the recall is also admissible to show that the defect was present in the plaintiff's vehicle when it left the hands of the manufacturer.[16]

Although there does not appear to be direct authority on point in Massachusetts law, the federal subsequent remedial measures exclusionary rule has generally been held inapplicable to third-party repairs.[17]

§ 4.6 Compromise and Offers to Compromise/Expressions of Sympathy or Apology/Payment of Medical Expenses/Offers to Plead Guilty

Compromise and Offers to Compromise/Expressions of Sympathy or Apology. As with subsequent repairs (§ 4.5, supra), a party's willingness to compromise a dispute may appear to a fact-finder as a tacit admission of the weakness of its position, but may simply reflect a desire to avoid litigation. Moreover admission of such evidence may discourage attempts to conciliate.

---

[14] See *doCanto v. Ametek, Inc.*, supra, 367 Mass at 781, 328 NE2d at 876 (general concession by defendant that design improvements were practical does not defeat the admissibility of the evidence to establish feasibility of redesign); *Schaeffer v. General Motors Corp.*, supra, 372 Mass at 176 n.3 (feasibility of safety warnings). But compare *Cameron v. Otto Bock Orthopedic Indus., Inc.*, 43 F3d 14 (1st Cir 1994) (plaintiff failed to satisfy "if controverted" condition of FRE 407 when manufacturer offered to stipulate to feasibility and did not deny that certain measures might have avoided accident).

[15] See *Santos v. Chrysler Corp.*, 430 Mass 198, 207-208, 715 NE2d 47, 55-56 (1999) (& citations).

[16] See *Carey v. General Motors Corp.*, 377 Mass 736, 744, 387 NE2d 583, 587-588 (1979).

[17] See Am.Jur.2d Evidence § 484.

Thus, a party's offer to compromise or acceptance of a settlement is not admissible to prove the validity or invalidity or the amount of the claim. Proposed Mass R Evid 408 reflects Massachusetts practice:

> **Compromise and Offers to Compromise**
> Evidence of (1) furnishing or offering or promising to furnish, or (2) accepting or offering or attempting to compromise a claim which was disputed as to either validity or amount, is not admissible to prove liability for, invalidity of, or amount of the claim or any other claim. Evidence of conduct or statements made in compromise negotiations is likewise not admissible. This rule does not require exclusion when the evidence is offered for another purpose, such as proving bias or prejudice of a witness, negativing a contention of undue delay, or proving an effort to obstruct a criminal investigation or prosecution.[1]

"This rule is founded in policy, that there may be no discouragement to amicable adjustment of disputes, by a fear, that if not completed, the party amicably disposed may be injured."[2]

The exclusion applies to offers and completed settlements with third parties as well.[3] The principle thus applies to settlements between plaintiff and a joint tortfeasor; but in mitigation of damages the defendant is entitled to place in evidence the amount of the settlement.[4] The judge should instruct the jury to determine the damages substantially caused by the defendant, and then the judge (not the jury) will make the appropriate reduction in any amount awarded.[5]

---

§ 4.6 [1] See also *Enga v. Sparks*, 315 Mass 120, 124, 51 NE2d 984, 987 (1943).

[2] *Strauss v. Skurnik*, 227 Mass 173, 175, 116 NE 404 (1917).

[3] See *Murray v. Foster*, 343 Mass 655, 659-660, 180 NE2d 311, 313-314 (1962) ("Evidence of a settlement entered into by the defendants with a third person not a party to the action [the owner of a trailer involved in the accident] for injuries arising out of the same accident would be inadmissible on the issue of the defendants' liability to the plaintiffs."); *Ricciutti v. Sylvania Electric Products, Inc.*, 343 Mass 347, 349, 178 NE2d 857, 859 (1961) (agreements between the defendant's insurer and other claimants who allegedly contracted berylliosis while in the defendant's employ). See also *Federico v. Ford Motor Co.*, 67 Mass App 454, 460-462, 854 NE2d 448, 454-455 (2006) (discussing use at trial of interrogatories answered by settling defendants).

[4] See *Morea v. Cosco, Inc.*, 422 Mass 601, 603, 664 NE2d 822, 824 (1996).

[5] The Court explained:

> The rule we adopt will tend to encourage a plaintiff to settle with one tortfeasor, knowing that the case against another tortfeasor will not be prejudiced by evidence of the settlement. Moreover, leaving the calculation to adjust for the settlement to the judge instead of to the jury, will facilitate the application of the offset that this court has directed be made to reflect a settlement with another joint tortfeasor.

Morea v. Cosco, Inc., supra, 422 Mass at 604, 664 NE2d at 825.

Evidence of a settlement or offer to compromise may be admitted (with limiting instructions) for a purpose *other than* to prove liability or the invalidity of the claim, such as to impeach the credibility of a witness.[6]

"While it is well settled that offers of settlement are inadmissible to establish liability, whether a particular discussion is in fact a settlement offer may require the resolution of conflicting testimony and is a preliminary question for the trial judge."[7] A unilateral statement made by a person who injured a child in an automobile accident to the child's father that he would "fix it up, everything" was, for example, held to be an admission of liability, not an offer to compromise, and thus admissible.[8]

Expressions of sympathy such as "I'm sorry" generally do not qualify as admissions of liability.[9] Similarly expressions of apology or

---

[6] See, e.g., *Dahms v. Cognex Corp.*, 455 Mass 190, 198-199, 914 NE2d 872, 880 (2009) (evidence of settlement negotiations admissible as relevant to whether work restrictions imposed on plaintiff subsequent to filing sexual harassment claim were retaliatory); *Global Investors Agent Corp. v. National Fire Ins. Co. of Hartford*, 76 Mass App 812, 821-822, 927 NE2d 480, 490-491 (2010) (testimony by defendants' claim representative regarding settlement offers made to plaintiffs prior to litigation admissible on claims of unfair and deceptive trade practices); *Cottam v. CVS Pharmacy*, 436 Mass 316, 327-328, 764 NE2d 814, 824 (2002) (settlement between physician witness, called by defendant, and plaintiff relevant to show possible bias against plaintiff). See also *Zucco v. Kane*, 439 Mass 503, 509-510, 789 NE2d 115, 120 (2003) (statements plaintiff made in workers' compensation settlement agreement properly admitted against her when she testified to contrary facts in medical malpractice action).

[7] *Marchand v. Murray*, 27 Mass App 611, 615, 541 NE2d 371, 374 (1989) (conversation in question was considered an offer to purchase and not offer of settlement).

[8] *Bernasconi v. Bassi*, 261 Mass 26, 28, 158 NE 341, 342 (1927). See also *Cassidy v. Hollingsworth*, 324 Mass 424, 426, 86 NE2d 663, 664 (1949) (statement made after accident that "I guess I owe you a fender" was admissible); *Dennison v. Swerdlove*, 250 Mass 507, 146 NE 27 (1925) (defendant's statement immediately after automobile accident that he would "adjust, the damage to your car" was not offer to compromise but admissible as admission of fault).

[9] See GL 233, § 23D: "Statements, writings or benevolent gestures expressing sympathy or a general sense of benevolence relating to the pain, suffering or death of a person involved in an accident and made to such person or to the family of such person shall be inadmissible as evidence of an admission of liability in a civil action." See also *Denton v. Park Hotel, Inc.*, 343 Mass 524, 528, 180 NE2d 70, 73 (1962) (such statements have "no probative value as an admission of responsibility or liability" and "[c]ommon decency should not be penalized by treating such statements as admissions."); *Lyons v. Levine*, 352 Mass 769, 225 NE2d 593 (1967); *Casper v. Lavoie*, 1 Mass App 809, 294 NE2d 466 (1973).

sympathy by a health care provider are inadmissible at trial of a malpractice or related claim, unless the declarant or defense expert testifies to contradictory facts or opinions.[10]

Proposed Mass R Evid 408's reference to a "claim which was disputed as to either validity or amount" assures that there is a ripe dispute that is the subject of the compromise. Thus a phone message from an employer to its employee asking that the latter "come up with a number" to settle their business differences was admissible because at the time there was no indication that a lawsuit was planned.[11]

Both Proposed Mass R Evid 408 and Fed R Evid 408 provide that statements (such as admissions of fact) made in the course of compromise negotiations are also inadmissible. Massachusetts case law appears not to extend the exclusion that far.[12] Where, however, the parties "understood at [the time of the negotiations] that what was said at that time was said without prejudice to either party," admissions of fact will not be admissible at trial.[13] Admissions made on the face of settlement documents, as distinguished from those made during negotiation, are admissible (and would be even if Proposed Mass R Evid 408 were adopted):

> The distinction between statements made during negotiations and statements attached to a settlement document is critical. The primary argument in favor of excluding statements made during settlement negotiations is that the probative value of admitting them is outweighed by the public policy repercussions of discouraging compromise by penalizing candor between bargaining parties. This logic does not apply, however, to factual statements included within the settlement document itself. While it may be difficult to negotiate without discussing the factual bases of a dispute, a valid settlement can be drafted easily without referring to them. Admitting factual statements contained in settlement agreements, therefore, would only discourage factual statements, not the agreements themselves.[14]

---

[10] GL 233, § 79L.

[11] *Hurwitz v. Bocian*, 41 Mass App 365, 371-372, 670 NE2d 408, 413 (1996).

[12] See *Puzo v. Puzo*, 342 Mass 775, 173 NE2d 268 (1961); *Calvin Hosmer, Stolte Co. v. Paramount Cone Co.*, 285 Mass 278, 281, 189 NE 192, 194 (1934); *Wagman v. Ziskind*, 234 Mass 509, 125 NE 633 (1920).

[13] *Garber v. Levine*, 250 Mass 485, 490, 146 NE 21, 22-23 (1925).

[14] *Zucco v. Kane*, 439 Mass 503, 510-511, 789 NE2d 115, 120-121 (2003) (citations omitted).

Statements made during the course of mediation are not admissible.[15]

Payment of Medical Expenses. Payment of, or offer to pay, medical expenses is inadmissible to prove liability for the underlying injury, again based primarily on the public policy of encouraging such payments. Proposed Mass R Evid 409 reflects Massachusetts practice:

> **Payment of Medical and Similar Expenses**
>
> Evidence of furnishing or offering or promising to pay medical, hospital, or similar expenses occasioned by an injury is not admissible to prove liability for the injury.[16]

Offers to Plead Guilty. Massachusetts practice bars the use in evidence in any criminal or civil proceeding of a withdrawn guilty plea or an offer to plead guilty. Proposed Mass R Evid 410 provides:

> **Inadmissibility of Pleas, Offers of Pleas, and Related Statement**
>
> [E]vidence of a plea of guilty, later withdrawn, or a plea of nolo contendere, or an offer to plead guilty or nolo contendere to the crime charged or any other crime, charged or any other crime, or statements made in connection with, and relevant to, any of the foregoing pleas or

---

[15] GL 233, 23C (discussed infra at § 5.4.10): "Any communication made in the course of and relating to the subject matter of any mediation and which is made in the presence of such mediator by any participant, mediator or other person shall be a confidential communication and not subject to disclosure in any judicial or administrative proceeding." See also GL 152, § 48(5), read in *Zucco v. Kane*, 55 Mass App 76, 81-83, 769 NE2d 313, 318-319 (2002) as possibly precluding admission of fact statements attendant to lump sum agreements in workers' compensation proceedings.

[16] See also *Gallo v. Veliskakis*, 357 Mass 602, 606, 259 NE2d 568, 570 (1970) (statement by owner of automobile to parent of passenger injured that owner was sorry about accident and would take care of medical bills was not an admission of liability and lacked probative value).

Proposed Mass R Evid 409, unlike Rule 408, does not bar admissions of liability made in conjunction with such offers.

See also GL 231, § 140B:

> **Advance payments or settlements of claims by insurers; effect upon liability; admissibility as evidence; credit upon judgment; notice of limitations to claimant by insurer; accrual of cause of action**
>
> Any person against whom a claim or suit for damages on account of bodily injury, property damage, or death is made, or if such person is insured against loss by reason of his liability to pay such damages the insurer of such person may advance money to, or pay bills incurred by or on behalf of, such claimant, or plaintiff, as the case may be, without affecting the question of liability for such damages, and evidence of such payments shall not be admissible at the trial of such suit on the issue of liability or to mitigate damages; but if, in such case, there shall be a judgment in favor of the plaintiff for money damages, the presiding judge of the court in which the judgment is entered shall, upon motion of the defendant, credit upon such judgment the amount of such payments.

> offers, is not admissible in any civil or criminal proceedings against the person who made the plea or offer. However, evidence of a statement made in connection with, and relevant to, a plea of guilty, later withdrawn, or a plea of nolo contendere, or an offer to plead guilty or nolo contendere to the crime charged or any other crime, is admissible in a criminal proceeding for perjury if the statement was made by the defendant under oath, on the record, and in the presence of counsel.[17]

Except in a prosecution for perjury, the bar created applies to any statement made in the course of the plea negotiations as long as it is relevant to the negotiations.

The Massachusetts rule differs from its federal counterpart Fed R Evid 410 (and Fed R Crim P 11(e)) in two regards.[18] First, the statements in question need not have been made to an attorney for the prosecuting authority to qualify for exclusion, as is explicitly required by Fed R Evid 410(4).[19] Second, the rule excludes only statements made during "plea negotiations," not the apparently broader "plea discussions" referred to in the federal rule.[20] For discussion of the admissibility of a guilty plea not withdrawn, see § 8.6.2, infra.

Even though neither Proposed Mass R Evid 410 nor Mass R Crim P 12(f) addresses the admissibility in evidence of a refusal to plead guilty, such refusal is not admissible when offered by defendant to prove consciousness of innocence.[21]

---

[17] Mass R Crim Pro 12(f) is identical. These provisions change prior law in the Commonwealth, at least as to the admissibility of withdrawn guilty pleas in subsequent civil cases. See *Morrissey v. Powell*, 304 Mass 268, 271, 23 NE2d 411, 414 (1939). For the preclusive effect of a guilty plea in a subsequent civil proceeding, see *Aetna Casualty & Surety Co. v. Niziolek*, 395 Mass 737, 481 NE2d 1356 (1985).

[18] The Massachusetts rules track the original version of Fed R Evid 410, but a 1979 amendment changed federal practice in these regards.

[19] See *Com. v. Wilson*, 430 Mass 440, 442-443, 720 NE2d 464, 466-467 (1999) (statements to detective). But see *Com. v. Mejia*, 88 Mass App 227, 237, 36 NE3d 612, 621 (2015) ("because the defendant's statements were made to someone who had no authority to negotiate a plea, the judge properly admitted them").

[20] *Id.*, 430 Mass at 443, 720 NE2d at 467. On the issue of what constitutes plea negotiations, see also *Com. v. Smiley*, 431 Mass 477, 482 n.3, 727 NE2d 1182, 1187 n.3 (2000) (because the prosecutor made no promises, commitments, or offers, and defendant did not give his statement only in consideration of a benefit offered by prosecutor, there were no plea negotiations); *Com. v. Luce*, 34 Mass App 105, 111-112, 607 NE2d 427, 430-431 (1993) (meetings between defendant, counsel, and government officers did not constitute plea bargaining). Defendant's statement to a friend in a recorded telephone conversation while in jail that he would be happy to receive a sentence of five years for the murder charge did not constitute an offer to plead. *Com. v. Boyarsky*, 452 Mass 700, 709, 897 NE2d 574, 581 (2008).

[21] See *Com. v. DoVole*, 57 Mass App 657, 662, 785 NE2d 416, 420 (2003).

§ 4.7 Liability Insurance

Evidence of insurance coverage or lack thereof is not admissible on the issue of negligence or liability. It may be admissible for other purposes such as proof of agency, ownership, or control where those issues are genuinely in dispute, or to demonstrate the bias of a witness. Proposed Mass R Evid 411 reflects Massachusetts practice:

Liability Insurance

Evidence that a person was or was not insured against liability is not admissible upon the issue whether he acted negligently or otherwise wrongfully. This rule does not require the exclusion of evidence of insurance against liability when offered for another purpose, such as proof of agency, ownership, or control, or bias or prejudice of a witness.[1]

"Exposing juries to [insurance coverage] information is condemned because it is not itself probative of any relevant proposition and is taken to lead to undeserved verdicts for plaintiffs and exaggerated awards which jurors will readily load on faceless insurance companies supposedly paid for taking the risk."[2] The exclusion covers:

- Evidence offered by the plaintiff that the defendant is insured.
- Evidence offered by the defendant that the plaintiff has received third-party compensation for his injury.
- Evidence offered by the defendant that he is not protected by insurance (considered a "plea of poverty" that might influence the jury to give defendant "compassionate but strictly unmerited relief from personal liability").
- Evidence offered by the plaintiff that he has no resort to insurance or other coverage for his loss.[3]

---

§ 4.7 [1] See also *Goldstein v. Gontarz*, 364 Mass 800, 807-814, 309 NE2d 196, 202-205 (1974) (extensive discussion of principles and authorities); *Leavitt v. Glick Realty Corp.*, 362 Mass 370, 372, 285 NE2d 786, 787-788 (1972). That a party carries liability insurance, either voluntarily or because a third party requires it to, is not relevant to the question of what risks and dangers it foresaw or should have foreseen. *Carrel v. National Cord & Braid Corp.*, 447 Mass 431, 448-449, 852 NE2d 100, 113-114 (2006).

[2] *Goldstein v. Gontarz*, supra, 364 Mass at 808, 309 NE2d at 202. But see *McDaniel v. Pickens*, 45 Mass App 63, 70, 695 NE2d 215, 219 (1998) (raising but not reaching the issue of "whether jurors have attained to such a level of sophistication that they can take insurance and related things in stride when properly instructed.").

[3] *Goldstein v. Gontarz*, supra, 364 Mass at 808-810, 309 NE2d at 202-204.

Evidence of a policy of indemnity insurance is admissible on the issue of control over the covered premises, if disputed, because the jury could properly infer that "the defendants would not have deemed it prudent to secure indemnity insurance on [an area] not within their control, or for the careless management or defective condition of which they could not be held responsible."[4] A blanket insurance policy covering more than one location is not, however, admissible to show control.[5]

Evidence of insurance coverage or lack thereof may be admissible to establish the bias of a witness. Where, for example,

> a defendant's expert in a particular malpractice action has appeared for numerous defendant physicians all insured by one or a group of liability insurers and expects further references from the same sources, a judge may admit such evidence as tending to prove the expert's biased mindset (with limiting instructions, probably, to guard against the jury's applying the fact of the insurance to the issue of the defendant physician's negligence or to other immediately extraneous matters). But where an expert has had no relation to any liability insurer apart from the fact that the defendant's insurer in the end footed his bill, a judge might decide to limit the cross-examination to exclude reference to the insurance altogether, and so avoid any collateral entanglements.[6]

The matter is one of discretion for the trial judge to weigh the probative force of the bias challenge against the risk of prejudicial effect.[7] Where counsel intends to pursue this subject, advance notice to the court and counsel is strongly advised.[8]

---

[4] *Perkins v. Rice*, 187 Mass 28, 30, 72 NE 323, 324 (1904).

[5] See *Camerlin v. Marshall*, 411 Mass 394, 398, 582 NE2d 539, 542 (1991) (& cases cited).

[6] *McDaniel v. Pickens*, supra, 45 Mass App at 67, 695 NE2d at 217-218. See also *Harris-Lewis v. Mudge*, 60 Mass App 480, 487-488, 803 NE2d 735, 741-742 (2004) (patient's insurance coverage was relevant in medical malpractice case to his credibility in denying cocaine use to his physician, as it established a compelling financial incentive to lie); *Com. v. Danis*, 38 Mass App 968, 650 NE2d 802 (1995) (showing that policy did not cover collision damage to prosecution witness' car was relevant to her possible bias in trial of vehicular offenses).

[7] *Masters v. Khuri*, 62 Mass App 467, 471, 817 NE2d 811, 815 (2004) (no error in excluding cross-examination of physician's experts regarding compensation received from insurer on previous occasions).

[8] *Id.*

Evidence of insurance coverage has been held inadmissible in intra-family tort actions even though jurors may wrongfully assume that one family member is seeking to deplete the assets of another family member and that institution of the lawsuit has disrupted family harmony.[9]

Ordinarily, evidence of collateral source payments (such as workers' compensation benefits) is excluded because jurors may be led to consider the plaintiff's claims unimportant or trivial, or to reduce a verdict in the plaintiff's favor believing that otherwise there would be unjust double recovery. In some limited circumstances, however, such evidence may be admissible as probative of a relevant proposition such as the credibility of a witness.[10]

---

[9] *Share v. Shore*, 385 Mass 529, 432 NE2d 526 (1982) (any possible prejudice should be dealt with by appropriate instructions).

[10] See *Goldstein v. Gontarz*, supra, 364 Mass at 809, 309 NE2d at 202; *Corsetti v. Stone Co.*, 396 Mass 1, 16-21, 483 NE2d 793, 801-804 (1985); *West v. Shawmut Design & Construction*, 39 Mass App 247, 655 NE2d 136 (1995) (& citations) (extensive discussion). See also *Harris-Lewis v. Mudge*, supra, 60 Mass App at 487-488, 803 NE2d at 741-742 (value of patient's contract with Boston Celtics and continued salary was relevant in medical malpractice case to his credibility in denying cocaine use to his physician, as it established a compelling financial incentive to lie). See generally *Fitzgerald v. Expressway Sewerage Construction, Inc.*, 177 F3d 71 (1st Cir 1999) (discussing Massachusetts collateral source rule).

CHAPTER 5

PRIVILEGES and DISQUALIFICATIONS

§ 5.1 Introduction

GL 233, § 20[1] provides for two disqualifications that bar testimony relating private conversations between spouses (see § 5.2.1, infra) and

---

§ 5.1 [1] Any person of sufficient understanding, although a party, may testify in any proceeding, civil or criminal, in court or before a person who has authority to receive evidence, except as follows:

> First, Except in a proceeding arising out of or involving a contract made by a married woman with her husband, a proceeding under chapter two hundred and nine D and in a

testimony of a minor child against a parent in certain circumstances (see § 5.3, infra). The statute also creates a privilege of a spouse not to testify against the other spouse in a criminal case (see § 5.2.2) and of a criminal defendant not to testify in the proceedings against him (see § 5.14, infra).[2]

Regarding these disqualifications and privileges, which deprive courts of probative evidence but are justified by policy concerns such as family harmony, the Supreme Judicial Court has observed:

> Testimonial privileges are exceptions to the general duty imposed on all people to testify.[3] Such privileges diminish the evidence before the court, and contravene the fundamental principle that the public has a right to every man's evidence. As such, they must be strictly construed,

---

prosecution begun under sections one to ten, inclusive, of chapter two hundred and seventy-three, any criminal proceeding in which one spouse is a defendant alleged to have committed a crime against the other spouse or to have violated a temporary or permanent vacate, restraining, or no-contact order or judgment issued pursuant to section eighteen, thirty-four B or thirty-four C of chapter two hundred and eight section thirty-two of chapter two hundred and nine, section three, three B, three C, four, or five of chapter two hundred and nine A, or sections fifteen or twenty of chapter two hundred and nine C, or a similar protection order issued by another jurisdiction, obtained by the other spouse, and except in a proceeding involving abuse of a person under the age of eighteen, including incest, neither husband nor wife shall testify as to private conversations with the other.

Second, Except as otherwise provided in section seven of chapter two hundred and seventy-three and except in any proceeding relating to child abuse, including incest, neither husband nor wife shall be compelled to testify in the trial of an indictment, complaint or other criminal proceeding against the other.

Third, the defendant in the trial of an indictment, complaint or other criminal proceeding shall, at his own request, but not otherwise, be allowed to testify; but his neglect or refusal to testify shall not create any presumption against him.

Fourth, An unemancipated, minor child, living with a parent, shall not testify before a grand jury, trial of an indictment, complaint or other criminal proceeding, against said parent, where the victim in such proceeding is not a member of said parent's family and who does not reside in the said parent's household. For the purposes of this clause the term "parent" shall mean the natural or adoptive mother or father of said child.

[2] For a case discussing the evolving right of privacy as it manifests itself in a privilege against disclosure of personal information in the course of litigation, see *Planned Parenthood of Massachusetts v. Blake*, 417 Mass 467, 476-479, 631 NE2d 985, 991-993 (1994).

[3] Proposed Mass R Evid 501provides:

Privileges Recognized Only as Provided
Except as otherwise provided by constitution or statue or by these or other rules promulgated by the Supreme Judicial Court of this Commonwealth, no person has a privilege to:

(1) refuse to be a witness;
(2) refuse to disclose any matter;
(3) refuse to produce any object or writing;
(4) prevent another from being a witness or disclosing any matter or producing any object or writing.

> and accepted only to the very limited extent that permitting a refusal to testify or excluding relevant evidence has a public good transcending the normally predominant principle of utilizing all rational means for ascertaining truth.[4]

Matters of privilege and disqualification in the federal courts are not specifically enumerated in the evidentiary rules but are governed by constitutional, statutory, or common law.[5] In diversity cases, the federal courts apply the state evidentiary rules of privilege and competence pursuant to *Erie Railroad Co. v. Tompkins*.[6] The Proposed Massachusetts Rules of Evidence, modeled on a draft of proposed federal rules rejected by Congress, do enumerate privileges and disqualifications, as discussed below.[7]

A party in a civil action may resist discovery on the basis of privilege.[8] Having done so, the party may not rely on the privileged information as evidence at trial. Conversely, a party may waive the privilege and then offer the information as evidence. A party following the latter course should waive the privilege before raising it as a bar to discovery, to allow his adversary sufficient time for discovery and preparation. "A waiver on the virtual eve of trial is insufficient and, depending on the circumstances, may justify an order barring the use of the privileged evidence."[9]

Evidentiary privileges and disqualifications, which exclude evidence in court proceedings, are to be distinguished from duties of confidentiality (such as that between physician and patient, see § 5.5.1, infra), and from "privileges" that serve as substantive defenses, such as the litigation privilege that immunizes statements made in the institution of or during the course of judicial proceedings from defamation liability.[10]

---

[4] *Three Juveniles v. Com.*, 390 Mass 357, 359-360, 455 NE2d 1203, 1205 (1983). See also *Com. v. Fitzpatrick*, 463 Mass 581, 598-600, 977 NE2d 505, 520-521 (2012) ("evidentiary privileges are to be narrowly construed and are generally waivable").

[5] See Fed R Evid 501.

[6] 304 US 64 (1938); Fed R Evid 501, 601. See, e.g., *Kowalski v. Gagne*, 914 F2d 299, 306-308 (1st Cir 1990) (Massachusetts spousal disqualification would apply in wrongful death diversity action).

[7] See Proposed Mass R Evid 501-512.

[8] Mass R Civ P 26(b)(1).

[9] *G.S. Enterprises, Inc. v. Falmouth Marine, Inc.*, 410 Mass 262, 270-271, 571 NE2d 1363, 1368 (1991).

[10] See *Harmon Law Offices, P.C. v. Attorney General*, 83 Mass App 830, 991 NE2d 1098, 1106 (2013) (& cases cited).

§ 5.2 Husband-Wife

GL 233, § 20 disqualifies spouses from testifying as to private conversations with each other (see § 5.2.1), and privileges a spouse from testifying against the other in any criminal proceeding (see § 5.2.2). A common-law disqualification that prevented a spouse from testifying as to impotency or non-access when the legitimacy of a child born in wedlock is in issue has been abandoned (see § 5.2.4).

§ 5.2.1 Disqualification of Spouses to Disclose Private Conversations

GL 233, § 20, provides that "neither husband nor wife shall testify as to private conversations with the other." The disqualification does not apply:

- in proceedings arising out of a contract between husband and wife;
- in proceedings to enforce support or a prosecution for non-support;[1]
- in any criminal proceeding in which one spouse is alleged to have committed a crime against the other or to have violated a court order protecting the other;
- in a proceeding, criminal or civil, involving abuse of a person under age 18.[2]

The disqualification applies in divorce cases, but not to mere abusive language addressed by one spouse to the other outside the context of a conversation.[3]

The rule is one of disqualification, not privilege. The spouses are forbidden (upon objection of the party against whom it is offered) to

---

§ 5.2 [1] In a prosecution for nonsupport "both husband and wife shall be competent witnesses to testify against each other to any relevant matters," and "any existing statute or rule of law prohibiting the disclosure of confidential communications between husband and wife" shall be inapplicable. GL 273, § 7.

[2] See *Com. v. Burnham*, 451 Mass 517, 520-521, 887 NE2d 222, 225-226 (2008); *Com. v. Winfield*, 76 Mass App 716, 724 n.5, 926 NE2d 550, 557 n.5 (2010), *habeas denied*, *Winfield v. O'Brien*, 775 F3d 1 (1st Cir 2014). The Supreme Judicial Court has not determined whether testimony produced in violation of the statutory spousal privilege or disqualification should be admissible for impeachment purposes. See *Com. v. Paszko*, 391 Mass 164, 191 n.31, 461 NE2d 222, 238 n.31 (1984).

[3] See *Fuller v. Fuller*, 177 Mass 184, 58 NE 588 (1900).

testify about the conversation, even if both wish the evidence to be received.[4] If no objection is made, testimony as to the conversation may be admitted for its full probative value.[5]

The disqualification applies only to conversations between persons validly married at the time of the conversation; conversations occurring before marriage are not included.[6] The disqualification does not terminate with the death of one of the spouses[7] unless the conversation may be admitted as a declaration of a deceased person within the terms of GL 233, § 65, discussed in § 8.20.1, infra. The disqualification applies only to oral conversations; written communications are not deemed "conversations" within the meaning of the statute.[8]

If a third person is present and hears the conversation, it is not "private" and the disqualification is inapplicable.[9] Whether a conversation between husband and wife that occurs in the proximity of other persons was "private" depends upon the distance of the other persons, whether they were within earshot, and whether they were paying attention to the conversation.[10] Whether a conversation in the presence of a

---

[4] See *Gallagher v. Goldstein*, 402 Mass 457, 459-460, 524 NE2d 53, 54-55 (1988) (testimony of husband regarding conversation with wife concerning her symptoms properly excluded in medical malpractice case on objection of defendant physician) (citing Text); *Kaye v. Newhall*, 356 Mass 300, 304, 249 NE2d 583, 585 (1969).

[5] *Miller v. Miller*, 448 Mass 320, 326, 861 NE2d 393, 399 (2007); *Com. v. Salyer*, 84 Mass App 346, 354-355, 996 NE2d 488, 495 (2013).

[6] *Com. v. Barronian*, 235 Mass 364, 366, 126 NE 833, 834 (1920).

[7] See *Dexter v. Booth*, 84 Mass (2 All) 559, 561 (1861).

[8] See *Com. v. Szczuka*, 391 Mass 666, 678 n.14, 464 NE2d 38, 46 n.14 (1984) (letters from defendant to wife). Compare Proposed Mass R Evid 504(b)(1) (discussed below) which substitutes the broader phrase "communications" and thus includes acts other than conversations "by which ideas may be transmitted from one person to another." See Advisory Committee Note to R 504(b)(1).

[9] *Com. v. Foxworth*, 473 Mass 149, 159-160, 40 NE3d 1003, 1012-1013 (2015); *Com. v. Perez*, 460 Mass 683, 698, 954 NE2d 1, 15 (2011); *Com. v. Paszko*, 391 Mass 164, 190 n.30, 461 NE2d 222, 238 n.30 (1984).

[10] See, e.g., *Com. v. Perez*, 460 Mass 683, 698, 954 NE2d 1, 15 (2011) (it could reasonably be inferred that third party present in small apartment could overhear phone conversation between defendant and his wife). Compare *Freeman v. Freeman*, 238 Mass 150, 161-162, 130 NE 220, 222 (1921) (testimony properly excluded because it did not appear that any passers-by on public street paid any attention to conversation or could even hear it) with *Linnell v. Linnell*, 249 Mass 51, 54, 143 NE 813, 814 (1924) (testimony regarding conversations properly admitted because daughter was in next room just across hall for first conversation and second conversation took place in train station waiting room).

child was "private" depends upon the child's intellectual ability to pay attention and understand what was being said.[11]

The subject matter of the conversation need not be of a confidential nature in order to fit within the disqualification. Business conversations between husband and wife are included.[12] By its terms, however, GL 233, § 20 does not disqualify a spouse from testifying to private conversations concerning the disputed transactions in an action arising out of or involving a contract between the spouses.[13]

Threats and verbal assaults are not considered "private conversations" and thus do not come within the disqualification.[14] "Whether the policy is to protect the marital relationship or to encourage confidence between spouses, or merely reflects legislative reticence concerning marital confidences, the purpose does not logically extend to words constituting or accompanying abuse, threats, or assaults of which the other spouse is the victim."[15] Spontaneous exclamations of pain are similarly not subject to the disqualification.[16] It has been suggested that the marital disqualification might not apply where the communications are made at a time when the spouses are jointly involved in criminal activity.[17]

The statutory disqualification covers the contents of the private conversation, but not the fact that a conversation occurred. "There is a plain line of demarcation between the occurrence of the fact of a private conversation between husband and wife, which [where relevant] may be competent, and a narration of the substance of that conversation by

---

[11] *Freeman v. Freeman*, 238 Mass 150, 161, 130 NE 220, 222 (1921) (conversation in front of nine-year-old daughter and younger siblings properly admitted). See also *Com. v. Stokes*, supra, 374 Mass at 595, 374 NE2d at 95.

[12] *Com. v. Hayes*, 145 Mass 289, 293, 14 NE 151, 153 (1887) (testimony of defendant concerning directions she gave husband, as her agent, relating to their business was properly excluded).

[13] See, e.g., *Hutchinson v. Hutchinson*, 6 Mass App 705, 710-711, 383 NE2d 82, 85-86 (1978) (action by husband for equitable relief seeking reconveyance of stock transferred to wife).

[14] See *Com. v. Foxworth*, supra, 473 Mass at 159-160, 40 NE3d at 1012-1013; *Com. v. Burnham*, 451 Mass 517, 523, 887 NE2d 222, 227 (2008); *Com. v. Gillis*, 358 Mass 215, 217, 263 NE2d 437, 439 (1970) (& cases cited).

[15] *Com. v. Gillis*, supra, 358 Mass at 217-218, 263 NE2d at 439-440. See also *Com. v. O'Brien*, supra, 377 Mass at 774, 388 NE2d at 661. But see *Sherry v. Moore*, 265 Mass 189, 194, 163 NE 906, 907 (1928) (statement by husband to wife that he wished she were dead was not "abusive language" and thus properly excluded).

[16] *Com. v. Jardine*, 143 Mass 567, 10 NE 250 (1887).

[17] See *Com. v. Walker*, 438 Mass 246, 254 n.4, 780 NE2d 26, 33 n.4 (2002) (& citations).

either of them, which is not competent."[18] The disqualification does not apply to evidence of, or reference to, the absence of a conversation.[19]

While spouses are forbidden to testify concerning the conversation, a third person who overheard it may testify about it. "The circumstance that the conversation was between a husband and wife while they were physically alone is no ground for objection. There is no rule of law that third persons who hear a private conversation between a husband and wife shall be restrained from testifying what it was."[20] Where the private statements of one spouse are repeated by the other to a third party, that party is disqualified from testifying to the statements.[21]

Characterizing GL 233, § 20, cl 1, as a "statutory preservation of a remnant of an outdated common-law concept," the Supreme Judicial Court has nonetheless left any reform of the disqualification to the Legislature:

> It seems imprudent to prohibit testimony as to a marital conversation when both parties to the conversation want disclosure and the interests of the marital unit would be furthered by disclosure. However, the Legislature has enacted a statute stating a clear and unambiguous preference for the marital disqualification. We have consistently ruled that the statute renders spouses incompetent to testify as to the contents of their private conversations with their marital partners. . . . While we agree with the plaintiff that many of the stated policy reasons for this statute are anachronistic and that those that are not outmoded, such as the preservation of marital confidentiality and harmony, are not furthered by the inadmissibility of this testimony, we must construe the statute as written. Were this strictly a common law rule, we would not hesitate to transform it from a rule of disqualification to one of privilege. However, given the existence of the statute, that decision is for the Legislature.[22]

---

[18] *Sampson v. Sampson*, 223 Mass 451, 458-459, 112 NE 84, 87 (1916). See also *Miller v. Miller*, 448 Mass 320, 326-327, 861 NE2d 393, 399 (2007) (timing of conversations relevant to when marriage became irretrievably broken); *Freeman v. Freeman*, supra, 238 Mass at 161, 130 NE at 222 (wife properly permitted to testify that she refrained from engaging in certain social affairs in consequence of conversation with husband).

[19] See *Com. v. Dodgson*, 80 Mass App 307, 315, 952 NE2d 961, 968-969 (2011).

[20] *Com. v. Wakelin*, 230 Mass 567, 574, 120 NE 209, 212 (1918) (witness permitted to relate conversation he recorded between husband and wife in jail cell). See also *Com. v. O'Brien*, 377 Mass 772, 774-775, 388 NE2d 658, 661 (1979) (attorney could testify to conversation in his presence).

[21] *Com. v. Garcia*, 89 Mass App 67, 72-73, 45 NE3d 602, 607-608 (2016).

[22] *Gallagher v. Goldstein*, supra, 402 Mass at 460-461, 524 NE2d at 55 (citations omitted).

The policies behind the disqualification may be outweighed by a criminal defendant's constitutional rights to confrontation and a fair trial.[23]

Proposed Mass R Evid 504(b)[24] is for the most part consistent with present practice concerning the disqualification of testimony from a spouse regarding private conversations with the other spouse.

§ 5.2.2 *Privilege of Spouse Not to Testify Against Other Spouse in Criminal Case*

Except in a prosecution for nonsupport or a proceeding relating to child abuse (including incest), "neither husband nor wife shall be compelled to testify in the trial of an indictment, complaint or other criminal proceeding against the other." GL 233, § 20, cl Second. The statutory privilege replaced the common-law prohibition preventing a spouse from being a witness in any case (civil or criminal) in which the

---

[23] See *Com. v. Sugrue*, 34 Mass App 172, 177-178, 607 NE2d 1045, 1048-1049 (1993) (private conversation in which defendant threatened to obtain custody of children in event of divorce was admissible in prosecution for indecent assault on defendant's son, as it provided evidence of motive for wife to lie about incident). Compare *Com. v. Perl*, 50 Mass App 445, 453-454, 737 NE2d 937, 944-945 (2000) (disqualification not overridden where defendant's purpose for introducing conversations with spouse was subject of other testimony and thus cumulative). See also *Com. v. Maillet*, 400 Mass 572, 578 n.8, 511 NE2d 529, 533 n.8 (1987).

[24] 504(b) provides:

Disqualified Communication

(1) ***General Rule.*** Neither husband nor wife shall testify as to confidential communications with the other.

(2) ***Definition.*** A communication is confidential if it is made by any person to his or her spouse and is not intended for disclosure to any other person.

(3) ***Exceptions.*** The foregoing disqualification of confidential communications does not apply:

(i) In a civil proceeding to a declaration of a deceased spouse if the court finds that it was made in good faith and upon the personal knowledge of the declarant.

(ii) In a proceeding arising out of or involving a contract made between a husband and wife.

(iii) In a proceeding under G.L. c. 273A, Uniform Reciprocal Enforcement of Support Act.

(iv) In any prosecution for nonsupport, desertion, or neglect of parental duty.

"In most respects this rule is proposed from current Massachusetts law." See Advisory Committee's Note to Rule 504. The Rule would, however, extend the disqualification to written communications.

other spouse was a party.[25] The privilege applies only to a spouse's testimony offered in a criminal trial.[26]

While application of the spousal disqualification discussed above is contingent upon marriage at the time of the conversation, availability of the privilege depends upon marriage *at time of testifying*.[27] The Supreme Judicial Court has refused to establish an analogous common-law privilege for unmarried persons who live together.[28]

The privilege is personal; it can be claimed or waived by the witness-spouse only, and may be waived over the objection of the other spouse.[29] The "spouse facing criminal prosecution [has] no voice in controlling the witness stand appearance of the other."[30] Consequently, the defendant-spouse has no standing to assert error in the admission of privileged testimony from the other spouse, or assert the waiver was invalid.[31] The privilege applies where the spouse is called as a witness *by* the defendant to testify *for him* as well as where the spouse is called to testify against the defendant.[32]

Because one spouse may testify against the other in a criminal case only if willing to do so, the Supreme Judicial Court has advised that "good trial practice" requires that the judge "satisfy himself, outside the presence of the jury, that the spouse who is about to testify against the other in a criminal proceeding knowingly waives his or her statutory privilege."[33]

Where it is clear that a witness, if called to testify, will invoke the privilege, the witness should not be called or, alternatively, should be questioned in the absence of the jury. "[The witness] should not be put

---

[25] *Com. v. Maillet*, 400 Mass 572, 575-576, 511 NE2d 529, 531-532 (1987).

[26] *Com. v. Cotto*, 471 Mass 97, 27 NE3d 1213, 1230-1231 (2015) (privilege inapplicable in evidentiary hearing pertaining to post-conviction motions).

[27] For a case in which it was found that the defendant married the victim with the intent to enable her to claim the spousal privilege and avoid testifying against him, see *Com. v. Szerlong*, 457 Mass 858, 864-866, 933 NE2d 633, 641-642 (2010) (applying forfeiture by wrongdoing doctrine to admit victim's hearsay statements).

[28] See *Com. v. Diaz*, 422 Mass 269, 273-274, 661 NE2d 1326, 1329 (1996).

[29] *Com. v. Stokes*, 374 Mass 583, 595, 374 NE2d 87, 96 (1978).

[30] *Com. v. Maillet*, supra, 400 Mass at 576, 511 NE2d at 532.

[31] *Com. v. Maillet*, supra; *Com. v. Rosa*, 412 Mass 147, 160-162, 587 NE2d 767, 775-776 (1992) (but spouse's testimony cannot be used where her decision to testify is found to have been involuntary) (citing Text); *Com. v. Garcia*, 89 Mass App 67, 71-72, 45 NE3d 602, 606-607 (2016) (but judge improperly advised witness the privilege was to refuse to testify only about conversations with the defendant).

[32] See *Com. v. Maillet*, supra, 400 Mass at 575-578, 511 NE2d at 531-533 (phrase "against the other" in GL 233, § 20, cl 2, refers to nature of proceeding and not content of spousal testimony).

[33] *Com. v. Stokes*, supra, 374 Mass at 595 n.9, 374 NE2d at 96 n.9.

in the position of having to exercise the privilege before the jury, lest they draw inferences adverse to the party against whom the witness is called to testify."[34]

By explicit words of the statute, the privilege does not apply "in any proceeding relating to child abuse." This has been held to render the privilege inapplicable even where the child victim is not related to either husband or wife and does not live with them.[35] Nor does the privilege apply in grand jury proceedings.[36] There is no privilege for a spouse not to testify against the other spouse in a civil action "even if that testimony may be highly destructive of the marital relationship."[37]

As with the spousal disqualification (see 5.2.1, supra), it has been recognized that the constitutional right to present a defense might be implicated in a case where the spousal privilege deprives the defendant of material evidence favorable to his defense.[38]

Proposed Mass R Evid 504(a)[39] is consistent with present practice in recognizing a privilege not to testify against one's spouse in a criminal proceeding, but would extend the privilege to nontrial settings such as the grand jury[40] and make explicit an exception for domestic abuse prosecutions. Federal practice is in accord with that of Massachusetts in

---

[34] *Com. v. Labbe*, 6 Mass App 73, 79, 373 NE2d 227, 232 (1978). See also *Com. v. Szerlong*, 457 Mass 858, 869 n.13, 933 NE2d 633, 644 n.13 (2010). But see *Com. v. DiPietro*, 373 Mass 369, 388-391, 367 NE2d 811, 823 (1977) (no error in permitting Commonwealth to call defendant's spouse in front of jury to assert privilege because Commonwealth was entitled to lay foundation for admission of spouse's prior testimony, especially in light of fact that defendant's own act in marrying the principal witness against him four days before trial compelled Commonwealth to resort to witness's prior testimony).

[35] See *Villalta v. Com.*, 428 Mass 429, 434, 702 NE2d 1148, 1152 (1998).

[36] *In re Grand Jury Subpoena*, 447 Mass 88, 98, 849 NE2d 797, 805 (2006) (but requiring spouse to testify before grand jury would not waive her right to invoke privilege at subsequent trial).

[37] See *Three Juveniles v. Com.*, 390 Mass 357, 361, 455 NE2d 1203, 1206 (1983).

[38] See *Com. v. Maillet*, supra, 400 Mass at 578 n.8, 511 NE2d at 533 n.8. See also *Com. v. Sugrue*, 34 Mass App 172, 177-178, 607 NE2d 1045, 1048-1049 (1993).

[39] Proposed Mass R Evid 504(a) provides:

> (a) ***Testimonial Privilege***
>
> (1) ***General Rule.*** In any criminal proceeding, neither husband nor wife shall be compelled to testify against the other.
>
> (2) ***Exceptions.*** The foregoing shall not apply in any prosecution for nonsupport, desertion, neglect of parental duty, or abuse of family or household member.

[40] See Advisory Committee Note to R 504(a)(1).

recognizing a privilege in the witness-spouse that may be asserted (or waived) only by that spouse and not the defendant.[41]

No comment may be made and no adverse inference drawn based on invocation of the privilege.[42]

§ 5.2.3 *Comparison Between the Statutory Disqualification and Privilege*

The following are the distinctions between the disqualification for private spousal conversations, GL 233, § 20, cl 1, and the privilege not to testify against a spouse in a criminal case, GL 233, § 20, cl 2:

(1) The disqualification applies in all actions, civil and criminal, and regardless of whether one of the spouses is a party or not; the privilege applies only in criminal cases where the spouse is the defendant.
(2) The disqualification affects only testimony concerning private conversations between the spouses; the privilege affects all testimony.
(3) The disqualification operates whether or not one or both spouses want to disclose the conversation; the privilege operates only if invoked (and not waived) by the witness-spouse.
(4) The disqualification prevents both spouses from testifying; the privilege excuses only the non-defendant spouse from testifying.
(5) The disqualification depends upon the existence of the marriage relationship at the time of the conversation; the privilege depends upon the existence of the relation at the time of trial.[43]

---

[41] See *Trammel v. United States*, 445 US 40 (1980).

[42] *Com. v. Szerlong*, 457 Mass 858, 869-870, 933 NE2d 633, 643-645 (2010).

[43] For further discussion of these differences, see *Com. v. Szerlong*, supra, 457 Mass at 859 n.3, 933 NE2d at 637 n.3; *Com. v. McCreary*, 12 Mass App 690, 695-697, 428 NE2d 361, 366 (1981) (judge apparently confused statutory disqualification and privilege).

§ 5.2.4 Abandonment of Lord Mansfield's Rule Disqualifying Spouses from Testifying as to Illegitimacy of Child

In *C. C. v. A. B.*,[44] the Supreme Judicial Court abandoned Lord Mansfield's Rule, a disqualification that prevented either husband or wife from testifying as to impotency or as to nonaccess between them where the legitimacy of a child born in lawful wedlock was in issue. Explaining that "[m]odern trends in the law, combined with changes in social attitudes, have brought into question the continuing validity of archaic rules which obfuscate the truth-seeking principles our system of jurisprudence strives to achieve."[45]

Proposed Mass R Evid 601, establishing a general rule of competence, would also abrogate the Rule.[46]

§ 5.3 Parent-Child

GL 233, § 20, was amended in 1986 to add the Fourth Clause providing that "[a]n unemancipated, minor child, living with a parent, shall not testify before a grand jury, trial of an indictment, complaint or other criminal proceeding, against said parent, where the victim in such proceeding is not a member of said parent's family and who does not reside in the said parent's household." Adoption of the disqualification followed the Supreme Judicial Court's refusal to recognize a common-law privilege permitting a child to refuse to testify against a parent in criminal proceedings.[1] Three dissenters argued (with apparent persuasion in the Legislature):

> The State should not make unrealistic demands on its citizens, especially its children. A requirement that an unemancipated minor child, living with his or her parents, must incriminate one or both of them is an unrealistic demand, at least when a family member is not a victim of the crime under investigation. The demand is unrealistic because it is insensitive to the needs of children, and to the nature of the normal relationship between children and their parents, involving, as it does, love, trust, loyalty, and dependency. This court should recognize a public policy against imposing on the conscience of a child responsibility for incriminating his or her parent. Society's interest in its children should

[44] 406 Mass 679, 550 NE2d 365 (1990).
[45] 406 Mass at 688, 550 NE2d at 371.
[46] See Advisory Committee Note to R 601.
§ 5.3 [1] See *Three Juveniles v. Com.*, 390 Mass 357, 455 NE2d 1203 (1983).

> be recognized as sufficiently important to outweigh the need for probative evidence in the administration of criminal justice in the circumstances presented by this case.[2]

The phrase "living with a parent" as used in GL 233, § 20, Fourth, is given its ordinary meaning: the disqualification applies only to a child who actually resides with the accused parent.[3]

The Supreme Judicial Court has declined to create a testimonial privilege under which parents could not be compelled to testify against their minor child as to confidential communications from the child, leaving the issue for consideration by the legislature.[4] Where the parent's privilege against self-incrimination is not involved, there is no bar to requiring a parent to testify in a child custody termination proceeding.[5]

§ 5.4 Attorney-Client

§ 5.4.1 Introduction

Where a person as a client or prospective client consults a member of the bar in his or her capacity as such, the communication in confidence of matters that are (or that the client reasonably supposes to be) necessary to the proper conduct of legal business is privileged at the option of the client.[1] As Proposed Mass R Evid 502(b) provides: "A client has a privilege to refuse to disclose and to prevent any other person from disclosing confidential communications made for the purpose of facilitating the rendition of professional legal services to the client . . ." The privilege is reinforced by an attorney's ethical duty to preserve the confidences and secrets of the client.[2]

The purpose of the privilege is "to encourage full and frank communication between attorneys and their clients and thereby promote

---

[2] 390 Mass at 366, 455 NE2d at 1209 (O'Connor, J, Hennessey, CJ, and Lynch, J, dissenting).

[3] See *In re Grand Jury Investigation*, 443 Mass 20, 819 NE2d 171 (2004) (rejecting argument that phrase should include children who are in marital home with mother while parents are separated and who receive frequent visits from father).

[4] See *In re Grand Jury Subpoena*, 430 Mass 590, 722 NE2d 450 (2000).

[5] *Adoption of Salvatore*, 57 Mass App 929, 930, 786 NE2d 858, 860-861 (2003).

§ 5.4 [1] See *In the Matter of a John Doe Grand Jury Investigation*, 408 Mass 480, 482, 562 NE2d 69 (1990); *Panell v. Rosa*, 228 Mass 594, 596, 118 NE 225, 226 (1918).

[2] See SJC Rule 3:07, Rules of Prof Conduct Rule 1.6 (as amended July 1, 2015); *Com. v. Downey*, 58 Mass App 591, 596-597, 793 NE2d 377, 381 (2003).

broader public interests in the observance of law and administration of justice. The privilege recognizes that sound legal advice or advocacy serves public ends and that such advice or advocacy depends upon the lawyer being fully informed by the client."[3] The Supreme Judicial Court has assigned "extraordinarily high value" to the privilege, which protects "the right of every citizen to obtain the thoughtful advice of a fully informed attorney concerning legal matters," even at the cost of resolving a murder investigation.[4] The Court has recently imposed procedures to protect against the disclosure of privileged communications when the Commonwealth seeks to seize emails of a defendant under indictment.[5] It has also ruled that the privilege protects a law firm from being compelled by grand jury subpoena from producing a cell phone its client had turned over to obtain legal advice, even in the face of probable cause to believe it contained evidence of crime.[6]

The court has recognized, however, that the privilege may have to yield to a constitutionally based claim of denial of the right of confrontation or to a fair trial.[7]

Similarly the attorney-client privilege may be overridden when it conflicts with an important public policy such as the legislative mandate to report possible child abuse provided in GL 119, § 51A.[8] The privilege is not overridden by the disclosure provisions of the public

---

[3] *Upjohn Co. v. United States*, 449 US 383, 389 (1981). For an extensive discussion of the privilege, see also *Commissioner of Revenue v. Comcast Corp.*, 453 Mass 293, 901 NE2d 1185 (2009); *Suffolk Construction Co., Inc. v. Division of Capital Asset Management*, 449 Mass 444, 870 NE2d 33 (2007); *Hanover Ins. Co. v. Rapo & Jepsen Ins. Services, Inc.*, 449 Mass 609, 870 NE2d 1105 (2007).

[4] *In the Matter of a John Doe Grand Jury Investigation*, supra, 408 Mass at 485, 562 NE2d at 69 (attorney-client privilege of deceased husband is not overridden by society's interest in ascertaining truth concerning murder of wife); *Com. v. Goldman*, 395 Mass 495, 501-502, 480 NE2d 1023, 1028 (1985) (privilege of prosecution witness not overridden in the interest of justice by defendant's need for testimony).

[5] *Preventive Medicine Associates, Inc. v. Com.*, 465 Mass 810, 992 NE2d 257 (2013) (setting out "taint team" procedures).

[6] *In re Grand Jury Investigation*, 470 Mass 399, 402-403, 22 NE3d 927, 931-932 (2015) (citing *Fisher v. United States*, 425 US 391 (1976)). "The *Fisher* rule serves to protect open communication between attorneys and clients by ensuring that a client does not sacrifice the protection that evidence otherwise would receive against compelled production by transferring it to an attorney." 470 Mass at 405, 22 NE3d at 933.

[7] *Com. v. Goldman*, supra, 395 Mass at 502 n.8, 480 NE2d at 1028 n.8; *Com. v. Michel*, 367 Mass 454, 460, 327 NE2d 720, 724 (1975), *new trial granted*, 381 Mass 447, 409 NE2d 1293 ("in certain circumstances assertion of an attorney-client privilege in such a way as to prevent the defense from exposing the bias of an important witness may deprive the defendant of his constitutional rights.").

[8] See *In re Grand Jury Investigation*, 437 Mass 340, 350-356, 771 NE2d 9, 17-20 (2002) (documents concerning private school's internal investigation of alleged abuse of students not protected by attorney client or work-product privilege).

records law, GL 4, § 7; GL 66, § 10, discussed infra at § 5.10[9] Confidential communications between public officers, employees, and governmental entities and their legal counsel undertaken for the purpose of obtaining legal advice are protected under the usual rules of attorney-client privilege.[10]

The privilege protects communications from client to attorney as well as from attorney to client.[11]

As with any doctrine that deprives the court of probative evidence, the attorney-client privilege is ordinarily strictly construed.[12] The burden of establishing that the privilege applies to a communication rests on the party asserting it. This burden extends to showing the existence of the privilege and that it has not been waived.[13]

§ 5.4.2 "Client" or "Prospective Client" Defined

It is not necessary that a fee be paid by the client or that the attorney be actually retained for the privilege to attach.[14] The privilege extends to "preliminary communications looking toward representation even if representation is never undertaken."[15] An attorney-client relationship need not rest on an express contract but may be implied when "(1) a person seeks advice or assistance from an attorney, (2) the advice or assistance sought pertains to matters within the attorney's professional competence, and (3) the attorney expressly or impliedly agrees to give or actually gives the desired advice or assistance."[16] The

---

[9] *Suffolk Construction Co., Inc. v. Division of Capital Asset Management*, 449 Mass 444, 450, 870 NE2d 33, 38 (2007).

[10] *Suffolk Construction Co., Inc. v. Division of Capital Asset Management*, supra.

[11] *McCarthy v. Slade Associates, Inc.*, 463 Mass 181, 190 n.21, 972 NE2d 1037, 1045 n.21 (2012).

[12] *In re Reorganization of Electric Mutual Liability Ins. Co.*, 425 Mass 419, 421, 681 NE2d 838, 840 (1997) (& citations). "A narrow construction of the privilege is particularly appropriate where information is being withheld from the government in a tax enforcement proceeding." *Commissioner of Revenue v. Comcast Corp.*, 453 Mass 293, 304, 901 NE2d 1185, 1195 (2009).

[13] *In re Reorganization of Electric Mutual Liability Ins. Co.*, supra, 425 Mass at 421, 681 NE2d at 840.

[14] *Foster v. Hall*, 29 Mass (12 Pick) 89, 94 (1831).

[15] *Com. v. O'Brien*, 377 Mass 772, 775-776, 388 NE2d 658, 661 (1979) (but defendant's request "Will you be my lawyer?" moments after shooting was not within privilege because not viewed as intended to be confidential).

[16] *Bays v. Theran*, 418 Mass 685, 690, 639 NE2d 720, 723 (1994) (preliminary consultations between condominium unit owner and attorney gave rise to attorney-client relationship). See also *Neitlich v. Peterson*, 15 Mass App 622, 624, 447 NE2d 671,

privilege applies even after the attorney/client relationship has ceased—"the mouth of the attorney shall be for ever sealed."[17] The privilege may extend to communications from the client's agent or employee to the attorney.[18]

Proposed Mass R Evid 502(a)(1) defines "client" as "a person, public officer, or corporation, association, or other organization or entity, either public or private, who is rendered professional legal services by a lawyer, or who consults a lawyer with a view to obtaining professional legal services." The rule adopts a "control group" test that limits the category of "representative of the client" to those "having authority to obtain professional legal services, or to act on advice rendered pursuant thereto, on behalf of the client."[19]

Confidential communications between law firm attorneys and the law firm's in-house counsel concerning a malpractice claim asserted by a current client of the firm are protected from disclosure to the client by the attorney-client privilege.[20]

A lawyer employed by an organization represents the organization through its duly authorized constituents; it follows that the power to assert or waive the privilege rests with the organization's management, and for a corporation is normally exercised by its officers and

---

672 (1983) (initiating letter to obtain legal services falls within privilege). But see *Mailer v. Mailer*, 390 Mass 371, 372-375, 455 NE2d 1211, 1213 (1983) (fact that wife had on one occasion five years earlier consulted husband's attorney concerning divorce did not establish attorney-client relationship requiring disqualification of attorney in subsequent divorce proceedings).

[17] *Hatton v. Robinson*, 31 Mass (14 Pick) 416, 421-422 (1833); *Foster v. Hall*, supra, 29 Mass at 94 (communications subject to privilege "cannot be disclosed at any future time").

[18] See *Ellingsgard v. Silver*, 352 Mass 34, 40, 223 NE2d 813, 817 (1967).

[19] See Proposed Mass R Evid 502(a)(2) and Advisory Committee Note. For discussion of the attorney-client privilege as it applies to corporate clients, compare *Upjohn Co. v. United States*, 449 US 383 (1981) (rejecting "control group" test and extending privilege to communications from employees concerning matters within the scope of their duties and made at direction of corporate superiors) with *United States v. Sawyer*, 878 F Supp 295 (D Mass 1995) (defendant had obligation to assist employer's in-house counsel with internal investigation of his activities, and thus was not "client"). For the related issue of limitations on an attorney's ex parte contacts with employees of a represented corporation, see *Messing, Rudavsky & Weliky, P.C. v. President and Fellows of Harvard College*, 436 Mass 347, 764 NE2d 825 (2002); *Clark v. Beverly Health and Rehabilitation Services, Inc.*, 440 Mass 270, 797 NE2d 905 (2003) (former employees).

[20] *RFF Family Partnership, LP v. Burns & Levinson, LLP*, 465 Mass 702, 991 NE2d 1066 (2013) (extensive discussion of the issue of first impression). Similarly, when a governmental entity employs an attorney to serve as its in-house legal counsel, confidential communications between the counsel and the entity's employees are protected under the usual rules of attorney client privilege. 465 Mass at 708, 991 NE2d at 1071.

directors.[21] A director whose interests are adverse to those of the corporation on a given issue, however, is not automatically entitled to access the corporation's confidential communications with counsel.[22]

§ 5.4.3 "Member of the Bar" Defined

Early Massachusetts case law holds that the would-be client takes the risk that the person whom he consults and discloses information to is not actually an attorney; if he is mistaken, there is no privilege.[23] Proposed Mass R Evid 502(a)(3) would, in fairness, extend the privilege to communications to persons "reasonably believed by the client to be authorized" to practice law.

Under the Rule, the privilege would also apply to communications made to a "representative of the lawyer," i.e., a person "used by the lawyer to assist the lawyer in the rendition of professional legal services."[24] The Supreme Judicial Court has extended the privilege to communications made to or shared with necessary agents of the attorney or the client, including experts consulted for the purpose of facilitating the rendition of legal advice, as well as communications with an attorney representing a client having a common interest.[25]

§ 5.4.4 "Communications"/"Facts" Distinguished

The privilege protects only those communications from the client made for the purpose of obtaining legal advice.[26] The communication

---

[21] *Clair v. Clair*, 464 Mass 205, 215-216, 982 NE2d 32, 41 (2013).

[22] *Chambers v. Gold Medal Bakery, Inc.*, 464 Mass 383, 395, 983 NE2d 683, 693 (2013).

[23] *Barnes v. Harris*, 61 Mass (7 Cush) 576 (1851) (disclosure to student in attorney's office not privileged even though client supposed him to be an attorney); *Foster v. Hall*, supra, 29 Mass at 98.

[24] Proposed Mass R Evid 502(a)(4).

[25] *Hanover Ins. Co. v. Rapo & Jepsen Ins. Services, Inc.*, 449 Mass 609, 616, 870 NE2d 1105, 1111 (2007).

[26] See *Purcell v. District Attorney for the Suffolk District*, 424 Mass 109, 115, 676 NE2d 436, 440 (1997) (question on remand as to whether tenant informed attorney of his intention to commit arson for purpose of receiving legal advice); *Judge Rotenberg Educational Center, Inc. v. Commissioner of Department of Mental Retardation*, 424 Mass 430, 457 n.26, 677 NE2d 127, 145 n.26 (1997) (general policy meeting not privileged because participants neither supplied counsel with information necessary to provide legal advice, nor sought legal advice); *Grant v. Lewis/Boyle, Inc.*, 408 Mass 269, 271-272, 557 NE2d 1136, 1138 (1990) (engineering expert previously retained by party

need not be made in regard to a lawsuit that has been or is to be brought; communications seeking legal advice are privileged regardless of whether litigation is involved.[27]

"The protection of the privilege extends only to *communications* and not to facts. A fact is one thing and a communication concerning that fact is an entirely different thing. The client cannot be compelled to answer the question, 'What did you say or write to the attorney?' but may not refuse to disclose any relevant fact within his knowledge merely because he incorporated a statement of such fact into his communication to his attorney."[28] An attorney's impressions about the truthfulness of his or her client are as much a part of the privileged information as the communication itself.[29]

The identity of an attorney's client and the source of payment for legal fees are generally not protected by the privilege, although details in billing statements may reveal confidential communications or the attorney's mental impressions of legal theories, which would be protected as work product (see § 5.4.10).[30]

The attorney-client privilege poses no obstacle to inquiry into promises or representations made to the Commonwealth's witnesses in exchange for their testimony.[31]

---

had provided no legal representation and possessed no confidential information). Proposed Mass R Evid 502(d)(4) would not apply the privilege to a communication to a lawyer in his capacity as attesting witness to a document.

[27] See *Foster v. Hall*, supra, 29 Mass at 99 ("the rule is not strictly confined to communications made for the purpose of enabling an attorney to conduct a cause in court, but does extend so as to include communications made by one to his legal advisor, whilst engaged and employed in that character, and when the object is to get his legal advice and opinion as to legal rights and obligations.").

[28] *Upjohn Co. v. United States*, supra, 449 US at 395-396; *Chambers v. Gold Medal Bakery, Inc.*, 464 Mass 383, 392, 983 NE2d 683, 690-691 (2013) (citing Text). For examples of protected "communications," see *Ellingsgard v. Silver*, supra, 352 Mass at 40, 223 NE2d at 817 (written statement relative to accident given by client to attorney); *Vigoda v. Barton*, 348 Mass 478, 485, 204 NE2d 441, 446 (1965) (letters written by defendant to attorneys seeking legal assistance in lawsuit).

[29] See *Com. v. Martinez*, 425 Mass 382, 391-392, 681 NE2d 818, 825 (1997).

[30] *Hanover Ins. Co. v. Rapo & Jepsen Ins. Services, Inc.*, 449 Mass 609, 619, 870 NE2d 1105, 1114 (2007).

[31] *Com. v Hardy*, 464 Mass 660, 668, 984 NE2d 727, 734 (2012) (a prosecutor's communication of any promises to a witness, whether or not made through the witness's attorney, is not privileged). see also § 6.15, infra.

§ 5.4.5 "In Confidence" Defined/Disclosure to Third Persons

The essence of the privilege is that it is recognized only to protect the confidential relation between attorney and client. The information contained within the communication need not itself be confidential; but to be deemed privileged the communication must be made "in confidence"—i.e., with the expectation that it will not be divulged.[32] Communications that are intended to be conveyed to others are not privileged.[33] Thus, "[w]hile an attorney's advice to his client on whether to accept the offer of the prosecution [of a plea arrangement] may be confidential, it is evident that the attorney's recitation of that offer is not confidential, for necessarily the offer is known to the prosecutor and it is likely to become the basis of a statement for the record in court."[34] Similarly,

> The attorney-client privilege, when properly applied, should present no obstacle to inquiring into promises, rewards, and inducements made by the Commonwealth to the witness or through counsel. The communication of such matters by the prosecutor is not privileged, and the details of what the prosecutor told counsel or the witness, or what counsel conveyed from the prosecutor to the witness, are subject to examination without violating attorney-client privilege. Other conversations between the witness and counsel, about whether to accept the terms offered by the prosecutor, or about the possible permutations of "consideration"

---

[32] *Commissioner of Revenue v. Comcast Corp.*, 453 Mass 293, 304, 305, 901 NE2d 1185, 1195, 1196 (2009) (communication between corporate tax counsel and outside tax accounting consultant which counsel conveyed to client was in confidence, even though some of the client information was public knowledge).

[33] *Com. v. O'Brien*, 377 Mass 772, 775-776, 388 NE2d 658, 661 (1979). Proposed Mass R Evid 502(a)(5) provides:

> A communication is "confidential" if not intended to be disclosed to third persons other than those to whom disclosure is made in furtherance of the rendition of professional legal services to the client or those reasonably necessary for the transmission of the communication.

See, e.g., *Com. v. Goulet*, 374 Mass 404, 418-419, 372 NE2d 1288, 1298 (1978) (error to allow claim of attorney-client privilege to prosecution witness asked on cross-examination if he caused his lawyer to send letter to victim threatening an injunction, because not intended to stop with lawyer but to be communicated to victim); *Peters v. Wallach*, 366 Mass 622, 627-628, 321 NE2d 806, 809 (1975) (client's grant of authority to attorney to settle case must be communicated to other party and thus not confidential); *Com. v. Anolik*, 27 Mass App 701, 709-710, 542 NE2d 327, 332 (1989) (attorney's testimony concerning real estate documents and insurance claim did not violate privilege because documents not intended to stop with attorney, but were meant to be passed along to third parties).

[34] *Com. v. Michel*, 367 Mass 454, 460-461, 327 NE2d 720, 724 (1975), *new trial granted*, 381 Mass 447, 409 NE2d 1293 (1980).

> and how each might affect the witness's future, may well be confidential in nature and subject to the attorney-client privilege. Whether that privilege might ever need to give way to the right of confrontation is an issue we need not decide in this case.[35]

Disclosure of the communication to a third person (other than a necessary agent of the attorney or client) destroys the privilege.[36] A narrow "derivative attorney-client privilege" can shield communications of a third party employed to facilitate communication between attorney and client, as where the third party functions as a translator.[37] Communications between an attorney and a third party are otherwise not within the attorney-client privilege.[38]

§ 5.4.6 *"Privileged at the Option of the Client"*

The privilege belongs to the client, not to the attorney, and thus the latter cannot disclose the communication unless released from the obligation by the former.[39] Proposed Mass R Evid 502(c) provides:

> The privilege may be claimed by the client, his guardian or conservator, the personal representative of a deceased client, or the successor, trustee, or similar representative of a corporation, association, or other

---

[35] *Com. v. Birks*, 435 Mass 782, 788, 762 NE2d 267, 273 (2002). See also *Com. v. Sullivan*, 435 Mass 722, 729-730, 761 NE2d 509, 515-516 (2002) (judge may have defined privilege too broadly by precluding inquiry into all conversation between immunized witness and his attorney).

[36] *Commissioner of Revenue v. Comcast Corp.*, 453 Mass 293, 304, 306-309, 901 NE2d 1185, 1196-1198 (2009). Regarding agency, compare *Com. v. Senior*, 433 Mass 453, 744 NE2d 614 (2001) (hospital personnel were not acting as agents for defense attorney when conducting blood tests at counsel's request) with *Jensen v. Daniels*, 57 Mass App 811, 818-819, 786 NE2d 1225, 1232 (2003) (nephew could not testify to statements deceased uncle made to attorney in nephew's presence where latter was present in his capacity as uncle's agent). See also *Blount v. Kimpton*, 155 Mass 378, 29 NE 590 (1892) ("[A]s between the client and attorney [communications] are still confidential, though made in the presence or hearing of a third party. The only effect of that is . . . that such third party may testify to them.").

[37] *DaRosa v. City of Bedford*, 471 Mass 446, 462-463, 30 NE3d 790, 804-805 (2015) (derivative attorney-client privilege).

[38] *Com. v. Noxon*, 319 Mass 495, 543-544, 66 NE2d 814, 844 (1946) (conversation between defense counsel and expert witness).

[39] *In the Matter of a John Doe Grand Jury Investigation*, 408 Mass 480, 483, 562 NE2d 68, 70 (1990) (privilege can be waived only by client, or in some instances by executor or administrator of client's estate); *Foster v. Hall*, 29 Mass (12 Pick) 89, 92-93 (1831). See also *Bermingham v. Thomas*, 3 Mass App 742, 326 NE2d 733 (1975) (third parties had no right to assert attorney-client privilege).

organization, whether or not in existence. The lawyer or the lawyer's representative or the person who was the lawyer or the lawyer's representative at the time of the communication is presumed to have authority to claim the privilege but only on behalf of the client.

The attorney-client privilege survives the client's death.[40] "A rule that would permit or require an attorney to disclose information given to him or her by a client in confidence, even though such disclosure might be limited to the period after the client's death, would in many instances . . . so deter the client from 'telling all' as to seriously impair the attorney's ability to function effectively."[41] The privilege may be exercised or waived in appropriate circumstances after the client's death by his executor or other personal representative.[42]

Individual directors are not entitled to waive the corporation's attorney-client privilege.[43] A trustee who seeks legal advice about a potential conflict of interest with the beneficiaries may claim the privilege to preclude the beneficiaries from discovering memoranda prepared by counsel.[44]

§ 5.4.7 Exceptions

Several exceptions to the attorney-client privilege have been carved out. The privilege does not apply to:

1. Information concerning the commission of a future crime or fraud.[45] The crime-fraud exception focuses not on the attorney's conduct but on whether the client sought services to

---

[40] *In the Matter of a John Doe Grand Jury Investigation*, supra, 408 Mass at 483, 562 NE2d at 70. See also *Swidler & Berlin v. United States*, 524 US 399 (1998).

[41] *In the Matter of a John Doe Grand Jury Investigation*, supra, 408 Mass at 485, 562 NE2d at 71.

[42] *In the Matter of a John Doe Grand Jury Investigation*, supra, 408 Mass at 483, 562 NE2d at 70. See also *District Attorney for Norfolk District v. Magraw*, 417 Mass 169, 172-173, 628 NE2d 24, 26 (1994) (probate judge had duty to remove husband as executor of wife's estate where, as suspect in her murder, husband had conflict of interest regarding waiver of privileges).

[43] *Clair v. Clair*, 464 Mass 205, 217, 982 NE2d 32, 42 (2013); *Symmons v. O'Keeffe*, 419 Mass 288, 298 n.10, 644 NE2d 631, 638 n.10 (1995).

[44] *Symmons v. O'Keeffe*, supra, 419 Mass at 301, 644 NE2d at 639-640.

[45] *In the Matter of a John Doe Grand Jury Investigation*, supra, 408 Mass at 486, 562 NE2d at 72 (& citations). See generally *Purcell v. District Attorney for the Suffolk District*, 424 Mass 109, 676 NE2d 436 (1997) (extensive discussion of crime-fraud exception).

enable or aid someone to commit a crime.[46] The crime-fraud exception is a narrow one, and the burden is on the party invoking it to demonstrate its applicability by a preponderance of the evidence.[47] The trial judge may rely on the Commonwealth's ex parte affidavit in determining whether the exception applies.[48]

2. Disputes between parties claiming through the same deceased client.[49]
3. Disputes between joint clients who share the same attorney.[50]
4. Directions given an attorney by a deceased client concerning the drafting of a will, to determine whether the instrument, presented for probate is the actual will.[51]
5. Disputes between client and attorney regarding collection of the fee or allegations of wrongful conduct against the attorney.[52] Although the attorney-client privilege is treated as

---

Compare *Matter of Wise*, 433 Mass 80, 88-89, 740 NE2d 946, 953-954 (2000) (attorney's revelation of confidences not justified where concerns were of civil, not criminal, nature).

SJC Rule 3:07, Rules of Prof Conduct, Rule 1.6(b)(1) provides: "A lawyer may reveal [and in certain defined circumstances] must reveal, such information to prevent the commission of a criminal or fraudulent act that the lawyer reasonably believes is likely to result, in death or substantial bodily harm, or in substantial injury to the financial interests or property of another, or to prevent the wrongful execution or incarceration of another." It should be emphasized that the ethical permissibility of an attorney's disclosure under Rule 1.6 does not resolve the separate question of whether the attorney can be compelled to testify regarding the matters. *In re Grand Jury Investigation*, 453 Mass 453, 455, 902 NE2d 929, 931 (2009).

[46] See *In re Grand Jury Investigation*, 453 Mass 453, 902 NE2d 929 (2009); *In re Grand Jury Investigation*, 437 Mass 340, 362, 771 NE2d 9, 25 (2002); *In re Ellis*, 425 Mass 332, 335-336, 680 NE2d 1154, 1158 (1997).

[47] *In re Grand Jury Investigation*, 437 Mass 340, 357, 771 NE2d 9, 21-22 (2002).

[48] *Id.*

[49] See *Panell v. Rosa*, 228 Mass 594, 596-597, 118 NE 225, 226-227 (1917); *Phillips v. Chase*, 201 Mass 444, 449, 87 NE 755, 758 (1909).

[50] See *Beacon Oil Co. v. Perelis*, 263 Mass 288, 293, 160 NE 892, 894 (1928); *Thompson v. Cashman*, 181 Mass 36, 62 NE 976 (1902).

[51] See *Sullivan v. Brabazon*, 264 Mass 276, 286, 162 NE2d 312, 316-317 (1928), citing *Doherty v. O'Callaghan*, 157 Mass 90, 93, 31 NE 726, 727 (1892).

[52] See *Com. v. Silva*, 455 Mass 503, 528-529, 918 NE2d 65, 89 (2009) (because defendant's claim of ineffective assistance of counsel accused trial counsel of telling him he had to testify and then failing to prepare him, and defendant and counsel were the only witnesses to the conversations, the attorney-client privilege must be deemed waived to permit counsel to disclose only those confidences necessary to rebut the charge); *Com. v. Brito*, 390 Mass 112, 119, 453 NE2d 1217, 1221 (1983) (trial counsel turned over portions of his files to the district attorney after defendant, in seeking new trial, asserted the ineffectiveness of trial counsel); *Zabin v. Picciotto*, 73 Mass App 141, 157-158, 896 NE2d 937, 955 (2008) (where client sues attorney for malpractice, the

> waived when the client charges the attorney with misconduct, "counsel's obligation may continue to preserve confidences whose disclosure is not relevant to the defense of the charge of his ineffectiveness as counsel."[53] The circumstances in which in-house counsel may pursue a claim for wrongful discharge are limited by the obligation to protect client confidences.[54]

Proposed Mass R Evid 502(d)[55] essentially incorporates the existing exceptions[56] and additionally removes communications between a

---

privilege is waived as to communications with all attorneys involved in the underlying litigation); *Com. v. Woodberry*, 26 Mass App 636, 637, 530 NE2d 1260, 1261 (1988) (if a client assails his attorney's conduct, the privilege as to confidential communications is waived because the lawyer has a right to defend himself). See also SJC Rule 3:07, Rules of Prof Conduct, Rule 1.6(b)(2).

[53] *Com. v. Brito*, supra, 390 Mass at 119, 453 NE2d at 1221. See also *Com. v. Woodberry*, supra, 26 Mass App at 637-640, 530 NE2d at 1261-1262 (attorney's testimony at hearing on defendant's motion to withdraw guilty pleas, covering entire range of discussions between attorney and client regarding pleas, was properly admitted because relevant to counsel's defense of charge of misconduct).

[54] See *GTE Products Corp. v. Stewart*, 421 Mass 22, 32, 653 NE2d 161, 167-168 (1995) (it must be established that claim can be proved without violation of confidentiality obligation).

[55] Rule 502(d) provides:

> ***Exceptions.*** There is no privilege under this rule:
>
> (1) *Furtherance of crime or fraud.* If the services of the lawyer were sought or obtained to enable or aid anyone to commit or plan to commit what the client knew or reasonably should have known to be a crime or fraud;
>
> (2) *Claimants through same deceased client.* As to a communication relevant to an issue between parties who claim through the same deceased client, regardless of whether the claims are by testate or intestate succession or by *inter vivos* transaction;
>
> (3) *Breach of duty by a lawyer or client.* As to a communication relevant to an issue of breach of duty by the lawyer to his client or by the client to his lawyer;
>
> (4) *Document attested by a lawyer.* As to a communication relevant to an issue concerning an attested document to which the lawyer is an attesting witness;
>
> (5) *Joint clients.* As to a communication relevant to a matter of common interest between or among two or more clients if the communication was made by any of them to a lawyer retained or consulted in common, when offered in an action between or among any of the clients; or
>
> (6) *Public officer or agency.* As to a communication between a public officer or agency and its lawyers unless the communication concerns a pending investigation, claim, or action and the court determines that disclosure will seriously impair the ability of the public officer or agency to process the claim or conduct a pending investigation, litigation, or proceeding in the public interest.

[56] The Supreme Judicial Court has confirmed that "the Proposed Massachusetts Rules of Evidence adequately define the crime-fraud exception to the lawyer-client privilege set forth in rule 502(d)(1)." *Purcell v. District Attorney for the Suffolk District*, 424 Mass 109, 112, 676 NE2d 436, 439 (1997).

public officer or agency and its lawyers from the protection of the privilege except in certain situations.

The Supreme Judicial Court has recently declined to adopt the "fiduciary" and the "current client" exceptions to the privilege.[57]

§ 5.4.8 Waiver

A client does not waive the attorney-client privilege by testifying at trial as to events that were a topic of a privileged communication.[58] A waiver may be found, however, where the client testifies as to the contents of a privileged communication.[59] The fact that a document may have been stolen or disclosed in bad faith does not result in a waiver where it can be shown that reasonable precautionary steps were taken.[60]

The Supreme Judicial Court has recognized as a general principle the concept of an "at issue" waiver, whereby a litigant implicitly waives the attorney-client privilege by injecting certain claims or

---

[57] *RFF Family Partnership, LP v. Burns & Levinson, LLP*, 465 Mass 702, 713-723, 991 NE2d 1066, 1074-1081 (2013).

[58] See *Com. v. Goldman*, 395 Mass 495, 498-502, 480 NE2d 1025, 1027-1029 (1985) (resolving long-standing conflict in the case law). See also *Com. v. Birks*, 435 Mass 782, 789 n.5, 762 NE2d 267, 273 n.5 (2002); *Neitlich v. Peterson*, 15 Mass App 622, 626-627, 447 NE2d 671, 673 (1983).

[59] *Com. v. Goldman*, supra, 395 Mass at 500, 480 NE2d at 1027; *Com. v. Woodberry*, 26 Mass App 636, 639, 530 NE2d 1260, 1262 (1988) ("By giving testimony concerning privileged communication about his plea decision the defendant waived his privilege and permitted counsel to introduce testimony as to all consultations relating to the same subject.").
Proposed Mass R Evid 510 provides:

> **Waiver of Privilege by Voluntary Disclosure**
> A person upon whom these rules confer a privilege against disclosure waives the privilege, if he or his predecessor while holder of the privilege voluntarily discloses or consents to disclosure of any significant part of the privileged matter. This rule does not apply if the disclosure itself is privileged.
>
> The Advisory Committee Note explains that under this rule "there is no waiver [where a party witness voluntarily takes the stand] unless the direct testimony discloses a 'significant part of the privileged matter.' " See also Proposed Mass R Evid 511: "A claim of privilege is not defeated by a disclosure which was (a) compelled erroneously or (b) made without opportunity to claim the privilege."

[60] See *In re Reorganization of Electric Mutual Liability Ins. Co.*, 425 Mass 419, 681 NE2d 838 (1997) (rejecting traditional view that once contents of document became public by any means, confidentiality is destroyed).

defenses into a case.[61] An "at issue" waiver also occurs where the client relies on a privileged communication as evidence.[62] This is not a blanket waiver, but is limited to what has been put "in issue"; and there can be no "at issue" waiver unless it is shown that the privileged information sought to be discovered is not available from any other source.[63] Where a client sues his attorney for malpractice, the privilege is waived as to communications with all attorneys involved in the underlying litigation.[64]

Massachusetts has adopted the common interest doctrine as an exception to waiver of the attorney-client privilege, thus extending the privilege to any privileged communication shared with another represented party's counsel in a confidential manner for the purpose of furthering a common legal interest.[65]

§ 5.4.9 Comment upon Claim of Privilege

Case law permits opposing counsel in a civil case to comment upon a party's claim of the attorney-client privilege and to argue to the jury that the claim is an implied admission that the privileged matter would be harmful to the party's case.[66] Counsel may similarly comment on the claim of privilege by a witness who is closely aligned with a party and has an interest in the outcome of the proceeding.[67]

---

[61] See *Darius v. City of Boston*, 433 Mass 274, 277-278, 741 NE2d 52, 53 (2001) (but where defendant asserts statute of limitations defense and plaintiff relies on discovery rule, no automatic waiver to determine whether attorney-client communications undermine plaintiff's reliance); *McCarthy v. Slade Associates, Inc.*, 463 Mass 181, 972 NE2d 1037 (2012) (defendants failed to show that the privileged information regarding plaintiff's reliance on the statue of limitations discovery rule was not available from another source, such as deposition of the plaintiff and discovery of title examination reports); *Clair v. Clair*, 464 Mass 205, 218-220, 982 NE2d 32, 43-44 (2013) (closely held companies waived privilege as to communications with corporate counsel when they asserted a breach of fiduciary duty counterclaim).

[62] See *Global Investors Agent Corp. v. National Fire Ins. Co. of Hartford*, 76 Mass App 812, 816-819, 927 NE2d 480, 487-489 (2010).

[63] *Id.*, 76 Mass App at 816-819, 927 NE2d at 487-489.

[64] *Zabin v. Picciotto*, 73 Mass App 141, 157-158, 896 NE2d 937, 955 (2008).

[65] See *Hanover Ins. Co. v. Rapo & Jepsen Ins. Servs., Inc.*, 449 Mass 609, 870 NE2d 1105 (2007).

[66] *Phillips v. Chase*, 201 Mass 444, 450, 87 NE 755, 758 (1909).

[67] *Neitlich v. Peterson*, 15 Mass App 622, 628, 447 NE2d 671, 674 (1983) (& cases cited) (but trial judge properly refused to permit comment because witness was not so aligned with defendant as to make defendant responsible for witness's claim of privilege).

Proposed Mass R Evid 512(a) would preclude an adverse comment or inference based upon a claim of privilege in a criminal case.[68]

It has been held that a party may be called before the jury even though it is known that the party will claim the attorney-client privilege.[69]

§ 5.4.10 Work Product

Mass R Civ P 26(b)(3) codifies the privilege first recognized in *Hickman v. Taylor*[70] to refuse discovery of documents prepared in anticipation of litigation by or for a party, his attorney, insurer, or agent.[71] "While the attorney-client privilege shields communications between attorney and client (and in some circumstances third parties), the work product doctrine protects an attorney's written materials and 'mental impressions,'"[72] as well as documents that a party's non-lawyer representative prepared, or obtained, in anticipation of litigation.[73]

The work product doctrine, a discovery limitation and not an evidentiary privilege, is "intended to enhance vitality of the adversary system of litigation by insulating counsel's work from intrusions, interferences, or borrowings by other parties."[74] In order to fit within

---

[68] Proposed Mass R Evid 512(a) provides:

> The claim of a privilege, whether in the present proceeding or upon a prior occasion, is not a proper subject of comment by judge or counsel in a criminal case. No inference may be drawn therefrom.

[69] *Kendall v. Atkins*, 374 Mass 320, 325-326, 372 NE2d 764, 767-768 (1978). But compare Proposed Mass R Evid 512(b) ("In criminal cases tried to a jury, proceedings shall be conducted to the extent practicable, so as to facilitate the making of claims of privilege without the knowledge of the jury.").

[70] 329 US 495 (1947).

[71] See generally *General Electric Co. v. Department of Environmental Protection*, 429 Mass 798, 711 NE2d 589 (1999), clarified in *DaRosa v. City of Bedford*, 471 Mass 446, 30 NE3d 790 (2015) (work product prepared on behalf of a government entity may be protected from disclosure by the "policy deliberation" exemption to the public records law, see § 5.10, infra).

[72] *Commissioner of Revenue v. Comcast Corp.*, 453 Mass 293, 312, 901 NE2d 1185, 1200 (2009) (extensive discussion).

[73] *Cahaly v. Benistar Property*, 85 Mass App 418, 424, 10 NE3d 659, 665 (2014). See, e.g., *Lindsey v. Ogden*, 10 Mass App Ct 142, 153-155, 406 NE2d 701, 710 (1980) (bank documents containing notations of party's accountants and tax attorney and their respective worksheets were within privilege).

[74] *Commissioner of Revenue v. Comcast Corp.*, supra, 453 Mass at 311, 901 NE2d at,1200. See also *McCarthy v. Slade Associates, Inc.*, supra, 463 Mass at 194, 972 NE2d at1048; *Ward v. Peabody*, 380 Mass 805, 817, 405 NE2d 973, 980 (1980).

the privilege, the materials must have been prepared in relation to litigation, pending or prospective.[75] Facts contained in the documents, as opposed to the attorney's mental impressions or legal theories, are not protected from disclosure.[76]

The qualified protection may be overcome upon a showing of "substantial need" for the materials (i.e., where the documents are central to the party's substantive claims) and inability to obtain their equivalent by other means.[77] However, in ordering discovery of such materials when the required showing has been made, "the court shall protect against disclosure of the mental impressions, conclusions, opinions, or legal theories of an attorney or other representative of a party concerning the litigation."[78] Such "opinion" work product is afforded greater protection than "fact" work product, and applies also to "other representatives" such as accountants as long as their work relates to the litigation.[79]

The privilege applies in a more limited fashion in criminal cases to documents that contain the "legal research, opinions, theories or conclusions of the adverse party or it attorney and legal staff, or statements of a defendant, signed or unsigned, made to the attorney for the defendant or the attorney's legal staff."[80] The work-product privilege has been extended to cover the notes of victim-witness advocates,

---

[75] *Commissioner of Revenue v. Comcast Corp.*, supra, 453 Mass at 315-316, 901 NE2d at,1203; *Com. v. Fall River Motor Sales, Inc.*, 409 Mass 302, 308-309, 565 NE2d 1205, 1210 (1991).

[76] *Cahaly v. Benistar Property*, supra, 85 Mass App at 425, 10 NE3d at 666. For more on the distinction between fact and opinion work product, see *DaRosa v. City of Bedford*, supra, 471 Mass at 446, 30 NE3d at 790.

[77] Mass R Civ P 26(b)(3) ("substantial need" and "unable without undue hardship to obtain the substantial equivalent of the materials by other means"). See also *Cahaly v. Benistar Property*, supra, 85 Mass App at 425, 10 NE3d at 665.

"Work product shielded by the doctrine is not privileged, but instead is given qualified protection from discovery . . . The qualifications in the rule speak, albeit more generally, to the concerns addressed by the concept of at issue waiver of the attorney-client privilege, that is, concerns about fairness where the party asserting the privilege affirmatively raises a claim or defense that makes information protected by the privilege material and relevant to the case and the particular information is vital to the opposing party." *McCarthy v. Slade Associates, Inc.*, 463 Mass 181, 194-195, 972 NE2d 1037, 1048-1049 (2012).

[78] Mass R Civ P 26(b)(3).

[79] *Commissioner of Revenue v. Comcast Corp.*, supra, 453 Mass at 304, 314, 901 NE2d at 1202 (2009); *Chambers v. Gold Medal Bakery, Inc.*, 464 Mass 383, 391 n.22, 983 NE2d 683, 691 n.22 (2013).

[80] See Mass R Crim P 14((a)(5) and *Com. v. Paszko*, 391 Mass 164, 187-188, 461 NE2d 222, 236-237 (1984) (Mass R Crim P 14(a)(5) protects only materials that reveal mental processes of attorney, but unlike federal doctrine, excludes statements of witnesses other than defendant and nonlegal reports from the definition of work product).

unless the notes contain exculpatory evidence or "statements" of witnesses (within the meaning of Mass R Crim P 14(d)). There is an affirmative duty on the prosecutor to review these notes and inquire about conversations with victims pursuant to the obligation to disclose exculpatory evidence.[81] A reciprocal discovery order requiring defendant to disclose statements of the Commonwealth's witnesses in his possession that defendant intends to use at trial does not violate the work product doctrine.[82]

Voluntary disclosure by the attorney or agent waives any work-product privilege. Inadvertent disclosure cases turn on whether reasonable precautions had been taken to prevent disclosure; if not, the privilege is waived.[83] The privilege is not waived merely because the party places the underlying matter in issue in its pleadings.[84]

Where mandated by law to disclose all facts concerning possible child abuse, relevant internal investigation reports are not shielded by the work-product privilege.[85] The crime-fraud exception (see § 5.4.7, supra) also applies to materials otherwise protected by the work-product doctrine.[86]

The work-product of a mediator, as well as any communications made in the course of a mediation, are protected against disclosure by GL 233, § 23C.[87]

---

[81] See *Com. v. Bing Sial Liang*, 434 Mass 131, 137, 747 NE2d 112, 118 (2001).

[82] *Com. v. Durham*, 446 Mass 212, 221, 843 NE2d 1035, 1043 (2006).

[83] See *Adoption of Sherry*, 435 Mass 331, 336, 757 NE2d 1097, 1102 (2001) (child's attorney gave retained psychologist permission to speak to court investigator and attorneys for father, with no limiting instructions, thereby waiving privilege).

[84] *Buster v. George W. Moore, Inc.*, 438 Mass 635, 653-654, 783 NE2d 399, 415 (2003).

[85] *In re Grand Jury Investigation*, 437 Mass 340, 356, 771 NE2d 9, 21 (2002).

[86] *In re Grand Jury Investigation*, supra, 437 Mass at 357 n.28, 771 NE2d at 21 n.28.

[87] GL 233, § 23C provides:

> **Work product of mediator confidential; confidential communications; exception; mediator defined**
>
> All memoranda, and other work product prepared by a mediator and a mediator's case files shall be confidential and not subject to disclosure in any judicial or administrative proceeding involving any of the parties to any mediation to which such materials apply. Any communication made in the course of and relating to the subject matter of any mediation and which is made in the presence of such mediator by any participant, mediator or other person shall be a confidential communication and not subject to disclosure in any judicial or administrative proceeding; provided, however, that the provisions of this section shall not apply to the mediation of labor disputes.
>
> For the purposes of this section a "mediator" shall mean a person not a party to a dispute who enters into a written agreement with the parties to assist them in resolving their disputes and has completed at least thirty hours of training in mediation and who either has four years of professional experience as a mediator or is accountable to a dispute

§ 5.4.11 Attorney as Witness

Except in limited circumstances, an attorney cannot take part in a trial in which he is to be a witness.[88]

§ 5.5 Physician-Patient; Psychotherapist-Patient; Social Worker-Client; Counselor-Victim; Court-Ordered Psychiatric Examination

No physician-patient, psychotherapist-patient, or social worker-client privileges existed at common law.[1] Privileges have been established by statute for communications between psychotherapist and patient, between social worker and client, and between sexual-assault or domestic-violence counselor and victim. A statutory disqualification renders inadmissible for certain purposes in a criminal case statements made by the defendant during a court-ordered psychiatric examination. In addition, a nonstatutory civil remedy has been recognized for breach of a physician's duty of confidentiality.

---

resolution organization which has been in existence for at least three years or one who has been appointed to mediate by a judicial or governmental body.

[88] See *Kendall v. Atkins*, 374 Mass 320, 323-325, 372 NE2d 764, 766-767 (1978) (discussion of propriety of calling opposing counsel as witness); SJC Rule 3:07, Rules of Prof Conduct, Rule 3.7; Superior Court Rule 12. Compare *Com. v. Patterson*, 432 Mass 767, 780, 739 NE2d 682, 693 (2001) (defense counsel's continued representation of defendant after it became obvious she should be called as witness in his defense rendered her representation constitutionally ineffective) and *Serody v. Serody*, 19 Mass App 411, 474 NE2d 1171 (1985) (judge did not abuse discretion in requiring wife's attorney to withdraw from case after husband's attorney gave notice he intended to call attorney as witness) with *Borman v. Borman*, 378 Mass 775, 785-792, 393 NE2d 847, 854-858 (1979) (judge erred in disqualifying law firm from representing husband merely because he was member of firm and, as litigant, would testify in proceeding; extensive discussion of applicable ethical rules and policy). For a case discussing the propriety of calling a judge as witness, see *Guardianship of Pollard*, 54 Mass App 318, 322-324, 764 NE2d 935, 939-940 (2002) (while judge cannot be called to testify on what ruling he might have made on a particular hypothesis, or what unexpressed reasons actuated decision, judge who formerly served as GAL could testify at guardianship trial).

§ 5.5 [1] *Com. v. Mandeville*, 386 Mass 393, 409, 436 NE2d 912, 922 (1982) (psychotherapist-patient); *Kramer v. John Hancock Mutual Life Ins. Co.*, 336 Mass 465, 467, 146 NE2d 357, 359 (1957) (physician-patient).

§ 5.5.1 *Physician-Patient Confidentiality*

Other than the psychotherapist-patient privilege discussed in § 5.5.2, infra, no statutory testimonial privilege applies to physicians and their patients.[2] A duty of confidentiality arising from the physician-patient relationship has been recognized by the Supreme Judicial Court, violation of which gives rise to a tort claim against the physician.[3] The duty covers medical facts communicated to or discovered by the physician[4] and proscribes out-of-court disclosure of such information without the patient's consent, except to meet a serious danger to the patient or to others.[5] A physician's duty of confidentiality to a patient has been read into administrative regulations concerning the profession.[6]

The Supreme Judicial Court has observed that "[w]hile there is no statutory patient-physician privilege per se, there is a legislatively created policy favoring the confidentiality of medical records [citing GL 111, §§ 70, 70E, pertaining to hospital records]."[7] The courts have, however, refused to create an exclusionary rule for disclosures in violation of the duty of confidentiality, relying instead on the damages remedy.[8]

GL 111, § 70F, providing that no facility shall disclose the results of an HIV test to anyone other than the patient without first obtaining his consent, may be overridden by the defendant's right to a fair trial.[9] In such cases, the *Bishop-Fuller* protocol (see § 5.5.4, infra) is to be used.

---

[2] *Com. v. Dube*, 413 Mass 570, 572 n.3, 601 NE2d 467, 468 n.3 (1992) (& citations); *Alberts v. Devine*, 395 Mass 59, 67, 479 NE2d 113, 118 (1985), *cert. denied sub nom, Carroll v. Alberts*, 474 US 1013 (1985).

[3] *Alberts v. Devine*, supra.

[4] *Alberts v. Devine*, supra, 395 Mass at 65, 479 NE2d at 118.

[5] *Alberts v. Devine*, supra, 395 Mass at 66-68, 479 NE2d at 119.

[6] See *Sugarman v. Board of Registration in Medicine*, 422 Mass 338, 662 NE2d 1020 (1996) (Board had authority to sanction psychiatrist who, as expert witness in custody case, released confidential report to press); *Hellman v. Board of Registration in Medicine*, 404 Mass 800, 537 NE2d 150 (1989).

[7] *Com. v. Senior*, 433 Mass 453, 457 n.5, 744 NE2d 614, 617 n.5 (2001) (but provision is made for release pursuant to court order).

[8] See *Com. v. Senior*, supra, 433 Mass at 457 n.5, 744 NE2d at 617 n.5; *Schwartz v. Goldstein*, 400 Mass 152, 154, 508 NE2d 97, 99 (1987). See also *Tower v. Hirshhorn*, 397 Mass 581, 585, 492 NE2d 728, 731-732 (1986) (neurologist had divulged confidential medical information without patient's consent to physician hired by insurer for defendant).

[9] See *Com. v. Maxwell*, 441 Mass 773, 779-781, 808 NE2d 806, 811-813 (2004) (records bearing on ability of victim-witness to perceive and remember events accurately). It is not a violation of § 70F for a physician, health care provider or institution, or laboratory to report such information to the department of health as required by law.

§ 5.5.2 Psychotherapist-Patient Privilege

GL 233, § 20B provides:

> Except as hereinafter provided, in any court proceeding and in any proceeding preliminary thereto and in legislative and administrative proceedings, a patient shall have the privilege of refusing to disclose, and of preventing a witness from disclosing, any communication, wherever made, between said patient and a psychotherapist relative to the diagnosis or treatment of the patient's mental or emotional condition. This privilege shall apply to patients engaged with a psychotherapist in marital therapy, family therapy, or consultation in contemplation of such therapy.
>
> If a patient is incompetent to exercise or waive such privilege, a guardian shall be appointed to act in his behalf under this section. A previously appointed guardian shall be authorized to so act.
>
> Upon the exercise of the privilege granted by this section, the judge or presiding officer shall instruct the jury that no adverse inference may be drawn therefrom.

The purpose of the statute is to "protect justifiable expectations of confidentiality that people who seek psychotherapeutic help have a right to expect."[10]

Section 20B defines "psychotherapist" as "a person licensed to practice medicine, who devotes a substantial portion of his time to the practice of psychiatry," and also includes licensed psychologists and psychiatric nurses.[11] "Communications" are defined as "conversations, correspondence, actions and occurrences relating to diagnosis or treatment before, during or after institutionalization, regardless of the patient's awareness of such conversations, correspondence, actions and occurrences, and any records, memoranda or notes of the

---

[10] *Com. v. Clancy*, 402 Mass 664, 667, 524 NE2d 395, 397 (1988). The privilege applies as well to "administrative proceedings" including investigations by licensing boards. See *Board of Registration in Medicine v. Doe*, 457 Mass 738, 743, 933 NE2d 67, 71 (2010).

[11] St 1989, c 373 removed the former requirement that a psychologist have a doctoral degree in psychology in order to be considered a "psychotherapist." See, e.g., *Com. v. McDonough*, 400 Mass 639, 644-645, 511 NE2d 551, 555-556 (1987). St 2000, c348 added to the list: "a graduate of, or student enrolled in, a doctoral degree program in psychology at a recognized educational institution . . . who is working under the supervision of a licensed psychologist." See also *Board of Registration in Medicine v. Doe*, 457 Mass 738, 743, 933 NE2d 67, 71-72 (2010) (pain management is a subspecialty of psychiatry and thus is included in definition of psychotherapist).

foregoing." "Patient" is defined as "a person who, during the course of diagnosis or treatment, communicates with a psychotherapist."

A psychotherapist-patient relationship forms the basis for the privilege under G.L. c. 233, § 20B.[12] The courts have further required that "some confidential relationship" exist between patient and psychotherapist before the privilege may be invoked.[13] Thus, where the facts suggested that the defendant did not consult the psychotherapist for treatment or diagnosis but rather to minimize the impact of the charges against him, the relationship was not that of patient and psychotherapist and the privilege would not apply.[14]

The Supreme Judicial Court has indicated that it is not inclined "to extend the patient-psychotherapist privilege beyond the bounds established by the Legislature."[15] Thus communications to therapists who do not meet the specifications of the statute do not fall within the privilege even though the therapist is working under the supervision of a qualifying psychotherapist.[16] Still open is the question of whether the privilege might apply to an agent or assistant of the psychotherapist in order to protect an existing confidential relationship.[17]

GL 112, § 129A requires licensed psychologists as well as their colleagues, agents, or employees (professional, clerical, academic, or therapeutic) to maintain the confidentiality of patient communications. Such communications are privileged from testimonial disclosure.[18]

---

[12] *Doe v. Sex Offender Registry Board*, 459 Mass 603, 643, 947 NE2d 9, 41 (2011).

[13] *Com. v. Mandeville*, 386 Mass 393, 409, 436 NE2d 912 (1982); *Com. v. Clemons*, 12 Mass App 580, 586-587, 427 NE2d 761, 765 (1981).

[14] See *Com. v. Berrio*, 407 Mass 37, 42-43, 551 NE2d 496, 500 (1990). But see *Robinson v. Com.*, 399 Mass 131, 503 NE2d 31 (1987) (judge erred in ruling that privilege did not apply because defendant had not been a "patient" undergoing "diagnosis or treatment" while conversing privately with staff psychiatrist at latter's initiation in hospital where critically ill infant victim was being treated).

[15] *Com. v. Rosenberg*, 410 Mass 347, 353, 573 NE2d 949, 953 (1991); *Com. v. Mandeville*, supra, 386 Mass at 409, 436 NE2d at 992-923.

[16] *Com. v. Rosenberg*, supra, 410 Mass at 353, 573 NE2d at 953; *Adoption of Diane*, 400 Mass 196, 200-201, 508 NE2d 837, 840 (1987); *Com. v. Mandeville*, supra, 386 Mass at 408-409, 436 NE2d at 922 (unlicensed community health center staff psychologist); *Com. v. Clemons*, supra, 12 Mass App at 584-587, 427 NE2d at 764 (unlicensed family therapist).

[17] *Com. v. Rosenberg*, supra, 410 Mass at 354, 573 NE2d at 954; *Com. v. Mandeville*, supra, 386 Mass at 409, 436 NE2d at 923; *Com. v. Clemons*, supra, 12 Mass App at 586-587, 427 NE2d at 765.

[18] See *Doe v. Sex Offender Registry Board*, supra, 459 Mass at 643 n.35, 947 NE2d at 41 n.35.

Proposed Mass R Evid 503 would broaden the definition of "psychotherapist" to include persons "reasonably believed by the patient to be [a licensed psychotherapist, psychologist, or social worker],"[19] and would extend the applicability of the privilege to "persons who are participating in the diagnosis or treatment under the direction of the psychotherapist, including members of the patient's family."[20] The rule also excepts from the "third persons" to whom disclosure destroys confidentiality those "persons present to further the interest of the patient in the consultation, examination, or interview, persons reasonably necessary for the transmission of the communication, or persons who are participating in the diagnosis and treatment under the direction of the psychotherapist, including members of the patient's family."[21]

GL 233, § 20B, establishes a privilege in the patient to refuse to disclose, and to prevent another witness from disclosing, communications with her psychotherapist.[22] As a privilege and not a disqualification, the patient must affirmatively exercise the privilege in order to prevent the psychotherapist from disclosing confidential communications at trial, and failure to do so precludes assertion of the privilege on appeal.[23] Where the patient's counsel questions the psychotherapist about privileged communications and records, the privilege is waived.[24] A psychotherapist has standing to raise the privilege on behalf of a patient.[25] The parent of a patient, however, has no right to

---

[19] Proposed Mass R Evid 503(a)(2).

[20] Proposed Mass R Evid 503(b).

[21] Proposed Mass R Evid 503(a)(3).

[22] *Com. v. Clancy*, supra, 402 Mass at 667, 524 NE2d at 397.

[23] *Com. v. Oliveira*, 438 Mass 325, 330-337, 780 NE2d 453, 457-462 (2002) (absent an affirmative assertion of the privilege, court must treat records as if they were unprivileged); *Adoption of Carla*, 416 Mass 510, 515, 623 NE2d 1118, 1121 (1993) (mother's failure to object at trial to testimony of psychotherapist precluded appellate review; mother's assertion of privilege in motion in limine insufficient to preserve appellate rights); *Com. v. Benoit*, 410 Mass 506, 518-519, 574 NE2d 347, 354-355 (1991); *Com. v. Hawkesworth*, 405 Mass 664, 672 n.6, 543 NE2d 691, 696 n.6 (1989) (failure to claim § 20B privilege at trial limits consideration on appeal to whether there was substantial likelihood of miscarriage of justice); *P.W. v. M.S.*, 67 Mass App 779, 786, 857 NE2d 38, 44 (2006).

[24] See *Care and Protection of Bruce*, 44 Mass App 758, 764-765, 694 NE2d 27, 31-32 (1998) (& citations).

[25] See *Com. v. Kobrin*, 395 Mass 284, 287 n.8, 479 NE2d 674, 677 n.8 (1985) (psychiatrist had standing to raise patient's claims of privilege when grand jury investigating Medicaid fraud demanded patient's records). See also Proposed Mass R Evid 503(c) ("The person who was the psychotherapist at the time of the communication is presumed to have authority to claim the privilege but only on behalf of the patient"). But see *Com. v. Oliveira*, 438 Mass 325, 332 n.8, 780 NE2d 453, 459 n.8 (2002)

assert the privilege on behalf of the child; pursuant to § 20B only the child or a guardian appointed by the court may do so.[26]

Like the attorney-client privilege (see § 5.4.6, supra), the psychotherapist-patient privilege survives the death of the patient and may be invoked or waived by the administrator or executor of the estate.[27]

GL 233, § 20B has been read to create only an evidentiary privilege applicable in various "proceedings"; "it does not mandate confidentiality, or prohibit disclosure, in other settings [unlike the broader confidentiality requirements that apply to other mental health professionals such as social workers, see GL 112, 135A, discussed at § 5.5.3, below]."[28]

The privilege protects only communications, not facts. Those parts of a psychiatric record that contain conclusions based on objective indicia rather than on communications from the patient may be admitted in evidence.[29] The privilege does not apply to notations in psychiatric records as to the patient's diagnosis where the notations do not reveal any communications from patient to psychotherapist.[30] Similarly a psychotherapist must disclose portions of records documenting times and lengths of patient appointments, fees, diagnoses, and treatment plans; but those portions of the records which reflect

("[A] provider's assertion of the privilege may be treated as only a temporary precaution pending confirmation of the patient's own intentions.").

[26] *Adoption of Diane*, supra, 400 Mass at 201-202, 508 NE2d at 840 (mother in adoption consent case could not challenge testimony of psychotherapists regarding communications with child); *Adoption of George*, 27 Mass App 265, 275, 537 NE2d 1251, 1258 (1989) (mother, whose interests in litigation conflict with those of the child, may not invoke privilege on child's behalf). See generally *Com. v. Pellegrini*, 414 Mass 402, 407-409, 608 NE2d 717, 721-722 (1993) (parents have no privacy right to exclude child's medical record).

[27] *District Attorney for Norfolk District v. Magraw*, 417 Mass 169, 172-174, 628 NE2d 24, 26-27 (1994).

[28] See *Com. v. Brandwein*, 435 Mass 623, 628-629, 760 NE2d 724, 728-729 (2002) (psychiatric nurse's disclosure to police that patient told her he had robbed bank did not fall within privilege).

[29] *Adoption of Seth*, 29 Mass App 343, 353, 560 NE2d 708, 713-714 (1990) ("To the extent that the psychiatrist's opinions may have been grounded on such a mixed foundation, the recommended approach would be for the [patient's] counsel to request a voir dire to determine the basis of the expert opinion.").

[30] *Adoption of Saul*, 60 Mass App 546, 552-553, 804 NE2d 359, 365 (2004). Treatment center records that do not disclose communications between the patient and therapist are thus not protected. See *Doe v. Sex Offender Registry Board*, 459 Mass 603, 643, 947 NE2d 9, 39-41 (2011) (Doe had refused to participate in treatment or answer questions by evaluators).

the patients' "thoughts, feelings, and impressions, or contain the substance of the psychotherapeutic dialogue" are protected.[31]

The privileged status of a communication is not lost by reason of being recorded in a hospital record otherwise admissible.[32] On the other hand, the fact that hospital records contain some references to psychiatric matters does not compel the conclusion that the entire record is privileged.[33]

The fact that the patient later repeated some of the confidential information to other persons does not necessarily defeat the privilege.[34] A prosecution witness retains the privilege as to protected communications not testified to on direct examination.[35]

Section 20B sets out six exceptions[36] to the privilege:

(a) where the psychotherapist determines that the patient is in need of treatment in a hospital for mental or emotional illness, or is a threat to himself or others, and discloses the communication for the purpose of placing or retaining the patient in a hospital or under arrest;[37]

---

[31] See *Com. v. Kobrin*, supra, 395 Mass at 294-295, 479 NE2d at 681. See also *Com. v. Neumyer*, 432 Mass 23, 731 NE2d 1053 (2000) (portions of rape crisis counseling center records setting forth time, date, and fact of communication were not protected by privilege); *Com. v. Clancy*, 402 Mass 664, 667, 524 NE2d 395, 397 (1988); *Com. v. Reynolds*, 67 Mass App 215, 223, 852 NE2d 1124, 1130-1131 (2006) (pharmacy records indicating names and dosages of medications prescribed to OUI defendant did not reveal privileged communications).

[32] See *Usen v. Usen*, 359 Mass 453, 455-456, 269 NE2d 442, 443-444 (1971). See also *Com. v. Rexach*, 20 Mass App 919, 478 NE2d 744 (1985) (patient's statements to psychiatrists contained in hospital records are protected).

[33] *Petitions of the Department of Social Services to Dispense with Consent to Adoption*, supra, 399 Mass at 287-288, 503 NE2d at 1280-1281.

[34] *See Robinson v. Com.*, 399 Mass 131, 135, 503 NE2d 31, 34 (1987).

[35] See *Com. v. Clancy*, supra, 402 Mass at 666-669, 524 NE2d at 397-398 ("a witness does not relinquish all protection by merely testifying to events falling within the subject matter of a privilege.").

[36] Proposed Mass R Evid 503(d)(1) through (6) incorporates these exceptions.

[37] See *Walden Behavioral Care v. K.I.*, 471 Mass 150, 27 NE3d 1244 (2015) (imminent harm exception applied at commitment hearing to statements patient made to treating psychiatrist at mental health facility; because the examination was not ordered by a court nor sought by the Commonwealth, exception discussed in fn. 38 below did not apply and thus no warnings were required). This exception is inapplicable to communications made by a defendant already in custody and undergoing examination for possible commitment as a sexually dangerous person. *Com. v. Lamb*, 365 Mass 265, 268-269, 311 NE2d 47, 50 (1974). Such communications are governed by exception (b).

(b) where the patient was informed that his communications would not be privileged in the context of a court-ordered examination, but such communications are admissible only on issues involving the patient's mental or emotional condition, and not as a confession or admission of guilt;[38]

(c) where the patient places his mental or emotional condition in issue in any proceeding except one involving child custody, adoption, or adoption consent, but only if the judge determines that "it is more important to the interests of

---

[38] See *Com. v. Johnston*, 467 Mass 674, 688-689, 7 NE3d 424, 437 (2014) (no dispute defendant had been warned that his interviews with Bridgewater State Hospital staff would not be privileged, rendering his statements and refusals admissible); *Com. v. Benoit*, 410 Mass 506, 518-519, 574 NE2d 347, 354-355 (1991); *Com. v. Buck*, 64 Mass App 760, 766, 835 NE2d 623, 628 (2005). For the nature of the warnings and waiver required, see *Adoption of Serena*, 64 Mass App 260, 262-263, 832 NE2d 701, 704 (2005). When a defendant places his mental state at issue at trial, where he raises a defense of lack of responsibility, he thereby waives the privilege. *Com. v. Harris*, 468 Mass 429, 451-452, 1 NE3d 95, 113 (2014) (extensive discussion). Thus, a defendant should be specifically warned as well that the contents of a competency evaluation report may be used against him should he decide to place his mental state at issue at trial. 468 Mass at 452, 1 NE3d at 114.

This exception and its notice requirement have been held applicable to court-ordered examinations in the context of:

- A sexually dangerous person determination. See *Petition of Sheridan*, 412 Mass 599, 604, 591 NE2d 193, 196 (1992); *Com. v. Barboza*, 387 Mass 105, 109, 438 N.E.2d 1064, 1070-1071 (1982); *Com. v. Lamb*, supra, 365 Mass 265, 311 NE2d 47. An offender waives his privilege regarding statements to SDP qualified examiners when he retains his own expert and seeks to admit his statements to that expert at trial. *Com. v. Connors*, 447 Mass 313, 319, 850 NE2d 1038, 1043 (2006). Records protected by the psychotherapist-patient privilege do not lose that status merely by virtue of their being "pertinent or helpful to the examiners" in making the diagnosis of a sexually dangerous person pursuant to GL 123A. See *Com. v. Callahan*, 440 Mass 436, 799 NE2d 113 (2003).
- An evaluation of defendant's competency to stand trial. See *Com. v. Harris*, supra, 468 Mass at 443, 1 NE3d at 107. See also GL 233, § 23B.
- A request to extend a juvenile's commitment beyond his 18th birthday. See *Department of Youth Services v. A Juvenile*, 398 Mass 516, 524-527, 499 NE2d 812, 817-818 (1986); *Com. v. Traylor*, 29 Mass App 584, 590 n.2, 563 NE2d 243, 247 n.2 (1990).
- A petition to dispense with need of the mother's consent to adoption of her child. See *Petition of the Department of Social Services to Dispense with Consent to Adoption*, 396 Mass 485, 487, 487 NE2d 184, 185-186 (1986).

Warnings are not required in the context of suicide assessment examinations conducted at the request of jail officials. *Com. v. Seabrooks*, 433 Mass 439, 450-451, 743 NE2d 831, 840-841 (2001).

justice that the communication be disclosed than that the relationship between patient and psychotherapist be protected";[39]

(d) where the patient is dead and his mental or emotional condition is placed in issue by a party claiming or defending through or as a beneficiary of the patient, but only if the judge determines that "it is more important to the interests of justice that the communication be disclosed than that the relationship between patient and psychotherapist be protected";

(e) in child custody, adoption, and adoption consent cases, where the judge determines that the evidence bears significantly on the patient's ability to provide suitable care or custody and that "it is more important to the welfare of the child that the communication be disclosed than that the relationship between patient and psychotherapist be protected";[40] and

(f) in any proceeding against the psychotherapist where disclosure is necessary to the defense.

---

[39] See, e.g., *Com. v. Hanright*, 465 Mass 639, 646-647, 989 NE2d 883, 889 (2013) (defendant waived privilege when he raised lack of criminal responsibility defense, spoke to his own mental health expert, and sought to have his statements admitted at trial); *Com. v. Brandwein*, 435 Mass 623, 630 n.8, 760 NE2d 724, 730 n.8 (2002) (psychiatric nurse's testimony at trial concerning defendant's statements was admissible where defense was lack of criminal responsibility); *Com. v. Seabrooks*, supra, 433 Mass at 447-449, 743 NE2d at 839-840 (where defendant introduced mental condition as element of defense of acute stress disorder, forensic psychologist properly disclosed defendant's communications made during examinations). See also *McMillan v. Massachusetts Society for the Prevention of Cruelty to Animals*, 24 Mass Lawyers' Weekly 509 (D Mass 1995) (plaintiff seeking emotional distress damages in GL 151B employment discrimination action must disclose her therapist's session notes during discovery, and therapist may be deposed).

A defendant's claim of lack of intent does not, without more, suffice to put in issue his mental or emotional condition for purposes of this exception to the privilege. *Com. v. Dung Van Tran*, 463 Mass 8, 16-21, 972 NE2d 1, 9-12 (2012) (defendant's testimony that he did not intend to set fire to home did not put his mental condition in issue, and thus incriminating statements made to hospital psychotherapist were inadmissible).

For an extensive discussion of the discovery procedures pursuant to Mass R Crim P 14(b)(2) regarding defendant's psychiatric records in anticipation of a defense of lack of criminal responsibility, see *Com. v. Sliech-Brodeur*, 457 Mass 300, 315-317, 930 NE2d 91, 103-105 (2010).

[40] See, e.g., *Adoption of Adam*, 23 Mass App 922, 925, 500 NE2d 816, 820 (1986); *Custody of a Minor (No. 3)*, 16 Mass App 998, 1002, 454 NE2d 924, 927 (1983). The judge may not delegate to the GAL the statutory duty to conduct an in camera review of the records and determine whether the exception for the welfare of the child applies. See *P.W. v. M.S.*, 67 Mass App 779, 785-786, 857 NE2d 38, 43-44 (2006).

The trial judge is required to treat the determinations in these exceptions with "meticulous observance," and the findings should be shown on the record or transcript.[41]

In addition to the statutory exceptions, the privilege is not infringed when a psychotherapist reports a suspected instance of child abuse as required by GL 119, § 51A.[42] The privilege § 20B confers is not absolute but "hedged," and by requiring reports pursuant to § 51A the Legislature "gave higher priority to the protection of children than the protection of psychotherapist-patient confidences."[43]

Finally, the psychotherapist-patient (as well as the social worker-client privilege discussed in the next section) may be overridden by the criminal defendant's constitutional rights. See § 5.5.4, infra.[44]

§ 5.5.3 Social Worker-Client Confidentiality and Privilege

Massachusetts law provides for both the confidentiality of communications between social worker and client as well as a privilege that attaches to certain of those communications.

GL 112, § 135A mandates the confidentiality of "all communications"[45] between a licensed social worker or a social worker employed in a state, county, or municipal government agency[46] and a client.[47] "No such social worker, colleague, agent, or employee of any social worker, whether professional, clerical, academic or therapeutic, shall disclose any information acquired or revealed in the course of or in connection with the performance of the social worker's professional

---

[41] *Usen v. Usen*, 359 Mass 453, 456-457, 269 NE2d 442, 444 (1971).

[42] GL 119, § 51A was so amended by St 2002, c107, § 1-4. See *Com. v. Souther*, 31 Mass App 219, 222-224, 575 NE2d 1150, 1153-1154 (1991) (patient not entitled to dismissal of indictments founded on report by psychotherapist filed on § 51A).

[43] *Id.*, 31 Mass App at 224, 575 NE2d at 1154.

[44] There is no public policy exception that overrides the privilege in investigations by the Board of Registration in Medicine. *Board of Registration in Medicine v. Doe*, 457 Mass 738, 745-746, 933 NE2d 67, 72-73 (2010).

[45] "Communications" include "conversations, correspondence, actions and occurrences regardless of the client's awareness of such conversations, correspondence, actions and occurrences and any records, memoranda or notes of the foregoing." GL 112, § 135.

[46] The confidentiality provisions of § 135A and the privilege provided for in § 135B apply to unlicensed persons employed by governmental agencies to perform social work. See *Bernard v. Com.*, 424 Mass 32, 673 NE2d 1220 (1996) (state trooper employed as peer counselor).

[47] A "client" is defined in GL 112, § 135 as "a person with whom a social worker has established a social worker-client relationship."

services, including the fact, circumstances, findings or records of such services." Disclosure is permitted in the following circumstances:

(a) where the communication falls within an exception to the privilege created by GL 135B, discussed below;
(b) upon express, written consent of the client or a guardian appointed to act in the client's behalf, and in the case of marital or family therapy, with the consent of each adult participant;
(c) upon the need to disclose information that is necessary to protect the safety of the client or others if the client presents a clear and present danger to himself, or has communicated to the social worker an explicit threat to kill or inflict serious bodily injury upon a reasonably identified victim or victims;[48]
(d) in order to collect amounts owed by the client for professional services rendered by the social worker or his employees;
(e) in order to initiate or give testimony in a care and protection proceeding or petition to dispense with consent to adoption;[49]
(f) where the social worker has acquired the information while acting as an elder protective services worker; and
(g) where the social worker has acquired the information while conducting an investigation into abuse of a disabled person.

GL 112, § 135B additionally creates a testimonial privilege that permits the client to refuse to disclose and to prevent a witness from disclosing in any court, legislative, or administrative proceeding any communication "relative to the diagnosis or treatment of the client's mental or emotional condition" between the client and a licensed

---

[48] The predecessor to § 135A more broadly excepted communications that reveal "the contemplation or commission of a crime or a harmful act." See *Com. v. Berrio*, 407 Mass 37, 40-41, 551 NE2d 496, 498-499 (1990). The Advisory Committee for the Proposed Massachusetts Rules of Evidence concluded, in rejecting this formulation, that this exception was "so ambiguous and broad as to drastically impair the value and meaning of the privilege." Advisory Committee Note to Proposed Rule 503.

[49] See, e.g., *Adoption of Diane*, 400 Mass 196, 198-200, 508 NE2d 837, 838-839 (1987); *Petition of the Department of Social Services to Dispense with Consent to Adoption*, 397 Mass 659, 662-664, 467 NE2d 866, 869-870 (1986) (exception applies to permit social worker to disclose information even if she was not party bringing the petition).

social worker, or a social worker employed in a state, county, or municipal governmental agency. The judge is required by the statute to instruct the jury that no adverse inference may be drawn from assertion of the privilege.

The privilege is "a legislative recognition that the confidentiality of a person's communications to a social worker is a necessity for successful social work intervention. . . . The purpose of enacting a social worker-client privilege is to prevent the chilling effect which routine disclosures may have in preventing those in need of help from seeking that help."[50]

By its terms, the privilege encompasses only those statements made for the purpose of diagnosis and treatment of the client's mental or emotional condition, as compared to the broader reference to "all communications" in § 135A.[51] Both §§ 135A and 135B apply only to the disclosure of "communications." Thus information contained in DSS records that was acquired through the personal observations of the social worker in the subject's home is not within the prohibition.[52] Like the psychotherapist-patient privilege, the social worker privilege is not self-executing—it must be affirmatively asserted by the client (or guardian).[53]

Neither § 135A nor § 135B prohibit the filing of a report of suspected child abuse.[54]

The privilege established by § 135B does not apply to the following communications:[55]

(a) where the social worker determines that the patient is in need of treatment in a hospital for mental or emotional illness, or is a threat to himself or others, and discloses the communication for the purpose of placing or retaining the patient in a hospital;

---

[50] *Com. v. Collett*, 387 Mass 424, 428, 439 NE2d 1223, 1226 (1982) (decided under predecessor statute).

[51] See *Com. v. Wojcik*, 43 Mass App 595, 608-609, 686 NE2d 452, 461-462 (1997).

[52] See *Allen v. Holyoke Hospital*, 398 Mass 372, 378, 496 NE2d 1368, 1372 (1986); *Custody of a Minor (No. 3)*, 16 Mass App 998, 454 NE2d 924 (1983).

[53] *Com. v. Oliveira*, 438 Mass 325, 330-331, 780 NE2d 453, 458 (2002); *Com. v. Pelosi*, 441 Mass 257, 261, 805 NE2d 1 (2004).

[54] St 2002, c107, § 1-4.

[55] The exceptions essentially track those applying to the psychotherapist-patient privilege discussed in § 5.5.2, supra.

(b) where the patient was informed that his communications would not be privileged in the context of a court-ordered examination, but such communications are admissible only on issues involving the patient's mental or emotional condition, and not as a confession or admission of guilt;

(c) where the patient places his mental or emotional condition in issue in any proceeding except one involving child custody, adoption or adoption consent, but only if the judge determines that "it is more important to the interests of justice that the communication be disclosed than that the relationship between client and social worker be protected";[56]

(d) where the client is dead and his mental or emotional condition is placed in issue by a party claiming or defending through or as a beneficiary of the client, but only if the judge determines that "it is more important to the interests of justice that the communication be disclosed than that the relationship between client and social worker be protected";

(e) in the initiation or giving of testimony in certain child protection proceedings;[57]

(f) in any proceeding whereby the social worker has acquired the information while conducting an investigation of child abuse pursuant to GL 119, § 51B;[58]

(g) in child custody, adoption, and adoption consent cases, where the judge determines that the evidence bears significantly on the client's ability to provide suitable care or custody and that "it is more important to the welfare of the

---

[56] See, e.g., *Com. v. Stroyny*, 435 Mass 635, 647-648, 760 NE2d 1202, 1212 (2002) (social worker could testify to defendant's statement where his mental condition was critical aspect of defense).

[57] *Adoption of Diane*, 400 Mass 196, 198-200, 508 NE2d 837, 838-839 (1987); *Petition of the Department of Social Services to Dispense with Consent to Adoption*, 397 Mass 659, 662-664, 467 NE2d 866, 869-870 (1986).

[58] In the context of criminal prosecutions, see also *Com. v. Pelosi*, 441 Mass 257, 805 NE2d 1 (2004), and *Com. v. Jones*, 404 Mass 339, 535 NE2d 221 (1989) (defendant entitled to have judge make in camera inspection of entire Department of Social Services (DSS) file for exculpatory evidence concerning alleged abuse); *Com. v. O'Brien*, 27 Mass App 184, 536 NE2d 361 (1989) (defendant entitled to DSS investigatory report on incident without any showing of particularized need); *Com. v. Pratt*, 42 Mass App 695, 679 NE2d 579 (1997) (reversible error to exclude defendant's evidence of lack of fresh complaint by complainant in her communications with DSS case worker). But see *Com. v. Hyatt*, 31 Mass App 488, 492-493, 579 NE2d 1365, 1368-1369 (1991) (raw file of DSS remains confidential).

child that the communication be disclosed than that the relationship between client and social worker be protected"; and

(h) in any proceeding brought by the client against the social worker and in any malpractice, criminal or license revocation proceeding in which disclosure is necessary or relevant to the claim or defense of the social worker.

The Legislature has thus determined that "while the preservation of the confidential relationship is an important objective, under certain circumstances, this goal must give way in favor of other societal interests," such as the protection of children.[59]

Communications to an "allied mental health professional" (AMHP) are privileged pursuant to GL 112, § 172.[60]

Proposed Mass R Evid 503 (discussed in § 5.5.2) combines the psychotherapist-patient and social worker-client privilege.

An earlier version of GL 112, § 135 prohibited disclosure of any information "acquired from persons consulting [the social worker] in his professional capacity" and was interpreted as extending the privilege to communications regardless of whether such persons were "clients" of the social worker or whether the social worker initiated the contact.[61] The current version of §§ 135A and 135B, as noted above, applies only to communications between client and social worker.

In addition to the statutory exceptions, the social worker-client privilege may in a criminal case have to yield to a defendant's constitutional right to use privileged communications in his defense. See § 5.5.4, infra.

---

[59] *Com. v. Collett*, supra, 387 Mass at 428, 434, 439 NE2d at 1226.

[60] See *Com. v. Vega*, 449 Mass 227, 866 NE2d 892 (2007) (subject to exceptions enumerated in § 172).

[61] See *Com. v. Collett*, supra, 387 Mass at 427-430, 439 NE2d at 1226-1228 (information obtained from interviews with victim's family members); *Allen v. Holyoke Hospital*, 398 Mass 372, 376-378, 496 NE2d 1368, 1371-1372 (1986) (communications to DSS social workers from child decedent's grandparents and foster parents fell within privilege and were not subject to discovery in wrongful death action). See also *In re Production of Records to Grand Jury*, 618 F Supp 440 (D Mass 1985) (recognizing, as matter of federal evidentiary law, a qualified privilege for DSS records containing communications made to social worker from either patient or third parties).

The federal courts now recognize a privilege protecting confidential communications between psychotherapist and patient.[62]

§ 5.5.4 *Privilege Overridden by Constitutional Rights*

Both the psychotherapist-patient and social worker-client privilege may be overridden by the defendant's rights under art. 12 of the Massachusetts Declaration of Rights to confront his accusers and to present relevant evidence in his favor. The Supreme Judicial Court has, in a series of decisions in rape and sexual abuse cases, confronted the difficult task of balancing these rights against the competing interest of confidentiality.[63]

Beginning with *Com. v. Stockhammer,*[64] defense counsel have been given restricted access to review a rape complainant's privileged files.[65] *Com. v. Figueroa*[66] extended the disclosure rule to privileged records concerning the condition of mental retardation or impairment of a complaining witness: "[D]efense counsel must also be allowed to search the records for evidence of how that impairment might affect her capacity to perceive, remember and articulate the alleged events. This type of evidence, like evidence of bias, prejudice, or motive to lie, can be used to impeach the credibility of the complaining witness."[67]

Com. v. Bishop,[68] emphasizing that the privileges for mental health records should be pierced only in those cases in which "there is

---

[62] See *Jaffee v. Redmond*, 518 US 1 (1996) (statements that defendant police officer made to licensed social worker in course of psychotherapy and notes taken during counseling sessions were protected from compelled disclosure in civil rights action).

[63] A judge has no authority to withhold records where the records are not privileged or where no privilege has been asserted. *Com. v. Oliveira*, 438 Mass 325, 337-338, 780 NE2d 453, 462 (2002). Mass R Crim P 17(a)(2) controls where no privilege is asserted. *Com. v. Lampron*, 441 Mass 265, 806 NE2d 72 (2004). See also *Com. v. Caceres*, 63 Mass App 747, 829 NE2d 1144 (2005) (defendant satisfied threshold requirement for showing of relevancy of records from rape counseling center).

[64] 409 Mass 867, 880-884, 570 NE2d 992, 1001-1003 (1991).

[65] See also § 6.15, supra.

[66] 413 Mass 193, 202-203, 595 NE2d 779, 785 (1992).

[67] See also *Com. v. Hrycenko*, 31 Mass App 425, 433-434, 578 NE2d 809, 814-815 (1991) (defense counsel must be permitted to examine DMH records concerning victim); *Com. v. Arthur*, 31 Mass App 178, 182, 575 NE2d 1147, 1149-1150 (1991) (DSS investigation records); *Com. v. Simcock*, 31 Mass App 184, 199-200, 575 NE2d 1137, 1145-1146 (1991) (notes concerning victim's therapy).

[68] 416 Mass 169, 617 NE2d 990 (1993). *Bishop* has been superseded by *Com. v. Dwyer,* discussed below, but remains an important part of the evolution of law in this area.

a reasonable risk that nondisclosure may result in an erroneous conviction,"[69] devised a five-step protocol for determining whether disclosure was required.[70]

In *Com. v. Fuller*[71] the court addressed the procedure to be followed and the standards to be applied when a defendant seeks access to the complainant's rape counseling records, which are privileged under GL 233, § 20J (see § 5.5.6, infra). While expressing general adherence to the procedures set forth in *Bishop*, the court subjected rape-counseling records to somewhat more stringent controls. The defendant must file a written motion seeking production and explaining in detail his reasons for doing so. Such a motion should be "the last step" in the defendant's pretrial discovery, exhausting all other potential sources for the information, and must contain a showing that the material sought is not available elsewhere. A judge should undertake an in-camera review of records privileged under § 20J only when the defendant's motion has demonstrated "a good faith, specific, and reasonable basis for believing that the records will contain exculpatory evidence which is relevant and material to the issue of the defendant's guilt." "Material evidence" means evidence that not only is admissible, but that "also tends to create a reasonable doubt that might not otherwise exist."[72] A credible showing that the complainant had previously fabricated allegations of sexual assault or a showing of bias against the defendant or credible evidence that the complainant has difficulty distinguishing fantasy from reality might suffice to warrant in camera

---

[69] 416 Mass at 177, 617 NE2d at 995.

[70] For extensive discussion of the *Bishop/Fuller* protocol, see *Com. v. Pelosi*, 441 Mass 257, 805 NE2d 1 (2004) and *Com. v. Pare*, 427 Mass 427, 693 NE2d 1002 (1998). On the admissibility of records once they are disclosed, compare *Com. v. Sheehan*, 435 Mass 183, 755 NE2d 1208 (2001) (trial court improperly excluded mental health records regarding post-incident treatment of 10-year-old complainant, which indicated that complainant had some tendency toward fantasizing) with *Com. v. Ramos*, 47 Mass App 792, 716 NE2d 676 (1999) (mental health records of victim properly excluded because they did not support defense theory that she falsely accused defendant in order to hurt her father). See also *Com. v. Beaudry*, 63 Mass App 488, 490-493, 826 NE2d 782, 786-787 (2005) (trial judge's time restrictions on use of victim's medical records were reasonable and did not prevent effective defense).

On the question of appellate review of a trial court's order sealing records after *in-camera* review, see *Com. v. Feliciano*, 442 Mass 728, 732-734, 816 NE2d 1205, 1208-1209 (2004). See also *Com. v. McCoy*, 443 Mass 1015, 823 NE2d 1246 (2005) (GL 211, § 3 not available to review technical errors in judge's finding that defendant had demonstrated relevance of privileged records).

[71] 423 Mass 216, 667 NE2d 847 (1996).

[72] 423 Mass at 226, 667 NE2d at 855.

inspection of the records.[73] Emphatically repeating the admonition in *Bishop*, there is to be no "unrestrained foray into confidential records in the hope that the unearthing of some unspecified information would enable [the defendant] to impeach the witness."[74]

By way of example, where a rape defendant's proffer demonstrated that the complainant formed the opinion that she was raped after speaking with a rape crisis counselor, that she had used alcohol and marijuana on the night of the incident, that she lied to her grandmother about the incident, and that she continued to socialize with defendant after the incident, constitutional principles required that defendant be afforded access to the record of the telephone conversation with the counselor.[75]

The *Bishop-Fuller* procedures were also applied with regard to requests for information protected by the domestic counselor privilege, GL 233, § 20K (see § 5.5.5, infra)[76] and the privilege protecting against release of HIV test results, GL 111, § 70F.[77] *Fuller's* heightened standard of relevance was applied to all cases in which a defendant seeks privileged treatment records, including those protected by the psychotherapist-patient privilege in GL 233, § 20B.[78]

In *Com. v. Dwyer*,[79] the Supreme Judicial Court again recalibrated the balance between the defendant's right of access to potentially exculpatory information and the alleged victim's right to privacy. Concluding that the trial judge should no longer be put in the role of examining records for possible use in the defense case, the Court replaced what it characterized as the "stringent" *Bishop/Fuller* protocols with one grounded in Mass R Crim P 17(a)(2) that gives defense counsel the opportunity to inspect presumptively privileged records, subject to a strict protective order.

At the outset, the party moving for the production of documents must establish: (1) that the documents are evidentiary and relevant; (2) that they are not otherwise procurable reasonably in advance of

---

[73] Compare *Com. v. Rushworth*, 60 Mass App 145, 149-150, 799 NE2d 1281, 1285 (2003) (defendant did not meet "high burden" under *Fuller* of demonstrating motive to lie).

[74] *Com. v. Fuller*, supra, 423 Mass at 226, 667 NE2d at 855.

[75] *Com. v. Neumyer*, 432 Mass 23, 731 NE2d 1053 (2000).

[76] *Com. v. Tripolone*, 425 Mass 487, 681 NE2d 1216 (1997).

[77] *Com. v. Maxwell*, 441 Mass 773, 779-781, 808 NE2d 806, 811-812 (2004).

[78] See *Com. v. Sheehan*, supra, 435 Mass at 185 n.1, 755 NE2d at 1210 n.1; *Com. v. Oliveira*, 431 Mass 609, 616-617, 728 NE2d 320, 326 (2000); *Com. v. Zane Z.*, 51 Mass App 135, 142-143, 743 NE2d 868, 873 (2001).

[79] 448 Mass 122, 859 NE2d 400 (2006).

trial by exercise of due diligence; (3) that the party cannot properly prepare for trial without such production and inspection in advance of trial and that the failure to obtain such inspection may tend unreasonably to delay the trial; and (4) that the application is made in good faith and is not intended as a general "fishing expedition." Where the records sought are presumptively privileged, the record holder and/or the subject of the records must be afforded notice and an opportunity to be heard.

If the judge orders issuance of a Rule 17(a)(2) summons, all presumptively privileged records must be retained in court under seal, and may be inspected only by defense counsel and subject to a protective order prohibiting copying or disclosure to any person, including the defendant. If counsel challenges the privilege designation of any record, a hearing must be held to determine if the record should be released from the protective order. Counsel may also move to modify the protective order to permit copying or disclosure to other persons (e.g., the defendant, an investigator, an expert) where necessary to prepare for trial.

A defendant seeking to introduce a presumptively privileged record at trial must file a motion in limine at or before the final pretrial conference. The judge may allow the motion only with oral or written findings that introduction at trial is necessary for the defendant to obtain a fair trial. Before permitting the introduction in evidence of such records, the judge shall consider alternatives to introduction, including an agreed to stipulation or introduction of redacted portions of the records.[80]

Third parties other than the complainant who may be referenced in the records sought do not have standing to participate in the hearings; their privacy is to be protected pursuant to the protective order.[81]

---

[80] For application of the *Dwyer* protocol, compare *Com. v. Bourgeois*, 68 Mass App 433, 862 NE2d 464 (2007) (child victim's mental health records indicating she had attempted suicide, was abusing drugs and alcohol, and was failing school, were not discoverable because not indicative of bias, motive to lie or fabrication) and *Com. v. Rivera*, 83 Mass App 581, 588-589, 987 NE2d 597, 603-604 (2013) (rape victim's treatment records from community health center were not subject to discovery because defense counsel failed to articulate specific relevance to victim's credibility) with *Com. v. Labroad*, 466 Mass 1037, 2 NE3d 869 (2014) (defendant made sufficiently particular showing as to relevancy of records of child's psychologist regarding her report of sexual assault).

[81] *Martin v. Com.*, 451 Mass 113, 123, 884 NE2d 442, 449-450 (2008) (applying the new procedures).

The *Dwyer* protocol, which applies whenever a defendant seeks inspection of statutorily privileged records of any third party,[82] applies prospectively to criminal cases tried after December 29, 2006.[83]

The Commonwealth has no obligation to seek information from the complainant concerning any mental health treatment she has received or any records which may exist; nor is the prosecutor under a duty to affirmatively facilitate the questioning of the complainant by defendant.[84] The Commonwealth has no right, comparable to the defendant's, to privileged documents for use at trial.[85]

The principle allowing a criminal defendant access to privileged records in certain cases has been held inapplicable to noncriminal proceedings.[86]

With regard to a criminal defendant's effort to seek discovery of the psychiatric treatment records of a Commonwealth witness with an eye towards obtaining information relevant to the witness's testimonial capacities, see *Com. v. Alcantara*, 471 Mass 550, 563-564, 31 NE3d 561, 573-574 (2015).

§ 5.5.5 Confidential Communications to Sexual Assault and Domestic Violence Counselors

GL 233, § 20J, provides:

> A sexual assault counsellor shall not disclose [a] confidential communication [defined as information transmitted in confidence by and between a victim of sexual assault and a sexual assault counsellor by a means which does not disclose the information to a person other than a person present for the benefit of the victim, or to those to whom disclosure of such information is reasonably necessary to the counselling and assisting of such victim], without the prior written consent of the victim; provided, however, that nothing in this chapter shall be construed to

---

[82] *Com. v. Sealy*, 467 Mass 617, 627, 6 NE3d 1052, 1060 (2014).

[83] *Com. v. Dwyer*, 448 Mass at 124, 859 NE2d at 404. The Supreme Judicial Court has declined an invitation to extend the protocol to rape-counseling records subject to the attorney-client privilege. See *Com. v. Sealy*, supra, 467 Mass at 625-628,, 6 NE3d at 1059-1061.

[84] See *Com. v. Beal*, 429 Mass 530, 709 NE2d 413 (1999); *Com. v. Dexter*, 50 Mass App 30, 34-35, 734 NE2d 332, 336 (2000).

[85] *Com. v. Callahan*, 440 Mass 436, 438 n.5, 799 NE2d 113, 115 n.5 (2003).

[86] See *Herridge v. Board of Registration in Medicine*, 420 Mass 154, 157, 648 NE2d 745, 747 (1995).

> limit the defendant's right of cross-examination of such counsellor in a civil or criminal proceeding if such counsellor testifies with such written consent.
>
> Such confidential communications shall not be subject to discovery and shall be inadmissible in any criminal or civil proceeding without the prior written consent of the victim to whom the report, record, working paper or memorandum relates.

A privilege for rape counseling records has also been recognized under federal law.[87]

Unlike the privileges pertaining to psychotherapists and social workers discussed earlier (see §§ 5.5.2 and 5.5.3, supra), the privilege created by GL 233, § 20J has no statutory exceptions (other than the consent of the victim) and has thus been characterized as "absolute."[88] Nor does the sexual assault counselor privilege require the victim to affirmatively exercise the privilege; rather, the statutory language prevents disclosure "without the prior written consent of the victim."[89]

Nonetheless, "in certain circumstances the absolute privilege expressed in § 20J . . . must yield to the constitutional right of a criminal defendant to have access to privileged communications."[90] *Com. v. Fuller*,[91] discussed in § 5.5.4, supra, established the procedure to be followed and the standards to be applied when a defendant seeks access to the complainant's rape counseling records.[92] These procedures are also to be followed with regard to requests for information protected by the domestic counselor privilege, GL 233, § 20K, set out immediately below.[93]

GL 233, § 20K, provides:

> A domestic violence victims' counselor shall not disclose . . . confidential communications without the prior written consent of the victim, except as hereinafter provided. Such confidential communication shall

---

[87] See *United States v. Lowe*, 948 F Supp 97 (D Mass 1996).

[88] See *Com. v. Stockhammer*, 409 Mass 867, 883, 570 NE2d 992, 1002 (1991); *Com. v. Jones*, 404 Mass 339, 342, 535 NE2d 221, 223 (1989).

[89] *Com. v. Oliveira*, 438 Mass 325, 331 n.7, 780 NE2d 453, 458 n.7 (2002).

[90] *Com. v. Two Juveniles*, 397 Mass 261, 266, 491 NE2d 234, 238 (1986). But see *Com. v. Giacalone*, 24 Mass App 166, 170, 507 NE2d 769, 772 (1987) (no sufficient showing made to justify resort to privileged records).

[91] 423 Mass 216, 667 NE2d 847 (1996).

[92] For a case holding that defendant was constitutionally entitled to access to rape counseling records, see *Com. v. Neumyer*, 432 Mass 23, 731 NE2d 1053 (2000), discussed supra at § 5.5.4.

[93] See *Com. v. Tripolone*, 425 Mass 487, 681 NE2d 1216 (1997).

not be subject to discovery in any civil, legislative or administrative proceeding without the prior written consent of the victim to whom such confidential communication relates. In criminal actions such confidential communications shall be subject to discovery and shall be admissible as evidence but only to the extent of information contained therein which is exculpatory in relation to the defendant; provided, however, that the court shall first examine such confidential communication and shall determine whether or not such exculpatory information is therein contained before allowing such discovery or the introduction of such evidence.

§ 5.5.6 Inadmissibility of Statements Made During Court-Ordered Psychiatric Examination

GL 233, § 23B, provides:

In the trial of an indictment or complaint for any crime, no statement made by a defendant therein subjected to [a court-ordered] psychiatric examination . . . for the purposes of such examination or treatment shall be admissible in evidence against him on any issue other than that of his mental condition, nor shall it be admissible in evidence against him on that issue if such statement constitutes a confession of guilt of the crime charged.[94]

The relationship between GL 233, § 23B, and the constitutional privilege against self-incrimination (see § 5.14, infra) is discussed in *Blaisdell v. Com.*,[95] holding that the protections afforded by § 23B to a defendant subjected to a compelled psychiatric examination are not

[94] See also discussion of exception (b) to GL 233, § 20B, in § 5.5.2, supra. For cases applying § 23B, see *Seng v. Com.*, 445 Mass 536, 545-547, 839 NE2d 283, 290-291 (2005) (any inculpatory statement during competency evaluation would be inadmissible); *Com. v. Harvey*, 397 Mass 803, 807-809, 494 NE2d 382, 385-386 (1986) (prosecutor's introduction of evidence obtained as result of court-ordered psychiatric examination was improper before defendant had introduced any evidence of mental impairment); *Com. v. Martin*, 393 Mass 781, 786-787, 473 NE2d 1099, 1103 (1985) (defendant's admissions during court-ordered psychiatric examination regarding his state of mind at time of shooting were improperly admitted). But see *Com. v. Williams*, 30 Mass App 543, 551, 571 NE2d 29, 33 (1991) (defendant may waive privilege by testifying about the matters).

[95] 372 Mass 753, 761-764, 364 NE2d 191, 198-199 (1977). See also *Com. v. Sliech-Brodeur*, 457 Mass 300, 315-317, 930 NE2d 91, 103-105 (2010) (Commonwealth was not entitled to pretrial discovery of defendant's psychiatric records maintained by expert witness testifying to lack of criminal responsibility).

coextensive with the greater protection afforded by the constitutional privilege. The Court established certain requirements in order to meet the constitutional mandate, such as construction of "confession" to include inculpatory statements falling short of a full acknowledgment of guilt.[96] The procedures mandated by the court[97] are now found in Mass R Crim P 14(b)(2).[98]

Nontestimonial evidence such as scientific and objective psychological test results obtained during a court-ordered examination are not privileged either under GL 233, § 23B, or the privilege against self-incrimination.[99]

Where a defendant presents expert testimony placing at issue his mental ability to voluntarily waive his *Miranda* rights and make a voluntary statement thereafter, he may be required to submit to an examination by the Commonwealth's expert, and the expert may testify based on the compelled communications with the defendant.[100]

§ 5.6 Priest-Penitent

There is no priest-penitent privilege at common law,[1] but a privilege is established by GL 233, § 20A, which provides:

> A priest, rabbi or ordained or licensed minister of any church or an accredited Christian Science practitioner shall not, without the consent of the person making the confession, be allowed to disclose a confession made to him in his professional character, in the course of discipline enjoined by the rules or practice of the religious body to which he belongs; nor shall a priest, rabbi or ordained or licensed minister of any church or an accredited Christian Science practitioner testify as to any communication made to him by any person in seeking religious or spiritual advice or comfort, or as to his given advice thereon in the course of his professional duties or in his professional character, without the consent of such person.

---

[96] 372 Mass at 763, 364 NE2d at 198-199.

[97] 372 Mass at 767-769.

[98] See generally *Com. v. Sliech-Brodeur*, 457 Mass 300, 309-326, 930 NE2d 91, 99-111 (2010).

[99] *Blaisdell v. Com.*, supra, 372 Mass at 759, 765-769, 364 NE2d at 196, 199, -202; *Com. v. Marshall*, 373 Mass 65, 68, 364 NE2d 1237, 1241 (1977). See also Mass R Crim P 14(b)(2)(B)(ii).

[100] *Com. v. Ostrander*, 441 Mass 344, 351-355, 805 NE2d 497, 504-506 (2004).

§ 5.6 [1] *Com. v. Drake*, 15 Mass 161 (1818).

The word "communication" in the statute is not limited to conversation and includes other acts by which ideas may be transmitted from one person to another.[2] A penitent may waive the privilege, and as a result the minister may be required to disclose confidential communications.[3]

The privilege applies only to communications made for a spiritual or religious purpose.[4] The privilege is waived where the penitent requests that the conversation be relayed to third parties.[5]

Unlike the psychotherapist-patient privilege (see § 5.5.2) the priest-penitent privilege is written in absolute terms without exceptions, indicating that the "legislative concern for the inviolability of the communications [protected] is more substantial"; consequently, courts should be cautious in accepting arguments of waiver by an executor or administrator of the deceased.[6]

Proposed Mass R Evid 505 would expand the privilege by including "other similar functionary of a religious organization" in its definition of "clergyman" as well as "an individual reasonably believed so to be by the person consulting him."[7] The Rule provides that a person holding the privilege may bar disclosure by third parties, 505(b), and

---

[2] *Com. v. Zezima*, 365 Mass 238, 241, 310 NE2d 590, 592 (1974) (defendant's display of gun to clergyman may have constituted "communication").

[3] See, e.g., *Com. v. Kane*, 388 Mass 128, 135-138, 445 NE2d 598, 602-603 (1983).

[4] *See Com. v. Vital*, 83 Mass App 669, 671-673, 988 NE2d 866, 870-871 (2013) (defendant's conversations with pastor were aimed at seeking his assistance to avoid criminal charges); *Com. v. Kebreau*, 454 Mass 287, 301-303, 909 NE2d 1146, 1158-1159 (2009) (defendant's inculpatory statements regarding sexual abuse of daughters made at a family meeting at church were not within privilege); *Com. v. Nutter*, 87 Mass App 260, 28 NE3d 1, 4 (2015) (defendant's statements to pastor over telephone regarding allegations of sexual abuse against him were not made for purpose of seeking spiritual guidance).

[5] *Com. v. Vital*, supra, 83 Mass App at 674, 988 NE2d at 871.

[6] See *Ryan v. Ryan*, 419 Mass 86, 95-96, 642 NE2d 1028, 1034-1035 (1994).

[7] Proposed Mass R Evid 505 provides:

Religious Privilege

(a) **Definitions**. As used in this rule:
   (1) A "clergyman" is a minister, priest, rabbi, accredited Christian Science practitioner, or other similar functionary of a religious organization, or an individual reasonably believed so by the person consulting him.
   (2) A communication is "confidential" if not intended for further disclosure except to other persons present in furtherance of the purpose of the communication.

(b) **General rule of privilege**. A person has a privilege to refuse to disclose and to prevent another from disclosing a confidential communication by the person to a clergyman in his professional character as spiritual advisor.

(c) **Who may claim the privilege**. The privilege may be claimed by the person, by his guardian or conservator, or by his personal representative if he is deceased. The

that the privilege survives the death of the claimant, 505(c), matters upon which GL 233, § 20A, is silent. The Supreme Judicial Court has declined to consider adoption of Proposed Mass R Evid 505's expanded definition of clergyman.[8]

By amendment of GL 119, § 51A in 2002, GL 233, § 20A does not prohibit the filing of a report of suspected child abuse.[9] The legislation provides as follows:

> Notwithstanding section 20A of chapter 233, a priest, rabbi, clergy member, ordained or licensed minister, leader of a church or religious body or accredited Christian Science practitioner shall report all cases of abuse under this section, but need not report information solely gained in a confession or similarly confidential communication in other religious faiths. Nothing in the general laws shall modify or limit the duty of a priest, rabbi, clergy member, ordained or licensed minister, leader of a church or religious body or accredited Christian Science practitioner to report a reasonable cause that a child is being injured as set forth in this section when the priest, rabbi, clergy member, ordained or licensed minister, leader of a church or religious body or accredited Christian Science practitioner is acting in some other capacity that would otherwise make him a reporter.

A religious order has no protection under the doctrine of "church autonomy" or other constitutional provision from complying with a subpoena seeking documents regarding a priest facing criminal prosecution.[10]

§ 5.7 Deliberations of Jurors and Judicial Officers/Extraneous Influences upon Jury Deliberations/Post-Verdict Interviews

The deliberations of judicial or quasi-judicial bodies may not be testified to by members of the bodies.[1] Nor are grand or petit jurors permitted to testify as to opinions expressed or discussions occurring

---

person who was the clergyman at the time of the communication is presumed to have authority to claim the privilege but only on behalf of the communicant.

[8] See *Com. v. Marrero*, 436 Mass 488, 495, 766 NE2d 461, 467-468 (2002) (declining privilege to manager of Christian rehabilitation center, to whom defendant made incriminating statements).

[9] St. 2002, c107, § 1-4.

[10] See *Society of Jesus of New England v. Com.*, 441 Mass 662, 808 NE2d 272 (2004).

§ 5.7 [1] *Day v. Crowley*, 341 Mass 666, 669-670, 172 NE2d 251, 253 (1961) (judge cannot properly state the unexpressed reasons which actuated his decision);

during deliberations: "To uphold the integrity of the verdict and to keep the jury free from unwarranted intrusions, juror testimony is generally not admissible to impeach the jury's verdict."[2] Jurors are competent witnesses to prove an error in the recording of their verdict.[3]

Although jurors may not testify as to the internal decision-making process of their deliberations, they may give testimony about extraneous influences (such as unauthorized views,[4] a juror's own research,[5] or facts communicated by a third party) that may have improperly tainted the deliberations. Proposed Mass R Evid 606(b), which tracks the federal rule, reflects Massachusetts practice:

> **(b) Inquiry into validity of verdict or indictment.**
>
> Upon an inquiry into the validity of a verdict or indictment, a juror may not testify as to any matter or statement occurring during the course of the jury's deliberations or to the effect of anything upon his or any other juror's mind or emotions as influencing him to assent to or dissent from the verdict or indictment or concerning his mental processes in connection therewith, except that a juror may testify on the

---

Philips v. Town of Marblehead, 148 Mass 326, 330, 19 NE 547, 549 (1889) (deliberations of selectmen acting in a quasi judicial capacity assessing value of land taken by the town).

[2] *Markee v. Biasetti*, 410 Mass 785, 789, 575 NE2d 1083, 1085 (1991). On the secrecy of grand jury proceedings, see GL 277, § 5; Mass R Crim P 5(d); *Globe Newspaper Co. v. Police Commissioner of Boston*, 419 Mass 852, 865-866, 648 NE2d 419, 428-429 (1995) ("The requirement that grand jury proceedings remain secret is deeply rooted in the common law of the Commonwealth. We have recognized that several interests are served by maintaining strict confidentiality, such as protection of the grand jury from outside influence, including influence by the news media; protection of individuals from notoriety and disgrace; encouragement of free disclosure of information to the grand jury; protection of witnesses from intimidation; and enhancement of free grand jury deliberations."). See also *Com. v. Dew*, 443 Mass 620, 627-628, 823 NE2d 771, 777-778 (2005) (judges have discretion to limit disclosure of grand jury minutes to defendants in order to protect persons mentioned, to avoid interfering with an investigation, and where the testimony is irrelevant).

[3] *Latino v. Crane Rental Co.*, 417 Mass 426, 429-430, 630 NE2d 591 (1994) (judge entitled to conduct inquiry of jury to determine whether they had agreed on special verdicts they announced); *Cassamasse v. J. G. Lamotte & Sons, Inc.*, 391 Mass 315, 318, 461 NE2d 785, 788 (1984). But see *Com. v. Brown*, 367 Mass 24, 27-29, 323 NE2d 902, 905 (1975) (proof other than testimony of jurors may be received to correct formal or clerical error in recording of verdict). See also *Carzis v. Hassey*, 6 Mass App 13, 15-16, 371 NE2d 1375, 1377 (1978) (verdicts regular on their face cannot be disturbed on basis of foreman's representations of jury's intentions).

[4] See § 4.2.5, supra.

[5] See *Com. v. Rodriguez*, 63 Mass App 660, 678, 828 NE2d 556, 568 (2005) (juror researched statute on Internet and raised it during deliberations). Trial judges are advised to reference Internet searches specifically when instructing jurors not to conduct their own research or investigations. *Id.*

> question whether extraneous prejudicial information was improperly brought to the jury's attention or whether any outside influence was improperly brought to bear upon any juror. Nor may his affidavit or evidence of any statement by him concerning a matter about which he would be precluded from testifying be received for these purposes.

Com. v. Fidler[6] set the original parameters for post-verdict inquiries into possible juror exposure to extraneous influence. When such a claim was brought to his or her attention, the judge was directed first to determine whether there was a serious question of possible prejudice. If the judge so determined, he or she was required to conduct a voir dire examination of the jurors, which may be conducted collectively, but if a juror indicated exposure to the extraneous material, individual voir dire was required to determine the extent of exposure and its possible prejudicial effect.[7]

---

[6] 377 Mass 192, 385 NE2d 513 (1979) (extensive discussion of authorities; judge properly refused to consider portions of juror affidavit concerning matters discussed during deliberations, but allegation that another juror referred to fact not in evidence indicated possibility of extraneous influence and entitled defendant to hearing).

[7] See *Com. v. Amran*, 471 Mass 354, 362-364, 29 NE3d 188, 196-197 (2015) (one juror exposed to redacted pages of defendant's statement). Compare *Com. v. Stewart*, 450 Mass 25, 39, 875 NE2d 846, 859 (2007) (judge acted properly in conducting voir dire to determine whether jurors had seen defendant in lockup), *Com. v. Kincaid*, 444 Mass 381, 828 NE2d 45 (2005) (trial judge properly determined that topic of alleged co-conspirator's flight was improperly introduced into deliberations from outside source and prejudiced defendant), *Com. v. Tennison*, 440 Mass 553, 555-560, 800 NE2d 285, 289-293 (2003) (judge handled alleged contamination involving co-defendant's contact with juror appropriately by conducting voir dire and removing juror), *Com. v. Guisti*, 434 Mass 245, 249-255, 747 NE2d 673, 678-681 (2001) (judge should have conducted post-verdict inquiry to determine whether juror posted email messages regarding case and received any responses that were communicated to other jurors), *aff'd after remand*, 449 Mass 1018, 867 NE2d 740 (2007), *Com. v. Francis*, 432 Mass 353, 369-371, 734 NE2d 315, 330-331 (2000) (court used proper procedures upon being advised of possible exposure to extraneous influences including presence of film crew and newspaper accounts of case), and *Com. v. Kamara*, 422 Mass 614, 664 NE2d 825 (1996) (court employed proper procedures upon being told by juror during deliberations that another juror had said she knew defendant was member of gang) with *Com. v. Richardson*, 469 Mass 248, 255, 13 NE3d 989, 986 (2014) (trial judge did not abuse discretion by denying defendant's motion for post-verdict voir dire where defendant failed to make colorable showing of possible juror connection to the prosecutor), *Com. v. Greineder*, 458 Mass 207, 246-248, 936 NE2d 372, 401-402 (2010) (jurors' experiment with banana and gloves to determine whether the latter was capable of making the pattern of dots found on defendant's glasses and jacket did not constitute extraneous influence), *Com. v. Pytou Heang*, 458 Mass 827, 857-859, 942 NE2d 927,951-953 (2011) (juror's letter asserting she and two others were pressured to convict by overbearing jurors did not constitute extraneous influence), *Com. v. Semedo*, 456 Mass 1, 21-24, 921 NE2d 57, 74-76 (2010) (post-trial voir dire of juror not warranted where juror sent letter alleging improprieties), *Com. v. Drumgold*, 423 Mass 230, 260-261, 668

A significant change to the Massachusetts Rules of Professional Conduct effective July 1, 2015 loosened these restrictions and allows attorneys to communicate with jurors after they are discharged unless prohibited by law or court order, or the juror has made known a desire not to communicate.[8] The lawyer must not of course engage in "misrepresentation, coercion, duress or harassment."

Most recently, *Com. v. Moore*[9] effectively removes court supervision from attorney-initiated post-verdict contact and communications with jurors, thus superseding *Fidler* (which the Court emphasized remains good law for the common-law principle barring inquiry into the contents of jury deliberations and thought processes, as opposed to extraneous influences). The restrictions of Massachusetts Rules of Professional Conduct 3.5 remain in force.

Evidence of a juror's racially or ethnically prejudiced comments during deliberations presents a "difficult case" of distinguishing extraneous factors from internal deliberative processes.[10] While juror bias is generally not an "extraneous matter" within the *Fidler* rule,[11] a juror affidavit asserting that three other jurors made racist verbal attacks on

---

NE2d 300, 320-321 (1996) (discussion among jurors about option of mistrial was not "extraneous influence"; court officer's remark did not qualify as extraneous influence so to warrant mistrial), *Com. v. Luna*, 418 Mass 749, 754, 641 NE2d 1050, 1053 (1994) (trial judge properly refused to allow post-verdict interviews of jurors based on claim that during deliberations juror indicated he was prejudiced against police officers, as that was not extraneous influence), *Com. v. Murphy*, 86 Mass App 118, 13 NE3d 1018 (2014) (extensive discussion) (no post-verdict inquiry required where danger of bias arising from juror's experience as customer of gas station subject to break-in was speculative), and *Com. v. Gerhartstreiter*, 82 Mass App 500, 512-513, 975 NE2d 890, 901-902 (2012) (judge properly allowed deliberations to resume after jurors confirmed they had not been exposed to media reports about the case).

For discussion of the problem of a juror conducting his own research and sharing it with others, see *Stagecoach Transport, Inc. v. Shuttle, Inc.*, 50 Mass App 812, 819-822, 741 NE2d 862, 868-870 (2001). For the steps that should be taken to address the problem of jurors' inappropriate use of social media such as Facebook and Twitter, see *Com. v. Werner*, 81 Mass App 689, 699-700, 967 NE2d 159, 167-169. (2012). For discussion of the issue of juror impartiality prior to empanelment, see § 1.9, supra.

[8] Rule 3.5, and Comment 3, Supreme Judicial Court Rule 3:07, 471 Mass 1429 (2015).

[9] 474 Mass 541, 52 NE3d 126 (June 16, 2016) (Although this case came down after the end date for this current edition, because of its importance it has been included.)

[10] See *Com. v. Tavares*, 385 Mass 140, 153-157, 430 NE2d 1198, 1208 (1982) (trial judge properly concluded that jury was impartial notwithstanding comments).

[11] See *Com. v. Grant*, 391 Mass 645, 651-653, 464 NE2d 33, 38 (1984) (daughter of juror in rape trial had been rape victim ten years earlier).

defendant throughout deliberations raised a question about defendant's fundamental right to a fair trial by an impartial jury and thus required a hearing to determine the truth of the assertions.[12]

Where the defendant files an affidavit from a juror alleging that racial or ethnic bias tainted the deliberations, the trial judge should conduct a hearing to determine the truth or falsity of the allegations.[13] If juror testimony is needed to ascertain whether racist statements were made, the judge may inquire of the jurors, but not into their subjective thought process, the content of their deliberations, or the effect the statement had. If it is determined such statements were made, the defendant bears the burden of proving the statements infected the deliberations with racial or ethnic bias, and then the Commonwealth must show beyond a reasonable doubt that the defendant was not prejudiced by the jury's exposure to the statements.[14]

Juror testimony more generally is admissible to establish the existence of an improper influence on the jury, but not to define the role it played in the jury's decisions.[15] "[A]ny inquiry into whether any juror was actually influenced would violate the principle expressed in *Com. v. Fidler* that inquiry into the subjective mental process of jurors is impermissible."[16] The judge reviewing the matter is to determine not the *actual* effect the extraneous material had on the jury's deliberations, but whether the it might have affected the verdict of a hypothetical average jury.[17]

---

[12] *Com. v. Laguer*, 410 Mass 89, 94-99, 571 NE2d 371, 375-377 (1991). Compare *Com. v. Delp*, 41 Mass App 435, 672 NE2d 114 (1996) (trial judge, viewing juror's post-verdict testimony concerning his bias against defendant because of his homosexuality, properly denied motion for new trial).

[13] *Com. v. McCowen*, 458 Mass 461, 494, 939 NE2d 735, 764 (2010) (extensive discussion).

[14] *Com. v. McCowen* 458 Mass at 496-497, 939 NE2d at 765-766.

[15] *Com. v. Fidler*, supra, 377 Mass at 196, 385 NE2d at 516.

[16] *Com. v. Smith*, 403 Mass 489, 497, 531 NE2d 556, 561 (1988). See also *Cassamasse v. J. G. Lamotte & Sons, Inc.*, 391 Mass 315, 317-318, 461 NE2d 785, 787 (1984).

[17] *Cassamasse v. J. G. Lamotte & Sons, Inc.*, supra, 391 Mass at 318, 461 NE2d at 787-788; *Com. v. Cuffie*, 414 Mass 632, 634-638, 609 NE2d 437, 438-440 (1993) (judge erred in inquiring into deliberative processes of jury to determine potential influence of juror who allegedly made unauthorized view of crime scene); *Fitzpatrick v. Allen*, 410 Mass 791, 796, 575 NE2d 750, 753 (1991); *Com. v. Fidler*, supra, 377 Mass at 201, 385 NE2d at 519; *Com. v. Kamara*, 37 Mass App 769, 643 NE2d 1056 (1994) (upon determining that highly prejudicial extraneous information concerning defendant's gang membership had entered jury room, judge erred in questioning individual jurors about its impact and refusing to order new trial based on their responses). Compare *Markee v. Biasetti*, 410 Mass 785, 789, 575 NE2d 1083, 1085 (1991) (because two jurors conducted outside investigations of the accident scene, jury could not be considered a "hypothetical average jury.").

A judge may, of course, inquire into a juror's ability to act impartially, and this is distinguishable from improper questions about a deliberating juror's thought processes.[18] Under any circumstances, a trial judge who decides to conduct questioning of jurors "must proceed with the utmost caution to avoid straying into revelation of the jury's thought process,"[19] recognizing that tensions among jurors are expected and are part and parcel of jury deliberations.[20] A judge cannot inquire into, or set aside, a recorded verdict because of a juror's *post hoc* statement that he disagreed with the verdict.[21]

Post-verdict interviews of jurors by counsel, litigants, or their agents must be conducted under the supervision and direction of the judge; the jurors may not be independently contacted. Counsel may, however, investigate unsolicited information to determine whether it should be brought to the judge's attention.[22] The judge must be provided with sufficiently clear, detailed, and reliable information to recognize the need for supervised post-verdict inquiry.[23] The trial judge has no duty to investigate the possibility of extraneous influences on the jury unless the court finds some showing to that effect, and the

---

[18] See *Com. v. Martinez*, 431 Mass 168, 179-180, 726 NE2d 913, 925 (2000). See also *Com. v. Guisti*, 434 Mass 245, 253-254, 747 NE2d 673, 680-681 (2001), *aff'd after remand*, 449 Mass 1018, 867 NE2d 740 (2007) (although juror bias is not extraneous matter, post-verdict inquiry may be appropriate to ensure fair trial).

[19] *Com. v. Bright*, 463 Mass 421, 442, 974 NE2d 1092, 1111 (2012).

[20] *Com. v. Carnes*, 457 Mass 812, 838, 933 NE2d 598, 618 (2010). See also *Com. v. Rodriguez*, 63 Mass App 660, 674, 828 NE2d 556, 565 (2005).

[21] *Com. v. Lassiter*, 80 Mass App 125, 130, 951 NE2d 961, 965 (2011). See also *Com. v. Alicea*, 464 Mass 837, 844-845, 985 NE2d 1197, 1204-1205 (2013) (transcript of jury poll showing one juror appeared to have responded "not guilty" was insufficient to show juror disagreed with verdict).

[22] *Com. v. Fidler*, supra, 377 Mass at 202-204, 385 NE2d at 520; *Com. v. Dixon*, 395 Mass 149, 153, 479 NE2d 159, 162-163 (1985). For discussion of the procedures for conducting post-verdict hearings where, although a defendant claims that the jury were exposed to an extraneous influence, there is also evidence that the defendant or someone acting on his behalf may have violated the *Fidler* principles, see *Com. v. Bresnahan*, 462 Mass 761, 971 NE2d 218 (2012).

[23] *Com. v. Lynch*, 439 Mass 532, 544-545, 789 NE2d 1052, 1061-1062 (2003) (defendant failed to make adequate showing that jurors were exposed to memorial buttons worn by victim's family); *Cassamasse v. J.G. Lamotte & Sons, Inc.*, supra, 391 Mass 318-319, 461 NE2d at 788 (affidavit of plaintiff's counsel containing hearsay conclusory statements from unidentified source insufficient); *Com. v. Taylor*, 32 Mass App 570, 579-580, 591 NE2d 1108, 1114-1115 (1992) (party requesting investigation must make colorable showing that extrinsic influence may have had impact on jury's impartiality).

party seeking post-verdict inquiry must show more than mere speculation.[24]

Once it is determined that the jury has been exposed to extraneous matter, the burden shifts to the non-moving party to show that there was no prejudice. The burden on the Commonwealth in a criminal case is to show beyond a reasonable doubt that no prejudice resulted to the defendant.[25] In a civil case, a lesser standard of "no reasonable likelihood of prejudice" is imposed.[26] Where, however, there was "active juror participation in an effort to resolve key issues by resort to material not in evidence," prejudice is presumed and a new trial must be granted.[27]

The disqualification of jurors and judicial officers to disclose deliberations should be distinguished from the disqualification of such persons from testifying in a proceeding in which they are acting.[28]

§ 5.8 Informers/Surveillance Location

Communications made to a district attorney or other prosecuting officer in order to secure the enforcement of law are privileged.[1] The identity of an informer is also privileged in both civil and criminal

---

[24] *Com. v. Rivera*, 464 Mass 56, 80-81, 981 NE2d 171, 191 (2013) (juror questions to prosecutor did not suggest extraneous influence). See also SJC Rule 3:07, Rules of Prof Conduct Rule 3.5(d), prohibiting the initiation of any communication with a juror and limiting the response to juror initiated communications. For the view that Rule 3.5(d) may violate a criminal defendant's constitutional rights, see Wilkins, *The New Massachusetts Rules of Professional Conduct: An Overview*, 82 Mass L Rev 261, 264 (1997).

[25] *Com. v. Bresnahan*, supra, 462 Mass at 774, 971 NE2d at 228; *Com. v. Kincaid*, 444 Mass 381, 386, 828 NE2d 45 (2005); *Com. v. Cuffie*, supra, 414 Mass at 637, 609 NE2d at 439.

[26] *Fitzpatrick v. Allen*, supra, 410 Mass at 794-795, 575 NE2d at 752.

[27] *Fitzpatrick v. Allen*, supra, 410 Mass at 796, 575 NE2d at 753 (jurors at medical malpractice trial consulted home reference medical book not in evidence); *Markee v. Biasetti*, supra, 410 Mass 789, 575 NE2d at 1085 (at least two jurors conducted unauthorized on-site investigation of accident scene).

[28] See Proposed Mass R Evid 605 ("The judge presiding at the trial may not testify in that trial as a witness.") and 606(a) ("A member of the jury may not testify as a witness before that jury in the trial of the case in which he is sitting as a juror.").

§ 5.8 [1] *District Attorney for Norfolk District v. Flatley*, 419 Mass 507, 509-510, 646 NE2d 127, 129-130 (1995). The common law privilege, while "absolute," is now subject to the public records statute, GL 66, § 10, discussed infra at § 5.10 Police have been considered members of the prosecution team for purposes of the privilege in private civil litigation. *Continental Assurance Co. v. Diorio-Volungis*, 51 Mass App 403, 411 n.15, 746 NE2d 550, 557 n.15 (2001).

cases.[2] The purpose is to encourage every citizen "to communicate to his government any information which he has of the commission of an offence against its laws."[3]

The informer privilege not only protects the release of the name of the informant, but also the disclosure of details that would in effect identify him.[4] The privilege does not apply where the informer's identity or the substance of the communication has already been disclosed.[5]

Where the disclosure of an informer's identity or of the contents of his communication is necessary to the defense of the criminal case, as where the informer was a participant in or witness to the crime, the privilege must give way.[6] Where, however, the informant did not participate in the crime and acted only as a tipster, the privilege will not be overridden.[7] For the stages of analysis of whether an informant's

---

[2] *Com. v. Bakoian*, 412 Mass 295, 306-307, 588 NE2d 667, 673-674 (1992); *Worthington v. Scribner*, 109 Mass 487 (1872) (defendants in malicious prosecution case could not be compelled to answer interrogatories concerning information given treasury officials regarding alleged illegal importation by plaintiff).

[3] *Worthington v. Scribner*, supra, 109 Mass at 488-489. See also *Hutchinson v. New England Tel. & Tel. Co.*, 350 Mass 188, 191, 214 NE2d 57, 59 (1966).

[4] See *Com. v. John*, 36 Mass App 702, 706, 635 NE2d 261, 264 (1994) (& citations).

[5] *Pihl v. Morris*, 319 Mass 577, 579-580, 66 NE2d 804, 806 (1946); *Com. v. McMiller*, 29 Mass App 392, 406, 560 NE2d 732, 739-740 (1990) (newspaper article disclosed informer's identity).

[6] See *Roviaro v. United States*, 353 US 53, 60-61(1957). See, e.g., *Com. v. Dias*, 451 Mass 463, 468-470, 886 NE2d 713, 718-719 (2008) (disclosure of informant's identity was required where informant participated in the controlled purchase of cocaine); *Com. v. Choice*, 47 Mass App 907, 711 NE2d 938 (1999) (court's refusal to allow defendant to cross-examine police witness regarding identity of "Hispanic gentleman" who allegedly directed undercover officer to defendant to purchase drugs was reversible error); *Com. v. Healis*, 31 Mass App 527, 529-532, 580 NE2d 1047, 1048-1050 (1991) (judge erred in denying defendant's motion for disclosure of informer where he was active participant in crime, the only non-government witness to events, and he had arranged meeting at which arrest occurred); *Com. v. Ennis*, 1 Mass App 499, 301 NE2d 589 (1973) (extensive discussion of issue; privilege inapplicable where informer had arranged sale of marijuana from defendant to police officer and was only other person present). See also *Com. v. Johnson*, 365 Mass 534, 544-545, 313 NE2d 571, 577-578 (1974) (discussion of informer privilege in context of trial court's refusal to elicit identity of other participants in crime from prosecution witness).

[7] See, e.g., *Com. v. Jordan*, 464 Mass 1004, 1005, 980 NE2d 454, 456 (2012) (disclosure of informant status of victim would have no bearing on defendant's self-defense defense); *Com. v. Maldonado*, 456 Mass 1012, 924 NE2d 258 (2010) (any potential testimony of tipster that another individual was seen in defendant's car hours before defendant was stopped was insufficient to justify piercing the privilege); *Com. v. Connolly*, 454 Mass 808, 913 NE2d 356 (2009), *habeas denied*, 2013 WL 139702 (D Mass 2013) (informant was not a participant in or percipient witness to the charged

identity should be disclosed or not, see *Com. v. Bonnett*, 472 Mass 827, 846-850, 37 NE3d 1064, 1081-1084 (2015). In some situations, knowledge of the informant's identity can offer substantial aid to the defense even if he cannot provide admissible testimony.[8]

Where defendant seeks disclosure of an informant to support an entrapment defense, the question is whether the defense has been appropriately raised by the introduction of some evidence of inducement.[9] Neither concern for the safety of the informant nor anticipation that he would assert his privilege against self-incrimination if called as a witness at trial can block disclosure of his identity where necessary to a fair defense.[10]

The privilege generally applies to prevent a criminal defendant from obtaining the identification of an informer where the issue is not guilt or innocence but rather the suppression of illegally obtained evidence.[11] Upon a sufficient preliminary showing to demonstrate that the affidavit in support of a warrant contained a deliberate or reckless misstatement of facts (under the principles discussed in *Franks v. Delaware*[12]), for example, the court may order disclosure of the informant. "The conflict between the government's interest in protection of the informant and a defendant's interest in proving that the affiant lied concerning either the existence of an informant or what the informant said may be resolved by the judge conducting a preliminary hearing at which the affiant testifies but without revealing the informant's identity. Further, if it appears necessary, the judge may hold an

---

crime and disclosure would not have been helpful to the defense); *Com. v. Signorine*, 404 Mass 400, 407-408, 535 NE2d 601, 606 (1989) (judge did not abuse discretion in limiting cross-examination of two prosecution witnesses regarding identity of confidential informant where evidence sought had no tendency to exculpate defendant); *Com. v. Figueroa*, 74 Mass App 784, 789-791, 911 NE2d 206, 211-213 (2009) (Commonwealth's case did not depend on any transactions with informant, and he was not a percipient witness to the incidents charged).

[8] *Com. v. Bonnett*, 472 Mass at 849, 37 NE3d at 1083.

[9] *Com. v. Elias*, 463 Mass 1015, 1016-1017, 978 NE2d 772, 775 (2012); *Com. v. Mello*, 453 Mass 760, 762, 905 NE2d 562, 565 (2009); *Com. v. Madigan*, 449 Mass 702, 871 NE2d 478 (2007) (defendant made sufficient showing to require disclosure of information concerning relationship between informant, police, and prosecutor). In exceptional circumstances, a defendant may make his showing of inducement by way of ex parte submissions to be reviewed in camera, but the Commonwealth must be permitted some opportunity to be heard in response. See *Com. v. Shaughessy*, 455 Mass 346, 916 NE2d 980 (2009).

[10] *Com. v. Dias*, 451 Mass 463, 470, 473, 886 NE2d 713, 719, 721 (2008).

[11] See *McCray v. Illinois*, 386 US 300 (1967); *Com. v. Snyder*, 413 Mass 521, 532-533, 597 NE2d 1363, 1369-1370 (1992).

[12] 438 US 154 (1978).

in-camera hearing in which he questions the affiant further, and, if he deems it appropriate, the informant himself."[13] Where the judge concludes that the defendant challenging the seizure of evidence should have the opportunity to question the informant, the Commonwealth presumably has the option of making disclosure or accepting dismissal of the charges.[14] The informant retains his Fifth Amendment right against self-incrimination if called as a witness.[15]

In the absence of a specific request by the defendant, the Commonwealth is not bound to disclose that it had used an informer or to disclose the identity of the informer.[16] Nor may the Commonwealth be required to inquire of a victim or witness whether he was an informant.[17] The Commonwealth has no affirmative duty to produce an informant not in custody; it's obligation is merely to provide defendant with last known address and to refrain from obstructing defendant's access to informant.[18]

In dual sovereignty situations, as where state and federal investigations interface, if the defendant is entitled to disclosure, the onus is on the Commonwealth to secure cooperation of the federal authorities.[19]

---

[13] *Com. v. Douzanis*, 384 Mass 434, 441, 425 NE2d 326, 331 (1981). See also *Com. v. Dias*, 451 Mass 463, 470-472, 886 NE2d 713, 719-721 (2008) (use of in camera hearings to determine whether disclosure is required); *Com. v. Amral*, 407 Mass 511, 554 NE2d 1189 (1990) (where defendant by affidavit asserts facts that cast reasonable doubt on veracity of material representations made by affiant concerning informer, judge must order in-camera hearing to interrogate affiant and, if necessary, informer, to determine whether *Franks* hearing is required). Compare *Com. v. Signorine*, 404 Mass 400, 405-407, 535 NE2d 601, 605-606 (1989) (defendant's affidavits failed to demonstrate that either affiant or informer made any misstatement of fact, and thus judge properly denied motion for disclosure of informer).

For discussion of the problem of police perjury regarding informants, see *Com. v. Lewin*, 405 Mass 566, 542 NE2d 275, 277 (1989); *Com. v. Nelson*, 26 Mass App 794, 536 NE2d 1094 (1989).

[14] *Com. v. Douzanis*, supra, 384 Mass at 442 n.13, 425 NE2d at 332 n.13.

[15] See *Com. v. Zuluaga*, 43 Mass App 629, 641 n.14, 686 NE2d 463, 472 n.14 (1997).

[16] *Com. v. Monteiro*, 396 Mass 123, 129, 484 NE2d 999, 1004 (1985); *Com. v. Ramos*, 30 Mass App 915, 917, 566 NE2d 1141, 1143 (1991).

[17] *Com. v. Jordan*, 464 Mass 1004, 1005, 980 NE2d 454, 456 (2012).

[18] See *Com. v. Gratereaux*, 49 Mass App 1, 725 NE2d 573 (2000). See also *Com. v. Manrique*, 31 Mass App 597, 599-602, 581 NE2d 1036, 1038-1039 (1991) (rejecting claim that defendant was denied access to informer); *Com. v. Curcio*, 26 Mass App 738, 746-749, 532 NE2d 699, 704-705 (1989).

[19] *Com. v. Bonnett*, 472 Mass 827, 845-846, 37 NE3d 1064, 1080 (2015).

Disclosure of an informant may be required in a prison disciplinary hearing[20] or probation revocation proceeding[21] where relevant to the defense.

Where the informant privilege is overcome and disclosure ordered, a protective order should ordinarily be entered ensuring that the identity of the informant not be used for any purpose beyond the reason for the disclosure.[22]

Proposed Mass R Evid 509 generally reflects present practice regarding the informer privilege.[23]

---

[20] See *Nelson v. Commissioner of Correction*, 390 Mass 379, 394 n.19, 456 NE2d 1100, 1109 n.19 (1983).

[21] *Com. v. Kelsey*, 464 Mass 315, 982 NE2d 1134 (2013) (informant was both a percipient witness to and active participant in alleged transaction).

[22] *Com. v. Shaughessy*, 455 Mass 346, 358, 916 NE2d 980, 989-990 (2009).

[23] Proposed Mass R Evid 509 provides:

Identity of Informer

(a) Rule of privilege. The United States or a state or subdivision thereof has a privilege to refuse to disclose the identity of a person who has furnished information relating to or assisting in an investigation of a possible violation of a law to a law enforcement officer or member of a legislative committee or its staff conducting an investigation.

(b) Who may claim. The privilege may be claimed by an appropriate representative of the public entity to which the information was furnished.

(c) Exceptions.

(1) Voluntary disclosure; informer a witness. No privilege exists under this rule if the identity of the informer or his interest in the subject matter of his communication has been disclosed by a holder of the privilege or by the informer's own action to those who would have cause to resent the communication, or if the informer appears as a witness for the government.

(2) Testimony on merits. If it appears from the evidence in the case or from other showing by a party that an informer may be able to give testimony necessary to a fair determination of the issue of guilt or innocence in a criminal case or of a material issue on the merits in a civil case to which the public entity is a party, and the informed public entity invokes the privilege, the judge shall give the public entity an opportunity to show in camera facts relevant to determining whether the informer can, in fact, supply that testimony. The showing will ordinarily be in the form of affidavits, but the judge may direct that testimony be taken if he finds that the matter cannot be resolved satisfactorily upon affidavit. If the judge finds that there is a reasonable probability that the informer can give the testimony, and the public entity elects not to disclose his identity, the judge on motion of the defendant in a criminal case shall dismiss the charges to which the testimony would relate, and the judge may do so on his own motion. In civil cases, he may make any order that justice requires. Evidence submitted to the judge shall be sealed and preserved to be made available to the appellate court in the event of an appeal, and the contents shall not otherwise be revealed without consent of the public entity. All counsel and parties shall be permitted to be present at every stage of proceedings under this subdivision except a showing *in camera*, at which no counsel or party shall be permitted to be present.

(3) Legality of obtaining evidence. If information from an informer is relied upon to establish the legality of the means by which evidence was obtained and the judge is not satisfied that the information was received from an informer reasonably believed to be reliable or credible, he may require the identity of the informer disclosed. The judge shall, on request of the public entity, direct that the disclosure be made *in camera*. All counsel and parties concerned with the issue of legality shall be permitted to be present at every stage of the proceedings under this subdivision except a disclosure *in camera*, at which no counsel or

A "surveillance location privilege" has been recognized which permits the prosecution in appropriate cases to withhold the exact location from which observations of criminal activity were made.[24] The privilege must give way when disclosure would provide "material evidence needed by the defendant for a fair presentation of his case to the jury."[25] A defendant seeking to overcome the surveillance location privilege must make an affirmative showing that disclosure of the information would provide evidence needed to defend the case; it is not enough simply to assert such a need.[26]

The Commonwealth's interest in preserving the confidentiality of a surveillance point cannot justify exclusion of the defendants from a portion of their trial during which a police officer testified concerning the location from which he observed the unlawful sales of drugs.[27]

§ 5.9 Journalists

Massachusetts does not recognize a privilege of a news reporter to refuse to disclose the identity of, or communications with, a confidential news source. No such privilege exists at common law or under either the federal or state constitutions.[1] The Supreme Judicial Court

---

party shall be permitted to be present. If disclosure of the identity of the informer is made *in camera*, the record thereof shall be sealed and preserved to be made available to the appellate court in the event of an appeal, and the contents shall not otherwise be revealed without consent of the public entity.

[24] See *Com. v. Lugo*, 406 Mass 565, 570-574, 548 NE2d 1263, 1265-1267 (1990).

[25] *Id.*, 406 Mass at 574 (disclosure required where prosecution's entire case rested on the officer's credibility and ability to observe from hidden location, his testimony was not corroborated in any respect, and inconsistencies existed as to location and whether it provided clear view). See also *Com. v. Hernandez*, 421 Mass 272, 275, 656 NE2d 1237, 1239 (1995) (disclosure of surveillance location required where testimony of observing officers was crucial to Commonwealth's case).

[26] See *Com. v. Grace*, 43 Mass App 905, 906, 681 NE2d 1265, 1267 (1997).

[27] *Com. v. Rios*, 412 Mass 208, 588 NE2d 6 (1992).

§ 5.9 [1] See *Branzburg v. Hayes*, 408 US 665 (1972); *In re John Doe Grand Jury Investigation*, 410 Mass 596, 598, 1991) (& citations); *Com. v. Corsetti*, 387 Mass 1, 438 NE2d 805 (1982) (newsman has no constitutional right to refuse to testify at criminal proceeding concerning information acquired in confidence); *In re Roche*, 381 Mass 624, 411 NE2d 466 (1980) (newsman not privileged by First Amendment to refuse to divulge at deposition in civil matter his confidential sources used in preparing investigative report); *In re Pappas*, 358 Mass 604, 266 NE2d 297 (1971) (no newsman's privilege under First Amendment to refuse to appear and testify before court or grand jury).

has declined to establish an evidentiary privilege by rule,[2] and the Legislature has failed on several occasions to enact a statutory press shield law.[3] Accordingly, a reporter must appear and testify when summonsed.

The Supreme Judicial Court has indicated, however, that "some protection" is provided by the First Amendment to the United States Constitution for any person who gathers information and prepares it for expression.[4] Three justices noted their "willingness to consider, in future cases, whether the central role a free discussion of public issues plays in a self-governing society requires, as a matter of Massachusetts practice, that persons addressing such issues be afforded more clearly defined protection against intrusive discovery than that provided by the discretionary supervision contemplated by Mass R Civ P 26(c)."[5]

While the Supreme Judicial Court has not adopted a shield against all sanctions for failure to provide confidential information, it has nonetheless recognized that "the availability of alternative remedies to compelled disclosure should be considered. Likewise, a judge is obliged to consider the effect of compelled disclosure on values underlying the First Amendment and art. 16. Thus, a judge has the authority to prevent 'harassing' or the needless disclosure of confidential relationships."[6] Moreover, the First Amendment protects reporters against grand jury investigations initiated or conducted in bad faith.[7]

In ruling on a motion to quash a subpoena issued to a news reporter to discover the identity of a confidential news source, a judge must balance the public interest in having every person's evidence against the public interest in the free flow of information.[8] The threshold inquiry is whether the unwilling witness has made "some showing that the asserted damage to the free flow of information is more than speculative or theoretical."[9] Such a showing is made where the witness demonstrates that he would not have received the information without

---

[2] See *Petition for the Promulgation of Rules Regarding the Protection of Confidential News Sources and Other Unpublished Information*, 395 Mass 164, 479 NE2d 154 (1985).

[3] See *In re Roche*, supra, 381 Mass at 635 n.13, 411 NE2d at 474 n.13; *Petition for the Promulgation of Rules*, supra, 395 Mass at 164, 479 NE2d at 157.

[4] *In re Roche*, supra, 381 Mass at 632, 411 NE2d at 472.

[5] *Id.*, 381 Mass at 638-639, 411 NE2d at 476.

[6] *Petition for the Promulgation of Rules*, supra, 395 Mass at 171-172, 479 NE2d at 158s.

[7] *Branzburg v. Hayes*, supra, 408 US at 707.

[8] *In re John Doe Grand Jury Investigation*, supra, 410 Mass at 599, 574 NE2d at 375 (judge properly allowed motions to quash grand jury subpoenas).

[9] *Id.*

the promise of anonymity to the source and that his future newsgathering ability would be impaired if he violated the promise.[10] In assessing the public interest in obtaining the evidence, the judge should consider the particular circumstances of the grand jury inquiry and the importance of the evidence sought. On several occasions the Supreme Judicial Court has affirmed the Superior Court's refusal to compel investigative news reporters to disclose confidential sources.[11]

§ 5.10 Public Records and Reports/"Governmental Privilege"

Public records (as defined by GL 4, § 7(26), as amended June 3, 2016, effective January 1, 2017) are subject to inspection and copying and thus are not privileged from disclosure.[1] "The primary purpose of [the statute] is to give the public broad access to government documents."[2] Massachusetts also has long recognized a common-law right of access to judicial records. Thus most records, including transcripts, evidence, memoranda, court orders, and even material relating to the issuance

---

[10] *Id.*, 410 Mass at 600, 574 NE2d at 376.

[11] See *Com. v. Bui*, 419 Mass 392, 402, 645 NE2d 689, 695 (1995); *In re John Doe Grand Jury Investigation*, supra, 410 Mass at 596-597, 574 NE2d at 373; *Sinnott v. Boston Retirement Board*, 402 Mass 581, 524 NE2d 100 (1988); *Ayash v. DanaFarber Cancer Institute*, 46 Mass App 384, 706 NE2d 316 (1999) (finding that reporter had made threshold showing against disclosure of sources, and remanding for performance of balancing test), *order on remand aff'd*, 443 Mass 367, 399-404, 822 NE2d 667, 695-696 (2005). See also *Wojcik v. Boston Herald, Inc.*, 60 Mass App 510, 803 NE2d 1261 (2004) (vacating Superior Court order compelling disclosure of reporters' sources because relevance of identities to libel case was not apparent).

§ 5.10 [1] See GL 66, § 10. The Public Records Act applies to state governmental entities and those of its political subdivisions; it does not include the legislature or the judiciary. Thus the Board of Bar Overseers and Bar Counsel, located in the judicial branch, are not subject to Public Records law. *Kettenbach v. Board of Overseers*, 448 Mass 1019, 863 NE2d 36 (2007). GL c. 41, § 97D requires police departments to maintain the confidentiality of reports regarding rape or sexual assault. *Com. v. George W. Prescott Publishing Co., LLC*, 463 Mass 258, 264, 973 NE2d 667, 673 (2012).

[2] *Harvard Crimson, Inc. v. President & Fellows of Harvard College*, 445 Mass 745, 749, 840 NE2d 518, 522 (2006) (public records law is applicable to documents held by public entities, not private ones). See generally *Suffolk Construction Co., Inc. v. Division of Capital Asset Management.*, 449 Mass 444, 870 NE2d 33 (2007) (extensive discussion of statute); *Lambert v. Executive Director of Judicial Nominating Council*, 425 Mass 406, 681 NE2d 285 (1997) (questionnaire completed by applicants for judicial appointment not public record); *Globe Newspaper Co. v. Police Commissioner of Boston*, 419 Mass 852, 648 NE2d 419 (1995); *District Attorney for Norfolk District v. Flatley*, 419 Mass 507, 646 NE2d 127 (1995). See also *Globe Newspaper Co. v. Commissioner of Education*, 439 Mass 124, 786 NE2d 328 (2003) (release of records within ten-day period is presumptively reasonable).

of search warrants, are presumptively public documents. The presumption may be overcome only on a showing of "good cause."[3] The Supreme Judicial Court has directed that a list of the names of jurors empanelled in any criminal case be included in the court file of the case, no later than the completion of the trial.[4]

GL 4, § 7(26) has, however, the following exemptions from disclosure:[5]

- Records "related solely to internal personnel rules and practices of the government unit, provided however, that such records shall be withheld only to the extent that proper performance of necessary governmental functions requires such withholding." § 7(26)(b)
- "Personnel and medical files or information; also any other materials or data relating to a specifically named individual, the disclosure of which may constitute an unwarranted invasion of personal privacy." § 7(26)(c)[6]

---

[3] The right of public access to judicial records is governed by overlapping constitutional, statutory, and common-law rules. See generally *Com. v. George W. Prescott Publishing Co., LLC*, 463 Mass 258, 263, 973 NE2d 667, 673 (2012) (once a search warrant and affidavit are returned to the court, they become public documents pursuant to GL c. 276, § 2B); *New England Internet Cafe, LLC v. Clerk of Superior Court*, 462 Mass 76, 966 NE2d 797 (2012). Inquest reports and transcripts of inquest proceedings become presumptively public documents after the grand jury returns an indictment or a no bill, or the district attorney certifies he will not present the case to a grand jury. See *In re Globe Newspaper Co., Inc.*, 461 Mass 113, 958 NE2d 822 (2011) (abrogating *Kennedy v. Justice of the District Court of Dukes County*, 356 Mass 367); GL 38, § 10. An unofficial "room recording" made by a court reporter is not a "judicial record" subject to public access. See *Com. v. Winfield*, 464 Mass 672, 985 NE2d 86 (2013).

[4] *Com. v. Fujita*, 470 Mass 484, 489, 23 NE3d 882, 887 (2015). Such a list is presumptively open to public access, and may be impounded only on good cause. Compare *Com. v. Silva*, 448 Mass 701, 864 NE2d 1 (2007) (concern for jurors' safety constituted good cause for order impounding names and addresses of jurors in murder trial involving gang violence).

[5] The custodian of the record has the burden to prove with specificity that an exemption applies. See *In re Subpoena Duces Tecum*, 445 Mass 685, 688, 840 NE2d 470, 473 (2006).

[6] Application of the privacy exemption requires a balancing between the claimed invasion of privacy and the interest of the public in disclosure. See *In re Subpoena Duces Tecum*, supra, 445 Mass at 688, 840 NE2d at 474 (exemption does not apply to videotaped interviews of school children pursuant to concluded criminal investigation of abuse complaints). Compare *Cape Cod Times v. Sheriff of Barnstable County*, 443 Mass 587, 823 NE2d 375 (2005) (records in sheriff's possession regarding reserve deputies were public records and disclosure of names and addresses of deputies would not constitute unwarranted invasion of privacy), *Worcester Telegram & Gazette Corp. v. Chief of Police of Worcester*, 436 Mass 378, 386, 764 NE2d 847, 854 (2002) and 58 Mass App 1, 787 NE2d 602 (2003) (records of internal affairs investigation of officer were not insulated from disclosure merely because designated part of "personnel file"; extensive

- "Inter-agency or intra-agency memoranda or letters relating to policy positions being developed by the agency; but this subclause shall not apply to reasonably completed factual studies or reports on which the development of such policy positions has been or may be based." § 7(26)(d)[7]

---

discussion of various mechanisms for determination of whether public records are exempt from disclosure), *Globe Newspaper Co. v. Police Comm'r of Boston*, supra, 419 Mass at 857-868, 648 NE2d at 425-430 (transcripts and audio tapes of citizen witness statements and police officer statements compiled by police internal affairs division not protected by privacy exemption), *Brogan v. School Committee of Westport*, 401 Mass 306, 516 NE2d 159 (1987) (individual absentee records of school employees not records of "personal nature" and not exempt from disclosure), *Pottle v. School Committee of Braintree*, 395 Mass 861, 482 NE2d 813 (1985) (names and addresses of employees of municipal school department not within privacy exemption), *Reinstein v. Police Comm'r of Boston*, 378 Mass 281, 292-293, 391 NE2d 881, 885-887 (1979) (privacy exemption not blanket exemption for all records of police department relating to discharge of firearms by officers), and *Antell v. Attorney General*, 52 Mass App 244, 752 NE2d 823 (2001) (records pertaining to 1991 inquiry into conduct of police chief, which did not result in criminal charges, not within privacy exemption) with *LeBlanc v. Com.*, 457 Mass 94, 96-97, 929 NE2d 1017, 1019 (2010) (autopsy reports are not public records), *Wakefield Teachers Association v. School Committee*, 431 Mass 792, 731 NE2d 63 (2000) (disciplinary decision and report by school superintendent concerning teacher's inappropriate notes to female students, resulting in teacher's four-week suspension, within privacy exemption), *Globe Newspaper Co. v. Chief Medical Examiner*, 404 Mass 132, 533 NE2d 1356 (1989) (reports of autopsies conducted by medical examiner exempt from disclosure), *Globe Newspaper Co. v. Boston Retirement Board*, 388 Mass 427, 446 NE2d 1051 (1983) (medical and personnel files pertaining to disability pensions exempt where they are of personal nature and relate to particular individual), *Viriyahiranpaiboon v. Department of State Police*, 52 Mass App 843, 756 NE2d 635 (2001) (inmate not entitled to copies of laboratory reports of blood tests relating to murder conviction, as reports were medical data about person's body and tests could reveal genetic markers), *Connolly v. Bromery*, 15 Mass App 661, 447 NE2d 1265 (1983) (written evaluations of faculty and courses by students at public university constitute "personnel files or information" and thus exempt from disclosure). See also *Com. v. Beauchemin*, 410 Mass 181, 185, 571 NE2d 395, 398 (1991) (judge erred in excluding complainant's school records during cross-examination because although exempt from public disclosure under § 7(26)(c), they were lawfully subpoenaed); *Georgiou v. Commissioner of Dep't of Industrial Accidents*, 67 Mass App 428, 854 NE2d 130 (2006) (privacy interest was implicated in determination of whether names and addresses of injured employees were within exemption).

Deletion of particular identifying details does not necessarily remove the documents from the exemption where "indirect identification" is still possible. See *Logan v. Commissioner of Dep't of Indus. Accidents*, 68 Mass App 533, 863 NE2d 559 (2007) (IME reports were exempt from disclosure under "medical files" exemption even with proposed redactions of the names of claimants).

[7] See generally *DaRosa v. City of Bedford*, 471 Mass 446, 30 NE3d 790 (2015).

- "Notebooks and other materials prepared by an employee of the Commonwealth which are personal to him and not maintained as part of the files of the governmental unit." § 7(26)(e)
- "Investigatory materials necessarily compiled out of the public view by law enforcement or other investigatory officials the disclosure of which materials would probably so prejudice the possibility of effective law enforcement that such disclosure would not be in the public interest." § 7(26)(f)[8]
- "Trade secrets or commercial or financial information voluntarily provided to an agency for use in developing governmental policy and upon a promise of confidentiality; but this subclause shall not apply to information submitted as required by law or as a condition of receiving a governmental contract or other benefit." § 7(26)(g)

---

[8] It has been emphasized that "[t]here is no 'blanket exemption' to public disclosure for records kept by police departments or for investigatory materials." *Worcester Telegram & Gazette Corp. v. Chief of Police of Worcester*, supra, 436 Mass at 383, 764 NE2d at 852 (records of internal affairs investigation of officer were subject to limited disclosure). Compare *In re Subpoena Duces Tecum*, supra, 445 Mass at 690, 840 NE2d at 475 (exemption does not apply to videotaped interviews of school children pursuant to concluded criminal investigation of abuse complaints), *Globe Newspaper Co. v. Police Comm'r of Boston*, supra, 419 Mass at 857-868, 648 NE2d at 425-430 (transcripts and audio tapes of citizen witness' and police officer statements compiled by police internal affairs division not protected by investigatory exemption; certain homicide hotline records within exemption), *District Attorney for Norfolk District v. Flatley*, supra, 419 Mass at 512, 646 NE2d at 130 (record did not show whether trial judge found whether district attorney met his burden of proof that documents were exempt from public disclosure as "law enforcement investigative materials."), *WBZ-TV4 v. District Attorney for the Suffolk District*, 408 Mass 595, 603, 562 NE2d 817, 822 (1990) (exemption does not operate to exclude from disclosure all information contained in law enforcement files, but requires case by case consideration of whether access would prejudice law enforcement), and *Com. v. Rafuse*, 61 Mass App 595, 813 NE2d 558 (2004) (exemption did not apply to witnesses' statements given in 10-year-old murder investigation sought by victim's mother in connection with wrongful death suit) with *Bougas v. Chief of Police of Lexington*, 371 Mass 59, 354 NE2d 872 (1976) (police reports and letters to police from private citizens regarding incident resulting in misdemeanor charges exempt from disclosure) and *Continental Assur. Co. v. Diorio-Volungis*, 51 Mass App 403, 411-413, 746 NE2d 550, 557-558 (2001) (exemption applied to materials sought by litigant seeking to establish that beneficiary was accessory to murder of insured).

The exception applies to investigatory materials, and not to court records. See *Republican Co. v. Appeals Court*, 442 Mass 218, 223 n.9, 812 NE2d 887, 893 n.9 (2004) (extensive discussion of process for impoundment of court records and subsequent review of impoundment order). Regarding the impoundment of court records, see generally *Boston Herald, Inc. v. Sharpe*, 432 Mass 593, 737 NE2d 859 (2000).

- Proposals and bids to enter into any contract or agreement until the time for the opening of bids. § 7(26)(h)
- Appraisals of real property until a final agreement is entered into, or litigation arising therefrom is terminated. § 7(26)(i)[9]
- Names and addresses of persons applying for firearm permits or firearm identification cards. § 7(26)(j)
- Materials related to tests and examinations. § 7(26)(l)
- Certain contracts for hospital or related health care services. § 7(26)(m)
- Records that are "specifically or by necessary implication exempted from disclosure by statute." § 7(26)(a)[10]

---

[9] See *Coleman v. Boston Redevelopment Authority*, 61 Mass App 239, 809 NE2d 538 (2004) (exemption is parcel-specific).

[10] A sampling of such exempting statutes follows:

Family Education Rights and Privacy Law (FERPA), 20 USC § 1232g. See *Champa v. Weston Public Schools*, 473 Mass 86, 39 NE3d 435 (2015) (settlement agreements between school and parents of special needs student were not a "public record" and thus not subject to disclosure).

GL 66A (Fair Information Practices Act) restricts access to "personal data" maintained by a state agency and not contained in a public record. See, e.g., *Allen v. Holyoke Hospital*, 398 Mass 372, 378-382, 496 NE2d 1368, 1372-1374 (1986) (DSS records containing social worker's personal observations of family of deceased child); *Torres v. Attorney General*, 391 Mass 1, 460 NE2d 1032 (1984) (information derived from DSS client's case file relating to his whereabouts on particular dates).

GL 46, § 2A restricts access to "records and returns of children born out of wedlock or abnormal sex births, or fetal deaths."

GL 71B, § 3, limits access to special education records to parents, guardians, or persons with custody of the child. But see *Com. v. Figueroa*, 413 Mass 193, 203, 595 NE2d 779, 785-786 (1992) and *Com. v. Gauthier*, 32 Mass App 130, 134-135, 586 NE2d 34, 37 (1992) (where information is relevant to witness's credibility, statutory privilege must yield to defendant's constitutional right to defend himself). For a discussion of the privacy protections for school records under the federal Individuals with Disabilities Education Act, see *Com. v. Nathaniel N*, 54 Mass App 200, 764 NE2d 883 (2002).

GL 71, § 34D, protects the confidentiality of student records. See generally *Com. v. Buccella*, 434 Mass 473, 751 NE2d 373 (2001) (student's homework assignments and tests did not come within definition of protected records). GL 4, § 7 (26)(c) also exempts certain school records from public disclosure. See *Com. v. Beauchemin*, 410 Mass 181, 185, 571 NE2d 395, 398 (1991).

GL 66, § 10 exempts from disclosure the home address and home telephone number of law enforcement, judicial, prosecutorial, department of youth services, correctional, and any other public safety and criminal justice personnel; the names of family members of such personnel; and the home address, telephone number, and place of employment or education of crime victims or persons involved in family planning services.

Several statutes limit access to criminal, probation, and juvenile records. See GL 6, §§ 167-178 (Criminal Offender Record Information System ["CORI"]); GL 94C, § 34 (providing for sealing of certain drug offense records); GL 119, § 60 (restricting admissibility of juvenile records and proceedings); GL 276, §§ 100, 100A-C (restricting access to probation records; providing for sealing, expungement, and inadmissibility of certain criminal records). GL 119, § 60, does not preclude use of a juvenile record in subsequent sentencing proceedings. *Department of Youth Services v. A Juvenile*, 384 Mass 784, 786-787, 429 NE2d 709, 711 (1981); *Com. v Rodriguez.*, 376 Mass 632, 634-641, 382 NE2d 725, 729-731 (1978) (juvenile records admissible in action, in lieu of sentence, for commitment as sexually dangerous person). The district attorney is permitted access to a juvenile's records for the purpose of making a determination whether to proceed with a petition for commitment as a sexually dangerous person, and the records may be admitted at trial on the petition. See *In re Kenney*, 66 Mass App 709, 714-715, 850 NE2d 590, 596 (2006). For a discussion of the constitutional limits on GL 119, § 60, when the information is relevant to a prosecution witness's bias, see § 6.15, infra. See also GL 119, § 60A, which opens to public inspection the records of certain youthful offender proceedings, and GL 6, § 178K et seq., the Sexual Offender Registration Act, which sets forth procedures for the dissemination of otherwise confidential information. In *Doe v. Attorney General*, 425 Mass 210, 680 NE2d 92 (1997), the Supreme Judicial Court held that the disclosure provisions of the Sexual Offender Registration Act prevailed over the confidentiality provisions of GL 119.

For discussion of the statutory framework pertaining to the maintenance of criminal history records, including the reforms adopted in 2010, and the statutes authorizing sealing and expungement, see *Com. v. Pon*, 469 Mass 296, 14 NE3d 182 (2014). See also *Com. v. Moe*, 463 Mass 370, 974 NE2d 619 (2012); *Com. v. Boe*, 456 Mass 337, 924 NE2d 239 (2010); *Com. v. Gavin G.*, 437 Mass 470, 772 NE2d 1067 (2002); *Com. v. Doe*, 420 Mass 142, 648 NE2d 1255 (1995); *Com. v. Balboni*, 419 Mass 42, 642 NE2d 576 (1994); *Com. v. S.M.F.*, 40 Mass App 42, 660 NE2d 701 (1996) (where sealing statutes are not applicable, trial courts retain inherent power to expunge criminal records). For discussion of the regulation authorizing dissemination of CORI information, see *Bellin v. Kelley*, 435 Mass 261, 755 NE2d 1274 (2001); *Reinstein v. Police Commissioner of Boston*, 378 Mass 281, 293-296, 391 NE2d 881, 888 (1979) (relationship between CORI and GL 66, § 10); *New Bedford Standard-Times Publishing Co. v. Clerk of Third District Court*, 377 Mass 404, 387 NE2d 110 (1979) (CORI's applicability to court records); *Globe Newspaper Co. v. District Attorney for Middle District*, 439 Mass 374, 788 NE2d 513 (2003) (CORI did not prevent disclosure of docket numbers in criminal cases involving municipal corruption); *Kordis v. Superintendent, Souza Baranowski Correctional Center*, 58 Mass App 902, 787 NE2d 613 (2003) (CORI's applicability to a prisoner's prison account transactions). For the right of an individual to inspect and copy his or her own criminal record information, see GL 6, § 175.

While expungement removes all traces of the matter, sealing does not operate to erase the fact of the prior conviction, and such conviction may thus be considered by the police when issuing or revoking firearms licenses. See *Rzeznik v. Chief of Police of Southampton*, 374 Mass 475, 480, 373 NE2d 1128, 1132 (1978). See also *Dickerson v. New Banner Inst., Inc.*, 460 US 103, 103 S Ct 986, 74 L Ed 2d 845 (1983) (provisions of federal gun control law that make it unlawful for person convicted of felony to ship firearm apply even though record is expunged under state law); *Com. v. Doe*, 420 Mass 142, 151 n.9, 648 NE2d 1255, 1260 n.9 (1995) (records sealed pursuant to Section 100C remain accessible to law enforcement personnel and courts).

- Records relating to the internal layout, security, safety, or vulnerability of buildings or persons, the disclosure of which in the reasonable judgment of the custodian is likely to jeopardize public safety. § 7(26)(n).

Materials privileged as work product (see § 5.4.10, supra) are not protected from disclosure under the public records statute unless the materials fall within an express statutory exemption.[11] When the materials are sought in discovery during litigation from a government entity, they may be protected by the "policy deliberation" exemption discussed above.[12]

A district court has no authority to direct expungement of a record from the statewide domestic abuse violence record keeping system maintained pursuant to GL 209, § 7. See *Vaccaro v. Vaccaro*, 425 Mass 153, 680 NE2d 55 (1997); *Smith v. Jones*, 67 Mass App 129, 137-138, 852 NE2d 670, 678-679 (2006) (judge has authority to expunge record from domestic violence registry only in the rare instance the order is determined to have been obtained through a fraud on the court). Sealed records may be admissible to establish bias of the witness. See § 6.15, infra.

The Supreme Judicial Court has recently eased the showing required to seal records of criminal proceedings resulting in a dismissal or nolle prosequi. Abrogating *Com. v. Doe*, 420 Mass 142, 648 NE2d 1255 (1995), a defendant seeking sealing under GL 276, § 100C, second par. (as amended in 2010) need only show that good cause exists. *Com. v. Pon*, 469 Mass 296, 312, 14 NE3d 182, 197 (2014). GL 276, § 100C is the exclusive remedy in all cases governed by it, but expungement may be appropriate in an exceptional case where the person charged was not only factually innocent, but was never the intended target of law enforcement. See *Com. v. Alves*, 86 Mass App 210, 215, 15 NE3d 247, 250 (2014). Compare *Com. v. Moe*, 463 Mass 370, 974 NE2d 619 (2012) (ordinary factual mistakes about the identity of the perpetrator do not justify expungement).

A criminal defendant is not entitled under the mandatory discovery provisions to the sealed criminal records of a prospective prosecution witness. *Wing v. Commissioner of Probation*, 473 Mass 368, 43 NE3d 286 (2015) (defendant's constitutional right to confrontation is not implicated where the prior conviction is sought only for purposes of impeachment).

The provisions of § 100C which automatically seal records of cases ending with acquittal or finding of no probable cause have been declared unconstitutional. See *Globe Newspaper Co. v. Pokaski*, 868 F2d 497 (1st Cir 1989) (extensive discussion of sealing statutes). A defendant who wishes to permanently seal the court records following his acquittal must file a motion at the conclusion of the trial, and in most cases will likely be unable to make out a prima facie case for sealing. See *Soe v. Sex Offender Registry Board*, 466 Mass 381, 397 n.12, 995 NE2d 73, 86 n.12 (2013).

[11] See *General Electric Co. v. Department of Environmental Protection*, 429 Mass 798, 711 NE2d 589 (1999). See also *Com. v. Fremont Inv. & Loan*, 459 Mass 209, 216 n.11, 944 NE2d 1019, 1024 n.11 (2011).

[12] *DaRosa v. City of Bedford*, 471 Mass 446, 30 NE3d 790 (2015) (extensive discussion).

The provisions of the public records statute do not override the attorney-client privilege between public officials and their counsel.[13] Nor does the public records statute override a court's inherent power to keep information confidential under a protective order.[14] A criminal defendant's right of access to relevant records is not constrained by the exemptions to the public records law.[15]

Reports required to be filed with governmental agencies pursuant to certain statutes are privileged. For example, an employer's report of an accident to the Division of Industrial Accidents required by GL 152, § 19, has been held privileged and inadmissible in a tort action arising out of the accident, and on grounds that indicate that many reports required by executive departments or administrative bodies may be similarly privileged.[16] Agreements for the payment of compensation filed under GL 152, § 6, are not admissible in evidence.[17] A statement by a workers' compensation claimant (either in writing or taken on a recording instrument) and given to the insurer is inadmissible unless a copy of the statement has been furnished to the claimant or his attorney upon request.[18] Medical records from an employer's or insurer's hospital or clinic are similarly inadmissible against the claimant unless provided upon request.[19] Information secured by the Department of Employment and Training is inadmissible except in limited circumstances.[20]

The following are open for inspection and not protected from disclosure:

- A corporation's certificate of condition and annual report, filed with the secretary of state of the Commonwealth.[21]

---

[13] *Suffolk Constr. Co., Inc. v. Division of Capital Asset Mgmt.*, 449 Mass 444, 870 NE2d 33 (2007).

[14] *Com. v. Fremont Inv. & Loan*, 459 Mass 209, 213, 944 NE2d 1019, 1023 (2011).

[15] See *Com. v. Wanis*, 426 Mass 639, 642, 690 NE2d 407, 411 (1998) and *Com. v. Rodriguez*, 426 Mass 647, 692 NE2d 1 (1998) (defendant is entitled to statements obtained from percipient witnesses that are contained in police department internal affairs records).

[16] *Gerry v. Worcester Consolidated Street Railway Co.*, 248 Mass 559, 566-568, 143 NE 694, 696 (1924).

[17] *Ricciutti v. Sylvania Electric Products, Inc.*, 343 Mass 347, 349, 178 NE2d 857, 859 (1961).

[18] GL 152, § 7B.

[19] GL 152, § 20A.

[20] GL 151A, § 46.

[21] *Union Glass Co. v. Somerville*, 228 Mass 202, 203-204, 117 NE 184, 185 (1917); *Brackett v. Com.*, 223 Mass 119, 127, 111 NE 1036, 1040 (1916).

- Communications to a board of assessors stating the value of corporate property.[22]
- An accident report filed by a motor vehicle operator as required by GL 90, § 26.[23] Such reports are generally admissible in personal injury actions.[24] A motorist may properly assert his privilege against self-incrimination in refusing to file an accident report where criminal charges are pending against him.[25]

In general, whether a particular report will be considered privileged depends upon the court's conclusion as to whether the legislature intended the document to be open to the public, whether it would be fair to permit it to be used, and whether permitting it to be put in evidence would tend to defeat the purpose of the statute by discouraging complete disclosure of information.[26]

The Supreme Judicial Court has refused to create a common-law evidentiary "governmental" privilege for documents relating to the development of policy in the executive branch.[27] Among the documents exempted from mandatory disclosure under the Public Records Act discussed above, however, are "inter-agency or intra-agency memoranda or letters relating to policy positions being developed by the agency."[28] This exemption protects such documents from disclosure only while policy is "being developed"—i.e., while the deliberative process is "ongoing and incomplete"; once the process is completed, the documents generated become publicly available.[29]

---

[22] *Union Glass Co. v. Somerville*, supra.

[23] *Lord v. Registrar of Motor Vehicles*, 347 Mass 608, 199 NE2d 316 (1964).

[24] *Genova v. Genova*, 28 Mass App 647, 653, 554 NE2d 1221, 1225 (1990). But see *Kelly v. O'Neil*, 1 Mass App 313, 317-319, 296 NE2d 223, 227 (1973) (hearsay rule limitations).

[25] See *Com. v. Sasu*, 404 Mass 596, 536 NE2d 603 (1989).

[26] *Carr v. Howard*, 426 Mass 514, 689 NE2d 1304 (1998) (incident reports protected by peer review committee privilege); *Gerry v. Worcester Consolidated Street Railway Co.*, supra, 248 Mass at 568, 143 NE at 697; *Swatch v. Treat*, 41 Mass App 559, 671 NE2d 1004 (1996) (proceeding before hearing panel of national association of social workers was protected by statute).

[27] See *Babets v. Secretary of Human Services*, 403 Mass 230, 526 NE2d 1261 (1988); *District Attorney for Norfolk District v. Flatley*, supra, 419 Mass at 510, 646 NE2d at 129.

[28] GL 4, § 7(26)(d).

[29] *Babets v. Secretary of Human Services*, supra, 403 Mass at 237 n.8, 526 NE2d at 1266 n.8. See also *General Electric Co. v. Department of Environmental Protection*, 429 Mass 798, 806, 711 NE2d 589, 595-596 (1999) (discussing policy deliberation exemption).

Bar discipline complaints are confidential.[30]

a. *Judicial Deliberation Privilege*

First recognized in 2012, a judicial deliberative privilege exists to protect judges from attempts by third parties to extract their deliberative processes or intra-court deliberative communications.[31] The privilege does not cover a judge's memory of non-deliberative events in connection with cases, nor inquiries into whether judge was subjected to improper extraneous influences or ex parte communications during the deliberative process. Communications about deliberative processes between judge and law clerk are confidential.[32]

b. *Medical Peer Review Committee Records*

GL 111, § 204 protects the confidentiality of proceedings, reports, and records of a hospital's medical peer review committee, and exempts them from disclosure under the public records statute.[33] The peer review privilege is not based on a confidential relationship, as the attorney-client privilege, but "instead is designed to foster a candid exchange of information regarding the quality of medical care."[34] Determining whether the privilege applies thus turns on the way the document was created and its purpose, rather than its content.[35]

For a discussion of "executive privilege" in the federal context, see *United States v. Nixon*, 418 US 683 (1974) (Watergate tapes case); *Clinton v. Jones*, 520 US 681, 703-704 (1997). See also Proposed Mass R Evid 508 (recognizing privileges created by the federal Constitution, 508(a), but providing that "[n]o other governmental privilege is recognized except as created by the Constitution or statutes of the Commonwealth." 508(b)).

[30] *Bar Counsel v. Farber*, 464 Mass 784, 985 NE2d 1155 (2013).

[31] See *In re Enforcement of Subpoena*, 463 Mass 162, 972 NE2d 1022 (2012).

[32] *In re Crossen*, 450 Mass 533, 560, 880 NE2d 352, 373 (2008).

[33] See *Com. v. Choate-Symmes Health Services, Inc.*, 406 Mass 27, 545 NE2d 1167 (1989); *Grande v. Lahey Clinic Hospital, Inc.*, 49 Mass App 77, 725 NE2d 1083 (2000) (peer review committee's consultant activities protected by privilege). For the history of the privilege, see *Carr v. Howard*, 426 Mass 514, 689 NE2d 1304 (1998).

[34] *Miller v. Milton Hospital & Medical Center*, 54 Mass App 495, 501, 766 NE2d 107, 112 (2002).

[35] *Id.; Board of Registration in Medicine v. Hallmark Health Corp.*, 454 Mass 498, 910 NE2d 898 (2009) (extensive discussion of statutory privilege).

Documents and records generated during the peer review process are not subject to subpoena or discovery, and may not be introduced into evidence; nor is any person who was in attendance at a committee meeting permitted to testify concerning its proceedings or findings.[36] An exception permits discovery of medical peer review materials where a committee member did not act "in good faith" and "in the reasonable belief" that his actions were warranted.[37] Documents and records otherwise available from original sources are not immune from subpoena, discovery or use in any such judicial or administrative proceeding merely because they were presented to the committee in connection with its proceedings.[38]

The privilege applies to communications between the hospital and credentialing organizations such as the Board of Registration in Medicine.[39] Where there are federal law claims as well as state law claims in the case, the state peer review privilege may not apply.[40]

The statute does not create a private right of action for a physician under investigation to sue the hospital for invasion of privacy for releasing protected peer review information to the public.[41]

§ 5.11 Tax Returns/Accountant Privilege

GL 62C, § 21 generally prohibits public employees from disclosing to anyone other than the taxpayer or his representative information set

---

[36] GL 111, § 204(a). See generally *Ayash v. Dana Farber Cancer Institute*, 443 Mass 367, 395-399, 822 NE2d 667, 691-693 (2005).

[37] GL 111, § 204(b). See *Pardo v. General Hospital Corp.*, 446 Mass 1, 8-13, 841 NE2d 692, 698-701 (2006) (exception not triggered by allegation that committee member initiated review for discriminatory reasons); *Vranos v. Franklin Medical Center*, 448 Mass 425, 436-440, 862 NE2d 11, 20-22 (2007) (suspicions about committee member's ulterior motives are not sufficient to invoke bad faith exception).

[38] GL 111, § 204(b).

[39] See *Vranos v. Franklin Medical Center*, 448 Mass 425, 435-436, 862 NE2d 11, 19 (2007) (physician not entitled to production of documents allegedly containing defamatory statements); *Vranos v. Skinner*, 77 Mass App 280, 293-294, 930 NE2d 156, 167-168 (2010) (letter sent by hospital president to physician suspending his staff privileges for disruptive behavior was a peer review document and thus could not serve as the basis for a defamation action).

[40] See *Gargiulo v. Baystate Health Inc.*, 279 FRD 62 (2012) (documents regarding comparable participants in hospital's medical residency program were not protected by the privilege in former resident's age and disability discrimination action).

[41] *Ayash v. Dana Farber Cancer Institute*, supra, 443 Mass at 383, 822 NE2d at 682-683.

forth in a tax return or document filed with the Commonwealth. The statute and its predecessor "embody the policy of the Commonwealth to preserve the confidentiality of State tax returns."[1] Exemptions permit disclosure in the context of tax and certain other enumerated investigations and proceedings.

Tax preparers[2] and accountants[3] are forbidden from disclosing (without consent) any information communicated by clients relating to and in connection with services rendered. The Internal Revenue Service Restructuring and Reform Act of 1998 creates a privilege for federally authorized tax practitioners to refuse to disclose client communications in noncriminal matters before the IRS or in federal court.[4]

The courts have recognized a privilege against the disclosure and use in evidence of state tax documents.[5] The privilege cannot be circumvented by inquiring of the individual who filed the return as to its contents.[6] The fact that municipal payroll records reveal information that could also be found in tax returns does not prevent disclosure of the payroll information as a public record.[7]

Although federal officials and certain other persons receiving tax information must preserve the confidentiality of tax returns,[8] copies of federal tax returns in the hands of the taxpayer are not absolutely privileged. Such returns may be discovered from the taxpayer on a sufficient showing of need.[9]

---

§ 5.11 [1] *Finance Commissioner of Boston v. Commissioner of Revenue*, 383 Mass 63, 71, 417 NE2d 945, 950 (1981) (extensive discussion of GL 62C, § 21).

[2] GL 62C, § 74.

[3] GL 112, § 87E (but exempting disclosures required in court proceedings and investigations).

[4] Internal Revenue Code § 7525.

[5] See *Leave v. Boston Elevated Railway Co.*, 306 Mass 391, 398-403, 28 NE2d 483, 487-489 (1940); *James Millar Co. v. Com.*, 251 Mass 457, 464, 146 NE 677, 678 (1925). See also *In re Hampers*, 651 F2d 19 (1st Cir 1981) (recognizing qualified privilege against disclosure of state tax records in federal grand jury proceeding).

[6] *James Millar Co. v. Com.*, supra, 251 Mass at 464, 146 NE at 679. But see *Com. v. Ventola*, 351 Mass 703, 221 NE2d 395 (1966) (defendant's admission that he failed to report alleged income admissible to impeach his testimony).

[7] *Hastings & Sons Publishing Co. v. City Treasurer of Lynn*, 373 Mass 812, 820 n.10, 375 NE2d 299, 304-305 n.10 (1978).

[8] See 26 USC § 6103.

[9] *Town Taxi, Inc. v. Police Commissioner of Boston*, 377 Mass 576, 586-588, 387 NE2d 129, 135-136 (1979) (& cases cited); *Finance Commissioner of Boston v. McGrath*, 343 Mass 754, 766-768, 180 NE2d 808, 816-817 (1962); *A.C. Vaccaro, Inc. v. Vaccaro*, 80 Mass App 635, 638-640, 955 NE2d 299, 303-304 (2011) (evidence of non-filing is not

§ 5.12 Political Vote

In order to encourage participation in the election process, the Supreme Judicial Court has concluded that good faith voters may not be asked to reveal the candidate for whom they cast their ballots.[1] So fundamental is society's interest in the secret ballot that the right at stake does not belong to the individual voter. Accordingly, the good faith voter may not waive the "privilege" and disclose his vote.[2] The question whether courts may require illegal voters to reveal the candidate for whom they voted has not been resolved.[3]

Proposed Mass R Evid 506 provides a privilege to refuse to disclose the tenor of one's vote in a political election, except where the court finds that the vote was cast illegally or where "disclosure should be compelled pursuant to the election laws of the Commonwealth."

§ 5.13 Trade Secrets

Massachusetts case law does not recognize a testimonial privilege as to trade secrets.[1] Mass R Civ P 26(c)(7), however, authorizes the issuance of a protective order during the discovery process providing that "a trade secret or other confidential research, development, or commercial information not be disclosed or be disclosed only in a designated way." And as noted in § 5.10, supra, the Public Records Act, GL 4, § 7(26)(g), exempts from disclosure "trade secrets or commercial or financial information voluntarily provided to an agency for use in developing governmental policy and upon a promise of confidentiality."

Proposed Mass R Evid 507 creates an evidentiary privilege "to refuse to disclose and to prevent other persons from disclosing a trade

---

within the privilege); *Com. v. Ianelli*, 17 Mass App 1011, 1013, 460 NE2d 203, 206 (1984) (no error in admitting defendant's tax returns through his accountant); *Com. v. Garabedian*, 8 Mass App 442, 446, 395 NE2d 467, 470 (1979) (federal income tax returns admissible in prosecution for failure to file state returns). For assertion of the privilege against self-incrimination with regard to tax returns, see § 5.14, infra.

§ 5.12 [1] *McCavitt v. Registrars of Voters of Brockton*, 385 Mass 833, 846-850, 434 NE2d 620, 629-631 (1982).

[2] *Id.*, 385 Mass at 849, 434 NE2d at 630.

[3] *Id.*, 385 Mass at 848 n.18, 434 NE2d at 630 n.18.

§ 5.13 [1] *Gossman v. Rosenberg*, 237 Mass 122, 124, 129 NE 424, 426 (1921).

secret" provided "the allowance of the privilege will not tend to conceal fraud or otherwise work injustice."

§ 5.14 Privilege Against Self-Incrimination

§ 5.14.1 Introduction

The privilege against self-incrimination derives from constitutional, statutory, and common-law sources. It is established by the Fifth Amendment to the United States Constitution,[1] which was held applicable to the states by way of the Fourteenth Amendment in *Malloy v. Hogan*.[2] It is also recognized by the Massachusetts Constitution in Part 1, Article 12,[3] and is provided for in GL 233, § 20(3)[4] and GL 231, § 63.[5] The privilege was also recognized at common law.[6] Neither the Federal Rules of Evidence nor the Proposed Massachusetts Rules of Evidence purport to deal with the privilege against self-incrimination.[7]

The effect of *Malloy v. Hogan* is to apply federal standards to the determination of whether a claim of Fifth Amendment privilege is

§ 5.14 [1] "No person . . . shall be compelled in any criminal case to be a witness against himself." US Const., amend v.

[2] 378 US 1 (1964).

[3] "No subject shall . . . be compelled to accuse, or furnish evidence against himself." Mass Const., pt 1, art. xii.

[4] "The defendant in the trial of an indictment, complaint, or other criminal proceeding shall, at his own request, but not otherwise, be allowed to testify; but his neglect or refusal to testify shall not create any presumption against him." GL 233, § 20(3).

That a defendant may need to testify in order to raise a self-defense or alibi does not violate the privilege. See *Com. v. Dame*, 473 Mass 524, 533 n.16, 45 NE3d 69, 78 n.16 (2016) (alibi); *Com. v. Beatrice*, 75 Mass App 153, 159, 912 NE2d 504, 510 (2009), *aff'd on other grounds*, 460 Mass 255 (2011) (self-defense).

[5] "[N]o party interrogated [by way of interrogatory] shall be obliged to answer a question or produce a document tending to criminate him. . . ." GL 231, § 63.

[6] See *Com. v. Brennan*, 386 Mass 772, 780, 438 NE2d 60, 65-66 (1982) (& citations).

[7] See Advisory Committee's Note to Proposed Mass R Evid 501 (constitutional privileges are "preserved without further reference"). But see Advisory Committee's Note to Proposed Mass R Evid 512, suggesting that the rule regarding comment upon or inference from the claim of privilege does purport to apply to self-incrimination contexts.

justified in state proceedings.[8] A state may of course interpret its own constitutional provisions to provide more protection than the federal decisions, but may not fall short of the federal standard in applying Fifth Amendment protections.[9] The Supreme Judicial Court has in fact "consistently held that art. 12 requires a broader interpretation than that of the Fifth Amendment."[10] "Our Constitution adds an additional element not found in most other jurisdictions. Art. 12 of the Declaration of Rights of the Massachusetts Constitution provides in part that no person shall 'be compelled to accuse, or furnish evidence against himself.'"[11]

§ 5.14.2 Availability of the Privilege

The privilege against self-incrimination is available when three conditions exist:

1. The person claiming the privilege must be under *governmental compulsion* to furnish evidence.
2. The evidence required must be *testimonial* in nature.
3. The evidence must have a *reasonable possibility of incriminating the witness in criminal proceedings*.

a. Governmental Compulsion

First, the person claiming the privilege must be under *governmental compulsion*[12] to furnish evidence. Absent such compulsion, the

---

[8] See *Com. v. Borans*, 388 Mass 453, 456, 446 NE2d 703, 705 (1983) (& citations).

[9] *Attorney General v. Colleton*, 387 Mass 790, 795-796, 444 NE2d 915, 918-919 (1982); *Com. v. Brennan*, supra, 386 Mass at 779-780, 438 NE2d at 65.

[10] *Opinion of the Justices to the Senate*, 412 Mass 1201, 1210, 591 NE2d 1073, 1078 (1992).

[11] *Id.*, 412 Mass at 1206, 591 NE2d at 1076. See also *Com. v. Mavredakis*, 430 Mass 848, 858, 725 NE2d 169, 177-178 (2000); *Com. v. Burgess*, 426 Mass 206, 217-219, 688 NE2d 439, 447-448 (1997).

[12] Statements extracted by private coercion are subject to suppression under Massachusetts due process standards. See § 12.3.

privilege does not apply.[13] The threat of the loss of one's livelihood may constitute compulsion.[14]

Public employees cannot be discharged simply because they invoke their privilege under the Fifth Amendment in response to questions from their employer; but they can be discharged for refusing to answer questions narrowly drawn and specifically related to their job performance, where the answers cannot be used against them in a criminal proceeding.[15] A *private* employer's threat to fire an employee who refuses to give a statement to police or submit to a police-conducted polygraph does not raise constitutional issues.[16]

---

[13] See *Selective Service System v. Minnesota Public Interest Research Group*, 468 US 841 (1984) (no coercion where legislative scheme requires persons who have failed to register with Selective Service to acknowledge their non-registration and thereby confess to crime in order to obtain financial aid, because non-registrants under no compulsion to seek financial aid); *Minnesota v. Murphy*, 465 US 420 (1984) (no coercion where probationer makes incriminating statements to probation officer even though probationer has general obligation to appear and answer questions truthfully); *United States v. Doe*, 465 US 605, 610-612 (1984) (contents of business records subpoenaed from respondent by grand jury are not privileged because records were voluntarily prepared by him and thus no compulsion); *South Dakota v. Neville*, 459 US 553, 562 (1983) (no coercion when motorist refuses to submit to blood-alcohol test); *Com. v. Hunt*, 462 Mass 807, 971 NE2d 768 (2012) (admission of evidence of defendant's refusal to participate in sex offender treatment programs would not violate his right against self-incrimination, since the risk of refusal—that it may be used in evidence in a SDP proceeding—is not severe enough to constitute compulsion); *Com. v. Delisle*, 440 Mass 137, 794 NE2d 1191 (2003) (no compulsion where probationer required by private counseling program to write incriminating letter); *Com. v. Harvey*, 397 Mass 351, 355-357, 491 NE2d 607, 610-611 (1986) (statements made by police officer during internal affairs investigation not result of overt threat or pressure, and thus not "compelled"). But see *Opinion of the Justices to the Senate*, 412 Mass 1201, 591 NE2d 1073 (1992) (proposed statute making defendant's refusal to submit to chemical analysis of breath admissible as evidence in criminal proceeding would violate art. 12 of Massachusetts Declaration of Rights because there is compulsion on subject to choose between two alternatives, both of which are capable of producing adverse evidence) and *Com. v. McGrail*, 419 Mass 774, 779, 647 NE2d 712, 715 (1995) (same/field sobriety test), discussed infra at § 5.14.2(b).

[14] See *Walden v. Board of Registration*, 395 Mass 263, 266, NE2d 665, 668 (1985) (& citations) (certification that applicant for renewal of license as registered nurse has complied with state tax laws treated as compelled, but no substantial threat of prosecution).

[15] See *Furtado v. Town of Plymouth*, 69 Mass App 319, 320 n.3 & 324 n.12, 867 NE2d 801, 802 n.3 & 805 n.12 (2007), *aff'd*, 451 Mass 529, 888 NE2d 357 (2008). See also § 5.14.2(c), infra. Cf. *City of Worcester v. Civil Service Commission*, 87 Mass App 120, 26 NE3d 196 (2015) (Civil Service Commission's determination that city did not have just cause to suspend or terminate tenured police officer for failing to testify at his disciplinary hearing was not arbitrary, capricious, or otherwise contrary to the law).

[16] See *Bellin v. Kelley*, 435 Mass 261, 272-273, 755 NE2d 1274, 1284 (2001).

A court-ordered psychiatric examination is considered compelled production,[17] but a defendant who testifies at trial or proffers expert testimony concerning his criminal responsibility based on his statements during the examination waives the privilege.[18] Requiring testimony to purge a contempt judgment is not compulsion for purposes of this privilege.[19]

A person may be required to produce documents voluntarily created even though they contain incriminating statements because the creation of those documents was not compelled.[20]

b. Testimonial Evidence/Act of Production Doctrine/Refusal Evidence

Second, the evidence required must be *testimonial* in nature.[21] "Testimonial evidence" is evidence "which reveals the subject's

---

[17] See *Estelle v. Smith*, 451 US 454, 468-469 (1981) (admission at penalty phase of capital trial of psychiatrist's damaging testimony on crucial issue of future dangerousness violated Fifth Amendment privilege against compelled self-incrimination because based on defendant's statements during examination to determine competency to stand trial); *Com. v. Harris*, 468 Mass 429, 11 NE3d 95 (2014) (inculpatory statements made during competency evaluation); *Seng* v. *Com.*, 445 Mass 536, 545-547, 839 NE2d 283, 290-291 (2005) (immunity provisions of statute governing statements made during court-ordered evaluation protected defendant's privilege against self-incrimination); *Com. v. Wayne*, 414 Mass 218, 228 n.11, 606 NE2d 1323, 1330 n.11 (1993); *Blaisdell v. Com.*, 372 Mass 753, 757-758, 364 NE2d 191, 195-196 (1977). There is no constitutional right to have the interview electronically recorded. *Com. v. Baldwin*, 426 Mass 105, 111 n.4, 686 NE2d 1001, 1005 n.4 (1997); *Com. v. Lo*, 428 Mass 45, 47-48, 696 NE2d 935, 938 (1998).

[18] *Com. v. Harris*, *supra*, 468 Mass at 448-449, 11 NE3d at 110-111; *Com. v. Sliech-Brodeur*, 457 Mass 300, 315-317, 930 NE2d 91, 104-105 (2010); *Com. v. Baldwin*, supra 426 Mass at 109-110, 686 NE2d at 1004. See also *Com. v. Ostrander*, 441 Mass 344, 351-355, 805 NE2d 497, 504-506 (2004) (waiver where defendant presents expert testimony placing at issue his mental ability to voluntarily waive *Miranda* rights and make a voluntary statement and is compelled to undergo examination by Commonwealth expert). Cf. *Doe v. Massachusetts Parole Board*, 82 Mass App 851, 861-862, 979 NE2d 226, 235 (2012) (paroled sex offender's claim that condition of parole requiring his psychotherapist to disclose treatment records constituted compelled waiver of his right against self-incrimination was rejected absent any allegation that he had been asked or compelled to disclose any prior crimes in therapy, or otherwise incriminate himself).

[19] See *In re Care & Protection Summons*, 437 Mass 224, 237-239, 770 NE2d 456, 467-468 (2002). See also *Com. v. Fallon*, 38 Mass App 366, 375, 648 NE2d 767, 772 (1995), *rev'd on other grounds*, 423 Mass 92 (financial records voluntarily obtained from the defendant under court order in the civil case could be admitted in criminal case).

[20] See *Com. v. Gelfgatt*, 468 Mass 512, 522 n.13, 1 NE3d 605, 614 (2014). But see discussion of the act of production doctrine in next section.

[21] *Com. v. Hughes*, 380 Mass 583, 588, 404 NE2d 1239, 1242 (1980).

knowledge or thoughts concerning some fact."[22] Where the subject himself is merely the source of real, physical, or identification evidence the privilege does not apply,[23] as in the following:

- Field sobriety tests.[24]
- Fingernail scrapings.[25]
- Handwriting exemplars.[26]
- Voice exemplars.[27]
- Extraction of blood sample from motorist.[28]
- Body examination.[29]
- Line-ups.[30]
- Booking photographs.[31]
- Videotape of booking procedure for OUI suspect.[32]
- Scientific tests such as CAT-scan and psychological tests.[33]
- Requirement that driver stop at scene after "hit and run."[34]
- An officer's request for a driver's or weapon license.[35]

---

[22] *Com. v. Brennan*, 386 Mass 772, 778, 438 NE2d 60, 64 (1982).

[23] See generally *Com. v. Gelfgatt*, supra, 468 Mass at 521, 11 NE3d at 613.

[24] *Pennsylvania v. Muniz*, 496 US 582 (1990); *Vanhouten v. Com.*, 424 Mass 327, 333-337, 676 NE2d 460, 464-466 (1997) (field sobriety tests and alphabet recitation); *Com. v. Brennan*, supra, 386 Mass at 776-779, 438 NE2d at 63-64 (breathalyzer and field sobriety tests); *Com. v. Brown*, 83 Mass App 772, 776-777, 989 NE2d 915, 919 (2013) (sobriety tests). See also *Com. v. Carey*, 26 Mass App 339, 340-341, 526 NE2d 1329, 1331 (1988) (videotape of defendant performing sobriety tests).

[25] *Cupp v. Murphy*, 412 US 291 (1973).

[26] *United States v. Mara*, 410 US 19 (1973); *Com. v. Buckley*, 410 Mass 209, 214-216, 571 NE2d 609, 612-613 (1991); *Com. v. Nadworny*, 396 Mass 342, 362-365, 486 NE2d 675, 687-688 (1985) (handwriting exemplar including defendant's declaration of right-handedness).

[27] *United States v. Dionisio*, 410 US 1 (1973).

[28] *Schmerber v. California*, 384 US 757 (1966); *Com. v. Beausoleil*, 397 Mass 206, 222-223, 490 NE2d 788, 795 (1986).

[29] *Com. v. Miles*, 420 Mass 67, 82 n.16, 648 NE2d 719, 729 n.16 (1995).

[30] *United States v. Wade*, 388 US 218 (1967). See also *Com. v. Burke*, 339 Mass 521, 159 NE2d 856 (1959) (forcing defendant to assume posture in court to aid identification not testimonial).

[31] *Com. v. Fryar*, 425 Mass 237, 250, 680 NE2d 901, 911 (1997). See also *United States v. Bullard*, 37 F3d 765, 768-769 (1st Cir 1995) (requiring defendant to wear hat for identification photograph).

[32] *Com. v. Mahoney*, 400 Mass 524, 527-528, 510 NE2d 759, 762 (1987).

[33] *Seng v. Com.*, 445 Mass 536, 545-547, 839 NE2d 283, 290-291 (2005) (competency evaluation); *Com. v. Trapp*, 396 Mass 202, 212, 485 NE2d 162, 169 (1985).

[34] *California v. Byers*, 402 US 424 (1971).

[35] *Com. v. Haskell*, 438 Mass 790, 796, 784 NE2d 625, 630 (2003).

- Compelled execution of forms authorizing disclosure of federal tax return information.[36]

In some instances, however, the manner in which these procedures are conducted may convert a non-testimonial exercise into a testimonial message. An order requiring defendant to supply a handwriting exemplar that would have shown his choice of spelling and thus link him in an incriminating way to a particular document was, for example, held to violate the Fifth Amendment.[37] Similarly a motorist's answer to the "sixth birthday" question during a field sobriety test was "testimonial" because it revealed his mental processes.[38]

The act of producing documents in response to a subpoena may have a compelled testimonial aspect because production may constitute an admission that the papers existed and were in the witness's possession.[39] In this regard, the Massachusetts Constitution provides broader protection than the federal Constitution, as art. 12 specifically protects a subject against being forced "to furnish evidence against himself."[40] Even though a subject's act of production would otherwise be within the privilege, as being compelled to enter a password or encryption key for a seized computer (thereby acknowledging control over the computer and its contents), the factual statements conveyed may fall within the exception for "foregone conclusions, i.e., the facts conveyed are already known to the government."[41]

---

[36] *Com. v. Burgess*, 426 Mass 206, 688 NE2d 439 (1997). See also *Com. v. Barnoski*, 418 Mass 523, 538 n.10, 638 NE2d 9, 18 n.10 (1994) (act of defendant rubbing hand through hair allegedly to remove gunshot residue); *Com. v. Billings*, 42 Mass App 261, 264 n.7, 676 NE2d 62, 64 n.7 (1997) (suspect's lifting of foot to show sole of sneaker); *Com. v. Billups*, 13 Mass App 963, 432 NE2d 105 (1982) (exposure of defendant's underwear and genital area).

[37] *United States v. Campbell*, 732 F 2d 1017, 1020-1021 (1st Cir 1984).

[38] See *Pennsylvania v. Muniz*, supra, 496 US at 593-594. See also *Com. v. Hughes*, supra, 380 Mass at 592, 404 NE2d at 1244 (order to produce gun violated defendant's Fifth Amendment privilege because it compelled implicit statements as to existence, location, and control of weapon); *Com. v. Ayre*, 31 Mass App 17, 21 & n.8, 574 NE2d 415, 418 n.8 (1991) (potential testimonial dimension to roadside sobriety tests); *Com. v. Carey*, supra, 26 Mass App at 341-342, 526 NE2d at 1331-1332 (testimonial component of OUI booking procedure).

[39] See *In re Grand Jury Investigation*, 470 Mass 399, 403, 22 NE3d 927, 931 (2015) (& citations) (law firm could not be compelled to produce cell phone containing documents and other materials turned over by client).

[40] *Id; Com. v. Gelfgatt*, 468 Mass 512, 524-526, 11 NE3d 605, 616-617 (2014). See also § 5.14.5.

[41] *Com. v. Gelfgatt*, supra, 468 Mass at 522-524, 11 NE3d at 614-615 (extensive discussion of "foregone conclusion" exception).

Where *a refusal* to submit to a test or procedure could be viewed as an implicit admission of guilt, the refusal may be deemed testimonial and the privilege applicable in Massachusetts. The refusal to take a field sobriety test or to submit to breathalyzer constitutes testimonial evidence under art. 12, and the admission of evidence of the refusal violates the state constitutional privilege.[42] A driver's "negotiation" with an officer about taking the test may be deemed the equivalent of a refusal and thus inadmissible.[43] Where the refusal is not attributable

---

[42] *Com. v. McGrail*, 419 Mass 774, 647 NE2d 712 (1995) (field sobriety test); *Opinion of the Justices to the Senate*, supra, 412 Mass at 1208-1211, 591 NE2d at 1077-1078 (breathalyzer). See also *Com. v. Lopes*, 459 Mass 165, 944 NE2d 999(2011) (consent form suggesting defendant's refusal did not violate privilege); *Com. v. Healy*, 452 Mass 510, 513-515, 895 NE2d 752, 755-757 (2008) (refusal evidence may not be considered on sentencing or at trial); *Com. v. Seymour*, 39 Mass App 672, 660 NE2d 679 (1996) (evidence that defendant refused breathalyzer inadmissible; prosecutor's closing argument commenting on refusal violated privilege); *Com. v. Ranieri*, 65 Mass App 366, 370-372, 840 NE2d 963, 967-968 (2006) (reversal required where evidence of defendant's refusal to recite alphabet during field sobriety test was admitted); *Com. v. Quinn*, 61 Mass App 332, 336 n.3, 810 NE2d 819, 822 n.3 (2004) (videotape of defendant's booking which depicts his refusal to take breathalyzer examination should not be admitted). Compare *South Dakota v. Neville*, supra, 459 US at 562 (evidence of motorist's refusal to submit to blood-alcohol test does not violate Fifth Amendment of federal constitution).

See also GL 90, § 24(1)(e), which provides: "Evidence that the defendant failed or refused to consent to [a blood alcohol] chemical test or analysis shall not be admissible against him in a civil or criminal proceeding. . . ." The statute does not preclude defendant from introducing in an appropriate case evidence as to his recantation of such refusal. See *Com. v. Jones*, 464 Mass 16, 20 n.6, 979 NE2d 1088, 1092 n.6 (2012).

Where defendant does not refuse the breathalyzer, but instead consents and then tries to avoid exhaling into the testing machine, there is no impediment to admissibility. See *Com. v. Curley*, 78 Mass App 163, 935 NE2d 772 (2010). For blood tests in the context of a prosecution for operating a vessel under the influence of alcohol. GL 90B, § 8A, see *Com. v. Thompson*, 87 Mass App 572, 32 NE3d 1273 (2015).

[43] See *Com. v. Grenier*, 45 Mass App 58, 695 NE2d 1075 (1998). For other forms of inadmissible refusal evidence, see *Com. v. Conkey*, 430 Mass 139, 714 NE2d 343 (1999) (*Conkey I*) (defendant's failure to provide finger and palm prints); *Com. v. Conkey*, 443 Mass 60, 71-72, 819 NE2d 176, 186-187 (2004) (*Conkey II*) (defendant refused to comply with police request to reduce his statements to writing); *Com. v. Hinckley*, 422 Mass 261, 661 NE2d 1317 (1996) (defendant's refusal to turn over sneakers during criminal investigation); *Com. v. Lydon*, 413 Mass 309, 313-315, 597 NE2d 36, 39-40 (1992) (defendant's refusal to allow police to swab hands for evidence that he had fired gun); *Com. v. Vermette*, 43 Mass App 789, 797-798, 686 NE2d 1071, 1076-1077 (1997) (defendant's refusal to consent to search of car); *Com. v. Martinez*, 34 Mass App 131, 608 NE2d 740 (1993) (rape defendant's failure to voluntarily offer to furnish district attorney with physical evidence). Compare *Mello v. Hingham Mutual Fire Insurance Co.*, 421 Mass 333, 656 NE2d 1247 (1995) (insured's refusal to submit to examination under oath not justified by privilege against self-incrimination). For discussion of the use of refusal evidence before a grand jury, see *Com. v. Rice*, 441 Mass 291, 309-310, 805 NE2d 26, 42 (2004), *habeas denied*, 564 F3d 523 (1st Cir 2009).

to any request or action by the police, it is not protected from admission as evidence.[44]

The prohibited element of compulsion in these cases arises because the defendant is given a choice between two alternatives, submission or refusal, both of which may produce evidence against him. Where the defendant has no choice but to comply, as with a warrant or court order, there is no such "Catch-22" and evidence of refusal may be admitted to show consciousness of guilt.[45] A defendant's volunteered statements made after consenting to the tests and while performing them are not products of compulsion and thus admissible.[46]

Refusal evidence may be admitted to correct a misimpression created by defendant's direct testimony[47] or to explain the loss of potentially incriminating evidence and put defendant's destruction of it in context.[48] Where defense counsel opens the door by raising the issue during cross-examination, refusal evidence may be admitted.[49]

In *Com. v. Zevitas*,[50] the court found that the statutorily mandated instruction concerning a defendant's failure to take a blood alcohol test had the same effect as the admission of refusal evidence and thus violated the privilege against self-incrimination. *Zevitas* has been held retroactively applicable.[51]

---

[44] *Com. v. Arruda*, 73 Mass App 901, 895 NE2d 783 (2008) (request was made by private medical personnel for purposes of treatment while defendant was in police custody).

[45] See *Com. v. Delaney*, 442 Mass 604, 814 NE2d 346 (2004) (defendant's refusal to submit to body search pursuant to warrant); *Com. v. Bly*, 448 Mass 473, 496-497, 862 NE2d 341, 360-361 (2007) (refusal to provide court-ordered hair sample). See also *Com. v. Johnston*, 467 Mass 674, 685-686, 7 NE3d 424, 435 (2014) (where officers were merely performing a community caretaking function regarding him and his vehicle, and no criminal prosecution was contemplated, defendant was not placed in "Catch-22").

[46] *Com. v. Brown*, 83 Mass App 772, 778, 989 NE2d 915, 920 (2013).

[47] See, e.g., *Com. v. Johnson*, 46 Mass App 398, 404-406, 706 NE2d 716, 722-723 (1999).

[48] *Com. v. O'Laughlin*, 446 Mass 188, 205-206, 843 NE2d 617, 631-632 (2006) (defendant's withdrawal of consent to search following officers' request to swab reddish stain, which disappeared on their return), *habeas granted on other grounds*, *O'Laughlin v. O'Brien*, 568 F3d 287 (1st Cir 2009).

[49] See *Com. v. Beaulieu*, 79 Mass App 100, 103-104, 944 NE2d 1057, 1060-1061 (2011).

[50] 418 Mass 677, 639 NE2d 1076 (1994). See also *Com. v. Gibson*, 82 Mass App 834, 836-837, 978 NE2d 1226, 1229 (2012) (judge erroneously instructed that "a person does not have to take a breathalyzer test," suggesting defendant had refused to submit).

[51] See *Com. v. D'Agostino*, 421 Mass 281, 657 NE2d 217 (1995); *Com. v. Koney*, 421 Mass 295, 657 NE2d 210 (1995). But compare *Com. v. Adams*, 421 Mass 289, 657 NE2d 455 (1995) and *Com. v. Madigan*, 38 Mass App 965, 650 NE2d 363 (1995) (no retroactive application where case was tried after *Opinion of the Justices* foreshadowed *Zevitas*).

Evidence that a sex offender refused treatment conditioned upon a waiver of confidentiality
has been held inadmissible in an SDP proceeding.[52]

c. *Reasonable Possibility of Incriminating the Witness in Criminal Proceedings*

Third, the evidence must have a *reasonable possibility of incriminating the witness in a criminal proceeding,*[53] including the sentencing stage.[54] It is not sufficient that the evidence may subject the witness to civil liability or otherwise adversely affect his pecuniary interest,[55] or might embarrass him or place him or his family in danger.[56] Nor may the witness refuse to testify about matters on which the statute of limitations has run.[57]

The privilege does not prevent disclosures from being used in noncriminal commitment proceedings,[58] or in child custody or

---

See also *Com. v. Downs*, 53 Mass App 195, 758 NE2d 1062 (2001) (rejecting defendant's argument that jury instruction not to consider absence of breathalyzer evidence could have opposite effect and thus violated privilege against self-incrimination); *Com. v. Carnell*, 53 Mass App 356, 759 NE2d 336 (2001) (failure to cure trooper's inaccurate testimony concerning defendant's refusal to take blood alcohol test required reversal).

[52] See *Com. v. Hunt*, 462 Mass 807, 971 NE2d 768 (2012) (admission of evidence of defendant's refusal to participate in sex offender treatment programs would not violate his right against self-incrimination; but the risk of unfair prejudice from such evidence substantially exceeds its probative value, and it should not be admitted). Compare *Com. v. Cahoon*, 86 Mass App 266, 15 NE3d 787 (2014) (distinguishing *Com. v. Hunt* because refusal of treatment was not connected to avoidance of adverse use of information disclosed during treatment).

Com. v. Mazzarino, 81 Mass App 358, 366-368, 963 NE2d 112, 119-120 (2012) (qualified examiners were properly permitted to testify that defendant refused to speak with them on advice of counsel).

[53] *Lefkowitz v. Turley*, 414 US 70 (1973).

[54] *Estelle v. Smith*, 451 US 454 (1981) (admission at sentencing stage of capital trial of statements made to psychiatrist violated defendant's right against self-incrimination).

[55] *United States v. Ward*, 448 US 242, 248-256 (1980) (statutory reporting requirement regarding oil spills did not violate Fifth Amendment because monetary fine was "civil" in nature).

[56] See *Com. v. Martin*, 423 Mass 496, 503, 668 NE2d 825, 831 (1996); *Com. v. Johnson*, 365 Mass 534, 543-544, 313 NE2d 571, 577 (1974).

[57] *In re DeSaulnier (No. 2)*, 360 Mass 761, 763-764, 276 NE2d 278, 280 (1971).

[58] See *Com. v. Barboza*, 387 Mass 105, 114, 438 NE2d 1064, 1067 (1982) (GL 123A proceeding for commitment as sexually dangerous person).

protection cases.[59] The privilege is not violated where the information sought may result not in a criminal prosecution but rather in loss of the witness's employment.[60] Thus a state may properly insist that public employees either answer questions (under an adequate grant of immunity from criminal prosecution, see § 5.14.7.b., infra) concerning the performance of their jobs or suffer loss of employment.[61] Police officers may be required to answer questions or submit to a polygraph examination in connection with the performance of their duties provided they are granted immunity from the use of their responses in a criminal prosecution.[62]

The threat of dismissal renders involuntary any incriminating statements made by the employee in response thereof, thus rendering the statements inadmissible under the Fifth Amendment in any subsequent criminal proceeding.[63] Where the employee invokes art. 12 of the Massachusetts Declaration of Rights, a grant of transactional

---

[59] *Care and Protection of Sharlene*, 445 Mass 756, 767, 840 NE2d 918, 926 (2006) (juvenile court judge entitled to draw negative inference from stepfather's intention to invoke privilege not to testify with respect to child's injuries); *In re Care & Protection Summons*, 437 Mass 224, 235, 770 NE2d 456, 466 (2002) (judge could draw inferences from parent's refusal to testify as to existence and location of child); *Custody of Two Minors*, 396 Mass 610, 616-618, 487 NE2d 1358, 1363 (1986).

[60] *Lefkowitz v. Turley*, supra, 414 US at 84-85.

[61] *Lefkowitz v. Turley*, supra, 414 US at 84; *Uniformed Sanitation Men Association, Inc. v. Commissioner of Sanitation*, 392 US 280, 284-285 (1968); *Gardner v. Broderick*, 392 US 273, 276-279 (1968); *Com. v. Dormady*, 423 Mass 190, 193-194, 667 NE2d 832, 834 (1996).

[62] See *Patch v. Mayor of Revere*, 397 Mass 454, 492 NE2d 77 (1986); *Baker v. Lawrence*, 379 Mass 322, 409 NE2d 710 (1979); *Reinstein v. Police Commissioner of Boston*, 378 Mass 281, 391 NE2d 881 (1979); *Broderick v. Police Commissioner of Boston*, 368 Mass 33, 330 NE2d 199 (1975); *Silverio v. Municipal Court of the City of Boston*, 355 Mass 623, 628-630, 247 NE2d 379, 382 (1969) (privilege did not bar dismissal of officer who refused to answer superior's questions concerning his testimony before grand jury where answers could not be used to prosecute him). See also GL 149, § 19B(2), excepting law enforcement agencies in the conduct of criminal investigations from the prohibition against requiring employees to submit to lie detector tests; *Furtado v. Town of Plymouth*, 451 Mass 529, 888 NE2d 357 (2008) (statutory exception applies to permit police department to order officer to submit to lie detector test in course of internal departmental investigation).

[63] See *Garrity v. New Jersey*, 385 US 493, 500, 87 S Ct 616, 17 L Ed 2d 562 (1967); *Carney v. City of Springfield*, 403 Mass 604, 607-608 n.5, 532 NE2d 631, 634 n.5 (1988) (this is form of "informal immunity" because although not under the umbrella of statutory immunity, statements compelled by the threat of job sanction are inadmissible in criminal proceedings). See also *Patch v. Mayor of Revere*, supra, 397 Mass at 456, 492 NE2d at 78.

immunity (see § 5.14.7.b., infra) with respect to the answers sought is required to supplant the privilege and compel the testimony.[64]

The Fifth Amendment has been applied to disciplinary proceedings in which a license might be revoked.[65]

A witness may not claim the privilege out of fear that he will be prosecuted for perjury for what he is about to say, but he may claim the privilege if his new testimony might suggest that he had previously perjured himself at a prior proceeding.[66] The privilege "does not condone perjury. It grants a privilege to remain silent without risking contempt, but 'it does not endow the person who testifies a license to perjury.' "[67] The Fifth Amendment privilege against self-incrimination is available to a person who claims innocence, since her answers may provide the government with incriminating evidence.[68]

At its most basic the privilege permits a criminal defendant to refuse to testify at trial. More generally it permits any person to refuse to furnish information that could be used against him in a criminal prosecution. A witness protected by the privilege "may rightfully refuse to answer unless and until he is protected at least against the use of his compelled answers and evidence derived therefrom in any subsequent criminal case in which he is a defendant. . . . Absent such protection, if he is nevertheless compelled to answer, his answers are inadmissible against him in a later criminal prosecution."[69]

The protection against self-incrimination extends beyond criminal investigations, privileging a witness not to answer official questions put to him in any other proceeding, civil or criminal, formal or informal, where the answers might incriminate him in future criminal proceedings.[70] It extends not only to evidence that would support a

---

[64] See *Baglioni v. Chief of Police of Salem*, 421 Mass 229, 656 NE2d 1223 (1995); *Com. v. Kerr*, 409 Mass 11, 14, 563 NE2d 1364, 1366-1367 (1990); *Carney v. City of Springfield*, supra, 403 Mass at 610-611, 532 NE2d at 635.

[65] See *Spevack v. Klein*, 385 US 511 (1967) (lawyer could not be disbarred on the ground that he claimed the privilege during an investigation into his professional conduct).

[66] *Com. v. Martin*, 423 Mass 496, 503-504, 668 NE2d 825, 830 (1996) (& citations).

[67] *United States v. Wong*, 431 US 174, 178 (1977). See also *Com. v. Steinberg*, 404 Mass 602, 607, 536 NE2d 606, 610 (1989).

[68] See *Ohio v. Reiner*, 532 US 17 (2001); *In re Proceedings Before a Grand Jury*, 55 Mass App 17, 768 NE2d 1102 (2002).

[69] *Minnesota v. Murphy*, 465 US 420, 426 (1984) (citations omitted).

[70] *Lefkowitz v. Turley*, supra, 414 US at 77; *Ainsworth v. Risley*, 244 F3d 209 (1st Cir 2001) (privilege in context of prison inmates).

conviction but to any information "which would furnish a link in the chain of evidence needed to prosecute" the claimant of the privilege.[71] It also protects a person from having to disclose the names of persons who could testify against him.[72]

The protection, however, must be confined to instances where the witness has "reasonable cause to apprehend danger from a direct answer. The witness is not exonerated from answering merely because he declares that in so doing he would incriminate himself—his say-so does not of itself establish the hazard of incrimination. It is for the court to say whether his silence is justified, and to require him to answer if 'it clearly appears to the court that he is mistaken.' "[73]

A person's right to be free from self-incrimination is a fundamental principle of our system of justice and, accordingly, it is to be "construed liberally in favor of the claimant."[74] It will be sustained where it is "evident from the implications of the question, in the setting in which it is asked, that a responsive answer to the question or an explanation of why it cannot be answered might be dangerous because injurious disclosure could result."[75]

To deny the privilege, it must be "*perfectly clear*, from a careful consideration of all the circumstances in the case, that the witness is mistaken, and that the answer[s] *cannot possibly* have such tendency to incriminate,"[76] and that there is no "real or substantial danger that the

---

[71] *Hoffman v. United States*, 341 US 479, 486 (1951); *Malloy v. Hogan*, 378 US 1, 11-12 (1964); *Com. v. Borans*, 388 Mass 453, 456, 446 NE2d 703, 705 (1983); *Taylor v. Com.*, 369 Mass 183, 187-188, 338 NE2d 823, 826 (1975).

[72] *Com. v. Prince*, 313 Mass 223, 229-231, 46 NE2d 755, 758-759 (1943), *aff'd*, 321 US 158 (1944).

[73] *Hoffman v. United States*, supra, 341 US at 486 (citations omitted). See, e.g., *In re Enforcement of Subpoena*, 435 Mass 1, 753 NE2d 145 (2001) (respondent, former member of Judicial Conduct Commission, was not placed at risk for criminal prosecution by compelled testimony and document production); *Republic of Greece v. Koukouras*, 264 Mass 318, 323, 162 NE 345, 347 (1928) (nothing indicating that a criminal offense was committed with which answers to the interrogatories would tend to connect the defendant).

[74] *Com. v. Borans*, supra, 388 Mass at 455, 446 NE2d at 704 (& citations).

[75] *Malloy v. Hogan*, supra, 378 US at 11-12; *Emspak v. United States*, 349 US 190, 198-199 (1955); *Hoffman v. United States*, supra, 341 US at 486-487.

[76] *Hoffman v. United States*, supra, 341 at 488. See also *Com. v. Cotto*, 471 Mass 97, 27 NE3d 1213, 1231-1232 (2015) (drug analyst's wife's invocation of Fifth Amendment privilege provided a valid ground to quash defendant's subpoena because her testimony would reveal her own drug use); *Com. v. Alicea*, 464 Mass 837, 841-842, 985 NE2d 1197, 1203 (2013) (witness was properly allowed to invoke privilege, where if defense theory was correct, his testimony could implicate him as the shooter and to drug charges); *Com. v. Lucien*, 440 Mass 658, 665, 801 NE2d 247, 254 (2004) (witness could invoke privilege involving swap of handguns where he had already pled guilty to

evidence supplied will lead to a charge of crime or to the securing of evidence to support such a charge."[77] The privilege extends not only to answers that would support a conviction in themselves, but also to answers that would furnish a link in the chain of evidence needed to prosecute.[78]

Any circumstance that eliminates a witness's exposure to prosecution—the running of the statute of limitations on the alleged crime, a conviction or acquittal for the alleged crime, the granting of a pardon—bars the privilege.[79] An individual prosecutor's

possession of only one of the two firearms involved); *Com. v. Dagenais*, 437 Mass 832, 838-840, 776 NE2d 1010, 1015-1017 (2002) (because witness was planning to assert mental incapacity defense at his own unrelated murder trial, testimony demonstrating his unimpaired ability to recall past events could undermine that defense and thus tend to incriminate him); *Com. v. Tracey*, 416 Mass 528, 538, 624 NE2d 84, 90 (1993) (since exact nature of relationship between witness and police was unclear, it was not perfectly clear that witness's testimony could not incriminate him); *In re Proceedings Before a Grand Jury*, 55 Mass App 17, 768 NE2d 1102 (2002) (notwithstanding Commonwealth's representation that witness was not target of investigation, as one of but two individuals in a position to have perpetrated the crime she could reasonably apprehend prosecution); *Com. v. LaBonte*, 25 Mass App 190, 196, 516 NE2d 1193, 1197 (1987) (claim of privilege should be allowed "if there was even slender ground for apprehending that testimony on the part of [the witness] might tend to incriminate him."). For the matter of whether an informant may assert the privilege if called to testify, see *Com. v. Dias*, 451 Mass 463, 473-474, 886 NE2d 713, 721-722 (2008).

[77] *Com. v. Joyce*, 326 Mass 751, 756, 97 NE2d 192, 196 (1951). See also *Leary v. United States*, 395 US 6, 16 (1969); *Com. v. Farley*, 443 Mass 740, 747-750, 824 NE2d 797, 804-806 (2005), *habeas denied*, 544 F3d 344 (1st Cir 2009) (defense counsel's question regarding witness's employment would tend to incriminate him as it was designed to establish he was a drug dealer); *Com. v. Freeman*, 442 Mass 779, 784-786, 817 NE2d 727, 733-734 (2004) (witness's answers to defense counsel's questions could have incriminated him because witness may have agreed to testify falsely for defendant and thus possibly conspired to commit perjury).

[78] *Com. v. Leclair*, 469 Mass 777, 782-783, 17 NE3d 1415, 419-420 (2014) (witness's admission to drug use could have provided witnesses and leads for subsequent criminal investigation).

[79] *Com. v. Borans*, supra, 388 Mass at 459, 446 NE2d at 707 (conviction; but witness does not lose privilege concerning other matters not included in conviction); *In re DeSaulnier (No. 2)*, supra, 360 Mass at 763, 276 NE2d at 280 (statute of limitations); *Com. v. Sueiras*, 72 Mass App 439, 446-448, 892 NE2d 768, 775-776 (2008) (juvenile witnesses had already been charged with and sentenced for crimes relating to their conduct at defendant's house; another was facing no charges); *Com. v. Crawford*, 12 Mass App 776, 784, 429 NE2d 54, 59 (1981) (guilty plea). But see *Com. v. Colantonio*, 31 Mass App 299, 305-306, 577 NE2d 314, 318 (1991) ("Although [the witness's] testimony could not expose him to prosecution for the crime to which he had pleaded guilty, testimony concerning the episode could expose him to prosecution for a related crime, such as conspiracy"; thus judge did not err in permitting witness to assert privilege); *Com. v. Wooden*, 70 Mass App 185, 873 NE2d 764 (2007) (judge properly

denial of intent to prosecute is not sufficient to undermine the privilege.[80]

When a witness informs the judge that he would exercise the privilege against self-incrimination, the judge must make an informed determination as to whether the witness has established a real risk of incrimination.[81] Usually this can be done in open court, but where there is a question about the propriety of the claim of privilege and insufficient information upon which the judge can rule, an *in-camera* hearing may be conducted.[82]

A witness may claim the privilege even though the sovereign that is seeking the testimony is not the same sovereign that may institute criminal proceedings. One jurisdiction within the federal structure may not, absent an immunity provision, compel a witness to give testimony that might incriminate him under the laws of another jurisdiction. The Fifth Amendment thus provides protection for a witness in a state proceeding against incrimination under federal (or another state's) law, and for a witness in a federal proceeding against incrimination under state law.[83] Fear of prosecution in a foreign country is beyond the scope of the Fifth Amendment.[84]

The federal government is not required, however, when it seeks to compel testimony, to grant immunity coextensive with the immunity the state would grant if it were seeking the testimony. Thus, a witness is not entitled to transactional immunity from the federal government on grounds that Massachusetts would grant the broader immunity.[85] See § 5.14.7.b, infra.

---

recognized that if witness were required to testify, he could be subjected to further criminal prosecution, including conspiracy, beyond the six charges arising from armed robbery that he had pled guilty to).

[80] *Com. v. Leclair*, supra, 469 Mass at 783-784, 17 NE3d 1415 at 420.

[81] *Com. v. Pixley*, 77 Mass App 624, 627, 933 NE2d 645, 649 (2010) (judge properly determined that witness would be required on cross-examination to incriminate himself regarding his history of drug dealing).

[82] See *Com. v. Martin*, 423 Mass 496, 504-505, 668 NE2d 825, 831-832 (1996); *Com. v. Alicea*, 464 Mass 837, 840, 985 NE2d 1197, 1202 (2013) (in camera hearing excluding defendant and defense counsel, but not prosecutor).

[83] *Murphy v. Waterfront Commission of New York*, 378 US 52 (1964).

[84] *United States v. Balsys*, 524 US 666 (1998) (resident alien subpoenaed to testify about wartime activities in Europe could not claim privilege based on fear of prosecution in Lithuania). See also *Com. v. Steinberg*, 404 Mass 602, 607-608, 536 NE2d 606, 610 (1989).

[85] See *In re Bianchi*, 542 F2d 98, 101 (1st Cir 1976).

The privilege does not generally extend to self-reporting schemes that primarily further noncriminal regulatory objectives.[86] But where there is a "real and appreciable" threat of incrimination, the privilege will apply.[87]

§ 5.14.3 *Assertion in Civil or Criminal Proceeding*

Although the privilege protects only against disclosures that might be used in a criminal proceeding, it can be asserted in any proceeding, civil or criminal, administrative or judicial, investigatory or adjudicatory.[88] The privilege also extends to a person subjected to custodial interrogation by law enforcement officials.[89]

Recognizing that the issuance of a summons to appear and testify before a grand jury is a form of compulsion, the Supreme Judicial Court has recently adopted (pursuant to its supervisory power) a rule requiring

---

[86] See, e.g., *California v. Byers*, 402 US 424, 433-444 (1971) (statute requiring motorist involved in accident to stop and furnish name and address does not violate privilege even though information could lead to prosecution) and *Com. v. Joyce*, 326 Mass 751, 97 NE2d 192 (1950) (same).

[87] See *Com. v. Sasu*, 404 Mass 596, 600-601, 536 NE2d 603, 605-606 (1989) (while criminal charges stemming from accident were pending against defendant and information requested on accident report included identity of operator, which was essential element of Commonwealth's case against him, furnishing of any information on report would have constituted "a link in the chain of evidence needed to prosecute"). See also *Leary v. United States*, 395 US 6, 16 (1969) (requirement to complete a tax form on the transfer of marijuana violates the privilege); *Grosso v. United States*, 390 US 62 (1968) (requirement to file form and pay excise tax on gambling proceeds violates privilege); *Marchetti v. United States*, 390 US 39 (1968) (required registration of persons liable for occupational tax relating to gambling violates privilege); *Albertson v. Subversive Activities Control Board*, 382 US 70 (1965) (required registration of members of Communist Party violates privilege).

[88] *Kastigar v. United States*, 406 US 441, 444 (1972). See also *United States v. Washington*, 431 US 181, 186 (1977); *Malloy v. Hogan*, 378 US 1, 11 (1964) (state gambling investigation); *Watkins v. United States*, 354 US 178, 188, 77 S Ct 1173, 1 L Ed 2d 1273 (1957) (congressional committee investigation); *In the Matter of a John Doe Grand, Jury Investigation*, 418 Mass 549, 551, 637 NE2d 858, 860 (1994) (grand jury); *Com. v. Tewolde*, 88 Mass App 423, 434-435, 38 NE3d 1027, 1037 (2015) (judge erred in determining defendant did not have privilege in grand jury proceeding because the incriminatory potential of the questions was apparent); *Wansong v. Wansong*, 395 Mass 154, 157, 478 NE2d 1270 (1985) (civil action); *Attorney General v. Colleton*, 387 Mass 790, 794, 444 NE2d 915, 917 (1982) (civil investigative demand by Attorney General).

[89] See *Miranda v. Arizona*, discussed in § 12.6, infra.

> that where, at the time a person appears to testify before a grand jury, the prosecutor has reason to believe that the witness is either a "target" or is likely to become one, the witness must be advised, before testifying, that (1) he or she may refuse to answer any question if a truthful answer would tend to incriminate the witness, and (2) anything that he or she does say may be used against the witness in a subsequent legal proceeding.[90]

Unlike a criminal case, invocation of the privilege in a civil case may result in sanctions against the litigant.[91] In determining the effect the claim of privilege should have on the case, "[t]he judge's task is to balance any prejudice to the other civil litigants which might result . . . against the potential harm to the party claiming the privilege if he is compelled to choose between defending the civil action and protecting himself from criminal prosecution."[92]

§ 5.14.4 *Required Records Exception*

A "required records" exception has been read into both the Fifth Amendment and art. 12 privileges, and applies where:

1. the purpose of the official inquiry is essentially regulatory;
2. the records sought are of a kind that the regulated party must customarily keep; and
3. the records themselves have assumed "public aspects" such that they are analogous to public documents.[93]

---

[90] *Com. v. Woods*, 466 Mass 707, 719-720, 1 NE3d 762, 772 (2013).

[91] See *Department of Revenue v. B. P.*, 412 Mass 1015, 1016, 593 NE2d 1305, 1306 (1992) (because paternity action is civil, compelling putative father to submit to testing or be subject to sanctions would not violate privilege against self-incrimination); *Wansong v. Wansong*, supra, 395 Mass at 157-158 (judge did not abuse discretion by dismissing plaintiff's complaint for divorce and imposing other discovery sanctions for plaintiff's refusal at deposition to answer questions about relationship with another woman).

[92] *Wansong v. Wansong*, supra, 395 Mass at 157-158 (citations omitted).

[93] See *In re Kenney*, 399 Mass 431, 437-442, 504 NE2d 652, 656-658 (1987) (enforcement of subpoena requiring attorney to produce certain records would not infringe on right against compulsory self-incrimination because documents met test for "required records"); *Stornanti v. Com.*, 389 Mass 518, 521-522, 451 NE2d 707, 710 (1983) (records required to be maintained by pharmacy under Medicaid program not privileged); *Metro Equipment Corp. v. Com.*, 74 Mass App 63, 68, 904 NE2d 432, 438-440 (2009) (payroll records requested by Attorney General under Minimum Fair Wage Law).

In such situations, there is said to be no compelled self-incrimination.[94]

§ 5.14.5 *Who May Claim the Privilege*

The privilege against self-incrimination is personal and may not be asserted by another party; thus, a defendant has no standing at trial to challenge a ruling of the judge regarding whether a witness has a valid privilege.[95]

Similarly, where the individual's papers are produced by a third party, the privilege does not apply because a "party is privileged from producing the evidence but not from its production."[96] A reciprocal discovery order requiring defendant to disclose statements of Commonwealth's witnesses does not implicate his right against self-incrimination.[97]

The Fifth Amendment privilege protects only natural persons, not organizations or corporations. Thus, the federal privilege cannot

---

[94] *In re Kenney*, supra, 399 at Mass 442, 504 NE2d at 658.

[95] *Com. v. Morganti*, 455 Mass 388, 403-404, 917 NE2d 191, 204-205 (2009); *Com. v. Molina*, 454 Mass 232, 238, 909 NE2d 19, 25 (2009); *Com. v. Simpson*, 370 Mass 119, 121, 345 NE2d 899, 902 (1976), *habeas denied*, *Simpson v. Matesanz*, 175 F3d 200 (1st Cir 1999); *Com. v. Lopez*, 87 Mass App 642, 649, 34 NE3d 750, 756 (2015) (defendant had no standing to assert that grand jury witness should have been provided counsel to advise him about the privilege). See also *Com. v. Smith*, 456 Mass 476, 488, 924 NE2d 270, 281 (2010) (a defendant lacks standing to challenge the Commonwealth's grant of immunity to a witness; see § 5.14.7(b), infra).

Nor is a defendant or counsel entitled to disclosure of the witness's testimony from an in camera hearing to determine whether the witness had a valid privilege. *Pixley v. Com.*, 453 Mass 827, 906 NE2d 320 (2009) (defense witness who asserted privilege). See also *Com. v. Martin*, 423 Mass 496, 668 NE2d 825 (1996). Similarly, a defendant has no right to review the transcript of the pretrial hearing at which a trial court rules that a witness did not have a valid Fifth Amendment privilege to avoid testifying before a grand jury. *Com. v. Clemente*, 452 Mass 295, 317-318, 893 NE2d 19, 40 (2008).

Where a trial judge rules that a defense witness has a valid privilege and excuses him from testifying, however, defendant has standing to challenge the merits of that ruling in his direct appeal. *Pixley v. Com.*, supra, 453 Mass at 833, 906 NE2d at 326.

[96] *Johnson v. United States*, 228 US 457, 458 (1913). See also *Fisher v. United States*, 425 US 391 (1976) (attorney could not claim privilege for tax records entrusted him by client); *Couch v. United States*, 409 US 322, 327-329 (1973) (no violation of privilege where petitioner's records were summoned from his accountant); *In re Grand Jury Subpoena (Mr. S)*, 662 F3d 65 (1st Cir 2011) (files subpoenaed from attorney were not subject to protection under client's Fifth Amendment privilege against self-incrimination, although they may fall within the attorney-client privilege).

[97] See *Com. v. Durham*, 446 Mass 212, 226-227, 843 NE2d 1035, 1046 (2006).

be claimed by an individual to avoid production of the records of an organization that he holds in a representative capacity as agent or custodian, even if the production may incriminate him.[98] Although a custodian may not resist a subpoena for corporate records on Fifth Amendment grounds, he may nonetheless claim the privilege to avoid giving oral testimony that might incriminate him, including answering questions concerning the whereabouts of the records.[99]

In *Com. v. Doe,*[100] however, the Supreme Judicial Court expanded the custodian's protection under the state constitution. Rejecting the "fiction" that the custodian acts only as a representative of the entity and thus cannot claim the privilege regarding the entity's papers, the Court held:

> The act of production is demanded *of the witness* and the possibility of self-incrimination is inherent in that act. The witness's status as a representative does not alter the fact that in so far as he is a natural person he is entitled to the protection of art. 12. It would be factually unsound to hold that requiring *the witness* to furnish corporate records, the act of which would incriminate him, is not *his act.* [The witness's] status as custodian of the corporation's records does not require that he lose his individual privilege under art. 12.[101]

Thus, the sole stockholder and custodian of corporate records in *Doe* could not be held in contempt for invoking his privilege under art. 12 in refusing to produce corporate documents that were asserted to be incriminatory.[102]

The personal privilege against self-incrimination possessed by individual representatives of a corporation does not extend to the corporation's papers and records. That privilege protects only those

---

[98] *Braswell v. United States,* 487 US 99 (1988) (custodian of corporate records; extensive discussion); *Bellis v. United States,* 417 US 85 (1974) (records of law firm partnership); *Campbell Painting Corp. v. Reid,* 392 US 286 (1968) (corporation cannot invoke privilege); *Rogers v. United States,* 340 US 367 (1951) (petitioner could not claim privilege with respect to books and records of Communist Party that she held in representative capacity, even though production might incriminate her personally); *In re Hampers,* 651 F2d 19 (1st Cir 1981) (state commissioner of revenue had no privilege to refuse production of state sales tax records); *In the Matter of a John Doe Grand Jury Investigation,* 418 Mass 549, 552, 637 NE2d 858, 860 (1994).

[99] *Braswell v. United States,* supra, 487 US at 113-114; *Curcio v. United States,* 354 US 118, 122-125,(1957).

[100] 405 Mass 676, 679, 544 NE2d 860, 862 (1989).

[101] 405 Mass at 679-680, 544 NE2d at 862.

[102] 405 Mass at 681, 544 NE2d at 863.

papers that are the private property of the person claiming the privilege, or in the possession of such person in a purely private capacity. The custodian retains the privilege against self-incrimination by compelled oral testimony and by an act of production, but the corporate records themselves are outside the protection.[103] If the custodian of the corporate records cannot produce the records without implicating his or her personal art. 12 rights, an alternate keeper of the records can be appointed to do so.[104]

Finally, even where *the contents* of the records sought are not protected, there are certain situations where the *act of producing them* is deemed "testimonial incrimination," and thus the Fifth Amendment is applicable.[105]

§ 5.14.6 Claim of the Privilege

The Fifth Amendment privilege against compelled self-incrimination is not self-executing; it may not be relied upon unless it is invoked in a timely fashion.[106] A "witness must claim his privilege in the outset, when the testimony he is about to give, will, if he answers

---

[103] *In the Matter of a John Doe Grand Jury Investigation*, supra, 418 Mass at 552-553, 637 NE2d at 861. See also *Metro Equipment Corp. v. Com.*, 74 Mass App 63, 68-69, 904 NE2d 432, 438-439 (2009) (payroll records requested by Attorney General under Minimum Fair Wage Law came within required records exception and thus custodian had no testimonial privilege).

[104] *In the Matter of a John Doe Grand Jury Investigation*, supra, 418 Mass at 554, 637 NE2d at 861.

[105] See *United States v. Hubbell*, 530 US 27, 35-37 (2000); *United States v. Doe*, 465 US 605 (1984) (because by producing business records, which were not themselves compelled testimony, owner would tacitly admit their existence and authenticity as well as his possession, act of producing documents was privileged and could not be compelled without a statutory grant of use immunity); *In re Grand Jury Investigation*, 470 Mass 399, 403, 22 NE3d 927, 931 (2015) (& citations) (law firm could not be compelled to produce cell phone containing documents and other materials turned over by client); *Com. v. Doe*, 405 Mass 676, 679, 544 NE2d 860, 862 (1989); *In re Kenney*, 399 Mass 431, 440-441, 504 NE2d 652, 658 (1987) ("Production of the documents is an admission that the records exist, that they are in the possession of the person and that they are authentic; such an admission could be incriminating."). See also § 5.14.2.

[106] *Roberts v. United States*, 445 US 552, 559 (1980); *Minnesota v. Murphy*, 465 US 420, 427-428 (1984). It has been suggested that one of the consequences of the broader protection of art. 12 of Massachusetts Declaration of Rights may include "the extent to which and the manner in which an applicant would have to assert the protection of art. 12, in contrast to the Fifth Amendment, in order to receive the benefit of her art. 12 rights." *Walden v. Board of Registration*, 395 Mass 263, 270 NE2d 665, 671 (1985). Nonetheless, art. 12 has not been held to be self-executing. See *Com. v. Harvey*, 397 Mass 351, 357 n.6, 491 NE2d 607, 611 n.6 (1986).

fully all that appertains to it, expose him to a criminal charge, and if he does not, he waives it altogether."[107]

Although a judge is not generally required by Massachusetts law to warn a witness at trial that he need not answer questions tending to incriminate him, in circumstances where the witness is ignorant, misinformed, or confused about his rights and there is danger to him in the testimony sought to be elicited, it is a "commendable practice" for the judge to intervene and advise the witness.[108] Where the witness is unrepresented and appears to need assistance, the better practice is to provide counsel to assist him.[109] The witness must himself claim the privilege, although in practice the witness's counsel (assuming the witness is represented) may usually claim the privilege for him.[110]

A claim of the privilege does not require any ritualistic formula or special combination of words. "Plainly a witness need not have the skill of a lawyer to invoke the protection of the Self-Incrimination Clause. If an objection to a question is made in any language that a [questioner] may reasonably be expected to understand as an attempt to invoke the privilege, it must be respected."[111]

A witness is not entitled to make a blanket assertion of the privilege, but should assert it with respect to particular questions and the possibly incriminating nature of each proposed question.[112]

Where it is known that a prosecution witness will claim the privilege in front of the jury, the witness should not be called to testify.

---

[107] *Com. v. Funches*, 379 Mass 283, 289, 397 NE2d 1097, 1100 (1979); *Com. v. Fallon*, 38 Mass App 366, 375, 648 NE2d 767, 773 (1995) (testimony from deposition and contempt hearing admissible in criminal case where defendant failed to assert privilege in previous proceedings).

[108] *Taylor v. Com.*, 369 Mass 183, 192, 338 NE2d 823, 828 (1975) (special caution is indicated where witness is juvenile). See also *Com. v. Slaney*, 345 Mass 135, 141-142, 185 NE2d 919, 924 (1962); *Com. v. LaFontaine*, 32 Mass App 529, 532, 591 NE2d 1103, 1105 (1992) (better practice is to dispense advice outside hearing of jury). But see *Webb v. Texas*, 409 US 95 (1972) (trial court's extended warning to defendant's only witness discouraged witness from testifying and deprived defendant of due process of law).

[109] See *Com. v. Funches*, supra, 379 Mass at 287, 397 NE2d at 1099; *Com. v. Holmes*, 34 Mass App 916, 609 NE2d 489 (1993) (no prejudicial error when judge interrupted testimony of defense witness at suppression hearing to appoint counsel to advise her of right against self-incrimination, with result that witness declined to testify any further and previous testimony was stricken).

[110] See *Jones v. Com.*, 327 Mass 491, 495 n.4, 99 NE2d 456, 458 n.4 (1951).

[111] *Quinn v. United States*, 349 US 155, 162-163 (1955). See also *Com. v. Dormady*, 423 Mass 190, 195, 667 NE2d 832, 835 (1996).

[112] *Com. v. Martin*, 423 Mass 496, 502, 668 NE2d 825, 830(1996); *Com. v. Sueiras*, 72 Mass App 439, 445, 892 NE2d 768, 774 (2008).

Questioning of a material witness in order to provoke a claim of privilege and thus raise improper inferences in the minds of the jurors constitutes prosecutorial misconduct necessitating reversal of the conviction.[113] Even in the absence of such misconduct there is reversible error "when the impression made on the jurors by the witness's demurral is thought to add the 'critical weight' that brings about the verdict of guilty."[114] In contrast, in a civil case a party may call a witness (even a party) knowing he will claim the privilege, and comment on the claim.[115]

Where there is doubt about what the prosecution witness will do, he may be called. "A prosecutor need not go on an assumption that a witness, if called, will balk at testifying, but may make the test by actually calling him."[116] The "sound practice," however, is to put the questions to the witness under oath in the absence of the jury in order to determine whether he or she should be called.[117] Reversal is not

---

[113] See *Com. v. Martin*, 372 Mass 412, 414, 362 NE2d 507, 508 (1977). But compare *Com. v. Phoenix*, 409 Mass 408, 428-429, 567 NE2d 193, 204-205 (1991) (although it may have been improper for judge to permit witness to claim privilege in front of jury, defendant suffered no prejudice since his theory was that witness had committed the crime charged). The courts have declined to adopt a corollary rule that would prohibit a jury from knowing that a witness was testifying despite the potential criminal ramifications of his testimony. See *Com. v. Oliveira*, 74 Mass App 49, 57-58, 904 NE2d 442, 449-450 (2009) (because of witness's inherent bias as a participant in the events giving rise to defendant's crime, his decision to testify despite possible criminal consequences provided proper rehabilitative evidence).

[114] *Com. v. Martin*, supra, 372 Mass at 414, 362 NE2d at 508; *Com. v. LaFontaine*, supra, 32 Mass App at 533, 591 NE2d at 1105-1106.

[115] See *Kaye v. Newhall*, 356 Mass 300, 305, 249 NE2d 583, 586 (1969) (& citations).

[116] *Com. v. Martin*, supra, 372 Mass at 420, 362 NE2d at 511. See also *Com. v. Fazio*, 375 Mass 451, 456, 378 NE2d 648, 652 (1978) ("The prosecutor was not obliged to guess at the time of his opening as to whether this previously cooperative individual would claim his Fifth Amendment privilege at trial, whether the claim ultimately would be upheld, and whether [the witness] would choose to suffer contempt rather than testify if the claim were not upheld.").

[117] *Com. v. Martin*, supra, 372 Mass at 421 n.17, 362 NE2d at 512 n.17; *Com. v. Fazio*, supra, 375 Mass at 460, 378 NE2d at 654; *Com. v. LaFontaine*, supra, 32 Mass App at 532-533, 591 NE2d at 1105-1106.

In the context of other privileges, the courts have not been as scrupulous. See, e.g., *Com. v. Kane*, 388 Mass 128, 135-140, 445 NE2d 598, 602-604 (1983) (no abuse of discretion where judge permitted prosecutor to question witness regarding conversation with defendant even though witness, a priest, had stated during voir dire that he would assert religious privilege; prosecutor could "reasonably have assumed that the priest might change his mind and testify, in light of the judge's admonishment"); *Com. v. DiPietro*, 373 Mass 369, 389, 367 NE2d 811, 823 (1977) ("The judge was not required to accept the defendant's statement that [the witness] would exercise the [spousal] privilege, [and]

required in every case where the jury hears a witness assert the privilege or otherwise refuse to testify.[118]

A criminal defendant has no right (either under the federal or state constitutions) to call a witness to the stand solely in order for the witness to invoke his privilege against self-incrimination, as the witness's invocation of the privilege would not furnish any probative evidence and would be likely to have an illegitimate impact on the jury's deliberations.[119] A trial judge may accept the representation of counsel that a prospective defense witness would assert the privilege.[120]

A defendant in a criminal trial effectively claims the privilege when he chooses not to testify, and no comment may be made upon or presumption drawn from this choice.[121]

§ 5.14.7 Overcoming the Privilege

When the privilege against self-incrimination applies, it may be overcome only by either: (1) a valid waiver of the privilege by the person who possesses it; or (2) a constitutionally adequate grant of immunity.[122]

---

the prosecutor was not precluded from calling her to the stand in the presence of the jury to inquire of her to the point where she claimed the privilege").

Proposed Mass R Evid 512(b) provides:

> **Claiming privilege without knowledge of jury.**
>
> In criminal cases tried to a jury, proceedings shall be conducted to the extent practicable, so as to facilitate the making of claims of privilege without the knowledge of the jury.

[118] See *Com. v. Fisher*, 433 Mass 340, 350, 742 NE2d 61, 70 (2001) (& citations).

[119] *Com. v. Gagnon*, 408 Mass 185, 194-198, 557 NE2d 728, 734-737 (1990); *Com. v. Hesketh*, 386 Mass 153, 155-160, 434 NE2d 1238, 1241-1243 (1982). See also *Com. v. Springfield Terminal Railway Co.*, 80 Mass App 22, 41-42, 951 NE2d 696, 712-713 (2011) (trial judge did not abuse her discretion by excluding potentially exculpatory out-of-court statements by defendant's corporate officer who asserted his Fifth Amendment privilege, where introduction would likely have placed his invocation before jury). Compare *Com. v. Rosario*, 444 Mass 550, 557-558, 829 NE2d 1135, 1141 (2005) (trial court erred in denying defendant's request to display alleged perpetrator before jury because it raised no problem of invocation of privilege).

[120] See *Com. v. Sanders*, 451 Mass 290, 294-296, 885 NE2d 105, 111-112 (2008) (witness was incarcerated out of state, and papers supported assertion of the privilege in that witness's testimony would implicate him in the murder). For a case asserting that police intimidated a defense witness into asserting his privilege, see *Com. v. McGee*, 467 Mass 141, 4 NE3d 258 (2014).

[121] See GL 233, § 20, Third, and § 5.14.8, infra.

[122] *Blaisdell v. Com.*, 372 Mass 753, 761, 364 NE2d 191, 198 (1977).

a. Waiver

An individual may waive the privilege expressly by affirmatively relinquishing the right against self-incrimination, as in the case of a *Miranda* waiver.[123] The term "waiver" as used in the context of self-incrimination also refers however to an implied waiver, or "waiver by testimony." This occurs when a witness who may claim the privilege does not do so and instead testifies or otherwise discloses the information.[124]

When a defendant in a criminal case voluntarily takes the stand, under Massachusetts law he waives his privilege against self-incrimination as to all facts relevant to the crime charged and thus renders himself open to cross-examination on such facts.[125] The defendant does not waive the privilege with respect to matters not pertinent to the issue, or improper for impeachment.[126] In the federal courts, the privilege is waived only as to matters reasonably related to the subject matter of direct examination.[127] The different approaches appear to reflect the distinction between the respective rules on the permissible scope of cross-examination.[128]

A defendant waives the self-incrimination privilege (as well as his psychotherapist-patient privilege, see § 5.5.2, supra) in his treatment records when he gives notice of his intent to offer expert testimony regarding his mental state and is thus subject to a court-ordered psychiatric examination.[129] A defendant may also be deemed to have waived the privilege when his own statements are offered into evidence by an expert on his behalf, as for example a psychiatrist testifying on the

---

[123] See § 12.6.4, supra.

[124] See generally *Garner v. United States*, 424 US 648, 653-654 (1976) (but noting that "waiver" is not appropriate term: if witness makes disclosures instead of claiming privilege, the government has not "compelled" him to incriminate himself); *Com. v. King*, 436 Mass 252, 258-261, 763 NE2d 1071, 1078-1079 (2002); *Com. v. Martin*, 423 Mass 496, 500, 668 NE2d 825, 829 (1996); *Taylor v. Com.*, 369 Mass 183, 189, 338 NE2d 823, 827-828 (1975).

[125] *Com. v. Judge*, 420 Mass 433, 445, 650 NE2d 1242, 1250 (1995) (privilege waived by testimony at suppression hearing as well as at trial); *Com. v. West*, 357 Mass 245, 249, 258 NE2d 22, 24 (1970), *overruled on other grounds Com. v. Maguire*,392 Mass 466, 467 NE2d 112 (1984); *Com. v. Mandile*, 17 Mass App 657, 661-662, 461 NE2d 838, 841 (1984). But see *Com. v. Poggi*, 53 Mass App 685, 687-688, 761 NE2d 983, 986 (2002) (defendant's desire to show jury tattoos was not "testimonial," and thus would not subject him to cross-examination).

[126] See *Com. v. Seymour*, 39 Mass App 672, 675-677, 660 NE2d 679, 681-682 (1996).

[127] See *Jenkins v. Anderson*, 447 US 231, 237 n.3 (1980) (& citations).

[128] See § 6.7, infra.

[129] *Com. v. Hanright*, 465 Mass 639, 989 NE2d 883 (2013).

issue of mental responsibility.[130] A defendant in a sexually dangerous person proceeding, however, has not injected his own mental state into the proceedings; rather, it is the Commonwealth that has done so by initiating the commitment proceedings and therefore the defendant has not waived his privilege and cannot be compelled (beyond examination by two "qualified examiners" pursuant to the statute) to be examined by the Commonwealth's own expert.[131]

A non-party witness who voluntarily testifies to a fact of an incriminating nature is held to have thereby waived his privilege as to subsequent questions seeking related facts.[132] Where the witness is ordered by the judge to answer after asserting his privilege, his answers do not waive the privilege.[133]

The doctrine of waiver by testimony is based on twin rationales: (1) that once a witness has testified to incriminating facts, there is little risk that further testimony about the same transaction will incriminate him further; and (2) that a witness should not be permitted unilaterally to select and choose which facts to reveal regarding the transaction.[134]

---

[130] See *Blaisdell v. Com.*, 372 Mass 753, 764-766, 364 NE2d 191, 197-200 (1977) (when defendant voluntarily submits to psychiatric examination and submits evidence of statements as basis for expert opinion, he waives privilege against self-incrimination with respect to court-ordered interrogation). See also *Com. v. Wayne*, 414 Mass 218, 226-232, 606 NE2d 1323, 1328-1332 (1993) (juvenile defendant who voluntarily chooses at transfer hearing to present expert psychiatric testimony that includes juvenile's own statements is not denied his constitutional privilege against self-incrimination if he is ordered to submit to examination by psychiatrist retained by Commonwealth); *Com. v. Connors*, 447 Mass 313, 319-320, 850 NE2d 1038, 1043 (2006) (defendant in SDP proceedings who seeks to present expert psychiatric evidence including his own statements is not denied his privilege against self-incrimination if he is required to submit to an examination by the Commonwealth's psychiatrist as a condition for admission of his evidence). For the privilege in competency evaluations, see *Seng v. Com.*, 445 Mass 536, 839 NE2d 283 (2005).

[131] *Com. v. Poissant*, 443 Mass 558, 564-566, 823 NE2d 350, 355-356 (2005).

[132] *Com. v. Martin*, supra, 423 Mass at 500, 668 NE2d at 829; *Com. v. Funches*, 379 Mass 283, 289-291, 397 NE2d 1097, 1100-1101 (1979).

[133] *Com. v. Leclair*, 469 Mass 777, 784-785, 17 NE3d 1415, 421 (2014). Similarly a witness who testifies involuntarily before the grand jury, after it is ruled that he has no valid privilege, does not thereby waive his privilege not to testify at trial. *Com. v. Clemente*, 452 Mass 295, 318 n.33, 893 NE2d 19, 40 n.33 (2008).

[134] *Taylor v. Com.*, supra, 369 Mass at 190, 338 NE2d at 828; *Com. v. King*, 436 Mass 252, 258-259, 763 NE2d 1071, 1078 (2002). See also *Loud v. Loud*, 386 Mass 473, 475-476, 436 NE2d 164, 166 (1982) (where husband chose to answer questions asked by wife's counsel about cohabitation with another woman, husband waived privilege for subsequent questions on same topic). See also *Com. v. Pelosi*, 55 Mass App 390, 397 n.11, 771 NE2d 795, 802 n.11 (2002), *remanded* 441 Mass 257, 805 NE2d 1 (2004) (doctrine of waiver by testimony in other privilege contexts).

In order for a waiver by testimony to occur, the witness must admit to at least one element of a crime.[135] Even when incriminating information is disclosed, however, there is no waiver as to further disclosures that pose a "real danger of legal detriment"—i.e., disclosures that would supply an additional link in the chain of evidence.[136] Moreover, by testifying with respect to one unlawful act, the witness does not thereby waive his privilege of refusing to reveal other unlawful acts.[137]

To constitute a valid waiver, the witness's testimony must have been given freely and voluntarily.[138] Waiver by testimony does not require that the witness's failure to invoke the privilege be knowing and

---

[135] *Com. v. Funches*, supra, 379 Mass at 291, 397 NE2d at 1101 (witness who testified that defendants had come to his house and told him they wanted to buy heroin had not admitted to element of crime and thus had not waived privilege). See also *McCarthy v. Arndstein*, 262 US 355, 359, 43 S Ct 562, 67 L Ed 1023 (1923) (if previous disclosure by witness is not incriminatory, he does not relinquish privilege of "stopping short in his testimony whenever it may fairly tend to incriminate him").

[136] *Com. v. Funches*, supra, 379 Mass at 290, 397 NE2d at 1101.

[137] *Com. v. Voisine*, 414 Mass 772, 784-785, 610 NE2d 926, 933 (1993) (witness who had pled guilty as accessory after fact to murder did not, by so pleading, waive privilege with respect to testifying in murder prosecution as to his own involvement in the murder, because testimony might furnish a link in chain of evidence needed to prosecute witness on additional charge as principal); *Com. v. Francis*, 375 Mass 211, 217, 375 NE2d 1221, 1225 (1978) (witness's testimony concerning breaking and entering did not constitute waiver of privilege for questions that would have incriminated him with respect to separate offenses of larceny and conspiracy).

[138] See *Garrity v. New Jersey*, 385 US 493 (1967) (where police officer testifies under threat of dismissal, testimony is not voluntary and thus inadmissible in subsequent criminal proceedings); *Com. v. Koonce*, 418 Mass 367, 378-379, 636 NE2d 1305, 1311 (1994) (witness's testimony at prior trial not voluntary because of his level of education and ignorance of the privilege); *Com. v. Ortiz*, 393 Mass 523, 530, 471 NE2d 1321, 1327 (1984) (juvenile did not waive privilege by testifying at prior hearing because testimony, against advice of counsel, not given freely and voluntarily); *Com. v. Turner*, 371 Mass 803, 810, 359 NE2d 626, 630-631 (1977) (witnesses who testified before grand jury about prior crimes in mistaken belief that crimes were within grant of immunity did not thereby waive privilege); *Taylor v. Com.*, supra, 369 Mass at 190-193, 338 NE2d at 827-829 (testimony of confused juvenile, unrepresented by counsel and not advised of rights by judge, "not so freely and voluntarily given as to effect a waiver of his privilege on later questioning"); *Com. v. Hammond*, 50 Mass App 171, 177, 736 NE2d 398, 403 (2000) (no waiver where recanting witness gave affidavit without consulting with counsel). Compare *Com. v. King*, 436 Mass 252, 259-260, 763 NE2d 1071, 1078 (2002) (victim's voluntary testimony at voir dire may have waived privilege for trial); *Com. v. Slonka*, 42 Mass App 760, 769, 680 NE2d 103, 109 (1997) (if witness's sworn statement to defense counsel about drug use with victim was given freely and voluntarily, then witness waived privilege); *Com. v. Weed*, 17 Mass App 463, 459 NE2d 144 (1984) (witness who testified at the grand jury after prosecutor had given her detailed recitation of rights had done so freely and voluntarily and thus could not invoke privilege at trial; but witness who had been misinformed by prosecuting attorney as to consequences of testimony before grand jury and at hearing on motion to suppress could not be deemed to have waived privilege).

intelligent; rather, waiver occurs where the prior incriminating testimony is given voluntarily.[139] A witness's ignorance of the privilege is a factor to be considered in determining whether the prior testimony was voluntarily given, but is not dispositive; and failure to advise the witness of the privilege does not in itself defeat a waiver.[140]

As a general rule waiver by testimony is limited to the proceeding in which it is given and does not extend to subsequent proceedings.[141] Testimony before a grand jury should not be considered a waiver of the witness's privilege against self-incrimination for the purpose of testifying at a subsequent trial on an indictment returned by that grand jury.[142] In certain circumstances where the witness testifies in a proceeding that was the "probable, logical, or natural continuation or outgrowth of the proceeding or inquiry" in which he previously waived the privilege, waiver by testimony may act as a continuing waiver as to matters previously addressed.[143] The admission of defendant's prior testimony from a previous trial against defendant at a subsequent trial does not implicate the privilege against self-incrimination.[144]

---

[139] *Com. v. King*, 436 Mass 252, 259-261, 763 NE2d 1071, 1078-1079 (2002).

[140] *Com. v. King*, supra (witness's testimony at voir dire may have waived her privilege despite failure of judge to advise her of privilege at start of voir dire testimony).

[141] *Com. v. King*, supra, 436 Mass at 258 n.6, 763 NE2d at 1078 n.6 (voir dire hearing held on day of trial is same proceeding); *Com. v. Borans*, 388 Mass 453, 457, 446 NE2d 703, 705 (1983) (witness's testimony at grand jury proceedings and at his own trial did not constitute waiver extending to his testimony at trial of another defendant); *Com. v. Sueiras*, 72 Mass App 439, 446, 892 NE2d 768, 775 (2008) (juveniles did not waive their right against self-incrimination at defendant's trial by testifying at their own show cause hearings); *Com. v. Fiore*, 53 Mass App 785, 789-790, 762 NE2d 905, 910 (2002) (since civil deposition was separate proceeding from criminal trial, no waiver).

[142] See *Com. v. Martin*, supra, 423 Mass at 500-501, 668 NE2d at 829-830. See also *Palaza v. Superior Court*, 393 Mass 1001, 464 NE2d 60 (1984).

[143] See *Com. v. Judge*, 420 Mass 433, 445,n.8, 650 NE2d 1242, 1250 n.8 (1995) (defendant who testified at suppression hearing waived privilege as if he had testified at trial); *Luna v. Superior Court*, 407 Mass 747, 751, 555 NE2d 881, 883 (1990) (prospective witness in criminal case who voluntarily submitted affidavit in conjunction with Commonwealth motion waived privilege against self-incrimination as to further proceedings in same case); *In re DeSaulnier (No. 2)*, 360 Mass 761, 765-766, 276 NE2d 278, 281 (1971) (indicating in dicta that witness who answered questions during preliminary inquiry on judicial misconduct could not assert privilege in later proceedings relating to same misconduct); *Com. v. Penta*, 32 Mass App 36, 44-46, 586 NE2d 996, 1001-1002 (1992) (prospective witness at criminal trial who voluntarily testified at two pretrial hearings involving same charges and same defendant waived privilege as to questions at trial seeking related facts).

[144] See *Com. v. Beauchamp*, 49 Mass App 591, 603-608, 732 NE2d 311, 323-326 (2000).

Unsworn statements made during police interrogation do not constitute "testimony" for purposes of the waiver doctrine so as to deprive the witness of the privilege during subsequent in-court testimony.[145] Nor do guilty pleas previously entered by the witness constitute "testimony."[146] Under federal law, neither a defendant's guilty plea nor statements at the plea colloquy function as a waiver of defendant's right to remain silent at sentencing proceedings.[147]

An individual undergoing police interrogation in custody does not waive the privilege by answering questions. He may claim the privilege at any stage of the interrogation; and if he indicates at any time prior to or during questioning that he wishes to remain silent or to consult with counsel, the interrogation must cease.[148]

An individual who asserts the privilege may, at a later time, waive it.[149]

b. Removal by Grant of Immunity/Corroboration Requirement

Neither a "practical unlikelihood of prosecution nor the prosecutor's denial of an intention to prosecute negates an otherwise proper invocation of the Fifth Amendment."[150] A constitutionally adequate grant of immunity does however bar the privilege and compel the testimony.[151]

The United States may compel testimony from an unwilling witness who invokes the Fifth Amendment privilege by conferring immunity pursuant to statute.[152] The immunity must be coextensive with the scope of the privilege, which has been held to require that the grant of immunity bar both the use and derivative use of the witness's testimony in any subsequent proceeding.[153]

---

[145] *Com. v. Dormady*, 423 Mass 190, 195 n.3, 667 NE2d 832, 835 n.3 (1996); *Taylor v. Com.*, supra, 369 Mass at 190-191, 338 NE2d at 828. See also *Com. v. Dias*, 451 Mass 463, 473-474, 886 NE2d 713, 722 (2008) (informant would not waive privilege by speaking with police).

[146] See *Com. v. Voisine*, 414 Mass 772, 784-785, 610 NE2d 926, 933 (1993).

[147] See *Mitchell v. United States*, 526 US 314 (1999).

[148] See § 12.6.1, infra.

[149] *Com. v. Barnes-Miller*, 59 Mass App 832, 834, 798 NE2d 569, 570 (2003).

[150] *Com. v. Borans*, 388 Mass 453, 459, 446 NE2d 703, 707 (1983).

[151] *United States v. Mandujano*, 425 US 564, 575 (1976).

[152] *Kastigar v. United States*, 406 US 441 (1972).

[153] *Kastigar v. United States*, supra, 406 US at 453 (transactional immunity, which completely bars prosecution for offense to which compelled testimony relates, is not constitutionally required).

The Commonwealth may compel testimony from an unwilling witness who invokes the privilege by conferring immunity in the manner prescribed by GL 233, §§ 20C-20I.[154] Article 12 of the Declaration of Rights of the Massachusetts Constitution has been read to require a broader grant of immunity than the Fifth Amendment. Thus a witness's privilege can be displaced only by a grant of transactional immunity, which bars prosecution for offenses to which the compelled testimony relates.[155] The statutory scheme provides for such transactional immunity.[156] Where immunity has been granted, a refusal to testify may result in a citation for contempt.[157]

A justice of the Supreme Judicial Court, Appeals Court, or Superior Court[158] may, upon request of the attorney general or a district attorney[159] and after a hearing, grant immunity for enumerated

---

[154] The Supreme Judicial Court has held that the statute "covers the entire subject of immunity," at least for witnesses in the specified proceedings, and has refused to recognize an inherent common-law authority of the Attorney General or a district attorney to grant immunity. See *Com. v. Dalrymple*, 428 Mass 1014, 1015-1016, 699 NE2d 344, 345-346 (1998) (& citations). GL 233, § 20F, relating to superior court orders granting immunity to witnesses in criminal proceedings, was repealed by St. 1988, c. 188, § 5.

[155] For comparison of the Commonwealth and federal immunities, see *In re Vaccari*, 460 Mass 756, 955 NE2d 266 (2011) (the fact that an effective state grant of transactional immunity only translates into use and derivative use immunity for federal purposes does not prevent an immunized person from being compelled to answer questions at state trial); *Com. v. Dormady*, 423 Mass 190, 194, 667 NE2d 832, 835 (1996) (transactional immunity required to compel police officer to answer questions during internal affairs investigation); *Attorney General v. Colleton*, 387 Mass 790, 444 NE2d 915 (1982) (immunity granted by GL 93A, § 6(7) is inadequate under art. 12 because it provides only use immunity).

[156] See GL 233, § 20G:

> A witness who has been granted immunity as provided [by this statute] shall not be prosecuted or subjected to any penalty or forfeiture for or on account of any transaction matter, or thing concerning which he is so compelled, after having claimed his privilege against self-incrimination, to testify or produce evidence, nor shall testimony so compelled be used as evidence in any criminal or civil proceeding against him in any court of the commonwealth, except in a prosecution for perjury or contempt committed while giving testimony or producing evidence under compulsion. . . .

See also *In re Pressman*, 421 Mass 514, 516, 658 NE2d 156, 158 (1995); *In re a John Doe Grand Jury Investigation*, 405 Mass 125, 129, 539 NE2d 56, 58 (1989).

[157] GL 233, § 20H. See, e.g., *Com. v. Santaniello*, 369 Mass 606, 341 NE2d 259 (1976).

[158] Judges in Juvenile Court do not have power to grant immunity to a witness. See *Com. v. Russ R.*, 433 Mass 515, 744 NE2d 39 (2001).

[159] An application for immunity may be signed by an assistant district attorney or assistant attorney general as well. See *Lindegren v. Com.*, 427 Mass 696, 695 NE2d 207 (1998).

crimes[160] to a witness called before a grand jury or criminal proceeding.[161] The district attorney has no power to grant immunity; therefore his assurance of immunity does not remove the privilege.[162] The district attorney does, however, have authority to withdraw charges and to thereby in effect confer immunity within his district.[163] Moreover, where a witness reasonably relies on a prosecutor's promise of immunity, the courts will enforce the promise to the same extent as a formal grant of immunity.[164]

Before a judge may grant immunity under the statutory scheme it must be found that the witness validly refused to answer questions or produce evidence on the ground that such testimony might tend to incriminate him.[165] The Supreme Judicial Court has rejected the contention that the Commonwealth must make an additional showing that the testimony sought is necessary to its investigation, although it has suggested that "certain rare circumstances may arise where the relevancy of a particular line of questioning may be slight or nonexistent, and where the need for the testimony may be outweighed by legitimate privacy interests."[166]

Under GL 233, § 20E, only the prosecutor may request an order of immunity. Accordingly, the defendant has no right under the statute to an order granting immunity to one of his witnesses.[167] Although the Supreme Judicial Court has acknowledged that in some unique circumstances "due process may require the granting by a judge of a

---

[160] The crimes as to which the witness is immunized are not only those crimes listed in § 20D but also any crime related to a transaction about which the witness is compelled to testify. See *In re a John Doe Grand Jury Investigation*, supra, 405 Mass at 129, 539 NE2d at 58-59 (defining the scope of transactional immunity). Immunity may only be granted to a grand jury witness when the grand jury is investigating one or more of the enumerated crimes. See *Petition of the District Attorney for the Plymouth District*, 391 Mass 723, 726-727, 464 NE2d 62, 65 (1984).

[161] GL 233, § 20D, 20E.

[162] *Grand Jurors for Middlesex County for the Year 1974 v. Wallace*, 369 Mass 876, 343 NE2d 844 (1976) (grand jury witnesses not required to testify on being given written offer of immunity signed by assistant district attorney).

[163] *Baglioni v. Chief of Police of Salem*, 421 Mass 229, 233, 656 NE2d 1223, 1225 (1995).

[164] See *Com. v. Dormady*, 423 Mass 190, 196-198, 667 NE2d 832, 836-837 (1996); *In re DeSaulnier (No. 2)*, 360 Mass 761, 764, 276 NE2d 278, 280 (1971). See also *Grand Jurors for Middlesex County for the Year 1974 v. Wallace*, supra, 369 Mass at 880, 343 NE2d at 845-846.

[165] GL 233, § 20E.

[166] *Petition of the District Attorney for the Plymouth District*, 395 Mass 1005, 1006, 479 NE2d 1370, 1371 (1985) (& citations).

[167] *Com. v. Curtis*, 388 Mass 637, 643, 448 NE2d 345, 348-349 (1983).

limited form of immunity" to a defense witness,[168] it has declined to recognize a defendant's constitutional right to such a judicial grant of immunity.[169] As of yet, the Court had not been presented with such a unique circumstance.[170] The Court has upheld the constitutionality of the immunity scheme.[171]

A defendant in federal court similarly has no right to obtain immunity for a defense witness, nor has the federal district court the general power to grant such immunity or order the government to request it.[172] In certain narrow circumstances, however, it has been held that the federal defendant's constitutional right to a fair trial may require that his witness be granted immunity.[173]

Although the assertion by a witness of his Fifth Amendment right may impair a defendant's ability to present an effective defense, the question whether to seek a grant of immunity "primarily involves

---

[168] *Com. v. Curtis*, supra, 388 Mass at 646, 448 NE2d at 350 (but Commonwealth established that it had a strong interest in opposing grant of immunity to witness who was potential suspect in continuing investigation); *Pixley v. Com.*, 453 Mass 827, 834 n.7, 906 NE2d 320, 326 n.7 (2009).

[169] *Com. v. Doherty*, 394 Mass 341, 343-346, 476 NE2d 169, 173 (1985) (barring unique circumstances, "any inquiry into the question of immunity is foreclosed if the prospective witness is an actual or potential target of prosecution"). See also *Com. v. Drew*, 447 Mass 635, 644-645, 856 NE2d 808, 816-817 (2006) (witness would not have been entitled to judicial immunity because her proffered testimony was cumulative and not exculpatory); *Com. v. Reynolds*, 429 Mass 388, 400, 708 NE2d 658, 667-668 (1999) (proffered testimony was not clearly exculpatory); *Com. v. Grimshaw*, 412 Mass 505, 512, 590 NE2d 681, 685-686 (1992) (fact that case involved battered-woman-syndrome defense did not create unique circumstance); *Com. v. Upton*, 390 Mass 562, 575-577, 458 NE2d at 725-726 (no showing that judicial grant of immunity was constitutionally required); *Com. v. Toney*, 385 Mass 575, 587-588, 433 NE2d 425, 433 (1982) (no showing that witness if called would invoke privilege or would testify to exculpatory facts); *Com. v. Cash*, 64 Mass App 812, 816-818, 836 NE2d 318, 322 (2005) (witness's recantation would be equivocal at best and only marginally exculpatory). Cf. *Com. v. Turner*, 393 Mass 685, 473 NE2d 679 (1985) (no substantial risk of miscarriage of justice in permitting two prosecution witnesses, defendant's alleged accomplices whose direct testimony was under grant of immunity, to invoke privilege against self-incrimination during cross-examination by defense counsel because testimony would have been collateral and cumulative).

[170] *Com. v. Vacher*, 469 Mass 425, 439, 14 NE3d 264, 277 (2014); *Com. v. Brewer*, 472 Mass 307, 311-314, 34 NE3d 314, 317-320 (2015) (no unique circumstances were found).

[171] *Id.*, 469 Mass at 441, 14 NE3d at 278.

[172] *United States v. Davis*, 623 F2d 188, 192-193 (1st Cir 1980).

[173] See *United States v. Davis*, supra, 623 F2d at 193 (& cases cited) (but no such showing where witness's testimony went merely to credibility of prosecution witness and was cumulative); *United States v. Drape*, 668 F2d 22, 26-27 (1st Cir 1982) (but no showing that witness's evidence would have been exculpatory and essential to defense).

public interest considerations best evaluated by the prosecutor."[174] A defendant lacks standing to challenge a grant of immunity to a prosecution witness,[175] and has no right to participate in the immunity hearing.[176]

A state witness may not be compelled to give testimony that may be incriminating under federal law unless the compelled testimony and its fruits cannot be used in any manner by federal officials in connection with a criminal prosecution against him.[177] The federal government is not required to grant transactional immunity to a Massachusetts witness on grounds that the Commonwealth would grant the broader immunity.[178]

Testimony given by a witness immunized pursuant to GL 233, §§ 20C-20I may not be used against him (for either substantive or impeachment purposes) in any criminal or civil proceeding in the Commonwealth,[179] except in a prosecution for perjury or contempt committed while giving testimony or producing evidence under compulsion.[180]

Nor may the immunized testimony be used against him in a prosecution in any other jurisdiction in the United States.[181] Testimony

---

[174] *Com. v. Curtis*, supra, 388 Mass at 645-646, 448 NE2d at 350. See also *Com. v. Pennellatore*, 392 Mass 382, 389, 467 NE2d 820, 824-825 (1984); *Com. v. Wooden*, 70 Mass App 185, 190-191, 873 NE2d 764, 769 (2007).

[175] *Com. v. Vacher*, supra, 469 Mass at 438-439, 14 NE3d at 277; *Com. v. Smith*, 456 Mass 476, 488, 924 NE2d 270, 281 (2010); *Com. v. Figueroa*, 451 Mass 566, 578, 887 NE2d 1041, 1049 (2008).

[176] *Com. v. Mercado*, 466 Mass 141, 150-152, 993 NE2d 661, 669-670 (2013) (judge properly closed hearing).

[177] *Murphy v. Waterfront Commission of New York*, 378 US 52, 79 (1964). See also *Com. v. Stone*, 369 Mass 965, 341 NE2d 284 (1976) (nothing that immunized witness may say before Hampden County grand jury could be used against him in federal proceeding).

[178] *In re Bianchi*, 542 F2d 99, 101 (1st Cir 1976); *Baglioni v. Chief of Police of Salem*, supra, 421 Mass at 234, 656 NE2d at 1226 (fact that state grant of transactional immunity only translates into use immunity for federal purposes does not preclude compelling person to answer questions).

[179] GL 233, § 20G; *New Jersey v. Portash*, 440 US 450 (1979). See also *Pillsbury Co. v. Conboy*, 459 US 248, 103 S Ct 608, 74 L Ed 2d 430 (1983) (grant of use immunity to grand jury witness did not preclude him from asserting Fifth Amendment privilege in deposition in subsequent civil case, even though deposition testimony sought closely tracked prior immunized testimony).

[180] GL 233, § 20G; *United States v. Apfelbaum*, 445 US 115 (1980) (if any part of immunized testimony is false, witness's entire testimony may be used against him at perjury trial); *In re Vaccari*, 460 Mass 756, 761, 955 NE2d 266, 270 (2011).

[181] *Com. v. Steinberg*, 404 Mass 602, 607, 536 NE2d 606, 610 (1989).

given pursuant to an immunity agreement in another jurisdiction may be used in non-criminal proceedings in the Commonwealth.[182]

A proper grant of immunity pursuant to the Massachusetts statute protects the witness from prosecution on the basis of the immunized testimony in any court of the Commonwealth, including the Juvenile Court.[183]

Under Massachusetts law a conviction cannot be based solely on the testimony of an immunized witness, and the judge should so instruct the jury.[184] The corroboration required need not be proof of defendant's actual participation in the crime; it need only provide support for the credibility of the immunized witness.[185] To provide the requisite credibility "there must be some evidence in support of the testimony of an immunized witness on at least one element of proof essential to convict the defendant."[186] The Supreme Judicial Court has refused to extend the corroboration requirement to testimony provided pursuant to an informal nonprosecution agreement.[187] The corroboration requirement does not apply to *non*-immunized witnesses and has not been so extended by the courts.[188]

---

[182] See *In re Pressman*, 421 Mass 514, 658 NE2d 156 (1995), 421 Mass 514, 658 NE2d 156 (federal grant of immunity to attorney does not foreclose use of immunized testimony in Massachusetts bar disciplinary proceeding); *Adoption of Astrid*, 45 Mass App 538, 543-544, 700 NE2d 275, 279 (1998) (statement given by mother in her home state under immunity agreement could be admitted in child custody proceeding in Commonwealth).

[183] *Com. v. Austin A.*, 450 Mass 665, 881 NE2d 117 (2008).

[184] See GL 233, § 20I. See also *Com. v. Shaheen*, 15 Mass App 302, 305-306, 445 NE2d 619, 622 (1983) (& cases cited). For discussion of the jury instructions to be given regarding an immunized witness, see *Com. v. Foxworth*, 473 Mass 149, 162, 40 NE3d 1003, 1014-1015 (2015) (judge was not required to instruct that jury should scrutinize immunized witness's testimony with great care if the government was not vouching for the witness's truthfulness); *Com. v. Gagliardi*, 29 Mass App 225, 240-242, 559 NE2d 1234 (1990); *Com. v. Kindell*, 44 Mass App 200, 207, 689 NE2d 845, 850 (1998).

[185] *Com. v. Fernandes*, 425 Mass 357, 681 NE2d 270 (1997); *Com. v. Asmeron*, 70 Mass App 667, 875 NE2d 870 (2007) (corroboration of juvenile witness in prostitution case).

[186] *Id.*, 425 Mass at 360, 681 NE2d at 272; *Com. v. Vacher*, 469 Mass 425, 440, 14 NE3d 264, 278 (2014).

[187] *Com. v. Thomas*, 439 Mass 362, 371-372, 787 NE2d 1047, 1056-1057 (2003) (but judges are encouraged to instruct juries to scrutinize the testimony of accomplices).

[188] See *Com. v. Davis*, 52 Mass App 75, 79-80, 751 NE2d 420, 424 (2001).

§ 5.14.8 Comment upon and Adverse Inference from Claim of Privilege

In a civil case, a party's claim of the privilege against self-incrimination can be commented upon by opposing counsel and an inference adverse to the party may properly be drawn.[189] Such an inference may be drawn against an employer where its employee has invoked the privilege,[190] and in certain circumstances against a litigant as a result of the invocation of the privilege by a nonparty witness.[191] A negative inference may be drawn against a party who fails to testify in a child custody proceeding,[192] and against the defendant from his failure to testify in an abuse prevention order proceeding.[193] Such adverse inference alone, however, cannot meet the opponent's burden.[194]

In a criminal case, the failure of the defendant to take the stand is not a proper subject for comment and "shall not create any presumption against him."[195] The Supreme Court elevated this rule to constitutional status and made it applicable to the states as well as the federal government in *Griffin v. California*.[196]

---

[189] *Frizado v. Frizado*, 420 Mass 592, 596, 651 NE2d 1206, 1210 (1995) (inference adverse to defendant may properly be drawn in domestic abuse prevention case, even if criminal proceedings are pending or might be brought); *Quintal v. Commissioner of Department of Employment & Training*, 418 Mass 855, 861, 641 NE2d 1338, 1342 (1994); *Department of Revenue v. B. P.*, 412 Mass 1015, 593 NE2d 1305 (1992) (& citations).

[190] See *Shafnacker v. Raymond James & Associates*, 425 Mass 724, 735-736, 683 NE2d 662, 670 (1997) (& citations).

[191] See *Lentz v. Metropolitan Property & Casualty Ins. Co.*, 437 Mass 23, 786 NE2d 538 (2002) (where adjuster and body shop employee invoked privilege at trial of claim against automobile insurer, jury could properly draw inference against plaintiff that all three collaborated in false claim, and judge properly so instructed; extensive discussion of topic).

[192] *Care & Protection of Quinn*, 54 Mass App 117, 123, 763 NE2d 573, 579 (2002). See also *In re Care & Protection Summons*, 437 Mass 224, 235, 770 NE2d 456, 466 (2002).

[193] *S.T. v. E.M.*, 80 Mass App 423, 429, 953 NE2d 269, 274 (2011); *Adoption of Cecily*, 83 Mass App 719, 727, 989 NE2d 532, 539 (2013).

[194] See *Frizado v. Frizado*, supra, 420 Mass at 596; *C.O. v. M.M.*, 442 Mass 648, 655, 815 NE2d 582, 589 (2004); *Scully v. Retirement Board of Beverly*, 80 Mass App 538, 544-545, 954 NE2d 541, 546 (2011).

[195] GL 233, § 20, Third. See generally *Com. v. Paradiso*, 368 Mass 205, 211, 330 NE2d 825, 828-829 (1975) (GL 233, § 20 must be read in conjunction with art. 12 of Declaration of Rights).

[196] 380 US 609 (1965). See also *Roberts v. United States*, 445 US 552(1980) (suggesting that judge, when sentencing, may not draw adverse inference from the defendant's refusal to assist in criminal investigation if failure is justified by timely claim of privilege against self-incrimination).

A comment is improper if it is reasonably susceptible of being interpreted as a comment on the defendant's failure to take the stand.[197] The prosecutor is permitted to emphasize the strong points of the Commonwealth's case and the weaknesses of the defendant's even though that may prompt some collateral reflection on the fact that the defendant declined to testify.[198]

Although a prosecutor may, when persuasive reasons exist, generally suggest a negative inference from a defendant's failure to offer evidence on a critical issue (see § 3.6, supra), the prosecutor may not comment upon the failure to admit evidence or to provide an explanation for the failure if such remarks could be taken as comments on defendant's right to silence and shift the burden of proof.[199]

---

[197] See *Com. v. Phoenix*, 409 Mass 408, 427, 567 NE2d 193, 203 (1991) (prosecutor's suggestion that defendant offered no proof of alibi); *Com. v. Sherick*, 401 Mass 302, 304-305, 516 NE2d 157, 158 (1987) (extensive discussion). Compare *Com. v. Gomes*, 443 Mass 502, 509-510, 822 NE2d 720, 726 (2005), *habeas denied*, 564 F3d 532 (1st Cir 2009) (prosecutor's remark that "the only one in this courtroom that I've heard say that it wasn't this [murder] defendant" was defense counsel was improper), *Com. v. Young*, 399 Mass 527, 505 NE2d 186 (1987) (prosecutor's closing argument which urged jury to draw inferences adverse to defendant because he sat impassively at trial was prejudicial and required reversal), *Com. v. Smith*, 387 Mass 900, 908-909, 444 NE2d 374, 381 (1983) (impermissible reference to defendant's silence at trial), and *Com. v. Botelho*, 87 Mass App 846, 852-853, 35 NE3d 417, 423-424 (2015) (prosecutor's comment that "the only testimony you heard from [regarding OUI defendant's intoxication] was [the police officer]" was improper as focusing the jury's attention on defendant's failure to testify), with *Com. v. Pena*, 455 Mass 1, 17-19, 913 NE2d 815, 828-829 (2009) (prosecutor's remarks were not comment on defendant's failure to testify, but directed at the absence of evidence of motive for the murder), *Com. v. Whitman*, 453 Mass 331, 346-348, 901 NE2d 1206, 1219-1220 (2009) (prosecutor's statement that defendant "didn't tell us" what his motive was for attacking victims, although appearing to be a comment on defendant's failure to testify, in context referred instead to his statement to police), *Com. v. Morales*, 440 Mass 536, 550-551, 800 NE2d 683, 695-696 (2003) (prosecutor's comment did not refer to defendant's failure to testify but to fact that in statement to police at time of arrest he never mentioned self-defense), *Com. v. Grant*, 418 Mass 76, 82-83, 634 NE2d 565, 569-570 (1994) (prosecutor's rhetorical questions inviting jurors to examine defendant's intent at time of shooting did not improperly focus attention on defendant's silence at trial), *Com. v. Walker*, 413 Mass 552, 560, 600 NE2d 583, 588 (1992) (comment by prosecutor as to who might be able to tell jury about what happened at murder scene was at worst oblique reference to defendant and was remedied by judge's instruction). See also § 13.2, infra.

[198] *Com. v. Elliott*, 87 Mass App 520, 525, 32 NE3d 345, 350-351 (2015) (comment "where's the evidence that this was a consensual affair? Where was it presented in this courtroom? There's nothing, nada, zip, zilch, zero evidence that this was consensual" did not improperly comment on rape defendant's failure to testify).

[199] See *Com. v. Elliott*, supra; *Com. v. Gaynor*, 443 Mass 245, 271-272, 820 NE2d 233, 255 (2005) (testimony of prosecution experts that DNA evidence had been preserved and was available for testing by defendant was a "sensitive area," but did not

"References to material facts as uncontradicted or uncontested invariably approach the border of the forbidden territory of speculation regarding the absence of testimony by the defendant."[200]

Similarly, the prosecutor may not question defendant about, nor comment upon, the fact that defendant "sat through" the Commonwealth's case.[201] "To use against the defendant his strategy to wait until after the prosecution had made its case before revealing his story would disparage the constitutional rights which allowed him that strategy."[202] Where defendant's sanity is in issue, the prosecutor may alert the jury to inconsistencies between his conduct at trial (such as sitting quietly) and his alleged mental illness.[203]

Improper comment referring to defendant's failure to testify may issue from the judge[204] or co-counsel[205] as well as the prosecutor. Such

---

constitute impermissible comment of defendant's failure to produce evidence); *Com. v. Silanskas*, 433 Mass 678, 700-701, 746 NE2d 445, 465-466 (2001); *Com. v. Lodge*, 431 Mass 461, 471-472, 727 NE2d 1194, 1204 (2000); *Com. v. Cancel*, 394 Mass 567, 573-576, 476 NE2d 610, 616 (1985) (impermissible comment on defendant's failure to call alibi witnesses); *Com. v. Hiotes*, 58 Mass App 255, 259-260, 789 NE2d 179, 182 (2003) (reversible error for prosecutor to suggest rape defendant had burden to produce psychiatric evidence to challenge victim's mental condition; *Com. v. Awad*, 47 Mass App 139, 143-144, 712 NE2d 601, 605 (1999).

[200] *Com. v. Buzzell*, 53 Mass App 362, 366-367, 759 NE2d 344, 349 (2001) (extensive discussion and review of cases).

[201] *Com. v. Martinez*, 431 Mass 168, 177-178, 726 NE2d 913, 923 (2000) (& citations). See also § 13.2, infra.

[202] *Id.*, 431 Mass at 177, 726 NE2d at 923. See also *Com. v. Gaudette*, 441 Mass 762, 808 NE2d 798 (2004) (reaffirming rule); *Com. v. Ewing*, 67 Mass App 531, 541-542, 854 NE2d 993, 1002 (2006), *aff'd*, 449 Mass 1035 (prosecutor's cross-examination of defendant concerning discovery materials he reviewed before trial raised impermissible inference that defendant conformed his testimony falsely to the evidence against him). But compare *Portuondo v. Agard*, 529 US 61,120 S Ct 1119 (2000) (prosecutor's comments during summation, calling jury's attention to fact that defendant had opportunity to hear other witnesses testify and to tailor his testimony, did not violate United States Constitution).

[203] See *Com. v. Hunter*, 427 Mass 651, 657, 695 NE2d 653, 655 (1998); *Com. v. Smiledge*, 419 Mass 156, 160, 643 NE2d 41, 44 (1994) (prosecutor's question to defense expert on mental disease as to whether he found it surprising defendant was able to sit quietly through trial not improper comment on failure to testify).

[204] See, e.g., *Com. v. Sneed*, 376 Mass 867, 872, 383 NE2d 843, 845-846 (1978) (charge gave jurors erroneous impression about defendant's election not to testify); *Com. v. Goulet*, 374 Mass 404, 410-414, 372 NE2d 1288, 1294-1296 (1978) (reversible error where judge's charge implied that testimony of defense witness should be devalued because defendant himself had not taken stand). See also *Com. v. Carrion*, 407 Mass 263, 269-272, 552 NE2d 558, 562-564 (1990) (although judge's embellishment on instruction regarding defendant's right not to testify "teeters on the brink of reversible error," viewed in context reversal not required).

[205] See *Com. v. Russo*, 49 Mass App 579, 731 NE2d 108 (2000). But see *Com. v. Vallejo*, 455 Mass 72, 75-82, 914 NE2d 22, 26-30 (2009) (comments by codefendant's

comments are subject to the same analysis as above—whether the statement could be fairly understood as permitting the jury to draw the forbidden adverse inference.[206] When the judge or prosecutor has made an improper comment it is not *per se* reversible error, but is subject to harmless error analysis.[207]

GL 278, § 23 precludes comment at trial upon the fact that the defendant failed to testify or offer evidence at the preliminary hearing.[208] The statute is not violated by pointing out inconsistencies between a defendant's testimony on the stand and a prior voluntary statement, including omissions from the prior statement where it would have been natural to include the omitted fact.[209]

Proposed Mass R Evid 512(a) would generally preclude both comment upon and an adverse inference from any claim of privilege.[210]

As the Supreme Court has recognized, "[e]ven without adverse comment, the members of a jury, unless instructed otherwise, may well

---

counsel during opening and closing statements, emphasizing that her client chose to speak to police, did not directly refer to defendant's failure to do so).

[206] *Com. v. Russo*, supra, 49 Mass App at 582-583, 731 NE2d at 111. For a case involving comment on the privilege in the form of an outburst by the victim on the witness stand, see *Com. v. Farnkoff*, 16 Mass App 433, 441-442, 452 NE2d 249, 255 (1983). See also *Com. v. Ries*, 337 Mass 565, 585, 150 NE2d 527, 541 (1958) (judge properly refused to permit defendant to comment in closing argument upon prosecution witness's invocation of privilege on cross-examination).

[207] See, e.g., *United States v. Hasting*, 461 US 499 (1983); *Com. v. Walker*, 421 Mass 90, 97-99, 653 NE2d 1080, 1084-1085 (1995); *Com. v. Paradiso*, 368 Mass 205, 209-213, 330 NE2d 825, 828-829 (1975); *Com. v. Ayre*, 31 Mass App 17, 23-24, 574 NE2d 415, 419 (1991). See also *Com. v. Pope*, 406 Mass 581, 588-591, 549 NE2d 1120, 1125-1126 (1990) (no substantial likelihood of miscarriage of justice where judge, at defendant's request, instructed jury as to defendant's right to remain silent).

[208] GL 278, § 23 provides:

> At the trial of a criminal case in the superior court, upon indictment, or in a district court, the fact that the defendant did not testify at any preliminary hearing in the first court, or that at such hearing he waived examination or did not offer any evidence in his own defense, shall not be used as evidence against him, nor be referred to or commented upon by the prosecuting officer.

See also *Grunewald v. United States*, 353 US 391 (1957) (prejudicial error for trial judge to permit defendant to be cross-examined regarding assertion of privilege before grand jury); *Com. v. Bennett*, 2 Mass App 575, 582 n.3, 317 NE2d 834 n.3 (1974) (citing Text).

[209] *Com. v. Rivera*, 425 Mass 633, 640, 682 NE2d 636, 642 (1997).

[210] Proposed Mass R Evid 512(a) provides:

> **Comment or inference not permitted.**
> The claim of a privilege, whether in the present proceeding or upon a prior occasion, is not a proper subject of comment by judge or counsel in a criminal case. No inference may be drawn therefrom.

draw adverse inferences from a defendant's silence."[211] Accordingly a defendant who chooses not to testify is constitutionally entitled upon request to an instruction that he is not compelled to testify and that no adverse inference may be drawn from his failure to do so.[212] Absent a request, no instruction is required.[213]

"No aspect of the charge to the jury requires more care and precise expression than that used with reference to the right of a defendant in a criminal case to remain silent and not be compelled to incriminate himself. . . . Even an unintended suggestion that might induce the jury to draw an unfavorable inference is error."[214] To avoid prejudice to the defendant, the judge in instructing the jury should avoid use of the phrase "the right not to incriminate oneself" and instead substitute "the right to remain silent."[215]

As a matter of federal constitutional law, the "no-adverse-inference" instruction may be given over the defendant's objection without violating his privilege.[216] Under Massachusetts law, however, the judge must accede to a defendant's request that the jury not be so instructed.[217]

---

[211] *Carter v. Kentucky*, 450 US 288, 301 (1981).

[212] *Id.*, 450 US at 305. See also Proposed Mass R Evid 512(c) which provides:

> Upon request, any accused in a criminal case against whom the jury might draw an adverse inference from a claim of privilege is entitled to an instruction that no inference may be drawn therefrom.

See also *Com. v. Botelho*, 87 Mass App 846, 848-851, 35 NE3d 417, 420-422 (2015) (extensive discussion, citations, and Model Instructions) (failure to instruct jury upon defendant's request that they could not draw an adverse inference from his decision not to testify required reversal of conviction). But see *Com. v. Gilchrist*, 413 Mass 216, 218, 597 NE2d 32 (1992) (defendant does not have right to specify the precise language of the judge's instruction, which is reviewed in context of entire charge).

[213] *Com. v. Zammuto*, 89 Mass App 80, 83-84, 46 NE3d 73, 77 (2016).

[214] *Com. v. Thomas*, 400 Mass 676, 679, 511 NE2d 1095, 1097-1098 (1987) (citations omitted).

[215] *Com. v. Charles*, 397 Mass 1, 9, 489 NE2d 679, 684-685 (1986) (& cases cited). See also *Com. v. Jenkins*, 416 Mass 736, 741, 625 NE2d 1344, 1347 (1993) (although reference to "no adverse inference" is preferable form of instruction, judge's instruction that jury "absolutely" not consider defendant's failure to testify was not reversible error); *Com. v. Powers*, 9 Mass App 771, 774, 404 NE2d 1260, 1263 (1980).

[216] See *Lakeside v. Oregon*, 435 US 333 (1978) (instruction does not constitute improper comment on failure to testify).

[217] *Com. v. Buiel*, 391 Mass 744, 746, 463 NE2d 1172, 1173 (1984). Compare *Com. v. Jackson*, 419 Mass 716, 731-732, 647 NE2d 401, 410 (1994) (no error in instructing jury in absence of defendant's request that judge not give instruction) and *Com. v. Rivera*, 441 Mass 358, 368-370, 805 NE2d 942, 951-952 (2004) (counsel did not sufficiently alert judge to omit reference). The former rule under *Com. v. Buiel*,

§ 5.15 Limitation on Privileges and Disqualifications in Proceedings Arising out of Abuse of Disabled Persons

In the case of an investigation of possible abuse against a disabled person, GL 19C, § 5 provides as follows:

> Any privilege created by statute or common law relating to confidential communications or any statute prohibiting the disclosure of information shall neither preclude the disclosure of such documents to the [Disabled Persons Protection] commission or its designated agency nor prevent the admission of such documents in any civil or disciplinary proceeding arising out of the alleged abuse or neglect of the disabled person; provided, however, that absent the written consent of an individual to whom the requested documents relate, any information which is protected by the attorney-client privilege, the psychotherapist-client privilege, or the clergy-penitent privilege shall not be subject to such disclosure.

---

which treated all errors in giving the charge over objection as requiring reversal, has been abrogated. See *Com. v. Rivera*, 441 Mass at 370-371, 805 NE2d at 952-953 (substituting harmless error standard). The Supreme Judicial Court has noted that "the instruction often functions as a double-edged sword, and that the effect of the instruction on the jury's deliberations is equivocal." *Com. v. Dussault*, 71 Mass App 542, 545, 883 NE2d 1243, 1247 (2008).

CHAPTER

6

WITNESSES

A. BASICS

§ 6.1 Attendance/Compulsory Process/Subpoenas/Discovery

In Massachusetts, subpoenas run throughout the Commonwealth and mandate attendance in court as long as accompanied by one day's witness fees and travel fare to and from court.[1] The form and process for the issuance of a subpoena in civil proceedings are set forth in Mass R Civ P 45, and for criminal matters in Mass R Crim P 17.[2]

In criminal cases, Massachusetts witnesses can be summoned into other states, and witnesses from other states can be summoned into

§ 6.1 [1] GL 233, §§ 1-3; GL 262, § 29.

[2] For the authority of an administrative agency to issue a summons in connection with an adjudicatory proceeding, see GL 30A, § 12 (discussed in § 14.3, infra).

Massachusetts, provided the other state in question has enacted reciprocal legislation and certain other conditions are met.[3]

Witness fees may be paid by the government on written ex parte application of an indigent criminal defendant.[4] A defendant indicted for a capital offense may have process issued at the expense of the Commonwealth without regard to proof of indigence.[5] Fees and mileage need not be tendered when a subpoena is issued on behalf of the United States, the Commonwealth, a political subdivision or agency, or an officer of a political subdivision or agency.[6]

Penalties, warrants, and contempt powers for failure of a witness to appear in accordance with a valid subpoena are found in both statutes and rules of court.[7]

Regarding the procedures and standards for the issuance of summonses to third parties for the production of documentary evidence and objects (known as a subpoena duces tecum), see Mass R Crim P 17(a)(2)[8] and Mass R Civ P 45(b). Regarding discovery within the

---

[3] GL 233, §§ 13A-B (Uniform Act to Secure the Attendance of Witnesses from Without a State in Criminal Proceedings); Mass R Crim P 17(d)(2). See generally *Matter of Rhode Island Grand Jury Subpoena*, 414 Mass 104, 605 NE2d 840 (1993) (& citations) (extensive discussion of issues of standing, privilege, and application of Uniform Act); *Com. v. Sellers*, 74 Mass App Ct 1119, 907 NE2d 1161 (2009).

[4] Mass R Crim P 17(b) and (c).

[5] GL 277, § 66.

[6] Mass R Civ P 45(c); Fed R Civ P 45(c). For discussion of the recovery of witness fees (including expert witness fees) as taxable costs by a successful civil litigant, see *Waldman v. American Honda Motor Co.*, 413 Mass 320, 597 NE2d 404 (1992); *City of Boston v. United States Mineral Products Co.*, 37 Mass App 933, 641 NE2d 132 (1994).

[7] See GL 233, §§ 5-11 (courts and nonjudicial tribunals); GL 3, § 28A (General Court); Mass R Civ P 45(f), Fed R Civ P 45(f), and Fed R Crim P 17(g) (contempt); Mass R Crim P 17(e) (warrant). Once a trial is underway, a witness who refuses to comply with a court order to testify is subject to punishment for civil contempt. See *Com. v. Viust*, 84 Mass App 308, 995 NE2d 1133 (2013).

[8] See generally *Com. v. Dwyer*, 448 Mass 122, 139-142, 859 NE2d 400, 415-416 (2006) (protocol for privileged documents, discussed in § 5.5.4, supra); *Com. v. Lampron*, 441 Mass 265, 806 NE2d 72 (2004) (extensive discussion of showing necessary for issuance); *Com. v. Hunt*, 86 Mass App 494, 17 NE3d 448 (2014). (defense counsel's conclusory affidavit was insufficient). The Commonwealth may not subpoena the production of records from a third party in advance of trial or an evidentiary hearing pursuant to GL c. 277, § 68, without first obtaining judicial approval pursuant to Mass R. Crim. P 17(a)(2). *Com. v. Odgren*, 455 Mass 171, 915 NE2d 215 (2009) (recordings of defendant's jailhouse telephone conversations); *Com. v. Hart*, 455 Mass 230, 243, 914 NE2d 904, 914-915 (2009) (recordings of defendant's telephone calls at correctional facility). See also *Com. v. Reed*, 444 Mass 803, 806-809, 831 NE2d 901, 904-906 (2005) (victim's medical records; *Com. v. Caceres*, 63 Mass App 747, 829 NE2d 1144 (2005) (victim's counseling records). For the procedures to obtain telephone records from a provider, see *Com. v. Chamberlin*, 86 Mass App 705, 20 NE3d 954 (2014).

Commonwealth for proceedings held in another jurisdiction, see GL 223A, § 11 ("A court of this Commonwealth may order a person who is domiciled or is found within this Commonwealth to give his testimony or statement or to produce documents or other things for use in a proceeding in a tribunal outside this Commonwealth.").[9]

A defendant in a state criminal proceeding is entitled to compulsory process to obtain witnesses in his or her favor under both the Sixth and Fourteenth Amendments to the United States Constitution and Article 12 of the Massachusetts Declaration of Rights.[10] A witness "necessary" to an adequate defense is one whose testimony is relevant, material, and not cumulative.[11]

The constitutional rights to call witnesses and present a defense are not absolute. "In the face of legitimate demands of the adversarial system, this right may be tempered according to the discretion of the trial judge. For example, a trial judge has the discretion to control the scope of the examination of witnesses, and can exclude witnesses whose testimony is cumulative, repetitive, or confusing."[12] The right to present testimony may be also lost by the failure to make timely disclosure of the intention to call the witness.[13]

In rare instances a defendant can obtain an ex parte order compelling production under Mass R Crim P 17(a)(2). See *Com. v. Mitchell*, 444 Mass 786, 831 NE2d 890 (2005).

[9] Construed in *Matter of a Rhode Island Select Commission Subpoena*, 415 Mass 890, 616 NE2d 458 (1993).

[10] See *Washington v. Texas*, 388 US 14 (1967); *Blazo v. Superior Court*, 366 Mass 141, 315 NE2d 857 (1974) (indigent defendants are entitled to compel attendance of witnesses at misdemeanor trials at public expense); *Com. v. Degrenier*, 40 Mass App 212, 214-215, 662 NE2d 1039, 1041-1042 (1996) (defendant had constitutional right to compel presence of inmate witness); *Com. v. Adderley*, 36 Mass App 918, 919-920, 629 NE2d 308, 310-311 (1994) (judge's refusal to issue bench warrant for defense witness deprived defendant of right to present defense).

[11] *Com. v. Degrenier*, supra, 40 Mass App at 215, 662 NE2d at 1041 (& citations).

[12] See *Com. v. Carroll*, 439 Mass 547, 552-553, 789 NE2d 1062, 1067 (2003) (evidence of coperpetrator's motive was irrelevant).

[13] See *Com. v. Durning*, 406 Mass 485, 494-498, 548 NE2d 1242, 1248-1250 (1990) (witness not listed on pretrial conference report); *Com. v. Chappee*, 397 Mass 508, 516-519, 492 NE2d 719, 724-726 (1986) (expert witnesses not disclosed to prosecution as required by pretrial agreement); *Com. v. Porcher*, 26 Mass App 517, 529 NE2d 1348 (1988) (alibi witness not disclosed as required by Mass R Crim P 14(b)). But compare *Com. v. Steinmeyer*, 43 Mass App 185, 681 NE2d 893 (1997) (trial court abused discretion in striking testimony of defense witness as sanction for defense counsel's failure to furnish prosecution with copy of witness's pretrial notes as required by pretrial conference agreement).

A defendant has no constitutional right to the testimony of a witness who validly asserts his privilege against self-incrimination,[14] nor to call a witness solely for the purpose of impeaching her with otherwise inadmissible prior inconsistent statements.[15] The defendant's constitutional right to prepare a defense is abridged where a prospective defense witness decides not to testify because of the prosecutor's threats to prosecute him.[16]

A criminal defendant has a right to testify in his own behalf, and the right not to testify.[17]

The right of defendant to testify on his own behalf is fundamental, and the decision whether to testify must be made in consultation with counsel; waiver must be knowing and intelligent.[18] The trial judge has discretion to permit a criminal defendant to make an unsworn statement in lieu of testifying under oath.[19]

---

[14] *Pixley v. Com.*, 453 Mass 827, 834, 906 NE2d 320, 326 (2009); *Com. v. Drumgold*, 423 Mass 230, 247-249, 668 NE2d 300, 313-314 (1996) (& citations); *Com. v. Wooden*, 70 Mass App 185, 188-189, 873 NE2d 764, 768 (2007). See § 5.14.6, supra.

[15] See *Com. v. Raposa*, 440 Mass 684, 692-693, 801 NE2d 789, 797 (2004); *Com. v. McAfee*, 430 Mass 483, 491 n.3, 722 NE2d 1, 9 n.3 (1999) (& citations); *Com. v. Elliot*, 430 Mass 498, 502-503, 721 NE2d 388, 392-393 (1999).

[16] See *Com. v. Turner*, 37 Mass App 385, 640 NE2d 488 (1994) (& citations). Compare *Com. v. Penta*, 423 Mass 546, 548-550, 669 NE2d 767, 769-770 (prosecution did not improperly prevent informer from testifying by requesting perjury prosecution warning in open court); *Com. v. Morales*, 440 Mass 536, 544, 800 NE2d 683, 691 (2003) (no intimidation where police officers inadvertently interrupted defense investigators' interview of witness).

[17] See *Com. v. Grissett*, 66 Mass App 454, 459, 848 NE2d 441, 445 (2006) (& citations). That trial counsel discouraged defendant from testifying is insufficient to establish a violation of the right to testify. *Com. v. McWilliams*, 473 Mass 606, 621, 45 NE3d 94, 109 (2016) (defense counsel erroneously advised defendant that five prior convictions—which were actually time-barred—could be used to impeach him).

To relieve "Dookhan" defendants from the untenable position of having to sacrifice their Fifth Amendment privilege against self-incrimination in order to obtain relief from the government misconduct surrounding the forensic drug laboratory, the testimony of the defendant at a hearing on a motion to withdraw a guilty plea is only admissible at a subsequent trial for impeachment purposes should the defendant choose to testify. *Bridgeman v. District Attorney for Suffolk County*, 471 Mass 465, 493, 30 NE3d 806, 829 (2015).

[18] See *Com. v. Smith*, 459 Mass 538, 550, 946 NE2d 95, 105 (2011); *Com. v. Garvin*, 456 Mass 778, 785-786, 926 NE2d 169, 176-177 (2010).

[19] See *Com. v. Gallagher*, 408 Mass 510, 518, 562 NE2d 80, 85-86 (1990) (& citations) (but defendant has no right to make statement); *Com. v. Mitchell*, 438 Mass 535, 548-549, 781 NE2d 1237, 1249 (2003). A foster parent's statutory right to be heard in an adoption proceeding does not include the right to submit an unsworn, written statement to the judge. *Adoption of Sherry*, 435 Mass 331, 337-338, 757 NE2d 1097, 1102-1103 (2001).

Defendants are entitled as of right to have access to witnesses who are in the custody of the Commonwealth, including the opportunity for an interview.[20] Witnesses may, however, refuse to grant an interview with defense counsel; if they chose to be interviewed, they have "the right to impose reasonable conditions on the conduct of the interview."[21] Regarding child witnesses, consent to be interviewed lies within the authority of the parents or, where custody has been so awarded, the Department of Social Services.[22] The Commonwealth has a duty to produce informers in custody; and for those not in custody, to provide whatever information it has about the informer's whereabouts.[23]

A criminal defendant may obtain in pretrial discovery the names and addresses of the Commonwealth's prospective witnesses as well as records of any prior convictions.[24] A court may issue a protective order restricting defendant's access to identifying information to ensure the safety of witnesses, providing that the restrictions do not impair defendant's rights to effective assistance of counsel and to a fair trial.[25] As part of the reciprocal discovery authorized by Mass R Crim P 14(a), a defendant may be required to furnish the Commonwealth with any statements of the Commonwealth's prospective witnesses in his or his attorney's possession that he intends to use at trial for any purpose including impeachment.[26]

---

[20] See generally *Com. v. Rivera*, 424 Mass 266, 271-272, 675 NE2d 791, 796 (1997), *habeas denied*, 596 F Supp 2d 162 (D Mass 2009); *Com. v. Penta*, 423 Mass 546, 669 NE2d 767 (1996).

[21] See GL 258B, § 3(m). Witnesses may decline to talk to either side or to both. *Com. v. Drew*, 447 Mass 635, 643, 856 NE2d 808, 816 (2006).

[22] See *Com. v. Adkinson*, 442 Mass 410, 416-420, 813 NE2d 506, 511-514 (2004) (extensive discussion); *Com. v. Barnes-Miller*, 59 Mass App 832, 834 n.2, 798 NE2d 569, 571 n.2 (2003); *Com. v. Giacobbe*, 56 Mass App 144, 775 NE2d 759 (2002) (extensive discussion) (allowing victim-witness advocate to be present when defense counsel interviewed child witnesses was reasonable).

[23] *Com. v. Penta*, supra, 423 Mass at 548-549, 669 NE2d at 769-770.

[24] GL 218, § 26A; Mass R Crim P 14(a). See generally *Com. v. Righini*, 64 Mass App 19, 831 NE2d 332 (2005). For the disclosure and securing of attendance of a witness in witness protection, see *Com. v. Platt*, 464 Mass 1006, 980 NE2d 452 (2012). For the problem of the attorney who may become a necessary witness at trial, see *Smaland Beach Association, Inc. v. Genova*, 461 Mass 214, 959 NE2d 955 (2012).

[25] *Com. v. Holliday*, 450 Mass 794, 802-804, 882 NE2d 309, 318-319 (2008).

[26] See *Com. v. Durham*, 446 Mass 212, 843 NE2d 1035 (2006).

GL 268, § 13B, makes it a crime to intimidate, influence, or otherwise interfere with a witness.[27]

§ 6.2 Sequestration

Sequestration of witnesses is designed to prevent perjury or tailoring of testimony by keeping them out of the courtroom during each other's testimony.[1] Unlike the federal practice where sequestration is mandatory upon the request of a party,[2] the sequestration of witnesses in the Massachusetts courts lies within the discretion of the trial judge.[3] Similarly left to the discretion of the judge is the modification or revocation of sequestration orders,[4] as well as the appropriate remedy for violation.[5]

---

[27] See generally *Com. v. Belle Isle*, 44 Mass App 226, 694 NE2d 5 (1998). See also *Com. v. Cruz*, 442 Mass 299, 309-310, 812 NE2d 1178, 1185-1186 (2004) (testimony of witnesses pursuant to cooperation agreements was not result of witness intimidation); *Com. v. Auguste*, 418 Mass 643, 646-648, 639 NE2d 388, 390-391 (1994) (questions regarding witness's fear of testifying, whether or not caused by defendant, are allowable at judge's discretion); *Com. v. Teixeira*, 76 Mass App 101, 920 NE2d 56 (2010) (extensive discussion of defendant's claim that police officer confronted him on day before trial and intimidated him into forgoing his right to testify); *Com. v. Belete*, 37 Mass App 424, 640 NE2d 511 (1994) (court interpreter is not "witness" for purposes of GL 268, § 13B).

§ 6.2 [1] See *Com. v. Collins*, 470 Mass 255, 270-272, 21 NE3d 528, 540-542 (2014); *Com. v. Jackson*, 384 Mass 572, 582, 428 NE2d 289, 295 (1981) (citing Text). With regard to sequestration of the jury, see *Com. v. McCowen*, 458 Mass 461, 476-477, 939 NE2d 735, 751-752 (2010).

[2] See Fed R Evid 615.

[3] Proposed Mass R Evid 615, which reflects Massachusetts practice, provides:

> **Exclusion of Witnesses**
> At the request of a party the court may order witnesses excluded so that they cannot hear the testimony of other witnesses, and it may make the order on its own motion. This rule does not authorize exclusion of (1) a party who is a natural person or (2) an officer or employee of a party which is not a natural person designated as its representative by its attorney, or (3) a person whose presence is shown by a party to be essential to the presentation of his cause.

Mass R Crim P 21 provides:

> Upon his own motion or the motion of either party, the judge may, prior to or during the examination of a witness, order any witness or witnesses other than the defendant to be excluded from the courtroom.

See also Com. v. Baker, 440 Mass 519, 534, 800 NE2d 267, 280 (2003); *Com. v. Vanderpool*, 367 Mass 743, 748, 328 NE2d 833, 837 (1975); *Com. v. Bonner*, 33 Mass App 471, 473-474, 601 NE2d 32, 33-34 (1992) (citing Text) (judge acted within discretion in denying motion to sequester child victim's mother); *Com. v. Sevieri*, 21 Mass App 745, 757, 490 NE2d 481, 488-489 (1986) (discretion should be exercised based on reasons

Parties to the case and prospective witnesses whose presence is essential to the management and presentation of the party's case, such as the police officer in charge of the investigation, are exempt from exclusion.[6]

The fact that witnesses are sequestered does not also require excluding the media.[7]

§ 6.3 Competency/Oath

"Any person of sufficient understanding, although a party, may testify in any proceeding, civil or criminal."[1] The only requirement of competency to testify as a witness in the Massachusetts courts is sufficient mental capacity to: (1) observe, remember, and give expression to that

---

related to particular case rather than as matter of general practice). The better practice in "capital cases" is to order sequestration. *Com. v. Watkins*, 373 Mass 849, 370 NE2d 701 (1977). Prospective witnesses may be excluded where appropriate. See, e.g., *Com. v. Jones*, 71 Mass App 568, 571-572, 884 NE2d 532, 535-536 (2008), *habeas dismissed*, Jones v. O'Brien, 2010 WL 2090335 (D Mass 2010) (defendant's girlfriend, charged as an accessory and awaiting her own trial).

[4] See *Com. v. Jackson*, supra, 384 Mass at 581-582, 428 NE2d at 295 (judge acted within discretion in allowing expert witness for prosecution to remain in courtroom to assist prosecution, and permitting police officer witness to resume testimony after hearing testimony of other witnesses, despite general sequestration order); *Com. v. Parry*, 1 Mass App 730, 735-736, 306 NE2d 855, 859-860 (1974) (judge did not abuse discretion by permitting witness to remain in courtroom and hear testimony of other witnesses after having initially ordered her to be sequestered).

[5] See *Com. v. Pope*, 392 Mass 493, 506, 467 NE2d 117, 126 (1984) (judge acted within discretion in deciding that counsel should be responsible for enforcing sequestration order); *Com. v. Gogan*, 389 Mass 255, 261-262, 449 NE2d 365, 369 (1983) (judge did not abuse discretion in denying motion for mistrial after police officer witnesses violated order not to discuss case with one another).

[6] Proposed Mass R Evid 615, supra. See also *Com. v. Ahart*, 464 Mass 437, 443, 983 NE2d 1203, 1208 (2013) (no error in excepting from sequestration police officer witness who is essential to management of the Commonwealth's case); *Com. v. Perez*, 405 Mass 339, 343, 540 NE2d 681, 683 (1989) (& cases cited). As to the propriety of allowing a police officer witness to sit at the Commonwealth's table during trial, see *Com. v. Auguste*, 414 Mass 51, 59-60, 605 NE2d 819, 824 (1992) (& citations); *Com. v. Duffy*, 36 Mass App 937, 939, 629 NE2d 1347, 1349 (1994).

Where inexperienced defense counsel mistakenly had defendant wait outside the courtroom in response to an order for sequestration, defendant's rights to be present at trial and confront witnesses were violated. See *Com. v. Nwachukwu*, 65 Mass App 112, 837 NE2d 301 (2005).

[7] See *Com. v. Clark*, 432 Mass 1, 7-9, 730 NE2d 872, 880-881 (2000).

§ 6.3 [1] GL 233, § 20.

which she has seen, heard, or evidenced; and (2) comprehend the difference between truth and falsehood.[2]

Except in quite clear cases of incompetency,[3] the modern trend is to let the witness testify and have the trier-of-fact make any proper discount for the quality of her testimonial faculties.[4] "The established safeguards of the Anglo-American legal system leave the veracity of a witness to be tested by cross-examination, and the credibility of his testimony to be determined by a properly instructed jury."[5] Inconsistencies or lapses in testimony, as well as the witness's inability to remember details of events, go to credibility and the weight of the evidence, not competence to testify.[6] A judge may find a witness competent even though his reliability is, in the judge's eyes, "marginally sufficient."[7]

---

[2] Proposed Mass R Evid 601 provides:

Competency In General; Disqualification

(a) General rule of competency. Every person is competent to be a witness except as otherwise provided in these rules.

(b) Disqualification of witness; interpreters. A person is disqualified to be a witness if the court finds that the proposed witness (1) lacked the capacity to perceive, or (2) is incapable of remembering, or (3) is incapable of expressing himself concerning the matter so as to be understood by the judge and jury either directly or through interpretation by one who can understand him, or (4) is incapable of understanding the duty of a witness to tell the truth. An interpreter is subject to all the provisions of these rules relating to witnesses.

See generally *Com. v. Brusgulis*, 398 Mass 325, 329, 496 NE2d 652, 655 (1986); *Com. v. Whitehead*, 379 Mass 640, 656, 400 NE2d 821, 833-834 (1980); *Com. v. Buzzell*, 79 Mass App 460, 947 NE2d 75 (2011) (a witness need not be a citizen or legal resident to testify; immigration status is not relevant to a witness's testimony).

[3] See, e.g., *Com. v. Brescia*, 471 Mass 381, 29 NE3d 837, 847 (2015). After defendant's two days of testimony, he was taken to the hospital and it was determined he had suffered a stroke during the night between. The judge ordered a new trial, and on appeal the Supreme Judicial Court affirmed, recognizing that the defendant's difficulty understanding and responding to questions on the second day undermined the fairness of the trial, and was exploited by the prosecutor's suggestion that defendant was prevaricating.

[4] *Com. v. Whitehead*, supra, 379 Mass at 656, 400 NE2d at 833-834.

[5] *Com. v. Colon*, 408 Mass 419, 443, 558 NE2d 974, 989 (1990) (quoting *Hoffa v. United States*, 385 US 293, 311 (1966)).

[6] See, e.g., *Com. v. Winquist*, 87 Mass App 695, 707, 35 NE3d 366, 377 (2015); *Com. v. Lamontagne*, 42 Mass App 213, 218, 675 NE2d 1169, 1173 (1997).

[7] *Demoulas v. Demoulas*, 428 Mass 555, 564, 703 NE2d 1149, 1159 (1998). See also *Com. v. Echavarria*, 428 Mass 593, 595-596, 703 NE2d 1137, 1139 (1998) (although witness was illiterate, recently arrived in the United States, and unable to speak English, he was "far from failing the not very stringent test of competence," and opposing counsel brought these deficiencies out on cross-examination); *Com. v. Tang*, 66 Mass App 53, 63, 845 NE2d 407, 415 (2006).

Witnesses have been deemed competent to testify although they were:

- Young children.[8]
- Emotionally disturbed or learning disabled.[9]
- Mentally ill or insane.[10]
- Of limited intelligence.[11]
- Alcoholic or under influence of drugs at time of event.[12]

It has been observed that "[in] recent years, there has been a tremendous explosion of the number of child abuse cases in the courts. Young children are being called upon frequently to be witnesses in such cases. Judges must carefully craft questions posed to child witnesses to ensure that they are indeed competent."[13]

Neither a child's inability to place events in a temporal framework, nor inconsistencies or lapses in the child's answers, renders the child incompetent to testify.[14] A formal oath for the child referring to

---

[8] See, e.g., *Com. v. Patton*, 458 Mass 119, 135-136, 934 NE2d 236, 250-251 (2010) (four-year-old child was competent to give videotaped statement in probation revocation hearing, where there was evidence that child understood she could get a spanking if she told a lie); *Com. v. Thibeault*, 77 Mass App 419, 423-431, 931 NE2d 1008, 1013-1018 (2010) (six-year-old witness was competent, even though she gave some hesitant, inconsistent, and equivocal answers and had difficulty explaining the consequences of failing to tell the truth); *Com. v. Trowbridge*, 419 Mass 750, 754-755, 647 NE2d 413, 417 (1995) (eight-year-old); *Com. v. LeFave*, 407 Mass 927, 941-942, 556 NE2d 83, 92-93 (1990) (day-care children); *Com. v. Dockham*, 405 Mass 618, 542 NE2d 591 (1989) (four-year-old); *Com. v. Murphy*, 57 Mass App 586, 591-592, 784 NE2d 1144, 1147-1148 (2003) (eight-year-old). For a discussion of special arrangements for the taking of testimony from a child witness, see § 6.4, infra. For extensive discussion of the issue of competency of a child declarant to make a spontaneous utterance, see *Com. v. Tang*, supra, 66 Mass App at 61-67, 845 NE2d at 414-418 (judge was not required to conduct voir dire examination of five-year-old who made spontaneous statements to police officer before admitting the statements under hearsay exception).

[9] See, e.g., *Com. v. Sylvia*, 35 Mass App 310, 619 NE2d 360 (1993) (witness mentally competent to testify even though she had suffered nervous breakdown and was under hospital treatment); *Com. v. Jimenez*, 10 Mass App 441, 409 NE2d 204 (1980) (15-year-old victim with learning disabilities and emotional problems).

[10] See, e.g., *Com. v. Zelenski*, 287 Mass 125, 129, 191 NE2d 355, 357 (1934); *Com. v. Piedra*, 20 Mass App 155, 159-160, 478 NE2d 1284, 1288 (1985).

[11] See, e.g., *Com. v. Whitehead*, supra, 379 Mass at 655-656, 400 NE2d at 833.

[12] See, e.g., *Com. v. Alicea*, 464 Mass 837, 845-846, 985 NE2d 1197, 1205-1206 (2013) (witness was competent to testify even though she admitted she used three bags of heroin on day of shooting); *Com. v. Sires*, 370 Mass 541, 546, 350 NE2d 460, 464 (1976) (witness an alcoholic under medication for hallucinations).

[13] *Com. v. Monzon*, 51 Mass App 245, 253, 744 NE2d 1131, 1138 (2001).

[14] See *Com. v. Trowbridge*, 419 Mass 750, 755, 647 NE2d 413, 418 (1995); *Com. v. Gamache*, 35 Mass App 805, 806-809, 626 NE2d 616, 618-620 (1994).

a deity or to "swearing" or "affirming" is not essential, although these traditions should not be abandoned without good reason.[15] Nor is it necessary that the child have a full understanding of the obligation of the oath; it is sufficient if she demonstrates an understanding of the difference between truth and falsehood and an awareness of the duty to tell the truth.[16] There is no requirement that the child be able to explain the concept of punishment for the telling of a lie.[17]

Unlike some jurisdictions, Massachusetts does not mandate a pretrial hearing to give the defendant an opportunity to show that a child's memory of events is the product of suggestive or coercive interview techniques. Such hearing is within the discretion of the judge.[18]

Ordinarily when an issue is raised as to the competency of a witness, the trial judge should require a voir dire examination.[19] "The judge is afforded wide discretion—indeed, is obliged—to tailor the competency inquiry to the particular circumstances and intellect of the witness."[20]

---

[15] See *Com. v. Murphy*, 57 Mass App 586, 592, 784 NE2d 1144, 1148 (2003); *Com. v. McCaffrey*, 36 Mass App 583, 589-590, 633 NE2d 1062, 1066 (1994).

[16] *Com. v. LeFave*, supra, 407 Mass 927, 941-942, 556 NE2d 83 (1990); *Com. v. Ike I.*, 53 Mass App 907, 909, 760 NE2d 781, 783 (2002). Compare *Com. v. Corbett*, 26 Mass App 773, 775-777, 533 NE2d 207, 209-210 (1989) (judge did not abuse discretion in ruling four-year-old witness incompetent to testify because her answers indicated confusion as to difference between truth and lie). See also *Com. v. Monzon*, supra, 51 Mass App at 248-253, 744 NE2d at 1135-1138 (judge should have questioned six-year-old further about her understanding of truth and lie); *Com. v. Murphy*, 48 Mass App 143, 718 NE2d 395 (1999) (discussing use of questions concerning child's religious training and beliefs on issue of her understanding of the importance of truth-telling).

[17] *Com. v. Brusgulis*, 398 Mass 325, 330, 496 NE2d 652, 655-656 (1986).

[18] See *Com. v. Allen*, 40 Mass App 458, 461-463, 665 NE2d 105, 108-109 (1996). See also *Com. v. Adkinson*, 442 Mass 410, 420-421, 813 NE2d 506, 514-515 (2004) (trial court's denial of voir dire to determine if child witnesses had been subject to suggestive interviewing techniques was not error in jury-waived trial); *Com. v. Thibeault*, 77 Mass App 419, 432, 931 NE2d 1008, 1018 (2010) (where record contained no evidence of coercion or coaching, no taint hearing was necessary).

[19] But see *Com. v. Calderon*, 65 Mass App 590, 594-595, 842 NE2d 986, 991 (2006) (judge not required to hold voir dire on eleven-year-old where defendant offered no evidence or argument challenging competence).

[20] *Com. v. Brusgulis*, supra, 398 Mass at 329-330, 496 NE2d at 655. See also *Com. v. Doucette*, 22 Mass App 659, 496 NE2d 837 (1986) (judge did not abuse discretion in conducting voir dire on his own and refusing to allow defense counsel to ask questions); *Com. v. Rockwood*, 27 Mass App 1137, 538 NE2d 40 (1989) (trial judge is not required to administer oath to child witness who undergoes voir dire to determine competency).

Upon a proper showing the judge may require an examination of the witness's mental condition by a qualified physician under the authority of GL 123, § 19.[21] The decision whether to employ an expert is entirely within the judge's discretion.[22] The judge is not empowered to order a psychiatric examination merely for purposes of assessing a witness's credibility.[23]

GL 233, § 23E provides alternative procedures for determining the competency of a witness with mental retardation where the court finds that the usual procedures will likely cause severe psychological or emotional trauma. The statute also provides alternative methods of taking the testimony, including videotape, but in a criminal proceeding the defendant has the right to be present during the taking of the testimony, to have an unobstructed view of the witness, and to have the witness's view of the defendant be unobstructed. § 23E(d).

Although competency is determined before a witness testifies, the judge may reconsider the decision (either sua sponte or on motion) if she entertains doubts about the correctness of the ruling.[24] "While the judge must be careful not to invade the jury's province of deciding the witness's credibility, he may consider whether the witness's performance on the stand demonstrates a lack of awareness of the obligation to tell the truth or an inability to observe, remember, and recount."[25]

---

[21] GL 123, § 19 provides:

> In order to determine the mental condition of any party or witness before any court of the Commonwealth, the presiding judge may, in his discretion, request the department [of Mental Health] to assign a qualified physician or psychologist, who, if assigned shall make such examinations as the judge may deem necessary.

For a discussion of the statute and the limitations on the judge's power thereunder, see *Com. v. Gibbons*, 378 Mass 766, 393 NE2d 400 (1979).

For the procedure to follow where a witness requests an accommodation due to a disability in order to testify, see *In re McDonough*, 457 Mass 512, 930 NE2d 1279 (2010).

[22] *Com. v. Trowbridge*, supra, 419 Mass at 755, 647 NE2d at 418. Compare *Com. v. Santos*, 402 Mass 775, 787-788, 525 NE2d 388, 395-396 (1988) (judge erred in not ordering competency evaluation of witness with Down's syndrome) with *Com. v. Hiotes*, 58 Mass App 255, 256, 789 NE2d 179, 180 (2003) (no abuse of discretion in denying motion to examine rape victim who acknowledged she occasionally talked to space people). See also *Com. v. Gamache*, supra, 35 Mass App at 809 (judge did not improperly delegate to psychiatrist determination of competence).

[23] See *Com. v. Polk*, 462 Mass 23, 33-34, 965 NE2d 815, 825 (2012); *Com. v. Widrick*, 392 Mass 884, 467 NE2d 1353 (1984).

[24] *Com. v. Brusgulis*, supra, 398 Mass at 331, 496 NE2d at 656.

[25] *Id.* But see *Com. v. Lamontagne*, 42 Mass App 213, 218-219, 675 NE2d 1169, 1173 (1997) (judge did not abuse discretion in refraining from sua sponte inquiry into child's competency).

Objections to the competency of a witness must generally be raised before the testimony is given.[26] The competency of a person to testify is a question "peculiarly for the trial judge, and his determination will be rarely faulted on appellate review."[27]

Competency in the context of a declarant making an excited utterance requires only that the assertion rest on personal knowledge.[28]

Particularized jury instructions regarding a witness's limited testimonial capacities have generally not been required.[29]

Despite the general rule of competency, certain witnesses under certain circumstances are precluded by law from testifying as to certain matters (e.g., spouses regarding private conversations with each other). In other circumstances, witnesses are privileged not to reveal, or privileged to prevent others from revealing, certain matters (e.g., confidential communications between attorney and client). These disqualifications and privileges are discussed in Chapter 5.

"Before testifying, every witness shall be required to declare that he will testify truthfully, by oath or affirmation administered in a form calculated to awaken his conscience and impress his mind with his duty to do so."[30] A judge may also remind a witness of the duty to tell the truth.[31]

§ 6.4 Special Arrangements for the Child Witness

GL 278, § 16D provides for alternative procedures for the taking of testimony if the court finds by a preponderance of the evidence "that the child witness is likely to suffer psychological or emotional trauma

---

[26] See *Com. v. Domanski*, 332 Mass 66, 73-74, 123 NE2d 368, 373 (1954); *Com. v. Sylvia*, 35 Mass App 310, 312, 619 NE2d 360 (1993). But see *Com. v. Whitehead*, supra, 379 Mass at 655, 400 NE2d at 833 (objection to competency made by "novel" method of motion to strike).

[27] *Com. v. Whitehead*, supra, 379 Mass at 656, 400 NE2d at 833-834.

[28] *Com. v. Figueroa*, 79 Mass App 389, 396, 946 NE2d 142, 149-150 (2011).

[29] See, e.g., *Com. v. Figueroa*, 413 Mass 193, 196-198, 595 NE2d 779, 781-783 (1992) (judge not required to give defendant's requested instruction regarding mentally retarded victim); *Com. v. Perkins*, 39 Mass App 577, 580, 658 NE2d 975, 977-978 (1995) (judge not required to give special instruction on credibility and suggestibility of child witness).

[30] Proposed Mass R Evid 603, which tracks FRE 603 and reflects Massachusetts practice. See also *Com. v. Stewart*, 454 Mass 527, 531, 911 NE2d 161, 167 (2009) (reversing conviction because trial court in murder trial should have ordered prosecution witness to take oath, and held him in contempt for failing to do so). A judge may remind a witness of the duty to tell the truth to maintain the integrity of the trial. See also § 6.17.

[31] See *Com. v. Molina*, 454 Mass 232, 240, 909 NE2d 19, 26 (2009).

as a result of testifying in open court, as a result of testifying in front of the defendant, or as a result of both."[1] A child can give videotaped testimony, but it must be taken in the defendant's presence.[2]

Although permitted by GL 278, § 16D, testimony by closed circuit television outside the presence of the defendant has been held violative of the art. 12 right to confront one's accusers "face to face."[3] Similarly, a special seating arrangement in the courtroom that results in the defendant being unable to see the face of the child witness during testimony, or that permits the witness to give testimony without facing the accused, violates art. 12.[4]

GL 278, § 16A mandates closure of proceedings during the testimony of minor complainants of sexual offenses, but the decisional law dictates a case-by-case determination of the necessity of closure.[5] GL 233, §§ 81, 82, and 83 provide for the admission of out-of-court statements of children not available or competent to testify relating to acts of sexual abuse. See § 8.21, infra.

A Probate and Family Court judge may conduct an in camera interview with a minor child in a custody matter, but is required to make an electronic recording.[6]

§ 6.5 Personal Knowledge

Competency to testify is to be distinguished from the separate requirement that a witness have personal knowledge of the matters he is testifying about. See Proposed Mass R Evid 602.[1] Testimony must be based on first-hand observations derived from the witness's own

---

§ 6.4 [1] See generally *Com. v. Dockham*, 405 Mass 618, 622-625, 542 NE2d 591, 594-595 (1989) (& cases cited).

[2] *Com. v. Tufts*, 405 Mass 610, 614-615, 542 NE2d 586, 589 (1989).

[3] See *Com. v. Bergstrom*, 402 Mass 534, 524 NE2d 366 (1988).

[4] See *Com. v. Amirault*, 424 Mass 618, 631-632, 677 NE2d 652, 662 (1997); *Com. v. Johnson*, 417 Mass 498, 631 NE2d 1002 (1994).

[5] See *Com. v. Martin*, 417 Mass 187, 191-196, 629 NE2d 297, 300-303 (1994) (& citations).

[6] See *Abbott v. Virusso*, 68 Mass App 326, 334-339, 862 NE2d 52, 59-62 (2007), *aff'd*, 450 Mass 1031 (2008).

§ 6.5 [1] Proposed Mass R Evid 602, which tracks the federal rule and reflects Massachusetts practice, provides:

Lack of Personal Knowledge
A witness may not testify to a matter unless evidence is introduced sufficient to support a finding that he has personal knowledge of the matter. Evidence to prove personal knowledge may, but need not, consist of the testimony of the witness himself. This rule is subject to the provisions of Rule 703, relating to opinion testimony by expert witnesses.

senses.[2] Thus, for example, a witness's testimony that she had an instinct or suspicion that the defendant had had sexual relations with the complainant cannot be admitted.[3]

A preliminary question to the witness is sometimes required to establish personal knowledge. In the absence of a showing of personal knowledge concerning the matter inquired into, the judge may exclude the question.[4] Lack of sufficient personal knowledge to testify about a matter may also be raised by a motion to strike.[5]

When an extrajudicial statement is offered for its truth (see Chapter 8), the proponent of the statement may be required to establish that the declarant had personal knowledge of the information contained in the statement.[6]

B. PRESENTING EVIDENCE

§ 6.6 Order of Presentations and Examination of Witnesses/ Role of the Trial Judge

Proposed Mass R Evid 611(a), which essentially tracks Fed R Evid 611(a) and reflects Massachusetts practice, provides:

See also *Com. v. Whitehead*, 379 Mass 640, 657, 400 NE2d 821, 833 (1980); *Malchanoff v. Truehart*, 354 Mass 118, 121-122, 236 NE2d 89, 92-93 (1968).

[2] *Com. v. Whitehead*, supra, 379 Mass at 657, 400 NE2d at 834; *Com. v. Irene*, 462 Mass 600, 606, 970 NE2d 291, 297 (2012) (it could fairly be inferred that witness was testifying from personal knowledge as to what he heard robber exclaim).

[3] See *Com. v. Martin*, 417 Mass 187, 189-190, 629 NE2d 297, 299-300 (1994). Compare *Com. v. Casali*, 459 Mass 139, 145-146, 943 NE2d 936, 940-941 (2011) (testimony of witness was based on personal knowledge, not instinct or suspicion), and *Com. v. Cintron*, 435 Mass 509, 521, 759 NE2d 700, 711 (2001) (witness's testimony that he learned of defendant's gang affiliations when they were in jail together and that he saw defendant with members of gang revealed personal knowledge) with *Com. v. Wilson*, 49 Mass App 429, 729 NE2d 1143 (2000) (daughter's testimony concerning reason for mother returning to marital residence after alleged assault was not shown to be based on personal knowledge).

[4] *See Com. v. LaCorte*, 373 Mass 700, 706-707, 369 NE2d 1006, 1011 (1977).

[5] *Com. v. Whitehead*, supra, 379 Mass at 657, 400 NE2d at 834; *Com. v. Boris*, 317 Mass 309, 318, 58 NE2d 8, 14 (1944).

[6] See *Com. v. Hurley*, 455 Mass 53, 64, 913 NE2d 850, 860 (2009) (as with any other witness, the declarant must have personal knowledge of the event in question, and must be competent); *Com. v. King*, 436 Mass 252, 254-255, 763 NE2d 1071 (2002); *Com. v. Crawford*, 417 Mass 358, 363, 629 NE2d 1332, 1334 (1994) (& citations).

> **Control by court.** The court shall exercise reasonable control over the mode and order of interrogating witnesses and presenting evidence on direct and cross-examination so as to (1) make the interrogation and presentation effective for the ascertainment of the truth, (2) avoid needless consumption of time, and (3) protect witnesses from harassment or undue embarrassment. The court has the discretion to admit evidence conditionally upon the representation that its relevancy will be established by evidence subsequently offered.

The party having the burden of proof is required to put in its entire affirmative case first. Thereafter, the opposing party rebuts and puts in its entire affirmative case. The party that presented first may then introduce evidence to rebut new matters. Nonetheless a broad discretion is conferred on the trial judge regarding the order of evidence in the interest of accommodating witnesses and the parties.[1]

Rebuttal is considered a matter of right where the proponent seeks to refute evidence of new facts presented by the opposing party.[2] "Rebuttal is legitimate when it responds to the opponent's case; [and the judge] has a nearly unreversible discretion to allow it."[3] There is no right to rebut evidence that was not unanticipated, or to present rebuttal evidence that merely supports the proponent's affirmative case.[4] Although courts are generally strict in forbidding affirmative evidence

---

§ 6.6 [1] See *Com. v. Lopez*, 433 Mass 406, 413-414, 742 NE2d 1067, 1073 (2001), *habeas petition denied in Lopez v. Massachusetts*, 480 F3d 591 (1st Cir 2007); *Com. v. Rancourt*, 399 Mass 269, 277, 503 NE2d 960, 965 (1987). Cf. *Finance Commission of Boston v. McGrath*, 343 Mass 754, 768, 180 NE2d 808, 817 (1962) (administrative body has discretion to determine order of testimony).

[2] *Com. v. Wood*, 302 Mass 265, 267, 19 NE2d 320, 322 (1939).

[3] *Com. v. Roberts*, 433 Mass 45, 51, 740 NE2d 176, 181 (2000) (citation omitted). See also *Com. v. Pagan*, 440 Mass 84, 89, 794 NE2d 1184, 1187-1189 (2003), *habeas denied*, 578 F Supp 2d 343 (D Mass 2008) (rebuttal evidence that defendant threatened to kill former girlfriend if he ever saw her with another man responded to defendant's testimony that he had no motive to kill victim); *Com. v. Upton U.*, 59 Mass App 252, 259, 795 NE2d 575, 580 (2003) (licensed social worker permitted to give rebuttal testimony concerning interviewing techniques and behavior patterns of sexually abused children). Compare *Com. v. Whitman*, 453 Mass 331, 342, 901 NE2d 1206, 1216 (2009) (proffered testimony did not rebut prosecution witnesses).

[4] *Com. v. Lopez*, supra, 433 Mass at 414, 742 NE2d at 1073 (proffered evidence cumulative and collateral). See also *Drake v. Goodman*, 386 Mass 88, 92, 434 NE2d 1211, 1214 (1982); *Urban Investment & Development Co. v. Turner Construction Co.*, 35 Mass App 100, 103-104, 616 NE2d 829, 832 (1993).

in rebuttal, the judge is accorded wide discretion to allow it.[5] Rebuttal evidence on a collateral matter may be admitted to impeach a witness's credibility.[6] A party would be well-advised to obtain the judge's ruling on the matter of his right to present a rebuttal witness before resting his case-in-chief.[7]

Where counsel opens a subject, opposing counsel may generally respond with evidence on the subject.[8]

A trial judge may, in certain limited circumstances, allow the Commonwealth to reopen its case after it has rested, but presumptively not where the defendant has also rested and filed a motion for a required finding of not guilty,[9] and not in order to permit the Commonwealth to supplement evidence on a missing element.[10] The decision whether to reopen a case cannot be made in an arbitrary or capricious manner, and good practice dictates that trial judges record their reasons for allowing or refusing a party's request to reopen.[11]

The usual procedure for interrogation of a witness[12] is that the party producing him conducts direct examination about all matters as

---

[5] See *Mason v. General Motors Corp.*, 397 Mass 183, 193, 490 NE2d 437, 443 (1986). See also *Drake v. Goodman*, supra, 386 Mass at 92-94, 43 NE2d at 1213-1215 (extensive discussion of issue); *Chadbourn v. Franklin*, 71 Mass (5 Gray) 312 (1855); *Teller v. Schepens*, supra, 25 Mass App at 350, 518 NE2d at 870; *Com. v. Guidry*, 22 Mass App 907, 909, 491 NE2d 281, 283 (1986).

[6] See *Com. v. Francis*, 432 Mass 353, 360, 734 NE2d 315, 323-324 (2000).

[7] See *Dahms v. Cognex Corp.*, 455 Mass 190, 204, 914 NE2d 872, 884 (2009).

[8] See, e.g., *Com. v. Stuckich*, 450 Mass 449, 459-460, 879 NE2d 105, 115 (2008) (since defense counsel opened on direct examination the topic of defendant's hiring of a lawyer and the advice lawyer gave him regarding responding to the charges, prosecutor could cross-examine on these matters); *Com. v. Stone*, 70 Mass App 800, 807, 877 NE2d 620, 626-627 (2007) (trial judge did not err in admitting trooper's testimony regarding defendant's prior assertion of *Miranda* rights in response to defense expert testimony regarding defendant's mental capacity to waive the warnings).

[9] See *Com. v. Hurley*, 455 Mass 53, 68-69, 913 NE2d 850, 863-864 (2009); *Com. v. Zavala*, 52 Mass App 770, 777-779, 756 NE2d 29, 36-37 (2001) (& cases cited).

[10] *Com. v. Costa*, 88 Mass App 750, 754, 42 NE3d 1162, 1166 (2015).

[11] *Com. v. Moore*, 52 Mass App 120, 126-127, 751 NE2d 901, 906 (2001); *Weber v. Coast to Coast Medical, Inc.*, 83 Mass App 478, 985 NE2d 1212 (2013) (trial court could open record and read parties' stipulations to jury to cure oversight in failing to inform them that parties had stipulated to plaintiff's receipt of right to sue letter).

[12] Mass R Civ P 43(g) provides: "Unless otherwise permitted by the court, the examination and cross-examination of any witness shall be conducted by one attorney only for each party. The attorney shall stand while so examining or cross-examining unless the court otherwise permits." See also Mass Superior Court Rule 69 (same rule applicable in criminal cases).

For a discussion of the propriety of permitting the questioning of witnesses by jurors, see *Com. v. Britto*, 433 Mass 596, 610-615, 744 NE2d 1089, 1103-1106 (2001); *Com. v. Urena*, 417 Mass 692, 632 NE2d 1200 (1994); *Com. v. Reeder*, 73 Mass App 750, 756-757, 901 NE2d 701, 706-707 (2009) (judge should not allow questions that are

to which he is to testify. The witness is then cross-examined by the opponent on the matters as to which he has testified and, under Massachusetts practice, on any other matters relevant to the case.[13] There may then be a redirect examination by the proponent and a re-cross-examination by the opponent; occasionally there are several redirect and re-cross-examinations.[14] The same witness may be called later as the opposing party's witness, in which case the original proponent conducts cross-examination. The court in its discretion may permit a witness to be recalled by either side to present new information, but the judge is not required to do so.[15] While the trial judge has wide discretion to impose reasonable limits on the length of witness examination, the judge may not impose arbitrary time limits on the taking of testimony in a manner that prevents the parties from presenting their entire case.[16]

A criminal defendant has a constitutional right to be present at all critical stages of the proceedings.[17]

Regarding the role of the trial judge, "[i]t is a part of the right of trial by jury as established by the law of this Commonwealth that each

---

inconsistent with the rules of evidence or defendant's due process rights). Judges have been advised to exercise particular care in posing questions from jurors in criminal cases involving subtle evidentiary issues. See *Com. v. Mendez*, 77 Mass App 905, 906-907, 929 NE2d 314, 316 (2010) (jury question opened door on testimony that violated first complaint doctrine).

[13] See § 6.7, infra.

[14] See § 6.9, infra.

[15] *Com. v. Forte*, 469 Mass 469, 488, 14 NE3d 900, 916 (2014) (recall is appropriate if the defendant would otherwise be unreasonably deprived of an opportunity to present newly discovered information material to the defense); *Adoption of Cecily*, 83 Mass App 719, 724-725, 989 NE2d 532, 537 (2013) (no error in refusing to allow mother to recall witness); *Com. v. Bradley*, 35 Mass App 525, 531, 622 NE2d 1386, 1390 (1993).

[16] See *Clark v. Clark*, 47 Mass App 737, 745-746, 716 NE2d 144, 152 (1999); *Chandler v. FMC Corp.*, 35 Mass App 332, 338, 619 NE2d 626, 629 (1993). See also *Guardianship of Brandon*, 424 Mass 482, 492-494, 677 NE2d 114, 122-123 (1997) (parties stipulated to time limits).

[17] See *Com. v. Campbell*, 83 Mass App 368, 983 NE2d 1227 (2013) (suppression hearing); *Com. v. Bacigalupo*, 49 Mass App 629, 731 NE2d 559 (2000) (where judge is called on to respond to deliberating jury's communication of legal significance). A defendant has no right to be part of the process in which a witness's claim of Fifth Amendment privilege is considered. *Com. v. Mercado*, 466 Mass 141, 151-152, 993 NE2d 661, 669-670 (2013); *Com. v. Alicea*, 464 Mass 837, 843, 985 NE2d 1197, 1204 (2013) (no right to attend *Martin* hearing). For the protocol to follow where a defendant fails to reappear for trial, see *Com. v. Zammuto*, 89 Mass App 80, 82-83, 46 NE3d 73, 76-77 (2016).

party is entitled to the assistance and protection of the judge throughout the trial."[18] The judge is "not a mere functionary to preserve order and lend ceremonial dignity to the proceedings but rather the directing and controlling mind at the trial."[19] In this regard a judge has "the right, and perhaps the duty . . . to intervene occasionally in the examination of witnesses" to clarify an issue or develop the most trustworthy testimony.[20] The judge may participate in the questioning of a witness "so long as the examination is not partisan in nature, biased, or a display of belief in the defendant's guilt."[21] "So far as possible, a judge should not dress down counsel before the jury, but when examination

---

[18] *Com. v. Bergstrom*, 402 Mass 534, 551, 524 NE2d 366, 376 (1988) (citation omitted). See also *Barrett v. Leary*, 34 Mass App 659, 614 NE2d 1035 (1993) (trial judge's presence in courtroom was required while videotape deposition of medical experts was played for jury). But compare *McSweeney v. Build Safe Corp.*, 417 Mass 610, 632 NE2d 1185 (1994) (reversal not required where counsel failed to object to judge absenting himself during videotaped testimony and there was no showing of prejudice arising from absence). Cf. *Com. v. Patry*, 48 Mass App 470, 722 NE2d 979 (2000) (defendant's constitutional right to public trial was violated by trial judge's giving of supplemental instructions to jury in deliberation room).

[19] *Adoption of Seth*, 29 Mass App 343, 350, 560 NE2d 708, 712 (1990). See, e.g., *Com. v. Mendez*, 77 Mass App 253, 257-258, 929 NE2d 975, 978 (2010) (judge could properly preclude any reference in closing argument to testimony as to victim's prior sexual conduct that was admitted in violation of the Rape Shield statute even without an objection).

[20] *Com. v. Festa*, 369 Mass 419, 422, 341 NE2d 276, 279 (1976). See also *Com. v. Rivera*, 441 Mass 358, 367-368, 805 NE2d 942, 950-951 (2004) (judge's interruptions of defense expert were made in thoughtful, courteous manner and with proper instruction to jury); *Com. v. Lucien*, 440 Mass 658, 663-664, 801 NE2d 247, 253-254 (2004) (judge did not improperly put words in witness's mouth or "rescue" prosecution when he interrupted defense inquiry and told witness not to speculate); *Com. v. Paradise*, 405 Mass 141, 157, 539 NE2d, 1006, 1016-1017 (1989); *Com. v. Powell*, 72 Mass App 22, 30, 888 NE2d 370, 376 (2008) (proper for judge to ask witness whether she harbored any doubt about her identification of defendant).

[21] *Com. v. Festa*, supra, 369 Mass at 422, 341 NE2d at 279. See also *Adoption of Norbert*, 83 Mass App 542, 546-548, 986 NE2d 886, 891-892 (2013) (trial judges questioning of witnesses in termination of parental rights proceeding, almost to the exclusion of attorneys, went beyond clarification and into substantive areas best left to counsel to develop, but did not deprive mother of impartial justice); *Com. v. Marangiello*, 410 Mass 452, 457-462, 573 NE2d 500, 503-506 (1991) (judge's questioning of the victim, who because of a handicap was testifying through interpreters, was not inappropriate where he properly determined there was need for clarification and his involvement was not overbearing); *Nancy P. v. D'Amato*, 401 Mass 516, 525, 517 NE2d 824, 829 (1988) (judge entitled to question witness not called as an expert as to her opinions); *Com. v. Watkins*, 63 Mass App 69, 823 NE2d 404 (2005) (scope of judge's questioning of eyewitness in jury-waived trial, which elicited testimony about the source of the witness's certainty, was proper); *Com. v. Gomes*, 54 Mass App 1, 763 NE2d 83 (2002) (judge's clarifying question of victim witness, leading to in-court identification, was proper); *Com. v. DeJesus*, 44 Mass App 349, 353, 691 NE2d 234, 238 (1998) (trial judge's brief take-over of cross-examination of prosecution witness, to ask seven

of witnesses veers off the point, it is not unreasonable for a trial judge to rein in counsel."[22] "[A] first-rate trial judge will find and tread the narrow path that lies between meddlesomeness on the one hand and ineffectiveness and impotence on the other."[23]

Massachusetts law permits the trial judge to comment on the evidence, provided of course that it is done in a fair and impartial manner and does not invade the jury's sole function to assess the credibility of witnesses and find the facts.[24] In order to avoid inadvertently conveying to the jury a suggestion about what the verdict should be, trial

---

simple questions clarifying description of robbery location, not prejudicial to defendant); *Com. v. Meadows*, 33 Mass App 534, 539-540, 602 NE2d 583, 586-587 (1992) (trial judge did not give robbery victim's testimony judicial imprimatur of credibility or undercut cross-examination when he intervened by questioning witness to clarify testimony). Compare *Com. v. Ragonesi*, 22 Mass App 320, 493 NE2d 527 (1986) (& citations) (reversal of convictions was required because of judge's extensive and excessive questioning of complainant at pretrial hearing) and *Com. v. Hassey*, 40 Mass App 806, 668 NE2d 357 (1996) (judge's examination of defense witness went beyond clarification and was partisan).

On the matter of judicial bias, see *City of Boston v. U.S. Gypsum Co.*, 37 Mass App 253, 256-259, 638 NE2d 1387, 1389-1391 (1994). For a discussion of the judge's role regarding a pro se litigant, see *Com. v. Jackson*, 419 Mass 716, 721-722, 647 NE2d 401, 405 (1995).

[22] *Com. v. Meadows*, supra, 33 Mass App at 536-537, 602 NE2d at 585. Compare *Com. v. Brown*, 462 Mass 620, 632-634, 970 NE2d 306, 316-318 (2012) (trial judge did not act unfairly in interrupting and admonishing defense counsel during his opening, closing, and cross-examination) and *Com. v. Keniston*, 423 Mass 304, 310, 667 NE2d 1127, 1132-1133 (1996) (no unfair prejudice where judge reprimanded defense counsel for theatrics) with *Com. v. Sylvester*, 388 Mass 749, 751-752, 448 NE2d 1106, 1107-1108 (1983) (judge's remarks disparaging defense counsel's skill, some with personal overtones, deprived defendant of a fair trial) and *Kuczynski v. Alfano*, 402 Mass 1001, 520 NE2d 150 (1988) (judge's repeated and combative interruptions of counsel and his sharp comments and questions to plaintiff's witnesses were not consistent with judge's role as impartial magistrate).

[23] *Com. v. Brown*, 462 Mass 620, 632, 970 NE2d 306, 317 (2012) (citation omitted).

[24] See GL 231, § 81 ("The courts [in civil actions] shall not charge juries with respect to matters of fact, but they may state the testimony and the law."). See also *Com. v. Moses*, 436 Mass 598, 603-605, 766 NE2d 827, 831-832 (2002) (although judge's instructions on deliberate premeditation used examples similar to evidence introduced by Commonwealth, no impermissible comment on evidence); *Com. v. Perez*, 390 Mass 308, 319, 455 NE2d 632, 638 (1983) (judge may state the evidence and discuss possible inferences to be drawn therefrom, but may not directly or indirectly express an opinion as to the credibility of particular witnesses); *Com. v. McColl*, 375 Mass 316, 321-322, 376 NE2d 562, 565-566 (1978) (& citations) (judge may properly engage in analysis of evidence). Compare *Com. v. Kane*, 19 Mass App 129, 138, 472 NE2d 1343, 1349-1350 (1984) (& citations) (judge improperly conveyed his own view of evidence); *Com. v. Borges*, 2 Mass App 869, 316 NE2d 627 (1974) (judge's comment during instructions, "You don't go around paying somebody else's doctor's bills if you didn't cause the reason for it," amounted to instruction as to inference which jury should

judges are advised to specifically inform the jury that they are not to read anything into the judge's voice inflections during instructions.[25]

Juror note-taking has a long history in the Commonwealth, dating to the Boston Massacre trial,[26] and may be permitted in the discretion of the trial judge.[27]

§ 6.6.1 *Right to Public Trial*

The testimony of witnesses "shall be taken orally in open court."[28] The right to a public criminal trial is protected by the Sixth Amendment to the U.S. Constitution,[29] and extends to jury selection.[30] Jurors should be informed, however, that they may request an opportunity to

---

draw from victim's testimony and had effect of throwing judge's opinion onto scales decisively against defendant). See also *Com. v. Armstrong*, 54 Mass App 594, 597-598, 766 NE2d 894, 897 (2002) (discussing limitations on judge's comments on evidence in context of bench trial); *Adoption of Tia*, 73 Mass App 115, 896 NE2d 51 (2008) (trial judge's comments prematurely assessing the evidence supporting termination of parental rights and urging settlement were improper but did not warrant reversal of bench trial ruling).

[25] See *Com. v. Moore*, 52 Mass App 120, 128-129, 751 NE2d 901, 907-908 (2001). See also *Com. v. Medina*, 64 Mass App 708, 719-720, 835 NE2d 300, 311-312 (2005) (record did not support defendant's contention that judge's gestures during closing argument prejudiced him, and instructions to jury cured any possible prejudice).

[26] See H.B. Zobel, The Boston Massacre 271 (1970), cited in *Com. v. Germain*, 381 Mass 256, 267 n.18, 408 NE2d 1358 (1980).

[27] *Com. v. Shea*, 460 Mass 163, 176-179, 950 NE2d 393, 404-406 (2011).

[28] Mass R Civ P 43(a) (unless otherwise provided by these rules). Evidence offered as a basis for a motion may, in the discretion of the court, be received by way of affidavit. Mass R Civ P 43(e); Mass R Crim P 13; Mass Superior Ct Rule 9, 9A, 61. A Probate and Family Court judge may conduct an in camera interview with a minor child in a custody matter. See *Abbott v. Virusso*, 68 Mass App 326, 334-339, 862 NE2d 52, 59-62 (2007), *aff'd*, 450 Mass 1031 (2008).

[29] "In all criminal prosecutions, the accused shall enjoy the right to a speedy and public trial . . ."

[30] See generally *Presley v. Georgia*, 558 US 209 (2010). Compare *Com. v. Lennon*, 463 Mass 520, 526-528, 977 NE2d 33, 37-39 (2012) (defendant failed to show closure of courtroom by exclusion of his sister during jury selection), *Com. v. Rogers*, 459 Mass 249, 263-264, 945 NE2d 295, 308-309 (2011) (removal of all spectators so there was room for the venire was not a closure of the courtroom, where the judge ordered the back door to remain open), *Com. v. Greineder*, 458 Mass 207, 219-234, 936 NE2d 372, 383-393 (2010) (individual voir dire was not improperly closed to the public), and *Com. v. Edward*, 75 Mass App 162, 169-174, 912 NE2d 515, 521-524 (2009) (closure of rape trial with minor victim under age 18) with *Com. v. White*, 85 Mass App 491, 11 NE3d 628 (2014) (closure of courtroom during statutory questioning of potential jurors was not de minimis); *Com. v. Downey*, 78 Mass App 224, 936 NE2d 442 (2010) (judge improperly closed courtroom during empanelment), *Com. v. Grant*, 78 Mass App 450, 940 NE2d 448 (2010) (trial judge should have made a factual determination

meet in camera with the judge with counsel present and on the record regarding matters that would be embarrassing or damaging if done in public.[31]

A defendant claiming the right has been violated bears the burden of proving the courtroom was closed.[32] The party seeking to close a criminal trial to the public must advance an overriding interest that is likely to be prejudiced; the closure must be no broader than necessary to protect that interest; the trial court must consider reasonable alternatives to closing the proceeding; and it must make findings adequate to support the closure.[33]

Use of a sign-in procedure for all attendees, taken for concerns about security or witness intimidation, does not rise to the level of a constitutional closure;[34] but the Supreme Judicial Court will exercise its supervisory power to preserve the presumption of openness in our courtrooms.[35] The exclusion of potential or sequestered witnesses is

---

and held a hearing to determine whether the courtroom was closed to the public during voir dire), *Com. v. Wolcott*, 77 Mass App 457, 459-465, 931 NE2d 1025, 1028-1032 (2010) (defendant's Sixth Amendment right to public trial was violated by full closure of courtroom during jury selection), *Com. v. Cohen*, 456 Mass 94, 921 NE2d 906 (2010) (closure of courtroom during jury selection was broader than necessary, requiring new trial), and *Com. v. Baran*, 74 Mass App 256, 292-297, 905 NE2d 1122, 1151-1154 (2009) (counsel failed to protect defendant's right to a public trial when the courtroom was closed during testimony of children in day care molestation case). See also § 1.9, supra.

For partial closure of the courtroom by ejecting certain individuals, see *Com. v. Caldwell*, 459 Mass 271, 281-284, 945 NE2d 313, 324-325 (2011) (setting forth proper procedures to inform counsel and make findings supporting removal, such as safety concerns).

Civil commitment hearings are presumptively open to the public. *Kirk v. Com.*, 459 Mass 67, 944 NE2d 135 (2011).

The First Amendment right of access to a criminal trial does not include a right to bring cameras in or make audio or video recordings. *Com. v. Winfield*, 464 Mass 672, 677, 985 NE2d 86, 91 (2013).

[31] *Com. v. Jaynes*, 55 Mass App 301, 770 NE2d 483 (2002), *habeas denied*, *Jaynes v. Mitchell*, 2015 WL881245 (D Mass 2015), relying on *Press-Enterprise Co. v. Superior Court of California*, 464 US 501, 511-512 (1984).

[32] *Com. v. Buckman*, 461 Mass 24, 27-29, 957 NE2d 1089, 1094-1096 (2011) (defendant failed to satisfy his burden that there was partial closure of the courtroom through exclusion of friends and family during jury selection); *Com. v. Torres*, 86 Mass App 272, 274-275, 15 NE3d 778, 782 (2014).

[33] *Presley v. Georgia*, supra, 558 US at 213-214; *Com. v. Alebord*, 467 Mass 106, 111 n.12, 4 NE3d 248, 254 n.12. (2014).

[34] *Com. v. Ray*, 467 Mass 115, 122-126, 4 NE3d 221, 229-231 (2014); *Com. v. Maldonado*, 466 Mass 742, 746-753, 2 NE3d 145, 150-155 (2014).

[35] *Com. v. Maldonado*, supra, 466 Mass at 751-752, 2 NE3d at 154.

not considered to be partial closure of the courtroom.[36] Although the Sixth Amendment right extends to some pretrial proceedings, such as suppression hearings, it does not extend to all such proceedings.[37]

Defense counsel may waive, with or without defendant's express consent, the right to public trial during jury selection, where waiver is a tactical decision as part of the defense strategy.[38] A procedural waiver may occur where counsel fails to object.[39] Where the defendant has procedurally waived his Sixth Amendment public trial claim by not raising it at trial, and later raises it in a collateral attack asserting ineffective assistance of counsel, the defendant is required to affirmatively show prejudice.[40]

§ 6.7 Scope and Extent of Cross-Examination

"Parties to litigation are entitled as a matter of right to the reasonable cross-examination of witnesses against them for the purpose of attempting to impeach or discredit their testimony. The scope of cross-examination, including to what extent the accuracy, veracity, and credibility of a witness may be tested, rests largely in the sound discretion of the judge, not subject to revision unless prejudice is shown to a party by reason of too narrow restriction or too great breadth of inquiry."[1] Once trial counsel has "opened up" a subject, opposing counsel must of

[36] See *Com. v. Collins*, 470 Mass 255, 270-272, 21 NE3d 528, 540-542 (2014) (exclusion during empanelment); *Com. v. Buckman*, supra, 461 Mass at 29 n.2, 957 NE2d at 1096 n.2.

[37] See *Com. v. Riley*, 86 Mass App 309, 313, 15 NE3d 1165, 1169 (2014).

[38] See *Com. v. Lavoie*, 464 Mass 83, 981 NE2d 192 (2013).

[39] *Com. v. Jackson*, 471 Mass 262, 28 NE3d 437 (2015) (closure of courtroom for 60 to 90 minutes during empanelment waived by failure to object, even though neither defense counsel nor defendant knew of closure); *Com. v. Wall*, 469 Mass 652, 672-673,15 NE3d 708, 724-725 (2014) (no objection when defendant's uncle was allegedly prevented from entering courtroom during empanelment, even though defense counsel was not aware of exclusion); *Com. v. Alebord*, supra, 467 Mass at 111-113, 4 NE3d at 254-255 (waiver by acquiescence of trial counsel); *Com. v. Morganti*, 467 Mass 96, 4 NE3d 241 (2014) (waiver by trial counsel's failure to object); *Com. v. Ray*, supra, 467 Mass at 121-122, 4 NE3d at 228 (defense counsel affirmatively acquiesced to judge's proposal to close courtroom); *Com. v. Hardy*, 464 Mass 660, 663-666, 984 NE2d 727, 731-733 (2012) (counsel's failure to object to closures of courtroom during jury selection); *Com. v. Dyer*, 460 Mass 728, 736-737, 955 NE2d 271, 281-282 (2011) (defendant waived his rights to public trial by consenting to partial closure).

[40] *Com. v. LaChance*, 469 Mass 854, 17 NE3d 1101 (2014).

§ 6.7 [1] *Com. v. Gagnon*, 408 Mass 185, 192, 557 NE2d 728, 733-734 (1990).

course be permitted to reasonably explore it.[2] Cross-examination on the same subject as direct examination is appropriate.[3]

Massachusetts practice defines a broad scope of cross-examination, as summarized in Proposed Mass R Evid 611(b): "A witness may be cross-examined on any matter relevant to any issue in the case, including credibility. In the interests of justice, the judge may limit cross-examination with respect to matters not testified to on direct examination."[4] This approach contrasts with the more restrictive scope of cross-examination in the federal courts. See Fed R Evid 611(b): "Cross-examination should be limited to the subject matter of the direct examination and matters affecting the credibility of the witness. The court may, in the exercise of discretion, permit inquiry into additional matters as if on direct examination."[5]

Thus, when a proponent produces a witness, the opposing counsel may cross-examine the witness as to all relevant aspects of the case, whether or not a particular aspect was elicited during direct examination.[6] This rule applies to the criminal defendant who chooses to testify in his own behalf: he thereby renders himself subject to cross-examination on all facts relevant to the crime.[7] Under Massachusetts

---

[2] *Com. v. Torres*, 437 Mass 460, 464, 772 NE2d 1046, 1050 (2002); *Com. v. Stuckich*, 450 Mass 449, 459-460, 879 NE2d 105, 115 (2008) (since defense counsel opened on direct examination the topic of defendant's hiring of a lawyer and the advice lawyer gave him regarding responding to the charges, prosecutor could cross-examine on these matters).

[3] *Kace v. Liang*, 472 Mass 630, 647-648, 36 NE3d 1215, 1229 (2015).

[4] See *Com. v. Bibby*, 35 Mass App 938, 940, 624 NE2d 624, 627 (1993) (citing Text); *Nuger v. Robinson*, 32 Mass App 959, 591 NE2d 1116 (1992) (trial court's ruling in contract action limiting scope of plaintiff's cross-examination of defendant to specific subjects raised on direct examination was reversible error). See also Mass R Civ P 43(b) (interrogation of hostile witness).

[5] In explaining the preference for the broader scope, Chief Justice Lemuel Shaw wrote:

> [W]here a witness is called to a particular fact, he is a witness to all purposes, and may be fully cross-examined to the whole case. . . . It is most desirable that rules of general practice, of so much importance and of such frequent recurrence, should be as few, simple and practical as possible, and that distinctions should not be multiplied without good cause. It would be often difficult, in a long and complicated examination, to decide whether a question applies wholly to new matter, or to matter already examined to in chief. [I]t would not be useful to engraft upon [practice] a distinction not in general necessary to attain the purposes of justice, in the investigation of the truth of facts, that it would be often difficult of application, and that all the practical good expected from it may be as effectually attained by the exercise of the discretionary power of the court.
>
> *Moody v. Rowell*, 34 Mass (17 Pick) 490, 499-500 (1836).

[6] *Nuger v. Robinson*, supra, 32 Mass App at 960, 591 NE2d at 1116-1117. Cross-examination must of course be limited to relevant matters. See, e.g., *Com. v. Haggett*, 79

practice, a party may put in its own affirmative case on cross-examination of the opposing party's witness, regardless of whether the matters were raised on direct.

GL 233, § 22 and Mass R Civ P 43(b) permit a party to call the adverse party (or an officer, director, or managing agent of an institutional party) as a witness and interrogate that witness by leading questions. In such case, the witness may be "cross-examined" by his own counsel only upon the subject matter of his examination-in-chief. The court may permit the use of leading questions when the adverse witness is examined.[8]

Both Proposed Mass R Evid 611(c) and Fed R Evid 611(c) broaden the concept of adverse party in this context to include "a witness identified with an adverse party." This approach is consistent with at least one decision of the Supreme Judicial Court, which upheld cross-examination of a witness called by a proponent to whom the witness is "essentially, although not technically, an adverse party."[9]

The judge has wide discretion to exclude cross-examination in the following circumstances:

- in collateral or remote areas.[10]
- where the proposed inquiry is repetitious or cumulative.[11]

Mass App 167, 173-176, 944 NE2d 601, 607-609 (2011) (cross-examination of victim's guidance counselor regarding her crisis intervention response to victim's report had no relevance, and was prejudicial).

[7] See, e.g, *Com. v. Bell*, 455 Mass 408, 421, 917 NE2d 740, 753 (2009) (defendant could be confronted with post-arrest statements that he failed to mention on direct examination because he cannot select the subjects on which he can be cross-examined); *Com. v. Judge*, 420 Mass 433, 445, 650 NE2d 1242, 1250 (1995). But compare *Com. v. McClendon*, 39 Mass App 122, 128-130, 653 NE2d 1138, 1142-1143 (1995) (even though defendant opened himself up to cross-examination by taking stand, prosecution not entitled to impeach his credibility by way of prior bad acts, see § 6.16.3, infra).

[8] *Westland Housing Corp. v. Scott*, 312 Mass 375, 383, 44 NE2d 959, 964 (1942). See § 6.10, infra.

[9] *Virta v. Mackey*, 343 Mass 286, 291, 178 NE2d 571, 574 (1961).

[10] See, e.g., *Com. v. Fuller*, 66 Mass App 84, 92-93, 845 NE2d 434, 441 (2006) (trial court properly prevented defense counsel from cross-examining mentally retarded rape victim regarding her parenting skills because it would have raised collateral issue of her sexual behavior); *Com. v. Fidler*, 23 Mass App 506, 516-517, 503 NE2d 1302, 1309 (1987); *Com. v. Shaheen*, 15 Mass App 302, 308, 445 NE2d 619, 623-624 (1983).

[11] See, e.g., *Com. v. Jackson*, 419 Mass 716, 722, 726-727, 647 NE2d 401, 405, 407-408 (1995); *Com. v. Carroll*, 360 Mass 580, 589, 276 NE2d 705, 711 (1971); *Com. v. Meadows*, 33 Mass App 534, 540, 602 NE2d 583, 587 (1992).

- to limit cross-examination that is too general or indefinite, particularly in non-jury trials.[12]

"The judge presiding over the trial of a case has the power to keep the examination of witnesses within the limits of common decency and fairness, and he has the duty to exercise that power promptly and firmly when it becomes necessary to do so."[13]

§ 6.8 Cross-Examination in Criminal Cases—Right of Confrontation

The extent of cross-examination assumes a constitutional dimension in criminal cases, where the defendant is guaranteed the right to confront the Commonwealth's witnesses by both the Sixth Amendment to the United States Constitution[1] and art. 12 of the Massachusetts Declaration of Rights.[2] "[T]he decisions of [the United States Supreme Court] and other courts throughout the years have constantly emphasized the necessity for cross-examination as a protection for defendants in criminal cases . . . There are few subjects, perhaps, upon which [the Supreme] Court and other courts have been more nearly unanimous than in their expressions of belief that the right of confrontation and cross-examination is an essential and fundamental requirement for the kind of fair trial which is this country's constitutional goal."[3] Where, for

---

[12] See, e.g., *Nancy P. v. D'Amato*, 401 Mass 516, 524, 517 NE2d 824, 829 (1988).

[13] *Com. v. Rooney*, 365 Mass 484, 495-496, 313 NE2d 105, 112-113 (1974). See also Proposed Mass R Evid 611(a) ("The court shall exercise reasonable control over the mode and order of interrogating witnesses and presenting evidence on direct and cross-examination so as to . . . (3) protect witnesses from harassment or undue embarrassment."); *Com. v. Blake*, 409 Mass 146, 156-162, 564 NE2d 1006, 1012-1016 (1991).

§ 6.8 [1] "In all criminal prosecutions, the accused shall enjoy the right . . . to be confronted with the witnesses against him." US Const., amend. vi.

[2] "[E]very subject shall have a right . . . to meet the witnesses against him face to face." Mass Const, Declaration of Rights art. 12. See *Com. v. Miles*, 420 Mass 67, 71, 648 NE2d 719, 723 (1995); *Com. v. Fuller*, 399 Mass 678, 684, 506 NE2d 852, 856 (1987).

[3] *Com. v. Tanso*, 411 Mass 640, 650, 583 NE2d 1247, 1253-1254 (1991) (citation omitted). See, e.g., *Com. v. Woodbine*, 461 Mass 720, 737-738, 964 NE2d 956, 970-971 (2012) (judge improperly restricted defendant's cross-examination of police officer who failed to record interrogation, requiring reversal of conviction).

example, the issue at trial is identification, the right to cross-examine an eyewitness must be scrupulously protected.[4]

Nonetheless, the right of confrontation is not absolute. A trial judge may curtail cross-examination if the questions are not relevant or the relevance is attenuated.[5] Defendant's right to cross-examine a witness about his current address and place of employment may be restricted when the judge determines that a threat to the witness's safety from disclosure of this information outweighs the defendant's need for it.[6] Questions as to how far cross-examination may go are committed to the trial judge's discretion, and the burden of showing an abuse of that discretion and resulting prejudice is on the defendant, with the reviewing court considering the cross-examination in its entirety.[7] Determining whether a defendant's constitutional right of cross-examination has been violated requires weighing the materiality of the witness's direct testimony and the degree of the restriction on cross-examination.[8]

---

[4] See *Com. v. Vardinski*, 438 Mass 444, 450-451, 780 NE2d 1278, 1285-1286 (2003) (reversing armed robbery conviction because judge restricted defendant's ability to cross examine eyewitness).

[5] See, e.g., *Com. v. Avalos*, 454 Mass 1, 8-9, 906 NE2d 987, 993 (2009) (judge properly prevented defense counsel from asking victim whether she had ever been physically abused by her mother, as it would have created its own trial and was only marginally relevant); *Com. v. Crouse*, 447 Mass 558, 571-575, 855 NE2d 391, 403-405 (2006) (excluding questions to officer called for limited purpose of rebutting attack on jail informant's testimony was proper and did not entirely bar inquiry on the matter); *Com. v. Jordan*, 439 Mass 47, 55, 785 NE2d 368, 375 (2003) (question to detective only marginally relevant to bias and credibility); *Com. v. Buckley*, 410 Mass 209, 221, 571 NE2d 609, 616 (1991); *Com. v. Souza*, 39 Mass App 103, 108, 653 NE2d 1127, 1131 (1995).

[6] See *Com. v. Francis*, 432 Mass 353, 357-358, 734 NE2d 315, 321-322 (2000) (& citations); GL 258B, § 3(h).

[7] *Com. v. Garcia*, 470 Mass 24, 35-36, 18 NE3d 654, 664-665 (2014) (judge did not abuse discretion in prohibiting defendant from presenting a child, for witness to identify and for jury to see); *Com. v. Fordham*, 417 Mass 10, 19-20, 627 NE2d 901, 906 (1994) (but while defendant bears burden of showing both abuse of discretion and prejudice, defendant ought not be required to prove what opposing witness's testimony would have been had cross-examination been permitted); *Com. v. O'Connor*, 407 Mass 663, 672, 555 NE2d 865, 870-871 (1990); *Com. v. Fuller*, supra, 399 Mass, at 684-685, 506 NE2d at 856.

[8] *Com. v. Knight*, 437 Mass 487, 496, 773 NE2d 390, 398-399 (2002); *Com. v. DeJesus*, 44 Mass App 349, 352, 691 NE2d 234, 237 (1998). Compare *Com. v. Reynolds*, 429 Mass 388, 390-392, 708 NE2d 658, 661-662 (1999) (reversible error to prevent defense counsel from cross-examining police officer concerning failure to pursue

"Where there is no opportunity to cross-examine a witness, because, for example, he is uncooperative, fails to appear, or invokes his privilege against self-incrimination, the striking of any direct testimony by that witness may be constitutionally required."[9]

---

leads concerning other possible suspects), *Com. v. Miles*, supra, 420 Mass at 71-75, 648 NE2d at 723-724 (error to exclude cross-examination of police officer concerning other suspect), and *Com. v. Rescia*, 44 Mass App 909, 688 NE2d 1026 (1998) (remand required where defendant not permitted to cross-examine victim at restitution hearing regarding specifics of property taken in purse) with *Com. v. Mercado*, 456 Mass 198, 203-204, 922 NE2d 140, 146 (2010) (limiting counsel's use of inflammatory photographs on cross-examination was proper where the disturbing visual evidence had minimal probative value), *Com. v. Perez*, 444 Mass 143, 148-150, 825 NE2d 1040, 1045-1046 (2005) (no improper limitation of defendant's cross-examination of detective regarding other possible suspects because he was extensively examined about adequacy of investigation), *Com. v. Sands*, 424 Mass 184, 189 n.7, 675 NE2d 370, 373 n.7 (1997) (no violation of art. 12 where defendant chose to avoid extensive questioning of trooper as matter of trial strategy), *Com. v. Barbosa*, 399 Mass 841, 845, 507 NE2d 694, 696 (1987) (rejecting defendant's contention that his confrontation right was denied because of the limited language skills of the deaf-mute victim and inability of the interpreter to interpret critical questions on cross-examination), *Com. v. Monlez*, 45 Mass App 802, 810, 702 NE2d 40, 46-47 (1998) (no error in refusing to allow defendant to cross-examine victim by showing her altered photo array), and *Com. v. Lloyd*, 45 Mass App 931, 702 NE2d 395 (1998) (judge properly refused to permit defendant to cross-examine victim about her alleged use of Prozac at time of incident). See also *Com. v. Conefrey*, 410 Mass 1, 8-14, 570 NE2d 1384, 1388-1391 (1991) (discussing the right to cross-examine in context of defendant representing himself); *Com. v. Massey*, 402 Mass 453, 523 NE2d 781 (1988) (discussing right to cross-examine during voir dire of witness to determine competency to testify).

[9] See *Com. v. Santiago*, 30 Mass App 207, 221, 567 NE2d 943, 951-952 (1991) (& citations). See, e.g., *Com. v. Kirouac*, 405 Mass 557, 560-564, 542 NE2d 270 (1989); *Com. v. Funches*, 379 Mass 283, 397 NE2d 1097 (1979) (trial judge erred in refusing to strike direct testimony of prosecution's chief witness who asserted privilege against self-incrimination on cross-examination); *Com. v. Johnson*, 365 Mass 534, 539-548, 313 NE2d 571, 576-581 (1974) (defendant's right to confrontation violated where judge, concerned with safety of the prosecution witness, refused to order him to answer questions on cross-examination); *Com. v. Brazie*, 66 Mass App 315, 847 NE2d 1100 (2006) (reversal required where child rape victim did not return to court to complete direct and was never subject to cross-examination). Compare *Com. v. Almeida*, 452 Mass 601, 607, 897 NE2d 14, 21 (2008) (reluctant witness's memory lapses did not deprive defendant of meaningful cross-examination); *Com. v. Brown*, 451 Mass 200, 206-208, 884 NE2d 488, 494 (2008) (although a jury should generally be afforded the fullest opportunity to observe all aspects of witness's demeanor, no violation of defendant's confrontation rights where judge allowed witness to give some nonverbal responses); *Com. v. Amirault*, 404 Mass 221, 234-235, 535 NE2d 193, 202-203 (1989) (child witness's lapse of memory was not comparable to a refusal to answer questions); *Com. v. Santiago*, supra, 30 Mass App at 221-222 (exclusion of police officer's testimony regarding defendant's inculpatory statements not required even though he could not remember, and made no notes of, any exculpatory statements). See also *Brown v. Ruane*, 630 F3d 62 (1st Cir 2011) (discussing federal standard for determining whether limits imposed on defense cross-examination violate the Confrontation Clause).

The right of "face to face" confrontation protected by art. 12 of the Massachusetts Declaration of Rights precludes witnesses from testifying outside the physical presence of the defendant and the jury.[10] Art. 12 also forbids a special courtroom seating arrangement that impedes the defendant's view of the faces of minor complainants as they testify.[11] Art. 12 is not violated, however, where the child's testimony is taken on videotape in the presence of the defendant upon a showing of a compelling need to do so.[12]

Because a proceeding pursuant to GL 209A alleging domestic abuse is civil, not criminal, the constitutional right to confront witnesses does not apply. A defendant against whom a domestic abuse prevention order is sought has a general right to cross-examine witnesses against him, but the judge in appropriate circumstances may limit and even deny cross-examination for good cause.[13] Similarly,

---

[10] See *Com. v. Bergstrom*, 402 Mass 534, 524 NE2d 366 (1988) (holding that GL 278, § 16D, which permits child witnesses in sexual assault cases to testify by closed-circuit television transmission, violates art. 12). Compare *Maryland v. Craig*, 497 US 836 (1990) (rejecting Sixth Amendment challenge to statutory procedure allowing use of one-way closed-circuit television to present testimony of child abuse victim). See also *Com. v. Nwachukwu*, 65 Mass App 112, 837 NE2d 301 (2005) (defendant's constitutional rights to be present at trial and confront witnesses were violated where defense counsel instructed defendant to wait outside courtroom in erroneous response to sequestration order).

[11] See *Com. v. LeFave*, 430 Mass 169, 170, 714 NE2d 805, 807 (1999); *Com. v. Amirault*, 424 Mass 618, 632, 677 NE2d 652, 662 (1997); *Com. v. Souza*, 44 Mass App 238, 689 NE2d 1359 (1998); *Com. v. Spear*, 43 Mass App 583, 686 NE2d 1037 (1997) (special seating arrangement allowing nine-year-old complainant to testify facing jury box and not defendant violated confrontation rights, even if defendant could see complainant's profile). Compare *Com. v. Sanchez*, 423 Mass 591, 596-598, 670 NE2d 377, 380-381 (1996) (no violation of confrontation right where judge seated child witness at table in front of jury box while defendant sat 20 feet away at counsel table); *Com. v. Johnson*, 417 Mass 498, 631 NE2d 1002 (1994). See also *Coy v. Iowa*, 487 US 1012 (1988) (Sixth Amendment violated when child witnesses were shielded from defendant by a screen).

[12] See *Com. v. Tufts*, 405 Mass 610, 542 NE2d 586 (1989); *Com. v. Dockham*, 405 Mass 618, 622-625, 542 NE2d 591, 594-595 (1989); *Com. v. Amirault*, 404 Mass 221, 240-243, 535 NE2d 193, 205-207 (1989).

[13] *Frizado v. Frizado*, 420 Mass 592, 596-598, 651 NE2d 1206, 1210-1211 (1995); *Silvia v. Duarte*, 421 Mass 1007, 657 NE2d 1262 (1995) (failure to allow defendant to cross-examine domestic abuse complainant not abuse of discretion given defendant's established history of violence directed at complainant); *F.A.P. v. J.E.S.*, 87 Mass App 595, 600-601, 33 NE3d 1245, 1250-1251 (2015) (defendant at hearing on temporary harassment prevention order was afforded extensive cross-examination of plaintiff's witnesses, and was ordered to "move on" only after the topic had been exhaustingly explored). But see *C.O. v. M.M.*, 442 Mass 648, 656-658, 815 NE2d 582, 589-591 (2004)

there is no constitutional right to confront witnesses in a divorce proceeding,[14] or in proceedings to terminate parental rights,[15] or in sex offender classification or sexually dangerous person commitment proceedings.[16] The right to cross-examine extends to witnesses only, and not to persons present in the courtroom as "demonstrative evidence" but who do not testify.[17]

In 2006, the Supreme Judicial Court departed from then-current practice in Massachusetts and most of the country (federal and state courts) when it upheld a reciprocal discovery order requiring a defendant to disclose to the Commonwealth statements of prosecution witnesses that the defendant intended to use for impeachment at trial, rejecting the contention that this violated defendant's right to confront and cross-examine.[18] Over a dissent by Chief Justice Marshall (joined by Justices Ireland and Cordy) observing that the effectiveness of cross-examination often depends on being able to confront a witness with a prior statement that he has not had the opportunity to shade his testimony around, the Court insisted that "criminal trials are matters of justice and not sporting events."[19]

For further discussion of the right to cross-examine to show bias, see § 6.15, infra. For discussion of the confrontation issue in regard to a non-testifying codefendant (the *Bruton* issue), see § 8.6.7, infra.

§ 6.9 Redirect and Re-Cross-Examination

The primary purpose of redirect examination is to give the witness who has been cross-examined an opportunity to explain, correct, or

---

(trial court's refusal to allow defendant to cross-examine witnesses in 209A proceeding, where there was no concern about harassment or intimidation of witnesses, violated defendant's constitutional and statutory rights).

[14] *White v. White*, 40 Mass App 132, 133, 662 NE2d 230, 232 (1996) (but judge lacked authority to take 22-year-old daughter's testimony outside presence of parties and attorneys to resolve conflicting testimony about father's alleged sexual misconduct).

[15] *Adoption of Thea*, 78 Mass App 818, 826, 942 NE2d 190, 196-197 (2011) (no face-to-face confrontation right was violated where institutionalized child was permitted to testify telephonically); *Adoption of Don*, 435 Mass 158, 167-169, 755 NE2d 721, 728-729 (2001) (seating arrangement that permitted children to testify against parents without facing them did not implicate art. 12).

[16] *Doe v. Sex Offender Registry Board*, 79 Mass App 683, 694, 948 NE2d 1268, 1276-1277 (2011).

[17] See *Com. v. Roderick*, 411 Mass 817, 820, 586 NE2d 967, 969 (1992).

[18] See *Com. v. Durham*, 446 Mass 212, 843 NE2d 1035 (2006).

[19] 446 Mass at 229, 843 NE2d at 1048.

modify evidence elicited from him on cross-examination.[1] Thus, a subject opened during cross-examination may be explored on redirect.[2] Introduction of parts of a statement on cross-examination generally permits detailed examination of the entire statement on redirect.[3]

The scope of redirect examination is within the discretion of the trial judge, and a party who claims an abuse of discretion assumes a heavy burden.[4] Such abuse will not be found where the party "opened the door" to the rebuttal.[5]

Redirect examination to explain testimony adduced on cross-examination is, however, treated as a matter of right.[6] Although the scope of inquiry on redirect is generally limited to those matters raised

---

§ 6.9 [1] See *Com. v. Wright*, 444 Mass 576, 583, 829 NE2d 1117, 1124 (2005); *Com. v. Olszewski*, 416 Mass 707, 718, 625 NE2d 529, 536 (1993), *habeas petition denied in Olszewski v. Spencer*, 466 F3d 47 (1st Cir 2006); *Com. v. Allen*, 395 Mass 448, 459, 480 NE2d 630, 638 (1985).

[2] See, e.g, *Com. v. Borgos*, 464 Mass 23, 979 NE2d 1095 (2012) (by suggesting during cross-examination of detective that the Commonwealth had paid witnesses to have a hotel room in exchange for their testimony, defense counsel opened the door to redirect eliciting that witnesses feared for their lives); *Com. v. Ridge*, 455 Mass 307, 323-324, 916 NE2d 348, 363-364 (2009) (by cross-examining prosecution witness about common use of duct tape in construction work, in murder trial involving victims bound by such tape, defense counsel opened the door to redirect from witness that he never knew defendant to have a construction job); *Com. v. Marrero*, 427 Mass 65, 68-69, 691 NE2d 918, 921-922 (1998); *Com. v. Johnson*, 412 Mass 318, 325, 588 NE2d 684, 688 (1992); *Com. v. Otsuki*, 411 Mass 218, 236, 581 NE2d 999, 1009-1010 (1991); *Com. v. Smith*, 403 Mass 489, 498-499, 531 NE2d 556, 561-562 (1988) (& citations). Compare *Com. v. Casali*, 459 Mass 139, 144-145, 943 NE2d 936, 940 (2011) (redirect sought by defense counsel would not have rehabilitated witness, but put evidence previously excluded before jury).

[3] *Com. v. Wright*, supra, 444 Mass at 583, 829 NE2d at 1123; *Com. v. Hoffer*, 375 Mass 369, 376, 377 NE2d 685, 690 (1978). See also § 1.7, supra.

[4] *Com. v. Gordon*, 407 Mass 340, 352, 553 NE2d 915, 921-922 (1990); *Com. v. Maltais*, 387 Mass 79, 92, 438 NE2d 847, 854 (1982).

[5] *Com. v. Garcia*, 470 Mass 24, 37, 18 NE3d 654, 666 (2014); *Com. v. Torres*, 86 Mass App 272, 279, 15 NE3d 778, 785 (2014).

[6] See *Com. v. Helfant*, 398 Mass 214, 222, 496 NE2d 433, 439-440 (1986) (defendant had right to explain why he lied to police); *Com. v. Mandeville*, 386 Mass 393, 400, 436 NE2d 912, 917-918 (1982) (defendant had right to explain damaging testimony elicited on cross-examination); *Com. v. Fatalo*, 345 Mass 85, 185 NE2d 754 (1962) (defendant had right to explain testimony developed on cross-examination that had impeached his alibi); *Com. v. Emence*, 47 Mass App 299, 713 NE2d 374 (1999) (reversible error to exclude defense counsel's question on redirect responding to prosecutor's suggestion of fabrication on cross); *Com. v. Charles*, 47 Mass App 191, 712 NE2d 613 (1999) (reversible error to prevent defendant from testifying, by way of rehabilitation, as to what police detective told her before taking taped statement, after defendant conceded on cross that statement omitted several facts testified to at trial). Compare

on cross-examination, the judge has discretion to allow redirect concerning matters not touched on in cross-examination.[7]

A defendant has no right to re-cross-examination unless the examination addresses a new matter brought out for the first time on redirect examination. Otherwise, re-cross-examination is allowed within the sound discretion of the trial judge.[8]

§ 6.10 Leading Questions

Leading questions are questions that suggest to the witness the answer desired by the examiner, and for that reason are generally objectionable on direct examination of one's own witness.[1] Mass R Evid 611(c), which is substantially identical to Fed R Evid 611(c), provides:

> Leading questions should not be used on the direct examination of a witness except as may be necessary to develop his testimony. Ordinarily leading questions should be permitted on cross-examination. When a party calls a hostile witness, an adverse party, *or a witness identified with an adverse party*, interrogation may be by leading questions (emphasis added).

The italicized phrase, as the Advisory Committee pointed out, is broader than Mass R Civ P 43(b) and GL 233, § 22, both of which confine the use of leading questions in this context to the adverse party or an officer, director, or managing agent of the adverse party.[2]

Martel v. MBTA, 403 Mass 1, 7, 525 NE2d 662, 665 (1988) (since no erroneous impression was created on cross-examination, judge did not err in excluding clarifying evidence on redirect); *Footit v. Monsees*, 26 Mass App 173, 182, 525 NE2d 423, 429 (1988) (judge properly limited efforts to rehabilitate witness on redirect that went to collateral matters).

[7] *Com. v. Allen*, supra, 395 Mass at 459, 480 NE2d at 638; *Com. v. Nawn*, 394 Mass 1, 5, 474 NE2d 545, 549 (1985); *Com. v. Rodriguez*, 75 Mass App 235, 245, 913 NE2d 880, 889 (2009) (no abuse of discretion in allowing Commonwealth to introduce testimony about school-zone measurement for first time on redirect).

[8] *Com. v. O'Brien*, 419 Mass 470, 476, 645 NE2d 1170, 1174 (1995); *Com. v. Riley*, 17 Mass App 950, 952, 457 NE2d 660, 662-663 (1983) (citing Text) (same ground had been well-plowed by the direct, cross, and redirect examination).

§ 6.10 [1] See *Com. v. Stewart*, 454 Mass 527, 531-532, 911 NE2d 161, 167-168 (2009) (prosecutor should not have been permitted to communicate Commonwealth's versions of events by means of leading questions to witness, who answered "No comment").

[2] But see *Virta v. Mackey*, 343 Mass 286, 291, 178 NE2d 571, 574 (1961) (judge had discretion to permit cross-examination of a witness called by a proponent to whom the witness was "essentially, although not technically, an adverse party").

Leading questions are permissible on direct examination in the following circumstances:

- When examining a hostile witness, including the adverse party.[3]
- If necessary to refresh the failing or confused memory of a friendly witness.[4]
- To elicit testimony from a witness of limited understanding due to age, mental disability, difficulty with the English language, or other similar reason.[5]
- In bringing out preliminary matters such as name, age, business, place of residence, and so on.[6]

The allowance of leading questions is almost wholly a matter within the court's discretion.[7] The judge may instruct the jury that facts suggested in leading questions, which are answered in the negative are not evidence.[8]

Although the use of leading questions in presenting evidence to a grand jury has been challenged on occasion, there appears to be no federal or state reported decisions in which an indictment was dismissed solely because the prosecutor used leading questions.[9]

---

[3] See § 6.7, supra. See also *Com. v. Ridge*, 455 Mass 307, 326-327, 916 NE2d 348, 365-366 (2009) (leading questions are proper where witness's testimony is evasive, ambiguous, or inconsistent); *Com. v. LaFrance*, 361 Mass 53, 57, 278 NE2d 394, 397 (1972); *Com. v. Greene*, 9 Mass App 688, 693, 404 NE2d 110, 113 (1980). Massachusetts practice also permits the use of leading questions when the adverse witness is then "cross-examined" by his own counsel. See *Westland Housing Corp. v. Scott*, 312 Mass 375, 383, 44 NE2d 959, 964 (1942).

[4] See *Com. v. Fiore*, 364 Mass 819, 825-826, 308 NE2d 902, 907-908 (1974); *DiMarzo v. S. & P. Realty Corp.*, 364 Mass 510, 512, 306 NE2d 432, 433-434 (1974). See also § 6.26, infra.

[5] See *Com. v. Carrion*, 370 Mass 408, 411, 348 NE2d 754, 756 (1976) (child witness); *Com. v. Baran*, 21 Mass App 989, 991, 490 NE2d 479, 480-481 (1986) (child witness); *Com. v. Clark*, 3 Mass App 481, 487, 334 NE2d 68, 72 (1975) (non-English-speaking witness).

[6] See *Moody v. Rowell*, 34 Mass (17 Pick) 490, 498 (1836).

[7] *Com. v. Mitchell*, 367 Mass 419, 326 NE2d 6 (1975); *DiMarzo v. S. & P. Realty Corp.*, supra, 364 Mass 512 ("We are aware of no decision in this Commonwealth in which exceptions have been sustained because of the allowance of leading questions."); *Dorfman v. TDA Industries, Inc.*, 16 Mass App 714, 719, 455 NE2d 457, 460 (1983) (remedy for abusive use of leading questions is committed to the broad discretion of trial judge).

[8] See *Com. v. Judge*, 420 Mass 433, 452 n.12, 650 NE2d 1242, 1254 n.12 (1995).

[9] See *Com. v. Martinez*, 420 Mass 622, 625-626, 651 NE2d 380, 382-383 (1995) (& citations).

§ 6.11 Questions Improper as to Form

The following are objectionable:

- Questions that are argumentative—i.e., that assume a material fact not in evidence.[1]
- Questions that communicate impressions by innuendo when the questioner has no evidence to support the innuendo.[2]
- Questions that imply the truth of a proposition the cross-examiner knows to be false.[3]
- Questions that are repetitious.[4]
- Questions that are overbroad and confusing.[5]
- Questions that are too vague or indefinite to likely be understood by the witness or jury.[6]
- Questions that ask a witness to comment on the credibility of another witness. See §§ 6.12 and 7.3.3, infra.

---

§ 6.11 [1] See *Cleary v. St. George*, 335 Mass 245, 250, 139 NE2d 180, 183-184 (1957); *Com. v. McHugh*, 17 Mass App 1015, 1016, 460 NE2d 613, 614 (1984).

[2] See *Com. v. Johnson*, 441 Mass 1, 802 NE2d 1025 (2004) (Text cited). See also *Com. v. Johnson*, 431 Mass 535, 540, 728 NE2d 281, 286 (2001) (principle applies to defense counsel and prosecutors alike); *Com. v. Fordham*, 417 Mass 10, 20-21, 627 NE2d 901, 906-907 (1994); *Com. v. Wynter*, 55 Mass App 337, 770 NE2d 542 (2002) (conviction reversed where prosecutor posed series of evocative and leading questions concerning alleged motive for shooting, none of which had any mooring in evidence in record); *Com. v. Peck*, 86 Mass App 34, 39-40, 12 NE3d 1020, 1025-1026 (2014); *Com. v. Howell*, 49 Mass App 42, 49, 725 NE2d 582, 588 (2000) (prosecutor improperly sought to create impression that defendant's father had attempted to intimidate victim into changing testimony); *Com. v. Syrafos*, 38 Mass App 211, 219, 646 NE2d 429, 434 (1995) ("The attempt to communicate impressions by innuendo through questions which are answered in the negative, . . . when the questioner has no evidence to support the innuendo, is an improper tactic which has often been condemned by the courts."). Compare *Com. v. Johnston*, 467 Mass 674, 7 NE3d 424 (2014) (prosecutor had record support for questions and argument); *Com. v. Jenkins*, 458 Mass 791, 795-796, 941 NE2d 56, 64 (2011) (prosecutor did not create misimpression by innuendo in asking defendant's mother a series of questions about keeping a gun for defendant, to which she responded negatively).

[3] See *Com. v. Martinez*, 431 Mass 168, 178-179, 726 NE2d 913, 924 (2000) (Text cited); *Com. v. Christian*, 430 Mass 552, 561, 722 NE2d 416, 424 (2000) (Text cited); *Com. v. Mahoney*, 400 Mass 524, 531-532, 510 NE2d 759, 763-764 (1987); *Com. v. McCoy*, 59 Mass App 284, 288-290, 795 NE2d 1183, 1187-1188 (2003) (prosecutor improperly tainted defendant with guilt by association with drug criminal).

[4] See *LaCroix v. Zoning Board of Appeals of Methuen*, 344 Mass 489, 183 NE2d 99 (1962); *Com. v. Roukous*, 2 Mass App 378, 382-383, 313 NE2d 143, 147 (1974).

[5] See *Com. v. Blake*, 409 Mass 146, 159, 564 NE2d 1006, 1014 (1991).

[6] See *Com. v. Tarver*, 369 Mass 302, 313, 345 NE2d 671, 680 (1975); *Footit v. Monsees*, 26 Mass App 173, 183, 525 NE2d 423, 430 (1988).

- Questions asking whether the witness "would be surprised" by certain facts.[7]
- Questions that the examiner has no reason to believe are relevant to the case and that are intended to degrade the witness.[8]
- A line of questioning when there is no reasonable expectation of being able to prove the matters referred to.[9]

Counsel should always have a good faith basis in fact for any question and be prepared to disclose it to the judge.[10] It is an error for a judge to overrule an objection where a prosecutor's leading questions offer extrajudicial testimony with no good faith basis through innuendo or insinuation.[11]

C. IMPEACHMENT

§ 6.12 Introduction

The credibility of a witness is a matter for the jury to weigh—"they may accept or reject, in whole or in part, the testimony presented to them."[1] A Massachusetts jury is not required to credit a witness's

---

[7] *Com. v. Johnson*, 441 Mass 1, 7 n.8, 802 NE2d 1025, 1030 n.8 (2004) (the witness's surprise is irrelevant).

[8] See *Com. v. Pagano*, 47 Mass App 55, 59, 710 NE2d 1034, 1037 (1999), *habeas granted on other grounds by Pagano v. Allard*, 218 F Supp 2d 26 (D Mass 2002); *Com. v. Murphy*, 57 Mass App 586, 784 NE2d 1144 (2003).

[9] See *Abramian v. President & Fellows of Harvard College*, 432 Mass 107, 123, 731 NE2d 1075, 1088-1089 (2000).

[10] *Com. v. Johnson*, supra, 441 Mass at 4-5, 802 NE2d at 1028 (but counsel need not lay an evidentiary foundation for the question); *Com. v. Bolling*, 462 Mass 440, 454, 969 NE2d 640, 652 (2012); *Com. v. Santiago*, 458 Mass 405, 411-412, 937 NE2d 965, 970 (2010).

[11] *Com. v. Peck*, supra, 86 Mass App at 39 n.10, 12 NE3d at 1026 n.10.

§ 6.12 [1] *Com. v. Fitzgerald*, 376 Mass 402, 411, 381 NE2d 123, 131 (1978). See also *Com. v. Forte*, 469 Mass 469, 14 NE3d 900 (2014) (although Commonwealth may not present knowingly false testimony, it need not make an independent credibility determination as to each witness and may leave for the jury the determination of whether the witness is telling the truth); *Com. v. Molina*, 454 Mass 232, 240, 909 NE2d 19, 26 (2009) (rejecting defendant's argument that prosecution witness's testimony should have been excluded because it lacked indicia of reliability); *Com. v. Hoffer*, 375 Mass 369, 377, 377 NE2d 685, 691 (1978) (rejecting contention that key prosecution witness's testimony was so inherently contradictory and had been so fully impeached that it was incredible as a matter of law).

testimony merely because he tells a plausible story and is not impeached.[2] "Various aspects of a witness's testimony on the stand, including his demeanor, whether his answers are consistent with prior statements, and whether he appears to be avoiding the questions asked, can affect the jury's determinations of credibility".[3]

Counsel may seek to discredit a witness in four basic ways:

1. Contradict his testimony. § 6.13, infra.
2. Challenge his testimonial faculties. § 6.14, infra.
3. Demonstrate that he has a bias, prejudice, or motive to lie in the particular case. § 6.15, infra.
4. Demonstrate that he has a bad character for truthfulness and veracity. § 6.16, infra.

Impeachment may be accomplished on cross-examination and, as to noncollateral matters (see § 6.13.1, infra), by the introduction of extrinsic evidence. As the Court put it long ago:

> [I]n cross-examination, an adverse party is usually allowed great latitude of inquiry, limited only by the sound discretion of the court, with a view to test the memory, the purity of principle, the skill, accuracy, and judgment of the witness; the consistency of his answers with each other, and with his present testimony; his life and habits, his feelings towards the parties respectively, and the like; to enable the jury to judge of the degree of confidence they may safely place in his testimony.[4]

A party may impeach its own witness. See § 6.18, infra. When hearsay evidence is admitted (see Chapter 8), the declarant's credibility may be attacked (and then supported) in any manner that would be permissible if the declarant had testified as a live witness.[5]

---

[2] See *Com. v. McInerney*, 373 Mass 136, 143-144, 365 NE2d 815, 820 (1977) (& cases cited).

[3] *Com. v. Brescia*, 471 Mass 381, 393, 29 NE3d 837, 847 (2015).

[4] *Hathaway v. Crocker*, 48 Mass (7 Met) 262, 266 (1843). Because impeachment of a witness "is, by its very nature, fraught with a host of strategic considerations," failure to impeach a witness does not generally constitute ineffective assistance of counsel. See *Com. v. Jenkins*, 458 Mass 791, 805, 941 NE2d 56, 71 (2011); *Com. v. Garvin*, 456 Mass 778, 791-792, 926 NE2d 169, 181 (2010); *Com. v. Jackson*, 78 Mass App 465, 472, 940 NE2d 460, 466 (2010).

[5] See *Com. v. Mahar*, 430 Mass 643, 648-650, 722 NE2d 461, 466-467 (2000) (adopting Proposed Mass R Evid 806). Proposed Mass R Evid 806, which tracks the federal rule, provides in pertinent part:

It is improper to ask a witness to comment (positively or negatively) on the credibility of another witness, or to ask whether another witness is lying.[6] Nor may counsel, in asking a question, express a personal belief in the credibility of the witness or indicate that he has knowledge independent of the evidence before the jury.[7] It is for the fact finder, not the witness, to determine the weight and credibility of testimony.

Attacking and Supporting Credibility of Declarant
When a hearsay statement . . . has been admitted in evidence, the credibility of the declarant may be attacked, and if attacked may be supported, by any evidence which would be admissible for those purposes if declarant had testified as a witness. . . .

See also *Com. v. Gray*, 463 Mass 731, 745-749, 978 NE2d 543, 554-557 (2012) (applying Mass Evidence Guide Section 806 to prior grand jury testimony impeaching hearsay identification at trial); *Com. v. Hudson*, 446 Mass 709, 722-723, 846 NE2d 1149, 1159-1160 (2006) (citing Text) (witness whose testimony is offered in form of prior recorded testimony may be impeached by a prior inconsistent statement); *Com. v. Springfield Terminal Railway Co.*, 80 Mass App 22, 41-42, 712, 951 NE2d 696 (2011) (but attack on declarant's credibility would have brought his exercise of Fifth Amendment privilege to attention of jury); *Com. v. Beatrice*, 75 Mass App 153, 160-161, 912 NE2d 504, 510-511 (2009), *aff'd*, 460 Mass 255 (victim's hearsay statement about a separate incident was not directly inconsistent with her 911 call).

[6] See *Com. v. Clemente*, 452 Mass 295, 335, 893 NE2d 19, 52 (2008); *Com. v. Stuckich*, 450 Mass 449, 459, 879 NE2d 105, 115 (2008); *Com. v. Martinez*, 431 Mass 168, 177-178, 726 NE2d 913, 923-924 (2000) (improper to ask defendant whether he was saying other witness was lying); *Com. v. Alphas*, 430 Mass 8, 17, 712 NE2d 575, 582 (1999); *Com. v. Belmer*, 78 Mass App 62, 67-68, 935 NE2d 327, 331-332 (2010) (improper to ask witness whether her own prior statement was "true" or whether she had "lied"); *Com. v. Pagano*, 47 Mass App 55, 59-60, 710 NE2d 1034, 1037-1038 (1999), *habeas granted on other grounds by Pagano v. Allard*, 218 F Supp 2d 26 (D Mass 2002); *Com. v. Krepon*, 32 Mass App 945, 948, 590 NE2d 1165, 1168 (1992); *Com. v. Carver*, 33 Mass App 378, 383, 600 NE2d 588, 592-593 (1992); *Com. v. Morris*, 20 Mass App 114, 119, 478 NE2d 750, 753-754 (1985) (improper for defendant to be asked on cross-examination: "There is no reason for [the alleged child victims] to lie, is there?"). Compare *Com. v. Ahart*, 464 Mass 437, 442-443, 983 NE2d 1203, 1207-1208 (2013) (police officer witness did not improperly vouch for prosecution witness when he testified that police had investigated his version of events and verified them); *Com. v. Grenier*, 415 Mass 680, 690, 615 NE2d 922, 927 (1993) (police officer's testimony that he told defendant in course of questioning that he did not believe him, and that defendant then became noticeably nervous, was not the same as testimony of witness who expresses an opinion about credibility of another witness).

[7] See, e.g, *Com. v. Andrade*, 468 Mass 543, 550-551, 11 NE3d 597, 603-604 (2014).

It is equally well-settled that an expert may not offer an opinion (directly or indirectly) on another witness's credibility.[8] This prohibition includes expert testimony explicitly linking a complainant's behavior to the typical behavior of abuse victims, or testimony profiling the typical perpetrator, which may tend to vouch for the credibility of the complaining witness.[9] A qualified examiner may, however, testify as to his opinion regarding the credibility of statements made by petitioner during the clinical examination as part of his evaluation of sexual dangerousness.[10]

The main evil of this line of questioning is that it "implies to the jury that differences in the testimony of the witness and any other witness could only be the result of lying and not because of misrecollection, failure of recollection or other innocent reason."[11] Admission of an interrogating police officer's repeated accusations that the defendant was lying during his recorded interview, played to the jury, runs afoul of this principle.[12] It is of course proper for counsel through questioning to point out inconsistencies between the witness's testimony and that of other witnesses.[13]

---

[8] See § 7.3, infra. See, e.g., *Com. v. Perry*, 432 Mass 214, 236-237, 733 NE2d 83, 102-103 (2000) (expert not permitted to testify to the effects of prolonged marijuana use on ability of witness to perceive and remember accurately); *Com. v. Velazquez*, 78 Mass App 660, 666-667, 941 NE2d 1136, 1141 (2011) (although Commonwealth's expert was not explicitly asked whether she believed child victim's allegations, her testimony conveyed her belief and vouched for her). Compare *Com. v. Quinn*, 83 Mass App 759, 989 NE2d 901 (2013) (defense witness therapist did not implicitly vouch for victim's credibility on cross-examination because she did not link general symptoms of abuse with victim's).

A defendant, however, was held entitled to offer expert evidence that those with dissociative memory disorder (which the evidence indicated may include the alleged victim) sometimes have a distorted memory of past events. See *Com. v. Polk*, 462 Mass 23, 36-37, 965 NE2d 815, 826 (2012) (an expert does not cross the line into impermissible opinion testimony by merely educating the jury about dissociative disorder).

[9] *Com. v. Quinn*, 469 Mass 641, 646-650, 15 NE3d 726, 731-733 (2014) (social worker's expert testimony suggested that behavioral characteristics of the victim were consistent with those of a sexual abuse victim and thus implicitly vouched for her testimony); *Com. v. Federico*, 425 Mass 844, 683 NE2d 1035 (1997); *Com. v. Aspen*, 85 Mass App 278, 282-285, 8 NE3d 782, 787-789 (2014).

[10] *In re Gammell*, 86 Mass App 8, 11-12, 12 NE3d 409, 412-413 (2014).

[11] *Com. v. Ward*, 15 Mass App 400, 401-402, 446 NE2d 89, 91 (1983).

[12] *Com. v. Amran*, 471 Mass 354, 360-36129 NE3d 188, 194 (2015); *Com. v. Santos*, 463 Mass 273, 288-289, 974 NE2d 1, 15 (2012).

[13] See, e.g., *Com. v. Johnson*, supra, 412 Mass at 326, 558 NE2d at 689; *Com. v. Alphas*, supra, 430 Mass at 18, 712 NE2d at 583.

Although a judge may summarize the evidence, discuss possible inferences to be drawn therefrom, and point out factors to be considered by the jury in weighing the credibility of witnesses, the judge may not (directly or indirectly) express an opinion as to the credibility of particular witnesses.[14]

Polygraph (lie detector) evidence may not be used to impeach a witness in Massachusetts.[15] Immigration status is not relevant to a witness's credibility, and is not admissible to impeach his testimony.[16]

"Impeachment of a witness is, by its very nature, fraught with a host of strategic concerns,"[17] and failure to impeach a witness generally does not, standing alone, constitute ineffective assistance of counsel.[18]

§ 6.13 By Contradiction

The testimony of W1 may be contradicted in three ways:

1. By testimony of W2 as to the same subject matter.
2. By evidence of a statement made by W1 prior to trial that is inconsistent with his testimony.
3. By inconsistent testimony of W1 given at the trial.

§ 6.13.1 Contradiction by W2

The testimony of W1 may be challenged by calling W2 to contradict it. Where W1 testifies the traffic signal was red at the time of the accident in litigation, W2 may be called to testify it was green.

---

[14] See *Com. v. Keniston*, 423 Mass 304, 313, 667 NE2d 1127, 1134 (1996); *Com. v. Perez*, 390 Mass 308, 319-321, 455 NE2d 632, 638-639 (1983); *Com. v. Ortiz*, 39 Mass App 70, 653 NE2d 1119 (1995) (instructing jury that quality of police officer's report was not important impermissibly implied that omissions had no impeachment value). Compare *Com. v. Mello*, 420 Mass 375, 388-389, 649 NE2d 1106, 1115-1116 (1995) (although challenged instruction may have impermissibly warned jury not to accept defendant's testimony, in context of entire charge it did not create substantial likelihood of miscarriage of justice). For an example of a general instruction to the jury on the credibility of witnesses, see *Com. v. Whitlock*, 39 Mass App 514, 521 n.5, 658 NE2d 182, 187 n.5 (1995).

[15] See § 7.8, infra.

[16] *Com. v. Buzzell*, 79 Mass App 460, 947 NE2d 75 (2011).

[17] *Com. v. Lally*, 473 Mass 693, 709, 46 NE3d 41, 56 (2016).

[18] *Com. v. Lally*, supra, 473 Mass at 709, 46 NE3d at 56; *Com. v. Valentin*, 470 Mass 186, 190, 23 NE3d 61, 67 (2014).

The right to present contradictory testimony is limited, however, to matters that are otherwise directly relevant to the issues in the lawsuit. W1 may be probed in cross-examination as to collateral facts that cast doubt on his credibility by suggesting that if he was wrong about one matter "other portions of his testimony also might be inaccurate,"[1] but the opponent must take the answer as it is given and generally cannot resort to extrinsic proof (such as testimony of W2) to contradict on those collateral matters.[2] Opposing counsel may seek to discredit W1's testimony that the signal was red by showing that W1's memory regarding the color of the hat he wore that day was faulty; but this can only be pursued on cross-examination—the opponent cannot call W2 to contradict on the hat's color because its only relevance is what it may tell us generally about W1's testimonial capacities.

The limitation on contradiction by extrinsic proof is premised upon a desire to avoid a proliferation of tangential issues as well as unfair surprise to the opposing party. As the Supreme Judicial Court long ago recognized, "if a different rule were adopted . . . the trial of a cause would branch out into collateral issues without limit."[3] The rule can be traced to the common-law *Hitchcock* doctrine:

> If the answer of witness is [about] a matter which you would be allowed on your part to prove in evidence—if it have such connection with the issue, that you would be allowed to give it in evidence—then it is a matter on which you may contradict him [with extrinsic evidence].[4]

---

§ 6.13 [1] *Com. v. Fleury-Ehrhart*, 20 Mass App 429, 434, 480 NE2d 661, 665 (1985).

[2] See *Leone v. Doran*, 363 Mass 1, 15, 292 NE2d 19, 30 (1973). See, e.g., *Com. v. Sherry*, 386 Mass 682, 693, 437 NE2d 224, 231 (1982) ("The out-of-court statement of the [rape] victim was . . . offered only to impeach her credibility generally and not as to her description of the events in issue. Consequently, [evidence of the statement] was collateral to all issues in the case, save the victim's credibility. The victim's testimony on matters not relevant to contested issues in the case cannot, as of right, be contradicted by extrinsic evidence.") (citing Text); *Com. v. Doherty*, 353 Mass 197, 213-214, 229 NE2d 267, 277 (1967) (extrinsic evidence contradicting prosecution witness's denial that she had known victim); *Com. v. Connolly*, 308 Mass 481, 495, 33 NE2d 303, 311 (1941) (extrinsic proof contradicting prosecution witness's denial that defendant clerk had been compelled to reprove him in unrelated matter); *Com. v. Wheeler*, 42 Mass App 933, 678 NE2d 168 (1997) (defendant's lack of belligerence at police station, shown on videotape, was collateral to issue of earlier assault).

[3] *Hathaway v. Crocker*, supra, 48 Mass (7 Metc) at 266. See also *Leone v. Doran*, supra, 363 Mass at 15, 292 NE2d at 30 (& citations).

[4] *Attorney-General v. Hitchcock*, 1 Exch 91, 99 (Eng 1847). For discussion of the doctrine in federal litigation, see *United States v. Pisari*, 636 F2d 855 (1st Cir 1981) (& citations).

Notwithstanding the general prohibition, a judge may in appropriate circumstances permit contradiction by extrinsic evidence even on collateral points.[5] When the matter is relevant to an issue in the lawsuit and not merely to the credibility of the witness, extrinsic proof can always be offered to contradict.[6]

§ 6.13.2 *Contradiction by Prior Inconsistent Statement*

a. General Considerations

The testimony of W1 may be challenged by showing that he made a contradictory statement (either oral or written) at some time prior to trial. This may be done on cross-examination and, for noncollateral matters (see previous section), by extrinsic proof such as the testimony of W2 who heard the statement. When the prior statement bears upon a central issue in the case, it has been held that the judge has no discretion to exclude extrinsic evidence of it,[7] even if it would otherwise be inadmissible.[8] A judge's refusal to permit such impeachment is reversible error.[9]

---

[5] See *Com. v. Bonds*, 445 Mass 821, 832 n.17, 840 NE2d 939, 949 n.17 (2006); *Com. v. Linton*, 456 Mass 534, 555, 924 NE2d 722, 741 (2010). See, e.g., *Com. v. Ferguson*, 425 Mass 349, 355-356, 680 NE2d 1166, 1170 (1997) (rebuttal testimony contradicting murder defendant on collateral issue of his treatment of female employees properly admitted because it cast serious doubt on his credibility); *Simon v. Solomon*, 385 Mass 91, 107, 431 NE2d 556, 567 (1982) (no error where exhibits admitted not likely to delay trial or confuse jury, and no unfair surprise to opponent). See also *Abramian v. President & Fellows of Harvard College*, 432 Mass 107, 120, 731 NE2d 1075, 1087 (2000); *Com. v. Pagan*, 440 Mass 84, 89-90, 794 NE2d 1184, 1187-1189 (2003), *habeas denied*, 578 F Supp 2d 343 (D Mass 2008).

[6] See *Hathaway v. Crocker*, supra, 48 Mass at 266 (W1 could be contradicted on his denial that he had told W2 that his son was a partner in business because son's partnership was central issue in case); *Com. v. Agular*, 78 Mass App 193, 205, 936 NE2d 16, 25-26 (2010) (citing Text).

[7] See *Com. v. Parent*, 465 Mass 395, 399-401, 989 NE2d 426, 430-431 (2013) (citing Text) (indecent assault victim's prior inconsistent statement to police officer was admissible to impeach her trial testimony, even though she did not remember making the statement).

[8] See *Schwartz v. Goldstein*, 400 Mass 152, 508 NE2d 97 (1987) (prior inconsistent statement of physician witness admissible for impeachment even though it constituted breach of confidentiality); *Com. v. Domaingue*, 397 Mass 693, 701-702, 493 NE2d 841, 847 (1986) (prior recorded statement obtained in violation of GL 272, § 99). Compare *Com. v. Street*, 56 Mass App 301, 309-310, 777 NE2d 184, 191 (2002) (victim's testimony on collateral matters could not be impeached with transcript of her grand jury testimony).

[9] See, e.g., *Com. v. Wray*, 88 Mass App 403, 405-409, 37 NE3d 1114, 1116-1119 (2015).

"The rule of evidence is well settled that if a witness either upon his direct or cross-examination testifies to a fact which is relevant to the issue on trial the adverse party, for the purpose of impeaching his testimony, may show that the witness has made previous inconsistent or conflicting statements, either by eliciting such statements upon cross-examination of the witness himself, or proving them by other witnesses."[10] The witness may be asked to explain inconsistencies between prior statements and trial testimony.[11]

With the exception of certain statutory limitations discussed below (§§ 6.13.2.c and 6.13.2.d), evidence of prior inconsistent statements may be gathered from a wide variety of sources including:

---

[10] *Robinson v. Old Colony Street Railway*, 189 Mass 594, 596, 76 NE 190, 191 (1905). See also *Com. v. Shea*, 460 Mass 163, 171-172, 950 NE2d 393, 401 (2011) ("A defendant may elicit extrinsic evidence of a material prior inconsistent statement of a prosecution witness for the limited purpose of impeachment."); *Com. v. Evans*, 439 Mass 184, 191-192, 786 NE2d 375, 383-384 (2003), *habeas petition denied in Evans v. Thompson*, 465 F Supp 2d 62 (D Mass 2006); *Evans v. Verdini*, 466 F3d 141 (1st Cir 2006).

For examples of such use of prior inconsistent statements, see *Com. v. Basch*, 386 Mass 620, 623, 437 NE2d 200, 203-204 (1982) (prior report of coroner contradicting time of death testified to); *Com. v. A Juvenile*, 361 Mass 214, 217-218, 280 NE2d 144, 147 (1972) (transcript of delinquency hearing in the District Court to impeach the credibility of Commonwealth witnesses in the Superior Court); *Com. v. Naylor*, 73 Mass App 518, 524, 899 NE2d 862, 868 (2009) (prior written statements of alibi witnesses contradicting the date of alibi); *Com. v. Campbell*, 37 Mass App 960, 963, 643 NE2d 462, 464 (1994) (citing Text) (prior inconsistent statement of alibi witness); *Com. v. Donnelly*, 33 Mass App 189, 196-198, 597 NE2d 1060, 1065-1066 (1992) (state trooper's diagrams of accident scene, which he had used to illustrate grand jury testimony, to impeach contradictory trial testimony); *Com. v. Cogswell*, 31 Mass App 691, 696-699, 583 NE2d 266, 269-271 (1991) (complaining witness's diary that contradicted testimony); *Com. v. Smith*, 26 Mass App 673, 679-680, 532 NE2d 57, 61-62 (1988) (victim's prior inconsistent statement to co-worker concerning name perpetrator was addressed by); *Com. v. Pimental*, 25 Mass App 971, 519 NE2d 795 (1988) (victim's prior inconsistent statement to police); *Com. v. Allen*, 22 Mass App 413, 417-423, 494 NE2d 55, 58-62 (1986) (transcript of telephone conversation between victim witness and emergency operator, offered to impeach testimony concerning identification of defendant).

Compare *Com. v. Clarke*, 418 Mass 207, 211-213, 635 NE2d 1197, 1200-1201 (1994) (no error in excluding written prior statements made by prosecution witness where witness admitted making the statements, which had been prepared by defense counsel, and statements were read to jury); *Com. v. McGowan*, 400 Mass 385, 390-391, 510 NE2d 239, 243 (1987) (judge properly refused to permit proof of prior statement where it did not bear directly on any central issue).

[11] See *Com. v. Dickinson*, 394 Mass 702, 706, 477 NE2d 381, 383-384 (1985). It is to be noted that "simply because a witness alters some portion of his testimony at the time of trial is not sufficient reason to conclude that the new testimony was false, or that the [proponent] knew or had reason to know that it was false." *Com. v. McLeod*, 394 Mass 727, 743, 477 NE2d 972, 984; *Com. v. Sullivan*, 410 Mass 521, 532, 574 NE2d 966, 973 (1991).

- Pretrial depositions and other discovery materials (see Mass R Civ P 26-37).
- Prior statements and reports of a witness that are in the possession of the adverse party (see Mass R Crim P 23).
- Transcripts of grand jury testimony (see Mass R Crim P 14(a)(1)(B)).
- Transcripts of prior hearings or trials.
- Accident and other reports.[12]
- Letters and documents.
- Witnesses who heard the oral statement.

Any materials in the possession of the prosecution that are of an exculpatory nature must be disclosed to the defendant.[13] Prior inconsistent statements of a prosecution witness that constitute exculpatory evidence must be disclosed in a timely fashion.[14]

Where there is evidence that a witness has made a prior inconsistent statement, the jury must be instructed on the use of such statements in assessing credibility.[15]

b. *Nature of the Inconsistency*

In order to be used to impeach a witness, it is not necessary that his prior statement be a complete, categorical, or explicit contradiction of his trial testimony.[16] It is sufficient if "taken as a whole, either by what it says or by what it omits to say, [it] affords some indication that the fact was different from the testimony,"[17] or that the statement's "implications tend in a different direction" from the trial testimony.[18]

---

[12] See *Genova v. Genova*, 28 Mass App 647, 554 NE2d 1221 (1990) (motorist's accident report filed under GL 90, § 26 admissible as prior inconsistent statement). See also GL 175, § 111F (requiring insurance companies to deliver to an injured party medical reports as to his examination by insurance doctors if said party furnishes, in exchange, copies of medical reports by his physicians).

[13] Mass R Crim P 14(a)(1)(C).

[14] See *Com. v. Hunt*, 84 Mass App 643, 653, 999 NE2d 1104, 1112 (2013); *Com. v. Vieira*, 401 Mass 828, 832, 519 NE2d 1320, 1322 (1988).

[15] See *Com. v. Kessler*, 442 Mass 770, 778, 817 NE2d 711, 717 (2004); *Com. v. Bruce*, 61 Mass App 474, 483-484, 811 NE2d 1003, 1010-1011 (2004) (judge should instruct on use of prior omissions as well as inconsistent statements).

[16] *Com. v. Simmonds*, 386 Mass 234, 242, 434 NE2d 1270, 1276 (1982).

[17] *Com. v. West*, 312 Mass 438, 440, 45 NE2d 260, 262 (1942).

[18] *Com. v. Pickles*, 364 Mass 395, 402, 305 NE2d 107, 111 (1973). See also *Com. v. Parent*, 465 Mass 395, 400, 989 NE2d 426, 432 (2013) (citing Text); *Com. v. Lopes*, 34

The inconsistency may lie not only in the prior assertion, but in an omission to speak as well. "A prior statement may be inconsistent . . . if by what it omits to say the facts look different than those suggested by the in-court testimony of the witness."[19] A police officer's trial testimony may thus be impeached with the officer's report omitting important details that it would have been natural to include.[20] Similarly, a witness's prior failure to dispute the accuracy of a statement made to her may bear upon the credibility of her contradictory trial testimony.[21] A prosecutor may cross-examine a defendant claiming self-defense about his failure to relate that explanation when later describing the fatal stabbing incident to his companions.[22]

In sum, "[d]eclarations or acts, or omissions to speak or to act when it would have been natural to do so if the fact were as testified to, may be shown by way of contradiction or impeachment of the testimony of a witness, when they fairly tend to control or qualify his testimony."[23]

It has generally been held that for purposes of impeachment there is no inconsistency between a present failure of memory on the

---

Mass App 179, 185-186, 608 NE2d 749, 753 (1993); *Com. v. Donnelly*, supra, 33 Mass App at 197, 597 NE2d at 1065 (citing Text); *Com. v. Tiexeira*, 29 Mass App 200, 202, 559 NE2d 408, 410 (1990). But see *Com. v. Accetta*, 422 Mass 642, 644-645, 664 NE2d 830, 831-832 (1996) (witness' statement to grand jury that defendant used recoil from pistol to break it free of victim was not inconsistent with trial testimony that victim held defendant's wrist); *Com. v. Hesketh*, 386 Mass 153, 160-161, 434 NE2d 1238, 1244 (1982) (judge has wide discretion to exclude prior statement where it is not plainly contradictory).

There is no inconsistency if the witness does not testify regarding the matters set forth in the prior statement. *Com. v. Niels N.*, 73 Mass App 689, 702-703, 901 NE2d 166, 177-178 (2009).

[19] *Com. v. Kindell*, 44 Mass App 200, 204, 689 NE2d 845, 848 (1998). See also *Com. v. Perez*, 460 Mass 683, 699-700, 954 NE2d 1, 15-16 (2011) (witness's electronic journal omitting reference to a visit from defendant on night of murder was properly admitted to contradict trial testimony); *Com. v. Kessler*, 442 Mass 770, 778, 817 NE2d 711, 717 (2004) (failure to mention something in an earlier statement is inconsistent with a later statement of fact when it would have been natural to include the fact in the initial statement).

[20] See, e.g., *Com. v. Ortiz*, 39 Mass App 70, 71-72, 653 NE2d 1119, 1120 (1995).

[21] *Com. v. Goldenberg*, 338 Mass 377, 385, 155 NE2d 187, 192 (1959).

[22] *Com. v. Niemic*, 472 Mass 665, 671-673, 37 NE3d 577, 583-584 (2015) (but cross-examination about his failure to report to the police and tell them he acted in self-defense was improper, as it would not have been natural for him to do that.)

[23] *Foster v. Worthing*, 146 Mass 607, 608, 16 NE 572, 574 (1888). For more on impeachment by silence, see §§ 6.13.2.e and 12.6.8, infra.

witness stand and a past existence of memory.[24] "Where a witness has no present memory as to the substance of the prior statement, its admissibility generally is precluded because opposing counsel would not have an opportunity for meaningful cross-examination of the witness at trial."[25] The rule is designed to avoid the admission of prior statements carrying dubious probative value but a high degree of risk that the jury would give affirmative testimonial value to the statement.[26]

But a witness who has actually made a statement contradictory to trial testimony cannot escape impeachment simply by saying he does not remember making the statement.[27] Where the witness recalls the underlying events to which the prior statement refers, the witness need not recall making the statement, provided there is evidence of it, such as a grand jury transcript.[28] And the judge may, upon determination that the witness is feigning memory loss, admit a statement as "inconsistent" with a claim of lack of memory.[29]

---

[24] *Com. v. Santos*, 463 Mass 273, 294, 974 NE2d 1, 19 (2012) (grand jury testimony by codefendant's sister that defendant had gun in his waistband should not have been admitted absent a finding that the sister's lack of memory at trial was feigned); *Com. v. Sanders*, 451 Mass 290, 302 n.10, 885 NE2d 105, 117 n.10 (2008) (citing Text) (witness's response at trial that she did not recall where the other two men went after the shooting cannot be inconsistent with her grand jury testimony unless judge finds her lack of memory is a pretext); *Com. v. Martin*, 417 Mass 187, 197, 629 NE2d 297, 303 (1994) (citing Text) (prior statement of witness not admissible where witness had no present memory of substance of prior statement).

[25] *Com. v. Martin*, supra n.9, 417 Mass at 197, 629 NE2d at 303. See also *Com. v. Johnson*, 49 Mass App 273, 278, 729 NE2d 306, 310-311 (2000); *Kirby v. Morales*, 50 Mass App 786, 790-791, 741 NE2d 855, 859 (2001) (when witness does not acknowledge having made inconsistent statement there is no meaningful opportunity for cross even if witness recalls the underlying event).

[26] See *Langan v. Pianowski*, 307 Mass 149, 151, 29 NE2d 700, 701 (1940).

[27] See *Langan v. Pianowski*, supra, 307 Mass at 152, 29 NE2d at 702.

[28] *Com. v. Daye*, 393 Mass 55, 73 n.17, 469 NE2d 483, 494 n.17 (1984). See also *Com. v. Parent*, supra, 465 Mass at 401, 989 NE2d at 432.

[29] The issue left open in *Com. v. Daye*, supra, 393 Mass at 73 n.17, 469 NE2d at 494 n.17, "whether, when the circumstances at trial indicate that a witness is falsifying a lack of memory, a judge may admit the statement as 'inconsistent' with the claim of lack of memory," was answered in the affirmative in *Com. v. Sinerio*, 432 Mass 735, 741-743, 740 NE2d 602, 607-608 (2000), which affirmed the admission of the victim's prior testimony at the probable cause hearing because the trial judge could properly have concluded that her trial testimony as to lack of memory was feigned. "[T]here is good reason for a judge to find the existence of inconsistency when the judge concludes that testimony asserting an inability to remember is false." *Id.*, 432 Mass at 742, 740 NE2d at 608. The determination that the witness's lack of memory is fabricated is for the judge; the jury should not be told of this finding. *Id.* See also *Com. v. Hanino*, 82 Mass App 489, 497, 975 NE2d 876, 884 (2012).

A witness's failure to recall certain details of a prior statement does not preclude impeachment by use of the statement at trial.[30] Leading questions may be used to refresh a witness's recollection concerning a prior conversation.[31]

A statement may be admitted as a prior inconsistent statement only if it can be clearly attributed to the witness.[32]

The fact that the prior inconsistent statement is in the form of an opinion does not necessarily preclude its use to impeach the witness. This is obviously true where the witness has expressed a contrary opinion on the stand. Thus a physician called by the defendant who minimized the plaintiff's injuries in his testimony could be contradicted by a prior statement that the plaintiff was "the worst accident case he handled in the last ten years."[33]

Where a lay witness testifies as to specific facts, evidence of a prior inconsistent opinion may be used only if the facts testified to lead directly to a contrary conclusion.[34] The prior inconsistent opinion is

[30] See *Com. v. Gil*, 393 Mass 204, 219-220, 471 NE2d 30, 41 (1984) (interview with a trooper). See also *Com. v. Granito*, supra, 326 Mass at 500, 95 NE2d at 543 ("It was open to the prosecution to show that at the time of his arrest, nine days after the robbery, the defendant's reply to [police] questions bearing on [his whereabouts at the time of the crime] was that he did not know. These replies were admissible to discredit the detailed alibi testified to at the trial. And the fact that the defendant testified in several instances that he did not remember being asked such questions or giving such answers did not deprive the Commonwealth of the right to put them in evidence."); *Com. v. Cappellano*, 17 Mass App 272, 278-279, 457 NE2d 1121, 1125 (1983) (witness's lack of memory of details of detective's interview in hospital did not preclude impeachment).

[31] See *Com. v. Hartford*, 346 Mass 482, 486-487, 194 NE2d 401, 404 (1963).

[32] See, e.g., *Com. v. Evans*, 438 Mass 142, 157, 778 NE2d 885, 898 (2002) (statement in assistant district attorney's memo not sufficiently attributable to detective); *Com. v. Fruchtman*, 418 Mass 8, 18, 633 NE2d 369, 374 (1994) (no error in excluding attempted impeachment where allegedly prior inconsistent statement in social worker's reports not shown to be based on communication by victim); *Pina v. McGill Development Corp.*, 388 Mass 159, 164, 445 NE2d 1059, 1062 (1983) (insurance forms containing prior statements not signed by witness). *Wingate v. Emery Air Freight Corp.*, 385 Mass 402, 405, 432 NE2d 474, 478 (1982) (evidence did not warrant inference that injury report contained statements made by witness); *Com. v. Beauregard*, 25 Mass App 983, 521 NE2d 404 (1988) (notation in hospital record, "Cannot identify assailant," could not be sufficiently attributed to victim).

[33] *McGrath v. Fash*, 244 Mass 327, 139 NE 303 (1923). See also *Schwartz v. Goldstein*, 400 Mass 152, 508 NE2d 97 (1987) (physician witness's prior statement that "he felt there was no malpractice" and "the case should be thrown out").

[34] See, e.g., *Com. v. Grossman*, 261 Mass 68, 71-72, 158 NE 338, 339 (1927) (prior statement by character witness that "it looked bad for [defendant]"); *Whipple v. Rich*, 180 Mass 477, 63 NE 5 (1902) (prior statement that railway driver was "not to blame" for accident properly admitted to impeach witness's testimony).

admissible for the limited purpose of impeachment even though the witness would not otherwise be permitted to state an opinion on the matter.[35]

c. Special Provisions for Impeachment in Criminal Cases

Like any witness, a criminal defendant who takes the stand may be impeached by use of a prior inconsistent statement.[36] Under federal constitutional standards, this may be accomplished even if the statement was obtained in violation of the *Miranda* safeguards (and thus otherwise inadmissible), provided the statement is voluntary and trustworthy.[37] Massachusetts law is in accord.[38]

In the context of the retrial of a criminal case, any admission the defendant made in the first trial, as well as any prior testimony that tends to contradict later testimony, is admissible in the second trial.[39] Moreover a defendant's testimony or affidavit in support of a motion to suppress evidence on Fourth Amendment grounds may be used as a prior inconsistent statement to impeach the defendant's later testimony at trial.[40]

There are, however, several limitations that apply specially to criminal cases. GL 233, § 23B[41] provides that any statement made by a

---

[35] See *Hogan v. Roche*, 179 Mass 510, 61 NE 57 (1901) (statements and conduct of witness indicating opinion on sanity of testator admissible to impeach witness who testified to facts tending to show testator was of unsound mind); *Com. v. Tiexeira*, supra n.8, 29 Mass App at 202, 559 NE2d at 410 (prior statement of lay witness admissible even though it involved inference drawn from her observations).

[36] *Com. v. Richotte*, 59 Mass App 524, 527, 796 NE2d 890, 893 (2003).

[37] *Harris v. New York*, 401 US 222, 91 S Ct 643, 28 L Ed 2d 1 (1971).

[38] See *Commonwealth v. Mahnke*, 368 Mass 662, 691-697, 335 NE2d 660, 678-681 (1975); *Com. v. Harris*, 364 Mass 236, 238-241, 303 NE2d 115, 117-118 (1973). See also § 12.6.7, infra.

[39] See *Com. v. Cassidy*, 29 Mass App 651, 655 n.4, 564 NE2d 400, 402 n.4 (1990) (citing Text).

[40] See *Com. v. Rivera*, 425 Mass 633, 637-638, 682 NE2d 636, 640-641 (1997); *Com. v. McCollum*, 79 Mass App 239, 256, 45 NE2d 937, 942-953 (2011) (defendant's failure to mention alleged police threats in his affidavit in support of his motion to suppress could be used to impeach his trial testimony that he had been threatened).

[41] "In the trial of an indictment or complaint for any crime, no statement made by a defendant therein subjected to psychiatric examination pursuant to sections fifteen or sixteen of chapter one hundred and twenty-three for the purposes of such examination or treatment shall be admissible in evidence against him on any issue other than of his mental condition, nor shall it be admissible in evidence against him on that issue if such statement constitutes a confession of guilt of the crime charged." GL 233, § 23B. See generally *Blaisdell v. Com.*, 372 Mass 753, 364 NE2d 191 (1977). See also *Com. v. Martin*, 393 Mass 781, 473 NE2d 1099 (1985) (defendant's statements made

criminal defendant pursuant to a psychiatric examination ordered by the court is inadmissible in evidence against him on any issue other than his mental condition. The statute has been read to preclude the use of the defendant's statements for purposes of impeachment.[42]

Any evidence given in a delinquency proceeding is rendered inadmissible against the child in any subsequent proceeding (except in a delinquency or sentencing proceeding involving the same person) by a broad confidentiality provision, GL 119, § 60 (discussed at § 5.10, supra).[43] The statute has been held to preclude the use against a defendant at a criminal proceeding of prior testimony given by the defendant and other witnesses at a prior delinquency hearing.[44] GL 119, § 60 does not appear to prevent the use of prior inconsistent testimony when offered by the juvenile to impeach prosecution witnesses in a subsequent proceeding.[45] For a discussion of the constitutional limits on GL 119, § 60, when the information is relevant to a witness's bias, see § 6.15, infra.

For a discussion of the limits on impeachment of a defendant by his prior silence, see § 12.6.8, infra.

d. Special Provisions for Impeachment in Tort Actions and Worker's Compensation Proceedings

Two statutory limitations affect the impeachment use of prior statements in tort actions.

---

during court-ordered psychiatric examination, which revealed his thought processes at time of shooting, were improperly admitted in violation of § 23B); *Com. v. Callahan*, 386 Mass 784, 438 NE2d 45 (1982) (defendant's inculpatory statements in course of court-ordered psychiatric examination constituted strong evidence of premeditation and thus were improperly admitted in violation of § 23B). See also § 5.5.6, supra.

[42] See *Blaisdell v. Com.*, supra, 372 Mass at 763, 364 NE2d at 197-198. See also Mass R Crim P 14(b)(2)(B)(iii) (restricting disclosure of incriminating statements made by defendant during course of court-ordered psychological examination); GL 233, § 20B (dealing with privileged communications between patient and psychotherapist, discussed at § 5.5.2, supra).

[43] See generally *Police Commissioner of Boston v. Municipal Court of the Dorchester District*, 374 Mass 640, 651-652, 374 NE2d 272, 288 (1978) (construing earlier version of statute).

[44] See *Com. v. Franklin*, 366 Mass 284, 291, 318 NE2d 469, 474 (1974) (Commonwealth cannot confront defense witnesses with prior testimony at delinquency proceeding); *Com. v. Wallace*, 346 Mass 9, 15-16, 190 NE2d 224, 228 (1963).

[45] See *Com. v. A Juvenile*, 361 Mass 214, 217-218, 280 NE2d 144, 146 (1972) (but deciding case on different ground).

GL 233, § 23A renders inadmissible in an action for personal injuries any signed written or recorded statement of a party concerning the event unless a copy of the statement was promptly provided to the party upon request prior to trial. The purpose of the statute is to enable a party before trial to ascertain what he has written to an adversary and "to disallow ambushes of injured persons by their adversaries, because statements are sometimes obtained before the injured person is represented . . . [a]nd it's not fair to permit a defendant at the trial to spring on the plaintiff such a statement."[46] Section 23A applies to written statements given by an injured person on his own accord as well as those solicited by the defendant or insurer.[47] The trial judge has some discretion to admit a statement notwithstanding the failure to strictly comply with the statute.[48] A similar statute applies to worker's compensation proceedings.[49]

GL 271, § 44 renders inadmissible in tort actions for personal injuries any settlement, general release, or statement in writing signed by a patient confined in a hospital or sanitarium that refers to any personal injuries for which the patient is confined if the statement was obtained within 15 days after the injuries were sustained. "The apparent purpose of the statute is to protect persons who might be weakened and vulnerable following injury and treatment and, therefore, unwittingly act against their best legal interests."[50] The statute excepts by its terms statements given to police or Registry of Motor Vehicle inspectors acting in the performance of their duty, as well as statements given to members of the patient's family or to his attorney, and it does not apply to worker's compensation proceedings under GL 152.

Several significant points distinguish GL 271, § 44 from GL 233, § 23A:

> (1) statements covered by § 44 are barred even though no demand for a copy thereof was made;

---

[46] See *Mazzoleni v. Cotton*, 33 Mass App 147, 149-150, 597 NE2d 59, 60-61 (1992) (quoting Superior Court Judge J. Harold Flannery).

[47] *Spellman v. Metropolitan Transit Authority*, 328 Mass 446, 104 NE2d 493 (1952).

[48] See *Mazzoleni v. Cotton*, supra (statement not furnished upon plaintiff's demand nonetheless admissible where it was ultimately furnished long before trial and plaintiff could demonstrate no prejudice from delay).

[49] See GL 152, § 7B.

[50] *Fahey v. Rockwell Graphic Systems, Inc.*, 20 Mass App 642, 655, 482 NE2d 519, 528 (1985).

(2) § 44 is not limited to statements of a "party" or one acting in his behalf (and thus arguably applies to a statement given by one passenger in an action brought by another passenger against the vehicle's operator); and

(3) § 44 applies only to written, and not tape-recorded, statements.[51]

e. *Impeachment by Silence or Failure to Come Forward*

A prior contradictory statement of a witness may consist of silence in circumstances where denial would be called for. "It is generally appropriate to impeach a witness by showing that he was silent in circumstances in which he naturally would have been expected to deny some asserted fact or that, in the circumstances, the witness would be expected to disclose some fact and did not do so."[52] Thus a witness testifying for the taxpayer in an abatement action could be impeached with evidence that he never expressed disapproval of the assessors' valuation when he participated in an earlier discussion on the subject in which the proposed valuation plan was distributed.[53]

It is for the court (and ultimately the jury) to determine whether the witness understood the statements made to him or in his presence, had the opportunity to reply to them, and conducted himself in such a manner that by his silence he must be deemed to have acquiesced in the statements.[54]

Where a witness has been impeached with evidence that she was silent in a circumstance naturally calling for expression, she may explain the silence on redirect.[55] The prior silence of the witness may in some circumstances give rise to an implication that his testimony is a recent contrivance.[56]

---

[51] See *Fahey v. Rockwell Graphic Systems, Inc.*, supra.

[52] *Com. v. Nickerson*, 386 Mass 54, 57, 434 NE2d 992, 994 (1982).

[53] *Assessors of Pittsfield v. W. T. Grant Co.*, 329 Mass 359, 108 NE2d 536 (1952). See also *Com. v. Azar*, 32 Mass App 290, 303, 588 NE2d 1352 (1992) (defendant's failure to offer explanation of child's death to mother was admissible to impeach defendant at trial).

[54] *Hill v. Crompton*, 119 Mass 376, 382 (1876).

[55] See *Com. v. Dyer*, 460 Mass 728, 744, 955 NE2d 271, 287 (2011).

[56] See, e.g., *Com. v. Heffernan*, 350 Mass 48, 51-52, 213 NE2d 399, 402-403 (1966) (defense counsel questioned prosecution witness's motive for not mentioning alleged bribe until he was arrested on unrelated charge).

In situations where the natural response of a person in possession of exculpatory evidence would be to come forward and disclose it to the police in order to avoid a mistaken prosecution of a relative or friend, the failure to do so might well cast doubt on the defense witness's subsequent exculpatory testimony at trial. The witness's silence in such circumstances may be used to impeach and suggest recent fabrication.[57] A prosecutor may also question a witness about the failure to come forward sooner to suggest an opportunity to collude.[58]

A proper foundation must be laid for such impeachment by establishing that the witness knew of the pending charges in sufficient detail to realize that his information was exculpatory, that he had reason to make the information available, and that he knew how to report it to the proper authorities.[59] The goal is "to establish that the witness's pretrial silence is in fact inconsistent with his trial testimony."[60] In the

---

[57] See, e.g., *Com. v. Gregory*, 401 Mass 437, 444-445, 517 NE2d 454, 459-460 (1988) (cross-examination of alibi witness concerning failure to report information to police); *Com., v. Brown*, 11 Mass App 288, 295-297, 416 NE2d 218, 224 (1981) (same).

[58] See, e.g., *Com. v. Passley*, 428 Mass 832, 840, 705 NE2d 269, 275 (1999).

[59] See *Com. v. DaSilva*, 471 Mass 71, 81-82, 27 NE3d 383, 393 (2015); *Com. v. Horne*, 466 Mass 440, 447-449, 995 NE2d 773, 781-782 (2013). See also *Com. v. Hart*, 455 Mass 230, 237-242, 914 NE2d 904, 910-914 (2009) (removing what had previously been the fourth foundational requirement, that neither the defendant nor his lawyer asked witness to refrain from reporting, abrogating *Com. v. Cintron*, 435 Mass 509, 759 NE2d 700 (2001) and *Com. v. Brown*, 11 Mass App 288, 416 NE2d 218 (1981); *Com. v. Gonzalez*, 68 Mass App 620, 630-631, 863 NE2d 958, 967-968 (2007) (prosecutor did not establish foundation that it would have been natural for defendant to contact police because he testified he had consulted with his attorney after he learned he was suspect).

[60] *Com. v. Brown*, supra, 11 Mass App at 296, 416 NE2d at 224. For more on the required foundation for this form of impeachment, see *Com. v. Washington*, 459 Mass 32, 41-44, 944 NE2d 98, 107-109 (2011) (Commonwealth made foundational showing to impeach alibi witness for failing to come forward with exculpatory evidence, and to argue point to jury); *Com. v. Daye*, 435 Mass 463, 476-477, 759 NE2d 313, 325-326 (2001); *Com. v. Cintron*, 435 Mass 509, 522-525, 759 NE2d 700, 711-713 (2001); *Com. v. Nickerson*, supra, 386 Mass at 57-58, 434 NE2d at 995 (pointing out that the examples in *Brown* of situations in which the witness would not be expected to come forward were not exhaustive: "A witness may have a particular reason for not wanting to deal with the police." 386 Mass at 58 n.4, 434 NE2d at 995 n.4); *Com. v. Rivera*, 62 Mass App 859, 863-864, 821 NE2d 928, 932 (2005) (improper for prosecutor to argue defense witness's testimony should be discounted because she did not call police at time of confrontation, where there was no evidence on whether she did call, and no foundation as to whether failure to call would support an inference of recent fabrication); *Com. v. Brissett*, 55 Mass App 862, 774 NE2d 1170 (2002) (reversing conviction for improper cross-examination of defendant and alibi witness); *Com. v. DeCoste*, 51 Mass App 691, 697-699, 748 NE2d 481, 486-487 (2001) (foundation sufficient even though witnesses, defendant's sister and mother, were apparently aware investigating officer told defendant he was likely to be charged and should get a lawyer); *Com. v.*

absence of an objection to the failure to lay a proper foundation, a defendant is entitled to relief on appeal only if the evidence and related argument created a substantial risk of a miscarriage of justice.[61]

If the witness is a party to the litigation, the silence may be offered as an adoptive admission, in which case it is admissible as probative evidence and not merely for impeachment, and admissible even if the party does not testify at trial.[62]

The use of silence to impeach a criminal defendant's own testimony presents a special situation raising constitutional questions.[63]

A statutory bar precludes reference to the fact that a criminal defendant failed to testify or offer evidence at the preliminary hearing on his case.[64] The statute prevents the prosecution from asking a defense witness whether he had testified at any prior court hearing on the case, even when offered to suggest that his testimony was recently contrived.[65] A violation of GL 278, § 23, may be harmless error.[66]

Lopes, 34 Mass App 179, 608 NE2d 749 (1993) (sufficient foundation laid where jury could draw inference that witness, who had been working toward degree in law enforcement, could reasonably be expected to provide police with information concerning shooting of one friend when another friend was charged).

[61] See *Com. v. Epsom*, 399 Mass 254, 259, 503 NE2d 954, 958 (1987). Compare *Com. v. Bassett*, 21 Mass App 713, 716-717, 490 NE2d 459, 462-463 (1986) (substantial risk of miscarriage of justice) with *Com. v. Liberty*, 27 Mass App 1, 6, 533 NE2d 1383, 1386-1387 (1989) (error not prejudicial).

[62] See § 8.6.5, infra.

[63] See § 12.6.8, infra.

[64] "At the trial of a criminal case in the superior court, upon indictment, or in a jury-of-six session in the district court, the fact that the defendant did not testify at any preliminary hearing in the first court, or that at such hearing he waived examination or did not offer any evidence in his own defense, shall not be used as evidence against him, nor be referred to or commented upon by the prosecuting officer." GL 278, § 23. See also *Com. v. Barber*, 14 Mass App 1008, 1010, 441 NE2d 763, 765 (1982). GL 278, § 23 has been read in conjunction with the constitutional protections against self-incrimination. See generally § 5.14.8, supra; *Com. v. Sherick*, 23 Mass App 338, 341-346, 502 NE2d 156, 158-161 (1987).

[65] See *Com. v. Palmarin*, 378 Mass 474, 392 NE2d 534 (1979); *Com. v. Morrison*, 1 Mass App 632, 635-637, 305 NE2d 518, 521 (1973) (statute violated when prosecutor elicited from defense witnesses that they had been present at probable cause hearing but had not testified or told the judge the exculpatory information they testified to at trial). Compare *Com. v. Egerton*, 396 Mass 499, 508, 487 NE2d 481, 486-487 (no violation where questions concerning alibi witnesses' failure to come forward did not relate to earlier court proceedings) and *Com. v. Cefalo*, 381 Mass 319, 337-338, 409 NE2d 719, 730-731 (1980) (no violation where prosecutor elicited from defense witness that he had been present at probable cause hearing but had not told his story to any representative of the Commonwealth at that time).

[66] See *Com. v. Maguire*, 375 Mass 768, 774, 378 NE2d 445, 449 (1978) (violation of statute not reversible error where "there was no basis on which the jury could reasonably infer that the defendant's failure to call [non-pivotal] witness indicated a

Another statutory bar, together with constitutional protections, prohibits comment on the defendant's failure to testify at trial.[67]

f. Mechanics of Impeachment/Extrinsic Proof

Massachusetts practice permits a witness to be examined concerning a prior statement without showing it to him or disclosing its contents at that time, but upon request, it must be shown or disclosed to opposing counsel.[68] "The purpose in not requiring disclosure during examination is to afford the advocate the tactical choice of not placing the witness on guard."[69] Permitting opposing counsel to examine the statement protects his interests and prevents selective quotation by the questioner.[70]

In many states and in the federal courts[71] a witness's prior inconsistent statement cannot be put into evidence by extrinsic proof unless the witness has been asked on the stand whether he made the statement and been given an opportunity to explain it. Massachusetts departs from this practice,[72] except in the case of impeachment of one's own witness.

---

failure to offer any evidence in his defense in the lower court"); *Com. v. Gagliardi*, 29 Mass App 225, 238-239, 559 NE2d 1234, 1243-1244 (1990) (improper impeachment of defense witness by reference to his refusal to answer questions before grand jury not sufficiently prejudicial to require new trial).

[67] See GL 233, § 20, discussed at § 5.14.8, supra.

[68] Proposed Mass R Evid 613(a), which tracks the federal rule, provides:

> **Prior Statements of Witnesses**
>
> (a) **Examining witness concerning prior statement**. In examining a witness concerning a prior statement by him, whether written or not, the statement need not be shown nor its contents disclosed to him at that time, but on request the same shall be shown or disclosed to opposing counsel.

See also *Hubley v. Lilley*, 28 Mass App 468, 471-472, 552 NE2d 573, 575-576 (1990).

[69] Advisory Committee Note to Proposed Mass R Evid 613.

[70] *Hubley v. Lilley*, supra, 28 Mass App at 472, 552 NE2d at 575-576.

[71] See Fed R Evid 613(b).

[72] Proposed Mass R Evid 613(b) provides:

> (b) **Extrinsic evidence of prior inconsistent statement of witness**. Extrinsic evidence of a prior inconsistent statement by a witness is admissible whether or not the witness was afforded an opportunity to explain or deny the inconsistency.

See also *Sirk v. Emery*, 184 Mass 22, 25, 67 NE 668, 669 (1903) (extrinsic evidence of prior inconsistent statement may be offered against opponent's witness without laying foundation calling attention to statement).

In this latter situation, GL 233, § 23 (see § 6.18, infra) provides that "before proof of such inconsistent statements is given, the circumstances thereof sufficient to designate the particular occasion shall be mentioned to the witness and he shall be asked if he has made such statements, and, if so, shall be allowed to explain them."

Thus, as a prerequisite to extrinsic proof, the party's own witness must be apprised of the time, place, and content of the prior statement, and asked the prescribed preliminary questions.[73] The designation of the circumstances of the prior statement is particularly important where a witness has made relevant statements on more than one occasion.[74] It is not necessary to give the witness an opportunity to explain the statement where he testifies he has no recollection, or denies, having made it.[75]

As with direct contradiction of a witness's testimony,[76] use of prior inconsistent statements is controlled by the doctrine limiting extrinsic proof to issues of primary relevance to the lawsuit. Thus W1 may be cross-examined about a prior statement contradicting his testimony that the traffic signal was red at the time of the accident, and, if W1 refuses to acknowledge having made the statement, opposing counsel can prove it through W2. But if the prior statement contradicts W1 on the color of the hat he wore on the day of the accident, opposing counsel will have to be satisfied with whatever she can get on cross-examination—if W1 denies having made the statement, that is generally the end of it:

> It is well settled that if a witness testifies to a fact that is relevant to the issue on trial, the adverse party, for the purpose of impeaching the

---

[73] See *Com. v. Scott*, 408 Mass 811, 824 n.14, 564 NE2d 370, 379 n.14 (1990); *Com. v. Champagne*, 399 Mass 80, 88, 503 NE2d 7, 13 (1987); *Hubley v. Lilley*, supra, 28 Mass App at 473 n.7, 552 NE2d at 576 n.7. Compare *Fishman v. Brooks*, 396 Mass 643, 650-651, 487 NE2d 1377, 1382 (1986) (not necessary to lay foundation where adverse party witness testified extensively on cross-examination by his own attorney and explained his positions as if he had been called as a witness on his own behalf); *Com. v. Charles*, 397 Mass 1, 7, 489 NE2d 679, 683-684 (1986) (Commonwealth permitted to impeach its own witness with proof of prior inconsistent statement in apparent absence of foundation). See also *Com. v. Perez*, 460 Mass 683, 699-701, 954 NE2d 1, 16-17 (2011) (error in Commonwealth failing to inform witness of prior inconsistent omission in her journal, and failing to give her opportunity to explain it before offering the journal, was harmless).

[74] See *Com. v. Ferrara*, 368 Mass 182, 192, 330 NE2d 837, 844 (1975).

[75] See *Com. v. Ferrara*, supra, 368 Mass at 193, 330 NE2d at 844 (denial must be unequivocal); *Com. v. Cappellano*, 17 Mass App 272, 278-279, 457 NE2d 1121, 1125 (1983).

[76] See § 6.13.1, supra.

> testimony, may show that the witness previously made inconsistent or conflicting statements by offering them through other witnesses. However, extrinsic evidence on a collateral matter may be introduced at trial for the purposes of impeachment only in the discretion of the judge.[77]

A prosecutor may question his own witness about a prior inconsistent statement made during an interview of the witness by the prosecutor. If extrinsic evidence is to be offered, the GL 233, § 23 foundation (see above) must be laid and, if no third person were present during the interview, the prosecutor would have to obtain leave to withdraw from the case in order to prove the statement.[78]

Prior inconsistent testimony may read by counsel or the witness.[79] On redirect examination, the witness who has been impeached by a prior inconsistent statement must be afforded the opportunity to explain or elaborate on the alleged inconsistencies.[80]

An audiotape may be used to impeach a witness.[81]

g. *Use of Statement Generally Limited to Impeachment/Exception for Substantive Use*

Massachusetts law has followed the traditional view that the witness's prior contradictory statement is admitted solely for its bearing on the credibility of the witness—to reveal to the fact finder that the account heard from the witness on the stand is but one of two (or more) inconsistent versions provided by him at different times.[82] The statement is deemed inadmissible hearsay (see Chapter 8) for any other

---

[77] *Com. v. Farley*, 443 Mass 740, 750-751, 824 NE2d 797, 806-807 (2005), *habeas denied*, 544 F3d 344 (1st Cir (Mass)) (prosecution witness's denial that he had ever been to victim's house raised a collateral issue; extrinsic evidence of his prior inconsistent statement was properly excluded). See also *Com. v. Parent*, 465 Mass 395, 401, 989 NE2d 426, 432 (2013).

[78] *Com. v. Johnson*, 412 Mass 318, 325-327, 588 NE2d 684, 688-689 (1992).

[79] *Com. v. Fort*, 33 Mass App 181, 186, 597 NE2d 1056, 1059 (1992).

[80] See *Hubley v. Lilley*, supra, 28 Mass App at 473, 552 NE2d at 576 (& cases cited).

[81] See *Com. v. Gordon*, 389 Mass 351, 353-356, 450 NE2d 572, 574-576 (1983) (guidelines for use of recorded testimony); *Com. v. Supplee*, 45 Mass App 265, 266-268, 697 NE2d 547, 548-549 (1998) (error to refuse to permit defense counsel to impeach witness with audiotape of her police interview).

[82] See generally *Com. v. Daye*, 393 Mass 55, 65-75, 469 NE2d 483, 496-499 (1984).

purpose and cannot be used to prove the facts asserted.[83] A party may not call a witness, who would provide no probative testimony, for the sole purpose of creating a basis for impeaching him with a prior inconsistent statement.[84]

The Massachusetts approach differs from that taken by both Fed R Evid 801(d)(1) and Proposed Mass R Evid 801(d)(1),[85] which afford full substantive effect for all probative purposes to prior inconsistent statements that were made under oath at an official proceeding and are offered against a declarant who is testifying at trial and subject to cross-examination concerning the statement.

In a significant move toward the federal approach, *Com. v. Daye*[86] ruled that a prior inconsistent statement made under oath before a grand jury[87] is admissible for all probative purposes provided that:

---

[83] See *Com. v. Rosa*, 412 Mass 147, 587 NE2d 767 (1992) (reversing conviction where prosecutor argued in closing as though prior inconsistent statements were substantive evidence) (Text cited); *Com. v. Costello*, 411 Mass 371, 377-378, 582 NE2d 938, 941-942 (1991) (reversing conviction for rape of child because only evidence against defendant was prior inconsistent statement of alleged victim); *Wheeler v. Howes*, 337 Mass 425, 427, 150 NE2d 1, 2 (1958); *Com. v. Frisino*, 21 Mass App 551, 553, 488 NE2d 51, 53 (1986) (where only evidence of defendant's participation in crime consisted of two unsworn out-of-court statements of witnesses who repudiated the statements at trial, a required finding of not guilty must follow). The limitation has more significance for the Commonwealth's case (where the burden of proof lies) than the defendant's. See *Com. v. Prunty*, 462 Mass 295, 315-318, 968 NE2d 361, 378-379 (2012).

[84] See *Com. v. Maldonado*, 466 Mass 742, 758-759, 2 NE3d 145, 158-159 (2014) (prosecution witness); *Com. v. McAfee*, 430 Mass 483, 489-491, 722 NE2d 1, 8-9 (1999); *Com. v. Benoit*, 32 Mass App 111, 586 NE2d 19 (1992) (prosecution witness); *Com. v. McGee*, 42 Mass App 740, 746, 679 NE2d 609, 612-613 (1997) (defense witness). Compare *Com. v. Hailey*, 62 Mass App 250, 252, 815 NE2d 1098, 1100 (2004) (witness could be impeached with prior grand jury testimony where he provided probative evidence in his trial testimony); *Com. v. Melo*, 67 Mass App 71, 77, 851 NE2d 1124, 1130 (2006) (witness provided testimony of assistance to Commonwealth's case).

[85] Proposed Mass R Evid 801(d)(1) provides:

> **Statements which are not hearsay**. A statement is not hearsay if—(1) **Prior statement by witness**. The declarant testifies at the trial or hearing and is subject to cross-examination concerning the statement, and the statement is (A) inconsistent with his testimony and was given under oath subject to the penalty of perjury at a trial, hearing, or other proceeding, or in a deposition.

[86] 393 Mass 55, 469 NE2d 483 (1984).

[87] The court deferred consideration of a more expansive admissibility of prior inconsistent statements. *Com. v. Daye*, supra, 393 Mass at 71, 469 NE2d at 483. Another portion of *Daye*, which dealt with the admissibility a police officer's attribution to a witness of a positive pretrial identification denied by the witness at trial, 393 Mass at 60-63, 469 NE2d at 487-489, has been overruled by *Com. v. Le*, 444 Mass 431, 828 NE2d 501 (2005). *Le* adopts Proposed Mass R Evid 801(d)(1)(C) allowing substantive use of the pretrial identification even if the identifying witness disclaims having made the identification at trial. See also *Com. v. Ragland*, 72 Mass App 815, 828, 894 NE2d

- the witness can be effectively cross-examined as to the accuracy of the statement,
- the statement was not coerced and was more than a mere confirmation or denial of the interrogator's assertion, and
- other evidence tending to prove the issue is presented.[88]

1147, 1157-1158 (2008), *habeas denied, Ragland v. St. Amand*, 2010 WL 5350677 (D Mass 2010); *Com. v. Cash*, 64 Mass App 812, 836 NE2d 318 (2005). For further discussion of this issue see § 11.1.1, infra.

[88] For application of the *Daye* requirements, see *Com. v. McGhee*, 472 Mass 405, 420-424, 35 NE3d 329, 343-345 (2015) (extensive discussion); *Com. v. DaSilva*, supra, 471 Mass at 76-79, 27 NE3d at 389-391 (all requirements met); *Com. v. Maldonado*, 466 Mass 742, 754-756, 2 NE3d 145, 155-156 (2014) (judge found all requirements met, including that grand jury testimony of 15-year-old was not coerced); *Com. v. Franklin*, 465 Mass 895, 906, 995 NE2d 319, 329 (2013) ("The relevant portions of Hill's sworn description of the defendant's confession before the 2007 grand jury were properly admitted as substantive evidence of the defendant's guilt because they were inconsistent with his testimony at trial, the defendant had an adequate opportunity to cross-examine Hill at trial, and Hill's prior grand jury testimony was in his own words and was not coerced."); *Com. v. Figueroa*, 451 Mass 566, 576-577, 887 NE2d 1040, 1048-1049 (2008) (judge found that witness's lack of memory was a recent fabrication, that he did not deny his testimony to the grand jury, that he recalled the events to which the statement related, that he did not refuse to answer questions posed by defense counsel, and that defense counsel was able to probe fully the inconsistent versions of events); *Adoption of Cecily*, 83 Mass App 719, 723-724, 989 NE2d 532, 536-537 (2013) (victim's maternal grandmother's inconsistent trial testimony permitted admission of grand jury testimony).

The court has since clarified that the corroboration requirement goes not to the admissibility of the prior statement but rather to the sufficiency of the Commonwealth's case. See *Com v. Clements*, 436 Mass 190, 193-195, 63 NE2d 55, 58-59 (2002), *habeas denied on other grounds*, 592 F3d 45 (1st Cir 2010):

> [The] requirement concerning additional corroborative evidence was described as a third prerequisite for the admissibility of prior grand jury testimony as substantive evidence, and, since the *Daye* opinion, we have characterized that opinion as necessitating three "requirements" for such "admissibility." In fact, of course, the first two relate to the admissibility of grand jury testimony, while the third concerns the sufficiency of evidence. Thus, only two factors must be satisfied for the evidence in question to be admitted for substantive purposes. Then, if that evidence concerns an element of the crime, there is a separate requirement that the Commonwealth must meet to sustain its burden on the element: there must be other corroborating evidence on the issue.

436 Mass at 193, 63 NE2d at 58 (witness's recanted photographic identification of defendant made to police five weeks after shooting was sufficient corroboration). For further discussion of the corroboration requirement, see *Com. v. Swafford*, 441 Mass 329, 338 n.11, 805 NE2d 931, 938 n.11 (2004) (statements made to police at crime scene); *Com. v. Noble*, 417 Mass 341, 343-347, 629 NE2d 1328, 1329-1331 (1994) (witness's grand jury testimony admissible for full probative value where it corroborates inferences already apparent from the circumstantial evidence of defendant's guilt); *Com. v. Ragland*, 72 Mass App 815, 824-827, 894 NE2d 1147, 1155-1157 (2008), *habeas denied, Ragland v. St. Amand*, 2010 WL 5350677 (D Mass 2010) (grand jury testimony was sufficiently corroborated by trial testimony concerning witness's interview with detective and by other witnesses; there is no requirement that the corroborating evidence come

The *Daye* Court concluded that "a fact finder should be permitted to prefer a grand jury statement made closer in time to the events at issue over contradictory trial testimony that the passage of time and intervening influences may have affected. The prior statement will have been made in an atmosphere of formality impressing upon the declarant the need for accuracy, and will be memorialized in a manner eliminating subsidiary inquiries into whether the statement was actually made that would unacceptably attenuate the statement's probative worth."[89]

Com. v. Sinerio[90] extended *Daye* to include the testimony of a witness who the trial judge determines is falsifying a lack of memory regarding the statement, as that may constitute an inconsistency with trial testimony and also indicate that effective cross-examination is possible.[91]

Although the grand jury testimony in *Daye* involved eyewitness identification, the rule has since been expanded to encompass inconsistent statements relating to other subjects as well.[92] The *Daye* exception has also been extended to a witness's prior testimony at a

---

from a different witness). Compare *Idaho v. Wright*, 497 US 805, 823 (1990) (rejecting corroboration as acceptable evidence of reliability of a hearsay statement).

[89] *Com. v. Daye*, supra, 393 Mass at 71-72, 469 NE2d at 494.

[90] 432 Mass 735, 745, 740 NE2d 602, 610 (2000).

[91] See, e.g., *Com. v. McGhee*, supra, 472 Mass at 423-424, 35 NE3d at 345 (judge acted within her discretion in finding that witness was feigning memory loss and was available for cross-examination); *Com. v. Silvester*, 89 Mass App 350, 355-356, 49 NE3d 252, 258 (2016) ("Here, in making his determination, the judge was able to observe [the witness's] demeanor and assess her credibility. The judge acted well within his discretion in finding that [she] feigned memory loss with regard to the events of [the crime]. . . . Contrary to the defendant's claim on appeal that the third foundational requirement was not met, [the witness] was available for cross-examination at trial and defense counsel cross-examined her skillfully. Specifically, the jury were able to observe [her] demeanor on the witness stand and to assess her credibility in light of her ability to remember details pertaining to her life but not those that had a bearing on the specific facts of this case."); *Com. v. Lopez*, 87 Mass App 642, 648, 34 NE3d 750, 755 (2015) (judge determined that witness was feigning lack of memory at trail, which was inconsistent with his grand jury testimony).

[92] See *Com. v. Clements*, 436 Mass 190, 192 n.2, 763 NE2d 55, 57 n.2 (2002), *habeas denied on other grounds*, 592 F3d 45 (1st Cir 2010). For cases admitting prior grand jury testimony for substantive purposes, see *Com. v. Berrio*, 407 Mass 37, 43-46, 551 NE2d 496, 500-501 (1990) (victim's recanted grand jury answers); *Com. v. Carrasquillo*, 54 Mass App 363, 765 NE2d 777 (2002) (victim's grand jury testimony identifying shooter); *Com. v. Rivera*, 37 Mass App 244, 246-250, 638 NE2d 1382, 1383-1386 (1994) (witness's grand jury testimony regarding defendant's location at time of crime); *Com. v. Donnelly*, 33 Mass App 189, 198, 597 NE2d 1060, 1066 (1992) (state

probable cause hearing.[93] The Supreme Judicial Court has refused to apply *Daye* to statements made in circumstances lacking the formality of grand jury proceedings.[94] The appeals court has expanded *Daye* to apply to testimony from a former trial,[95] and to c. 209A affidavits that result in the issuance of an abuse protective order.[96] It has been suggested that the same principles would apply on the civil side to the admission of prior inconsistent evidence given at a deposition.[97]

The trial judge may find it necessary to conduct a voir dire to determine whether the requirements are met, but that is not required in

---

trooper's accident scene diagrams used to illustrate testimony before grand jury admissible by defendant as prior inconsistent statement for probative value); *Com v. Tiexeira*, 29 Mass App 200, 203-204, 559 NE2d 408, 410-411 (1990) (witness's grand jury answers linking the defendant to the victim's injuries). But compare *Com. v. Santos*, 463 Mass 273, 294, 974 NE2d 1, 19 (2012) (grand jury testimony by codefendant's sister that defendant had gun in his waistband should not have been admitted absent a finding that the sister's lack of memory at trial was feigned; absence of memory at trial is not evidence of an inconsistent statement); *Com. v. Ridge*, 455 Mass 307, 326-327, 916 NE2d 348, 365-366 (2009) (misuse of prior grand jury testimony, through use of leading questions, was not prejudicial); *Com. v. Stewart*, 454 Mass 527, 533, 911 NE2d 161, 168 (2009) (prior grand jury testimony by prosecution witness was not admissible as substantive evidence where Commonwealth was permitted to ask witness leading questions regarding the testimony to which the witness responded "no comment," denying opportunity for meaningful cross-examination); *Com. v. Accetta*, 422 Mass 642, 645, 664 NE2d 830, 832 (1996) (speculative testimony before grand jury not admissible under *Daye*). See also *Wright v. Marshall*, 656 F3d 102 (1st Cir 2011) (defendant was not denied effective assistance by trial counsel's failure to make particular objections to admission of grand jury testimony pursuant to *Daye*).

For admission of grand jury nonidentification evidence to impeach a witness unavailable at trial (by assertion of privilege), where witness's hearsay statement identifying the defendant was admitted at trial, see *Com. v. Gray*, 463 Mass 731, 745-749, 978 NE2d 543, 554-557 (2012) (applying Mass Evidence Guide Section 806).

[93] See *Com. v. Sinerio*, supra, 432 Mass at 741-745, 740 NE2d at 607-610 (2000); *Com. v. Jenkins*, 34 Mass App 135, 144, 607 NE2d 756, 762 (1993), *aff'd*, 416 Mass 736, 625 NE2d 1344 (1994) (prior testimony at probable cause hearing and grand jury); *Com. v. Fort*, 33 Mass App 181, 184-185, 597 NE2d 1056, 1058-1059 (1992) (testimony at probable cause hearing). See also *Com. v. Janovich*, 55 Mass App 42, 46-48, 769 NE2d 286, 291-292 (2002) (extending doctrine of substantive admission to probationary hearings for prior inconsistent testimony at preliminary surrender hearing).

[94] See *Com. v. Swafford*, 441 Mass 329, 338 n.11, 805 NE2d 931, 938 n.11 (2004) (statements made to police at crime scene); *Com. v. Weaver*, 395 Mass 307, 311, 479 NE2d 682, 685 (1985); *Com. v. Johnson*, 49 Mass App 273, 278, 729 NE2d 306, 310-311 (2000) (witness's sworn affidavit submitted in support of application for protective order); *Com. v. Frisino*, supra, 21 Mass App at 554, 488 NE2d at 53-54 (unsworn extrajudicial statements).

[95] *Com. v. Newman*, 69 Mass App 495, 497-498, 868 NE2d 946, 948 (2007).

[96] *Com. v. Belmer*, 78 Mass App 62, 64-67, 935 NE2d 327, 329-331 (2010).

[97] *Com. v. Ragland*, 72 Mass App 815, 823 n.9, 894 NE2d 1147, 1154 n.9 (2008), *habeas denied*, *Ragland v. St. Amand*, 2010 WL 5350677 (D Mass 2010).

all cases.[98] The *Daye* decision suggests that "[b]efore offering a prior inconsistent statement as probative evidence, counsel should ask for a voir dire, during which the witness should be reminded of the circumstances in which the statement was made and given an opportunity to explain the inconsistency."[99] This hearing has been construed as a mechanism for determining whether the conditions for admissibility have been met, and not an opportunity for the witness to explain the inconsistency in order to prevent the jury from hearing the prior statement.[100] Moreover, the witness's disavowal at trial of statements made to the grand jury does not render the statements inadmissible, but rather presents an issue of credibility for the jury.[101]

Since the *Daye* exception applies only where the declarant is testifying at trial and subject to cross-examination concerning the prior statement, it is not affected by *Crawford v. Washington*.[102]

Unless the prior inconsistent statement was made before a grand jury or at a probable cause hearing or falls within another exception to the hearsay rule,[103] the judge on request will instruct the jury that the statement shall not be considered as evidence for its truth, but only as it affects the weight to be accorded the witness's testimony. Failure to make the request for such instruction allows consideration of the statement for all probative purposes and precludes a claim of error on appeal.[104] Although a limiting instruction may be of dubious value because it is "unrealistic to believe that a jury properly discriminates

---

[98] See *Com. v. DaSilva*, 471 Mass 71, 76, 27 NE3d 383, 389 (2015).

[99] *Com. v. Daye*, supra, 393 Mass at 74 n.21, 469 NE2d at 495 n.21. A voir dire is not necessary where the trial testimony provides enough information for the judge to make the required findings. *Com. v. Maldonado*, 466 Mass 742, 755-756, 2 NE3d 145, 156 (2014).

[100] *Com. v. Fort*, 33 Mass App 181, 185-186, 597 NE2d 1056, 1059 (1992).

[101] *Com. v. Noble*, 417 Mass 341, 347, 629 NE2d 1328, 1331 (1994).

[102] 541 US 36 (2004) (discussed in Chapter 8, infra). See also *Com. v. DaSilva*, 471 Mass 71, 78-79, 27 NE3d 383, 391 (2015) (witness did not deny making the statements to the grand jury, judge found witness was feigning memory loss, and witness did not refuse to answer questions posed by defense counsel, giving defendant an opportunity to effectively cross-examine); *Com. v. Figueroa*, 451 Mass 566, 576-577, 887 NE2d 1040, 1048 (2008).

[103] See Chapter 8. If, for example, the witness who made the prior statement is a party to the action, the statement is admissible for all probative purposes under the admissions exception to the hearsay rule. See § 8.6. Because a victim of crime is not a party in criminal proceedings, the victim's prior inconsistent statements are admissible only as to credibility. See *Com. v. Kennedy*, 389 Mass 308, 314, 450 NE2d 167, 172 (1983).

[104] See *Com. v. Ashley*, 427 Mass 620, 627-628, 694 NE2d 862, 868 (1998); *Schwartz v. Goldstein*, 400 Mass 152, 154, 508 NE2d 97, 99 (1987); *Com. v. Luce*, 399 Mass 479, 482-483, 505 NE2d 178, 180 (1987); *Com. v. Gil*, 393 Mass 204, 220, 471 NE2d 30 (1984); *Com. v. Keaton*, 36 Mass App 81, 88, 628 NE2d 1286, 1290 (1994);

limited admissibility,"[105] a request that the evidence be limited to impeachment ensures a directed verdict if there is no other evidence of the fact asserted and the fact is essential to the claim.[106]

When a witness confronted with a prior inconsistent statement adopts the earlier statement as the truth, the statement acquires full probative value.[107] If, however, the witness later contradicts his adoption of the prior inconsistent statement, it does not acquire full probative value.[108]

§ 6.13.3 Self-Contradictory Statements Made at Trial

The testimony of a witness may be impeached by contradictory testimony of that witness given at the same proceeding. Where a witness gives conflicting testimony on direct and cross-examination, the general rule is that it is for the jury to determine which version to believe. Where, however, the witness on cross-examination is asked to make a choice between his contradictory statements and he affirmatively repudiates his testimony on direct, the witness is "bound by" that choice and the jury is not entitled to believe the repudiated version.[109]

Genova v. Genova, 28 Mass App 647, 652, 554 NE2d 1221, 1224 (1990). See also Proposed Mass R Evid 105 (discussed at § 1.5, supra).

[105] See Advisory Committee Note to Proposed Mass R Evid 801(d)(1).

[106] See, e.g., *Desmond v. Boston Elevated Railway Co.*, 319 Mass 13, 64 NE2d 357 (1946).

[107] *Com. v. Jones*, 432 Mass 623, 627, 737 NE2d 1247, 1252 (2000); *Com. v. Rivera*, 37 Mass App 244, 250, 638 NE2d 1382, 1385 (1994); *Com. v. Tiexeira*, 29 Mass App 200, 202, 559 NE2d 408, 410 (1990).

[108] *Com v. Jones*, 432 Mass 623, 627, 737 NE2d 1247, 1252 (2000).

[109] See *Sullivan v. Boston Elevated Railway Co.*, 224 Mass 405, 406-407, 112 NE 1025 (1916); *Donovan v. Johnson*, 301 Mass 12, 16 NE2d 62 (1938). For cases applying the *Sullivan* rule, see *Harlow v. Chin*, 405 Mass 697, 706 n.11, 545 NE2d 602, 608 n.11 (1989); *Krasnow v. Fenway Realty Co.*, 352 Mass 781, 227 NE2d 501 (1967); *Osborne v. Boston Consolidated Gas Co.*, 296 Mass 441, 444, 6 NE2d 347, 348 (1937). Compare *Sira v. Shields*, 360 Mass 874, 277 NE2d 825 (1972) (no conclusive election by witness among possibly conflicting accounts so as to remove matter from the province of the jury); *Yanowitz v. Augenstern*, 343 Mass 513, 515, 179 NE2d 592, 593 (1962) (plaintiff witness refused to elect one of two dates on which fall occurred); *Ballon v. Boston & M.R.R.*, 341 Mass 696, 698, 171 NE2d 857, 858-859 (1961) (plaintiff witness did not definitively elect one version of accident over other); *Stinson v. Soble*, 301 Mass 483, 487, 17 NE2d 703, 705 (1938) (variance of five mph in testimony concerning speed of vehicle not a "material difference" for purposes of *Sullivan* rule); *Com. v. Geisler*, 14 Mass App 268, 273 n.6, 438 NE2d 375, 378 n.6 (1982) (& cases cited) (defendant not entitled to have testimony struck because the witness was not clearly asked to make a definite choice between his contradictory statements).

The rule has been applied to nonparty witnesses.[110] For further discussion of the concept of "binding testimony," see § 2.11, supra.

§ 6.14 By Challenging Testimonial Faculties

The credibility of W1's testimony is dependent upon his or her ability to:

- accurately perceive the event in question;
- reliably remember what was perceived;
- correctly articulate the former in court; and
- testify truthfully.

Each of these faculties, both in general and in regard to the particular case, are open to challenge on cross-examination.[1] Questions may for example be asked concerning the witness's use of alcohol, illegal drugs, or medication at the time of the events about which he or she is testifying.[2] Questions may similarly be addressed regarding a mental impairment if it is shown that it might affect perception, memory, or communication.[3] The victim's prior misidentification of the perpetrator may raise questions about the accuracy of his perceptions and thus can be explored on cross-examination.[4]

The parties are entitled to reasonable latitude on cross-examination concerning testimonial faculties, with discretion as to scope and extent left to the trial judge.[5] There must be some indication that the matter is relevant to credibility before it can be used to

---

[110] See *Pahigian v. Manufacturers' Life Insurance Co.*, 349 Mass 78, 83, 206 NE2d 660, 664 (1965); *Morris v. Logden*, 343 Mass 778, 179 NE2d 821 (1962).

§ 6.14 [1] See *Com. v. Carrion*, 407 Mass 263, 273-274, 552 NE2d 558, 564-565 (1990); *Com. v. Caine*, 366 Mass 366, 369, 318 NE2d 901, 905 (1974).

[2] See *Com. v. Alcantara*, 471 Mass 550, 564-565, 31 NE3d 561, 574 (2015) (use of legal or illegal drugs); *Com. v. Daley*, 439 Mass 558, 564, 789 NE2d 1070, 1076 (2003); *Morea v. Cosco, Inc.*, 422 Mass 601, 604, 664 NE2d 822, 825 (1996); *Com. v. Carrion*, supra, 407 Mass at 273-274, 552 NE2d at 564-565 (& cases cited).

[3] See *Com. v. Gibbons*, 378 Mass 766, 771 n.9, 393 NE2d 400, 404 n.9 (1979); *Com. v. Caine*, supra.

[4] See, e.g., *Com. v. Franklin*, 366 Mass 284-290, 318 NE2d 469, 472-474 (1974).

[5] See, e.g., *Com. v. Carrion*, supra, 407 Mass at 273, 552 NE2d at 565 (judge did not abuse discretion in excluding question concerning prosecution witness's use of drugs in prison when defense counsel had already elicited that she was heroin addict); *Com. v. Russell*, 38 Mass App 199, 203-204, 646 NE2d 760, 763 (1995) (no error in excluding questions regarding prosecution witness's drug use at time of testimony where there was extensive evidence before jury about her use of drugs at time of incident).

impeach, and the burden is on the cross-examiner to demonstrate this.[6] Expert testimony may be necessary to establish the relevance to credibility.[7]

Extrinsic proof raising a substantial question about the witness's testimonial abilities may be admissible.[8] In appropriate circumstances, defense counsel may be permitted to search otherwise confidential and privileged records for evidence of how mental impairment might affect a victim witness's capacity to perceive, remember, and articulate the alleged events.[9]

Various challenges to the honesty and truthfulness of the witness are discussed in the sections that follow.

§ 6.15 By Proving Bias, Prejudice, or Motive to Lie

A witness may be impeached by showing facts indicating his bias, prejudice, or motive to lie against or in favor of one side. Such

---

[6] *Com. v. Arce*, 426 Mass 601, 604, 690 NE2d 806, 808-809 (1998) (question regarding eyewitness's drug use properly excluded because such use, standing alone, did not relate to capacity to perceive or recall); *Com. v. Adrey*, 376 Mass 747, 752, 383 NE2d 1110, 1112-1113 (1978) (no showing that question concerning witness's pattern of drug addiction or treatment was relevant to credibility, where counsel had already elicited that witness was under influence of drugs at time of incident); *Com. v. Caine*, supra, 366 Mass at 370, 318 NE2d at 905 (no showing that question concerning witness's commitment to state hospital was relevant to credibility); *Com. v. Beattie*, 29 Mass App 355, 366-367, 560 NE2d 714, 721 (1990) (no showing that questions relating to witness's hospitalization and psychiatric history were relevant to credibility); *Com. v. Williams*, 25 Mass App 210, 218, 517 NE2d 176, 181 (1987) (no showing that line of questions concerning witness's use of medication was relevant to credibility).

[7] See *Com. v. Lloyd*, 45 Mass App 931, 702 NE2d 395 (1998) (defendant needed to demonstrate that use of Prozac impairs ability to perceive or remember).

[8] See *Com. v. Fayerweather*, 406 Mass 78, 82-84, 546 NE2d 345, 347-348 (1989) (hospital psychiatric report on complainant's mental status); *Com. v. Barber*, 261 Mass 281, 290, 158 NE 840, 843 (1927) (evidence that defense witness was drunk on morning of incident).

[9] See *Com. v. Figueroa*, 413 Mass 193, 203, 595 NE2d 779, 785-786 (1992) (records concerning the complaining witness's condition of retardation); *Com. v. Gauthier*, 32 Mass App 130, 134-136, 586 NE2d 34, 37-38 (1992) (special education records). But compare *Com. v. Jones*, 34 Mass App 683, 615 NE2d 207 (1993) (defendant not automatically entitled to access records). The proponent of the impeaching evidence must show at trial that the mental impairment of the witness may lead to unreliability in his reporting of the events. See *Com. v. Despres*, 70 Mass App 645, 875 NE2d 864 (2007) (testimony of mentally retarded victim's caretakers regarding his tendency to fabricate was properly excluded). See also § 5.5.4, supra.

impeachment is commonly predicated on either the relationship between the witness and a party, or the interest (financial or otherwise) that the witness has in the outcome of the litigation.[1]

Because the presence of bias, prejudice, or motive to lie can so significantly affect a witness's credibility, each may be demonstrated by extrinsic proof as well as on cross-examination.[2] There is no

---

§ 6.15 [1] For recognized grounds of bias or interest, see *Com. v. McGee*, 467 Mass 141, 154, 4 NE3d 256, 266 (2014) (Commonwealth witness received financial support from prosecutor); *Com. v. Elangwe*, 85 Mass App 189, 7 NE3d 1102 (2014) (financial interest of complaining witness because of pending civil action); *Com. v. Sok*, 439 Mass 428, 434-435, 788 NE2d 941, 948 (2003) (gang membership of prosecution witnesses); *Com. v. Daley*, 439 Mass 558, 564, 789 NE2d 1070, 1076 (2003) (defendant's probationary status); *Com. v. Martin*, 434 Mass 1016, 750 NE2d 1009 (2001) (reversible error to preclude counsel from cross-examining complaining witness concerning complaints defendant had lodged against her); *Com. v. Moorer*, 431 Mass 544, 728 NE2d 288 (2000) (possible racial bias of victim); *Com. v. Dixon*, 425 Mass 223, 228-229, 680 NE2d 84, 88-89 (1997) (fact that it was necessary to arrest witnesses to ensure they would appear to testify could be basis for inference of bias in favor of defendant); *Com. v. Frate*, 405 Mass 52, 54, 537 NE2d 1235, 1236 (1989) (cross-examination of witness concerning representation of other clients in similar circumstances was relevant to bias and interest in outcome of lawsuit); *Com. v. Omonira*, 59 Mass App 200, 203-204, 794 NE2d 1248, 1251-1252 (2003) (spouse's knowledge of potential deportation consequences attending husband's conviction); *Com. v. Barboza*, 54 Mass App 99, 109-110, 763 NE2d 547, 555-556 (2002) (witness's consultation with civil attorney regarding suit against defendant); *Com. v. Hall*, 50 Mass App 208, 211-213, 736 NE2d 425, 428-430 (2000) (evidence of police brutality in effecting defendant's arrest).

For discussion of the problem of the "contingent fee witness" who testifies in the hope of an award of compensation from the proceeds of defendant's forfeited assets, see *Com. v. Luna*, 410 Mass 131, 139-140, 571 NE2d 603, 608 (1991). For the witness testifying in anticipation of a monetary reward upon defendant's conviction, see *Com. v. Miranda*, 458 Mass 100, 111-112, 934 NE2d 222, 231-232 (2010) (precluding, under Court's supervisory powers, prosecutors from providing, or participating in providing, monetary awards to witnesses contingent on conviction; and adopting procedural safeguard including pretrial disclosure and jury instruction about heightened scrutiny of testimony); *Com. v. Molina*, 81 Mass App 855, 857-860, 969 NE2d 738, 740-742 (2012) (instructions on heightened scrutiny were sufficient). For the witness who has been paid by police to engage in controlled buys, see *Com. v. Hughes*, 82 Mass App 21, 24-29, 969 NE2d 1149, 1153-1155 (2012) (defendant is entitled to jury instruction that the testimony of fee-paid witness must be scrutinized with particular care).

[2] See *United States v. Abel*, 469 US 45, 52 (1984) ("The 'common law of evidence' allowed the showing of bias by extrinsic evidence, while requiring the cross-examiner to 'take the answer of the witness' with respect to less favored forms of impeachment."). See, e.g., *Com. v. Colon*, 408 Mass 419, 443-445, 558 NE2d 974, 989-990 (1990) (plea agreement admitted in evidence to illuminate witness's incentives to please the prosecution); *Com. v. Aguiar*, 400 Mass 508, 513-514, 510 NE2d 273, 276-277 (1987) (judge erred in precluding cross-examination and extrinsic testimony suggesting bias).

requirement that the opponent cross-examine on the matter as a foundation prior to offering extrinsic evidence.[3]

Cross-examination to show bias, prejudice, or motive to lie is a matter of right that in criminal cases assumes constitutional dimension under the confrontation clause of the Sixth Amendment to the United States Constitution and art. 12 of the Declaration of Rights.[4] Evidence tending to show that an important government witness is so influenced is exculpatory within the meaning of *Brady v. Maryland*, 373 US 83 (1963) and must be disclosed to defendant.[5]

The defendant has the right to bring to the jury's attention any " 'circumstance which may materially affect' the testimony of an adverse witness which might lead the jury to find that the witness is under an 'influence to prevaricate.' "[6] "If, on the facts, there is a possibility of bias, even a remote one, the judge has no discretion to bar all inquiry in to the subject."[7] A criminal defendant has the right to establish by

---

[3] See *Com. v. Brown*, 394 Mass 394, 397, 476 NE2d 184, 186-187 (1985); *Com. v. Gabbidon*, 17 Mass App 525, 531, 459 NE2d 1263, 1268 (1983).

[4] See *Com. v. Grenier*, 415 Mass 680, 686, 615 NE2d 922, 925 (1993) (& citations).

[5] See *Com. v. Hill*, 432 Mass 704, 715-716, 739 NE2d 670, 679 (2000) (agreement for leniency). This would include any communication that suggests preferential treatment in return for that witness's testimony. 432 Mass at 716, 739 NE2d at 680. But see *Com. v. Fuller*, 394 Mass 251, 262-264, 475 NE2d 381, 389 (1985) (judge found that district attorney's office made no deal with either witness and in no way attempted to influence their testimony at trial).

[6] *Com. v. Haywood*, 377 Mass 755, 760, 388 NE2d 648, 652 (1979). See, e.g., *Com. v. Stockhammer*, 409 Mass 867, 873-877, 570 NE2d 992, 996-999 (1991) (cross-examination of rape complainant designed to uncover evidence of motive to lie to avoid exposure of sexual relationship); *Com. v. Koulouris*, 406 Mass 281, 285, 547 NE2d 916, 918 (1989) (witness's involvement in pending federal forfeiture proceeding for defendant's house); *Com. v. Barnes*, 399 Mass 385, 393, 504 NE2d 624, 630 (1987) (pending charges against the witness); *Com. v. Elliot*, 393 Mass 824, 828, 473 NE2d 1121, 1124 (1985) (right to demonstrate witness's motive to lie is particularly important in rape cases because the "right to cross-examine a complainant . . . to show a false accusation may be the last refuge of an innocent defendant"); *Com. v. Ahearn*, 370 Mass 283, 287, 346 NE2d 907, 910 (1976) (defendant had applied for civil complaints against officers prior to the filing of charges); *Com. v. Michel*, 367 Mass 454, 459-460, 327 NE2d 720, 723-724 (1975), *new trial granted*, 381 Mass 447 (1980) (witness's deal with prosecutor); *Com. v. Morin*, 52 Mass App 780, 784, 756 NE2d 37, 41 (2001) (reversing conviction because trial court limited defendant's cross-examination of complainant designed to suggest fear of abusive boyfriend as motive to lie); *Com. v. Civello*, 39 Mass App 373, 375-377, 656 NE2d 1262, 1263-1264 (1995) (cross-examination on bias designed to show that complainant knew her accusations could result in defendant's removal from her home).

[7] *Com. v. Allison*, 434 Mass 670, 681, 751 NE2d 868, 883 (2001), quoting *Com. v. Bui*, 419 Mass 392, 400, 645 NE2d 689 (1995). There is discretion, however, to impose reasonable limits to avoid cumulative or unduly prejudicial material, as discussed below.

extrinsic proof, as well as cross-examination, any circumstance that could suggest prosecutorial favoritism toward one of its witnesses.[8]

Frequently the proffered evidence of bias takes the form of charges pending against the prosecution witness that, it is argued, provide an incentive to "please the prosecution."[9] (For testimony pursuant to a plea agreement, see § 6.15.1, infra). A defendant has a constitutional right to inquire on cross-examination whether the witness expects more favorable treatment from the government in return for his testimony.[10] Defendant is entitled to question the witness about a pending charge even if the Commonwealth has offered no inducements to the witness, although in certain circumstances the judge may limit examination.[11] It is incumbent on defense counsel "to furnish some persuasive explanation why the arrest [or pending charge] might indicate bias or a motive to lie."[12]

Such questioning allows proper rehabilitation by the prosecutor.[13]

Thus although an arrest, indictment, or the pendency of charges are generally not admissible to impeach a witness,[14] where relevant to particularized bias or motive to lie these matters may be developed on cross-examination.[15] Other related matters relevant to bias are a prosecution witness's past cooperation with the Commonwealth that led to

---

[8] See *Com. v. O'Neil*, 51 Mass App 170, 179-180, 744 NE2d 86, 92-93 (2001).

[9] See, e.g., *Com. v. Andrade*, 468 Mass 543, 549-550, 11 NE3d 597, 603 (2014) (defense counsel during cross-examination of immunized prosecution witness suggested that he fabricated his testimony to curry favor with the Commonwealth to obtain favorable treatment on pending drug charges).

[10] *Com. v. Williams*, 456 Mass 857,872-874, 926 NE2d 1162, 1174-1176 (2010) (discussing required offer of proof regarding pending and dismissed charges). Compare *Com. v. Schand*, 420 Mass 783, 792-793, 653 NE2d 566, 573 (1995) (prosecutor's commitment to be "fair" to witness with regard to pending charges is not a promise of favorable treatment); *Com. v. Winfield*, 76 Mass App 716, 726-727, 926 NE2d 550, 558-559 (2010), *habeas denied*, *Winfield v. O'Brien*, 775 F3d 1 (1st Cir 2014) (voir dire failed to show bias on the part of mother against defendant, notwithstanding pending 25-count indictment for uttering false prescriptions).

[11] See *Com. v. Hamilton*, 426 Mass 67, 72, 686 NE2d 975, 979 (1997).

[12] *Com. v. McGhee*, 472 Mass 405, 426, 35 NE3d 329, 347 (2015). See also *Wing v. Commissioner of Probation*, 473 Mass 368, 376-377, 43 NE3d 286, 293 (2015) (defendant failed to demonstrate nexus between witness's sealed criminal records and potential bias.)

[13] *Com. v. Andrade*, supra, 468 Mass at 550, 11 NE3d at 603.

[14] See § 6.16, infra.

[15] See, e.g., *Com. v. Magdalenski*, 471 Mass 1019, 30 NE3d 830 (2015) (cross-examination regarding application for criminal complaint filed by defendant against prosecution witness should have been permitted as relevant to possible motive to lie) and cases collected in *Com. v. Smith*, 26 Mass App 673, 675-676, 532 NE2d 57, 59-60 (1988).

favorable treatment,[16] and a witness's invocation of the privilege against self-incrimination and subsequent grant of immunity.[17]

The use of unrelated criminal charges pending against a defense witness for the purpose of demonstrating a generalized bias against the prosecution has been rejected as not sufficiently probative given

---

A judge has discretion to preclude such inquiry of a prosecution witness when the witness gave a statement to police before his arrest and his trial testimony is consistent with that statement. *Com. v. Roby*, 462 Mass 398, 412, 969 NE2d 141, 154 (2012) (where witness has made statements that predates the charge, there must typically be a material change in the witness's testimony to render it subject to impeachment); *Com. v. Martinez*, 431 Mass 168, 180-181, 726 NE2d 913, 926 (2000); *Com. v. Hamilton*, 426 Mass 67, 72, 686 NE2d 975, 979 (1997); *Com. v. Hrabak*, 57 Mass App 648, 652, 785 NE2d 410, 413-414 (2003); *Com. v. Grant*, 49 Mass App 169, 174, 727 NE2d 1207, 1211-1212 (2000) (& citations); *Com. v. DiMuro*, 28 Mass App 223, 228-229, 548 NE2d 896, 899-900 (1990) (judge did not abuse discretion in curtailing cross-examination on charges pending against chemist witness where he formed his opinion and wrote his report concluding that substance was cocaine before charges were brought against him).

For cases reversing convictions because the trial judge unduly restricted cross-examination concerning pending charges, see *Com. v. Colon*, 408 Mass 419, 443-445, 558 NE2d 974, 989-990 (1990); *Com. v. Henson*, 394 Mass 584, 586-590, 476 NE2d 947, 950-952 (1985); *Com. v. Connor*, 392 Mass 838, 840-842, 467 NE2d 1340, 1344 (1984); *Com. v. Martinez*, 384 Mass 377, 379-381, 425 NE2d 300, 302-303 (1981); *Com. v. Moore*, 50 Mass App 730, 735-736, 741 NE2d 86, 91 (2001); *Com. v. Dean*, 17 Mass App 943, 457 NE2d 286 (1983); *Com. v. Lewis*, 12 Mass App 562, 569-573, 427 NE2d 934, 940 (1981). Compare *Com. v. McGhee*, supra, 472 Mass at 424-426, 35 NE3d at 345-347 (defense counsel failed to raise bias); *Com. v. Evans*, 439 Mass 184, 188-189, 786 NE2d 375, 382 (2003), *habeas petitions denied in Evans v. Thompson*, 465 F Supp 2d 62 (D Mass 2006) and *Evans v. Verdini*, 466 F3d 141 (1st Cir 2006) (no abuse of discretion in prohibiting defense counsel from specifying precise charges pending during cross-examination of prosecution witness and instead substituting "serious felony charges"); *Com. v. Walker*, 438 Mass 246, 253, 780 NE2d 26, 32 (2002) (no abuse of discretion in barring defense counsel from asking prosecution witness whether she knew she avoided potential life sentence by testifying, where judge allowed related questions); *Com. v. Castro*, 438 Mass 160, 778 NE2d 900 (2002) (no abuse of discretion in refusing to allow defense counsel to cross-examine prosecution witness on pending unrelated federal charges where there had been no communication between state and federal authorities and witness had no expectation of leniency in federal case); *Com. v. McPherson*, 74 Mass App 125, 128, 904 NE2d 488, 491 (2009) (judge properly limited cross-examination of immunized witness regarding the details of charges that had nothing to do with case against defendant); *Com. v. Santiago*, 54 Mass App 656, 662-663, 767 NE2d 619, 623-624 (2002) (no error in curtailing cross-examination about three misdemeanors carrying small punishment where promise of leniency in exchange for testimony is hard to imagine). See also *Com. v. Ellis*, 432 Mass 746, 739 NE2d 1107 (2000) (any error in precluding cross regarding charge dismissed against witness was not prejudicial).

[16] See *Com. v. Rodwell*, 394 Mass 694, 699-700, 477 NE2d 385, 389 (1985).

[17] See *Com. v. Voisine*, 414 Mass 772, 785-786, 610 NE2d 926, 934 (1993).

the prejudicial nature of the evidence.[18] There is, however, some room for judicial discretion in allowing such questions when they evoke a particularized bias of the witness, as when there is a "link between the witness's entanglement with law enforcement and the main case on trial."[19]

In any of its forms, proposed evidence of bias must be sufficiently probative to justify its admission.[20] Where it is not clear that a proffered question is relevant to bias, the cross-examiner must be prepared to explain the relevance.[21] As in other contexts, the questioner must be prepared to state a good faith basis for questions concerning bias.[22] The judge may conduct a voir dire to determine whether the alleged grounds of bias are valid, or speculative.[23]

Reasonable concerns about harassment of the witness or confusion of the issues may justify limitations on cross-examination where

---

[18] See *Com. v. Smith*, 26 Mass App 673, 675-678, 532 NE2d 57, 59-61 (1988); *Com. v. Liberty*, 27 Mass App 1, 533 NE2d 1383 (1989).

[19] *Com. v. Sholley*, 48 Mass App 495, 502, 726 NE2d 415, 421 (2000) (& citations) (though relevant to possible bias, evidence of bad acts here may have led jury to infer defendant's bad character).

[20] See, e.g., *Com. v. Avalos*, 454 Mass 1, 7-8, 906 NE2d 987, 992 (2009) (defendant's marital difficulties with witness too tenuous to demonstrate bias); *Com. v. Dejarnette*, 75 Mass App 88, 101-102, 911 NE2d 1280, 1291 (2009) (judge properly excluded speculative avenues of inquiry regarding witness's willingness to post bond for another alleged drug dealer in unrelated cases); *Com. v. Bussell*, 79 Mass App 460, 462, 947 NE2d 75, 77-78 (2011) (no connection between witness's immigration status and her possible bias). *Com. v. Bui*, 419 Mass 392, 401, 645 NE2d 689, 694-695 (1995) (defendant's bias theory too tenuous); *Com. v. Weichel*, 403 Mass 103, 105-106, 526 NE2d 760, 761-762 (1988) (proffered evidence had little relevance to bias and invited misuse by the jury); *Michnik-Zilberman v. Gordon's Liquor, Inc.*, 390 Mass 6, 15-16, 453 NE2d 430, 436 (1983) (evidence of witness's settlement with plaintiff three years earlier not sufficiently probative of bias); *Com. v. Gittens*, 55 Mass App 148, 155-156, 769 NE2d 777, 783-784 (2002) (no plausible showing that police officer's testimony was influenced by "code of silence"); *Com. v. Souza*, 39 Mass App 103, 108-109, 653 NE2d 1127, 1131 (1995) (defendants failed to adequately connect victims' mothers' recovered memories of sexual abuse to possible bias against defendants); *Com. v. Stokes*, 38 Mass App 752, 761, 653 NE2d 180, 185 (1995) (release of witness despite warrant for her arrest insufficient to demonstrate police bias against defendant).

[21] See, e.g., *Com. v. Taylor*, 455 Mass 372, 378-381, 916 NE2d 1000, 1006-1007 (2009) (defendant made no proffer of how questioning witness about why he did not testify at trial of another participant in home invasion might reveal bias); *Com. v. Armstrong*, 54 Mass App 594, 600-601, 766 NE2d 894, 899-900 (2002).

[22] See *Com. v. Dixon*, 425 Mass 223, 227-228, 680 NE2d 84, 88 (1997) (Commonwealth's information, although derived from questionable sources, nonetheless sufficed to permit questioning); *Com. v. Santiago*, 458 Mass 405, 411-412, 937 NE2d 965, 970 (2010) (questions concerning a witness's fear of testifying are proper with a good faith basis).

[23] *Com. v. Meas*, 467 Mass 434, 449-451, 5 NE3d 864, 877-878 (2014).

the evidence is only marginally relevant to possible bias.[24] The right to cross-examine to show bias or prejudice is not infringed by reasonable limitations as, for example, where the matter sought to be elicited has been sufficiently aired.[25] "When a possibility of bias exists, however, even if remote, the evidence is for the jury to hear and evaluate."[26]

Because of its importance in weighing credibility, impeachment by showing bias, prejudice, or motive to lie is permissible even where it reveals confidential, privileged, or other inadmissible matters.[27] Thus, bias may be explored even though it involves:

- Prior sexual conduct of the victim.[28]
- Privileged matters.[29]

---

[24] See *Com. v. Johnson*, 431 Mass 535, 540, 728 NE2d 281, 285 (2000) (possible racial bias of principal prosecution witness).

[25] *Com. v. Smiledge*, 419 Mass 156, 159, 643 NE2d 41, 44 (1994). See, e.g., *Com. v. Sealy*, 467 Mass 617, 623-625, 6 NE3d 1052, 1057-1059 (2014) (judge had already permitted extensive inquiry into victim's alleged motive to lie to improve immigration status); *Com. v. Ahart*, 464 Mass 437, 440-441, 983 NE2d 1203, 1206-1207 (2013) (exclusion of cumulative questions was proper); *Com. v. Mora*, 82 Mass App 575, 579-580, 976 NE2d 196, 201 (2012) (defense was permitted to elicit testimony regarding informant's motive to fabricate, and additional questions along same lines were properly excluded); *Com. v. Talbot*, 444 Mass 586, 598-590, 177, 180-181 (2005); *Com. v. Palacios*, 66 Mass App 13, 19-20, 845 NE2d 382, 388 (2006).

[26] *Com. v. Henson*, 394 Mass 584, 587, 476 NE2d 947, 950-951 (1985). See, e.g., *Com. v. Kindell*, 84 Mass App 183, 993 NE2d 1222 (2013) (reversing conviction because trial judge refused to permit cross-examination of Commonwealth's sole witness regarding animosity towards defendant and motive to lie).

[27] *Davis v. Alaska*, 415 US 308 (1974).

[28] See *Com. v. Joyce*, 382 Mass 222, 415 NE2d 181 (1981) (rape shield statute, GL 233, § 21B (see § 4.4.3.b, supra) does not preclude evidence of complaining witness's prior sexual conduct where relevant to bias or motive to lie); *Com. v. Mountry*, 463 Mass 80, 86-88, 972 NE2d 438, 444-445 (2012) (judge properly excluded evidence that victim had sexual intercourse with her boy friend five days before where defendant failed to make requisite showing that victim had tried to conceal her relationship in order to avoid confronting her disapproving parents).

[29] For psychiatric records, see *Com. v. Figueroa*, 413 Mass 193, 203, 595 NE2d 779, 785-786 (1992), *Com. v. Stockhammer*, 409 Mass 867, 570 NE2d 992 (1991), *Com. v. Bishop*, 416 Mass 169, 617 NE2d 990 (1993), and § 5.5.4, supra. For attorney-client privilege, see *Com. v. Sullivan*, 435 Mass 722, 728-730, 761 NE2d 509, 515-516 (2002) (extensive discussion of defendant's ability to cross-examine immunized witness regarding conversations with his attorney concerning immunity agreement), *Com. v. Michel*, 367 Mass 454, 459-460, 327 NE2d 720, 724-725 (1975), and § 5.4, supra. For insurance coverage, see *Dempsey v. Goldstein Brothers Amusement Co.*, 231 Mass 461, 464-465, 121 NE 429, 430 (1919) (no error in allowing question on cross-examination eliciting that defendant's medical expert was retained by insurance company and thus suggesting bias, even though evidence of insurance coverage is usually inadmissible), and § 4.7, supra.

- Prior bad acts of the defendant.[30]
- Prior arrest.[31]
- Juvenile record of the witness.[32]

Examination of a witness concerning possible bias toward a *non*-party is within the discretion of the judge and is not a matter of right.[33] It is permissible to show that the witness is in the employ of the real party in interest.[34]

The bias or interest of a witness may be shown by evidence of prior statements or conduct.[35] An expert witness is not immune from impeachment by evidence of bias or interest.[36]

---

[30] See *Com. v. Wright*, 411 Mass 678, 685, 584 NE2d 621, 626 (1992), *habeas denied, Wright v. Marshall*, 656 F3d 102 (1st Cir 2011); (relationship of defendant and witness's mother could be shown to establish bias); *Com. v. Aguiar*, 400 Mass 508, 513-514, 510 NE2d 273, 276-277 (1987) (& citations) (evidence of motive to prevaricate admissible even though it reveals otherwise inadmissible fact such as witness's criminal activity).

[31] See *Com. v. Allen*, 29 Mass App 373, 376-378, 560 NE2d 704, 706-707 (1990) (& citations) (extensive discussion of use of prior arrests to establish bias).

[32] See *Com. v. Bembury*, 406 Mass 552, 556-561, 548 NE2d 1255, 1258-1261 (1990) (if information contained in juvenile record indicates witness's testimony may be product of official pressure or inducement, record may be used to impeach despite GL 119, § 60); *Com. v. Ferrara*, 368 Mass 182, 330 NE2d 837 (1975) (juvenile or criminal records). But see *Com. v. Santos*, 376 Mass 920, 384 NE2d 1202 (1978) (no absolute right to use sealed juvenile records; judge must balance defendant's need to cross-examine on bias against confidentiality interest).

[33] See *Com. v. D'Agostino*, 344 Mass 276, 280, 182 NE2d 133, 136 (1962) (no error in excluding question concerning prosecution witness's relationship to owner of restaurant where assault occurred); *Com. v. Harrison*, 342 Mass 279, 286, 173 NE2d 87, 92 (1961) (no error in excluding question concerning friendly relationship between prosecution witness and deputy police chief).

[34] See *Stevens v. Stewart-Warner Speedometer Corp.*, 223 Mass 44, 47, 111 NE 771, 773 (1916).

[35] See, e.g., *Omansky v. Shain*, 313 Mass 129, 131, 46 NE2d 524, 526 (1943) (plaintiff and defendant's wife took trip together); *Tasker v. Stanley*, 153 Mass 148, 26 NE 417 (1891) (statement); *Com. v. While*, 32 Mass App 949, 590 NE2d 716 (1992) (statement of child victim's mother that even if defendant did not commit the rape, she still hoped "all sorts of nasty things happen to him"); *Com. v. Gabbidon*, 17 Mass App 525, 530-532, 459 NE2d 1263, 1268-1269 (1983) (statements).

[36] See, e.g., *Com. v. Perkins*, 39 Mass App 577, 581, 658 NE2d 975, 978 (1995) (& citations) (prosecutor could show bias of defense expert by using statements from published article in which expert appeared to endorse pedophilia).

§ 6.15.1 *Testimony Pursuant to a Plea Agreement*

The testimony of a prosecution witness pursuant to a plea agreement founded on the witness's promise of truthful testimony poses special problems regarding motive to lie as well as the appearance that the prosecution is vouching for witness's truthfulness. *Com. v. Ciampa*[37] imposes prophylactic measures including redacting references in the plea agreement to witness's obligation to tell the truth. When a prosecution witness testifies pursuant to a plea agreement containing such a promise, the judge should warn the jury that the government does not know whether the witness is actually telling the truth, and that the "truthful testimony" requirement cannot bear on their ultimate credibility determination.[38]

---

[37] 406 Mass 257, 547 NE2d 314 (1989) (reversing convictions because judge failed to redact repeated references in written plea agreement to witness's obligation to tell the truth and failed to instruct jury adequately on incentives that could have influenced witness's testimony). See also *Com. v. Chaleumphong*, 434 Mass 70, 74, 746 NE2d 1009, 1014 (2001) (extending *Ciampa* proscriptions against vouching to police witnesses). Compare *Com. v. Walker*, 438 Mass 246, 252, 780 NE2d 26, 31-32 (2002) (nonprosecution agreement with defendant's wife was sufficiently redacted even though references to "complete" testimony remained).

[38] See *Com. v. Rosario*, 460 Mass 181, 188-191, 950 NE2d 407, 414-417 (2011), *habeas denied, Rosario v. Roden*, 2014 WL 7409584 (D Mass 2014). See also *Com. v. Roman*, 470 Mass 85, 100, 18 NE3d 1069, 1080-1081 (2014) (failure to warn that the government did not know whether the witness was telling the truth, standing alone, is not reversible error); *Com. v. Arriaga*, 438 Mass 556, 578-579, 781 NE2d 1253, 1273 (2003) (no particular words required as long as jury cautioned to give special attention to such testimony); *Com. v. Lindsey*, 48 Mass App 641, 724 NE2d 327 (2000) (failure to instruct, together with prosecutor's vouching for witness, required reversal). Compare *Com. v. Smiley*, 431 Mass 477, 486-487, 727 NE2d 1182, 1190 (2000) (no *Ciampa* instruction required because witness did not have agreement with government); *Com. v. James*, 424 Mass 770, 785-786, 678 NE2d 1170, 118-1182 (1997) (no special instruction required where no discussion before jury that agreement with Commonwealth was contingent on veracity of his testimony); *Com. v. Figueroa*, 83 Mass App 251, 982 NE2d 1202 (2013) (no *Ciampa* instruction required regarding testimony of victim's mother pursuant to nonprosecution agreement where prosecutor did not suggest witness had special obligation to tell the truth and no portion of agreement was before jury). See also *Com. v. Perez*, 460 Mass 683, 694 n.17, 954 NE2d 1, 12 n.17 (2011) (not improper for prosecutor to try to rehabilitate witness who has been impeached by reference to nonprosecution agreement); *Com. v. Almeida*, 452 Mass 601, 608 n.8, 897 NE2d 14, 22 n.8 (2008) (not improper for witness to testify that he generally understands obligations under plea agreement).

For appropriate instructions regarding a plea agreement that does *not* include an explicit requirement that the witness testify truthfully, see *Com. v. Burgos*, 462 Mass 53, 74, 965 NE2d 854 (2012). For general instructions regarding a cooperating witness, see *Com. v. McGee*, 467 Mass 141, 154-155, 4 NE3d 256, 266-267 (2014).

Where a *Ciampa* instruction is warranted, the following rules apply:

> A prosecutor may generally bring out on direct examination the fact that a witness has entered into a plea agreement and understands his obligations under it, but any attempts to bolster the witness by questions concerning his obligation to tell the truth should await redirect examination, and are appropriate only after the defendant has attempted to impeach the witness's credibility by showing the witness struck a deal with the prosecution to obtain favorable treatment. A prosecutor in closing argument may then restate the witness's agreement, but commits reversible error if she suggests that the government has special knowledge by which it can verify the witness's testimony. To guard against an implied representation of credibility, the judge must specifically and forcefully tell the jury to study the witness's credibility with particular care. Where the jury are aware of the witness's promise to tell the truth, the judge also should warn the jury that the government does not know whether the witness is telling the truth.[39]

A properly redacted nonprosecution agreement between the Commonwealth and the witness may be admitted in evidence if accompanied by appropriate instructions.[40] While reference to the "truthful testimony" provisions of such plea agreements should be avoided, a prosecutor may use direct examination to bring out the fact that the witness has entered into a plea agreement and generally understands his obligations under it.[41] Ordinarily, however, the prosecutor's questions concerning a requirement for truthful testimony should be reserved for re-direct, and the better practice is for prosecutor to seek permission before eliciting such testimony.[42] *Ciampa*

---

[39] *Com. v. Webb*, 468 Mass 26, 32, 8 NE3d 270, 274-75 (2014) (citations and internal quotations omitted).

[40] See *Com. v. Conkey*, 430 Mass 139, 147, 714 NE2d 343, 351 (1999); *Com. v. Rivera*, 430 Mass 91, 98, 712 NE2d 1127, 1133 (1999) (timing of admission of plea agreement is in judge's discretion, and it can be admitted on direct examination when it is clear that defendant will challenge credibility on cross). Compare *Com. v. Marrero*, 436 Mass 488, 501, 766 NE2d 461, 471 (2002) (judge should have redacted signatures of ADA who prosecuted case and witness's attorney, as well as repeated references to obligation to tell truth).

[41] See *Com. v. Martinez*, 425 Mass 382, 398, 681 NE2d 818, 829 (1997).

[42] But see *Com. v. Webb*, supra, 468 Mass at 32-34, 8 NE3d at 275-276 and *Com. v. Rolon*, 438 Mass 808, 813-815, 784 NE2d 1092, 1098-1099 (2003) (no improper vouching where prosecutor elicited testimony on direct in response to defense counsel's attack on witness's credibility during opening).

For other cases dealing with the issues raised by these plea agreements, see *Com. v. Charles*, 428 Mass 672, 680-681, 704 NE2d 1137, 1145 (1999); *Com. v. Gordon*, 422

permits questions on redirect regarding the truth requirement when the agreement is raised on cross.[43]

Thus if on cross-examination defense counsel attacks the witness's credibility based on her incentive to help the government under the agreement, the prosecution on redirect may attempt to bolster the witness by questions concerning her specific obligation under the agreement to tell the truth.[44] No reference should be made to the name of the court or judge who actually granted the immunity; nor should reference be made to the signatures of attorneys;[45] the prosecutor may elicit only that the witness has been granted immunity and the sanctions for untruthful testimony.[46] The Commonwealth is permitted to argue in closing that immunity can be considered by the jury as an indication that the witness was telling the truth,[47] but may not vouch for the credibility of the witness.[48]

Com. v. Davis[49] mandated the *Ciampa* measures even in absence of an express plea agreement where there is a "more amorphous arrangement" between witness and prosecution for some non-specific consideration:

Mass 816, 833-835, 666 NE2d 122, 134-135 (1996); *Com. v. Brousseau*, 421 Mass 647, 653-655, 659 NE2d 724, 728-729 (1996); *Com. v. Fuller*, 421 Mass 400, 413, 657 NE2d 1251, 1258-1259 (1995); *Com. v. Grenier*, 415 Mass 680, 686-687, 615 NE2d 922, 925-926 (1993); *Com. v. Evans*, 415 Mass 422, 427-428, 614 NE2d 653, 657 (1993); *Com. v. Marangiello*, 410 Mass 452, 462-465, 573 NE2d 500 (1991); *Com. v. Sullivan*, 410 Mass 521, 524-525, 574 NE2d 966, 969 (1991) (*Ciampa distinguished*); *Com. v. DeCicco*, 51 Mass App 159, 744 NE2d 95 (2001) (even assuming prosecutor misled jury by stating accomplice witness would be tried for murder and there was no plea deal, no prejudicial error); *Com. v. Holmes*, 46 Mass App 550, 707 NE2d 1094 (1991) (language of *Ciampa* plea agreement distinguished). Cf. *Com. v. Prater*, 431, Mass 86, 98, 725 NE2d 233, 244 (2000) (judge should instruct jury not to consider accomplice's guilty plea as evidence against defendant).

[43] *Com. v. Rosario*, 460 Mass 181, 188-191, 950 NE2d 407, 414-417 (2011), *habeas denied, Rosario v. Roden*, 2014 WL 7409584 (D. Ma. 2014).

[44] *Com. v. Martinez*, 458 Mass 684, 699, 940 NE2d 422, 435 (2011); *Com. v. Rivera*, 430 Mass 91, 96-97, 712 NE2d 1127, 1132 (1999); *Com. v. Dyous*, 436 Mass 719, 725-727, 767 NE2d 51, 58-59 (2002); *Com. v. Marrero*, 436 Mass 488, 499-501, 766 NE2d 461, 470-472 (2002).

[45] *Com. v. Webb*, supra, 468 Mass at 34, 8 NE3d at 276.

[46] *Com. v. Rolon*, supra, 438 Mass at 814-815, 784 NE2d at 1099.

[47] *Com. v. Sullivan*, 435 Mass 722, 726-727, 761 NE2d 509, 513-514 (2002); *Com. v. Caldwell*, 459 Mass 271, 279-280, 945 NE2d 313, 322-323 (2011) (prosecutor, responding to defense arguments, properly argued that the witness with plea agreement would not risk lying under oath). See also § 13.2, infra.

[48] *Com. v. Webb*, supra, 468 Mass at 35-36, 8 NE3d at 277. See also 13.2, infra.

[49] 52 Mass App 75, 751 NE2d 420 (2001) (reversing conviction because of judge's misleading response to jury question concerning possible leniency toward witness facing charges).

> By allowing Thornton to testify without making any express advance promises, the Commonwealth could presumably craft a reward post hoc that conformed to the quality of the service. This approach has the added advantage of permitting a prosecutor to tout the fact to the jury that no specific promises have been made to the witness. Needless to say, this tactic provides a witness who faces pending charges with an even stronger motive to lie than a witness with whom a bargain is made before trial. The need for cautionary instruction, therefore, is even more acute in situations like the present case.[50]

Regarding the extent to which defense counsel may inquire into conversations between the immunized witness and his attorney concerning the immunity agreement and the negotiations leading up to it, the Supreme Judicial Court has observed:

> The attorney-client privilege, when properly applied, should present no obstacle to inquiring into promises, rewards, and inducements made by the Commonwealth either directly to the witness or through counsel. The communication of such matters by the prosecutor is not privileged, and the details of what the prosecutor told counsel or the witness, or what counsel conveyed from the prosecutor to the witness, are subject to examination without violating attorney-client privilege. Other conversations between the witness and counsel, about whether to accept the terms offered by the prosecutor, or about the possible permutations of "consideration" and how each might affect the witness's future, may well be confidential in nature and subject to attorney-client privilege.[51]

The Court left for another day the issue of whether the privilege might ever have to give way to the right of confrontation in this context.[52]

---

[50] 52 Mass App at 78 n.7, 751 NE2d at 423 n.7. But compare *Com. v. Correia*, 65 Mass App 597, 601, 843 NE2d 84, 88 (2006) (*Ciampa* measures not required because there was no agreement, explicit or otherwise; "the mere fact that [witness] may have expected and, in fact, received favorable treatment by not being charged, did not amount to a deal."); *Com. v. Rebello*, 450 Mass 118, 121-124, 876 NE2d 851, 855-857 (2007) (judge found there was no undisclosed, tacit agreement that contemplated dismissal of charges after witness testified). For agreements not to charge the witness, see *Com. v. Iago I.*, 77 Mass App 327, 334, 931 NE2d 47, 53 (2010).

[51] *Com. v. Birks*, 435 Mass 782, 788, 762 NE2d 267, 273 (2002). See also *Com. v. Hardy*, 464 Mass 660, 668, 984 NE2d 727, 734 (2013).(trial judge improperly excluded cross-examination as to whether prosecutor had made promise to witness as inducement to testify); *Com. v. Sullivan*, supra, 435 Mass at 728-730, 761 NE2d at 515-516; § 5.4.5, supra.

[52] *Com. v. Birks*, supra, 435 Mass at 788, 762 NE2d at 273.

§ 6.16 By Proving Bad Character

The credibility of a witness may be impeached by attacking his or her character for truthfulness. Under Massachusetts practice, this impeachment may take two forms: (1) evidence of the general reputation of the witness for truthfulness and veracity; and (2) evidence that the witness has been convicted of a crime. A third mode of character impeachment, cross-examination of the witness regarding prior bad acts, is not permitted, but would be if Proposed Mass R Evid 608(b) were adopted.[1]

§ 6.16.1 General Character for Truthfulness and Veracity

W1's credibility may be attacked by testimony of W2 that W1 has a poor reputation for truthfulness and veracity among those who know him.[2] This mode of impeachment is limited to:

- Reputation for truth and veracity, *not* character in general.[3]
- Evidence of general reputation, *not* specific acts of lying or misconduct.[4]

Reputation in this context has been defined as follows: "Has the subject been so much discussed and considered that there is in the public mind a uniform and concurrent sentiment which can be stated as a fact?"[5]

Massachusetts practice does not permit opinion evidence from W2 regarding W1's truthfulness.[6] Indeed it is the longstanding rule

---

§ 6.16 [1] See generally *Com. v. Daley*, 439 Mass 558, 562-564, 789 NE2d 1070, 1075-1076 (2003) (citing Text).

[2] See *Eastman v. Boston Elevated Railway Co.*, 200 Mass 412, 86 NE 793 (1909).

[3] See, e.g., *Com. v. Cancel*, 394 Mass 567, 572-573, 476 NE2d 610, 615 (1985) (evidence that witness was a member of a street gang improperly admitted to attack his credibility).

[4] See, e.g., *Com. v. Arthur*, 31 Mass App 178, 180, 575 NE2d 1147, 1149 (1991).

[5] *Com. v. Baxter*, 267 Mass 591, 593, 166 NE 742, 743 (1929). See also *Com. v. Dockham*, 405 Mass 618, 631, 542 NE2d 591, 599 (1989) (& citations).

[6] See *Com. v. Dockham*, supra, 405 Mass at 631, 542 NE2d at 599; *Eastman v. Boston Elevated Railway Co.*, supra (question as to whether W2 would believe W1 under oath was properly excluded); *Com. v. Edgerly*, 13 Mass App 562, 576, 435 NE2d 641, 649-650 (1982) (& citations). Evidence concerning particular bad acts is also inadmissible for this purpose. See *Com. v. Olsen*, 452 Mass 284, 293, 892 NE2d 739, 745 (2008).

that a witness, either lay or expert, may not offer an opinion regarding the credibility of another witness. See § 6.12, supra. Such opinion evidence would be allowed by Proposed Mass R Evid 608(a),[7] modeled on the federal rule. In support of the allowance of opinion testimony the Advisory Committee expressed its belief "that in practice the distinction between opinion and reputation testimony in this context is often difficult to preserve."[8]

The impeaching witness must have personal knowledge of W1's reputation for truth and veracity, and a sufficient foundation must be demonstrated. A witness who has knowledge of the opinions of only a few members of W1's community is not qualified to testify to his general reputation. "It is what is said of the person under inquiry in the common speech of his neighbors and members of his community or territory of repute, from which his reputation for truth or falsehood arises, and not what the impeaching witness may have heard others say who numerically may be few and insignificant."[9] The information

---

[7] Proposed Mass R Evid 608(a) provides:

Evidence of Character and Conduct of Witness
(a) **Opinion and reputation evidence of character**. The credibility of a witness may be attacked or supported by evidence *in the form of opinion or reputation*, but subject to these limitations: (1) the evidence may refer only to character for truthfulness or untruthfulness, and (2) evidence of truthful character is admissible only after the character of the witness for truthfulness has been attacked by opinion or reputation or otherwise (emphasis added).

[8] Advisory Committee Note to 608(b). See also *Com. v. Belton*, 352 Mass 263, 269, 225 NE2d 53, 57 (1967). In a related context, a request to adopt Proposed Mass R Evid 405(a), permitting character witnesses for the defense to testify in the form of opinion, has been declined. See *Com. v. Walker*, 442 Mass 185, 812 NE2d 262 (2004).

[9] *F. W. Stock & Sons v. Dellapenna*, 217 Mass 503, 506, 105 NE 378, 379 (1914). See also *Com. v. Olsen*, 452 Mass 284, 292, 892 NE2d 739, 745 (2008) (defendant did not lay proper foundation for witnesses proffered to testify that prosecution witness had reputation of being a pathological liar). Compare *Com. v. Baxter*, supra, 267 Mass at 593, 166 NE at 743 (stranger to community who was hired as investigator by a party and inquired of only five persons not qualified to testify that witness's reputation for truthfulness was bad), *Com. v. DiGiacomo*, 57 Mass 312, 324, 782 NE2d 1094, 1104 (2003) (reputation evidence of child victim properly excluded where it consisted not of general reputation but the private opinions of a few persons reporting a specific instance of lying); *Com. v. Phachansiri*, 38 Mass App 100, 109, 645 NE2d 60, 66 (1995) (testimony based on community of 10 to 12 adults properly excluded), *Com. v. Healey*, 27 Mass App 30, 39-40, 534 NE2d 301, 306-307 (1989) (judge properly excluded testimony of defense witness in sexual abuse case concerning victim's poor reputation in community for truth and veracity because the sources of knowledge were insufficient and foundation inadequate), and *Com. v. Gomes*, 11 Mass App 933, 416 NE2d 551 (1981) (judge properly excluded testimony concerning victim's poor reputation for truthfulness where based on views of only five people, and on remarks from a few other teachers in school community) with *Com. v. Arthur*, supra, 31 Mass App at 179-181, 575 NE2d at 1148-1149 (evidence of complainant witness's reputation for lying

upon which the impeaching witness bases her testimony as to reputation must be current and not too attenuated.[10]

At common law, the reputation of the witness being impeached had to be drawn from the community where he resided, but GL 233, § 21A makes admissible reputation where the witness works or has his business associations as well.[11] This has been held to include the school community to which a student belongs.[12]

Although not explicitly mandated by the caselaw,[13] the foundation for testimony from the impeaching witness may be established as follows:

1. Are you familiar with W1's general reputation for truth and veracity in the community in which he or she resides (or works)?
2. What is that reputation?

On cross-examination, a character witness's knowledge of W1's reputation may be tested by asking for specifics regarding the events that formed the basis for that reputation.[14] "The credibility of the witness is tested in the following manner—if the witness states that he has

---

and exaggerating, presented by two eighth-grade classmates and drawn from her middle school class of 150, was improperly excluded; the foundation established a discrete, identifiable community of middle school students, 50 or 60 of whom had expressed views about the victim's reputation for veracity, and an impeaching witness who knew complainant for six years and was in position to know of her reputation).

[10] See *Com. v. Moore*, 379 Mass 106, 115, 393 NE2d 904, 910 (1979) (no error in excluding testimony that W1's reputation for veracity was poor where impeaching witness, W1's former wife, had moved out of the community seven years before trial); *Com. v. Phachansiri*, supra, 38 Mass App at 109, 645 NE2d at 66 (evidence of defendant's reputation for truthfulness five years earlier properly excluded).

[11] Proposed Mass R Evid 608(a) "does not alter G.L. c. 233, § 21A, as regards the source or basis of reputation evidence." Advisory Committee Note to 608.

[12] See *Com. v. Arthur*, supra, 31 Mass App at 179, 575 NE2d at 1148.

[13] See *Wetherbee v. Norris*, 103 Mass 565 (1870) and *F. W. Stock & Sons v. Dellapenna*, supra, 217 Mass at. 506-507, 105 NE at 379.

[14] See *Com. v. Arthur*, supra, 31 Mass App at 180, 575 NE2d at 1148-1149 (& citations). Proposed Mass R Evid 405(a) provides:

> **Methods of Proving Character**
>
> (a) **Reputation or opinion**. In all cases in which evidence of character or a trait of character is admissible, proof may be made by testimony as to reputation or by testimony in the form of an opinion. *On cross examination, inquiry is allowable into relevant specific instances of conduct* (emphasis added).

Proposed Mass R Evid 608(b) (discussed at § 6.16.3, infra) permits cross-examination of a character witness regarding specific instances of conduct probative of the truthfulness of the witness whose character is being testified about.

not heard of the report of prior misconduct, his professed knowledge of the defendant's reputation in the community may be doubted by the jury or, if he states that he has heard of the report but still testifies that the defendant's reputation is good in the community, the jury may consider whether the witness is fabricating or whether the community standards in regard to character are too low."[15] The thrust of such cross-examination goes to the weight of the character evidence, and not to its admissibility.[16] The reputation witness may not be asked, however, if he would change his mind if he knew the adverse facts because that suggests the existence of facts not in evidence.[17]

§ 6.16.2 *Prior Convictions*

W1 may be impeached by evidence that he has been convicted of a crime or crimes. In this mode of impeachment, the jury is implicitly asked to infer a readiness to lie from the witness's prior involvement in criminal activity.[18] A conviction may be admissible for this purpose even though the underlying crime does not reflect directly on the defendant's truth-telling abilities, as a perjury conviction would.[19]

---

[15] *Com. v. Montanino*, 27 Mass App 130, 137, 535 NE2d 617, 621 (1989) (Commonwealth had right to cross-examine defendant's character witnesses about whether they had heard reports of prior misconduct concerning the character trait testified about). See also *Com. v. Brown*, 411 Mass 115, 117-118, 579 NE2d 153, 154-155 (1991) (Commonwealth had right to cross-examine defense witnesses testifying to defendant's reputation for truthfulness regarding allegedly false statements made by defendant regarding his military record); *Com. v. Deveau*, 34 Mass App 9, 14 n.2, 606 NE2d 921, 924 n.2 (1993) (prosecutor on cross-examination may inquire of witness who has testified to defendant's reputation if witness has heard rumors inconsistent with good reputation to which the witness has vouched on direct). See generally *Michelson v. United States*, 335 US 469 (1948).

[16] See *Com. v. Arthur*, supra, 31 Mass App at 180, 575 NE2d at 1148-1149.

[17] See *Com. v. Deveau*, supra, 34 Mass App at 14 n.2, 606 NE2d at 924; *Com. v. Kamishlian*, 21 Mass App 931, 933-934, 486 NE2d 743, 746 (1986).

[18] See *Com. v. Fano*, 400 Mass 296, 302-303, 508 NE2d 859, 863-864 (1987) ("a defendant's earlier disregard for the law may suggest to the fact finder similar disregard for the courtroom oath"); *Com. v. Sheeran*, 370 Mass 82, 89, 345 NE2d 362, 367 (1976) ("it is not irrational to infer that a thief may also be a liar"); *Brillante v. R. W. Granger & Sons, Inc.*, 55 Mass App 542, 545, 772 NE2d 74, 77 (2002) ("One who has been convicted of crime is presumed to be less worthy of belief than one who has not been so convicted.").

[19] See, e.g., *Com. v. Smith*, 450 Mass 395, 407-408, 879 NE2d 87, 97 (2008) (witness's conviction for sexual conduct for a fee was admissible to impeach her; GL 233, § 21 is not limited to crimes involving dishonesty or false statement because the underlying theory is that the witness' earlier disregard for the law may suggest a similar disregard for the courtroom oath); *Com. v. Paulding*, 438 Mass 1, 11-12, 777 NE2d 135,

The logic of impeachment by prior convictions has not escaped criticism over the years.[20]

Impeachment of witnesses by prior convictions is available in both civil and criminal cases[21] and is controlled by GL 233, § 21,[22] which prescribes the following time limits[23] after which convictions cannot be used to impeach a witness:

> (1) Misdemeanors cannot be used after five years from the date the sentence was imposed unless the witness has subsequently been convicted of a crime within five years of the time he testifies.[24]
>
> (2) Felony convictions resulting in (a) no sentence, (b) a suspended sentence, (c) a fine, or (d) a sentence to a correctional institution other than a state prison cannot be used after ten years from the date of conviction or sentence, whichever is applicable, unless the witness has subsequently been convicted of a crime within ten years of the time he testifies.
>
> (3) Felony convictions resulting in a sentence to state prison cannot be used after ten years from the expiration of the minimum term of imprisonment unless the witness has subsequently been convicted of a crime within ten years of the time he testifies.
>
> (4) Traffic violations for which a fine only was imposed shall not be used unless the witness was convicted of another crime or crimes within five years of the time he testifies.[25]

143-144 (2002) (drug possession and assault and battery); *Com. v. Kowalski*, 33 Mass App 49, 50, 595 NE2d 798, 799-800 (1992) (& citations) (distribution of heroin and accessory after fact to armed robbery).

[20] See, e.g., *Com. v. DiMarzo*, 364 Mass 669, 682, 308 NE2d 538, 546 (1974) (Hennessey, J, concurring) ("Prior convictions, even as applied only to the credibility issue, have little or no probative value in most instances.").

[21] It has been held that the use of convictions for impeachment infringes neither the state nor federal constitutional rights of criminal defendants. See *Com. v. Drumgold*, 423 Mass 230, 249, 668 NE2d 300, 314 (1996); *Com. v. Diaz*, 383 Mass 73, 417 NE2d 950 (1981) (& cases cited).

[22] For discussion of the statute and its legislative history, see generally *Com. v. Harris*, 443 Mass 714, 825 NE2d 58 (2005).

[23] Regarding the operation of the time limits, see generally *Com. v. Leftwich*, 430 Mass 865, 869, 724 NE2d 691, 696 (2000) (prior conviction admissible even though just a few days from being time-barred); *Com. v. Gladney*, 34 Mass App 151, 154-155, 607 NE2d 750, 752 (1993); *Com. v. Childs*, 23 Mass App 33, 35, 499 NE2d 299 (1986).

[24] A plea of guilty tendered pursuant to a pretrial diversion program does not revitalize a stale conviction. See *Com. v. Jackson*, 45 Mass App 666, 669-670, 700 NE2d 848, 851-852 (1998).

[25] See, e.g., *Com. v. Burnett*, 417 Mass 740, 632 NE2d 1206 (1994) (judge properly excluded witness's prior conviction for "operating to endanger" for which only a

When the defendant is the witness being impeached, the last clause of GL 233, § 21 extends the time limitations for "any period during which the defendant was a fugitive from justice."

Federal and out-of-state convictions are admissible under GL 233, § 21 provided that the convictions come within the statute.[26] In order to be used to impeach, a conviction must be a final judgment.[27] A guilty plea constitutes a conviction within the explicit terms of the statute. GL 233, § 21, second paragraph.[28] A conviction based on a plea of nolo contendere is not admissible for impeachment.[29]

For felony crimes, a finding of guilty constitutes a conviction within the meaning of GL 233, § 21 even if no sentence is imposed; for misdemeanors, the conviction alone in the absence of a sentence may not be used to impeach.[30] Probation on a conviction of a misdemeanor is not a sentence for purposes of the statute.[31] A fine is a sentence within the meaning of the statute.[32]

An adjudication of juvenile delinquency based on a criminal offense may be used for impeachment in the same manner as a criminal

---

fine had been imposed); *Com. v. Johnson*, 431 Mass 535, 541, 728 NE2d 281, 286-287 (2001) (defendant was improperly impeached with conviction of operating uninsured vehicle, for which only fine was imposed).

[26] See *Attorney General v. Pelletier*, 240 Mass 264, 310-312, 134 NE 407, 420 (1922) (federal crime); *Com. v. Gladney*, supra, 34 Mass App at 155, 607 NE2d at 753 (& citations). See also *Com. v. Bourgeois*, 391 Mass 869, 882-883, 465 NE2d 1180, 1189 (1984) (conviction in foreign country; burden falls on defendant to show that the conviction was obtained in proceedings so fundamentally unfair that the conviction should be excluded).

[27] See *Wilson v. Honeywell*, Inc., 409 Mass 803, 808-809, 569 NE2d 1011, 1014-1015 (1991). A conviction at a bench trial in the district court was not "final" for purposes of impeachment if the defendant filed an appeal under the former *de novo* system. *Wilson v. Honeywell, Inc.*, supra. A suspended sentence is a final judgment for purposes of the statute. *Com. v. Sheeran*, 370 Mass 82, 88, 345 NE2d 362, 366 (1976). A prior conviction based on a plea of guilty is a final judgment even though, subsequent to the trial in which it was used to impeach, a motion was made to withdraw the plea and the conviction was vacated. See *Com. v. DiGiambattista*, 59 Mass App 190, 199, 794 NE2d 1229, 1236 (2003), *rev'd on other grounds*, 442 Mass 423, 813 NE2d 516 (2004).

[28] See *Com. v. DiGiambattista*, supra, 59 Mass App at 199, 794 NE2d at 1236.

[29] *Olszewski v. Goldberg*, 223 Mass 27, 111 NE 404 (1916). See also Mass R Crim P 12(f) and Proposed Mass R Evid 410, discussed at § 4.6, supra.

[30] See *Com. v. Devlin*, 365 Mass 149, 163, 310 NE2d 353, 362 (1974) (& cases cited).

[31] See *Com. v. Stewart*, 422 Mass 385, 387, 663 NE2d 255, 257 (1996); *Com. v. Rossi*, 19 Mass App 257, 259, 473 NE2d 708, 710 (1985). See also *Com. v. Edgerly*, 13 Mass App 562, 569-571, 435 NE2d 641, 646-647 (1982) (adjudication of paternity and support order is not "conviction").

[32] See *Com. v. Ortiz*, 47 Mass App 777, 781, 716 NE2d 659, 663-664 (1999) (& citations).

conviction in a subsequent delinquency or criminal proceeding.[33] Where the juvenile record is relevant to bias or prejudice, the court may be required to put aside any concern for confidentiality and admit it to preserve the accused's constitutional right of confrontation.[34]

Probation violations may not be used to impeach a witness's character for truthfulness, but may be used to show bias on the part of the witness who might want to curry favor with the prosecution.[35]

Suggestions in earlier cases that a conviction followed by a pardon is not admissible for impeachment[36] appear to have been undercut.[37]

---

[33] GL 119, § 60, as amended in 1991, provides:

> An adjudication of any child as a delinquent child . . . shall not be received in evidence or used against such child for any purpose in any proceedings in any court except in subsequent delinquency or criminal proceedings against the same person; . . . provided, however, that adjudication of delinquency by reason of the child having committed an offense against the commonwealth may be used for impeachment purposes in subsequent delinquency or criminal proceedings in the same manner and to the same extent as prior criminal convictions.

See *Com v. Beatrice*, 57 Mass App 1114, 785 NE2d 427 (2003) (1991 amendment permits use of juvenile adjudications for impeachment); *Com. v. Ortiz*, 53 Mass App 168, 180 n.15, 757 NE2d 1113, 1124 n.15) (2001) (emphasizing use of "may" in proviso). See also *Com. v. Scott*, 463 Mass 561, 571-573, 977 NE2d 490, 500-501 (2012) (prosecutor improperly questioned defendant about his juvenile record after agreeing before trial not to introduce such record, but defendant opened the door by testifying he filed application for gun permit answering he had no criminal convictions).

The 1991 amendment brings Massachusetts closer in line with the federal rule, which provides juvenile adjudications are "generally not admissible" to impeach but may be used to impeach a witness other than the accused if admission if "necessary for a fair determination of the issue of guilt or innocence." Proposed Mass R Evid 609(e) reflects pre-1991 practice:

> (e) **Juvenile adjudications**. Evidence of a juvenile adjudication is not admissible, except by constitutional requirement or as otherwise provided by statute.

The application of GL 119, § 60, to the use of prior testimony for impeachment is discussed at § 6.13.2, supra.

[34] See § 6.15, supra. See also *Com. v. A Juvenile* (No. 2), 384 Mass 390, 394, 425 NE2d at 297 (& citations); *Com. v. Ferrara*, 368 Mass 182, 186-190, 330 NE2d 837, 840-843 (1975) (witness may have been motivated by desire to please authorities). For a discussion of the factors to be weighed in deciding whether to permit the use of juvenile records to impeach a prosecution witness in such a situation, see *Com. v. Santos*, 376 Mass 920, 924-926, 384 NE2d 1202, 1204-1206 (1978).

[35] See *Com. v. Roberts*, 423 Mass 17, 20-21, 666 NE2d 475, 478 (1996).

[36] See *Rittenberg v. Smith*, 214 Mass 343, 101 NE 989 (1913).

[37] See *Com. v. Vickey*, 381 Mass 762, 771, 412 NE2d 877, 882 (1980) and *Commissioner of the MDC v. Director of Civil Service*, 348 Mass 184, 193-196, 203 NE2d 95, 98-103 (1964). But see *Com. v. Childs*, 23 Mass App 33, 36-37, 499 NE2d 299 (1986) (suggesting that GL 127, § 152, providing for automatic sealing of criminal records of offenses for which a pardon has been granted, may preclude use of such convictions for impeachment).

Proposed Mass R Evid 609(d) would resolve the unsettled case law by providing that "[w]here a conviction has been followed by a pardon, both the conviction, if otherwise admissible, and the pardon shall be admissible."[38] Records that have been sealed or expunged under GL 94C, §§ 34, 35, 44, or GL 276, §§ 100A, 100B, 100C (discussed in § 5.10, infra) may not be admitted in evidence or used in any way in court proceedings, and thus may not be used for impeachment.[39]

A conviction resulting in a jail sentence cannot be used to impeach a defendant[40] (or revive a stale conviction) unless he was represented by counsel or waived counsel in the prior proceeding; but a presumption relieves the Commonwealth of the burden to affirmatively show such representation or waiver.[41] The Commonwealth does not have to come forward with proof on that point unless the defendant first makes a showing that the prior conviction was obtained without representation or waiver.[42]

Subject to the time limitations of GL 233, § 21, the conviction may be for any type of crime regardless (as noted above) of its logical relevance to the matter of credibility. The courts have repeatedly emphasized, however, that the trial judge has the discretion to exclude a defendant's prior conviction, even if it falls within the requirements of the statute, where the danger of unfair prejudice outweighs the

---

[38] Compare Fed R Evid 609(c) (excluding impeachment use of convictions followed by pardons where the latter is based on a finding of rehabilitation or innocence).

[39] Proposed Mass R Evid 609(g) forbids use of a sealed conviction "except by constitutional requirement or as otherwise provided by statute."

[40] The courts have left open the question whether a nonparty witness may be impeached by uncounseled convictions, see *Com. v. Napier*, 417 Mass 32, 33, 627 NE2d 913, 914 (1994) and *Com. v. Puleio*, 394 Mass 101, 104, 474 NE2d 1078, 1080-1081 (1985), as well as the use of uncounseled convictions to impeach a witness in a civil case. See *Carey v. Zayre of Beverly, Inc.*, 367 Mass 125, 324 NE2d 619 (1975); *Walter v. Bonito*, 367 Mass 117, 123 n.1, 324 NE2d 624, 627 n.1 (1975).

[41] See *Com. v. Saunders*, 435 Mass 691, 695-696, 761 NE2d 490, 493-494 (2002); *Com. v. McMullin*, 76 Mass App 904, 905, 923 NE2d 1062, 1064 (2010).

[42] A docket sheet indicating counsel had been appointed satisfies the burden in absence of contrary evidence. *Com. v. Stewart*, 422 Mass 385, 386, 663 NE2d 255, 257 (1996). As to other methods available to the Commonwealth to establish either representation or waiver, see *Com. v. Napier*, supra, 417 Mass at 33, 627 NE2d at 914; *Com. v. Delorey*, 369 Mass 323, 328-331, 339 NE2d 746, 749-750 (1975).

The use of an uncounseled conviction is constitutional error, *Com. v. Stewart*, supra, 422 Mass at 386, 663 NE2d at 257; but it may be harmless beyond a reasonable doubt. *Com. v. Delorey*, supra, 369 Mass at 327, 339 NE2d at 748. Compare *Com. v. Brown*, 2 Mass App 76, 83, 308 NE2d 794, 798 (1974) (error harmless) with *Com. v. Proctor*, supra, 403 Mass at 149, 526 NE2d at 767-768 and *Com. v. Barrett*, 3 Mass App 8, 322 NE2d 89 (1975) (error not harmless).

probative value of the conviction for purposes of impeachment.[43] "The admission of evidence of a prior conviction, particularly a conviction of a crime not involving the defendant's truthfulness and one closely related to or identical to the crime with which the defendant is charged, may well divert the jury's attention from the question of the defendant's guilt to the question of the defendant's bad character. Moreover, the mere threat of the admission of evidence of a defendant's prior conviction of a crime may discourage him from testifying."[44] "Impeachment of a defendant's credibility by means of prior convictions is always subject to possible misconstruction by a jury, who may improperly regard the impeachment as substantive evidence of guilt, despite careful limiting instructions."[45]

The trial judge's ruling admitting evidence of a prior conviction may be reviewed on appeal on the question of whether there was an abuse of discretion because the probative value of the conviction for impeachment purposes was outweighed by the danger of unfair prejudice.[46] Reversal is required where it appears that the judge was unaware of his discretion to exclude convictions.[47]

The substantial similarity of the crime charged and the conviction offered for impeachment is a strong factor weighing against admission because of the risk that the jury will engage in prejudicial propensity logic.[48] Indeed it has been observed that "[g]enerally, a prior conviction must be substantially similar to the charged offense for the prejudicial effect to outweigh the probative value of prior conviction

---

[43] See *Com. v. Maguire*, 392 Mass 466, 470, 467 NE2d 112, 115 (1984); *Com. v. Little*, 453 Mass 766,772, 906 NE2d 286, 292 (2009).

[44] *Com. v. Maguire*, supra, 392 Mass at 466, 467 NE2d at 114-115.

[45] *Com. v. Childs*, supra, 23 Mass App at 38, 499 NE2d at 302.

[46] See, e.g., *Com. v. Gallagher*, 408 Mass 510, 516-517, 562 NE2d 80, 84-85 (1990) (upholding decision to admit convictions for breaking and entering, larceny, and receiving stolen property in murder trial); *Com. v. Feroli*, 407 Mass 405, 407-408, 553 NE2d 934, 935-936 (1990) (upholding decision to admit convictions for armed robbery in murder trial).

[47] See *Com. v. Ruiz*, 400 Mass 214, 508 NE2d 607 (1987) (& citations).

[48] *Com. v. Maguire*, supra, 392 Mass at 471, 467 NE2d at 1180-1181; *Com. v. Little*, supra, 453 Mass at 772-775, 906 NE2d at 292-295 (conviction reversed where judge denied defendant's motion in limine to exclude substantially similar prior convictions for drug offenses; the similarity of the crimes should have raised a "red flag"). See also *Walter v. Bonito*, supra n.32, 367 Mass at 124, 324 NE2d at 628. Compare *Com. v. King*, 445 Mass 217, 226-227, 834 NE2d 1175, 1186-1187 (2005) (armed robbery conviction was sufficiently dissimilar to sexual offenses being tried).

evidence."[49] Where the prior crime is identical to the one being tried, does not bear directly on truthfulness, and there are other convictions which could be used to impeach the defendant, impeachment should usually not be allowed.[50] Nonetheless, the admission of a conviction substantially similar to the crime for which the defendant is on trial is not *per se* error,[51] and the admission of similar crimes has been upheld on numerous occasions.[52]

---

[49] *Com. v. Drumgold*, 423 Mass 230, 250, 668 NE2d 300, 314 (1996). See also *Com. v. Preston*, 27 Mass App 16, 23, 534 NE2d 787, 791-792 (1989) ("It is at least difficult, if not impossible, to show an abuse of discretion [in the admission of prior convictions] in the absence of a 'substantial similarity' between the offenses being tried and the prior convictions.").

[50] See *Com. v. Bly*, 444 Mass 640, 654, 830 NE2d 1048, 1059 (2005).

[51] See *Com. v. Bly*, supra, 444 Mass at 654, 830 NE2d at 1059; *Com. v. Whitman*, 416 Mass 90, 94, 617 NE2d 625, 628 (1993); *Com. v. Fano*, 400 Mass 296, 304, 508 NE2d 859, 864 (1987).

[52] See, e.g., *Com. v. Crouse*, 447 Mass 558, 565-566, 855 NE2d 391, 398 (2006) (no abuse of discretion in admitting prior convictions for rape, aggravated rape, breaking and entering while armed with a knife, assault in a dwelling while armed with a screwdriver, and assault and battery by means of a knife and screwdriver, even though substantially similar to the charged murder); *Com. v. Deberry*, 441 Mass 211, 224-225, 804 NE2d 911, 921 (2004) (no abuse of discretion in admitting prior conviction for assault with dangerous weapon in prosecution for assault and battery and malicious destruction of property); *Com. v. Whitman*, supra, 416 Mass at 94-95 (conviction for assault with intent to commit rape admitted in murder prosecution arising out of defendant's alleged sexual assault); *Com. v. Mahoney*, 405 Mass 326, 330, 540 NE2d 179, 182 (1989) (in prosecution for breaking and entering, judge did not abuse discretion in denying defendant's motion in limine to bar use of prior convictions for armed robbery, kidnapping and assault by means of a deadly weapon, inasmuch as prior crimes were not so similar to crime charged as to require exclusion); *Com. v. Andrews*, 403 Mass 441, 456, 530 NE2d 1222, 1230-1231 (1988) (substantial difference between armed robbery and murder, even if that murder is committed in course of armed robbery); *Com. v. Smith*, 403 Mass 489, 497-498, 531 NE2d 556, 561-562 (1988) (armed robbery convictions admitted in trial on armed assault); *Com. v. Walker*; 401 Mass 338, 345-346, 516 NE2d 1143, 1148-1149 (1987) (unarmed robbery, larceny, and assault convictions admitted in trial on murder and armed robbery); *Com. v. Cordeiro*, 401 Mass 843, 855, 519 NE2d 1328, 1335 (1988) (no abuse of discretion where judge admitted prior conviction for assault by means of dangerous weapon at trial for aggravated rape even though both incidents involved use of knife); *Com. v. Weaver*, 400 Mass 612, 618-619, 511 NE2d 545, 549 (1987) (convictions for assaultive crimes sufficiently dissimilar to firearm possessory offense); *Com. v. Boyer*; 400 Mass 52, 56-59, 507 NE2d 1024, 1026-1028 (1987) (conviction for prostitution in trial on prostitution charges); *Com. v. Reid*, 400 Mass 534, 537-540, 511 NE2d 331, 333-335 (1987) (defendant on trial for rape of a child without force and assault and battery on child properly impeached by evidence of 14 prior convictions, five of which involved assaults or threats); *Com. v. Chartier*; 43 Mass App 758, 762, 686 NE2d 1055, 1058 (1997) (conviction for violating domestic abuse order admitted in trial for same offense); *Com. v. Nutile*, 31 Mass App 614, 621, 582 NE2d 547, 551-552 (1991) (conviction for possession of cocaine admitted in trial on cocaine trafficking); *Com. v. Dwyer*, 22 Mass App 724, 726-728, 497 NE2d 1103, 1104-1106 (1986) (finding no abuse of discretion even

No numerical limits have been imposed on the use of prior convictions for impeachment;[53] but a judge may determine that the admission of additional convictions constitutes "piling on" that would add nothing to the case.[54]

The duty of the judge to exercise discretion regarding impeachment by prior convictions also applies to witnesses other than the defendant.[55] Where a declarant's out-of-court statement is admitted, evidence of his prior convictions may be admitted as if he had testified live.[56]

The defendant may seek an order prohibiting use of his prior convictions by filing a motion in limine,[57] but is not required to make a motion in order to object to the introduction of prior convictions at trial.[58] Because a ruling on a defendant's motion to bar the use of convictions for impeachment may affect counsel's conduct of the entire trial, it is desirable for the trial judge to rule on it at "an early

---

though "[m]ost of the offenses could be viewed as similar in nature to that under consideration to the extent they reveal a propensity for assaultive behavior"; judge could properly consider defense counsel's declared intent to impeach credibility of victim with prior convictions for assault crime).

Compare *Com. v. Sanchez*, 405 Mass 369, 378-379, 540 NE2d 1316, 1322-1323 (1989) (judge properly exercised discretion in rape and sexual assault trial when he "carefully excluded the defendant's prior convictions of crimes involving homosexual rapes of minors and admitted for impeachment purposes the conviction of a crime dissimilar to the ones being tried [arson]"); *Com. v. Guilfoyle*, 396 Mass 1003, 485 NE2d 679 (1985) (reversal required where trial judge stated that he was admitting the prior conviction because of the similarity between it and crime charged).

[53] See *Com. v. White*, 48 Mass App 658, 661, 724 NE2d 726, 729 (2000) (Commonwealth could impeach defendant with 23 prior convictions); *Com. v. Brown*, 451 Mass 200, 202-205, 884 NE2d 488, 491-493 (2008) (permitting use of 14 convictions against defendant where none were substantially similar to the charged offenses).

[54] See *Com. v. Pierce*, 66 Mass App 283, 289-290, 846 NE2d 1189, 1194 (2006).

[55] See *Com. v. Manning*, 47 Mass App 923, 714 NE2d 843 (1999) (& citations) (alibi witness); *Com. v. Robinson*, 78 Mass App 714, 716 n.1, 942 NE2d 980, 984 n.1 (2011) (judge properly prevented defense counsel from impeaching prosecution witness with prior convictions of malicious destruction of property, as there was risk the jury would use them to infer that the witness, rather than the defendant, set the fatal fire charged).

[56] See *Com. v. Moses*, 436 Mass 598, 7602-7603, 766 NE2d 827 (2002) (following Proposed Mass R Evid 806, discussed at § 6.12, supra). For a case discussing (but not permitting) the use of a third-party's conviction to impeach a witness, see *Com. v. Supplee*, 45 Mass App 265, 268, 697 NE2d 547, 549-550 (1998).

[57] See, e.g., *Com. v. Gallagher*, 408 Mass 510, 516, 562 NE2d 80, 84-85 (1990). For discussion of the showing required for such a motion in limine, see *Com. v. Dwyer*, supra, 22 Mass App at 726-728, 497 NE2d at 1104-1106.

[58] See *Com. v. Ruiz*, supra, 400 Mass at 215-216, 508 NE2d at 608.

moment."[59] A judge is not required to exercise discretion to exclude a conviction absent timely objection or motion in limine.[60]

Where defendants have testified in reliance upon representations or pretrial agreements by prosecutors that convictions would not be offered at trial, failure to comply has resulted in reversals on appeal.[61] Unlike federal practice, the Massachusetts courts have not required a defendant to testify in order to preserve for review the claim that a motion to exclude convictions was improperly denied.[62] Under federal practice, a defendant who does testify and preemptively introduces his prior convictions on direct examination may not claim on appeal that such admission was error.[63] Massachusetts does not appear to have ruled on this matter.

The mode of impeachment under GL 233, § 21 is by production of the record of criminal conviction. A witness's conviction can be proven only by the court record or a certified copy of the record; it cannot be shown by cross-examination without production of record.[64] Prior convictions may be elicited during direct examination for tactical

---

[59] *Com. v. Diaz*, supra, 383 Mass at 81, 417 NE2d at 955. But see *Com. v. Pina*, 406 Mass 540, 550, 549 NE2d 106, 112-113 (1990) (advance ruling not required).

[60] See *Com. v. Bly*, 444 Mass 640, 653, 830 NE2d 1048, 1059 (2005).

[61] See, e.g., *Com. v. Felton*, 16 Mass App 63, 448 NE2d 1304 (1983) and *Com. v. Lavin*, 42 Mass App 711, 713-714, 679 NE2d 590, 592 (1997).

[62] See *Com. v. Crouse*, 447 Mass 558, 564, 855 NE2d 391, 397-398 (2006) (declining to adopt *Luce v. United States*, 469 US 38 (1984)); *Com. v. King*, 445 Mass 217, 227 n.9, 834 NE2d 1175, 1186 n.9 (2005); *Com. v. Gonzalez*, 22 Mass App 274, 277-280, 493 NE2d 516, 518-520 (1986) (comparing the federal rule and discussing the record required for review in a case where defendant does not testify). But see *Com. v. Preston*, 27 Mass App 16, 24, 534 NE2d 787, 792 (1989) ("It may not be necessary in our practice for a defendant to testify to preserve for appellate review the correctness of the denial of a [motion in limine to exclude prior convictions]. We think, however, that such an issue is not preserved for appellate review where a defendant neither presses for a ruling on the [motion in limine] nor testifies.").

[63] *Ohler v. United States*, 529 US 753 (2000).

[64] See *Com. v. Walters*, 472 Mass 680, 705, 37 NE3d 980, 1002 (2015); *Com. v. Puleio*, 394 Mass 101, 104, 474 NE2d 1078, 1080-1081 (1985); *Com. v. Atkins*, 386 Mass 593, 600, 436 NE2d 1203, 1207 (1982); *Com. v. Clifford*, 374 Mass 293, 305, 372 NE2d 1267, 1275 (1978) (citing Text). But see *Com. v. Ferguson*, 365 Mass 1, 11 n.8, 309 NE2d 182, 188 n.8 (1974) (no error where prosecutor was permitted to read prior convictions from the original records instead of introducing certified copies); *Com. v. Smith*, 342 Mass 180, 185-186, 172 NE2d 597, 601-602 (1961) (no error where prosecutor was permitted to argue that fact that criminal record was not introduced did not mean that defendant did not have one, where defense counsel had argued that if defendant had a criminal record, prosecution would have introduced it).

Proposed Mass R Evid 609(b) would permit proof by the record of conviction "or in such other manner as the court may approve." Where the prior crime is being admitted for a purpose other than impeachment under the statute, mode of proof is not so limited. See § 4.4.6, supra.

purposes.[65] It is proper to ask, for purposes of identification, whether the witness on the stand is the same person as the one whose name appears on the court record.[66] Indeed it is necessary to establish in this manner or another that the witness is in fact the person referred to in the court record; mere identity of name is not sufficient.[67]

The record of conviction must be properly authenticated to be admissible for impeachment, but this may be accomplished under the provisions of Mass R Civ P 44, Mass R Crim P 39 & 40, and GL 233, § 69. While the trial judge may choose to, he is not obliged to actually admit the records of conviction into evidence. The impeachment is complete upon reading the records and establishing that the witness was the subject of the convictions.[68]

Even where the fact of the defendant's convictions are already established through his testimony, certified copies of the convictions may be admitted into evidence.[69] When admitted, the record of conviction may be taken by the jury into the deliberations.[70] Where certified copies of the prior convictions are admitted, care must be taken to avoid including extraneous material that could cause prejudice.[71] Details of the underlying crimes should not be referred to or inquired into.[72] The better practice is to avoid mention of the crimes for which the defendant was indicted where he was only convicted of lesser offenses.[73]

---

[65] See *Com. v. Bly*, supra, 444 Mass at 655-656, 830 NE2d at 1060; *Com. v. Garcia*, 443 Mass 824, 835, 824 NE2d 864, 872 (2005), *habeas denied, Garcia v. Russo*, 844 F Supp 2d 187 (D Mass 2011). See also § 6.18, infra.

[66] See *Com. v. Millyan*, 399 Mass 171, 184 n.10, 503 NE2d 934, 941 n.10 (1987).

[67] *Com. v. Rondoni*, 333 Mass 384, 386, 131 NE2d 187, 188 (1955); *Com. v. Doe*, 8 Mass App 297, 299, 393 NE2d 426, 429 (1979) ("Slight confirmatory evidence is needed to establish identity of persons where there is identity of names.").

[68] *Com. v. Thomas*, 439 Mass 362, 364, 787 NE2d 1047, 1052 (2003).

[69] See *Com. v. White*, 27 Mass App 789, 795, 543 NE2d 703, 707 (1989).

[70] *Com. v. Rondoni*, supra, 333 Mass at 386, 131 NE2d at 188.

[71] See *Com. v. Ford*, 397 Mass 298, 300-301, 490 NE2d 1166, 1168 (1986) (docket entries showing defaults, warrants, arrests, and violations of probation were erroneously admitted); *Com. v. Kowalski*, 33 Mass App 49, 51, 595 NE2d 798, 800 (1992) (error in admitting unexpurgated records of convictions, including docket entries showing defaults, warrants, and surrender for probation violation); *Com. v. White*, supra, 27 Mass at 795, 543 NE2d at 707 (error to include extraneous material consisting of victims' names, probation surrender and default); *Com. v. Clark*, 23 Mass App 375, 380-383, 502 NE2d 564, 567-569 (1987).

[72] *Com. v. Bly*, supra, 444 Mass at 651-655, 830 NE2d at 1058-1060.

[73] *Com. v. Kowalski*, supra, 33 Mass App at 50, 595 NE2d at 799-800 (but no abuse of discretion where prosecutor was permitted to read to jury charges of armed robbery and robbery when defendant's conviction was for accessory after fact).

The trial judge (unless the defendant moves otherwise) should advise the jury of the nature of the conviction; revealing only the fact that the defendant had a prior conviction increases the risk of prejudice since it allows the jury to speculate as to what the conviction was for.[74]

The length of the sentence imposed for the conviction should not be included, as the "mention of the sentence has the potential to cause unfair prejudice to the witness by inviting the jury to speculate about the details and seriousness of the conviction and consider the conviction for reasons other than credibility."[75] Where, however, the length of the sentence is relevant for a purpose other than impeachment, it need not be excluded.[76]

In sum:

> When a party uses a prior conviction to impeach a witness, that party is limited to establishing the identity of the witness as the person named in the record. If the witness answers in the negative or equivocates on the answer then the questioner can use the facts contained in the record of conviction to establish the identity of the witness as the person named in the record of conviction. Those facts, however, do not include the details of the conviction, e.g., the victim's name or circumstances surrounding the event.[77]
>
> [A]ll that is introduced is the fact of the conviction—neither side may seek to introduce the particulars of how the offense was committed or the circumstances surrounding it. Instead, the evidence of prior convictions is extremely brief and is introduced in almost clinical fashion, usually just a single question asking the witness to acknowledge the date, the court, and the technical term for the offense committed.[78]

Once admitted, the record of conviction is conclusive, and matters of explanation, extenuation, or aggravation are not admissible.[79] If, however, one side is permitted to go into the matter, the other side must

---

[74] See *Com. v. Ioannides*, 41 Mass App 904, 668 NE2d 845 (1996).

[75] *Com. v. Kalhauser*, 52 Mass App 339, 342-343, 754 NE2d 76, 79 (2001) (modifying *Com. v. Ortiz*, 47 Mass App 777, 781, 716 NE2d 659, 664 (1999)); *Com. v. Eugene*, 438 Mass 343, 352-353, 780 NE2d 893, 900-901 (2003) (adopting *Kalhauser* approach to exclude reference to sentence).

[76] See, e.g., *Com. v. Bly*, supra, 444 Mass at 652, 830 NE2d at 1058 (length and consecutive nature of defense witness's sentences were relevant to his motive to lie to take blame off defendant).

[77] *Com. v. Kalhauser*, supra, 52 Mass App at 343-344, 754 NE2d at 80-81.

[78] *Com. v. Harris*, 443 Mass 714, 727 n.12, 825 NE2d 58, 69 n.12 (2005).

[79] See *Com. v. McGeoghean*, 412 Mass 839, 843, 593 NE2d 229, 231-232 (1992); *Com. v. Maguire*, supra, 392 Mass at 471 n.10, 467 NE2d at 155 n.10 ("the proponent of

also be allowed to do so.[80] The witness should be allowed on redirect to explain any inconsistency between his testimony on direct and cross relating to the prior conviction.[81]

Where a prior conviction is admitted for impeachment under the statute, the judge should clearly instruct the jury that it is relevant solely in evaluating the credibility of the witness.[82] It is improper for a prosecutor to attempt to exploit the admission for substantive purposes.[83]

The limitations on the introduction of prior crimes may be lifted if the defendant opens the subject of his prior record.[84] But where defendant discloses prior convictions during direct examination in order

---

the witness may not undertake in rehabilitation of the witness to show the circumstances of the conviction"); *Lamoureux v. New York & N. H. & H. Railroad*, 169 Mass 338, 340, 47 NE 1009, 1010 (1897) (the guilt or innocence of the witness cannot be retried, and "it is impracticable to introduce what may be a long investigation of a wholly collateral matter into a case to which it is foreign"); *Com. v. Velasquez*, 48 Mass App 147, 152-153, 718 NE2d 398, 403 (1999) (there is "good reason, as well, not to permit a prosecutor offering a prior conviction of defendant to delve into the circumstances of the conviction for purposes of luxuriating in the prior bad acts of that defendant").

[80] *Com. v. McGeoghean*, supra, 412 Mass at 842-843, 593 NE2d at 231-232 (where cross-examination goes beyond simply establishing that witness is person named in record of conviction, proponent of witness may, in judge's discretion, inquire about those collateral matters in effort to rehabilitate witness); *Com. v. Callahan*, 358 Mass 808, 265 NE2d 382 (1970).

[81] *Com. v. Donovan*, 17 Mass App 83, 86-88, 455 NE2d 1217, 1219-1221 (1983).

[82] See *Com. v. Gallagher*, supra, 408 Mass at 516, 562 NE2d at 84-85. For an example of a proper instruction, see *Com. v. Rivera*, 425 Mass 633, 647 n.14, 682 NE2d 636, 646 (1997):

> You have heard evidence that [the defendant] was previously convicted of a crime. You may consider that information only for the purpose of helping you decide whether or not to believe his testimony and how much weight, if any, to give it. You may not draw any inference of guilt against [the defendant] because of his prior convictions. The fact that he was once found guilty of another crime does not mean that he is guilty of this charge. And you must not consider that prior conviction to be any indication of his guilt. You may consider his prior convictions solely to help you in deciding and determining whether or not he is a truthful witness.

See also *Com. v. Riccard*, 410 Mass 718, 723-724, 575 NE2d 57, 60-61 (1991) (reversing conviction because judge gave contradictory instructions on jury's use of prior convictions in determining credibility of witnesses); *Com. v. Bassett*, 21 Mass App 713, 490 NE2d 459 (1986) (reversing conviction because judge's instructions allowed jury to use prior convictions to establish propensity of defendant for violence and threats); *Com. v. Felton*, 16 Mass App 63, 448 NE2d 1304 (1983) (reversing conviction because judge failed to give immediate limiting instruction).

[83] See, e.g., *Com. v. Roberts*, 378 Mass 116, 126-127, 389 NE2d 989, 996 (1979) (suggesting defendant's propensity for violence).

[84] See, e.g., *Com. v. Daley*, 439 Mass 558, 564-565, 789 NE2d 1070, 1076 (2003) (defendant opened subject of his drug dealing); *Com. v. Roderick*, 429 Mass 271, 274-275, 707 NE2d 1065, 1068-1069 (1999) (when witness denied ever having carried or used a firearm in the past, he opened the door to the admission of his prior conviction

to preempt the effect of their being brought out on cross, the prosecution should not be permitted to explore the underlying details of the crimes.[85]

GL 233, § 21 applies only where the past crime is being used to impeach the credibility of a witness at trial. Where evidence of a prior conviction is offered for another purpose, neither GL 233, § 21 nor its restrictions—i.e., the time limitations or the requirement that proof be by certified copy of court record—apply.[86] Thus the statute is inapplicable where the prior crime is used circumstantially to motive, intent, plan, etc. (see § 4.4.6, supra); or where the conviction is offered as an element of the crime charged, as in the case of a second offense of operating under the influence;[87] or where the conviction is relevant to parental fitness;[88] or where the conviction specifically rebuts the witness's testimony.[89] In these situations, the conviction may be established without the court record, and the evidence is admissible whether the defendant takes the stand as a witness or not.

The proper route for a defendant seeking to obtain prior convictions of prospective prosecution witnesses for possible use at trial is to request the judge to order the probation department to produce them.[90]

---

for gun possession); *Com. v. Oliveira*, 74 Mass App 49, 52-54, 904 NE2d 442, 446-447 (2009) (when defendant testified that he was a peaceful, nonviolent man who wished to avoid conflict, he opened the door to the Commonwealth offering prior assault convictions to rebut, even though the convictions would otherwise have been excluded because they involved the same victim, his ex-wife); *Com. v. Graham*, 62 Mass App 642, 647-648, 818 NE2d 1069, 1074 (2004) (citing Text) (defendant opened door to cross-examination about prior convictions when he testified on direct examination about the underlying altercation).

The fact that a witness has committed a crime may also be disclosed where it is referred to in a prior inconsistent statement otherwise admissible. *Com. v. West*, 312 Mass 438, 440-441, 45 NE2d 260, 262 (1942). But compare *Gonzalez v. Spates*, 54 Mass App 438, 444-445, 766 NE2d 77, 82-83 (2002) (plaintiff not entitled to introduce defendant driver's 18-year-old drug distribution conviction to show driver had been untruthful in initial response to interrogatory).

[85] See *Com. v. Bly*, supra, 444 Mass at 655-656, 830 NE2d at 1060.

[86] See *Care & Protection of Frank*, 409 Mass 492, 495, 567 NE2d 214, 217 (1991) (& cases cited).

[87] See *Com. v. Fortier*, 258 Mass 98, 155 NE 8 (1927) (prior conviction may be established by cross-examination of defendant without production of the record).

[88] See *Care & Protection of Frank*, supra; *Adoption of Irwin*, 28 Mass App 41, 545 NE2d 1193 (1989).

[89] See *Com. v. Lavoie*, 47 Mass App 1, 4-6, 710 NE2d 1011, 1014-1015 (1999). For other evidentiary uses of a judgment of conviction, see § 8.6.2, infra.

[90] See Mass R Crim P 14(a)(2); *Com. v. Martinez*, 437 Mass 84, 95, 769 NE2d 273, 283 (2002).

A trial judge has discretion, despite the rape-shield statute (GL 233, § 21B), to admit evidence of the rape complainant's prior convictions for prostitution where relevant to the witness's bias or motive to fabricate.[91]

Proposed Mass R Evid 609[92] would modify present practice in several regards.[93] Most notably, the rule imposes a fixed time limit of 15 years from the date of conviction (or five years from the date of expiration of the minimum sentence imposed), after which evidence of the conviction is not admissible.[94] While the discretion accorded the judge under 609(a) to exclude a conviction offered to impeach a criminal defendant is consistent with present practice, 609(a) allows no discretion to exclude a conviction offered against any witness other than the accused, which would change current practice.[95]

Fed R Evid 609 adopts an approach different from both GL 233, § 21, and Proposed Mass R Evid 609. The federal rule limits the crimes that can be used for impeachment to those punishable by death

---

[91] See *Com. v. Harris*, 443 Mass 714, 825 NE2d 58 (2005), discussed at § 4.4.3.b, infra.

[92] Proposed Mass R Evid 609 provides:

Impeachment By Evidence of Conviction of Crime

(a) **General rule**. For the purpose of impeaching the credibility of a witness, evidence that be has been convicted of a crime is admissible. In a criminal case, the court shall have the discretion to exclude evidence of a prior conviction offered to impeach the credibility of the accused if it finds that its probative value is outweighed by the danger of unfair prejudice. There shall be no discretion to exclude a prior conviction offered to impeach the credibility of any other witness. A plea of guilty or a finding or verdict of guilty shall constitute a conviction.

(b) **Type of evidence**. The evidence of conviction shall be by the original or certified copy of the record of conviction, or in such other matter as the court may approve.

(c) **Time limits**. Evidence of a conviction is not admissible under this rule after fifteen years from the date conviction, or five years from the date of expiration of the minimum term of confinement imposed by the court for that conviction, whichever is greater.

(d) **Effect of pardon**. Where a conviction has been followed by a pardon, both the conviction, if otherwise admissible, and the pardon shall be admissible.

(e) **Juvenile adjudications**. Evidence of a juvenile adjudication is not admissible, except by constitutional requirement or as otherwise provided by statute.

(f) **Pendency of appeal**. The pendency of an appeal therefrom does not render evidence of a conviction inadmissible. Evidence of the pendency of an appeal is admissible.

(g) **Sealed records**. Notwithstanding any other provisions of this rule, no evidence of a conviction shall be used or admissible, if the record of such has been sealed under the law of the jurisdiction where it occurred, except by constitutional requirement or as otherwise provided by statute.

[93] See generally *Com. v. Diaz*, 383 Mass 73, 80-82, 417 NE2d 950, 955-956 (1981).

[94] Proposed Mass R Evid 609(c).

[95] See *Com. v. Burnett*, 417 Mass 740, 743 n.1, 632 NE2d 1206 n.1 (1994) and *Com. v. Bucknam*, 20 Mass App 121, 123-124, 478 NE2d 747, 749-750 (1985).

or imprisonment for more than one year and those involving dishonesty or false statement. With regard to the former category (but not the latter), the judge is afforded discretion to exclude the conviction if the probative value is outweighed by the risk of prejudice. This discretion applies to both criminal defendants and other witnesses, although with a more favorable balancing standard employed for the accused. The federal rule establishes a ten-year time limit on the use of a conviction, but permits the judge to admit a conviction over ten years old if the probative value substantially outweighs its prejudicial effect.[96]

The mere fact that a witness has been arrested or indicted is not admissible for impeachment.[97] Such evidence may be admissible if the fact of arrest or indictment shows bias or motive to lie.[98] Special problems arise where mug shots, which reveal prior arrests, are used at trial for identification purposes.[99]

§ 6.16.3 Prior Bad Acts

Massachusetts practice does not permit a witness to be impeached (either on cross-examination or by extrinsic proof) by use of specific acts of misconduct showing the witness to be untruthful (unless the act resulted in a criminal conviction, as discussed in the previous section).[100] The Supreme Judicial Court has recently declined the invitation to abandon this long-standing limitation on the type of

---

[96] For more discussion of the federal approach, see *Walter v. Bonito*, 367 Mass 117, 123 n.2, 324 NE2d 624, 628 n.2 (1975).

[97] *Com. v. Roby*, 462 Mass 398, 412, 969 NE2d 141, 154 (2012) (murder indictment); *Com. v. Baldwin*, 385 Mass 165, 178, 431 NE2d 194, 202-203 (1982); *Com. v. Haywood*, 377 Mass 755, 759-760, 388 NE2d 648, 651-652 (1979). See also § 6.16.3, infra. Special statutory provisions permit the admission of such records in sexually dangerous persons proceedings. See GL 123A, § 14(c) and *Com. v. Mazzarino*, 81 Mass App 358, 368-369, 963 NE2d 112, 120-121 (2012).

[98] See § 6.15, supra. See also *Com. v. Roby*, supra, 462 Mass at 412, 969 NE2d at 154.

[99] See § 4.4.2, supra.

[100] See *Com. v. Avalos*, 454 Mass 1, 10-11, 906 NE2d 987, 994 (2009) (judge properly excluded questions about witness's admission in her diary to prior instances of lying and forgery); *Com. v. Olsen*, 452 Mass 284, 293, 892 NE2d 739, 745 (2008) (specific acts of untruthfulness not admissible); *Com. v. Costa*, 69 Mass App 823, 830, 872 NE2d 750, 756 (2007) (& citations); *Com. v. Buzzell*, 79 Mass App 460, 463, 947 NE2d 75, 78 (2011) (judge acted properly in preventing defendant from cross-examining victims about allegedly providing false information to obtain Social Security numbers); *Com. v. Podkowka*, 445 Mass 692, 696, 840 NE2d 476, 480 (2006) (victim's mother's acts of bad parenting); *Com. v. Dew*, 443 Mass 620, 628-629, 823

admissible evidence of untruthful character.[101] Such matters may be explored where the opposing party opens the subject on direct examination.[102]

"The reasons generally given [for the rule against impeachment by bad acts] are: That proof of separate instances of falsehood may have existed without impairing his general reputation for truthfulness. Or that the impeached witness is not required to be prepared to meet particular acts of which he has had no notice, although he is presumed to be capable of supporting his general reputation. Or that the attention of jurors will be distracted from the real issue to be tried by the introduction of collateral issues, which also would tend to prolong the trial unduly."[103]

Application of the principle that prior bad acts may not be used to impeach a witness's credibility forecloses impeachment by showing that the witness has testified falsely in a collateral proceeding,[104] or has made false accusations in the past.[105] Under a "narrow exception" to the rule, the fact that a rape complainant has made prior false allegations of rape may be admissible to challenge her credibility.[106]

Proposed Mass R Evid 608(b)[107] would bring Massachusetts into line with federal practice by permitting cross-examination (but not extrinsic proof) concerning specific instances of conduct of the witness that are deemed probative of untruthfulness.

NE2d 771, 778-779 (2005) (citing Text) (excluding defendant's evidence that witness had sold him drugs on unrelated occasion); *Com. v. Bregoli*, 431 Mass 265, 275, 727 NE2d 59, 69 (2000) (witness's arrest for assaulting girlfriend); *Com. v. Andrews*, 403 Mass 441, 459, 530 NE2d 1222, 1232 (1988) (witness's receipt of welfare payments while employed); *Com. v. Hightower*, 400 Mass 267, 271, 508 NE2d 850, 853 (1987) (defendant's lying to sister who put up his bail); *Com. v. Johnson*, 41 Mass App 81, 669 NE2d 212 (1996) (defaults not admissible).

[101] *Com. v. Almonte*, 465 Mass 224, 241, 988 NE2d 415, 428 (2013) (refusing to adopt Fed R Evid 608(b)).

[102] See, e.g., *Com. v. Perez*, 390 Mass 308, 316-319, 455 NE2d 632, 637-638 (1983) (defense counsel introduced subject of the defendant's supplying drugs); *Com. v. Key*, 381 Mass 19, 28-29, 407 NE2d 327, 334 (1980); *Com. v. McClendon*, 39 Mass App 122, 128, 653 NE2d 1138, 1141 (1995).

[103] *F. W. Stock & Sons v. Dellapenna*, 217 Mass 503, 506, 105 NE 378, 379 (1914).

[104] See *Com. v. Frey*, 390 Mass 245, 249, 454 NE2d 478, 480 (1983).

[105] *Com. v. Martin*, 467 Mass 291, 310-311, 4 NE3d 1236, 1252-1253 (2014) (citing Text) (evidence of unrelated prior false accusations was properly excluded); *Com. v. Trenholm*, 14 Mass App 1038, 442 NE2d 745 (1982).

[106] See *Com. v. LaVelle*, 414 Mass 146, 151, 605 NE2d 852, 856 (1993) (citing Text) and *Com. v. Bohannon*, 376 Mass 90, 378 NE2d 987 (1978), discussed in § 4.4.3, supra.

[107] Proposed Mass R Evid 608(b) provides:

§ 6.17 Impeachment by Religious Belief/Oaths, and Affirmations

A witness may not be impeached by evidence of his disbelief in God. GL 233, § 19.[1] Proposed Mass R Evid 610, reflecting Massachusetts practice, provides:

> **Religious Beliefs or Opinions**
> Evidence of the beliefs or opinions of a witness on matters of religion is not admissible for the purpose of showing that by reason of their nature his credibility is impaired or enhanced.[2]

Proposed Mass R Evid 603 provides:

> **Oath or Affirmation**
> Before testifying, every witness shall be required to declare that he will testify truthfully, by oath or affirmation administered in a form calculated to awaken his conscience and impress his mind with his duty to do so.

(b) **Specific instances of conduct**. Specific instances of the conduct of a witness, for the purpose of attacking or supporting his credibility, other than conviction of crime as provided in Rule 609, may not be proved by extrinsic evidence. They may, however, in the discretion of the court, if probative of truthfulness or untruthfulness, be inquired into on cross-examination of the witness (1) concerning his character for truthfulness or untruthfulness, or (2) concerning the truthfulness or untruthfulness of another witness as to which character the witness being cross-examined has testified. The giving of testimony, whether by an accused or any other witness, does not operate as a waiver of his privilege against self-incrimination when examined with respect to matters which related only to credibility.

§ 6.17 [1] GL 233, § 19 provides:

> A person believing in any other than the Christian religion may be sworn according to the appropriate ceremonies of his religion. A person not a believer in any religion shall be required to testify under the penalties of perjury, and evidence of his disbelief in the existence of God may not be received to affect his credibility as a witness.

[2] See also *Com. v. Dahl*, 430 Mass 813, 822-824, 724 NE2d 300, 307-308 (2000) (improper to allow witness to testify that she was considering becoming a nun, and to permit her to testify while holding rosary beads); *Com. v. Rodriguez*, 57 Mass App 368, 374-375, 782 NE2d 1129, 1133-1134 (2003) (improper for prosecutor to suggest complainant would not likely make false accusations because she kept Bibles in every window); *Com. v. Murphy*, 48 Mass App 143, 145-146, 718 NE2d 395, 398 (1999) (prosecutor's questioning of child complainant regarding her religious training improperly sought to enhance her credibility). Compare *Com. v. Kartell*, 58 Mass App 428, 436-437, 790 NE2d 739, 746-747 (2003) (evidence of defendant's religious beliefs and practices admissible where not used to impeach credibility but to establish jealousy as motive for shooting); *Com. v. Murphy*, supra, 48 Mass App at 145, 718 NE2d at 398 (the effort to establish a child's competency to testify, and specifically her understanding of the importance of truth-telling, a question concerning her belief in God and whether she recognizes the oath as a promise to God may be appropriate).

As to the method of administering oaths and affirmations, see GL 233, §§ 15-19; Mass R Civ P 43(d). The better practice is for judge to explain fully the witness's option to affirm instead of taking traditional oath.[3]

§ 6.18 Impeachment of One's Own Witness

Massachusetts practice permits impeachment of one's own witness, but in a restricted form. GL 233, § 23, provides:

> The party who produces a witness shall not impeach his credit by evidence of bad character, but may contradict him by other evidence, and may also prove that he has made at other times statements inconsistent with his present testimony; but before proof of such inconsistent statements is given, the circumstances thereof sufficient to designate the particular occasion shall be mentioned to the witness, and he shall be asked if he has made such statements, and, if so, shall be allowed to explain them.[1]

Thus impeachment of one's own witness is limited to direct contradiction (discussed in § 6.13.1, supra) and proof of prior inconsistent statements (discussed in § 6.13.2, supra). The prohibition against impeachment by evidence of bad character excludes use of prior convictions (discussed in § 6.16.2, supra) or reputation for untruthfulness (discussed in § 6.16.1, supra). The latter prohibition applies to any witness who is called by the proponent, even if the witness is the opposing party called under the provisions of GL 233, § 22 (discussed at § 6.7, supra).[2]

Regarding the restrictions of the statute, the Supreme Judicial Court has observed:

> We are aware that there is much sentiment and strong argument for allowing a party to impeach his own witness just as he can attack the opposition's, and particularly does the argument appear cogent when one's witness is the adverse party, for here the fiction that by offering a

---

[3] See *Adoption of Fran*, 54 Mass App 455, 466-467, 766 NE2d 91, 100-101 (2002).

§ 6.18 [1] See also *Com. v. Barbosa*, 463 Mass 116, 132, 972 NE2d 987, 999 (2012) (Commonwealth entitled to question its own witness about prior inconsistent statements).

[2] See *Walter v. Bonito*, 367 Mass 117, 120-123, 324 NE2d 624, 626-628 (1975) (& citations). See also Mass R Civ P 43(b) (forbidding impeachment of an adverse party called by proponent "by evidence of bad character").

> witness one "vouches" for him is most vacuous. But regardless of what the degree of our own enthusiasm might be for such a rule, we do not consider ourselves free to adopt it by decision in defiance of the statute as previously interpreted.[3]

For impeachment by prior inconsistent statements, GL 233, § 23 adds to the usual mode of proof[4] the additional requirement that a foundation be laid by bringing the statement to the attention of the witness with sufficient circumstances to designate the particular occasion on which it was made, asking the witness if he made the statement, and allowing him to explain it.

As is generally the case,[5] the prior inconsistent statement of one's own witness is admitted for the limited purpose of challenging the witness's credibility, and not for its truth.[6] It is generally presumed that the judge's limiting instructions are understood and followed by the jury.[7] GL 233, § 23, does not create a right to call a witness whom the party knows will offer no relevant testimony for the sole purpose of impeaching that witness with a prior inconsistent statement.[8]

Although the witness who claims a lack of memory regarding the subject generally cannot be impeached by prior statements,[9] the prior statements of one's own witness may in appropriate circumstances be used to refresh recollection.[10] And if the witness goes beyond asserting a lack of memory by way of a denial, impeachment may be allowed.[11] Massachusetts practice has not required that the party calling the

---

[3] *Walter v. Bonito*, supra n.1, 367 Mass at 121, 324 NE2d at 627.

[4] See § 6.13.2.f.

[5] See § 6.13.2.g, supra.

[6] *Com. v. Rosa*, 412 Mass 147, 156, 587 NE2d 767, 772-773 (1992); *Com. v. Thompson*, 362 Mass 382, 386, 286 NE2d 333, 335 (1972); *Com. v. Anselmo*, 33 Mass App 602, 609, 603 NE2d 227, 232 (1992).

[7] *Com. v. Rosa*, supra, 412 Mass at 159-160, 587 NE2d at 774-775 (but prosecutor's argument emphasizing the substantive use of the testimony overcomes the presumption).

[8] See *Com. v. McAfee*, 430 Mass 483, 489-491, 722 NE2d 1, 8-9 (1999); *Com. v. Butler*, 62 Mass App 836, 847, 821 NE2d 501, 511 (2005).

[9] See § 6.13.2(b) and *Com. v. Reddick*, 372 Mass 460, 463, 362 NE2d 519, 521 (1977).

[10] See § 6.26, infra. See, e.g., *Com. v. Hartford*, 346 Mass 482, 487, 194 NE2d 401, 404 (1963); *Jensen v. McEldowney*, 341 Mass 485, 487, 170 NE2d 472, 473 (1960).

[11] See, e.g., *Com. v. Cobb*, 379 Mass 456, 463-464, 405 N.E.2d 97, 102 (1980); *Com. v. Reddick*, supra, 372 Mass at 463, 362 NE2d at 521; *Com. v. Greene*, 9 Mass App 688, 692-693, 404 NE2d 110, 113 (1980).

witness be surprised by his testimony before being allowed to impeach him with a prior statement under GL 233, § 23.[12]

The tactical use of prior convictions on direct examination to minimize the impact on the jury is not regarded as impeachment for purposes of the GL 233, § 23 prohibition, and may be permitted within the judge's discretion.[13] It has similarly been held that the prosecutor may bring out on direct examination of its own witness the fact that he is testifying pursuant to an agreement for leniency.[14]

Proposed Mass R Evid 607[15] would bring Massachusetts into line with federal practice by permitting impeachment of a witness by any party without regard to who called him and without further limitations. The reasoning behind lifting the restrictions of GL 233, § 23 is that it is unrealistic to assume that the party calling a witness thereby vouches for his credibility, given the reality that a litigant rarely has a free choice in selecting witnesses.[16]

D. REHABILITATION

§ 6.19 Introduction

A witness who has been impeached may be rehabilitated in a variety of ways:

- Where W1 has been contradicted by the testimony of W2, by impeaching W2.
- Where W1 has been impeached by challenging his character for veracity, by evidence of W1's good character for veracity.
- Where W1 has been impeached on the ground that his testimony is a recent contrivance, by proof of W1's prior consistent statement.

---

[12] See *Com. v. Bray*, 19 Mass App 751, 758, 477 NE2d 596, 601 (1985) (citing *Brooks v. Weeks*, 121 Mass 433 (1877)).

[13] See *Com. v. McTigue*, 384 Mass 814, 429 NE2d 707 (1981); *Com. v. Coviello*, 378 Mass 530, 392 NE2d 1042 (1979); *Com. v. Blodgett*, 377 Mass 494, 502-503, 386 NE2d 1042, 1046 (1979); *Com. v. Bandy*, 38 Mass App 329, 337, 648 NE2d 440, 445 (1995).

[14] *Com. v. Griffith*, 404 Mass 256, 265-266, 534 NE2d 1153, 1158-1159 (1989).

[15] Proposed Mass R Evid 607, which tracks the federal rule, provides:

Who May Impeach
The credibility of a witness may be attacked by any party, including the party calling him.

[16] See Advisory Committee Note to Proposed Mass R Evid 607.

- By evidence denying or explaining the impeaching evidence.
- By proving facts bearing on the merits of the case that tend to make W1's testimony more credible.

For reasons of efficiency and logic, evidence enhancing credibility is generally not admissible to bolster the testimony of a witness who has not been impeached. The attempt at impeachment need not be successful in order to open the door to rehabilitation; where "the opponent has insinuated the lack of truthfulness of the witness through attempted, though unsuccessful, impeachment, the party who put on the witness may adduce evidence to establish his good character and truthfulness."[1]

In two situations discussed below—prior identification and "fresh complaint"—prior consistent statements are admissible even in the absence of any attempt at impeachment. See § 6.25, infra.

§ 6.20 By Impeaching the Impeacher

The same rules apply to impeachment of W2 (who impeached W1) as apply to the impeachment of W1.[1] It should be noted, however, that because impeachment of an impeaching witness is remote from the merits of the controversy, the trial judge may exclude some of this evidence on the ground that it is too collateral.

§ 6.21 By Evidence of W1's Good Character for Veracity

Evidence of W1's good character for veracity is not admissible unless and until his character for veracity has been attacked.[1] Such an attack has occurred when:

---

§ 6.19 [1] *Com. v. Haraldstad*, 16 Mass App 565, 571, 453 NE2d 472, 475 (1983).

§ 6.20 [1] See, e.g., *Com. v. Lawton*, 82 Mass App 528, 536-538, 976 NE2d 160, 168-169 (2012) (once defense counsel put victim's credibility in issue by calling forensic interviewer to introduce victim's prior inconsistent statements, Commonwealth had right to rehabilitate victim's testimony through cross-examination of interviewer).

§ 6.21 [1] *Com. v. Sheline*, 391 Mass 279, 288, 461 NE2d 1197, 1204 (1984); *Com. v. Clark*, 23 Mass App 375, 378-380, 502 NE2d 564, 567-568 (1987).

- Records of W1's conviction for a crime have been introduced.[2]
- Evidence of bad reputation for truthfulness and veracity has been introduced.[3]

Impeachment by contradiction or by prior inconsistent statement does not constitute an attack on W1's character for veracity and thus does not permit rehabilitation by character evidence.[4]

Rehabilitation is limited to evidence of reputation for truthfulness and veracity. W1's testimony may not be bolstered by evidence from W2 in the form of an opinion that W1 is truthful.[5]

Proposed Mass R Evid 608(a)[6] would bring Massachusetts into line with federal practice by expanding the avenues of rehabilitation to include opinion evidence of W1's good character for truthfulness, and 608(b)[7] would permit inquiry on cross-examination of W1 into specific instances of conduct showing him to be truthful. Like its federal counterpart, Proposed Mass R Evid 608(a) does not permit rehabilitation until W1's character for truthfulness has been "attacked by opinion or reputation or otherwise."

Both the case law and the Proposed Rules permit a witness who testifies to W1's good reputation for truthfulness to be cross-examined as to specific acts of untruthfulness committed by W1.[8]

---

[2] See *Gertz v. Fitchburg Railroad Co.*, 137 Mass 77 (1884).

[3] See *Quinsigamond Bank v. Hobbs*, 77 Mass (11 Gray) 250 (1858). Older precedent would permit rehabilitation whenever, in an effort to impeach, W2 is asked to testify as to W1's character for veracity, even where the answer is that W1's character is good. *Com. v. Ingraham*, 73 Mass (7 Gray) 46, 48 (1856) ("in the manner in which the answer is given, though in language apparently favorable to the witness, yet there might be conveyed the impression of doubt and uncertainty as to his reputation").

[4] *Com. v. Sheline*, supra, 391 Mass at 288-289, 461 NE2d at 1204 (& cases cited); *Gertz v. Fitchburg Railroad Co.*, supra; *Com. v. Clark*, supra, 23 Mass App at 380, 502 NE2d at 567-568.

[5] See *Com. v. Montanino*, 409 Mass 500, 502-505, 567 NE2d 1212, 1213-1215 (1991) (police officer improperly permitted to testify to typical manner in which sexual abuse victims report crime because that had same effect as stating opinion that victim testified truthfully).

[6] See § 6.16.1, supra.

[7] See § 6.16.3, supra.

[8] See *Com. v. Brown*, 411 Mass 115, 118, 579 NE2d 153, 155 (1991); Proposed Mass R Evid 405(a) and 608(b).

§ 6.22 By Proof of Prior Consistent Statement

Prior statements of a witness consistent with his testimony at trial are generally not admissible to bolster his testimony.[1] "The reason for the rule is that the testimony of a witness in court should not need—and ought not—to be 'pumped up' by evidence that the witness said the same thing on some prior occasion."[2]

When, however, W1 is impeached on the ground that his testimony is a recent contrivance[3] or was the product of bias or undue influence, or that the facts described in the testimony have been concealed under conditions that warrant the belief that the witness would have disclosed them if true, then prior consistent statements made at a time before the motivation to falsify existed may be introduced to fortify his testimony.[4]

---

§ 6.22 [1] But see § 6.25, infra.

[2] *Com. v. Kindell*, 44 Mass App 200, 202-203, 689 NE2d 845, 847 (1998). See also *Com. v. Gaudette*, 441 Mass 762, 768-770, 808 NE2d 798, 804-805 (2004) (improper for prosecutor to suggest witness's testimony was credible because she had not been impeached with her pretrial statement to police, implying prior consistent statement); *Com. v. Foreman*, 52 Mass App 510, 513-514, 755 NE2d 279, 282 (2001) (complaint for protective order and supporting affidavit were improperly admitted as prior consistent statements).

[3] A claim of recent contrivance of course goes to the credibility of the witness and is not ground for exclusion of the testimony. See *Com. v. Gurney*, 13 Mass App 391, 406, 433 NE2d 471, 480 (1982) (citing Text).

[4] *Com. v. Lessieur*, 472 Mass 317, 323-326, 34 NE3d 321, 327-330 (2015) (three witnesses permitted to testify to prosecution witness's prior consistent statements that defendant killed the victim in response to defense cross-examination suggesting recent fabrication); *Com. v. Barbosa*, 463 Mass 116, 129, 972 NE2d 987, 997 (2012) (but no suggestion here of recent fabrication); *Com. v. Almeida*, 452 Mass 601, 616, 897 NE2d 14, 27 (2008); *Com. v. Novo*, 449 Mass 84, 93-94, 865 NE2d 777, 785 (2007) (prior consistent statement of victim's mother prepared on the advice of her attorney before her arrest); *Com. v. Arriaga*, 438 Mass 556, 579-580, 781 NE2d 1253, 1273-1274 (2003); *Com. v. Dargon*, 74 Mass App 330, 337, 906 NE2d 1002, 1008 (2009) (victim's prior consistent statements alleging sexual assault to rebut claim of recent contrivance, i.e., asserting victim's silence when conversing with neighbors, family members, police officers, and medical providers), *aff'd on other grounds*, 457 Mass 387, 930 NE2d 707 (2010). See also *Com. v. Diaz*, 422 Mass 269, 274-275, 661 NE2d 1326, 1329-1330 (1996) (testimony from witness's lawyer on circumstances under which witness first told prosecutor about murders admissible to rebut implication of recent fabrication); *Com. v. Fryar*, 425 Mass 237, 252, 680 NE2d 901, 912 (1997) (witness properly rehabilitated with consistent testimony from first trial); *Com. v. Sullivan*, 410 Mass 521, 527, 574 NE2d 966, 970 (1991) (prosecution witness's 19-page handwritten statement made ten months before plea agreement admissible to counter allegation that witness's testimony was product of inducement); *Com. v. Kater (Kater III)*, 409 Mass 433, 448, 567 NE2d 885, 894 (1991) (application to post-hypnotic testimony); *Com. v. Mayfield*, 398 Mass 615, 629-630, 500 NE2d 774, 783 (1986) (prior consistent statement of witness admissible where defendant raised inference that his trial testimony resulted

The trial judge has considerable discretion in determining whether a suggestion of recent fabrication has been made.[5] Prior consistent statements have been held admissible even where the assertion of recent contrivance was not explicit.[6] The judge may admit a prior consistent statement on direct examination, prior to any impeachment, when a claim of recent contrivance is inevitable on cross-examination.[7] Only those portions of the prior statement that are consistent with the witness's trial testimony should be admitted.[8]

In order to be admitted, it must be demonstrated that the statement was made *prior* to the intervention of the pernicious impulses or the motivation to contrive; otherwise the statement is not probative in

---

from coercion by investigating officers); *Com. v. Worcester*, 44 Mass App 258, 260-262, 690 NE2d 451, 453-454 (1998) (detective properly permitted to testify to witness's interview statement where defense counsel had raised on cross-examination inference that she received inducements from Commonwealth); *Com. v. Graves*, 35 Mass App 76, 87-88, 616 NE2d 817, 824 (1993) (rape victim properly allowed on redirect to read from her handwritten statement given to police shortly after incident where defense counsel had suggested on cross that her testimony about defendant's use of a knife was recent contrivance). Compare *Com. v. Henry*, 37 Mass App 429, 433, 640 NE2d 503, 507 (1994) (defendant's out-of-court statement denying guilt not admissible where no suggestion in prosecutor's cross of recent contrivance); *Com. v. Avila*, 454 Mass 744, 757, 912 NE2d 1014, 1025-1026 (2009) (improper to admit witness's oral and written statements to police, as there was risk jury would treat them as a form of credibility-enhancing prior consistent statement). Cf. *Com. v. Parreira*, 72 Mass App 308, 317-318, 891 NE2d 257, 265 (2008) (defendant's cross-examination of rape victim about whether she told her boyfriend about it opened the door to the prosecution inquiring on redirect concerning the conversation).

[5] See, e.g, *Com. v. Andrews*, 403 Mass 441, 455, 530 NE2d 1222, 1230 (1988 (implication of fabrication); *Com. v. Diemer*, 57 Mass App 677, 687-688, 785 NE2d 1237, 1246 (2003) (where witness was subjected to forceful cross-examination focusing on discrepancies in witness's versions of events, insinuating fabrication, prior consistent statement was properly admitted).

[6] See, e.g., *Com. v. Brookins*, 416 Mass 97, 617 NE2d 621 (1993) (judge erred in excluding defendant's prior consistent statement where, although prosecutor did not explicitly argue defendant's testimony was contrived, cross-examination focused on defendant's exposure to materials that informed him of Commonwealth's probable evidence and strongly implied he tailored his testimony to the evidence); *Com. v. Pickles*, 364 Mass 395, 400-401, 305 NE2d 107, 110-111 (1973) (jury might have "inferred" that witness's testimony was recent fabrication from cross-examination concerning her deal with prosecutor).

[7] See *Com. v. Barbosa*, 457 Mass 773, 797-798, 933 NE2d 93, 114-115n (2010) (defense counsel made plain in opening statement that he would attack credibility of witness by suggesting recent contrivance); *Com. v. Knight*, 437 Mass 487, 496-498, 773 NE2d 390, 399-400 (2002) (judge knew it was inevitable and necessary for defense to impeach witness with claim of recent contrivance based on plea agreement); *Com. v. Rivera*, 430 Mass 91, 100, 712 NE2d 1127, 1134 (1999); *Com. v. Martinez*, 425 Mass 382, 397, 681 NE2d 818, 828-829 (1997).

[8] *Com. v. Jiles*, 428 Mass 66, 73-74, 698 NE2d 10, 14-15 (1998).

dispelling these suggestions.[9] This "limitation serves to exclude, as inherently untrustworthy, self-serving statements made by a witness after the witness has a reason to build up his position, knowing that repetitions of his claims may be helpful later to blunt the force of an accusation that he is fabricating his testimony or is expressing a bias."[10]

The ultimate "test [of admissibility] should remain one of probative value—whether the prior consistent statement has a logical tendency to meet and counter the suggestion that the witness has recently contrived his testimony for purposes of trial."[11] While as a matter of practice the theory advanced by the party opposing introduction of the prior statement is generally used as the basis for deciding when the motive to fabricate arose, the trial judge need not accept that theory.[12]

When admitted, the prior consistent statement is admissible only to show that the witness's testimony is not the product of the asserted

---

[9] *Tome v. United States*, 513 US 150, 156 (1995) (reading the "prevailing common-law" temporal requirement into Fed R Evid 801(d)(1)(B)). See *Com. v. Tennison*, 440 Mass 553, 563, 800 NE2d 285, 295 (2003); *Com. v. DiLego*, 387 Mass 394, 399, 439 NE2d 807, 810 (1982); *Com. v. Zukoski*, 370 Mass 23, 27, 345 NE2d 690, 693 (1976). Compare *Com. v. Maioli*, 11 Mass App 179, 181-183, 414 NE2d 1017, 1019 (1981) (transcript of prosecution witness's grand jury testimony properly admitted to rebut inference that witness had falsified testimony to obtain favorable disposition of criminal charge brought against him shortly before trial, where it appeared that the witness was unaware of a default warrant on the charge outstanding against him at time he testified before grand jury) with *Com. v. McLaughlin*, 433 Mass 558, 567, 744 NE2d 47, 54 (2001) (defendant's statement properly excluded because made at time he had interest in exonerating himself); *Com. v. Gaudette*, 56 Mass App 494, 500, 778 NE2d 988, 993 (2002) (defense failed to show statements were made before witness had motive to fabricate); *Com. v. Foreman*, 52 Mass App 510, 513-514, 755 NE2d 279, 282 (2001) (complaint for protective order and supporting affidavit improperly admitted as prior consistent statements, because witness had motive to fabricate at time she made statements).

[10] *Com. v. Healey*, 27 Mass App 30, 35 n.5, 534 NE2d 301, 304 n.5 (1989) (letter written by child abuse victim to defendant referring to abuse was admissible where defendant had tried to show on cross-examination that victim had earlier denied abuse and changed her story under pressure from social worker).

For discussion of the difficulty in some contexts of fixing a particular moment in time that a motive to fabricate may have emerged, see *Com. v. Healey*, supra, 27 Mass App at 37, 534 NE2d at 305-306 (& cases cited); *Com. v. Bougas*, 59 Mass App 368, 374-375, 795 NE2d 1230, 1235-1236 (2003) (judge has broad discretion to identify point in time).

[11] *Com. v. Darden*, 5 Mass App 522, 530, 364 NE2d 1092, 1096 (1977). See also *Com. v. Kindell*, supra, 44 Mass App at 202-205, 689 NE2d at 848-849 (judge acted within discretion in admitting prior statements of witness that completed what he said to authorities, even though statements were made after motive to fabricate arose); *Com. v. Williams*, 56 Mass App 337, 344, 777 NE2d 821, 827 (2002) (statement relevant to show victim had not puffed up claims on eve of trial even if made after motive to fabricate).

[12] *Com. v. Williams*, supra, 56 Mass App at 344 n.8, 777 NE2d 821, 827 n.8.

bias or is not recently contrived; it is not admissible substantively to prove the truth of the facts asserted.[13] Both Proposed Mass R Evid 801(d)(1)(B)[14] and its federal counterpart[15] remove this limitation and give full substantive effect to a prior consistent statement offered to rebut the charge of recent fabrication as long as the declarant is testifying at trial and subject to cross-examination concerning the statement. The Massachusetts courts have not adopted this expanded admissibility.[16]

Nonetheless, it has been recognized that prior consistent statements are likely to significantly influence the jury as substantive evidence, despite limiting instructions, and thus trial judges are advised that such statements "should be allowed only with caution, and where the probative value for the proper purpose is clear."[17] Courts should "scrupulously avoid improper [cumulative] bolstering."[18]

Prior consistent statements are *not* admissible where W1 has been impeached only in the following manner:

- Testimony of W2 contradicting W1's testimony.[19]
- Prior statements of W1 inconsistent with his trial testimony.[20]

---

[13] *Com. v. Diaz*, 422 Mass 269, 275, 661 NE2d 1326, 1330 (1996); *Com. v. Zukoski*, supra, 370 Mass at 27, 345 NE2d at 693; *Com. v. Cruz*, 53 Mass App 393, 401, 759 NE2d 723, 731 (2001).

[14] Proposed Mass R Evid 801(d)(1) provides:

> **A statement is not hearsay if**—The declarant testifies at the trial or hearing and is subject to cross-examination concerning the statement, and the statement is . . . (B) consistent with his testimony and is offered to rebut an express or implied charge against him of recent fabrication or improper influence or motive. . . ."

[15] Fed R Evid 801(d)(1)(B).

[16] See *Com. v. Cruz*, supra, 53 Mass App at 401 n.10, 759 NE2d at 732 n.10.

[17] *Com. v. Cruz*, supra, 53 Mass App at 400, 759 NE2d at 731 (statements made by victim's mother to police, alleging defendant's physical abuse of victim, could not be admitted as prior consistent statement).

[18] *Com. v. Lessieur*, 472 Mass 317, 325, 34 NE3d 321, 329 (2015).

[19] See *Com. v. Reid*, 384 Mass 247, 259-260, 424 NE2d 495, 502-503 (1981).

[20] See *Com. v. Hatzigiannis*, 88 Mass App 395, 400, 37 NE3d 1108, 1113 (2015); *Com. v. McBrown*, 72 Mass App 60, 64, 888 NE2d 976, 980 (2008) (citing Text); *Com. v. Bruce*, 61 Mass App 474, 481-482, 811 NE2d 1003, 1008-1009 (2004) (impeachment of witness by prior inconsistent statement or omission, standing alone, does not entitle adverse party to introduce prior consistent statements). But see *Com. v. Seng*, 456 Mass 490, 496-499, 924 NE2d 285, 292-294 (2010) (while generally impeachment by prior inconsistent statements does not entitle the adverse party to introduce prior consistent statements of the witness, the proponent may rehabilitate the witness with questions designed to explain the inconsistency, even though prior consistent statements are implicated) (citing Text); *Com. v. Walker*, 370 Mass 548, 570-571, 350 NE2d 678, 694 (1976) (Commonwealth properly permitted to read into record portion of

- Evidence of W1's bad reputation for veracity.

Since a witness's prior consistent statements are relevant only to credibility and admissible only to show that the witness's in-court testimony is not recently contrived, such statements may not be admitted unless the declarant actually testifies.[21] For the admissibility of prior consistent identifications, see § 6.25.1, infra. For the overlap between this doctrine and the rule of verbal completeness, see § 1.7, supra.[22]

§ 6.23 By Evidence Denying or Explaining the Impeaching Evidence

When W1 has been impeached, the party who called W1 may introduce evidence that explains or contradicts the impeachment evidence. Thus where W1 has been impeached with a self-contradictory statement or silence in circumstances calling for disclosure, his proponent may elicit from him an explanation of the contradiction or silence.[1]

---

witness's prior testimony consistent with her trial testimony to put in context portions read by defendant that appeared to be inconsistent); *Com. v. Manrique*, 31 Mass App 597, 599-602, 581 NE2d 1036, 1038-1039 (1992) (prosecutor properly permitted to elicit statement in trooper's police report where defense had shown trooper's grand jury testimony inconsistent with trial testimony); *Com. v. Horne*, 26 Mass App 996, 998, 530 NE2d 353, 356 (1988) ("If it can be made to appear that the inconsistent statement was the product of a peculiar and transient bias or pressure of some kind, the prior consistent statement may be admitted to shore up the consistent in-court statement.").

Fed R Evid 801(d)(1)(B) was amended in 2014 to expand the substantive use of prior consistent statements to rehabilitate a witness "when attacked on another ground" in addition to recent fabrication, including inconsistency. See 5 Weinstein's Federal Evidence § 801.22[1][bb].

[21] *Com. v. Delaney*, 34 Mass App 732, 740, 616 NE2d 111, 117 (1993).

[22] See also *Com. v. Aviles*, 461 Mass 60, 75-76, 958 NE2d 37, 51 (2011).

§ 6.23 [1] See *Com. v. Seng*, 456 Mass 490, 496-499, 924 NE2d 285, 292-294 (2010) (proponent may rehabilitate the witness with questions designed to explain the inconsistency, even though prior consistent statements are implicated); *Com. v. Rodriquez*, 454 Mass 215, 221-222, 908 NE2d 734, 739 (2009) (citing Text); *Com. v. Cintron*, 435 Mass 509, 521, 759 NE2d 700, 711 (2001) (Commonwealth entitled to inquire about reasons motivating witness's inconsistent statements); *Com. v. Errington*, 390 Mass 875, 880, 460 NE2d 598, 602 (1984); *Com. v. Watkins*, 377 Mass 385, 391 n.11, 385 NE2d 1387, 1391 n.11 (1979) (prosecution witness permitted to explain why she had made contradictory statement to police); *Com. v. Young*, 73 Mass App 479, 484-485, 899 NE2d 838, 843-844 (2009), *habeas denied*, 2012 WL 3638824 (D. Mass 2012) (impeached witness properly allowed to explain why he had recanted his earlier identification of defendant); *Com. v. Charles*, 47 Mass App 191, 712 NE2d 613 (1999) (reversible error to prevent defendant from testifying, by way of rehabilitation, as to

Similarly a witness may explain, modify, or correct damaging testimony that was elicited on cross-examination,[2] such as why she waited seven years before reporting the rape.[3] Where the rehabilitation relates to an issue collateral to the merits of the lawsuit, the judge may impose reasonable limits on redirect examination.[4]

§ 6.24 By Proof of Facts Tending to Make Witness's Testimony Credible

A witness's testimony may be corroborated by other admissible evidence of the material facts.[1] Ordinarily, however, a witness may not be accredited before his credibility has been impeached. Thus, evidence whose purpose is not to prove material facts but merely to bolster credibility generally may not be admitted unless and until there has been an attack on credibility.[2]

It has been held, nonetheless, that corroborating evidence (other than the witness's own prior consistent statements, see § 6.22, supra)

---

what police detective told her before taking taped statement, after defendant conceded on cross that statement omitted several facts testified to at trial).

Such testimony may not be admissible if it reveals the defendant's bad acts. See *Com. v. Hynes*, 40 Mass App 927, 928, 664 NE2d 864, 866 (1996) (& citations). But compare *Com. v. Mitchell*, 38 Mass App 184, 195-196, 646 NE2d 1073, 1079 (1995) (witness could explain that he had lied to police out of fear of the defendant who had stabbed him just a few months earlier).

[2] Com. v. Mandeville, 386 Mass 393, 399-400, 436 NE2d 912, 917 (1982). See, e.g., *Com. v. Jackson*, 384 Mass 572, 584-585, 428 NE2d 289, 296-297 (1981) (prosecutor permitted to elicit facts underlying grants of immunity to witness "to correct any mistaken conclusions the jury may have drawn from defendant's questions as well as to rehabilitate the witness"); *Com. v. Mendes*, 441 Mass 459, 469-470, 806 NE2d 393, 404 (2004), *habeas denied, Mendes v. Brady*, 656 F3d 126 (1st Cir 2011) (redirect to counter suggestion of bias); *Com. v. Emence*, 47 Mass App 299, 713 NE2d 374 (1999) (error to refuse to permit witness, whom prosecutor on cross suggested was fabricating his testimony, to explain why he would have particularly recalled complainant being with him at time of alleged attack).

[3] *Com. v. Hall*, 66 Mass App 390, 394-395, 848 NE2d 781, 785-786 (2006).

[4] See *Footit v. Monsees*, 26 Mass App 173, 182, 525 NE2d 423, 429 (1988) (& cases cited).

§ 6.24 [1] See *Com. v. Grammo*, 8 Mass App 447, 455, 395 NE2d 476, 482-483 (1979) (& citation).

[2] See *Krupp v. Craig*, 247 Mass 273, 142 NE 69 (1924) (error to admit insurance policy to corroborate witness's testimony concerning address at particular point in time); *Com. v. Haraldstad*, 16 Mass App 565, 571, 453 NE2d 472, 475 (1983).

may be admitted as a matter of discretion.[3] Where the "whiff of [the witness's] bias was inherent in his position as an alleged participant in the crime," rehabilitative evidence may be introduced even though no attack on credibility has occurred.[4]

§ 6.25 Prior Identification and Fresh Complaint

The general rule that prior consistent statements of a witness are not admissible to bolster his credibility unless he is impeached has two important exceptions:

§ 6.25.1 Prior Identification

Where a witness identifies the defendant in a criminal case during his direct testimony, he or others may also testify to his prior consistent identification to corroborate the courtroom identification. See § 11.1, infra.[1]

---

[3] See, e.g., *Com. v. DeBrosky*, 363 Mass 718, 725, 297 NE2d 496, 501 (1973) (hotel registration records admissible to corroborate testimony that defendants were at hotels on particular days); *Com. v. Galvin*, 310 Mass 733, 747, 39 NE2d 656, 663-664 (1942) (witness permitted to testify he had bankbook with him to corroborate testimony that he had consulted it to refresh his recollection as to date he made a particular payment to defendant). But compare *Com. v. Rego*, 360 Mass 385, 391, 274 NE2d 795, 799 (1971) (exclusion of check to corroborate testimony of alibi witness as to presence of defendant at her home).

[4] See *Com. v. Haraldstad*, supra, 16 Mass App at 571-572, 453 NE2d at 476. "If a witness in one case will be a defendant in another case based on the same facts, the presumption that the witness testifies truthfully falls away, and evidence enhancing credibility, if otherwise competent, may be admitted." 16 Mass App at 571, 453 NE2d at 475.

§ 6.25 [1] See also *Com. v. Barbosa*, 463 Mass 116, 130-132, 972 NE2d 987, 998-1000 (2012) (citing Proposed Mass R Evid 801(d)(1)(C), creating hearsay exception for prior statements of identification, based on rationale that the prior identification occurred under nonsuggestive circumstances and closer in time to the event); *Com. v. Adams*, 458 Mass 766, 770-774, 941 NE2d 1127, 1130-1133 (2011); *Com. v. McCoy*, 456 Mass 838, 850, 926 NE2d 1143, 1158 (2010) (victim's statements to SANE nurse were admissible regarding defendant's identification).

§ 6.25.2 *Fresh Complaint/First Complaint*

Where the defendant is charged with a sexual assault, evidence of a "fresh complaint" by the complaining witness had long been admissible as part of the Commonwealth's case in chief to corroborate her testimony (but with a limiting instruction that it could not be used to establish the truth of the complaint). There was no requirement that the complaining witness already have been impeached, or that the complaint be a spontaneous utterance.[2] The fresh complaint doctrine was justified on the ground that a victim's failure to make a prompt complaint might be viewed by the jury as inconsistent with the charge of sexual assault, and that in the absence of evidence of complaint the jury might assume that none was made.[3]

Recognizing that Massachusetts was one of only two states that admitted such evidence even absent an attack on the complainant's credibility, the Supreme Judicial Court began an extended reconsideration of the doctrine in *Com. v. Licata*[4] and *Com. v. Montanez*[5] that culminated in a reformulation of the doctrine in *Com. v. King*[6].

> Under the new ["first complaint"] doctrine, to be applied only in sexual assault cases tried after the issuance of the rescript in this opinion, the recipient of a complainant's first complaint of an alleged sexual assault may testify about the fact of the first complaint and the circumstances surrounding the making of that first complaint. The witness may also testify about the details of the complaint. The complainant may likewise testify to the details of the first complaint (i.e., what she told the first complaint witness), as well as why the complaint was made at that particular time. Testimony from additional complaint witnesses is not admissible.
>
> First complaint testimony may be admitted for a limited purpose only, to assist the jury in determining whether to credit the complainant's testimony about the alleged sexual assault. The testimony may not

---

[2] See § 8.7, infra.

[3] For discussion of the history and rationale of the fresh complaint doctrine, see *Com. v. King*, 445 Mass 217, 228-231, 834 NE2d 1175, 1187-1190 (2005); *Com. v. Quincy Q.*, 434 Mass 859, 867-868, 753 NE2d 781, 791 (2001); *Com. v. Sherry*, 386 Mass 682, 691 n.5, 437 NE2d 224, 229 n.5 (1982); *Com. v. Bailey*, 370 Mass 388, 391-397, 348 NE2d 746, 748-752 (1976).

[4] 412 Mass 654, 591 NE2d 672 (1992).

[5] 439 Mass 441, 445 n.5, 788 NE2d 954, 959 n.5 (2003).

[6] 445 Mass 217, 834 NE2d 1175 (2005). See also *Com. v. McCoy*, 456 Mass 838, 844-845, 926 NE2d 1143, 1153 (2010) (summarizing changes in fresh complaint doctrine brought by *Com. v. King*).

> be used to prove the truth of the allegations. The jury must be so instructed. The timing by the complainant in making a complaint will not disqualify the evidence, but is a factor the jury may consider in deciding whether the first complaint testimony supports the complainant's credibility or reliability. First complaint testimony is not relevant and therefore not admissible under the doctrine where neither the fact of the sexual assault nor the complainant's consent is at issue, as in cases where the identity of the assailant is the only contested issue.[7]

Such evidence remains necessary in sexual assault cases, the Court ruled, "to counterbalance or address inaccurate assumptions regarding stereotypes about delayed reporting of a sexual assault or about sexual assault victims in general,"[8] and does not violate the defendants's right of confrontation where the declarant victim testifies at trial and is subject to cross-examination.[9]

Com. v. King changed prior doctrine in several significant ways:

- The previous requirement for "promptness" or "freshness" as a condition of admissibility[10] is replaced by a rule admitting the "first complaint." The timing of the complaint and its ostensible delay are a matter for the jury to weigh in assessing the complainant's credibility.[11]

---

[7] 445 Mass at 218-219, 834 NE2d at 1181. Regarding the last sentence above, compare *Com. v. Letkowski*, 83 Mass App 847, 857-858, 991 NE2d 1106, 1114-1115 (2013) (first complaint testimony was admissible even though main issue at trial was defendant's criminal responsibility, because defendant had not stipulated to the rape).

The decision applies prospectively only. *Com. v. King* 445 Mass at 248, 834 NE2d at 1201.

[8] 445 Mass at 240, 834 NE2d at 1196.

[9] 445 Mass at 236, 834 NE2d at 1193.

[10] Under prior practice the preliminary question of whether a complaint was sufficiently "fresh" or "prompt" was for the trial judge. *Com. v. Montanino*, 409 Mass 500, 508, 567 NE2d 1212, 1216 (1991). If admitted, the jury was instructed that they may disregard the evidence if they find the complaint was not made "reasonably promptly." *Com. v. Sherry*, supra, 386 Mass at 691, 437 NE2d at 229. There was no absolute rule as to the time within which a sexual assault victim must make a complaint for that complaint to be a seasonable fresh complaint. *Com. v. Amirault*, supra, 404 Mass at 228, 535 NE2d at 198 (complaint made by child victim 18 months after alleged assault properly admitted as reasonably prompt in exceptional circumstances of case).

[11] 445 Mass at 241-242, 834 NE2d at 1196-1197.

- The evidence is limited to one witness—the first person told of the assault. Multiple witnesses are no longer permitted.[12]
- The "first complaint" witness may testify to the details of the alleged victim's first complaint of sexual assault[13] and the circumstances surrounding that complaint as part of the

---

[12] 445 Mass at 242-243, 834 NE2d at 1197; *Com. v. Roby*, 462 Mass 398, 408-409, 969 NE2d 142, 151-152 (2012) (trial court erred in allowing cumulative first complaint testimony of child victims after allowing their mother to testify as substituted first complaint witness); *Com. v. Hoyt*, 461 Mass 143, 156-158, 958 NE2d 834, 846-848 (2011).

Even where the multiple witnesses merely testify to a conversation with the victim, without reporting the details, the first complaint rule is violated. See *Com. v. McCoy*, 456 Mass 838, 846-847, 926 NE2d 1143, 1154-1155 (2010) (the fact of the conversation itself is the equivalent of saying the victim repeated her account, allowing fresh complaint testimony through the back door); *Com. v. Monteiro*, 75 Mass App 489, 914 NE2d 981 (2009) (same). It may be necessary to conduct a *voir dire* to designate the first complaint witness. *Com. v. Stuckich*, 450 Mass 449, 454-456, 879 NE2d 105, 111-112 (2008) (conflicting evidence as to who received first complaint).

The Commonwealth is also limited to just *the first complaint* received by the witness. *Com. v. Stuckich*, supra, 450 Mass at 454-456, 879 NE2d at 111-112 (multiple items of letter, conversation, and journal entry could not be admitted); *Com. v. Arana*, 453 Mass 214, 901 NE2d 99 (2009) (convictions reversed because of erroneous admission of victims' repeated complaints of sexual abuse); *Com. v. Lyons*, 71 Mass App 671, 885 NE2d 848 (2008) (trial court erred in allowing officer who responded to complainant's emergency call to testify to her report after a tape recording of her call had already been admitted). Compare *Com. v. Morris*, 82 Mass App 427, 439, 974 NE2d 1152, 1163 (2012) (defendant himself elicited multiple complaints on cross-examination of victim); *Com. v. Grant*, 78 Mass App 450, 463, 940 NE2d 448, 458-459 (2010) (even if victim should not have been permitted on direct examination to testify she told several people other than her first complaint witness about the rape, defendant's strategy was to discredit her with prior inconsistent statements, thus no substantial risk of miscarriage of justice); *Com. v. Revells*, 78 Mass App 492, 495-496, 940 NE2d 481, 484-485 (2010) (no violation of multiple witness rule where child victim's mother testified to simultaneous written and oral statements by victim). For a case involving an assertion that the nonverbal conduct of witnesses after they spoke to the victim amounted to impermissible multiple complaint testimony, see *Com. v. Niels N.*, 73 Mass App 689, 699-701, 901 NE2d 166, 175-177 (2009).

Testimony from two first complaint witnesses was allowed where each testified to disclosures made years apart, concerning different periods of time and escalating levels of abuse, see *Com. v. Kebreau*, 454 Mass 287, 292-296, 909 NE2d 1146, 1152-1155 (2009); and where evidence of multiple reports of a victim's allegations was presented as a fair response to the defendant's cross-examination, and necessary to present an accurate picture of the Commonwealth's case. See *Com. v. Saunders*, 75 Mass App 505, 509-510, 915 NE2d 229, 232-233 (2010). Under prior practice there was no *per se* rule as to how many fresh complaint witnesses could testify, and often several did. See, e.g., *Com. v. Davis*, 54 Mass App 756, 764-765, 767 NE2d 1110, 1117-1118 (2002) (numerous excited utterances and fresh complaints).

[13] The courts have read "first complaint" to refer to the first complaint of *sexual assault*, thus permitting such testimony after a prior complaint of non-sexual physical abuse. See *Com. v. Rivera*, 83 Mass App 581, 584-585, 987 NE2d 597, 600-601 (2013).

prosecution's case-in-chief. Law enforcement officials as well as investigatory, medical, or social work professionals may testify to the complaint only where they are in fact the first to have heard of the assault (and not where they have been told of the alleged crime after previous complaints or an official report).[14]

- The "first complaint" witness may also testify to the circumstances surrounding the complaint, including observations of the complainant during the complaint, the events or conversations that culminated in the complaint, the timing of the complaint, and other relevant conditions that might help a jury assess the veracity of the complainant's allegations or assess the specific defense theories as to why the complainant is making a false allegation.[15]
- The complainant may also testify to the details of the complaint and why the complaint was made at that particular time,[16] but only if the complaint witness is produced at trial and testifies concerning the complaint.[17]
- In limited circumstances a judge may permit the testimony of a complaint witness other than the very "first," as where the first person told of the alleged assault is unavailable, incompetent, or too young to testify meaningfully.[18]

---

[14] 445 Mass at 243, 834 NE2d at 1198. A witness may not testify that police told her the victim had been raped. *Com. v. McCoy,* 456 Mass 838, 844-845, 926 NE2d 1143, 1154 (2010).

[15] 445 Mass at 246, 834 NE2d at 1199-1200. A "complaint" may consist of a report that merely hints at inappropriate sexual conduct. See *Com. v. Wallace,* 76 Mass App 411, 414-415, 922 NE2d 834, 837-838 (2010).

[16] Prior practice precluded such testimony from the complainant. See *Com. v. Peters,* 429 Mass 22, 30, 705 NE2d 1118, 1123 (1999).

[17] 445 Mass at 245 n.24, 834 NE2d at 1199 n.24. See also *Com. v. Haggett,* 79 Mass App 167, 171, 944 NE2d 601, 605-606 (2011) (victim's testimony regarding her reporting assault to teacher and guidance counselor was inadmissible, where Commonwealth chose not to produce the first complaint witness). The complainant cannot testify that she told others in addition to the first complaint witness about the alleged assault, as such testimony is essentially the same as permitting those other witnesses to testify, allowing fresh complaint testimony "through the back door." *Com. v. Stuckich,* 450 Mass 449, 456-457, 879 NE2d 105, 112-113 (2008); *Com. v. Hanino,* 82 Mass App 489, 495-496, 975 NE2d 876, 882 (2012).

[18] 445 Mass at 243-244, 834 NE2d at 1198. Such substitution requires justification from the prosecutor in a motion in limine. See, e.g., *Com. v. Murungu,* 450 Mass 441, 879 NE2d 99 (2008) (allowing victim's mother to testify to victim's description of assault in lieu of first complaint witness because the latter was defendant's sister, who displayed a bias in his favor, and victim's report to her did not constitute a complaint but an expression of concern); *Com. v. Thibeault,* 77 Mass App 419, 421-423, 931 NE2d

The Court retained that aspect of prior doctrine that permits the first complaint witness to testify to the details of the complaint, thus continuing to depart from practice elsewhere which limits testimony to the fact of the complaint only.[19] "[I]t is beneficial to provide jurors with more, not less, information concerning the initial complaint," and defendant is free to cross examine both the complaint witness and the complainant about any discrepancies.[20]

The *Com. v. King* Court modified the instructions to be given to the jury to conform to the reformulated doctrine:

> In sexual assault cases we allow testimony by one person the complainant told of the alleged assault. We call this "first complaint" evidence. The complainant may have reported the alleged sexual assault to more than one person. However, our rules normally permit testimony only as to the complainant's first report. The next witness will testify about the complainant's "first complaint." You may consider this evidence only for specific limited purposes: to establish the circumstances in which the complainant first reported the alleged offense, and then to determine whether that first complaint either supports or fails to support the complainant's own testimony about the crime. You may not consider this testimony as evidence that the assault in fact occurred.[21]

1008, 1011-1012 (2010) (trial court properly substituted victim's mother as first complaint witness, where father was unavailable for trial). These exceptions do not amount to a relaxation of the first complaint rule "so that the Commonwealth may pick and choose among various complaint witnesses to locate the one with the most complete memory, the one to whom the complainant related the most details, or the one who is likely to be the most effective witness." *Com. v. Murungu*, 450 Mass at 446, 879 NE2d at 104. See also *Com. v. McGee*, 75 Mass App 499, 915 NE2d 235 (2009) (Commonwealth could not substitute police officer who interviewed rape victim for neighbor to whom victim made first report).

[19] 445 Mass at 244, 834 NE2d at 1198. See *Com. v. Licata*, 412 Mass 654, 657-659, 591 NE2d 672, 673-675 (1992) ("When a witness is limited to testifying only that the victim made a complaint, the jury must rely on that witness's interpretation of the victim's statements. In our view, the better approach remains one which allows a jury to make their own interpretation based on the details of the statements.").

[20] *Com. v. King*, supra, 445 Mass at 247, 834 NE2d at 1200-1201.

[21] The courts have long recognized the considerable risk that the jury will use the evidence for substantive purposes. See *Com. v. Trowbridge*, 419 Mass 750, 761, 647 NE2d 413, 421 (1995); *Com. v. Lavalley*, 410 Mass 641, 646, 574 NE2d 1000, 1003-1004 (1991); *Com. v. Swain*, 36 Mass App 433, 442, 632 NE2d 848, 854 (1994). See also *Com. v. Edward*, 75 Mass App 162, 166-167, 912 NE2d 515, 519-520 (2009) (instruction regarding limited use was adequate); *Com. v. Haggett*, 79 Mass App 167, 172-173, 944 NE2d 601, 606 (2011) (instructions were necessary even though Commonwealth called no first complaint witness, because alleged victim gave testimony regarding reports to teacher and guidance counselor).

> The purpose of this "first complaint" evidence is to assist you in your assessment of the credibility and reliability of the complainant's testimony here in court. In assessing whether this "first complaint" evidence supports or detracts from the complainant's credibility or reliability, you may consider all the circumstances in which the first complaint was made. The length of time between the alleged crime and the report of the complainant to this witness is one factor you may consider in evaluating the complainant's testimony, but you may also consider that sexual assault complainants may delay reporting the crime for a variety of reasons.[22]

These instructions are to be given to the jury contemporaneously with the first complaint testimony, and again during the final instructions.[23]

There can be no fresh complaint testimony without a fresh complaint witness. "[T]he fresh complaint doctrine is not operative until fresh complaint testimony *from someone other than the complainant* is properly introduced."[24] The victim need not remember her complaint to permit testimony by a first complaint witness.[25]

---

[22] 445 Mass at 247-248, 834 NE2d at 1199. Under prior practice, where a defendant was charged with other offenses that are tried together with the alleged sexual offense, the defendant was entitled to an instruction that the fresh complaint shall be considered only in relation to the sexual offense. *Com. v. Barbosa*, 399 Mass 841, 849, 507 NE2d 694, 698-699 (1987); *Com. v. Blow*, 370 Mass 401, 404-406, 348 NE2d 794, 796 (1976); *Com. v. Mareschi*, 38 Mass App 562, 566-569, 649 NE2d 1132, 1135-1137 (1995) (because of nature of crimes, impossible to segregate facts only corroborating rape claim). But see *Com. v. Lanning*, 32 Mass App 279, 286, 589 NE2d 318, 323 (1992) (fact that victim's complaint "might have pertained to acts outside the information provided by the bill of particulars did not require its exclusion, especially in view of the ongoing nature of the defendant's acts").

Defendant is not entitled to a specific instruction that fresh complaint evidence could be used to impeach as well as support the victim's testimony. See *Com. v. Kachoul*, 69 Mass App 352, 358, 868 NE2d 153, 158 (2007).

[23] *Com. v. King*, supra, 445 Mass at 247-248, 834 NE2d at 1200-1201; *Com. v. Garcia*, 89 Mass App 67, 74, 45 NE3d 602, 609 (2016).

[24] *Com. v. Buelterman*, 68 Mass App 829, 830-831, 865 NE2d 809, 810-811 (2007) (emphasis added) (defendant was not entitled to a fresh-complaint limiting instruction where victim testified that she confided in a friend a couple of years after the incidents that defendant had touched her inappropriately; but noting the self-corroboration and hearsay issues surrounding such testimony, 68 Mass App at 831-833, 865 NE2d at 811-812).

[25] *Com. v. Dale*, 86 Mass App 187, 190-192, 15 NE3d 232, 236-237 (2014) (any discrepancy between the memory of the victim and the witness goes to the weight, not admissibility, of the first complaint testimony).

The fresh complaint doctrine does not strictly prohibit the admission of evidence that, while barred by that doctrine, is otherwise independently admissible (e.g., falling within a hearsay exception),[26] or offered for a legitimate purpose other than to corroborate the complainant's testimony, such as to rehabilitate an impeached witness or to rebut a charge of bias or motive to lie.[27] In such cases, the judge

---

[26] Compare *Com. v. Dargon*, 457 Mass 387, 399-401, 930 NE2d 707, 719-721 (2010) (victim's statements to SANE nurse, recorded on form that was part of a sexual assault evidence kit, were independently admissible under hospital records statute, and served a purpose other than to corroborate the victim, i.e., establishing the essential elements of the crime and laying the foundation for the admission of physical evidence contained in the rape kit) and *Com. v. Starkweather*, 79 Mass App 791, 799-803, 950 NE2d 461, 468-471 (2011) (police sergeant's testimony regarding rape victim's comment that his gun appeared similar to one used by defendant had independent significance concerning identification of the gun present in defendant's vehicle; other officer's reference to victim's statement at the hospital was offered in connection with victim's demeanor; other police testimony related to the investigation and was admissible in response to the defense theory of the case) with *Com. v. McCoy*, 456 Mass 838, 848-849, 926 NE2d 1143, 1156 (2010) (SANE nurse's testimony regarding conversation with victim fell within no hearsay exception) and *Com. v. Monteiro*, 75 Mass App 489, 494-497, 914 NE2d 981, 985-987 (2009) (no independent hearsay exceptions found to apply to additional complaints).

[27] See, e.g., *Com. v. Aviles*, 461 Mass 60, 71-73, 958 NE2d 37, 48-49 (2011) (child victim's testimony that she had complained to her grandmother that defendant had raped her three years after she first complained to her mother about inappropriate touchings became independently admissible when defendant suggested on cross-examination that victim had fabricated the accusations); *Com. v. Kebreau*, 454 Mass 287, 297-299, 909 NE2d 1146, 1155-1157 (2009) (testimony was offered to rebut questions raised by defendant on cross-examination regarding inconsistencies in victim's testimony, and to rehabilitate the witness on redirect) (citing Text); *Com. v. Arana*, 453 Mass 214, 224-229, 901 NE2d 99, 107-111 (2009) (evidence that victim in police station following the alleged assault was reluctant to make a statement and was upset and crying was non-hearsay demeanor evidence admissible to rebut suggestion that she had fabricated her complaint for purposes of a civil lawsuit against the defendant); *Com. v. Lawton*, 82 Mass App 528, 536-537, 976 NE2d 160, 168-169 (2012) (once defendant put SAIN interviewer on stand to introduce victim's prior inconsistent statements, Commonwealth had right to rehabilitate with further abuse disclosures); *Com. v. Hanino*, 82 Mass App 489, 496-498, 975 NE2d 876, 883-884 (2012) (victim's testimony about conversation with uncle and brother was relevant to rebut defense contention that she had recanted; police officers' testimony about victim's reports was admissible for impeachment as prior inconsistent statement of witness who judge found feigned memory loss). See also *Com. v. Roby*, 462 Mass 398, 410, 969 NE2d 142, 152 (2012) (evidence regarding computer images of naked women that defendant allegedly showed victims was properly admitted to provide context to first complaint testimony of mother); *Com. v. Flint*, 81 Mass App 794, 805-806, 968 NE2d 928, 938 (2012) (admission of other conversations beyond first complaint were relevant as evidence of the circumstances surrounding the first complaint). Judges should, however, be cautious about admitting multiple complaint testimony merely to "provide context" for other evidence. See *Com. v. Place*, 81 Mass App 229, 232, 961 NE2d 597, 600 (2012).

should carefully balance the probative value and risks of prejudice, as usual. But the existence of a potential alternative evidentiary basis for admission of repetitive complaints, such as an independent exception to the hearsay rule, does not guarantee admissibility; the evidence must serve a purpose other than to repeat the fact of the complaint and thereby unfairly corroborate the complainant's accusations, the concerns underlying the first complaint rule.[28] Once a defendant opens the door to evidence beyond the scope of the doctrine, the Commonwealth is permitted to explore the contents and context of the statements in more detail.[29]

The circumstances giving rise to police involvement in the sexual assault case, and the details of the investigative process after victim's complaint is made, are usually not relevant to the issue of defendant's guilt, and should not be admitted in the Commonwealth's case-in-chief.[30] Testimony regarding reports to law enforcement officers or prosecutors,[31] as well as testimony indicating that the victim was interviewed pursuant to the sexual abuse intervention network (SAIN), is potentially extremely prejudicial, as it vouches for the victim's claims, and should not be admitted.[32]

---

[28] See *Com. v. Ramsey*, 76 Mass App 844, 848-850, 927 NE2d 506, 510-511 (2010) (hospital records containing multiple repetitions of victim's allegations of incest were improperly admitted, even though the records fell within the statutory hearsay exception); *Com. v. McGee*, 75 Mass App 499, 502-504, 915 NE2d 235, 238-240 (2009) (although complainant's statements to nurse qualified as spontaneous utterances, because of potential prejudice to defendant, great caution must be exercised in admitting both first complaint and spontaneous utterances that are in the nature of a complaint).

[29] *Com. v. Torres*, 86 Mass App 272, 277-278, 15 NE3d 778, 784 (2014).

[30] *Com. v. Arana*, supra, 453 Mass at 226-227, 901 NE2d at 109 (but where defendant vigorously argued that the police investigation demonstrated bias, incompetence, and complicity in complainants' support of their civil law suit, evidence of the timing and circumstances of the investigation was properly admitted).

[31] See *Com. v. Stuckich*, supra, 450 Mass at 457, 879 NE2d at 113 ("The fact that the Commonwealth brought its resources to bear on this incident creates the imprimatur of official belief in the complainant. It is unnecessary and irrelevant to the issue of the defendant's guilt, and is extremely prejudicial."); *Com. v. Revells*, 78 Mass App 492, 498-499, 940 NE2d 481, 486-487 (2010) (testimony that victim told the police "everything that she told the jury here today" was error, as it constituted self-corroboration and lent an official imprimatur to her complaint); *Com. v. Place*, 81 Mass App 229, 232-233, 961 NE2d 597, 600 (2012). But compare *Com. v. Morris*, 82 Mass App 427, 440, 974 NE2d 1152, 1164 (2012) (prosecutor elicited testimony concerning victim's complaints to police at the request of the defense).

[32] *Com. v. Monteiro*, 75 Mass App 489, 493-494, 914 NE2d 981, 985 (2009). Nor should testimony regarding the investigative response of a witness to the complainant's report be admitted. *Com. v. Haggett*, 79 Mass App 167, 173-175, 944 NE2d 601,

Testimony regarding the victim's demeanor and physical condition does not implicate the first complaint doctrine.[33] The reaction of third persons to an alleged sexual molestation, however, may not be admitted as fresh complaint testimony.[34]

The courts have rejected the argument that first complaint testimony should not be admitted where there is a percipient witness (in addition to the victim) to the sexual assault.[35]

Six years after *Com. v. King*, the Supreme Judicial Court assessed the continued viability of the first complaint doctrine and determined to retain it, but with modification of the scope of appellate review: the admission of evidence in violation of the established parameters will always be deemed error; where a defendant has objected to the admission, the appellate court will then determine whether the error was prejudicial, and where there was no objection, whether the error created a substantial risk of a miscarriage of justice.[36] Where the inconsistencies contained in cumulative complaint testimony were more important to the defense strategy than the Commonwealth's case, there is no prejudicial harm to the defendant.[37]

Although only those details to which the victim has testified generally at trial are admissible as corroboration by way of evidence of a fresh complaint,[38] "[f]resh complaint testimony need not replicate precisely the victim's own testimony, nor must it be sanitized to match the victim's testimony exactly. Some inconsistency between a fresh complaint witness's testimony and a complainant's testimony is expected, and will often aid the jury in determining whether the fresh

---

607-609 (2011) (cross-examination of victim's guidance counselor regarding her crisis intervention response to victim's report had no relevance, and was prejudicial).

[33] *Com. v. Santos*, 465 Mass 689, 699-701, 991 NE2d 1049, 1058-1060 (2013) (mother's testimony regarding demeanor of child victim); *Com. v. McCoy*, 456 Mass 838, 846, 926 NE2d 1143, 1154 (2010); *Com. v. Flint*, 81 Mass App 794, 806, 968 NE2d 928, 938 (2012).

[34] See *Com. v. Figueroa*, 413 Mass 193, 198, 595 NE2d 779, 783 (1992); *Com. v. Montanez*, supra, 439 Mass at 448-449, 788 NE2d at 961 (improper for victim to testify to action guidance counselor took after her complaint, as it served only as self-corroboration; improper for victim's mother to testify that she was shocked by daughter's revelations); *Com. v. Calderon*, 65 Mass App 590, 595, 842 NE2d 986, 992 (2006) (improper for social worker to testify about subsequent steps department took to investigate victim's allegations).

[35] *Com. v. Hartnett*, 72 Mass App 467, 470-473, 892 NE2d 810-812 (2008).

[36] *Com. v. Aviles*, 461 Mass 60, 71-73, 958 NE2d 37, 48-49 (2011).

[37] *Com. v. Lenane*, 80 Mass App 14, 19-20, 951 NE2d 361, 366 (2011).

[38] *Com. v. Licata*, supra, 412 Mass at 659 n.8, 591 NE2d at 675 n.8; *Com. v. Baran*, 74 Mass App 256, 289-290, 905 NE2d 1122, 1149 (2009).

complaint testimony ultimately supports the complainant's story."[39] Defense counsel can of course exploit such inconsistencies during cross-examination and closing argument.[40]

The trial judge retains the usual discretionary authority to exclude new details where their potential prejudice outweighs their probative value.[41] First complaint witnesses may not testify to details which "add substantively to the complainant's account, and details which are so graphic, colorful, or gruesome as to have an important effect on the jury may be excluded."[42] Thus, a police officer should not have been permitted to testify to potentially prejudicial details of the complaint not included in the victim's own testimony.[43] But the fact that a fresh complaint witness gave detailed testimony regarding an incident about which the child complainant had testified more generally did not render the evidence inadmissible.[44]

---

[39] *Com. v. King*, supra, 445 Mass at 235, 834 NE2d at 1192 (citing *Com. v. Scanlon*, 412 Mass 664, 670, 592 NE2d 1279, 1283 (1992)). See also *Com. v. Rivera*, 83 Mass App 581, 586, 987 NE2d 597, 602 (2013).

[40] *Com. v. King*, supra, 445 Mass at 245, 834 NE2d at 1199; *Com. v. Rivera*, supra, 83 Mass App at 587,, 987 NE2d at 602.

[41] *Com. v. Rivera*, supra, 83 Mass App at 586 n.6, 987 NE2d at 602 n.6.

[42] *Com. v. Snow*, 30 Mass App 443, 446, 569 NE2d 838, 840 (1991).

[43] See *Com. v. Scanlon*, supra, 412 Mass at 670, 592 NE2d at 1283.

[44] See *Com. v. LeFave*, 407 Mass 927, 941, 556 NE2d 83, 92 (1990). Compare *Com. v. Flebotte*, 417 Mass 348, 351, 630 NE2d 265, 267 (1994) (error to allow fresh complaint testimony as to acts not testified to by child victim), *Com. v. Kirouac*, 405 Mass 557, 564-565, 542 NE2d 270, 274-275 (1989) (videotape of police interview with child victim that included serious criminal conduct not mentioned in her testimony could not be admitted), *Com. v. Demars*, 38 Mass App 596, 650 NE2d 368 (1995) (victim's father's testimony that victim put male doll's face on genitals of female doll exceeded scope of victim's testimony), *Com. v. Kerr*, 36 Mass App 505, 632 NE2d 1244 (1994) (detective's testimony relating defendant's threatening statement to complainant and that complainant thought defendant was going to shoot her exceeded permissible scope), and *Com. v. Sugrue*, 34 Mass App 172, 607 NE2d 1045 (1993) (testimony of fresh complaint witnesses concerning incidents other than one testified to by victim was clearly outside permissible bounds of corroborative evidence) with *Com. v. Kirkpatrick*, 423 Mass 436, 444-445, 668 NE2d 790, 795-796 (1996) (police officer's testimony regarding incident of anal sex barely went beyond victim's testimony), *Com. v. Upton U.*, 59 Mass App 252, 256-258, 795 NE2d 575, 578-579 (2003) (fresh complaint testimony differed only slightly from victim's), *Com. v. Freitas*, 59 Mass App 903, 794 NE2d 636 (2003) (discrepancy inconsequential), *Com. v. Molle*, 56 Mass App 621, 631-632, 779 NE2d 658, 667 (2002) (detective permitted to summarize fresh complaint in his own words), *Com. v. Gichel*, 48 Mass App 206, 208-209, 718 NE2d 1262, 1265 (1999) (although fresh complaint testimony added detail of penetration not testified to by victim, it did not exceed permissible scope of her general testimony; but fresh complaint evidence relating to defendant's direction of dog to lick victim should not have been admitted), *Com. v. Caracino*, 33 Mass App 787, 791-792, 605 NE2d 859,

Fresh complaint evidence may not be used to fill gaps in the prosecution's case.[45] The trial judge must closely watch the details of fresh complaint testimony "to ensure that the limited hearsay exception allowing fresh complaint testimony is not used to put inadmissible and prejudicial evidence into the case."[46] A fresh complaint witness may not testify regarding the credibility of the complainant.[47] Nor may the doctrine be used to admit the prior statements of a witness *other than the victim*.[48]

The complaint must be "voluntary" to be admissible, but it may be deemed so even though elicited in part by questions provided they were not suggestive or leading.[49] Fresh complaint evidence has been admitted where the complaint was written rather than oral.[50]

862-863 (1993) (abuse specialist properly testified to child's complaint describing penile penetration, although victim testified only to digital and lingual penetration), and *Com. v. Tingley*, 32 Mass App 706, 709-712, 594 NE2d 546, 548-550 (1992) (additional details and variances between fresh complaint testimony and child victim's did not render testimony inadmissible, but testimony as to incidents not testified to by child improperly admitted).

[45] See *Com. v. King*, supra, 445 Mass at 234, 834 NE2d at 1192; *Com. v. Scanlon*, supra, 412 Mass at 670, 592 NE2d at 1283; *Com. v. Gardner*, 30 Mass App 515, 527, 570 NE2d 1033, 1040 (1991) (judge erred in permitting jury to use fresh complaint testimony to supply explanation for failure of complainant to report assault at earlier time).

[46] *Com. v. Lagacy*, 23 Mass App 622, 629, 504 NE2d 674, 679 (1987).

[47] See *Com. v. Powers*, 36 Mass App 65, 627 NE2d 953 (1994) and § 6.12, supra.

[48] *Com. v. Hatzigiannis*, 88 Mass App 395, 401, 37 NE3d 1108, 1113 (2015).

[49] See, e.g., *Com. v. Amirault*, supra, 404 Mass at 228, 535 NE2d at 198-199 (fresh complaint properly admitted even though child made statements following investigatory interview); *Com. v. McGrath*, supra, 364 Mass at 246-250, 303 NE2d at 111-113 (police questioning); *Com. v. Hanger*, 357 Mass 464, 258 NE2d 555 (1970) (1,500-word account of conversation between police officer and complainant admissible despite fact it was elicited by questions from officer); *Com. v. Caracino*, 33 Mass App 787, 789-791, 605 NE2d 859, 861-862 (1993) (child's complaints properly admitted even though one made in response to pointed questions from abuse specialist in district attorney's office, and other in response to request that she repeat story to mother); *Com. v. Davids*, supra, 33 Mass App at 425-426, 600 NE2d at 1009 (child's complaint properly admitted even though result of persistent questioning by aunt); *Com. v. Lanning*, supra, 32 Mass App at 285, 589 NE2d at 323 (complaint made in course of interviews by social worker and investigator); *Com. v. Tingley*, supra, 32 Mass App at 709, 594 NE2d at 548 (mother's inquiry was sufficiently broad that the child's reply had a spontaneity that did not indicate mere acquiescence). But compare *Com. v. Howell*, 57 Mass App 716, 721, 785 NE2d 1256, 1261-1262 (2003) (complaint not spontaneous but result of grilling by mother and grandmother).

[50] See *Com. v. Scanlon*, supra, 412 Mass at 668-669, 592 NE2d at 1282-1283 (note to friend); *Com. v. Graves*, 35 Mass App 76, 87-88, 616 NE2d 817, 824 (1993) (rape victim, who had been referred to portion of her written statement given to police in order to rebut defense counsel's assertion of recent fabrication, properly allowed to

Despite the apparent anomaly of applying the logic of the fresh complaint doctrine to non-forcible, consensual statutory rape cases, the courts have permitted fresh complaint testimony in such cases.[51] The courts have, however, been unwilling to expand the doctrine beyond cases involving sexual assaults.[52]

It has been held that the "defendant's right to show lack of fresh complaint is correlative with the Commonwealth's duty to show that such complaint was made."[53] Defendant is not, however, entitled to an instruction drawing the jury's attention to the victim's failure to complain.[54]

Regarding the use of an expert to present fresh complaint testimony, the Supreme Judicial Court has cautioned: "Notwithstanding the theoretical right of a qualified fresh complaint witness also to testify to the general characteristics of sexually abused children, prosecutors would be well advised to avoid such juxtaposition and, if it occurs, trial judges should be alert to its considerable prejudicial potential."[55] For further discussion of the problem of bolstering with regard to expert testimony, see §§ 7.3, 7.5, and 7.6, infra.

---

read entire statement under doctrine of fresh complaint); *Com. v. Lanning*, supra, 32 Mass App at 286, 589 NE2d at 323 (note given to investigator); *Com. v. Lagacy*, supra, 23 Mass at 625, 504 NE2d at 677 (police officer read victim's written statement to jury). In appropriate circumstances, a tape recording or videotape of the victim's complaint is admissible. See *Com. v. Lavalley*, supra, 410 Mass at 645, 574 NE2d at 1003; *Com. v. Jerome*, 36 Mass App 59, 627 NE2d 948 (1994).

[51] See *Com. v. McCutcheon*, 51 Mass App 715, 718-720, 748 NE2d 489, 492-493 (2001) (& citations).

[52] See *Com. v. Gichel*, 48 Mass App 206, 211-212, 718 NE2d 1262, 1267 (1999) (posing a child in violation of GL 272, § 29A(a) and (b)).

[53] *Com. v. Pratt*, 42 Mass App 695, 701-702, 679 NE2d 579, 582-583 (1997) (reversible error to exclude evidence of lack of fresh complaint by complainant in communication to DSS case worker).

[54] See *Com. v. Medina*, 64 Mass App 708, 718, 835 NE2d 300, 311 (2005). For a case dealing with defense counsel's strategic use of fresh complaint testimony in an attempt to discredit the victims' credibility, see *Com. v. Fanara*, 47 Mass App 560, 715 NE2d 62 (1999).

[55] *Com. v. Swain*, 36 Mass App 433, 444-445, 632 NE2d 848, 856 (1994). See also *Com. v. Brouillard*, 40 Mass App 448, 665 NE2d 113 (1996) (reversing convictions because fresh complaint testimony was presented by treating therapist, improperly bolstering complainants' credibility).

E. REVIVED AND ENHANCED TESTIMONY

§ 6.26 Present Recollection Revived

In the event that a witness has difficulty recalling the events about which he is asked to testify, there are three techniques that may be employed to elicit the information.

First, leading questions may be used to aid the memory of the witness.[1]

Second, the witness's memory may be stimulated by use of an item that revives his or her recollection, as discussed in this section.

Third, when the memory of the witness is beyond revival, a document embodying his or her forgotten knowledge may be admissible under the doctrine of past recollection recorded, an exception to the hearsay prohibition.[2]

When a witness is unable to testify as to facts of which he apparently has knowledge, his recollection may be refreshed by showing him a writing or object that then permits him to recall the events from his own memory. The witness may use the writing to refresh his failing memory, but the testimony which the witness gives must be the product of the revived present recollection.[3] Refreshing of the witness's recollection must occur within the presence of the jury to allow an opportunity to assess whether the witness actually remembers the statement or is being prompted to give a particular answer.[4] Counsel may refresh a witness's recollection only if her memory clearly is exhausted.[5]

Anything may be used to refresh a witness's memory including (in the oft-cited words of Learned Hand) "a song, a scent, a photograph,

---

§ 6.26 [1] See § 6.10, supra.

[2] See § 8.10, infra. The determination of whether the doctrine of present recollection revived or past recollection recorded is applicable is a question within the sound discretion of the trial judge. *Com. v. Pickles*, 364 Mass 395, 402, 305 NE2d 107 (1973); *Com. v. Dougherty*, 343 Mass 299, 306, 178 NE2d 584 (1961). For an excellent comparison of the two, see *United States v. Riccardi*, 174 F2d 883 (3d Cir 1949).

[3] *Com. v. Hoffer*, 375 Mass 369, 376, 377 NE2d 685, 690-691 (1978). Compare *Com. v. Walker*, 42 Mass App 14, 19, 674 NE2d 249, 252 (1997) (judge, in refusing to permit defense counsel to show nine-year-old witness social worker's report, could reasonably conclude that witness would not likely understand that document was only being used to refresh recollection).

[4] See generally *Com. v. Woodbine*, 461 Mass 720, 730-732, 964 NE2d 956, 965-966 (2012); *Com. v. Quincy Q.*, 434 Mass 859, 871, 753 NE2d 781, 793 (2001); *Com. v. O'Brien*, 419 Mass 470, 478-479, 645 NE2d 1170, 1175 (1995).

[5] *Com. v. McGee*, 469 Mass 1, 15, 11 NE3d 1043, 1053 (2014).

an allusion, even a past statement known to be false."[6] Most often it is a writing of some kind, and any writing that in fact refreshes the memory of the witness may be used by him for that purpose,[7] even if it is itself inadmissible.[8] An item typically employed in this manner is a transcript of the witness's grand jury testimony.[9]

It is not necessary that the writing be contemporaneous with the event it records or even that it have been made by the witness.[10] A witness may not, of course, be permitted to refer to a writing to refresh his recollection with reference to a matter about which he never had any knowledge.[11] Before attempting to refresh a witness's recollection, it must be established that his memory is clearly exhausted.[12]

The evidence admitted is the testimony of the witness, not the memorandum or object used to refresh recollection.[13] It is error,

---

[6] *United States v. Rappy*, 157 F2d 964, 967 (2d Cir 1946). See also *Com. v. Quincy Q.*, supra, 434 Mass at 870-872, 753 NE2d at 792-793 (videotape of child complainant's prior statement); *Com. v. Cheek*, 374 Mass 613, 617-618, 373 NE2d 1161 (1978) (conversation overheard by witness); *Com. v. Hartford*, 346 Mass 482, 487, 194 NE2d 401 (1963) (witness's own prior statement); *Kuklinska v. Maplewood Homes, Inc.*, 336 Mass 489, 495, 146 NE2d 523, 527 (1957) (expert witness used United States Geological Survey map to refresh recollection).

[7] *Com. v. O'Brien*, supra, 419 Mass at 478, 645 NE2d at 1175.

[8] *Com. v. Woodbine*, supra, 461 Mass at 732-736, 964 NE2d at 966-970 (but judge must assure the witness's memory is not based on a *Miranda*-suppressed statement). Nor need the writing be an original. *Com. v. Ford*, 130 Mass 64, 66 (1881).

[9] See, e.g., *Com. v. Silva*, 401 Mass 318, 328, 516 NE2d 161, 168 (1987); *Com. v. Daye*, 393 Mass 55, 65 n.11, 469 NE2d 483, 490 n.11 (1984).

[10] *Com. v. McDermott*, 255 Mass 575, 580-581, 152 NE 704, 705-706 (1926). See also *Gordon v. Medford*, 331 Mass 119, 124, 117 NE2d 284, 287 (1954) (plaintiff properly permitted to refresh his memory as to items of damage from paper prepared by another plaintiff); *Com. v. Levine*, 280 Mass 83, 91, 181 NE 851, 854 (1932) (immaterial that witness did not prepare ledger he used to refresh recollection).

[11] See *Kaplan v. Gross*, 223 Mass 152, 156, 111 NE 853, 855 (1916).

[12] *Com. v. O'Brien*, supra, 419 Mass at 478, 645 NE2d at 1175; *Com. v. Woodbine*, 461 Mass 720, 731-732, 964 NE2d 956, 966 (2011) (in this way, the jury is made aware of the limitations of the witness's memory and the areas that could not initially be recalled); *Com. v. Jenkins*, 458 Mass 791, 796 n.4, 941 NE2d 56, 65 n.4 (2011) (witness did not assert lack of memory, and negative responses are not the equivalent). See also *Com. v. Baldwin*, 385 Mass 165, 178-179, 431 NE2d 194, 202-203 (1982) (not sufficient if recollection is simply different from what examiner wishes it to be); *Com. v. Hennigan*, 11 Mass App 979, 417 NE2d 1232 (1981) (no error in refusing to allow tape recording to be used to refresh witness's recollection where witness had no failure of memory, but his testimony was unequivocal).

[13] See *Com. v. Daye*, supra, 393 Mass at 65 n.11, 469 NE2d at 490 n.11; *Com. v. Bookman*, 386 Mass 657, 662 n.8, 436 NE2d 1228, 1232 n.8 (1982); *Com. v. A Juvenile*, 361 Mass 214, 217, 280 NE2d 144, 146 (1972).

therefore, to show the writing to the jury or to permit the witness to read the document into the record under the guise of refreshing his recollection.[14]

A frequently recurring question is whether a police officer on the stand is reading from his or her notes rather than testifying from recollection refreshed by those notes.[15] Regarding expert witnesses, there is a "somewhat less rigid application of the rule concerning refreshed memory" where the witness is not likely to remember details of the many cases they review: "When a witness asks to consult his or her notes . . . that generally can be taken to mean that the witness's memory is exhausted, but could be refreshed by reviewing the notes."[16]

Opposing counsel may seek to impeach the witness by invoking his prior inconsistent statements on the subject, thus permitting the fact finder to conclude that the testimony actually derived entirely from review of the document, or by introducing the document itself into evidence to show that it could not have aided the witness as claimed.[17]

Under Massachusetts practice, opposing counsel is not entitled to inspect a writing used to refresh a witness's recollection on the stand before it is shown to the witness, but is entitled to do so afterwards and before cross-examination so that he may raise the question of whether it refreshes the witness's memory as claimed.[18] Opposing counsel may not, as of right, examine documents used by a witness to refresh his recollection *prior to* taking the stand, but the judge may permit such examination as a matter of discretion.[19] A document used by a witness

---

[14] See *Com. v. Daye*, supra; *Com. v. McDuffie*, 16 Mass App 1016, 455 NE2d 461 (1983) (error to admit medical report used by prosecution witnesses to refresh recollection of rape victim's statement).

[15] See, e.g., *Com. v. Woodbine*, supra, 461 Mass at 730-731, 964 NE2d at 966; *Com. v. Pike*, 324 Mass 335, 339-340, 86 NE2d 519, 521 (1949); *Com. v. Pickles*, 364 Mass 395, 401-402, 305 NE2d 107, 111 (1973) (no error in permitting police officer on direct examination to read from notes of conversation with defendant because, although judge did not distinguish between present recollection revived and past recollection recorded, it appears judge acted properly on basis of latter doctrine).

[16] *Adoption of Larry*, 434 Mass 456, 459 n.3, 750 NE2d 475, 480 n.3 (2001).

[17] *Com. v. Woodbine*, supra, 461 Mass at 732, 964 NE2d at 966.

[18] *Com. v. O'Brien*, supra, 419 Mass at 478, 645 NE2d at 1175.

[19] See *Leonard v. Taylor*, 315 Mass 580, 583-584, 53 NE2d 705, 707 (1944) (discussed at § 6.27, infra). Documents used by a witness to refresh recollection prior to taking the stand may also be sought through pretrial discovery where appropriate. See Mass R Civ P 26-37; Mass R Crim P 14.

to refresh recollection and provided to opposing counsel may be introduced by the latter to show that it could not or did not aid the witness in any legitimate way.[20]

A document used to refresh the memory of a witness *prior to* trial and examined upon demand by opposing counsel at trial may become admissible at the option of the party who produced the document under the doctrine of *Leonard v. Taylor*.[21] The doctrine does not, however, apply to the examination of documents used by the witness *while testifying* at trial. Neither inspection of such a document by opposing counsel in court nor use of it during cross-examination makes the document admissible in evidence at the option of the proponent.

When materials otherwise protected by the work product doctrine are used by the examiner to refresh a witness's recollection on the stand, the protection afforded by the work product doctrine is waived and the opponent's attorney is entitled to inspect the writing.[22]

Proposed Mass R Evid 612[23] (which is in substance the same as Fed R Evid 612) is consistent with present practice in providing that the adverse party is entitled to examine any writing or object used by the witness while testifying to refresh his memory, but leaving the time of inspection to the court's discretion. Items used by the witness before

---

[20] *Bendett v. Bendett*, supra, 315 Mass at 62, 52 NE2d at 5.

[21] See § 6.27, infra.

[22] See *Com. v. O'Brien*, supra, 419 Mass at 478, 645 NE2d at 1175.

[23] Proposed Mass R Evid 612 provides:

Writing or Object Used to Refresh Memory

(a) **While testifying**. If, while testifying, a witness uses a writing or object to refresh his memory, an adverse party is entitled to have the writing or object produced at the trial, hearing, or deposition in which the witness is testifying. ["This rule leaves the time of inspection to the court's discretion." Advisory Committee Note to R 612]

(b) **Before testifying**. If, before testifying, a witness uses a writing or object to refresh his memory for the purpose of testifying and the court in its discretion determines that the interests of justice so require, an adverse party is entitled to have the writing or object produced, if practicable, at the trial, hearing, or deposition in which the witness is testifying.

(c) **Terms and conditions of production and use**. A party entitled to have a writing or object produced under this rule is entitled to inspect it, to cross-examine the witness thereon, and to introduce in evidence those portions which relate to the testimony of the witness. If production of the writing or object contains matters not related to the subject matter of the testimony the court shall examine the writing or object in camera, excise any portions not so related, and order delivery of the remainder to the party entitled thereto. Any portion withheld over objections shall be preserved and made available to the appellate court in the event of an appeal. If a writing is not produced, made available for inspection, or delivered pursuant to order under this rule, the court shall make any order justice requires, except that in criminal cases when the state elects not to comply, the order shall be one striking the testimony or, if the court in its discretion determines that the interests of justice so require, declaring a mistrial. ["The provisions for inspection, cross-examination, and introduction are for the limited purpose of showing that the writing or object did not or could not have refreshed the witness's memory." Advisory Committee Note to R 612]

testifying may under the rule be ordered produced within the discretion of the court. The party obtaining the writing or object may use it to cross-examine the witness and may introduce into evidence those portions that relate to the witness's testimony.

In criminal cases, the right to inspect prior statements or notes used to refresh recollection is further provided by way of decisional law and court rules. Notes used by a witness to refresh recollection prior to taking the stand may be inspected in the discretion of the trial judge without a formal demand and, where the request occurs during voir dire (and thus not in a situation where counsel may be "grandstanding"), "there are substantial reasons for exercising discretion in favor of the inspection."[24]

§ 6.27 Documents Called For and Examined by a Party at Trial

Under long-standing Massachusetts practice, where one party at trial calls for a document from the other party and in response to the call receives and examines it, the document may be put in evidence by the party who produced it even if it would have been otherwise inadmissible.[1] The rule originally reflected concern with "the disastrous effect upon a jury in a perfectly good case or defense of a bold and dramatic demand by opposing counsel for the production of a document at some critical moment of the trial. It may be impossible to refuse without creating an impression of evasion and concealment, and even if the demand is acceded to it may be practically impossible to prevent the same impression without showing the document itself to the jury."[2]

Application of the rule is not dependent upon the giving of a notice to produce the document prior to the trial.[3] There must, however, be a demand at trial for the document in order to trigger the rule.[4]

---

[24] *Com. v. Marsh*, 354 Mass 713, 721-722, 242 NE2d 545, 550 (1968). Compare *Com. v. Walker*, 370 Mass 548, 562-563, 350 NE2d 678, 689 (1976) ("Where notes, memoranda, tapes or the like have not been used to refresh a witness's recollection, they, likewise, are not automatically to be made available to the defense."); *Com. v. Guerro*, 357 Mass 741, 756-757, 260 NE2d 190, 199 (1970) (judge not required to order production of entire file of notations and worksheet of police officer witnesses where there was no indication they were used to refresh recollection). See also Mass R Crim P 23.

§ 6.27 [1] See *Leonard. v. Taylor*, 315 Mass 580, 53 NE2d 705 (1944).

[2] *Leonard v. Taylor*, supra, 315 Mass at 582-583, 53 NE2d at 706.

[3] *Leonard v. Taylor*, supra, 315 Mass at 581, 53 NE2d at 706.

[4] See *Com. v. Kenneally*, 10 Mass App 162, 179, 406 NE2d 714, 725 (1980).

The rule making documents called for and examined at trial admissible at the option of the producing party does not apply to documents used by a witness to refresh his recollection *while* testifying (see § 6.26, supra).[5] It does apply to documents used for that purpose by the witness *before* trial.[6] The logic of this distinction has been questioned.[7] Nonetheless, Proposed Mass R Evid 612 carries forward the distinction.[8]

The rule is of limited applicability in criminal cases. It has been held inapplicable where the defendant demands to inspect prior statements of a prosecution witness in the possession of the Commonwealth.[9] Similarly, neither defense counsel's request to see the notes referred to by a prosecution witness to refresh his recollection at trial nor counsel's use of them in cross-examination make the notes admissible at the option of the Commonwealth.[10] Further, the judge has discretion to permit inspection of a prosecution witness's notes without a formal demand (thus not triggering the rule); and where the request is on a voir dire there are substantial reasons for exercising discretion in favor of the inspection.[11] Application of the rule has also been questioned in the case where a defense attorney requests and obtains a police report at trial.[12]

The rule does not apply unless the document produced is found by the judge to be the one demanded by the opponent.[13]

The wisdom of the rule making admissible a document called for and examined at trial has long been questioned, "chiefly on the

---

[5] See *Nussenbaum v. Chambers & Chambers, Inc.*, 322 Mass 419, 424, 77 NE2d 780, 783-784 (1948).

[6] *Leonard v. Taylor*, supra, 315 Mass at 583, 53 NE2d at 707.

[7] See *Com. v. Marsh*, 354 Mass 713, 721-722, 242 NE2d 545, 551 (1968) ("It is an artificial distinction to allow inspection of notes on the stand to refresh recollection [without rendering the notes admissible] and to decline it where the witness inspects his notes just before being called to the stand.").

[8] The Rule is set out in § 6.26, supra. The Advisory Committee states that Proposed Mass R Evid 612(b), providing that the judge has discretion to order production of a document used by a witness before testifying, "does not change the practice under *Leonard v. Taylor*, which held that a demand for a writing used prior to trial made such writing admissible at the option of the party producing it, though it would have otherwise been incompetent. *Leonard v. Taylor*, supra, is considered to be disciplinary in nature in order to discourage the 'bravado' demand, and does not impair appropriate discovery."

[9] See *Com. v. Ellison*, 376 Mass 1, 22-23, 379 NE2d 560, 571 (1978).

[10] *Com. v. Beaulieu*, 333 Mass 640, 648-650, 133 NE2d 226, 231-232 (1955).

[11] *Com. v. Marsh*, supra, 354 Mass at 721, 242 NE2d at 551.

[12] See *Com. v. Kenneally*, supra, 10 Mass App at 179, 406 NE2d at 725.

[13] See *O'Connell v. Kennedy*, 328 Mass 90, 95-96, 101 NE2d 892, 895-896 (1951).

grounds that it is a survival of the notion that a lawsuit is a contest in sportsmanship; that the rule is contrary to modern tendencies; and that it results in the admission of otherwise incompetent evidence."[14] And the current status of the rule has been questioned by the Supreme Judicial Court.[15] Moreover, because the rule is designed to avoid prejudicial impact on the jury, there is serious question as to whether it should apply at all in jury-waived cases.

§ 6.28 Hypnotically Enhanced Testimony

Testimony of a witness that has been enhanced or aided by use of hypnotism may not be admitted as probative evidence in the trial of a criminal case in the Massachusetts courts. "Hypnosis simply lacks general acceptability by experts in the field as a reliable method of enhancing the memory of a witness."[1]

A witness may, however, testify based on what he knew before hypnosis.[2] "Before admitting proffered testimony, the judge must be satisfied by a preponderance of the evidence presented at a hearing that the testimony is based on prehypnotic memory."[3] The judge's findings on the issue of separating pre-hypnotic memory from post-hypnotic memory are accorded substantial deference and will be accepted absent clear error.[4]

A criminal defendant has a constitutional right to testify to facts remembered after hypnosis.[5]

---

[14] *Leonard v. Taylor*, supra, 315 Mass at 582, 53 NE2d at 706.

[15] See *Com. v. Ellison*, supra, 376 Mass at 22, 379 NE2d at 570.

§ 6.28 [1] *Com. v. Kater (Kater I)*, 388 Mass 519, 520-521, 447 NE2d 1190, 1193 (1983); *Com. v. Kater (Kater III)*, 409 Mass 433, 567 NE2d 885 (1991).

[2] *Kater III*, supra, 409 Mass at 439, 567 NE2d 889; *Com. v. Kater (Kater VII)*, 432 Mass 404, 416-417, 734 NE2d 1164, 1176-1177 (2000), *habeas petition denied in Kater v. Maloney*, 459 F3d 56, 65-67 (1st Cir 2006).

[3] *Kater III*, supra. For a description of the required procedures, see 409 Mass at 441-442, 567 NE2d at 890-891.

[4] *Com. v. Kater*, 412 Mass 800, 802, 592 NE2d 1328, 1329-1330 (1992) (*Kater IV*) (court properly suppressed testimony by witnesses identifying defendant's automobile where there was no evidentiary basis to conclude they could have identified automobile prior to hypnosis).

[5] *Rock v. Arkansas*, 483 US 44 (1987); *Kater I*, supra, 388 Mass at 528-529 n.6, 447 NE2d 1197 n.6.

F. DEMEANOR EVIDENCE

§ 6.29 Demeanor Evidence

The trier of fact may consider the demeanor of a witness on the stand as evidence.[1] Demeanor may be considered not only on questions of credibility but also on other issues including the fitness of a parent contesting custody of a child,[2] the age of the witness,[3] a criminal defendant's mental condition or sanity,[4] and intelligence or competence to perform particular work.[5] The demeanor of a victim may also constitute demonstrative evidence that may be considered by a jury.[6]

Within appropriate limits, closing argument is permitted with respect to the demeanor of testifying witnesses, including parties.[7] Closing argument by a prosecutor on the demeanor of a criminal defendant who has not testified is dangerous and may be inappropriate in several respects. Remarks reasonably susceptible of being interpreted as comment on the defendant's failure to take the stand are impermissible.[8] Evidence of guilt may not be implied from a defendant sitting impassively and calmly in the courtroom.[9] A prosecutor

---

§ 6.29 [1] See, e.g., *Breton v. Breton*, 332 Mass 317, 125 NE2d 121 (1955). Demeanor evidence regarding a defendant's response to police questioning is also admissible. See *Com. v. Elangwe*, 85 Mass App 189, 199, 7 NE2d 1102, 1110-1111 (2013).

[2] *O'Brien v. O'Brien*, 347 Mass 765, 197 NE2d 192 (1964).

[3] *Com. v. Hollis*, 170 Mass 433, 435, 49 NE 632, 633 (1898).

[4] *Com. v. Zagrodny*, 443 Mass 93, 819 NE2d 565 (2004) (defendant usually has the right to appear at trial in unmedicated state or, if medicated, to introduce evidence of the effect of the medication); *Com. v. Smiledge*, 419 Mass 156, 643 NE2d 41 (1994) (expert may be asked questions regarding defendant's demeanor during trial, if relevant to sanity issues); *Com. v. Gurney*, 413 Mass 97, 595 NE2d 320 (1992) (where defense was diminished capacity to form specific intent to commit crime, error to exclude evidence that defendant was taking antipsychotic medication during trial that affected his outward appearance); *Com. v. Louraine*, 390 Mass 28, 34-38, 453 NE2d 437, 442-444 (1983) (under the facts of the case, to compel defendant asserting insanity defense to appear before jury in a medicated state was reversible error).

[5] *Leistritz v. American Zylonite Co.*, 154 Mass 382, 28 NE 294 (1891); *Keith v. New Haven & Northampton Co.*, 140 Mass 175, 3 NE 28 (1885).

[6] *Com. v. Roderick*, 411 Mass 817, 819, 586 NE2d 967, 969 (1992) (not error to permit non-testifying victim to sit in spectator section where jury could observe her conduct, including noises she made).

[7] *Com. v. Houghton*, 39 Mass App 94, 654 NE2d 932 (1995) (prosecutor's comment on victim's crying after testifying did not raise a substantial risk of miscarriage of justice) (Text cited); *Com. v. White*, 2 Mass App 258, 265, 311 NE2d 81, 86 (1974).

[8] For a more extensive discussion, see § 5.4.8.

[9] *Com. v. Young*, 399 Mass 527, 505 NE2d 186 (1987); *Com. v. Borodine*, 371 Mass 1, 11, 353 NE2d 649, 656 (1976), *habeas denied*, *Borodine v. Douzanis*, 592 F2d 1202, 1210-1211 (1st Cir 1979).

may not suggest that normal courtroom behavior demonstrates a consciousness of guilt.[10] It is improper for a prosecutor to suggest that he has particular knowledge of a defendant's appearance that is unknown to the jury.[11] It has been held proper to comment on affirmative behavior of a defendant plainly visible in the courtroom.[12]

---

[10] *Com. v. Valliere*, 366 Mass 479, 494, 321 NE2d 625, 635 (1974); *Com. v. Pullum*, 22 Mass App 485, 488, 494 NE2d 1355, 1358 (1986) (error to permit prosecutor to argue that defendant's failure to bare his teeth during trial demonstrated consciousness of guilt, when he was not asked to do so).

[11] *Com. v. Kater*, 388 Mass 519, 533, 447 NE2d 1190, 1199 (1983) (not proper to argue defendant wore long-sleeved shirts to trial to hide hairy arms in absence of evidence he had hairy arms).

[12] *Com. v. Smith*, 387 Mass 900, 907, 444 NE2d 374, 380 (1983) (squirming, smirking, laughing).

CHAPTER

7

OPINION and EXPERT EVIDENCE

A. OPINION RULE—GENERAL PRINCIPLES

§ 7.1 Federal Rule and Proposed Massachusetts Rule 701

Federal Rule 701 and Proposed Mass R Evid 701 allow somewhat greater latitude than traditional Massachusetts practice in the reception of opinions by lay witnesses. They are identical and provide:

> If the witness is not testifying as an expert, his testimony in the form of opinions or inferences is limited to those opinions or inferences which are (a) rationally based on the perception of the witness and (b) helpful to a clear understanding of his testimony or the determination of a fact in issue.

The intent of Rule 701 is to liberalize the admissibility of lay opinion testimony subject to the sound discretion of the trial judge. Rule 701 recognizes that lay witnesses may communicate their observations in the form of opinions or inferences that can be helpful to the trier of fact. The shorthand expression rule, discussed infra, is a reflection of a similar pragmatic approach. To the extent that Rule 701 is more flexible, its adoption might cause relaxation in practice of the stricter aspects of the opinion rule in Massachusetts—e.g., the limitations on lay opinion testimony on matters such as sanity.

§ 7.2 Massachusetts Practice

§ 7.2.1 When Lay Opinion Testimony Is Admissible

The opinion rule traditionally required that a lay witness testify as to facts known or observed by him and not give an opinion based on those facts.[1] The rule has long been relaxed in Massachusetts by allowing lay opinion based upon the practical necessity that evidence as to some matters may be otherwise difficult or impossible to obtain.[2] Lay opinion testimony is permissible when two conditions are met: "first, that the subject matter to which the testimony relates cannot be reproduced or described to the jury precisely as it appeared to the witness at the time; and second, that the facts upon which the witness is called to express his opinion, are such as men in general are capable of comprehending and understanding."[3] The witness must have personal knowledge of the facts on which the opinion is based and the opinion must be one which lay persons in general are capable of drawing.[4] The personal knowledge requirement leads to the conclusion that when a witness's testimony concerning a given fact is based only partly on her own observations of the fact testified to, and partly on what she has concluded based on statements by others, her testimony as to that fact constitutes an inadmissible opinion.[5]

Admissible lay opinions are often called "shorthand expressions." The rule under which such opinions are admitted is sometimes called the collective facts doctrine. Such conclusions of fact are admissible even if they were not reached at the time of the observation.[6]

The purpose of the traditional opinion rule was to reserve for the jury the function of making inferences whenever that is feasible. The rule provided that where: (1) the witness can cast his knowledge in the form of facts; and (2) the jury is equipped to draw the inference from such facts, the witness may not usurp the province of the jury by drawing the inference.[7]

---

§ 7.2 [1] The Supreme Judicial Court sometimes articulates the rule in this way. *Com. v. Molina*, 454 Mass 232, 243, 909 NE2d 19, 28 (2009) ("Lay witnesses are allowed to testify only to facts that they observed and may not give an opinion on those facts.").

[2] *Com. v. Sandler*, 368 Mass 729, 335 NE2d 903 (1975); *Com. v. Tracy*, 349 Mass 87, 95, 207 NE2d 16, 21 (1965).

[3] *Com. v. Vitello*, 376 Mass 426, 459-460, 381 NE2d 582, 601 (1978); *Com. v. Sturtivant*, 117 Mass 122 (1875).

[4] *Com. v. Smith*, 17 Mass App 918, 920-921, 456 NE2d 760, 763 (1983) (Text cited).

[5] *Com. v. Prater*, 431 Mass 86, 93-94, 725 NE2d 233, 240-241 (2000) (witness's conclusion as to who was present at crime scene was improperly based on what she heard others say about it).

[6] *Copithorn v. Boston & M.R.R. Co.*, 309 Mass 363, 366-367, 35 NE2d 254, 255-256 (1941).

[7] See *Com. v. Austin*, 421 Mass 357, 366, 657 NE2d 458, 463 (1995) (error to allow non-expert to testify that defendant was the man in videotape when tape was available to jury).

The implication of the traditional rule—that there is a clear distinction between fact and opinion—is not warranted by logic, experience, or the reported decisions. All testimony is to some extent an assertion of inference, or opinion, drawn by the witness from his or her perceptions. Courts tend to call testimony "fact" if it describes the witness's experience in terms of the most elemental logical ingredients that human nature and the English language permit—in terms of the words heard and the acts seen by the witness and of other sensory experiences of the witness. The further testimony goes in the direction of articulating inferences drawn from such elemental ingredients, the more likely it is to be ruled an "opinion."[8]

Lay and expert witnesses are precluded from giving an opinion that involves a conclusion of law or in regard to a mixed question of fact and law.[9]

The opinion rule applies to most hearsay declarations. Evidence as to a hearsay declaration, although within a hearsay exception, is barred if the declaration is in the form of improper opinion. It should be remembered, however, that the opinion rule does not apply to statements by a party opponent (see § 8.2.5) or to reputation evidence (see § 8.15). Also, the courts are likely to be somewhat more lenient in

---

[8] See *Com. v. Molina*, 454 Mass 232, 243, 909 NE2d 19, 28 (2009) (judge properly allowed forensic scientist to give lay opinion that knife blade and knife handle were a mechanical match in that jutting out spot on one matched indentation on the other, and properly advised jury that witness could not testify that the blade came from that handle). The words in which the witness casts her testimony are not conclusive with respect to whether she has testified to facts or opinion. See, e.g., *Doherty v. Belmont*, 396 Mass 271, 485 NE2d 183 (1985) (plaintiff's testimony she "presumed" she tripped over spot where pipe had been removed held not unduly speculative, when in other testimony she stated she tripped over a bump, and any uncertainty goes to weight of evidence, not admissibility).

[9] *Com. v. Canty*, 466 Mass 535 (2013) (lay witness may offer opinion regarding defendant's level of intoxication, but not whether he operated vehicle while intoxicated or whether his ability to operate vehicle safely was impaired, because the latter opinions come too close to an opinion on guilt or innocence) (Text cited); *DiMarzo v. American Mutual Ins. Co.*, 389 Mass 85, 103-104, 449 NE2d 1189, 1201 (1983) (witness properly testified to existence of custom and usage as a factual matter, but legal effect of custom or usage may not be proven by opinion); *Perry v. Medeiros*, 369 Mass 836, 343 NE2d 859 (1976) (barring opinion interpreting building code and stating whether certain condition was in violation thereof); but see *Ford v. Boston Housing Authority*, 55 Mass App 623, 773 NE2d 471 (2002) (expert could testify that locked door was in noncompliance with State building code) (Text cited); *Com. v. Brady*, 370 Mass 630, 351 NE2d 199 (1976) (insurance agent precluded from testifying as to the legal sufficiency of defendant's coverage).

cases where the declarant did not have the aid of an attorney in phrasing his declaration in non-opinion form.[10]

§ 7.2.2 *Examples of "Shorthand Expressions" and Permissible Lay Opinions*

Facts from which the jury is to draw an inference often cannot be described in testimony as precisely as they appeared to the witness. This may be because the witness's perception was a "composite" one—such as the perception of speed—that registered in the mind only in the form of a conclusion. Or it may be because the witness possessed certain knowledge—such as the mannerisms of a drunken person—that can reasonably be translated into language only in conclusory terms. In such cases, if the jury is to get the information at all, the witness must be permitted to articulate his or her knowledge in the form of conclusions.

Testimony as to speed may be a shorthand expression. Speed is an inference from distance, time, sound, dust trail, and so on; yet the knowledge of a witness who perceived a moving automobile cannot meaningfully be cast in a form more elemental than speed. A conclusion as to speed conveys a definite conception of facts and is one that jurors in general are capable of drawing. A witness may give his estimate in terms of miles per hour[11] or in terms of comparison between two vehicles—e.g., that one vehicle was moving "considerably faster" than another.[12] The trial judge must determine whether a witness had an adequate opportunity to observe a vehicle to express an estimate as to its speed in terms of miles per hour.[13]

The observations of a witness as to the manner of operation of a motor vehicle are also admissible.[14]

---

[10] *Old Colony Trust Co. v. Shaw*, 348 Mass 212, 217-218, 202 NE2d 785, 790 (1964).

[11] *Snow v. Sulkoski*, 345 Mass 766, 186 NE2d 822 (1962) and *Com. v. Charland*, 338 Mass 742, 157 NE2d 538 (1959).

[12] *Sax v. Horn*, 274 Mass 428, 174 NE 673 (1931).

[13] *Gonzalez v. Spates*, 54 Mass App 438, 766 NE2d 77 (2002) (within trial judge's discretion to conclude that "a few seconds" was not adequate to permit expression of speed in miles per hour).

[14] *Cushman v. Boston, W. & N.Y. Street Railway Co.*, 319 Mass 177, 179, 65 NE2d 6, 8 (1946) (bus started with unusual jerk or jolt worse than witness had ever experienced before); *McGrath v. Fash*, 244 Mass 327, 139 NE 303 (1923) (truck appeared to be "out of control of driver").

Matters relating to distance, size, color, weight, time, and other similar phenomena are within the doctrine of shorthand expressions.[15]

The human features, likewise, are not capable of accurate description so as to enable the jury to determine whether the person the witness saw is the person the jury has before it. Thus, witnesses are permitted to testify as to the identity of persons whom they have seen.[16] Whether a witness should be permitted to give an opinion regarding the identify of a person in a photograph depends upon whether "there is some basis for concluding that the witness is more likely to correctly identify the defendant from the photograph than is the jury."[17] Relevant factors include: (1) the condition of the picture, (2) the familiarity of the witness with the person's appearance at the time the picture was taken, and (3) whether the person was disguised or altered his appearance after the photograph was taken.

Witnesses may also describe the emotional, mental, or physical condition of another in terms of summary description.[18]

---

[15] See *Com. v. Olszewski*, 401 Mass 749, 519 NE2d 587 (1988) (police officer testified that chrome strip came from defendant's vehicle); *Com. v. Robertson*, 357 Mass 559, 259 NE2d 553 (1970) (sound was like that of people wrestling and falling to floor); *Com. v. LePage*, 352 Mass 403, 418, 226 NE2d 200, 210 (1967) (officer described footprints in snow as "fresh"); *Com. v. Cataldo*, 326 Mass 373, 94 NE2d 761 (1950) (dust was "similar to the dust one might get on oneself from the mortar on bricks"); *Com v. Damelio*, 83 Mass App 32, 38, 979 NE2d 792, 798 (2012) (police officer's opinion that bag contained "around three ounces" of marijuana); *Com. v. Brusgulis*, 41 Mass App 386, 670 NE2d 207 (1996) (car tracks in snow were from small car); *Com. v. Lopes*, 34 Mass App 179, 608 NE2d 749 (1993) (testimony that defendant had a gun because of way he held his hand in his pocket).

[16] *Com. v. Gagnon*, 16 Mass App 110, 127-128, 449 NE2d 686, 696 (1983) (where defendants had altered their appearance, there was no error in allowing police detective to testify that photographs taken by bank surveillance camera included photographs of the defendants); *Com. v. Bourgeois*, 391 Mass 869, 465 NE2d 1180 (1984) (Supreme Judicial Court explicitly agreed with Appeals Court on this issue).

[17] *Com. v. Pleas*, 49 Mass App 321, 326, 729 NE2d 642, 646 (2000); *Com v. Vacher*, 469 Mass 425, 14 NE3d 264 (2014) (error to allow detective to identify defendant as person in photograph, where detective had no special familiarity with defendant that jury lacked and there was no evidence that defendant's appearance had changed since photographs were taken); *Com. v. Pearson*, 77 Mass App 95, 105, 928 NE2d 961, 969 (2010) (woman who had known defendant for several years and had information about his clothes and jewelry that jury did not have identified him from photographs).

[18] See, e.g., *Com. v. Fuller*, 66 Mass App 84, 845 NE2d 434 (2006) (where caseworker did not give any expert opinion that victim's mental retardation precluded her from consenting to sexual intercourse, testimony of caseworker who had worked with victim for over eight years that she had limited mental abilities and that described daily caretaking that caseworker provided and limitations victim had in caring for herself was permissible) (Text cited); *Proulx v. Basbanes*, 354 Mass 559, 238 NE2d 531 (1968) (nervous condition of plaintiff described); *Luz v. Stop & Shop, Inc. of Peabody*,

This includes whether a person was drunk or intoxicated.[19]

A lay witness, however, may not testify that he or she has a disease, the diagnosis of which requires expert knowledge.[20] Similarly, he or she may not testify as to the cause of a physical or mental condition when that cause is a matter of expert medical knowledge.[21] A criminal defendant may, however, testify to his feelings and recent history of psychiatric care to support an insanity defense.[22]

A witness should attempt to relate the words of the parties to a conversation as accurately as he can remember them. This does not mean, however, that a witness is required to recite an oral conversation verbatim. He may give the substance of the conversation.[23] A witness may testify to his understanding of his friends' and associates' expressions and use of language.[24] The trial judge should instruct the jury

---

348 Mass 198, 208, 202 NE2d 771, 777 (1964) (driver of car characterized as "confused"); *Com. v. Harrison*, 342 Mass 279, 285, 173 NE2d 87, 93 (1961) (defendant described as "angry" and "upset"); *Kane v. Fields Corner Grille, Inc.*, 341 Mass 640, 647, 171 NE2d 287, 292 (1961) (person described as "boisterous" and having "an arrogant manner"); *Vieira v. East Taunton Street Railway Co.*, 320 Mass 547, 70 NE2d 841 (1947) (person had "failed" mentally or physically within a given period of time). But see *Maimonides School v. Coles*, 71 Mass App 240, 881 NE2d 778 (2008) (only the witnesses to a will, testator's treating physician, and qualified experts may give opinions on testamentary capacity); *Com. v. Despres*, 70 Mass App 645, 875 NE2d 864 (2007) (court had discretion to conclude that clinician had insufficient intimate and lengthy experience caring for victim to give lay opinion on his mental disability).

[19] *Com. v. Rarick*, 87 Mass App 349, 353, n.5, 30 NE3d 116, 120 (2015) (field sobriety tests form a basis for a lay opinion concerning sobriety, not an expert opinion); *Com. v. Orben*, 53 Mass App 700, 761 NE2d 991 (2002) (testimony witness was "concerned that something was wrong" constituted proper lay opinion that defendant was intoxicated; second witness who knew defendant well was properly permitted to testify that defendant was intoxicated, although she did not see him and only heard him speak); *Com. v. Atencio*, 12 Mass App 747, 429 NE2d 37 (1981) (Text cited).

[20] *Com. v. White*, 329 Mass 51, 106 NE2d 419 (1952) (syphilis).

[21] *Jones v. Spering*, 334 Mass 458, 136 NE2d 217 (1956) (cause of nervous breakdown).

[22] *Com. v. Guadalupe*, 401 Mass 372, 516 NE2d 1159 (1987) (error to exclude defendant's testimony that he heard noises, had visited a mental health clinic shortly before crime, and felt better now because he was seeing a psychiatrist). Opinion evidence regarding insanity is discussed in more detail at § 7.6.4(g).

[23] *Com. v. Bonomi*, 335 Mass 327, 347, 140 NE2d 140, 156 (1957); *Com. v. Solomonsen*, 50 Mass App 122, 735 NE2d 411 (2000) (where witness did not appear to understand the word "substance," it was permissible to ask him for the "meaning" of what the defendant had said, but court notes it is not inviting questions or answers that edge into interpretation).

[24] *Com. v. Dyous*, 436 Mass 719, 729, 767 NE2d 51, 61 (2002) (meaning of the phrase "wet them up" was to kill people); *Com. v. Henderson*, 434 Mass 155, 160, 747 NE2d 659, 663 (2001) (parties maintained an affectionate relationship for several years and victim's understanding of defendant's expressions was admissible); *Commonwealth v. Anderson*, 425 Mass 685, 687, n.5, 682 NE2d 859, 862 (1997) ("cap him"

that a witness's understanding of language is not dispositive and that they are free to find the meaning of the language as a factual matter.[25]

§ 7.3 Opinions on Ultimate Issues

§ 7.3.1 Federal Rule and Proposed Mass Rule 704

The Federal Rules of Evidence have explicitly abolished the ultimate issue rule, with the exception of testimony regarding sanity in a criminal case. Proposed Mass R Evid 704 is identical to paragraph (a) of the Federal Rule, but does not have the exception in paragraph (b) for psychiatric testimony in criminal cases. Fed R Evid 704 provides:

Opinion on Ultimate Issue

> (a) Except as provided in subdivision (b), testimony in the form of an opinion or inference otherwise admissible is not objectionable because it embraces an ultimate issue to be decided by the trier of fact.
>
> (b) No expert witness testifying with respect to the mental state or condition of a defendant in a criminal case may state an opinion or inference as to whether the defendant did or did not have the mental state or condition constituting an element of the crime charged or of a defense thereto. Such ultimate issues are matters for the trier of fact alone.

There are two basic reasons for the relaxation of the ultimate issue rule: (1) the rule proved difficult to apply in that the distinction between ultimate and non-ultimate issues was often impossible to make; and (2) the rationale for the rule—that such testimony usurped the province of the jury—was not justified in that the jury is free to disregard opinion testimony and draw its own conclusions. Rule 704 follows the basic approach of modern opinion rules, which is to admit opinions when admission is helpful to the trier of fact.

---

meant to fire pistol or shoot); *Commonwealth v. Strahan*, 39 Mass App Ct 928, 929, 657 NE2d 234, 236 (1995) (ship's mate "took the defendant's remarks as a threat to sink the boat").

[25] *Com. v. Henderson*, 434 Mass 155, 160, n.9, 747 NE2d 659, 663 (2001).

§ 7.3.2 Massachusetts Practice: Opinion on Ultimate Issue Is Generally Permissible

Massachusetts has always made exceptions to strict enforcement of the rule that a witness may not give an opinion on the ultimate issue in a case. In recent years the rule has been relaxed generally. The Supreme Judicial Court has repeatedly held that an expert may testify on matters within the witness's field of expertise whenever it will aid the jury in reaching a decision, even if the opinion touches on the ultimate issues.[1]

Decisions under the traditional opinion rule give no clear guidelines as to what constitutes an "ultimate issue." Insofar as this rule has meaning, it seems to preclude a witness from giving an opinion as to the legal significance of facts in issue in such a manner as to interfere with the province of the jury.[2] Neither the rationales nor the holdings of the decided cases have been consistent. There is a wide variety of decisions ruling that opinions reaching the ultimate issue are admissible.[3]

---

§ 7.3 [1] See, e.g., *Com. v. Cruz*, 413 Mass 686, 689, 602 NE2d 1089, 1091 (1992) (in murder case where defense was inability to form intent, error to exclude expert testimony that defendant's blood alcohol level would have severely affected his judgment); *Sacco v. Roupenian*, 409 Mass 25, 564 NE2d 386 (1990) (whether defendant doctor should have diagnosed breast cancer); *Martel v. MBTA*, 403 Mass 1, 525 NE2d 662 (1988) (whether driver could have prevented accident).

[2] See *Com. v. Coleman*, 366 Mass 705, 322 NE2d 407 (1975) (medical examiner improperly allowed to testify that death was a homicide, but error not prejudicial); *DeCanio v. School Committee of Boston*, 358 Mass 116, 260 NE2d 676 (1970) (proper to exclude expert testimony that suspension and dismissal of probationary teachers "would have no legitimate educational purpose" as such was opinion on ultimate issue of whether statutes in issue were patently arbitrary); *Foley v. Hotel Touraine Co.*, 326 Mass 742, 96 NE2d 698 (1951) (treasurer of corporate defendant precluded from testifying whether assistant manager had "ostensible authority" to represent hotel); *Peterson v. Foley*, 77 Mass App 348, 356, 931 NE2d 478, 486 (2010) (error to permit officer to testify who was at fault in automobile accident); *Grassi Design Group, Inc. v. Bank of America, N.A.*, 74 Mass App 456, 908 NE2d 393 (2009) (expert affidavits contained improper legal conclusions and legal argument); *Dalrymple v. Town of Winthrop*, 50 Mass App 611, 740 NE2d 204 (2000) (plaintiff's testimony in sex discrimination and retaliation claim that she believed defendants were angry because she filed complaints and wanted to punish her was a statement of the obvious rather than prejudicial opinion on ultimate issue); *Com. v. Amcan Enterprises, Inc.*, 47 Mass App 330, 712 NE2d 1205 (1999) (expert's affidavit that words and logo did not deceive consumers improperly stated the ultimate fact and conclusion of law).

[3] See *Com. v. Roderigues*, 462 Mass 415, 428, 968 NE2d 908, 920 (2012) (pediatrician's testimony that baby's injuries were not "accidental" and could not have been caused by someone stepping on him in recliner); *Com. v. Cyr*, 425 Mass 89, 96, 679 NE2d 550, 556 (1997) (medical examiner's testimony re: presence of "defensive

The Supreme Judicial Court has suggested that where opinion testimony on the ultimate issue is permitted, the trial judge should instruct the jury that the witness's interpretation is not dispositive of the matter.[4]

Despite relaxation of the ultimate issue rule as a general matter, there are a number of areas where witnesses are not permitted to express opinions that would invade the province of the jury.[5] We discuss them in the following sections.

§ 7.3.3 *Opinions About Credibility of Witnesses*

A witness is not permitted to express an opinion on the credibility of other witnesses.[6] A statement that a witness has made before trial,

---

wounds"); *Com. v. Allen*, 395 Mass 448, 480 NE2d 630 (1985) (physician's opinion on cause of defendant's black eyes); *Everett v. Bucky Warren, Inc.*, 376 Mass 280, 380 NE2d 653 (1978) (opinion of neurosurgeon with extensive experience in sports medicine as to relative safety of two types of hockey helmets); *Ford v. Boston Housing Authority*, 55 Mass App 623, 773 NE2d 471 (2002) (expert could testify that locked door was in noncompliance with State building code) (Text cited); *Foreign Car Center, Inc. v. Salem Suede, Inc.*, 40 Mass App 15, 21, 660 NE2d 687, 693 (1996) (error to exclude expert testimony regarding whether company's manufacturing and emissions control equipment was "reasonable and appropriate"); *Welch v. Keene Corp.*, 31 Mass App 157, 575 NE2d 766 (1991) (opinion about appropriate warnings on dangerous product); *Gleason v. Source Perrier, S.A.*, 28 Mass App 561, 553 NE2d 544 (1990) (opinions of doctor as to details of how glass fragment entered plaintiff's eye improperly excluded); *Burns v. 21 Combined Insurance Co. of America*, 6 Mass App 86, 373 NE2d 1189 (1978) (medical expert properly permitted to give opinion regarding date of plaintiff's total disability).

[4] *Com. v. Henderson*, 434 Mass 155, 160, n.9, 747 NE2d 659, 663 (2001) (Text cited).

[5] *Lind v. Domino's Pizza. LLC*, 87 Mass App 650, 663, 37 NE3d 1, 13 (2015) (expert witness could not provide legal conclusion on whether defendant's security plans were negligent); *See* also *Matteo v. Livingstone*, 40 Mass App 658, 663, 666 NE2d 1309, 1313 (1996) ("Although the orthodox rule has sustained considerable erosion, and opinion evidence may now come much closer to the ultimate issue if it will aid the jury, experts are still foreclosed from expressing an opinion on commonplace conclusions that juries may reach without expert assistance.") (Text cited).

[6] *Com. v. Stuckich*, 450 Mass 449, 879 NE2d 105 (2008) (prosecutor may not ask defendant if other witnesses were "lying," or ask another witness if she believed victim's allegations); *Com. v. Perry*, 432 Mass 214, 236, 733 NE2d 83, 102 (2000) (expert opinion that chronic marijuana use affects memory was properly excluded as comment on credibility, where expert had not observed effect of drug consumption on witness and there was no evidence linking witness's memory problems to her drug use); *Com. v. Reed*, 417 Mass 558, 631 NE2d 552 (1994) (defendant not entitled to offer expert testimony on either witness's ability or willingness to tell the truth, hence defendant not entitled to discovery of witness's psychiatric files in order to obtain expert testimony on his veracity) (Text cited); *Com. v. Sires*, 413 Mass 292, 304, 596 NE2d

however, that commented on the credibility of another witness may be admissible.[7] The special problems of "vouching" by expert witnesses in child abuse cases are discussed in § 7.6.4.c.

§ 7.3.4 Opinions About Guilt of Criminal Defendant

Opinions concerning the identity of a suspect or a perpetrator of a crime are normally inadmissible in a criminal trial.[8] Such evidence may be admissible for an oblique purpose, however.[9] This evidence must be approached with caution, and it is not permitted for an officer to explain his actions by "a general expression of the officer's opinion of guilt, followed by a recital of all the evidence against the defendant."[10] The prosecutor should proceed "by inquiring of the officer the reason for each specific omission or decision."[11] Because it amounts to a comment on the guilt of a defendant, it is impermissible for a police officer testifying as an expert to state that a given set of facts constituted a drug transaction, or that he observed a drug transaction taking place.[12] A persuasive argument may be made that prosecutors should not be permitted to circumvent this rule by asking the

---

1018, 1026 (1992) (not error to exclude expert's testimony about defendant's state of mind on morning after killing, where it could have been viewed as opinion that defendant told the truth as to how much alcohol he drank). See *Com. v. McIntyre*, 430 Mass 529, 538, 721 NE2d 911, 919 (1999) (emergency room nurse's opinion of the victim's level of consciousness did not amount to an opinion on credibility)(Text cited).

[7] *Com. v. Colon*, 64 Mass App 303, 832 NE2d 1154 (2005) (defendant's answer during police interrogation was admissible, where officer had asked why victim would accuse him of sexually abusing her and he answered "Maybe she's mad at me. She's kind of evil and she lies a lot.").

[8] *Com. v. Perez*, 460 Mass 683, 954 NE2d 1 (2011) (error to permit witness to give opinion that defendant had killed the victim); *Com. v. Lennon*, 399 Mass 443, 445, 504 NE2d 1051, 1053 (1987) (opinion by victim's wife that defendant was her husband's killer should have been excluded); *Com. v. Garcia*, 46 Mass App 466, 707 NE2d 328 (1999) (officer not qualified to give legal opinion on whether he had probable cause, court notes defendant's argument that question approached comment on his guilt).

[9] See *Com. v. Lodge*, 431 Mass 461, 727 NE2d 1194 (2000) (when defendant puts in issue the quality of police judgment or investigation, police may explain why their action was correct under the circumstances); *Com. v. Miller*, 361 Mass 644, 282 NE2d 394 (1972) (evidence that police knew certain people suspected defendant was admissible, not to prove guilt, but for limited purpose of justifying undercover activity, and thus to rebut entrapment claim).

[10] *Com. v. Lodge*, supra, 431 Mass at 467.

[11] *Id.*

[12] *Com. v. Rodriguez*, 456 Mass 578, 592, 925 NE2d 21, 32 (2010) (officer's belief that defendant was guilty cannot be admitted through indirect expressions; error to

officer whether the observations he made were "consistent with" a drug transaction.[13] Nonetheless, the courts have allowed testimony where the officer's statement is limited to the fact that what he observed was "consistent with" a drug transaction.[14] Given the apparent confusion created by these cases, and the continued elicitation of such testimony by prosecutors, the present authors believe it is time for the appellate courts to resolve this problem with a clear statement that the "consistent with" language is unacceptable as an opinion on the defendant's guilt. The equivocation in the present law does not send a clear signal to either trial judges or prosecutors.[15]

---

admit officer's radio transmission that was code for recovering drugs from a buyer); *Com. v. Barbosa*, 421 Mass 547, 658 NE2d 966 (1995) (narcotics officer's testimony that drug transaction had taken place constituted comment on defendant's guilt and should not have been admitted); *Com. v. DeJesus*, 87 Mass App 198, 26 NE3d 1134 (2015) (improper to ask officer hypothetical question that closely tracks the facts of the case so that it becomes a non-hypothetical comment on the actual actors); *Com. v. Grissett*, 66 Mass App 454, 848 NE2d 441 (2006) (testimony by officer that cocaine seized from defendant was "far more than a user would carry on his person," and that "It's clearly in my opinion for drug distribution," was improper and presented in conclusory form in terms of whether defendant had committed the offense) (Text cited); *Com. v. Cavanaugh*, 63 Mass App 111, 823 NE2d 429 (2005) (error to allow police sergeant to testify that defendant was engaged in drug dealing); *Com. v. Ortiz*, 50 Mass App 304, 737 NE2d 482 (2000) (undercover officer's testimony that he believed defendant was a "runner" was improper).

[13] *Com. v. Tanner*, 45 Mass App 576, 581, 700 NE2d 282, 286 (1998) ("such semantical differences almost certainly make no difference to jurors"). As the court noted in *Tanner*, "The better practice in drug cases, especially when an expert is a percipient witness, is to confine opinion testimony to the explanation of specific unusual or cryptic conduct, without stating, in any form, whether such conduct amounts to a criminal offense." 45 Mass App at 581, 700 NE2d at 287. See also *Com. v. Gant*, 51 Mass App 314, 321, 745 NE2d 371, 377 (2001) ("we have viewed semantic locutions such as 'consistent with' to serve no educative function").

[14] *Com. v. MacDonald*, 459 Mass 148, 163, 945 NE2d 260, 271 (2011) (permissible to ask expert witness hypothetical question based on facts in evidence to elicit opinion that facts were "consistent with" a drug transaction; court distinguishes between such testimony by expert witnesses and percipient witnesses, noting in the latter case the line between "specific observations and expert generalizations [becomes] blurred"; court emphasizes expert may not *directly* express views on defendant's guilt).

[15] Consider *Com. v. Lobo*, 82 Mass App 803, 810, 978 NE2d 807, 812 (2012) (permitting officer to testify that possession of 22 grams of cocaine hidden in defendant's private parts coupled with absence of smoking paraphernalia was more consistent with distribution than personal use); *Com. v. Madera*, 76 Mass App 154, 163, 920 NE2d 312, 320 (2010) (permitting testimony by officer that "my opinion is absolutely that the first items there (sic) for possession with intent to distribute it" because "the opinion did not stand alone but was based upon a series of opinions, properly expressed, that began with a question in proper form"); *Com. v. Delgado*, 51 Mass App 661, 747 NE2d 1265 (2001), where the witness testified that given the quantity found, the defendant "would be a distributor of heroin." The trial judge then interrupted to ask,

It is not permissible to ask an expert for an opinion regarding the defendant's intent.[16] On the other hand, it has been held that it is not an impermissible comment on the guilt of the defendant, or an improper invasion of the province of the jury, for an arson expert to give an opinion that a fire was intentionally set.[17]

The prosecution may not offer syndrome evidence regarding the characteristics of perpetrators of crime. See § 7.6.5.b.

"I take it by that you mean that would be consistent with somebody who might be distributing, correct?" 51 Mass App at 663. After noting that the witness's answer was an improper opinion on the defendant's guilt, the appellate court held that the trial judge had "transformed the answer into a statement which satisfied existing rules of evidence on the subject," and therefore there was no error. *Id.* The court goes on to say that it would have been "better practice" to strike the improper response and tell the jury to disregard it, but that it was within the trial court's discretion to handle it as it did. 51 Mass App at 664. The court notes that even if this were error, it was harmless given other evidence. Finally, the court concludes with an approving citation to *Com. v. Tanner*, supra, and urges that expert testimony should be "explanatory" and "not be presented in conclusory form indicating that a defendant did or did not commit a particular offense." 51 Mass App at 664-665. See also *Com. v. Lopez*, 55 Mass App 741, 774 NE2d 667 (2002) (officer initially testified that, based on the facts, his opinion was that drugs were intended for distribution, then prosecutor asked whether his opinion was the facts were "consistent with distribution"—the court concludes there was no error because officer was not a percipient witness). *Delgado* and *Lopez* treated the "consistent with" amendment as a sufficient antidote for the fact that the witness has already testified that in his opinion the defendant committed the crime charged. This is meaningless formalism.

[16] *Com. v. Sepheus*, 468 Mass 160, 9 NE3d 800 (2014) (ineffective assistance of counsel for defense lawyer to bring out on cross-examination that officer thought defendant was a dealer); *Com. v. Hamilton*, 459 Mass 422, 945 NE2d 877 (2011) (error to allow police officer to testify that he interpreted defendant's words as a "threat"); *Com. v. Dessources*, 74 Mass App 232, 238, 905 NE2d 586, 591 (2009) (error to permit officer to testify that defendant possessed drugs with intent to sell); *Com. v. Acosta*, 81 Mass App 836, 842, 969 NE2d 720, 725 (2012) (testimony of narcotics expert that defendant possessed 3.16 grams of cocaine in five twist bags with intent to sell was "wholly speculative," "inherently flawed and legally incompetent"); *Com. v. Santiago*, 41 Mass App 916, 670 NE2d 199 (1996) (permissible to ask veteran detective whether a given amount of heroin was inconsistent with personal use, but error to permit him to testify that heroin "was intended for" distribution).

[17] *Com. v. Lugo*, 63 Mass App 204, 824 NE2d 481 (2005). See also *Com. v. Cheromcka*, 66 Mass App 771, 786, 850 NE2d 1088, 1101 (2006) (in case alleging misuse of public funds, permissible for accounting expert to testify it was "unusual" for petty cash fund to contain large amounts of money and for employee to contribute her personal funds to it for two years).

§ 7.3.5 *Rape and Sexual Abuse Cases*

In rape and sexual abuse cases, if the expert witness limits his testimony to observations made during his physical examination, and expresses no opinion on whether the alleged victim was "raped," the testimony is clearly admissible.[18] When the witness goes beyond that, however, there are significant inconsistencies in the reported decisions concerning whether expert testimony improperly reached the ultimate issue. One line of cases appears to hold clearly that an expert witness may not express an opinion directly on the question of whether a rape, forcible assault, or sexual assault occurred.[19] Despite those cases, however, on occasion opinions touching in one way or another on the ultimate issue have been permitted.[20]

---

[18] *Com. v. Crichlow*, 30 Mass App 901, 565 NE2d 816 (1991). See *Com. v. Wise*, 39 Mass App 922, 655 NE2d 643 (1995) (where medical records included notation "here for molestation rape evaluation" and contained heading "Record of Possible Sexual Assault," but contained no opinion by medical provider about whether sexual assault occurred, not error to admit them).

[19] *Com. v. Jewett*, 442 Mass 356, 368, 813 NE2d 452, 462 (2004) ("[I]n the absence of special circumstances, an expert may not be asked whether a rape or sexual assault has occurred."); *Com. v. Federico*, 425 Mass 844, 849, 683 NE2d 1035, 1039 (1997) (expert's testimony suggesting that sexual abuse had in fact occurred was inadmissible); *Com. v. Colin C.*, 419 Mass 54, 643 NE2d 19 (1994) (error to permit expert testimony that children were sexually abused, noting distinction in cases between expert testimony relating generally to behavioral characteristics of sexual assault and sexual abuse victims, and testimony that an alleged victim was in fact sexually assaulted); *Com. v. Gardner*, 350 Mass 664, 216 NE2d 558 (1966) (reversible error where gynecologist allowed to give opinion that there had been "forcible entry" in rape prosecution); *Com. v. LaCaprucia*, 41 Mass App 496, 671 NE2d 984 (1996) (error to permit expert to give characteristic sexual profile testimony that presented defendant's family situation as prone to sexual abuse).

[20] See *Com. v. Montmeny*, 360 Mass 526, 276 NE2d 688 (1971) (permissible for the prosecutor to ask a physician whether the observations he had made during his physical examination were "consistent with the history" [of rape] he had taken from the victim); *Com. v. Lanning*, 32 Mass App 279, 288, 589 NE2d 318, 324 (1992) (error, if any, was harmless where doctor testified hymenal ring was intact, leading to conclusion full penetration had not occurred, but observations were consistent with insertion of tip of penis into complainant's genitalia); *Com. v. Lewandowski*, 22 Mass App Ct 148, 491 NE2d 670 (1986) (prosecution's expert, a pediatrician, properly permitted to testify that results of his examination of the victim were consistent with sexual molestation); *Com. v. Howard*, 355 Mass 526, 246 NE2d 419 (1969) (doctor's testimony that the probable cause of a widening in the private area of a girl was male organ penetration, interpreted as equivalent to testimony that the physical condition observed was consistent with male penetration, held no error).

B. EXPERT TESTIMONY

§ 7.4 General Principles

§ 7.4.1 Federal Rule and Proposed Mass Rule 702

Federal R Evid 702 provides:

> If scientific, technical, or other specialized knowledge will assist the trier of fact to understand the evidence or to determine a fact in issue, a witness qualified as an expert by knowledge, skill, experience, training, or education, may testify thereto in the form of an opinion or otherwise, if (1) the testimony is based upon sufficient facts or data, (2) the testimony is the product of reliable principles and methods, and (3) the witness has applied the principles and methods reliably to the facts of the case.

Proposed Mass R Evid 702 provides:

> If scientific, technical, or other specialized knowledge will assist the trier of fact to understand the evidence or to determine a fact in issue, a witness qualified as an expert by knowledge, skill, experience, training, or education, may testify thereto in the form of an opinion or otherwise.

Proposed Mass R Evid 702 codifies existing Massachusetts case law, providing that prior to the admission of expert testimony the judge must determine whether the situation is a proper one for expert testimony and whether the proposed expert is properly qualified.[1] These determinations are governed by Proposed Mass R Evid 104(a).[2] The

---

§ 7.4 [1] See, e.g., *Simon v. Solomon*, 385 Mass 91, 105, 431 NE2d 556, 566 (1982) (court refers with approval to standard of admissibility of expert testimony as stated in Fed R Evid 702 and 704); *Terrio v. McDonough*, 16 Mass App 163, 175-176, 450 NE2d 190, 198 (1983) (expert testimony as to rape trauma syndrome, an area of specialized medical knowledge, properly admitted to assist jury in understanding evidence; court cited Proposed Mass R Evid 702).

[2] Proposed Mass R Evid 104(a) provides:

> **Questions of admissibility generally**. Preliminary questions concerning the qualification or competency of a person to be a witness, the existence of a privilege, or the admissibility of evidence shall be determined by the court, subject to the provisions of subdivisions (b) and (f). In making its determination it is not bound by the rules of evidence except those with respect to privileges, the existence of a conspiracy, and on questions arising in hearings on motions to suppress evidence.

three final requirements of the Federal Rule that are not set forth in the Proposed Mass Rule are also consistent with Massachusetts practice, as discussed below.[3]

The test used under the Rules in determining whether the situation is a proper one for expert testimony, as under case law, is whether the testimony will assist the trier of fact in determining a fact in issue or in understanding the evidence.[4] This decision is dependent on the facts of the case in question. Clearly, the testimony would be permitted where the inference to be drawn or opinion to be given is one for which more than the equipment of everyday experience is required. Additionally, when the testimony will be of assistance, it will be admissible, in the judge's discretion, even though the matter may be within the knowledge of the trier of fact. Where lay jurors are as capable as the expert of assessing the facts, expert testimony may be excluded.[5]

Expert testimony may be appropriate in the discretion of the trial judge, even though not necessary.[6]

---

[3] *Com. v. Ortiz*, 463 Mass 402, 411, 974 NE2d 1079, 1087 (2012) (the five foundational requirements for expert testimony in a criminal case are: (1) the expert testimony will assist the trier of fact, (2) the witness is qualified as an expert in the relevant area of inquiry, (3) the expert's opinion is based on facts or data of a type reasonably relied on by experts to form opinions in the relevant field, (4) the process or theory underlying the opinion is reliable, and (5) the process or theory is applied to the particular facts of the case in a reliable manner. The trustworthiness of the expert is not a foundational requirement, but an issue to be decided by the jury.)

[4] *Com. v. Portillo*, 462 Mass 324, 330, 968 NE2d 395, 401 (2012) (where parties cannot agree on English-language translation of recording in a foreign language, parties may present testimony from expert translators so jury may resolve the issue).

[5] *Com. v. Nerette*, 432 Mass 534, 735 NE2d 1242 (2000) (proper to reject testimony from defense psychologist on voluntariness of confession, where expert relied almost entirely on information furnished by defendant, conducted no testing, and had neither listened to audio tape of confession nor watched videotape made after statement); *Com. v. Little*, 453 Mass 766, 768, 906 NE2d 286, 289 (2009) (Text cited); *Com. v. Miranda*, 441 Mass 783, 793, 809 NE2d 487, 495 (2004) (Text cited); *Com. v. Peppicelli*, 70 Mass App 87, 872 NE2d 1142 (2007) (not abuse of discretion to exclude expert testimony regarding objective standards on the use of firearm in self-defense); *OneBeacon Ins. Group v. RSC Corp.*, 69 Mass App 409, 868 NE2d 644 (2007) (where jury heard evidence as to amount of rain and speed of winds and could reach conclusion about adequacy of tarpaulin protection without testimony about statistical likelihood of such storms, not error to exclude testimony from meteorologist that storm was so unusual in ferocity as to be "act of God" for which preparation was useless).

[6] *Bernier v. Boston Edison Co.*, 380 Mass 372, 403 NE2d 391 (1980).

§ 7.4.2 *When Expert Testimony Is Required*

Findings of fact as to technical matters beyond the scope of ordinary experience are not warranted in the absence of expert testimony supporting such findings. Expert evidence regarding the standard of care and whether it has been breached is required in professional malpractice actions,[7] but not in bar disciplinary proceedings to establish a rule violation or a standard of care.[8] Expert

[7] *Anderson v. Attar*, 65 Mass App 910, 841 NE2d 1286 (2006) (expert is required when jurors are not competent from their own knowledge and experience to determine whether dentist was negligent); *Frullo v. Landenberger*, 61 Mass App 814, 814 NE2d 1105 (2004) (in legal malpractice case, expert required to prove effect of attorney's negligence on plaintiff's prospects in underlying case); *Goldberg v. Northeastern University*, 60 Mass App 707, 805 NE2d 517 (2004) (expert required to establish that there was negligence in the creation, staffing, and operation of a medical facility); *Atlas Tack Corp. v. Donabed*, 47 Mass App 221, 712 NE2d 617 (1999) (expert required to establish standard of care of reasonable engineer); *Harris v. Magri*, 39 Mass App 349, 656 NE2d 585 (1995) (expert required on standard of care in legal malpractice action, whether viewed as negligence claim or contract claim); *Edwards v. Boland*, 41 Mass App 375, 670 NE2d 404 (1996) (expert testimony may afford sufficient basis for application of res ipsa loquitur doctrine in medical malpractice cases); *Broderick v. Gibbs*, 1 Mass App 822, 296 NE2d 708 (1973) (possible disbelief of expert testimony as to good medical practice cannot fill void left by absence of expert testimony of bad medical practice). But see *LeBlanc v. Logan Hilton Joint Venture*, 463 Mass 316, 331, 974 NE2d 34, 45 (2012) (where design team of architects actually knew of deficiencies but failed to fulfill its contractual duty to report them, and where deficiencies presented an obvious risk to safety, evidence of professional negligence was sufficient without expert opinion); *Cottam v. CVS Pharmacy*, 436 Mass 316, 326, 764 NE2d 814, 823 (2002) (plaintiff not required to call expert witness on breach of duty to warn of side effects by pharmacist, question was adequacy of the warning, not technical performance by pharmacist); *Global NAPs, Inc. v. Awiszus*, 457 Mass 489, 501, 930 NE2d 1262, 1272 (2010) (expert testimony not required to prove that failure to file timely appeal violated standard of care); *Matter of Tobin*, 417 Mass 81, 628 NE2d 1268 (1994) (expert testimony not required to prove ethical violations by lawyers); *Collins v. Baron*, 392 Mass 565, 569, 467 NE2d 171, 173-174 (1984) (admission of defendant doctor may be sufficient to justify a finding of negligence); *Kelly v. Brigham & Women's Hospital*, 51 Mass App 297, 745 NE2d 969 (2001) (expert not required to establish negligence in wrongful autopsy claim); *Fall River Savings Bank v. Callahan*, 18 Mass App 76, 82-83, 463 NE2d 555, 560-561 (1984) (trial judge in legal malpractice case involving conveyancing may obviate the need for, or supplement, expert testimony by resort to opinions, standard texts, and articles in law reviews). Cf. *Sullivan v. Utica Mutual Insurance Co.*, 439 Mass 387, 403, 788 NE2d 522, 536 (2003) (expert testimony required to establish standard of care owed by liability insurer in overseeing defense of third-party claim; admissions by insurance company's agents as to standard of care were the functional equivalent of expert testimony).

[8] *In re Crossen*, 450 Mass 533, 571, 880 NE2d 352, 380 (2008) (generally expert testimony is not appropriate in bar disciplinary proceedings because fact finder does not need such assistance).

testimony is required to make a finding of sexual dangerousness,[9] to explain sophisticated medical issues,[10] in some circumstances to establish the existence of emotional distress,[11] to establish engineering

---

[9] *In re Johnstone*, 453 Mass 544, 903 NE2d 1074 (2009); *Com. v. Bruno*, 432 Mass 489, 735 NE2d 1222 (2000) (expert evidence is required to temporarily commit offender as sexually dangerous person); *Com. v. Dube*, 59 Mass App 476, 796 NE2d 859 (2003) (*Bruno* requires conclusion that expert testimony is required to meet Commonwealth's burden of proof at trial on merits of sexually dangerous person charge); *Com. v. Boyer*, 61 Mass App 582, 812 NE2d 1235 (2004) (same; preliminary report submitted at probable cause hearing and subsequently recanted at trial was insufficient evidence to prove beyond a reasonable doubt that defendant was a sexually dangerous person).

[10] *Reckis v. Johnson & Johnson*, 471 Mass 272, 28 NE3d 445 (2015) (expert testimony required to establish medical causation); *Com. v. Scott*, 464 Mass 355, 982 NE2d 1166 (2013) (conviction requiring proof of impairment of an organ reversed where medical records established Grade II hepatic laceration of liver, but no expert explained effect of same on liver's ability to function); *Sparrow v. Demonico*, 461 Mass 322, 960 NE2d 296 (2012) (medical evidence is required to establish an incapacity to contract); *Matsuyama v. Birnbaum*, 452 Mass 1, 28, 890 NE2d 819, 841 (2008) (expert testimony required to assess damages under proportional method in "loss of chance" medical malpractice case); *Com. v. Kirkpatrick*, 423 Mass 436, 447, 668 NE2d 790, 797 (1996) (expert testimony required to establish likelihood of transmission of sexually transmissible disease); *Department of Revenue v. Sorrentino*, 408 Mass 340, 557 NE2d 1376 (1990) (error to admit human leukocyte antigen test results without expert testimony that proper testing procedures were employed); *Com. v. Kennedy*, 389 Mass 308, 313-314, 450 NE2d 167, 171-172 (1983) (exhibition of a child to jury for comparison with features of alleged father should not be allowed absent expert testimony concerning the probability that specific physical characteristics were inherited); *Com. v. Shellenberger*, 64 Mass App 70, 831 NE2d 375 (2005) (in motor vehicle homicide prosecution, error to admit evidence of amphetamines in defendant's body without reliable evidence of amount or concentration of the drug and expert testimony that such a concentration would impair her ability to operate a motor vehicle); *Com. v. Lloyd*, 45 Mass App 931, 702 NE2d 395 (1998) (expert required to explain effects of Prozac on perception and memory). But see *Com. v. Moran*, 439 Mass 482, 789 NE2d 121 (2003) (expert not required to explain terms "laparoscopy" and "sigmoidoscopy" before hospital record containing terms could be admitted—nature of procedures was clear from record itself).

[11] *Sullivan v. Boston Gas Co.*, 414 Mass 129, 138, 605 NE2d 805, 810 (1993) (expert medical testimony may be required to establish showing of objective corroboration of emotional distress in negligent infliction of emotional distress case). But see *Cady v. Marcella*, 49 Mass App 334, 729 NE2d 1125 (2000) (expert not required in intentional infliction of emotional distress claim where other evidence established that mental distress was caused by wrongful attachment of plaintiffs' property); *Bresnahan v. McAuliffe*, 47 Mass App 278, 712 NE2d 1173 (1999) (under circumstances of case, involving negligent infliction of emotional distress, expert testimony not required to establish objective evidence requirement).

propositions,[12] and often to prove causation.[13] There is, however, no bright line test for determining when expert testimony is required.[14]

---

[12] *Enrich v. Windmere Corp.*, 416 Mass 83, 87, 616 NE2d 1081, 1084 (1993) (presence of defect in electric fan could not be inferred in absence of expert testimony); *Stewart v. Worcester Gas Light Co.*, 341 Mass 425, 435, 170 NE2d 330, 337 (1960) (expert required to establish propriety of a "dresser coupling" in gas pipe close to house); *Esturban v. Mass Bay Transportation Authority*, 68 Mass App 911, 865 NE2d 834 (2007) (expert required to establish that narrow escalator constituted a defective and dangerous design). But see *Smith v. Ariens Co.*, 375 Mass 620, 625, 377 NE2d 954 (1978) (expert testimony is not always required to establish liability in design defect case, jury could find that protuberances on snowmobile were a defect based on their lay knowledge); *Petchel v. Collins*, 59 Mass App 517, 796 NE2d 886 (2003) (expert not required to prove that propane tanks wrapped by customers were flammable and explosive in moving truck).

[13] *Aetna Life & Casualty Insurance Co. v. Com.*, 50 Mass App 373, 737 NE2d 880 (2000) (expert testimony required to prove that absence of chair with arms caused back injury in worker's compensation claim); *Lally v. Volkswagen Aktiengesellschaft*, 45 Mass App 317, 322, 698 NE2d 28, 34 (1998) (expert required to prove that paraplegic's injury was caused by striking open glove box door during crash); *Triangle Dress, Inc. v. Bay State Service, Inc.*, 356 Mass 440, 252 NE2d 889 (1969) (expert required to prove cause of fire in air conditioner). But see *Nemet v. Boston Water & Sewer Comm'n*, 56 Mass App 104, 110, 775 NE2d 750, 755 (2002) (expert not required to establish causation for flooding).

[14] See, *Com. v. Rosa*, 468 Mass 231, 9 NE3d 832 (2014) (expert not required to explain "street jargon" used by defendant in telephone call); *Com. v. Bundy*, 465 Mass 538, 989 NE2d 496 (2013) (expert testimony not required to introduce evidence of operation of Xbox, Web camera, and accessories that allowed defendant to broadcast child masturbating on television screen); *Morgan v. Laboratory Corp. of America*, 65 Mass 816, 844 NE2d 689 (2006) (expert not required to establish negligence in reporting lab results where failure to report was not result of deliberated judgment on the part of physician or skilled staff, or result of a failure to institute policies and procedures for reporting of life-threatening results, but was merely an alleged inadequacy in the actual reporting of indisputably urgent test results); *Com. v. Oliveira*, 431 Mass 609, 728 NE2d 320 (2000) (expert testimony not required as basis for prosecutor's argument that some women stay in abusive relationships for a variety of social and economic reasons); *Com. v. Trowbridge*, 419 Mass 750, 647 NE2d 413 (1995) (trial judge not required to employ expert to determine whether eight-year-old victim was competent to testify); *Com. v. Dockham*, 405 Mass 618, 542 NE2d 591 (1989) (no expert testimony required to sustain judge's conclusion that child witness would suffer emotional trauma if he testified in open court); *Pitts v. Wingate At Brighton, Inc.*, 82 Mass App 285, 972 NE2d 74 (2012) (expert testimony not required for lay jurors to appreciate that allowing nursing home patient to fall to floor could cause broken bone); *Campbell v. Cape & Islands Healthcare Services, Inc.*, 81 Mass App 252, 961 NE2d 1096 (2012) (where provision of Code of Mass Regulations with respect to drawing blood was admitted in evidence, there was no requirement that a witness give opinion testimony that Code was violated in order for judge to instruct jury on the significance of failure to comply with safety regulation in negligence case); *Com. v. Berendson*, 73 Mass App Ct 395, 400, 897 NE2d 1276, 1281 (2008) (expert testimony not required to support prosecutor's closing argument that rape is a crime of violence and degradation, not sexual pleasure); *Figueiredo Case*, 49 Mass App 906, 729 NE2d 1122 (2000) (expert not required to explain straightforward corporate tax return) (Text cited); *Com. v. Adames*, 41 Mass App

The failure to consult with and employ expert witnesses may amount to ineffective assistance of counsel in criminal cases.[15] However, where the decision not to call experts at trial is a reasonable tactical choice, failure to do so does not amount to ineffective assistance.[16]

14, 668 NE2d 848 (1996) (expert testimony not required to lay foundation for police officer's testimony that bill dusted with fluorescent powder glowed under ultraviolet light); *Town of Shrewsbury v. Commissioner of Environmental Protection*, 38 Mass App 946, 648 NE2d 1287 (1995) (DEP not required to base its decision that a composting operation created a condition of air pollution upon scientific evidence).

[15] *Com. v. LaBrie*, 473 Mass 754, 46 NE3d 519 (2016) (failure to consult oncologist where defendant was charged with attempted murder for failing to provide chemotherapy); *Com. v. Baker*, 440 Mass 519, 526, 800 NE2d 267, 274 (2003) (defendant was prejudiced by change in prosecution theory requiring expert response and failure of defense counsel to take steps to secure expert testimony after learning of the change); *Com. v. Alvarez*, 433 Mass 93, 740 NE2d 610 (2000) (ineffective assistance to fail to provide expert medical records concerning head injuries); *Com. v. Roberio*, 428 Mass 278, 700 NE2d 830 (1998) (failure to investigate insanity defense); *Com. v. Martin*, 427 Mass 816, 821, 696 NE2d 904, 907 (1998) (ineffective assistance not to insist upon confirmatory test, rather than relying upon screening test, to prove presence of LSD); *Com. v. Haggerty*, 400 Mass 437, 509 NE2d 1163 (1987) (murder conviction reversed where counsel failed to investigate whether victim's death was caused by heart problems, rather than beating by defendant, the sole defense available); *Com. v. Baran*, 7 Mass App 256, 275, 905 NE2d 1122, 1139 (2009) (ineffective assistance not to employ expert with respect to interviewing of alleged child sexual assault victims).

[16] *Com. v. Drayton*, 473 Mass 23, 31, 38 NE3d 247, 254 (2015) (where effects of alcohol, drugs, and sleep deprivation on testimony were thoroughly explored on cross-examination, failure to call an expert was not ineffective); *Com. v. Riley*, 467 Mass 799, 7 NE3d 1060 (2014) (counsel was not ineffective in failing to investigate reliability of femoral blood analysis of clonidine in victim's body, where defense presented well thought out case that death resulted from pneumonia rather than drug overdose); *Com. v. Watson*, 455 Mass 246, 257, 915 NE2d 1052, 1061 (2009) (decision not to request funds for eyewitness identification expert was strategic and not manifestly unreasonable); *Com. v. Caillot*, 454 Mass 245, 264, 909 NE2d 1, 18 (2009) (question of whether it was physically impossible to blow out rear passenger windows with bullets was not abstruse and expert was not required to belabor it); *Com. v. Morgan*, 453 Mass 54, 899 NE2d 770 (2009) (where defense counsel used prosecution expert to support defense theory of case, not ineffective to call defense expert); *Com. v. Frank*, 433 Mass 185, 740 NE2d 629 (2001) (reasonable not to call expert in order to avoid potentially damaging cross-examination); *Com. v. Cormier*, 427 Mass 446, 451, 693 NE2d 1015, 1019 (1998) (fact that defense counsel consulted with experts does not mean that it was ineffective assistance not to call them as witnesses). See also, *Com. v. Spray*, 467 Mass 456, 5 NE3d 891 (2014) (not ineffective assistance of counsel to fail to explore expert testimony for insanity defense where counsel had no facts that would have put her on notice of need to obtain psychiatric evaluation); *Com. v. Carr*, 464 Mass 865, 874, 986 NE2d 380, 398 (2013) (not error to deny funds to defendant for identification expert on effect of 30-year delay in trial on witnesses' memories, where witnesses were familiar with defendant before crime); *In re Edwards*, 464 Mass 454, 984 NE2d 276 (2013) (trial judge is bound by determination by CPCS as to hourly rate of expert witness, but retains authority to determine if total amount billed was reasonably necessary to provide defendant with as effective a case as he would have had if financially

Where a new scientific test is developed after a conviction, a defendant may be entitled to a new trial.[17]

§ 7.4.3 Expert Testimony Is Not Binding on Trier of Fact

Experts' conclusions are not binding on the trier of fact, who may decline to adopt them in whole or in part.[18] As a corollary, where testimony from various experts is conflicting, it is for the trier of fact to determine which expert's testimony to accept, if any.[19] The trial judge's disagreement with expert testimony does not constitute a sufficient ground for excluding it.[20]

---

able to pay); *Com. v. Alicea*, 464 Mass 837, 850, 985 NE2d 1197, 1209 (2013) ("claim of ineffective assistance of counsel for failure to call an expert witness is generally doomed" without affidavits to disclose content of omitted expert testimony).

[17] *Com. v. Meggs*, 30 Mass App 111, 565 NE2d 1249 (1991) (defendant sought new trial based on new tests that determine the blood grouping of semen donors; court held issue should not have been decided on affidavits alone, remanded for evidentiary hearing). Where an indigent defendant fails to make a sufficient showing that expert assistance is reasonably likely to uncover evidence that might warrant a new trial, he is not entitled to the post-conviction appointment of experts at state expense. *Com. v. Morgan*, 453 Mass 54, 64, 899 NE2d 770, 778 (2009).

[18] The Supreme Judicial Court recommended language for a jury instruction on evaluating expert testimony in *Com. v. Hinds*, 450 Mass 1, 12 n.7, 875 NE2d 488, 496 (2007). See *Police Dept. of Boston v. Kavaleski*, 463 Mass 680, 694, 978 NE2d 55, 66 (2012) (Civil Service Commission could discredit expert testimony of psychiatrist on fitness of job applicant even in the absence of contrary expert testimony); *In re Wyatt*, 428 Mass 347, 360, 701 NE2d 337, 346 (1998) (experts' opinions that petitioner was a sexually dangerous person were not entitled to conclusive weight, even though no contrary opinions were offered). See *Com. v. Guiliana*, 390 Mass 464, 457 NE2d 275 (1983) (court acknowledged power of jury to disregard expert testimony, but nevertheless exercised its extraordinary power in a first degree murder case under GL 278, § 33E, to set aside the conviction and order a new trial because of a substantial likelihood of miscarriage of justice). But cf. *New Boston Garden Corp. v. Board of Assessors of Boston*, 383 Mass 456, 471-472, 420 NE2d 298, 307-308 (1981) (while Appellate Tax Board is not bound by expert testimony, it must have basis in evidence for alternative finding). *Pollard v. Conservation Comm'n of Norfolk*, 73 Mass App 340, 897 NE2d 1242 (2008) (administrative agency must have basis in the record for rejection of uncontradicted expert testimony). Opinions of experts may be given presumptive effect by statute. Under MGL c. 15, § 11A, the conclusion of the impartial physician that an employee's disability has as its predominant contributing cause an injury arising during the course of employment must be accepted as true in the absence of contradictory medical evidence. *Case of May*, 67 Mass App 209, 852 NE2d 1120 (2006).

[19] *Com. v. Lyons*, 426 Mass 466, 688 NE2d 1350 (1998) (conflicting opinions regarding competence of defendant).

[20] *Com. v. Roberio*, 428 Mass 278, 700 NE2d 830 (1998) (error for court to deny new trial motion because he did not believe expert, credibility was for the jury); *Com. v. O'Brien*, 423 Mass 841, 854, 673 NE2d 552, 561, 562 (1996) (even when sitting

The purpose of standard instructions on expert testimony is to remind the jury that they are the sole judges of credibility and to counteract the possibility that jurors may believe they cannot reject an expert witness's testimony. Nonetheless, in the absence of a request for such an instruction, or an objection to the court's failure to give one, it has been held that there was no substantial risk of a miscarriage of justice where the court failed to instruct the jury on its role in evaluating expert testimony.[21]

The Appeals Court has held that the doctrine that the trier of fact is not required to accept even an uncontradicted expert opinion leads to the conclusion that the opinion is not binding on the party who called the expert.[22] The court noted that the expert is not a party and not an agent for the party and that, "in theory, the expert testifies impartially to assist the trier of fact about matters not in common knowledge."[23] See § 2.2 for a discussion of judicial admissions.

§ 7.4.4 Degree of Certitude Required of Expert

When an expert is asked for her conclusions, it is traditional to ask whether she has an opinion "to a reasonable degree of [medical or other professional] certainty." It may be argued that this phrase has no intelligible meaning, given that there should not be any degrees of "certainty." The definition of "reasonable" is never supplied and the word may well mean different things to lawyers and scientists. It has been held that this formulaic phrase is not essential and that an expert need not recite "magic words" for her opinion to be admissible, as long as the opinion is expressed with sufficient firmness and clarity.[24]

---

without a jury, judge should recognize the difference between the admissibility and the weight of the evidence); cf. *Com. v. Pallotta*, 36 Mass App 669, 634 NE2d 915 (1994) (error to exclude defendant's expert testimony on criminal responsibility; court notes, however, that there could be cases where an expert's opinion is transparently so wrong or misdirected that it could be excluded even in the absence of conflicting testimony).

[21] *Com. v. Harbin*, 435 Mass 654, 760 NE2d 1216 (2002) (judge's general instruction that it was for the jury to accept or reject any parts of any witness's testimony was adequate given no request for specific instruction; failure to request such an instruction was not ineffective assistance of counsel where it was a strategic choice not to emphasize the expert's testimony).

[22] *Turners Falls Ltd. v. Board of Assessors*, 54 Mass App 732, 767 NE2d 629 (2002).

[23] 54 Mass App at 738.

[24] *Com. v. Rodriguez*, 437 Mass 554, 563, 773 NE2d 946, 954 (2002) (cross-examiner did not ask whether expert's opinions were held "to a reasonable degree of medical certainty"); *Anderson v. Paulo*, 74 Mass App 635, 641, 909 NE2d 47, 51 (2009)

Nonetheless, in *Com. v. Pytou Heang*, the court held that a firearms identification expert should express opinions to a "reasonable degree of ballistic certainty."[25] The court concluded that in this field, "The phrase 'reasonable degree of scientific certainty' should also be avoided because it suggests that forensic ballistics is a science, where it is clearly as much an art as a science."[26] The formalism of this solution is apparent if one asks what meaning it would have for the expert to express an opinion to a "reasonable degree of artistic certainty."

The fact that a witness expresses his opinion by stating that given causes of a condition are "consistent with" his observations does not render the testimony inadmissible.[27] Where other evidence is introduced tending to prove the cause, such expert testimony is relevant to show that the expert or scientific evidence is not inconsistent with the claimed cause.

Where an expert's opinion is based on facts in evidence, that it relies on extrapolations made from those facts will not render the testimony inadmissible.[28] Where an expert's opinion is sufficiently

---

(negative answer to whether expert had a "reasonable degree of scientific certainty" did not render opinion inadmissible: "The purpose of such 'wooden phrases' is to ensure that the expert testimony is not based on speculation."); *Bailey v. Cataldo Ambulance Service, Inc.*, 64 Mass App 228, 233, 832 NE2d 12, 16 (2005) (plaintiff's medical records provided sufficient expert evidence of causation where doctor had written that the accident "presumably set off" chronic pain syndrome, that doctor "feels" that plaintiff suffers from chronic muscle spasm that began at time of accident and that doctor's "impression" was that plaintiff's chronic muscle spasm began at time of accident) and cases cited therein; *Resendes v. Boston Edison Co.*, 38 Mass App 344, 352, 648 NE2d 757, 763 (1995) (expert's characterization of his opinion as a "reasonable explanation" of how accident occurred did not render it inadmissible).

[25] *Com. v. Pytou Heang*, 458 Mass 827, 848, 942 NE2d 927, 945 (2011).

[26] *Id.*, 458 Mass at 849, 942 NE2d at 946.

[27] *Com. v. Torres*, 469 Mass 398, 14 NE3d 253 (2014) (expert's opinion was admissible where he testified that defendant's sandal was consistent with bloody footprint at crime scene, that it "could have" made the impression, but he could not give a "more definitive conclusion."); *Com. v. Roy*, 464 Mass 818, 822, 985 NE2d 1164, 1170 (2013) (medical examiner's testimony was not speculative although he did not state what caused blunt force trauma to victim's skull); *Com. v. Ruell*, 459 Mass 126, 943 NE2d 447 (2011) (medical examiner's opinion about weapons that were consistent with victim's wounds was not mere speculation, but properly based on her training and experience); *Com. v. Azar*, 32 Mass App 290, 302, 588 NE2d 1352, 1361 (1992) (doctor's testimony that injuries were consistent with victim's chest having been compressed and her body shaken was not "speculative").

[28] *Com. v. Johnson*, 410 Mass 199, 571 NE2d 623 (1991) (extrapolation method for estimating total weight of drugs in multiple bags); *Sacco v. Roupenian*, 409 Mass 25, 564 NE2d 386 (1990) (expert deduced that cancer could have been diagnosed at time of defendant doctor's exam, by working back from size of tumor he observed, using the rate of "doubling time" of breast cancer, trial court erred in rejecting evidence as

grounded in the evidence, that certain facts were unknown to the expert or that mistakes were made in some of the expert's assumptions does not render the testimony inadmissible, but rather goes to the weight of the evidence.[29]

However, an expert's opinion that is a "mere guess or conjecture . . . in the form of a conclusion from basic facts that do not tend toward that conclusion any more than toward a contrary one has no evidential value."[30] An opinion expressed as a mere assertion of a possibility of a causal connection is insufficient alone to sustain a finding.[31]

"far-fetched"); *Com. v. Crapps*, 84 Mass App 442, 997 NE2d 444 (2013) (affirms conviction based on estimated weight using extrapolation method; Judge Milkey in concurrence argues for greater transparency and precision in use of extrapolation, including disclosure of algorithms and underlying assumptions employed and taking into account the sample size employed, whether selection of samples was truly random, and variation among weight of samples).

[29] *Com. v. DelValle*, 443 Mass 782, 824 NE2d 830 (2005) (doctor who did not perform autopsy, but who testified on basis of report, diagrams, and photographs, had sufficient information to testify regarding cause of death, severity of force necessary to cause injuries, and that they could have been inflicted by "stomping") (Text cited); *Simmons v. Monarch Mach. Tool Co., Inc.*, 413 Mass 205, 212, 596 NE2d 318, 323 (1992) (some facts unknown); *Sullivan v. First Massachusetts Financial*, 409 Mass 783, 791, 569 NE2d 814, 820 (1991) (some assumptions incorrect); *Anderson v. Paulo*, 74 Mass App 635, 640, 909 NE2d 47, 51 (2009) (although witness characterized his opinion as "preliminary," Appeals Court found it was adequately grounded in facts) (Text cited); *Curcuru v. Rose's Oil Service, Inc.*, 66 Mass App 200, 846 NE2d 401 (2006) (expert's testimony that propeller shaft was bent, based on visual examination and other evidence, rather than measurement with instruments, had adequate factual basis) (Text cited). Cf. *Board of Assessors of Boston v. Ogden Suffolk Downs*, 398 Mass 604, 499 NE2d 1200 (1986) (witness examined property in 1982, opinion as to value in 1979 was properly struck due to blatant error of overlooking in excess of $2,000,000 in improvements between 1979 and 1982).

[30] *Toubiana v. Priestly*, 402 Mass 84, 91, 520 NE2d 1307, 1312 (1988); *Com. v. Daye*, 435 Mass 463, 474, 759 NE2d 313, 324 (2001) (where there were insufficient facts in evidence to establish the precise position of the shooter, the victim and the gun at the instant of the shooting, calculations by a pathologist about the height from which the gun was fired had no basis in the evidence); *Santos v. Chrysler Corp.*, 430 Mass 198, 205, 715 NE2d 47, 54-55 (1999) (NHTSA fatal accident reporting system data provided inadequate basis for expert statistical opinion; opinion held speculative); *Van Brode Group v. Bowditch & Dewey*, 36 Mass App 509, 520, 633 NE2d 424, 430 (1994) (expert prediction of dramatic new profits to be realized in a business turnaround from a historic record of losses, based on only one month of profitability, was properly excluded in the discretion of the trial judge).

[31] *Goffredo v. Mercedes-Benz Truck Co.*, 402 Mass 97, 103, 520 NE2d 1315, 1318 (1988) (directed verdict was proper where witness expressed opinion in terms of possibilities, rather than probabilities); *Curreri v. Isihara*, 80 Mass App 193, 197, 952 NE2d 393, 397 (2011) (judge correctly excluded testimony that cancer was "possibly stage 1" at time of alleged malpractice, but testimony that cancer was "no worse than stage 2" was admissible); *Fidalgo v. Columbus McKinnon Corp.*, 56 Mass App 176, 775

§ 7.4.5 Procedural Matters

Expert testimony is subject to specific notice requirements. Whether failure to give the opposing party notice of anticipated expert testimony prior to trial constitutes a significant enough abuse of discovery requirements for the testimony to be barred depends upon the individual circumstances of the case.[32] Whether a continuance is required due to late notice of an expert also depends upon the circumstances.[33]

NE2d 803 (2002) (evidence based on speculation and stated in terms of possibilities); *Patterson v. Liberty Mutual Insurance Co.*, 48 Mass App 586, 723 NE2d 1005 (2000) (testimony regarding medical causation must be expressed in terms of probability, not possibility). Cf. *Blood v. Lea*, 403 Mass 430, 530 NE2d 344 (1988) (medical expert's assessment of a "probable" causal link between alleged negligent act and injury was sufficient to submit case to trier of fact).

[32] Compare *In re LiBassi*, 449 Mass 1014, 867 NE2d 332 (2007) (barring testimony); *Com. v. Chappee*, 397 Mass 508, 492 NE2d 719 (1986) (barring testimony); *Barron v. Fidelity Magellan Fund*, 57 Mass App 507, 784 NE2d 634 (2003) (barring testimony) (Text cited), with *Kace v. Liang*, 472 Mass 630, 36 NE3d 1215 (2015) (allowing testimony); *Grassi Design Group, Inc. v. Bank of America, N.A.*, 74 Mass App 456, 908 NE2d 393 (2009) (court troubled by exclusion of expert reports that was tantamount to dismissal where expert affidavits were plaintiffs' only evidence in response to summary judgment motion and continuance could have remedied prejudice to defendants, but judgment affirmed because reports were insufficient to oppose summary judgment in any event); *Com. v. Almeida*, 452 Mass 601, 609, 897 NE2d 14, 22 (2008) (defendant did not demonstrate prejudice from disclosure of chemist's blood spatter diagrams only at trial); *Hammell v. Shooshanian Eng'g Assocs., Inc.*, 73 Mass App 634, 900 NE2d 891 (2009) (where expert changed opinion because of new information received two weeks before trial, not error to admit it where opposing party was not prejudiced); *Com. v. Paiva*, 71 Mass App 411, 882 NE2d 863 (2008) (barring testimony was reversible error); *Resendes v. Boston Edison Co.*, 38 Mass App 344, 648 NE2d 757 (1995) (allowing testimony, noting that opposing party did not object to expert until lobby conference immediately before empanelment of jury and had not sought either a continuance or a deposition of the expert during the month before trial in which it had notice he would be called); *Beaupre v. Cliff Smith & Assoc.*, 50 Mass App 480, 738 NE2d 753 (2000) (allowing expert testimony from witness opponent knew was treating physician).

[33] Compare *Com. v. Nester*, 32 Mass App 983, 594 NE2d 542 (1992) (error to deny defendant a continuance during trial to obtain expert to rebut unexpected evidence from Commonwealth's expert, whose testimony had gone significantly further than her report) with *Com. v. Figueroa*, 74 Mass App 784, 911 NE2d 206 (2009) (substitution of different trooper to testify as drug trade expert on day of trial was permissible where court conducted lengthy voir dire, one trooper's testimony was likely not substantially different from the other's, and testimony was not overwhelmingly powerful in relation to other evidence); *Com. v. MeMaria*, 46 Mass App 114, 703 NE2d 1203 (1999) (not error to deny continuance where no bad faith or carelessness by prosecutor and no material prejudice resulted from denial), and *Com. v. Bandy*, 38 Mass App 329, 648 NE2d 440 (1995) (not error where continuance was denied when defendant was on notice on the prior trial day that expert would probably be required). See

A criminal defendant may obtain discovery of relevant laboratory data from public forensic laboratories.[34]

A party may not obtain expert testimony by summoning an involuntary witness solely for the expertise he may bring to the trial, in the absence of any personal knowledge on his part related to the issues before the court.[35] A court does have discretionary power to require, without payment of expert fees, that an expert witness testify as to an opinion already formed; however, such power is exercised sparingly, and only when necessary for the purposes of justice.[36] In criminal cases, the court may provide funds for the payment of expert fees for indigent defendants.[37]

Fed R Evid 706 and Proposed Mass R Evid 706 provide that the court may appoint experts on its own motion or on the motion of any party. See § 7.8. A provision for nonpartisan experts is made for testimony before the Industrial Accident Board. GL 152, § 11A.

Where a party does not challenge the admissibility of scientific evidence at trial, the issue is waived and the appellate court will review it only for a substantial risk of a miscarriage of justice.[38]

§ 7.5 Foundation for Expert Testimony

Expert opinion is the product of special knowledge applied to the particular facts of the case in dispute. Thus, as foundation for expert opinion evidence, it must be established that: (1) the scientific principles

---

Com. v. Nolin, 448 Mass 207, 859 NE2d 843 (2007) (delaying forensic dentist's testimony by several days during trial and authorization of funds for defendant to hire his own expert rendered harmless delay in disclosure of expert's report); *Com. v. Stote*, 433 Mass 19, 739 NE2d 261 (2000) (defendant not prejudiced by prosecution's late pretrial disclosure of chemical report, despite his contention that he was unable to hire expert regarding the information).

[34] *Com. v. Lewis*, 468 Mass 1001, 8 NE3d 735 (2014) (discovery is not limited to items included within automatic discovery rule; Commonwealth failed to show that providing maintenance and calibration records for machines used for weighing and analyzing drugs would be unduly burdensome).

[35] *Bagley v. Illyrian Gardens, Inc.*, 401 Mass 822, 519 NE2d 1308 (1988); *Com. v. Vitello*, 367 Mass 224, 327 NE2d 819 (1975).

[36] *Bagley v. Illyrian Gardens, Inc.*, supra, 401 Mass at 827, 519 NE2d at 1311 (& citations).

[37] G.L. c. 261, §§ 27A-27G; *Diatchenko v. District Attorney for Suffolk District*, 471 Mass 12, 27 NE3d 349 (2015) (approving fees for expert for parole-eligible, indigent juvenile homicide offender in connection with parole proceeding).

[38] *Com. v. Enimpah*, 81 Mass App 657, 663, 966 NE2d 840, 845 (2012) (affirming conviction where defendant failed to object to DNA evidence at trial).

and methodology on which the expert's opinion is based are reliable; (2) the witness is qualified with special knowledge; and (3) the witness has sufficient knowledge of the particular facts to bring his expertise meaningfully to bear.

§ 7.5.1 Determination of Reliability by Trial Court

For scientific evidence to be admissible, the court must determine that the body of scientific or expert knowledge on which the witness's testimony is based is sufficiently reliable. The classic definition of the standard was articulated in *Frye v. United States*,[1] where it was held that, "while courts will go a long way in admitting expert testimony deduced from a well-recognized scientific principle or discovery, the thing from which the deduction is made must be sufficiently established to have gained general acceptance in the particular field in which it belongs."[2]

In *Daubert v. Merrell Dow Pharmaceuticals, Inc.*,[3] the United States Supreme Court held that Fed R Evid 702 abandoned the *Frye* test in the federal courts. The Court held that the "general acceptance" standard of the *Frye* test had not been silently incorporated into Rule 702. The Court reasoned that the doctrine would be at odds with the "liberal thrust" of the Federal Rules of Evidence and their "general approach of relaxing the traditional barriers to 'opinion' testimony."[4]

In *Daubert*, the Court emphasized that Fed R Evid 702 continues to impose on trial judges the obligation to make an initial determination of whether scientific testimony and evidence is relevant and reliable. The Court noted that the subject of such testimony must be "scientific . . . knowledge," which requires that inferences or assertions must be derived by the scientific method. The Court suggested several guidelines that might be used in assessing such testimony, although it indicated that none of the individual guidelines were strict requirements. The Court indicated that it would be relevant to determine:

---

§ 7.5 [1] *Frye v. United States*, 293 F 1013, 1014 (DC Cir 1923).

[2] The requirement of general acceptance in the scientific community was intended to ensure "that those most qualified to assess the general validity of a scientific method will have the determinative voice" as to whether such evidence may be accepted in trials. *Com. v. Lykus*, 367 Mass 191, 202, 327 NE2d 671, 678 (1975) (permitting expert testimony as to voice identification based on voice print spectrogram or on aural comparison and analysis). The premise of the requirement was that those most qualified are not judges, but scientists with specialized knowledge.

[3] *Daubert v. Merrell Dow Pharmaceuticals, Inc.*, 509 US 579, 113 S Ct 2786 (1993).

[4] 509 US at 588.

1. whether or not a given theory or technique had been tested;
2. whether or not a given theory or technique had been subjected to peer review and publication;
3. whether a particular scientific technique had a known or potential rate of error;
4. whether there were standards controlling the operation of the technique; and
5. whether the theory or technique did have general acceptance in the relevant scientific community. The Court emphasized that the inquiry envisioned by Rule 702 is a flexible one.[5]

The decision for the trial judge is the threshold one of whether testimony is sufficiently reliable to be admissible. The Court concluded that risks of inappropriate scientific evidence are further minimized through the adversary system by vigorous cross-examination and the presentation of contrary evidence, and by careful instruction to jurors by trial judges on the burden of proof.

In *Com. v. Lanigan*,[6] the Supreme Judicial Court held that the general acceptance standard of the *Frye* test is not the exclusive means by which the admissibility of scientific evidence is to be determined in Massachusetts courts.[7] The Court held that the "ultimate test . . . is the reliability of the theory or process underlying the expert's testimony."[8] The Court stated that the trial judge has a "gatekeeper role" in determining whether the process or theory underlying a scientific expert's opinion lacks reliability, and concluded:

> We accept the basic reasoning of the *Daubert*, opinion because it is consistent with our test of demonstrated reliability. We suspect that general acceptance in the relevant scientific community will continue to be the significant, and often the only, issue. We accept the idea, however, that a proponent of scientific opinion evidence may demonstrate the reliability or validity of the underlying scientific theory or process by some other means, that is, without establishing general acceptance.[9]

---

[5] 509 US at 593-594.

[6] *Com. v. Lanigan*, 419 Mass 15, 641 NE2d 1342 (1994) (*Lanigan II*).

[7] The *Frye* test had been subjected to substantial criticism. See *Com. v. Mendes*, supra, 406 Mass 201, 212, 547 NE2d 35, 41 (1989) (Liacos, CJ, dissenting) and authorities cited therein. The rule was inherently conservative and was questioned on the ground that it may bar otherwise reliable probative evidence simply because the scientific community had not yet adequately digested and approved of its foundation.

[8] 419 Mass at 24.

[9] *Lanigan II*, supra, 419 Mass at 26, 641 NE2d at 1349.

In *Com. v. Patterson*,[10] the Supreme Judicial Court went further than the "suspicion" it had articulated in *Lanigan II* and declared that, "*Lanigan*'s progeny make clear that general acceptance in the relevant community of the theory and process on which an expert's testimony is based, on its own, continues to be sufficient to establish the requisite reliability for admission in Massachusetts courts regardless of other *Daubert* factors."[11] The Court relied upon the language it had used in several cases, including *Com. v. Sands*,[12] where it had stated that "a party seeking to introduce scientific evidence may lay a foundation either by showing that the underlying scientific theory is generally accepted within the relevant scientific community, or by showing that the theory is reliable or valid through other means."

The "other means" that may be relied upon to establish reliability are flexible. Neither *Lanigan II* nor *Daubert* established a specific checklist or test for determining the reliability of the principles or methodology upon which expert testimony is based. Thus, in *Adoption of Hugo*,[13] the court rejected the argument that the reliability of the testimony of a clinical social worker could only be established by one of the five factors discussed in *Lanigan II*.[14]

Where general acceptance is relied upon to establish reliability, the court must determine what the relevant community is for the purpose of determining whether the theory or method has been accepted. In *Com. v. Patterson*, supra, the Court stated that with respect to technical forensic evidence, the relevant scientific community must be sufficiently broad to permit the potential for dissent.[15] It held that the

---

[10] *Com. v. Patterson*, 445 Mass 626, 840 NE2d 12 (2005).

[11] *Com. v. Patterson*, supra, 445 Mass at 641. See *Com. v. Powell*, 450 Mass 229, 877 NE2d 589 (2007) (bloodstain analysis and the "string method" are generally accepted).

[12] *Com. v. Sands*, 424 Mass 184, 185-186, 675 NE2d 370, 371 (1997) (evidence of a Horizontal Gaze Nystagmus (HGN) field sobriety test is not admissible in the absence of expert testimony, because its underlying assumption—that there is a correlation between intoxication and nystagmus—is not within the common experience of jurors).

[13] *Adoption of Hugo*, 428 Mass 219, 234, 700 NE2d 516, 526 (1998).

[14] In *Hugo* the court approved a methodology that consisted of using knowledge gained from the expert's training and experience, reviewing the case file, interviewing the parties, and gathering information from service providers, the same methods used by the child's and DSS's experts. See also *Higgins v. Delta Elevator Service Corp.*, 45 Mass App 643, 700 NE2d 833 (1998) (criticizing a jury instruction regarding the reliability of expert testimony which supplied four specific criteria similar to the *Daubert* factors; court rejected plaintiff's argument that it was error to limit the jury's reliability determination to consideration of those factors).

[15] *Com. v. Patterson*, 445 Mass at 643.

"fingerprint examiner community" (including independent and retired examiners and scientists from other fields who study the underlying premises of fingerprint examination) constituted the relevant scientific community for determining the admissibility of fingerprint evidence.[16] In *Patterson*, the Court concluded that the trial judge had an adequate basis for concluding that the overall theory and method of fingerprint comparison was generally accepted in the relevant community, and thus did not need to examine the other *Daubert* factors.[17] This does not fully address the question, however, of what a trial court is obligated to do when the proponent of expert or scientific evidence establishes general acceptance but the opponent offers persuasive evidence that other factors demonstrate unreliability. Challenges to forensic science evidence that has long been accepted without serious critical review raise this question. The Court has said that the general acceptance standard "does not preclude a party from requesting a hearing on the belief that the science in a particular field has advanced to the point where previously accepted expert testimony would no longer be considered reliable."[18] The Court has not yet, however, specifically identified what standard a party must meet to justify a hearing under such circumstances, or to justify the conclusion that previously accepted expert testimony is no longer reliable. Given that knowledge is constantly expanding, and that scientific principles are frequently modified in light of new discoveries or theories, it is inconsistent with the reliability requirement to permit any theories or methods to be "grandfathered" as admissible evidence.

Patterson also reaffirmed that the procedure that the Court adopted in *Lanigan* "includes ensuring not only the reliability of the abstract theory and process underlying an expert's opinion, but the particular application of that process."[19] Thus having held that the general theory and method of finger print comparison were reliable; the Court conducted a separate inquiry with respect to whether the specific application of the theory and method to the facts of the case was reliable. It follows, for example, that it is necessary to establish

---

[16] *Id.*, 445 Mass at 641.

[17] *Id.*, 445 Mass at 644.

[18] *Com. v. Sliech-Brodeur*, 457 Mass 300, 327, n.39, 930 NE2d 91, 112 (2010); *Com. v. Nelson*, 460 Mass 564, 578, 953 NE2d 164, 176 (2011). A request for a hearing should be accompanied by an affidavit or other materials demonstrating that the testimony in question should no longer be routinely admitted. *Com. v. Vasquez*, 462 Mass 827, 845, 971 NE2d 783, 798 (2012) (Text cited).

[19] *Patterson*, 445 Mass at 648. *See also Com. v. Gaynor*, 443 Mass 245, 820 NE2d 233 (2005).

a foundation for introducing results from measuring devices by showing that the device has been calibrated or otherwise shown to be accurate.[20]

In *Kumho Tire Co., Ltd. v. Carmichael*,[21] the United States Supreme Court held that Rule 702 imposes a "gatekeeping" obligation on the trial court to determine that all expert testimony, not just that from scientific experts, is reliable. In so doing, trial courts may apply the factors suggested in *Daubert*, or employ other criteria, depending upon the circumstances. The Court again emphasized that the test of reliability is "flexible."[22] In *Canavan's Case*,[23] the Supreme Judicial Court held that expert conclusions based on personal observations or clinical experience must be subject to *Lanigan* analysis.[24] The Court held that conclusions of a physician that a plaintiff suffered from multiple chemical sensitivity caused by exposure to chemicals at work should have been excluded because the doctor's methodology did not withstand analysis.[25] The decision in *Canavan's Case* implies that a trial judge must perform a gatekeeper role with regard to the reliability of all expert testimony, although the Court was not required to reach that conclusion to decide that case. Historically some types of testimony were exempted from reliability review. For example, experts who developed their own particular techniques based on accepted

---

[20] *Com. v. Podgurski*, 81 Mass App 175, 185, 961 NE2d 113, 122 (2012) (error to admit testimony based on in-court measuring of drug weight by detective without evidence establishing the accuracy of the scale). See § 7.5.5 for foundation requirements for blood alcohol tests.

[21] *Kumho Tire Co., Ltd. v. Carmichael*, 526 US 137, 119 S Ct 1167 (1999) (admissibility of testimony of tire failure analyst).

[22] 562 US at 141.

[23] *Canavan's Case*, 432 Mass 304, 733 NE2d 1042 (2000).

[24] Prior to *Canavan's Case*, the Appeals Court had held in *Ducharme v. Hyundai Motor America*, 45 Mass App 401, 698 NE2d 412 (1998), that the trial court had properly excluded the testimony of the plaintiff's expert with regard to whether a vehicle would have satisfied the requirements of a particular Federal Motor Vehicle Safety Standard. The expert had conceded that he had not employed any of the objective criteria specified in the test protocol. The court found that his opinion, based on a post-collision examination of the vehicle and crash test reports involving other Hyundai automobiles, was speculative and properly excluded "pursuant to the judge's 'gatekeeper' function against unreliable expert testimony." 45 Mass App at 407, 698 NE2d at 416.

[25] See *Case of Wolovick*, 69 Mass App 523, 868 NE2d 1271 (2007) (testimony of doctor that multiple chemical sensitivity is not recognized by AMA or CDC provided adequate basis for rejecting employee's claim that symptoms were caused by exposure to volatile organic compounds, but judge properly refused to exclude evidence about MCS as a matter of law, because scientific knowledge is constantly evolving).

instruments or theories generally were allowed to give their opinions.[26] In addition, where an expert's testimony did not involve the use of a scientific technique or test, the validity of which might be subject to dispute, the *Frye* test was not employed.[27] In the post *Daubert/Lanigan* world the continuing vitality of some of these previous decisions is questionable.[28]

Nonetheless, there are some circumstances in which the reliability inquiry is unnecessary, or less rigorous. In *Palandjian v. Foster*,[29] the Supreme Judicial Court held that expert testimony regarding the standard of care in malpractice actions is generally not subject to a reliability analysis, because it is based on an expert's knowledge of the care provided by other professionals in the field, not on scientific theory or research. A reliability inquiry is required, however, when the witness incorporates scientific facts into a description of the standard of care.[30] In *Com. v. Sands*,[31] the Court suggested that if the subject matter of expert testimony is understandable to jurors, separate expert testimony on the reliability of the theory behind it may not be required:

---

[26] See, e.g., *Com. v. Cifizzari*, 397 Mass 560, 492 NE2d 357 (1986) (affirming admission of expert testimony making an identification from bite marks); *Com. v. Devlin*, 365 Mass 149, 310 NE2d 353 (1974) (identification of dismembered torso by x-ray comparisons).

[27] See *Com. v. Avellar*, 416 Mass 409, 418, 622 NE2d 625, 630 (1993) (testimony by pediatrician that father's response upon seeing deceased son's body constituted an inappropriate grief reaction did not involve scientific testing methods, *Frye* test inapplicable); *Com. v. Ghee*, 414 Mass 313, 320, 607 NE2d 1005, 1010 (1993) (expert testimony on the basis of photographic techniques that witness could identify a latent fingerprint, and testimony that by comparing stripes running lengthwise in plastic bags, expert could conclude that one bag was made on the same day as others, constituted physical comparisons that experts made using their knowledge of particular techniques; *Frye* test did not apply).

[28] It would appear difficult to reconcile *Canavan's Case* with the decision in *Com. v. Gordon*, 422 Mass 816, 666 NE2d 122 (1996) (chemist's testimony that orthotolidine procedure was a presumptive test for the presence of blood, among other iron-containing substances, but that based on her observations she could rule out false positive test results when she observed a brilliant blue color on the filter paper used in the test, was admissible and not subject to the *Frye* test).

[29] *Palandjian v. Foster*, 446 Mass 100, 842 NE2d 916 (2006).

[30] Thus in *Palandjian*, the Court concluded that the plaintiff did not establish a foundation of reliability for the claim that the defendant physician should have realized that a history of gastric cancer in second degree relatives increased the risk for such cancer.

[31] *Com. v. Sands*, 424 Mass 184, 185-186, 675 NE2d 370, 371 (1997) (evidence of a Horizontal Gaze Nystagmus (HGN) field sobriety test is not admissible in the absence of expert testimony, because its underlying assumption—that there is a correlation between intoxication and nystagmus—is not within the common experience of jurors).

> Expert testimony on the scientific theory is needed if the subject of expert testimony is beyond the common knowledge or understanding of the lay juror. If jurors can evaluate an expert's testimony with common sense and experience and can understand the underlying methods or theories of the testimony, then the expert's qualifications and the logical basis of the testimony can be effectively tested through cross-examination and rebuttal evidence.[32]

In *Com. v. Goodman*,[33] the court followed *Sands* in concluding that in determining the reliability of a fire inspector's methodology (which it characterized as "simplicity itself"), the trial judge could "look to his own common sense, as well as the depth and quality of the proffered expert's education, training, experience, and appearance in other courts." In *Com. v. Bradway*,[34] the Appeals Court held that where the Legislature had mandated the admissibility of reports of "qualified examiners" in trials to determine sexual dangerousness, no hearing on the reliability of such expert testimony was necessary. The court held it was within the province of the Legislature to determine the admissibility of such evidence.

The reliability requirement should be applied rigorously where there is reason to challenge social science evidence and forensic science evidence previously accepted by Massachusetts courts.[35] The Supreme Judicial Court has not been entirely consistent on this point, however. In *Com. v. Shanley*,[36] the Court noted that a *Lanigan* hearing may not always be required where expert testimony of the same type has been accepted as reliable in the past in Massachusetts appellate cases. At the same time the Court observed, "However, we have not 'grandfathered' any particular theories or methods for all time, especially in areas where knowledge is evolving, and new understandings may be expected as more studies and tests are conducted."[37] The opinion in *Com. v. Pytou Heang*,[38] however, suggests that the Supreme Judicial Court has in effect grandfathered as admissible some forensic

---

[32] 424 Mass at 186, 675 NE2d at 371.

[33] *Com. v. Goodman*, 54 Mass App Ct 385, 391, 765 NE2d 792, 796 (2002).

[34] *Com. v. Bradway*, 62 Mass App 280, 816 NE2d 152 (2004).

[35] But see *Com. v. Murphy*, 59 Mass App 571, 576, 797 NE2d 394, 399 (2003) (*Lanigan* hearing not necessary for expert testimony concerning the authorship of handwriting, given that Massachusetts courts have long accepted such testimony as reliable). This result is at odds with conclusions reached by some of the federal courts. See, e.g., *United States v. Hines*, 55 F Supp 2d 62 (D Mass 1999).

[36] *Com. v. Shanley*, 455 Mass 752, 919 NE2d 1254 (2010).

[37] 455 Mass at 763, n.15, 919 NE2d at 1264.

[38] *Com. v. Pytou Heang*, 458 Mass 827, 942 NE2d 927 (2011).

evidence, at least where a trial judge has admitted expert testimony that has long been accepted. The opinion first set out a thorough and persuasive critique of the reliability of firearms identification evidence.[39] The principal problems the court identified are (1) that "there is little scientific proof supporting the theory that each firearm imparts 'unique' individual characteristic toolmarks onto projectiles and cartridge cases"; and (2) "that the matching of individual characteristics, regardless of the technique used, is highly subjective."[40] Nonetheless, the court held that the trial court had not abused its discretion in admitting the evidence, subject to conditions, despite declining to conduct a *Daubert-Lanigan* hearing, for the reasons that (1) the trial court has wide discretion to determine the reliability of expert testimony; and (2) firearms identification testimony has long been deemed admissible.[41]

Given the weight the court put on the abuse of discretion standard of review in *Pytou Heang*, it is evident that where recent scientific criticism challenges the reliability of traditionally accepted forensic evidence, in Massachusetts the responsibility for significant change in its admissibility falls on the shoulders of trial judges. Presumably, the appellate courts will show the same deference to trial courts' decisions excluding questionable evidence as the court showed to the admissibility determination in *Pytou Heang*.

The Supreme Judicial Court has directed that parties must file pretrial motions to challenge the reliability of expert or scientific testimony on reliability grounds.[42] Where the reliability of scientific or

---

[39] The discussion is based on the 2008 Report on Ballistic Imaging of the National Research Council and other recent scholarly sources.

[40] *Com. v. Pytou Heang*, supra, 458 Mass at 842, 942 NE2d at 941.

[41] *Com. v. Pytou Heang*, supra, 458 Mass at 844, 942 NE2d at 942. The court noted that the pedigree of firearms identification testimony goes back to the decision of Oliver Wendell Holmes admitting the evidence in *Com. v. Best*, 180 Mass 492, 62 NE 748 (1902). Given intervening scientific developments, why the century old opinion of Holmes has any persuasive value is hard to imagine, despite the continuing general utility of comparison photographs. See *Com. v. Pytou Heang*, supra, 458 Mass at 848, n.30, 942 NE2d at 945. The trial court's conditions were merely that the witness could testify "to a degree of scientific certainty" that the subject weapon fired the projectiles recovered from the victims, but that he also must admit that he could not exclude the possibility that they were fired by another nine millimeter firearm. *Id.*, 458 Mass at 844, 942 NE2d at 942.

[42] *Com. v. Fernandez*, 458 Mass 137, 150-151, n.20, 934 NE2d 810, 821 (2010) (timing of motion in limine filed immediately before trial considered in finding no abuse of discretion in admitting field tests for narcotics for limited purpose despite weak authority in support; "Given more ample warning, a more searching *Lanigan* analysis would have been appropriate."); *Com. v. Bly*, 448 Mass 473, 487, n.8, 489, 862

other principles or methodology is disputed for the first time at trial and the court entertains the challenge, it should hold a voir dire examination of the experts for the purpose of determining reliability. Jurors should not be permitted to hear the testimony of any expert in support of the validity of a given scientific procedure until after the court has made its determination that the expert's testimony will be admitted.[43]

The existence of a stipulation between the parties as to the admissibility of a scientific test is not always sufficient to justify its admission.[44] However, where evidence has been received pursuant to a stipulation, a challenge to the admissibility of the evidence on appeal must demonstrate a substantial likelihood of a miscarriage of justice to obtain a reversal.[45]

In *Canavan's Case*, the Supreme Judicial Court adopted the abuse of discretion standard of review of reliability determinations made by the trial court, following the federal practice.[46] The Court reasoned that this standard reflects the reality that the admissibility of a particular scientific method may vary from case to case and may change due

---

NE2d 341, 354, 355 (2007) (where defendant offered evidence regarding reliability at trial that he had not offered at hearing on motion in limine, court would not consider it, absent a motion to reopen the in limine ruling outside presence of jury, but court would consider the issue in first degree murder case under substantial likelihood of miscarriage of justice standard); *Com. v. Sparks*, 433 Mass 654, 746 NE2d 133 (2001) (murder defendant waived appellate claim that DNA testing kits used by Cellmark were not reliable); *Driscoll v. Providence Mutual Fire Ins. Co.*, 69 Mass App 341, 867 NE2d 806 (2007) (*Lanigan* challenge is waived when raised for first time on appeal; parties cannot challenge expert evidence where they have stipulated to its admissibility); *Com. v. Pasteur*, 66 Mass App 812, 826, 850 NE2d 1118, 1132 (2006) (defendant's only pretrial objection to testimony was based on prosecution's failure to provide written notice of pathologist's opinion and grounds therefor, and at voir dire of witness, made no inquiry relevant to methodology, thus objection on reliability grounds was waived); *Com. v. Julien*, 59 Mass App 679, 797 NE2d 470 (2003) (defendant cannot preserve error in admission of unreliable expert testimony by means of a motion to strike).

[43] *Com. v. Curnin*, 409 Mass 218, 565 NE2d 440 (1991).

[44] *Com. v. Mendes*, 406 Mass 201, 547 NE2d 35 (1989); *Com. v. Walker*, 392 Mass 152, 466 NE2d 71 (1984) (polygraph evidence as to witnesses inadmissible, even if all parties stipulate to admissibility).

[45] *Com. v. Phoenix*, 409 Mass 408, 420, 567 NE2d 193, 200 (1991) (conviction affirmed where genetic allotype blood testing admitted following stipulation that such testing has general acceptance in scientific community).

[46] See *General Electric Co. v. Joiner*, 522 US 136, 118 S Ct 512 (1997). *Kumho* declared that the same standard applies to review of the method by which trial courts determine reliability. See *Salvas v. Wal-Mart Stores, Inc.*, 452 Mass 337, 893 NE2d 1187 (2008) (reversing trial court's exclusion of expert testimony, concluding that statistician's methodology was reliable).

to the evolving nature of scientific knowledge. The Court has held that when a party preserves only a limited basis for objecting to expert evidence, an appellate court will review only that basis.[47] Where a criminal defendant fails to object to scientific evidence at trial on the ground that tests performed were not generally accepted, and does not request a voir dire hearing to make that determination, an appellate court will review the issue only to determine if admission of the evidence created a substantial risk of a miscarriage of justice.[48]

Examples of scientific evidence that have passed the reliability hurdle, or have been held admissible without an explicit finding with respect to reliability, are discussed in § 7.6 infra.

Based upon a lack of sufficient acceptance in the scientific community, a number of types of evidence have been held properly excluded.[49]

§ 7.5.2 *Expert's Qualifications*

An expert witness must show to the trial court's satisfaction that he or she possesses sufficient special knowledge and experience to be able to give competent aid to the jury in construing the particular facts of the case in dispute. "The crucial issue is whether the witness has sufficient education, training, experience and familiarity with the

---

[47] *Vassallo v. Baxter Healthcare Corp.*, 428 Mass 1, 11, 696 NE2d 909, 917 (1998) (declining to reach the defendants' objections to experts under *Lanigan II* asserted on appeal in silicone breast implant case). See *Tarpey v. Crescent Ridge Dairy, Inc.*, 47 Mass App 380, 713 NE2d 975 (1999) (plaintiff acknowledged that use of polyclonal antibodies for immunohistochemistry testing was generally accepted, so burden was on plaintiff to show that use of monoclonal antibodies was based on new scientific theory, and plaintiff could not rely upon unsupported assertions to do so).

[48] *Com. v. Daye*, 411 Mass 719, 741, 587 NE2d 194, 207 (1992).

[49] *Federico v. Ford Motor Co.*, 67 Mass App 454, 854 NE2d 448 (2006) (trial judge justified in concluding there was no reliable scientific foundation for expert's theory that transient electronic signals could have affected cruise control of vehicle and caused it to accelerate); *Com. v. Soares*, 51 Mass App 273, 745 NE2d 362 (2001) (trial judge had properly afforded no weight to psychologist's testimony because record did not establish reliability of test on which he had relied, the Gudjonsson Suggestibility Scale (GSS)); *Rotman v. National Railroad Passenger Corp*, 41 Mass App 317, 669 NE2d 1090 (1996) (expert testimony that trauma exacerbated preexisting optic neuritis was not supported by evidence indicating that the opinion was either generally accepted or otherwise had scientific validity); *Croall v. MBTA*, 26 Mass App 957, 526 NE2d 1320 (1988) (rejecting expert testimony concerning "microbursts" of wind).

subject matter of the testimony."[50] The witness need not have encountered precisely the same facts before.[51]

It is not essential that an expert be a specialist within his profession. The Supreme Judicial Court has held: "There is no requirement that testimony on a question of discrete knowledge come from an expert qualified in that subspecialty rather than from an expert more generally qualified."[52] The Court has held repeatedly that a medical

---

[50] *Letch v. Daniels*, 401 Mass 65, 68, 514 NE2d 675-677 (1987) (testimony of orthodontist permissible in dental malpractice action against defendant pedodontist).

[51] *McLaughlin v. Board of Selectmen of Amherst*, 422 Mass 359, 662 NE2d 687 (1996) (error to exclude testimony of real estate expert because she had not bought, sold, or owned land in the locality about which she intended to testify); *Marchand v. Murray*, 27 Mass App 611, 616, 541 NE2d 371, 374 (1989) (questions of whether economist had previously evaluated fast food franchises, as opposed to other types of restaurants or businesses, did not preclude testimony).

[52] *Com. v. Crouse*, 447 Mass 558, 569, 855 NE2d 391, 401 (2006) (expert in cause and origin of fires was qualified to give opinion on lapse of time from when fire was set until fire alarm sounded) (Text cited). See *Com. v. Scesny*, 472 Mass 185, 195, 34 NE3d 17, 27 (2015) (state lab criminalist properly allowed to testify concerning drainage and disturbance of stains she would have expected to see on victim's pants); *Com. v. Fryar*, 425 Mass 237, 251, 680 NE2d 901, 911 (1997) (supervising chemist in state police lab, who had taken courses on blood spatter patterns, was competent to testify on physics of blood spattering and knife's ability to inflict wounds). See *Adoption of Hugo*, 428 Mass 219, 700 NE2d 516 (1998) (licensed social worker experienced in working with children and families qualified to testify in adoption case, despite lack of specific clinical experience with foster care and adoption problems); *Com. v. Avellar*, 416 Mass 409, 415, 622 NE2d 625, 629 (1993) (court had discretion to allow board-certified physician in emergency medicine and pediatrics to testify that father's response to viewing the child after death demonstrated an inappropriate grief response); *Com. v. Mahoney*, 406 Mass 843, 852, 550 NE2d 1380, 1385-1386 (1990) (testimony of chemist was admissible that substance on victim's shirt and defendant's footwear was consistent with "residual stomach contents," although expert had no particular training in chemical analysis of same); *Keville v. McKeever*, 42 Mass App 140, 151, 675 NE2d 417, 426 (1997) (psychiatrist who had treated 10 to 20 patients who suffered from dementia, but did not hold himself out as an expert in dementia, was properly qualified to render opinion that person was suffering from severe dementia); *Com. v. Estep*, 38 Mass App 502, 649 NE2d 775 (1995) (permissible to allow chemist, who had testified that paint on wood chip matched paint on ax handle, to also testify that the wood on both items matched); *Cronin v. McCarthy*, 22 Mass App 448, 494 NE2d 411 (1986) (police officers permitted to give opinions that, at point of impact, decedent's vehicle was in defendant's lane, although officers lacked training and experience in accident reconstruction). But see *Com. v. Despres*, 70 Mass App 645, 875 NE2d 864 (2007) (within court's discretion to conclude that crisis clinician with degree in human services and assistant director of respite facility with degree in psychology, both of whom lacked advanced degrees, had insufficient skills, knowledge, or experience to give opinion on victim's mental disability and its relationship to his ability to perceive, remember, and articulate events); *Com. v. Barresi*, 46 Mass App 907, 705 NE2d 639 (1999) (physician who generally treated the elderly and had limited experience with sexually transmitted diseases was properly excluded from testifying about the likelihood of the transmission of chlamydia).

expert need not be a specialist in the area concerned or be practicing in the same field as a medical malpractice defendant in order to give an opinion.[53] The standard used to judge the qualifications of an expert before a medical malpractice tribunal is "extremely lenient."[54] The tribunal should consider a proffered opinion if a trial judge might properly rule the expert to be qualified, even though if that exercise of discretion were in the tribunal's province, it would find the expert not qualified.[55]

Whether a person who might qualify as an expert in one subject is qualified to give an expert opinion in another somewhat related subject will depend upon the circumstances of the case.[56]

---

[53] *Letch v. Daniels*, supra, and cases cited therein.

[54] *Heyman v. Knirk*, 35 Mass App 946, 626 NE2d 5 (1994) (tribunal should have accepted opinion by podiatrist, not a physician, in case involving foot surgery by orthopedic surgeon).

[55] *Blake v. Avedikian*, 412 Mass 481, 482, 590 NE2d 183, 184 (1992) (& citations).

[56] Compare *Reckis v. Johnson & Johnson*, 471 Mass 272, 28 NE3d 445 (2015) (professor of pharmacology and toxicology qualified to give opinion that ibuprofen caused toxic epidermal necrolysis, although not a physician who had treated the condition); *Com. v. Gomes*, 459 Mass 194, 205, 944 NE2d 1007, 1017 (2011) (forensic chemist was qualified to give opinion about "fracture match" between two pieces of tape) (Text cited); *Com. v. Avila*, 454 Mass 744, 764, 912 NE2d 1014, 1030 (2009) (medical examiner was properly allowed to testify that bullet was deformed as a result of striking pavement after leaving body); *Com. v. Ruiz*, 442 Mass 826, 817 NE2d 771 (2004) (EMT was properly permitted to testify that victim was suffocating and lung may have been collapsing); *Com. v. Rice*, 441 Mass 291, 298, 805 NE2d 26, 35 (2004) (permissible for State Police chemist to opine on the life expectancy of sperm cells); *Com. v. Frangipane*, 433 Mass 527, 744 NE2d 25 (2001) (certified social worker was qualified to testify to existence of dissociative memory loss and recovered memory experiences among sexually abused children, but not to process by which trauma victim stores and retrieves, or dissociates traumatic memory); *Com. v. Simmons*, 419 Mass 426, 646 NE2d 97 (1995) (chemist with experience in blood pattern analysis was properly qualified as an expert on that subject); *Com. v. Thayer*, 418 Mass 130, 634 NE2d 576 (1994) (licensed and experienced psychiatric social worker was qualified to testify regarding behavior characteristics of sexually abused children; medical doctor was not required); *Timmons v. MBTA*, 412 Mass 646, 591 NE2d 667 (1992) (vocational rehabilitation counselor qualified to give opinion about plaintiff's impairment of earning capacity between accident and trial based on adequate medical records, but not qualified to testify about permanence of injury absent medical evidence on the issue) (Text cited); *Com. v. Cantres*, 405 Mass 238, 540 NE2d 149 (1989) (identification of drug does not require chemist; police officer or user may testify to identity of substance if court makes determination he has sufficient experience to do so); *Com. v. Griffith*, 404 Mass 256, 534 NE2d 1153 (1989) (no error for prosecution's ballistics expert to testify that blow to defendant's arm would not have caused gun to discharge accidentally); *Com. v. Garabedian*, 399 Mass 304, 503 NE2d 1290 (1987) (not error to permit psychiatrists to testify about organophosphate intoxication, on issue of whether defendant suffered from mental disease or defect); *Drake v. Goodman*, 386 Mass 88, 434 NE2d 1211 (1982) (attending orthopedic surgeon properly allowed to testify that plaintiff's clenched fist

Where the court has determined that an expert has sufficient qualifications to render an opinion, further questions and criticisms by the opponent as to the witness's education, training, knowledge, and professional experience are said to go to the weight of the testimony and not its admissibility.[57]

Knowledge of details—e.g., points of medicine, law, real estate values—gained through reading the works of others may contribute to the opinion of an expert witness, though the sources from which the

---

caused by psychological, not physical, problem); *Howe v. Marshall Contractors, Inc*, 38 Mass App 981, 651 NE2d 1245 (1995) (not error to allow vocational expert to testify that plaintiff was permanently disabled and, in practical effect, unemployable where opinion was predicated on ample testimony from physicians); *Com. v. Azar*, 32 Mass App 290, 301, 588 NE2d 1352, 1360 (1992) (forensic pathologist qualified to give opinions regarding deceased infant, although not a "pediatric pathologist"); *Moore v. Fleet Refrigeration*, 28 Mass App 971, 552 NE2d 127 (1990) (error to assume that social worker was not qualified to give opinion on psychological matters, particularly where judge did not even permit testimony on her credentials); and *Com v. Sullivan*, 17 Mass App 981, 459 NE2d 117 (1984) (medical examiner, although not a ballistics specialist, properly allowed to extrapolate from nature of wound the approximate distance from which shotgun was fired) with *Com. v. Gray*, 463 Mass 731, 755, 978 NE2d 543, 561 (2012) ("police officer who has been qualified as a 'gang expert' cannot, without more, be deemed an expert qualified to interpret the meaning of rap music lyrics"); *Com. v. Olszewski*, 401 Mass 749, 519 NE2d 587 (1988) (police officer not permitted to testify "within a reasonable degree of police certainty" that a chrome strip originally came from victim's automobile, because court does not recognize such a standard; error held not prejudicial because same testimony could be given by witness as a lay person); *Com. v. Weichell*, 390 Mass 62, 78, 453 NE2d 1038, 1048 (1983) (expertise in the area of photography does not qualify a witness to testify on the subject of human perception; also, ability of person to perceive is within the common experience of a jury); *Com. v. Seit*, 373 Mass 83, 91-92, 364 NE2d 1243, 1249 (1977) (ballistician not allowed to testify whether bullet wound to forehead would cause victim to spin around where witness had no expertise in area of physiology or pathology); *Com. v. Guinan*, 86 Mass App 445, 17 NE3d 439 (2014) (trooper qualified as accident reconstruction expert was not qualified to give opinion on computer-assisted, motor-driven power steering system); *Crown v. Kobrick Offshore Fund, Ltd.*, 85 Mass App 214, 222, 8 NE3d 281, 288 (2014) (court could preclude stock broker who had never testified as an expert and had never managed any investment fund from testifying about a fund's pre-investment trading activity); *Moncy v. Planning Bd. of Scituate*, 50 Mass App 715, 741 NE2d 82 (2001) (historian not qualified to render an opinion on the legal status of a roadway); *Com. v. Neverson*, 35 Mass App 913, 619 NE2d 344 (1993) (no error in court's refusal to allow professor of physics and biomechanics, lacking medical qualifications, to testify regarding effect on child of fall from a given height); *McNeill v. American Cyanamid Co.*, 3 Mass App 738, 326 NE2d 366 (1975) (metallurgist not allowed to give opinion as to manufacture or processing of molded compound).

[57] See *Com. v. Portillo*, 462 Mass 324, 330, n.3, 968 NE2d 395, 401 (2012) (translator need not be "certified interpreter" or "qualified interpreter" under G.L. c. 221C, § 1, to qualify as an expert, if she is fluent in the foreign language and in English, and if her knowledge will assist jury in making an accurate English translation); *Letch v. Daniels*, 401 Mass 65, 69, 514 NE2d 675 (1987).

knowledge was obtained are inadmissible as hearsay.[58] Where the expert draws upon hearsay sources for his generalized knowledge and evaluation of specific facts and states such to be the basis, in part, of his opinion, this will not necessarily make the hearsay admissible.[59]

The trial judge as a preliminary question of fact must pass on the qualifications of an expert.[60] The record must be clear about whether a given witness is called as an expert or as a lay witness. Otherwise, the proponent of the witness may be relieved of satisfying the requirements of offering him as an expert, the court may fail to make necessary findings, the jury may not be properly instructed on the considerations that apply in evaluating expert testimony and appellate review of the admissibility of the evidence will be more difficult.[61]

The better practice is for the trial judge to make an explicit finding on the qualifications of the expert at the time any objection is made to the solicitation of his opinion. However, the fact that the court heard the witness's qualifications and then permitted the testimony has been held to imply a finding that the witness qualified as an expert.[62] The judge need not entertain the proffer of a witness as an expert or make the preliminary finding that the witness is qualified as an expert before the jury.[63] It is error for the judge to expressly leave the question of whether a witness has qualified as an expert to the jury.[64] However, once the judge does make a preliminary finding that a witness is qualified to render expert opinion, the jury is entitled to continue to evaluate the witness's qualifications and to take them into

---

[58] *Kuklinska v. Maplewood Homes, Inc.*, 336 Mass 489, 496, 146 NE2d 523, 528 (1957) (geological survey); *Johnson v. Lowell*, 240 Mass 546, 550, 134 NE 627, 629 (1922) (real estate); *Barker v. United States Fidelity & Guaranty Co.*, 228 Mass 421, 117 NE 894 (1917) (foreign law); *Finnegan v. Fall River Gas Works Co.*, 159 Mass 311, 34 NE 523 (1893) (medicine); *Donahue v. Draper*, 22 Mass App 30, 491 NE2d 260 (1986) (business executives' compensation).

[59] *National Bank of Commerce v. New Bedford*, 175 Mass 257, 261, 56 NE 288, 290 (1900), where Holmes, CJ, said, "An expert may testify to value, although his knowledge of details is chiefly derived from inadmissible sources, because he gives the sanction of his general experience. But the fact that an expert may use hearsay as a ground of opinion does not make the hearsay admissible."

[60] *Leibovich v. Antonellis*, 410 Mass 568, 574 NE2d 978 (1991).

[61] See *Com. v. Wolcott*, 28 Mass App 200, 207-208, 548 NE2d 1271, 1275 (1990) (police officer was improperly permitted to testify concerning tactics and organization of Jamaican gangs, where he was not identified and qualified as an expert).

[62] *Leibovich v. Antonellis*, supra.

[63] *Com. v. Phillips*, 452 Mass 617, 636, n.13, 897 NE2d 31, 47 (2008); *Com. v. Richardson*, 423 Mass 180, 184, 667 NE2d 257, 261 (1996) (Text cited).

[64] *Com. v. Boyd*, 367 Mass 169, 326 NE2d 320 (1975); *Winthrop Products Corp. v. Elroth Co.*, 331 Mass 83, 117 NE2d 157 (1954).

account in determining how much or whether to credit the expert's testimony.[65] The trial courts have discretion in determining whether or not experts are qualified, and the decision, being one of fact, will not be reversed unless there is no evidence to warrant the conclusion.[66]

Opposing counsel cannot preclude the sponsor of an expert from producing evidence to establish his expertise by stipulating or conceding the expert's qualifications.

§ 7.5.3 *Expert's Knowledge of Particular Facts*

Proposed Mass R Evid 703 provides:

> **Bases of Opinion Testimony By Experts**
>
> The facts or data in the particular case upon which an expert bases an opinion or inference may be those perceived by or made known to him at or before the hearing. If of a type reasonably relied upon by experts in the particular field in forming opinions or inferences upon the subject, the facts or data need not be admissible in evidence.

The second sentence of the rule goes further than current Massachusetts law. Under current state law an expert witness may base her opinion about the particular facts of the case upon: (1) facts observed by herself; (2) evidence already in the record or which the parties represent will be presented during the course of the proceedings, which facts may be assumed to be true in questions put to the witness; and (3) facts or data not in evidence, including hearsay, if the facts or data

---

[65] *Leibovich v. Antonellis*, supra.

[66] *In re Will of Crabtree*, 449 Mass 128, 152, 865 NE2d 1119, 1138 (2007) (trial judge acted within his discretion in concluding that proposed expert lacked qualifications to testify about reasonableness of trustees' fees); *Com. v. Benoit*, 410 Mass 506, 520, 574 NE2d 347, 355 (1991); *El Chaar v. Chehab*, 78 Mass App 501, 508, 941 NE2d 75, 81 (2010) (decision that Imam was not an expert in Lebanese law was within trial court's discretion) (Text cited); *Prudential Insurance Co. v. Board of Appeals of Westwood*, 23 Mass App 278, 502 NE2d 137 (1986) (trial court had discretion to refuse to qualify town police sergeant as expert on traffic conditions in a zoning case). Cf. *McLaughlin v. Board of Selectmen*, supra, 422 Mass 359, 662 NE2d 687 (appropriate to reverse trial judge where exclusion of expert was based on improper factor that real estate expert was required to have practical knowledge and sales experience in the area in which she proposed to evaluate property) (Text cited); *Com. v. Banuchi*, 335 Mass 649, 655, 141 NE2d 835, 839 (1957) (judge was reversed where expert's testimony was excluded because of misunderstanding of relevance of testimony on issues of fact).

are independently admissible and constitute a permissible basis for an expert to consider in formulating an opinion.[67] An expert's opinion may be based on a combination of facts derived from those various sources.

Fed R Evid 703 was identical with Proposed Mass R Evid 703 but has been amended since the latter was drafted. See § 7.5.3.c below.

Whether an expert has sufficient knowledge of the particular facts of the dispute to be qualified to render an opinion is in the discretion of the trial court, which will seldom be reversed with respect to such determinations.[68] We discuss the various sources of facts in turn.

a. Personal Observation

Where an expert witness has personally observed the facts on which his opinion is based, he may bring his general knowledge to bear upon those facts and render expert opinions.[69] Questions put to

---

[67] *Sacco v. Roupenian*, 409 Mass 25, 564 NE2d 386 (1990); *Department of Youth Services v. A Juvenile*, 398 Mass 516, 499 NE2d 812 (1986) (modifying Massachusetts law, which had previously foreclosed an expert from gaining knowledge about the particular facts of the case from facts or data that were themselves not in evidence). See *Com. v. Hinds*, 450 Mass 1, 875 NE2d 488 (2007) (error to instruct jury that it must disregard opinion of expert unless it finds that facts assumed by witness have been proven by Commonwealth beyond a reasonable doubt).

[68] *Aleo v. SLB Toys USA, Inc.*, 466 Mass 398, 995 NE2d 740 (2013) (opinion of expert as to whether deceased could have been injured going down slide into pool was properly excluded where expert's tests did not sufficiently replicate conditions of the accident, hence opinion was not based on sufficient facts or data); *Com. v. McDonough*, 400 Mass 639, 648, 511 NE2d 551, 557 (1987) (court did not err in excluding proposed defense experts on question of whether victim could distinguish real episodes of sexual abuse from imagined ones, based on witnesses' lack of knowledge of victim's mental and emotional condition); *Minkina v. Frankl*, 86 Mass App 282, 292, 16 NE3d 492 (2014) (expert's opinion that client would have received greater recovery from trial than arbitration was speculative where based on no statistical evidence); *Masters v. Khuri*, 62 Mass App 920, 817 NE2d 809 (2004) (trial court had discretion to permit experts to testify that time recorded for blood tests reflected time results were received rather than time when blood was drawn) (Text cited).

[69] *Com. v. Benoit*, 410 Mass 506, 574 NE2d 347 (1991) (pathologist who was present at autopsy, although he did not perform it, was competent to testify as to autopsy results); *Com. v. Freiberg*, 405 Mass 282, 540 NE2d 1289 (1989) (medical examiner competent to testify that injuries could have been caused by a stove, based upon photographs of stove and personal observations of victim during autopsy); *Adoption of Frederick*, 405 Mass 1, 537 NE2d 1208 (1989) (psychiatrist's interview with mother provided sufficient basis for opinion regarding her "intellectual shortcomings"); *Com. v. Pikul*, 400 Mass 550, 511 NE2d 336 (1987) (expert who performed autopsy may testify that injuries observed could have been caused in a particular way or by a specified instrumentality); *Fourth Street Pub, Inc. v. National Union Fire Ins. Co.*, 28 Mass App 157,

such an expert need not be in hypothetical form, nor must the inquiry of the expert on direct examination call for the reasons upon which his opinion is based.[70] The witness's straightforward factual observations, however, should not be characterized as expert testimony or supplied in an answer to a hypothetical question.[71] The trial court has broad discretion in determining the admissibility of testimony based on personal observations made at some time in the past.[72]

Where an expert has examined an item of real evidence and either intentionally or negligently destroyed or lost it, upon request of the opposing party the court should preclude the expert's testimony based on the examination. The rule is necessary to avoid the unfair advantage that might result were the testimony received.[73]

b. *Facts in Evidence, Hypothetical Questions*

The expert witness may base his opinion on facts that are in evidence at the trial.[74] Counsel may elicit this opinion by posing a hypothetical question incorporating such facts, but it is not necessary to do so. The requirement of employing hypothetical questions was eliminated by Proposed Mass R Evid 705, discussed below, which was approved by the Supreme Judicial Court in *Department of Youth Services v. A Juvenile*.[75]

Counsel may still find it advisable, for tactical reasons or for clarity of presentation, to employ hypothetical questions. An expert may testify in response to a hypothetical question whether she has personally observed the subject in dispute or not.[76]

161, 547 NE2d 935, 937-938 (1989) (error to exclude fire expert's testimony based on examination of scene, although there were inadequacies in investigation).

[70] *City Welding & Manufacturing Co. v. Gidley-Eschenheimer Corp.*, 16 Mass App 372, 451 NE2d 734 (1983) (Text cited).

[71] *Com. v. Burgess*, 450 Mass 422, 436, 879 NE2d 63, 76 (2008).

[72] *Com. v. Rosenberg*, 410 Mass 347, 355, 573 NE2d 949, 954 (1991) (no error to admit testimony of doctor who examined defendant on one occasion over three years before trial, where doctor had reviewed defendant's records since that time). See *Stark v. Patalano Ford Sales, Inc.*, 30 Mass App 194, 200, 567 NE2d 1237, 1241 (1991) (expert's examination of truck six years after delivery, in breach of warranty case, was sufficient—weaknesses in testimony went to its weight, not admissibility).

[73] See § 9.5.2.

[74] Cf. *Hanover Ins. Co. v. Talhouni*, 413 Mass 781, 789, 604 NE2d 689, 694 (1992) (doctor properly permitted to testify on the basis of deposition testimony and medical records, where facts on which the doctor relied were later testified to at trial).

[75] *Department of Youth Services v. A Juvenile*, 398 Mass 516, 499 NE2d 812 (1986).

[76] See, e.g., *Davis v. Seller*, 329 Mass 385, 108 NE2d 656 (1952).

In a properly constructed hypothetical question, counsel sums up the facts, evidence of which has previously been introduced or may fairly be expected to be introduced, and asks the expert to state his opinion on the assumption that the facts are true.[77] Where the question is based on evidence yet to be introduced, failure to produce such evidence will, of course, vitiate the opinion.

The scope of hypothetical questions is within the sound discretion of the trial judge.[78] The judge may allow separate hypothetical questions designed to elicit the opinion of the expert rather than requiring one question to sum up the whole issue.[79] The question need not include all relevant facts; the effect of omission of relevant facts upon the expert's opinion may be tested on cross-examination.[80] The trial judge may require that certain facts be included in a hypothetical question, however.[81] Failure to include sufficient facts in the hypothetical question may also destroy the value of the expert's opinion based thereon.[82] If counsel employs a hypothetical question, one based on assumptions not in evidence is improper.[83]

A question is also improper where it contains a material misstatement of facts,[84] or is confusing and creates a prejudicial ambiguity in the answer.[85] The jury should, on request, be instructed that it may give weight to the expert's opinion only if it finds all of the necessary assumed facts to be true.[86]

Where testimony has been in conflict, it is improper to ask an expert: "Basing your opinion on all the testimony you have heard given in this case, what is the cause of X's condition?" This requires the witness to perform the jury's function of believing or disbelieving testimony and gives the jury no opportunity to discard the opinion if the wrong facts have been assumed as its basis.[87] It is improper for a prosecutor to describe its theory of how a crime was physically committed in the form of a hypothetical question and then ask an expert whether

---

[77] *Com. v. Burgess*, 450 Mass 422, 434, 879 NE2d 63, 75 (2008).

[78] *Com. v. Merola*, 405 Mass 529, 542 NE2d 249 (1989).

[79] *Com. v. Noxon*, 319 Mass 495, 538, 66 NE2d 814, 841 (1946).

[80] *Com. v. Burke*, 376 Mass 539, 382 NE2d 192 (1978); *Foreign Car Center, Inc. v. Salem Suede, Inc.*, 40 Mass App 15, 21, 660 NE2d 687, 693 (1996) (Text cited).

[81] *O'Brien v. Wellesley College*, 346 Mass 162, 173, 190 NE2d 879, 886 (1963).

[82] *Bearse v. Fowler*, 347 Mass 179, 196 NE2d 910 (1964).

[83] *Roddy v. Fleischman Distilling Sales Corp.*, 360 Mass 623, 277 NE2d 284 (1971); *Hopping v. Whirlaway, Inc.*, 37 Mass App 121, 637 NE2d 866 (1994).

[84] *Buck's Case*, 342 Mass 766, 770-771, 175 NE2d 369, 372-373 (1961).

[85] *Molloy v. Kizelewicz*, 343 Mass 402, 179 NE2d 247 (1961).

[86] *Com. v. Rodriguez*, 437 Mass 554, 561, 773 NE2d 946, 953 (2002) (Text cited).

[87] *Connor v. O'Donnell*, 230 Mass 39, 119 NE 446 (1918).

it is "consistent" with his observations. The expert's opinion, which essentially evaluates the credibility of the Commonwealth's theory of the case, may threaten the independence of the jury's decision.[88]

c. Facts and Data Not in Evidence but Which Would Be Admissible

As noted above, in *Department of Youth Services v. A Juvenile*,[89] the Supreme Judicial Court held that an expert may gain his knowledge of the facts in dispute from material that is not in evidence, but which would be admissible in evidence. In reaching this decision, the Court considered whether to adopt proposed Mass R Evid 703, which provides that an expert may base an opinion on inadmissible evidence if it is of a type reasonably relied upon by experts in the field in forming opinions. The proposed rule was identical with Fed R Evid 703 as it read at the time the proposed rules were drafted. Fed Rule 703 was amended in 2000 to add a third sentence:

> Facts or data that are otherwise inadmissible shall not be disclosed to the jury by the proponent of the opinion or inference unless the court determines that their probative value in assisting the jury to evaluate the expert's opinion substantially outweighs their prejudicial effect.

The Court concluded in *Department of Youth Services v. A Juvenile* that allowing an expert to rely on facts not admissible in evidence would constitute a radical departure from prior practice and raise a serious potential for abuse. The Court was concerned that experts recounting the bases for their opinions may put before the jury material inadmissible in evidence that it would otherwise not hear. This is the same concern that later led to the amendment of the federal rule. As a result of its concerns, the Supreme Judicial Court declined to adopt the full reach of the proposed rule. It did, however, decide that permitting an expert to base an opinion on facts that would be admissible in evidence was a reasonable modification that would eliminate the necessity of producing exhibits and witnesses whose sole function would be to construct a proper foundation for an expert's opinion. The Court held, "If the facts or data are admissible and of the sort that experts in

---

[88] *Com. v. Burgess*, 450 Mass 422, 436, 879 NE2d 63, 76 (2008).
[89] *Department of Youth Services v. A Juvenile*, 398 Mass 516, 499 NE2d 812 (1986).

that specialty reasonably rely on in forming their opinions, then the expert may state that opinion without the facts or data being admitted in evidence."[90]

Subsequently the Supreme Judicial Court substantially broadened its view of what information may be relied upon by an expert in forming her opinion. In *Com. v. Markvart*,[91] examiners who prepared reports under the sexually dangerous person statute, GL c 123A, § 13, were provided police reports and witness statements from a previous case and relied upon them in making their assessment of the prisoner. The Court acknowledged that such reports were hearsay and could not be admitted in evidence, but held that the examiners properly relied upon them because the "facts" in the reports would themselves be admissible. The Court held that, "It is not the form of the presentation to

---

[90] 398 Mass at 532, 499 NE2d at 821. For other cases following *Department of Youth Services*, see *Com. v. Johnston*, 467 Mass 674, 7 NE3d 424 (2014) (no substantial miscarriage of justice where state's expert witness was allowed to summarize in his testimony written statements of witnesses concerning the defendant's mental state, because it was cumulative; statements defendant made to defense psychiatrist were properly excluded on direct examination of the expert); *Com. v. Bins*, 465 Mass 348, 989 NE2d 404 (2013) (improper for DNA supervisor at crime laboratory to testify to contents of charts showing results of analysis of unknown DNA samples from crime scene and known DNA samples from defendant and victims, where supervisor did not perform tests on the known samples and was not the technical reviewer for those tests, because an expert cannot testify to test results where she lacks personal knowledge of the tests); *Com. v. O'Brien*, 423 Mass 841, 851, 673 NE2d 552, 560 (1996) (proper for expert to rely on admissible evidence not offered but furnished to him by prosecutor); *Com. v. Daye*, 411 Mass 719, 742, 587 NE2d 194, 207 (1992) (expert's testimony concerning analysis of bullet lead was admissible, although radiation testing was performed by a technician); *Anthony's Pier Four, Inc. v. HBC Associates*, 411 Mass 451, 480, 583 NE2d 806, 824-825 (1991) (expert's opinion on value of real estate based on "comparables" was admissible where he spoke to a party involved in each transaction and their testimony would have been independently admissible); *Com. v. Duarte*, 56 Mass App 714, 780 NE2d 99 (2002) (proper to allow deputy laboratory director to testify at *Lanigan* hearing that testing followed laboratory's standard operating procedures based on review of analyst's notes, although she did not conduct or observe the testing); *Com. v. Hill*, 54 Mass App 690, 767 NE2d 1078 (2002) (proper to allow laboratory analyst to testify to her conclusions about DNA testing, although she did not personally conduct the tests or supervise them); *Adoption of Kirk*, 35 Mass App 533, 623 NE2d 492 (1993) (social worker's diagnosis of father as paranoid schizophrenic was properly based on witness's knowledge of his psychiatric history as contained in hospital records); *Adoption of Seth*, 29 Mass App 343, 560 NE2d 708 (1990) (psychiatrist's testimony may be based on reports of treatment by others only where that information is independently admissible).

[91] *Com. v. Markvart*, 437 Mass 331, 771 NE2d 778 (2002).

the expert that governs whether an opinion may be based thereon, but the nature of the facts or data contained in that presentation."[92]

For example, if the pathologist who performed an autopsy does not testify, his report and the facts reported in it are inadmissible. A different expert witness who did not perform or attend the autopsy may give his opinion on a variety of matters based on the original pathologist's report, such as the cause of death, whether wounds were entrance or exit wounds, elapsed time between injury and death, the amount of force required to cause an injury, characteristics of the object probably used to inflict the injury, and the effect of certain types of injuries on a victim. The witness may not, however, refer on direct examination to the findings of the autopsy report. It is permissible, however, for the cross-examiner to ask about the underlying facts or data on which the opinions are based, for the purpose of testing the merit of the witness's opinions, even though such facts would otherwise be inadmissible.[93]

Although medical records regarding treatment and history that would be admissible in evidence may form the basis of expert opinion, when they involve a diagnosis that is controversial or involves difficulties in interpretation, the judge may preclude the use of such material as a foundation for an expert opinion.[94]

---

[92] *Id.*, 437 Mass at 337, n.4, 771 NE2d at 783. The *Markvart* rationale is somewhat problematic. The form of the presentation may well affect one's confidence level with respect to whether the "facts or data" reported in the presentation are true. If the information as presented to the expert would be inadmissible hearsay, that might reflect some level of concern about its reliability. *Markvart* indicated that a trial judge must examine the material relied upon by the expert, and possibly conduct a voir dire, to determine whether there is any manner in which the facts or data could be presented that would render them admissible. The Court, however, provided no specific guidance as to how the judge should decide this issue.

[93] *Com. v. Nardi*, 452 Mass 379, 388, 893 NE2d 1221, 1229 (2008) (expert's opinion based on report is admissible, but report is not); *Com. v. Avila*, 454 Mass 744, 759-763, 912 NE2d 1014, 1027-1030 (2009) (substitute medical examiner could not testify to conclusion of autopsy report that wound was a "shored exit wound" (a wound created when a bullet exits a body shored up against another surface), but could give his own opinion as to the nature of the wound if there was an independent basis for it); *Com. v. Rivera*, 464 Mass 56, 981 NE2d 171 (2013) (although error on authentication grounds to admit autopsy photos, substitute witness properly relied on photos, which could have been authenticated by a different witness). See §§ 8.4.2 and 8.12.2 for more detailed discussion of the Confrontation Clause issues.

[94] *Com. v. Waite*, 422 Mass 792, 803-804, 665 NE2d 982, 990 (1996) (not error to exclude opinion offered on the basis of a written preliminary diagnosis by another physician, which was considered to be only an "initial impression").

d. Misconduct by Forensic Scientists

Misconduct by forensic scientists may lead to a variety of post-conviction remedies, including a new trial,[95] permission to withdraw a guilty plea,[96] and retesting of alleged drugs.[97]

§ 7.5.4 Disclosure of Bases of Opinion

a. Under Rule 705

In *Department of Youth Services v. A Juvenile,*[98] the Supreme Judicial Court approved the rule articulated in Proposed Mass R Evid 705, Disclosure of Facts or Data Underlying Expert Opinion:

---

[95] *Com. v. Gaston*, 86 Mass App 568, 18 NE3d 1118 (2014) (defendant entitled to new trial on drug charge where forensic scientist Annie Dookhan, who signed drug certificates although she had not properly tested the substances in question, was confirmatory chemist and misconduct was discovered after trial). See *Com. v. Curry*, 88 Mass App 61, 63, 35 NE3d 435, 438 (2015) (defendant who originally elected a trial, or a retrial following withdrawal of guilty plea, is not entitled to *Scott* presumption of misconduct, but may present evidence on the issue; evidence did not show that Dookhan mixed substances from different suspects or adulterated anything other than samples, rather than the original substances seized from suspects).

[96] *Bridgeman v. District Attorney for Suffolk District*, 471 Mass 465, 30 NE3d 806 (2015) (defendants granted new trials due to Dookhan misconduct cannot be charged with more serious offenses or given more severe sentences); *Com. v. Cotto*, 471 Mass 97, 27 NE3d 1213 (2015) (where Commonwealth did not conduct thorough investigation of misconduct of forensic scientist Sonja Farak, defendant was not entitled to *Scott's* conclusive presumption because he could not show that misconduct was systemic, but would be entitled to have alleged drugs retested if samples still existed; given that samples no long existed, either Commonwealth must conduct a thorough investigation of Farak's malfeasance, or defendant would be entitled to have other random samples retested to determine time frame of misconduct; then judge should reconsider issue of whether defendant would have pleaded guilty if he knew of Farak's misconduct); *Com. v. Scott*, 467 Mass 336 (2014) (actions by forensic scientist Annie Dookhan constituted government misconduct of systemic magnitude such that drug certificates signed by her created a conclusive presumption that egregious government misconduct occurred in the defendant's case; defendant entitled to withdraw guilty plea as involuntary where he could show that misconduct preceded the entry of guilty plea and there was a reasonable probability that he would not have pleaded guilty had he known of misconduct). See *Ferrara v. United States*, 456 F3d 278 (1st Cir 2006).

[97] *Com. v. Ware*, 471 Mass 85, 27 NE3d 1204 (2015) (where Commonwealth did not conduct thorough investigation of misconduct of forensic scientist Farak, defendant was entitled to post-conviction relief of having alleged drugs in his case retested).

[98] *Department of Youth Services v. A Juvenile*, 398 Mass 516, 499 NE2d 812 (1986).

> The expert may testify in terms of opinion or inference and give his reasons therefor, without prior disclosure of the underlying facts or data, unless the court requires otherwise. The expert may in any event be required to disclose the underlying facts or data on cross-examination.

The rule is virtually identical with Fed R Evid 705.

The rule allows a witness to state his opinion or inferences he has drawn from the evidence, without first setting out during direct examination the underlying facts or data on which the testimony is based. The rule not only eliminates the necessity for posing a hypothetical question to expert witnesses, but also allows counsel to structure an expert examination by beginning with the expert's conclusions if it seems desirable to do so.

In *Department of Youth Services v. A Juvenile*, the Court specifically noted that the use of the word "may" in the second sentence of the rule does not permit a judge to exclude questions designed to elicit the underpinnings of the expert's opinion. It would appear, therefore, that opposing counsel has a clear right to examine the expert on the bases of his opinion.[99]

The proponent of an expert may introduce the basis for the expert's opinion on direct examination, insofar as it consists of evidence that has been or will be admitted in the case, the personal knowledge of the witness, the witness's training and experience and protocols generally accepted in the witness's field of expertise. To the extent the expert has relied upon facts or data not in evidence that would be admissible and are of the sort that experts in that specialty reasonably rely upon in forming opinions, the proponent may not elicit such information on direct examination.[100] Where an expert has stated the

---

[99] But see *Com. v. Anestal*, 463 Mass 655, 668, 978 NE2d 37, 47 (2012) (where "information known to expert does not form the basis of the expert's opinion, does nothing to clarify or discredit the expert's opinion, and serves only to focus on the defendant's prior bad acts, the balance—after a weighing of prejudice against probative value—plainly favors exclusion") (Text cited).

[100] *Com. v. Chappell*, 473 Mass 191, 204, 40 NE3d 1031, 1042 (2015) (the limitation on the reference on direct examination to material not in evidence relied upon by the expert "is a common-law evidentiary rule that operates in both civil and criminal cases and applies to both sides"); *Com. v. Jones*, 472 Mass 707, 37 NE3d 589 (2015) (where witness was not present at hospital, testimony about her "understanding" about how rape kit swabs were collected was hearsay); *Com. v. Greineder*, 464 Mass 580, 583, 984 NE2d 804, 807 (2013) (expert may not present on direct examination specific information on which he relied if the facts or data in question are not in evidence); *Com. v. Barbosa*, 457 Mass 773, 784, 933 NE2d 93, 105 (2010) (DNA analyst may not disclose opinion or data of nontestifying colleague on direct examination); *Com. v. Durand*, 457 Mass 574, 931 NE2d 950 (2010) (expert may not testify on direct

information on which he relied, such facts are not admitted to prove their truth, and the trier of fact may not rely on them in making findings.[101] In criminal cases, where the basis for a prosecution expert's testimony constitutes admissible hearsay, and the statements are testimonial, the Confrontation Clause prohibits the proponent from eliciting them on direct examination.[102] In any event, the opponent may elicit the basis of the expert's opinion on cross-examination. Where a criminal defendant introduces testimonial hearsay through cross-examination, there is no Confrontation Clause violation.[103] Under the federal rule, whether the expert may testify on direct examination to the basis for an opinion where the basis consists of inadmissible evidence is determined by balancing the probative value of such evidence in assisting the jury to assess the opinion against the risk of prejudice that disclosure would cause.

---

examination to content of literature she has reviewed; even though contents of studies are not testimonial and there is no Confrontation Clause violation, they are hearsay); *Com. v. McNickle*, 434 Mass 839, 857, 753 NE2d 133, 145 (2001) (it would not be admissible for a witness from Cellmark to testify about other analysts' observations of a control dot, but there was no error in admitting such testimony where defendant had insisted on a further foundation for the witness's expert opinion based on the observation of the dot by others, and defendant intended to bring out on cross-examination that the dot had been observed by the other analysts, not the witness); *Com. v. Jaime*, 433 Mass 575, 577-578, 745 NE2d 320, 322 (2001) (error to permit Commonwealth psychiatrist to testify that he based his opinion of defendant in part on statements by others that he was in a jovial mood the day before the murder and with respect to the length of his unemployment); *Grant v. Lewis/Boyle, Inc.*, 408 Mass 269, 272-273, 557 NE2d 1136, 1138-1139 (1990) (although proper for doctor to testify that he relied on the reports of other physicians in reaching his opinion, not proper for him to introduce their out-of-court diagnoses unless they came within an exception to hearsay rule) (Text cited); *Care and Protection of Martha*, 407 Mass 319, 324, 553 NE2d 902, 905 (1990) (inappropriate to admit hearsay statements by minors regarding alleged sexual abuse made to psychotherapist, where therapist had developed plan for the children and court's role was to evaluate the plan); *Com. v. Martin*, 17 Mass App 717, 461 NE2d 1244 (1984) (expert's testimony as to inculpatory statements by defendant, otherwise inadmissible, constitutes reversible error, even absent objection).

[101] *Com. v. Sepheus*, 468 Mass 160, 9 NE3d 800 (2014) (officer's testimony that a basis for his expert opinion was information furnished by a reliable informant was not admissible for the truth of that information and did not implicate the Confrontation Clause); *Com. v. Brown*, 449 Mass 747, 768, 872 NE2d 711, 728 (2007) (psychiatrist's disclosure as basis for his opinion on sanity that defendant told him he had smoked marijuana and drunk alcohol before shootings did not provide evidentiary basis for instruction on intoxication); *Care and Protection of Rebecca*, 419 Mass 67, 83, 643 NE2d 26, 35 (1994) (statements by alleged sexual abuse victims to expert witness were not admissible for their truth) (Text cited); .

[102] *Com. v. Barbosa*, 457 Mass at 785, 933 NE2d at 106.

[103] *Id.*

b. Statutory Admissibility of Hearsay in Child Abuse and Neglect Reports

Hearsay that forms the basis for opinions may be rendered admissible by statute in particular instances.[104] The Supreme Judicial Court has recognized that it is error to admit hearsay from GL 119, § 24 reports unless there is "an opportunity to refute the investigator *and the investigator's sources* through cross-examination and other means."[105]

§ 7.6 Subject Matter of Expert Testimony

§ 7.6.1 *Introduction*

The circumstances under which expert testimony might be employed are bounded only by the limits of imagination. Expert testimony is admissible when it relates to matters within the witness's field of expertise and the evidence will aid the jury in reaching a decision.[1] The court should consider among other things whether the inference

---

[104] See, e.g., GL 119, §§ 21 and 24 (reports regarding child abuse and neglect); *Custody of a Minor (No. 2)*, 378 Mass 712, 723, 393 NE2d 379, 386 (1979); *Adoption of Kenneth*, 31 Mass App 946, 580 NE2d 392 (1991); *Custody of Tracy*, 31 Mass App 481, 579 NE2d 1362 (1991). See *Adoption of Paula*, 420 Mass 716, 724-725, 651 NE2d 1222, 1229 (1995) (GL 119, § 24 reports, as well as testimony of investigator, are admissible in proceeding dispensing with parents' consent to adoption); *Adoption of Mary*, 414 Mass 705, 610 NE2d 898 (1993); *Adoption of Sean*, 36 Mass App 261, 630 NE2d 604 (1994) (guardian ad litem reports containing hearsay are admissible in proceedings to dispense with consent for adoption under GL 215, § 56A).

[105] *Adoption of Carla*, 416 Mass 510, 514, 623 NE2d 1118, 1120 (1993) (emphasis added). See *Care and Protection of Rebecca*, 419 Mass 67, 82, 643 NE2d 26, 35 (1994) (hearsay in § 24 report which is inadmissible under *Adoption of Carla* may not be used to bolster reliability determination in order to admit hearsay under GL 233, § 83); *Adoption of Iris*, 43 Mass App Ct 95, 680 NE2d 1188 (1997) (requiring parents to call court investigator on direct examination, denial of right to conduct cross-examination, was error); *In re Leo*, 38 Mass App 237, 646 NE2d 1086 (1995) (where party was given opportunity to call as witnesses the sources in investigator's report, but refused to do so, he waived right to complain of hearsay in § 24 report); *Care and Protection of Inga*, 36 Mass App 660, 634 NE2d 591 (1994) (hearsay accusations of child from GL 119, § 51A report inadmissible where child does not testify and judge has no other means to assess accuracy of statements).

§ 7.6 [1] See, e.g., *Murphy v. Boston Herald, Inc.*, 449 Mass 42, 68-69, 865 NE2d 746, 766 (2007) (admission of expert testimony regarding journalistic standards was within trial court's discretion in public official libel case, although failure to abide by established standards is not alone sufficient to demonstrate actual malice, because plaintiff was entitled to prove defendant's state of mind through circumstantial evidence and "a reporter's apparent reckless lack of care may be one factor in the actual malice inquiry"); *Com. v. Crawford*, 429 Mass 60, 65, 706 NE2d 289, 293 (1999) (error

to be drawn or the material to be understood is something for which more than the equipment of everyday experience is required.[2] Examples of the subjects of expert testimony are provided in the next section.

Some of the cases cited in the following sections are illustrative of varying results that may occur on superficially similar subjects. As stated above, expert testimony may be essential in certain areas; in others it may not be necessary although appropriate. In these latter situations the discretion of the trial judge seems to be given great weight on the question of the propriety of such evidence.[3]

§ 7.6.2 *Physical Sciences*

a. Speed Detection

In *Com. v. Whynaught*,[4] the Court, based on reported decisions from other jurisdictions that had taken judicial notice of the underlying scientific principles at issue, took judicial notice that the radar speedmeter was an accurate and reliable means of measuring velocity. Radar evidence is admissible when the prosecution can demonstrate the accuracy of the particular device on which the defendant's speed was measured.

---

to decline to receive expert testimony regarding voluntariness of confession, despite judge's claim to be familiar with PTSD and battered woman's syndrome).

[2] *Com. v. Cruz*, 413 Mass 686, 691, 602 NE2d 1089, 1092 (1992) (in absence of expert testimony, jury would not have known what effect a given blood alcohol level would have on defendant's mental processes in case where defense was diminished capacity); *Harlow v. Chin*, 405 Mass 697, 714, 545 NE2d 602, 612 (1989) (expert on medical economics permitted to give opinion on future medical expenses); *Com. v. Boudreau*, 362 Mass 378, 380, 285 NE2d 915, 917 (1972) (doctor may give an opinion, where layman could not, that brain injury was caused by blows around the head); *Coyle v. Cliff Compton, Inc.*, 31 Mass App 744, 749, 583 NE2d 875, 878 (1992) (exclusion of expert testimony about standards of installation of overhead doors was proper—jurors could comprehend the matter without it); *Adams v. U.S. Steel Corp.*, 24 Mass App 102, 506 NE2d 893 (1987) (judge properly excluded testimony of safety engineer on whether hole in parking lot was dangerous).

[3] See, e.g., *Goldhor v. Hampshire College*, 25 Mass App 716, 521 NE2d 1381 (1988) (within court's discretion to exclude expert testimony that termination from an academic position makes it difficult to be hired elsewhere in the academic community).

[4] *Com. v. Whynaught*, 377 Mass 14, 384 NE2d 1212 (1979).

b. Firearms Identification

Evidence regarding firearms identification has traditionally been held to be admissible.[5] Recent challenges, however, have explored the validity of some of the premises on which such evidence relies.[6] Nonetheless, the Supreme Judicial Court held in *Com. v. Pytou Heang*[7] that it was not an abuse of discretion to admit such evidence. The court set forth guidelines for future cases with respect to discovery, background information to be supplied to the jury by the expert and the degree of certitude to which opinions should be expressed ("reasonable degree of ballistic certainty").[8]

---

[5] *Com. v. Daye*, 411 Mass 719, 587 NE2d 194 (1992) (bullet fragments from victim's body identified as manufactured by the same party on approximately the same date as bullet found in defendant's basement; although there was conflicting evidence at trial from experts as to whether methods of conducting elemental analysis of bullet lead were accepted in the relevant scientific community, the defendant had not challenged at trial the admissibility of the prosecution expert's testimony and the Supreme Judicial Court found no substantial risk of a miscarriage of justice); *Com. v. Ellis*, 373 Mass 1, 364 NE2d 808 (1977) (spent projectile in victim's car identified as coming from same gun which had been used to fire shots into tree, by person who sold weapon to defendant; although murder weapon itself was never found, deviation from traditional methods of obtaining comparison bullets went to weight, not admissibility of evidence); *Com. v. Giacomazza*, 311 Mass 456, 42 NE2d 506 (1942) (evidence admissible that a particular projectile was fired from a particular barrel, based on rifling marks). See also *Com. v. Johnson*, 463 Mass 95, 107, 972 NE2d 460, 470 (2012) (affirming admissibility of gunshot residue evidence).

[6] See *Com. v. Lykus*, 451 Mass 310, 323, 885 NE2d 769, 779 (2008) (discussing the 2003 report by the National Research Council (NRC) that compositional analysis of bullet lead (CABL) is sufficiently reliable to support testimony that bullets that are analytically indistinguishable increases the probability that they came from the same compositionally indistinguishable volume of lead (CIVL), but that the "available data do not support any statement that a crime bullet came from, or is likely to have come from, a particular box of ammunition, and references to 'boxes' of ammunition in any form is seriously misleading"); *United States v. Monteiro*, 407 F Supp 2d 351 (D Mass 2006); *United States v. Green*, 405 F Supp 2d 104 (D Mass 2005); Adina Schwartz, A Systemic Challenge to the Reliability and Admissibility of Firearms and Toolmark Identification, 6 Colum. Sci. & Tech. L. Rev. 2 (2005).

[7] *Com. v. Pytou Heang*, 458 Mass 827, 942 NE2d 927 (2011). See § 7.5.1 for a further discussion of this case. See also *Com. v. Fritz*, 472 Mass 341, 349, 34 NE3d 705, 712 (2015) (no *Daubert-Lanigan* hearing required); *Com. v. McGee*, 467 Mass 141, 4 NE3d 256 (2014) (permissible for expert to testify that defendant's weapon was in class of weapons that could have fired bullet, even though class was large); *Com. v. Carnes*, 81 Mass App 713, 967 NE2d 148 (2012) (testimony permitted that shell casing found at scene came from same weapon that was test fired, to a reasonable degree of ballistic certainty).

[8] *Com. v. Pytou Heang*, 458 Mass at 846, 942 NE2d at 944.

c. Trace Evidence

Trace evidence refers to the analysis of small items or particles that have been left at a crime scene or another relevant location. Expert testimony regarding such evidence has generally been held to be admissible.[9] With regard to the weight to be attached to such evidence, however, it is important to differentiate between testimony which provides a definitive identification of an item as having come from a particular source, and testimony which is limited to concluding that an item might have come from a given source, although there are other sources which could have generated the same item. Hair comparison testimony based on microscopic analysis (as opposed to DNA analysis) falls in the latter category.

d. Fingerprints

In *Com. v. Patterson*,[10] the Supreme Judicial Court held that "the underlying theory and process of latent fingerprint identification, and the ACE-V method in particular, are sufficiently reliable to admit expert opinion testimony regarding the matching of a latent impression with a full fingerprint." "ACE-V" is a common method of fingerprint comparison (analysis, comparison, evaluation, and verification).

The holding that fingerprint comparison is generally reliable does not mean that all fingerprint comparison evidence is admissible. The *Patterson* Court also held that the reliability of the specific expert testimony in the case had not been established. The Court found that the government had not demonstrated the reliability of the expert's claim to be able to identify four partial latent prints that he believed

---

[9] *Com. v. Sullivan*, 410 Mass 521, 574 NE2d 966 (1991) (photos of microscopic comparison of hairs were admissible); *Com. v. Tarver*, 369 Mass 302, 345 NE2d 671 (1975) (microscopic comparison of hair samples in order to exclude classes of suspects; record demonstrated that microscopic examination was accepted by the relevant scientific community).

[10] *Com. v. Patterson*, 445 Mass 626, 628, 840 NE2d 12, 15 (2005). The Court conducted a reliability analysis, in comparison with its earlier decision in *Com. v. Ghee*, 414 Mass 313, 607 NE2d 1005 (1993) (photographic techniques employed to identify latent fingerprint of defendant on a shotgun; court specifically held that *Frye* test was not relevant, expert had made a physical comparison using his knowledge of a particular technique).

had been made at the same time by the same hand, by comparing their cumulative similarities with the defendant's known fingerprints.[11]

In *Com. v. Gambora*,[12] the Supreme Judicial Court acknowledged that the 2009 Report of the National Research Council for the National Academy of Sciences (NAS) has raised important questions about the reliability of fingerprint evidence that deserve consideration.[13] The Court declared that, "[t]estimony to the effect that a print matches, or is 'individualized' to, a known print . . . should be presented as an opinion, not a fact, and opinions expressing absolute certainty about, or the infallibility of, an 'individualization' of a print should be avoided."[14] The Report stated that ridge identification does not "guarantee that prints from two different people are always sufficiently different that they cannot be confused, or that two impressions made by the same finger will also be sufficiently similar to be discerned as coming from the same source."[15] The Report stressed that comparison involves subjective judgments by the examiner and that two examiners do not always reach the same result. The Report recognized that there is an issue of unintentional examiner bias. The Report concluded, "merely following the steps of ACE-V does not imply that one is proceeding in a scientific manner or producing reliable results."[16] It was also critical of claims of absolute certainty by fingerprint examiners. In *Com. v. Joyner*,[17] the Court discussed additional research that followed the Report. The Court rejected the defendant's argument that fingerprint evidence is insufficient to identify a perpetrator in the

---

[11] The expert had relied on cumulative similarities because he was not able to match any of the individual latent prints to an individual known print. *Com v. Patterson*, supra, 445 Mass at 628, 633.

[12] *Com. v. Gambora*, 457 Mass 715, 933 NE2d 50 (2010).

[13] The court declined to undertake that consideration in *Gambora* because the fingerprint examiner did not claim to be able to state with absolute certainty that a particular latent print matched a known print and that the ACE-V method was error free. Moreover, the court found that any error with respect to individualization testimony would have been harmless in this case.

[14] *Com. v. Gambora*, 457 Mass at 729, n.22. See *Com. v. Wadlington*, 467 Mass 192, 4 NE2d 296 (2014) (it would be error for Commonwealth to elicit testimony that error rate for ACE-V methodology "should be zero").

[15] *Com. v. Gambora*, 457 Mass 724-725, 933 NE2d 58 (2010).

[16] *Id.*, 457 Mass at 726, 933 NE2d at 59.

[17] *Com. v. Joyner*, 467 Mass 176, 4 NE3d 282 (2014).

absence of a standard by which the expert measures the probability that two sets of fingerprints came from the same source.[18]

e. Voice Recognition

The Supreme Judicial Court held that voice identification based on visual analysis of spectograms (voice prints) was generally accepted in the relevant scientific community in *Com. v. Lykus*.[19] As reported in new trial proceedings in *Lykus*, in 1979 the National Research Council (NRC), at the request of the FBI, prepared a report titled "On the Theory and Practice of Voice Identification." The NRC concluded that the assumption relied upon for spectrographic identification, that intraspeaker variability is less than interspeaker variability is "not adequately supported by scientific theory and data." The NRC also found that estimates of error rates then available did not take into sufficient account real-life situations and "do not constitute a generally adequate basis for a judicial or legislative body to use in making judgments concerning the reliability and acceptability of aural-visual voice identification in forensic applications."[20] As noted on the new trial appeal, "Based on the NRC report the FBI discontinued offering voice identification testimony in judicial proceedings."[21] Nonetheless, the Supreme Judicial Court concluded that the NRC report "did not repudiate the use of the underlying science in the court room, but instead recommended a series of prophylactic measures for its use."[22]

---

[18] *Id.*, 467 Mass at 183-184, 4 NE3d at 290-291 (the Court distinguished fingerprint evidence from DNA evidence, where evidence of a match or nonexclusion is inadmissible in the absence of statistical evidence concerning the likelihood of a match in the general population, see *Com. v. Mattei*, 455 Mass 840, 920 NE2d 845 (2010)).

[19] *Com. v. Lykus*, 367 Mass 191, 327 NE2d 671 (1975). Justice Kaplan dissented on this point, emphasizing that scientific opinion was divided on the reliability of the technique.

[20] See *Com. v. Lykus*, 451 Mass 310, 322-323, 885 NE2d 769, 779 (2008) (overruling grant of new trial on basis of newly discovered evidence).

[21] *Id.* (citing D.L. Faigman, M.J. Saks, J. Sanders & E.K. Cheng, Modern Scientific Evidence: the Law and Science of Expert Testimony § 37.1, at 8 (2006)).

[22] *Lykus*, 451 Mass 331, 885 NE2d 785. The measures included instructions by the trial judge on the problems in the forensic use of voice spectrogram analysis and the presentation of expert testimony critical of the analysis.

f. Handwriting

A witness with sufficient knowledge of the alleged author's hand to enable the witness to give an opinion as to the authorship of the specimen in dispute may give an opinion regarding the authorship of a piece of handwriting. Whether the witness has such knowledge as to enable him to give an opinion is a preliminary question of fact for the trial judge.[23] The most usual method of identifying handwriting is to have some person testify on the basis of having seen writings of the alleged author in the past and being familiar with his handwriting.[24]

Where a genuine specimen (the standard) of the alleged author's handwriting has been obtained, an expert may give his opinion as to whether the genuine specimen and the specimen in dispute are by the same hand.[25] If such specimen is admitted in evidence, the court or jury may compare it with the disputed document to determine the authenticity of the latter.[26] But a lay witness may not do so; nor may he offer an opinion in such event as to the authenticity of the disputed document based on his familiarity with the writing of the purported author.[27] In *Com. v. O'Connell*,[28] the Court acknowledged that where the witness had only seen the person sign his name on one prior occasion, that would ordinarily not be sufficient to qualify her to give a lay opinion about the genuineness of a signature. However, the Court concluded that where the witness had 20 years of experience in the banking business comparing signatures she could qualify as an expert on the issue. The opinion does not address the question of whether expert testimony regarding handwriting would be vulnerable to a *Lanigan* reliability attack.

The Appeals Court has held that a *Lanigan* hearing is not necessary for expert testimony concerning the authorship of handwriting,

---

[23] *Com. v. Ryan*, 355 Mass 768, 247 NE2d 564 (1969). See also § 9.3.2.

[24] See *Pataskas v. Judeikas*, 327 Mass 258, 98 NE2d 265 (1951); *Sheinkopf v. Eskin*, 4 Mass App 826, 350 NE2d 469 (1976).

[25] See *Priorelli v. Guidi*, 251 Mass 449, 146 NE 770 (1925) (handwriting specimen obtained from defendant while she was on the witness stand).

[26] *Com. v. O'Laughlin*, 446 Mass 188, 209, 843 NE2d 617, 634 (2006), *conviction vacated on other grounds*, *O'Laughlin v. O'Brien*, 568 F3d 287 (1st Cir 2009); *Okoli v. Okoli*, 81 Mass App 371, 963 NE2d 730 (2012) (trier of fact can determine authenticity of handwriting when there are genuine specimens with which to compare it).

[27] *Noyes v. Noyes*, 224 Mass 125, 112 NE 850 (1916).

[28] *Com. v. O'Connell*, 438 Mass 658, 667, 783 NE2d 417, 425-426 (2003).

given that Massachusetts courts have long accepted such testimony as reliable.[29] This result is at odds with conclusions reached by some of the federal courts.[30]

The genuineness of the specimen itself is to be determined by the trial judge before it can be used in evidence as a basis of comparison by the expert witness or by the trier of fact.[31] In criminal cases, such a preliminary determination of fact by the trial judge must be made, but the same issue will be submitted to the jury if the genuineness of the specimen is disputed.[32] The genuineness of the standard may be established by direct or circumstantial evidence but not by the opinion of witnesses, lay or expert.[33]

Fed R Evid 901 and Proposed Mass R Evid 901 would allow non-expert opinion as to the genuineness of handwriting where familiarity was not acquired for purposes of litigation. The Rules would also permit comparisons by the trier of fact or by experts with specimens that have been authenticated.

g. *Polygraph Examination*

Evidence regarding polygraph examinations was held inadmissible prior to the *Lanigan* decision.[34] The issue of whether such evidence might be admissible under *Lanigan* standards has been noted by the Supreme Judicial Court, but not resolved.[35] The Court has said:

---

[29] *Com. v. Murphy*, 59 Mass App 571, 576, 797 NE2d 394, 399 (2003).

[30] See, e.g., *United States v. Hines*, 55 F Supp 2d 62 (D Mass 1999).

[31] *Davis v. Meenan*, 270 Mass 313, 169 NE 145 (1930).

[32] *Com. v. Tucker*, 189 Mass 457, 473-474, 76 NE 127, 132-133 (1905).

[33] *Com. v. Di Stasio*, 297 Mass 347, 362, 8 NE2d 923, 931 (1937).

[34] *Com. v. Mendes*, 406 Mass 201, 204, 547 NE2d 35, 37 (1989) (holding that polygraph evidence had failed to gain sufficient general acceptance among scientific authorities to be admissible). *Mendes* reversed a line of authority that had permitted polygraph evidence under certain limited conditions. See *Com. v. Vitello*, 376 Mass 426, 381 NE2d 582 (1978); *Com. v. A Juvenile*, 365 Mass 421, 313 NE2d 120 (1974). *Mendes* was followed in *Com. v. Tanso*, 411 Mass 640, 583 NE2d 1247 (1992).

[35] The issue of whether polygraph test results might be admissible after *Lanigan II* was noted in *Com. v. Stewart*, 422 Mass 385, 389, 663 NE2d 255 (1996) (issue not reached because defendant made no showing regarding the reliability of polygraph evidence) and *Com. v. Kent K.*, 427 Mass 754, 763, 696 NE2d 511, 518 (1998) (juvenile made no attempt to meet "demanding Stewart standard").

"[R]eliability will be established by proof in a given case that a qualified tester who conducted the test had in similar circumstances demonstrated, in a statistically valid number of independently verified and controlled tests, the high level of accuracy of the conclusions that the tester reached in those tests."[36]

h. Accident Reconstruction

Testimony by experts is frequently offered, but not always admitted, in the litigation of automobile accidents.[37] The same is true of boating cases.[38] The event data recorder (EDR) installed in

---

[36] *Com. v. Duguay*, 430 Mass 397, 402, 720 NE2d 458, 463 (1999) (polygraph evidence excluded), citing *Com. v. Stewart*, supra. See also *Com. v. Martinez*, 437 Mass 84, 88, 769 NE2d 273, 278 (2002) (because polygraph evidence is inadmissible, defendant's offer to take polygraph test, offered as "consciousness of innocence," was inadmissible).

[37] *Hallett v. Town of Wrentham*, 398 Mass 550, 499 NE2d 1189 (1986) (police officer's testimony about cause of skid marks properly excluded because jury had as much knowledge as officer to draw conclusion); *Bernier v. Boston Edison Co.*, 380 Mass 372, 403 NE2d 391 (1980) (expert permitted to give opinion on speed and on how a light pole was caused to fall when it was struck by a motor vehicle); *Turcotte v. DeWitt*, 332 Mass 160, 124 NE2d 241 (1955) (no expert testimony permitted as to whether certain wheel marks, which had been described to jury, were caused by automobiles involved in collision); *Reardon v. Marston*, 310 Mass 461, 38 NE2d 644 (1941) (Registry of Motor Vehicles inspector can testify that skid marks on road showed that defendant's brakes were not in good working order); *Jackson v. Anthony*, 282 Mass 540, 185 NE 389 (1933) (where two automobiles collided, causing very extensive damage not only to the bodies of the cars but to their structural parts, the manner of the happening of the accident was a matter upon which expert repairmen could give an opinion). *Com. v. Addy*, 79 Mass App 835, 950 NE2d 883 (2011) (trooper's conclusions were based on his observations; court rejects defendant's objection that trooper failed to use "scientific methods, analysis, or mathematical calculations" in the absence of any explanation for why they were necessary in this case); *Peterson v. Foley*, 77 Mass App 348, 931 NE2d 478 (2010) (accident reconstruction is based on laws of physics, mathematical formulae and technical matters; officer without training was not qualified to give opinion about cause of accident); *Rothkopf v. Williams*, 55 Mass App 294, 770 NE2d 493 (2002) (proper to admit accident reconstruction testimony based on accident report, testimony of witnesses and exhibits, and expert's own observations, calculations, and measurements of scene). See *Lally v. Volkswagen Aktiengesellschaft*, 45 Mass App 317, 698 NE2d 28 (1998) (testimony of accident reconstruction expert admitted without objection; objection to video shown to illustrate his opinion properly overruled on ground there was no prejudice because video was cumulative).

[38] Compare *New England Glass Co. v. Lovell*, 61 Mass (7 Cush) 319 (1851) (whether bales of goods could be washed out of a hole in the hull of a wreck was not the subject of expert knowledge) and *Sargent v. Massachusetts Accident Co.*, 307 Mass 246, 29 NE2d 825 (1940) (probability of survival in a canoe descent of rapids in a Canadian river was a subject for expert testimony).

automobiles with airbags has been found to be reliable.[39] The device measures and records the severity (delta force) and duration of a crash and four other factors for a five-second period before a crash—vehicle speed, engine revolutions per minute, whether the brakes have been applied, and the throttle position.

i. Construction Cases

There are no bright line standards for determining whether expert testimony is admissible in cases dealing with construction and related problems.[40]

j. Computer Simulations

Computer-generated models or simulations have been treated like other scientific tests. In *Commercial Union Insurance Co. v. Boston Edison Co.*,[41] admissibility was held to be conditioned on a sufficient showing that: "(1) the computer is functioning properly; (2) the input

---

[39] *Com. v. Zimmerman*, 70 Mass App 357, 873 NE2d 1215 (2007) (affirming conclusion of reliability based on testimony by expert and general acceptance) (Text cited).

[40] See *Roberts v. Southwick*, 415 Mass 465, 614 NE2d 659 (1993) (majority and dissenting justices disagree about whether exclusion of expert testimony regarding the force required to pull down stacked sheet rock was harmless error); *Wilson v. Boston Redevelopment Authority*, 371 Mass 841, 359 NE2d 1306 (1977) (expert allowed to opine on whether a grate over an elevator shaft had ever been secured thereto); *Stimpson v. Wellington Service Corp.*, 355 Mass 685, 246 NE2d 801 (1969) (expert testimony was not required, although admissible, to support the inference that if an overloaded truck drives over a buried pipe, one end of the pipe would be depressed and the other end would rise); *Thomas v. Tom's Food World, Inc.*, 352 Mass 449, 226 NE2d 188 (1967) (expert testimony not required to show hazard of individual walking down greasy wooden ramp at 45-degree grade while carrying a quarter of beef); *Merwin v. DeRaptellis*, 338 Mass 118, 153 NE2d 893 (1958) (expert testimony was not necessary for a jury to find that a clicking sound of a marble stair tread, when stepped upon, indicated that the tread was loose and could slip out of place); *Scully v. Joseph Connolly Ice Cream Sales Corp.*, 336 Mass 392, 145 NE2d 826 (1957) (expert testimony that construction and maintenance of booth in ice cream parlor were improper was properly excluded because such question was easily comprehended by the jury); *Johnson v. Orange*, 320 Mass 336, 69 NE2d 587 (1946) (where jury had viewed place where plaintiff fell, court excluded expert testimony as to whether construction of driveway was unusual and improper); *Harrington v. Boston Elevated Railway Co.*, 229 Mass 421, 118 NE 880 (1918) (whether a given temporary subway structure was properly constructed was matter for expert testimony).

[41] *Commercial Union Insurance Co. v. Boston Edison Co.*, 412 Mass 545, 549, 591 NE2d 165, 168 (1992).

and underlying equations are sufficiently complete and accurate (and disclosed to the opposing party, so that they may challenge them); and (3) the program is generally accepted by the appropriate community of scientists." A variety of different computer simulation cases from other jurisdictions are noted in *Commercial Union*.[42]

k. Cause of Fires

In *Com. v. Goodman*,[43] the court held that the testimony of a fire inspector that a fire was deliberately set was admissible. The expert located the origin of the fire by examining burn patterns and concluded that arson was the cause after ruling out the possibility of an electrical fire. The court held that the foundation of the expert's methodology was "simplicity itself" and that the trial judge could "look to his own common sense, as well as the depth and quality of the proffered expert's education, training, experience, and appearance in other courts" to judge its reliability.[44]

l. "Fracture Matching"

The Supreme Judicial Court has approved expert testimony with respect to "fracture matching," the "'physical match' or 'jigsaw match' that occurs when a substance or an item has been broken into one or more pieces, and the jagged ends are observed to fit together."[45] The court found, based solely on the testimony of the expert witness, a Boston Police criminalist, that "fracture matching" was generally accepted and had been subjected to peer review and publication, although no such articles were offered to the court. It would seem, however, that a substantial question could be raised about the underlying theory that an item broken or torn by human action will not be fractured in exactly the same way twice. The court reasoned that "the application of human force is not precisely reproducible, and the characteristics of a

---

[42] See also *Schaeffer v. General Motors Corp.*, 372 Mass 171, 177, 360 NE2d 1062, 1066-1067 (1977).

[43] *Com. v. Goodman*, 54 Mass App Ct 385, 765 NE2d 792 (2002).

[44] 54 Mass App at 391.

[45] *Com. v. Gomes*, 459 Mass 194, 204, 944 NE2d 1007, 1016 (2011) (criminalist was properly allowed to give opinion that end of piece of tape from gun "matched" end of tape from roll in defendant's apartment).

break or tear will be different every time."[46] The question, however, is not whether one could intentionally reproduce a given break pattern, but what the likelihood is that the pattern would reoccur randomly. Given the absence of a database, it would seem the answer to that question might be in the realm of common sense and not expert testimony. Although the witness might be useful in demonstrating the way in which she believes the pieces fit together, it seems doubtful that her opinion that they are a "match" would be helpful to the jury, which could just as easily come to its own conclusion on the matter.

§ 7.6.3 *Biological Sciences*

a. Anatomy and Anthropology

The Supreme Judicial Court has upheld the admissibility of identification by means of x-ray comparison of bones and joints.[47] The Court specifically held that the testimony was not subject to a *Frye* analysis because it did not involve a "scientific instrument" or "scientific theory," and the experts relied on experienced-based knowledge.

A medical examiner is permitted to testify regarding the course of a projectile through a victim's body and the position of body at the time of the shooting.[48]

b. Time of Death

Several methods of estimating the time of death have been held admissible.[49]

---

[46] *Id.*

[47] *Com. v. Gilbert*, 366 Mass 18, 314 NE2d 111 (1974); *Com. v. Devlin* 365 Mass 149, 310 NE2d 353 (1974).

[48] *Com. v. Festo*, 251 Mass 275, 146 NE 700 (1925).

[49] See *Com. v. Bennett*, 424 Mass 64, 674 NE2d 237 (1997) ("12-12-12 rule"—during the first 12 hours after death, rigor begins to form, then it is generally complete and stays on full rigor for the next 12 hours, over the last 12 hours rigor starts to wane and eventually disappears; court finds that there is substantial authority demonstrating the reliability of time of death evidence, citing *Com. v. Haas*, infra); *Com. v. Campbell*, 378 Mass 680, 393 NE2d 820 (1979) (estimate based upon observations of corpse by medical examiner and a prison medic; Court held that a medical opinion regarding time of death is not objectionable merely because it was not based on objective scientific evidence, suggested in dictum that a rectal thermometer could have provided objective evidence); *Com. v. Haas*, 373 Mass 545, 563, 369 NE2d 692 (1977) (estimate of time of death formulated at the scene without benefit of scientific

c. Blood Spatter

Experts have been permitted to testify concerning the analysis of blood patterns in order to deduce how the blood was deposited on surfaces and the movement of persons during an incident.[50] In *Com. v. Powell*,[51] the Court affirmed a finding of the reliability of bloodstain analysis and the "string method" to determine the area of origin of bloodstains, based on general acceptance in the relevant scientific community of pathologists, medical examiners, crime laboratory personnel, police officers, and attorneys practicing criminal law.[52]

d. Odontology

Identification by comparing bite marks with dental impressions has been held admissible. In *Com. v. Cifizzari*,[53] the Supreme Judicial Court indicated that the witnesses' testimony merely aided the jury in comparing photographs of the bite marks with the dental impressions. The Court held that in order to admit such testimony, including the opinion that no two people have the same bite mark, there was no need to establish that such evidence has gained general acceptance in the scientific community. The Court concluded it would be sufficient to establish the reliability of the procedures involved, such as x-rays, models, and photographs. This decision may be questionable under the reliability principles under *Lanigan*.

---

testing was admissible; Court found, without citations, that there is substantial authority demonstrating the reliability of time of death evidence).

[50] See *Com. v. Evans*, 469 Mass 834, 849, 17 NE3d 1084 (2014) (expert properly allowed to testify in blunt force injury case that assailant would not necessarily have blood spatter on his body); *Com. v. Fryar*, 425 Mass 237, 680 NE2d 901 (1997); *Com. v. Simmons*, 419 Mass 426, 646 NE2d 97 (1995).

[51] *Com. v. Powell*, 450 Mass 229, 877 NE2d 589 (2007). See also *Com. v. Vasquez*, 462 Mass 827, 844, 971 NE2d 783, 798 (2012) (National Academy of Science report of 2009 did not conclude that blood spatter analysis is unreliable; that it is more subjective than scientific goes to the weight of the evidence, not admissibility).

[52] Cf. *Com. v. Lodge*, 431 Mass 461, 469, 727 NE2d 1194, 1202 (2000) (testimony that when blood drops it forms a teardrop, the tail of which indicates the direction in which it is falling, with the tail farther from the person bleeding, was within experienced homicide investigator's general experience and did not rise to the level of expert blood spatter testimony).

[53] *Com. v. Cifizzari*, 397 Mass 560, 492 NE2d 357 (1986).

e. DNA

In the landmark case, *Com. v. Lanigan,*[54] the Court held that DNA evidence was properly admitted where the probability of a random DNA match was based on the "ceiling principle" recommended in a 1992 report by a committee of the National Research Council of the National Academy of Sciences (NRC Report). The Court found the ceiling principle was a conservative approach to determining the likelihood of a match, and was sufficiently reliable to be admissible.[55]

---

[54] *Com. v. Lanigan*, 413 Mass 154, 596 NE2d 311 (1992) (*Lanigan II*).

[55] For further development of DNA-related issues, see *Com. v. Cassino*, 474 Mass 85, 48 NE3d 27 (2016) (where statistical likelihood of finding victim's DNA on defendant's shoes was less than one in one million, failure to introduce statistical evidence as required by *Mattei* would not have influenced verdict); *Com. v. Lally*, 473 Mass 693, 703, 46 NE3d 41, 51 (2016) (ineffective assistance of counsel not to object to DNA evidence without statistics where "jury heard evidence that PCR testing could result in 'numbers in the billions, trillions,' but did not hear that the results in this case (with less than a full profile) could be significantly less"); *Com. v. Cole*, 473 Mass 317, 327, 41 NE3d 1073, 1084 (2015) (testimony regarding computer generated population statistics is not hearsay and admission does not violate Confrontation Clause; statistics must be challenged on reliability grounds under *Lanigan*); *Com. v. Kostka*, 471 Mass 656, 31 NE3d 1116 (2015) (under the circumstances present, DNA of defendant's twin was not sufficiently relevant to require twin to furnish a buccal swab over his objection); *Com. v. Arzola*, 470 Mass 809, 817, 26 NE3d 185 (2015) (analysis of unknown bloodstain on shirt lawfully seized from defendant did not constitute a "search" where the loci examined disclosed only identity and sex; if Commonwealth were to obtain more information from those loci, use the DNA profile for a purpose other than identification, or analyze different loci that contained more personal genetic information, Court would revisit issue of whether a search occurred); *Com. v. DiCicco*, 470 Mass 720, 728, 25 NE3d 859 (2015) (affirming exclusion of expert opinions "based solely on peaks identified as potential alleles in the context of very limited data obtained from low-level DNA"); *Com v. Sullivan*, 469 Mass 340, 14 NE3d 205 (2014) (judge did not abuse discretion in awarding new trial to defendant where new DNA tests contradicted testimony of state chemist at trial that there was blood on defendant's jacket and that hair found in jacket was consistent with hair of victim); *Com. v. Fitzpatrick*, 463 Mass 581, 601, 977 NE2d 505, 522 (2012) (evidence of testing that resulted in inconclusive DNA results was admissible where defendant made *Bowden* defense and testing was relevant to adequacy of police investigation); *Com. v. Bizanowicz*, 459 Mass 400, 945 NE2d 356 (2011) (rejecting defendant's claim that there is significant debate in scientific community concerning preferable statistical method of describing likelihood of confirmatory match after a cold hit database match; trial judge did not abuse discretion in finding no *Lanigan* hearing was necessary); *Com. v. Linton*, 456 Mass 534, 559, 924 NE2d 722, 743 (2010) (raising question of whether *Mattei* requirement of statistical evidence applies to Y-STR testing where such calculations are not available; evidence was admitted without objection and court finds no substantial likelihood of miscarriage of justice); *Com. v. Mattei*, 455 Mass 840, 846, 920 NE2d 845, 851 (2010) (expert testimony that tests could not exclude defendant as potential source of DNA, absent statistical evidence explaining the import of that result, was more prejudicial than probative); *Com. v. Bly*, 448 Mass 473, 862 NE2d 341 (2007) (conclusion by trial court that

In *Com. v. McNickles*, supra, the Court discussed the relevance of DNA evidence where the test fails to provide a positive identification of the defendant as the source of the DNA found on a rectal swab from the victim. The prosecution's experts had testified that PCR test results on a strip at the DQA1 site demonstrated the presence of the allele 4.2/3, from which it concluded that the contributor was a homozygous 4.2/3 at the DQA1 site. The defendant was a homozygous

---

Bode Technology Group database was reliable was within its discretion; discovery afforded to defendant was adequate given other available methods of challenging database); *Com. v. O'Laughlin*, 446 Mass 188, 843 NE2d 617 (2006), *conviction vacated on other grounds*, *O'Laughlin v. O'Brien*, 568 F3d 287 (1st Cir 2009) (where defendant's expert's affidavit challenged only the State Police laboratory's threshold for reportable DNA results and cited to no study or criteria supporting that challenge, defendant was not entitled to a reliability hearing before DNA evidence could be introduced); *Com. v. Gaynor*, 443 Mass 245, 820 NE2d 233 (2005) (affirming trial court's findings that Cellmark's methodology in reporting tests of a mixed sample with an identifiable primary contributor in the same way it reports tests of a single source sample is reliable and that Cellmark's methodology for dealing with technical artifacts is reliable; rejecting challenge based on Cellmark's failure to follow conservative recommendations of test kit manufacturers; affirming use of product rule in mixed sample cases with identifiable primary contributor; concluding that Cellmark's population database was adequate); *Com. v. McNickles*, 434 Mass 839, 753 NE2d 131 (2001) (with respect to RFLP tests, expert's testimony concerning "likelihood ratios"—comparing probability that defendant was a contributor to the sample with probability that he was not a contributor—was properly admitted; expert offered testimony both on the assumption that victim's DNA was part of the RFLP sample, and that it was not—this properly presented statistical analyses for the full range of possibilities presented by the forensic evidence; evidence of PCR test was properly admitted where, despite small sample size, there was evidence that the control dot had activated); *Com. v. Rosier*, 425 Mass 807, 685 NE2d 739 (1997) (Polymerase chain reaction (PCR)-based DNA tests at short tandem repeat (STR) loci are scientifically reliable); *Com. v. Sok*, 425 Mass 787, 683 NE2d 671 (1997) (PCR-based DNA tests at DQA1, PM, and D1S80 loci generally meet test of reliability, case remanded to determine if technique used followed appropriate protocols); *Com. v. Fowler*, 425 Mass 819, 685 NE2d 746 (1997) (based upon 1996 NRC Report, product rule is permissible in calculating DNA profile frequencies, ceiling principle is not required; RFLP method of analysis found to be scientifically reliable); *Com. v. Thad T.*, 59 Mass App 497, 796 NE2d 869 (2003) (DNA expert may give qualitative testimony that to a reasonable degree of scientific certainty, the defendant is the source of DNA found on victim's clothing; no *Lanigan* hearing was required for this portion of the testimony, which did not involve a new theory but merely the interpretation of the unique nature of the DNA profile found); *Com. v. Rocha*, 57 Mass App 550, 784 NE2d 651 (2003) (approving admissibility of testimony that DNA evidence established that defendant's "probability of paternity" was 99.7%); *Com. v. Teixeira*, 40 Mass App 236, 662 NE2d 726 (1996) (contention on appeal that prosecution had not established proficiency of DNA laboratory, a significant variable noted in the NRC Report, would not justify reversal either on the ground that there was a substantial risk of a miscarriage of justice or on the "clairvoyance exception" that constitutional error had not yet been fully developed where the point was not raised in the trial court). For Confrontation Clause issues raised by DNA evidence, see § 8.12.2.

4.2/3 at that site, although two other suspects were not. In the general population, that trait is found in 1/1000 Caucasians, 1/100 African Americans and 1/83 Hispanics. The Court held that this descriptive information regarding the contributor of the DNA was relevant and properly admissible, where it was not presented to the jury as a complete identification of the defendant, or as a "match," and where the Commonwealth did not exaggerate the significance of the evidence or otherwise suggest that the PCR-based testing had identified the defendant as the perpetrator.[56]

In 2012, the legislature passed a statute that permits access to forensic and scientific evidence by a convicted person who has been incarcerated and who asserts factual innocence. The statute makes it possible for convicted persons to obtain DNA analysis of relevant samples that were previously not tested.[57]

---

[56] The Supreme Judicial Court has taken a case-by-case approach to the admissibility of inconclusive DNA evidence. See *Com. v. Almonte*, 465 Mass 224, 988 NE2d 415 (2013) (DNA analyst's testimony that testing was "inconclusive" (because sample was too small) with respect to whether victim was a contributor to minor DNA profile from blood on defendant's hands was properly admitted where adequacy of criminal investigation was an issue, but improper for witness to add that results of the testing "could go either way" in relation to whether victim's DNA was in the sample because it might mislead jury into thinking it was a close question; but under circumstances of case, error did not create substantial likelihood of miscarriage of justice); *Com. v. Mathews*, 450 Mass 858, 882 NE2d 833 (2008) (testimony that DNA testing was inconclusive was relevant to respond to defendant's attack on integrity of police investigation and its use of forensics); *Com. v. Nesbitt*, 452 Mass 236, 254, 892 NE2d 299, 313 (2008) (where defendant failed to challenge admission of inconclusive DNA evidence, court determined it did not create a substantial likelihood of a miscarriage of justice; court stressed that "for inconclusive DNA evidence to be admissible, it must be probative of an issue of consequence in the case," noting risk of prejudice in suggesting defendant was linked to blood found when that was not the case). Cf. *Com. v. Grinkley*, 75 Mass App 798, 917 NE2d 236 (2009) (error to permit statistical testimony regarding product rule where DNA evidence came from mixed sample to which victim was primary contributor and defendant was possible contributor in five loci where DNA from additional contributor was detected).

[57] G.L. c. 278A. See *Com. v. Wade*, 467 Mass 496, 5 NE3d 816 (2013) (motion under § 3 of statute requesting a hearing requires only a limited, threshold inquiry in which court does not make credibility determinations or consider weight of the evidence, moving party need not demonstrate a reasonable probability of a more favorable result in event of a new trial, but need only show that test results could be material to identity of person who committed the crime; where evidence was not originally subjected to analysis because of decision by trial counsel, movant need only show that a reasonably effective attorney would have sought testing, not that every reasonably effective attorney would have done so; statute does not require a showing under ineffective assistance of counsel standard; assertion of factual innocence does not require movant to aver specific facts supporting innocence on any conceivable theory of guilt); *Com. v. Clark*, 472 Mass 120, 136, 34 NE3d 1, 15 (2015) (statute should be construed

f. Screening Tests

In the ordinary course, screening tests that require further confirmatory tests in order to definitively establish the presence of drugs or biological material in a sample should not be admitted in order to prove the presence of the material in question in the absence of confirmatory tests.[58] The Supreme Judicial Court has concluded that "the presumption of reliability that attaches to the content of hospital records is defeated where the record explicitly indicates that the results of a toxicology screen are 'presumptive based on screening methods and have not been confirmed by a second independent chemical method.'"[59] In *Com. v. Fernandez*,[60] however, the Supreme Judicial Court held it was not an abuse of discretion to admit field tests as "cumulative or incremental" evidence rather than "conclusive" evidence of the presence of cocaine, where the defendant's motion in limine was only made immediately before trial. The court cautioned that with greater warning a more searching *Lanigan* analysis would have been appropriate; that until an appellate case in Massachusetts accepts such tests as reliable, they must be evaluated according to one of the *Lanigan* methods; and that general acceptance requires more than the

"in a manner generous to the moving party"); *Com. v. Coutu*, 88 Mass App 686, 703, 42 NE3d 622, 638 (2015) (strength of evidence in underlying case against defendant is not a factor); *Com. v. Donald*, 468 Mass 37, 8 NE3d 727 (2014) (where evidence was previously subjected to DNA test using older methodology, GL c. 278A permits access to testing using newer technique, but petitioner must show that such technology did not exist at time of trial or provide explanation why requested testing was unavailable at trial).

[58] See Com. *v. Johnson*, 59 Mass App 164, 794 NE2d 1214 (2003) (error to admit hospital record report of "rapid urine screening test" that was positive for presence of drugs, where report stated that a second method was required to obtain confirmed analytical result and no second test was performed). But see *Com. v. Duguay*, 430 Mass 397, 402, 720 NE2d 458, 462 (1999) (orthotolidine test results are admissible, although numerous substances other than human blood will yield positive test results). See also *Com. v. Nadworny*, 396 Mass 342, 359, 486 NE2d 675, 686 (1985) (no error to admit testimony of pathologist despite lack of certainty as to time and cause of death; noting cases going both ways on whether evidence of presence of blood is admissible when it cannot be said whether it is animal or human, admission not error here where no prejudice shown); *Com. v. Wright*, 411 Mass 678, 584 NE2d 621 (1992) (fact that chemist could not determine if blood found on murder victim's kitchen floor was human affected weight of evidence, but not admissibility).

[59] *Com. v. Wall*, 469 Mass 652, 669, 15 NE3d 708 (2014) (results of hospital toxicological screen for drugs were improperly admitted absent an independent chemical test, but where no objection was made, error did not raise a substantial likelihood of a miscarriage of justice).

[60] *Com. v. Fernandez*, 458 Mass 137, 150-151, 934 NE2d 810, 821 (2010).

New York case and state regulation proffered in *Fernandez.*[61] In *Com. v. MacDonald,*[62] the Supreme Judicial Court affirmed the admission of testimony by an experienced narcotics officer who identified the contents of a plastic bag as marijuana, without opening the bag, based on its appearance and feel. The court treated the officer as an expert, but not a "forensic expert" who was obliged to follow the State Police protocol for forensic testing. There was no mention in the opinion of *Lanigan,* and no detailed analysis of the reliability of the officer's method.[63]

g. Medical Causation

Physicians are frequently called as expert witness to testify regarding the cause of a given condition. Such a witness must have a sufficient knowledge of the particular facts of the case to give a reliable opinion.[64] Medical causation may in some cases be proved by medical records that are admissible under 233 MGL § 79G, without calling a live witness.[65]

In *Case of Hicks,*[66] the Appeals Court held that a medical expert's testimony that optic neuritis was caused by a flu vaccination was admissible, despite the lack of scientific or epidemiological studies showing a statistically significant relationship between receipt of the vaccine and optic neuritis. The court held that the administrative judge had

---

[61] *Id.*, 458 Mass at 151, n.20, 934 NE2d at 821.

[62] *Com. v. MacDonald*, 459 Mass 148, 945 NE2d 260 (2011). In accord, *Com. v. Damelio*, 83 Mass App 32, 979 NE2d 792 (2012).

[63] The court suggested that in the future it would be preferable for an officer to open the bag in order to smell the substance inside. In *MacDonald*, the trial for distribution of marijuana took place just three weeks after the Supreme Court decision in *Melendez-Diaz*. The analyst who did the test on the plant material had left the crime lab and no other analyst was available on the day of the trial. Relying on the testimony of an officer rather than a toxicological analysis raises several questions. An officer who is introduced to the jury through a recitation of his experience and credentials will hardly be perceived as a lay witness. Is there really a basis for distinguishing between "experts" and "forensic experts" with respect to whether protocols must be followed? Other than the officer's own testimony, should there be some other source for the assertion that marijuana "twigs and seeds" are uniquely distinctive? Should the court at least know the error rate for identification of marijuana by police officers based on sight and touch before admitting such testimony?

[64] See *Smith v. Bell Atlantic*, 63 Mass App 702, 829 NE2d 228 (2005) (plaintiff's treating physician, a physiatrist, lacked sufficient knowledge of her personal and professional day-to-day activities to testify that defendant's failure to make accommodations for her caused post polio syndrome that resulted in total disability) (Text cited).

[65] *Bailey v. Cataldo Ambulance*, 64 Mass App 228, 832 NE2d 12 (2005).

[66] *Case of Hicks*, 62 Mass App 755, 820 NE2d 826 (2005).

not abused her discretion in admitting the evidence based on case studies published in ophthalmology and medical journals, some authored by the witness in question, and the witness's methodology of differential diagnosis. The court held that differential diagnosis was a reliable methodology in which one identifies the cause of a medical problem by eliminating the likely causes until the most probable one is isolated.

h. Adolescent Brain

In the murder trial of a juvenile, the defense is permitted to call an expert to testify "regarding the development of adolescent brains and how this could inform an understanding of [a] particular juvenile's capacity for impulse control and reasoned decision-making" at the time of the crime.[67] Such an expert, however, is not permitted to testify that a fifteen year-old is incapable of forming the intent required for murder simply by being fifteen. Such testimony would contradict the legislative judgment that such youths may be capable of murder.[68]

§ 7.6.4 *Behavioral Sciences*

a. Battered Woman's Syndrome (BWS)

Evidence of a history of abuse and expert testimony regarding such abuse are admissible by statute in criminal cases where the defendant claims to have been a victim of abuse. GL 233, § 23F.[69] The statute allows expert testimony on: the common patterns in abusive relationships; the nature and effects of abuse and typical responses thereto; how those effects relate to the perception of the imminent nature of the threat of death or serious bodily harm; the relevant facts and circumstances that form the basis for the opinion; and evidence of

---

[67] *Com. v. Okoro*, 471 Mass 51, 66, 26 NE3d 1092 (2015) (affirming trial court's admission of such testimony).

[68] *Id.*

[69] *Com. v. Crawford*, 429 Mass 60, 706 NE2d 289 (1999) (defendant abused by victim entitled to present evidence on BWS and PTSD with respect to voluntariness of confession). See *Com. v. Morris*, 82 Mass App 427, 974 NE2d 1152 (2012) (domestic violence is a proper subject matter for expert testimony). With respect to syndrome evidence generally, see Mark S. Brodin, Behavioral Science Evidence in the Age of Daubert: Reflections of a Skeptic, 73 U Cin L Rev. 867 (Spring, 2005).

whether the defendant displayed characteristics common to victims of abuse. The statute is gender neutral.

Given the passage of this statute in 1994, the Massachusetts appellate courts have not found an occasion to determine explicitly whether the theory on which battered woman's syndrome is based is scientifically reliable. In *Com. v. Pike*, the Supreme Judicial Court noted: "The reliability of expert testimony concerning battered woman syndrome has gained acceptance and, when properly presented, is considered admissible to show self-defense . . . to explain a victim's erratic behavior . . . and to prove that a defendant's statements to police were not voluntary."[70] The Court also held that in appropriate circumstances evidence of BWS may constitute newly discovered evidence following a criminal conviction, although the condition may have existed at or prior to trial. This is because one characteristic of the syndrome is an inability of the woman to perceive herself as abused or to gain help by communicating the abuse to others. In *Com. v. Conaghan*,[71] defendant claimed in a post-sentence motion to withdraw her plea to manslaughter that as a result of BWS she had been unable to assist her counsel in preparing a defense. The Court held that the motion was improperly denied in the absence of an examination by an expert and ordered an appointment under GL 123, § 15(a). The Appeals Court has noted that such evidence has been admitted in numerous jurisdictions.[72]

In *Com. v. Rodriquez*,[73] the Court reversed a manslaughter conviction where evidence of the history of abuse had been excluded, employing a traditional self-defense analysis. The Court did not decide the issue of the admissibility of evidence of battered woman's syndrome as such. It did note that when self-defense is at issue with respect to a crime involving the use of force against another, "where there is evidence of a pattern of abuse of the defendant by the victim, expert testimony on common patterns in abusive relationships and the typical emotional and behavioral responses of persons who are battered may be admissible."

---

[70] *Com. v. Pike*, 431 Mass 212, 221-222, 726 NE2d 940, 948 (2000) (footnote and citations omitted).

[71] *Com. v. Conaghan*, 433 Mass 105, 740 NE2d 956 (2000).

[72] *Com. v. Goetzendanner*, 42 Mass App Ct 637, 679 NE2d 240 (1997).

[73] *Com. v. Rodriquez*, 418 Mass 1, 10, 633 NE2d 1039, 1042 (1994).

In *Com. v. Goetzendanner*, supra[74] the court addressed the question of whether expert testimony regarding BWS is admissible when the alleged victim of a crime claims to have been abused. It held that such evidence of battered woman's syndrome may be admitted "to enlighten jurors about behavioral or emotional characteristics common to most victims of battering and to show that an individual victim or victim witness has exhibited similar characteristics." The purpose of the evidence is to explain what might otherwise seem to be counterintuitive behavior by a victim, which could diminish her credibility. The court ruled that evidence of the syndrome is not limited to those situations expressly authorized by statute.[75]

b. *Rape Trauma Syndrome*

Expert testimony concerning rape trauma syndrome has been held sufficiently reliable to be admissible.[76]

c. *Sexually Abused Children*

Expert testimony concerning the characteristics of sexually abused children has been held admissible as "beyond the common knowledge of jurors and of assistance in assessing a victim witness's testimony and credibility."[77] In *Com. v. Dockham*, the Court relied upon

---

[74] *Com. v. Goetzendanner*, 42 Mass App at 646, 679 NE2d at 246.

[75] See *Com. v. Adkinson*, 80 Mass App 570, 954 NE2d 564 (2011) (ordering new trial based on substantial evidence that defendant was incompetent to stand trial due to BWS); *R.H. v. B.F.*, 39 Mass App 29, 37-38, 653 NE2d 195, 200 (1995) (in custody dispute, expert testimony that mother suffered from battered woman's syndrome was admissible when father put in issue mother's use of force against him).

[76] *Com. v. Mamay*, 407 Mass 412, 553 NE2d 945 (1990) (medical community has generally recognized existence of rape trauma syndrome; questions of whether sexual assault and battery victims are affected by the syndrome and whether it applies in the context of a trust relationship were within professional knowledge and experience of witness); *Terrio v. McDonough*, 16 Mass App Ct 163, 450 NE2d 190 (1983) (RTS evidence admissible in civil suit for sexual assault and battery). See concurring opinion by Liacos, CJ, in *Mamay* questioning whether evidence was sufficient to conclude there was a scientific basis for the testimony regarding the behavior of sexual assault victims in a trust relationship. 407 Mass at 427, 553 NE2d at 954.

[77] *Com. v. Dockham*, 405 Mass 618, 629, 542 NE2d 591, 598 (1989); *Com. v. Hudson*, 417 Mass 536, 540, 631 NE2d 50, 52 (1994) (citing *Dockham*; further noting that expert testimony is not admissible to prove that victim was in fact sexually abused, court held that testimony regarding symptoms of posttraumatic stress disorder (PTSD) was admissible and relevant to jury's assessment of victim's testimony and credibility; testimony established that victim's stomachaches and nightmares were

decisions from other jurisdictions to demonstrate admissibility on the ground that the testimony addressed issues beyond the common knowledge of jurors, but did not discuss the scientific basis for the he testimony or its general acceptance in the scientific community. In *Com. v. Frangipane*,[78] the Court indicated that a hearing with respect to reliability would likely be required before a retrial if the Commonwealth were to offer evidence in a child sexual abuse case regarding dissociative memory loss and recovered memory.

The appellate courts have recognized there is a substantial danger that such testimony may amount to impermissible vouching for the credibility of the complainant. An expert may not directly opine on whether an alleged victim was in fact subjected to sexual abuse. The Supreme Judicial Court has concluded that an expert may not directly refer to or compare the behavior of specific child complainants to the general characteristics of sexual abuse victims. The Court has warned that opinion testimony may constitute impermissible vouching even when it does not explicitly link an opinion to a child witness, and the danger of implicit vouching is greater when the witness testifies both as a direct witness who examined the complainant and as an expert, particularly when the witness offers fresh complaint testimony.[79]

---

typical symptoms of PTSD, and that PTSD could result from a traumatic event such as sexual abuse). See dissent by O'Connor, J and Liacos, CJ, arguing that stomachaches and nightmares are not "behavior" which might reflect negatively on the victim's credibility and thus need to be explained; PTSD evidence was wrongly used to prove that the victim was in fact sexually assaulted. 417 Mass at 543, 631 NE2d at 54.

[78] *Com. v. Frangipane*, 433 Mass 527, 744 NE2d 25 (2001).

[79] See *Com. v. Quinn*, 469 Mass 641, 15 NE3d 726 (2014) (therapist's testimony that victim was not malingering with respect to symptoms of anxiety and depression related to problems at school, which she treated before victim made allegations defendant had sexually abused her, was properly admitted; testimony regarding symptoms of sexually abused children and victim's symptoms constituted improper vouching despite fact that therapist did not link them, where witness had treated the child and jury would have taken testimony to mean that complainant's behavior was consistent with that of a teenager who had been sexually abused as a child; defense did not open door to vouching by eliciting testimony on cross-examination that complainant was a troubled girl whose testimony may not be reliable and suggesting that allegations were not credible where victim had consulted therapist for eight months without claiming sexual abuse); *Com. v. Quincy Q.*, 434 Mass 859, 753 NE2d 781 (2001) (testimony from expert who did not provide fresh complaint testimony that child's physical examination was normal and that majority of girls examined for possible sexual abuse have no recognizable traces of physical contact was permissible and did not amount to vouching for witness); *Com. v. Pare*, 427 Mass 427, 693 NE2d 1002 (1998) (error to admit social worker's reference to child's "truthful" disclosures); *Com. v. Federico*, 425 Mass 844, 849, 683 NE2d 1035, 1039 (1997) (testimony of one expert improperly admitted, could be understood as indicating that sexual abuse occurred in the case; testimony of second expert who stated lack of physical trauma was not "inconsistent" with abuse

was permissible); *Com. v. Trowbridge*, 419 Mass 750, 647 NE2d 413 (1995) (testimony that symptoms and physical condition of child at issue were consistent with the type of non-violent sexual abuse that was alleged came impermissibly close to an endorsement of child's credibility; expert testimony that mother's animosity could have influenced child to make false accusations of sexual abuse was properly excluded as an impermissible comment on the credibility of the child witness); *Care and Protection of Rebecca*, 419 Mass 67, 643 NE2d 26 (1994) (expert's testimony that children had been sexually abused, identifying the persons who had abused them, and opining that their mother was present amounted to testimony that he believed children and was inadmissible); *Com. v. Colin C.*, 419 Mass 54, 643 NE2d 19 (1994) (expert testimony that victims were sexually abused was essentially a statement vouching for their credibility); *Com. v. Montanino*, 409 Mass 500, 504, 567 NE2d 1212, 1214 (1991) (error to admit police officer's testimony that most sexual assault victims provide more complete details of the incident in later as compared to initial interviews—would be taken by jury as endorsement of victim's credibility) (Text cited); *Com. v. Ianello*, 401 Mass 197, 515 NE2d 1181 (1987) (no error in exclusion of testimony by defendant's expert, a psychologist, which amounted to opinion on veracity of minor rape victim); *Com. v. Aspen*, 85 Mass App 278, 8 NE3d 782 (2014) (doctor's testimony was equivalent to vouching where she cherry-picked general characteristics of victims that were similar to the complainant's, leaving others out, and gave profile testimony relating to intra-family sexual abuse that mirrored the complainant's family makeup and dynamic); *Com. v. Morris*, 82 Mass App 427, 433, 974 NE2d 1152, 1159 (2012) (mere fact that expert's description of possible behavior of abuse victims is consistent with that of the victim does not render it impermissible vouching); *Com. v. Velazquez*, 78 Mass App 660, 666, 941 NE2d 1136, 1140 (2011) (reversible error to allow doctor, appearing as expert, to testify that child demonstrated with dolls "what happened to her" and doctor effectively communicated to jury she believed child); *Com. v. Baran*, 74 Mass App 256, 279, 905 NE2d 1122, 1141 (2009) (ineffective assistance of counsel not to object to impermissible vouching by experts); *Com. v. Bougas*, 59 Mass App 368, 375, 795 NE2d 1230, 1236 (2003) (in questionable decision, court holds that prosecution's testimony that children often delay disclosure of sexual abuse was admissible, but defense offer of testimony that children enmeshed in serious family turmoil often fabricate allegations of sexual abuse was properly excluded because it "brands the class of which the alleged victim is a member as untrustworthy"); *Com. v. Deloney*, 59 Mass App 47, 56-57, 794 NE2d 613, 621-622 (2003) ("expert testimony that describes what a typical victim looks or acts like, and that suggests that child victims in a particular case have acted typically when compared to a 'norm' of child victims, may not be admitted. . . . We recognize the apparent oddity that under this approach, the more numerous the similarities between the individual child victim and a 'standard' child victim created by an expert witness, the more likely it is that the expert testimony will be excluded. That is because our concern is not with relevance. . . . The concern we address is the fear that the jury's responsibility ultimately to decide for itself whether the children are telling the truth will give way to expert opinion that paints the child witness as a victim."); *Com. v. Colon*, 49 Mass App 289, 729 NE2d 315 (2000) (expert testimony that absence of physical findings did not rule out sexual abuse and that only 15 to 20 percent of girls with confirmed sexual abuse histories showed physical signs of vaginal penetration did not amount to opinion on complainant's credibility); *Com. v. Spear*, 43 Mass App 583, 593, 686 NE2d 1037, 1044 (1997) (direct comparison between general characteristics of child victims and complainants was improper); *Com. v. LaCaprucia*, 41 Mass App 496, 671 NE2d 984 (1996) (school counselor's description of her observations of complainant, coupled with her observations of her experience with other

The large number of appellate decisions on this point demonstrates the ongoing difficulty that trial judges apparently have controlling the questioning by prosecutors of experts on child sexual abuse.

In *Com. v. Rather*,[80] the court suggested guidelines for cases in which either side intends to offer expert evidence as to patterns of disclosure of child abuse victims. The guidelines include: (1) early notification to trial judge; (2) voir dire of the expert witness; (3) specific advice to the witness not to render an opinion as to the credibility of the alleged victim or the general veracity of sexually abused children; (4) jury instructions on the role of experts, including, on request, that expert testimony is not affirmative evidence of sexual abuse and that the expert did not assess the credibility of the alleged victim; (5) proponent of the testimony should not imply in closing argument that expert vouched for credibility of victim.

d. Battered Child Syndrome

Expert testimony concerning the battered child syndrome has been held sufficiently reliable to be admissible.[81] In *Estelle v. McGuire*,[82] the United States Supreme Court reviewed the admission

---

traumatized children amounted to impermissible vouching); *Com. v. Allen*, 40 Mass App 458, 665 NE2d 105 (1996) (not error to allow therapist to testify about general symptoms associated with sexual abuse where prosecution brought out the fact that witness was the child's treating therapist only briefly at the end of testimony; not error to allow doctor to testify that complainant's hymen was a normal shape and that the majority of girls examined with regard to a finding of sexual abuse have a normal exam); *Com. v. Perkins*, 39 Mass App 577, 583, 658 NE2d 975, 979 (1995) (where expert testified as to general characteristics of sexually abused children and then answered a series of hypothetical questions regarding particularized behavior of children that matched children in the case, testimony was tantamount to endorsement of credibility of complaining witnesses, and admission was error); *Com. v. McCaffrey*, 36 Mass App 583, 591, 633 NE2d 1062, 1067 (1994) (allowing psychologist to testify as both behavioral expert and treating therapist may have amounted to vouching for victim's credibility by suggesting that therapist had accepted child as a patient to be treated because she accepted her allegations as true).

[80] *Com. v. Rather*, 37 Mass App 140, 150, 638 NE2d 915, 920 (1994).

[81] *Com. v. Day*, 409 Mass 719, 724, 569 NE2d 397, 399-400 (1991) (battered child syndrome is "a well recognized medical diagnosis, dependent on inferences, not a matter of common knowledge, but within the area of expertise of physicians whose familiarity with numerous instances of injuries accidentally caused qualifies them to express with reasonable probability that a particular injury or group of injuries is not accidental or is not consistent with the explanation offered therefor but is instead the result of physical abuse by a person of mature strength"); *Adoption of Iris*, 43 Mass App 95, 101 n.8, 680 NE2d 1188 (1997); *Com. v. Collins*, 26 Mass App 1021, 533 NE2d 214 (1989) (finding "shaken infant syndrome" to be a recognized medical diagnosis).

[82] *Estelle v. McGuire*, 498 US 1119, 111 S Ct 1071 (1991).

under California law of evidence that an alleged child murder victim suffered from "battered child syndrome." The Court ruled that the evidence of prior abuse was relevant to prove that someone had intentionally, as opposed to accidentally, harmed the child, although there was no direct evidence linking the prior incidents to defendant. The Court held there was no constitutional due process violation in the admission of such evidence.

e. Eyewitness Identification

Expert testimony on the capacity of eyewitnesses to make identifications is not admissible as of right. It is, however, admissible in the proper exercise of discretion by the trial judge.[83] In *Com. v. Gomes,*[84] the Supreme Judicial Court specifically stated that the model jury instructions were "not intended in any way to preclude expert testimony." The Court added, "Expert testimony may be important to elaborate on the generally accepted principles in a model instruction and to explain how other variables relevant to the particular case can affect the accuracy of the identification. A judge may also allow an expert to challenge the generally accepted principles we incorporated, and, where the judge finds the expert's challenge to be persuasive, the judge may modify the model instruction accordingly."[85] In *Com. v. Sowers,*[86] the Court found no error in the admission of an ophthalmologist's testimony that a victim, who was legally blind, could identify a person from a certain distance, stating that the testimony dealt with only the clarity and distinctness of the victim's vision, not the reliability of the identification in issue. In *Com. v. Zimmerman*[87] the Court held that it was error for the trial judge to deny funds for an expert on eyewitness identification based on the argument that such testimony

---

[83] *Com. v. Borgos*, 464 Mass 23, 35, 979 NE2d 1095, 1105 (2012) (whether to permit expert testimony on eyewitness identification remains within discretion of trial judge); *Com. v. Bly*, 448 Mass 473, 495, 862 NE2d 341, 360 (2007) (affirming denial of expert testimony); *Com. v. Ashley*, 427 Mass 620, 624 n.3, 694 NE2d 862, 866 (1998) (court refused to adopt Commonwealth's argument that expert testimony on eyewitness identification is never admissible); *Com. v. Francis*, 390 Mass 89, 453 NE2d 1204 (1983) (extensive review of authorities on expert testimony on eyewitness identification).

[84] *Com. v. Gomes*, 470 Mass 352, 378, 22 NE3d 897, 918 (2015) (proposing new eyewitness identification instruction).

[85] *Id.*

[86] *Com. v. Sowers*, 388 Mass 207, 446 NE2d 51 (1983).

[87] *Com. v. Zimmerman*, 441 Mass 146, 804 NE2d 336 (2004).

was of questionable admissibility. The Court held that the judge should also have considered the desirability or necessity of the testimony to the defendant's case. In a concurring opinion, Justice Cordy, joined by Justice Ireland, concluded that expert testimony on cross-racial identification should be admissible and rests on a reliable basis. For an example of a case where expert testimony was admitted by the trial judge see *Com. v. Daniels.*[88]

f. Hypnotically Aided Testimony

Hypnotically aided testimony has been rejected.[89] Where a witness has been hypnotized, testimony must be based on pre-hypnotic memory to be admissible. The trial court must determine the substance of a witness's pre-hypnotic memory and compare it to the proposed trial testimony, then exclude from evidence details "remembered" for the first time after hypnosis.[90]

g. Insanity

In Massachusetts, persons not expert in mental disease may testify only as to facts observed and may not draw the conclusion of sanity or insanity.[91] A witness qualified in the treatment of mental diseases may give an opinion on the criminal responsibility of the defendant.[92]

---

[88] *Com. v. Daniels*, 445 Mass 392, 409 n.29, 837 NE2d 683 (2005).

[89] *Com. v. Kater*, 388 Mass 519, 447 NE2d 1190 (1983) (*Kater I*) (rejecting hypnotically aided testimony).

[90] *Com. v. Kater*, 432 Mass 404, 734 NE2d 1164 (2000) (*Kater VII*); *Com. v. Kater*, 412 Mass 800, 592 NE2d 1328 (1992) (*Kater IV*); *Com. v. Kater*, 409 Mass 433, 567 NE2d 885 (1991) (*Kater III*); *Com. v. Kater*, 394 Mass 531, 476 NE2d 593 (1985) (*Kater II*); and cases cited therein. See also § 6.27.

[91] *Com. v. Monico*, 396 Mass 793, 488 NE2d 1168 (1986) (Text cited).

[92] *Com. v. Berry*, 466 Mass 763, 770 (2014) (not error for trial judge to refuse to strike testimony of expert that included inaccurate definition of the law with respect to insanity defense, where trial judge later advised jury that it should take the law from the judge and gave jury correct instruction with respect to insanity defense); *Com. v. Sliech-Brodeur*, 457 Mass 300, 326, 930 NE2d 91, 111 (2010) (not error for judge to decline to hold *Lanigan* hearing on reliability of methodology of psychiatrist who examined defendant and reviewed wide variety of material related to her personal and medical history, as well as circumstances of crime charged). See *Com v. Gerhartsreiter*, 82 Mass App 500, 509, 975 NE2d 890, 899 (2012) (expert may express opinion on defendant's mental condition without referring to *McHoul* standard); *Com. v. Montanez*, 55 Mass App 132, 144-146, 769 NE2d 784, 795-796 (2002) (unless Commonwealth offers rebutting information on retrial, court should admit evidence of dissociative

Although an expert is allowed to give an opinion on the ultimate issue of criminal responsibility, she is not required to do so. An expert may testify as to her observations of the defendant and supply psychiatric explanations for a defendant's actions, without providing an opinion on criminal responsibility.[93]

Under the Federal Rules, an expert may not express an opinion on the ultimate issue of whether the defendant had a mental state or condition constituting an element of the crime charged or of a defense thereto. Fed R Evid 704(b).[94]

In Massachusetts, a doctor without a specialty in psychiatry who has examined a criminal defendant may testify as to his observations, diagnosis, and treatment of the defendant's condition. However, he may not render an opinion on criminal responsibility if he is not specially qualified in the treatment of mental diseases.[95] A witness may be so qualified without possessing a medical degree—the issue is the witness's experience and the probative value of the testimony.[96]

Expert testimony is not required to raise an insanity defense. The issue may be presented on the facts of the case, through prosecution witnesses, by lay testimony of observations of the defendant, or a combination of such evidence.[97] A criminal defendant may testify himself as to the symptoms he suffered from and to the fact that he felt better after psychiatric care.[98]

---

trance disorder (DTD), based on evidence that it is a research category in DSM-IV, although not a diagnostic category, that it has been subject to peer review articles, and that it employs generally accepted testing instruments).

[93] *Com. v. Kappler*, 416 Mass 574, 585, 625 NE2d 513, 519 (1993).

[94] See § 7.3.1 for text of the rule.

[95] *Com. v. Monico*, supra.

[96] *Com. v. Monico*, supra (psychologist may give opinion on criminal responsibility).

[97] *Com. v. Guadalupe*, 401 Mass 372, 516 NE2d 1159 (1987); *Blaisdell v. Com.*, 372 Mass 753, 765, 364 NE2d 191, 201-202 (1977). In *Guadalupe*, the Court held that failure to give notice of an insanity defense pursuant to Mass R Crim P 14(b)(2) will not bar evidence on the issue unless the defendant has refused to submit to a court-ordered psychiatric examination. In accord, *Com. v. Dotson*, 402 Mass 185, 521 NE2d 395 (1988).

[98] *Com. v. Guadalupe*, supra. Cf. *Com. v. Seabrooks*, 425 Mass 507, 681 NE2d 1198 (1997) (nature of crime itself, suicide attempt, and defendant's testimony that "he freaked out" and "lost control" were not enough to raise insanity defense); *Com. v. Johnson*, 422 Mass 420, 663 NE2d 559 (1996) (suicidal ideation, absent more, provides insufficient basis for finding of lack of criminal responsibility; bizarre or inexplicable nature of crime alone does not provide foundation for insanity defense).

Once the defendant has raised the issue of insanity, the prosecution must prove that a defendant is sane beyond a reasonable doubt.[99] The prosecution need not present expert testimony to meet its burden of proving sanity.[100] Where a defendant intends to offer psychiatric testimony, or where there is a reasonable likelihood that he will, the court may order the defendant to submit to a psychiatric examination so that the prosecution may obtain expert testimony.[101] The Commonwealth is also entitled to discovery of the defendant's medical and psychiatric records in connection with the examination.[102] An examination may also be ordered when the defendant places at issue his mental ability voluntarily to waive his *Miranda* rights and make a voluntary statement.[103] In each case in which the defendant's criminal responsibility is raised, the court should give a jury instruction permitting the jury to consider the "presumption of sanity," the fact that a great majority of people are sane, and the probability that any particular person is sane.[104] The Commonwealth is not precluded from offering expert testimony on the issue of sanity, even if the defendant does not raise the issue.[105]

---

[99] *Com. v. Keita*, 429 Mass 843, 712 NE2d 65 (1999) (rejecting suggestion that burden of proving insanity should be placed upon the defendant).

[100] *Com. v. Keita*, supra (evidence of the defendant's conduct after his arrest, although "thin," was sufficient along with presumption of sanity to carry Commonwealth's burden); *Com. v. Kappler*, supra (although defendant introduced testimony from experts who concluded he was not criminally responsible, and prosecution's experts failed to reach that ultimate issue, evidence was sufficient for jury to find defendant was sane).

[101] Mass R Crim P 14(b)(2)(B); *Blaisdell v. Com.*, 372 Mass 753, 364 NE2d 191 (1977); *Com. v. Harris*, 468 Mass 429, 11 NE3d 95 (2014) (where defendant gave notice of intent to offer expert testimony regarding mental impairment, based in part on his statements, and then offered expert witness testimony at trial, he waived the constitutional privilege against self-incrimination and opened the door to rebuttal evidence of a prior court-ordered competency exam of defendant); *Com. v. Brown*, 75 Mass App 361, 365, 914 NE2d 332, 335 (2009) (Commonwealth need not request examination under Rule 14(b)(2)(B) to rebut defendant's evidence, but can offer expert's opinion based on an examination that took place previously). In *Com. v. Stockwell*, 426 Mass 17, 686 NE2d 426 (1997), it was held that the trial judge had not abused his discretion by denying the defendant's request to videotape the examination by the Commonwealth's psychiatrist.

[102] *Com. v. Hanright*, 465 Mass 639, 989 NE2d 883 (2013) (Mass R. Crim. P. 14(b)(2)(B) permits pretrial discovery by Commonwealth of a defendant's medical and psychiatric records in connection with a Rule 14(b)(2)(B) psychiatric examination).

[103] *Com. v. Ostrander*, 441 Mass 344, 352, 805 NE2d 497, 504 (2004).

[104] *Com. v. Keita*, supra.

[105] *Com. v. Contos*, 435 Mass 19, 26, 754 NE2d 647, 654 (2001).

An expert who testifies at trial may be asked questions regarding the defendant's demeanor during the trial, if relevant to the sanity issues involved.[106]

In a homicide case, where a defendant presents expert testimony that his mental condition impaired his ability to form specific intent, the defendant is entitled to a jury instruction on the question of whether his mental condition impaired his ability to engage in deliberate premeditation.[107] Although Massachusetts does not recognize a "diminished capacity" defense, a defendant also may produce expert testimony on whether impairment of his mental processes precluded him from being able to deliberately premeditate and whether he acted with extreme atrocity or cruelty.[108]

In a civil case, a judge has discretion to admit testimony from physicians who are not psychiatrists concerning a party's mental capacity.[109]

In a will case, an attesting witness can give his opinion as to sanity formed at the time of execution of the will, but not his opinion as to sanity formed either before or after that time.[110] The testator's attending physician can give his opinion, even if he is not a qualified expert in mental disease.[111]

h. Sexual Dangerousness

Pursuant to statute in Massachusetts, the district attorney or the attorney general may petition the Superior Court to have persons who have been convicted of certain sexual crimes designated as sexually dangerous persons and committed to a treatment center.[112] If the person is scheduled to be released from custody prior to a probable cause

---

[106] *Com. v. Hunter*, 427 Mass 651, 655, 695 NE2d 653, 657 (1998) (not error to permit government expert to comment on defendant's demeanor during showing of Vietnam film in case where insanity claim was based on PTSD); *Com. v. Smiledge*, 419 Mass 156, 643 NE2d 41 (1994).

[107] *Com. v. Ward*, 426 Mass 290, 688 NE2d 227 (1997).

[108] *Com. v. Candelario*, 446 Mass 847, 848 NE2d 769 (2006) (even though such testimony is permissible, it was not ineffective of counsel to choose not to call such an expert here for tactical reasons).

[109] *Barshak v. Buccheri*, 406 Mass 187, 547 NE2d 23 (1989).

[110] *Williams v. Spencer*, 150 Mass 346, 23 NE 105 (1890).

[111] *Duchesneau v. Jaskoviak*, 360 Mass 730, 277 NE2d 507 (1972).

[112] MGL Ch. 123A, §§ 12-15.

hearing, the court may order him temporarily committed to the treatment center. Expert testimony is required to justify a temporary commitment, but the evidence need not be in the form of live testimony.[113] If the court determines at a hearing that there is probable cause to believe the person is sexually dangerous, he may be committed to the treatment center initially for a period of 60 days for observation. At the hearing on probable cause, the judge must determine whether the Commonwealth's evidence satisfies all the elements of proof necessary to prove the case, and find that the evidence "is not so incredible, insubstantial, or otherwise of such a quality that no reasonable person could rely on it. . . ."[114] If the court finds probable cause, it may order the person to be examined by two "qualified examiners" whose reports are admissible at the trial of the petition.[115] The defendant is entitled to retain a psychologist or psychiatrist to perform an examination on his behalf and, if indigent, is entitled to court funds to pay for the cost of such examination.[116] The defendant is not required to submit to an interview by the two court appointed examiners. If he refuses to do so, however, the testimony of a defense expert is inadmissible.[117]

---

[113] *Com. v. Bruno*, 432 Mass 489, 735 NE2d 1222 (2000) (temporary commitment).

[114] *Com. v. Reese*, 438 Mass 519, 524, 781 NE2d 1225, 1230 (2003) (concluding that trial judge substituted his own opinion of expert's credibility rather than determining whether a reasonable fact finder could credit expert).

[115] *Com. v. Felt*, 466 Mass 316, 994 NE2d 374 (2013) (where a qualified examiner declined to conduct personal interview that defendant agreed to attend as part of a § 13(a) examination, examiner's report was inadmissible, but dismissal of Commonwealth's petition was improper where other examiner conducted interview and found defendant sexually dangerous). The statute requires that a qualified examiner have two or more years of experience with diagnosis or treatment of sexually aggressive offenders. It is error to permit testimony from an examiner who does not meet the requirement. *In re LeSage*, 76 Mass App 566, 924 NE2d 309 (2010).

[116] G.L. c. 123A § 13. See *In re Santos*, 461 Mass 565, 962 NE2d 726 (2012) (§ 9 requires admission of petitioner's expert reports on same basis as reports of qualified examiners); *Com. v. Starkus*, 69 Mass App 326, 867 NE2d 811 (2007) (not error to exclude defense expert's report where he failed to provide discovery of underlying data on which conclusions were based; report not admissible as report of qualified examiner where expert was not designated as qualified examiner by Commissioner of Correction).

[117] *Com. v. Connors*, 447 Mass 313, 850 NE2d 1038 (2006) (to allow testimony by defense expert would put the Commonwealth at a disadvantage because it could not effectively rebut it); *Com. v. Mazzarino*, 81 Mass App 358, 963 NE2d 112 (2012) (where defendant cross-examined qualified examiners to show that it was difficult for them to assess him without examining him, it was permissible for prosecution to elicit testimony that defendant declined to be examined on advice of counsel in order to eliminate suggestion that lack of examination was due to examiners' negligence or bias).

The statute provides in §§ 9 and 14 that the reports of the qualified examiners "shall be admissible" in a hearing or trial if proper notice is given to the opposing party. In *Com. v. Markvart*,[118] however, the Supreme Judicial Court held that such reports function as the equivalent of the direct testimony of an expert witness and must be redacted to eliminate inadmissible hearsay. An expert witness may not put inadmissible evidence before the jury merely in order to explain the basis of his opinion, unless it is elicited on cross examination, and that principle would be violated if the reports of qualified examiners could be admitted containing such inadmissible evidence.[119] The Appeals Court has held that the qualified examiners are permitted to testify concerning the credibility of the defendant's statements to the examiner.[120]

In *Com. v. Bradway*,[121] the Appeals Court held that where the Legislature had mandated the admissibility of reports of "qualified examiners" in trials to determine sexual dangerousness, no hearing on the reliability of such expert testimony was necessary. The court held it was within the province of the Legislature to determine the admissibility of such evidence. The Appeals Court has held, however, that this does not eliminate the reliability requirement for evidence other than that of the qualified examiners.[122]

The Commonwealth is not entitled to have the defendant submit to an examination by its own expert. The fact that the defendant is entitled to have an expert other than the two qualified examiners appointed by the court does not entitle the Commonwealth to a separate expert.[123]

---

[118] *Com. v. Markvart*, 437 Mass 331, 771 NE2d 778 (2002) (examiners preparing such reports may rely on hearsay evidence if the facts or data contained therein would be otherwise admissible, but references to such material in the reports must be redacted before they are presented to the jury) (Text cited); *Com. v. Starkus*, supra.

[119] This holding in *Markvart* was not overruled in *In re Mchoul*, 445 Mass 143, 833 NE2d 1146 (2005), where the Court held that other multiple hearsay in reports made admissible by the sexually dangerous person statutes was admissible; *Com. v. Starkus*, supra (layered hearsay is admissible in record under G.L. c. 123A, § 14(c)).

[120] *In re Gammell*, 86 Mass App 8, 12 NE3d 409 (2014).

[121] *Com. v. Bradway*, 62 Mass App 280, 816 NE2d 152 (2004).

[122] *In re Gammell*, 86 Mass App 8, 12 NE3d 409 (2014) (defendant's penile plethysmograph evidence was not admissible over Commonwealth's objection absent a *Daubert-Lanigan* hearing).

[123] *Com. v. Poissant*, 443 Mass 558, 823 NE2d 350 (2005).

Expert testimony is required to commit someone as a sexually dangerous person.[124] If both the qualified examiners conclude that the defendant is not sexually dangerous, the Commonwealth cannot rely upon other sources of expert testimony, including the report of the Community Access Board, to meet its burden of proof at the trial.[125] The Appeals Court has held, however, that if at least one of the qualified examiners concludes that the defendant is sexually dangerous, testimony from that examiner is not required at trial and the finder of fact may find sexual dangerousness on the basis of a representative of the community access board.[126]

Expert testimony is permitted, in the discretion of the Board, but not required in proceedings before the Sex Offender Registry Board.[127] Under certain circumstances the Board should furnish funds to an alleged offender to obtain expert testimony.[128]

In *In re Ready*,[129] the court affirmed the trial court's rejection, on reliability grounds, of the Abel Assessment for Sexual Interest (AASI) test. The test purports to measure a subject's relative sexual interest in people of different ages and genders. In proceedings to commit someone as a sexually dangerous person, the "personality disorders" upon

---

[124] *In re Johnstone*, 453 Mass 544, 903 NE2d 1074 (2009); *Com. v. Dube*, 59 Mass App 476, 796 NE2d 859 (2003) (applying *Bruno* requirement to permanent commitment); *Com. v. Boyer*, 61 Mass App 582, 812 NE2d 1235 (2004) (same; preliminary report submitted at probable cause hearing and subsequently recanted at trial was insufficient evidence to prove beyond a reasonable doubt that defendant was a sexually dangerous person).

[125] *In re Johnstone*, 453 Mass 544, 903 NE2d 1074 (2009).

[126] *In re Souza*, 87 Mass App 162, 27 NE3d 395 (2015).

[127] *Doe v. Sex Offender Registry Board*, 470 Mass 102, 18 NE3d 1081 (2014) (opinion of expert testifying on behalf of sex offender need not be accepted by the hearing examiner even where board does not present contrary expert testimony).

[128] *Doe v. Sex Offender Registry Board*, 466 Mass 594 (2013) (error for board to fail to consider effect of gender on recidivism, and abuse of discretion to deny motion for funds for an expert witness on that issue); *Doe v. Sex Offender Registry Board*, 452 Mass 764, 897 NE2d 1001 (2008) (Board has discretion to grant funds to indigent sex offender for expert witness or report, even though Board itself does not intend to rely on expert witness); *Doe v. Sex Offender Registry Board*, 452 Mass 784, 897 NE2d 992 (2008) (not an abuse of discretion to deny funds where one was not needed to shed light on report regarding penile plethysmography); *Doe v. Sex Offender Registry Board*, 447 Mass 779, 857 NE2d 492 (2006) (Board was not required to furnish funds to indigent sex offender to retain an expert and could classify him as a level three sex offender without expert testimony).

[129] *In re Ready*, 63 Mass App 171, 824 NE2d 474 (2005).

which the Commonwealth may rely are not limited to those described in APA, Diagnostic and Statistical Manual of Mental Disorders (4th Ed.) (DSM-IV).[130]

i. False Confessions

The Supreme Judicial Court has had no occasion to rule squarely on the question of when expert testimony regarding false confessions is admissible. In *Com. v. Hoose*,[131] the Court stated that expert testimony on false confessions may be admissible in some cases, for example, where defendant directly attacks the veracity of his statements to police and several false confession factors are present. The Court has yet to affirm the admission of such evidence in a case, however.[132]

j. Recovered Memory, Dissociative Amnesia, and Dissociative Disorder

The Supreme Judicial Court held that testimony in a case alleging child sexual abuse regarding recovered memory and dissociative amnesia was reliable, despite controversy in the field.[133] The Court noted that the diagnosis was included in DSM-IV and found that there had been a sufficient number of peer reviewed studies to support a finding

---

[130] *In re Souza*, supra, 87 Mass App at 162, 27 NE3d at 395.

[131] *Com. v. Hoose*, 467 Mass 395, 5 NE3d 843 (2014) (research on false confessions has progressed significantly since *Robinson* decision; not error to exclude expert where data base of proven false confessions was sample size of 150–200 false confessions, no research showed how frequently dispositional factors also occurred in true confessions [but court notes lack of prevalence data alone may not be sufficient to rule evidence unreliable], only some of recognized dispositional factors and no situational factors contributing to false confessions were present, and defendant offered no other evidence directly attacking the substantive reliability of his statements).

[132] *Com. v. Tolan*, 453 Mass 634, 648, 904 NE2d 397, 409-410 (2009) (suggesting that whether to preclude testimony touching on "the alleged relationship between various interrogation techniques and false confessions" was within the trial court's discretion, but no confession was made in this case); *Com. v. Robinson*, 449 Mass 1, 864 NE2d 1186 (2007) (defendant failed to establish that expert testimony regarding false confessions had a reliable basis; Court notes that competent scientific evidence regarding the psychological manipulation of a defendant and its relation to false confessions may well be useful); *Com. v. DiGiambattista*, 442 Mass 423, 437, 813 NE2d 516, 526-527 (2004) (authorities from other jurisdictions are split on admissibility).

[133] *Com. v. Shanley*, 455 Mass 752, 919 NE2d 1254 (2010). See an earlier discussion of recovered memory in *Com. v. Frangipane*, 433 Mass 527, 744 NE2d 25 (2001).

of reliability. In a later case, the Court ruled that defendant was not required to introduce expert testimony that an alleged victim of child sexual abuse had dissociative memory to establish the relevance of an expert's testimony that those with dissociative memory sometimes have a distorted memory of past events.[134] The Court noted that because the alleged victim could not be required to submit to an examination, and medical records may not exist or be available to the defendant, it may be impossible for a defendant to obtain an expert diagnosis of such a condition. It was sufficient to introduce evidence that the alleged victim had demonstrated behavior consistent with a dissociative memory disorder in order to permit a reasonable inference that she had the disorder and that her memory might be affected by it.

§ 7.6.5 *Law Enforcement*

a. General Issues

Law enforcement officers may be permitted to render opinions about instrumentalities and evidence of crime.[135] The government frequently offers such evidence in drug cases.[136] Law enforcement

---

[134] *Com. v. Polk*, 462 Mass 23, 965 NE2d 815 (2012).

[135] See *Com. v. Boyarsky*, 452 Mass 700, 716, 897 NE2d 574, 585 (2008) (detective was properly permitted to testify which of two nearly identical shoes could have created footprint, even though subject matter may have been within the knowledge of jury) (Text cited); *Com. v. Miller*, 435 Mass 274, 755 NE2d 1266 (2001) (medical examiner properly allowed to testify that that victim's killing was a "sexually related death"); *Com. v. Luna*, 418 Mass 749, 754, 641 NE2d 1050, 1053 (1994) (assistant district attorney permitted to testify regarding materiality of defendant officer's statements in prosecution for perjury and filing false police reports); *Com. v. Schutte*, 52 Mass App 796, 801, 756 NE2d 48, 53 (2001) (police officer permitted to testify to administration of field sobriety tests); *Com. v. Pope*, 19 Mass App 627, 476 NE2d 969 (1985) (police officer permitted to testify that paper with notations was a bookmaker's gambling memorandum); *Com. v. LaBella*, 17 Mass App 973, 458 NE2d 763 (1984) (no error in the admission of a state trooper's opinion describing habits of bookmakers and significance of evidence seized); *Com. v. Kimball*, 16 Mass App 974, 453 NE2d 465 (1983) (judge had discretion to admit police officer's opinion on footprints and tracks) (Text cited). Cf. *Com. v. Goguen*, 361 Mass 846, 279 NE2d 666 (1972) (testimony of vexillologist as to contemporary use and treatment of American flag properly excluded; flag on seat of pants could be found not to articulate any idea of redeeming social importance).

[136] See *Com. v. Little*, 453 Mass 766, 769, 906 NE2d 286, 290 (2009) (facts of cases were more consistent with distribution than personal use of drugs); *Com. v. Miranda*, 441 Mass 783, 793, 809 NE2d 487, 496 (2004) (narcotics officer was properly allowed to testify about the role of "lookouts" in drug transactions); *Com. v. Wilson*, 441

officers may not, however, phrase their testimony in such a manner as to constitute an opinion on the guilt of the defendant. See § 7.3.4.

The Appeals Court has held that evidence that a dog tracked a scent from the crime scene to the home of the defendant is admissible, "due to its widely recognized reliability," relying upon pre-*Lanigan* precedent.[137]

b. *Syndrome Evidence About Perpetrator of Crime*

Expert testimony offered by the government regarding the expected characteristics of perpetrators of crime is not admissible. Reported cases have rejected such testimony in child abuse and sexual abuse cases.[138] In drug cases the courts have struggled to distinguish inadmissible profile testimony from admissible modus operandi testimony.[139]

Mass 390, 401, 805 NE2d 968, 979 (2004) (officer properly allowed to testify that possession of one-half ounce of marijuana individually packaged in twenty small bags, money, pager, and cellular telephone, but no smoking paraphernalia, was consistent with intent for "street distribution"); *Com. v. Gollman*, 436 Mass 111, 762 NE2d 847 (2002) (experienced narcotics investigator properly allowed to testify that amount of cocaine found on defendant, under the circumstances, was not consistent with personal use); *Com. v. Johnson*, 413 Mass 598, 603, 602 NE2d 555, 558 (1992) (narcotics officer permitted to testify that manner in which cocaine was packaged was consistent with intent to distribute); *Com. v. Munera*, 31 Mass App 380, 578 NE2d 418 (1991) (opinion admissible that method of carrying cocaine was consistent with dealer's sample; explanation of "stash pads" permissible to rebut defendant's claim of simple lifestyle inconsistent with dealing drugs, but court notes that expert evidence about drug profiles is suspect if offered to prove that because defendant fit profile he must be guilty of particular offense).

[137] *Com. v. Hill*, 52 Mass App Ct 147, 153, 751 NE2d 446, 450 (2001) (no reference in opinion to *Lanigan*), citing *Commonwealth v. LePage*, 352 Mass 403, 418-419, 226 NE2d 200 (1967).

[138] *Com. v. Federico*, 425 Mass 844, 850, 683 NE2d 1035, 1039 (1997) (child abuse); *Com. v. Day*, 409 Mass 719, 569 NE2d 397 (1991) (child battering); *Com. v. Poitras*, 55 Mass App 691, 774 NE2d 647 (2002) (such testimony cannot be deemed harmless error when the prosecution's case is not strong); *Com. v. Roche*, 44 Mass App 372, 691 NE2d 946 (1998) (error to admit expert's profile of "abusive male"); *Com. v. LaCaprucia*, 41 Mass App 496, 499, 671 NE2d 984, 987 (1996) (error to permit expert to give characteristic sexual profile testimony that presented defendant's family situation as prone to sexual abuse).

[139] Compare *Com. v. Johnson*, 76 Mass App 80, 84, 918 NE2d 876, 880 (2010) (error to allow testimony that users of crack cocaine would not have $3,500 needed to buy 98 grams of cocaine and would buy cocaine as soon as they had $20), *aff'd*, 461 Mass 1012, 965 NE2d 176 (2012); *Com. v. James*, 54 Mass App 908, 909, 763 NE2d 1127, 1129 (2002) (cautioning prosecution not to offer "profile" testimony describing the

It is also improper to offer profile testimony concerning the parent in a petition to dispense with the need for a parent's consent for adoption.[140]

§ 7.6.6 *Foreign Law*

Expert testimony is admissible in certain situations to prove what the law is in other jurisdictions.[141] Where the point in dispute between experts is a question of settled law, the judge should instruct the jury about the applicable law on the subject, and not permit it to return a verdict premised on an erroneous view of the law. In such a case, the

---

activities of "people selling crack cocaine in the area [under investigation]" from officer who was also a percipient witness), and *Com. v. Jackson*, 45 Mass App 666, 700 NE2d 848 (1998) (officer's statement that it was very common for drug buyers to refuse to identify sellers because of fear of retribution was an inadmissible description of characteristic of drug buyers, rather than permissible explanation of modus operandi of drug sales) with *Com. v. Pike*, 430 Mass 317, 718 NE2d 855 (1999) (expert testimony regarding methods of doctors and drug users in drug diversion schemes was more akin to description of modus operandi of such actors than profile testimony, and hence admissible); *Com. v. Frias*, 47 Mass App 293, 712 NE2d 1178 (1999) (expert testimony regarding mid-level drug transactions was modus operandi, not profile, evidence); *Com. v. Robinson*, 43 Mass App 257, 682 NE2d 903 (1997) (testimony about characteristics of two-person street drug transactions was admissible so long as it was more akin to description of modus operandi rather than profile of a drug dealer) and *Com. v. Dennis*, 33 Mass App 666, 604 NE2d 48 (1992) (defendant's conviction of trafficking reversed on other grounds, but court indicated that experienced narcotics officer's testimony as to how street level dealers conduct their business was admissible, court concluding it was more akin to a description of the dealers' modus operandi, than a "profile" of a drug dealer). See also *Com. v. Caraballo*, 81 Mass App 536, 540, 965 NE2d 194, 198 (2012) (to allow officer to testify that people who followed defendant into building appeared to be drug-dependent, but that defendant's appearance was different, suggested inference that defendant was selling drugs, but was not improper).

[140] *Adoption of Fran*, 54 Mass App 455, 465, 766 NE2d 91 (2002) (permitting evidence regarding behavior by cults where witness had not used general group characteristics to determine whether specific acts had occurred in the past, but instead "used facts about behavior of group members to reach conclusions about the group's nature and likely future course"); *Adoption of Keefe*, 49 Mass App 818, 733 NE2d 1075 (2000) (profile evidence regarding Munchausen Syndrome by Proxy (MSBP), namely that the perpetrators are typically the children's mothers, that they are often health care professionals, and that the father in MSBP cases is often emotionally or physically absent, was improper).

[141] See *Sullivan v. First Massachusetts Financial Corp.*, 409 Mass 783, 793, 569 NE2d 814, 821 (1991) (affirming trial court's discretion to admit expert testimony on question of whether a bank qualified for subchapter S status under federal tax law).

judge's instruction on the point of law, or his or her ruling in a trial to the court, will be subject to appellate review in the same manner as any other instruction or ruling.[142]

§ 7.6.7 *Value*

Testimony as to the value of property, business interests, investments, and the like may be given by properly qualified experts.[143] An expert may base his opinions on value in part upon "trustworthy sources of information."[144]

The determination of value is a question of fact and the trial judge's determination will be affirmed on appeal, unless clearly erroneous. The judge is free to determine what weight to give to expert testimony with respect to value, may reject expert opinions and determine value based on other evidence, but may not reach a valuation materially at odds with the totality of the circumstances.[145]

In assessing the value of real property, whether it is appropriate to use the capitalization of income method of valuation rather than sale

---

[142] *Romano v. Weiss*, 26 Mass App Ct 162, 524 NE2d 1381 (1988) (leaving open the question of whether the same approach is required if the legal point is the subject of uncertainty).

[143] See, e.g., *Anthony's Pier Four, Inc. v. HBC Associates*, 411 Mass 451, 479, 583 NE2d 806, 824 (1991) (real estate development); *Dewan v. Dewan*, 30 Mass App 133, 566 NE2d 1132 (1991) (value of pension); *Foley v. Foley*, 27 Mass App 221, 537 NE2d 158 (1989) (expert on value of real estate brokerage business improperly excluded); *Cataldo v. Zuckerman*, 20 Mass App 731, 744, 482 NE2d 849, 858 (1985) (testimony by CPA properly admitted on value of party's share of developer's equity in several projects). For a discussion of proof of value based on the sale price of similar land, see § 4.4.9.b.

[144] *Olympia & York State v. Board of Assessors*, 428 Mass 236, 700 NE2d 533 (1998) (appraiser could rely upon his staff for market data); *McLaughlin v. Board of Selectmen of Amherst*, 422 Mass 359, 662 NE2d 687 (1996) (error to exclude opinion of real estate appraiser on real estate value, although witness had no brokering experience in the particular locality involved); *Analogic Corp. v. Peabody Board of Assessors*, 45 Mass App 605, 700 NE2d 548 (1998) (appraiser may rely on admissible data from interested parties).

[145] *Adams v. Adams*, 459 Mass 361, 945 NE2d 844 (2011) (error for special master to use direct capitalization of income method, rather than a variant of the discounted cash flow method, to value an interest in a partnership; error to accept unmodified expert's opinion of present value of future payments although special master had adjusted downward several constituent variables; not necessarily error to reject both parties' experts' opinion as to taxes, but court was required to supply reasonable explanation of its choices); *Haskell v. Versyss Liquidating Trust*, 75 Mass App 120, 912 NE2d 481 (2009) (upholding trial court's valuation of stock).

prices depends on the circumstances.[146] In *Clifford v. Algonquin Gas Transmission Co.*,[147] it was held that the trial court had properly admitted expert testimony on the value of a large tract of land based on the "lot" method of appraising a potential subdivision. The Court reasoned that the admissibility of such testimony turns on the particular facts and the extent to which a development has progressed toward completion, and that a trial judge is afforded discretion to determine whether a proposed subdivision plan is too speculative or remote as to preclude its submission to the jury. Under appropriate circumstances, a trial judge also has the discretion to permit expert testimony valuing land pursuant to the depreciated reproduction cost (DRC) method, for special purpose properties, although the method is disfavored.[148]

The Supreme Judicial Court has recognized that "traditional lost profits analysis as a measure of damages may not be an adequate model for analyzing harm cause by misappropriation of the trade secrets of a 'start-up' business."[149] It invited parties to test other theories of damages in such cases in the Massachusetts courts.

Testimony as to value is usually given by experts, but it may also be given by non-experts who are particularly familiar with the property in question. Admission of such opinion testimony by non-experts is a matter of sound judicial discretion upon establishment of a proper foundation of competency.[150]

At one time, it was thought that an owner was presumed to have sufficient familiarity with his property to testify to its value. It is clear, however, that an owner, like any other witness, must be particularly

---

[146] See *Olympia & York State v. Board of Assessors*, supra (capitalization of income); *Pepsi-Cola Bottling Co. v. Board of Assessors of Boston*, 397 Mass 447, 491 NE2d 1071 (1986) (sale price had been adversely affected by uneconomic lease, "comparable" sales differed materially from subject property); *Board of Assessors of Boston v. Diab*, 396 Mass 560, 487 NE2d 491 (1986) (error to reject sale price in favor of capitalization of income method where decision was based on error of law regarding tax factors).

[147] *Clifford v. Algonquin Gas Transmission Co.*, 413 Mass 809, 816, 604 NE2d 697, 702 (1992).

[148] See *Correia v. New Bedford Redevelopment Authority*, 375 Mass 360, 366-367, 377 NE2d 909 (1978); *Lodge No. 65 v. Lawrence Redevelopment Authority*, 33 Mass App 701, 604 NE2d 715 (1992).

[149] *Lightlab Imaging, Inc. v. Axsun Technologies, Inc.*, 469 Mass 181, 193, 13 NE3d 604 (2014) (trial judge had discretion to exclude expert's opinion based on the "first mover advantage"; and to conclude that expert's opinion on future loss profits based on yet uninvented products was too speculative).

[150] *Menici v. Orton Crane & Shovel Co.*, 285 Mass 499, 504, 189 NE 839, 841 (1934); *Com. v. Shagoury*, 6 Mass App 584, 594, 380 NE2d 708, 714 (1978) (Text cited).

familiar with property to testify as to its value.[151] A fortiori, an officer of a corporation must show particular familiarity with the land or property owned by the corporation to testify as to its value.[152]

The recent assessed valuations of real estate are, by statute, admissible in eminent domain proceedings as evidence of fair market value of the property.[153]

A person can testify as to the value of his own services even though he has never been paid for them.[154] However, if it appears that the opinion of the value of the witness's services is based primarily on the opinions of others as to such value, the evidence is inadmissible.[155] In any event, testimony as to value of services is admissible only if such services are shown to have some market value.[156] A finding as to the fair value of such services may be made without expert testimony.[157]

§ 7.7 Statutory Provisions for Expert Testimony

Massachusetts statutes provide for the discretionary admissibility of expert opinion evidence in certain cases. We discuss a number of these statutes in the following sections.

---

[151] *Von Henneberg v. Generazio*, 403 Mass 519, 524, 531 NE2d 563, 566 (1988); *Blais-Porter, Inc. v. Simboli*, 402 Mass 269, 272, 521 NE2d 1013, 1016 (1988); *Epstein v. Board of Appeal of Boston*, 77 Mass App 752, 933 NE2d 972 (2010) (reversing summary judgment in zoning aggrievement matter where trial court rejected testimony of owner who had substantial familiarity with property); *Turner v. Leonard*, 17 Mass App 909, 455 NE2d 1215 (1983) (error to admit owner's testimony as to value of automobile absent evidence of familiarity with vehicle) (Text cited).

[152] *Newton Girl Scout Council, Inc. v. Massachusetts Turnpike Authority*, 335 Mass 189, 198, 138 NE2d 769, 773 (1956).

[153] GL 79, § 35; *Bennett v. Brookline Redevelopment Authority*, 342 Mass 418, 173 NE2d 815 (1961); *Stewart v. Burlington*, 2 Mass App 712, 319 NE2d 921 (1974) (construing the 1969 amendment to § 35). For discussion of the permissible methods of valuation by experts as to so-called specialized use properties, see *Correia v. New Bedford Redevelopment Authority*, 375 Mass 360, 377 NE2d 909 (1978) and *Saxon Theatre Corp. of Boston v. Hayden*, 7 Mass App 695, 389 NE2d 1020 (1979).

[154] *Berish v. Bornstein*, 437 Mass 252, 273, 770 NE2d 961, 979 (2002).

[155] *Downey v. Union Trust Co. of Springfield*, 312 Mass 405, 416, 45 NE2d 373, 380 (1942).

[156] *Williamson v. Feinstein*, 311 Mass 322, 41 NE2d 185 (1942); *Matloff v. Chelsea*, 308 Mass 134, 31 NE2d 518 (1941). See also *Elbaum v. Sullivan*, 344 Mass 662, 183 NE2d 712 (1962).

[157] *Berish v. Bornstein*, supra.

§ 7.7.1 *Obscenity Cases*

GL 272, § 28F, provides that in actions to suppress an allegedly obscene book, "the court may receive the testimony of experts and may receive evidence as to the literary, artistic, political or scientific character of said book and as to the manner and form of its dissemination." This statute makes permissible expert testimony that would not have been admissible under the common-law criteria set forth above.[1]

Section 28F, however, has been construed strictly as to the type of expert testimony it makes permissible.[2] The concept of the statute may not be extended into other types of proceedings.[3]

§ 7.7.2 *Treatises*

GL 233, § 79C, provides that in actions of contract or tort for malpractice or error in treatment by specified medical practitioners, facts and opinions from authoritative treatises are admissible.[4] The party

---

§ 7.7 [1] Cf. *Com. v. United Books, Inc.*, 389 Mass 888, 894-896, 453 NE2d 406, 411-413 (1983) (reversible error to exclude qualified expert's testimony on contemporary community standards and question of serious artistic, social, political, and scientific value of film); *Com. v. Dane Entertainment Services, Inc.* (*No. 2*), 389 Mass 917, 452 NE2d 1135 (1983) (same). Compare *Com. v. Dane Entertainment Services, Inc.* (*No. 1*), 389 Mass 902, 910-915, 452 NE2d 1126, 1131-1134 (1983) (no error to exclude investigator's testimony as to community standards; although court may have ruled otherwise, it affirmed judge's discretion); *Attorney General v. Book Named* "John Cleland's Memoirs of a Woman of Pleasure," 349 Mass 69, 206 NE2d 403 (1965) (expert literary testimony admitted and utilized by appellate court in two latter cases to determine whether books were hard-core pornography); *Com. v. Isenstadt*, 318 Mass 543, 62 NE2d 840 (1945) (testimony of literary and other experts properly excluded).

[2] *Attorney General v. Book Named* "Forever Amber," 323 Mass 302, 81 NE2d 663 (1948) (§ 28F does not permit testimony of psychiatrist that book had no tendency to incite lascivious thoughts or did not violate current sex mores). Cf. *District Attorney v. Three Way Theatres Corp.*, 371 Mass 391, 357 NE2d 747 (1976) (injunctive proceedings under GL 272, § 30; error for judge to require expert testimony on the subject of community standards for proof of obscenity).

[3] *Supreme Malt Products Co. v. Alcoholic Beverages Control Commission*, 334 Mass 59, 63-64, 133 NE2d 775, 779 (1956) (psychiatric testimony to effect that retail price of liquor has nothing to do with alcoholism was properly excluded in proceeding challenging minimum price law).

[4] See *Ramsland v. Shaw*, 341 Mass 56, 63-64, 166 NE2d 894, 900 (1960) (even where defendant admitted authoritativeness of treatise, trial judge has discretion to exclude same as irrelevant); *Reddington v. Clayman*, 334 Mass 244, 134 NE2d 920 (1956) (biographical data in front of treatise cannot be used to establish authoritativeness of author; nor can court take judicial notice of same).

intending to use a text must give 30 days' notice prior to trial. In *Mazzaro v. Paull*,[5] the Court suggested that a *Who's Who* might be used to establish the expertise of authors of medical treatises, if the requirements of the Commercial Lists Statute, GL 233, § 79B, were met.

In *Simmons v. Yurchak*,[6] the court held that § 79C did not authorize the admission of a videotape produced by the American Medical Association. The court acknowledged that videotapes are now frequently used for informational and instructional purposes and that exclusion was not compelled by the fact that they were not mentioned in the statute, because they did not exist when it was drafted in 1949. However, the court reasoned that published written works have "an imprimatur of reliability" as a result of the careful, professional criticism attendant to the editorial and publishing process. Lacking information about whether similar care is taken in the production of videotapes, the court concluded that it should be left to the legislature to indicate whether videotapes are admissible under § 79C.

In actions other than malpractice actions the use of treatises is governed by Proposed Mass R Evid 803(18), discussed in § 8.14.

§ 7.7.3 Physicians' Reports

GL 233, § 79G, permits medical opinions regarding diagnosis, treatment, prognosis, and causation to be introduced in the form of written reports that would otherwise constitute hearsay. The statute requires that notice of the intention to offer a report into evidence be provided no less than ten days before its introduction at trial. The opposing party is then free to summon into court at his own expense the author of the report, for the purposes of cross-examination. For the text of the statute and additional discussion, see § 8.11.3.

§ 7.7.4 Blood and Genetic Marker Tests

GL 209C, § 17, provides for the administration of tests to establish paternity. Section 17 applies to all blood or genetic marker tests that may be used to attempt to establish paternity. The statute provides, inter alia, that agencies accredited pursuant to Title IV, Part D of

---

[5] *Mazzaro v. Paull*, 372 Mass 645, 363 NE2d 509 (1977). See § 8.13 for discussion.

[6] *Simmons v. Yurchak*, 28 Mass App 371, 551 NE2d 539 (1990).

the Social Security Act, as well as a court, have authority to order testing if there is a "proper showing" that the parties had intercourse during the probable period of conception.[7] An affidavit from the mother or the putative father is sufficient for such a showing. In *G. E. B. v. S. R. W.*,[8] the court held that proof of intercourse to trigger the statute is judged by a preponderance of the evidence standard and it refused to read a clear and convincing evidence standard into the statute.

The statute by its terms applies only to establishing the paternity of children born out of wedlock. Under § 17, such tests may be introduced not only to exclude the possibility of a putative father's paternity, but also to establish the statistical probability of a putative father's paternity.[9] The statute provides that if the mother was married to someone other than the putative father during the probable period of conception, notice to that spouse is required before testing may be ordered. Upon a showing that there is a statistical probability of paternity of 97 percent or greater, the statute establishes a rebuttable presumption that the putative father is the father. Despite the rule barring spouses from testifying as to non-access where the legitimacy of a child born during wedlock is issue[10] scientific evidence is not only admissible but may also conclusively establish non-paternity.[11]

Under § 17, blood and genetic marker tests may not be used as evidence of the occurrence of intercourse between the mother and the putative father. Reports of such tests are not admissible and are not sufficient to prove paternity unless there is sufficient other evidence of intercourse between the mother and putative father during the period of probable conception.[12]

Section 17 provides that the refusal by a party to submit to a blood test is admissible in evidence. In *Department of Revenue v. B. P.*,[13] the Court held that there was no constitutional impediment to the admission in evidence in a civil action of a party's refusal to take such tests

---

[7] An order is not necessary for the tests to be admissible where parties voluntarily consent to submit to such tests and the other requirements of the statute are met even though the tests were not taken pursuant to a court order. *Department of Revenue v. Sorrentino*, 408 Mass 340, 344, 557 NE2d 1376, 1379 (1990).

[8] *G.E.B. v. S.R.W.*, 422 Mass 158, 661 NE2d 646 (1996).

[9] The use of blood tests to exclude the possibility of paternity has long been held reliable, even in the absence of a statute. *Com. v. Sasville*, 35 Mass App 15, 22, 616 NE2d 476, 481 (1993) (citing *Com. v. Stappen*, 336 Mass 174, 143 NE2d 221 (1957)).

[10] *Taylor v. Whittier*, 240 Mass 514, 138 NE 6 (1922) (Lord Mansfield rule).

[11] *Symonds v. Symonds*, 385 Mass 540, 432 NE2d 700 (1982).

[12] *Department of Revenue v. Sorrentino*, 408 Mass 340, 345 n.1, 557 NE2d 1376, 1379 n.1 (1990).

[13] *Department of Revenue v. B. P.*, 412 Mass 1015, 593 NE2d 1305 (1992).

and stated that there was no constitutional bar to the imposition of other sanctions for failure to comply with discovery orders under Dist/ Mun Cts R Civ P 37(b)(2).

The statute provides for the payment and apportionment of costs of the test and for the payment by the Commonwealth for costs for indigent parties.

A report of the results of blood or genetic marker tests on the issue of paternity is not admissible in evidence unless offered through the testimony of an expert who describes and establishes the adequacy of the testing procedures used.[14]

At present, there is no statute permitting a court to require a criminal defendant in a paternity action to submit to blood tests. It would appear that a refusal to submit to blood testing in a criminal proceeding would not be admissible in evidence, based on the defendant's constitutional right not to furnish evidence against himself.[15]

Under Mass R Civ P 35(a) and Mass R Dom Rel P 35(a), a court may order a physical or mental examination, including blood or genetic marker tests.[16] The Supreme Judicial Court has held that probable cause to believe either that a man is or is not the father of a child is sufficient to meet the constitutional standard for ordering parties to submit to blood tests.[17]

The court does not have the power to require a blood test in a proceeding for non-support of a minor child under GL 273, § 1, but expert testimony of blood grouping tests showing the exclusion of the defendant as the father of the child whose support is sought is admissible. The presumption of legitimacy of a child born during wedlock may be rebutted by such an exclusionary blood grouping.[18] Where there is evidence of a blood grouping test properly administered that

---

[14] *Department of Revenue v. Sorrentino*, supra; *Com. Beausoleil*, 397 Mass 206, 490 NE2d 788 (1986).

[15] See *Opinion of the Justices*, 412 Mass 1201, 591 NE2d 1073 (1992) (declaring unconstitutional proposed legislation that would have rendered admissible the refusal to submit to blood tests in connection with the charge of driving under the influence).

[16] *Symonds v. Symonds*, 385 Mass 540, 432 NE2d 700 (1982) (results of such tests are admissible in annulment and divorce proceedings, even in absence of statutory authority).

[17] *A. R. v. C. R.*, 411 Mass 570, 576, 583 NE2d 840, 844 (1992) (leaving open question of whether something less than probable cause might also suffice to justify court-ordered blood testing in civil proceedings). See *R. R. K. v. S. G. P.*, 400 Mass 12, 18, 507 NE2d 736, 740 (1987) (concurring op, Liacos, CJ) ("improper in the extreme" for a judge to order parties to submit to psychological evaluations and to blood tests based solely on the unsworn, unverified complaint of plaintiff).

[18] *Symonds v. Symonds*, supra; *Com. v. Stappen*, 336 Mass 174, 143 NE2d 221 (1957).

definitely excludes the paternity of the alleged father, he must be adjudged not to be the father as a matter of law.[19]

§ 7.7.5 *Blood Alcohol Tests*

GL 90, § 24(1)(e), provides for blood and breath testing of drivers for the presence of alcohol. It permits an inference that a defendant is intoxicated if the percentage of alcohol in the blood is .08% or greater. The test gives rise to a "permissive inference" of intoxication at that level, rather than a "presumption," as the former version of the statute had provided. The case law had already indicated that a jury should not be charged in terms of presumptions with respect to such evidence.[20] If the Commonwealth chooses to proceed only on an impaired ability to operate theory, however, it may not offer evidence of a breathalyzer reading of .08 or higher without expert testimony on the significance of that level of blood alcohol as it pertains to impairment.[21]

The constitutionality of GL 90, § 24(1)(f), which requires an immediate suspension of the right to operate a motor vehicle when an arrestee refuses to submit to a test and where the terms of § 24(1)(f) have been complied with, was upheld against a claim of denial of due process of law absent a hearing prior to suspension.[22]

The statute provides that the Commonwealth may offer as prima facie evidence of blood alcohol percentage a signed, sworn statement of a chemist of the Department of State Police or the Department of Public Health. The Confrontation Clause, however, is probably a bar to the use of a certificate in lieu of live testimony in a criminal case.[23]

---

[19] *Symonds v. Symonds*, supra; *Com. v. D'Avella*, 339 Mass 642, 162 NE2d 19 (1959).

[20] See *Com. v. Moreira*, 385 Mass 792, 434 NE2d 196 (1982).

[21] *Com. v. Colturi*, 448 Mass 809, 864 NE2d 498 (2007); *Com. v. Hubert*, 453 Mass 1009, 902 NE2d 368 (2009) (admission of breathalyzer evidence without expert was not harmless error where prosecution was based on impairment). *Com. v. Douglas*, 75 Mass 643, 650, 915 NE2d 1111, 1118 (2009) (applying Colturi requirement of expert to blood test evidence); *Com. v. Filoma*, 79 Mass App 16, 943 NE2d 477 (2011) (reversing alcohol related convictions because expert never explained connection between levels of blood alcohol content and impairment).

[22] *Mackey v. Montrym*, 443 US 1, 99 S Ct 2612 (1979) (upholding 90-day suspension in former version of statute).

[23] The constitutionality of the various prima facie provisions permitting proof of disputed facts in criminal cases by certificates prepared for use at trial is placed in

The statutory and regulatory requirements of § 24(1)(e) apply only to testing at the direction of the police, not to blood alcohol assessments made by physicians as part of medical evaluation and treatment.[24]

In *Com. v. Brooks*[25] and in *Com. v. Bernier*[26] the Court engaged in an extensive discussion of the legal and chemical meaning of the terms of § 24 with particular reference to the so-called breathalyzer. In subsequent cases, the Court rejected a number of constitutional arguments against the use of breathalyzer evidence where breath samples or test ampoules had not been preserved for the defendant's experts to test.[27]

The reliability of the instrumentation employed and the specific procedures followed present legitimate issues that may be contested in individual cases involving breathalyzer evidence. The court must make a preliminary finding in a given case that the breathalyzer test result is sufficiently reliable to go to the jury.[28] Performance of simulator tests is a common method for establishing the reliability of the machines.[29]

Problems of reliability are specifically addressed by GL 90, § 24K, and regulations promulgated thereunder, 501 Code Mass Regs, § 2.14. The regulations stipulate that testing shall be performed by the

---

grave doubt by *Melendez-Diaz v. Massachusetts*, 557 US 305, 129 S Ct 2527 (2009), holding that such certificates are "testimonial" for purposes of the Sixth Amendment Confrontation Clause. See § 8.12.2.

[24] *Com. v. Dyer*, 77 Mass App 850, 853, n.5, 934 NE2d 293, 297 (2010).

[25] *Com. v. Brooks*, 366 Mass 423, 319 NE2d 901 (1974).

[26] *Com. v. Bernier*, 366 Mass 717, 322 NE2d 414 (1975). Further discussion of the scientific principles underlying the use of a breathalyzer is found in *Com. v. Neal*, 392 Mass 1, 464 NE2d 1356 (1984).

[27] Com v. Neal, supra; Com. v. Doyle, 392 Mass 23, 465 NE2d 1192 (1984).

[28] *Com. v. Durning*, 406 Mass 485, 548 NE2d 1242 (1990). See *Com. v. Marley*, 396 Mass 433, 486 NE2d 715 (1985) (delay in administration of breathalyzer test was not unreasonable and did not require exclusion of results, nor was defendant entitled to a jury instruction on the effect of delay, in absence of scientific evidence to support claim that delay was harmful); *Com. v. Neal*, supra (potential effect of radio frequency interference on S & W model 900A breathalyzer units is sufficient to require that admission of results be conditioned on demonstration to trial judge of the accuracy of the particular unit at the time test was performed).

[29] See *Com. v. Durning*, supra (no requirement that a simulator test be performed immediately after the breathalyzer examination of defendant, simulations performed 19 days before and 13 days after the defendant's, together with certification of the device 11 days before and a beam attenuator test 5 days after, were sufficient); *Com. v. Dolliver*, 52 Mass App 278, 752 NE2d 827 (2001) (simulator reading within .01 was within zone of tolerance); *Com. v. Cochran*, 25 Mass App 260, 517 NE2d 498 (1988) (where simulator deviation exceeds the permissible tolerance according to the testimony, test results are inadmissible).

police using the breathalyzer equipment and that the mandatory calibration of a breathalyzer prior to each use shall be deemed to be a test of the device. The regulations were found to be in compliance with the statutory mandate in *Morris v. Com*[30] where the Court rejected a challenge based on the assertion that delegation of the testing to the police was improper and that the regulations should have provided a fixed period or regular interval for "periodic" testing. In *Com. v.* Barbeau,[31] the Court had held that breathalyzer test results were inadmissible where the Commonwealth had not offered any evidence that a periodic testing program existed.

The regulations require that the breathalyzer must not only be tested each time it is used, but that the operator must change the simulator solution in the device, run calibration analyses, and record test results in a prescribed manner.[32] The Supreme Judicial Court has upheld the regulation that requires that when two breath samples differ within + /0.02 blood alcohol content units, only the lower blood alcohol level may be introduced in evidence.[33] If the difference between the two samples is greater, the evidence is inadmissible.[34] An officer must observe the suspect for 15 minutes prior to administering the test.[35]

For the results of a breathalyzer examination to be admissible, the analysis must be performed by a certified operator. GL 90, § 24K. The Secretary of Public Safety may delegate the process of certification to

---

[30] *Morris v. Com*, 412 Mass 861, 593 NE2d 241 (1992).

[31] *Com. v. Barbeau*, 411 Mass 782, 585 NE2d 1392 (1992).

[32] See *Com. v. Smith*, 35 Mass App 655, 661, 624 NE2d 604, 608 (1993); *Com. v. Livers*, 420 Mass 556, 650 NE2d 791 (1995) (Commonwealth was required to have a periodic testing program of devices, but statute did not require adoption of regulations for periodic testing of devices); *Com. v. Costa*, 88 Mass App 750, 42 NE3d 1162 (2015) (it was of no moment that one cylinder of dual cylinder breathalyzer device was used for periodic calibration and the other for calibration during defendant's test); *Com. v. Rollins*, 65 Mass App 694, 843 NE2d 118 (2006) (where breathalyzer failed to meet calibration standard because it was given insufficient time to warm up and it functioned properly once the "ready" light had come on, initial failure to meet standard did not result in decertification of machine); *Com. v. Kelley*, 39 Mass App 448, 657 NE2d 1274 (1995) (neither statutes nor regulations require certification by Office of Alcohol Testing of known value of simulator solution every time a device is used).

[33] *Com. v. Steele*, 455 Mass 209, 914 NE2d 886 (2009).

[34] *Com. v. Hourican*, 856 Mass App 408, 10 NE3d 646 (2014) (interpreting 501 Code Mass Regs § 2.14(4)).

[35] *Com. v. Pierre*, 72 Mass App 230, 890 NE2d 152 (2008) (evidence was insufficient to comply with then current version of regulation, which required observation to make sure suspect did not put anything into his mouth).

the Criminal Justice Training council.[36] The qualifications of a police officer as an expert to testify as to breathalyzer test results is discussed in *Com. v. Shea*.[37] A defendant is entitled to call a properly qualified expert to testify about various particulars of breathalyzer examination and the effect of alcohol upon the body.[38]

"Retrograde extrapolation," is a calculation that attempts to determine from a given reading at the time of the test what the operator's blood alcohol level would have been earlier at the time of the alleged offense. Reliability of retrograde extrapolation analysis under *Lanigan II* was established in *Com. v. Senior*.[39] Testimony regarding retrograde extrapolation, however, is not required to prove a per se violation of the operating under the influence statute (more than .08% blood alcohol), as long as the test is conducted within a reasonable period of time after the driver's last operation of the vehicle. The Court has identified three hours as a reasonable time, although it noted that a greater or lesser time might be appropriate given the particular facts of a case.[40]

In *Douillard v. LMR, Inc.*,[41] the Court held that plaintiff could rely on expert opinion as some evidence of whether a person would have

---

[36] *Com. v. Smigliano*, 427 Mass 490, 694 NE2d 341 (1998).

[37] *Com. v. Shea*, 356 Mass 358, 252 NE2d 336 (1969) (officer's infirmities in knowledge and skill in administering test go to weight and not admissibility of testimony).

[38] *Com. v. Smythe*, 23 Mass App 348, 502 NE2d 162 (1987) (error to exclude proposed testimony regarding installation, maintenance, testing, calibration and operation of machine, whether or not defendant on videotape displayed the clinically observable signs expected of an individual with a 0.17 percent blood alcohol content, the amount of alcohol a person of defendant's size would need to consume during relevant time period to obtain a 0.17 reading, what defendant's blood alcohol content would have been if he had consumed only the amount of alcohol he claimed). But see *Com. v. Connolly*, 394 Mass 169, 474 NE2d 1106 (1985) (where defendant refused to take breathalyzer, it was proper for trial court to exclude evidence from expert regarding what blood alcohol level a person of defendant's size would have had after consuming a given amount of alcohol, and of the effect of that amount of alcohol on his person).

[39] *Com. v. Senior*, 433 Mass 453, 744 NE2d 614 (2001). In *Baudanza v. Comcast of Massachusetts I, Inc.*, 454 Mass 622, 633, n.13, 912 NE2d 458, 467 (2009), the Court distinguished *Douillard v. LMR, Inc.*, 433 Mass 162 (2001) (admitting retrograde extrapolation), from *Kirby v. Morales*, 50 Mass App 786 (2001) (excluding retrograde extrapolation), on the ground that in the former case there was independent evidence of the driver's reaction to alcohol, but in the latter case no evidence of the driver's own reaction to alcohol was offered.

[40] *Com. v. Colturi*, 448 Mass 809, 864 NE2d 498 (2007); *Com. v. Dacosta*, 85 Mass App 386, 10 NE3d 174 (2014) (55 minutes was a reasonable time).

[41] *Douillard v. LMR, Inc.*, 433 Mass 162, 740 NE2d 618 (2001).

exhibited signs of intoxication two hours before an elevated blood alcohol level was measured. The Court noted that the opponent had not challenged the reliability of such evidence in connection with the summary judgment motion that was the subject of the appeal, and that such a challenge might be made at trial. The Court also reserved the question of whether expert testimony would be sufficient to establish that a drinker showed signs of intoxication in the absence of other evidence.[42]

In *Baudanza v. Comcast of Massachusetts I, Inc.*,[43] the Supreme Judicial Court held that expert testimony that a driver was impaired based on a blood alcohol level of .04 did not meet the *Lanigan* reliability requirements. On voir dire, the witness testified regarding experiments on low level blood alcohol, but did not provide the number of such experiments or the size of the sample in any of them, and offered no evidence of epidemiological studies of the effects of low level blood alcohol.

In *Com. v. Brennan*,[44] the Court held that the use of a breathalyzer and field sobriety tests to determine intoxication does not involve testimonial communication; hence, introduction of such tests is not barred by the Fifth Amendment to the United States Constitution or by art. 12 of the Massachusetts Declaration of Rights. In *Com. v. Brazelton*[45] the Court held that there is no constitutional right to consult with counsel before deciding whether or not to submit to a breathalyzer examination.

---

[42] See *Kirby v. Morales*, 50 Mass App 786, 741 NE2d 855 (2001) (holding such expert testimony inadmissible where evidence was uncertain as to elapsed time between last beer customer drank at bar and the accident, as to amount of alcohol consumed by customer after leaving bar, and with respect to customer's reactions to alcohol consumption in general).

[43] *Baudanza v. Comcast of Massachusetts I, Inc.*, 454 Mass 622, 631, 912 NE2d 458, 466 (2009).

[44] *Com. v. Brennan*, 386 Mass 772, 438 NE2d 60 (1982).

[45] *Com. v. Brazelton*, 404 Mass 783, 537 NE2d 142 (1989). However, in *Opinion of the Justices*, 412 Mass 1201, 591 NE2d 1073 (1992), the Justices expressed the view that under art. 12 of the Declaration of Rights, a proposed amendment to the statute would be unconstitutional that would have made the refusal to consent to such an examination admissible in evidence. The Justices noted that although the use of test results does not involve testimonial evidence, a refusal to take a test is testimonial and an arrestee is constitutionally entitled to refuse to furnish such evidence against himself, under the Declaration of Rights. It should be noted that the United States Supreme Court had earlier held that the admission in evidence of a refusal to submit to a breathalyzer test does not violate the Fifth Amendment to the United States Constitution. *South Dakota v. Neville*, 459 US 553, 103 S Ct 916 (1983). For a further discussion of the difference between testimonial and non-testimonial material and the protection afforded by the privilege against self-incrimination, see § 5.14.2b.

An earlier version of GL 90, § 24(1)(e), had provided that when no evidence of the blood alcohol level is presented at trial, the trial judge must instruct the jury that a person has a legal right not to take the test, that there might be a number of reasons why a person would not take the test and why a test would not be administered, and that the jury is not allowed to speculate as to the reason for the absence of the test. Jury instructions pursuant to this statute were held unconstitutional in *Com. v. Zevitas*.[46] The Court reasoned that the trial judge was, in effect, informing the jury that the defendant had refused the test and that a jury would be likely to draw inferences adverse to the defendant. The Court held that the question was the same, for all practical purposes, as the issue the Justices had considered in *Opinion of the Justices*, supra, and that this portion of the statute would compel an accused to furnish evidence against himself, in violation of art. 12 of the Declaration of Rights.

Collateral comments made by a defendant during a discussion with the police about the breathalyzer may be admissible in evidence where no evidence is offered that the defendant refused the test.[47] Determining whether or not one has "consented" to a breathalyzer examination is a question of whether the person gave actual consent, as opposed to having been forced to submit to the testing. It is not essential that the Commonwealth demonstrate that the decision to submit to the test was "knowing, voluntary, and intelligent," as is required when demonstrating a waiver of constitutional rights.[48]

In addition to the provision in GL 90, § 24(1)(e), that the defendant shall be afforded "a reasonable opportunity, at his request and at his expense, to have another such test or analysis made by a person or a physician selected by him," a correlative right for private examination is provided in GL 263, § 5A. The statutes require that the police afford a person in custody a reasonable opportunity to obtain an

---

[46] *Com. v. Zevitas*, 418 Mass 677, 639 NE2d 1076 (1994).

[47] *Com. v. Sands*, 424 Mass 184, 189, 675 NE2d 370, 373 (1997) (not error to admit statement, "I'm not drunk, but I'm over."). See *Com. v. Conroy*, 396 Mass 266, 485 NE2d 180 (1985) (error for trooper to testify that defendant was offered a breathalyzer examination, when no such test results were offered at trial, because it implied that defendant had refused the examination; error was ruled harmless in the circumstances of the case).

[48] *Com. v. Carson*, 72 Mass App 368, 892 NE2d 347 (2008) (evidence was sufficient to find lack of consent); *Com. v. Davidson*, 27 Mass App 846, 545 NE2d 55 (1989).

independent examination, and inform him of his right to do so.[49] An indigent defendant has no constitutional right to have a private test or examination at public expense under either GL 90, § 24(1)(e), or GL 263, § 5A.[50]

Although the police are not required to assist an arrestee in obtaining an independent blood test, they may not prevent or hinder his reasonable and timely attempt to do so. GL 263, § 5A, together with the statutory right to prompt release on bail, GL 276, §§ 42, 57, 58, require that the police promptly telephone a bail commissioner and inform him that an arrestee has requested an independent medical examination or allow the detainee to do so directly. The bail commissioner is obliged to respond promptly.[51] It is required that an arrested party inform the police that he wishes to exercise his right under § 5A

---

[49] See *Com. v. Lopes*, 459 Mass 165, 944 NE2d 999 (2011) (admitting form in evidence without redacting language indicating defendant was informed of right to receive independent medical examination did not violate privilege against self-incrimination, but it was not relevant and better practice requires such redaction); *Com. v. Rosewarne*, 410 Mass 53, 571 NE2d 354 (1991) (police not required to assist defendant in obtaining independent test, not required to drive him to hospital); *Com. v. Durning*, 406 Mass 485, 548 NE2d 1242 (1990) (requirement was met where defendant was given a reasonable opportunity to obtain an independent blood test, although he was unsuccessful in locating a physician to perform one); *Com. v. Marley*, 396 Mass 433, 486 NE2d 715 (1985) (police waited until after taking defendant from two-hour stay at hospital to police station before advising him of rights under GL 263, § 5A, no violation because statute requires advice of rights only "upon being booked"; but see concurring opinion by Liacos, CJ, which would have found a violation and applied a standard of reasonableness to the giving of notice of rights); *Com. v. Lindner*; 395 Mass 144, 478 NE2d 1267 (1985) (police not responsible for loss or destruction of defendant's blood sample left at hospital).

[50] *Com. v. Tessier*, 371 Mass 828, 360 NE2d 304 (1977).

[51] *Com. v. King*, 429 Mass 169, 706 NE2d 685 (1999) (six-hour guideline for providing a bail hearing does not apply once an independent medical exam is requested, because the evidence will be destroyed during that length of time; violation of rights occurred when bail commissioner refused to come to station because arrestee had refused breathalyzer). Compare *Com. v. O'Brien*, 434 Mass 615, 750 NE2d 1000 (2001) (after permitting defendant to post bail, holding him in protective custody when he could not locate anyone to pick him up, because officers felt he could not safely walk home in his inebriated condition, did not impermissibly interfere with his exercise of statutory rights); *Com. v. Priestley*, 419 Mass 678, 646 NE2d 754 (1995) (although there was no evidence that defendant was advised by police that he could make contact with bail commissioner, evidence showed he made numerous telephone calls, obtained advice from his lawyer, and talked with friends; hence, defendant was not prevented from seeking bail on his own); *Com. v. Maylott*, 43 Mass App 516, 684 NE2d 10 (1997) (permissible to require arrestee to complete booking procedure before allowing him to exercise statutory rights).

to an independent examination or blood tests to support a finding of an obstruction of his rights under the statute.[52]

In *Com. v. King*, supra, the Court held that dismissal is the presumptive remedy for a violation of the statute. The Court concluded:

> the violation itself is prima facie evidence that the defendant has been prejudiced in that his opportunity to obtain and present potentially exculpatory evidence has been restricted or destroyed. This presumption of prejudice, however, may be overcome by overwhelming evidence of intoxication . . . or by other evidence indicating that the omission was not prejudicial in the circumstances.[53]

In *Com. v. Neal*,[54] the Court held that this statutory right of a second test discharges the due process obligation of the Commonwealth to preserve breath samples and breathalyzer ampules for retesting by the defendant.

In *Irwin v. Ware*[55] the Court held that a doctor's letter as to blood alcohol analysis was not admissible under GL 233, § 78, as a business record, and that there was insufficient evidence to authenticate the blood samples analyzed—i.e., to show the blood to be that of the motor vehicle operator.

---

[52] *Com. v. Finelli*, 422 Mass 860, 666 NE2d 144 (1996); *Com. v. Falco*, 43 Mass App 253, 682 NE2d 900 (1997) (holding arrestee for six and one-half hours without bail hearing, because he refused breathalyzer, where he was advised of right to telephone call and independent medical exam and requested neither, did not violate his rights).

[53] 429 Mass at 180-181, 706 NE2d at 693-694. See *Com. v. Ames*, 410 Mass 603, 574 NE2d 986 (1991) (police offered defendant a blood test when he was at hospital, although they did not specifically mention § 5A right, court found defendant would not have exercised right, hence no prejudice); *Com. v. McIntyre*, 36 Mass App 193, 629 NE2d 355 (1994) (not error to refuse to dismiss for failure to notify defendant of rights where he was an attorney who knew of right to have an independent examination and requested one). In *Com. v. King*, the court did not explicitly state whether a remedy other than dismissal is appropriate when the Commonwealth overcomes the presumption of prejudice. In *Com. v. Hampe*, 419 Mass 514, 646 NE2d 387 (1995), the court had suggested that where dismissal is inappropriate, ordinarily the results of the breathalyzer should be suppressed as well as any police testimony about events occurring after the violation of the right. Because the *King* presumption in favor of dismissal is not based on an exclusionary rule analysis, but rather on the prejudice to the defendant's right to establish his innocence, it is not clear that suppression would still be appropriate where no prejudice exists.

[54] *Com. v. Neal*, 392 Mass 1, 464 NE2d 1356 (1984).

[55] *Irwin v. Ware*, 392 Mass 745, 748-752, 467 NE2d 1292, 1296-1298 (1984).

§ 7.7.6 Sexually Dangerous Persons

Several statutes treat the admissibility of expert testimony with regard to proceedings to commit sexually dangerous persons. See § 7.6.4.h.

§ 7.8 Court-Appointed Experts

Proposed Mass R Evid 706, Court Appointed Experts, provides:

> **(a) Appointments**. The court may on its own motion or on the motion of any party enter an order to show cause why expert witnesses should not be appointed, and may request the parties to submit nominations. The court may appoint any expert witness agreed upon by the parties and may appoint expert witnesses of its own selection. An expert witness shall not be appointed by the court unless he consents to act. A witness so appointed shall advise the parties of his findings and conclusions, if any; his deposition may be taken by any party; and he may be called to testify by the court or by any party. He shall be subject to cross-examination by each party, including a party calling him as a witness.
>
> **(b) Compensation**. Expert witnesses so appointed are entitled to reasonable compensation in whatever sum the court may allow. Except as otherwise provided by law, the compensation shall be paid by the parties in such proportion and at such time as the court directs, and thereafter charged in like manner as other costs.
>
> **(c) Disclosure of appointment**. The fact that the court appointed the expert witness shall not be disclosed to the jury.
>
> **(d) Parties' experts of own selection**. Nothing in this rule limits the parties in calling expert witnesses of their own selection.

The purpose of section (a), which is identical with the federal rule, is to make available nonpartisan expert testimony. The rule makes explicit a power that has been implicit in Massachusetts for years and does not disturb statutory schemes for appointment of experts.[1]

Where the court appoints an expert, both parties should have an opportunity to cross-examine the witness.[2]

---

§ 7.8 [1] See *Abodeely v. County of Worcester*, 352 Mass 719, 227 NE2d 486 (1967); GL 123, § 15. See also Mass R Crim P 41.

[2] *Abdeljaber v. Gaddoura*, 60 Mass App 294, 801 NE2d 290 (2004) (error for Housing Court to base decision on report of housing specialist appointed by court after trial ended, without notice to parties).

Proposed Mass R Evid 706(b) provides for reasonable compensation of the appointed expert. This section diverges from the federal rule to accommodate state practice.[3] Rule 706(c), which also diverges from the federal rule, prohibits disclosure to the jury through any source of the fact that the court has appointed the witness. Federal Rule 706(c) leaves this matter to the discretion of the court.[4] Rule 706(d), which is the same as the federal rule, makes it clear that the appointment of an expert by the court does not preclude the parties from calling their own expert witnesses.

---

[3] Fed R Evid 706(b) provides:

(b) Compensation. Expert witnesses so appointed are entitled to reasonable compensation in whatever sum the court may allow. The compensation thus fixed is payable from funds which may be provided by law in criminal cases and civil actions and proceedings involving just compensation under the fifth amendment. In other civil actions and proceedings the compensation shall be paid by the parties in such proportion and at such time as the court directs, and thereafter charged in like manner as other costs.

[4] Fed R Evid 706(c) provides:

(c) Disclosure of appointment. In the exercise of its discretion, the court may authorize disclosure to the jury of the fact that the court appointed the expert witness.

CHAPTER

8

HEARSAY

A. THE HEARSAY RULE

§ 8.1 Definition of Hearsay

The hearsay rule forbids the admission in evidence of extrajudicial statements offered to prove the truth of the matters asserted in the statements.[1] The definitions in the Proposed Massachusetts Rules of Evidence and the Federal Rules are consistent with the Massachusetts articulation of the hearsay rule.[2] Proposed Mass R Evid 801 provides:

> **(a) Statement**. A "statement" is (1) an oral or written assertion or (2) nonverbal conduct of a person, if it is intended by the person as an assertion.
>
> **(b) Declarant**. A "declarant" is a person who makes a statement.
>
> **(c) Hearsay**. "Hearsay" is a statement, other than one made by the declarant while testifying at the trial or hearing, offered in evidence to prove the truth of the matter asserted.

Fed R Evid 801 is identical. Thus, hearsay is a statement made outside the trial or hearing in which it is introduced, offered to prove the truth of the assertions made in the statement.[3] For example, if a police officer testifies on the stand that Mr. Jones told him that the defendant shot the victim, the testimony is hearsay. The assertion is that the defendant shot the victim and the evidence is introduce to prove that. The person who made the extrajudicial statement, Mr. Jones in the example, is the "declarant." For a statement to be hearsay, it must have been made by a person.[4]

A "statement" can be either an oral or written assertion or the nonverbal conduct of a person, if he intends it to be an assertion.[5] To

---

§ 8.1 [1] In certain proceedings, the proscription against hearsay may be relaxed. See § 1.2.

[2] *Com. v. Keizer*, 377 Mass 264, 269 n.4, 385 NE2d 1001, 1004 n.4 (1979) (definition of hearsay) (Text cited); *Opinion of the Justices*, 412 Mass 1201, 1209, 591 NE2d 1073, 1077 (1992) (conduct as an assertion) (Text cited); *Com. v. Diaz*, 426 Mass 548, 689 NE2d 804 (1998) (statement offered to prove the truth of an assertion is not admissible "to show the general atmosphere of what was occurring"); *Com. v. Boothby*, 64 Mass App 582, 834 NE2d 1202 (2005) (statement to police officer by passenger in automobile that had rolled over and crashed that he was ninety per cent sure that defendant had been driving was hearsay).

[3] See *Com. v. McCoy*, 456 Mass 838, 846, 926 NE2d 1143, 1154 (2010) (testimony by mother of alleged victim that police told her that her daughter had been raped was hearsay).

[4] *Com. v. Thissell*, 457 Mass 191, 198, n.13, 928 NE2d 932, 938 (2010) (discussing issues arising from use of computer generated and computer stored records); *Com. v. Royal*, 89 Mass App 168, 46 NE3d 583 (2016) (trooper's statement that registry check indicated defendant's license was suspended was hearsay; record was computer stored, not computer generated); *Com. v. Perez*, 89 Mass App 51, 56, 44 NE3d 886, 891 (2016) (bank date and time stamp on withdrawal slip was not hearsay; record was computer generated).

[5] Nonverbal conduct that is not intended as an assertion is not hearsay. *Com. v. Baez*, 69 Mass App 500, 868 NE2d 1251 (2007) (testimony that people were pointing to defendant and another man when officer arrived at scene was not offered to prove

determine whether the declarant intended nonverbal conduct to be an assertion, one should ask whether the declarant engaged in the conduct for its own sake, or in order to communicate something. If the captain of a ship assigns a sailor to be a lookout, we may infer that the captain thinks the sailor has good eyesight. But the captain makes the assignment for the simple purpose of getting the job done, not for the purpose of communicating his opinion of the sailor's eyesight. Thus there is no assertion. If a captain pins a medal on a sailor's chest, he does so to communicate that the sailor has done something deserving of a medal. Pinning the medal is an assertion.

An implied assertion in a statement may be classified as hearsay.[6] Testimony concerning the "gist" of an out of court assertion is also hearsay.[7] An extrajudicial statement may contain within it one or more other statements that also constitute assertions offered for their truth. In such multiple hearsay problems, each layer of hearsay must be independently admissible.[8] Current Massachusetts law is in accord with Proposed Mass R Evid 805:

> Rule 805. Hearsay Within Hearsay
>
> Hearsay included within hearsay is not excluded under the hearsay rule if each part of the combined statements conforms with an exception to the hearsay rule provided by law or in these rules.[9]

---

that the people pointing were accusing defendant of participating in a robbery, but to call officer's attention to ongoing incident in which other man was holding defendant down) (Text cited). Nonverbal conduct may constitute circumstantial evidence of the actor's state of mind. See, e.g., § 4.2.1 (consciousness of guilt and consciousness of liability). For a discussion of the intent of nonverbal conduct in the context of first complaint evidence, see *Com. v. Niels N.*, 73 Mass App 689, 901 NE2d 166 (2009).

[6] *Com. v. Ashman*, 430 Mass 736, 742, 723 NE2d 510, 515 (2000) (testimony by witnesses—that after speaking with murder victim on an earlier occasion at defendant's apartment, they telephoned police—created possible inference that victim had told them that defendant had abused or threatened to abuse her, and thus was equivalent to hearsay statement by victim).

[7] *Com. v. Occhiuto*, 88 Mass App 489, 498, 38 NE3d 783, 791 (2015) (admission of hearsay gist violated defendant's Confrontation Clause rights).

[8] *Com. v. Cassidy*, 470 Mass 201, 216, 21 NE3d 127 (2014) ("chain" of statements was inadmissible); *Com. v. Caillot*, 449 Mass 712, 871 NE2d 1056 (2007) (statement by co-defendant in police report that his girlfriend told him that another person had admitted shooting defendant's cousin was inadmissible multiple hearsay).

[9] Proposed Fed R Evid 805 is essentially the same and provides: "Hearsay included within hearsay is not excluded under the hearsay rule if each part of the combined statements conforms with an exception to the hearsay rule provided in these rules."

To analyze potential multiple hearsay problems, one should identify all the declarants, and then determine whether there is an exception to the hearsay rule for each declarant. The requirement that each level of hearsay be independently admissible may be modified by statute.[10]

The principal reason for the hearsay rule is that extrajudicial statements, unlike statements in court, are not immediately tested by cross-examination. Thus, there may be no way to determine whether extrajudicial statements accurately and fully depict the matters asserted. Hearsay evidence is nevertheless admissible in many instances, either because the extrajudicial statements were made under circumstances that ensure accuracy or because no better evidence is available. Hearsay statements are not admissible merely because they may have been made under oath.[11]

To determine whether extrajudicial statements are admissible, one should follow the following steps:

1. Identify the words or conduct in question.
2. Identify the declarant(s).
3. Determine whether the declarant intended to make an assertion. Whether there is an assertion depends upon the intent of the *declarant*.
4. Determine whether the party is offering the evidence in order to prove the truth of the assertion. The purpose for which evidence is offered depends upon the intent of the *party* (as a practical matter, the intent of the lawyer making the offer).
5. If the words or conduct are assertive, and the party is offering the evidence to prove the truth of the assertion, the evidence is hearsay.
6. Determine whether the evidence is exempt from the hearsay rule (§§ 8.5, 8.6), or falls within an exception to the rule (§§ 8.7-8.25).

§ 8.2 Extrajudicial Statements That Are Not Hearsay

Extrajudicial statements offered to prove something other than the truth of the statement are not hearsay. When the issue is simply

---

[10] See § 7.5.4.b.

[11] *Moran v. School Committee of Littleton*, 317 Mass 591, 595, 59 NE2d 279, 281 (1945) (affidavits are hearsay).

whether given words were spoken, not whether they were true, a statement is not hearsay.[1] The variety of other purposes for which extrajudicial statements may be offered is endless, and many do not fall neatly within any particular category. For example, in *Com. v. Koney*,[2] the Commonwealth sought to prove that the defendant had received notice that his driver's license had been revoked. A police officer had testified that he received a Massachusetts identification card from the defendant, and the Court concluded that the card could not be offered for the hearsay purpose of proving that the defendant actually was the person named on the card and lived at the address on the card. It could, however, be offered for the more limited purpose of establishing that the defendant held himself out to be a person of that name, residing at that address, and hence was connected with the address to which the notices of revocation had been mailed.[3] Some out-of-court statements are offered to prove not the truth of the statements, but that they were made and they were false.[4]

---

§ 8.2 [1] *Com. v. Aguiar*, 78 Mass App 193, 205, 936 NE2d 16, 25 (2010) (witness's testimony that defendant had made no admissions, contradicting previous witness who claimed defendant had admitted to assault, was not hearsay).

[2] *Com. v. Koney*, 421 Mass 295, 303, 657 NE2d 210, 215 (1995).

[3] For additional examples, see *Com. v. Siny Van Tran*, 460 Mass 535, 550, 953 NE2d 139, 155 (2011) (airline passenger manifest and "ticket inquiry" form were properly admitted as business records; defendants' names on the records were not offered to prove the truth of the assertion that defendants were the travelers, but merely as evidence that they or someone else had used their names when purchasing the tickets); *Com. v. Sullivan*, 410 Mass 521, 526, 574 NE2d 966, 970 (1991), a police officer testified that D's sister told him that V left her apartment in a cab. The statement was not offered to prove that V left in a cab, for she had not. It was offered to prove that D told his sister to claim that V left in that way, evidence of his consciousness of guilt, and an effort to cover up his crime. In *Com. v. Gabbidon*, 398 Mass 1, 494 NE2d 1317 (1986), there was testimony that after a shooting, D became known by nicknames, such as "Top Ranking," "Rankin," and "General," whereas before he was "just another person." The Court held that the nicknames were not hearsay, and were admissible as relevant to D's motives for the shooting. In *Com. v. Sullivan*, 123 Mass 221 (1877), the Court held that if the existence of an event described in an extrajudicial statement is proved otherwise, the statement is admissible to prove that the event occurred before the statement. In *Com. v. Serrano-Ortiz*, 53 Mass App 608, 760 NE2d 1251 (2002) (Text cited), statements of a participant in a drug transaction apparently designed to establish the bona fides of the buyer were admissible, not for their truth, but to establish the nature and context of the transaction and the relationship of the declarant to the defendant.

[4] *Com. v. Brum*, 438 Mass 103, 116, 777 NE2d 1238, 1250 (2002) (statement of defendant's brother was admissible to show that both brother and defendant had given identically false accounts of the same precise details, in order to prove joint venture that continued after the crime).

Previous statements by a witness may be either consistent or inconsistent with her present testimony. Where such statements are offered for the truth of their assertions, they would constitute hearsay. Where offered simply to impeach or to bolster credibility, they are not offered for a hearsay purpose. The use and admissibility of such evidence is discussed in § 6.13.2 (prior inconsistent statements) and § 6.22 (prior consistent statements).

In the following sections, we discuss several types of extrajudicial statements offered for something other than their truth. The various categories should be viewed as illustrative, rather than exhaustive.

§ 8.2.1 Speech Evidencing Condition of Speaker

An extrajudicial declaration is not hearsay if it is offered to prove that the declarant was conscious at the time of the declaration.[5] Nor is it hearsay if it is offered as proof of a cry of distress or emotion.[6]

§ 8.2.2 Statement Offered as Proof of Notice, Knowledge, Motive

An extrajudicial statement is not hearsay when offered to prove that the person to whom it was addressed had notice or knowledge of the contents of the statement.[7] A party's knowledge of the contents of

---

[5] *Hayes v. Pitts-Kimball Co.*, 183 Mass 262, 67 NE 249 (1903).

[6] *Com. v. Tracy*, 349 Mass 87, 96, 207 NE2d 16, 21 (1965).

[7] *Pardo v. General Hospital Corp.*, 446 Mass 1, 841 NE2d 692 (2006) (memorandum and letter were admissible in employment discrimination action to show that employer had notice of complaints regarding plaintiff's job performance and to show the state of mind of supervisor to explain actions he took regarding plaintiff) (Text cited); *Com. v. Torres*, 442 Mass 554, 575, 813 NE2d 1261, 1278 (2004) (in order to explain why defendant had suddenly accused infant's mother of abusing the children, after denying any knowledge of such abuse, it was permissible to admit officer's statement to defendant that mother blamed him for child's death which officer made at beginning of interview in which defendant changed his story); *Com. v. Bush*, 427 Mass 26, 691 NE2d 218 (1998) (witness's statements to defendant about victim were admissible to prove reasons for defendant to be angry, to anticipate a confrontation, and to arm himself); *McNamara v. Honeyman*, 406 Mass 43, 546 NE2d 139 (1989) (in medical malpractice action, the statement of decedent's boyfriend to ward attendant that she told him she had attempted to choke herself admissible to show notice to the hospital staff of the danger of suicide, but not to prove that she actually had tried to harm herself); *Com. v. Porro*, 74 Mass App 676, 684, 909 NE2d 1184, 1191 (2009) (evidence that defendant's supervisor told him there was not enough money to fix scratches in government car was not hearsay when offered to prove his state of mind in not reporting

statements must be material for them to be admissible on this basis.[8]

On occasion courts have found it necessary to permit testimony relating to the investigative background that led to the taking of specific action by police officers.[9] There are three requirements for the admissibility of such testimony. First, the evidence must come through the testimony of a police officer testifying only on the basis of personal knowledge. Second, the testimony must be limited to the facts required to establish the state of the officer's knowledge. Third, the police action or state of police knowledge must be relevant to an issue in the case.[10] The rationale for allowing such testimony is that it makes the discovery of the identity of the suspect, or the presence of an officer at a scene, "seem more natural and less mysterious."[11] The cost of

---

accident to vehicle) (Text cited); *Com. v. Thevenin*, 33 Mass App 588, 603 NE2d 223 (1992) (statement to D by friend prior to alleged rape that V had "crabs" admissible to show D's disinclination to have contact with her).

[8] *Com. v. Pleasant*, 366 Mass 100, 315 NE2d 874 (1974); *Com. v. Stokes*, 38 Mass App 752, 653 NE2d 180 (1995) (defendant's evidence of out-of-court statement by witness to police officers, otherwise hearsay, was not admissible to show that police had ignored the information, as evidence of their bias, where interview with witness did not contain exculpatory evidence and defendant's account of her statements lacked reasonable guarantee of trustworthiness).

[9] *Com. v. Gaynor*, 443 Mass 245, 820 NE2d 233 (2005); *Com. v. Doyle*, 83 Mass App 384, 984 NE2d 297 (2013) (in questionable decision, court affirms admissibility of evidence that when officers arrived at bank, witness pointed to other side of street where defendant was running away carrying a large bag, on ground that evidence was relevant to explain why officers went after defendant rather than stopping to speak to witness).

[10] *Com. v. Arana*, 453 Mass 214, 227, 901 NE2d 99, 109 (2009) (circumstances and timing of police involvement were relevant as response to defense theory that complainants pursued charges to support civil lawsuit); *Com. v. Rosario*, 430 Mass 505, 721 NE2d 903 (1999) (Text cited). See *Com. v. LaVelle*, 414 Mass 146, 155, 605 NE2d 852, 858 (1993) (extrajudicial statements regarding informant's past relationship with police were admissible as relevant to state of police knowledge that led them to use that person as an informant and to seek out defendant as a possible drug trafficker); *Com. v. Cohen*, 412 Mass 375, 393, 589 NE2d 289, 300 (1992) (testimony that defendant's father told police that defendant was not home while he pointed to another room in the apartment and allowed the police to enter was admissible to show state of police knowledge that impelled approach to defendant).

[11] *Com. v. Rivera*, 83 Mass App 581, 987 NE2d 597 (2013) (conversation about formation of plan to rescue victim from abusive domestic partner was not hearsay where admitted to describe physical ending of relationship and explain presence of police officer); *Com. v. Rupp*, 57 Mass App 377, 783 NE2d 475 (2003) (*Rosario* criteria were met where testimony was limited to fact that 911 call was "regarding a firearm" and it was introduced to explain why police had come to address and acted the way they did); *Com. v. Doyle*, 67 Mass App 846, 856, n.15, 858 NE2d 1098, 1106-1107 (2006) (in drug case where defendant asserted entrapment defense, proper to allow officer to testify on cross-examination that defendant was targeted by police because

eliminating the mystery, however, may be the introduction of inculpatory hearsay accusations that cannot be cross-examined. The Supreme Judicial Court has recognized that this kind of testimony "carries a high probability of misuse."[12] The Court has directed that "disclosure of the substance of a conversation ordinarily is not required, and should be curtailed because of its prejudicial potential."[13]

The trial court should carefully scrutinize the prosecution's claim that the evidence is offered for the purpose of explaining police actions.[14] The specific details of the police investigation, when based upon hearsay statements by third parties, "are seldom needed and present the likelihood of serious prejudice."[15] "For this reason a statement that an officer acted 'upon information received,' or 'as a consequence of a conversation,' or words to that effect—without further detail—satisfy (sic) the purpose of explaining police conduct."[16] The admission of unnecessary and prejudicial hearsay details has been held to amount to reversible error.[17]

---

others identified him as a cocaine trafficker, where judge gave limiting instruction that information could not be used for its truth and did not go to the state of mind or predisposition of the defendant).

[12] *Com. v. Rosario*, supra, 430 Mass at 509.

[13] *Id.* See *Com. v. Wilson*, 441 Mass 390, 400, 805 NE2d 968, 978 (2004) (prejudicial effect outweighed probative value of hearsay radio dispatch to explain why officer frisked defendant); *Com. v. Erdely*, 430 Mass 149, 713 NE2d 965 (1999) (to explain why police did not permit detainee to speak with his girlfriend during interrogation, testimony should have been limited to hearsay statement by girlfriend that she did not want to see him; it was error to allow testimony that she said she thought he was responsible for murder); *Com. v. Tanner*, 66 Mass App 432, 848 NE2d 430 (2006) (reversible error to allow officer to testify he asked person in custody where he got his drugs from and then went directly back into restaurant and arrested defendant).

[14] See *Com. v. Johnson*, 60 Mass App 243, 800 NE2d 1063 (2003) (hearsay identifications of defendant as assailant were improperly admitted to explain why police attention focused on him); *Com. v. James*, 54 Mass App 908, 763 NE2d 1127 (2002) (where jury is already aware of the police agenda at the time of the incident, it would likely be error on retrial to permit hearsay description of defendant from police radio); *Com. v. Parkes*, 53 Mass App 815, 762 NE2d 895 (2002) (reversing conviction because of improper admission of hearsay complaints trooper testified were received against defendant); *Com. v. Randall*, 50 Mass App 26, 733 NE2d 579 (2000) (reversing conviction where claim that hearsay statements were offered to explain state of police knowledge was belied by use prosecutor made of statements in closing argument).

[15] *Com. v. Solo*, 45 Mass App 109, 113, 695 NE2d 683, 687 (1998).

[16] *Com v. Rosario*, 430 Mass at 510 (citations omitted).

[17] *Com. v. Arias*, 81 Mass App 342, 963 NE2d 100 (2012) (reversible error to allow officers to testify to hearsay that defendant was known to carry a firearm and would be driving a certain car).

Where a defendant raises the defense of entrapment, a detailed explanation of what led the police to him may be more relevant.[18] When the defendant offers evidence of conversations between the police agent and the defendant, it is not hearsay because the statements are not offered to prove their truth, but to prove inducement and the defendant's state of mind.[19]

The defendant may offer evidence regarding information the police received in order to suggest that the police investigation of the crime was inadequate, and thus that the evidence introduced at trial by the prosecution is unreliable or insufficient to prove guilt beyond a reasonable doubt.[20] Evidence that the police were told about a suspect other than the defendant or were told of other exculpatory information is not hearsay when offered to show that the police had such knowledge and took inadequate steps to investigate it.[21] Whether such information is admissible is subject to an analysis of whether its probative value is outweighed by the risk of prejudice or diversion of the jury's attention to collateral matters. Such out-of-court statements cannot be offered for the purpose of proving that a third party committed the crime, or that other exculpatory information was in fact true.[22] When a defendant makes a *Bowden* defense, the Commonwealth may rebut it by offering evidence of statements made to the police that explain why the police focused their investigation on the

---

[18] See *Com. v. Miller*, 361 Mass 644, 658, 282 NE2d 394, 403-404 (1972) (evidence that drug pushers had mentioned defendant's name was relevant to government's good faith where defendant alleged shocking and offensive entrapment). But see *Com. v. Urena*, 42 Mass App 20, 674 NE2d 253 (1997) (officer's testimony that informant stated following his arrest that defendant was his drug source was hearsay and not admissible to explain state of police knowledge that impelled the approach to defendant, who made entrapment defense).

[19] *Com. v. Podgurski*, 81 Mass App 175, 184, 961 NE2d 113, 121 (2012).

[20] This defense is popularly known as the *Bowden* defense. See *Com. v. Bowden*, 379 Mass 472, 399 NE2d 482 (1980).

[21] *Com. v. Ridge*, 455 Mass 307, 316, 916 NE2d 348, 358 (2009); *Com. v. Silva-Santiago*, 453 Mass 782, 802. 906 NE2d 299, 315 (2009).

[22] When the defendant is making a third-party culprit defense, such out-of-court statements are hearsay when offered to prove the truth of their assertions. *Com. v. Buckman*, 461 Mass 24, 32, 957 NE2d 1089, 1097 (2011). If the evidence does not fall within a recognized hearsay exception, it is nonetheless admissible "only if, in the judge's discretion, 'the evidence is otherwise relevant, will not tend to prejudice or confuse the jury, and there are other "substantial connecting links" to the crime.'" *Com. v. Bizanowicz*, 459 Mass 400, 418, 945 NE2d 356, 370 (2011), citing *Com. v. Santiago*, 453 Mass at 801, and *Com. v. Rice*, 441 Mass 291, 305, 805 NE2d 26 (2004). This exception allowing for the admissibility of hearsay evidence is constitutionally based. *Com. v. Drayton*, 473 Mass 23, 35, 38 NE3d 247, 258 (2015). See § 8.25, infra. See also *Com. v. Wood*, 469 Mass 266, 14 NE3d 140 (2014) (strained credulity that badly injured

defendant. Thus, a *Bowden* defense is a double-edged sword. Determining the proper scope of rebuttal evidence is a "delicate and difficult task," because of the risk such testimony might be used for substantive purposes in violation of the hearsay rule, might result in the admission of improper prior consistent statements, or might constitute opinion testimony by police officers on the guilt of the defendant or the credibility of witnesses.[23]

Statements of a victim of a crime made prior to the event may be admissible in order to prove a motive or relevant state of mind of the defendant, if there is evidence they were communicated to the defendant.[24] Where there is no evidence that the defendant learned of a statement, the statement constitutes hearsay and demonstrates only

---

victim of crime was a third-party culprit—hearsay statements were inadmissible); *Com. v. Smith*, 461 Mass 438, 961 NE2d 566 (2012) (evidence was inadmissible that victim feared a woman who could not be identified and feared "stuff in his past" because any links between the unknown persons and the murder were entirely speculative); *Com. v. Walker*, 460 Mass 590, 611, 953 NE2d 195, 213 (2011) (where defendants were African-American males, statement by unknown person to officer that Hispanic males left suspects' car, dropped something and fled was not admissible for its truth because not clear whether declarant observed the crime or got information from another person, or whether he observed participants well enough to identify them as Hispanics).

[23] *Com. v. Avila*, 454 Mass 744, 912 NE2d 1014 (2009) (approving under circumstances of the case oral testimony about statements of witnesses to police, but holding it was error to permit introduction in evidence of officer's lengthy handwritten notes of principal witness's statements).

[24] *Com. v. Watkins*, 473 Mass 222, 238, 41 NE3d 10, 25 (2015) (evidence was sufficient to show that defendant knew that victim wanted to fight him); *Com. v. Tassinari*, 466 Mass 340, 995 NE2d 42 (2013) (statements by victim to relative concerning victim's hopes for a divorce and dissatisfaction with marriage were admissible under state of mind exception because defendant was aware of her state of mind); *Com. v. Franklin*, 465 Mass 895, 992 NE2d 319 (2013) (evidence was sufficient for jury to infer that defendant knew of victim's threats and thus threats were admissible evidence of victim's state of mind); *Com. v. Bins*, 465 Mass 348, 989 NE2d 404 (2013) (hearsay declarations by murder victim were admissible to show her state of mind, that her marriage was failing and that she suffered from and fought against the defendant's aggressive behavior rather than submitting to it, which was relevant because defendant was aware of her feelings and they provided him with a motive to kill victim because of his loss of control over his home; judge gave repeated limiting instructions that jury could not use the evidence to prove bad character or prior bad acts by defendant); *Com. v. Sharpe*, 454 Mass 135, 141, 908 NE2d 376, 382 (2009) (sufficient evidence established that defendant was aware of victim's statements regarding her intention to move and their finances); *Com. v. Mendes*, 441 Mass 459, 466, 471, 806 NE2d 393, 401, 405 (2004) (victim wife's note, "I'm going to move out tonight," was evidence of husband's motive to kill her; statements to others suggesting she was upset with husband were evidence of her state of mind toward him; other evidence indicated that state of mind had been communicated to him) (Text cited); *Com. v. Qualls*, 440 Mass 576, 585, 800 NE2d 299, 306 (2003) (Court properly admitted witness's testimony that victim told defendant hours before being shot, "I am the one who stabbed your cousin."); *Com. v.*

the victim's state of mind. Unless the defendant has placed it in issue, the state of mind of the victim has no independent relevance. Statements that merely go to prove the victim's state of mind, rather than the defendant's, will not be admissible in evidence.[25] Direct evidence that the defendant was aware of the victim's statements is not required; circumstantial evidence is sufficient.[26]

Statements of a victim indicating prior assaults or threats by the defendant, or expressing fear of the defendant, are not relevant or admissible to prove a motive, even if known to the defendant. They are

---

Cyr, 433 Mass 617, 744 NE2d 1082 (2001) (victim's pleadings in probate court in custody dispute provided motive for murder); *Com. v. Seabrooks*, 425 Mass 507, 511 n.5, 681 NE2d 1198, 1202 (1997) (victim's intention to require child support for defendant to see his child); *Com. v. Qualls*, 425 Mass 163, 680 NE2d 61 (1997) (victim's statements reflecting hostility toward defendant are inadmissible unless communicated to defendant); *Com. v. Cyr*, 425 Mass 89, 679 NE2d 550 (1997) (statements of victim relative to her desire to seek custody of children); *Com. v. Cruz*, 424 Mass 207, 675 NE2d 764 (1997) (police testimony that domestic violence victim indicated defendant had broken her door lock and that she would apply for a restraining order and move away from him was admissible where evidence showed that defendant knew victim, victim had tried to separate herself from him, and victim had communicated to him her desire to be rid of him); *Com. v. Fiore*, 364 Mass 819, 308 NE2d 902 (1974) (V's challenging remark to group of which D was a member admissible to demonstrate state of mind of the group prior to assault on V).

[25] *Com. v. Lodge*, 431 Mass 461, 727 NE2d 1194 (2000) (statements demonstrating "hostile relationship" between defendant and victim are generally inadmissible, unless defendant was aware of them and they provided a motive for the crime); *Com. v. Vinnie*, 428 Mass 161, 172, 698 NE2d 896, 906 (1998) (victim's state of mind irrelevant if unknown to defendant); *Com. v. Taylor*, 426 Mass 189, 687 NE2d 631 (1997) (victim's stated impression that defendant was mad at her and "hated" her went only to her state of mind, not relevant or admissible); *Com. v. Olszewski*, 401 Mass 749, 519 NE2d 587 (1988) (V's statement to W that she would tell police of D's involvement in robberies inadmissible in absence of evidence it was communicated to D). See *Com. v. Richardson*, 59 Mass App 94, 793 NE2d 1278 (2003) (victim's state of mind was not relevant to any issue in case); *Com. v. Demars*, 38 Mass App 596, 650 NE2d 368 (1995) (evidence that victim's father had concerns about sexual abuse of his daughter after speaking with someone about the defendant was evidence of father's state of mind, but that was not relevant to determination of defendant's guilt).

[26] *Com. v. Purcell*, 423 Mass 880, 673 NE2d 53 (1996) (defendant's niece properly permitted to testify that she had told defendant to get his things and leave, jury was warranted in inferring that defendant knew of victim's state of mind); *Com. v. Todd*, 394 Mass 791, 477 NE2d 999 (1985) (not error to allow V's mother to testify that prior to shooting, V tore up marriage license for V and D—inference is permissible that if V was willing to tell third parties of deteriorating relationship, she told D); *Com. v. Borodine*, 371 Mass 1, 8-9, 353 NE2d 649, 654 (1976) (V's statements she intended to leave D were admissible, jury could infer V communicated feelings to D); *Com. v. Williams*, 30 Mass App 543, 503 NE2d 1 (1991) (same).

inadmissible as hearsay.[27] Although it is an error to admit evidence of the victim's fear of the defendant, such error may be deemed harmless on appeal where there was substantial other admissible evidence of a violent or abusive relationship between the victim and the defendant.[28]

A defendant may open the door to the victim's extrajudicial statements if he raises an issue to which the evidence would constitute logical rebuttal—e.g., by making a claim the victim committed suicide,[29] that the victim would have willingly gone with him, or that the victim and the defendant were on friendly terms. Under such circumstances, the extrajudicial statements of the victim may be proof of her state of mind, the relevance of which has been put in issue by the defendant.[30] Where a statement is offered to prove the effect it had on the listener's state of mind, that state of mind must be relevant to an issue properly in the case.[31]

Statements offered to prove notice or knowledge frequently do contain assertions that the proponent would like the jury to accept, although the evidence would be hearsay if offered for that purpose. If a limiting instruction would not cure the potential harm, a court may in appropriate cases decline to accept such evidence as more prejudicial than probative.[32]

---

[27] *Com. v. Wilson*, 427 Mass 336, 348, 693 NE2d 158, 170 (1998); *Com. v. Arce*, 426 Mass 601, 690 NE2d 806 (1998); *Com. v. Magraw*, 426 Mass 589, 690 NE2d 400 (1998); *Com. v. Jenner*, 426 Mass 163, 686 NE2d 1313 (1997); *Com. v. Seabrooks*, supra; *Com. v. Qualls*, supra; *Com. v. Cyr*, supra; *Com. v. Andrade*, 422 Mass 236, 239, 661 NE2d 1308, 1311 (1996).

[28] *Com. v. Squailia*, 429 Mass 101, 706 NE2d 636 (1999); *Com. v. Vinnie*, supra; *Com. v. Wilson*, supra.

[29] *Com. v. Silanskas*, 433 Mass 678, 697, 746 NE2d 445, 463 (2001) (statements indicated victim was seeking to save his life, not end it).

[30] *Com. v. Magraw*, supra.

[31] *Com. v. Weichel*, 403 Mass 103, 526 NE2d 760 (1988) (evidence that other prisoners told D that guards had assaulted inmates could be relevant to D's state of mind on a self-defense theory, but admissible only if there was sufficient evidence of self-defense to raise the issue).

[32] *Com. v. Diaz*, 453 Mass 266, 267, 901 NE2d 670, 681 (2009) (police statements during taped interrogation that "people" had identified defendant might have been offered to show defendant's response, but it was unlikely that a limiting instruction would have cured hearsay problem that statements amounted to accusations by out of court witnesses); *Com. v. Harris*, 409 Mass 461, 567 NE2d 899 (1991) (statement that members of D's group were carrying knives was relevant to V's state of mind where D claimed V was the aggressor, but evidence was unfairly prejudicial because declarant had not seen knives and thus her statement appeared to be based on her assessment of D's character).

§ 8.2.3 Conversations Evidencing the Nature of a Place or a Thing

A difficult group of cases is that in which extrajudicial conversations are admitted in evidence to prove the nature of a place or thing associated with the conversations.[33] Such extrajudicial declarations are treated as not hearsay in spite of the fact that the implications of the declarations must be believed for the declarations to have probative value. Such evidence may be admitted where there is a patent absence of motive to falsify on the part of the declarant and there is a large volume of independent items of evidence that can be consistent with one another only if the hypothesis is true.

§ 8.2.4 Verbal Acts

Some physical acts have legal significance only when accompanied by words that characterize the act. Without the characterization, such a physical act may be legally ambiguous. The words that accompany such acts are admissible to resolve such ambiguities. They are admitted under what is known as the verbal act doctrine. For example, A hands B a pen and says, "This pen is a gift." The statement is admissible to show that the pen was a gift, not a loan or the return of B's pen. Where A moves from one town to another, his declaration at that time of his intention to make the second town his home would be

[33] *Com v. Mullane*, 445 Mass 702, 711, 840 NE2d 484 (2006) (conversation between undercover agent and masseuse regarding "extras" was not hearsay to prove the establishment was one of ill fame); *Com. v. Niemic*, 427 Mass 718, 725, 696 NE2d 117, 122 (1998) (statement of merchant to defendant to put away knife and leave store so there would be no trouble admissible to show by merchant's reaction that object was a weapon, not merely a fishing knife) (Text cited); *Com. v. Massod*, 350 Mass 745, 217 NE2d 191 (1966) (proved telephone was "apparatus" for registering bets by testimony of policeman as to words heard on that telephone); *Com. v. Mendes*, 78 Mass App 474, 484, 940 NE2d 467, 475 (2010) (officer's testimony about incoming calls to defendants' cell phones were not hearsay, but were offered to prove that "defendants had organized and equipped themselves to sell, and not merely to use, drugs"); *Com. v. DePina*, 75 Mass App 842, 850, 917 NE2d 781, 788 (2009) (police officer's testimony that he answered defendant's cell phone and unidentified caller requested "a big fifty" was admissible as evidence of nature of phone as instrument used in drug distribution) (Text cited). But cf. *Com. v. Lopera*, 42 Mass App 133, 136, 674 NE2d 1340 (1997) (statements by alleged prostitute that defendant kept apartment where she worked a shift were not admissible to show nature of the place, because declarant knew she was talking to a police officer and it could not be said that there was a patent absence of motive to falsify) (Text cited).

admissible to prove change of residence.[34] Many declarations admissible under the verbal act doctrine would also be admissible as a declaration of mental condition, a hearsay exception. See § 8.8.

§ 8.2.5 Operative Words

Some extrajudicial statements are equivalent to actions and have independent legal significance. For example, given words may constitute a contract, a tort, or a crime. Such words are admissible under the operative words doctrine. For example, defamatory statements, words constituting an offer or acceptance of a contract, or words constituting the crime of obstruction of justice are admissible.[35]

---

[34] See *Salem v. Lynn*, 54 Mass (13 Metc) 544 (1847) (statement must refer to an act about to be done; statements in relation to a past act are inadmissible); *Com. v. McCray*, 40 Mass App 936, 665 NE2d 127 (1996) (error to exclude defendant's testimony that complainant, in response to his request for sex, answered affirmatively, statement constituted verbal act of consent and explained the character of actions that followed) (Text cited).

[35] See *Com. v. Stewart*, 454 Mass 527, 535, 911 NE2d 161, 170 (2009) (husband's solicitation of others to murder his wife was not hearsay); *Com. v. Rodriguez*, 454 Mass 215, 219, 908 NE2d 734, 738 (2009) (informant's testimony that another person solicited him to commit a murder by putting a wire around victim's neck was not hearsay); *Com. v. McLaughlin*, 431 Mass 241, 246, 726 NE2d 959, 964 (2000) (witness's testimony, concerning his agreement with others to use his car during an attempted murder, was not hearsay, but words used were operative facts in formation of conspiracy); *Com. v. Walter*, 388 Mass 460, 466, 446 NE2d 707, 711 (1983) (advertisement admitted not for truth, but to prove its publication in violation of statute); *Salvi v. Suffolk County Sheriff's Dept.*, 67 Mass App 596, 604-605, 855 NE2d 777, 785 (2006) (co-workers' statements to homosexual plaintiff referencing homophobic remarks made by other co-workers were admissible to prove hostile work environment simply because they were made to plaintiff, regardless of whether the co-workers quoted had made the underlying statements or not); *Shimer v. Foley, Hoag & Eliot LLP*, 59 Mass App 302, 795 NE2d 599 (2003) (admissibility of contract offer was not limited under operative words doctrine to contract actions or to situation where offer was accepted; in malpractice action, making of offer and its terms had independent legal significance and it was error to exclude evidence on hearsay grounds) (Text cited); *Com. v. Sepulveda*, 50 Mass App 909, 737 NE2d 929 (2000) (officer's testimony that cooperating witness said to defendant on telephone that "she wanted 125 grams of cocaine" was not offered to prove truth of the statement, but fact that she placed the order); *Fahey v. Rockwell Graphic Systems, Inc.*, 20 Mass App 642, 482 NE2d 519 (1985) (D's employee's statements to P that guard on a machine should be removed not hearsay, admissible as the operative fact of P's negligent instruction case); *Telecon, Inc. v. Emerson-Swan, Inc.*, 17 Mass App 671, 672-673, 461 NE2d 1227, 1228 (1984) (words of modification of contract admissible) (Text cited).

Such statements are also referred to in some of the cases as "verbal acts."[36]

§ 8.2.6 *State of Mind*

Many types of statements reflect circumstantially on the state of mind of the speaker. Such statements may be offered as evidence of state of mind without implicating the hearsay rule if the statements either do not contain assertions or are offered without regard to whether the assertions are true.[37] For example, evidence in a hearing on mental competency that the declarant said, "I am Napoleon," is not offered to prove that the speaker is Napoleon, but rather as evidence of his insanity.

Where a statement is offered to prove the contents of the assertion it contains respecting the declarant's state of mind, it must qualify under the hearsay exception for declarations as to mental condition to be admissible. See § 8.8.

---

[36] See *Com. v. Perez*, 89 Mass App 51, 55, 44 NE3d 886, 890 (2016) (statements on withdrawal slips from bank).

[37] See *Com. v. Romero*, 464 Mass 648, 652, n.5, 984 NE2d 853, 856 (2013) (in addition to being a statement by a party opponent, defendant's statement that another man had shown him a gun earlier in the day was admissible for non-hearsay purpose of showing defendant's state of mind, that is, that he knew gun was in his vehicle because he had seen it) (Text cited); *Com. v. Montanez*, 439 Mass 441, 788 NE2d 955 (2003) (victim's previous accusation of abuse against defendant was admissible as evidence of her state of mind, relevant to explanation for her delay in reporting abuse and timing of her disclosure); *Com. v. Silanskas*, 433 Mass 678, 693, 746 NE2d 445, 460 (2001) (statements by victim's wife, a joint venturer with murder defendant, that victim was alive and living in a monastery at a time when Commonwealth's evidence indicated his body was in the family freezer were not offered for their truth); *Com. v. Trowbridge*, 419 Mass 750, 760, 647 NE2d 413, 421 (1995) (error to admit multiple hearsay in statement by grandmother to doctor following gynecological exam that child had told grandmother "that's what it felt like when her father touched her," despite limiting instruction that statement was offered not for its truth but for what led the child to talk to the doctor); *Com. v. Mazzone*, 55 Mass App 345, 770 NE2d 547 (2002) (letter by complainant describing alleged criminal acts by defendant was not admissible as state of mind testimony, its purpose was to prove truth of its contents and corroborate complainant's oral testimony) (Text cited); *Keville v. McKeever*, 42 Mass App 140, 152, 675 NE2d 417, 427 (1997) (proper to admit transcript of unrelated proceeding in which incapacitated transferor was unable to give his correct age, as evidence of his state of mind) (Text cited); *Com. v. White*, 32 Mass App 949, 590 NE2d 716 (1992) (statement demonstrating declarant's bias improperly excluded).

§ 8.2.7 *Silence*

Under some circumstances, a person's silence may be as probative as a statement. Of course, silence may also be ambiguous in the absence of cross-examination. Silence is admissible against a hearsay objection if used as circumstantial evidence to support an inference, but inadmissible if offered as an implicit assertion. Where a witness is shown a photo spread and asked if he can identify a suspect, his silence in response is equivalent to an assertion that he cannot, and is therefore hearsay.[38] On the other hand, in *Silver v. New York Central Railroad Co.*,[39] to prove that a Pullman car was not cold, a porter was permitted to testify that no passenger other than the plaintiff had complained of the temperature. The people who made no complaint did not remain silent in order to assert anything.[40]

§ 8.3 Hearsay Admitted Without Objection

Hearsay admitted without objection may be considered by the jury and may be given any probative value it possesses.[1] See also § 1.3.4.

---

[38] *Com. v. Baker*, 20 Mass App 926, 928, 479 NE2d 193, 195 (1985).

[39] *Silver v. New York Central Railroad Co.*, 329 Mass 14, 19, 105 NE2d 923, 926 (1952).

[40] *Jacquot v. William Filene's Sons Co.*, 337 Mass 312, 317, 149 NE2d 635, 639 (1958) (evidence of no complaint on sale of 500 fingernail kits apparently received without objection); *Foreign Car Center, Inc. v. Salem Suede, Inc.*, 40 Mass App 15, 19, 660 NE2d 687, 692 (1996) (evidence that neither employees nor owners of other nearby businesses had complained of symptoms caused by odors or emissions from company was not admissible where it was not shown that they were similarly situated to plaintiffs in case or that mechanism for receiving complaints existed).

§ 8.3 [1] *Com. v. Clemente*, 452 Mass 295, 330, 893 NE2d 19, 48 (2008) (where defendant failed to request limiting instruction with respect to statements by codefendant, judge could not surmise that defendant had not made a strategic decision to allow admission of somewhat helpful statements against him); *Com. v. Washington*, 449 Mass 476, 869 NE2d 605 (2007) (trial judge not required to give sua sponte limiting instruction regarding statement by joint venturer where hearsay testimony is not objected to and no limiting instruction is requested); *Com. v. Jones*, 439 Mass 249, 261-262, 786 NE2d 1197, 1208 (2003) (hearsay not objected to in murder trial reviewed only to determine if admission created a substantial likelihood of miscarriage of justice); *Com. v. Ragland*, 72 Mass App 815, 827, 894 NE2d 1147, 1157 (2008) (when admitted without objection, evidence is substantive and probative for all purposes, including as corroborative evidence). Cf. *Com. v. Stovall*, 22 Mass App 737, 498 NE2d 126 (1986) (court expressed concern about prospect of affirming conviction if only evidence were inadmissible hearsay).

A general objection to a question may not be sufficient to preserve a hearsay objection.[2] An objection on an incorrect ground may not preserve a hearsay objection.[3]

When it becomes apparent through subsequent examination that a witness's earlier testimony was not based on personal knowledge, but on hearsay, a motion to strike should be allowed.[4]

Where an extrajudicial statement is admitted for any non-hearsay purpose, the opponent is entitled to an instruction to the jury as to the limited purpose for which such evidence is admitted.[5] The failure to do so may result in the admission of the evidence for all purposes.[6]

§ 8.4 General Principles Governing Exceptions to Hearsay

§ 8.4.1 Rationale for Hearsay Exceptions

The common-law exceptions to the hearsay rule in almost every case are based on two elements: (1) a strong necessity for the evidence the rule would otherwise exclude; and (2) a guarantee of trustworthiness in the circumstances surrounding the making of the particular

---

[2] See *Com. v. Cancel*, 394 Mass 567, 476 NE2d 610 (1985) (general objection to hearsay accusation against D insufficient because until D's response was related it was unclear whether he had unequivocally denied it, or whether it would be admissible as an adoptive admission; after W testified to D's denial, D was obliged to renew objection or move to strike).

[3] *Com. v. Raymond*, 424 Mass 382, 388 n.5, 676 NE2d 824, 829 n.5 (1997) (objection based on authenticity is insufficient to preserve a hearsay objection); *Blake v. Hendrickson*, 40 Mass App 579, 666 NE2d 164 (1996) (on appeal, court considers only the grounds asserted at trial in opposition to hearsay evidence); *Genova v. Genova*, 28 Mass App 647, 649, 554 NE2d 1221 (1990) (objection that testimony was "self-serving" did not preserve hearsay objection).

[4] *Giannasca v. Everett Aluminum, Inc.*, 13 Mass App 208, 212, 431 NE2d 596, 598-599 (1982).

[5] See *Com. v. Deanne*, 458 Mass 43, 53, 934 NE2d 794, 802 (2010) (where recorded conversation between defendant and others was admitted, court properly instructed jury that it could consider as evidence only defendant's statements, that statements of others were admitted only to make conversation understandable, and that statements by others were untrue, false, or speculative).

[6] *Genova v. Genova*, supra, 28 Mass App at 652, 554 NE2d at 1224; *Com. v. Fitzpatrick*, 14 Mass App 1001, 441 NE2d 559 (1982) (no duty on judge to give limiting instruction on his own motion). Cf. *G.E.B. v. S.R.W.*, 422 Mass 158, 167, 661 NE2d 646, 654 (1996) (record did not make clear in nonjury trial whether letter was offered for a hearsay purpose or for a proper non-hearsay purpose; decision admitting the evidence over a general objection affirmed, court assumed that ruling was based on the proper ground).

declaration for which an exception is created.[1] In order for any hearsay statement to be admissible, the declarant must have personal knowledge of the subject matter of his statement.[2] The only exception to that requirement is that statements by a party opponent are admissible even though the declarant lacked personal knowledge.[3]

Some hearsay evidence may be deemed more reliable than others. The Federal Rules of Evidence, through the catchall exception, permit the admissibility of some hearsay evidence, although it does not fall within the recognized exceptions, where there exist special indicia of reliability. See Fed R Evid 807. No such provision is included in the Proposed Massachusetts Rules of Evidence. The Supreme Judicial Court has specifically declined to adopt this general exception. See § 8.25.

Efforts to dilute or enforce the exclusionary aspects of the hearsay rule raise special problems with regard to criminal proceedings. The right of confrontation provided by the Sixth Amendment to the United States Constitution, art. 12 of the Massachusetts Declaration of Rights, and the hearsay rule, safeguard similar values. The United States Supreme Court substantially changed the test for determining if hearsay evidence violates the Confrontation Clause in *Crawford v. Washington*,[4] discussed in detail in § 8.4.2. We provide a general overview of Confrontation Clause problems in that section and then note specific cases relevant to specific hearsay exceptions in the following sections. While the confrontation right and the hearsay rule are not

---

§ 8.4 [1] *Com. v. Almeida*, 433 Mass 717, 746 NE2d 139 (2001) (admission of statements made by child complainant while sleeping ran counter to central principle that hearsay evidence be reliable) (Text cited).

[2] See *Aleo v. SLB Toys USA, Inc.*, 466 Mass 398, 995 NE2d 740 (2013) (statements in police report and hospital record by persons regarding manner in which deceased went down slide into pool were properly excluded where there was no evidence that declarants had personal knowledge of the matter). See § 6.5 for the personal knowledge requirement for live witnesses.

[3] See § 8.6.5.

[4] *Crawford v. Washington*, 124 S Ct 1354 (2004). The Confrontation Clause does not apply at probation revocation hearings. *Com. v. Wilcox*, 446 Mass 61, 67, 841 NE2d 1240, 1248 (2006); *Com. v. Nunez*, 446 Mass 54, 841 NE2d 1250 (2006) (although Confrontation Clause does not apply at probation revocation hearings, such hearsay must be reliable to be admissible). Strict evidentiary rules do not apply at restitution hearings and hearsay is admissible if reliable. *Com. v. Casanova*, 65 Mass App 750, 756, 843 NE2d 699, 705 (2006).

identical, the essential right both principles protect is the right of effective cross-examination.[5]

Our discussion of hearsay exceptions follows the general outline and order of the Proposed Mass Rules of Evidence and the Federal Rules of Evidence. With respect to each exception we indicate whether current Massachusetts law is consistent with the Rules, or differs from them.

Statutes may create additional exceptions to the hearsay rule. These statutes supersede the common-law exceptions to the hearsay rule only to the extent to which the statutes would admit evidence not within a common-law exception.[6] Such exceptions are incorporated into Proposed Mass R of Evid 802, which provides: "Hearsay is not admissible except as provided by law or by these rules or by other rules prescribed by the Supreme Judicial Court." Fed R Evid 802 takes a similar approach. The more significant statutory exceptions are discussed below.

§ 8.4.2 The Confrontation Clause

The admissibility of out-of-court statements against the defendant in a criminal case requires a two-step inquiry. First the court must determine whether the statement is admissible under the hearsay rules. If so, the court must consider whether admission is prohibited by the Confrontation Clause.[7] A criminal defendant has a constitutional right to confront the witnesses against him, under art. 12 of the Massachusetts Declaration of Rights and the Sixth Amendment to the

---

[5] See *White v. Illinois*, 502 US 346, 356, 112 S Ct 736, 743 (1992); *Com. v. Canon*, 373 Mass 494, 507-513, 368 NE2d 1181, 1188-1192 (1977) (Liacos, J, dissenting); Liacos, *The Right of Confrontation and the Hearsay Rule: Another Look*, 34 Am Trial LJ 153 (1972); Liacos, *The Right of Confrontation*, 33 Am Trial LJ 243 (1970).

[6] By way of illustration, consider: GL 79, § 35 (assessed value of real estate); GL 152, § 20B (medical reports of deceased physician); GL 175, § 4 (commissioner of insurance report of examination of insurance company); GL 185C, § 21 (housing inspection report); GL 233, § 65 (declarations of deceased persons); GL 233, § 65A (answers of deceased party to interrogatories); GL 233, § 66 (declarations of testator); GL 233, § 70 (judicial notice of law); GL 233, § 79 (hospital records); GL 233, § 79B (commercial lists); GL 233, § 79C (medical treatises in malpractice actions); GL 233, § 79F (public way); GL 233, § 79G (medical and hospital bills and reports); GL 233, § 79H (medical reports of deceased physicians); Mass R Civ P 32(a)(3) (depositions); Mass R Crim P 35(g) (depositions).

[7] *Com. v. Linton*, 456 Mass 534, 548, 924 NE2d 722, 735 (2010).

United States Constitution.[8] The rights provided by the state and federal constitutional provisions are equivalent.[9] GL 263, § 5, provides the same protection.[10] The Supreme Judicial Court has determined that in probation revocation and pretrial release dangerousness hearings the use of reliable hearsay evidence does not violate the Confrontation Clause.[11]

In *Crawford v. Washington*,[12] the United States Supreme Court substantially revised the test for determining whether the admission of statements made out of court violates the Confrontation Clause. The Court held in *Crawford* that where a statement made out of court is "testimonial" and offered to prove the truth of assertions in the statement,[13] it is inadmissible unless the defendant has an opportunity to cross-examine the declarant. The Court did not provide a comprehensive definition of what statements should be deemed testimonial but did declare that statements made at earlier court proceedings and statements made during police interrogations are testimonial.[14] The Court suggested that dying declarations might not implicate the Confrontation Clause because they were an exception to it at common law.[15] The Court also suggested in dictum that business records and statements made in furtherance of a conspiracy, on the other hand, are

---

[8] *Pointer v. Texas*, 380 US 400, 85 S Ct 1065, 13 L Ed 2d 923 (1965) (Sixth Amendment applicable to the states).

[9] *Com. v. Childs*, 413 Mass 252, 260, 596 NE2d 351 (1992); *Com. v. Siegfriedt*, 402 Mass 424, 430, 522 NE2d 970, 974-975 (1988) (holding that state law does not impose a stricter standard).

[10] For a general discussion of the history and meaning of the Confrontation Clause, see *Opinion of the Justices to Senate*, 406 Mass 1201, 1205-1210, 547 NE2d 8, 10-12 (1989); *Com. v. Bergstrom*, 402 Mass 534, 541-548, 524 NE2d 366, 371-375 (1988).

[11] *Abbott A. v. Commonwealth*, 458 Mass 24, 933 NE2d 936 (2010) (dangerousness hearing); *Com. v. Durling*, 493 Mass 108, 551 NE2d 1193 (1990) (probation revocation hearing).

[12] *Crawford v. Washington*, 541 US 36, 124 S Ct 1354 (2004).

[13] *Id.*, 541 US at 59-60 n.9; *Com. v. Sepheus*, 468 Mass 160, 9 NE3d 800 (2014) (officer's testimony that a basis for his expert opinion was information furnished by a reliable informant was not admissible for the truth of that information and did not implicate the Confrontation Clause); *Com. v. Pytou Heang*, 458 Mass 827, 854, 942 NE2d 927, 949 (2011) (co-defendant's statement was offered for its falsity, not its truth, and to show that co-defendant and defendant supplied similar false explanations of their movements, thus no Confrontation Clause violation); *Com. v. Pelletier*, 71 Mass App 67, 879 NE2d 125 (2008) (statements not offered for the truth of their assertions do not implicate the Confrontation Clause).

[14] 541 US at 52.

[15] 541 US at 56, n.6. The Supreme Judicial Court has determined that the Confrontation Clause does not apply to dying declarations. See § 8.19.

not testimonial.[16] In *Melendez-Diaz v. Massachusetts*, 129 S Ct 2527 (2009), however, the Court distinguished between business records and official records that are prepared in the ordinary course of business and those which are prepared for use at trial. The latter are testimonial and implicate the Confrontation Clause.[17] Under *Crawford*, the cross-examination requirement will be satisfied whenever the declarant appears at trial and is available for cross-examination regarding his prior statements, or where the defendant had a meaningful opportunity to cross-examine the declarant at an earlier proceeding regarding the statements.[18]

The United States Supreme Court elaborated on what constitutes a testimonial statement in *Davis v. Washington*.[19] The Court ruled on the admissibility of a "911" call and in a separate case the admissibility of a domestic battery victim's written statements in an affidavit given

---

[16] 541 US at 56.

[17] See *Com. v. Irene*, 462 Mass 600, 618, 970 NE2d 291, 305 (2012) (where statements in hospital records demonstrate on their face that they were included for the purpose of medical treatment, they are not testimonial); *Com. v. Siny Van Tran*, 480 Mass 535, 552, 953 NE2d 139, 156 (2011) (airline passenger manifest and "ticket inquiry" form were not testimonial); *Com. v. Zeininger*, 459 Mass 775, 947 NE2d 1060 (2011) (annual certification and accompanying diagnostic records attesting to proper functioning of breathalyzer machine are not testimonial because they are created as part of a regulatory program for routine maintenance of all breathalyzer machines); *Com v. Albino*, 81 Mass App 736, 967 NE2d 645 (2012) (copies of letters from Sex Offender Registration Board to defendant, maintained as business records by police department, were not testimonial); *Com. v. Fox*, 81 Mass App 244, 961 NE2d 611 (documents of Sex Offender Registration Board that identified defendant as a sex offender were not testimonial because they are kept in the ordinary course of SORB's affairs); *Com. v. McMullin*, 76 Mass App 904, 923 NE2d 1062 (2010) (certified copies of records of convictions from Registry of Motor Vehicles and District Court were not testimonial); *Com. v. Dyer*, 77 Mass App 850, 853, 934 NE2d 293, 297 (2010) (hospital tests of blood alcohol content conducted for purpose of evaluation and treatment are not testimonial); *Com. v. Lampron*, 65 Mass App 340, 346, n.6, 839 NE2d 870 (2005) (hospital records containing opinions that patient was intoxicated were admissible because notations were made for purposes of treatment and not in anticipation of their use in investigation and prosecution of crime).

[18] See *Com. v. Hurley*, 455 Mass 53, 66, 913 NE2d 850, 861 (2009) (sufficient for defendant to have had opportunity to cross-examine declarant about facts described in excited utterances, opportunity to cross-examine about the excited utterances themselves not required; opportunity to cross-examine declarant at detention hearing with respect to underlying facts was adequate, except with regard to facts included in excited utterances introduced at trial but not testified to at detention hearing by declarant, admission of those portions of her statements at trial violated Confrontation Clause but was harmless in circumstances of this case).

[19] *Davis v. Washington*, 126 S Ct 2266 (2006).

to a police officer.[20] The Court again eschewed an effort to provide a universal definition of what constitutes a testimonial statement. It did hold, however, that:

> Statements are nontestimonial when made in the course of police interrogation under circumstances objectively indicating that the primary purpose of the interrogation is to enable police assistance to meet an ongoing emergency. They are testimonial when the circumstances objectively indicate that there is no such ongoing emergency, and that the primary purpose of the interrogation is to establish or prove past events potentially relevant to later criminal prosecution.[21]

The Court recognized that there are various types of police interrogation and clarified that by "interrogation" in *Crawford* it had in mind "interrogations solely directed at establishing the facts of a past crime, in order to identify (or provide evidence to convict) the perpetrator."[22] The Court further held, "The product of such interrogation, whether reduced to a writing signed by the declarant or embedded in the memory (and perhaps notes) of the interrogating officer, is testimonial."[23]

The 911 caller in *Davis* appeared to have made the call during the events she was describing and was asking for emergency assistance. The Court held that her initial statements were not testimonial.[24] The Court noted, however, that an emergency call might evolve into

---

[20] The opinion was rendered in two consolidated cases, *Davis v. Washington* and *Hammon v. Indiana*. The Supreme Judicial Court followed the *Davis* analysis in *Com. v. Galicia*, 447 Mass 737, 857 NE2d 463 (2006). In a case where police responded to a domestic violence call, the Court held that the statements made during the 911 call that was made as the domestic assault was taking place were nontestimonial, and thus admissible, but that the statements made to the responding officers after the emergency had passed were testimonial and inadmissible. See *Com. v. Lao*, 450 Mass 215, 877 NE2d 557 (2007) (victim's statements in 911 call alleging that defendant had tried to run her over with his car were likely testimonial under *Crawford* where she was not reporting emergency situation but was making a solemn declaration for the purpose of establishing a fact; victim's statements to officer who came to investigate following 911 call were also likely testimonial as having been made during police "interrogation").

[21] 126 S Ct at 2273-2274.

[22] 126 S Ct at 2276.

[23] *Id.*

[24] See *Com. v. Baez*, 69 Mass App 500, 868 NE2d 1251 (2007) (any "statements" inherent in testimony that when officer arrived at scene people were pointing to defendant and another man holding him down were spontaneous and made while an emergency was ongoing and the scene not secure, hence not testimonial).

testimonial statements, once the emergency has ended. The Court indicated that a trial judge should review such calls through in limine procedures and redact from what is presented in evidence those portions of a call that have become testimonial.

In the second case before the Court the police had responded to a call of a domestic dispute. When they arrived the husband was still on the premises and his wife appeared frightened, but there was no disturbance in progress. The officers questioned the wife about what had happened and kept her husband separate from her when he tried to participate in the conversation. Ultimately the officers obtained a battery affidavit from the wife. The Court held that the statement was testimonial because the purpose of the officers' questions had been to investigate a possible crime and the declarant's statements related to how potentially criminal past events had begun and progressed. The fact that the setting in *Crawford* was more formal was not a sufficient basis to distinguish the statements in this case.

The Supreme Court continued to elaborate on the definition of testimonial statements in *Michigan v. Bryant.*[25] The Court held that, under the circumstances present in the case, statements by a shooting victim to police were not testimonial but in response to an ongoing emergency, where the location of the perpetrator was unknown to police at the time they located the victim. Even where the threat to the first victim has been neutralized, there may be an ongoing threat to the police and the public. Determining whether statements are testimonial requires an objective evaluation "of the circumstances in which the encounter occurred and the statements and actions of the parties."[26] The issue is not the subjective purpose that the parties to the conversation had, but what purpose reasonable participants would have had. The inquiry must account for the purpose of both the declarant and the interrogator. Relevant factors may include: the type of weapon employed, the severity of injuries to known victims, whether the encounter between the declarant and the police was formal or informal, and the possible existence of mixed motives on the part of either or both participants.[27]

---

[25] *Michigan v. Bryant,* _______ U S _______ , 131 S Ct 1143 (2011).

[26] *Id.*, 131 S Ct at 1156. The Supreme Judicial Court applied the ongoing emergency analysis in *Com. v. Beatrice*, 460 Mass 255, 951 NE2d 26 (2011) and *Com. v. Middlemiss*, 465 Mass 627, 989 NE2d 871 (2013).

[27] The Court's opinion raised a number of questions and identified open issues. It suggested that in addition to ongoing emergencies there may be other circumstances in which statements are not procured with a primary purpose of creating an

In *Ohio v. Clark*,[28] the Supreme Court decided that statements that a three-year-old made to his preschool teachers identifying the defendant as the one who had physically abused him were not testimonial. The Court noted that the existence of an emergency is not the touchstone of the inquiry about whether a statement is testimonial. Other circumstances may demonstrate that a statement was not made with the primary purpose of creating "an out-of-court substitute for trial testimony."[29] The Court took into account the informality of the situation and the interrogation, the fact that the statements were made to teachers, not police, that the teachers were dealing with an ongoing emergency involving child abuse, the age of the declarant, and historical evidence that such statements were admissible at common law in concluding that the primary purpose of the statements was not to create a substitute for trial testimony. The Court declined to adopt a categorical rule excluding statements to persons other than law enforcement officers from the reach of the Confrontation Clause. It rejected the defendant's argument that the teachers' status as mandatory reporters of child abuse made the statements testimonial.

As stated above, the United States Supreme Court applied *Crawford* to forensic reports in *Melendez-Diaz v. Massachusetts*.[30] The Court held that such certificates were equivalent to affidavits, that they contain "testimonial statements" and that the analyst who prepares them is a "witness" against the defendant. The Court noted that such certificates were clearly prepared for use as evidence at a later trial. The Court rejected any distinction under the Confrontation Clause between a "witness" who prepares such a certificate and "conventional witnesses" who have personal knowledge of some element of a defendant's guilt. The Court further indicated that although the government need not necessarily call all persons who handled the evidence to establish a sufficient chain of custody, any chain of custody testimony that is introduced must (if the defendant objects) be introduced live.[31] The decision abrogated the earlier decision of the Supreme Judicial

---

out-of-court substitute for trial testimony. The question is open whether statements made to someone other than law enforcement personnel may be testimonial. In a footnote, the opinion suggested that apart from the Confrontation Clause, the Due Process Clause may constitute a bar to "unreliable evidence." 131 S Ct at 1162, n.13.

[28] *Ohio v. Clark*, ___ US ___, 135 S Ct 2173 (2015).

[29] *Id.*, 135 S Ct at 2180.

[30] *Melendez-Diaz v. Massachusetts*, 129 S Ct 2527 (2009).

[31] *Melendez-Diaz*, 129 S Ct at 2532, n.1, slip op. at 4.

Court in *Com. v. Verde*[32] that the admission of such drug certificates did not violate the Confrontation Clause.[33]

The Supreme Judicial Court provided definitions for the terms "testimonial" and "police interrogation" in *Com. v. Gonsalves.*[34] The case arose from an alleged assault and battery and involved spontaneous utterances from the victim to a police officer and to her mother. The Court held that "statements made in response to questioning by law enforcement agents are *per se* testimonial, except when the questioning is meant to secure a volatile scene or to establish the need for or provide medical care."[35] The Court concluded that such statements are testimonial based on its definition of "interrogation." Following the suggestion of the Supreme Court in *Crawford*, the Supreme Judicial Court gave "interrogation" a common sense, rather than technical, meaning. It held that "interrogation must be understood expansively to mean all law enforcement questioning related to the investigation or prosecution of a crime."[36] The Supreme Judicial Court specified that this would include " 'investigatory interrogation,' such as preliminary fact gathering and assessment whether a crime has taken place."[37] In *Gonsalves*, statements made in response to the investigating officer's questions at a time when the scene was secure and there was no apparent need for medical attention were deemed made during interrogation and hence testimonial. Statements made by the alleged victim to her mother in her bedroom at a time when neither had called the police or spoken of seeking police assistance were held to be not testimonial.[38]

---

[32] *Com. v. Verde*, 444 Mass 279, 827 NE2d 701 (2005).

[33] For further discussion of the implications of *Melendez-Diaz*, see § 8.12.2.

[34] *Com. v. Gonsalves*, 445 Mass 1, 833 NE2d 549 (2005).

[35] *Id.* See *Com. v. Burgess*, 450 Mass 422, 879 NE2d 63 (2008) (victim's response "No, it's not" to officer's initial inquiry whether "everything was okay" was not testimonial as it was part of officer's attempt to comprehend and deal with what appeared to be a volatile situation; subsequent statements by victim to officer on that occasion and others on a prior occasion were testimonial per se as responsive to police interrogation not meant to secure a volatile situation); *Com. v. Gonzalez*, 68 Mass App 620, 863 NE2d 958 (2007) (officer's questioning of witness was not designed to secure the scene or obtain medical care).

[36] *Com. v. Gonsalves*, 445 Mass 1, 833 NE2d 549 (2005).

[37] *Id.* See *Com. v. Gonzalez*, 68 Mass App 620, 863 NE2d 958 (2007) (officer's questioning of witness was not designed to secure the scene or obtain medical care).

[38] See also, *Com. v. Middlemiss*, 465 Mass 627, 989 NE2d 871 (2013) (911 call by shooting victim identifying shooter who was at large were not testimonial); *Com. v. Beatrice*, 460 Mass 255, 951 NE2d 26 (2011) (911 call by alleged victim immediately after domestic assault was not testimonial, where ongoing emergency continued while she made call from another apartment in same building where defendant was "packing his

The *Gonsalves* Court had also held that if a statement is not testimonial *per se*, the trial judge must determine whether it is nonetheless "testimonial in fact by evaluating whether a reasonable person in the declarant's position would anticipate his statement being used against the accused in investigating and prosecuting a crime."[39] The test is an objective one that focuses on the specific circumstances in which an out-of-court statement is made.

---

stuff" in their apartment); *Com. v. Foley*, 445 Mass 1001, 833 NE2d 130 (2005) (in domestic assault case, officer's initial inquiries at the scene designed to locate husband and determine whether victim wife required medical care were not interrogation and not testimonial; later questions after husband was in custody and wife declined medical care were interrogation and testimonial); *Com. v. Rodriguez*, 445 Mass 1003, 833 NE2d 134 (2005) (statements by youth and his sister to officers that their father had assaulted the boy were testimonial per se, because made in response to investigatory interrogation at a secure scene); *Com. v. Simon*, 456 Mass 280, 298, 923 NE2d 58, 74 (2010) (statements by victim to 911 dispatcher reporting serious medical emergency and discussing shooting and robbery when it was unclear if perpetrator was still in the vicinity were not testimonial; statements providing details of shooting not relevant to medical emergency, securing crime scene or protecting emergency personnel responding, and statements that assailant worked out at a given gym, were testimonial per se); *Com. v. Tang*, 66 Mass App 53, 845 NE2d 407 (2006) (questions to young boy in house after a shooting for purpose of determining if anyone else was present were not testimonial); *Com. v. Williams*, 65 Mass App 9, 836 NE2d 335 (2005) (statements by alleged domestic assault victim to police officers were not made at a volatile scene where defendant was outside the apartment and downstairs).

[39] *Id.* See *Com. v. Celester*, 473 Mass 553, 563, 45 NE3d 539, 548 (2016) (statement by victim of shooting to bystander that the kid he was with shot him was not testimonial in fact because his injuries were so grave they would "preclude a reasonable person . . . from anticipating any nonimmediate future event, including a police investigation or a prosecution of the perpetrator," citing *Com. v. Nesbitt*, 452 Mass 236, 249, 892 NE2d 299 (2008)); *Com. v. Linton*, 456 Mass 534, 549, 924 NE2d 722, 737 (2010) (victim's statements to her father following domestic assault were not made with anticipation they would be used in prosecution where she did not report the crime to the police or the court); *Com. v. Robinson*, 451 Mass 672, 679, 888 NE2d 926, 932 (2008) (where victim followed his attackers to a dwelling, waited outside until police arrived, then as police escorted defendants from building ran toward them and stated, "That's the two guys," statement was a spontaneous utterance and not testimonial because witness was describing events as they unfolded and a reasonable person in his position would not have anticipated that statement would be used in prosecuting the crime); *Com. v. Lao*, 450 Mass 215, 877 NE2d 557 (2007) (victim's statements to daughter that defendant tried to run her over with his car likely were not testimonial given nothing in record to suggest that declarant had any reasonable expectation they would be used prosecutorially at some later date); *Com. v. Burton*, 450 Mass 55, 63, 876 NE2d 411, 418 (2007) (conversation in apartment among joint venturers immediately after fleeing from home invasion and murder was not one in which participants would have reasonably foreseen their statements being used in investigation or prosecution of crime, hence statements were not testimonial); *Com. v. Figueroa*, 79 Mass App 389, 397, 946 NE2d 142, 150 (2011) (statements by elderly sexual assault victim to nurse were not testimonial in fact where declarant understood questions were about her medical condition and would not have anticipated her statements would be used in

In *Com. v. Simon*,[40] the Supreme Judicial Court recognized that it was necessary to modify the *Gonsalves* rule, based on the later decision of the Supreme Court in *Davis*. To the extent the emergency exception applies, statements are not testimonial per se and cannot be deemed testimonial in fact.

Citing *Com. v. Galicia*'s summary of *Davis*, the Court articulated the factors that determine whether the emergency exception applies as, "(1) whether the 911 caller was speaking about 'events *as they were actually happening* rather than describ[ing] past events'; (2) whether any reasonable listener would recognize that the caller was facing an 'ongoing emergency'; (3) whether what was asked and answered was, viewed objectively, 'necessary to be able to *resolve* the present emergency, rather than simply to learn . . . what had happened in the past,' including whether it was necessary for the dispatcher to know the identity of the alleged perpetrator; and (4) the 'level of formality' of the interview."[41]

The *Crawford* test replaced the rule of *Ohio v. Roberts*,[42] and its progeny, under which a hearsay statement satisfied the Confrontation Clause if it was "reliable," which requirement was met if it fell within a "firmly rooted" hearsay exception or otherwise possessed "particularized guarantees of trustworthiness."[43] The biggest change that *Crawford* made is that hearsay evidence that was previously admissible because it was considered reliable under one of these tests will now be inadmissible if the hearsay is testimonial and the cross-examination requirement is not satisfied.[44]

Under *Roberts*, in the case of prior testimony, the Confrontation Clause also required that the declarant be unavailable at trial for the testimony to be admissible. Unavailability was not required by the Confrontation Clause in the case of other hearsay exceptions, although various hearsay rules themselves require unavailability as a

---

investigating and prosecuting a crime); *Com. v. Patterson*, 79 Mass App 316, 320, 946 NE2d 130, 134 (2011) (five-year-old child's statement as officer walked into domestic disturbance that "He pushed Mommy into the wall. He had a gun," was not testimonial as nothing suggested statement was made for any purpose other than to secure aid).

[40] *Com. v. Simon*, 456 Mass 280, 297, 923 NE2d 58, 73 (2010).

[41] *Com. v. Galicia*, 447 Mass at 743-744, 857 NE2d at 469-470 (emphasis in original).

[42] *Ohio v. Roberts*, 448 US 56, 100 S Ct 2531 (1980).

[43] See *Idaho v. Wright*, 497 US 805, 110 S Ct 3139 (1990).

[44] See *Com. v. Sena*, 441 Mass 822, 832 n.10, 809 NE2d 505, 514 (2004) (under *Crawford*, "the imprecise test of 'reliability' does not satisfy the Confrontation Clause of the Sixth Amendment to the United States Constitution").

prerequisite to admissibility. *Crawford* requires that testimonial statements of a witness who does not testify at trial cannot be admitted unless he is unavailable to testify and the defendant had a prior opportunity for cross-examination.[45]

The unavailability requirement derives from a constitutional preference for face-to-face accusation and recognizes that the Sixth Amendment establishes a rule of necessity to justify the hearsay use of testimonial statements by absent declarants. In order to use testimonial hearsay statements from a witness who does not testify at trial, the Commonwealth must establish that the witness is unavailable and that it has made a good faith and diligent effort to locate the witness and produce him at trial.[46] Whether a court will rule that the Commonwealth has made a sufficient showing involves a fact-based determination and will depend upon what reasonableness requires under the circumstances.[47]

---

[45] *Davis*, 126 S Ct at 2273; *Crawford*, 124 S Ct at 1367-1369; *Com. v. Sena*, 441 Mass 822, 832, 809 NE2d 505, 514 (2004).

[46] *Com. v. Sena*, supra (prosecution's efforts to locate witness in Puerto Rico were adequate); *Com. v. Ross*, 426 Mass 555, 689 NE2d 816 (1998) (fact that witness was in another country did not establish unavailability where defendant raised the issue in a pretrial hearing and Commonwealth made no showing it had inquired of witness whether she would return or offered to pay her plane fare).

[47] Compare *Barber v. Page*, 390 US 719, 88 S Ct 1318 (1968) (insufficient showing of unavailability where witness was incarcerated in federal prison and state made no effort to produce him at trial); *Mancusi v. Stubbs*, 408 US 204, 92 S Ct 2308 (1972) (absent witness living in Sweden and beyond reach of court's process was sufficiently "unavailable"); *Ohio v. Roberts*, supra (witness within United States who could not be located after good faith effort was "unavailable," although not every potential lead had been exhausted); *Com. v. Robinson*, 451 Mass 672, 888 NE2d 926 (2008) (Commonwealth made good faith efforts, including looking for witness in two cities and locating his brother, even though it did not exhaust every lead); *Com. v. Childs*, supra (although Commonwealth had computer information suggesting witness was in Florida and did not exhaust all available means of locating him, efforts taken were sufficient to demonstrate unavailability); *Com. v. Robinson*, 69 Mass App 576, 870 NE2d 102 (2007) (showing inadequate where Commonwealth did not supply dates for efforts to locate witness or for service of summonses and failed to use many potential sources of information, resorting to witness's family only on eve of trial); *Com. v. Perez*, 65 Mass App 259, 838 NE2d 604 (2005) (Commonwealth's efforts to procure attendance of witness were adequate, even though when missing witness finally appeared voluntarily prosecutor failed to take further action on a capias that had already issued and witness disappeared again before he was called to the stand); *Com. v. Florek*, 48 Mass App 414, 722 NE2d 20 (2000) (when Commonwealth knew that witness was in another state at a specified address, but did not enlist efforts of local police to find him, attempt to telephone him, or summons him under Uniform Act, there was insufficient showing of unavailability); *Com. v. Lopera*, 42 Mass App 133, 674 NE2d 1340, 1343 (1997) (declarant's supposed declarations against penal interest not admissible because witness not shown to be unavailable where she was subpoenaed for prior trial

The evidence must demonstrate that the witness is unavailable at the time of trial. In *Com. v. Bohannon*,[48] the Court held that rulings 8 and 13 months before trial that it would be an undue hardship to require an out-of-state witness to return to Massachusetts did not establish unavailability at trial.[49] It has been held that it is not unreasonable for the Commonwealth to commence its efforts to locate a witness shortly before trial.[50]

Where a witness has been located out of state, in determining unavailability the court should consider whether the Commonwealth has made recourse to the Uniform Act to Secure the Attendance of Witnesses from without a State in Criminal Proceedings, GL 233, § 13A.[51] Earlier recourse to the Uniform Act to produce the witness in the past, however, will not establish his unavailability at the time of trial.[52]

We discuss the application of the Confrontation Clause to individual hearsay exceptions infra.

§ 8.4.3 *Impeachment of Declarant*

Proposed Mass R Evid 806 and Fed R Evid 806 provide for the impeachment of hearsay statements admitted as exceptions to the hearsay rule or as vicarious admissions admitted under Rule 801(d)(2)(C), (D), or (E). The Supreme Judicial Court has adopted

---

date, but not actual trial date, and prosecutor did not describe specific steps taken by police or DA's Office to attempt to locate witness); *Com. v. Hunt*, 38 Mass App 291, 647 NE2d 433 (1995) (witness was unavailable where he lived in England, had been contacted by prosecutor, and had refused to come to United States to testify); *Com. v. Cook*, 12 Mass App 920, 423 NE2d 1056 (1981) (mere out-of-court refusal by witness to testify is insufficient).

[48] *Com. v. Bohannon*, 385 Mass 733, 434 NE2d 163 (1981).

[49] Compare *Com. v. Siegfriedt*, 402 Mass 424, 522 NE2d 970 (1988) (where second trial began within a week of a mistrial, not error to rely on finding made in first trial that witness could not be located, together with testimony that police made additional fruitless efforts to locate witness, and to use testimony from probable cause hearing).

[50] *Com. v. Childs*, supra, 413 Mass at 261, 596 NE2d at 356.

[51] *Barber v. Page*, supra, 390 US at 719, 88 S Ct at 1318; *Com. v. Bohannon*, supra, 385 Mass at 733, 434 NE2d at 163.

[52] *Id.* Cf. *Com. v. Roberio*, 440 Mass 245, 249, 797 NE2d 364, 368 (2003) (where government made adequate, but unsuccessful, steps to locate witness prior to trial, discovery of witness in custody in another state during trial did not change his status as unavailable, where lengthy delay would have been required to obtain his presence in Massachusetts).

Rule 806.[53] The rule, which seems essentially consistent with common practice, provides:

Attacking and Supporting Credibility of Declarant

When a hearsay statement, or a statement defined in Rule 801(d)(2), (C), (D) or (E), has been admitted in evidence, the credibility of the declarant may be attacked, and if attacked may be supported, by any evidence which would be admissible for those purposes if declarant had testified as a witness. Evidence of a statement or conduct by the declarant at any time, inconsistent with his hearsay statement, is not subject to any requirement that he may have been afforded an opportunity to deny or explain. If the party against whom a hearsay statement has been admitted calls the declarant as a witness, the party is entitled to examine him on the statement as if under cross-examination.[54]

B. EXCEPTIONS TREATED AS NON-HEARSAY BY THE PROPOSED RULES

§ 8.5 Prior Statements by Witnesses

Proposed Mass R Evid 801(d)(1) provides:

(d) Statements which are not hearsay. A statement is not hearsay if—

(1) Prior statement by witness. The declarant testifies at the trial or hearing and is subject to cross-examination concerning the statement, and the statement is (A) inconsistent with his testimony and was given under oath subject to the penalty of perjury at a trial, hearing, or other proceeding, or in a deposition, or (B) consistent with his testimony and is offered to rebut an express or implied charge against him of recent fabrication or improper influence or motive, or (C) one of identification of a person after perceiving him . . .

This is virtually identical with the Fed R Evid 801(d)(1)(C). It differs from current Massachusetts law in certain respects, as we discuss in the

[53] *Com. v. Gray*, 463 Mass 731, 745, 978 NE2d 543, 554 (2012) (error to exclude defendant's offer of prior inconsistent statements, namely, identifying a different person, from grand jury testimony to impeach witness whose hearsay identification of defendant was admitted in prosecution's case at trial); *Com. v. Mahar*, 430 Mass 643, 722 NE2d 461 (2000) (Text cited).

[54] See § 6.12.

next subsections. The Rule provides that if such statements are admissible they are deemed to be non-hearsay. It makes no practical difference whether they are described as non-hearsay or as hearsay that fits within an exception to the hearsay rule.

§ 8.5.1 Prior Inconsistent Statements by Witnesses

The general rule under Massachusetts law is that prior inconsistent statements are not admissible as substantive evidence of the matters asserted, but are admissible only for the impeachment purpose of demonstrating the inconsistency of the witness's accounts. The Supreme Judicial Court has recognized an exception for grand jury testimony under oath, provided the witness can be effectively cross-examined as to the accuracy of the statement, the statement was not coerced and was more than a mere confirmation or denial of the interrogator's assertion, and other evidence tending to prove the issue is presented. Under these circumstances, the prior inconsistent statement may be admissible as substantive evidence.[1] The Court has extended the exception to prior testimony from a probable cause hearing where the trial court is warranted in concluding that a witness has falsified a lack of memory in trial testimony. In such cases the corroboration requirement that applies to grand jury testimony need not be met as a condition of admissibility.[2] For a fuller discussion of these issues, see § 6.13.2.

---

§ 8.5 [1] *Com. v. Daye*, 393 Mass 55, 469 NE2d 483 (1984); *Com. v. DaSilva*, 471 Mass 71, 27 NE3d 383 (2015) (that witness was summonsed to grand jury and threatened with contempt if he did not answer questions does not establish coercion with the meaning of *Daye*); *Com. v. Maldonado*, 466 Mass 742, 754-755 (2014) (prior inconsistent statement made under oath at a grand jury may be admitted substantively at trial where the witness can be effectively cross-examined, the statement was not coerced, and was more than a mere confirmation or denial of an allegation by the interrogator; this principle encompasses grand jury testimony of a witness who a judge determines is falsifying a lack of memory; a voir dire is not necessary where direct and cross-examination provide a sufficient basis for trial court's determination of admissibility); *Com. v. Figueroa*, 451 Mass 566, 887 NE2d 1040 (2008) (grand jury testimony is testimonial hearsay, but when used as a prior inconsistent statement at trial and defendant is able to cross-examine witness at that time, there is no Confrontation Clause violation).

[2] *Com. v. Sineiro*, 432 Mass 735, 740 NE2d 602 (2000); *Com. v. Newman*, 69 Mass App 495, 868 NE2d 946 (2007) (substantive use of witnesses' testimony from co-defendant's trial, where judge found they were feigning memory loss at defendant's trial, did not violate defendant's Confrontation Clause rights where they were subject to cross-examination at defendant's trial).

§ 8.5.2 *Prior Consistent Statements by Witnesses*

Massachusetts law does not permit prior consistent statements to be admitted to prove the truth of assertions in the statements. To the extent that prior consistent statements may be admitted, it is only for the purpose of rehabilitating the witness. See § 6.22.

§ 8.5.3 *Statements of Identification*

The Supreme Judicial Court adopted Rule 801(d)(1)(C) in *Com. v. Le.*[3] Thus statements of identification made prior to trial are admissible to prove the truth of the statements. For a fuller discussion of these issues, see § 11.1.

§ 8.6 Statements by a Party-Opponent

§ 8.6.1 *General Principles*

Proposed[1] Mass R Evid 801(d)(1)(2) provides:

> **(d) Statements which are not hearsay**. A statement is not hearsay if—
>
> **(2) Admission by party-opponent**. The statement is offered against a party and is (A) his own statement, in either his individual or a representative capacity or (B) a statement of which he has manifested his adoption or belief in its truth, or (C) a statement by a person authorized by him to make a statement concerning the subject, or (D) a statement by his agent or servant concerning a matter within the scope of his agency or employment, made during the existence of the relationship, or (E) a statement by a coconspirator of a party during the course and in furtherance of the conspiracy.

The Rule is identical with Fed R Evid 801(d)(2) as originally adopted, although the federal rule has been amended subsequently.[2] The Rule is consistent with current Massachusetts law.

---

[3] *Com. v. Le*, 444 Mass 431, 828 NE2d 501 (2005).

§ 8.6 [1] See also §§ 2.2-2.5 (judicial admissions).

[2] The federal rule was amended in 1997 to add an additional sentence relative to proof of the relationships necessary as foundations for admissibility under C–E:

Any extrajudicial statement made by a party may be admitted in evidence against that party when offered by an opponent, and will not be excluded on the ground it constitutes hearsay.[3] Statements of others for which a party is vicariously responsible are similarly admissible.[4] Conduct of a party intended as an assertion is treated as a statement and when offered by an opponent is not barred by the hearsay rule.[5] Conduct of a party that was not intended as an assertion may be relevant because it suggests a state of mind of the party inconsistent with the position he has taken in the litigation. Proof of such conduct is admissible as circumstantial evidence, but because no assertion or statement was made, the evidence is simply not governed by the hearsay rule. The admissibility of such evidence is properly analyzed as a question of relevance.[6]

Traditionally, the extrajudicial statements of a party have been labeled "admissions." The term, however, is misleading. There is no requirement that an extrajudicial statement of a party be incriminating, inculpatory, or inconsistent with his perceived interests at the time it was made to be admissible.[7] Any statement of a party is admissible against him when offered by an opponent,[8] if not objectionable on

---

The contents of the statement shall be considered but are not alone sufficient to establish the declarant's authority under subdivision (C), the agency or employment relationship and scope thereof under subdivision (D), or the existence of the conspiracy and the participation therein of the declarant and the party against whom the statement is offered under subdivision (E).

[3] *Com. v. Marshall*, 434 Mass 358, 365, 749 NE2d 147, 155 (2001) (Text cited). Statements of the opponent obtained through formal discovery proceedings are admissible against a hearsay objection. See Mass R Civ P 32(a)(2), 33(b), and 36(b).

[4] See § 8.6.6. (vicarious admissions).

[5] *Com. v. Marrero*, 436 Mass 488, 496, 766 NE2d 461, 468 (2002) (shaking of head was communicative).

[6] See, e.g., § 4.2.1 (consciousness of guilt and consciousness of liability).

[7] *Com. v. Spencer*, 465 Mass 32, 987 NE2d 205 (2013) (statements by a party opponent need not be inculpatory to be admissible) (Text cited).

[8] Parties who are not opponents in a pleadings sense may have adverse positions on a given issue. In some circumstances, evidence offered by one such party of a statement by the other may be admissible as a statement by a "party opponent." *Flood v. Southland Corp.*, 416 Mass 62, 71, 616 NE2d 1068 (1993); *Com. v. Lester*, 70 Mass App 55, 62, 872 NE2d 818, 825 (2007) (criminal defendants in a given case may occupy sufficiently adverse positions) (Text cited); cf. *Care and Protection of Sophie*, 449 Mass 100, 865 NE2d 789 (2007) (Text cited) (extrajudicial statements by children were admissible against the children themselves in a care and protection case, but not against their father, necessitating reversal of a temporary order granting custody to DSS). An unusual case led to an interesting ruling based on who the real adversaries in interest were in *Genova v. Genova*, 28 Mass App 647, 554 NE2d 1221 (1990). The plaintiff sued her own husband as a result of injuries suffered in an auto accident. At trial, the Court

grounds other than hearsay.[9] Such statements are admissible without regard to whether the party against whom they are offered testifies in his own behalf. Both oral and written statements are admissible.[10]

Both the Proposed Mass Rules of Evidence and the Federal Rules of Evidence treat admissions as non-hearsay. Authorities differ as to whether statements by a party-opponent are hearsay. The contention that they are not hearsay is based on the view that their admissibility is the result of the adversary system, rather than satisfaction of the conditions of the hearsay rule, and that no guarantee of trustworthiness is required in the case of an admission.[11] It may be noted that a party cannot logically assert a lack of opportunity to cross-examine himself as the basis of excluding evidence of his own extrajudicial statements. The contention that such statements are hearsay is based on the fact that the statement or assertive conduct, the truth of which is important, occurred while the party was not a sworn witness in the case at bar. This theoretical difference is of no practical importance.

Statements of a party-opponent need not be made on personal knowledge to be admissible. Nor are such statements subject to the opinion rule.[12]

Statements of a party-opponent differ from the exception to the hearsay rule for declarations against interest (§ 8.21) in that: (1) the latter must be against the declarant's interest when made, whereas the former need not be;[13] (2) the latter can be offered by the

---

allowed the defendant husband's counsel to introduce his prior statement, which was more favorable to the defense position than his trial testimony. The Appeals Court reasoned that it could be received as an admission, because the insurance company was the real party in interest on the defense side, and the husband stood to benefit if his wife won the case. It should perhaps be noted that there were alternative grounds relied upon to support the Court's ruling that the statement was admissible.

[9] Certain statements of a party would be admissible as against a hearsay objection, but are excluded for policy reasons. See, e.g., § 4.6 (offers of compromise and withdrawn guilty pleas).

[10] See, e.g., *Com. v. Morgan*, 422 Mass 373, 379, 663 NE2d 247, 252 (1996) (defendant's oral statements to fellow prisoner are admissible) (Text cited); *Com. v. Pero*, 402 Mass 476, 524 NE2d 63 (1988) (written notes from D to co-conspirator regarding the cutting of cocaine and directions for its distribution).

[11] Adv Com Note to Fed R Evid 801(d)(2).

[12] *Hallett v. Rimer*, 329 Mass 61, 106 NE2d 427 (1952) (to prove defendant's gross negligence witness testified that defendant had said he had had "one too many"); *LaPlante v. Maguire*, 325 Mass 96, 89 NE2d 1 (1949) (to disprove defendant's negligence, witness testified that plaintiff had said "he didn't believe any of them were going too fast"); *Federico v. Ford Motor Co.*, 67 Mass App 454, 461, 854 NE2d 448, 455 (2006) (Text cited).

[13] This is true in spite of the loose language ("admission against interest") used in cases such as *Stern v. Stern*, 330 Mass 312, 316-317, 113 NE2d 55, 58 (1953).

declarant's estate, the opponent, or a third person, whereas admissions can be offered only by the party-opponent; (3) the latter are admissible only when the declarant is unavailable, whereas the former are admissible without regard to any unavailability of the party-declarant; and (4) admissions need not be based on the firsthand knowledge of the declarant, but declarations against interest are not admissible unless the declarant was speaking on the basis of firsthand knowledge.

Statements made by a party opponent are not conclusive proof. Where the trier of fact believes that a statement by a party was made, the statement is not binding on the party, but is only some evidence of the facts asserted.[14] Unlike a judicial admission (see § 2.2), it is error for the court to charge the jury that an evidentiary admission is conclusive on the party making the statement.[15] The same rule applies to one's answers to the interrogatories of the party opponent.[16]

§ 8.6.2 *Guilty Pleas*

A guilty plea to a criminal charge and statements made by the criminal defendant during the taking of the plea are admissible against him in a later civil trial in which the former defendant is a party.[17] Neither the plea nor the statements constitute conclusive proof of the facts admitted, however.[18] A withdrawn guilty plea is not admissible in later proceedings.[19] See § 4.6.

The Supreme Judicial Court has accepted the principles of Proposed Mass R Evid 803(22), substantively identical to Fed R Evid 803(22), which provides a hearsay exception for evidence of a final judgment of a criminal conviction, following either a trial or guilty

---

[14] *Brown v. MTA*, 345 Mass 636, 189 NE2d 214 (1963).

[15] *Tully v. Mandell*, 269 Mass 307, 168 NE 923 (1929).

[16] *Chaplain v. Dugas*, 323 Mass 91, 80 NE2d 9 (1948).

[17] *Aetna Casualty v. Niziolek*, 395 Mass 737, 481 NE2d 1356 (1985).

[18] *Department of Revenue v. W. Z. Jr.*, 412 Mass 718, 592 NE2d 1297 (1992). A conviction following a guilty plea does not bar the defendant from contesting the underlying facts in later civil litigation under principles of collateral estoppel, although a conviction after a trial on the merits will preclude the defendant from relitigating the issues. *Aetna Casualty v. Niziolek*, supra. In disciplinary proceedings involving lawyers, however, a plea of guilty to an earlier criminal charge is conclusive evidence of guilt. *In re Admission to Bar of Com.*, 444 Mass 393, 828 NE2d 484 (2005).

[19] Mass R Crim P 12(f); Proposed Mass R Evid 410; Fed R Crim P 11(e)(6); Fed R Evid 410.

plea, to prove any fact essential to sustain the judgment.[20] See § 8.16. Such a conviction, however, is not conclusive proof of such facts.

An "admission to sufficient facts" is admissible in a later civil action, but does not constitute conclusive proof of the relevant facts. The party may introduce evidence to contradict an earlier admission and may be questioned about the reasons for entering the admission in the criminal case.[21] The Supreme Judicial Court has ruled that, "An admission to sufficient facts, absent a subsequent finding of guilt, does not constitute substantial evidence from which a finder of fact in a collateral civil proceeding can determine that the alleged misconduct has indeed occurred."[22]

Where a motorist has been issued a citation and the clerk has found him "responsible," the fact that he pays a fine and foregoes an appeal to the judge will not be admissible against him in later civil proceedings. In *LePage v. Bumila*,[23] the Court reasoned that because many people choose to pay traffic fines simply to avoid the inconvenience of contesting them, such conduct could not fairly be taken as an assertion that the person had actually committed the violation.[24]

It is merely a straightforward application of the rule admitting statements of a party-opponent that the testimony of a defendant in a criminal trial will be admissible against him in later trials where a conviction is followed by a reversal and a new trial.[25] In the absence of a

---

[20] *Flood v. Southland Corp.*, 416 Mass 62, 70, 616 NE2d 1068 (1993).

[21] *Burns v. Com.*, 430 Mass 444, 720 NE2d 798 (1999); *Hopkins v. Medeiros*, 48 Mass App 600, 724 NE2d 336 (2000).

[22] *Santos v. Director of the Division of Employment Security*, 398 Mass 471, 473, 498 NE2d 118 (1986). For a discussion of what effect should be given to an admission to sufficient facts in the state district courts, see *Com. v. Duquette*, 386 Mass 834, 438 NE2d 334 (1982); *Doe v. Sex Offender Registry Board*, 452 Mass 764, 778, 897 NE2d 1001, 1012 (2008) (CWOF means that defendant admitted and judge found that prosecution had sufficient facts to warrant finding of guilty, admissible in civil action); *Davis v. Allard*, 37 Mass App 508, 641 NE2d 121 (1994) (admission to sufficient facts on crimes of operating under the influence and operating an automobile to endanger life and safety are admissible in evidence as testimonial admissions in later civil action). In *Com. v. Hector H.*, 69 Mass App 43, 865 NE2d 1178 (2007) the court held that admissions to sufficient facts, followed by adjudications of delinquency (i.e., convictions), with respect to the underlying charges, rendered moot the juvenile's appeal of the revocation of probation based on those charges. The court also concluded "the evidentiary force of the admissions conclusively validates the earlier findings of probation violations." 69 Mass App at 46-47, 865 NE2d at 1181.

[23] *LePage v. Bumila*, 407 Mass 163, 552 NE2d 80 (1990).

[24] *Id.*

[25] *Com. v. Marley*, 396 Mass 433, 486 NE2d 715 (1985); *Com. v. Beauchamp*, 49 Mass App 591, 598, 732 NE2d 311, 319 (2000) (Text cited).

transcript, any competent witness to the testimony from the first trial may recount the defendant's statements.[26]

§ 8.6.3 Civil Pleadings and Certain Statements by Vulnerable Parties

GL 231, § 87 provides: "In any civil action pleadings shall not be evidence on the trial."[27] But, except as to mere formal allegations, pleadings in one case are admissible as statements by a party in other cases, even if there is no evidence that they were dictated or approved by the party against whom they are offered.[28] If a pleading is amended, the superseded pleading cannot be introduced in evidence as an admission at the trial of the case, nor can the differences between the original and the amended pleading be commented upon in argument.[29]

In an action for personal injury, a party's written statements or his or her statements taken on a recording instrument that are given to the other party, or his representative, are inadmissible in evidence and may not be referred to at the trial unless a copy of the recorded statement or a verbatim written transcript of such statement is furnished to the party making it within ten days of written request therefor.[30] Written and signed settlements, general releases, and statements made by hospitalized patients within 15 days of their injuries are inadmissible

---

[26] *Com. v. Marley*, supra (assistant district attorney present at first trial could testify at second) (Text cited).

[27] Cf. Mass R Civ P 15; Fed R Civ P 15.

[28] *DiMare v. Capaldi*, 336 Mass 497, 504, 146 NE2d 517, 520 (1957); *Hibernia Savings Bank v. Bomba*, 35 Mass App 378, 620 NE2d 787 (1993) (pleadings from another case are admissible, but are not "judicial admissions" and are not binding against a party) (see § 2.4.2); *Pinshaw v. Metropolitan District Commission*, 33 Mass App 733, 737, 604 NE2d 1321, 1324 (1992) (Text cited). Cf. *Maney v. Maney*, 340 Mass 350, 164 NE2d 146 (1960) (allegations of unliquidated damage in prior proceeding in writ, declaration, or probate notice of claim not an admission as to true value of party's claim).

[29] *Harrington v. MTA*, 345 Mass 371, 187 NE2d 818 (1963); *Stoney v. Soar*, 322 Mass 408, 76 NE2d 645 (1948).

[30] GL 233, § 23A; *Spellman v. MTA*, 328 Mass 446, 104 NE2d 493 (1952). But see *Mazzoleni v. Cotton*, 33 Mass App 147, 597 NE2d 59 (1992) (statement not furnished upon demand for same admissible in discretion of trial court where statement was ultimately furnished in discovery long before trial and plaintiff could demonstrate no prejudice from delay). GL 152, § 7B, has similar provisions as to workmen's compensation proceedings.

and may not be referred to.[31] The statute does not apply, however, to tape-recorded statements.[32]

No statement made by a defendant during the course of a psychiatric examination under GL 123, §§ 15 and 16 shall be admissible on any issue other than that of his mental condition; nor shall any statement be admissible on that issue if the statement constitutes a confession of guilt for the crime charged.[33] See also § 5.14.6.

§ 8.6.4 Safety Standards

The fact that a company has provided a written rule of care for the conduct of its employees is admissible on the standard of care required if that rule was designed for the protection of persons in the position of the plaintiff.[34] Evidence of violation of safety standards or regulations promulgated by governmental organizations, trade associations, industry groups, or governmental and nongovernmental testing organizations may be admitted as evidence of negligence. In products liability cases, such evidence may be admitted under theories of admissibility other than that of an admission of a party.[35]

Evidence of violation of safety standards entered into by contract is admissible against a party to the contract.[36]

---

[31] GL 271, § 44.

[32] *Fahey v. Rockwell Graphic Systems, Inc.*, 20 Mass App 642, 656, 482 NE2d 519, 528 (1985).

[33] GL 233, § 23B. For discussion of the relationship of the statute to the privilege against self-incrimination, see *Blaisdell v. Com*, 372 Mass 753, 364 NE2d 191 (1977).

[34] *Stevens v. Boston Elevated Railway Co.*, 184 Mass 476, 69 NE 338 (1904).

[35] See, e.g., *Afienko v. Harvard Club of Boston*, 365 Mass 320, 312 NE2d 196 (1974) (violation of Department of Labor and Industries regulations admissible); *Campbell v. Leach*, 352 Mass 367, 225 NE2d 594 (1967) (violation of Department of Public Safety regulations admissible); *Woodcock v. Trailways of New England, Inc.*, 340 Mass 36, 40-41, 162 NE2d 658, 662-663 (1959) (violation of Interstate Commerce Commission (ICC) regulations admissible); *Torre v. Harris-Seybold Co.*, 9 Mass App 660, 404 NE2d 96 (1980) (extensive discussion of principles and authorities).

[36] *Corsetti v. Stone Co.*, 396 Mass 1, 11 n.8, 483 NE2d 793 (1985) (contract provides evidence of the standards the parties considered material to due care); *Banaghan v. Dewey*, 340 Mass 73, 162 NE2d 807 (1959) (contract between owner of building and defendant elevator company); *Kushner v. Dravo Corp.*, 339 Mass 273, 158 NE2d 858 (1959) (defendant's contract with Metropolitan District Commission). Compare *Ted's Master Service, Inc. v. Farina Brothers Co.*, 343 Mass 307, 178 NE2d 268 (1961) (contract not admissible; contained no relevant safety standards); *Clough v. New England Telephone & Telegraph Co.*, 342 Mass 31, 172 NE2d 113 (1961) (violation of safety rule not proximate cause of injury). It was held that this does not apply to a rule that is only

§ 8.6.5 Statements Adopted by a Party-Opponent

A statement made by a third person that has been affirmatively adopted by a party to a lawsuit may be admitted against that party as her own statement.[37] Such statements are often referred to as "adoptive admissions," but the statement does not have to be against the party's interest for the principle to apply. Mass R Evid 801(d)(2)(B) provides for the admission of such statements.

Silence in the presence of a statement is admissible against the silent party as an admission of the truth of the statement only when: (1) the person to whom the statement is made hears and understands it and has sufficient knowledge to reply to it; and (2) the statement is made under circumstances in which the ordinary person would contradict it if it were false.[38]

Where a statement is properly admitted as an adoptive admission, the Supreme Judicial Court has held there is no violation of the Confrontation Clause, although the maker of the original statement is not

---

given to employees orally, for the dangers of abuse in admitting evidence of such rules is too great. *Gerry v. Worcester Consolidated Street Railway Co.*, 248 Mass 559, 564-565, 143 NE 694, 696 (1924). If the rule or regulation is printed, oral testimony as to its contents will not be allowed. *Passanessi v. C. J. Maney Co.*, 340 Mass 599, 604, 165 NE2d 590, 593 (1960). See Ch. 10, Best Evidence Rule.

[37] *Zucco v. Kane*, 439 Mass 503, 508, 789 NE2d 115, 119 (2003) (plaintiff's signature on workers' compensation lump-sum agreement was an adoption of the agreement's contents); *Com. v. Gray*, 80 Mass App 98, 951 NE2d 931 (2011) (questioning, but not deciding, whether signature of defendant on booking memo established that he supplied the address on the form or adopted it as his statement) (Text cited).

[38] *Com. v. Shea*, 460 Mass 163, 170, 950 NE2d 393, 400 (2011) (adoption found where girl saw defendant on street arguing with two other men and she said to defendant, "That's messed up that you did that to Dymond [the victim]. Why would you do it? She was only fourteen,?" and defendant did not respond but gave her a "blank look"); *Com. v. Braley*, 449 Mass 316, 867 NE2d 743 (2007) (defendant's joint venturer described shooting to his girlfriend and defendant did not contest the account); *Com. v. Gonzalez*, 443 Mass 799, 824 NE2d 843 (2005) (presence of defendant during reenactment of a murder by co-participants rendered the communicative aspect of their conduct admissible as an adoptive admission) (Text cited); *Com. v. Silanskas*, 433 Mass 678, 694, 746 NE2d 445, 461 (2001) (silence in response to statements made in defendant's presence by victim's wife, a joint venturer with murder defendant, describing alleged details of victim's death); *Brown v. Com.*, 407 Mass 84, 90, 551 NE2d 531, 534 (1990) (silence in response to accusation of crime by coworker); *Com. v. Brown*, 394 Mass 510, 515, 476 NE2d 580, 583 (1985) (admission by silence inferred where witness could not recall which of two defendants made individual statements in incriminating conversation at which both were present); *Com. v. Galazka*, 84 Mass App 907, 997 NE2d 453 (2013) (defendant's mother's statement that defendant was 24 was an adoptive admission where defendant was present, heard and understood it, and would have refuted it if not true because rape victim was present and he had previously told her he was 17).

produced for cross-examination and his unavailability is not established.[39] The analysis by the Supreme Judicial Court predated the Supreme Court's decision in *Crawford v. Washington*, supra, and was premised on the argument that the hearsay exception for adoptive admissions was "firmly rooted" and thus met the prior test. It could be argued that *Crawford* requires cross-examination rather than reliability for out-of-court declarations deemed "testimonial." It would seem, however, that because an "adoptive admission" is taken to be the party's own statement that cross-examination of the original maker of the statement would be unnecessary for admissibility. The party has become the declarant by adopting the statement and cannot insist upon an opportunity to cross-examine himself.[40]

The Supreme Judicial Court has indicated that evidence of an adoptive admission is "to be received with caution."[41] The Court has described its attitude as "general wariness of adoptive admissions."[42] In *Leone v. Doran*,[43] the Court indicated it is "not inclined to extend the scope of the doctrine of admission by silence," and it refused to allow evidence of silence in response to an accusation made in a telephone conversation.[44]

A statement made in the presence of a party, but not directed to him, may not require a reply. His silence in such circumstances may not amount to an adoption.[45] Nor does a statement that does not constitute in any way an accusation of guilt or liability require a reply.[46] If one is in a situation in which one believes oneself not entitled to speak,

---

[39] *Com. v. Babbitt*, 430 Mass 700, 723 NE2d 17 (2000) (hearsay exception for adoptive admissions is "firmly rooted").

[40] See *United States v. Lafferty*, 387 F Supp 2d 500, 510-511 (W.D. Pa. 2005).

[41] *Com. v. Babbitt*, supra; *Com. v. Mackenzie*, 413 Mass 498, 506, 597 NE2d 1037, 1043 (1992) (noting that the meaning of a response, or lack thereof, to an accusatory statement is often ambiguous) (Text cited); *Com. v. Boris*, 317 Mass 309, 58 NE2d 8 (1944) (evidence of defendant's silence should have been excluded because he could not be expected to deny allegation that ran against third person).

[42] *Com. v. Rembiszewski*, 363 Mass 311, 293 NE2d 919 (1973) (defendant could not be expected to reply to doctor's comment about x-ray results, while feigning incoherence and when he had been advised of *Miranda* rights).

[43] 363 Mass 1, 292 NE2d 19 (1973).

[44] *Id.*

[45] *Com. v. Rembiszewski*, supra; *Com. v. Stevenson*, 46 Mass App 506, 511, 707 NE2d 385, 389 (1999) (defendants' mere presence in vicinity of conversation in which they were not participants did not establish that they could hear, let alone understand and respond to the allegations made).

[46] *Com. v. Thompson*, 431 Mass 108, 116, 725 NE2d 556, 564 (2000) (fact that defendant, when told of wife's death by police, made no response and stared silently at floor for 30 seconds should not have been admitted to prove consciousness of guilt);

one's silence is not an adoptive admission.[47] Similarly, silence is inadmissible as evidence if the person reasonably believes that the assertion has already been denied.[48]

If instead of remaining silent when a statement requiring contradiction is made the party makes an equivocal reply or a reply that partially admits the statement, the statement and the reply are admissible in evidence.[49] See § 12.6.8. On the other hand, where the witness to the conversation cannot remember whether the party made a response to the statement, there is nothing, by way of silence or otherwise, that signifies the party's acceptance of the statement.[50] Where the party unequivocally denied the statement, the statement is hearsay if offered to prove that it was true, and inadmissible.[51]

In *Com. v. MacKenzie*,[52] when the police confronted the defendant with a lengthy statement by his co-defendant, his apparent acceptance of portions of the statement did not justify admitting the statement in

---

Com. v. Wallace, 346 Mass 9, 14-15, 190 NE2d 224, 227 (1963) (statement by wife of deceased that "I could kill you!" was an emotional outburst; failure to reply did not constitute an adoptive admission).

[47] *Com. v. Kenney*, 53 Mass (12 Metc) 235 (1847).

[48] *Refrigeration Discount Corp. v. Catino*, 330 Mass 230, 112 NE2d 790 (1953).

[49] *Com. v. Williams*, 450 Mass 645, 880 NE2d 768 (2008) (where co-defendant said to third party in three-way telephone conversation that he and defendant "were kicking his ass nigger," defendant's reply, "Yo, chill, chill" could be found not to constitute a denial); *Com. v. Sullivan*, 436 Mass 799, 768 NE2d 529 (2002) (accomplice stated to third party that someone got shot, defendant interjected, "What are you telling him for? Be quiet."); *Brown v. Com.*, supra (coworker asked D if he "did it," and he sarcastically replied "yeah, right"); *Com. v. Jones*, 400 Mass 544, 547, 511 NE2d 17, 19 (1987) (D and alleged accomplice conversed with W, whether *D*'s comments and tears constituted adoption of accomplice's statements was properly question for jury); *Com. v. Earltop*, 372 Mass 199, 361 NE2d 220 (1977) (statement made to D, "you have a gun," to which he replied, "so what if I do"); *Com. v. Sazama*, 339 Mass 154, 158 NE2d 313 (1959) (evasive or equivocal reply admissible, but not if intended to assert right to counsel). *Com. v. Kruah*, 47 Mass App 341, 712 NE2d 1182 (1999) (whether apology encompassed a particular wrong, when made after request for apology in connection with series of problems, was question for jury) (Text cited).

[50] *Com. v. Jenkins*, 458 Mass 791, 795, 941 NE2d 56, 64 (2010).

[51] *Com. v. Spencer*, 465 Mass 32, 987 NE2d 205 (2013) (accusations against the defendant by another and unequivocal denials of the accusations by the defendant are inadmissible as hearsay) (Text cited); *Com. v. Womack*, 457 Mass 268, 272, 929 NE2d 943, 948 (2010) (where an objection was not preserved, error is reviewed under substantial likelihood of a miscarriage of justice standard; where error was preserved, the prejudicial error standard; court rejects harmless beyond a reasonable doubt standard, overruling *Com. v. Diaz*, 453 Mass 266, 901 NE2d 670 (2009) to the extent it applied the beyond a reasonable doubt standard to a defendant's denial of an accusation (as opposed to exercising the right to remain silent)).

[52] *Com. v. MacKenzie*, supra.

its entirety.[53] In *MacKenzie*, the defendant waived his objections to the inadmissible portions, however, by virtually conceding admissibility of testimony and failing to distinguish between admissible and inadmissible portions of the statement.

Ordinarily, statements in letters are not to be taken as admitted if they are not contradicted.[54]

If a defendant, while under arrest, is charged with a crime by a statement made in his presence and he makes an equivocal reply, a reply susceptible of being interpreted as an admission, or a reply not likely to be made by an innocent man, the statement and the reply may be admissible. However, admissibility of such evidence depends upon whether a violation of defendant's right to counsel or privilege against self-incrimination is involved. These problems are discussed in § 12.6.8 (confessions).

§ 8.6.6 Vicarious Admissions

There are a variety of situations in which a statement of a third person may be admitted against a party who is held to have responsibility for the statement, although he did not make it. These situations are covered by Proposed Mass R Evid 801(d)(2). We discuss with respect to specific issues the extent to which Massachusetts case law has adopted or differs from the Rule.

a. Statements of an Agent Offered Against Principal

It has long been the rule in Massachusetts that a statement made by an agent who was authorized to make a statement concerning the subject by the principal are admissible against the principal.[55] Massachusetts law is consistent with Proposed Mass R Evid 801(d)(2)(C).

In *Ruszcyk v. Secretary of Public Safety*,[56] the Supreme Judicial Court adopted Proposed Mass R Evid 801(d)(2)(D) and abrogated the prior common-law rule under which an agent's extrajudicial statement

---

[53] *Com. v. MacKenzie*, supra.

[54] *Wagman v. Ziskind*, 234 Mass 509, 125 NE 633 (1920). But see *Elwell v. Athol*, 325 Mass 41, 88 NE2d 635 (1949).

[55] *McNicholas v. New England Telephone & Telegraph Co.*, 196 Mass 138, 142, 81 NE 889 (1907); *Blake v. Hendrickson*, 40 Mass App 579, 666 NE2d 164 (1996) (letters by plaintiff's counsel were properly admitted as vicarious statements of agent).

[56] *Ruszcyk v. Secretary of Public Safety*, 401 Mass 418, 517 NE2d 152 (1988).

might be admitted against the principal only where the agent had actual authority to make the statement offered.[57]

Ruszcyk represents a substantial departure from prior law and changes the analysis from an inquiry into the agent's specific authorization to speak about the subject matter in question to an inquiry into his general authority to act in the area.[58] The universe of statements that are potentially admissible is much broader under the new rule than the old. However, the change does not mean that every statement by an agent concerning matters within the general scope of her duties will be admissible against the principal. In *Ruszcyk*, the Court directed trial judges to make an additional determination whether the probative value of the statement is substantially outweighed by the danger of unfair prejudice before admitting it, as suggested by Proposed Mass R Evid 403 and Fed R Evid 403:

> This determination, which should take place outside the hearing of the jury, see Proposed Mass R Evid 104(c), takes into account the particular circumstances of each case, including the credibility of the witness; the proponent's need for the evidence, e.g., whether the declarant is available to testify; and the reliability of the evidence offered, including consideration of whether the statement was made on firsthand knowledge and of any other circumstances bearing on the credibility of the declarant. In short, this approach rejects a rigid per se rule in favor of a flexible, fact-sensitive standard applied on a case-by-case basis.[59]

Personal knowledge is not required, although it may be taken into account in determining whether the probative value of the evidence is outweighed by danger of prejudice, and considered as well by the trier of fact in determining the weight to be given to the statement.

---

[57] *Id.* See also *Chan v. Chen*, 70 Mass App 79, 85, 872 NE2d 1153, 1159 (2007) (statements of agents who were self-dealing, and hence had conflict of interest with principal, should not be imputed to principal); *Herson v. New Boston Garden Corp.*, 40 Mass App 779, 667 NE2d 907 (1996) (affirming finding under *Ruszcyk* that hearsay was properly excluded where subject matter of statements was not within declarant's scope of employment).

[58] *Com. v. Keo*, 467 Mass 25, 3 NE3d 55 (2014) (recognizing that after *Ruszcyk* earlier decision in *Com. v. Arsenault*, 361 Mass 287, 280 NE2d 129 (1972), holding that defendant is not entitled to introduce prosecutor's closing argument from prior trial as admission by Commonwealth "is no longer sound precedent," but concluding that it was not admissible under the facts of this case, over dissent by three Justices).

[59] *Ruszcyk v. Secretary of Public Safety*, 401 Mass at 422-423. See also *Thorell v. ADAP, Inc.*, 58 Mass App 334, 339, 789 NE2d 1086, 1091 (2003) (reversing summary judgment where court failed to make findings required to determine whether declaration should have been admitted as vicarious admission).

Under Massachusetts law, out-of-court statements of an alleged agent are inadmissible to prove his agency.[60] The alleged agent can be called as a witness and the agency established by his testimony,[61] and it may be established by other competent evidence.[62]

b. Statements of Co-Conspirators and Participants in Joint Ventures

The extrajudicial statements of a co-conspirator or a fellow participant in a joint venture are admissible against the other conspirators or participants if the statements are made during the pendency of the cooperative effort and in furtherance of its goal.[63] Although generally statements must be made during the conspiracy to be admissible, if they surround the history of the conspiracy they may be admissible even if they predate the conspiracy.[64]

---

[60] See *Poulin v. H. A. Tobey Lumber Corp.*, 337 Mass 146, 148 NE2d 277 (1958); *DuBois v. Powdrell*, 271 Mass 394, 397, 171 NE 474, 475-476 (1930).

[61] *Eastern Paper & Box Co. v. Herz Manufacturing Corp.*, 323 Mass 138, 80 NE2d 484 (1948); *Campbell v. Olender*; 27 Mass App 1197, 543 NE2d 708 (1989).

[62] Under Fed Rule 801(d)(2), the out-of-court statement of an agent is admissible on the existence of the agency relationship and the scope thereof, but is not alone sufficient to prove it. The Proposed Massachusetts Rules of Evidence do not address this specific issue.

[63] *Com. v. Rousseau*, 465 Mass 372, 990 NE2d 543 (2013) (joint venturer's statements to reporter to publicize fire they had set were part of the ongoing criminal enterprise and admissible against defendant); *Com. v. Stewart*, 454 Mass 527, 536, 911 NE2d 161, 170 (2009) (husband's statements to daughter were relevant to establishing his alibi and in furtherance of joint venture; killer's statement to another that he had "offed" woman who lived in house they were passing by revealed the crime to someone not a member of joint venture and was not in furtherance of it); *Com. v. Reaves*, 434 Mass 383, 388, 750 NE2d 464, 469 (2001) ("classic pattern of a criminal joint venture"); *Com. v. Colon-Cruz*, 408 Mass 533, 543, 562 NE2d 797, 806 (1990) (statements made while attempting to conceal evidence and avoid detection were admissible); *Com. v. Borans*, 379 Mass 117, 145-148, 393 NE2d 911, 928-930 (1979) (extensive discussion of authorities; rule applies to joint ventures as well as to co-conspirators); *Com. v. Beckell*, 373 Mass 329, 366 NE2d 1252 (1977) (statement must be made in furtherance of conspiracy; this exception does not violate *Bruton* rule); Proposed Mass R Evid 801(d)(2)(E); Fed R Evid 801(d)(2)(E).

[64] *Com. v. Carriere*, 470 Mass 1, 18 NE3d 326 (2014) (statements probative of defendant's intent to kill his wife and joint venturers' actions in furtherance of that intent several months later were not too remote to be admissible; testimony regarding joint venturers' participation in unrelated theft several years earlier was too remote); *Com. v. Stewart*, 454 Mass 527, 535, 911 NE2d 161, 170 (2009) (statement indicative of husband's intent to kill wife was admissible although made before joint venture was formed); *Com. v. McLaughlin*, 431 Mass 241, 248, 726 NE2d 959, 965 (2000) (co-conspirator's statement, 15 months before conspiracy was formed, that he had a "contract" on his wife was probative of his intent to kill someone and that he acted on it by enlisting the assistance of others in the conspiracy; statement was admissible against

Under Massachusetts law, the existence of the conspiracy or joint venture must be proved by means other than the extrajudicial statement in question, as a condition of the statement's admissibility.[65] The existence of the conspiracy or joint venture and the party's involvement in the conspiracy must be proved by a preponderance of the evidence.[66]

The court need not make a preliminary finding that the joint criminal enterprise existed before admitting the evidence; it may be admitted subject to a later motion to strike if the proponent of the evidence fails to prove the opponent was part of a conspiracy or joint enterprise.[67] The existence of the conspiracy may be proved by circumstantial evidence.[68] The prior acquittal in a separate trial of the alleged co-conspirator who made the statement does not render it inadmissible.[69]

When a statement of a co-conspirator or joint venturer has been admitted, the court should instruct the jury that they may consider the statement against the party only if they determine on the basis of other evidence, by a preponderance of the evidence, that a conspiracy or joint venture existed, that the declarant and the party were members of it at the time of the statement, and that the statement was made during the course of the conspiracy or joint venture and in furtherance of the conspiracy or joint venture.[70] The Supreme Judicial Court has

---

co-conspirators; trial judge has discretion to exclude such evidence if it is too remote); *Com. v. Melanson*, 53 Mass App 576, 760 NE2d 794 (2002).

[65] *Com. v. Colon-Cruz*, supra; *Com. v. Bongarzone*, 390 Mass 326, 340, 455 NE2d 1183, 1192 (1983). The Massachusetts common law rule differs from Fed R Evid 801(d)(2), where the statement itself may be taken into account in determining whether a conspiracy existed and whether the defendant was a member of it. Even under the federal rule, the statement alone is not sufficient to prove the existence of the conspiracy. See *Bourjaily v. United States*, 483 US 171, 107 S Ct 2775 (1987).

[66] *Com. v. McLaughlin*, supra; *Com. v. Leftwich*, 430 Mass 865, 724 NE2d 683 (2000).

[67] *Com. v. Collado*, 426 Mass 675, 690 NE2d 424 (1998); *Com. v. Colon-Cruz*, supra.

[68] *Com. v. Soares*, 384 Mass 149, 159, 424 NE2d 221, 227 (1981); *Com. v. Cartagena*, 32 Mass App 141, 144, 586 NE2d 43, 45 (1992).

[69] *Com. v. Anselmo*, 33 Mass App 602, 603 NE2d 227 (1992).

[70] *Com. v. Caldwell*, 459 Mass 271, 287, 945 NE2d 313, 328 (2011); *Com. v. McLaughlin*, supra; *Com. v. Soares*, 384 Mass 149, 159-160, 424 NE2d 221, 227 (1981). Cf. *Com. v. Fernandes*, 427 Mass 90, 692 NE2d 3 (1998) (error in failing to give charge did not create substantial risk of miscarriage of justice where defendant did not request it); *Com. v. Cartagena*, supra (error in failing to give charge did not create substantial risk of miscarriage of justice, where D did not request it).

clarified that the standard of proof for the jury to find these preliminary facts is the preponderance of the evidence standard.[71] For the hearsay statements of a co-venturer to be admissible, the jury does not have to be instructed, however, that joint venture is a theory on which it might find the party criminally liable.[72]

A statement or confession by a co-conspirator or joint venturer made after the termination of the common enterprise does not come within this exception and may be admitted as against the declarant only. In a criminal case, admission of such a statement against the declarant may require a severance where the declarant does not testify and the remaining defendants have no opportunity to cross-examine him on the statement.[73] However, statements made during a period in which the conspirators were still acting to conceal evidence of their crime and to avoid detection and detention may be held to be during the pendency of the conspiracy and therefore admissible.[74] Statements made after the declarant has been apprehended and incarcerated are held to be after the termination of the conspiracy and not admissible.[75]

---

[71] *Com. v. Bright*, 463 Mass 421, 434, 974 NE2d 1092, 1105 (2012).

[72] *Com. v. Leftwich*, 430 Mass 838, 846, 724 NE2d 683, 691 (2000).

[73] See *Com. v. Bongarzone*, supra, 390 Mass at 326, 340, 455 NE2d at 1183, 1192, and § 8.6.7.

[74] *Com v. Wood*, 469 Mass 266, 14 NE3d 140 (2014) (jury could find that statements by one joint venturer to his girlfriend were made to frighten her from speaking to police and therefore during the venture and in furtherance of it); *Com v. Wright*, 444 Mass 576, 829 NE2d 1117 (2005) (statement that participant did not know if he had shot the victim was admissible when made as joint venturers were sharing information about what happened, "deepening their relationship" and discussing whether to dispose of their weapons); *Com. v. Raposa*, 440 Mass 684, 801 NE2d 789 (2004) (diversionary statements made after murder by joint venturer were admissible); *Com. v. Marrero*, 436 Mass 488, 766 NE2d 461 (2002) (co-joint venturers found together hours after the crime); *Com. v. Hardy*, 431 Mass 387, 727 NE2d 836 (2000) (statements were made while conspirators were attempting to dispose of murder weapon); *Com. v. Freeman*, 430 Mass 111, 712 NE2d 1135 (1999) (statement that "the cops are on the way" was admissible, having been made while defendant was trying to evade arrest); *Com. v. Winquist*, 87 Mass App 695 (2015) (statements made two years after crime was committed were admissible where evidence showed a new agreement to conceal evidence).

[75] *Com. v. Santos*, 463 Mass 273, 291, 974 NE2d 1, 16 (2012) (statement made to police after declarant was arrested was not made during pendency of joint enterprise; statements made after the crime that tended to exculpate declarant and distance him from acts of other joint venturers, shifting blame to them, were not in furtherance of the joint venture and thus inadmissible); But see *Com. v. Leach*, 73 Mass App 758, 764, 901 NE2d 708, 714 (2009) (even though defendants were in custody, statements made shortly after crime for the purpose of concealing it fell within the exception).

§ 8.6.7 *Statements by Co-Defendant in Criminal Cases (**Bruton** Problems)*

In *Bruton v. United States*,[76] the Court held that where a co-defendant does not testify, the admission of his confession implicating the defendant denies the non-confessing defendant's Sixth Amendment right of confrontation.[77] The Court held that limiting instructions are not sufficient to cure the problem and that the appropriate remedy is to sever the trials where the government is not willing to forego use of the statement. The Supreme Judicial Court has held that:

> According to *Bruton*, severance is constitutionally required where: a co-defendant's extrajudicial statements are offered in evidence at a joint trial; the statements are "clearly inadmissible" as against the defendant; the co-defendant is not subject to cross-examination because he does not testify; and, finally, there is a substantial possibility that, in determining the defendant's guilt, the jury relied on the co-defendant's "powerfully incriminating extrajudicial statements" notwithstanding any limiting instructions from the judge.[78]

If the co-defendant's statement incriminates the defendant, severance is required even though the Commonwealth argues to the jury that the statement should not be believed.[79]

For the Bruton rule to be invoked, the co-defendant's extrajudicial statement must inculpate the defendant.[80] Where the statement does not name the defendant, or explicitly identify him, the inculpatory connection may be established by the content of the statement taken together with other evidence in the case.[81] However, where the

---

[76] *Bruton v. United States*, 391 US 123, 88 S Ct 1620 (1968).

[77] *Id.*

[78] *Com. v. Pontes*, 402 Mass 311, 314, 522 NE2d 931, 933 (1988) (citing *Bruton v. United States*, supra, 391 US at 128 and n.3, 135-136).

[79] *Com. v. Hawkesworth*, 405 Mass 664, 674, 543 NE2d 691, 697 (1989) (rejecting argument that admission was harmless because full weight of Commonwealth's case was contrary to statement).

[80] *Com. v. Akara*, 465 Mass 245, 988 NE2d 430 (2013) (no *Bruton* violation of defendant's rights where witness first testified that co-defendant asked her whether "they [were] going to get away with it," but on cross after reviewing her grand jury testimony corrected her trial testimony to say that co-defendant had asked "Did I get away with it"; as such co-defendant had implicated only himself).

[81] *Com. v. Bacigalupo*, 455 Mass 485, 918 NE2d 51 (2009) (*Bruton* problem was not cured by witness who recounted co-defendant's confession testifying that co-defendant said he committed crime with a "friend" rather than using defendant's

challenged statement does not directly inculpate the defendant, an appropriate limiting instruction may be sufficient to protect the defendant's rights.[82] Other evidence should be considered to determine "if the risk of contextual implication is pressing enough to invalidate the effect of limiting instructions."[83] Where the co-defendant's statement is equivocal, *Bruton* may not apply.[84]

The prosecution may not put a non-testifying co-defendant's statement before the jury indirectly. It is improper to cross-examine a testifying defendant about statements he allegedly made to the non-testifying co-defendant, where the only basis for asking the questions is the inadmissible statement of the co-defendant.[85]

The Supreme Court has suggested that a confession so heavily edited that it eliminates any reference to the non-testifying defendant may be admissible.[86] The Court has held, however, that simply

---

name); *Com. v. Johnson*, 412 Mass 318, 588 NE2d 684 (1992) (despite lack of objection, substantial likelihood of miscarriage of justice found where jury could have concluded defendant was the person referred to in co-defendant's statement). See *Com. v. Dwyer*, 448 Mass 122, 130, 859 NE2d 400, 408 (2006) (though *Bruton* did not govern the case because trials of co-defendants had been severed, unfair to allow use of co-defendant's confession to impeach defendant's testimony that he had no knowledge that co-defendant had assaulted victim, by showing he knew co-defendant had been forced to confess).

[82] *Com. v. Rivera*, 464 Mass 56, 69, 981 NE2d 171, 183 (2013) (co-defendant's statement was redacted to remove references to defendant and would incriminate him only if jury accepted other evidence placing defendant at the crime); *Com. v. Vasquez*, 462 Mass 827, 971 NE2d 783 (2012) (co-defendant's statement made no reference to defendant and was admissible, reference to fact that "other members" favored killing the victim would not be deemed to refer directly to defendant where several people were involved); *Com. v. Vallejo*, 455 Mass 72, 914 NE2d 22 (2009) (co-defendant's statement did not implicate defendant expressly or when linked with other evidence); *Com. v. Dosouto*, 82 Mass App 474, 477, 975 NE2d 870, 872 (2012) (co-defendant implicated himself without identifying any compatriots); *Com. v. McAfee*, 430 Mass 483, 488, 722 NE2d 1, 7 (1999) (co-defendant's statement did not identify defendant as shooter, nor claim to have seen him at crime scene); *Com. v. Wilson*, 46 Mass App 292, 296, 705 NE2d 313, 316 (1999) (declarant's statement, "we stabbed him," did not explicitly identify the defendant).

[83] *Com. v. James*, 424 Mass 770, 780, 678 NE2d 1170, 1178 (1997) (noting that statement that does nothing more than raise an association between defendants is not sufficient by itself to give rise to *Bruton* challenge). See *Richardson v. Marsh*, 481 US 200 (1987).

[84] *Com. v. Santiago*, 30 Mass App 207, 215, 567 NE2d 943 (1991) (co-defendants' jailhouse remark, "We are all f - d," was equivocal, not necessarily incriminating).

[85] *Com. v. Francis*, 432 Mass 353, 363, 734 NE2d 315, 325 (2000). See *Douglas v. Alabama*, 380 US 415, 85 S Ct 1074 (1965) (error for prosecution to call co-defendant to stand and ask him about statement under the guise of cross-examination after he refused to answer any questions on direct).

[86] *Richardson v. Marsh*, 481 US 200 (1987).

replacing inculpating references to the defendant with a blank space, or the word "deleted" is insufficient to protect the defendant's rights.[87]

Decisions subsequent to *Bruton* have made it clear that if the declarant takes the stand and is available for cross-examination at trial, there is no violation of the confrontation right even if he denies making the statement or confession.[88] The opportunity to cross-examine a testifying co-defendant who by his silence may have "adopted" the statements of a non-testifying declarant is not, for *Bruton* purposes, the equivalent of cross-examining the declarant.[89]

The Confrontation Clause does not permit the use of the non-testifying co-defendant's confession incriminating the defendant, even where the defendant himself has confessed and his own statement is introduced in evidence.[90] Introduction of such a statement may, however, constitute harmless error in some circumstances. The Supreme Judicial Court applies a "stringent test" to determine if the error was harmless beyond a reasonable doubt.[91] The test is whether any "spillover" created by those portions of statements that do not perfectly interlock, "was without effect on the jury and did not contribute to the verdict."[92] In *Com. v. Adams*,[93] the Court rejected the prosecution's argument that because the confession of each co-defendant contained sufficient evidence from which the jury could infer that he intended to commit the crime, the *Bruton* error was harmless. Reversal was required where each defendant's confession had portrayed the other as the mastermind and himself as a reluctant follower.

There is no violation of the Confrontation Clause where the co-defendant's statement is independently admissible against the defendant as an admission by a fellow participant in a joint enterprise or conspiracy, or as an admission by silence by the defendant who was

---

[87] *Gray v. Maryland*, 523 US 185, 118 S Ct 1151 (1998).

[88] *Nelson v. O'Neill*, 402 US 622, 91 S Ct 1723, 29 L Ed 2d 222 (1971). Cf. *California v. Green*, 399 US 149, 90 S Ct 1930, 26 L Ed 2d 489 (1970); *Dutton v. Evans*, 400 US 74, 91 S Ct 210, 27 L Ed 2d 213 (1970). The significance of these three cases is discussed in Liacos, *The Right of Confrontation and The Hearsay Rule: Another Look*, 34 Am Trial LJ 153 (1972).

[89] *Com. v. Bongarzone*, 390 Mass 326, 344, 455 NE2d 1183, 1194 (1983).

[90] *Cruz v. New York*, 481 US 186, 193 (1987).

[91] *Com. v. Dias*, 405 Mass 131, 136, 539 NE2d 59, 63 (1989); *Com. v. Sinnott*, 399 Mass, 863, 872, 507 NE2d 699, 705 (1987); *Com. v. Twing*, 39 Mass App 75, 653 NE2d 1123 (1995) (*Bruton* violation found harmless).

[92] *Com. v. Cunningham*, 405 Mass 646, 649, 543 NE2d 12, 14 (1989); *Com. v. Libran*, 405 Mass 634, 642, 543 NE2d 5, 10 (1989).

[93] *Com. v. Adams*, 416 Mass 55, 617 NE2d 594 (1993).

present at the time the statement was made.[94] The fact that a co-defendant's statement inculpating the defendant may have been against the co-defendant's penal interest will not render it admissible in violation of the defendant's Confrontation Clause rights protected by *Bruton*.[95] Where a non-testifying co-defendant's statements are not offered to prove the truth of assertions made in the statements, the Confrontation Clause is not implicated.[96]

C. HEARSAY EXCEPTIONS FOR WHICH THE AVAILABILITY OF THE DECLARANT IS IMMATERIAL

The hearsay exceptions in this section apply whether or not the declarant is available to testify at the proceeding.

§ 8.7 Spontaneous Exclamations

Proposed Mass Rules of Evidence 803(1) and (2) provide:

> The following are not excluded by the hearsay rule, even though the declarant is available as a witness:
>
> **(1) Present sense impression.** A statement describing or explaining an event or condition made while the declarant was perceiving the event or condition, or immediately thereafter, except when such statement is made under circumstances that indicate its lack of trustworthiness.
>
> **(2) Excited utterance.** A statement relating to a startling event or condition made while the declarant was under the stress of excitement caused by the event or condition.

The Rules are identical to the federal rules, except for the qualifying language concerning trustworthiness in (1). Massachusetts has not adopted the present sense impression exception,[1] but the exception

---

[94] *Com. v. Collado*, 426 Mass 675, 690 NE2d 424 (1998); *Com. v. Brown*, 394 Mass 510, 515, 476 NE2d 580, 583 (1985).

[95] *Lilly v. Virginia*, 527 US 116, 119 S Ct 1887 (1999).

[96] *Com. v. Caillot*, 454 Mass 245, 255, 909 NE2d 1, 11 (2009).

§ 8.7 [1] For a discussion of the rationale of this exception, see *Houston Oxygen Co. v. Davis*, 139 Tex 1, 161 SW2d 474 (1942). Note that under this exception there need not be an exciting or startling event; nor need it be demonstrated that the declarant was excited. The theory of reliability under this exception is that spontaneous and routine

for excited utterances is generally consistent with Massachusetts law. There is a variation in how the rule is applied in state and federal practice, as we discuss below.

A statement made under the impulse of excitement or shock is admissible if its utterance was spontaneous to a degree that reasonably negated premeditation or possible fabrication.[2] A spontaneous

---

remarks contemporaneously describing an event to another in a position to verify the description are sufficiently trustworthy to be admitted.

[2] *Com. v. Tassinari*, 466 Mass 340, 995 NE2d 42 (2013) (statements by victim to friend while scared and crying after near violent incident with defendant); *Com. v. Irene*, 462 Mass 600, 605, 970 NE2d 291, 296 (2012) (statements of robber after taxi driver fired gun at him, to the effect of "I got hit"); *Com. v. Linton*, 456 Mass 534, 549, 924 NE2d 722, 736 (2010) ("physical attack that leaves the declarant unconscious is an external shock sufficiently startling"); *Com. v. Simon*, 456 Mass 280, 923 NE2d 58 (2010) (victim's statements to 911 dispatcher made shortly after he and his brother were shot and while agitated about their medical condition); *Com. v. Nesbitt*, 452 Mass 236, 892 NE2d 299 (2008) (statements by stabbing victim during 911 call requesting assistance and responding to dispatcher's questions about whether assailant was still present and statement at scene to neighbor that "Ralph did this to me . . . don't let me die"); *Com. v. Robinson*, 451 Mass 672, 680, 888 NE2d 926, 933 (2008) (victim followed his attackers to a dwelling, waited outside until police arrived, then as police escorted defendants from building ran toward them and stated, "That's the two guys"); *Com. v. Bianchi*, 435 Mass 316, 757 NE2d 1087 (2001) (victim's statement to police immediately after assault, while still shaking, crying, and bleeding); *Com. v. Snell*, 428 Mass 766, 777, 705 NE2d 236, 244 (1999) (domestic abuse victim's complaint to neighbor immediately after assault, while highly distraught); *Com. v. Whelton*, 428 Mass 24, 26, 696 NE2d 540, 544 (1998) (victim's daughter's statement to police shortly after assault); *Com. v. Giguere*, 420 Mass 226, 648 NE2d 1279 (1995) (telephone call from murder victim's wife to police immediately after the shooting); *Com. v. Cohen*, 412 Mass 375, 589 NE2d 289 (1992) (several exclamations of shooting victims shortly after the event); *Com v. Young*, 401 Mass 390, 517 NE2d 130 (1987) (statement shortly after a shooting by one who saw it, "That security guard killed that boy.") (Text cited); *Com. v. Fuller*, 399 Mass 678, 506 NE2d 852 (1987) (statement by child abuse victim to mother in car en route to doctor, a few moments after incident); *Com. v. Williams*, 399 Mass 60, 503 NE2d 1 (1987) (statement by stabbing victim within three minutes of event, while still in shock, admissible, although he had been able to telephone police, calm down, and stop mumbling); *Com. v. Rivera*, 397 Mass 244, 248, 490 NE2d 1160, 1163 (1986) (victim's statement to mother within minutes after rape, "Oh yes, my God, I will never forget that face."); *Com. v. Davis*, 54 Mass App 756, 767 NE2d 1110 (2002) (victim's statements immediately following sexual assault); *Com. v. Brown*, 46 Mass App 279, 705 NE2d 631 (1999) (911 calls describing home invasion and assault) (Text cited); *Com. v. Napolitano*, 42 Mass App 549, 678 NE2d 447 (1997) (admitting victim's statements to witness and EMTs who came to her aid respecting details of her boyfriend's attempt to drown her, although she later recanted them); *Com. v. Rockett*, 41 Mass App 5, 667 NE2d 1168 (1996) (unknown voice calls defendant's first name as burglar flees from stabbing occupant of premises) (Text cited); *Com. v. Alvarado*, 36 Mass App 604, 634 NE2d 132 (1994) (alleged victim's statements to police, while very emotional, that defendant had hit and bit her just before police arrived at her apartment were admissible, despite victim's later testimony denying that defendant had bitten her and claiming that she had arranged for a friend to bite her); *Com. v. Tiexeira*,

utterance is sufficient by itself to support a conviction in a criminal case.[3]

The declarant need not have been a participant in the underlying exciting event; a bystander's statements would be admissible.[4] The declarant must have personal knowledge of the subject of her statement, but the foundation for this may be contained within the statement itself.[5] The existence of the underlying exciting event may also be proved by the statement itself.[6] A variety of circumstances may qualify as sufficiently startling to trigger a spontaneous utterance.[7] The declarant is competent if her assertions are based on personal knowledge.[8]

Earlier cases sometimes justified the admissibility of such statements by labeling them part of the "res gestae" of the event. The Supreme Judicial Court has disapproved the use of this term, which is ambiguous, confusing and unnecessary, and prefers that such declarations be referred to as spontaneous exclamations or utterances.[9]

Statements need not be strictly contemporaneous with the exciting cause to be admissible, provided that the underlying event has not

---

29 Mass App 200, 205, 559 NE2d 408, 411 (1990) (statement by W to D shortly after his encounter with V, "Why did you have to hit him with the club? Why couldn't you just—if you wanted—to him, why couldn't you use your own hands?"). See *Com. v. Capone*, 39 Mass App 606, 659 NE2d 1196 (1996) (declarant's intoxication went to the weight of the evidence, but did not render it insufficiently reliable for admission). Whether statements offered as spontaneous utterances, or under other rules of evidence, may be precluded by the first complaint rule is discussed in § 6.25.2. See *Com. v. Kastner*, 76 Mass App 131, 138, n. 11, 920 NE2d 79, 85 (2010).

[3] *Com. v. Moquette*, 439 Mass 697, 791 NE2d 294 (2003) (child victim's statement that defendant struck him with a belt was sufficient for conviction, although uncorroborated and child recanted accusation at trial); *Com. v. Leavey*, 60 Mass App 249, 800 NE2d 1073 (2004) (spontaneous utterance of victim was sufficient for conviction, even though she recanted her accusation at trial).

[4] *Com. v. Harbin*, 435 Mass 654, 657, 760 NE2d 1216, 1220 (2002) (eyewitness to murder).

[5] *Com. v. Correa*, 437 Mass 197, 770 NE2d 435 (2002) (admitting statement by unidentified girl in crowd after a beating, "Why did Sammy have to do that?"—plausible inference that declarant saw the incident is a sufficient foundation); *Com. v. Harbin*, supra (Text cited).

[6] *Com. v. King*, 436 Mass 252, 255, 763 NE2d 1071, 1075 (2002).

[7] In addition to the foregoing cases, see *Com. v. Whitney*, 63 Mass App 351, 826 NE2d 219 (2005) (11:00 p.m. call to victim's sleeping wife that victim, who was known for punctuality, had not arrived at work, could be found to be a startling event that triggered her spontaneous statement that he had left home at 9:30).

[8] *Com. v. Figueroa*, 79 Mass App 389, 396, 946 NE2d 142, 149 (2011) (trial court did not err in refusing defense request for competency examination of elderly victim of alleged sexual assault).

[9] *Com. v. Sellon*, 380 Mass at 229 n.14, 402 NE2d at 1337 n.14; *Com. v. McLaughlin*, 364 Mass 221, n.3, 303 NE2d 338, 346 n.3 (1973).

lost its sway and been dissipated.[10] A statement may be considered spontaneous and admissible, although made in response to questions.[11]

Where the circumstances do not demonstrate that a statement was spontaneous and made without an opportunity for reflection that would undermine its reliability, it may be excluded.[12] The fact that the

---

[10] *Com. v. Linton*, 456 Mass 534, 549, 924 NE2d 722, 736 (2010) (domestic assault victim's statement to her father twenty minutes later, when she was still hysterical); *Com. v. Ruiz*, 442 Mass 826, 817 NE2d 771 (2004) (statement made ten minutes later); *Com. v. Marshall*, 434 Mass 358, 364, 749 NE2d 147, 154 (2001) (despite passage of two hours, victim was still "very upset," "crying and nervous" and "in fear"); *Com. v. Tevlin*, 433 Mass 305, 318, 741 NE2d 827, 838 (2001) (statement made by elderly woman one-half hour after assault that caused crushed aorta and loss of sensation in legs was made while she was still in pain and emotional distress); *Com. v. Grant*, 418 Mass 76, 634 NE2d 565 (1994) (statements of shooting victim where due to circumstances of shooting and provision of medical treatment she had been close to hysterical from the time of the shooting to her interview by police 60 minutes later); *Com. v. Crawford*, 417 Mass 358, 629 NE2d 1332 (1994) (child's statement within hours of murder that "Daddy shot Mummy," court takes into account fact that child had remained in the presence of alleged perpetrator until shortly before she made the statement); *Com. v. Brown*, 413 Mass 693, 602 NE2d 575 (1992) (statements made five hours after scalding episode by child victim); *Com. v. Fuller*, supra, 399 Mass at 682, 506 NE2d at 855; *Com v. Puleio*, 394 Mass 101, 104-105, 474 NE2d 1078, 1081 (1985) (following a shot and a scream, someone ran into bar, asked bartender to telephone police, she did so and then went outside and asked who shot—at first there was no answer, then someone named the defendant); *Com. v. Hampton*, 351 Mass 447, 221 NE2d 766 (1966) (statement made five to six minutes after stabbing); *Com. v. Ivy*, 55 Mass App 851, 774 NE2d 1100 (2002) (time lapse from when alleged assault victim escaped from apartment until she made statement at hospital of four and one-half hours); *Com. v. Carter*, 54 Mass App 629, 630, 767 NE2d 100, 101 (2002) (admission of statement was within "wide discretion" of trial judge, despite fact that declarant "appeared controlled and guarded, and that there was no testimony that she was visibly upset, distraught, hysterically sobbing, or in shock"); *Com. v. Tracy*, 50 Mass App 435, 737 NE2d 930 (2000) (mother's statement to police that her son might return to crime scene and injure someone was made under spell of her learning that he had a gun and might return to the scene after he was released to her custody from police station; statement was made within 48 minutes of his release).

[11] *Com. v. Ruiz*, 442 Mass 826, 817 NE2d 771 (2004); *Com. v. Kenney*, 437 Mass 141, 151, 769 NE2d 1231, 1240 (2002).

[12] See *Com. v. McCoy*, 456 Mass 838, 926 NE2d 1143 (2010) (alleged rape victim's statements to SANE nurse two hours after alleged assault, where, although nurse described declarant as upset, distraught, tearful, and labile, statement was developed in question and answer format, declarant had previously given statement to police, and declarant did not display "a degree of excitement sufficient to conclude that her statement was a spontaneous reaction to the exciting event rather than the product of reflective thought"); *Com. v. Negron*, 441 Mass 685, 808 NE2d 294 (2004) (officer testified that alleged victim of domestic violence "did not appear upset" but was just "very concerned for her safety"); *Com. v. Evans*, 438 Mass 142, 154, 778 NE2d 885, 896 (2002) (victim's negative identification of defendant was the product of deliberation, based on reluctance to get involved); *Com. v. McLaughlin*, 433 Mass 558, 565, 744

declarant had a motive to lie, however, goes only to the weight to be accorded his statements, not to their admissibility.[13]

In *Com. v. Santiago*,[14] the Supreme Judicial Court abrogated the previous requirement that a spontaneous utterance must tend to qualify, characterize, or explain the underlying event to be admissible. The Court instead indicated that the nexus between the statement and the event that produced it is a factor to be taken into account in determining whether the declarant was still under the sway of the event at

---

NE2d 47, 53 (2001) (although statement was made shortly after altercation with victim, defendant had sufficient time, as well as strong motive, to fabricate story); *Com. v. DiMonte*, 427 Mass 233, 692 NE2d 45 (1998) (facsimile describing alleged assault sent several hours later, some contents of which suggested a premeditated message); *Com. v. Gilbert*, 423 Mass 863, 673 NE2d 46 (1996) (defendant's statement the day after his wife's death that she had killed herself was lacking the spontaneity that would have negated possible fabrication); *Com. v. Trowbridge*, 419 Mass 750, 647 NE2d 413 (1995) (child's statements to teacher on Friday afternoons that she did not want to visit her father where there was no evidence that the child was under the influence of any startling or exciting event); *Com. v. Burnett*, 417 Mass 740, 632 NE2d 1206 (1994) (statements by second driver in motor vehicle homicide made 90 minutes after accident where there was no testimony that declarant was excited or upset); *Com. v. Reid*, 384 Mass 247, 258-259, 424 NE2d 495, 502 (1981) (statement made after declarant made two telephone calls and after considerable time lag); *Com. v. Gonzalez*, 68 Mass App 620, 863 NE2d 958 (2007) (witness's statement to officer that if he repeated what witness told him he would deny it demonstrated that statement was a product of reflection); *Com. v. Dunn*, 56 Mass App 89, 775 NE2d 745 (2002) (where declarant made statement as part of a preconceived plan it could not qualify as a spontaneous utterance); *Com. v. Newell*, 55 Mass App 119, 769 NE2d 767 (2002) (declarant intentionally left something out of his story); *Com. v. Pierowski*, 54 Mass App 707, 711, 767 NE2d 625, 628 (2002) (statement of alleged victim "elicited by persistent questioning of the police officer, after [she] had unambiguously attempted to avoid the attention given to her"); *Com. v. Santiago*, 52 Mass App 667, 755 NE2d 795 (2001) (where exciting event was arrest of her boyfriend, and declarant had reason to expect the arrest, she had ample time, opportunity and motive to contrive a story); *Com. v. Hardy*, 47 Mass App 679, 716 NE2d 109 (1999) (statement by robbery and assault victim, although he was sobbing and in physical pain, was not made while he was still under influence of exciting event); *Com. v. Joubert*, 38 Mass App 943, 647 NE2d 1238 (1995) (child's statements to aunt that father had touched her sexually where there was nothing in record to show circumstances of the touching or when it occurred); *Com. v. Bandy*, 38 Mass App 329, 648 NE2d 440 (1995) (defendant's exculpatory statements to nurses a month after accident and shortly after he was served with a citation). Compare *Com. v. Santos*, 402 Mass 775, 785, 525 NE2d 388, 394 (1988) (suggestive police station identification was not a spontaneous utterance) with *Com. v. Mendrala*, 20 Mass App 398, 480 NE2d 1039 (1985) (*V*'s identification of attacker shortly after event, at end of police chase, admissible as spontaneous exclamation, although not under exception for identifications, because did not meet requirements of *Com. v. Daye*, 393 Mass 55, 469 NE2d 483 (1984)).

[13] *Com. v. Joyner*, 55 Mass App 412, 771 NE2d 193 (2002).

[14] *Com. v. Santiago*, 437 Mass 620, 625, 774 NE2d 143, 147 (2002).

the time of the statement.[15] The federal practice requires that the statement must tend to qualify, characterize, or explain the underlying event to be admissible.

Whether admission of a spontaneous utterance when the declarant is not available to be cross-examined would violate the Confrontation Clause will depend upon the circumstances.[16] In *Com. v. Gonsalves*,[17] the Supreme Judicial Court held that spontaneous utterances made to an investigating police officer in response to questions by the officer could be testimonial and thus offend the Confrontation Clause under *Crawford v. Washington*, supra. The Court explained in *Gonsalves* that the determination of whether statements are testimonial for the purpose of Confrontation Clause analysis is separate and distinct from the question of whether they meet the requirements of the hearsay exception for spontaneous utterances. Massachusetts law, with respect to the admissibility of spontaneous utterances remains unchanged, but, to be admissible, such statements must also satisfy the constitutional requirements of the Confrontation Clause.[18]

The case of *Com. v. Harris*,[19] illustrates a problem analytically distinct from, but easily confused with, this hearsay exception. The statement of an unidentified bystander ("Shoot that m . . . f . . . !"), made immediately before a shooting, was admitted. The statement is not hearsay, because no assertion was made. The statement is admissible because statements and other circumstances attending the commission of a crime was committed are admissible to give the jury the benefit of the complete occurrence.[20]

---

[15] 437 Mass at 626, 774 NE2d at 148. See *Com. v. Figueroa*, 79 Mass App 389, 395, 946 NE2d 142, 149 (2011) (court considers fact that victim's statement both characterized and explained sexual assault in determining that victim was still under influence of startling event and statement was not product of reflective thought).

[16] Older cases holding that there was no Confrontation Clause violation under the analysis of *Ohio v. Roberts*, supra, do not answer the question of whether such evidence would be admissible under *Crawford v. Washington*, supra. For the earlier case law, see *White v. Illinois*, 502 US 346, 112 S Ct 736 (1992) and *Com. v. Whelton*, 428 Mass 24, 27, 696 NE2d 540, 545 (1998).

[17] *Com. v. Gonsalves*, 445 Mass 1, 833 NE2d 549 (2005).

[18] *Com. v. Smith*, 460 Mass 385, 951 NE2d 674 (2011) (woman's exclamation upon running from apartment, "He has a gun. He's wrapping it in a black sock," qualified as spontaneous utterance and nontestimonial because made during course of ongoing emergency). For additional cases, see § 8.4.2.

[19] *Com. v. Harris*, 376 Mass 201, 380 NE2d 642 (1978).

[20] See *Com. v. Murphy*, 356 Mass 604, 254 NE2d 895 (1970); *Com. v. Ward*, 45 Mass App 901, 694 NE2d 395 (1998) (statement by participant in drug transaction that he was selling drugs; also admissible as statement by joint venturer) (Text cited).

§ 8.8 Then Existing Mental, Emotional, or Physical Condition

Proposed Mass R Evid 803(3) creates a hearsay exception for:

> (3) **Then existing mental, emotional, or physical condition.** A statement of the declarant's then existing state of mind, emotion, sensation, or physical condition (such as intent, plan, motive, design, mental feeling, pain, and bodily health), but not including a statement of memory or belief to prove the fact remembered or believed unless it relates to the execution, revocation, identification, or terms of declarant's will.

The federal rule is identical. The Rule comports with current Massachusetts law.

Expressions of present pain, whether articulate or inarticulate and whether or not made to a physician, are admissible in Massachusetts.[1]

Statements of a person as to his present friendliness, hostility, intent, knowledge, or other mental condition are admissible to prove such mental condition.[2]

State of mind evidence is frequently offered to prove that the declarant did a certain act. To prove that the declarant did the act it is circumstantially relevant to show that at a time before or after the alleged act, not unreasonably remote from the act, the declarant declared a state of mind from which the act can be inferred.[3]

---

§ 8.8 [1] *Com. v. Irene*, 462 Mass 600, 607, 970 NE2d 291, 298 (2012) (statements of robber after taxi driver fired gun at him, to the effect of "I got hit" were admissible as expressions of present pain). Cf. *Simmons v. Yurchak*, 28 Mass App 371, 374, 551 NE2d 539, 542 (1990) (trial court may exclude such evidence where the evidence is untrustworthy and the danger of prejudice outweighs its probative value).

[2] *Com. v. Keo*, 467 Mass 25, 3 NE3d 55 (2014) (statement "crip killer" on bedroom wall of another was admissible as evidence of declarant's state of mind, but attributing import of those words to defendant would be "problematic"; no prejudice where defendant blamed the other for the murder with which defendant was charged); *Com. v. Horton*, 434 Mass 823, 828, 753 NE2d 119, 125 (2001) (statement that declarant wanted another to extend credit for drugs and needed money was indicative of his state of mind and relevant to his intent to rob); *Com. v. Borodine*, 371 Mass 1, 353 NE2d 649 (1976).

[3] *Com. v. Britt*, 465 Mass 87, 987 NE2d 558 (2013) (statement of victim that he intended to "meet" defendant was admissible under state of mind exception as proof of victim's intent; word "meet" did not necessarily improperly imply that defendant intended to meet victim, but might have meant victim intended to see or find defendant); *Com. v. Ortiz*, 463 Mass 402, 409, 974 NE2d 1079, 1085 (2012) (victim's daughter's testimony that victim told her that she was going to a restaurant to pick up the

Hearsay declarations may be admissible to prove the state of mind of a victim of a crime where that state of mind was known to the defendant and was relevant to an issue in the case. See § 8.2.2.

State of mind that merely amounts to a memory or belief as to past facts is excluded from this exception.[4]

§ 8.9 Statements for Purposes of Medical Diagnosis or Treatment

Proposed Mass R Evid 803(4) creates a hearsay exception for:

> **(4) Statements for Purposes of Medical Diagnosis or Treatment** Statements made for purposes of medical diagnosis or treatment and describing medical history, or past or present symptoms, pain, or sensations, or the inception or general character of the cause or external source thereof insofar as reasonably pertinent to diagnosis or treatment.

Fed R Evid 803(4) is identical. The Rule differs from Massachusetts law in that the declaration need not have been made to a physician nor

---

defendant was admissible as victim's present intent; court rejects argument that statement conveyed multiple hearsay that defendant told victim he would meet her at restaurant); *Com. v. Avila*, 454 Mass 744, 766, 912 NE2d 1014, 1032 (2009) (defendant's telephone call to victim's landlady the night before the murder suggesting she did not let victim into her house because a very dangerous person was looking to kill him could be understood as indicative of defendant's intent or plan to kill victim; any ambiguity in statement went to its weight); *Com. v. Fernandes*, 427 Mass 90, 692 NE2d 3 (1998) (threat to kill another); *Com. v. Caldron*, 383 Mass 86, 417 NE2d 958 (1981) (error to exclude defendant's statements in argument with co-defendant immediately after robbery, to the extent they revealed defendant's lack of intention to rob another); *Com. v. Trefethen*, 157 Mass 180, 31 NE 961 (1892) (intention to commit suicide); *Com. v. Vermette*, 43 Mass App 789, 801, 686 NE2d 1071, 1079 (1997) (intention to lie and falsely confess to a shooting). See *Mutual Life Insurance Co. v. Hillmon*, 145 US 285 (1892) (letters stating that declarant intended to travel to a certain destination with another).

[4] See, e.g., *Com. v. Whitman*, 453 Mass 331, 342, 901 NE2d 1206, 1216 (2009) (witnesses' testimony that defendant told them he was hearing voices was within state of mind exception, but testimony that defendant said he had heard voices in the past was inadmissible). *Com. v. Bianchi*, 435 Mass 316, 327, 757 NE2d 1087, 1095 (2001) ("suicide note purporting to explain past conduct is not admissible under state of mind exception"); *Com. v. Pope*, 397 Mass 275, 281, 491 NE2d 240, 244 (1986) (suicide note, "I killed Jimmy," inadmissible because went to past conduct, not intent to act); *Com. v. Lowe*, 391 Mass 97, 104-106, 461 NE2d 192, 197-198 (1984) (discussion of distinction between statements of memory and belief, which are inadmissible, and statements of present state of mind, which are admissible); *Custody of Jennifer*, 25 Mass App 241, 517 NE2d 187 (1988) (hearsay statements of alleged child abuse victims not admissible on "state of mind" theory—constituted statements of memory or belief to prove fact remembered).

have been made primarily for the purpose of obtaining treatment. The federal rule would allow admission of statements made solely for the purpose of enabling a physician to testify. The Rule also implies the possible admission of statements as to how the injuries were suffered. Last, the rule suggests that statements made by one other than the patient may also qualify as an exception to the hearsay rule.

Under current Massachusetts law, a physician may testify as to statements of past pain, symptoms, and condition made to him when he was consulted by the declarant for purposes of diagnosis and treatment.[1] If the primary purpose of such statements was to obtain medical treatment, they are admissible even if made after the commencement of the litigation.[2] Testimony as to such statements may also be admissible to show the basis of the doctor's expert testimony.[3] Narration of circumstances—e.g. a patient's story of how injuries were suffered—is not admissible, even if made to a physician.[4]

The Supreme Judicial Court suggested in dictum in *Bouchie v. Murray*,[5] that statements as to medical history based on personal knowledge of the declarant may be admissible as an exception to the hearsay rule even if the declarant is not the patient. In *Bouchie*, however, it was made clear that such statements would qualify only if made to a physician consulted for treatment and only if the statements were pertinent to diagnosis and treatment. Additionally, the Court suggested that in such instances it must be shown that the circumstances in which the statements were made would "guarantee" the trustworthiness of the statements. Rule 803(4) would go beyond the expanded limits of the common-law exception suggested by the *Bouchie* dictum.

In *White v. Illinois*,[6] the Court held that the admission of declarations made during medical examinations under the hearsay exception did not violate the Confrontation Clause, despite the failure of the prosecution to produce the declarant at trial or to demonstrate unavailability of the witness.[7] This conclusion is no longer binding under

---

§ 8.9 [1] *Com. v. Comtois*, 399 Mass 668, 675, 506 NE2d 503, 508 (1987) (Text cited).

[2] *Barber v. Mirriam*, 93 Mass (11 All) 322 (1865).

[3] *Uberto v. Kaufman*, 348 Mass 171, 202 NE2d 822 (1964); *Kramer v. John Hancock Mutual Life Insurance Co.*, 336 Mass 465, 146 NE2d 357 (1957).

[4] *Com. v. Arana*, 453 Mass 214, 231, 901 NE2d 99, 112 (2009).

[5] 376 Mass 524, 381 NE2d 1295 (1978).

[6] *White v. Illinois*, 502 US 346, 112 S Ct 736 (1992).

[7] See § 8.4.2 for a fuller discussion of the Confrontation Clause.

Crawford v. Washington,[8] and the Confrontation Clause analysis will depend upon the circumstances of individual cases or classes of cases. To the extent that statements made during medical examinations may be deemed testimonial, cross-examination would be required as a prerequisite to admissibility.

In *Com. v. DeOliveira*,[9] the Court held that statements made by a six-year-old girl to an emergency room pediatrician disclosing that she had been anally raped were made for the purpose of medical evaluation and treatment, not the investigation of crime, and were not testimonial. The doctor had spoken with the police before conducting the examination, knew there was an allegation that she had been sexually abused, and was aware of the possibility that he might be summonsed to testify about his findings in a criminal case. The Court first found that the examination by the doctor was not police interrogation and thus the statements were not testimonial per se. It then examined the particular circumstances of the examination and the statements by the child. The Court concluded that the child had understood the doctor's question (what happened that brought you to the hospital) to be a medical one and that a reasonable person in her position and with her knowledge would not have anticipated that the answer would be used in a criminal prosecution.[10]

§ 8.10 Past Recollection Recorded

Proposed Mass R Evid 803(5) creates a hearsay exception for:

> (5) **Recorded recollection**. A memorandum or record concerning a matter about which a witness once had knowledge but now has insufficient recollection to enable him to testify fully and accurately, shown to have been made or adopted by the witness when the matter was fresh in his memory and to reflect that knowledge correctly. If admitted, the

---

[8] *Crawford v. Washington*, 124 S Ct 1354 (2004).

[9] *Com. v. DeOliveira*, 447 Mass 56, 849 NE2d 218 (2006).

[10] The Court noted that it was not declaring that the lack of comprehension of criminal prosecution by young children renders any statement by a young child non-testimonial. The Court expressed hesitation that the United States Supreme Court would accept a rule of "such encompassing latitude." 447 Mass at 64. The Court also explicitly left open the larger questions of whether, and in what circumstances, statements by children to medical professionals might be considered testimonial when they concerned matters other than sexual abuse, and when statements by adults to medical professionals might be considered testimonial. 447 Mass at 67.

memorandum or record may be read into evidence but may not itself be received as an exhibit unless offered by an adverse party.

Fed R Evid 803(5) is identical. The Rule is in accord with current Massachusetts practice, except that under the Rule only the opposing party may offer the document itself in evidence.

A witness often has difficulty in recalling the events about which he is asked to testify. In such instances, either of two doctrines may be utilized to procure his knowledge for the jury's consideration: "present recollection revived" and "past recollection recorded."

Under the doctrine of present recollection revived, the witness has some memory of the events he observed but is unable to testify without the assistance of some stimulus to that memory. The stimulating factor may be a writing or any object that revives his memory. See § 6.26 for a detailed discussion of this doctrine. Reviving the present memory of a witness does not implicate the hearsay rule.

The doctrine of past recollection recorded permits the reading into evidence of a record or memorandum a witness made when he had a memory of the event in question. The proponent must show that the witness had personal knowledge of the facts, has insufficient recollection to testify fully and accurately, made or adopted a writing or memorandum when the events were fresh in his mind, and the memorandum accurately described the events. The proponent may not introduce the writing itself in evidence, but may read it to the finder of fact. It is within the judge's discretion to permit the proposing party to introduce the writing itself in evidence.[1]

It is not necessary that the memorandum be made in the regular course of business.[2] A prior recorded recollection may be introduced if a witness is not able to testify fully regarding the subject matter. A

---

§ 8.10 [1] *Com. v. Nolan*, 427 Mass 541, 694 NE2d 350 (1998) (witness remembered some details of her statement, but not others); *Com. v. Dougherty*, 343 Mass 299, 306, 178 NE2d 584, 588 (1961) (witness read document to jury); *Fisher v. Swartz*, 333 Mass 265, 130 NE2d 575 (1955) (overruling *Bendett v. Bendett*, 315 Mass 59, 52 NE2d 2 (1943) on the matter of admitting the writing in evidence); *Com. v. Galvin*, 27 Mass App 150, 152, 535 NE2d 623, 625 (1989) (Text cited). Cf. *Com. v. McDuffie*, 16 Mass App 1016, 455 NE2d 461 (1983) (error to allow report in evidence as past recollection recorded where transcript showed witnesses used report to refresh recollection); *Com. v. Murphy*, 6 Mass App 335, 343, 375 NE2d 366, 372 (1978) (where memo refreshed witness's recollection, no error in refusal of judge to allow it to be read in evidence).

[2] *Guiffre v. Carapezza*, 298 Mass 458, 11 NE2d 433 (1937).

complete failure of recollection is not required.[3] Inability to remember a single, inconsequential detail, or part of a report, however, does not mandate admission of the entirety of a witness's prior statement.[4] The traditional requirement that the memorandum be made at or about the time of the event recorded has been somewhat relaxed by the case law.[5]

It is not necessary that the witness be the author of the memorandum as long as he saw and approved it when his memory of events was fresh. However, a document that the witness has never seen or approved is not admissible.[6] Although the witness must assert that the record was accurate when made, it is not required that the witness

---

[3] *Guiffre v. Carapezza*, supra (where witness had made list of 49 household goods taken by defendant, it was not necessary for her to attempt to remember all the items before permitting counsel to read the list).

[4] *Com. v. Munoz*, 461 Mass 126, 958 NE2d 1167 (2011) (large portions of police reports were improperly read into evidence where witness testified only that he had forgotten details of certain conversations and did not assert he lacked a revivable recollection of other aspects of case discussed in reports); *Com. v. Seng*, 456 Mass 490, 924 NE2d 285 (2010) (opposing party could not introduce previous statement where witness testified that her recollection was not faulty).

[5] *Catania v. Emerson Cleaners, Inc.*, 362 Mass 388, 286 NE2d 341 (1972) (where trial took place four years after accident in question, signed statement of witness given eight months after accident and remembered as better and true recollection was admissible not only to impeach but as past recollection recorded); *Ralston v. Anthony*, 5 Mass App 859, 364 NE2d 1289 (1977) (memorandum drafted by an attorney for a party some time after negotiations completed admissible as past recollection recorded). Compare *Com. v. Evans*, 438 Mass 142, 157, 778 NE2d 885, 898 (2002) (memorandum made four to six weeks after conversation was not shown to be made while events were still fresh in maker's memory) and *Kirby v. Morales*, 50 Mass App 786, 741 NE2d 855 (2001) (deposition testimony given a year after the events at issue was not made at time when events were fresh in witness's memory), with *Com. v. Rodriguez*, 50 Mass App 405, 737 NE2d 910 (2000) (permissible to introduce at second trial as prior recollection recorded victim's testimony from first trial regarding fabric of attacker's jacket).

[6] *Com. v. Evans*, 439 Mass 184, 190, 786 NE2d 375, 383 (2003) (grand jury minutes were not adopted by witness) (Text cited); *Com. v. Bookman*, 386 Mass 657, 662-665, 436 NE2d 1228, 1231-1233 (1982) (transcript of grand jury testimony of witness improperly admitted as past recollection recorded absent evidence or a finding that witness adopted transcript as accurate at or about the time of the event). See *Com. v. Fryar*, 414 Mass 732, 745, 610 NE2d 903, 911 (1993) (where witness was not shown her grand jury testimony for one year, she did not adopt it as accurate at or about the time of events and it was inadmissible); *Com. v. Campbell*, 60 Mass App 215, 222, 800 NE2d 1055, 1061 (2003) (witness's signature on car rental form was not a sufficient foundation that he once had knowledge of the license number and that it was accurately recorded by him or another).

adopt the statement as true or accurate at the time of trial—indeed, for the rule to come into play he would not be able to do so because of a failure of recollection.[7]

The original memorandum must be produced or its absence accounted for.[8] A witness must, at the time he wrote or saw and approved the memorandum, have had personal knowledge of the events recorded; if he did not, he may not testify.[9] However, if A has reported events to B, who has recorded them, the record made by B may be used if A will testify that he reported correctly and if B will testify that he recorded correctly. Allowing admission of such memoranda merely represents a double application of the principle of past recollection recorded.[10]

§ 8.11 Regular Business Entries

Proposed Mass Rules 803(6) and (7) create hearsay exceptions for:

> **(6) Records of Regularly Conducted Activity.** A memorandum, report, record, or data compilation, in any form, of acts, events, conditions, opinions, or diagnoses, made at or near the time by, or from information transmitted by, a person with knowledge, if kept in the course of a regularly conducted business activity, and if it was the regular practice of that business activity to make the memorandum, report, record, or data compilation, all as shown by the testimony of the custodian or other qualified witness, unless the source of information or the method of circumstances of preparation indicate lack of trustworthiness. The term "business" as used in this paragraph includes business, institution, association, profession, occupation, and calling of every kind, whether or not conducted for profit.
>
> **(7) Absence of Entry in Records Kept in Accordance with the Provisions of Paragraph (6).** Evidence that a matter is not included in the memoranda, reports, records, or data compilations, in any form, kept in accordance with the provisions of paragraph (6), to prove the nonoccurrence or nonexistence of the matter, if the matter was of a kind of which

---

[7] *Com. v. Morgan*, 449 Mass 343, 868 NE2d 99 (2007) (where alibi witness testified he told police he was unsure of the date when he was with defendant at time he made prior statement, it did not qualify as past recollection recorded).

[8] *Whitney v. Sawyer*, 77 Mass (11 Gray) 242 (1858).

[9] *Kent v. Garvin*, 67 Mass (1 Gray) 148 (1854).

[10] *Com. v. Galvin*, supra (Text cited).

a memorandum, report, record, or data compilation was regularly made and preserved, unless the sources of information or other circumstances indicate lack of trustworthiness.

The corresponding federal rules are identical. Rule 803(6) differs from Massachusetts practice in several respects. First, it would allow the admission of opinions contained in business records rather than only medical opinions (diagnoses), as is provided by GL 233, §§ 78 and 79. Second, hospital records other than those described under GL 111, § 70, would come within the rule. Third, questions of admissibility as to both business and medical records would be decided conclusively by the trial judge pursuant to Proposed Mass R Evid 104 (Fed R Evid 104 is the same for these purposes). Proposed Mass R Evid 104 does not provide for the continuation of the practice whereby the jury may reconsider the admissibility of business records, as is now provided by § 78 (a similar requirement is not found in § 79 as to hospital records). Fourth, the rule does not explicitly require, as does § 78, that the record be "made in good faith;" nor does it require that the record be made "before the beginning of the civil or criminal proceeding." (§ 79 does not have these limitations of § 78.). Fifth, the provisions of §§ 78 and 79 as to the admissibility of certified copies are lacking; but see Proposed Mass R Evid 1003 and Fed R Evid 1003 (duplicates admissible to same extent as original). Sixth, the explicit language of § 79 (not found in § 78) precluding the admissibility of any evidence "which has reference to the question of liability" is not found in the rule. Rule 803(7) is consistent with Massachusetts practice.[1]

The admission in evidence of business entries is principally controlled at present by two Massachusetts statutes and two common-law rules. Proposed Mass R Evid 803(6) would combine the two statutory exceptions into one and modify them. The statutory rules were designed to liberalize the rather strict common-law rules pertaining to the admissibility of business entries. The common-law rules are still extant but are of only occasional utility. These exceptions to the hearsay rule overlap one another. If evidence can be brought within any one of them, it is admissible.

---

§ 8.11 [1] *McNamara v. Honeyman*, 406 Mass 43, 54, n.10, 546 NE2d 139, 146 (1989); Mass Guide to Evidence, § 803(7).

§ 8.11.1 *Statutory Exceptions: MGL 233, § 78*

Section 78 of GL 233 provides for the admissibility of ordinary business records. Four preliminary findings by the judge have to be made to admit such records: (1) the entry was made in good faith; (2) in the regular course of business; (3) before the action was begun; and (4) it was the usual course of business to make the entry at the time of the event recorded or within a reasonable time thereafter. The admission of the records in civil cases imports the necessary preliminary findings by the judge.[2]

In 1982, the legislature adopted GL 233, § 79J, which provides a method for the use of certified copies of business records. While the statute does not vary the prerequisites of admissibility of a business record set forth in GL 233 § 78 (from the point of view of the hearsay rule), it does provide for a method of authentication and use of copies of such records comparable to that provided for hospital records in the second paragraph of GL 233, § 79 (see § 8.11.2).

Under § 78, the unavailability of the declarant is not required for the record to be admissible. The section applies to criminal as well as civil cases. The section removes the objection not only to the hearsay rule but also to the best evidence rule to some extent.

The prerequisites of admissibility, and the nature of material in a purported business record that may qualify within the statutory exception, are discussed in both the main and the concurring opinion (joined in by the Court) in *Wingate v. Emery Air Freight Corp.*[3] The fact that a business record itself is admissible does not mean that every statement in a record is admissible. Where records contain multiple hearsay, each level of hearsay must satisfy an exception to the hearsay

---

[2] *Sawyer & Co. v. Southern Pacific Co.*, 354 Mass 481, 238 NE2d 357 (1968). But cf. *Fisher v. Swartz*, 333 Mass 265, 266, 130 NE2d 575, 577 (1955) (no such finding can be implied where record revealed no attempt to bring record within the statute). See *Friedman v. Kurker*, 14 Mass App 152, 157-158, 438 NE2d 76, 79 (1982) (where parties stipulated to admissibility of business records, fact there was evidence of some inaccuracies in same did not bar their use for all purposes) (Text cited). Of course, redacting business records for use at trial does not undermine the fact that they were originally prepared in the ordinary course of business. *Bank v. Thermo Elemental Inc.*, 451 Mass 638, 661, n.28, 888 NE2d 897, 916 (2008).

[3] *Wingate v. Emery Air Freight Corp.*, 385 Mass 402, 408, 432 NE2d 474, 479 (1982). See *Salvas v. Wal-Mart Stores, Inc.*, 452 Mass 337, 358, 893 NE2d 1187, 1205-1206 (2008) ("Business records have a special place in our law of evidence . . . Courts attach [a] presumption of reliability to business records because businesses themselves rely on their accuracy.").

rule to be admissible.[4] Whether the person who made entries on a business record had personal knowledge of the facts is a matter affecting the weight rather than the admissibility of the record.[5] However, "unless statements on which the preparer relies fall within some other exception to the hearsay rule, the proponent must show that all the persons in the chain of communication, from the observer to the preparer, reported the information as a matter of business duty or business routine."[6] In the case of records of loans that have been assigned from one financial institution to another, it is not necessary to provide testimony from a witness with personal knowledge regarding the maintenance of the predecessor institution's business records. In *Beal*

---

[4] See *Wingate v. Emery Air Freight Corp.*, supra; *Kelly v. O'Neil*, 1 Mass App 313, 296 NE2d 223 (1973); § 8.1.

[5] *McLaughlin v. CGU Ins. Co.*, 445 Mass 815, 819, 840 NE2d 935 (2006).

[6] *Wingate v. Emery Air Freight Corp.*, 385 Mass 402, 406, 432 NE2d 474, 478 (1982); *Tosti v. Ayik*, 394 Mass 482, 476 NE2d 928 (1985) (proper to exclude personnel memo regarding investigation into plaintiff's conduct where no showing it was made in the regular course of business); *Irwin v. Ware*, 392 Mass 745, 748-751, 467 NE2d 1292, 1296 (1984) (letter reporting blood test results not shown to be a business record made in the regular course of business); *Burke v. Memorial Hospital*, 29 Mass App 948, 558 NE2d 1146 (1990) (memorandum in personnel file not a business record because not placed in file as part of the regular practice of employer); *Alcan Aluminum v. Carlton Aluminum*, 35 Mass App 161, 617 NE2d 1005 (1993) (exhibit listing expenses of plaintiff, based on plaintiff's records, was inadmissible where records themselves were not introduced and it was undisputed that exhibit did not constitute a business record). Compare *Com. v. LaPlante*, 416 Mass 433, 441, 622 NE2d 1357, 1362 (1993) (foundation for invoice must be laid by witness from company issuing invoice, rather than keeper of records at company where order was picked up) with *Quinn Brothers, Inc. v. Wecker*, 414 Mass 815, 611 NE2d 234 (1993) (invoices from vendors offered as evidence of costs constituted business records of the customer where they were maintained as part of the customer's business records with checks written against them). But see *Com. v. Amaral*, 78 Mass App 671, 674, 941 NE2d 1143, 1146 (2011) (rejecting hearsay objection to admissibility of account information identifying defendant as associated with given login name from Yahoo as a business record, where defendant argued that Yahoo simply entered whatever information the user supplied; court concludes that business record is admissible even though preparer relied upon statements of others, because personal knowledge of entrant affects only weight of record, not admissibility). This opinion is based on citations to the Note to Mass G Evid § 803(6)(A) and *Wingate v. Emery Air Freight Corp.*, supra. In fact *Amaral* appears to be at odds with these sources. Although *Wingate* notes that the business record statute provides that the personal knowledge of the preparer affects the weight of the evidence, the court went on to say, "It does not follow, however, that the preparer may rely on statements that are not themselves a part of the regular course of business recordkeeping. The preparer's hearsay sources must carry the same indicia of reliability, arising from regularity and business motives, that bring his own act of recording the information within the statutory exception." 385 Mass at 406, 432 NE2d at 478. The Notes to the Mass Guide make the same point. In *Amaral*, the person who opened an account with Yahoo was under no business duty to report accurately his or her name.

Bank, SSB v. Eurich,[7] the Supreme Judicial Court held that the reliance by the successor institution on the predecessor's records is deemed to render the records the equivalent of the successor's own records. The foundation for the admissibility of a business record does not have to be established through one who prepared the record.

In *Com. v. Trapp*,[8] the Court explicitly held that "the extra assurance of unbiased assertions guaranteed by the requirement that a record must have been made before a proceeding began is a necessary component of the Massachusetts business records exception." The Court refused to adopt Proposed Mass R Evid 803(6) to the extent that it eliminates this requirement.[9]

In criminal cases, the judge, after finding the four preliminary facts and admitting the evidence, must instruct the jury that it should disregard the evidence if it fails to find any one of the preliminary facts. Failure to resubmit the question to the jury will not be reversible error, however, in the absence of an objection or request by the defendant.[10] In the absence of evidence to the contrary, the admission of such records by the judge in a criminal case also imports a finding by him that the conditions of admissibility contained in the statute have been satisfied.[11]

---

[7] *Beal Bank, SSB v. Eurich*, 444 Mass 813, 819, 831 NE2d 909, 914 (2005) (also holding that computer printouts maintained by bank's servicing agent, introduced through bank's default loan manager, were admissible without separate foundation testimony from the agent). The Court's discussion makes clear that in adopting this rule the Court was concerned with the difficulty that an assignee of debt would have in collecting the debt if the rule were otherwise.

[8] *Com. v. Trapp*, 396 Mass 202, 208 n.5, 485 NE2d 162, 166 n.5 (1985).

[9] See *DiMarzo v. American Mutual Insurance Co.*, 389 Mass 85, 105-106, 449 NE2d 1189, 1202 (1983) (records made during pendency of action lacked sufficient indicia of reliability to fall within ambit of statute); *Simon v. Solomon*, 385 Mass 91, 106-107 n.10, 431 NE2d 556, 567 n.10 (1982) (telephone records made after suit commenced not admissible under § 78 but could be used for impeachment purposes); *Com. v. Reyes*, 19 Mass App 1017, 476 NE2d 978 (1985) (telephone records—not objectionable that the actual document introduced in evidence was produced after commencement of litigation where the record itself was stored in the regular course of business before litigation began). Cf. *American Velodur Metal, Inc. v. Schinabeck*, 20 Mass App 460, 481 NE2d 209 (1985) (where party was entitled to attorneys' fees from opponent, not error to admit under this exception billing records of law firm, although prepared after litigation commenced).

[10] *Com. v. Stubbs*, 4 Mass App 777, 341 NE2d 695 (1976); *Com. v. Devlin*, 335 Mass 555, 563, 141 NE2d 269, 273 (1957).

[11] *Com. v. Monahan*, 349 Mass 139, 170, 207 NE2d 29, 44 (1965); *Com. v. Greenberg*, 339 Mass 557, 579, 160 NE2d 181, 187 (1959).

Among other documents, bills of lading, way bills, delivery sheets, and invoices are admissible.[12] Computer printouts are admissible under § 78.[13] Specifications from an engineering department also have qualified as business records.[14]

Police records may constitute business records under § 78, although they would not be admissible against defendants in criminal cases.[15] Records of the probation office of the probate court qualify under § 78.[16] Official records are discussed in § 8.12.

Employer's reports of injury received by a worker's compensation insurer are not business records of the insurer.[17] Nor do wage reports received by the Department of Public Welfare from the employer of an employee constitute business records of the Department.[18] A school file consisting of reports received as to the victim of a crime is not a business record of the school.[19]

Some hospital medical records not admissible under § 79 (see § 8.11.2) have been held admissible under § 78.[20] Business records of hospitals are, of course, within the scope of § 78.[21]

---

[12] *Wiley & Foss, Inc. v. Saxony Theatres*, 332 Mass 172, 124 NE2d 903 (1955); *Chadwick & Carr Co. v. Smith*, 293 Mass 293, 295, 199 NE 903, 904 (1936).

[13] *Com. v. Reed*, 23 Mass App 294, 502 NE2d 147 (1986) (that the witness does not understand how the system works is irrelevant to admissibility, but may go to the weight of the evidence); *Com. v. Hogan*, 7 Mass App 236, 250-251, 387 NE2d 158, 167 (1979).

[14] *Ricciutti v. Sylvania Electric Products, Inc.*, 343 Mass 347, 349, 178 NE2d 857, 860 (1961).

[15] *Adoption of Paula*, 420 Mass 716, 727, 651 NE2d 1222, 1230 (1995) (report of police officers' firsthand observations of conditions in home) (Text cited); *Com. v. Sellon*, 380 Mass 220, 402 NE2d 1329 (1980) (police log showing time telephone call was received); *Com. v. Albino*, 81 Mass App 736, 967 NE2d 645 (2012) (carbon copies of letters from Sex Offender Registration Bureau to defendant that were retained by police department in the regular course of business were business records of the police department). But compare *Kelly v. O'Neil*, 1 Mass App 313, 296 NE2d 223 (1973), holding that § 78 does not authorize admission of statements of second-level hearsay—i.e., statements made by third persons that are incorporated into a police officer's report—and that accident reports filed by a motor vehicle operator are not business records.

[16] *Furtado v. Furtado*, 380 Mass 137, 402 NE2d 1024 (1980). See also *Sawyer & Co. v. Southern Pacific Co.*, supra (government records may be considered business records).

[17] *Wingate v. Emery Air Freight Corp.*, 385 Mass 402, 432 NE2d 474 (1982).

[18] *Com. v. Hussey*, 14 Mass App 1015, 441 NE2d 783 (1982).

[19] *Com. v. Wilson*, 12 Mass App 942, 426 NE2d 162 (1981).

[20] *Com. v. Hogg*, 365 Mass 290, 311 NE2d 63 (1974) (hospital receipt for bullets taken from victim's body). But see *Com. v. Irene*, 462 Mass 600, 610, 970 NE2d 291, 300 (2012) (defendant's statement in hospital record that was not pertinent to diagnosis and treatment could not be offered as a business record, hospital medical records are not admissible under § 78 but must be offered under § 79 or § 79G).

[21] *Brockton Hospital v. Cooper*, 345 Mass 616, 188 NE2d 922 (1963).

Opinions contained in business records offered under § 78 are not admissible.[22] Proposed Mass R Evid 803(6) and Fed R Evid 803(6) allow statements of opinion.

Opinions in hospital and medical records regarding the diagnosis, prognosis, or causation of a medical condition may be admissible under MGL 233, § 79G. See § 8.11.3.

§ 8.11.2 Statutory Exceptions: MGL 233, § 79

Section 79, GL 233 provides for the admissibility of hospital records. The admissibility of hospital records in worker's compensation proceedings is governed by GL 152, § 20. The word "records" in § 79 has been construed to include technical reports.[23]
The oft-stated purpose of § 79 is primarily to relieve physicians and nurses working at hospitals from the inconvenience of attending court as witnesses to facts ordinarily recorded in hospital records.[24] Thus, hospital records containing facts relevant to medical history or treatment are admissible without need for and despite the absence of testimonial corroboration.[25] Although the presence of the maker of the

---

[22] *Julian v. Randazzo*, 380 Mass 391, 403 NE2d 931 (1980) (following the same rule as applied to official records offered as an exception to the hearsay rule); *Burke v. Memorial Hospital*, 29 Mass App 948, 558 NE2d 1146 (1990) (performance evaluations in personnel records constituted inadmissible opinions); *Wiik v. Rathore*, 21 Mass App 399, 487 NE2d 235 (1986) (doctor's opinion in medical record regarding cause of injury was inadmissible opinion). But see *Vassallo v. Baxter Healthcare Corp.*, 428 Mass 1, 18, 696 NE2d 909, 921 (1998) (scientific studies containing primarily factual data, although including some interpretations of data, were properly admitted as against a general objection to the studies as a whole where opponent made no request to strike those portions containing opinions).

[23] See *Com. v. Franks*, 359 Mass 577, 270 NE2d 837 (1971) (laboratory reports); *Kramer v. John Hancock Mutual Life Insurance Co.*, 336 Mass 465, 146 NE2d 357 (1957) (electrocardiograms); *Whipple v. Grand-champ*, 261 Mass 40, 158 NE 270 (1927) (x-rays taken in the course of diagnosis and treatment together with the evaluative reports of the doctors).

[24] *Com. v. Gogan*, 389 Mass 255, 263, 449 NE2d 365, 370 (1983); *Com. v. Bohannon*, 385 Mass 733, 749, 434 NE2d 163, 173 (1982). Once the records have been certified and delivered to the clerk's office, all or portions thereof may be offered in evidence by the proponent. The adversary may object on completeness grounds and request a ruling that other portions be admitted. The records are subject to redaction as necessary. *Com. v. Francis*, 450 Mass 132, 139, 876 NE2d 862, 870 (2007).

[25] *Com. v. Gogan*, supra, 389 Mass at 264, 449 NE2d at 270; *Com. v. Copeland*, 375 Mass 438, 377 NE2d 930 (1978). But compare *Diaz v. Eli Lilly & Co.*, 14 Mass App 448, 440 NE2d 518 (1982) (diagnostic statements in record that involve difficulties of interpretation, or are unusual or controversial, may lack sufficient indicia of reliability to be admitted as part of record); *Com. v. Ennis*, 2 Mass App 864, 314 NE2d 922 (1974)

record is not required, the statute does not limit the admissibility of hospital records to those cases where the preparers of the reports are absent. The report is admissible, even if it would be cumulative.[26]

In *Bouchie v. Murray*,[27] the Court set out a four-part test to determine whether material contained in a hospital record is admissible under § 79:

> First, the document must be the type of record contemplated by G.L. c. 233, § 79. Second, the information must be germane to the patient's treatment or medical history . . . Third, the information must be recorded from the personal knowledge of the entrant or from a compilation of the personal knowledge of those who are under a medical obligation to transmit such information. Fourth, voluntary statements of third persons appearing in the record are not admissible unless they are offered for reasons other than to prove the truth of the matter contained therein or, if offered for their truth, come within another exception to the hearsay rule or the general principles discussed supra.[28]

The source of the information in the record must have personal knowledge of the facts.[29] For application of the statute, see *Doyle v. Dong*.[30]

(no error to exclude diagnostic statements that could not be understood without expert testimony and that posed problems of multiple-level hearsay).

[26] *Com. v. McNickles*, 22 Mass App 114, 123, 491 NE2d 662, 669 (1986).

[27] *Bouchie v. Murray*, 376 Mass 524, 531, 381 NE2d 1295, 1300 (1978).

[28] The reference to "general principles" apparently refers to information from a person with reason to know of the patient's medical history by reason of his or her relationship to the patient, which the Court indicated should be admissible if the circumstances guaranteed its trustworthiness.

[29] *Aleo v. SLB Toys USA, Inc.*, 466 Mass 398, 995 NE2d 740 (2013) (statements in hospital record regarding manner in which deceased went down slide into pool were properly excluded where statements were not made based on personal knowledge of the recorders or by persons with personal knowledge who had an obligation in the course of their employment to transmit medical information to recorders).

[30] *Doyle v. Dong*, 412 Mass 682, 591 NE2d 1084 (1992) (reference in hospital record to throat culture results from a second hospital was admissible, although source of note was never explained); *Com. v. Hartman*, 404 Mass 306, 316, 534 NE2d 1170, 1177 (1989) (proper to redact defendant's "self-diagnosis" from hospital record where he failed to establish it was within any exception to hearsay rule); *Com. v. Dunne*, 394 Mass 10, 17, 474 NE2d 538, 543 (1985) (record excluded where defendant made no attempt to demonstrate that psychological evaluation of alleged rape victim taken to hospital for physical exam fit within meaning of "treatment and medical history"; record also included potential hearsay statements of victim's mother); *Com. v. Sargent*, 24 Mass App 657, 512 NE2d 285 (1987) (not error to admit results of blood alcohol test not ordered by physician nor used in treating defendant where test was conducted as part of normal procedure on every trauma patient). Cf. *Com. v. Perry*, 385 Mass 639,

Most of the litigation involving § 79 deals with the clause that excludes "evidence which has reference to the question of liability."[31] The rule is that those parts of the hospital record that relate mainly to the treatment and medical history of the patient are admitted in evidence even if incidentally the facts recorded may bear on the question of liability.[32] References to alcohol are generally admissible.[33] Hospital records containing medical tests of blood alcohol content are admissible to show that a defendant had consumed intoxicating liquor shortly before his arrest for driving under the influence.[34] The results of screening tests that have not been confirmed may be excluded from evidence.[35]

In *Com. v. DiMonte*,[36] the Court concluded that "unqualified statements in the wife's hospital record that report the ultimate conclusion of the crime charged—an assault and battery—should be redacted," but "more fact-specific references to the reported cause of the wife's

---

641-644, 433 NE2d 446, 448-450 (1982) (judge may require the entire relevant portion of a record to be placed in evidence, or none of it; where defendant had successfully caused exclusion of part of records, no error to exclude related portions, even if otherwise admissible under hearsay exception) (Text cited).

[31] There is a similar clause in GL 46, § 19; see § 8.12.2.

[32] *Com. v. Cole*, 473 Mass 317, 324, 41 NE3d 1073, 1081 (2015) (statements that patient had fallen to floor and onto a knife were relevant to treatment); *Com. v. Dargon*, 457 Mass 387, 393, 930 NE2d 707, 715 (2010) (victim's statements on sexual assault evidence collection form were admissible under § 79 although used both to decide whether declarant needed medical attention and to gather information for crime laboratory; statements recounting how she sustained injuries were for purpose of obtaining medical treatment although incidental to liability; error to admit printed language on form containing conclusory terms such as "assault" and "assailant").

[33] *Com. v. Gogan*, 389 Mass 255, 263, 449 NE2d 365, 370 (1983) (references in record to defendant's intoxication and belligerence related to treatment and hence properly admitted); *Leonard v. Boston Elevated Railway Co.*, 234 Mass 480, 125 NE 593 (1920) (patient had the odor of alcohol on his breath and vomited a fluid smelling like whiskey).

[34] *Com. v. Dube*, 413 Mass 570, 574, 601 NE2d 467, 469 (1992) (& citations); *Com. v. McCready*, 50 Mass App 521, 739 NE2d 270 (2000); *Com. v. St. Hilaire*, 43 Mass App Ct 743, 686 NE2d 1045 (1997) (preliminary findings of reliability of testing apparatus not required where testing administered at hospital and results recorded in hospital record). Cf. *Com. v. Sheldon*, 423 Mass 373, 667 NE2d 1153 (1996) (where information concerning alcohol in defendant's blood was not obtained pursuant to a hospital protocol or any medical goal, but rather to prove whether or not defendant was intoxicated, it would not be admissible under § 79).

[35] *Com. v. Wall*, 469 Mass 652, 669, 15 NE3d 708 (2014) ("the presumption of reliability that attaches to the content of hospital records is defeated where the record explicitly indicates that the results of a toxicology screen are 'presumptive based on screening methods and have not been confirmed by a second independent chemical method.'").

[36] *Com. v. DiMonte*, 427 Mass 233, 242, 692 NE2d 45, 52 (1998).

injuries are part of her medical history and are relevant to treatment." The Court concluded it was not error to admit the latter statements, although incidental to liability. An entry of diagnosis of "Cerebral hemorrhage (traumatic in origin)" is admissible as a specification of the type of injury.[37] But an entry that "While patient was running along the road she was run over by an automobile" is not.[38]

The broad language of § 79 allows copies of original records to be admitted, as well as original records; gives the court discretion to admit certified copies without requiring the attendance of a witness; and applies to records of state and federal hospitals outside the Commonwealth of Massachusetts but within the United States or its territories. A party may obtain hospital records pertaining to another person by procuring a judicial order under the authority of GL 111, § 70. Where records are obtained upon such order, the medical provider delivers certified copies to the court clerk, pursuant to GL 233, § 79.[39] Discovery as to such matters in criminal cases may be sought under Mass R Crim P 14.

In *Com. v. Lampron*,[40] the Appeals Court considered whether hospital records containing notations that the patient had been intoxicated were admissible over a Confrontation Clause objection in a prosecution for driving under the influence of liquor. The court applied *Com. v. Gonsalves*[41] and held that the statements were made for purposes of treatment and not in anticipation of their use in investigation and prosecution of a crime. As a result they were deemed not testimonial and were admissible.

---

[37] *Caccamo's Case*, 316 Mass 358, 362, 55 NE2d 614, 616 (1944).

[38] *Inangelo v. Pettersen*, 236 Mass 439, 128 NE 713 (1920). *Com. v. Dwyer*, 448 Mass 122, 137, 859 NE2d 400, 412-413 (2006) (ineffective assistance of defense counsel not to object to medical report including prejudicial history suggesting complainant's sister had been abused by defendant and statements containing ultimate conclusions about the crimes charged); Compare *Com. v. Baldwin*, 24 Mass App 200, 509 NE2d 4 (1987) (error to admit that portion of record stating "Diagnosis: Sexual molestation") with *Com. v. McNickles*, 22 Mass App 114, 123, 491 NE2d 662, 669 (1986) (not error to admit record containing notation "alleged rape").

[39] For alternative methods of discovery of hospital and medical records, see Mass R Civ P 26, 30, and 34. See also Mass R Civ P 35 (providing for physical and mental examination of persons).

[40] *Com. v. Lampron*, 65 Mass App 340, 839 NE2d 870 (2005).

[41] *Com. v. Gonsalves*, 445 Mass 1, 833 NE2d 549 (2005).

§ 8.11.3 *Statutory Exceptions: MGL 233, § 79G*

Section 79G of GL 233 provides a broad hearsay exception for medical and dental records prepared and offered according to its terms. The statute provides for the admissibility of records reflecting diagnosis and prognosis and opinions with respect to the causation of conditions and disability or incapacity caused by conditions. It has been held that an opinion concerning causation contained in records admitted under § 79G is adequate proof and that a live witness is not required in addition to the record.[42] Such records are also admissible as evidence of the fair and reasonable charge for services and the necessity of services or treatments.[43] The statute covers reports prepared in anticipation of litigation.[44] Records and reports that meet the requirements of the statute are admissible in both criminal and civil cases.[45] The statute requires pretrial notice to the opponent of an intention to offer such records. It has been held that the attestation required by the statute must accompany the record when it is offered at trial, but need not be attached to the copy furnished to opposing counsel prior to trial.[46]

In *Gompers v. Finnell*,[47] the plaintiff offered hospital records accompanied by a form drafted for use under § 79G, on which the authorized agent of the hospital certified under the penalties of perjury that particular services had been rendered to the injured person and that charges were necessary, fair, and reasonable. In addition, the authorized agent of the hospital, not a physician, had typed in that the personal injuries for which the services were rendered were sustained as a result of the accident at issue in the litigation. The Court held that

---

[42] *Bailey v. Cataldo Ambulance Service, Inc.*, 64 Mass App 228, 234, 832 NE2d 12, 17 (2005).

[43] *Law v. Griffith*, 457 Mass 349, 930 NE2d 126 (2010) (medical bills are admissible under § 79G to prove reasonableness of cost of services rendered even though amounts actually paid by plaintiff's insurer and accepted by medical providers were significantly lower than amounts providers had billed; evidence concerning possibility of payments by third parties and range of payments accepted by providers as payment in full is also admissible under § 79G on question of reasonable charge for and value of medical services; under collateral source rule, however, evidence of amounts actually paid to plaintiff's medical providers is inadmissible).

[44] *O'Malley v. Soske*, 76 Mass App 495, 923 NE2d 552 (2010); *Com. v. Schutte*, 52 Mass App 796, 756 NE2d 48 (2001).

[45] *Com. v. Schutte*, supra.

[46] *Knight v. Maersk Container Service Co.*, 49 Mass App 254, 728 NE2d 968 (2000).

[47] *Gompers v. Finnell*, 35 Mass App 91, 616 NE2d 490 (1993).

this constituted an extraneous opinion by the hospital's agent, not admissible under § 79G, and that it was error not to redact it. In *Ortiz v. Stein*,[48] the Court held that an affidavit setting out opinions on the liability of the defendant in a medical malpractice case, by a physician who had neither treated nor examined the plaintiff, would not be admissible under the statute. The Court reasoned that it could not find an intent to make such a radical change in the trial of such claims in the absence of a clear statutory expression.

The authority of a trial court to afford the same treatment to similar records is not limited by the statute. In *Phelps v. MacIntyre*,[49] the Court affirmed the admission of a bill of an ambulance service under the procedures of the statute, although ambulance services are not included in its terms. The Court held that the trial judge had discretion to admit the bill under its authority to adopt appropriate common-law rules of evidence.

There is no hearsay exception comparable to § 79G in either the Proposed Massachusetts Rules of Evidence or the Federal Rules of Evidence. In *Grant v. Lewis/Boyle, Inc.*,[50] the Court decided it was unnecessary to adopt Rule 803(6) with respect to physician's reports, given the existence of § 79G.

§ 8.11.4 Common-Law Exceptions

Entries made in the regular course of business are admissible in evidence.[51] Admissibility is subject to the following limitations:

(1) The witness must be dead or otherwise unavailable. This limitation does not apply to dispatch sheets kept by railroads or steamship companies.[52] The Supreme Judicial Court has refused to extend this principle beyond dispatch sheets. Thus, records kept in a hospital are inadmissible under this exception and the person keeping the record cannot

---

[48] *Ortiz v. Stein*, 31 Mass App 643, 582 NE2d 560 (1991).

[49] *Phelps v. MacIntyre*, 397 Mass 459, 462, 491 NE2d 1067, 1069 (1986).

[50] *Grant v. Lewis/Boyle, Inc.*, 408 Mass 269, 557 NE2d 1136 (1990).

[51] *Welsh v. Barrett*, 15 Mass (15 Tyng) 379 (1819).

[52] *Hines v. Eastern Steamship Lines*, 245 Mass 385, 139 NE 823 (1923); *Donovan v. Boston & M.R.R*, 158 Mass 450, 33 NE 583 (1893). The dispatcher keeping the sheet is allowed to testify as to the information received from station agents along the line without producing station agents or accounting for their absence, and the sheets themselves are admissible in evidence.

testify as to information therein contained received from another hospital employee unless the other employee is unavailable.[53] However, such records are likely to be admissible under GL 233, §§ 78 or 79, discussed above.

(2) The entry must be regular (i.e., not isolated) and in the course of business (i.e., not a personal diary). But there need not be any duty to a third person to keep the entry.[54]

(3) The entry must be made ante litem motam, and there must be no motive to misrepresent.

(4) The evidence contained in the entry must be within the personal knowledge of the person making the entry.[55]

§ 8.12 Official Records

Proposed Mass R Evid 803(8) creates a hearsay exception for:

> **(8) Public Records and Reports**. Records, reports, statements, or data compilations, in any form, of public offices or agencies, setting forth (A) the activities of the office or agency, or (B) matters observed pursuant to duty imposed by law as to which matter there was a duty to report, excluding, however, in criminal cases matters observed by police officers and other law enforcement personnel, or (C) in civil actions and proceedings and against the Commonwealth in criminal cases, factual findings resulting from an investigation made pursuant to authority granted by law, unless the sources of information or other circumstances indicate lack of trustworthiness.

Fed R Evid 803(8) is identical. The language of the Rule would both widen and narrow the common-law exception. Under the Rule, factually based conclusions and opinions are admissible.[1] However, law enforcement reports are not admissible against the defendant in criminal cases.

---

[53] *Delaney v. Framingham Gas Co.*, 202 Mass 359, 88 NE 773 (1909).

[54] *Kennedy v. Doyle*, 92 Mass (10 All) 161 (1865) (baptismal record).

[55] *Household Fuel Corp. v. Hamacher*, 331 Mass 653, 655, 121 NE2d 846, 848 (1954).

§ 8.12 [1] *Beech Aircraft Corp. v. Rainey*, 488 US 153, 109 S Ct 439 (1988) (conclusions concerning cause of airplane crash admissible).

§ 8.12.1 Common-Law Rules

Official records may be admitted in evidence in certain instances as evidence of the truth of the facts recorded therein, under a common-law exception to the hearsay rule. Not every official record will qualify under this exception, which provides that an official record of a primary fact made by a public officer in the performance of official duty may be introduced in evidence as proof of the facts recorded.[2]

Evaluative reports and other official records may be admissible by virtue of a specific statutory exception, apart from the common-law exception. A sampling of such statutes is given below.

The fact that a private party has filed a document with a government agency may make it a "public record" in the sense that it is available for public inspection, or with regard to whether it is privileged.[3] This will not make a document an official record, however, for the purpose of coming within this common-law exception to the hearsay rule.[4] This is because a record must have been prepared by a public official acting within the scope of his duty before it falls within this exception.[5] One should note that whether or not a report is admissible under a statute or the common law, an official record may be available

---

[2] *Com. v. Slavski*, 245 Mass 405, 140 NE 465 (1923) (extensive listing of types of records admissible). See, e.g., *Lodge v. Congress Taxi Association*, 340 Mass 570, 165 NE2d 94 (1960) (plaintiff established identity of owner of taxi as being defendant through Boston police records pertaining to licensing of hackneys); *Adoption of George*, 27 Mass App 265, 537 NE2d 1251 (1989) (DSS case records admissible, not restricted by requirement applicable to business records that records be generated prior to commencement of proceedings). Cf. *Jacobs v. Hertz Corp.*, 358 Mass 541, 265 NE2d 588 (1970) (allegation in complaint in court record about registration of vehicle was not official record of primary fact).

[3] See *Lord v. Registrar of Motor Vehicles*, 347 Mass 608, 199 NE2d 316 (1964) (accident reports filed with the Registry of Motor Vehicles are "public records").

[4] *Kelly v. O'Neil*, 1 Mass App 313, 319, 296 NE2d 223, 226 (1973) (accident report filed with police department not an official record within hearsay exception); *Genova v. Genova*, 28 Mass App 647, 654, 554 NE2d 1221, 1225 (1990) (dissenting op. by Brown, J).

[5] See *Com. v. Shangkuan*, 78 Mass App 827, 830, 943 NE2d 466, 470 (2011) (finding that return of service on a c. 209A order is a public record) (Text cited); *Com. v. Williams*, 63 Mass App 615, 827 NE2d 1281 (2005) (worker's compensation claim filing prepared by worker and attorney was neither a business record nor a public record) (Text cited); *Com. v. Kirk*, 39 Mass App 225, 654 NE2d 938 (1995) (identification of defendant in GL 209A order was merely a replication of complainant's assertion in her affidavit that defendant was her abuser and could not be regarded as a record of a "primary fact made by a public officer in the performance of official duty") (Text cited).

for use for non-hearsay purposes—e.g., to show constructive notice, recording, or as the source of admissions or prior inconsistent statements.[6]

The fact that a document may be admissible under the official records exception does not, of course, mean that all multiple hearsay statements contained within the document are admissible. Such multiple hearsay statements must fall within a separate hearsay exception to be admissible.[7]

Where the official record is offered as an exception to the hearsay rule, both the common-law and the statutory exceptions require that the recorded statement of fact be made by one who has a duty to do so. The duty may be imposed by a foreign law, and the official may be a foreign official. The duty need not be imposed directly by statute.

Statements of opinion, judgmental observations, and the results of investigations do not come within the common-law exception.[8]

The fact that the official has a duty generally to keep records is not sufficient. It must be shown that he has a public duty to record that particular type of fact.[9] A duty to record facts is ordinarily not construed to include expressions of opinion, conclusions, or statements as to causes and effects.[10] Thus, where a statute requires a medical examiner's report to contain "every fact tending to show the condition of the body and the cause and manner of death," the portion of a report that gives, in addition to such facts, the conclusion of the medical examiner as to the cause of death is inadmissible.[11]

---

[6] *Com. v. Williams*, supra (worker's compensation claim filing prepared by worker and attorney was admissible to show that statutorily required filing had been made and to prove contents of same).

[7] See, e.g., *Sklar v. Beth Israel Deaconess Medical Center*, 59 Mass App 550, 556, n.8, 797 NE2d 381, 386 (2003) (patient's statement to investigator for Board of Allied Health Professions was second-level hearsay and thus inadmissible).

[8] *Julian v. Randazzo*, 380 Mass 391, 403 NE2d 931 (1980) (recognizing also that police investigative reports may be treated as official records or as business records under GL 233, § 78, and applying the same limitation under either theory of admissibility); *Matoon v. City of Pittsfield*, 56 Mass App 124, 775 NE2d 770 (2002); *Herson v. New Boston Garden Corp.*, 40 Mass App 779, 792, 667 NE2d 907, 917 (1996) (evaluative reports are not admissible); *Adoption of George*, supra (appropriate to screen expressions of opinion, evaluation, or judgment from DSS records before admission).

[9] *Building Inspector of Chatham v. Kendrick*, 17 Mass App 928, 456 NE2d 1151 (1983) (minutes of meetings of zoning board of appeals admissible only to show specific matters that statute requires to be recorded; error to admit as evidence of truth of statements made to board) (Text cited).

[10] *Passanessi v. C. J. Maney Co.*, 340 Mass 599, 603, 165 NE2d 590, 593 (1960).

[11] *Jewett v. Boston Elevated Railway Co.*, 219 Mass 528, 107 NE 433 (1914); *Amory v. Com.*, 321 Mass 240, 72 NE2d 549 (1947) (details in annual report of Metropolitan

Reports of conclusions may be made admissible by statute, allowing them to be introduced in evidence.[12] Such conclusions or opinions may not only become admissible under a statute but may also be given the qualitative force of prima facie evidence.[13]

§ 8.12.2 *Statutory Rules*

GL 111, § 13, now repealed, provided that a certificate of the result of chemical analysis of narcotic drugs may be admitted in evidence as prima facie evidence of the composition, quality, and net weight of the narcotic or other drug present. In *Melendez-Diaz v. Massachusetts*,[14] however, the United States Supreme Court held that admitting such certificates in the place of live testimony and an opportunity to cross-examine the analyst would violate the Confrontation Clause. The Court held that such certificates amounted to testimonial hearsay and were clearly prepared for use as evidence at a later trial. The Court further indicated that although the government need not necessarily call all persons who handled the evidence to establish a sufficient chain of custody, any chain of custody testimony that is introduced must (if the defendant objects) be introduced live.[15] The decision abrogated the earlier decision of the Supreme Judicial Court in *Com. v. Verde*[16] that the admission of such drug certificates did not violate the Confrontation Clause.

The dissenting Justices in *Melendez-Diaz* questioned which of the various "analysts" that may be involved in drug testing must be called

---

District Water Commission held inadmissible). See *Rice v. James Hanrahan & Sons*, 20 Mass App 701, 706, 482 NE2d 833, 837 (1985) (environmental regulations barring insulation were not records of primary facts.).

[12] *Shamlian v. Equitable Accident Co.*, 226 Mass 67, 115 NE 46 (1917).

[13] *Miles v. Edward O. Tabor, M.D., Inc.*, 387 Mass 783, 787, 443 NE2d 1302, 1304 (1982) (death certificate admitted under GL 46, § 19, is not conclusive but only prima facie evidence); *Pahigian v. Manufacturers' Life Ins. Co.*, 349 Mass 78, 85, 206 NE2d 660, 665 (1965). Cf. *Resendes v. Boston Edison Co.*, 38 Mass App 344, 354, 648 NE2d 757, 764 (1995) (GL 82, § 40, which provides that failure to give a "dig safe" notice is prima facie evidence of negligence, did not authorize the admission in evidence of a written DPU decision that a contractor had failed to give such notice where the statute did not explicitly provide that the DPU document or record was admissible in evidence, hence no error where trial judge redacted conclusions from report).

[14] *Melendez-Diaz v. Massachusetts*, 129 S Ct 2527 (2009). Following the Supreme Court's decision, the Massachusetts legislature repealed the statute in 2012.

[15] *Melendez-Diaz*, 129 S Ct at 2532, n.1, slip op. at 4.

[16] *Com. v. Verde*, 444 US 279, 827 NE2d 701 (2005).

as live witnesses under the majority's decision.[17] The dissenters also raised concerns about the constitutionality of some "burden-shifting statutes" under which the prosecution is required to give notice of its intent to offer a certificate in lieu of testimony from an analyst and the defendant must then object or forfeit his Confrontation Clause rights.[18] The majority opinion stated that the simplest of these statutes, which require the defendant to do no more than assert his Confrontation Clause objection prior to trial, were constitutional, but declined to speculate about the constitutionality of statutes that required more, such as putting the burden of issuing a subpoena for the analyst on the defendant.[19]

The original scientist or analyst who prepared a forensic report or certificate is not always available to testify at the trial. The prosecution may attempt to satisfy the Confrontation Clause by calling a substitute witness. If the substitute performs her own tests on or analysis of the material in question, her testimony should not raise hearsay issues. To the extent she testifies on the basis of the work performed by the original analyst, however, there may be hearsay and Confrontation Clause problems. Similar issues arise when a witness compares the results of material tested in one laboratory with material tested in a different laboratory.

In *Bullcoming v. New Mexico*,[20] the Court held that admission of a certificate by an unavailable analyst violated the Confrontation Clause where another analyst, familiar with the testing device and the laboratory's testing procedures, had been called as a witness to validate the report. The testifying analyst had neither observed nor participated in the test in question. The Court rejected the argument that the analyst who had performed the test was a "mere scrivener" who simply transcribed the results generated by a gas chromatograph machine.[21] In a concurring opinion, Justice Sotomayor explained that this case could be distinguished from one in which the testifying analyst offers an

---

[17] *Melendez-Diaz*, 129 S Ct at 2544.

[18] *Melendez-Diaz*, 129 S Ct at 2557.

[19] *Melendez-Diaz*, 129 S Ct at 2541. Some of the latter issues might have been resolved in *Briscoe v. Virginia*, where the Supreme Court initially granted certiorari to review a burden-shifting statute. Subsequently, however, the Court merely vacated the lower court opinion and remanded for further proceedings in light of *Melendez-Diaz*, without further discussion. *Briscoe v. Virginia*, ___US___, 130 S Ct 1316 (2010).

[20] *Bullcoming v. New Mexico*, 131 S Ct 2705 (2011).

[21] The Court explained that in addition to reporting the results, the certification asserted that the analyst had received the blood sample with the seal unbroken, had checked that the forensic report number and sample number corresponded, had adhered to a precise protocol and that nothing had affected the integrity of the sample or the validity of the analysis.

independent opinion based on underlying testimonial reports that are not introduced into evidence. She noted that under FRE 703 the testifying expert may rely on facts or data that are not admissible in evidence if they are of a type that experts in the field would reasonably rely on.

In *Williams v. Illinois*,[22] in a badly splintered opinion in a rape case, the Court held that an analyst could testify that there was a match between a DNA sample from the defendant examined by another analyst (who testified) and a sample purportedly from the victim analyzed by a different lab operated by Cellmark (whose report was not admitted in evidence and from which no analyst testified). The opinion by Justice Alito, in which three other Justices joined, concluded that references in business records (shipping manifests) from Cellmark that identified the DNA sample it analyzed as coming from semen found on vaginal swabs of the victim were not admitted in evidence to prove the truth of such statements, but in order to demonstrate the basis for the testifying expert's opinion. Justice Alito's opinion also concluded that even had the Cellmark report itself been introduced into evidence, there would have been no Confrontation Clause violation. He reasoned that a DNA report generated before any suspect was identified was not made for the purpose of obtaining evidence to be used against the eventual defendant, "but for the purpose of finding a rapist who was on the loose."[23] Justice Thomas's concurring opinion created a majority for affirming the conviction only on the latter ground, although he concluded there was no violation of the Confrontation Clause because the statements in Cellmark's report lacked the "formality and solemnity" to be considered "testimonial."[24] Four Justices dissented in an opinion by Justice Kagan, concluding that the substance of the Cellmark report had been admitted in evidence, and that it was a report made to establish a fact in a criminal proceeding, namely the identity of the victim's attacker. The dissenters concluded that *Bullcoming* required a finding that the Confrontation Clause had been violated.[25]

As noted above in § 8.4.2, the Supreme Judicial Court has held that art. 12 of the Massachusetts Declaration of Rights and the Sixth

---

[22] *Williams v. Illinois*, 132 S Ct 2221 (2012). In *Com. v. Tassone*, 83 Mass App 197, 982 NE2d 534 (2013), further app rev granted, 465 Mass 1102, 987 NE2d 594 (2013), the court followed *Williams* and approved testimony by a chemist finding a match between DNA analyzed by the state laboratory and DNA found on eyeglasses analyzed by Cellmark.

[23] *Id.*, 132 S Ct at 2228.

[24] *Id.*, 132 S Ct at 2255 (concurring op. by Thomas, J.).

[25] *Id.*, 132 S Ct at 2266 (dissenting op. by Kagan, J.).

Amendment to the United States Constitution provide equivalent protection with regard to cross-examination under the Confrontation Clause. In *Com. v. Tassone*,[26] however, the Court underlined that the Massachusetts common law of evidence is more protective of confrontation rights than the constitutional guarantees. It proceeded to use the common law to analyze the admissibility of an expert's testimony about the laboratory results of tests in which he had not participated. The expert had testified that the DNA profile from a known saliva sample of the defendant matched a DNA profile from a swab taken from eyeglasses left at the crime scene. The expert had no affiliation with the laboratory that did the analysis of the swab from the eyeglasses. The Court held that the expert's testimony was inadmissible under the Massachusetts common law of evidence because the defendant lacked a meaningful opportunity to cross-examine regarding the laboratory work, procedures, or protocols of the laboratory that examined the eyeglasses. The Court noted that the case could be distinguished from *Williams v. Illinois*, and declined to reach the question of whether the United States Supreme Court would find a Confrontation Clause violation in this case.

Other recent Massachusetts cases dealing with substitute analysts have established that where the testifying witness is expressing an independent opinion, albeit based in part on the report of the absent doctor or scientist, that opinion is admissible, but reporting the findings of the absent analyst would violate the Confrontation Clause.[27]

---

[26] *Com. v. Tassone*, 468 Mass 391, 11 NE3d 67 (2014).

[27] See *Com. v. Chappell*, 473 Mass 191, 201, 40 NE3d 1031, 1040 (2015) ("critical issue . . . is whether the defendant is able to cross-examine the expert in a meaningful way regarding possible flaws relating to the underlying data that forms the basis of his or her opinion"; substitute DNA analyst who was supervisor's of lab's DNA analysts and second reader and technical reviewer in this case was properly allowed to testify); *Com. v. Jones*, 472 Mass 707, 37 NE3d 589 (2015) (where witness was not present at hospital, testimony based on rape kit inventory list violated Confrontation Clause because defendant could not cross-examine nurse who collected swabs); *Com. v. Reavis*, 465 Mass 875, 992 NE2d 304 (2013) (that original medical examiner had left the office and moved out of the Commonwealth was an adequate reason for calling a substitute medical examiner to testify at trial; substitute examiner could offer opinion on cause of death, time elapsed between injury and death, force required to inflict the injury, and effect that certain types of injuries would have on victim, based on review of autopsy report by original medical examiner and review of autopsy photographs, but may not testify to facts in underlying autopsy report where that report has not been admitted in evidence); *Com. v. Greineder*, 464 Mass 580, 984 NE2d 804 (2013) (defendant's rights were not violated by testimony of DNA expert, although expert relied on DNA test results obtained by a nontestifying analyst; Court reviews recent history of Confrontation Clause jurisprudence with respect to scientific evidence); *Com. v. Rivera*, 464 Mass 56, 981 NE2d 171 (2013) (substitute medical examiner); *Com. v. Leng*,

Determining whether the testifying witness is expressing an independent opinion or is serving as a conduit for the conclusions of the absent witness who performed the original examination is to say the least a difficult matter, as suggested by the different conclusions reached by Justices Alito and Kagan in *Williams v. Illinois*, supra. The issues include the nature of the original data that has been preserved, and what the witness does with the original data that allows her to claim to be expressing an "independent opinion." These issues require an in depth understanding of the applicable science and laboratory equipment and procedures in each case.

The logic of the Court in *Melendez-Diaz* compels the conclusion that other statutes permitting the introduction of a certificate to prove the results of a laboratory analysis run afoul of the Confrontation

---

463 Mass 779, 979 NE2d 199 (2012) (substitute medical examiner); *Com. v. Whitaker*, 460 Mass 409, 421, 951 NE2d 873, 883 (2011) (error to permit fingerprint examiner to testify that two other examiners verified and concurred with his opinion); *Com. v. Bizanowicz*, 459 Mass 400, 945 NE2d 356 (2011) (where testifying chemist was not expressing his own opinion, using report of chemist who performed tests as a basis for his opinion, but was merely reciting the results of absent chemist's tests and presenting that chemist's factual findings, the "testimony introduced factual findings through the hearsay notes of a nontestifying expert, and should not have been admitted"); *Com. v. Rogers*, 459 Mass 249, 264, 945 NE2d 295, 309 (2011) (testifying medical examiner properly based his independent opinion on cause of death on autopsy report of another medical examiner, photographs, notes from the EMT and emergency room doctors, toxicology reports, and other material; it was improper however for him to testify to length and depth of stab wound and source of bleeding, underlying factual findings presumably from autopsy report); *Com. v. Housen*, 458 Mass 702, 940 NE2d 437 (2011) (medical examiner based his own opinion on independently admissible hearsay from autopsy report and photographs in evidence and did not merely recite opinion of absent medical examiner who had performed autopsy; error to permit testimony about details of autopsy report during direct exam, but error was harmless); *Com. v. McCowen*, 458 Mass 461, 482, 939 NE2d 735, 755 (2010) (DNA expert who testified had performed tests on some samples, but others were performed by different analyst; her opinion on likelihood that defendant was a contributor to DNA on victim was proper because expert is entitled to rely on hearsay report of other analyst; error to admit chart containing hearsay allele numbers from testing by other analyst, but no substantial likelihood of miscarriage of justice because numbers were meaningless without testifying analyst's expert opinion); *Com. v. Barbosa*, 457 Mass 773, 933 NE2d 93 (2010) (DNA analyst may base her opinion on tests performed by different analyst, but informing jury that nontestifying analyst shares testifying analyst's opinion violates hearsay rule and Confrontation Clause; court collects cases from other jurisdictions); *Com. v. Taskey*, 78 Mass App 787, 941 NE2d 713 (2011) (analyst who conducted DNA test was unavailable for trial; supervisor testified she had reviewed all the raw data, all the absent analyst's worksheets, and her compliance with procedural protocols; supervisor's independent analysis and opinions were admissible, but admitting chart of absent analyst's findings violated Confrontation Clause, although error was harmless); and see cases reviewed in Taskey.

Clause and previous decisions sustaining them are now questionable.[28] Even before *Melendez-Diaz*, Massachusetts courts had held that forensic reports that involved opinions and conclusions requiring the exercise of judgment and discretion, rather than mere "primary facts," were not admissible as public records and were testimonial in nature, and hence their admission would violate the Confrontation Clause.[29] It is doubtful, however, whether the distinction the Massachusetts courts draw between "opinions" and "primary facts" withstands scrutiny. The United States Supreme Court has characterized the purported distinction between "fact" and "opinion" as arbitrary and rejected such an analysis with respect to the admissibility of public records.[30] With respect to the Confrontation Clause, the distinction the Supreme Court drew in *Melendez-Diaz* was between records that were prepared for use in litigation and other records.[31]

---

[28] See *Com. v. Lee*, 466 Mass 1028, 998 NE2d 768 (2013) (violation of Confrontation Clause to admit without live testimony certificate from Registry of Motor Vehicles attesting to fact that defendant had received notice that his license had been suspended); *Com. v. Carr*, 464 Mass 865, 875, 986 NE2d 380, 399 (2013) (statements re: cause of death in death certificate are testimonial in fact); *Com. v. Emeny*, 463 Mass 138, 972 NE2d 1003 (2012) (statements in an autopsy report are testimonial and admission of such statements violates Confrontation Clause); *Com. v. Mercado*, 456 Mass 198, 922 NE2d 140 (2010) (hearsay and Confrontation Clause violation for substitute examiner to testify on direct to findings from report regarding manner in which bullet penetrated body causing internal bleeding); *Com. v. Depina*, 456 Mass 238, 922 NE2d 778 (2010) (admission of ballistics certificates without accompanying testimony from a ballistician who performed the analysis violates Confrontation Clause).

[29] *Com. v. Nardi*, 452 Mass 379, 393, 893 NE2d 1221, 1232 (2008) (findings in autopsy report with respect to presence and location of facial trauma, extent of heart disease and opinion with respect to cause of death were matters of opinion and testimonial).

[30] *Beech Aircraft Corp. v. Rainey*, 488 US 153, 167 109 S Ct 439, 448 (1988) (interpreting Fed R Evid 803(8)).

[31] For Massachusetts cases drawing this distinction, see *Com. v. Parenteau*, 460 Mass 1, 948 NE2d 883 (2011) (certificate of Registry of Motor Vehicles, issued after defendant was charged with operating a motor vehicle without a license, was testimonial in nature for purpose of establishing that notice of license revocation was mailed on an earlier date, in contrast with one that might have been created at the time notice was mailed and maintained in Registry's files for administrative purposes); *Com. v. Nutter*, 87 Mass App 260, 28 NE3d 1 (2015) (RMV record kept in the ordinary course of business was not testimonial); *Com. v. Bigley*, 85 Mass App 507, 11 NE3d 1086 (2014) (RMV and Board of Probation records kept in the ordinary course of business are not testimonial); *Com. v. Lopes*, 85 Mass App 341, 10 NE3d 146 (attestation in RMV record that defendant's license had not been reinstated was created for purposes of trial, but any error cured because RMV agent testified and was cross-examined); *Com. v. Reddy*, 85 Mass App 104, 5 NE3d 1254 (2014) (return of service on a 209A order is not testimonial); *Com. v. Burton*, 82 Mass App 912, 978 NE2d 796 (2012) (fingerprint records are not testimonial); *Com. v. Ellis*, 79 Mass App 330, 945 NE2d 983 (2011) (in

Following the decision in *Melendez-Diaz*, numerous convicted defendants against whom forensic certificates had been admitted under *Verde* raised a Confrontation Clause challenge to their admission on appeal. Some had preserved the issue at the trial level, others had not objected to the introduction of the certificates. The Supreme Judicial Court ultimately held that even unpreserved errors based on *Melendez-Diaz* are entitled to a favorable standard of review, under which the issue is "whether the record establishes beyond a reasonable doubt that the error complained of did not contribute to the verdict obtained."[32] "[I]t is not enough for the Commonwealth to show that the evidence apart from the certificate was '"sufficient" to convict the defendant' or that the certificate was '"consistent" with the admissible evidence.' Rather, the other evidence that the substance possessed was [a drug] would have to be so overwhelming as to 'nullify any effect' the admission of the certificate '"might have had" on the fact finder or the [verdicts].'"[33] "The analysis of the strength of the Commonwealth's other evidence is significant only if, and to the extent that, it can bring us to the conclusion that the admission of the . . . certificates had little or no effect in proving that element."[34]

Among the factors the courts may consider in assessing whether the admission of such certificates was harmless error are "the importance of the evidence in the prosecution's case; the relationship between the evidence and the premise of the defense; who introduced the issue at trial; the frequency of the reference; whether the erroneously admitted evidence was merely cumulative of properly admitted evidence; the availability or effect of curative instructions; and the weight or quantum of evidence of guilt."[35]

OUI fourth offense prosecution: certified records of conviction are made to establish fact of adjudication, not as evidence in future trials, and thus are not testimonial; probation record was prepared for use in trial and thus testimonial; RMV records kept in ordinary course of business of RMV are maintained independent of any prosecutorial purpose and not testimonial); *Com. v. McLaughlin*, 79 Mass App 670, 677, 948 NE2d 1258, 1265 (2011) (certification by hospital record keeper is not testimonial).

[32] See *Chapman v. California*, 386 US 18, 24 (1967). In *Com. v. Melendez-Diaz*, 460 Mass 238, 950 NE2d 867 (2011) the Supreme Judicial Court held, however, that a convicted person was not entitled to retroactive application of the Supreme Court's decision in *Melendez-Diaz* on collateral review.

[33] *Com. v. Rodriguez*, 456 Mass 578, 591, 925 NE2d 21, 32 (2010) (citations omitted); *Com. v. Vasquez*, 456 Mass 350, 356-362, 923 NE2d 524, 530-535 (2010) (objection to admissibility of certificates would have been futile, given *Verde* decision).

[34] *Com. v. Vasquez*, 436 Mass at 363, 923 NE2d at 535.

[35] *Com. v. Fluellen*, 456 Mass 517, 526, 924 NE2d 713, 721 (2010), quoting previous cases.

In *Com. v. Loadholt*,[36] the Supreme Judicial Court cited previous cases that established that there is no absolute requirement for expert testimony in gun cases. In the case of a revolver, a jury may infer that it is a firearm capable of being fired where the weapon and cartridges are introduced into evidence and the revolver was loaded at the time of the seizure, although it is not clear that the same inference can be drawn in the case of a semiautomatic pistol. However, the Court held in *Loadholt* that when a certificate has been introduced and relied upon by the Commonwealth to prove the weapon is operable, more independent evidence is required to conclude the certificate did not contribute to the verdict and to render its admission harmless.[37] The inquiry is fact specific and the courts have held that admission of a ballistics certificate to prove a gun was operable was harmless error in some cases,[38] and that the Commonwealth failed to carry the burden of establishing harmless error in others.[39] Proof of unlawful possession of ammunition merely requires evidence that it was designed for use in a firearm, not that it is actually capable of being fired. Hence it has

---

[36] *Com. v. Loadholt*, 456 Mass 411, 433, 923 NE2d 1037, 1056 (2010).

[37] In accord, *Com. v. Muniz*, 456 Mass 166, 171, 921 NE2d 981, 986 (2010).

[38] Examples include *Com. v. Ramsey*, 466 Mass 489, 995 NE2d 1110 (2013) (admissions of ballistics certificate was harmless where defense counsel agreed judge could tell jury none of the elements of firearms charge were in dispute); *Com. v. Depina*, 456 Mass 238, 249, 922 NE2d 778, 788 (2010) ("overwhelming" evidence that weapon could be fired—seized revolver contained four live rounds of ammunition and one spent casing with no projectile and a "striker mark" on it; when box containing weapon came back from State Police where it was sent for testing it contained three additional spent projectiles and their casings); *Com. v. Pittman*, 76 Mass App 905, 923 NE2d 1083 (2010) (officer's testimony that gun was loaded when he found it, he submitted it to lab with two rounds of ammunition, lab's practice is to fire one and send empty casing back, he received spent casing back, and fact that prosecutor did not mention certificate in closing, rendered admission of certificate harmless); *Com. v. Mendes*, 75 Mass App 390, 397, 914 NE2d 348 (2009) (proof of three audible shots, three empty casings, and the smell of gunpowder rendered admission of certificate harmless).

[39] See, e.g., *Com. v. Barbosa*, 461 Mass 431, 961 NE2d 560 (2012) (evidence insufficient to make admission of certificate harmless although officer testified firearm was "authentic," officer cleared weapon of ammunition to make it safe, jury was able to inspect the weapon, firearm was loaded when seized (but no spent casing was found in weapon's chamber), trooper testified that out of six live rounds sent for analysis five were returned as well as a spent casing marked "test" and trooper stated it appeared ballistician had fired a test round, which was speculation on trooper's part); *Com. v. McCollum*, 79 Mass App 239, 249, 945 NE2d 937, 948 (2011) ("presence of ammunition, without direct evidence that a weapon's firing mechanism is functional, is insufficient" to establish introduction of certificate was harmless); *Com. v. Morales*, 76 Mass App 663, 925 NE2d 551 (2010) (that gun was loaded, had serial number scratched off, was carried by defendant in small of his back, and that defendant carried extra ammunition did not establish that it was operable).

been easier to establish that the admission of a certificate was harmless in possession of ammunition cases.[40]

In narcotics cases, the issue of whether admission of a certificate was harmless similarly depends upon the facts. The courts have found that the error was harmless in some cases,[41] and that the

---

[40] *Com. v. Loadholt*, 456 Mass 411, 431, 923 NE2d 1037, 1054 (2010) (no requirement of functionality with respect to ammunition, only that it was designed for use in a firearm; boxed ammunition found was same caliber as that found loaded in weapon); *Com. v. Muniz*, 456 Mass 166, 173, 921 NE2d 981, 987 (2010) (evidence included the gun, magazines, and officer's testimony that cartridges were found in the magazine); *Com. v. McCollum*, 79 Mass App 239, 249, 945 NE2d 937, 948 (2011) (testimony of officer that bullets were .44 caliber ammunition rendered admission of certificate harmless).

[41] Examples include *Com. v. Ramsey*, 466 Mass 489, 995 NE2d 1110 (2013) (admission of drug certificate was harmless where defendant admitted on the stand he had possessed cocaine and parties agreed the substance was cocaine); *Com. v. Mendes*, 463 Mass 353, 358, 974 NE2d 606, 611 (2012) (defendants' testimony that substances were cocaine and marijuana, coupled with circumstantial evidence introduced by prosecution, sufficed to render admission of certificate harmless; under facts of case, defendants' testimony was not in response to content of certificates); *Com. v. Connolly*, 454 Mass 808, 831, 913 NE2d 356, 375 (2009), *habeas denied*, 2013 WL 139702 (D. Mass 2013) (admission of certificate harmless where defendant told undercover officer substance was crack cocaine and experienced detectives identified it as crack cocaine and conducted positive field tests; ball of cocaine was in evidence and jury could determine themselves it weighed more than four ounces); *Com. v. Marte*, 84 Mass App 136, 993 NE2d 1201 (2013) (admission of certificate was harmless error for hand to hand sales where experienced officer conducted field tests, pattern of sales existed in response to undercover officers request for cocaine, defendant boasted of product's quality, sale price corresponded with market price, and manner of packaging and sale was typical of street-level cocaine distribution); *Com. v. Hopkins*, 79 Mass App 412, 415, 946 NE2d 153, 155 (2011) (admission of certificate harmless given admission of earlier trial testimony where defendant admitted substance was cocaine); *Com. v. DeMatos*, 77 Mass App 727, 732, 933 NE2d 992, 997 (2010) (certificate harmless as to composition of drugs based on defendant's admissions regarding cocaine and overwhelming evidence of narcotics; harmless as to weight where defendant did not deny amount, said three ounces was no big deal, and jury could determine weight exceed half an ounce); *Com. v. Villatoro*, 76 Mass App 645, 925 NE2d 45 (2010) (defendant admitted substance was marijuana, trained officer recognized odor of marijuana); *Com. v. Greco*, 76 Mass App 296, 921 NE2d 1001 (2010) (pills were in prescription bottle with names of defendant and drug store and stamped with brand name that judge could identify as a specific controlled drug through judicial notice and prosecution did not emphasize lab certificates); *Com. v. Rodriguez*, 75 Mass App 235, 244, 913 NE2d 880, 888 (2009) (admission of certificate to prove weight was not harmless on trafficking charge, but certificates with respect to identity of cocaine on other charges were harmless, based on defendant's admission to drug dealing, his attempt to swallow the drugs, expert testimony regarding significance of packaging and the swallowing of drugs, seizure of drug paraphernalia and suspected cocaine in defendant's basement, uncontested testimony regarding field testing as cocaine, and defense itself, which raised possibility of a cocaine binge).

Commonwealth failed to make the requisite proof of harmless error in others.[42]

---

[42] Examples include *Com. v. Montoya*, 464 Mass 566, 572, 984 NE2d 793, 799 (2013) (evidence included defendant's statement to police that he was selling cocaine, drug canine alerted to vehicle, detective testified that substance appeared to be cocaine and was typically packaged, and that substance was secreted in complex electronic "hide" in vehicle); Com. *v. Johnson*, 461 Mass 1012, 965 NE2d 176 (2012) (only evidence substance was cocaine was certificate, expert never gave his opinion that it was cocaine); *Com. v. Billings*, 461 Mass 362, 960 NE2d 900 (2012) (admission of certificate was not harmless where officer claimed no expertise in narcotics identification and result of field test was not in evidence); *Com. v. King*, 461 Mass 354, 960 NE2d 894 (2012) (evidence did not show officer was an expert with respect to cocaine and provided no objective criteria for his conclusion substance was "rock," no specific information about nature of field test was provided); *Com. v. Nelson*, 460 Mass 564, 953 NE2d 164 (2011) (that pills were in prescription bottle with defendant's name on it, labeled with name of the drug in question, did not render admission of certificate harmless error; admission of certificate identifying marijuana was not harmless error where officers were not asked directly to identify the substance based on their experience); *Com. v. Fernandez*, 458 Mass 137, 152, 934 NE2d 810, 822 (2010) (admission of certificate was not harmless where field tests were admitted for limited purpose of providing only incremental or cumulative evidence); *Com. v. Rodriguez*, 456 Mass 578, 591, 925 NE2d 21, 32 (2010) (no independent evidence, no field test); *Com. v. Fluellen*, 456 Mass 517, 526, 924 NE2d 713, 721 (2010) ("certificates crystallized the Commonwealth's otherwise entirely circumstantial case," there was no other evidence concerning identity of the substance, thus admission was not harmless, despite fact that "the defense was constructed around an admission that the substance was cocaine, and the character of the substance was not a contested issue at trial"); *Com. v. Charles*, 456 Mass 378, 923 NE2d 519 (2010) (prosecution's evidence was not sufficient to demonstrate harmless error, despite fact that defense counsel at trial referred to substances as "drugs," "marijuana," and "crack cocaine,"—defendant did not stipulate to the composition of the substances); *Com. v. Vasquez*, 456 Mass 350, 363-368, 923 NE2d 524, 535-539 (2010) (none of testifying officers had any experience with chemical analysis, there was no field test, officer familiar with crack cocaine testified he relied on lab test; presence of weapons, cellular telephones, and cash is evidence of distribution, but not that substance is a particular drug); *Com. v. Marte*, 84 Mass App 136, 993 NE2d 1201 (2013) (admission of certificate not harmless for trafficking in excess of 200 grams where there was no field test and little evidence bearing on composition of substance seized); *Com. v. Davis*, 83 Mass App 484, 985 NE2d 1216 (2013) (CI tasting substance, officer's testimony concerning appearance and packaging of substance, presence of large amount of cash, and ledger of defendant were not sufficient to establish harmless error); *Com. v. Mendes*, 78 Mass App 474, 78 Mass App 940 (2010) (in assessing whether erroneous admission of certificate was harmless, court need not consider testimony from defense case that both defendants used drugs—court could not determine whether defendants' testimony was a response to admission of certificates and hence tainted by the error), *rev. granted*, 459 Mass 1104, 942 NE2d 968 (2011); *Com. v. Morales*, 76 Mass App 663, 925 NE2d 551 (2010) (unlikely that form of packaging is proof that substance is a particular drug); *Com. v. Melendez-Diaz*, 76 Mass App 229, 921 NE2d 108 (2010) (on remand from Supreme Court, Appeals Court concludes officers' testimony that substance looked like cocaine plus circumstantial evidence of distribution did not render error in admitting drug certificates harmless); *Com. v. DePina*, 75 Mass App 842, 852, 917 NE2d 781, 790 (2009) (although officer identified substance

The appeals court has held that defense counsel may waive a defendant's Confrontation Clause right to confront the analyst and permit the prosecution to introduce a drug analysis certificate into evidence. The court held that no colloquy between the judge and the defendant is required "so long as the waiver occurs in the presence of the defendant, the defendant does not object, and the waiver objectively appears to further legitimate trial strategy."[43]

GL 46, § 19, provides for the admissibility of birth, marriage, and death records.[44] The troublesome clause in § 19—as in § 79, dealing with hospital records—is that forbidding the use in evidence of anything in a record of death "which has reference to the question of liability for causing the death."[45] Proposed Mass R Evid 803(9) (Records of vital statistics) incorporates this statutory language.[46] Fed R Evid 803(9) provides a similar exception but without the limitation as to statements relating to cause of death.

In *Trump v. Burdick*,[47] an action against a taxi driver for the death of a passenger, the clause was held not to bar that part of the death certificate that said, inter alia, "Cause of death . . . Accident, 9/1/44; Taxi Cab; Injuries to Side of Head, Ear and Arm." In *Wadsworth v. Boston Gas Co.*,[48] the Court stated that where the hospital records (GL 233, § 79) and the death certificate (GL 49, § 19) recited that the injury or death came about from the inhalation of illuminating gas, this alone did not impute fault. Also, in finding no error, the Court relied on the rule stated in *Trump*, supra, that where the words have reference to the injuries of the deceased they are admissible even though incidentally they may have some bearing on liability. However, it has been stated

---

as cocaine, which he had seen "a thousand times," judge did not make required finding that officer's experience permitted him to offer opinion that substance was cocaine; despite considerable circumstantial evidence, court cannot conclude certificates had only a slight effect on jury).

[43] *Com. v. Myers*, 82 Mass App 172, 183, 971 NE2d 815, 823 (2012).

[44] See *Com. v. Lykus*, 406 Mass 135, 144, 546 NE2d 159, 165 (1989) (death certificate is prima facie evidence of time of death); *Com. v. Garabedian*, 399 Mass 304, 308, 503 NE2d 1290, 1293 (1987) (death certificate is prima facie evidence of identity of deceased).

[45] See *Com. v. Lannon*, 364 Mass 480, 306 NE2d 248 (1974), for a discussion of the history of this insertion in the statute.

[46] See also Proposed Mass R Evid 803(12) and Fed R Evid 803(12).

[47] *Trump v. Burdick*, 322 Mass 253, 76 NE2d 768 (1948).

[48] *Wadsworth v. Boston Gas Co.*, 352 Mass 86, 223 NE2d 807 (1967).

that the better and safer course is to delete from the death certificate admitted in a criminal trial such words as "homicide," "suicide," or "accident."[49]

Other statutes may allow official statements in evidence.[50] For example, GL 79, § 35, allows evidence of assessed valuation of the real estate taken by eminent domain to be admitted. Admission of these official statements of value as evidence of value was not permissible at common law.[51] The use of such evidence is wholly dependent on the statute.[52] Similarly, GL 90, § 30, provides that certified copies of records of the Registry of Motor Vehicles pertaining to applications, certificates, and licenses issued may be admissible to prove the facts contained therein.[53] Again, this hearsay exception is wholly statutory and will not be extended beyond the terms of the statute.[54]

GL 123A, § 14(c), authorizes the admissibility of a variety of public records in evidence at a trial on whether one is a sexually dangerous person.[55] In *Com. v. Markvart*,[56] the Court held that the phrase "police reports relating to such person's prior sexual offenses" did not authorize the admission of police reports on charges that had not led to a conviction. In *Com. v. Given*,[57] the Court distinguished *Markvart* and held that a reference in a police report to a sexual assault on which the

---

[49] *Com. v. Griffin*, 8 Mass App 276, 279-280, 392 NE2d 1220, 1223 (1979) (judge properly excluded word "accident" from autopsy report offered by defendant); *Com. v. Ellis*, 373 Mass 1, 364 NE2d 808 (1977); *Com. v. Lannon*, supra.

[50] MGL c. 90, 24 (4) authorized the introduction in evidence of certain public records to prove prior convictions for driving under the influence. The statute did not foreclose the proof of such convictions by other means, however. *Com. v. Bowden*, 447 Mass 593, 855 NE2d 758 (2007). In 2005, the statute was amended to provide explicitly that an expanded list of records might be used to prove the prior convictions. For discussion of the provisions of the amendment, see *Com. v. Maloney*, 447 Mass 577, 855 NE2d 765 (2006).

[51] *Bennett v. Brookline Redevelopment Authority*, 342 Mass 418, 173 NE2d 815 (1961).

[52] *Wenton v. Com.*, 335 Mass 78, 138 NE2d 609 (1956).

[53] *Com. v. Blake*, 52 Mass App 526, 755 NE2d 290 (2001).

[54] *Carney v. Carrier*, 333 Mass 382, 130 NE2d 879 (1955) (notations with Registry stamp on letter of inquiry as to ownership of automobile did not come within exception).

[55] But see *Com v. Hunt*, 462 Mass 807, 821, 971 NE2d 768, 780 (2012) (unsubstantiated rumors defendant mentioned in his own correspondence with DOC were not admissible in sexually dangerous person trial under G.L. c. 123A, § 14(c), because prisoner's own correspondence did not constitute an "incident report" and there was no evidence there had in fact been an incident).

[56] *Com. v. Markvart*, 437 Mass 331, 771 NE2d 778 (2002).

[57] *Com. v. Given*, 441 Mass 741, 808 NE2d 788 (2004).

defendant had been neither charged nor convicted was admissible under § 14(c) as part of a report of a prior sexual offense to which the person had pleaded guilty.[58]

In the case of *In re McHoul*,[59] the Court held that multiple hearsay is admissible if contained in reports that are admissible either in commitment proceedings under § 14(c) or proceedings for release under §§ 6A and 9. *McHoul*, however, did not overrule *Markvart's* holding that multiple hearsay in the reports of the qualified examiners (which are admissible under c. 123A §§ 9 and 14) must be redacted unless it is independently admissible. That rule is based on the fact that the qualified examiners' reports function as the equivalent of an expert witness's direct testimony, and such testimony cannot be used as a vehicle for the admission of inadmissible evidence.[60]

In *Given*, the Supreme Judicial Court also held that the Confrontation Clause of the Sixth Amendment to the United States Constitution and of Article 12 of the Massachusetts Declaration of Rights does not apply to hearsay admitted under Section 14(c) because the commitment proceedings in which it applies are civil rather than criminal. The Court held that admission was subject to satisfaction of the principles of due process, but that due process required no more than that the evidence be "reliable."[61] The Court noted the recent rejection by the United States Supreme Court of the reliability standard in favor of a requirement of cross-examination in Confrontation Clause determinations in *Crawford v. Washington*,[62] but concluded that "[U]nlike the Confrontation Clause, due process demands that evidence be reliable in substance, not that its reliability be evaluated in 'a particular manner.' " *Id.*

Section 14(c) permits the admission of the report itself over a hearsay objection, but it does not render admissible multiple hearsay contained within the report.[63]

[58] See *Com. v. Starkus*, 69 Mass App 326, 867 NE2d 811 (2007) (interpreting *Given* to justify admission of police report concerning uncharged alleged sexual assault of victims other than those in the crime charged, relevant to show a pattern of conduct).

[59] *In re McHoul*, 445 Mass 143, 833 NE2d 1146 (2005).

[60] *McHoul*, 445 Mass at 148, n.4.

[61] 441 Mass at 746-747, 808 NE2d at 794.

[62] *Crawford v. Washington*, 124 S Ct 1354 (2004).

[63] *Com. v. Boyer*, 58 Mass App 662, 792 NE2d 677 (2003) (hearsay report by unidentified declarant of statement by defendant was inadmissible).

§ 8.12.3 *Authentication*

Generally, proof of official records is made by a certified copy of the original record, as provided in GL 233, § 76. The method of authenticating official written statements is almost always a matter of some precision. Statutes are specific in their requirements, and these requirements—involving attestations, certificates, affidavits, and seals—are rigidly insisted upon. For the requirements in Massachusetts courts, see GL 233, §§ 69, 75-77, 79, 79A.[64] It should be noted that the proper authentication of a public record does not compel the conclusion that its contents are admissible to prove the truth of assertions made therein, if it does not otherwise come within this exception to the hearsay rule.[65] Except where provided to the contrary by statute, there is no authority in a public officer to provide anything other than the entire official statement.[66]

Apart from the statutory modes of documentary proof, the authenticity of an official written statement may be proved by the testimony of a person with personal knowledge of the recorded statement.[67] For further discussion see Chapter 9.

A public officer usually has no authority to give a certificate that a record does not exist. But such authority is expressly given in Mass R Civ P 44(b) and Mass R Crim P 40(b). Any person who has searched the records can testify that he has so searched and has found no record.[68]

Proposed Mass R Evid 803(10) creates a hearsay exception, even though the declarant is available as a witness, for:

> **(10) Absence of public record or entry**. To prove the absence of a record, report, statement, or data compilation, in any form, or the nonoccurrence or nonexistence of a matter of which a record, report, statement, or data compilation, in any form, was regularly made and preserved by a public office or agency, evidence in the form of a certification in

---

[64] Cf. Mass R Civ P 44; Mass R Crim P 39, 40. See *Com. v. Deramo*, 436 Mass 40, 45, 762 NE2d 815, 819 (2002) (error to admit photocopy of records without original attestation) (Text cited); *Com. v. Key*, 381 Mass 19, 31, 407 NE2d 327, 335-336 (1980) (interpreting the requirements of GL 233, § 69).

[65] *Rice v. James Hanrahan & Sons*, 20 Mass App 701, 482 NE2d 833 (1985).

[66] *Wayland v. Ware*, 109 Mass 248, 250 (1872).

[67] *Kaufman v. Kaitz*, 325 Mass 149, 89 NE2d 505 (1949).

[68] *Blair's Foodland, Inc. v. Shuman's Foodland*, 311 Mass 172, 175, 40 NE2d 303, 306 (1942).

> accordance with Rule 902, or testimony, that diligent search failed to disclose the record, report, statement, or data compilation, or entry.

Fed R Evid 803(10) is identical and comparable provisions are found in Fed R Civ P 44(b) and Fed R Crim P 27.

§ 8.13 Commercial Lists

Proposed Mass R Evid 803(17) creates a hearsay exception for:

> **(17) Market reports, commercial publications.** Market quotations, tabulations, lists, directories, or other published compilations, generally used and relied upon by the public or by persons in particular occupations.

Fed R Evid 803(17) is identical.

Under current Massachusetts law, a similar hearsay exception is provided by statute. GL 233, § 79B, provides:

> Statements of facts of general interest to persons engaged in an occupation contained in a list, register, periodical, book or other compilation, issued to the public, shall, in the discretion of the court, if the court finds that the compilation is published for the use of persons engaged in that occupation and commonly is used and relied upon by them, be admissible in civil cases as evidence of the truth of any fact so stated.[1]

The statute has been applied in a variety of contexts.[2] Unlike this statute, Rule 803(17) would apply in criminal, as well as civil, cases.

---

§ 8.13 [1] The statute is discussed in *Torre v. Harris-Seybold Co.*, 9 Mass App 660, 404 NE2d 96 (1980), and *Mazzaro v. Paull*, 372 Mass 645, 363 NE2d 509 (1977).

[2] *Jordan Marsh Co. v. Board of Assessors of Malden*, 359 Mass 106, 267 NE2d 912 (1971) (publication entitled "Operating Results of Department and Specialty Stores" held properly admitted by Appellate Tax Board in abatement proceeding); *Petition of Boat Demand, Inc.*, 160 F Supp 833, 834 (D Mass 1958) (pamphlet entitled "Fire Protection Standards for Motor Craft" issued by the National Fire Protection Association); *Boston Consolidated Gas Co. v. Dep't of Public Utilities*, 327 Mass 103, 97 NE2d 521 (1951) (*Handy's Indices*, a book useful in the determination of reproduction cost in rate-making). Market quotations are also admissible under GL 106, § 2-724. But see *Fall River Savings Bank v. Callahan*, 18 Mass App 76, 83, 463 NE2d 555, 561 (1984) (title standards adopted and published by the Massachusetts Conveyancers' Association were expressions of professional opinion, not statements of fact, and hence were improperly admitted under § 79B).

In *Reddington v. Clayman,*[3] the plaintiff unsuccessfully offered medical treatises in evidence under GL 233, § 79C (see § 8.14). To prove their authoritativeness, he offered a directory of medical specialists and an English edition of *Who's Who* but did not offer these latter texts under § 79B. The Court implied, but did not decide, that these latter texts might be admissible under this section.[4] Subsequently, the Supreme Judicial Court has emphasized that in order to use a *Who's Who* under § 79B to qualify a treatise under § 79C, the offering party must offer evidence to persuade the trial judge that the *Who's Who* is, as required by the statute: (1) issued to the public; (2) published for persons engaged in the applicable occupation; and (3) commonly used and relied on by such persons.[5] On the requisite preliminary findings for admission under § 79B, see also *Ricciutti v. Sylvania Electric Products, Inc.*,[6] and *Torre v. Harris-Seybold Co.*, supra.

§ 8.14 Learned Treatises

In *Com. v. Sneed,*[1] the Supreme Judicial Court adopted Proposed Mass R Evid 803(18), establishing a new exception[2] for learned treatises, rendering admissible:

> To the extent called to the attention of an expert witness upon cross-examination, statements contained in published treatises, periodicals, or pamphlets on a subject of history, medicine, or other science or art, established as a reliable authority by the testimony or admission of the witness or by other expert testimony or by judicial notice. If admitted, the statements may be read into evidence but may not be received as exhibits.

---

[3] *Reddington v. Clayman*, 334 Mass 244, 134 NE2d 920 (1956).

[4] See also *Ramsland v. Shaw*, 341 Mass 56, 64, 166 NE2d 894, 900 (1960).

[5] *Mazzaro v. Paull*, 372 Mass 645, 363 NE2d 509 (1977) (also exhorting trial judges to consider the remedial purpose of § 79C and not to frustrate legitimate attempts to qualify authoritative treatises by use of § 79B).

[6] *Ricciutti v. Sylvania Electric Products, Inc.*, 343 Mass 347, 350-351, 178 NE2d 857, 860 (1961).

§ 8.14 [1] *Com. v. Sneed*, 413 Mass 387, 394-397, 597 NE2d 1346, 1350-1351 (1992). Cf. *Evans v. Lorillard Tobacco Co.*, 465 Mass 411, 990 NE2d 997 (2013) (error to allow plaintiff's counsel to confront defense expert with federal judge's findings in published opinion by characterizing them as conclusions of an "expert," judicial opinion may not be treated as a published treatise under Proposed Mass R Evid 803 (18)).

[2] Prior to *Sneed*, the only permitted use of treatises was pursuant to GL 233, § 79C.

Fed R Evid 803(18) is the same as the proposed Massachusetts rule except that it also provides that such a treatise is admissible to the extent relied on by the expert in direct examination. Proposed Mass R Evid 803(18) as adopted by the Court in *Sneed* does not allow the admission of a learned treatise in evidence as part of a party's case in chief since its applicability is related to cross-examination only.[3]

In *Com. v. Sneed*, the Court offered the following guidance for the use of treatises:

> Proposed Rule 803(18) requires that an opponent of the expert witness bring to the witness's attention a specific statement in a treatise that has been established, to the judge's satisfaction, as reliable authority. The witness should be given a fair opportunity to assess the statement in context and to comment on it, either during cross-examination or on redirect examination. The judge, of course, will have to determine the relevance and materiality of the statement and should consider carefully any claimed unfairness or confusion that admission of the statement may create.

The Court further noted: "We can imagine a situation in which, in fairness, portions of a learned treatise not called to the attention of a witness during cross-examination should be admitted on request of the expert's proponent in order to explain, limit, or contradict a statement ruled admissible under rule 803(18)."[4]

The trial judge must determine whether the proposed treatise is a reliable authority. The Supreme Judicial Court has explained:

> With regard to a "treatise," we have held that "the rule contemplates that an authored treatise, and not the statements contained therein," must be established as reliable. As to a periodical or journal, however, "[i]n these days of quantified research, and pressure to publish, an article does not reach the dignity of a 'reliable authority' merely because some editor, even a most reputable one, sees fit to circulate it." Accordingly, a statement within "an article in a journal or periodical would be

---

[3] See *Kace v. Liang*, 472 Mass 630, 645, 36 NE3d 1215, 1227 (2015) (improper for plaintiff to use treatise on redirect examination of defendant doctor, who was not testifying as an expert); *Com. v. Johnson*, 59 Mass App 164, 794 NE2d 1214 (2003); *Com. v. Reese*, 438 Mass 519, 781 NE2d 1225 (2003); *Brusard v. O'Toole*, 429 Mass 597, 710 NE2d 588 (1999). The Appeals Court has held that once a statement from a treatise has been admitted during cross-examination of the opponent's expert, it may be used for all substantive purposes, including during a subsequent examination of the proponent's expert and in final argument. *Federico v. Ford Motor Co.*, 67 Mass App 454, 460, 854 NE2d 448, 454 (2006).

[4] *Com. v. Sneed*, supra, 413 Mass at 396 n.8, 597 NE2d at 1351 n.8.

admissible . . . if an opponent of the expert witness establishes that the author of the . . . article is 'a reliable authority.'"[5]

The only other circumstances in which the contents of learned treatises are admissible in evidence to prove the truth of their assertions is as provided in GL 233, § 79C. That statute is discussed in §§ 7.7.2 and 8.13.

§ 8.15 Reputation

Reputation evidence may or may not be hearsay. It is hearsay if offered for a purpose that requires a belief that the reputation truthfully reflects the reputed facts; otherwise, it is not. Evidence of the plaintiff's bad reputation, for example, is not hearsay when offered by the defendant to mitigate damages in a defamation case.[1] Similarly, in a homicide case, evidence of the decedent's reputation for quarrelsomeness is not hearsay when offered to prove that the defendant acted in self-defense in reasonable fear of great bodily harm.[2] In such cases, it is the reputation itself, not the truth of the reputation, that is in issue. See § 4.4.4.

Hearsay use of reputation evidence is most commonly encountered in cases involving a person's pedigree or character. An infrequent instance of hearsay use of reputation evidence involves the establishment of a public or general right—e.g., the ownership or location of boundaries of public lands.[3]

§ 8.15.1 Family History

Proposed Mass R Evid 803(19) creates a hearsay exception for:

(19) Reputation concerning personal or family history. Reputation among members of his family by blood, adoption, or marriage, or

---

[5] *Kace v. Liang*, 472 Mass 630, 643, 36 NE3d 1215, 1226 (2015) (Internet web pages from Johns Hopkins and Mayo Clinic did not qualify as reliable authorities because they did not reference particular authors).

§ 8.15 [1] See, e.g., *Clark v. Brown*, 116 Mass 504 (1875).

[2] See, e.g., *Com. v. Dilone*, 385 Mass 281, 285-286, 431 NE2d 576, 579 (1982); *Com. v. Gibson*, 368 Mass 518, 333 NE2d 400 (1975); *Com. v. Edmonds*, 365 Mass 496, 313 NE2d 429 (1974).

[3] See *Inhabitants of Enfield v. Woods*, 212 Mass 547, 99 NE 331 (1912). Cf. Proposed Mass R Evid 803(20) and Fed R Evid 803(20) (reflecting this exception but extending it to include reputation evidence of boundaries of private lands).

among his associates, or in the community, concerning a person's birth, adoption, marriage, divorce, death, legitimacy, relationship by blood, adoption, or marriage, ancestry, or other similar fact of his personal or family history.

Fed R. 803(19) is identical.[4] Rule 803(19) states the family reputation exception more broadly than the common-law rule. There is no requirement in the Rule concerning "unavailability" and no requirement that a writing offered to establish reputation be ante litem motam.

Under current Massachusetts law, family reputation, such as appears in the family Bible and in inscriptions on tombstones, may be admissible to prove the truth of the matters reputed.[5] The matters that can be proved in this way are limited to birth, death, marriage, and the relationships between persons. And, contrary to the rule in some jurisdictions, the evidence can be used in cases other than "pedigree cases"; it can be used in any action in which reputed family fact is relevant.[6] To be admissible under this exception, the writing must have been created ante litem motam and be of such nature that any errors would have been corrected by members of the family. There is some question as to the admissibility of family reputation evidence if persons with personal knowledge of the disputed fact are available as witnesses. Any member of the family may testify to reputation within a family as to births, marriages, and deaths of members of the family.[7]

§ 8.15.2 Character

Proposed Mass R Evid 803(21) creates a hearsay exception for:

(21) Reputation as to character. Reputation of a person's character among his associates or in the community.

---

[4] Other provisions of the Proposed Mass Rules of Evidence and the Federal Rules of Evidence relating to the admissibility of evidence of family history and relationships are Rule 803(11) (records of religious organizations), Rule 803(12) (marriage, baptismal, and similar certificates), Rule 803(13) (family records), Rule 803(16) (statements in ancient documents), and Rule 803(23) (judgments as to matters of personal, family, or general history or as to boundaries). See also Rule 803(19) (public records of vital statistics).

[5] *North Brookfield v. Warren*, 82 Mass (16 Gray) 171 (1860).

[6] *Id.*

[7] *Butrick v. Tilton*, 155 Mass 461, 29 NE 1088 (1892).

The use of reputation evidence to prove character is discussed at § 4.4.4 (character as evidence of an act) and § 6.16 (character to impeach). See also Proposed Mass R Evid 404(a), 405(a), 608(a), and the parallel federal rules.

§ 8.16 Judgments in Criminal Cases

An exception to the hearsay rule for judgments in criminal cases is provided for by Proposed Mass R Evid 803(22), which would allow:

> Evidence of a final judgment, entered after a trial or upon a plea of guilty (but not upon a plea of nolo contendere), adjudging a person guilty of a crime punishable by death or confinement in excess of one year, to prove any fact essential to sustain the judgment, but not including, when offered by the Commonwealth in a criminal prosecution for purposes other than impeachment, judgments against persons other than the accused. The pendency of an appeal may be shown but does not affect admissibility.

Fed R of Evid 803(22) is essentially the same.

This hearsay exception was adopted by the Supreme Judicial Court in *Flood v. Southland Corp.*[1] As the Rule itself makes clear, a conviction based on a plea by one party cannot be used in evidence by the Commonwealth against another, other than to impeach the convicted person if he or she appears as a witness.[2] In *Com. v. Santiago*,[3] the Appeals Court relied on *Com. v. Tilley*,[4] and an earlier decision in the case, *Com. v. Santiago*,[5] to hold that a criminal defendant may not introduce a guilty plea of another from a case in which the defendant was not a party. The decision is based primarily on a relevance argument, and does not discuss the hearsay exception recognized in *Flood v. Southland Corp.*, supra. The admissibility of evidence under Rule 803(22) would not depend on whether the person convicted is a party to the case in which the evidence is offered.

---

§ 8.16 [1] *Flood v. Southland Corp.*, 416 Mass 62, 70, 616 NE2d 1068 (1993).

[2] *Com. v. Powell*, 40 Mass App 430, 665 NE2d 99 (1996).

[3] *Com. v. Santiago*, 50 Mass App 762, 741 NE2d 465 (2001).

[4] *Com. v. Tilley*, 327 Mass 540, 99 NE2d 749 (1951).

[5] *Com. v. Santiago*, 425 Mass 491, 681 NE2d 1205 (1997).

D. EXCEPTIONS REQUIRING THAT THE DECLARANT BE UNAVAILABLE

The hearsay exceptions in this section may only be used when live testimony from the declarant is not available at the proceeding.

§ 8.17 Definition of Unavailability

Proposed Mass R Evid 804(a) provides:

> **(a) Definition of unavailability**. "Unavailability as a witness" includes situations in which the declarant—
>
> (1) is exempted by ruling of the court on the ground of privilege from testifying concerning the subject matter of his statement; or
>
> (2) persists in refusing to testify concerning the subject matter of his statement despite an order of the court to do so; or
>
> (3) testifies to a lack of memory of the subject matter of his statement; or
>
> (4) is unable to be present or to testify at the hearing because of death or then existing physical or mental illness or infirmity; or
>
> (5) is absent from the hearing and the proponent of his statement has been unable to procure his attendance by process or other reasonable means.
>
> A declarant is not unavailable as a witness if his exemption, refusal, claim of lack of memory, inability, or absence is due to the procurement or wrongdoing of the proponent of his statement for the purpose of preventing the witness from attending or testifying.

Fed R Evid 804(a) is identical except for section (5).[1] The Rule takes a broad view of what constitutes unavailability and goes, beyond the case law.

---

§ 8.17 [1] Section (5) of the federal rule contains an additional clause "(or in the case of a hearsay exception under subdivision (b)(2), (3) or (4), his attendance or testimony)." The absence of this clause in the Proposed Mass Rule means that as to statements offered as declarations against interest under Proposed Mass R Evid 804(b)(3), statements of belief of impending death under 804(b)(2), and statements of personal or family history under 804(b)(4), no attempt to procure testimony by deposition or interrogatories is required by the proposed Massachusetts rule before the declarant is deemed "unavailable."

Current Massachusetts law provides that the "unavailability" of a witness may be established by a showing of death,[2] illness,[3] or an inability to locate the witness after due and diligent search.[4] However, the mere absence of the witness from the jurisdiction without a showing that he cannot be found or that a deposition cannot be taken is an insufficient showing of unavailability.[5] The issue is not the physical presence of a witness, but the availability of her testimony. Therefore, a valid claim of privilege by a witness makes her "unavailable."[6] A criminal defendant, however, may not offer his own prior grand jury testimony by claiming he is unavailable at trial by asserting his privilege against self-incrimination.[7]

The Supreme Judicial Court discussed in detail the burden on the Commonwealth to establish unavailability due to illness in a criminal case in *Com. v. Housewright*.[8] The prosecution must provide sufficiently detailed up-to-date information that permits the judge to make an independent evaluation of the risk to the witness of testifying in court. A conclusory statement by the doctor that the risk is unacceptable is insufficient. The judge may seek additional information beyond that provided in a letter from a doctor, such as a supplemental letter or affidavit, telephoning the doctor, a deposition of the doctor, or a court

---

[2] *Com. v. Mustone*, 353 Mass 490, 233 NE2d 1 (1968).

[3] *Com. v. Roberio*, 440 Mass 245, 797 NE2d 364 (2003); *Com. v. Dorsica*, 88 Mass App 776, 42 NE3d 1184 (2015) (mere fact that witness had gone into labor four days previously did not establish unavailability due to illness or infirmity).

[4] *Com. v. Charles*, 428 Mass 672, 678, 704 NE2d 1137, 1143 (1999) (declarant was a fugitive from prosecution as a co-defendant in the same case).

[5] *Ibanez v. Winston*, 222 Mass 129, 109 NE 814 (1915); *Com. v. David*, 82 Mass App 52, 970 NE2d 334 (2012) (defendant's evidence that another person had admitted that drugs found in defendant's apartment belonged to her was inadmissible as a declaration against interest, because declarant was not called as a witness and did not invoke Fifth Amendment privilege and defendant made no showing he was unable to procure her presence, thus unavailability was not shown); *Ruml v. Ruml*, 50 Mass App 500, 508, 738 NE2d 1131, 1139 (2000) (husband's self-imposed exile from jurisdiction during divorce trial did not establish unavailability for his introduction of transcripts of his testimony from contempt hearing).

[6] *Com. v. DiPietro*, 373 Mass 369, 367 NE2d 811 (1977) (wife's claim of statutory privilege under GL 233, § 20); *Com. v. Galloway*, 404 Mass 204, 208, 534 NE2d 778 (1989) (claim of privilege against self-incrimination). Cf. *Com. v. Charles*, supra (assumed that fugitive witness would exercise Fifth Amendment privilege if located because he would be a co-defendant in case on trial).

[7] *Com. v. Labelle*, 67 Mass App 698, 856 NE2d 876 (2006).

[8] *Com. v. Housewright*, 470 Mass 665, 25 NE3d 273 (2015) (Commonwealth did not make good faith effort to produce witness where it waited until day of trial to inform Court and defendant that witness was ill; judge's reliance on doctor's letter without detail regarding witness's medical condition or consideration of whether witness could be deposed violated defendant's Confrontation Clause rights).

hearing. The judge should consider the probability of an adverse health consequence, its severity, the importance of the testimony, and the extent to which live testimony would likely differ from the prior recorded testimony. Live testimony is more likely to differ if the previous testimony was recorded at a pretrial hearing, rather than an earlier trial of the same case. If testimony presents an unacceptable risk, the judge should consider whether a continuance would reduce the risk and would otherwise serve the interests of justice. The judge should also consider other means of obtaining live testimony, such as a deposition. The Commonwealth has an obligation to inform the court promptly when it learns of a witness's illness, so that the various necessary steps may be taken.

The Massachusetts courts have adopted Rule 804(a)(5). Thus, a witness will be found to be unavailable if the witness "is absent from the hearing and the proponent of a statement has been unable to procure the declarant's attendance . . . by process or other reasonable means."[9] The Supreme Judicial Court has not yet adopted Rule 804(a)(2), providing that a witness is unavailable if he or she "persists in refusing to testify concerning the subject matter of his [or her] statement despite an order of the court to do so."[10]

§ 8.18 Former Testimony

Proposed Mass R Evid 804(b)(1) provides that the following is not excluded by the hearsay rule if the declarant is unavailable as a witness:

> **(1) Former testimony**. Testimony given as a witness at another hearing of the same or a different proceeding, or in a deposition taken in compliance with law in the course of the same or another proceeding, if the party against whom the testimony is now offered, or in a civil action or proceeding, a predecessor in interest, had an opportunity and similar motive to develop the testimony by direct, cross, or redirect examination.

---

[9] *Com. v. Charles*, 428 Mass 672, 678, 704 NE2d 1137 (1999); *Com. v. Pittman*, 60 Mass App 161, 168, 800 NE2d 322, 328 (2003) (issue is not whether witness made reasonable efforts to be present but rather whether the party made reasonable efforts to procure her attendance).

[10] *Com. v. Fisher*, 433 Mass 340, 355, 742 NE2d 61, 73 (2001).

Fed R Evid 804(b)(1) is identical. The Rule is consistent with current Massachusetts law.[1]

Prior testimony of a presently unavailable witness is admissible if it was given under oath in a proceeding where the issues were substantially the same as in the current proceeding and the party against whom it is offered had an opportunity and a similar motive to cross-examine the witness.[2] The prior testimony rule has been applied to testimony given in a previous trial between the same parties;[3] testimony from a probable cause hearing;[4] testimony from the probable cause portion of a juvenile transfer proceeding;[5] testimony from a motion to suppress,[6] and testimony from a former civil trial where the defendant in a later criminal proceeding had been an adverse party to the witness.[7] Provided that the requirements of the rule are met, there is no principled reason why testimony from other types of proceedings would not be similarly admissible.

---

§ 8.18 [1] Insofar as previous testimony contains prior inconsistent statements, Proposed Mass R Evid 801(d)(1) and Fed R Evid 801(d)(1) would go further than the common law and allow prior inconsistent statements given under oath in a trial, hearing, proceeding, or deposition to be admitted for their truth, where the declarant testifies at trial and is subject to cross-examination concerning his former statements. See § 6.13.2 (prior inconsistent statements).

[2] *Com v. Trigones*, 397 Mass 633, 638, 492 NE2d 1146, 1149-1150 (1986); *Com. v. Hurley*, 455 Mass 53, 913 NE2d 850 (2009) (in some circumstances motive to cross-examine at detention hearing may differ from motive at trial, thus there is no per se rule that detention hearing testimony of unavailable witness is always admissible at trial; in this case motive was sufficiently similar); *Com. v. Arrington*, 455 Mass 437, 917 NE2d 734 (2009) (pretrial detention hearing testimony of complainant was not reliable because she was heavily medicated; although defendant had similar motive to cross-examine complainant at pretrial detention hearing, he lacked reasonable opportunity to do so where defense counsel was legitimately concerned that her medical condition substantially compromised her ability to respond to questions) (Text cited); *Com. v. Johnson*, 435 Mass 113, 135, 754 NE2d 685, 702 (2001) (finding cross-examination at voir dire directed to similar issue as raised at trial—whether defendant made certain statements attributed to him); *Martin v. Roy*, 54 Mass App 642, 767 NE2d 603 (2002) (holding inadmissible testimony from deposition in another action where instant party against whom it was offered had not been a party); *Kirby v. Morales*, 50 Mass App 786, 741 NE2d 855 (2001) (deposition testimony not admissible against defendant not a party at time of deposition, with no notice of deposition).

[3] *Com. v. Clark*, 363 Mass 467, 470, 295 NE2d 163, 165-166 (1973); *Com. v. Gallo*, 275 Mass 320, 175 NE2d 718 (1931).

[4] *Com. v. Salim*, 399 Mass 227, 503 NE2d 1267 (1987); *Com. v. Bohannon*, 385 Mass 733, 434 NE2d 163 (1982).

[5] *Com. v. Ortiz*, 393 Mass 523, 471 NE2d 1321 (1984).

[6] *Com. v. Trigones*, 397 Mass 633, 492 NE2d 1146 (1986).

[7] *Com. v. Canon*, 373 Mass 494, 368 NE2d 1181 (1977).

Deposition testimony is admissible under the rule, pursuant to Mass R Civ P 32(a)(3) and Mass R Crim P 35(g).[8] Where a videotaped deposition has been taken pursuant to Mass R Civ P 30(a), it is not necessary to establish the witness's unavailability to use the deposition at trial.[9] The Court further held in *Roche* that the admissibility of the deposition does not automatically quash a subpoena by the opposing party for the live testimony of the witness, because that would improperly restrict the opponent's right of cross-examination.

The Supreme Judicial Court has declined to adopt a general rule that would allow the admission against the Commonwealth of prior recorded grand jury testimony from a witness unavailable at trial.[10] The court noted that witnesses are usually handled differently at the grand jury than they would be at trial, and the Commonwealth may lack the opportunity (due to incomplete information at that stage of proceedings) and a similar motivation to develop the testimony as it would have at trial. The court suggested that it "is likely to be very difficult for defendants offering grand jury testimony to satisfy the 'opportunity and similar motive' test."[11] However, at a minimum, the defendant would have to establish that the government had a "similar motive" to develop the issues germane to the trial at the time of the grand jury testimony.[12] Grand jury testimony of unavailable witnesses may not be offered by the government against a criminal defendant, because he has had no opportunity to cross-examine or question the witness.[13]

---

[8] See *Shear v. Gabovitch*, 43 Mass App Ct 650, 666 n.17, 685 NE2d 1168, 1180 (1997) (error to refuse to admit deposition where witness was living in Florida, not amenable to Massachusetts process); *Caron v. General Motors Corp.*, 37 Mass App 744, 643 NE2d 471 (1994) (trial court properly excluded deposition testimony from out-of-state expert where proponent had not demonstrated he made a reasonable effort to secure expert's presence at trial, and opinions expressed during deposition were in response to objectionable questions and possibly speculative).

[9] *Roche v. MBTA*, 400 Mass 217, 508 NE2d 614 (1987).

[10] *Com. v. Clemente*, 452 Mass 295, 313, 893 NE2d 19, 37 (2008) (defendant did not make showing that Commonwealth had opportunity and similar motive to develop witness's testimony at grand jury). See *Com. v. Martinez*, 384 Mass 377, 381-385, 425 NE2d 300, 303-305 (1981); *Com. v. Meech*, 380 Mass 490, 403 NE2d 1174 (1980). A criminal defendant, however, may not offer his own prior grand jury testimony by claiming he is unavailable at trial by asserting his privilege against self-incrimination. *Com. v. Labelle*, 67 Mass App 698, 856 NE2d 876 (2006).

[11] *Com. v. Clemente*, 452 Mass at 315. 893 NE2d at 38.

[12] *Com. v. Clemente*, 452 Mass at 315, 893 NE2d at 38, citing *United States v. Omar*, 104 F3d 519, 523 (1st Cir 1997); *Com. v. Martinez*, supra; *Com. v. Meech*, supra. See *United States v. Salerno*, 505 US 317, 112 S Ct 2503 (1992) (admissibility of grand jury testimony against the government under Fed R Evid 804(b)(1) requires proof of similar motive; requirement may not be avoided to ensure "adversarial fairness").

[13] *Com. v. Meech*, supra, 380 Mass at 494, 403 NE2d at 1178.

Admissibility of prior testimony depends upon a reliable record or report of the former testimony. A stenographic transcript is the preferable way of establishing its content; the use of such a transcript is authorized under GL 233, § 80.[14] In the absence of such a transcript, a witness who can state the testimony with substantial accuracy may testify as to the testimony of the unavailable witness.[15]

In criminal cases, the use of former testimony from a witness unavailable at trial implicates the Confrontation Clause. Testimony given at earlier proceedings is "testimonial" evidence and squarely governed by the Confrontation Clause under *Crawford v. Washington*.[16] It is inadmissible unless the witness is unavailable and an opportunity for cross-examination was provided previously. For prior testimony to be admissible, it must have been given "in a proceeding addressed to substantially the same issues as in the current proceeding, with reasonable opportunity and similar motivation on the prior occasion for cross-examination of the declarant by the party against whom the testimony is now being offered."[17] Where cross-examination has been denied and the prior testimony admitted, a reversal of a conviction is required unless the error was harmless beyond a reasonable doubt. The prosecution bears the burden of proving that admission of the uncross-examined testimony was not a substantial factor in the jury's decision to convict.[18]

The Supreme Judicial Court has held that a meaningful opportunity to cross-examine is sufficient to admit previous testimony, even though no cross-examination was conducted.[19] A defendant may not be adequately prepared to cross-examine a witness against him when the matter is first reached at a preliminary hearing. However, the court may set a reasonable deadline by which cross-examination must be conducted or waived.[20] Where a defendant has cross-examined the

---

[14] See *Com. v. Mustone*, supra. See also Mass R Civ P 80; Fed R Civ P 80.

[15] *Com. v. Bohannon*, supra, 385 Mass at 746-747, 434 NE2d at 171-172 (Text cited); *Com. v. Di Pietro*, 373 Mass 369, 392-393, 367 NE2d 811, 825 (1977) (Text cited).

[16] *Crawford v. Washington*, 124 S Ct 1354 (2004).

[17] *Com. v. Trigones*, 397 Mass 633, 638, 492 NE2d 1146, 1149-1150 (1986).

[18] *Com. v. DiBenedetto*, 413 Mass 37, 605 NE2d 811 (1992).

[19] *Com. v. Tanso*, 411 Mass 640, 647, 583 NE2d 1247, 1252 (1992).

[20] *Com. v. Tanso*, supra (where defendant claimed inability to cross-examine at hearing, failure of court to set deadline or to rule that defendant had enjoyed a reasonable opportunity to cross-examine precluded later use of the testimony).

unavailable witness at the time the previous testimony was given, the issue becomes whether the examination permitted or conducted was constitutionally adequate.[21]

Where the prior reported testimony was involuntarily given, its use at trial would offend fundamental fairness, and it is not admissible.[22]

§ 8.19 Dying Declarations

Proposed Mass R Evid 804(b)(1) provides that the following is not excluded by the hearsay rule if the declarant is unavailable as a witness:

> **(2) Statement under belief of impending death.** In a prosecution for homicide or for unlawful procurement of an abortion or in a civil action or proceeding, a statement made by a declarant while believing that the declarant's death was imminent, concerning the cause or circumstances of what he believed to be his impending death.

---

[21] See, e.g., *Com. v. Housewright*, 470 Mass 665, 677, 25 NE3d 273 (2015) (Court acknowledged that motive to cross-examine at a detention hearing may be different than at trial, e.g., where cross-examiner did not challenge declarant's accuracy or credibility, but focused solely on challenging whether the defendant was dangerous); *Com. v. Sena*, 441 Mass at 833, 809 NE2d at 515 (that earlier cross-examination did not cover every detail and possible avenue of impeachment that counsel would later choose to pursue does not mean that defendant lacked requisite opportunity for cross-examination, nor does fact that subsequent trial involved additional evidence against defendant mean that opportunity for cross-examination at earlier trial was inadequate to satisfy the Confrontation Clause); *Com. v. Roberio*, 440 Mass 245, 250, 797 NE2d 364, 368 (2003) (cross-examination at prior trial was adequate, even though attorney in first trial had been found ineffective; use to which testimony was put did not relate to issue on which prior counsel was ineffective); *Com. v. DiBenedetto*, 413 Mass 37, 605 NE2d 811 (1992) (restricting cross-examination of witness to the area in which he had been promised immunity by the prosecution was a denial of right to cross-examine requiring reversal); *Com. v. Siegfriedt*, supra (cross-examination sufficient despite defendant's claim he only learned later of witness's real name and that he had overstated his employment status while testifying); *Com. v. Trigones*, supra (prior testimony sufficiently reliable, even though defendant did not adequately pursue opportunity to cross-examine on bias); *Com. v. Taylor*, 32 Mass App 570, 591 NE2d 1108 (1992) (cross-examination adequate, although improperly restricted by judge on one issue). If an adequate opportunity to cross-examine was available at the earlier hearing, the fact that the cross-examination produced evidence detrimental to the defendant does not render such testimony unreliable. *Com. v. Florek*, 48 Mass App 414, 418, 722 NE2d 20, 24 (2000) (defendant argued that he would have forgone some of the cross-examination if he had known Commonwealth would later drop a portion of the indictment; evidence was nonetheless admissible).

[22] *Com. v. Rosa*, 412 Mass 147, 161, 587 NE2d 767, 775 (1992) (remanding for determination of voluntariness of W's waiver of spousal privilege).

Fed R Evid 804(b)(2) is the same except that it does not include the phrase "or for unlawful procurement of an abortion," which was included in the Massachusetts version to conform to GL 233, § 64. Both versions of the Rule apply to civil matters as well as criminal matters.

Since the admissibility of a statement under Rule 804(b)(2) depends not on a showing of the death of the declarant but simply on a showing of the declarant's "unavailability"—as more broadly defined in Rule 804(a)—this exception is broader than the common-law dying declaration exception. Rule 804(b)(2) may be more restrictive than current Massachusetts law in that it appears to preclude statements relating to the death of one other than the declarant.

The current Massachusetts common-law hearsay exception for dying declarations provides that: (1) in a prosecution for homicide (2) committed upon declarant, (3) declarant's statement in regard to the manner in which he met his death is admissible (4) provided he believes at the time of the statement that he is to die immediately and (5) provided he does die within a very short time.[1] Each of these five elements is necessary. The trial judge must make the finding that the necessary elements are present in order to admit the evidence.[2] In *Com. v. Key*,[3] the Court modified the common-law rule that precluded the admissibility of a dying declaration relating to the death of one other than the declarant. The Court held that where multiple homicides result from one felonious act, the dying declaration of one victim should be admitted to prove the homicides of the other victims.

The declarant's apprehension of death may be inferred from circumstances, even if he has made no explicit statement on the matter.[4] Older cases required that the proponent show that "all hope of recovery [had] gone from the mind of the declarant," but the modern view is that it is sufficient to show that the declarant believed death was imminent and actually died within a short time.[5]

---

§ 8.19 [1] *Com. v. Vona*, 250 Mass 509, 146 NE 20 (1925).

[2] *Com. v. Green*, 420 Mass 771, 781, 652 NE2d 572, 579 (1995).

[3] *Com. v. Key*, 381 Mass 19, 407 NE2d 327 (1980).

[4] *Com. v. Moses*, 436 Mass 598, 602, 766 Mass 827, 830 (2002) (declarant had been shot four times, two bullets pierced his chest, one of which lodged in his spine—he asked EMT if he were going to die and she replied that "it didn't look too good" for him); *Com. v. Key*, supra, 381 Mass at 24, 407 NE2d at 332.

[5] *Com. v. Gonzalez*, 469 Mass 410, 14NE3d 282 (2014) (statement in ambulance identifying perpetrator by woman stabbed eight times with profuse bleeding and breathing difficulties, pale and distraught, pleading "Please, don't let me die," was dying declaration; court rejects stricter requirement of older cases requiring that "all hope of recovery has gone from the mind of the declarant"; requirement that victim die satisfies necessity requirement and requirement that declarant feared death was

Whether the elements of a dying declaration are established is initially a preliminary question of fact for the trial judge.[6] If the judge finds that the declaration is admissible, he must instruct the jury that it can reconsider the question of admissibility and may consider the declaration as probative evidence only if it finds the existence of the preliminary facts by a preponderance of the evidence.[7]

The Supreme Judicial Court has held that if a statement qualifies as a dying declaration it is not subject to the Confrontation Clause, whether it is testimonial or not. The rule is based on the fact that dying declarations were treated as an exception to the right of confrontation at common law.[8]

§ 8.20 Declarations of Deceased Persons

§ 8.20.1 GL 233, § 65

The statute provides:

> In any action or other civil judicial proceeding, a declaration of a deceased person shall not be inadmissible in evidence as hearsay or as private conversation between husband and wife, as the case may be, if the court finds that it was made in good faith and upon the personal knowledge of the declarant.[1]

---

imminent ensures that statement is trustworthy) (Text cited). See *Com. v. Middlemiss*, 465 Mass 627, 989 NE2d 871 (2013) (statements identifying his attacker to police officer made by murder victim after he was shot five times and lay fatally wounded in pool of blood, and was told by officer that he might "succumb," qualified as a dying declaration); *Com. v. Gaskins*, 419 Mass 809, 647 NE2d 429 (1995) (victim's statements did not constitute dying declarations where there was no evidence that he believed he was facing imminent death).

[6] *Com. v. Cantor*, 253 Mass 509, 149 NE 205 (1925).

[7] *Com. v. Green*, supra, 420 Mass at 781, 652 NE2d at 579 (Text cited); *Com. v. Key*, supra, 381 Mass at 22, 407 NE2d at 330-331. Cf. *Com. v. Mayne*, 38 Mass App 282, 287, 647 NE2d 89, 93 (1995) (where trial judge failed to instruct jury it must find that victim believed his death was imminent, but defendant failed to object, there was no substantial risk of a miscarriage of justice—statement was introduced by prosecution as a prior inconsistent statement of its own witness and defense counsel did not request a limiting instruction, and victim made statement after having been shot seven times and lay bleeding on the floor having stated he was dying).

[8] *Com. v. Gonzalez*, supra; *Com. v. Middlemiss*, 465 Mass 627, 989 NE2d 871 (2013); *Com. v. Nesbitt*, 452 Mass 236, 249, 892 NE2d 299 (2008).

§ 8.20 [1] Section 65 applies to proceedings before the Industrial Accident Board. *Stanton's Case*, 331 Mass 378, 119 NE2d 388 (1954). It also applies to disbarment proceedings. *In re Keenan*, 287 Mass 577, 192 NE 65 (1934). Cf. *In re Troy*, 364

This statute does not apply to criminal cases.[2] The federal rules have no specific comparable provision. Proposed Mass R Evid 804(b)(5) specifically incorporates this hearsay exception:

> **(5) Declaration of a deceased person.** In a civil action or proceeding, a declaration of a deceased person, if the court finds that it was made in good faith and upon personal knowledge of the declarant.

To render evidence admissible under § 65, the trial judge must find that the statement in question was made in good faith and on personal knowledge. It is error to leave this preliminary finding to the jury.[3] These factual findings by the trial court generally will be affirmed if there is any evidence to support them.[4]

Where the trial judge has admitted the statement, it will be assumed the preliminary facts were found, unless the record demonstrates otherwise.[5] Where the statement was excluded at trial, the court's decision will be affirmed unless the record demonstrates proof of the material facts.[6] Where a statement of a deceased person has been introduced for another purpose, its use will be limited to that purpose, where the preliminary findings required by GL 233, § 65, have not been made.[7]

Mass 15, 23, 306 NE2d 203, 164 (1973) (assumed to apply in judicial misconduct proceeding). As to the effect of § 65 on what would otherwise be a privilege for private conversations between spouses, see § 5.2.

[2] *Com. v. Cormier*, 427 Mass 446, 449 n.1, 693 NE2d 1015, 1018 n.1 (1998).

[3] *Horan v. Boston Elevated Railway Co.*, 237 Mass 245, 129 NE 355 (1921).

[4] *Kelley v. Jordan Marsh Co.*, 278 Mass 101, 106, 179 NE 299, 302 (1932). For illustrative cases, see *Barbosa v. Hopper Feeds, Inc.*, 404 Mass 610, 537 NE2d 99 (1989) (statement after accident of deceased co-worker to W that he advised P on proper operation of machine not made in good faith because of incentive for declarant to avoid blame himself); *Old Colony Trust Co. v. Shaw*, 348 Mass 212, 217-219, 202 NE2d 785, 789-790 (1964) (declarant's general duties as bookkeeper permitted conclusion that a specific memo was written in good faith, on personal knowledge). Compare *Anselmo v. Reback*, 400 Mass 865, 513 NE2d 1270 (1987) (failure to diagnose cancer case, videotape of deceased, answering questions from her attorney, made without notice to known potential defendants, held inadmissible for failure to afford defendants cross-examination as provided in GL 233, §§ 46, 47, and Mass R Civ P 27 (a)), with *Cusher v. Turner*, 22 Mass App 491, 495 NE2d 311 (1986) (failure to diagnose cancer case, tape recording, and diary of decedent regarding her mental and physical health properly admitted).

[5] *Warren v. Ball*, 341 Mass 350, 356, 170 NE2d 341, 345 (1960); *Horan v. Boston Elevated Railway Co.*, supra; *Mitchell v. Hastings & Koch Enterprises, Inc.*, 38 Mass App 271, 274, 647 NE2d 78, 81 (1995).

[6] *Virta v. Mackey*, 343 Mass 286, 178 NE2d 571 (1961).

[7] *Flanagan v. John Hancock Mutual Life Insurance Co.*, 349 Mass 405, 208 NE2d 497 (1965) (declarations of deceased insured in application for insurance policy

The requirement of a finding that the statement was made in good faith was held to include a requirement that the court find that the statement was in fact made by the declarant.[8] The requirement of personal knowledge is held to exclude most declarations of opinion. The requirement has been held to exclude opinion evidence that depends upon the expert qualifications of the declarant, even if the opinion is based on personal observation.[9]

The "personal knowledge" requirement does not exclude a class of "shorthand expression" opinion statements[10] that would not be improper if uttered on the witness stand.[11] When the form of the statement leaves doubt as to whether the statement is one of fact or opinion, the judge must decide in which sense the declaration was made.[12]

The declarations of a deceased person that otherwise qualify are admissible whether made orally or in writing and need not be reproduced in the exact words used by the declarant.[13]

GL 233, § 65A permits answers to interrogatories to be admitted in favor of the personal representative of the answering party where such party dies during the pendency of the litigation.[14] Note that since the answers to the interrogatories have been obtained by the adverse party, § 65A dispenses with the necessity of showing "good faith."

The statute does not make admissible a declaration of a deceased person that is inadmissible for other reasons.[15]

---

admitted on behalf of insurer as part of contract were not received under GL 233, § 65, and therefore could not be used by plaintiff for truth of matter).

[8] *Slotofski v. Boston Elevated Railway Co.*, 215 Mass 318, 102 NE 417 (1913).

[9] *Middlesex Supply, Inc. v. Martin & Sons*, 354 Mass 373, 237 NE2d 692 (1968); *Buck's Case*, 342 Mass 766, 772, 175 NE2d 369, 373 (1961).

[10] See §§ 7.2.1 and 7.2.2.

[11] *Samuel Cohen Shoe Co. v. Cohen*, 329 Mass 281, 107 NE2d 817 (1952); *Eldredge v. Barton*, 232 Mass 183, 122 NE 272 (1919).

[12] *Shamgochian v. Drigotas*, 343 Mass 139, 177 NE2d 580 (1961). See also *Old Colony Trust Co. v. Shaw*, supra.

[13] *Bellamy v. Bellamy*, 342 Mass 534, 174 NE2d 358 (1961); *Desrosiers v. Germain*, 12 Mass App 852, 858, 429 NE2d 385, 388-389 (1981) (oral statements).

[14] *Thornton v. First National Stores, Inc.*, 340 Mass 222, 163 NE2d 264 (1960) (interrogatories admissible under either section§ 65 or § 65A).

[15] *Taylor v. Whittier*, 240 Mass 514, 138 NE 6 (1922) (under the law of the time testimony as to a declaration by a husband (deceased at the time of the trial) was inadmissible because it tended to prove the illegitimacy of a child born to his wife while she was married to him). The legal rule regarding the disqualification of the testimony of spouses as to illegitimacy has been changed. See § 5.2.4.

§ 8.20.2 GL 233, § 66

The statute provides:

> If a cause of action brought against an executor or administrator is supported by oral testimony of a promise, or a statement made by the testator or intestate of the defendant, evidence of statements, written or oral, made by the decedent, memoranda and entries written by him, and evidence of his acts and habits of dealing tending to disprove or to show the improbability of the making of such promise or statement, such testimony shall be admissible.

The two preliminary requirements regarding the admission of evidence under § 65 do not apply to evidence admissible under § 66. Thus, no finding of good faith is required.[16] The single preliminary requirement to the admission of evidence under § 66 is that oral testimony of a statement of the deceased be presented by the party suing the executor or administrator. For an application of these words of the statute, see *Huebener v. Childs.*[17] The kinds of evidence this section admits are very broadly described.

§ 8.20.3 Other Statutes

Medical reports of deceased physicians are admissible under separate statutes: GL 233, § 79H (actions of tort); and GL 152, § 20B (workmen's compensation proceedings). Both statutes allow medical opinion evidence to be admitted in the discretion of the judge or hearing member, but § 79H bars any statement that "has reference to the question of liability." GL 152, § 20B, is broader than GL 233, § 79H, in two respects. First, it provides for discretionary admission of medical reports of deceased physicians and also reports of physicians who are "incapacitated" or "disabled." Second, § 20B was amended by St 1977, c 777, to delete the limitation on admissibility relating to the question of liability.

---

[16] *Rothwell v. First National Bank of Boston*, 286 Mass 417, 190 NE 812 (1934).
[17] *Huebener v. Childs*, 180 Mass 483, 62 NE 729 (1902).

§ 8.21 Declarations Against Interest

Proposed Mass R Evid 804(b)(1) provides that the following is not excluded by the hearsay rule if the declarant is unavailable as a witness:

> **(3) Statement against interest.** A statement which was at the time of its making so far contrary to the declarant's pecuniary or proprietary interest, or so far tended to subject him to civil or criminal liability, or to render invalid a claim by him against another, that a reasonable man in his position would not have made the statement unless he believed it to be true. A statement tending to expose the declarant to criminal liability and offered to exculpate the accused is not admissible unless corroborating circumstances clearly indicate the trustworthiness of the statement.

Fed R Evid 804(b)(3) is the same. The Rule is consistent with current Massachusetts law.

Under Massachusetts law, statements of a declarant against his own pecuniary or proprietary interest at the time the statements are made have long been admissible for the truth of the matters asserted under the circumstances herein described.[1] The common law did not recognize a statement that rendered the declarant subject to prosecution for a crime, a "declaration against penal interest," as being within the scope of this exception to the hearsay rule. Statements against penal interest were recognized as admissible under this exception to the hearsay rule in *Com. v. Carr.*[2]

Declarations against interest are statements made by witnesses, not parties to the litigation or their privies or representatives.[3] The declarant need not utter the statement if it is made by another and adopted by him.[4]

Under *Crawford v. Washington*,[5] a testimonial statement that qualifies as a declaration against interest would not be admissible, under the Confrontation Clause, against a criminal defendant unless the declarant was subject to cross-examination.

---

§ 8.21 [1] *Cunningham v. Davis*, 175 Mass 213, 56 NE 2 (1900).

[2] 373 Mass 617, 369 NE2d 970 (1977).

[3] Such latter statements may be admissible as statements by a party-opponent. See § 8.6. See also, *Com. v. McLaughlin*, 433 Mass 558, 744 NE2d 47 (2001) (defendant could not offer his own prior statement as a declaration against interest) (Text cited).

[4] *Com. v. Tague*, 434 Mass 510, 516, 751 NE2d 388, 394 (2001) (statement of another adopted by smiling and nodding; for adoption by silence, declarant must have heard and understood the statement, have had an opportunity to respond, and the context must be one in which he would be expected to deny an accusation if untrue).

[5] *Crawford v. Washington*, 124 S Ct 1354 (2004).

Whether a statement is sufficiently adverse to the declarant's penal interest to be admissible is judged by whether the statement subjected the declarant to criminal liability to the extent that he would not have made the statement unless it were true.[6] In *Com. v. Drew*,[7] the Court questioned whether the statement, which admitted little other than presence at a murder, was sufficiently inculpatory. However, the Court noted that the exception was "not so narrow as to preclude all declarations but direct admissions of guilt."[8] The Court reasoned that "it is not the fact that the declaration is against interest but the awareness of that fact by the declarant which gives the statement significance."[9] Because a layman might have believed he would be incriminated by an admission of presence at a murder scene, the Court indicated the statement was probably a declaration against penal interest. Courts have found statements insufficiently incriminating in a variety of circumstances.[10]

The United States Supreme Court has held that only those statements within a longer narrative that are individually self-incriminating are admissible under Fed R Evid 804(b)(3). In *Williamson v. United States*,[11] the Court held that non-self-inculpatory

---

[6] See *Com. v. Charles*, 428 Mass 672, 679, 704 NE2d 1137, 1144 (1999) (admission that accident for which an insurance claim had been made was fictional was against penal interest); *Com. v. Pope*, 397 Mass 275, 280, 491 NE2d 240, 243 (1986) (suicide note confessing to a murder was inadmissible because declarant had already decided to kill himself and would not be motivated by penal consequences of statement).

[7] *Com. v. Drew*, 397 Mass 65, 74, 489 NE2d 1233, 1239-1240 (1986).

[8] *Id.*

[9] *Id.*

[10] *Com. v. Burnham*, 451 Mass 517, 887 NE2d 222 (2008) (statements by child victim's mother that she did not see bruises on child on day she died, made to detective and to friend whom she requested not to talk to police, might have evidenced consciousness of guilt, but were too ambiguous to clearly tend to subject declarant to criminal liability so that a reasonable person would not have made them unless she believed them to be true, nor were they corroborated by circumstances indicating trustworthiness); *Com. v. Slonka*, 42 Mass App Ct 760, 770, 680 NE2d 103, 110 (1997) (witness's interview statement to defense counsel that he smoked "a couple of bowl fulls" with victim was not made under circumstances suggesting declarant's awareness that statement was against penal interest); *Com. v. Hearn*, 31 Mass App 707, 583 NE2d 279 (1991) (statement that essentially exculpated declarant/defendant and admitted only uncontested facts was not against penal interest); *Com. v. Fernandes*, 30 Mass App 335, 338, 568 NE2d 604, 607 (1991) (affirming exclusion of statement in part because the incriminating declaration was "clearly affected by the exigencies of the plea bargaining"); *Com. v. Marple*, 26 Mass App 150, 524 NE2d 863 (1988) (court questioned whether a statement qualified as against penal interest where declarant spoke after he believed his case was already lost).

[11] *Williamson v. United States*, 512 US 594, 114 S Ct 2431, 129 L Ed 2d 476 (1994).

statements are not admissible as declarations against interest, even if made within a broader narrative that is generally self-inculpatory.[12]

The Supreme Judicial Court has indicated that a statement by a co-defendant that seeks to shift blame to the defendant and exonerate or minimize the role of the co-defendant does not satisfy the test as a statement against penal interest.[13]

Fed R Evid 804(b)(3) and Proposed Mass R Evid 804(b)(3), as adopted in *Com. v. Carr*, supra, provide: "A statement tending to expose the declarant to criminal liability and offered to exculpate the accused is not admissible unless corroborating circumstances clearly indicate the trustworthiness of the statement." The Supreme Judicial Court has held that corroboration of trustworthiness is also required when the government seeks to introduce a statement against penal interest by an unavailable declarant that would inculpate the defendant.[14]

The Supreme Judicial Court has declared that in assessing whether a statement is sufficiently corroborated, a court should "not be stringent," and where the issue is close, a court should favor admission, relying on the good sense of the jury to correct any prejudicial impact.[15] The question is not whether the trial judge is satisfied that the statement is actually true, but whether there is some reasonable

---

[12] The Appeals Court followed *Williamson* in *Com. v. Marrero*, 60 Mass App 225, 800 NE2d 1048 (2003), in holding that only those portions of a longer narrative that are actually against the declarant's penal interest are admissible. See also *Com. v. Dejarnette*, 75 Mass App 88, 99, 911 NE2d 1280, 1289 (2009) (although it may be necessary to admit "necessary surrounding context" to avoid distortion, it is error to admit an entire statement because there are portions that are declarations against interest).

[13] *Com. v. Francis*, 432 Mass 353, 363, n.9, 734 NE2d 315, 325 (2000). See *Com. v. Lopera*, 42 Mass App 133, 674 NE2d 1340 (1997) (statements by alleged prostitute that she gave defendant a portion of her fee and that defendant kept the apartment in question were not sufficiently against declarant's penal interest to be admissible).

[14] *Com. v. Charles*, 428 Mass 672, 679, 704 NE2d 1137, 1144 (1999). See *Com. v. Pope*, 397 Mass 275, 280, 491 NE2d 240, 243 (1986). Such a statement may not be admissible under the Confrontation Clause if the declarant does not testify and the statement explicitly identifies the defendant. See § 8.6.7. The appeals court has suggested that there may be a requirement of corroboration for inculpatory statements in civil matters, but it does not appear that there is any doctrinal basis for such a suggestion. See *Zinck v. Gateway Country Store, Inc.*, 72 Mass App 571, 575, 893 NE2d 364, 368 (2008).

[15] *Com. v. Charles*, supra, 428 Mass at 679-680, 704 NE2d at 1144 (Text cited); *Com. v. Drew*, 397 Mass 65, 75 and n.10, 489 NE2d 1233, 1241 and n.10 (1986); *Com. v. Gagnon*, 408 Mass 185, 194, 557 NE2d 728, 734 (1990); *Com. v. Galloway*, 404 Mass 204, 208, 534 NE2d 778, 781 (1989) (reversing trial court's exclusion of statement); *Com. v. Fiore*, 53 Mass App 785, 762 NE2d 905 (2002) (letter from alternative culprit, written in prison, indicating that he "may" have started a fire was sufficiently corroborated).

likelihood that the statement could be true.[16] In making the determination, the court should take into account the degree of disinterestedness of the witnesses giving corroborating testimony, the plausibility of that testimony in the light of the rest of the proof, the credibility of the declarant and the credibility and probative quality of his statement, the timing of the declaration, the relationship between the declarant and the witness, the reliability and character of the declarant, whether the statement was made spontaneously, whether other people heard the out-of-court statement, whether there is any apparent motive for declarant to misrepresent the matter, and whether and in what circumstances the statement was repeated.[17] The judge should not base her determination, however, on the credibility of the witness who testifies as to the making of the statement by the declarant, because the jury should assess that witness's credibility.[18] Where the proponent of the evidence has failed to make a record of corroborating evidence, an appellate court will affirm a trial court's exclusion of the evidence.[19]

In a criminal trial, due process requirements may dictate that when the defendant seeks to introduce reliable declarations against penal interest that exculpate him, he be allowed to adduce such evidence even if it would not qualify as an exception to the hearsay rule under state law.[20] Where there is insufficient evidence of trustworthiness or reliability, and insufficient corroboration demonstrating trustworthiness, constitutional due process principles do not require the admission of a hearsay statement that would exculpate the accused.[21]

---

[16] *Com. v. Drew*, supra, 397 Mass at 75-76, 489 NE2d at 1241. But see *Com. v. DiToro*, 51 Mass App 191, 744 NE2d 672 (2001) (statements lack sufficient corroboration where there was no showing that one declarant had basis for knowing whether defendant was involved in the crime and second declarant's statement was vague and lacked detail and this declarant had a relationship with defendant).

[17] *Com. v. Drew*, supra, 397 Mass at 75-76, 489 NE2d at 1241. See *Com. v. Weichell*, 446 Mass 785, 847 NE2d 1080 (2006) (trial court erred in finding that trustworthiness had been corroborated).

[18] *Com. v. Carriere*, 470 Mass 1, 17, 18 NE3d 326 (2014); *Com. v. Drew*, supra, 397 Mass at 76, 489 NE2d at 1241; *Com. v. Nutbrown*, 81 Mass App 773, 779, 968 NE2d 418, 424 (2012) (error for court to exclude declaration against penal interest based on trustworthiness of witness, rather than trustworthiness of declarant).

[19] *Com. v. Morgan*, 449 Mass 343, 868 NE2d 99 (2007); *Com. v. Dew*, 443 Mass 620, 823 NE2d 771 (2005); *Com. v. Piper*, 426 Mass 8, 686 NE2d 191 (1997); *Com. v. Burgos*, 36 Mass App 903, 627 NE2d 471 (1994) (where declarant was identified only by first name, no efforts were made to locate him, and nothing was offered to bolster his statement, it was not error to exclude it).

[20] *Green v. Georgia*, 442 US 95, 99 S Ct 2150 (1979); *Chambers v. Mississippi*, 410 US 284, 93 S Ct 1038, 35 L Ed 2d 297 (1973).

[21] *Com. v. Drew*, supra.

Declarations of a landowner, now deceased, made during his ownership in disparagement of his title are admissible.[22]

Declarations of deceased persons are more liberally admitted under GL 233, § 65, than as declarations against interest. See § 8.20.1. However, unlike the statutory exception, this common-law exception applies to both civil and criminal cases.

§ 8.22 Declarations of Pedigree

Proposed Mass R Evid 804(b)(4) provides that the following is not excluded by the hearsay rule if the declarant is unavailable as a witness:

> **(4) Statement of personal history**. (A) A statement concerning the declarant's own birth, adoption, marriage, divorce, legitimacy, relationship by blood, adoption, or marriage, ancestry, or other similar fact of personal or family history, even though declarant had no means of acquiring personal knowledge of the matter stated; or (B) a statement concerning the foregoing matters, and death also, of another person, if the declarant was related to the other by blood, adoption, or marriage or was so intimately associated with the other's family as to be likely to have accurate information concerning the matter declared.

Fed R Evid 804(b)(4) is the same. Unavailability under the Rule is more broadly defined that at common law by virtue of Rule 804(a). The Rule broadens the common law scope of whose statements are admissible by including declarants who are not family members.

Under current Massachusetts law, declarations of pedigree are distinguishable from reputation of pedigree in that the declarant is known and meets certain qualifications. Thus, an entry in a family Bible, mentioned as an example under reputation of pedigree, may also be a declaration of pedigree if the person making the entry can be

---

[22] *Rowell v. Doggett*, 143 Mass 483, 10 NE 182 (1887). Other hearsay exceptions created by the rules of evidence may be a basis for admission of evidence pertaining to ownership or boundaries of land. See, e.g., Proposed Mass R Evid 803(14) and Fed R Evid 803(14) (records of documents recorded in a public office that affect an interest in property); Fed R Evid 803(15) (statements in documents affecting an interest in property; this exception is not adopted by the Proposed Massachusetts Rules of Evidence); Proposed Mass R Evid 803(16) and Fed R Evid 803(16) (statements in ancient documents); Proposed Mass R Evid 803(20) and Fed R Evid 803(20) (reputation concerning boundaries or customs affecting lands); Proposed Mass R Evid 803(23) and Fed R Evid 803(23) (inter alia judgments pertaining to boundaries; no common-law equivalent in Massachusetts).

identified and meets the qualifications. This exception to the hearsay rule applies to the same facts and in the same kinds of actions as the exception for reputation of pedigree. Also, the declaration must have been made ante litem motam. The persons who can be declarants are limited to blood members of the family whose pedigree is in question or spouses of blood members.

§ 8.23 Forfeiture by Wrongdoing

Fed R of Evidence 804(b)(6) provides that the following is not excluded by the hearsay rule if the declarant is unavailable as a witness:

> **(6) Forfeiture by wrongdoing**. A statement offered against a party that has engaged or acquiesced in wrongdoing that was intended to, and did, procure the unavailability of the declarant as a witness.

There is no similar provision in the Proposed Mass Rules of Evidence.

In *Com. v. Edwards*,[1] the Supreme Judicial Court adopted the doctrine of forfeiture by wrongdoing, but did not adopt Fed R 804(b)(6) as such. Where a trial court finds that a party has procured the unavailability of a witness through wrongdoing, the hearsay rule does not preclude admission of out of court statements by the witness. In criminal cases such action by the defendant also constitutes a forfeiture of Confrontation Clause objections to hearsay statements of the witness.[2] The Court noted that the rule "has its foundation in the maxim that no one shall be permitted to take advantage of his own wrong . . ."[3] The Court found that the doctrine applies where the trial court makes findings that: (1) the witness is unavailable; (2) the party was involved in, or responsible for, procuring the unavailability of the witness; and (3) the party acted with the intent to procure the witness's unavailability.[4]

---

§ 8.23 [1] *Com. v. Edwards*, 444 Mass 526, 830 NE2d 158 (2005).

[2] The United States Supreme Court has held that where hearsay evidence is admitted under the doctrine of forfeiture by wrongdoing, Confrontation Clause objections are extinguished on essentially equitable grounds. *Crawford v. Washington*, 541 US 36, 62, 124 S Ct 1354 (2004).

[3] *Com. v. Edwards*, 444 Mass at 534, citing *Reynolds v. United States*, 98 US 145, 159, 25 L Ed 244 (1878).

[4] *Com. v. Edwards*, 444 Mass at 540. The Court referenced "the defendant" because *Edwards* was a criminal case and the Confrontation Clause was implicated. The doctrine applies as well to the prosecution in criminal cases and to any party in a civil case.

The doctrine unquestionably applies where a party murders, threatens, or intimidates a witness or commits a criminal act in order to procure the witness's unavailability. The party's conduct does not have to consist of a criminal act, however, for the doctrine to apply.[5] The *Edwards* Court held that collusion with a witness to ensure that the witness will not be heard at trial is sufficient involvement by a party to justify invocation of the doctrine. Noting that a party must contribute to the witness's unavailability in "some significant manner," the Court held that a sufficient causal link would exist where: (1) a defendant puts forward to a witness the idea to avoid testifying, either by threats, coercion, persuasion, or pressure; (2) a defendant physically prevents a witness from testifying; or (3) a defendant actively facilitates the carrying out of the witness's independent intent not to testify.[6]

Collusion may apply where a party engages in a joint effort with the witness to secure unavailability, although the witness had previously decided "on his own" not to testify. Merely informing a witness of his constitutional right to remain silent, however, is not sufficient to constitute forfeiture.[7] Where a party has colluded with a witness to procure his unavailability, the fact that the witness was ultimately rendered unavailable through means different than those originally contemplated will not absolve the party of the forfeiture, as long as the method by which the witness becomes unavailable is a logical outgrowth or foreseeable result of the collusion. No independent wrongdoing is required for the doctrine to apply, the intentional procurement of a witness's unavailability through collusion is considered a per se wrongdoing sufficient to trigger the doctrine.[8]

The standard of proof in finding that a party procured the unavailability of a witness is preponderance of the evidence. The trial judge must conduct a hearing before making a finding, if requested by a party. The parties must be allowed to present evidence, including

---

[5] *Com. v. Szerlong*, 457 Mass 858, 933 NE2d 633 (2010).

[6] *Com. v. Edwards*, 444 Mass at 541.

[7] *Id.*, n.23.

[8] The Supreme Judicial Court held that *Edwards* was consistent with *Giles v. California*, 554 US 353, 128 S Ct 2678 (2008) with respect to the requirement that the defendant intended to prevent the witness from testifying in *Com. v. Szerlong*, 457 Mass 858, 933 NE2d 633 (2010) (where defendant and victim had no plans to marry before incident that gave rise to criminal complaint, even if idea to marry originated with victim, defendant's agreement to marry justified inference that he intended to make her unavailable to testify; making witness unavailable need not have been defendant's sole purpose or primary purpose, so long as it was a purpose in marrying her).

live testimony, but the judge may also consider hearsay evidence, including out of court statements by the unavailable witness.

In *Com. v. Szerlong*, the court also stated that where a court finds forfeiture by wrongdoing, or otherwise finds good cause to dispense with a defendant's right of confrontation, "due process requires that any hearsay admitted against the defendant be reliable."[9]

§ 8.24 Victims of Child Abuse

§ 8.24.1 Statements by Alleged Victims of Child Abuse

The Supreme Judicial Court has considered whether an exception to the hearsay rule should be created for extrajudicial declarations by children alleged to be victims of child abuse. In *Opinion of the Justices*,[1] the Court held that proposed legislation, which would have created such an exception for child sexual abuse, was unconstitutional, in violation of the Confrontation Clause in art 12 of the Declaration of Rights. The legislation would have permitted out-of-court statements to be admitted for their truth under a variety of circumstances, including where the child was unavailable as a witness for any of several reasons, including a refusal to testify, and there was corroborative evidence of sexual contact. The Court found significant that under the bill such statements did not have to be made under oath, there was no explicit requirement of good faith and due diligence in establishing unavailability, and concluded that a refusal to testify could not be equated with that measure of necessity which justifies other hearsay exceptions. The Court held that the criteria for determining the reliability of admissible statements under the legislation were inadequate and that the exception as drafted did not have the same guarantees of reliability as other hearsay exceptions.

In 1990, the Legislature passed three statutes creating hearsay exceptions for statements by child abuse victims, c. 233 GL §§ 81, 82, and 83. These statutes were evidently drafted with an eye toward responding to the concerns of the Supreme Judicial Court in *Opinion of the Justices*, supra.

---

[9] *Com. v. Szerlong*, 457 Mass at 866, 933 NE2d at 642 (finding hearsay reliable given circumstances under which declarant's statements were made).

§ 8.24 [1] 406 Mass 1201, 547 NE2d 8 (1989).

Section 81[2] governs the admissibility of such statements in criminal proceedings and was discussed at length in *Com. v. Colin C.*[3] The

---

[2] The statute provides:

§ 81. Admissibility in Criminal Proceeding of Out-of-Court Statement of Child Abuse Victim: Unavailability of Victim; Reliability of Statement.

(a) an out-of-court statement of a child under the age of ten describing an act of sexual contact performed on or with the child, the circumstances under which it occurred, or which identifies the perpetrator shall be admissible as substantive evidence in any criminal proceeding; provided, however, that the statement is offered as evidence of a material fact and is more probative on the point for which it is offered than any other evidence which the proponent can procure through reasonable efforts; the person to whom the statement was made or who heard the child make the statement testifies; the judge funds pursuant to subsection (b) that the child is unavailable as a witness: and the judge finds pursuant to subsection (c) that the statement is reliable.

(b) The proponent of such statement shall demonstrate a diligent and good faith effort to produce the child and shall bear the burden of showing unavailability. A finding of unavailability shall be supported by specific finding on the records, describing facts with particularity, demonstrating that:

(1) the child is unable to be present or to testify because of death or physical or mental illness or infirmity; or
(2) by a ruling of the court, the child is exempt on the ground of privilege from testifying concerning the subject matter of such statement; or
(3) the child testifies to a lack of memory of the subject matter of such statement; or
(4) the child is absent from the hearing and the proponent of such statement has been unable to procure the attendance of the child by process or by other reasonable means; or
(5) the court finds, based upon expert testimony from a treating psychiatrist, or clinician, that testifying would be likely to cause severe psychological or emotional trauma to the child; or
(6) the child is not competent to testify.

(c) If a finding of unavailability is made, the out-of-court statement shall be admitted if the judge further finds: (1) after holding a separate hearing, that such statement was made under oath, that it was accurately recorded and preserved, and there was sufficient opportunity to cross-examine; or (2) after holding a separate hearing and, where practicable and where not inconsistent with the best interests of the child, meeting with the child, that such statement was made under circumstances inherently demonstrating a special guarantee of reliability.

For the purposes of finding circumstances demonstrating reliability pursuant to clause (2) of subsection (c), a judge may consider whether the relator documented the child witness's statement, and shall consider the following factors:

(i) the clarity of the statement, meaning, the child's capacity to observe, remember, and give expression to that which such child has seen, heard, or experienced; provided, however, that a finding under this clause shall be supported by expert testimony from a treating psychiatrist, psychologist, or clinician;
(ii) the time, content and circumstances of the statement;
(iii) the child's sincerity and ability to appreciate the consequences of such statement.

(d) An out-of-court statement which is admissible by common law or by statute shall remain admissible notwithstanding the provisions of this section.

[3] *Com. v. Colin C.*, 419 Mass 54, 643 NE2d 19 (1994).

defendant made a challenge to the facial constitutionality of the statute. However, the Supreme Judicial Court did not reach that issue because it reversed the defendant's conviction on other grounds. Under *Crawford v. Washington*,[4] notwithstanding the statute, hearsay statements by child abuse victims that are testimonial would be inadmissible under the Confrontation Clause unless the child were unavailable and the defendant had been furnished an opportunity for cross-examination. See § 8.4.2.

In *Colin C.*, the Supreme Judicial Court stated that in addition to the procedures and protections set forth in the statute, it would impose certain other requirements before such hearsay could be admitted in criminal cases. It seems unlikely that these conditions would be sufficient to overcome a Confrontation Clause objection under *Crawford*.[5]

Section 82, which governs all civil cases except for care and protection cases, is substantially identical to § 81, with the exception that § 82 specifically directs the judge to consider the existence of corroborating evidence in determining whether the out-of-court statement is reliable under subsection (c). The Supreme Judicial Court upheld the constitutionality of § 82 in *Adoption of Quentin*,[6] suggesting that although they may not be required in every civil case, the better part of caution would be for judges to employ the procedures discussed in *Com. v. Colin C.*, supra, in § 82 proceedings.[7]

---

[4] *Crawford v. Washington*, 541 US 36, 124 S Ct 1354 (2004).

[5] The Supreme Judicial Court required that before the statute can be invoked, the Commonwealth must give prior notice to a criminal defendant that it will seek to use such hearsay statements, in order to provide a meaningful opportunity to respond to hearsay allegations. Second, the Commonwealth must show by proof beyond a reasonable doubt that there is a compelling need for the use of the hearsay. Third, the Court required that any separate hearing regarding the reliability of the out-of-court statement be on the record, and that the judge's determination of reliability be supported by specific findings on the record. The Court noted that where possible, without causing severe emotional trauma to the child witness, the defendant and counsel should be given the opportunity to be present at the hearing. Fourth, the Court noted that where the judge determines that a child witness was unavailable because she was incompetent to testify, the judge's reasons for finding the witness incompetent should not be those that call into question the reliability of the out-of-court statements. Finally, the Court required that in order to admit such hearsay statements for substantive purposes, there must be other independently admitted evidence that corroborated the out-of-court statements. See *Com. v. Jaubert*, 38 Mass App 943, 647 NE2d 1238 (1995) (hearsay by alleged child sexual abuse victim was not admissible where the trial judge made none of the requisite findings required by § 81).

[6] *Adoption of Quentin*, 424 Mass 882, 678 NE2d 1325 (1997).

[7] See *F.A.P. v. J.E.S.*, 87 Mass App 595, 33 NE3d 1245 (2015) (requirements of § 82 need not be met for admission of reliable hearsay in hearing on harassment prevention order); *Adoption of Arnold*, 50 Mass App 743, 741 NE2d 456 (2001) (statements

This hearsay exception "applies to statements made where the child was under the age of ten when she made the statements, regardless of her age at the time of trial."[8] There is no absolute bar against admitting statements from an incompetent child; the child's competence is a factor for the judge to consider in determining whether the statements are reliable.[9] The statute provides that the unavailability of the child may be established in various ways, including testimony by a treating psychiatrist or clinician that testifying would be likely to cause severe psychological or emotional trauma to the child.[10]

Section 83 governs care and protection proceedings.[11] Section 83 was discussed at length in *Care and Protection of Rebecca*.[12] The Court rejected the claim that the statute violated due process and equal protection provisions of the Fourteenth Amendment to the United States Constitution and art. 12 of the Massachusetts Declaration of Rights. The Court also rejected the claim that § 83 contained an implicit requirement that a judge find that the child witness is unavailable before admitting such evidence. The Court noted that such a

---

were properly admitted); *Adoption of Tina*, 45 Mass App 727, 701 NE2d 671 (1998) (trial court's findings were inadequate to demonstrate reliability of child's hearsay statements); *Edward E. v. Department of Social Services*, 42 Mass App 478, 678 NE2d 163 (1997) (holding that circumstances of the case did not demonstrate the reliability of the child's statements).

[8] *In re Adoption of Daisy*, 460 Mass 72, 73, 948 NE2d 1239 (2011).

[9] *In re Adoption of Olivette*, 79 Mass App 141, 944 NE2d 1068 (2011) (affirming trial court's conclusion that statements were reliable, despite child's cognitive limitations; court suggests trial judges should consider the benefit of a voir dire of the child declarant, but holds statements may be admissible even in the absence of a voir dire).

[10] For discussion of whether the testifying psychiatrist must be treating the child witness, how much involvement in treatment is necessary, and qualifications of such an expert, see *In re Adoption of Daisy*, 77 Mass App 768, 934 NE2d 252 (2010), *aff'd on other grounds*, *In re Adoption of Daisy*, 460 Mass 72, 948 NE2d 1239 (2011).

[11] The statute provides:

> § **83. Admissibility in Proceeding to Place Child in Foster Care of Out-of-Court Statement of Child Abuse Victim.**
>
> (a) Any out-of-court statement of child under the age of ten describing any act of sexual contact performed on or with the child, the circumstances under which it occurred, or which identifies the perpetrator offered in an action brought under subparagraph C of section twenty-three or section twenty-four of chapter one hundred and nineteen shall be admissible; provided, however, that the person to whom the statement was made, or who heard the child make the statement testifies, and the judge finds that the statement is offered as evidence of a material fact and is more probative on the point for which it is offered that any other evidence with the proponent can procure through reasonable effort.
>
> (b) An out-of-court statement admissible by common law or by statute shall remain admissible notwithstanding the provisions of this section.

[12] *Care and Protection of Rebecca*, 419 Mass 67, 643 NE2d 26 (1994).

requirement was explicitly set forth in §§ 81 and 82, and that its absence from § 83 would be deemed to be intentional by the Legislature. The Court did conclude, however, that there is an implicit requirement in the statute that a judge assess the reliability of such out-of-court statements in connection with deciding how much weight to afford to them. The Court noted that the judge is required "to treat this evidence with caution."[13] It noted that the person through whom the statement is introduced is subject to cross-examination concerning the circumstances in which the statement was made and related matters, and also noted that the legislation does not foreclose a judge from holding a voir dire to assess the child's capacity to remember and relate and the child's ability to perceive the necessity of telling the truth. The Court stated that in determining the weight to give to such statements, a judge should consider whether other admissible evidence corroborated the existence of child abuse. Finally, the Court required that a judge's reason for relying on § 83 evidence must appear clearly in the specific and detailed findings required in a care and protection case.

In *Com. v. Costello*,[14] the Court declined to recognize prior inconsistent statements by alleged child sexual abuse victims as substantive evidence. The Commonwealth had not argued for such an exception to the ordinary rule limiting the use of such statements to impeachment purposes; however, the Court recognized that some other states allow such evidence. The Court noted that Massachusetts has no general exception to the hearsay rule for statements by child sexual abuse victims.

It should be noted that statements by alleged child sexual abuse victims might be admissible as spontaneous exclamations (see § 8.7), or as fresh complaint evidence (see § 6.25). Solicitude for the sensitivity of such victims as witnesses may also be shown by making special arrangements for the receipt of their testimony, consistent with protecting the rights of the defendant. See § 6.8.

§ 8.24.2 *Reports Regarding Child Abuse and Neglect*

Hearsay statements in reports regarding child abuse and neglect have been made admissible by statute.[15] The Appeals Court has

---

[13] *Id.* 419 Mass at 79.

[14] *Com. v. Costello*, 411 Mass 371, 582 NE2d 938 (1991).

[15] GL 119, §§ 21 and 24. See *Adoption of Paula*, 420 Mass 716, 724-725, 651 NE2d 1222, 1229 (1995) (GL 119, § 24 reports, as well as testimony of investigator, are

assumed, without deciding, that reports containing hearsay by a court-appointed special advocate (CASA) are admissible as analogous to investigator's reports under § 21. The Supreme Judicial Court has decided that where a CASA has been formally appointed as a guardian ad litem, the report is admissible.[16]

The Supreme Judicial Court has recognized, however, that it is error to admit hearsay from GL 119, § 24 reports unless there is "an opportunity to refute the investigator *and the investigator's sources* through cross-examination and other means."[17]

§ 8.25 The Catchall Exception

Fed R Evid 807 provides a catchall exception not included as part of the Proposed Massachusetts Rules of Evidence:

> **Residual Exception**
>
> A statement not specifically covered by Rule 803 or 804 but having equivalent circumstantial guarantees of trustworthiness, is not excluded by the hearsay rule, if the court determines that (A) the statement is offered as evidence of a material fact; (B) the statement is more probative on the point for which it is offered than any other evidence which the proponent can procure through reasonable efforts; and (C) the general

---

admissible in proceeding dispensing with parents' consent to adoption); *Adoption of Mary*, 414 Mass 705, 610 NE2d 898 (1993); *Adoption of Sean*, 36 Mass App 261, 630 NE2d 604 (1994) (guardian ad litem reports containing hearsay are admissible in proceedings to dispense with consent for adoption under GL 215, § 56A); *Adoption of Arthur*, 34 Mass App 914, 609 NE2d 486 (1993) (same); *Adoption of Kenneth*, 31 Mass App 946, 580 NE2d 392 (1991); *Custody of Tracy*, 31 Mass App 481, 579 NE2d 1362 (1991).

[16] *Adoption of Georgia*, 433 Mass 62, 739 NE2d 694 (2000); *Guardianship of Pollard*, 54 Mass App 318, 764 NE2d 935 (2002).

[17] *Adoption of Carla*, 416 Mass 510, 514, 623 NE2d 1118, 1120 (1993) (citing *Custody of Michel*, 28 Mass App 260, 266, 549 NE2d 440 (1990), emphasis added in *Carla*). See *Care and Protection of Rebecca*, 419 Mass 67, 82, 643 NE2d 26, 35 (1994) (hearsay in § 24 report which is inadmissible under *Adoption of Carla* may not be used to bolster reliability determination in order to admit hearsay under GL 233, § 83); *Adoption of Iris*, 43 Mass App Ct 95, 680 NE2d 1188 (1997) (requiring parents to call court investigator on direct examination, denial of right to conduct cross-examination, was error); *In re Leo*, 38 Mass App 237, 646 NE2d 1086 (1995) (where party was given opportunity to call as witnesses the sources in investigator's report, but refused to do so, he waived right to complain of hearsay in § 24 report); *Care and Protection of Inga*, 36 Mass App 660, 634 NE2d 591 (1994) (hearsay accusations of child from GL 119, § 51A report inadmissible where child does not testify and judge has no other means to assess accuracy of statements).

> purposes of these rules and the interests of justice will best be served by the admission of the statement into evidence. However, a statement may not be admitted under this exception unless the proponent of it makes known to the adverse party sufficiently in advance of the trial or hearing to provide the adverse party with a fair opportunity to prepare to meet it, his intention to offer the statement and the particulars of it, including the name and address of the declarant.

The Supreme Judicial Court has stated, "we do not regard the common-law hearsay exceptions as frozen in their established contours, and have been prepared on suitable occasions to venture forth."[1] The Court consistently, however, has refused to adopt the general exception to the hearsay rule embodied in Fed R Evid 807.[2]

The Supreme Judicial Court has recognized, however, that there is a narrow "constitutionally based hearsay exception, rooted in the United States Supreme Court's decision in *Chambers v. Mississippi*, 410 U.S. 284, 302, 93 S. Ct. 1038, 35 L. Ed. 2d 297 (1973)."[3] The exception is appropriate where state evidentiary rules conflict with the compulsory process clause of the Sixth Amendment or the due process clause of the Fourteenth Amendment. The Supreme Judicial Court has recognized this exception in the case of third-party culprit evidence, where appropriate safeguards are met.[4] It has also held that an affidavit prepared with an awareness of the preparer's precarious medical condition, exculpatory with respect to a criminal defendant, might be admissible if found to be sufficiently trustworthy.[5]

---

§ 8.25 [1] *Com. v. Meech*, 380 Mass 490, 497, 403 NE2d 1174, 1179 (1980).

[2] *Com. v. Drayton*, 473 Mass 23, 33, 38 NE3d 247, 256 (2015) (treatise cited); *Com. v. Semedo*, 422 Mass 716, 665 NE2d 638 (1996) (recorded statements of eyewitnesses to assault, although reliable and trustworthy, were hearsay and not admissible); *Com. v. Costello*, 411 Mass 371, 377, 582 NE2d 938, 942 (1991); *Com. v. Pope*, 397 Mass 275, 281, 491 NE2d 240, 244 (1986).

[3] *Com. v. Drayton*, 473 Mass 23, 33, 38 NE3d 247, 256 (2015).

[4] See *Commonwealth v. Silva-Santiago*, 453 Mass 782, 801, 804 n.26, 906 NE2d 299 (2009); § 8.2.2, n.22.

[5] *Com. v. Drayton, supra* (remanded for hearing on trustworthiness where affidavit contradicted prosecution's sole eyewitness to crime, was critical to the defense, although inadmissible as a dying declaration was consistent with underlying rationale for that exception, was corroborated by other evidence in case, and affiant had made similar statements on multiple occasions).

CHAPTER

9

AUTHENTICATION

§ 9.1 In General

The materiality of any evidence depends upon its authenticity. The evidence must be the thing its proponent represents it to be. This is so whether the evidence is a witness, a viewed parcel of land, a gun, photograph, or document. Witnesses identify themselves. A thing, however, rarely authenticates itself. If it does not authenticate itself, its authenticity must be stipulated or proved as a preliminary fact. Such proof of authenticity usually takes the form of testimony from a qualified witness that either: (1) the thing is what its proponent represents it to be; or (2) circumstances exist that imply that the thing is what its proponent represents it to be.[1]

§ 9.2 Proposed Mass Rules and Federal Rules Regarding Authenticity

The basic principle that underlies all methods of authentication is set forth in Proposed Mass R Evid 901(a), identical to Fed R Evid 901(a), and reflects current Massachusetts law:

> **General provision**. The requirement of authentication or identification as a condition precedent to admissibility is satisfied by evidence sufficient to support a finding that the matter in question is what its proponent claims.

The role of the trial judge in jury cases is to determine whether there is evidence sufficient, if believed, to convince the jury by a preponderance of the evidence that the item in question is what the proponent claims it to be. If so, the evidence should be admitted, if it is otherwise admissible. It remains for the jury to determine whether the item is in fact what the proponent claims it to be.

The requirement of Rule 901(a) can be met through a wide variety of means. Proposed Mass R Evid 901(b) provides a non-exhaustive list of examples:

> **(b) Illustrations**. By way of illustration only, and not by way of limitation, the following are examples of authentication or identification conforming with the requirements of this rule:

---

§ 9.1 [1] *Com. v. LaCorte*, 373 Mass 700, 704, 369 NE2d 1006, 1009 (1977) (Text cited); *Com. v. Wheeler*, 42 Mass App 933, 935, 678 NE2d 168, 171 (1997) (Text cited). An appropriate objection must be made to preserve an objection based on authentication grounds. *Com. v. Emeny*, 463 Mass 138, 145, 972 NE2d 1003, 1010 (2012) ("overall objection" to admission of autopsy photos, based on risk of prejudice, does not preserve objection on authentication grounds for appeal).

(1) Testimony of witness with knowledge. Testimony that a matter is what it is claimed to be.

(2) Nonexpert opinion on handwriting. Nonexpert opinion as to the genuineness of handwriting, based upon familiarity not acquired for purposes of litigation.

(3) Comparison by trier or expert witness. Comparison by the trier of fact or by expert witnesses with specimens which have been authenticated.

(4) Distinctive characteristics and the like. Appearance, contents, substance, internal patterns, or other distinctive characteristics, taken in conjunction with circumstances.[1]

(5) Voice identification. Identification of a voice, whether heard first hand or through mechanical or electronic transmission or recording, by opinion based upon hearing the voice at any time under circumstances connecting it with the alleged speaker.

(6) Telephone conversations. Telephone conversations, by evidence that a call was made to the number assigned at the time by the telephone company to a particular person or business, if (A) in the case of a person, circumstances, including self-identification, show the person answering to be the one called, or (B) in the case of a business, the call was made to a place of business and the conversation related to business reasonably transacted over the telephone.

(7) Public records or reports. Evidence that a writing authorized by law to be recorded or filed and in fact recorded or filed in a public office, or a purported public record, report, statement, or data compilation, in any form, is from the public office where items of this nature are kept.

(8) Ancient documents or data compilations. Evidence that a document or data compilation, in any form, (A) is in such condition as to create no suspicion concerning its authenticity, (B) was in a place where it, if authentic, would likely be, and (C) has been in existence 20 years or more at the time it is offered.

(9) Process or system. Evidence describing a process or system used to produce a result and showing that the process or system produces an accurate result.

(10) Methods provided by statute or rule. Any method of authentication or identification provided by a rule of the Supreme Judicial Court of this Commonwealth or by a statute or as provided in the Constitution of the Commonwealth.

---

§ 9.2 [1] *Com. v. Siny Van Tran*, 460 Mass 535, 546, 953 NE2d 139, 152 (2011) (passenger manifest and "ticket inquiry" were authenticated by distinctive internal codes used only by United Airlines) (Text cited).

Fed R Evid 901(b) is identical, with the exception of paragraph (10), where the references are to the parallel federal authorities.

The methods of authentication provided by Proposed Mass R 901 largely reflect current Massachusetts law. The process of authenticating objects, documents, and analogous items of evidence—e.g., computer printouts, voice identification, and telephone conversations—is often affected not only by common-law rules or statutes but also by a number of rules of court. The primary rules in this regard are Mass R Civ P 44, Fed R Civ P 44, Mass R Crim P 39-40, and Fed R Crim P 27. Rules pertaining to discovery procedures also offer a method of establishing the authenticity of evidence that is likely to be offered at trial. See, e.g., Mass R Civ P 26, 30, 34, 36, and 37. Mass R Civ P 36 may be particularly helpful in that it provides a pretrial procedure to establish the genuineness of documents served on the adversary in accordance with its provisions.

We discuss particular examples of authentication below and note where current Massachusetts law varies from the Proposed Rules.

§ 9.3 Documents

§ 9.3.1 In General

Most authenticity problems relate to documents.[1] A document may be authenticated by the following evidence other than the document itself:

1. By a judicial admission on behalf of the opponent, see § 2.2.
2. By testimony (a) of the writer of the genuine document; (b) of a witness who saw the genuine document written or who is familiar with the handwriting on the document; (c) of document experts, see § 7.6.2.f; or (d) of a witness who offers information as to circumstantial facts.[2]

---

§ 9.3 [1] *Evans v. Lorillard Tobacco Co.*, 465 Mass 411, 990 NE2d 997 (2013) (relevance of documents may be established by category, but authenticity of a document generally must be decided individually; authenticity of exhibits may be established by stipulation).

[2] For example, see *Com. v. Nardi*, 452 Mass 379, 396, 893 NE2d 1221, 1235 (2008) (testimony of witness that photocopy was of check she cashed and identifying her signature was sufficient to authenticate photocopy) (Text cited); *Frick Co. v. New England Insulation Co.*, 347 Mass 461, 468-469, 198 NE2d 433, 438 (1964) (bill authenticated by variety of facts as well as by direct testimony).

3. By miscellaneous statutes and rules, including the authenticating certificates provided for in numerous Massachusetts statutes and rules, see § 9.3.3.

§ 9.3.2 *Selected Authenticating Circumstances*

There are a number of circumstances that occur frequently and have been recognized by the courts as tending to authenticate a document. Authentication by circumstantial evidence is not limited to the configurations set forth here. Rather, proof of any circumstances that would support a finding of genuineness will serve to authenticate a document or other item of evidence.

a. Age

The rule providing that the age of the document provides evidence of authenticity should be distinguished from the ancient document hearsay exception, which relates to the truth of the assertions in documents.

Age alone authenticates a document when the following requirements are met:

1. The document must be at least 30 years old.[3] The age of the document is determined from the date of execution to the date of the offer in evidence. This is an arbitrary requirement. The 30 years of existence must be proved by extrinsic evidence; the date on the face of the document and even the appearance of age of the document as a rule are not sufficient. Proposed Mass R Evid 901(b)(8) would liberalize authentication under the ancient document rule by reducing the required age to 20 years. The other requirements (honest and ancient appearance and appropriate custody) would remain intact.
2. The document must present an honest and ancient appearance.[4]

---

[3] *Drury v. Midland Railroad*, 127 Mass 571 (1879); *Tolman v. Emerson*, 21 Mass (4 Pick) 160 (1826).

[4] *Green v. Chelsea*, 41 Mass (24 Pick) 71 (1883).

3. The document must come from a place of custody where a genuine document of its kind would be likely to be found.[5]
4. In some states, it is held that where the document is a deed to land the person relying upon authentication by age must be in possession. While there is language in some cases indicating a similar requirement in Massachusetts,[6] it is likely that today possession is not a requirement and that Massachusetts will follow the modern trend toward admissibility upon proof of any proper confirmatory circumstances.[7]

b. Contents and Handwriting

Where the nature of the contents of the document or other circumstantial facts indicate its authenticity, the document may be held to be authentic.[8] Thus, for example, where a letter is sent by A to B containing information that B presumably does not know and, in the course of post, A receives a letter purporting to be sent by B and containing an answer to A's inquiries or an indication that B now knows the information conveyed by A's letter, this is usually sufficient authentication of the return letter as a letter from B.[9]

Authenticity of a document may be inferred from the authenticity of the signature on the document.[10] For a discussion of proof of handwriting, see § 7.6.2.f.

c. Custody

Where a document that is a public record is produced from the custody of a person upon whom the law places a duty to keep custody of the document, the document is sufficiently authenticated. Even

---

[5] *Whitman v. Shaw*, 166 Mass 451, 44 NE 333 (1896).

[6] See, e.g., *Phillips v. Watuppa Reservoir Co.*, 184 Mass 404, 68 NE 848 (1903).

[7] See *Cunningham v. Davis*, 175 Mass 213, 56 NE 2 (1900); *Boston v. Richardson*, 105 Mass 351, 371-372 (1870).

[8] *Irving v. Goodimate Co.*, 320 Mass 454, 70 NE2d 414 (1946); *Com. v. Williams*, 63 Mass App 615, 827 NE2d 1281 (2005) (fact that filer received benefits and his attorney received fees was sufficient to authenticate workers' compensation form as having been filed) (Text cited).

[9] *Connecticut v. Bradish*, 14 Mass (14 Tyng) 296, 300 (1817).

[10] *Simpson v. Davis*, 119 Mass 269 (1876).

private documents, such as business records, may be authenticated by testimony as to their proper custody.[11]

§ 9.3.3 Self-Authentication, Official Certificates and Seals; Miscellaneous Statutes and Rules

Proposed Mass R Evid 902 provides:

Self-Authentication
Extrinsic evidence of authenticity as a condition precedent to admissibility is not required with respect to the following:

(1) Domestic public documents under seal. A document bearing a seal purporting to be that of the United States, or of any State, district, Commonwealth, territory, or insular possession thereof, or the Panama Canal Zone, or the Trust Territory of the Pacific Islands, or of a political subdivision, department, officer, or agency thereof, and a signature purporting to be an attestation or execution.[12]

(2) Domestic public documents not under seal. A document purporting to bear the signature in his official capacity of an officer or employee of any entity included in paragraph (1) hereof, having no seal, if a public officer having a seal and having official duties in the district or political subdivision of the officer or employee certifies under seal that the signer has the official capacity and that the signature is genuine.[13]

(3) Foreign public documents. A document purporting to be executed or attested in his official capacity by a person authorized by the laws of a foreign country to make the execution or attestation, and accompanied by a final certification as to the genuineness of the signature and official position (A) of the executing or attesting person, or (B) of any foreign official whose certification of genuineness of signature and official position relates to the execution or attestation or is in a chain of

---

[11] *Com. v. Duddie Ford, Inc.*, 28 Mass App 426, 435, 551 NE2d 1211, 1212 (1990) (loan documents provided by customer not admissible to prove truth of contents, but admissible to show what was on record at and relied upon by bank in making loan, when properly authenticated by bank officer); *W. A. Robinson, Inc. v. Burke*, 327 Mass 670, 100 NE2d 366 (1951).

[12] This is to the same effect as GL 233, § 69 and Mass R Crim P 39(a). See *Rossi v. Rossi*, 348 Mass 796, 206 NE2d 53 (1965). See also *Com. v. Key*, 381 Mass 19, 31, 407 NE2d 327, 335-336 (1980). The Proposed Rule, however, applies broadly to all public documents.

[13] This is to the same effect as Mass R Civ P 44(a)(1) and Mass R Crim P 40(a)(1) requiring "double certification" for public records other than those kept in the Commonwealth.

certification of genuineness of signature and official position relating to the execution or attestation. A final certification may be made by a secretary of embassy or legation, consul general, consul, vice consul, or consular agent of the United States, or a diplomatic or consular official of the foreign country assigned or accredited to the United States. If reasonable opportunity has been given to all parties to investigate the authenticity and accuracy of official documents, the court may, for good cause shown, order that they be treated as presumptively authentic without final certification or permit them to be evidenced by an attested summary with or without final certification.[14]

(4) Certified copies of public records. A copy of an official record or report or entry therein, or of a document authorized by law to be recorded or filed and actually recorded or filed in a public office, including data compilations in any form, certified as correct by the custodian or other person authorized to make the certification, by certificate complying with paragraph (1), (2), or (3) of this rule or complying with any law of the United States or of this Commonwealth.[15]

(5) Official publications. Books, pamphlets, or other publications purporting to be issued by public authority.[16]

(6) Newspapers and periodicals. Printed materials purporting to be newspapers or periodicals.[17]

(7) Trade inscriptions and the like. Inscriptions, signs, tags, or labels purporting to have been affixed in the course of business and indicating ownership, control, or origin.[18]

---

[14] This is to the same effect as Mass R Civ P 44(a)(2) and Mass R Crim P 40(a)(2) concerning "official records." See *Com. v. Martinez*, 425 Mass 382, 395, 681 NE2d 818, 828 (1997). The Proposed Rule, however, covers the broader area of foreign public documents.

[15] Copies of public records are authenticated when certified under the provisions of paragraph (1), (2), or (3). See GL 233, § 79A (copies of public records shall be admitted in evidence equally with the originals when certified by the person in charge thereof).

[16] This paragraph is not inconsistent with, but would broaden current Massachusetts statutes and rules. See GL 233, § 75 (limited to printed copies of legislative and administrative bodies); GL 30A, § 6 (documents in the Massachusetts register); Mass R Civ P 44(a)(1) and Mass R Crim P 40(a)(1) (official records kept within the Commonwealth). Cf. *Bowes v. Inspector of Buildings of Brockton*, 347 Mass 295, 197 NE2d 676 (1964) (municipal ordinances and maps may be authenticated by testimony of city clerk).

[17] Current Massachusetts statutes and rules do not contain a similar provision; however, it can be implied from GL 233, § 79D (allowing for admissibility of copies of such materials if made in machines of a public library or university in the Commonwealth and certified by the person in charge thereof).

[18] This is to the same effect as existing Massachusetts law. See *Smith v. Ariens Co.*, 375 Mass 620, 377 NE2d 954 (1978).

(8) Acknowledged documents. Documents accompanied by a certificate of acknowledgement executed in the manner provided by law by a notary public or other officer authorized by law to take acknowledgements.[19]

(9) Commercial paper and related documents. Commercial paper, signatures thereon, and documents relating thereto to the extent provided by general commercial law.[20]

(10) Presumptions created by law. Any signature, document, or other matter declared by any law of the United States or this Commonwealth to be presumptively or prima facie genuine or authentic.[21]

(11) Certified copies of hospital, dispensary or clinic, or sanitarium records. A copy of a record kept by any hospital, dispensary or clinic, or sanitarium, if certified by the person in custody thereof to be true and complete.[22]

Fed R Evid 902 is identical with the exceptions of paragraph (4), (10), (11), and (12). Paragraphs (4) and (10) reference the parallel federal authorities. However, Fed R Evid 902 paragraphs (11) and (12), concerning domestic and foreign records of regularly conducted activity, are not included in the proposed Mass R Evid 902.[23] Proposed

[19] This is to a similar effect as GL 233, § 73 (concerning in state and out of state oaths and affidavits administered or taken by a notary public and certified under his official seal). *See* Wigmore § 2165 (Chad rev 1978). Cf. *Kirby v. Kirby*, 338 Mass 263, 155 NE2d 165 (1959).

[20] This is to the same effect as Massachusetts law by virtue of the Uniform Commercial Code.

[21] This paragraph addresses statutes that deal with matters not covered by specific provisions of the rule. See, e.g., GL 9, § 11 (Great Seal); GL 233, § 77 (copies of records of banks and trust companies); GL 233, § 79A (private records); GL 233, § 79G (medical and hospital bills); GL 233, § 80 (stenographic transcripts).

[22] This is to the same effect as GL 233, § 79 (concerning admissibility into evidence of records and copies of hospitals and certain institutions). Cf. *Custody of Two Minors*, 19 Mass App 552, 560, 476 NE2d 235, 240-241 (1985) (admission of hospital record certified before notary, but without affidavit or statement under penalties of perjury, not error).

[23] Fed R Evid 902 paragraphs (11) and (12) are as follows:

> **(11) Certified domestic records of regularly conducted activity**. The original or a duplicate of a domestic record of regularly conducted activity that would be admissible under Rule 803(6) if accompanied by a written declaration of its custodian or other qualified person, in a manner complying with any Act of Congress or rule prescribed by the Supreme Court pursuant to statutory authority, certifying that the record:
>
> (A) was made at or near the time of the occurrence of the matters set forth by, or from information transmitted by, a person with knowledge of those matters;
> (B) was kept in the course of the regularly conducted activity; and
> (C) was made by the regularly conducted activity as a regular practice.

Mass R Evid 902(11), concerning certified copies of hospital, dispensary or clinic, or sanitarium records is not contained in Fed R Evid 902.

In accordance with proposed Mass R Evid 901(b)(10), which recognizes any method of authentication provided by statute or by other rules of court, Massachusetts' other "self-authenticating" methods are as follows:

- GL 233, § 68, provides that "[a] signature to an attested instrument or writing, except a will, may be proved in the same manner as if it were not attested."[24]
- GL 233, § 76, requires that state and municipal records other than records of the department of telecommunications and energy relating to common carriers and records of the registry of motor vehicles, be attested under seal.[25]
- GL 233, § 76A (records of Securities and Exchange Commission must be attested under a certificate of a member).
- GL 233, § 76B (printed copies of rate schedules of Interstate Commerce Commission that show an ICC number and date admissible without certification).

A party intending to offer a record into evidence under this paragraph must provide written notice of that intention to all adverse parties, and must make the record and declaration available for inspection sufficiently in advance of their offer into evidence to provide an adverse party with a fair opportunity to challenge them.

(12) Certified foreign records of regularly conducted activity. In a civil case, the original or a duplicate of a foreign record of regularly conducted activity that would be admissible under Rule 803(6) if accompanied by a written declaration by its custodian or other qualified person certifying that the record:

(A) was made at or near the time of the occurrence of the matters set forth by, or from information transmitted by, a person with knowledge of those matters;
(B) was kept in the course of the regularly conducted activity; and
(C) was made by the regularly conducted activity as a regular practice.

The declaration must be signed in a manner that, if falsely made, would subject the maker to criminal penalty under the laws of the country where the declaration is signed. A party intending to offer a record into evidence under this paragraph must provide written notice of that intention to all adverse parties, and must make the record and declaration available for inspection sufficiently in advance of their offer into evidence to provide an adverse party with a fair opportunity to challenge them.

[24] See *Brigham v. Palmer*, 85 Mass (3 All) 450 (1862), for a statement of the common-law rule as to authentication of an attested document.

[25] *Com. v. Cuevas*, 87 Mass App 205, 27 NE3d 411 (2015) (attested copy of judgment of criminal conviction from New York was properly admitted).

- GL 233, § 77 (copies of records of banks and trust companies doing business in the Commonwealth must have an affidavit acknowledged before notary public or clerk of court under seal of same).[26]
- GL 233, § 78 (business records); § 79D (newspapers and photographic prints); § 79E (reproductions of public or business records); § 79J (business records and photocopies thereof may be certified by affidavit).[27]

It must also be noted that where a statute requires that a record be attested, the original attestation of the appropriate official must appear on the document offered in evidence. A photocopy of an attested document is not itself an attested document. As the Supreme Judicial Court explained in *Com. v. Deramo*[28]

> Merely making a copy of the original attestation along with a copy of the underlying record does not serve the purpose of the attestation requirement, as the copied attestation no longer signifies that the official in question is vouching for the authenticity of the copy that has just been made.

Other pertinent rules and statutes involving authentication by judicial admission are discussed in §§ 2.3, 2.4. Note also that a statute in a specialized area may make a document prima facie genuine—e.g., GL 106, § 1-202 (certain third-party documents prima facie genuine).

---

[26] *Com. v. Perez*, 89 Mass App 51, 59, 44 NE3d 886, 893 (2016) (this statute is not the exclusive means of authenticating bank records).

[27] *Com. v. Monahan*, 349 Mass 139, 167, 207 NE2d 29, 46 (1965) (interpreting §§ 77, 78, and 79E); *Ricciutti v. Sylvania Electric Products, Inc.*, 343 Mass 347, 349, 178 NE2d 857, 859-860 (1961) (records admitted under § 78).

[28] *Com. v. Deramo*, 436 Mass 40, 48, 762 NE2d 815, 821 (2002) (Text cited). Unless the statute specifically requires it, attestation does not require a handwritten signature; a stamped signature is adequate. *Com. v. Martinez-Guzman*, 76 Mass App 167, 920 NE2d 322 (2010).

§ 9.4 Telephone Conversations

Massachusetts law is consistent with Proposed Mass Rules 901(b)(5) and (6), supra.[1] There are a variety of circumstances that will suffice to authenticate the identity of a person with whom a witness has had a telephone conversation. It is sufficient if the witness testifies that she recognizes the voice on the other end of the telephone, regardless of who initiated the conversation.[2] The witness need not have met the individual to be identified in person, if she has had previous telephone conversations and there is evidence of circumstances attending those calls tending to establish the individual's identity.[3] In *Com. v. Carpinto,*[4] the victim of obscene and threatening telephone calls was unable to identify the speaker at the time she received the calls. However, she recorded them on her answering machine and was later able to identify the voice as that of the defendant, after she heard him speaking in court. This was the first time she had heard him speak in her presence in several years. The court held that where a recording of a telephone conversation exists and is deemed an accurate representation, a witness may offer identification testimony upon a showing that she is familiar with the speaker's voice.

Other circumstantial evidence may suffice to authenticate the identity of a person on the telephone, even where the witness does not recognize the voice.[5] When the witness has telephoned a number listed in the directory as belonging to a certain business or entity and the person answering takes the call on behalf of the entity, there is sufficient proof to admit the evidence of the call as one to that entity.[6] When the witness has called the listed number of a specific individual,

---

§ 9.4 [1] The Rules were cited with approval in *Com. v. Anderson*, 404 Mass 767, 770, 537 NE2d 146, 148 (1989) and *Com. v. Mezzanotti*, 26 Mass App 522, 527, 529 NE2d 1351, 1355 (1988) (citing Proposed Mass R Evid 901(b)(5) to support identification of voice heard through a wall where baseboard had been removed).

[2] *Com. v. Leonardi*, 413 Mass 757, 604 NE2d 23 (1992) (victim could identify telephone caller as defendant from hearing voice during earlier assault); *Com. v. Perez*, 411 Mass 249, 262, 581 NE2d 1010, 1018 (1991).

[3] *Com. v. Anderson*, 404 Mass at 770, 537 NE2d at 148 (1989); *Com. v. Hartford*, 346 Mass 482, 487-488, 194 NE2d 401, 404-405 (1963) (other circumstances were sufficient evidence of identity of speaker).

[4] *Com. v. Carpinto*, 37 Mass App 51, 636 NE2d 1349 (1994).

[5] See *Com. v. Anderson*, supra; *Com. v. Hartford*, supra; *Com. v. Loach*, 46 Mass App 313, 705 NE2d 642 (1999); *Com. v. Wojcik*, 43 Mass App 595, 606, 686 NE2d 452, 460 (1997).

[6] *Bond Pharmacy, Inc. v. Cambridge*, 338 Mass 488, 490-491, 156 NE2d 34, 36-37 (1959); *Pietroforte v. Yellow Cab of Somerville, Inc.*, 19 Mass App 961, 473 NE2d 1148 (1985).

the person answering says he is that individual, and there is evidence that no other person is at that number, the conversation is admissible as a call with that individual.[7]

Testimony that a witness made a call to an address not stated, and the person answering claimed to be a certain individual, is not sufficient to authenticate that the call was with that person.[8] When a witness has received an incoming call from a person claiming to be A, without more, this is insufficient evidence to admit the call as a conversation with A.[9]

When a court has admitted evidence that a telephone conversation was had with a given party, it ultimately remains an issue for the jury to determine whether the call was with that party.[10]

§ 9.5 Real Evidence

§ 9.5.1 Authenticity, Chain of Custody

An item of real evidence must be authenticated, or "identified," as the thing or event its proponent represents it to be.[1] Authentication is usually accomplished by the testimony of a witness who testifies that the object is what it purports to be.[2] If the object is one the witness can identify by observation, his testimony that he recognizes it will be sufficient. If not, it may be necessary for him to have placed an identifying mark or label thereon, or to otherwise create a "chain of custody" that will help him authenticate the object.[3]

---

[7] *Massachusetts N.E. Street Railway v. Plum Island Beach Co.*, 255 Mass 104, 114, 151 NE 84, 86-87 (1926).

[8] *Virta v. Mackey*, 343 Mass 286, 291, 178 NE2d 571, 574 (1961).

[9] *Com. v. Gettigan*, 252 Mass 450, 148 NE 113 (1925); *Com. v. Howard*, 42 Mass App 322, 677 NE2d 233 (1997).

[10] *Com. v. Hartford*, 346 Mass 482, 488, 194 NE2d 401, 405 (1963).

§ 9.5 [1] *Com. v. LaCorte*, 373 Mass 700, 704, 369 NE2d 1006, 1009 (1977).

[2] *Com. v. Drayton*, 386 Mass 39, 48, 434 NE2d 997, 1005 (1982) (Text cited); *Com. v. Leneski*, 66 Mass App 291 (2006) (testimony by person who "burned" a CD was sufficient to authenticate it).

[3] *Com. v. Hogg*, 365 Mass 290, 311 NE2d 63 (1974); *Com. v. Tofanelli*, 67 Mass App 61, 851 NE2d 1111 (2006) (detective's testimony that white pill inscribed with a "K" was the same one he received in drug transaction was sufficient to authenticate it); *Com. v. Herring*, 66 Mass App 360, 847 NE2d 1119 (2006) (affirming authentication of cocaine rocks on basis of officer's testimony that they were the same ones seized from defendant's apartment, where he had opened the bags, examined and counted the rocks).

The fact that there may be weaknesses in the identification or chain of custody of evidence usually goes to the weight rather than the admissibility of the evidence.[4]

§ 9.5.2 Destruction of Real Evidence

Neither the Massachusetts Proposed Rules nor the Federal Rules address the issue of what is to be done when an item of evidence that once existed has disappeared. When significant physical items are lost or destroyed, intentionally or accidentally, before trial, fairness may require the taking of remedial measures to avoid the possibility that the party who had access to the evidence may obtain an improper advantage. Remedies for the spoliation of evidence are limited to appropriately tailored sanctions in the underlying action in which the evidence would have been offered. There is no tort cause of action for spoliation of evidence, although if a third-party witness agrees to preserve an item of evidence there may be a remedy in contract.[5]

a. Criminal Cases

In a criminal case when potentially exculpatory real evidence is discarded, lost, returned to its owner, or destroyed (including during destructive testing by experts), a defendant may seek to have the charges dismissed, or to preclude the prosecution from relying on the evidence in question. In deciding what, if any, sanctions are appropriate, the court must weigh the culpability of the government, the materiality of the evidence, and the potential for prejudice.

In *Com. v. Williams*,[6] the Supreme Judicial Court reviewed the previous cases with respect to the loss or destruction of potentially exculpatory evidence. It first analyzed the issue as one of constitutional due

---

[4] *Com. v. Viriyahiranpaiboon*, 412 Mass 224, 230, 588 NE2d 643, 648 (1992); *Com. v. Andrews*, 403 Mass 441, 530 NE2d 1222 (1988); *Com. v. Best*, 50 Mass App 722, 740 NE2d 1065 (2001); *Com. v. Jordan*, 50 Mass App 369, 737 NE2d 511 (2000); *Com. v. Colon*, 33 Mass App 304, 309, 598 NE2d 1143, 1146 (1992). Compare *Irwin v. Ware*, 392 Mass 745, 750-751, 467 NE2d 1292, 1296-1298 (1984) (failure to produce specific evidence to establish chain of custody; evidence of blood test results improperly admitted).

[5] *Fletcher v. Dorchester Mutual Ins. Co.*, 437 Mass 544, 773 NE2d 420 (2002).

[6] *Com. v. Williams*, 455 Mass 706, 919 NE2d 685 (2010) (defendant failed to establish reasonable probability that a lost opportunity to observe Cellmark DNA testing was exculpatory).

process under *Brady v. Maryland*, 373 US 83 (1963), which imposed a duty on the government to furnish exculpatory evidence to a criminal defendant. The Court established that the correct analysis imposes an initial burden on a defendant to establish "a reasonable probability, based on concrete evidence rather than a fertile imagination," that access to lost or destroyed material would have produced evidence favorable to his cause. Where the defendant fails to meet this initial burden, the analysis is complete and the defendant is entitled to no remedy.[7] If the defendant does meet the burden of establishing that the evidence was probably exculpatory, then the Court must conduct a balancing test with respect to government culpability, materiality, and prejudice to determine the remedy.[8]

The *Williams* Court also indicated that a criminal defendant might have a remedy independent of the constitutional claim. Where "the Commonwealth has acted in bad faith or recklessly, resulting in the loss or destruction of evidence, the defendant may be independently entitled to a remedy even without meeting the [constitutional] test."[9] Even a negligent loss or destruction of evidence might permit the defendant to argue that an inadequate or incompetent investigation gave rise to reasonable doubt. The Court had no reason to explore the scope of any remedy for bad faith in *Williams*, where no such

---

[7] 455 Mass at 718, 919 NE2d at 694. In accord, *Com. v. Meas*, 467 Mass 434, 5 NE3d 864 (2014) (defendant did not establish reasonable probability that videotape from store near murder, lost by police, was exculpatory where two other tapes were in evidence and other identification evidence by witnesses existed); *Com. v. Carr*, 464 Mass 855, 986 NE2d 380 (2013) (affirming trial court's decision that missing evidence was neither exculpatory nor of demonstrable benefit to defendant); *Com. v. Marinho*, 464 Mass 115, 120, 981 NE2d 648, 654 (2013) (defendant presented no evidence of content of missing witness statement, thus claim it would have been inconsistent with trial testimony was speculative); *Com. v. Sanford*, 460 Mass 441, 951 NE2d 922 (2011) (remanding for further factfinding on issues under *Williams* standard); *Com. v. McIntyre*, 430 Mass 529, 536, 721 NE2d 911, 918 (1999) (balancing other factors is not necessary when defendant fails to meet initial burden). Cf. *Com. v. Ocasio*, 434 Mass 1, 746 NE2d 469 (2001) (lost evidence doctrine inapplicable to defendant's motion to suppress based on lost search warrant).

[8] *Com. v. Meas*, 467 Mass 434, 5 NE3d 864 (2014) (defendant was not prejudiced because he was able to cast doubt on cross-examination on thoroughness and accuracy of police investigation and received missing evidence instruction); *Com. v. DiBenedetto*, 427 Mass 414, 419, 693 NE2d 1007, 1011 (1998) (no prejudice shown where Commonwealth failed to make available evidence per pretrial conference report, prosecution expert wiped away blood on sneaker during test, but defense expert found blood on other sneaker); *Com. v. Willie*, 400 Mass 427, 432, 510 NE2d 258, 261-262 (1987) (remanding for hearing by trial judge on prejudice).

[9] 455 Mass at 718, 919 NE2d at 695.

claim was made. In a footnote, however, the Court seemed to invite future criminal defendants to argue that the spectrum of remedies available under the spoliation doctrine in civil cases might be applied in the criminal context.[10]

The inquiry into what remedy, if any, is available for the loss or destruction of evidence is highly fact specific and some cases have provided relief,[11] while others have not.[12] Whether a defendant is entitled

---

[10] 455 Mass at 719 n.10, 919 NE2d at 695.

[11] See, e.g., *Com. v. Kater*, 432 Mass 404, 421, 734 NE2d 1164, 1179 (2000) (*Kater VII*) (affirming trial court's exclusion of testimony of witness who performed improper destructive tool mark test); *Com. v. Harwood*, 432 Mass 290, 733 NE2d 547 (2000) (affirming trial court's order suppressing testimony of prosecution witness as remedy for lost letter that might have been exculpatory); *Com. v. Gliniewicz*, 398 Mass 744, 500 NE2d 1324 (1986) (defendants entitled to new trial where evidence altered by Commonwealth's experts, comparable testing no longer possible, destruction of items was either intended or condoned by Commonwealth, evidence was material and its destruction prejudicial); *Com. v. Rodriguez*, 50 Mass App 405, 737 NE2d 910 (2000) (affirming trial court's instruction to jury to resolve all doubts created by missing evidence in defendant's favor); *Com. v. White*, 47 Mass App 430, 713 NE2d 987 (1999) (Commonwealth destroyed cocaine after request by defendant to preserve, and defendant demonstrated discrepancy between purity of sample from controlled buy and purity of stash; defendant thus demonstrated prima facie case for claim that police had diluted drugs to enhance quantity; case remanded for resentencing on a lesser quantity); *Com. v. Sasville*, 35 Mass App 15, 616 NE2d 476 (1993) (dismissal required where Commonwealth failed to notify defendant that fetus was being preserved following abortion performed on alleged rape victim, then allowed fetus to be destroyed without opportunity for defendant to conduct blood tests). Cf. *Com. v. Fitzgerald*, 402 Mass 517, 524 NE2d 72 (1988) (defendant entitled to new trial in rape case based on newly discovered medical bill proving vasectomy—due diligence demonstrated in part by proof insurance company had destroyed its records). Compare *Com. v. Holman*, 27 Mass App 830, 544 NE2d 598 (1989) (defendant not entitled to dismissal of charge of operating under influence of liquor, despite erasure of arguably exculpatory videotape of booking) with *Com v. Cameron*, 25 Mass App 538, 520 NE2d 1326 (1988) (conviction of operating under influence of liquor reversed, defendant not entitled to dismissal, but error to refuse to allow defendant to question about and comment upon Commonwealth's failure to produce videotape of booking).

[12] See, e.g., *Com. v. Narea*, 454 Mass 1003, 907 NE2d 644 (2009) (single Justice did not abuse discretion in holding the trial court's ruling that Commonwealth could not introduce testimony concerning "buy money" that had been placed back in circulation was too extreme); *Com. v. Clemente*, 452 Mass 295, 309, 893 NE2d 19, 34 (2008) (defendant's arguments that fanny pack that had been returned to owner might have disclosed gunshot residue or evidence that it contained a weapon were speculative); *Com. v. Laguer*, 448 Mass 585, 601, 863 NE2d 46, 60 (2007) (defendant could not show that lost fingerprint evidence would have been favorable to his case); *Com. v. Murphy*, 442 Mass 485, 813 NE2d 820 (2004) (defendant failed to establish that missing footwear impression on piece of linoleum from crime scene would have produced favorable evidence); *Com. v. Dinkins*, 440 Mass 715, 802 NE2d 76 (2004) (defendant did not establish that gun and missing shell casings would have helped his case); *Com. v. O'Day*, 440 Mass 296, 798 NE2d 275 (2003) (grenade simulator found in defendant's residence was properly destroyed for safety reasons); *Com. v. Cintron*, 438 Mass 779,

784 NE2d 617 (2003) (loss of box on which latent fingerprint was found was not prejudicial where fingerprint had been photographed); *Com. v. Simpson*, 434 Mass 570, 577, 750 NE2d 977, 987 (2001) (destruction of van arguably relevant to ballistics testimony—bad faith not shown, defendant had nine months to view van, had photos of bullet holes); *Com. v. Lopez*, 433 Mass 406, 742 NE2d 1067 (2001) (Commonwealth's destruction of truck, despite court order to preserve it, did not require sanctions where there was no reasonable possibility it contained material exculpatory evidence); *Com. v. Kater*, 432 Mass 404, 417, 734 NE2d 1164, 1177 (2000) (*Kater VII*) (cumulative prejudicial effect of lost items did not warrant reversal); *Com. v. Woodward*, 427 Mass 659, 679, 694 NE2d 1277, 1292 (1998) (prosecution was responsible for medical examiner's failure to preserve tissue samples, the lost evidence was material, but there was not sufficient prejudice to warrant dismissal of the indictment); *Com. v. Eakin*, 427 Mass 590, 696 NE2d 499 (1998) (no prejudice when city destroyed house containing alleged building code violations, because defendants had opportunity to photograph it and have it examined by expert prior to demolition); *Com. v. Hunter*, 426 Mass 715, 690 NE2d 815 (1998) (dismissal not required by destruction of fingerprint during testing where defendant had been furnished enlarged photos of same, or by loss of police notes of witness interview, no bad faith shown); *Com. v. Taylor*, 426 Mass 189, 687 NE2d 631 (1997) (no reversible error based on failure of prosecution's expert to cut sneakers into sections before testing for presence of gasoline, in order to determine where on sneaker it was found); *Com. v. Nom*, 426 Mass 152, 686 NE2d 1017 (1997) (dismissal not required by standard procedure of recording over tape of police telephone calls where defendant could not establish reasonable possibility it contained favorable evidence); *Com. v. Waters*, 420 Mass 276, 649 NE2d 724 (1995) (conviction affirmed; court considered, among other factors, that defendant had been permitted to depose a number of witnesses as mitigation of police error in losing tapes of radio and telephone calls); *Com. v. Otsuki*, 411 Mass 218, 230, 581 NE2d 999, 1007 (1991) (conviction affirmed, despite missing bullet fragments); *Com. v. Troy*, 405 Mass 253, 540 NE2d 162 (1989) (conviction affirmed against argument that potentially exculpatory blood samples were not retained); *Com. v. Richenburg*, 401 Mass 663, 668, 518 NE2d 1143 (1988) (D's claim of error rejected, in part, because D made no request for smear slides he later argued were improperly discarded); *Com. v. Shipps*, 399 Mass 820, 836, 507 NE2d 671, 682 (1987) (better practice is to photograph stages of destructive testing, but error, if any, was harmless here); *Com. v. Mattei*, 455 Mass 840, 860, 920 NE2d 845, 862 (2010) (police failure to seize roll of duct tape from scene where victim's mouth had been sealed by duct tape did not call for sanctions); *Com. v. Upton U.*, 59 Mass App 252, 795 NE2d 575 (2003) (failure to videotape SAIN interview with child did not amount to destruction of evidence); *Com. v. North*, 52 Mass App Ct 603, 755 NE2d 312 (2001) (accidental taping over of videotape that was only marginally probative); *Com. v. Simmarano*, 50 Mass App 312, 737 NE2d 488 (2000) (destruction of "911" tapes after 90 days pursuant to established archive procedures, with no showing that evidence was exculpatory, did not require relief; court cautions Commonwealth that routine destruction of potentially exculpatory evidence after a short time creates an unnecessary risk of sanctions and that in future cases court may not deem such destruction benign); *Com. v. Beauchamp*, 49 Mass App 591, 611, 732 NE2d 311, 329 (2000) (destruction of gun and knife since time of first trial, 24 years earlier, was not result of culpable conduct by Commonwealth, nor could defendant show that objects themselves could have been exculpatory); *Com. v. Noonan*, 48 Mass App 356, 720 NE2d 828 (1999) (negligent disposal of hat that had been photographed and tested for trace evidence with negative results was "foolish," but not error to deny motion to

to a missing evidence instruction in a criminal case is within the trial court's discretion once the defendant has shown that the evidence might have been exculpatory and the balancing factors have been considered. If the court gives such an instruction, it should generally permit, rather than require, a negative inference against the Commonwealth.[13]

There are special circumstances attendant to defense requests for access to, and the Commonwealth's responsibility for preserving evidence from a homicide victim's body. In *Com. v. Woodward*,[14] the Court noted that, "Autopsy procedures are inherently destructive. . . ." Under the circumstances of the case, the Court held that the defendant was not entitled to relief based on the claims of lost body parts, delay in supplying defense attorneys with medical information, and the denial of a motion for an independent autopsy. The Court noted that whatever due process rights a defendant might have to an independent autopsy must be balanced against the statutory right of the victim's family to return of the body following the medical examiner's autopsy. It concluded that a defendant would have to show cause and a specific need in a motion for access to a victim's body. The Court suggested that "the optimal balancing and reconciliation of each party's interests could have been by allowing [defendant's] expert to be present at the [medical examiner's] autopsy."[15]

---

dismiss); *Com. v. Burns*, 43 Mass App 263, 683 NE2d 284 (1997) (dismissal not required by destruction of fingerprints, where defendant could point to no evidence showing they were exculpatory, or by destruction of original police notes where summary was provided); *Com. v. Chase*, 42 Mass App 749, 679 NE2d 1021 (1997) (no error where prosecution negligently released truck involved in homicide before defense inspection, with result it was repaired before seen by defense); *Com. v. Mitchell*, 38 Mass App 184, 646 NE2d 1073 (1995) (conviction affirmed although Commonwealth did not do blood tests on murder weapon, a knife, and fingerprint tests on knife handle destroyed ability to do blood testing later, court noted that absence of defendant's blood on knife was of marginal materiality); *Com. v. Greenberg*, 34 Mass App 197, 609 NE2d 90 (1993) (conviction affirmed where defendant's jacket was lost by Commonwealth, but jury was shown photo of jacket and told that chemists found no blood or accelerants on it). Cf. *Com. v. DeCicco*, 44 Mass App 111, 688 NE2d 1010 (1998) (under circumstances, no ineffective assistance of counsel based on lawyer's failure to inspect evidence apparently lost by prosecution).

[13] *Com. v. Kee*, 449 Mass 550, 558, 870 NE2d 57, 66 (2007).

[14] *Com. v. Woodward*, 427 Mass 659, 676, 694 NE2d 1277, 1290 (1998).

[15] *Id.*, 427 Mass at 676 n.29.

b. Civil Cases

In civil cases, the Supreme Judicial Court has held that where an item of physical evidence has been lost, destroyed, or materially altered by an expert, where he knew or should have known that the item in its original form might be material to litigation, an opposing party is entitled to an order precluding the expert from testifying about the appearance of the item before its disappearance or alteration and from expressing any opinion based thereon.[16] In *Bolton v. MBTA*,[17] the Appeals Court extended the rule to cover the destruction of evidence by the party after inspection by its expert.

In a civil case, a judge has broad discretion to fashion a remedy for the spoliation of evidence by a party. Available remedies include the exclusion of evidence offered by the party responsible for spoliation,[18] allowing the aggrieved party to present evidence about the pre-accident condition of the lost evidence and the circumstances surrounding the spoliation, and instructing the jury on the inferences that can be drawn from spoliation.[19]

Where a plaintiff loses all ability to press her cause of action as a result of the destruction or loss of records by the defendant, an appropriate sanction may include a default against the defendant.[20]

Sanctions for spoliation of evidence cannot be justified where the threat of a lawsuit is not sufficiently apparent that a reasonable person would realize the possible importance of the evidence to the resolution

---

[16] *Nally v. Volkswagen of America, Inc.*, 405 Mass 191, 197-198, 539 NE2d 1017, 1021 (1989).

[17] *Bolton v. MBTA*, 32 Mass App 654, 593 NE2d 248 (1992).

[18] *Scott v. Garfield*, 454 Mass 790, 797, 912 NE2d 1000, 1007 (2009) (defendant knew there would likely be litigation and negligently discarded columns of porch where railings collapsed; court properly precluded defendant from offering any evidence as to columns, permitted plaintiffs to inquire as to their unavailability and instructed jury they could draw adverse inference from their unavailability); *Wiedmann v. The Bradford Group*, 444 Mass 698, 831 NE2d 304 (2005) (affirming preclusion of defendant's evidence where plaintiff had notified defendant of potential claim and requested records that were subsequently destroyed); *Westover v. Leiserv, Inc.*, 64 Mass App 109, 831 NE2d 400 (2005) (preclusion of all of party's evidence with respect to a product was too severe where other similar examples of the product existed and could be examined to determine identity of manufacturer and whether there was a design defect).

[19] *Gath v. M/A-Com, Inc.*, 440 Mass 482, 488, 802 NE2d 521, 527 (2003) (affirming steps taken by trial judge).

[20] See *Keene v. Brigham & Women's Hospital, Inc.*, 439 Mass 223, 786 NE2d 824 (2003) (approving default against hospital in action for recovery for neonatal sepsis and meningitis where hospital lost records of 20-hour period of child's care).

of the potential dispute.[21] Sanctions for spoliation are also not appropriate against those parties in a case who played no role in the spoliation.[22]

§ 9.6 Photographs and Tapes

Photographs, maps, plans, and so on may be used as independent evidence or as substitutes for the narrative of a witness on the stand. Maps, photographs, and similar objects professing scientific accuracy are admitted in evidence as exhibits. It is a preliminary question of fact to be found by the trial judge whether the exhibit is sufficiently verified by proof that it is a true representation of the subject. If the offered exhibit is so verified, its admission or exclusion is not a matter of discretion but is governed by the usual rules of law as to admissibility of relevant evidence.[1]

Although a photograph is ordinarily authenticated by having a witness testify that it is a fair and accurate representation of something the witness actually saw,[2] a photograph may also be authenticated through circumstantial evidence "sufficient to support a finding that the matter in question is what its proponent claims."[3] Indeed, on occasion the foundation has been held to be implicit in a witness's testimony describing the scene pictured in a photo, even when the witness was not directly asked if the photo accurately depicted the scene.[4] If a photograph admittedly shows an object as being different from its condition at the relevant time, it may be admitted if witnesses can

---

[21] *Kippenhan v. Chaulk Services, Inc.*, 428 Mass 124, 127, 697 NE2d 527, 530 (1998).

[22] *Kippenhan v. Chaulk Services, Inc.*, supra (plaintiff in action against ambulance attendants and manufacturer of stretcher was not foreclosed from offering evidence about condition of stretcher prior to its loss by ambulance company). In *Nally v. Volkswagen of America, Inc.*, supra, the court had suggested that the rule barring testimony from an expert would apply without regard to whether the expert's conduct occurred before or after she was retained by a party to the case.

§ 9.6 [1] *Horowitz v. Bokron*, 337 Mass 739, 742, 151 NE2d 480, 483 (1958); *Howe v. Boston*, 311 Mass 278, 281, 41 NE2d 1, 3 (1942).

[2] *Com. v. Rodriguez*, 457 Mass 461, 476, 931 NE2d 20, 35 (2010) (where medical examiner who conducted autopsy did not testify, autopsy photographs could not be authenticated by substitute witness, error to admit them) (Text cited); *Com. v. Durand*, 457 Mass 574, 586 n.13, 931 NE2d 950, 961 (2010) (suggesting that autopsy photos may be authenticated by police officer who attended if medical examiner who conducted autopsy is not available).

[3] *Com. v. Figueroa*, 56 Mass App 641, 646, 779 NE2d 669, 673 (2002).

[4] *Com. v. Sheeran*, 370 Mass 82, 345 NE2d 362 (1976).

supplement the photograph by oral testimony explaining the differences.[5] Where an item of physical evidence cannot be produced at trial, a photograph of a similar item may be admitted as an exemplar when it is made clear to the jury that it is not a photograph of the actual item.[6]

Films and videotapes are admissible in evidence "if they are relevant, they provide a fair representation of that which they purport to depict, and they are not otherwise barred by an exclusionary rule."[7] In *Mahoney*, the Court held that a videotape of a booking was properly authenticated by the arresting officer who viewed the tape prior to trial and testified as to the procedure used in the videotaping process and the contents of the tape.[8] It is a mistake, however, to assume that videotapes and films necessarily constitute an objective portrayal of historical reality. Analysis of the extent to which videotapes and films may distort reality or advance a particular point of view requires a nuanced approach to how they are made and the extent to which they require interpretation.[9]

---

[5] *Renzi v. Paredes*, 452 Mass 38, 52, 890 NE2d 806, 817 (2008) (witness adequately authenticated digital photographs used as demonstrative aid as a substantial likeness of original X-rays); *Com. v. Sullivan*, 410 Mass 521, 533, 574 NE2d 966, 973 (1991) (photos of comparison hair samples properly admitted; witness adequately explained differences resulting from focusing error); *Com. v. Glanden*, 49 Mass App 250, 728 NE2d 953 (2000) (where photo of defendant identified by victim had been taken ten days before assault, it was admissible where she explained the difference in his appearance as due to hair growth).

[6] *Com. v. Housewright*, 470 Mass 665, 23 NE3d 273 (2015) (permissible to admit exemplar photo of Derringer similar to the actual gun in question).

[7] *Com. v. Mahoney*, 400 Mass 524, 527, 510 NE2d 759, 761-762 (1987). See *Com. v. Corliss*, 470 Mass 443, 23 NE3d 92 (2015) (no abuse of discretion for judge to exclude expert's videotape where there was an insufficient showing that floor level and surveillance camera positioning were the same during videotaping as they had been during the event; court notes it also would have been within judge's discretion to admit the videotape).

[8] See *Com. v. Lawson*, 425 Mass 528, 682 NE2d 845 (1997) (videotape made one and one-half years after crime, which was never represented to be a fair and accurate representation of the scene at the relevant time, was properly excluded); *Com. v. Carey*, 26 Mass App 339, 526 NE2d 1329 (1988) (videotape of field sobriety test was admissible, but testimonial statements by defendant on tape would not be if violated *Miranda* rights).

[9] See, e.g., Jessica Silbey, "Cross-Examining Film," 8 U. Md. L. J. Race, Religion, Gender & Class 17 (2008); *Com. v. Nhut Huynh*, 452 Mass 481, 895 NE2d 471 (2008) (noting extent to which videotape of event required interpretation).

Use of videotape or film at trials may be expected to increase.[10] Videotapes or films may, of course, be inadmissible on hearsay grounds, as violations of the Confrontation Clause, or for other substantive reasons.[11]

Audiotapes if properly authenticated are admissible to prove the content of prior speech, if not objectionable for substantive reasons.[12] In *Com. v. Gordon*,[13] the Court established guidelines for the use of audiotapes.[14] A judge may require it to be edited to include only relevant material. The proponent of the evidence must bring to court a recording that provides an adequate, audible, and coherent rendition of the material, and ensure that proper equipment is provided for playing it. The judge may allow a properly authenticated transcript to be provided to the jury as an aid to understanding the recording, but the lack of a transcript is not a sufficient reason to refuse to admit audiotapes.

---

[10] See *Com. v. Simmons*, 419 Mass 426, 646 NE2d 97 (1995) (videotape that provided panoramic views of apartment where murder was committed was admissible; videotape demonstrated that apartment was not quite as blood-drenched as photographs in evidence might have suggested); *Com. v. Lavalley*, 410 Mass 641, 574 NE2d 100 (1991) (not error to admit videotape of fresh complaint by victim); *Com. v. Mulica*, 401 Mass 812, 820-821, 520 NE2d 134, 138-139 (1988) (not error to exclude in first trial documentary film of Vietnam War, but on remand trial court should exercise broad discretion to consider admitting film either as evidence illustrating Vietnam experience similar to defendant's, relevant to diagnosis of post-traumatic stress syndrome (PTSD), or as chalk to illustrate expert's explanation of PTSD); *Case of Viveiros*, 53 Mass App 296, 758 NE2d 1066 (2001) (in workers' compensation case, videotape depicting tasks the job required; objection that claimant had a faster work pace than that depicted went to weight, not admissibility).

[11] See, e.g., *Com. v. Bergstrom*, 402 Mass 534, 547, 524 NE2d 366, 374 (1988) (statute that allows victim of sexual abuse to testify outside of courtroom through videotape or simultaneous transmission violates confrontation rights).

[12] *Com. v. Freiberg*, 405 Mass 282, 540 NE2d 1289 (1989) (not error to play 911 tape twice, over objection it was inflammatory); *Com. v. Silva*, 401 Mass 318, 516 NE2d 161 (1987) (security system tape recording of sounds during a larceny properly admitted); *Com. v. Fernette*, 398 Mass 658, 664, 500 NE2d 1290, 1294 (1986) (not error to admit taped confession, although recorder was turned off several times during interview; in future better practice is to stop recorder only for purpose of changing tapes); *Com. v. Wheeler*, 42 Mass App 933, 678 NE2d 168 (1997) (not error to exclude 911 tape where it was not authenticated by the evidence) (Text cited); *Com. v. Jerome*, 36 Mass App 59, 627 NE2d 948 (1994) (incomplete recording of fresh complaint interviews may render tapes inadmissible, but no error here in absence of prejudice to defendant); *Com. v. Carpenter*, 22 Mass App 911, 491 NE2d 1077 (1986) (proper to admit cassette copy, rather than original reel-to-reel tape of electronic surveillance).

[13] *Com. v. Gordon*, 389 Mass 351, 355-356, 450 NE2d 572, 575-576 (1983).

[14] The best evidence rule with respect to documents does not apply to oral communications. Therefore, a tape recording is not required to prove what was said; any competent witness may testify to what she heard. *Com. v. Gordon*, supra.

§ 9.7 Process or System

A device may record on paper an impression that the human senses have not perceived or cannot perceive—e.g., an x-ray picture. The testimony of a witness who identifies an x-ray as that of the person and bone in issue and shows that the picture was taken by a qualified technician in the standard manner upon a machine in good operating condition will serve to verify and admit the x-ray.[1] The same type of testimony is required to verify other scientific recording devices—e.g., electrocardiograms.[2]

X-rays or recordings taken of normal persons may be admitted as a basis of comparison to aid the jury in understanding the nature of the injury or disease in issue.[3] X-rays, coupled with expert testimony, may also be used to identify a body.[4]

Current Massachusetts law is consistent with Proposed Mass R Evid 901(b)(9), supra, and these methods may be employed to authenticate a variety of technological or scientific processes—e.g., the ordinary operation of computers. With respect to computer simulations, see § 7.6.2.j.

§ 9.8 Emails and Internet Communications

Emails and other forms of Internet communication are increasingly being offered as evidence in court. Admissibility, however, relies upon the same basic principles of authentication that apply to other evidence. The proponent must offer sufficient proof that the email in question is what he or she claims it is, e.g., an email from a particular person. Sufficient proof is evidence of whatever nature sufficient to convince the trier of fact by a preponderance of the evidence that the item is what the proponent claims.[1]

The Supreme Judicial Court has said, "Evidence that the defendant's name is written as the author of an email or that the electronic

---

§ 9.7 [1] *Doyle v. Singer Sewing Machine Co.*, 220 Mass 327, 107 NE 949 (1915).

[2] *Kramer v. John Hancock Mutual Life Ins. Co.*, 336 Mass 465, 146 NE2d 357 (1957).

[3] *McGrath v. Fash*, 244 Mass 327, 139 NE 303 (1923).

[4] *Com. v. Devlin*, 365 Mass 149, 310 NE2d 353 (1974).

§ 9.8 [1] *Com. v. Purdy*, 459 Mass 442, 447, 945 NE2d 372, 379 (2011) (Text cited); *Com. v. Oppenheim*, 86 Mass App 359, 16 NE3d 502 (2014) (rejecting argument that reasonable doubt standard and human practice rule applied to questions of authenticity in criminal cases).

communication originates from an e-mail or a social networking Web site such as Facebook or MySpace that bears the defendant's name is not sufficient alone to authenticate the electronic communication as having been authored or sent by the defendant. There must be some 'confirming circumstances' sufficient for a reasonable jury to find by a preponderance of the evidence that the defendant authored the e-mails."[2] A variety of types of circumstantial evidence may be sufficient to establish "confirming circumstances."[3] Neither expert testimony nor exclusive access to the computer in question by the subject are required to authenticate a particular person as the author of an email.[4]

---

[2] *Com. v. Purdy*, supra, 459 Mass at 450, 945 NE2d at 381. See *Com. v. Salyer*, 84 Mass App 346, 996 NE2d 488 (2013) (counsel was ineffective in failing to object on authentication grounds to allegedly harassing MySpace messages that could not be linked to defendant).

[3] *Com. v. Purdy*, supra (where emails originated from an account bearing defendant's name, which he acknowledged he used, and emails were found on hard drive of defendant's computer, which he acknowledged he used and for which he had the necessary passwords, confirming circumstances were sufficient); *Com. v. Johnson*, 470 Mass 300, 21 NE3d 937 (2014) (recipient of email testified he had exchanged emails with defendants on their account for years, he understood them to be from defendant 1 on defendant 2's behalf, they were signed using defendant 1's typical signature, and referenced recipient's responses to inquiries); *Com. v. Foster F.*, 86 Mass App 734, 20 NE3d 967 (2014) (communications themselves provided confirming circumstances and juvenile appeared at place and time his Facebook messages said he would); *Com. v. Amaral*, 78 Mass App 671, 674, 941 NE2d 1143, 1147 (2011) (emails were authenticated as coming from defendant by facts that defendant appeared at place and time email said he would, that when trooper called number provided in email defendant answered, and photograph provided in email was of defendant). Cf., *Com. v. Williams*, 456 Mass 857, 868, 926 NE2d 1162, 1172 (2010) (evidence was insufficient to authenticate MySpace messages as coming from defendant's brother; although messages apparently came from his MySpace page, no evidence established he sent it, how secure such a page is, who can access it, whether codes are required, etc.; Court reasons such a message is similar to an incoming call from a person claiming to be "A," without more, insufficient to authenticate call as made by "A").

[4] *Com. v. Purdy*, 459 Mass at 451 n.7, 945 NE2d at 381.

CHAPTER

10

THE BEST EVIDENCE RULE

§ 10.1 Proposed Mass R Evidence and Fed R Evidence 1001–1008

The Proposed Mass Rules and the Federal Rules are identical and provide as follows:

Rule 1001. Definitions

For purposes of this article the following definitions are applicable:

(1) Writings and recordings. "Writings" and "recordings" consist of letters, words, or numbers, or their equivalent, set down by handwriting, typewriting, printing, photostating, photographing, magnetic impulse, mechanical or electronic recording, or other form of data compilation.

(2) Photographs. "Photographs" include still photographs, x-ray films, video tapes, and motion pictures.

(3) Original. An "original" of a writing or recording is the writing or recording itself or any counterpart intended to have the same effect by a person executing or issuing it. An "original" of a photograph includes the negative or any print therefrom. If data are stored in a computer or similar device, any printout or other output readable by sight, shown to reflect the data accurately, is an "original."

(4) Duplicate. A "duplicate" is a counterpart produced by the same impression as the original, or from the same matrix, or by means of photography, including enlargements, and miniatures, or by mechanical or electronic recording, or by chemical reproduction, or by other equivalent techniques which accurately reproduces the original.

Rule 1002. Requirement of Original

To prove the content of a writing, recording, or photograph the original writing, recording, or photograph is required, except as otherwise provided in these rules or by statute.

Rule 1003. Admissibility of Duplicates

A duplicate is admissible to the same extent as an original unless (1) a genuine question is raised as to the authenticity of the original or (2) in the circumstances it would be unfair to admit the duplicate in lieu of the original.

Rule 1004. Admissibility of Other Evidence of Contents

The original is not required, and other evidence of the contents of a writing, recording, or photograph is admissible if—

(1) Originals lost or destroyed. All originals are lost or have been destroyed, unless the proponent lost or destroyed them in bad faith; or

(2) Original not obtainable. No original can be obtained by any available judicial process or procedure; or

(3) Original in possession of opponent. At a time when an original was under the control of the party against whom offered, he was put on notice, by the pleadings or otherwise, that the contents would be a subject of proof at the hearing, and he does not produce the original at the hearing; or

(4) Collateral matters. The writing, recording, or photograph is not closely related to a controlling issue.

Rule 1005. Public Records

The contents of an official record, or of a document authorized to be recorded or filed and actually recorded or filed, including data compilations in any form, if otherwise admissible, may be proved by copy, certified as correct in accordance with Rule 902 or testified to be correct by a witness who has compared it with the original. If a copy which complies with the foregoing cannot be obtained by the exercise of reasonable diligence, then other evidence of the contents may be given.

Rule 1006. Summaries

The contents of voluminous writings, recordings, or photographs which cannot conveniently be examined in court may be presented in the form of a chart, summary, or calculation. The originals, or duplicates, shall be made available for examination or copying, or both by other parties at reasonable time and place. The court may order that they be produced in court.

Rule 1007. Testimony or Written Admission of Party

Contents of writings, recordings, or photographs may be proved by the testimony or deposition of the party against whom offered or by his written admission, without accounting for the non-production of the original.

Rule 1008. Functions of Court and Jury

When the admissibility of other evidence of contents of writings, recordings, or photographs under these rules depends upon the fulfillment of a condition of fact, the question whether the condition has been fulfilled is ordinarily for the court to determine in accordance with the provisions of Rule 104. However, when an issue is raised (a) whether the asserted writing ever existed, or (b) whether another writing, recording, or photograph produced at the trial is the original, or (c) whether other evidence of contents correctly reflects the contents, the issue is for the trier of fact to determine as in the case of other issues of fact.

The Proposed Rules are largely consistent with current Massachusetts practice, but there are some differences. As we discuss below, Massachusetts currently does not apply the best evidence rule to photographs, videotapes, or digital images stored on a computer hard drive; generally does not treat "duplicates" as defined in the rules as admissible; and does not apply the best evidence rule to writings so simple that the possibility of error in recalling their contents is negligible.

§ 10.2 The Rationale for the Rule

The best evidence rule requires that where the contents of a writing or recording are to be proved, the party must either produce the original or show a sufficient excuse for its nonproduction.[1] The contents of a writing or recording are at issue: (1) when the writing or recording has legal significance, e.g., a contract, will, deed; or (2) where the contents of the writing or recording establish facts at issue, e.g., a confession, factual averments in a letter, a diary. Where a piece of evidence is not deemed to be a writing or recording, or where the item is not introduced to prove its contents, the best evidence rule has no applicability.[2]

Where the document is an electronic record, a printout is admissible in evidence, but the electronic record cannot be proved by oral testimony of its contents.[3]

---

§ 10.2 [1] See, e.g., *Com. v. Koney*, 421 Mass 295, 303, 657 NE2d 210, 215 (1995) (police officer testified that defendant gave him original identification card and officer made photocopy and returned original to defendant; photocopy was admissible, evidence accounted for non-production of original and no contention was made that photocopy was inaccurate or fraudulent); *Com. v. Silva*, 61 Mass App 28, 807 NE2d 170 (2004) (officer's testimony that he believed there was a written policy for inventory searches did not establish existence of the policy; it was necessary to introduce written policy itself). In a questionable decision, the Supreme Judicial Court held in *Com. v. Nardi*, 452 Mass 379, 397, 893 NE2d 1221, 1235 (2008), that the best evidence rule had no application where the prosecution sought to prove that the signature on a check had been forged subsequent to the purported maker's death. The court reasoned that the Commonwealth was not attempting to prove the "truth" of the contents, but rather to prove that they were "false." The best evidence rule, however, does not come into play only when the proponent seeks to prove the truth of the contents of a writing; it is equally applicable when the proponent intends to prove the contents are false. The Commonwealth was attempting to prove the contents of the check, including the date, the payee and the signature (albeit forged) of the maker. The allegation that the signature was forged would seem to give all the more reason for insisting on the original. The *Nardi* decision was based on *Com. v. Lenahan*, 50 Mass App 180, 185-186, 736 NE2d 405 (2000), which also incorrectly limited the best evidence rule to proof of the truth of the contents of a writing. In that case, the appeals court erred by mischaracterizing *Com. v. Koney*, supra, 421 Mass at 295, 303, 657 NE2d at 210, 215, by conflating the best evidence rationale for the decision (Commonwealth had adequately accounted for non-production of original) with the hearsay rationale (identification card was not hearsay because not offered for truth of assertions contained thereon). There is no "best evidence rule" with respect to physical objects not produced in court. The existence or condition of a tangible object may be described by witnesses without producing the article itself. *Com. v. Pope*, 103 Mass 440 (1869).

[2] See *Com. v. DeJesus*, 87 Mass App 198, 26 NE3d 1134 (2015) (in questionable decision, court concludes original bills were not required because the contents of the currency were not at issue, even though the serial numbers were used to prove bills found on defendant were the same ones police had given to undercover agent, court holds photocopy of currency used in undercover transaction was admissible in evidence; court leaves open question of whether currency constitutes a "writing").

[3] *Com. v. Salyer*, 84 Mass App 346, 356 n.10, 996 NE2d 488, 497 (2013) (oral testimony to prove the contents of an electronic record violates the best evidence rule; "The best evidence rule does not forbid the use of 'copies' of electronic records (including emails and text messages and other computer data files), because there is no 'original' in the traditional sense.").

Under the Proposed Mass Rules and the Federal Rules, the application of this rule extends to recordings and photographs. Massachusetts case law, however, has rejected extension of the best evidence rule to photographs.[4]

The best evidence rule is designed to: (1) protect against the possibility of error, which is proverbially very large in the repetition by memory of the contents of documents, particularly documents with legal significance; and (2) secure for the court the peculiarities of handwriting, paper, ink, and so on that may have great bearing on the genuineness of the document. The requirement that the original document must be produced does not apply to writings so simple in their nature that the possibility of error is negligible—e.g., the label on a whiskey bottle.[5]

Expert testimony as to the contents of complicated accounts is admissible[6] but only if the books and documents upon which the testimony is based are produced in court and made available for purposes of cross-examination.[7]

The significance of the best evidence rule has declined appreciably in recent decades. The rule predates the invention of photocopy machines and computers, and also the modern discovery rules. Most potential best evidence problems are probably resolved today by stipulations between attorneys who have satisfied themselves during discovery that there is no necessity to insist upon the production at trial of original documents.

---

[4] *Renzi v. Paredes*, 452 Mass 38, 52, 890 NE2d 806, 817 (2008) (use of digital photograph rather than original X-ray would not violate best evidence rule); *Com. v. Weichell*, 390 Mass 62, 77, 453 NE2d 1038, 1047 (1983) (noting contrary Proposed Mass R Evid 1002); *Com. v. Leneski*, 66 Mass App 291 (2006) (best evidence rule does not apply to photographs, videotapes or digital images stored on a computer hard drive; properly authenticated compact disc copy of video recorded initially directly onto computer hard drive was admissible; court notes that such a disc would be an "original" under Mass Proposed Evidence Rule 1001(3); testimony by person who "burned" the CD was sufficient to authenticate it).

[5] *Com. v. Blood*, 77 Mass (11 Gray) 74 (1859).

[6] *Com. v. Baker*, 368 Mass 58, 84, 330 NE2d 794, 808 (1975); *Com. v. Greenberg*, 339 Mass 557, 581-582, 160 NE2d 181, 197 (1959).

[7] *Cabel v. United States*, 113 F2d 998, 1001 (1st Cir 1940). See Proposed Mass R Evid 1006; Fed R Evid 1006.

§ 10.3 Cases in Which Production of Original Is Excused

§ 10.3.1 Where Document Is Lost or Destroyed

Where the original document is alleged to be lost or destroyed or otherwise unavailable, production may be excused if the trial judge finds that the original has become unavailable otherwise than through the serious fault of the proponent, provided that, where appropriate, reasonable search has been made for it.[1] It is a preliminary question of fact whether these requirements have been sufficiently established. It is for the trial judge to decide this matter and his decision ordinarily will be sustained.[2] Thus, where evidence warranting a finding that the original once existed is introduced, the judge must assume its existence and allow secondary evidence if he decides the preliminary questions of fact in favor of proponent.[3] But the ultimate questions of whether an original document ever existed or whether secondary evidence correctly reflects the content of the original are questions for the jury.[4]

If the document was destroyed by the proponent, secondary evidence of the contents ordinarily will not be admitted, there being a presumption that if the proponent destroyed the document it contained matter unfavorable to him.[5] The proponent can overcome this presumption by showing a satisfactory reason for destruction to refute culpable negligence or fraudulent or improper intent—e.g., that proponent had no reason to anticipate the need for the document[6] or that the destruction was inadvertent.

---

§ 10.3 [1] *Com. v. Ocasio*, 434 Mass 1, 746 NE2d 469 (2001) (after affirming finding that original search warrant had existed, remanding for findings by motion judge as to whether it became unavailable otherwise than through serious fault of Commonwealth and whether a reasonable search had been made for it); *Com. v. Revells*, 78 Mass App 492, 940 NE2d 481 (2010) (express best evidence findings not required to admit oral testimony regarding letter from child victim to mother that was "part and parcel" of single oral and written communication from child to mother, existence of letter and its basic contents were not disputed and there was no dispute about loss of letter, absence of serious fault by Commonwealth, or whether reasonable search for letter had been made); *Com. v. Fay*, 14 Mass App 371, 439 NE2d 855 (1982) (photocopy of confession properly admitted where prosecution could not find original and testimony indicated copy did not differ from the original).

[2] *Smith v. Brown*, 151 Mass 338, 24 NE 31 (1890).

[3] *Fauci v. Mulready*, 337 Mass 532, 540-543, 150 NE2d 286, 291-293 (1958).

[4] See Proposed Mass R Evid 1008.

[5] *Capitol Bank & Trust Co. v. Richman*, 19 Mass App 515, 521-522 & n.7, 475 NE2d 1236, 1240-1241 n.7 (1985) (citing Text).

[6] *Smith v. Holyoke*, 112 Mass 517 (1873).

GL 233, §§ 79D and 79E, provide for the use in evidence of photographic reproductions of certain lost or destroyed documents. These statutes recognize the practical necessity of destruction of certain business or public records as part of the regular course of business.

§ 10.3.2 Where Document Is in Control of Adversary

Where the document is in control of the opponent, the proponent can introduce secondary evidence of the contents of the document only if he gives the opponent sufficient notice to produce the document at the trial and the opponent fails to produce it. The only notice required is notice enough to give time to get the document to the courtroom. Thus, if the opponent has the document in court, oral notice at the trial is enough.[7] In certain cases that involve the contents of documents, the pleadings themselves are notice to produce and no other notice is necessary.[8]

If proper notice to produce is given and the opponent does not produce the original, the proponent can produce secondary evidence.[9] Case law provides that the opponent cannot thereafter bring forth the original or otherwise offer evidence of the contents of the document,[10] but this limitation is not contained in either Fed R Evid 1004(3) or Proposed Mass R Evid 1004(3). If the document is in court or readily available, it is within the power of the court to order the opponent to produce it or be held in contempt.[11] Failure of the opponent to produce a material document within his control is a proper basis for comment by the proponent and for an inference by the jury that the document, if produced, would be unfavorable to the opponent.

The fact that the privilege against self-incrimination covers production by the opponent of the document does not excuse the proponent from giving notice as the foundation for the use of secondary evidence. Nor does the opponent's privilege prevent the proponent

---

[7] See § 1.8.2 for the effect of such notice on admissibility of the document for the opponent.

[8] *Com. v. Slocomb*, 260 Mass 288, 157 NE 350 (1927). The principles stated in this paragraph are incorporated in Proposed Mass R Evid 1004(3) and Fed R Evid 1004(3).

[9] *Fisher v. Swartz*, 333 Mass 265, 271, 130 NE2d 575, 579 (1955); *Cregg v. Puritan Trust Co.*, 237 Mass 146, 129 NE 428 (1921).

[10] *Gage v. Campbell*, 131 Mass 566 (1881).

[11] *Kincaide v. Cavanagh*, 198 Mass 34, 84 NE 307 (1908). Cf. Mass R Civ P 34.

from putting in secondary evidence of the contents of the document.[12] Despite some of the language in the *Perry* case, it would seem appropriate in light of United States Supreme Court decisions to give the defendant notice to produce in writing or, if notice is given orally, to give notice out of the presence of the jury in order to avoid the possibility of appearing to infringe upon his right to remain silent.[13]

Insofar as the use of secondary evidence is concerned, a subpoena duces tecum has the effect of a notice to produce.[14] Nevertheless, the usual practice is to give notice in addition to having the subpoena served.

§ 10.3.3 *Where Document Is in Control of Third Person*

Where the document is in the control of some third person and the person is within the jurisdiction, a subpoena duces tecum must be issued ordering him to bring the document into court. If the person is outside of the jurisdiction, his absence is sufficient excuse for nonproduction and permits the introduction of secondary evidence.[15]

§ 10.3.4 *Where Document Is a Public Record*

Where the document is a Massachusetts public record, a certified copy is by statute competent evidence if the record itself was competent.[16] Additionally, see Mass R Civ P 44 which deals with the proof of

---

[12] *Com. v. Perry*, 254 Mass 520, 528, 150 NE 854, 858 (1926).

[13] See *Griffin v. California*, 380 US 609 (1965).

[14] *Cregg v. Puritan Trust Co.*, supra.

[15] Cf. Proposed Mass R Evid 1004(2). The language of the rule ("The original is not required . . . [if] . . . [n]o original can be obtained by any available judicial process or procedure. . . .") requires that even if the original is in the possession of a person outside the jurisdiction, an effort must be made to obtain the original by such judicial process as may be available before a claim of unavailability sufficient to permit the introduction of secondary evidence will be allowed. An example of such judicial process authorizing depositions to be taken outside the Commonwealth to obtain testimony of documents is found in GL 223A, § 10.

[16] GL 233, § 76. *Com. v. Rauseo*, 50 Mass App 699, 740 NE2d 1053 (2001). See also GL 233, §§ 69, 75-76B, 79A, 79D, and 79E, all of which contain provisions making copies of one kind or another equally competent with specific classes of original public documents. Compare *Com. v. Rondoni*, 333 Mass 384, 131 NE2d 187 (1955) (copy of document properly admitted under GL 233, § 69) with *Rossi v. Rossi*, 348 Mass 796, 206 NE2d 53 (1965) (same statute; copies improperly admitted).

official records, both domestic and foreign. The rule specifically provides in subdivision (b) for proof of "lack of record."[17] Mass R Civ P 44 follows prior Massachusetts practice except that as to records kept within the Commonwealth no double certification is required.[18]

§ *10.3.5 Proof of Contents of Deeds by Means of the Registry*

a. Massachusetts Deeds

GL 233, § 76, cited above, has no practical application to the proof of deeds by means of copies in the registry. There are two reasons for this.[19]

First, the registry copy of a deed is itself secondary evidence and may be inadmissible as such. In Massachusetts, the best evidence rule applies in full force to any deed of which either party is a grantee.[20] The rule does not apply, however, where the grantee is not a party to the action, and it is immaterial that the grantee and the original deed are available.[21]

Second, if the registry copy would itself be admissible, there is a common-law procedure simpler than that provided by GL 233, § 76,

---

[17] The language of Mass R Civ P 44(b) is as follows:

> A written statement that after diligent search no record or entry of a specified tenor is found to exist in the records designated by the statement, authenticated as provided in subdivision (a)(1) of this rule in the case of a domestic record, or complying with the requirements of subdivision (a)(2) of this rule for a summary in the case of a foreign record, is admissible as evidence that the records contain no such record or entry.

Subdivision (c) of Rule 44 also provides: "This rule does not prevent the proof, by any other method authorized by law, of the existence of, or the lack of, an official record, or of entry, or of lack of entry therein." (For further discussion, see § 8.12).

[18] Compare, e.g., GL 233, § 76 (requiring, except as to certain records of the Department of Public Utilities, certification of the genuineness of the signature of the attesting officer). In this regard, Mass R Civ P 44 also differs from Fed R Civ P 44, which retains the double certification requirement for domestic records. As to criminal matters, Mass R Crim P 40 is the same as Mass R Civ P 44. Cf. Fed R Crim P 27 (incorporating by reference the provisions of Fed R Civ P 44). Proposed Mass R Evid 1005 applies to criminal matters as well as to civil proceedings.

[19] See also official written statements exception to the hearsay rule, § 8.12.

[20] *Com. v. Emery*, 68 Mass (2 Gray) 80 (1854). Cf. *Gleason v. Galvin*, 374 Mass 574, 373 NE2d 357 (1978) (harmless error to admit certified registry copy in absence of dispute as to its accuracy).

[21] *Scanlan v. Wright*, 30 Mass (13 Pick) 523 (1833).

for getting a copy of the registry copy of a Massachusetts deed into evidence. The copy of the registry copy, verified only by the registrar's attestation, is admissible in evidence to prove the contents of the original deed.[22] Proposed Mass R Evid 1005 would apply to recorded instruments as well as to official records.[23] Rule 1005 carries forward the certification aspects of *Scanlan v. Wright*, supra, and adds two alternative methods of verifying the accuracy of a copy of such a recorded instrument.

Where a party seeks to prove the contents of a deed not made directly to him or the other party as grantee, the original evidence of a deed acknowledged and recorded in accordance with the statutes is the certified copy from the registry instead of the deed itself.[24]

b. Foreign Deeds

Proof of the contents of a deed recorded in a sister slate or in a foreign country is within the official written statements exception to the hearsay rule.[25] Proof is required that the foreign law imposed the duty of keeping a deed registry upon the person who copied the deed and that it imposes the duty of giving certified copies upon the person who made the copy. The duty to make the certified copy is usually presumed from the duty to keep the documents. The great seal, together with the attestation of the secretary of state of the foreign state or country, would have to be affixed to the document to show that the person certifying the copy was the present incumbent of the office of registrar and that the signature and seal appearing on the document were genuine.

The above cumbersome manner of proof is not, in practice, used to prove the contents of deeds registered in sister states. The method for proving the nonjudicial records of sister states is set out in 28 USC § 1739. To make a recorded deed admissible under this statute, affirmative evidence must be introduced that the person signing the paper produced in court is its custodian under the laws of the sister state. Evidence must also be introduced regarding what effect is given in the sister state to the paper produced in court. Observe that this statute

---

[22] *Scanlan v. Wright*, supra.

[23] Cf. Mass R Civ P 44 (applies to official records only).

[24] *Samuels v. Borrowscale*, 104 Mass 207 (1870).

[25] See § 8.12; Proposed Mass R Evid 803(14); Fed R Evid 803(14).

requires the paper to be sealed by "the keeper" of the records and attested by "the presiding justice" of a court.[26]

The admissibility of copies of foreign deeds would also be affected by Proposed Mass R Evid 1005, in interplay with both Proposed Mass R Evid 803(14) and 902. Rule 1005 would seem to apply to copies of deeds. Unlike Mass R Civ P 44 (applying only to official records), Rule 1005 applies not only to official records but also to a "document authorized to be recorded or filed and actually recorded or filed." A deed, mortgage, or other instrument so recorded or filed that affects "an interest in property" is admissible as a hearsay exception under Proposed Mass R Evid 803(14). A certified copy of such an instrument may be authenticated under Proposed Mass R Evid 902(4).[27]

Proposed Mass R Evid 1005 recognizes the certification procedures of Rule 902(4) but provides alternatively that a copy may be admitted if "testified to be correct by a witness who has compared it with the original." Rule 1005 provides further: "If a copy which complies with the foregoing cannot be obtained by the exercise of reasonable diligence, then other evidence of the contents may be given."

The evidentiary rules, while creating a clear preference for certified or compared copies, would provide for a more flexible approach to the proof of such records than has hitherto been allowed under local or federal statutes or case law.

§ 10.3.6 Miscellaneous Statutes

GL 233, §§ 77-79A, 79D, and 79E, provide for the admissibility of certified copies and identified photographic reproductions of records of hospitals, banks, trust companies, insurance companies, and other businesses and of photographic reproductions of newspapers. GL 233, § 79J provides for certification by affidavit and the use of certified photocopies of business records, which are required "to be produced in court by any party." Certified business records, or certified copies thereof, may now be deposited with the clerk of court for use in evidence, if the record is otherwise admissible.[28]

---

[26] See *Willock v. Wilson*, 178 Mass 68, 59 NE 757 (1901) for an indication of how strictly this requirement is enforced. But cf. *Portland Maine Publishing Co. v. Eastern Tractors Co.*, 289 Mass 13, 193 NE 888 (1935).

[27] See § 9.3.3.

[28] See § 8.11. See *Com. v. Monahan*, 349 Mass 139, 167, 207 NE2d 29, 46 (1965) (photostatic reproductions of checks properly admitted under GL 233, § 79E); *Com. v.*

§ 10.4 Originals and Duplicates

§ 10.4.1 Multiple Originals

Where a lease or other instrument is executed in multiple copies, each of which is intended by the parties to have legal effect, each of the copies so executed is considered an original.[1] Production of any such "original" is sufficient without accounting for the other.[2] The fact that a copy is mechanically reproduced by letterpress or otherwise does not give it the legal significance of an original unless circumstances showing such intent are established—e.g., a carbon copy of a letter is not an original.[3] But any such copy of a libelous handbill or newspaper that had publication might be so treated. The statutes cited above in §§ 10.3.4 and 10.3.6 may make mechanically reproduced copies equally admissible with the original documents where the prerequisites of the statute are satisfied.

Where there are multiple originals, production of all of them must be properly excused before secondary evidence is admissible.[4]

§ 10.4.2 Duplicates

Proposed Mass R Evid 1001(4) defines certain documents as "duplicates." Rather than focusing on the intent of the parties, these rules emphasize the accuracy of the reproductive process. Proposed Mass R Evid 1003 provides that duplicates are admissible to the same extent as originals unless a genuine question is raised as to the authenticity of

---

Gogan, 389 Mass 255, 264, 449 NE2d 365, 370 (1983) (certified copy of hospital record admissible under GL 233, § 79, "without need for and despite the absence of, testimonial corroboration"); *Com. v. Hubbard*, 371 Mass 160, 175-176, 355 NE2d 469, 479 (1976) (while records of hospital at Massachusetts Correctional Institution at Norfolk may be hospital records within meaning of GL 233, § 79, uncertified photocopies unauthenticated by any other means—e.g., by testimony of a witness—were properly excluded); *Com. v. Johnson*, 371 Mass 862, 870-871, 359 NE2d 1286, 1291-1292 (1977) (Rhode Island Hospital records kept in accordance with Rhode Island law, properly certified, admissible under GL 233, § 79); *Deutsche Bank Nat. Trust Co. v. Gabriel*, 81 Mass App 564, 965 NE2d 875 (2012) (GL 233, § 79A superseded earlier common law authority requiring original).

§ 10.4 [1] See Proposed Mass R Evid 1001(3).

[2] *Quinn v. Standard Oil Co. of New York*, 249 Mass 194, 144 NE 53 (1924).

[3] See *Augur Steel Axle & Bearing Co. v. Whittier*, 117 Mass 451 (1875) (letterpress copy treated as secondary evidence).

[4] *Peaks v. Cobb*, 192 Mass 196, 77 NE 881 (1906).

the original or in the circumstances of the case it would be unfair to admit the duplicate in lieu of the original.[5]

While copies subsequently produced manually, whether typed or handwritten, are not within the definition of a duplicate given by the rules, copies that meet the requirements of Rules 1001(4) and 1003 are for all practical purposes given the status of originals. Thus, the Rules considerably modify the common-law approach so as to make such copies freely admissible.

§ 10.5 Limitations and Exceptions to the Rule

The best evidence rule applies only to the proof of the *contents* of *documents*. There is no general rule requiring proof of the nature of tangible items by the "best evidence" and in Massachusetts the rule has no applicability to photographs.[1] The rule does not apply to proof of a document's existence, its execution, or transactions with it. Thus, the fact that a note was sold and delivered can be proved without production of the document.

The rule does not apply to the proof of an oral utterance even if the oral utterance was previously or subsequently written down.

An admission on the witness stand by the opponent as to the contents of a document is admissible to prove the contents of the document even if other secondary evidence would be inadmissible under the best evidence rule. This is in accord with Proposed Mass R Evid 1007. In Massachusetts, however, an admission by the opponent outside court and reported by a witness on the stand is also admissible, even if other secondary evidence would be excluded.[2] Proposed Mass R Evid 1007 does not go this far and therefore would be more restrictive than prior Massachusetts practice in this regard. However, where

---

[5] See *Com. v. Amaral*, 78 Mass App 671, 941 NE2d 1143 (2011) (rejecting best evidence objection to introduction of printed copies of email communications from defendant to trooper on ground that Yahoo servers or the computer drive constituted the original, noting "significance of best evidence rule has declined appreciably in recent decades" (Treatise cited), and that statute permits admission of duplicate "computer data file or program file").

§ 10.5 [1] See *Com. v. Balukonis*, 357 Mass 721, 260 NE2d 167 (1970) (best evidence rule does not apply to composite picture of defendants); *Com. v. Valleca*, 358 Mass 242, 263 NE2d 468 (1970) (best evidence rule does not preclude picture of purloined item).

[2] *Smith v. Palmer*, 60 Mass (6 Cush) 513 (1850).

conviction of prior crime is used to impeach the opponent or any other witness, the record of conviction may not be proved by the opponent's admission.[3]

If the requirements of the best evidence rule as to the excuse for nonproduction of the original and any multiple original documents have been met, any secondary evidence is admissible. There is no preference for an immediate copy over a copy of a copy or for a copy over oral testimony based on recollection. There are no degrees of secondary evidence so far as admissibility is concerned.[4] Proposed Mass R Evid 1004 is in accord with prior Massachusetts practice.

---

[3] See §§ 6.16.2

[4] *Bellamy v. Bellamy*, 342 Mass 534, 537, 174 NE2d 358 (1961).

CHAPTER

11

EYEWITNESS IDENTIFICATION EVIDENCE

§ 11.1 Use and Admissibility of Identification Evidence

In criminal cases where eyewitnesses are available, it is common practice for the prosecution to ask the witnesses to identify the defendant in the courtroom. In *Com. v. Crayton,*[1] however, the Supreme Judicial Court held that, absent good reason to allow it, a witness who has not previously identified the defendant should not be permitted to make a first-time identification in the courtroom. The Court reasoned that an in-court identification of the defendant sitting at counsel table is similar to a suggestive one-on-one showup, and may even be more suggestive, because the witness has greater reason to conclude the authorities believe the defendant is the perpetrator. The Court concluded that the fact that the jury would witness the identification and defense counsel would have contemporaneous cross-examination (as compared to a showup) did not justify admitting a suggestive identification. The Court declined to place a burden on the defendant to avoid a suggestive in-court identification by proposing alternative procedures.

The Court stated that good reason for an in-court first-time identification would exist where the eyewitness was familiar with the defendant before the commission of the crime, or where the arresting officer was an eyewitness to the crime and the identification merely confirms that the defendant was the person arrested.

The Court placed the burden on the prosecution to move in limine to admit an in-court identification of the defendant when there has been no out-of-court identification. Once it does so, the burden is on the defense to show that the in-court identification would be unnecessarily suggestive and that there is not good reason to allow it. The opinion reminded prosecutors that when they realize during trial preparation that an eyewitness has not made a previous identification, they may conduct a non-suggestive out-of-court procedure before the witness takes the stand. The Court's new rules apply prospectively to trials that commence after the issuance of this opinion, and only to in-court identifications of the defendant by eyewitness present during the crime.

---

§ 11.1 [1] *Com. v. Crayton*, 470 Mass 228, 21 NE3d 157 (2014), abrogating *Com. v. Bol Choeurn*, 446 Mass 510, 845 NE2d 310 (2006), *Com. v. Carr*, 464 Mass 855, 877, 986 NE2d 380 (2013), and *Com. v. Napolitano*, 378 Mass 599, 604, 393 NE2d 338 (1979). See, *Moore v. Illinois*, 434 US 220 (1977) (evidence excluded where defendant, not represented by counsel, was identified by victim at preliminary hearing after she was told she was going to view a suspect, observed him called up to the bench, and heard the prosecutor recite the evidence against him).

In *Com. v. Collins*,[2] decided the same day as *Crayton*, the Court considered the question of whether an in-court identification should be permitted where the witness has participated in an earlier nonsuggestive identification procedure, but did not make an unequivocal identification of the defendant. It concluded that the *Crayton* rule should apply under those circumstances. Relying on scientific studies, the Court was concerned that a witness would regard the defendant's prosecution as confirmation that he was the perpetrator and might develop an artificially inflated level of confidence in his or her in-court identification. There is also a concern that the perceived confirmatory feedback would cause the witness's memory to "improve" with respect to details regarding her observation of the crime. Such factors might cause the jury to give more weight to the in-court identification than the earlier equivocal response of the witness to a pretrial identification procedure.

The Court adopted the same procedures for in-court identifications in the *Collins* scenario as it had in *Crayton*. With respect to "good reason" for allowing an in-court identification, however, the Court said that the example of previous familiarity with the defendant recognized in *Crayton* would not suffice under *Collins*. To establish good reason where the witness has previously failed to make a positive identification, the prosecution would have to show "that the in-court identification is more reliable than the witness's earlier failure to make a positive identification and that it poses little risk of misidentification despite its suggestiveness."[3]

Where an in-court identification is permitted, defense counsel presumably will continue to have the option suggested in cases prior to *Crayton* to request that it be conducted under less suggestive circumstances, for example, by having the defendant sit in the courtroom rather than at counsel table.[4] Whether such arrangements would be prudent, of course, is a strategic question.

---

[2] *Com. v. Collins*, 470 Mass 255, 21 NE3d 528 (2014) (where defendant failed to object to in-court identification, Court found no substantial risk of miscarriage of justice in light of partial pretrial identification and compelling evidence of defendant's guilt).

[3] *Id.*, 470 Mass at 265, 21 NE3d at 536-537. The Court provided as an example a case in which a domestic violence victim only failed to identify the defendant in the earlier procedure out of fear or unwillingness to cooperate with the police.

[4] See *Com. v. Napolitano*, 378 Mass 599, 604 n.8, 393 NE2d 338 (1979); *Com. v. Cincotta*, 379 Mass 391, 395, 398 NE2d 478 (1979).

Opportunities contrived to allow witnesses improperly to observe the defendant in the courtroom may lead to suppression of an identification.[5]

A person suspected or accused of a crime may be the subject of police-initiated identification procedures, either formal or informal in nature. Through the process of observation of such a person (or his photograph) by the victim or a witness, the person so viewed may either be exculpated or inculpated. The Supreme Judicial Court has recognized that, "[E]yewitness identification of a person whom the witness had never seen before the crime or other incident presents a substantial risk of misidentification and increases the chance of a conviction of an innocent defendant," and that "[S]tudies conduct[ed] by psychologists and legal researchers . . . have confirmed that eyewitness testimony is often hopelessly unreliable."[6] As a result, "[W]henever eyewitness evidence is introduced against an accused," the Court requires "the utmost protection against mistaken identifications."[7]

Requiring a person to participate in a lineup or show-up does not violate the privilege against self-incrimination guaranteed by the Fifth Amendment.[8] Nor does compelled participation violate the Fourth Amendment so long as there is probable cause to detain the suspect.[9]

In *Com. v. Rosario*,[10] the Supreme Judicial Court held that the defendant was entitled to display a third party to the jury to be identified by another witness as the perpetrator of the crime. The fact that the person to be displayed would have asserted his Fifth Amendment right

---

[5] See *Martin v. Donnelly*, 391 F Supp 1241 (D Mass 1974) (contrived confrontation in courtroom prior to arraignment of defendant, apparently calculated to bolster identifications by witnesses and made without knowledge of defendant or his counsel, violated *Wade-Gilbert*); *Com. v. Donovan*, 392 Mass 649-651, 467 NE2d 199-200 (1984) (identification initiated by a police officer without notice to counsel while defendant was seated in courtroom awaiting his probable cause hearing violated *Wade-Gilbert*); *Com. v. Wheeler*, 3 Mass App 387, 389 n.1, 331 NE2d 815, 816 n.1 (1975) (trial judge suppressed identification of defendant seated in dock because he was not satisfied that victim's presence in courtroom on that occasion was "accidental").

[6] *Com. v. Vardinski*, 438 Mass 444, 450, 780 NE2d 1278, 1285 (2003).

[7] *Id.*

[8] *United States v. Wade*, 388 US 218, 222 (1967) ("compelling the accused merely to exhibit his person for observation by a prosecution witness prior to trial involves no compulsion of the accused to give evidence having testimonial significance"); *Com. v. Holland*, 410 Mass 248, 259, n.10, 571 NE2d 625, 632, n.10 (1991).

[9] See *United States v. Crews*, 445 US 463 (1980); *Dunaway v. New York*, 442 US 200 (1979); *Com. v. Napolitano*, 378 Mass 599, 607, 393 NE2d 338, 344 (1979) (absent probable cause, suspect cannot be detained for investigatory purposes).

[10] *Com. v. Rosario*, 444 Mass, 550, 829 NE2d 1135 (2005).

to remain silent if questioned did not provide sufficient justification to exclude this highly probative evidence on the critical issue of identification of the perpetrator.

§ *11.1.1 Use at Trial of Pretrial Identifications*

Testimony regarding out-of-court identifications is addressed in the Proposed Mass Rules of Evidence and the Federal Rules of Evidence only in Rule 801(d)(1)(c), which is identical in both sets of rules and provides:

> A statement is not hearsay if . . . the declarant testifies at the trial or hearing and is subject to cross-examination concerning the statement and the statement is . . . one of identification of a person after perceiving him.

Rule 801(d)(1)(c) was adopted by the Supreme Judicial Court in *Com. v. Le.*[11] It renders statements of identification made prior to trial admissible to prove the truth of the statements and eliminates a hearsay objection to such statements. In other respects, the principles that control identification evidence have their origin in constitutional or common law.

If the subject of an identification procedure is brought to trial, a pretrial identification of the defendant by a witness may be offered for both substantive and impeachment purposes, as long as the requirements of the Confrontation Clause are met and the defendant has been afforded an opportunity for meaningful cross-examination. In *Com. v. Le*,[12] the Supreme Judicial Court held that a pretrial identification of the defendant might be used as substantive evidence, even though the witness has denied or is unable to recall making the pretrial identification.[13] The decision adopts Proposed Mass R Evid 801(d)(1)(C), which is identical with the Federal Rule, and overrules

---

[11] *Com. v. Le*, 444 Mass 431, 828 NE2d 501 (2005).

[12] *Id.*

[13] See *Com. v. Young*, 73 Mass App 479, 899 NE2d 838 (2008) (victim's identification of defendant at hospital following shooting); *Com. v. Silvester*, 89 Mass App 350, 357, 49 NE3d 252, 259 (2016) (admitting videotape of identification of photo at police station); *Com. v. Machorro*, 72 Mass App 377, 892 NE2d 349 (2008) (officer's testimony that victim identified defendant at scene was admissible, although she could not identify him at trial and was not asked if she made identification at scene).

Com. v. Daye[14] to the extent that *Daye* required that the witness acknowledge the pretrial identification for it to be admitted for substantive purposes and not merely to impeach a witness who fails to make an identification at trial.

The Court relied upon recent federal cases to conclude that Confrontation Clause concerns no longer barred substantive use of the pretrial identification where the witness also testifies at the trial. The Confrontation Clause will be deemed satisfied as long as the identifying witness is subject to cross-examination concerning the pretrial statements of identification.[15] Confrontation Clause rights might be violated were a trial judge to limit cross-examination of a witness, or if a witness were to assert a privilege and decline to answer questions. In the ordinary case, however, the Court reasoned that the jury would have the prior identification before it in any event for impeachment purposes, and that jurors would be able to determine whether the identification was in fact made, and what weight to give it, by weighing the testimony and credibility of the various witnesses. Where the witness who made the identification does not appear at trial, testimony

---

[14] *Com. v. Daye*, 393 Mass 55, 60-63, 469 NE2d 483 (1984).

[15] *United States v. Owen*, 484 US 554 (1988). It is unfortunate that the Supreme Judicial Court relied so heavily on the specific facts and language of *Owen* in developing its rationale in *Le* for overruling *Daye*. In *Owen*, the witness, who had suffered a serious head injury, had a bare memory of making the prior identification, but no memory of his basis for it, no recollection of seeing his attacker, and no recollection of what might have been said to him that might have made the previous identification impermissibly suggestive. Despite being shown records that documented it, he was unable to recall having identified someone else as his attacker at one point. *Owen* is the low-water mark of what suffices for adequate cross-examination, with the US Supreme Court explicitly adopting the standard that all that is required is that the witness "is placed on the stand, under oath, and responds willingly to questions." *Owen* 484 US at 561. The Supreme Judicial Court has previously shown sensitivity to the need for vigorous cross-examination in cases that hinge on eyewitness identification testimony. See, e.g., *Com. v. Vardinski*, 438 Mass 444, 450, 780 NE2d 1278, 1285 (2003) ("Where the issue at a criminal trial is identification, the right to cross-examine must be scrupulously protected. This is so because while many, if not the majority of, criminal cases turn on eyewitness identification of the defendant . . . '[e]yewitness identification of a person whom the witness had never seen before the crime or other incident presents a substantial risk of misidentification and increases the chance of a conviction of an innocent defendant.' " [citation omitted]). Neither the US Supreme Court's decision in *Owen*, nor the decision of the Supreme Judicial Court in *Le* makes a persuasive argument that the risk of convicting an innocent defendant is any less where cross-examination is limited by a severe memory impairment on the part of the witness than it is by an error on the part of the trial judge with respect to the permissible scope of the examination.

concerning an identification is ordinarily hearsay and it is error to admit it.[16] Where the identification falls within an exception to the hearsay rule, and it is not testimonial, it may be admitted and does not violate the Confrontation Clause.[17]

Massachusetts courts have recognized identifications made both through visual and auditory perception.[18]

In *Le*, the court did not define what constitutes an "identification." In *Com. v. Adams*,[19] however, the court held that a statement by an eyewitness to the police that his brother had fired shots at the victim constituted an "identification." The court rejected the argument that Rule 801(d)(1)(C) applies only to identification procedures and does not include the simple articulation of a name based on the witness's familiarity with the person in question. The court reasoned that requiring a declarant to "go through the motions" of an identification procedure where he knows the suspect well would "elevate form over substance." The court added, "It is illogical to allow for substantive purposes a pretrial identification that consists of a witness's selection of a photograph of someone he does not know from a lineup, but to exclude a more reliable pretrial *statement* of identification by a witness who knows the individual well."[20]

The court's broad definition of an "identification" for the purpose of admitting hearsay statements as substantive evidence is based on a fundamental misunderstanding of the rationale behind Rule 801(d)(1)(C). The unreliability of identification testimony by witnesses

---

[16] *Com. v. Delong*, 72 Mass App 42, 888 NE2d 956 (2008) (given remainder of testimony admitting testimony in absence of witness was harmless).

[17] *Com. v. Robinson*, 451 Mass 672, 679, 888 NE2d 926, 932 (2008) (where victim followed his attackers to a dwelling, waited outside until police arrived, then as police escorted defendants from building ran toward them and stated, "That's the two guys," statement was a spontaneous utterance and not testimonial because witness was describing events as they unfolded and a reasonable person in his position would not have anticipated that statement would be used in prosecuting the crime).

[18] *Com. v. Torres*, 367 Mass 737, 738-740, 327 NE2d 871, 873-874 (1975) (pretrial voice identification of defendant by blind victim, who did not identify defendant at trial, was admissible for probative purposes where defendant's constitutional right of confrontation was satisfied); *Com. v. Pacheco*, 12 Mass App 109, 120-121, 421 NE2d 1239, 1247 (1981) (pretrial voice identification of defendant by blind victim, who did not attempt to identify defendant at trial, was admissible for probative purposes). See, however, § 11.2.2[d] for cases recommending caution with respect to voice identifications. An identification must be based on perceptions by one of the five natural senses. An identification based on extrasensory perception, or a person's "energy," is inadmissible. *Com. v. Coutu*, 88 Mass App 686, 694, 42 NE3d 622, 632 (2015).

[19] *Com. v. Adams*, 458 Mass 766, 941 NE2d 1127 (2011).

[20] *Id.*, 458 Mass at 770, 941 NE2d 1131. See also *Com. v. Ready*, 68 Mass App 440, 446-450, 862 NE2d 456 (2007).

who were unfamiliar with the subject before the incident in question has been well documented in both the case law and the scholarly literature. The problems may include a limited opportunity or poor environment for perception of the subject in the first instance; confounding factors of fear, excitement, and distraction; cross-racial identification issues; a myriad of ways in which the police may intentionally or inadvertently influence identifications; frailties of human memory, and a variety of other factors. Nonetheless, such evidence has probative value. Rule 801(d)(1)(C) admits earlier statements of identification in addition to courtroom identifications to attempt to use more probative evidence in an area where the risk of error is high, whether from honest mistake or intentional or inadvertent suggestion.

An accusation by a witness who knew the defendant well before the incident is a very different matter. The credibility and reliability of such evidence is subject to the same risks as all testimony, but it is not part of the class of identification testimony by a witness previously unfamiliar with the subject. Accusations by witnesses who know a subject well are different from identifications by witnesses unfamiliar with the subject, but they are not inherently more reliable. The risk of mistaken identification may be less, but the danger of false accusation based on motive or bias is greater. There is no more reason to admit such accusations than there is to admit any other hearsay evidence, and the *Adams* decision is an unwarranted and unfortunate expansion of the identification exception.[21]

A special problem may be presented where the proponent of identification evidence argues that training on the part of the witness supports the reliability of the identification. The Supreme Judicial

---

[21] Although the court in Adams purports to be clarifying a Massachusetts common law rule, it also acknowledges that it has "adopted" FRE 801(d)(1)(C). The *Adams* decision clearly extends the exception beyond the intent of the drafters of the Federal Rule. The cases cited in the Advisory Committee Note to the Federal Rule, for example, all refer to prior identification procedures. The Committee quotes from *Gilbert v. California*, 388 US 263 (1967), a line-up case, to approve the receipt of evidence "both by the witness and third parties at the prior identification." The expanded scope for the identification exception seriously undermines the hearsay rule and the requirements of the presently recognized exceptions for spontaneous exclamations and the substantive use of prior inconsistent statements. Such an expansion of the identification exception was rejected by the courts in *United States v. Kaquatosh*, 242 F Supp 2d 562 (ED Wis 2003) and *State v. Shaw*, 2005 SD 105, 705 NW2d 620 (2005), which limit the rule to identifications made at an identification procedure. Although there are also contrary federal cases, as noted in *Kaquatosh*, the reasoning of the court in *Kaquatosh* distinguishing between accusations and identifications is compelling. See Michael H. Graham, Handbook of Federal Evidence § 801.13 at 115 (2001).

Court has declared, "Prosecutors who intend to offer evidence of specialized training to bolster the credibility of witnesses whose ability to make an accurate identification has been (or will be) challenged at trial, should give advance warning to the defendant and the trial judge. Its admissibility must be considered with some care. A voir dire of the witness may be undertaken to ascertain the probative value of the testimony and to determine whether that value is outweighed by its likely prejudice."[22]

Prior to the decision in *Com. v. Le,* the Supreme Judicial Court had recognized the arguments in favor of assigning full probative value to a pretrial identification in more limited circumstances. The Court had held that substantive use of a pretrial identification was particularly appropriate "where the witness, because of the time lapse before trial, is unable to make an in-court identification but clearly recollects having positively identified the defendant earlier."[23] The Court had noted that, "A pretrial identification is regarded as having equal or greater testimonial value than one made in court because the circumstances of the earlier identification often were less suggestive and because that identification occurred closer to the time of the offense,"[24] and that "it is appropriate to recognize the possibility that fear will motivate a person who has made a pretrial identification to disclaim the ability to do so at trial."[25]

Decisions that predated *Com. v. Le* in which testimony concerning pretrial identifications was held admissible are still good law. An identification made under oath before the grand jury and inconsistent with trial testimony may be used substantively.[26] Where grand jury testimony of a witness who has since recanted his identification of the defendant is used for substantive evidence, the requirement that it be

---

[22] *Com. v. Johnson*, 463 Mass 95, 111, 972 NE2d 460, 472-473 (2012) (court finds no error in testimony that eyewitness who identified defendant had special training in "observation" in military, where defense counsel did not object).

[23] *Com. v. Swenson*, 368 Mass 268, 272, n.3, 331 NE2d 893, 896 (1975).

[24] *Com. v. Torres*, 367 Mass at 739, 327 NE2d at 873 (1975).

[25] *Com. v. Warren*, 403 Mass 137, 141, 526 NE2d 250, 252 (1988). See also *Com. v. Almonte*, 444 Mass 511, 829 NE2d 1094 (2005); *Com. v. McAfee*, 430 Mass 483, 493, 722 NE2d 1 (1999) ("Where a testifying witness in a criminal case identifies the defendant at trial, evidence that the witness made a prior extrajudicial identification of the defendant is admissible both to corroborate the in-court identification and as substantive evidence of the defendant's guilt."); *Com. v. Weichell*, 390 Mass 62, 71, 453 NE2d 1038, 1044 (1983) ("Since juries may have trouble making the distinction between corroboration evidence and substantive evidence, the elimination of this distinction is salutary.").

[26] *Com. v. Daye*, supra, 393 Mass at 73-74, 469 NE2d at 493 (adopting in part proposed Mass R Evid 801(d)(1)(A)). See also *Com. v. Jenkins*, 34 Mass App 135, 145,

corroborated to constitute evidence sufficient for conviction may be met by evidence of other pretrial identification of the defendant by the witness.[27] Evidence that a witness, under oath and subject to cross-examination, identified the defendant at a probable cause hearing is admissible at trial if the witness is "unavailable" at trial.[28]

Pretrial identifications continue to be admissible to corroborate an in-court identification at trial,[29] or to impeach a witness who disclaims a prior identification.[30]

Evidence of an extrajudicial identification procedure is limited to the identification procedure itself.[31] Testimony concerning an extrajudicial identification may include what the witness said as to the suspect's physical characteristics or clothing.[32] The extent of information allowable to put an identification in meaningful context will vary from case to case.[33] It may not, however, include the witness's comments

---

607 NE2d 756, 762 (1993), *superseded on another issue*, *Com. v. Jenkins*, 416 Mass 736, 625 NE2d 1344 (1993) (witness's prior identifications of defendant at probable cause hearing and grand jury proceedings, acknowledged by witness at trial, admissible for full probative value).

[27] *Com. v. Clements*, 436 Mass 190, 763 NE2d 55 (2002) (earlier photographic identification was sufficient corroboration).

[28] *Com. v. Furtick*, 386 Mass 477, 480, 436 NE2d 396, 398 (1982) (but record did not establish "unavailability"). See also *Com. v. Mendrala*, 20 Mass App 398, 400-401, 480 NE2d 1039, 1041 (1985) (although witness's failure to acknowledge a pretrial identification of defendants precluded its admission under *Com. v. Daye*, the identification was nevertheless admissible under the spontaneous utterance exception to the hearsay rule).

[29] See, e.g., *Com. v. Barbosa*, 463 Mass 116, 131, 972 NE2d 987, 999 (2012) (a pretrial identification is admissible even though witness has also made an in-court identification); *Com. v. Gunter*, 427 Mass 259, 692 NE2d 515 (1998); *Com. v. Weaver*, 395 Mass 307, 310, 479 NE2d 682, 685 (1985). For a discussion of the use of a prior identification to bolster trial testimony even before the identifying witness has been impeached, see § 6.25.

[30] See, e.g., *Com. v. Swenson*, supra, 368 Mass at 273-274, 331 NE2d at 897 (testimony of officer who had presented array of photographs was admissible to impeach witness who testified at trial that he had not identified defendant's photograph in pretrial procedure).

[31] *Com. v. Britto*, 433 Mass 596, 609, 744 NE2d 1089, 1102 (2001) (error to permit officer to testify to witness's comments re degree of certainty with respect to identification made in police car during ride home from station).

[32] *Com. v. Martinez*, 431 Mass 168, 175-176, 726 NE2d 913, 922 (2000) (rejecting Commonwealth's argument that the verbal completeness doctrine justified admission of declarant's description of number of shots fired, gun carried, and behavior of defendant).

[33] *Com. v. Spray*, 467 Mass 456, 470, 5 NE3d 891, 903 (2014) (Commonwealth argued that witness's hearsay statement that knife belonged to defendant was an extrajudicial "identification"; court assumes, without deciding, it was error to admit testimony where declarant did not see defendant use the knife to commit a crime and it

that go beyond identification of the defendant, such as how many shots were fired, the color of the gun, and the defendant's behavior after the murder.[34]

A prior identification by the witness of someone *other than* the defendant may be brought out to impeach an in-court identification.[35] Similarly, the failure of the witness to identify the defendant in a photographic array or lineup has impeachment value if the witness makes a subsequent identification of the defendant.[36] When defendant has introduced photos of other persons who fit the description of the perpetrator given by a witness, the prosecution may introduce, in rebuttal, evidence that the witness was shown those photos and did not identify the persons in them.[37]

§ *11.1.2 Composite Drawings and Sketches*

Composite drawings and sketches are admissible for substantive purposes unless prepared under suggestive circumstances.[38] Based on the rationale behind Proposed Mass R Evid 801(d)(1)(C) and the identical Federal Rule, a composite sketch is defined as not hearsay, even though it contains assertions and is offered to prove the truth of those assertions.[39]

---

was not clear when he last saw defendant in custody of the knife, but that error did not create substantial likelihood of miscarriage of justice); *Com. v. Walker*, 460 Mass 590, 608, 953 NE2d 195, 211 (2011) (not error to permit evidence of eyewitness's statement that the person in a certain photograph looked like the person who drove the car and fired shots at individuals on the sidewalk, but was error to admit his statement that the car was a "black Toyota" because that was extraneous to the identification); *Com. v. Adams*, 458 Mass 766, 772, 941NE2d 1127, 1132 (2011).

[34] *Com. v. Martinez*, supra.

[35] See *Com. v. Roselli*, 335 Mass 38, 40, 138 NE2d 607, 608 (1956).

[36] See, e.g., *Com. v. Santana*, 465 Mass 270, 988 NE2d 825 (2013) (prosecutor's failure to disclose to defendant juvenile witness's inability to identify defendant during earlier voir dire was error of constitutional dimension); *Com. v. Paszko*, 391 Mass 164, 171-172, 461 NE2d 222, 228 (1984); *Com. v. Correia*, 381 Mass 65, 79-80, 407 NE2d 1216, 1226 (1980).

[37] *Com. v. Howell*, 49 Mass App 42, 50, 725 NE2d 582, 588 (2000).

[38] See *Com. v. Weichell*, 390 Mass 62, 68-73, 453 NE2d 1038, 1044-1045 (1983) (but noting that the court "would not, at this time, sustain a conviction where such composite constituted the only evidence of identification, absent a more general acceptance of such evidence or a greater demonstration of its reliability." 390 Mass at 72 n.8, 453 NE2d at 1044-1045 n.8.); *Com. v. Thornley*, 400 Mass 355, 359-361, 509 NE2d 908, 911-912 (1987) (*Thornley I*); *Com. v. Kater*, 409 Mass 433, 443, 567 NE2d 885, 891 (1991) (*Kater III*).

[39] *Com. v. Weichell*, 390 Mass at 71-72.

The Appeals Court has noted that working with composite sketches requires caution:

> A composite is by its very nature imprecise. Even if the descriptions on which it is based are accurate, these descriptions cannot be perfectly reflected in what is essentially a drawing. Identification of a suspect from the composite (often . . . on the basis of the judgment of one person) adds an additional element of uncertainty. Thus, it is vital that the identification from the composite not become the product of a self-fulfilling prophecy. Procedures applied from this point forward must be designed truly to test the hypothetical identification, not merely to endorse a preconceived view that a given suspect is actually the perpetrator.[40]

The artist who prepares a composite sketch should not be permitted to vouch for the reliability of the witness's identification.[41]

§ 11.1.3 Identifications Following Hypnosis

Identification evidence concerning matters not remembered before hypnosis is inadmissible.[42]

§ 11.1.4 Mug Shots

Because of the risk of prejudice to the defendant inherent in the admission of photographs of the "mug shot" variety (see § 4.4.2),

---

[40] *Com. v. Poggi*, 53 Mass App 685, 693, 761 NE2d 983, 989 (2002).

[41] See *Com. v. Orton*, 58 Mass App 209, 211, 788 NE2d 1009, 1012 (2003) (error to permit police sketch artist to testify that time it took to prepare sketch was within time frame in which he felt comfortable, after testifying that if it goes either too quickly or too long, it renders the identification questionable).

[42] See *Com. v. Kater*, 432 Mass 404, 734 NE2d 1164 (2000) (*Kater VII*); *Com. v. Kater III*, supra, 409 Mass at 437-439, 567 NE2d 888-889 (statement of the procedures to be used by the trial judge to determine whether proffered identification testimony of a witness who had been subjected to hypnosis was based on the witnesses' prehypnotic memory; declining to adopt an absolute prohibition of all posthypnotic identifications); *Com. v. Dodge*, 391 Mass 636, 462 NE2d 1363 (1984); *Com. v. Brouillet*, 389 Mass 605, 451 NE2d 128 (1983); *Com. v. Watson*, 388 Mass 536, 447 NE2d 1182 (1983); *Com. v. Kater*, 388 Mass 519, 447 NE2d 1190 (1983) (*Kater II*). See also § 6.27.

judges and prosecutors are required to "use reasonable means to avoid calling the jury's attention to the source of [such] photographs used to identify the defendant."[43]

While there is no per se rule excluding mug shots, their introduction into evidence is limited by the following criteria: (1) the prosecution must show some need to introduce the mug shots; (2) the mug shots, to the extent possible, should not indicate a prior record; and (3) the mug shots should not call attention to their origins and implications.[44]

---

[43] *Com. v. Cruz*, 445 Mass 589, 839 NE2d 324 (2005) (rejecting argument that photos improperly conveyed defendant's criminal history to jury where photos had been sanitized, bore no indication that they were mug shots and judge gave appropriate cautionary instruction); *Com. v. Richardson*, 425 Mass 765, 682 NE2d 1354 (1997) (not error to admit over objection front and side views of defendant without separating them where all information on photos was sanitized and trial judge determined photos should go to jury in same condition as viewed by witness; judge did not err in not giving curative instruction where none was requested); *Com. v. Cohen*, 412 Mass 375, 382, 589 NE2d 289, 294-295 (1992) (phrase "mug shot" should not have been used by prosecutor in his opening); *Com. v. Blaney*, 387 Mass 628, 638, 442 NE2d 389, 395 (1982); *Com. v. DeJesus*, 71 Mass App 799, 887 NE2d 283 (2008) (although photographs themselves lacked usual indicia of mug shots, police testimony that photographs were compiled from database of those with prior arrest history required that they be treated as mug shots; such testimony was inappropriate; failure of defense counsel to object was not ineffective assistance under circumstances of case); *Com. v. Gee*, 36 Mass App 154, 628 NE2d 1296 (1994) (admission of unsevered and unsanitized mug shots was reversible error where identity was main issue in case, jury could have reasonably inferred from photograph that defendant had been involved in prior misconduct, and jury instruction was not adequate to cure error); *Com. v. Payton*, 35 Mass App 586, 623 NE2d 1127 (1993) (no abuse of discretion in allowing unsevered mug shots in evidence where profile shot was of some assistance in identifying perpetrator and trial counsel did not object for tactical reasons); *Com. v. Bassett*, 21 Mass App 713, 720, 490 NE2d 459, 463 (1986) (references to identification of defendant from "mug book" improperly suggested that he had a prior criminal record).

[44] *Com. v. McAfee*, 430 Mass 483, 722 NE2d 1 (1999); *Com. v. Martin*, 63 Mass App 587, 827 NE2d 1263 (2005); *Com. v. Gee*, supra, 36 Mass App at 157-158 (citations omitted). Compare *Com. v. Weaver*, 400 Mass 612, 620, 511 NE2d 545, 550 (1987) (evidence of a photographic identification should not have been admitted where identification was not a live issue at trial and the evidence tended to show that defendant had had prior trouble with the criminal law) and *Com. v. Smith*, 21 Mass App 619, 622-623, 489 NE2d 203, 205 (1986) (reversible error to admit police photograph of defendant where his presence at scene of crime was not disputed) with *Com. v. McPherson*, 74 Mass App 125, 904 NE2d 488 (2009) (opinion does not indicate whether photos were mug shots, but holds not error to introduce photographic array where witness had previously met defendant only once or twice); *Com. v. Holmes*, 32 Mass App 906, 909-910, 584 NE2d 1150, 1154 (1992) (no error in admission of mug shots where *Com. v. Blaney* procedures were strictly followed and identification was live issue at trial). Cf. *Com. v. McNickles*, 22 Mass App 114, 122, 491 NE2d 662, 668 (1986) (rape defendant charged on joint enterprise theory was not entitled to instruction that the

The defendant may be allowed to call the jury's attention to otherwise prejudicial information accompanying a mug shot, if it is relevant to challenging an identification based on the photograph.[45]

§ 11.2 Constitutional Issues

"[E]yewitness identification often plays a major, if not a determinative, role in the trial of criminal offenses, and the dangers of mistaken identification are great and the result possibly tragic. . . ."[1] Pretrial confrontations arranged by the police between the accused and the victim or witnesses to a crime to obtain identification evidence are "peculiarly riddled with innumerable dangers and variable factors which might seriously, even crucially, derogate from a fair trial."[2] The overriding danger inherent in such confrontations is that they might cause unreliable or mistaken identifications.[3]

Decisions of the United States Supreme Court and of the Massachusetts courts have therefore developed legal principles based largely on the Fifth, Sixth, and Fourteenth Amendments to the United States Constitution that are designed to lessen the dangers of misidentification. These principles sometimes require that identification evidence be excluded from evidence at trial, as discussed below.

An eyewitness identification may also be suppressed on the grounds that it was the product of conduct violative of the Fourth Amendment, such as an illegal arrest.[4]

---

jury should draw no negative inferences concerning defendant from the victim's photographic identification of defendant's alleged companion). See also *Com. v. Austin*, 421 Mass 357, 365, 657 NE2d 458, 463 (1995) (videotape depicting another bank robbery admissible even though not amenable to sanitation procedures).

[45] See *Com. v. Vardinski*, 438 Mass 444, 780 NE2d 1278 (2003) (reversible error not to allow defendant to challenge witness's level of confidence in his identification by showing that after viewing photograph on computer he had seen printout which included notation of defendant's prior arrest for illegal possession of a firearm).

§ 11.2 [1] *Com. v. Dickerson*, 372 Mass 783, 789, 364 NE2d 1052, 1056 (1977).

[2] *United States v. Wade*, 388 US 218, 228 (1967).

[3] *Id.*; *Manson v. Brathwaite*, 432 US 98, 111-114 (1977).

[4] See *United States v. Crews*, 445 US 463 (1980); *Com. v. Cao*, 419 Mass 383, 644 NE2d 1294 (1995) (field interrogation was not "seizure" for purposes of determining whether resulting photograph was admissible in subsequent identification procedure); *Com. v. Manning*, 44 Mass App 695, 693 NE2d 704 (1998) (although photo used in identification of defendant by witness was taken following illegal arrest, suppression was not required because purpose of arrest was not to gather evidence for unrelated crime, illegal arrest was not flagrant police misconduct, and photo was taken pursuant to standard police procedure).

§ 11.2.1 Right to Counsel

The right to counsel, guaranteed by the Sixth Amendment, extends to each critical stage of a criminal proceeding, which has been held to include a lineup (or other physical confrontation) occurring *after* the defendant has been indicted or adversary criminal proceedings have been otherwise initiated. Conducting such a lineup in the absence of defense counsel or a valid waiver thereof thus constitutes a denial of the right to counsel, and the evidence of identification that results from the lineup is inadmissible at trial.[5] The right to have counsel present does not apply to a lineup or other corporeal identification conducted *prior to* the initiation of adversary judicial criminal proceedings by way of indictment, information, arraignment, or preliminary hearing.[6]

The right to have counsel present does not apply to a photographic identification, even if the prosecution has already initiated adversary criminal proceedings.[7] The Court reasoned that a photographic identification procedure was not a critical stage of the criminal proceeding and that, inasmuch as the accused himself would

---

[5] *United States v. Wade*, 388 US 218 (1967); *Gilbert v. California*, 388 US 263 (1967); *Moore v. Illinois*, 434 US 220 (1977) (extending rule of per se inadmissibility to a one-on-one confrontation at a preliminary hearing held to determine whether accused should be bound over to the grand jury and to set bail); *Com. v. Donovan*, 392 Mass 647, 467 NE2d 198 (1984) (applying rule of per se inadmissibility to an identification initiated by a police officer without notice to counsel while defendant was seated in courtroom awaiting his probable cause hearing); *Com. v. Cooper*, 356 Mass 74, 80-84, 248 NE2d 253, 258-259 (1969) (discussion of *Wade-Gilbert* doctrine). Compare 18 USC § 3502 (1968), which purports to override *Wade* but is of doubtful constitutional validity.

[6] See *Kirby v. Illinois*, 406 US 682 (1972) (plurality refused to apply *Wade-Gilbert* rule to robbery victim's one-on-one station house identification of an uncounseled suspect after his arrest but before judicial proceedings have been initiated); *Com. v. Simmonds*, 386 Mass 234, 237-238, 434 NE2d 1270, 1273-1274 (1982) (neither Sixth Amendment nor art. 12 of Massachusetts Declaration of Rights entitles defendant to assistance of counsel at lineup occurring prior to indictment or formal charge); *Com. v. Smallwood*, 379 Mass 878, 884-885, 401 NE2d 802, 806 (1980) (complaint and arrest warrant procedures do not constitute initiation of adversary proceedings); *Com. v. Clifford*, 374 Mass 293, 302, 372 NE2d 1267, 1274 (1978) (per se rule of exclusion is inapplicable where defendant has been arrested but no criminal complaint, indictment, or other formal charge has been issued against him); *Com. v. Key*, 19 Mass App 234, 237-239, 472 NE2d 1381, 1384 (1985) (right to counsel did not extend to courtroom identification of defendant following his arrest but just before his arraignment).

[7] See *United States v. Ash*, 413 US 300 (1973).

not be present at the procedure, counsel was not needed to protect the accused from being misled or to counterbalance possible prosecutorial overreaching.[8]

There is likely no right to have counsel present at a post-lineup interview with the witness.[9]

The right to counsel may be waived.[10] But "[o]nce the right to counsel arises in connection with an identification procedure the person in custody must specifically and seasonably be informed of that right before the procedure commences," and waiver must be knowing and intelligent.[11] Merely advising a suspect of his *Miranda* rights does not suffice.[12]

The primary purpose of ensuring defense counsel's presence at pretrial identification procedures is to avoid suggestive influences (either intentional or unintentional) that may result in a mistaken identification.[13] Moreover, "because of the potential for prejudice at a pretrial lineup, there is a critical need for counsel at that stage to 'assure a meaningful confrontation at trial.' "[14] When counsel is present, counsel's role depends on the setting in which the prosecution conducts the identification procedure. At trial or at a probable cause hearing, of course, "counsel has the responsibility, by way of

---

[8] See also *Com. v. Jackson*, 419 Mass 716, 729 n.13, 647 NE2d 401, 409 n.13 (1995). But see *Com. v. Torres*, 367 Mass 737, 740, 327 NE2d 871, 874 (1975) (suggesting that right to counsel would apply to live voice identification procedure).

[9] See *Com. v. Tanso*, 411 Mass 640, 653-654, 583 NE2d 1247, 1255-1256 (1992); *Com. v. Charles*, 397 Mass 1, 6, 489 NE2d 679, 683 (1986) (although it was unnecessary to decide the issue, "the cases holding that defense counsel does not have a right to be present at a post-lineup interview would appear to represent the better reasoned view").

[10] See *Com. v. Davis*, 380 Mass 1, 8, 401 NE2d 811, 816 (1980) (defendant who, after arrest, was warned of his right to counsel before participating in lineup and signed a consent form validly waived his right to counsel).

[11] *Com. v. Cooper*, supra, 356 Mass at 83, 248 NE2d at 259.

[12] *Com v. Cooper*, supra; *Com. v. Mendes*, 361 Mass 507, 509-510, 281 NE2d 243, 245 (1972) ("The police, contrary to well-established law which we are required to apply, did not inform the defendant of his right to counsel *at the lineup*, and in these circumstances the defendant could not make a knowing and intelligent waiver of his *Wade* rights."); *Com. v. Guillory*, 356 Mass 591, 593, 254 NE2d 427, 429 (1970). Cf. *Com. v. Santos*, 402 Mass 775, 782-783, 525 NE2d 388, 393 (1988) (no waiver of constitutional rights occurred when defendant assented to one-on-one confrontation).

[13] *United States v. Wade*, supra, 388 US at 228-239; *Com. v. Napolitano*, 378 Mass 599, 604, 393 NE2d 338, 342 (1979) (counsel is present to "ferret out" any suggestive influences he perceives in the identification procedures); *Com. v. Clifford*, supra, 374 Mass at 302, 372 NE2d at 1274 (the "better practice" is to give the attorney a meaningful opportunity to become acquainted with the case and the prospective witnesses prior to the lineup).

[14] *Com. v. Cooper*, supra, 356 Mass at 82, 248 NE2d at 259 (citation omitted).

cross-examination, to bring to the attention of the trier of facts any circumstances which tend to cast doubt upon a witness's identification testimony."[15] It must be emphasized that the *Wade-Gilbert* rule of per se inadmissibility, founded on the Sixth Amendment right to counsel, is separate from and independent of any issue concerning the fairness of an identification premised on due process standards (discussed in § 11.2.2).[16]

§ 11.2.2 Due Process

Of wider application than the *Wade-Gilbert* rule of per se inadmissibility is the requirement that *any* identification procedure conducted at *any* time in investigative process (whether before or after the initiation of formal proceedings) conform to standards of fundamental fairness.[17] Under due process standards evolved from the Fifth and Fourteenth Amendments, evidence of a pretrial identification is inadmissible if obtained in a manner so impermissibly suggestive as to give rise to a substantial likelihood of mistaken identification.[18] As the Supreme Judicial Court has observed:

> The law has not taken the position that a jury can always be relied on to discount the value of an identification by a proper appraisal of the unsatisfactory circumstances in which it may have been made. On the contrary, this court, like others, has read the Constitution to require that where the conditions are shown to have been highly and unnecessarily suggestive, the identification should not be brought to the attention of the jury.[19]

---

[15] *Com. v. Jones*, 362 Mass 497, 500-501, 287 NE2d 599, 602 (1972).

[16] *Com. v. Donovan*, supra, 392 Mass at 648-650, 467 NE2d at 199 (& citations).

[17] See *Com. v. Simmonds*, 386 Mass 234, 239, 434 NE2d 1270, 1274 (1982) (due process considerations are applicable to lineup conducted prior to arrest); *Com. v. Chase*, 372 Mass 736, 743, 363 NE2d 1105, 1110 (1977) (due process considerations are applicable to informal identification procedures conducted prior to arrest).

[18] See *Kirby v. Illinois*, 406 US 682, 690-691 (1972) (pre-indictment stationhouse show-up); *Simmons v. United States*, 390 US 377 (1968) (pre-indictment photographic identification); *Stovall v. Denno*, 388 US 293 (1967) (hospital room show-up); *Com. v. Odware*, 429 Mass 231, 707 NE2d 347 (1999); *Com. v. Dinkins*, 415 Mass 715, 720-721, 615 NE2d 570, 573 (1993); *Com. v. Botelho*, 369 Mass 860, 343 NE2d 876 (1976) (suppressing identifications; extensive discussion of due process analysis).

[19] *Com. v. Marini*, 375 Mass 510, 519, 378 NE2d 51, 57 (1978) (citations omitted).

a. Unnecessarily Suggestive

Utilizing a totality of the circumstances approach, the court under the due process test must determine whether the identification procedure was: (1) suggestive; (2) unnecessary (i.e., because there was no exigent circumstance or other justification); and (3) unreliable. Only if all three elements are found will the identification be suppressed.[20] The Supreme Judicial Court has emphasized that the constitutional issue in identification cases is not whether "the witness was or might be mistaken but whether any possible mistake was or would be the product of improper suggestions made by the police."[21]

The first two elements require an analysis of both the prejudicial nature of the challenged procedure and the circumstances that necessitated resort to it. Thus, in *Stovall v. Denno*, supra, where the handcuffed black suspect was brought into the victim's hospital room by white police officers who asked if he was "the man," the court concluded that the concededly suggestive procedure was nonetheless "imperative" because it was unclear how long the victim would live.[22] "The evil to be avoided is *needless* suggestiveness."[23]

b. Reliability Factors

If the court concludes that the identification was unnecessarily suggestive, under United States Supreme Court doctrine it must then

---

[20] See *Manson v. Brathwaite*, 432 US 98 (1977); *Com. v. Melvin*, 399 Mass 201, 205, 503 NE2d 649, 652 (1987).

[21] *Com. v. Andrews*, 427 Mass 434, 438, 694 NE2d 329, 333 (1998); *Com. v. Rancourt*, 399 Mass 269, 276 n.10, 503 NE2d 960, 965 n.10 (1987) (& citations). See also *Com. v. Warren*, 403 Mass 137, 140, 526 NE2d 250, 252 (1988).

[22] See also *Simmons v. United States*, 390 US at 384-385 (arguably suggestive display of photographs was not "unnecessary" because a serious felony had been committed, the perpetrators were still at large, and it was essential for FBI to determine whether they were on the right track); *Com. v. Dickerson*, 372 Mass 783, 790, 364 NE2d 1052, 1058 (1977) (hospital room confrontation was not "unnecessarily" suggestive because it took place in the immediate aftermath of the crime as part of reasonable police investigation); *Com. v. Barnett*, 371 Mass 87, 91-94, 354 NE2d 879, 882-883 (1976) (hospital confrontation arranged by police between victim and defendant while both were being treated for gunshot wounds was not violative of due process).

[23] *Com. v. O'Loughlin*, 17 Mass App 972, 458 NE2d 767 (1984). Compare *Com. v. Kazonis*, 356 Mass 649, 255 NE2d 333 (1970) (confrontation at police headquarters two months after robbery was conducted in a manner so impermissibly suggestive and conducive to misidentification as to amount to a denial of due process; the procedure could not be justified by urgency, efficient police work, or some other relevant factor).

determine whether the evidence was nonetheless reliable. Reliability is "the linchpin" in determining the admissibility of identification testimony under federal standards.[24]

The factors to be considered regarding reliability include:

1. the opportunity the witness had to view the criminal at the time of the crime;
2. the witness's degree of attention;
3. the accuracy of the witness's prior description of the criminal;
4. the level of certainty demonstrated by the witness at the confrontation; and
5. the length of time between the crime and the confrontation.

(These factors are also relevant in determining whether there is an independent basis for an in-court identification when the pretrial identification has been ruled inadmissible. See § 11.2.3.) "[O]f most importance are the victim's attentiveness and opportunity to observe the assailant during the commission of the crime."[25] "Against these factors is to be weighed the corrupting effect of the suggestive identification itself."[26]

The Supreme Judicial Court has, however, rejected the "reliability test" set forth in *Manson v. Brathwaite* and has held that identification procedures that are unnecessarily suggestive require per se exclusion under the due process requirements of the Massachusetts Declaration of Rights.[27] Persuaded that "the dangers present whenever eyewitness evidence is introduced against an accused require the utmost protection against mistaken identifications,"[28] the court has ruled that once a defendant meets the burden of demonstrating (by a preponderance of the evidence) that the identification was unnecessarily suggestive, the prosecution is barred from using the evidence at trial. Regarding

---

[24] *Manson v. Brathwaite*, supra, 432 US at 114. See also *Neil v. Biggers*, 409 US 188 (1972). Even if there have been unnecessarily suggestive procedures, identification evidence is admissible if it possesses sufficient indicia of reliability to reduce the possibility of irreparable mistaken identification. See, e.g., *Com. v. Dickerson*, supra, 372 Mass at 790-791, 364 NE2d at 1057-1058 (the suggestiveness of the hospital confrontation was overridden by the facts that the witness had had ample opportunity to observe the assailant and promptly gave the police a description that fit the defendant).

[25] *Com. v. Riley*, 26 Mass App 550, 554, 530 NE2d 181, 184 (1988).

[26] *Manson v. Brathwaite*, supra, 432 US at 114.

[27] *Com. v. Johnson*, 420 Mass 458, 461, 650 NE2d 1257, 1259 (1995); *Com. v. Day*, 42 Mass App 242, 676 NE2d 467 (1997).

[28] *Com. v. Johnson*, supra, 420 Mass at 465, 650 NE2d at 1261.

other identifications the witness may have made of the defendant, only those which the prosecution can show by clear and convincing evidence are not the product of the suggestive confrontation—i.e., that have an independent source—are admissible at trial. See § 11.2.3.

c. Types of Identification Procedures

Significant to the issue of suggestiveness is the type of identification procedure used, as well as what the police did when using the particular procedure. There are essentially four identification procedures: (1) lineup, (2) photographic array, (3) informal pre-arrest procedures, and (4) one-on-one confrontation either in person or by photograph.

The lineup is the preferred procedure, especially when defense counsel is present.[29] The police are not required, however, to use a lineup over other identification procedures, even where the accused is already in custody.[30] Where there is evidence that a defendant has altered his appearance to avoid identification, the state may require him to undo the alteration.[31]

Although (as noted in § 11.1) absent probable cause the police may not detain an individual for investigatory purposes or require him to participate in a lineup,[32] the police may seek to arrange a noncustodial and informal pre-arrest identification procedure. "Informal identification procedures during the initial investigatory stages of the criminal process may free innocent suspects and allow the police to follow other more productive leads."[33] Such a procedure is permissible where the witness views the suspect in a non-suggestive setting that does not isolate the suspect from others.[34] A suspect need

[29] *Com. v. Storey*, 378 Mass 312, 318-319, 391 NE2d 898, 903 (1979); *Com. v. Marini*, supra, 375 Mass at 519, 378 NE2d at 57.

[30] *Com. v. Jackson*, 419 Mass 716, 729 n.13, 647 NE2d 401, 409 n.13 (1995).

[31] *Com. v. Cinelli*, 389 Mass 197, 205-207, 449 NE2d 1207, 1213 (1983) (where there was evidence that defendant had been relatively clean shaven on the day of the crime, compelling him to shave his full beard prior to a lineup did not violate his right of due process).

[32] *Com. v. Napolitano*, 378 Mass 599, 607, 393 NE2d 338, 344 (1979). A subject may agree voluntarily to participate in a lineup. See, e.g., *Com. v. Simmonds*, 386 Mass 234, 238, 434 NE2d 1270, 1274 (1982). Evidence that a defendant was requested to voluntarily submit to a lineup but refused should not be admitted. See *Com. v. Holland*, 410 Mass 248, 256-261, 571 NE2d 625, 630-633 (1991).

[33] *Com. v. Napolitano*, supra, 378 Mass at 606, 393 NE2d at 343.

[34] See, e.g., *Com. v. Napolitano*, supra, 378 Mass at 605-608, 393 NE2d 343-344 (1979) (defendant identified while being arraigned on unrelated charge; evidence was admissible even though defendant was in prisoner's dock because he sat with two

not be advised that an informal identification procedure is taking place.[35]

Out-of-court one-on-one confrontations, whether in person or by photograph, pose particularly serious dangers of suggestiveness and are thus generally disfavored.[36] Nonetheless, evidence produced by a one-on-one confrontation is not subject to a rule of per se exclusion.[37] Rather, whether the evidence is admissible under the controlling due process standard will depend on when, where, and why the confrontation occurred.[38] One-on-one confrontations have been held permissible where there are exigent circumstances or where they represent an effort to provide the witness with an opportunity to view the suspect in the immediate aftermath of the crime.[39] Even where there has been a

---

other males in the busy courtroom and the police did not direct the witness's attention to the dock); *Com. v. Chase*, 372 Mass 736, 741-745, 363 NE2d 1105, 1111-1112 (1977) (defendant identified in a public lounge; evidence was admissible even though defendant, a bartender, had a prominent role at lounge, because there were approximately 25 patrons and two bartenders and the police made no suggestion to witness concerning identification of the defendant); *Com. v. Soares*, 76 Mass App 612, 615, 924 NE2d 768, 770 (2010) (two witnesses together in police car identified defendant from group of men on street; not unduly suggestive because first witness to identify defendant was a stranger to him, second witness knew defendant and had already pointed him out to police outside presence of first witness); *Com. v. Huan Lieu*, 50 Mass App 162, 735 NE2d 1263 (2000) (identification of defendant while standing among several other Asian men in courthouse corridor was not improperly suggestive).

[35] See *Com. v. Chase*, supra, 372 Mass at 743, 363 NE2d at 1111; *Com. v. Napolitano*, supra, 378 Mass at 605, 393 NE2d at 343.

[36] *Stovall v. Denno*, 388 US 293, 302 (1967); *Com. v. Johnson*, 420 Mass 458, 461, 650 NE2d 1257, 1259 (1995); *Com. v. Santos*, 402 Mass 775, 781, 525 NE2d 388, 392 (1988).

[37] *Com. v. Martin*, 447 Mass 274, 850 NE2d 555 (2006); *Com. v. Johnson*, supra, 420 Mass at 461, 650 NE2d at 1259; *Com. v. Otsuki*, 411 Mass 218, 234, 581 NE2d 999, 1008 (1991); *Com. v. Freiberg*, 405 Mass 282, 295, 540 NE2d 1289, 1298 (1989); *Com. v. Pacheco*, 12 Mass App 109, 118, 421 NE2d 1239, 1245 (1981) (voice identification; the "use of a single taped voice raises suspicion of a constitutional violation, but that factor alone will not constitute sufficient ground for exclusion of the out of court identification").

[38] *Stovall v. Denno*, supra, 388 US at 302.

[39] See *Com. v. Bresilla*, 470 Mass 422, 23 NE3d 75 (2015) (approving showup within one hour of firing of semiautomatic firearm in crowd late at night); *Com. v. Figueroa*, 468 Mass 204, 9 NE3d 812 (2014) (although showup with handcuffed defendant near police van, flanked by plain clothes officers, was suggestive, it was not unnecessarily so when it was within two and one-half hours of shooting); *Stovall v. Denno*, supra, 388 US at 302 (hospital room confrontation with victim in critical condition); *Com. v. Phillips*, 452 Mass 617, 629, 897 NE2d 31, 42 (2008) (although defendant was in police wagon, in handcuffs, flanked by two police officers and illuminated by "take-down" lights, show-up was not unduly suggestive where crime was violent, need for public safety was critical and prompt identification would be more accurate); *Com. v. Thompson*, 427 Mass 729, 735, 696 NE2d 105, 109 (1998) (identifications were justified because they constituted efficient police investigation in the immediate aftermath

substantial time lapse between the crime and the confrontation, the identification may nonetheless be admissible if it is determined that, in the totality of circumstances, it was not unnecessarily suggestive.[40] First time in-court showups are inadmissible unless justified by good reason.[41]

Whether an out-of-court identification procedure is unnecessarily or impermissibly suggestive involves an inquiry into whether "good reason exists for the police to use a one on one identification procedure."[42] "Relevant to the good reason examination are the nature of

---

of a crime); *Com. v. Austin*, 421 Mass 357, 657 NE2d 458 (1995) (witnesses were shown videotape depicting another bank robbery); *Com. v. Eagles*, 419 Mass 825, 833-834, 648 NE2d 410, 416 (1995) (field identification outside of defendant's residence); *Com. v. Freiberg*, supra, 405 Mass at 295, 540 NE2d at 1298 (field identification by witness who had observed defendant burying victim in backyard of house); *Com. v. Santos*, supra, 402 Mass at 783-784, 525 NE2d at 393-394 (field confrontation immediately after defendant's apprehension); *Com. v. Melvin*, 399 Mass 201, 206 n.7, 503 NE2d 649, 653 n.7 (1987) (& citations); *Com. v. Leaster*, 395 Mass 96, 102-103, 479 NE2d 124, 128-129 (1985) (& citations) (parking lot confrontation in immediate aftermath of crime); *Com. v. Howell*, 394 Mass 654, 660, 477 NE2d 126, 131 (1985) (show-up at hospital within one or two hours of incident); *Com. v. Barnett*, 371 Mass 87, 91-94, 354 NE2d 879, 883-884 (1976) (confrontation occurred while both witness and suspect were in same hospital for wounds received during the crime; it makes no difference that witness's life was not in such jeopardy as to make confrontation imperative); *Com. v. Amaral*, 81 Mass App 143, 960 NE2d 902 (2012) (show-up was not unnecessarily suggestive where in immediate aftermath and locale of attempted armed robbery police apprehended suspect that met eyewitness descriptions); *Com. v. Wen Chao Ye*, 52 Mass App 850 (2001) (late evening show-up within 90 minutes of robbery in same lighting conditions, where perpetrator had threatened to kill victim); *Com. v. Rogers*, 38 Mass App 395, 402-405, 647 NE2d 1228, 1232-1233 (1995) (defendants brought to window of victim's ambulance). But compare *Com. v. Johnson*, supra, 420 Mass at 461, 650 NE2d at 1259 (show-up conducted 18 hours after crime was unnecessarily suggestive).

[40] *Com. v. Martin*, supra (even though defendant was in presence of police during show-up in parking lot and victim's father was nearby, suggesting to her that he had called defendant to the attention of police, show-up was not unduly suggestive where victim had gone driving with police to look at suspects over four days and motion judge found that victim was not susceptible to pressure from authority figures such as her father); *Com. v. Walker*, 421 Mass 90, 95, 653 NE2d 1080, 1083 (1995) (quick identification of a recently spotted at large suspect proper even though 16 days lapsed between crime and show-up); *Com. v. Pearson*, 87 Mass App 720, 723, 34 NE3d 1257, 1261 (2015) (show-up soon after chance encounter with suspect 53 days after crime was proper); *Com. v. Hill*, 64 Mass App 131, 831 NE2d (2005) (officer who investigated breaking and entering held driver the following day for fifteen minutes after traffic violation stop so victim could be brought to the scene for a show-up; held not improper because car and driver fit the descriptions of witnesses and lapse of 24 hours did not support finding of unnecessary suggestiveness); *Com. v. Levasseur*, 32 Mass App 629, 635-637, 592 NE2d 1350, 1354-1355 (1992) (victim requested show-up, which occurred nearly six months after crime, after she had described assailant and selected defendant's photograph).

[41] *Com. v. Crayton*, 470 Mass 228, 21 NE3d 157 (2014). See § 11.1.

[42] *Com. v. Austin*, supra, 421 Mass at 361-362, 657 NE2d at 461. (But see dissenting opinion of O'Connor, J, joined by Liacos, CJ: "The question . . . is not 'whether

the crime involved and corresponding concerns for public safety; the need for efficient police investigation in the immediate aftermath of a crime; and the usefulness of prompt confirmation of the accuracy of investigatory information, which, if in error, will release the police quickly to follow another track."[43] Neither the absence of exigent circumstances nor the fact that the police had ample time to conduct a lineup automatically renders a one-on-one confrontation unconstitutional.[44]

Single-photograph identifications have been upheld in circumstances similar to one-on-one confrontations.[45]

Because it has been recognized that one-on-one identifications may be less reliable than identifications based on a lineup where evidence of the former has been admitted the defendant is entitled to that portion of the pattern jury instruction (see § 11.3, infra) stating that "an identification made by picking the defendant out of a group

---

good reason exists for the police to use a one on one identification procedure' [but whether the procedure was] 'so impermissibly or unnecessarily suggestive and conducive to irreparable misidentification as to deprive the defendant of his due process rights.'" *Com. v. Austin* 421 Mass at 368.

[43] *Com. v. Austin*, 421 Mass at 362. See *Com. v. Meas*, 467 Mass 434, 5 NE3d 864 (2014) ("very good justification" for show-up where crime involved firearm not found at scene, presenting public safety concerns and need for efficient investigation and show-ups were conducted within one hour of shooting; fact that show-up at night was well illuminated and suspects, known gang members, were in handcuffs was not impermissibly suggestive; that one witness out of five was told police had apprehended someone matching description he gave was not necessarily impermissibly suggestive, and witnesses were cautioned that persons viewed might be innocent); *Com. v. Leaster*, supra, 395 Mass at 103, 479 NE2d at 129 ("Of course, if there are special elements of unfairness, indicating a desire on the part of the police to 'stack the deck' against the defendant, an identification resulting from a one on one confrontation would be inadmissible.")

[44] See *Com. v. Leonardi*, 413 Mass 757, 761, 604 NE2d 23, 26 (1992); *Com. v. Leaster*, supra, 395 Mass at 103, 479 NE2d at 129 (& citations); *Com. v. Libby*, 21 Mass App 650, 656, 489 NE2d 702, 706 (1986) (the fact that a lineup could have been conducted does not itself render the one-on-one confrontation unlawful).

[45] See *Simmons v. United States*, supra, 390 US at 383-384; *Com. v. Venios*, 378 Mass 24, 29, 389 NE2d 395, 398 (1979); *Com. v. Nolin*, 373 Mass 45, 51, 364 NE2d 1224, 1228 (1977) (single photograph shown to victim who was seriously wounded and near death); *Com. v. Martinez*, 67 Mass App 788, 837 NE2d 1096 (2006) (permissible to display single photo to undercover officer involved in narcotics purchase, where photo was taken immediately after purchase and was shown to officer to confirm that correct person was photographed and would be arrested); *Com. v. Laaman*, 25 Mass App 354, 361, 518 NE2d 861, 865 (1988) (display of driver's license photo three hours after armed attack on two State troopers; "[s]ome suggestiveness is permitted in such cases in order to speed detection of the offender or to exonerate the suspect"). But see *Com. v. Moon*, 380 Mass 751, 758, 405 NE2d 947, 952 (1980) (photographs of only one person should not be shown to witnesses in the absence of exigent circumstances).

of similar individuals is generally more reliable than one which results from the presentation of a defendant alone to the witness."[46]

d. Voice Identification

Voice identifications have been treated as suspect, and "police and prosecutors are warned to take particular pains to avoid suggestive conditions in making arrangements for out-of-court tests where a witness tries to match live voices with his recollections of a voice heard in the usually stressful original setting."[47] The preferred precautionary procedures for conducting voice identifications include avoiding one-on-one auditions, not having the witness view the speaker as he listens to the voice, and not choosing for repetition the words used by the perpetrator at the scene of the crime.[48]

---

[46] *Com. v. Cuffie*, 414 Mass 632, 639-640, 609 NE2d 437, 440-441 (1993).

[47] *Com. v. Marini*, 375 Mass 510, 516-519, 378 NE2d 51, 55-56 (1978) (one-on-one voice identification of defendant by victim at trial was unnecessarily suggestive). See also *Com. v. Torres*, 367 Mass 737, 740-741, 327 NE2d 871, 874 (1975); *Com. v. Enos*, 26 Mass App 1006, 530 NE2d 805 (1988) ("Although voice identification evidence has been accepted under circumstances thought appropriate or sufficiently hedged with safeguards (e.g., the presence of counsel), the cases manifest apprehension about its too free use to identify a defendant.").

[48] *Com. v. Marini*, supra, 375 Mass at 517, 375 NE2d at 56. But compare *Com. v. Chamberlin*, 86 Mass App 705, 20 NE3d 954 (2014), review granted on different issue, 471 Mass 1106 (2015) (one-on-one procedure where police specifically mentioned defendant to witnesses before the identifications, and identifications were not performed until several years after witnesses had last spoken with defendant, were not unduly suggestive where witnesses had known defendant for twenty years and one had a child by him); *Com. v. Saunders*, 50 Mass App 865, 744 NE2d 74 (2001) (not necessary to meet all prongs of *Marini* test, where victim heard voice accidentally at police station, without looking at defendant as he spoke, words were not the same as during the crime and identification took place within hours of the crime, identification was admissible); *Com. v. DeMaria*, 46 Mass App 114, 118, 703 NE2d 1203, 1206 (1999) (it would have been better not to refer to defendant by same number in voice identification procedure as in preceding visual lineup, but where witness testified she was not influenced by number, it was not unduly suggestive); *Com. v. Burgos*, 36 Mass App 903, 904, 627 NE2d 471, 473 (1994) (*Marini* precautions do not apply in a "show-up"). For a case following the *Marini* procedures, see *Com. v. Miles*, 420 Mass 67, 78-81, 648 NE2d 719, 727-729 (1995). See also *Com. v. Carpinto*, 37 Mass App 51, 636 NE2d 1349 (1994) (identification of voice on taped telephone call). See § 9.4.

e. Photographic Arrays and Police Conduct and Suggestiveness

Any identification procedure may become unnecessarily suggestive due to the way in which the police conduct it.[49] Whether photographic arrays are unnecessarily suggestive depends upon the

---

[49] See, e.g., *Com. v. Weichell*, 390 Mass 62, 72-73, 453 NE2d 1038, 1045 (1983) (identification by composite will be set aside if the process was so impermissibly suggestive as to give rise to a substantial likelihood of irreparable misidentification).

For cases finding undue suggestiveness, see *Foster v. California*, 394 US 440 (1969) (identification improperly admitted where witness identified defendant only after police first displayed defendant to witness in a three-man lineup in which defendant stood out from the others due to his height and jacket similar to that worn by robber, and then police permitted a one-on-one confrontation); *Com. v. Santos*, 402 Mass 775, 780-785, 525 NE2d 388, 391-394 (1988) (one-on-one stationhouse identification unconstitutionally suggestive in light of suggestibility of moderately retarded identifying witness; testimony corroborating the unconstitutional identification must also be suppressed); *Com. v. Moon*, 380 Mass 751, 756-759, 405 NE2d 947, 951-952 (1980) (identification evidence suppressed where victim identified defendant after police named defendant in victim's presence and then showed victim a single photograph of defendant); *Com. v. Marks*, 12 Mass App 511, 514-516, 426 NE2d 1172, 1176 (1981) (where two witnesses were permitted to view defendant jointly with result that mother identified him in the presence of her daughter, who then also identified him, there was risk of suggestiveness and judge was required to make findings as to whether daughter's identification had an independent source or was otherwise reliable).

For cases finding no impermissible suggestion, see *Com. v. Forte*, 469 Mass 469, 14 NE3d 900 (2014) (two witnesses were shown, separately, a restaurant videotape from the time of the crime and both identified the defendant as the man they had seen; they were then separately shown a photographic array from which they identified defendant's picture; court rejected defense argument that procedure was unnecessarily suggestive and encouraged women to pick photo of man who resembled man in videotape, rather than man they had seen at time of crime); *Com. v. Meas*, 467 Mass 434, 5 NE3d 864 (2014) (fact that show-up at night was well illuminated and suspects, known gang members, were in handcuffs was not impermissibly suggestive; that one witness out of five was told police had apprehended someone matching the description he gave was not necessarily impermissibly suggestive, and witnesses were cautioned that persons viewed might be innocent); *Com. v. Andrews*, 427 Mass 434, 438, 694 NE2d 329, 333 (1998) (detective's question whether perpetrator might have been light-skinned black man, rather than Hispanic as initially described by witness, was not impermissibly suggestive where police had no suspect in mind); *Com. v. Leonardi*, 413 Mass 757, 761-762, 604 NE2d 23, 26 (1992) (although it would have been better if detective had not told victim that he was bringing in someone who fit description given by victim, statement did not create special element of unfairness); *Com. v. Tanso*, 411 Mass 640, 651-653, 583 NE2d 1247, 1254-1255 (1992) (identification procedures used in three separate police lineups not unnecessarily suggestive; the "fact that each person in the lineup may not have closely resembled the defendant does not render the lineup impermissibly suggestive"); *Com. v. Simmonds*, 386 Mass 234, 239-240, 434 NE2d 1270, 1275 (1982) (lineup not unduly suggestive even though only three of seven participants were clean-shaven, defendant among them, and witnesses had described the assailant as clean-shaven; and even though several participants wore

composition of the array and the circumstances under which they are shown to witnesses.[50]

---

regulation police pants); *Com. v. Toney*, 385 Mass 575, 586-587, 433 NE2d 425, 432-433 (1982) (mentioning of defendant's name by police not, by itself, unduly suggestive and thus did not taint the in-court identification); *Com. v. Clifford*, 374 Mass 293, 303-304, 372 NE2d 1267, 1275 (1978) (lineup not impermissibly suggestive even though defendant wore a jacket similar to one used during the crime); *Com. v. Florek*, 48 Mass App 414, 722 NE2d 20 (2000) (that defendant was surrounded by police officers and asked to remove his shirt at the time of showup did not render request unnecessarily suggestive); *Com. v. Drane*, 47 Mass App 913, 712 NE2d 1162 (1999) (illumination of defendant's face by flashlight during nighttime show-up was not suggestive); *Com. v. O'Loughlin*, 17 Mass App 972, 458 NE2d 767 (1984) (one-on-one confrontation that allowed the victim to listen to defendant's voice as part of the identification process not unduly suggestive where confrontation occurred within three hours of crime and defendant spoke in a normal conversation rather than uttering the words spoken by victim's assailant during crime). See also *Com. v. Lopes*, supra, 362 Mass at 453-454, 287 NE2d at 121-122 (& citations) (nothing inherently suggestive about use of "two-way mirror" to view suspect).

[50] For cases finding photographic identifications impermissibly suggestive, see *Com. v. Riccard*, 410 Mass 718, 722-723, 575 NE2d 57, 60 (1991) (display of defendant's photograph to witness during meeting with prosecutor days before trial unnecessarily suggestive); *Com. v. Thornley*, 406 Mass 96, 98-101, 546 NE2d 350, 351-353 (1989) (*Thornley II*) (photographic identification impermissibly suggestive where defendant's picture was only one in array showing him wearing eyeglasses); *Com. v. Poggi*, 53 Mass App 685, 693, 761 NE2d 983, 990 (2002) (array of only six pictures, showing only head and shoulders, was impermissibly suggestive where only defendant wore a dark shirt and had a goatee, features described by the witnesses); *Com. v. Alicea*, 464 Mass 837, 847, 985 NE2d 1197, 1207 (2013) (identification was not suggestive where witness first identified defendant from among nine photos, later told police she was certain, consistently described defendant's appearance, and had known defendant for one year before incident, even though police may have shown her defendant as one of only two photos in a second array before she expressed certitude); *Com. v. Borgos*, 464 Mass 23, 32, 979 NE2d 1095, 1103 (2012) (identifications were not unduly suggestive based on unreliability of witnesses); *Com. v. Cavitt*, 460 Mass 617, 631, 953 NE2d 216-228 (2011) (identification of person on computer screen that witness passed while leaving police station was not impermissibly suggestive where witness had just been viewing thousands of photos on a different screen, police did not call his attention to the second screen, his viewing of it was inadvertent, and he did not hear any comments by second witness who was viewing that screen at the time); *Com. v. Watson*, 455 Mass 246, 915 NE2d 1052 (2009) (photographic array was not unduly suggestive although officer woke witness up in hospital, witness was groggy from being awakened and effects of medication, officer told witness photo of suspect was in array, officer did not follow DOJ Guidelines, officer administering array was involved in investigation and knew who suspect was); *Com. v. LaFaille*, 46 Mass App 144, 150, 704 NE2d 206, 210 (1999) (two photos of defendant in single array shown to witness 29 days following crime); *Com. v. Day*, 42 Mass App 242, 676 NE2d 467 (1997) (giving witnesses opportunity to view for 20 to 30 minutes a police flyer containing the same photograph of defendant which was used in the array from which they made an identification, where flyer advised that defendant had shot someone, was impermissibly suggestive);

Com. v. Gordon, 6 Mass App 230, 239, 374 NE2d 1228, 1231 (1978) (showing victim an array of photographs that included only one depiction of a person with braided hair such as victim had described to police was unnecessarily suggestive; but identification evidence was nonetheless admissible as reliable).

For cases finding that photographic identifications were not impermissibly suggestive, see *Com. v. Arzola*, 470 Mass 809, 26 NE3d 185 (2015) (although only defendant wore gray shirt in photos, face was focal point of photo and witness said identification was based on hair, complexion, and eyes); *Com. v. LaFaille*, 430 Mass 44, 712 NE2d 590 (1999) (inadvertent duplication of defendant's photograph in array did not render it suggestive); *Com. v. Miles*, 420 Mass 67, 77-78, 648 NE2d 719, 727 (1995) (nine photograph arrays did not distinguish defendant on basis of age, not otherwise unduly suggestive); *Com. v. Jackson*, 419 Mass 716, 728-730, 647 NE2d 401, 408-409 (1995) (post-identification statements by police did not render photographic identification suggestive); *Com. v. Wallace*, 417 Mass 126, 129, 627 NE2d 935, 938 (1994) (duplication of defendant's photograph in successive arrays not sufficient to compel suppression of resulting identification); *Com. v. Dinkins*, 415 Mass 715, 720-721, 615 NE2d 570, 573 (1993) (same; no substantial risk of miscarriage of justice where witness asked to see defendant's photograph after another eyewitness selected it in his presence); *Com. v. Downey*, 407 Mass 472, 478-479, 553 NE2d 1303, 1307 (1990) (photographic arrays not unnecessarily suggestive even though a "look-alike" photograph was removed); *Com. v. Melvin*, 399 Mass 201, 503 NE2d 649 (1987) (photographic array not impermissibly suggestive even though defendant's photograph was the only one depicting a person wearing a sling, and the witness had observed the intruder injure his shoulder while escaping from the scene of the crime); *Com. v. Shipps*, 399 Mass 820, 831, 507 NE2d 671, 679 (1987) (identification of defendant from photographs of two persons shown to witness not so suggestive as to give rise to a substantial likelihood of misidentification); *Com. v. Paszko*, 391 Mass 164, 167-171, 461 NE2d 222, 227-228 (1984) (photographic arrays not unduly suggestive even though defendant's photograph was only one shown in both arrays); *Com. v. Porter*, 384 Mass 647, 656-658, 429 NE2d 14, 21 (1981) (showing of one more photograph, taken from officer's pocket, after witness had been unable to identify defendant's photograph from among a group shown to him, was merely a continuation of an ongoing process and was not unduly suggestive); *Com. v. Cincotta*, supra, 379 Mass at 393-394, 398 NE2d at 480 (witness not unduly influenced by choice of defendant's photograph made by other witness); *Com. v. Clark*, 378 Mass 392, 399-401, 393 NE2d 296, 301 (1979) (photographic array not impermissibly suggestive even though defendant's photograph was one of two snapshots in a group including 11 "mug shots"); *Com. v. Mobley*, 369 Mass 892, 344 NE2d 181 (1976) (photographic array not impermissibly suggestive even though defendant was only person depicted wearing a ski cap and such a cap was worn by the robber); *Com. v. Manning*, 44 Mass App 695, 693 NE2d 704 (1998) (although defendant's photo was the only one in array of nine photos which witness had not previously seen, array was not unduly suggestive where judge credited witness's testimony that he did not realize the other eight photos were from prior array); *Com. v. Caldwell*, 36 Mass App 570, 579-580, 634 NE2d 124, 130 (1994) (although police had to reconstruct array after 10 to 12 photographs were lost, no showing of impermissible suggestiveness); *Com. v. Ayles*, 31 Mass App 514, 517-518, 580 NE2d 394, 397 (1991) (photograph identification not unduly suggestive even though police officer told rape victim that he "had a good idea of who did it" before displaying the photographs to her); *Com. v. Laaman*, 25 Mass App 354, 361, 518 NE2d 861, 865 (1988) (photographic identification not unduly suggestive even though police mentioned suspect's name inadvertently).

In *Commonwealth v. Silva-Santiago*,[51] the Supreme Judicial Court articulated a protocol that should be followed in out-of-court photographic identifications to reduce the risk of unnecessary suggestiveness and misidentification. The protocol is based on guidelines propagated by the United States Department of Justice.[52] The Court has so far declined to hold that the failure to follow the protocol renders an identification inadmissible, but both in *Silva-Santiago* and later in *Com. v. Watson*[53] the Court has emphasized its "expectation that the identification protocol . . . will be employed in the regular course of administering photographic arrays." The Court instructed:

> What is practicable in nearly all circumstances is a protocol to be employed before a photographic array is provided to an eyewitness, making clear to the eyewitness, at a minimum, that he will be asked to view a set of photographs; the alleged wrongdoer may or may not be in the photographs depicted in the array; it is just as important to clear a person from suspicion as to identify a person as the wrongdoer; individuals depicted in the photographs may not appear exactly as they did on the date of the incident because features such as weight, head, and facial hair are subject to change; regardless of whether an identification is made, the investigation will continue; and the procedure requires the administrator to ask the witness to state, in his or her own words, how certain he or she is of any identification.[54]

In *Watson* and *Silva-Santiago* the Court also suggested that the better practice is a double-blind procedure in which the officer who administers the photographic array does not know the identity of the suspect. It did not adopt a rule that an identification is unnecessarily suggestive when the double-blind procedure is not followed, recognizing that it might not be practical in all situations.

In *Com. v. Walker*,[55] the Court discussed, as it had in *Silva-Santiago*, the question of whether sequential, rather than simultaneous, display of photographs should be required for admissibility of a photographic identification. After reviewing the recent research and literature on the subject, the Court once again stated that it is too soon

---

[51] *Com. v. Silva-Santiago*, 453 Mass 782, 906 NE2d 299 (2009) (photographic array was not unduly suggestive; given the present state of research, simultaneous, rather than sequential, display of photos goes to weight of identification, not admissibility).

[52] United States Department of Justice, Eyewitness Evidence: A Guide for Law Enforcement (1999).

[53] *Watson*, 455 Mass at 252, 915 NE2d at 1058.

[54] *Id.*

[55] *Com. v. Walker*, 460 Mass 590, 602-603, 953 NE2d 195, 207 (2011).

to conclude that sequential display is so plainly superior that an identification arising from a simultaneous display is unnecessarily suggestive. The Court announced that it would convene a study committee to determine how best to deter unnecessarily suggestive procedures and to review model jury instructions. The Court declined to find that the photo array in *Walker* was unduly suggestive because it included only suspects. The Court indicated that in the future, absent exigent or extraordinary circumstances, police should not show a witness a photographic array with fewer than five fillers for every suspect photograph. It declined to address, however, whether a failure to do so will render an identification inadmissible. The *Walker* Court also declined to require trial judges to serve as gatekeepers to exclude unreliable eyewitness testimony even where a defendant is unable to establish unnecessary suggestiveness. It noted that New Jersey had adopted such a procedure and indicated the issue should be reviewed by the study committee it would appoint in Massachusetts.[56]

There is a line of authority supporting the proposition that where the pretrial identification of the suspect "is the product of something other than improper action by the state, due process does not require the suppression of it or its repetitions."[57] Thus, identification evidence from an accidental confrontation is unobjectionable.[58] Similarly, the fact that a witness has observed the defendant's likeness in the media does not, absent police involvement and misconduct, taint an identification.[59]

---

[56] *Id.*, 460 Mass at 606, 953 NE2d at 209-219.

[57] *Com. v. Wheeler*, 3 Mass App 387, 392, 331 NE2d 815, 818 (1975) (original identification was utterly independent of the police). See also *Com. v. Holland*, 410 Mass 248, 253, 571 NE2d 625, 629 (1991) (what is forbidden by the Due Process Clause is that a witness be "subjected *by the State* to an identification so unnecessarily suggestive") (emphasis added).

[58] See *Com. v. Otsuki*, supra, 411 Mass at 233-234, 581 NE2d at 1008 (witness's observation of wanted poster portraying defendant was accidental and not the result of improper police conduct); *Com. v. Leaster*, 362 Mass 407, 410-411, 287 NE2d 122, 125 (1972) (& citations); *Com. v. McMaster*, 21 Mass App 722, 725 n.2, 490 NE2d 464, 468 n.2 (1986).

[59] See *Com. v. Jules*, 464 Mass 478, 488, 984 NE2d 266, 274 (2013) (witness's identification of defendant in newspaper photograph was not unduly suggestive where witness saw photo only two days after incident and could not recall reading headline or text of article); *Com. v. Sylvia*, 456 Mass 182, 190, 921 NE2d 968, 976 (2010) (that witnesses saw media coverage of defendant's arrest, when he was dressed differently than at time of crime, did not impermissibly taint their later identifications); *Com. v. Otsuki*, supra, 411 Mass at 234-235, 581 NE2d at 1009 (witness identified defendant from a newspaper photograph); *Com. v. Colon-Cruz*, 408 Mass 533, 542, 562 NE2d 797, 805 (1990) ("If police have not in any way manipulated press reports,

The Supreme Judicial Court has held, however, that an in-court identification of a defendant may be excluded where it is the product of an earlier suggestive confrontation with the defendant, even though government agents had no hand in causing the confrontation.[60] The court's decision was not based on constitutional grounds but on common law principles of fairness, which dictate that an unreliable identification arising from especially suggestive circumstances should not be admitted. In *Com. v. Johnson*,[61] the court said that in the case of an out of court identification that was especially suggestive where government agents were not involved, a judge must weigh the probative value of the identification against the danger of unfair prejudice. The "probative value of the identification depends on the strength of its source independent of the suggestive circumstances of the identification."[62] "The danger of unfair prejudice arises because the accuracy of an identification tainted by suggestive circumstances is more difficult for a jury to evaluate."[63] The ultimate measure is the reliability of the identification.

To trigger a reliability analysis, "the circumstances surrounding the identification need only be so suggestive that there is a substantial risk that they influenced the witness's identification of the defendant, inflated his or her level of certainty in the identification, or altered his or her memory of the circumstances of the operative event. Where the independent source of an identification is slim, this level of suggestiveness may be sufficient to support a finding of inadmissibility; where the independent source is substantial, a greater level of suggestiveness would be needed to support a finding that the danger of unfair prejudice substantially outweighs the probative value of the

---

then simple exposure to the media is not sufficient ground to suppress an identification."). See also *Com. v. Currier*, 15 Mass App 929, 445 NE2d 158 (1983) (original identification of the defendant by the victim was made as a result of an encounter arranged by a friend of the victim); *Com. v. Mattias*, 8 Mass App 786, 788-789, 397 NE2d 1134, 1136 (1979) (first witness recognized defendant on a public street; second witness had accidental encounter with defendant).

[60] *Com. v. Jones*, 423 Mass 99, 666 NE2d 994 (1996). But see *Com. v. Bly*, 448 Mass 473, 494, 862 NE2d 341, 359 (2007) (circumstances of the case did not equate to the degree of unreliability present in *Jones*).

[61] *Com. v. Johnson*, 473 Mass 594, 45 NE3d 83 (2016). See *Com. v. McWilliams*, 473 Mass 606, 45 NE3d 94 (2016) (finding that photographic identification was not unreliable).

[62] *Com. v. Johnson*, 473 Mass at 601, 45 NE3d at 91.

[63] *Id.*, 473 Mass at 600, 45 NE3d at 90 (citing scientific studies).

identification."[64] The court also held in *Johnson* that where a judge excludes an identification as unreliable where law enforcement agents were not involved, no in court identification by that witness is admissible.[65]

f. Application to Other Identification Evidence

The due process principles discussed in this section apply principally to the direct identification of the defendant as the person who committed a crime. Defendants have unsuccessfully argued that these same principles should govern other identification evidence.[66] While rejecting this argument, the Supreme Judicial Court has nonetheless recognized that in an extreme case, the degree of suggestiveness in the identification procedures involving inanimate objects or persons other than the perpetrator might be so great as to violate due process.[67] Accordingly, law enforcement officers should exercise care to avoid unduly suggestive procedures. The court has also recognized that "it would be desirable to conduct a voir dire on a challenge based on a claimed suggestive 'confrontation' in the identification of an inanimate object."[68]

§ 11.2.3 Fruits of Illegal Identification Procedures—In-Court Identification

If evidence of a pretrial identification is suppressed because the accused's right to counsel was abridged (see § 11.2.1, supra) or because the procedure is found to have been impermissibly suggestive (see

---

[64] *Id.*, 473 Mass at 604, 45 NE3d at 93.

[65] *Id.*, 473 Mass at 603, 45 NE3d at 92.

[66] See *Com. v. Spann*, 383 Mass 142, 146-148, 418 NE2d 328, 331-332 (1981) (pretrial photographic identification of deceased victim); *Com. v. Simmons*, 383 Mass 46, 48-52, 417 NE2d 1193, 1195-1196 (1981) (pretrial one-on-one identification of automobile allegedly driven by victim's assailant). See also *Com. v. Shipps*, 399 Mass 820, 833, 507 NE2d 671, 680 (1987) (photographic identification of defendant's gun was not unnecessarily suggestive).

[67] *Com. v. Bresilla*, 470 Mass 422, 23 NE3d 75 (2015) (nothing fundamentally unfair or suggestive about procedures employed to identify jacket); *Com. v. Spann*, supra, 383 Mass at 148, 418 NE2d at 332; *Com. v. Simmons*, supra, 383 Mass at 51-52, 417 NE2d at 1196. See also *Com. v. Jones*, 25 Mass App 55, 62, 514 NE2d 1337, 1341 (1987).

[68] *Com. v. Simmons*, supra, 383 Mass at 53 n.3, 417 NE2d at 1197 n.3.

§ 11.2.2, supra), the question arises as to whether the witness will nonetheless be permitted to make an in-court identification. Generally, evidence derived even indirectly from a constitutional violation is subject to suppression as "the fruit of the poisonous tree."[69] The test for determining the admissibility of such derivative evidence is whether it "has been come at by exploitation of [the initial] illegality or instead by means sufficiently distinguishable to be purged of the primary taint."[70]

An in-court identification must therefore be excluded if it is the product of the illegal pretrial procedure. Current law, however, states that if it can be established that the in-court identification has an independent origin, such as the opportunity the witness had to observe the perpetrator at the time of the crime, it may be admitted.[71] The Supreme Judicial Court has noted that there is a question whether that doctrine will survive the decisions in *Com. v. Crayton* and *Com. v. Collins*, *supra*, given their reasoning that an in-court identification is equivalent to a suggestive show-up.[72] Until that is resolved, the issue is whether the witness's observations made during the course of the crime fixed in his mind the features of the offender and thus provided an independent source for the identification at trial.[73] The prosecution bears the burden of demonstrating by "clear and convincing evidence" that the in-court identification is based upon observations of the suspect other than the tainted pretrial identification.[74]

Several factors have been set forth as germane to the determination of whether a subsequent identification has an independent origin:

---

[69] See *Wong Sun v. United States*, 371 US 471 (1963).

[70] 371 US at 488. See also *United States v. Crews*, 445 US 463, 472-473 (1980) (in-court identification rested on witness's independent recollection of her initial encounter with the assailant and was not the product of defendant's illegal arrest or pretrial identifications); *Com. v. Crowe*, 21 Mass App 456, 462-465, 488 NE2d 780, 785-787 (1986) (extensive discussion of derivative evidence doctrine and authorities). Compare *Com. v. Lyons*, 397 Mass 644, 646-649, 492 NE2d 1142, 1145-1146 (1986) (the fact that defendant's identification was obtained as a result of an arrest on a warrant issued in violation of G.L. 218, § 35A, but otherwise lawful, does not require suppression of the resulting identification).

[71] *United States v. Wade*, 388 US 218, 239-241 (1967); *Com. v. Johnson*, 420 Mass 458, 467, 650 NE2d 1257, 1260-1261 (1995) (per se approach excluding impermissibly suggestive identifications notwithstanding their reliability does not render inadmissible a subsequent identification shown to come from an independent source); *Com. v. Hill*, 38 Mass App 982, 652 NE2d 621 (1995) (same).

[72] *Com. v. Johnson*, 473 Mass 594, 602, 45 NE3d 83, 92 (2016).

[73] *Com. v. Ross*, 361 Mass 665, 676, 282 NE2d 70, 77 (1972), *vacated on other grounds*, 410 US 901 (1973).

[74] *United States v. Wade*, supra, 388 US at 240; *Com. v. Johnson*, supra, 420 Mass at 463-464, 650 NE2d at 1260-1261; *Com. v. Bodden*, 391 Mass 356, 359, 461 NE2d 803, 806 (1984).

1. the prior opportunity to observe the alleged criminal act;
2. the existence of any discrepancy between the witness's description of the perpetrator and the defendant's actual personal characteristics;
3. any prior identification of another person as the perpetrator;
4. the identification of the defendant by picture prior to the impermissible procedure;
5. the failure to identify the defendant on a prior occasion; and
6. the length of time between the alleged act and the identification procedure.[75]

These factors are similar to those used to measure the reliability of a pretrial identification under the *Biggers-Brathwaite* test discussed above.[76] "The crucial determination in both instances is whether the identification sought to be admitted in evidence is the product of the witness's observations at the time of the crime or is instead the product of improper suggestions by the police."[77]

Application of these factors depends upon the context of the particular case, and each factor is not necessarily entitled to equal weight.[78] The extent of the witness's opportunity to observe the perpetrator at the time of the crime is probably the most important single factor, as the firmer the contemporaneous impression, the less the witness is subject to be influenced by subsequent events.[79] A witness's knowledge of and opportunity to observe the subject prior to the incident is also relevant to the determination of whether a subsequent identification has an independent source.[80]

These principles regarding derivative identification evidence apply whether the primary illegality involves the denial of the defendant's right to counsel or right to due process.[81] When, however, the

[75] *United States v. Wade*, supra, 388 US at 241.

[76] See *Com. v. Thornley*, 406 Mass 96, 98 n.2, 546 NE2d 350, 352 n.2 (1989) (*Thornley II*); *Com. v. Crowe*, 21 Mass App 456, 468 n.13, 488 NE2d 780, 788 n.13 (1986) ("The independent source and the reliability tests are essentially the same.").

[77] *Com. v. Wheeler*, 3 Mass App 387, 392, 331 NE2d 815, 818 (1975).

[78] *Com. v. Ross*, supra, 361 Mass at 671, 282 NE2d at 74.

[79] *Id.* at 671-672; *Com. v. Bodden*, supra, 391 Mass at 361, 461 NE2d at 807; *Com. v. Mendes*, supra, 361 Mass at 511, 281 NE2d at 246; *Com. v. Botev*, 79 Mass App 281, 284, 945 NE2d 956, 960 (2011) (witnesses saw perpetrator at close range for 45 seconds, gave only relative identifications at photo array but then picked defendant from sizeable crowd a year after incident).

[80] *Com. v. Crowe*, supra, 21 Mass App at 466, 488 NE2d at 787.

[81] Compare *United States v. Wade*, supra, 388 US at 242, and *Gilbert v. California*, 388 US 263, 272 (1967) (remanding to determine whether in-court identification had

primary illegality involves denial of the defendant's right to counsel, the prosecution is not entitled to show that the witness's *pretrial* identification had an independent source.[82]

We collect below cases finding that the in-court identification had an independent source,[83] and cases finding no independent source.[84]

---

a source independent of a lineup identification conducted in the absence of counsel), with *Com. v. Moon*, 380 Mass 751, 756-759, 405 NE2d 947, 951-952 (1980) (judge properly determined that naming defendant in presence of victim and then showing victim a single photograph of defendant was so violative of due process as to taint any subsequent in-court identification), and *Com. v. Jackson*, 377 Mass 319, 329-332, 386 NE2d 15, 21-22 (1979) (concluding that there was sufficient evidence to warrant a finding that witness's in-court identification had a source independent of an impermissibly suggestive pretrial photographic procedure).

[82] See *Moore v. Illinois*, 434 US 220, 226, 231-232 (1977); *Gilbert v. California*, supra, 388 US at 272-274 ("Only a per se exclusionary rule as to such testimony can be an effective sanction to assure that law enforcement authorities will respect the accused's constitutional right to the presence of his counsel at the critical lineup.").

[83] *Com. v. Castro*, 438 Mass 160, 778 NE2d 900 (2002) (witness had seen defendant on many prior occasions); *Com. v. Holland*, 410 Mass 248, 256, 571 NE2d 625, 630 (1991) (witness had opportunity to observe assailant close up and face-to-face while he stood over her for some time in well lit parking lot); *Com. v. Freiberg*, 405 Mass 282, 295, 540 NE2d 1289, 1298 (1989) (witness, with excellent vision, observed defendant for more than three minutes on sunny day from unobstructed view); *Com. v. Bodden*, supra, 391 Mass at 359-363, 461 NE2d at 806-807 (witness had opportunity to "quite easily" observe defendant at time of crime for a period of several minutes, and thus, trial judge properly concluded that in-court identification rested on independent recollection even though witness failed to identify defendant positively when he first saw him after crime); *Com. v. Cooper*, 356 Mass 74, 84-85, 248 NE2d 253, 260 (1969) (witnesses had ample opportunity to observe offenders and ample capacity to remember what they observed, and one witness selected defendant's photograph before the suggestive lineup); *Com. v. Hill*, 38 Mass App 982, 652 NE2d 621 (1995) (officer's initial encounter with defendant provided basis for in-court identification independent of later suggestive identification); *Com. v. Ayles*, 31 Mass App 514, 518-520, 580 NE2d 394, 397-398 (1991) (police officer's post-identification statement to victim that person whose photograph she selected was a suspect in other assaults on women did not taint in-court identification where her prior identification was made with certitude and without undue hesitation).

[84] *Com. v. Thornley*, 406 Mass 96, 101, 546 NE2d 350, 353 (1989) (*Thornley II*) (Commonwealth failed to demonstrate that lineup and courtroom identification were based on source independent of suggestive photographic identification); *Com. v. A Juvenile*, 402 Mass 275, 280, 521 NE2d 1368, 1372 (1988) (Commonwealth did not meet heavy burden of proving that proffered in-court identification would be free of taint of suggestive pretrial procedure); *Com. v. Martin*, 63 Mass App 587, 827 NE2d 1263 (2005) (trial judge's failure to consider the effect of the show-up itself and a confirming subsequent photo array on the in-court identification, together with judge's failure to consider witness's error in initial description of her attacker, rendered finding of independent source erroneous as matter of law); *Com. v. Botelho*, 369 Mass 860, 868-870, 343 NE2d 876, 882 (1976) (where witness's observation of assailant was over a substantial distance in dim lighting when she was influenced by alcohol, her description of the gunman immediately after incident was very general, she failed to identify

§ 11.3 Challenging Identification Evidence

§ 11.3.1 Motion to Suppress

When an allegedly impermissible pretrial identification has occurred, the defendant must seasonably raise the issue by filing a motion to suppress the evidence before trial.[1] A defendant who fails to make a pretrial motion is not entitled to object to an in-court identification at trial.[2] If the defendant's pretrial motion to suppress is denied, it is not necessary to object to the identification at trial to preserve the issue for appeal.[3]

A defendant has a right to be informed of the details of any out-of-court identification and may request a voir dire of the relevant witnesses to obtain such details. The Supreme Judicial Court has emphasized that "full exploration of the circumstances surrounding eyewitness identification is necessary to ensure a fair trial."[4]

When a timely motion is filed, the practice is to hold a pretrial hearing or voir dire examination in the absence of the jury to determine the

---

picture of defendant, and on a prior occasion she stated that defendant was positively not the assailant, court was warranted in finding that subsequent in-court identifications of defendant were tainted by suggestive confrontation at courthouse); *Com. v. Kazonis*, 356 Mass 649, 653, 255 NE2d 333, 336 (1970) (highly unlikely that in-court identification more than two years after crime could have occurred independently of suggestive police station confrontation); *Com. v. White*, 11 Mass App 953, 417 NE2d 44 (1981) (in-court identification should have been suppressed as lacking source independent of suggestive out-of-court identification where witness's description was at variance with defendant's height and weight and she failed to identify defendant's photograph prior to suggestive show-up).

§ 11.3 [1] Mass R Crim P 13; Mass Superior Court R 61; Fed R Crim P 12(b)(3).

[2] See *Com. v. Cooper*, 356 Mass 74, 78-79, 248 NE2d 253, 257 (1969) (decided under Superior Court Rule 101, the predecessor of Rule 61), and *Com. v. Stanley*, 363 Mass 102, 104, 292 NE2d 694, 697 (1973).

[3] *Com. v. Martin*, 447 Mass 274, 279, 850 NE2d 555, 560 (2006).

[4] *Com. v. Dougan*, 377 Mass 303, 316-317, 386 NE2d 1, 9-10 (1979) (conviction reversed because defendant had been denied any opportunity to explore the identification process). See also *Com. v. Dickerson*, 372 Mass 783, 789, 364 NE2d 1052, 1056-1057 (1977) ("In a case suggestive of unfairness in the confrontation process, failure to allow full development [on cross-examination] of the circumstances surrounding the identification might well warrant setting aside the verdict of guilt."). Compare *Com. v. Leaster*, 395 Mass 96, 104-105, 479 NE2d 124, 129-130 (1985) (newly discovered evidence suggesting a different version of the pretrial identification than was testified to at trial did not entitle defendant to new trial), with *Com. v. Wilson*, 46 Mass App 292, 705 NE2d 313 (1999) (voir dire unnecessary where prosecutor had accurately informed defense counsel of the information). Cf. *Com. v. Botticelli*, 51 Mass App 802, 748 NE2d 1006 (2001) (fact that government lost the photo array that had been shown to witnesses did not in itself justify striking the testimony of the witnesses).

admissibility of pretrial and in-court identifications.[5] While a judicial determination outside the jury's presence of the admissibility of identification evidence is the preferred proceeding, the due process clause of the Fourteenth Amendment of the United States Constitution does not demand that the trial judge conduct an evidentiary hearing whenever a defendant contends that an improper identification occurred.[6]

On a motion to suppress identification evidence, it is the defendant's burden to prove by a preponderance of the evidence that the pretrial procedure was so unnecessarily suggestive and conducive to mistaken identity as to deny the defendant due process of law.[7] Upon such a showing, the prosecution may not offer the identification in evidence. If the court excludes evidence of the pretrial identification and the prosecution desires to offer an in-court identification, it must (as discussed in § 11.2.3, supra) show by clear and convincing evidence that the proffered identification has a source independent of the suggestive procedure.

§ 11.3.2 Cross-Examination and Closing Argument

It should be added that a ruling admitting evidence of a pretrial identification does not end the matter. The testimony presented to the jury is subject to cross-examination on the question of the fairness and reliability of the procedure, and the matter will almost certainly be addressed in closing argument.[8] "Where identification evidence has not been suppressed, its infirmities are a matter for consideration by the

---

[5] See, e.g., *Com. v. Dickerson*, 372 Mass at 788. But see *Com. v. Hicks*, 377 Mass 1, 6-7, 384 NE2d 1206, 1210 (1979) (voir dire unnecessary at second trial where court had before it the transcript from the voir dire held during first trial). *Com. v. Powell*, 72 Mass App 22, 27 888 NE2d 370, 374 (2008) (not error to deny separate evidentiary hearing, but integration of motion to suppress and trial on merits should be avoided because it creates potential to confuse or misapply rules of evidence and burdens of proof, creates misunderstanding of the procedures to be followed, gives appearance that challenged evidence has been accepted on the merits, and denies to both parties rights to pursue interlocutory appeal before jeopardy attaches).

[6] See *Walkins v. Sowders*, 449 US 341, 345-349 (1981); *Com. v. Walker*, 421 Mass 90, 94, 653 NE2d 1080, 1083 (1995). See also *Com. v. Simmons*, 383 Mass 46, 47, 417 NE2d 1193, 1194 (1981) (although not constitutionally required, better practice is to conduct a voir dire to determine whether witness's pretrial identification of motor vehicle was unduly suggestive).

[7] *Com. v. Odware*, 429 Mass 231, 235, 707 NE2d 347, 351 (1999).

[8] *Com. v. Burnett*, 371 Mass 87, 94, 354 NE2d 879, 884 (1976).

jury. The defendant [is] entitled not only to inform the jury of procedures used which might have been somewhat suggestive, but also to establish the existence of fairer procedures which the police chose to ignore."[9]

§ 11.3.3 *Jury Instructions*

A defendant who fairly raises the issue of mistaken identification at trial is ordinarily entitled to jury instructions on the factors relevant to reliability. Even though no eyewitness makes a positive identification of the defendant as the perpetrator, a defendant is entitled, upon request, to jury instructions providing guidance where eyewitnesses have provided a physical description of the perpetrator or his clothing, or have identified a photograph in an array as someone who looks like the perpetrator.[10]

A new proposed version of a model identification instruction was published provisionally by the Supreme Judicial Court in its Appendix

---

[9] *Com. v. Rodriguez*, 378 Mass 296, 308, 391 NE2d 889, 896 (1979) (citations omitted) (judge improperly excluded evidence regarding pretrial identification procedures employed by the police). See also *Com. v. Colon-Cruz*, 408 Mass 533, 542 n.3, 562 NE2d 797, 805 n.3 (1990) ("Defense counsel took ample advantage of his remedy [for the admission of identification evidence]: on cross-examination he thoroughly explored [the witness's] exposure to the press and the consequent reliability of his identification."); *Com. v. Naylor*, 73 Mass App 518, 899 NE2d 862 (2009) (defense lawyer's failure to point out that defendant's appearance on date of incident was dramatically different from that in photo identified by witness amounted to ineffective assistance); *Com. v. Vardinski*, 53 Mass App 307, 758 NE2d 1087 (2001) (reversible error not to allow defendant to challenge witness's level of confidence in his identification by showing that after viewing photograph on computer he had seen printout which included notation of defendant's prior arrest for illegal possession of a firearm); *Com. v. Enos*, 26 Mass App 1006, 530 NE2d 805 (1988) ("When the voice identification is of a person other than the defendant, we may rely on cross-examination and argument to illuminate weaknesses in the identification, whether by reason of suggestion or conditions for observation."); *Com. v. Allen*, 22 Mass App 413, 417-423, 494 NE2d 55, 58-61 (1986) (judge erred in excluding a partial transcript of a telephone conversation between the victim and a police emergency operator that the defense offered to impeach the victim's testimony concerning his initial identification). But see *Com. v. Montez*, 45 Mass App 802, 810, 702 NE2d 40, 46 (1998) (no violation of defendant's rights where court refused to allow defense counsel to present photo array to witness with only eyes and noses exposed).

[10] *Com. v. Franklin*, 465 Mass 895, 912, 992 NE2d 319, 332 (2013); *Com. v. Navarro*, 86 Mass App 780, 21 NE3d 982 (2014) (burden is on defendant to request the instruction).Where there is no positive or partial identification of the defendant, whether to give identification, or failure to identify, instructions is left to the sound discretion of the trial judge. *Com. v. Johnson*, 470 Mass 389, 398, 22 NE3d 155 (2015).

to *Com. v. Gomes*,[11] as modified with respect to cross-racial identifications by *Com. v. Bastaldo*.[12] These opinions were informed by the findings of the Supreme Judicial Court Study Group on Eyewitness Evidence.[13] The Court concluded that a number of scientific principles were "so generally accepted" that trial courts should instruct juries with respect to them. Principles will be considered "so generally accepted" when "there is a near consensus in the relevant scientific community adopting that principle."[14] The *Gomes* opinion identified five new principles that should be added to the model jury instruction:

(1) Human memory does not function like a video recording but is a complex process that consists of three stages: acquisition, retention, and retrieval.
(2) An eyewitness's expressed certainty in an identification, standing alone, may not indicate the accuracy of the identification, especially where the witness did not describe that level of certainty when the witness first made the identification.
(3) High levels of stress can reduce an eyewitness's ability to make an accurate identification.
(4) Information that is unrelated to the initial viewing of the event, which an eyewitness receives before or after making an identification, can influence the witness's later recollection of the memory or of the identification.
(5) A prior viewing of a suspect at an identification procedure may reduce the reliability of a subsequent identification procedure in which the same suspect is shown.[15]

In *Bastaldo*, the Court provided a new instruction on cross-racial identifications. The opinion discussed the difficulty of defining "race." Given that difficulty, the Court concluded it would be inappropriate to ask judges to determine whether a reasonable juror would perceive an

---

[11] *Com. v. Gomes*, 470 Mass 352, 22 NE3d 897 (2015). The opinion invited comments on the provisional instruction before the final model instruction is issued.

[12] *Com. v. Bastaldo*, 472 Mass 16, 32 NE3d 873 (2015) (adopting the following for the model instruction: "If the witness and the person identified appear to be of different races, you should consider that people may have greater difficulty in accurately identifying someone of a different race than someone of their own race.")

[13] The Report and Recommendations of the Study Group are available at: http://perma.cc/WY4M-YNZN.

[14] *Com. v. Gomes*, 470 Mass at 367, 22 NE3d at 909.

[15] *Id.*, 470 Mass at 369-376, 22 NE3 at 911-916.

identification to be cross-racial. As a result, the Court directed that in future cases a cross-racial identification instruction should be given unless all parties agree that there was no cross-racial identification.

The Court found that there was not as yet a consensus in the relevant scientific community that people are less accurate at recognizing the face of someone of a different ethnicity. Thus, it left the decision whether to add ethnicity to the cross-racial instruction to the discretion of the trial judge.[16]

The new jury instructions have no retroactive application. Model instructions were initially set out in *Com. v. Rodriguez*,[17] and have been added to and revised subsequently.[18]

In *Com. v. Pressley*,[19] the Court held that the judge's refusal to instruct the jury on the possibility of a good faith mistake in the identification of defendant by the victim constituted reversible error.[20] A

---

[16] The Court noted that, "Where the persons involved in the identification self-identify as being of the same race but different ethnicity, and look as categorically different as people of different races, a cross-ethnic instruction will generally be appropriate . . ." *Com. v. Bastaldo*, 472 Mass at 29.

[17] *Com. v. Rodriguez*, 378 Mass 296, 302, 310-311, 391 NE2d 889, 892-893, 897-898 (1979).

[18] *Com. v. Hallet*, 427 Mass 552, 558, 694 NE2d 845, 849 (1998) (criticizing the *Rodriguez* language that invited the jury to consider "the length of time that passed between the occurrence of the crime and the next opportunity any identification witness had to see the defendant," on the ground such language "implies inappropriately that the witness saw the defendant at the crime scene."); *Com. v. Santoli*, 424 Mass 837, 680 NE2d 1116 (1997) (revising a portion of the charge which had suggested that jurors take into account the confidence of the witness in her identification in assessing its reliability).

[19] *Com. v. Pressley*, 390 Mass 617, 457 NE2d 1119 (1983).

[20] See *Com. v. Franklin*, 465 Mass 895, 992 NE2d 319 (2013) (counsel was not ineffective for failing to request eyewitness identification instruction where one witness acknowledged she was not sure of her identification and other witness was significantly impeached; instruction would not likely have affected verdict); *Com. v. Rodriguez*, 457 Mass 461, 474, 931 NE2d 20, 34 (2010) (no substantial likelihood of miscarriage of justice based on counsel's failure to request "honest but mistaken" instruction and judge's failure to give it); *Com. v. Pires*, 453 Mass 66, 71 899 NE2d 787, 792 (2009) (trial judge's instruction that "you may consider whether or not the witness might simply be mistaken" was not error, but in future the better course is to use *Pressley* language that a witness might be "honest but mistaken" in his identification of defendant); *Com. v. Molina*, 81 Mass App 855, 868, 969 NE2d 738, 747 (2012), *further app rev granted on other issue*, 463 Mass 1112, 979 NE2d 224 (not an error to fail to give instruction on honest but mistaken identification where defendant did not request it); *Com. v. Williams*, 58 Mass App 139, 788 NE2d 580 (2003) (failure to give instruction was reversible error where evidence against defendant was not overwhelming and identity was sole contested issue); *Com. v. Williams*, 54 Mass App 236, 240, 764 NE2d

judge is not required, however, to give all the suggested instructions set out in *Rodriguez*; they may be modified as the evidence at trial requires.[21]

889, 893 (2002) (in deciding whether trial judge should have given requested identification instructions, Appeals Court takes evidence in light most favorable to the defendant; reversible error not to give *Pressley* instruction where prosecution's evidence lay almost exclusively in eyewitness identification of defendant and defendant's testimony to contrary was not implausible); *Com. v. Richards*, 53 Mass App 333, 758 NE3d 1095 (2001) (erroneous refusal to give *Pressley* instruction was not harmless error); *Com. v. Spencer*, 45 Mass App 33, 39, 695 NE2d 677, 681 (1998) ("constancy in the testimony of identification witnesses by itself is insufficient reason to deny a requested *Pressley* charge where, in the circumstances of the case, the accuracy of the identification might reasonably be questioned by the jury and independent evidence linking the defendant to the alleged crime is not overwhelming"). Cf. *Com. v. Sanders*, 451 Mass 290, 309, 885 NE2d 105, 121 (2008) (failure to request "honest but mistaken" instruction was not ineffective assistance as "manifestly unreasonable" decision where defendant was known to identification witnesses and defense counsel argued they lied); *Com. v. Olavarria*, 71 Mass App 612, 885 NE2d 139 (2008) (failure to seek "honest but mistaken" instruction did not create substantial risk of miscarriage of justice where defense counsel focused on defense of misidentification throughout the trial); *Com. v. Montez*, 45 Mass App 802, 811, 702 NE2d 40, 47 (1998) (not ineffective assistance of counsel not to request *Pressley* instruction where jury was apprised by other means of possibility of good faith mistake in identification); *Com. v. Carter*, 423 Mass 506, 515, 669 NE2d 203, 209 (1996) (not ineffective assistance of counsel for defense lawyer to request a *Rodriguez/Pressley* jury instruction, rather than making different tactical choices for handling eyewitness testimony).

[21] *Com v. Gomes, supra*, 470 Mass at 377, 22 NE3d at 917. See also *Com. v. Jackson*, 419 Mass 716, 732-733, 647 NE2d 401, 410-411 (1995) (although instructions varied from recommended model, they made clear to jury that identification was subject to error and suggestion). Compare *Com. v. Hallet*, 427 Mass 552, 694 NE2d 845 (1998) (reversible error not to charge on presenting defendant to witness for identification, one-on-one confrontation, and failure to make identification, when these issues were relevant to case), and *Com. v. Monteiro*, 51 Mass App 552, 747 NE2d 721 (2001) (in case where undercover officer alleging sale of narcotics was the only eyewitness, error not to charge jury with respect to opportunity to observe, subsequent identification by the witness, and that picking out person from a group is generally more reliable than a show-up), and *Com. v. Caramanica*, 49 Mass App 376, 729 NE2d 656 (2000) (error for court to charge that "very few people come into court with an intention to mislead," and "accuracy means more than honesty"), with *Com. v. Walker*, supra, 421 Mass at 99-103, 653 NE2d at 1085-1087 (omission of portion of charge addressing suggestive one-on-one confrontation and error in instruction regarding length of time between crime and identification did not create substantial risk of miscarriage of justice), and *Com. v. Elam*, 412 Mass 583, 587, 591 NE2d 186, 189 (1992) (no error in refusal to charge jury on possibility of good faith mistake in identification), and *Com. v. McMaster*, 21 Mass App 722, 726-728, 490 NE2d 464, 469-470 (1986) (omission of certain portions of *Rodriguez* charge did not create substantial risk of miscarriage of justice). See also *Com. v. Walker*, 33 Mass App 915, 916-917, 597 NE2d 72, 72-73 (1992) (error for judge to instruct jury on identification, including factors relating to misidentification, where defense is that crime never occurred; but no prejudice).

§ 11.3.4 Harmless Error

When identification evidence has been wrongly admitted into evidence, either in violation of the defendant's right to counsel or in violation of due process, reversal is not mandatory; the error may be harmless beyond a reasonable doubt.[22] Whether an error is harmless depends on a variety of factors, including whether the erroneously admitted evidence was merely cumulative of other evidence properly before the jury; the "essential question is whether the error had or might have had an effect on the jury and whether the error contributed to or might have contributed to the verdict."[23] For more on the standards for harmless error, see *Chapman v. California*.[24]

§ 11.4 Expert Testimony

Expert testimony concerning eyewitness identification is not admissible as of right, but is admissible in the proper exercise of discretion by the trial judge. See § 7.6.4.e.

---

[22] See *Moore v. Illinois*, 434 US 220, 232, 98 S Ct 458, 54 L Ed 2d 424 (1977); *United States v. Wade*, 388 US 218, 242 (1967); *Gilbert v. California*, 388 US 263, 274 (1967); *Com. v. Thornley*, 406 Mass 96, 101, 546 NE2d 350, 353-354 (1989) (*Thornley II*); *Com. v. Morgan*, 30 Mass App 685, 691-693, 573 NE2d 989, 993 (1991).

[23] *Com. v. Thornley II*, supra, 406 Mass at 101-102, 546 NE2d at 354.

[24] *Chapman v. California*, 386 US 18 (1967).

CHAPTER

12

CONFESSIONS and INCRIMINATING STATEMENTS

In General

Several doctrines (sometimes overlapping) control the admissibility of confessions and incriminating statements: (1) the voluntariness standard under the Due Process Clause; (2) the *Miranda* doctrine under the Fifth Amendment; (3) the right to counsel approach under the Sixth Amendment; (4) the "fruit of the poisonous tree" doctrine under the Fourth Amendment; and (5) miscellaneous nonconstitutional exclusionary rules. We begin with a discussion of the Commonwealth's "humane practice" regarding confessions.

§ 12.1 The "Humane Practice" Doctrine

Pursuant to the practice followed in the Commonwealth for many years (and cited with approval by the United States Supreme Court in *Jackson v. Denno*[1]), a confession may be admitted in evidence only after

§ 12.1 [1] 378 US 368, 378-385 (1964).

a preliminary hearing in the absence of the jury and a judicial determination of its voluntariness.[2] If the judge concludes that the confession was involuntary, it is excluded. If the judge determines that the confession was voluntary, it will be admitted, but the jury instructed that they are not to consider it unless they are satisfied that it was the voluntary act of the defendant.[3] Thus, the defendant is given two opportunities to challenge a confession: first before the judge who may decide to exclude it; and then before the jury who may decide to disregard it.[4]

The defendant bears the burden of going forward at the suppression hearing with evidence that his statement was involuntary. It is then the Commonwealth's burden to prove voluntariness beyond a reasonable doubt.[5] If the judge concludes that the defendant's statement was voluntary beyond a reasonable doubt (and thus admits it), that conclusion must appear affirmatively with "unmistakable clarity" from the record.[6] If the voluntariness of the statement becomes a live issue at trial, the judge must instruct the jury to disregard it unless the

---

[2] See *Com. v. Crawford*, 429 Mass 60, 65, 706 NE2d 289, 293 (1999); *Com. v. Tavares*, 385 Mass 140, 149-150, 430 NE2d 1198, 1204-1205 (1982). See also Proposed Mass R Evid 104(c) ("Hearings on the admissibility of confessions shall in all cases be conducted out of the hearing of the jury.").

[3] *Com. v. Tavares*, supra, 385 Mass at 149-150, 430 NE2d at 1205. See also Proposed Mass R Evid 104(f) ("In a criminal case tried to a jury, if the court admits evidence of a confession . . . it shall submit for determination by the jury the respective questions of the voluntariness of the confession. . . .") The judge should not inform the jury of his determination of voluntariness, as this would "diminish the benefit of independent jury determination required by our long-established humane rule." *Com. v. Tavares*, supra, 385 Mass at 152 n.18, 430 NE2d at 1206 n.18. See also *Com. v. Chung*, 378 Mass 451, 460 n.12, 392 NE2d 1015. 1021 n.12 (1979).

[4] While the hearing and determination before the judge is constitutionally mandated, see *Jackson v. Denno*, supra, the "second prong" of the humane practice, jury reconsideration, is not. See *Lego v. Twomey*, 404 US 477, 489-490 (1972); *Com. v. Cole*, 380 Mass 30, 40, 402 NE2d 55, 62 (1980) (& citations). See also *Com. v. Griffin*, 345 Mass 283, 286, 186 NE2d 909, 910-911 (1963) (in a jury-waived trial, such duplication is unnecessary); *Com. v. Parker*, 412 Mass 353, 589 NE2d 306 (1992) (*Parker II*) (defendant's motion to suppress confession, which was denied at first trial, could be denied on retrial without conducting hearing where defendant raised no new issues and applicable law had not changed).

For an extensive discussion of the treatment of confessions and admissions under the "humane practice," see *Com. v. Bright*, 463 Mass 421, 428-434, 974 NE2d 1092, 1101-1106 (2012); *Com. v. Paszko*, 391 Mass 164, 179-183, 461 NE2d 222, 232-234 (1984) and *Com. v. Tavares*, supra, 385 Mass at 149-153, 430 NE2d at 1204-1206.

[5] *Com. v. Hilton*, 450 Mass 173, 177, 877 NE2d 545, 550 (2007); *Com. v. O'Brian*, 445 Mass 720, 724, 840 NE2d 500, 504 (2006).

[6] See *Com. v. Fernette*, 398 Mass 658, 662-663, 500 NE2d 1290, 1293 (1986). But see *Com. v. Mello*, 420 Mass 375, 381-383, 649 NE2d 1106, 1112-1113 (1995) (failure of judge to make specific findings of fact to support denial of defendant's motion to

Commonwealth has met its burden of proving beyond a reasonable doubt that the statement was voluntary. The instruction must inform the jury that they are to disregard the statement if they find it involuntary—permissive language indicating that they "may" disregard it is inadequate.[7] The Commonwealth is thus required to prove the voluntariness of a confession beyond a reasonable doubt to both the judge and the jury.[8]

The judge is required to conduct a preliminary hearing *sua sponte* and make a determination of voluntariness whenever there is credible evidence placing the voluntariness of the confession in issue.[9] A mere assertion by counsel does not amount to the "credible evidence" required to trigger a voir dire.[10] Where credible psychiatric evidence of mental impairment or insanity is presented, the judge has an obligation to hold a voir dire to determine voluntariness and to instruct the

suppress confession did not warrant new trial; judge's denial implied resolution of factual and credibility issues in favor of Commonwealth); *Com. v. Brady*, 380 Mass 44, 52, 410 NE2d 695, 700 (1980) ("Although we have stated that it is both prudent and desirable for a judge to make a record of facts found in a voir dire hearing on the admissibility of evidence, we have not held that 'unmistakable clarity' mandates an absolute requirement that such a record be made.").

[7] *Com. v. Sunahara*, 455 Mass 832, 836, 920 NE2d 831, 835 (2010). Regarding the instructions to be given the jury on its determination of voluntariness, see *Com. v. Anderson*, 445 Mass 195, 206-208, 834 NE2d 1159, 1168-1169 (2005) (while customary and preferable, judge is not required to refer specifically to factors like intoxication); *Com. v. Jordan*, 439 Mass 47, 56-57, 785 NE2d 368, 376-377 (2003) (it is advisable for the judge to recite some of the factors for the jury to consider).

[8] *Com. v. Tavares*, supra, 385 Mass at 151-152, 430 NE2d at 1206 (& citations). The Supreme Judicial Court has refused to impose a unanimity requirement on the jury's determination of voluntariness. See *Com. v. Watkins*, 425 Mass 830, 836, 683 NE2d 653, 657 (1997).

[9] See *Com. v. Harris*, 371 Mass 462, 467-472, 358 NE2d 982, 989 (1976) (evidence that defendant confessed only after having been beaten by police); *Com. v. Van Melkebeke*, 48 Mass App 364, 720 NE2d 834 (1999) (evidence that defendant was "extremely intoxicated" at time of statement); *Com. v. Collins*, 11 Mass App 126, 133-134, 414 NE2d 1008, 1012 (1981) (defendant forced to lie naked with hands handcuffed during time he gave statements). Compare *Com. v. Stroyny*, 435 Mass 635, 646-647, 760 NE2d 1202, 1211 (2002) (evidence that defendant was greatly distressed at hospital at time of incriminating statements was insufficient to mandate hearing); *Com. v. Benoit*, 410 Mass 506, 512-513, 574 NE2d 347, 351-352 (1991) (no evidence of involuntariness presented at suppression hearing); *Com. v. Pavao*, 46 Mass App 271, 274-275, 705 NE2d 307, 310-311 (1999) (lack of affirmative credible evidence of involuntariness).

[10] See *Com. v. Watkins*, 33 Mass App 7, 15 n.8, 595 NE2d 786, 791 n.8 (1992).

jury to consider the voluntariness of the confession even in the absence of a request from defendant.[11] Defendant may of course decide for strategic reasons not to challenge the voluntariness of his statement.[12]

The judge has no duty to ask the jury to pass on voluntariness unless it is made a live issue at trial.[13] Where voluntariness is an issue, the judge must submit all relevant evidence to the jury.[14] A defendant is entitled to present expert testimony (at both the suppression hearing and trial) on the issue of voluntariness in appropriate cases.[15]

---

[11] *Com. v. Sheriff*, 425 Mass 186, 192-196, 680 NE2d 75, 79-81 (1997); *Com. v. Callahan*, 401 Mass 627, 631 n.5, 519 NE2d 245, 248 n.5 (1988) (judge properly submitted to jury question of effect of defendant's mental state as described in psychiatric testimony); *Com. v. Louraine*, 390 Mass 28, 39, 453 NE2d 437, 445 (1983) (in light of evidence of insanity, court must determine whether confession was product of rational intellect, even where the confession was spontaneously made while defendant was not in custody). Compare *Com. v. Benoit*, 410 Mass 506, 513-516, 574 NE2d 347, 352-353 (1991) (insufficient evidence of psychosis, intoxication, or injury to raise issue of voluntariness); *Com. v. Brady*, 380 Mass 44, 49, 410 NE2d 695, 699-700 (1980) (mere evidence of drinking alcohol or using drugs does not trigger judge's obligation to inquire into voluntariness of confession absent defendant's objection). The fact that defendant raises an insanity defense does not automatically trigger the voluntariness procedure. *Com. v. Brown*, 449 Mass 747, 766-767, 872 NE2d 711, 726-727 (2007), *habeas denied*, *Brown v. O'Brien*, 666 F3d 818 (1st Cir 2012).

[12] See, e.g., *Com. v. Brown*, 449 Mass 747, 767, 872 NE2d 711, 727 (2007) *habeas denied, Brown v. O'Brien,* 666 F3d 818 (1st Cir 2012) (defense counsel's strategy was to question whether the statements were made); *Com. v. Zagrodny*, 443 Mass 93, 97, 819 NE2d 565, 570-571 (2004) (defense counsel made strategic choice not to challenge voluntariness); *Com. v. Laurore*, 437 Mass 65, 81, 769 NE2d 725, 736 (2002) (trial counsel's failure to request voir dire was tactical decision); *Com. v. Serino*, 436 Mass 408, 411-414, 765 NE2d 237, 241-243 (2002) (defendant's trial strategy was not to contest admission of statements).

[13] *Com. v. Caillot*, 454 Mass 245, 263-264, 909 NE2d 1, 17-18 (2009) (trial counsel was not ineffective in failing to request instruction, because the issue of voluntariness was not a live issue when statements were admitted); *Com. v. Greco*, 76 Mass App 296, 302 921 NE2d 1001, 1006-1007 (2010) (merely raising the issue in closing argument is insufficient, as that is not evidence); *Com. v. LaCava*, 438 Mass 708, 719-720, 783 NE2d 812, 821-822 (2003) (trial counsel's waiver of instruction was part of trial strategy); *Com. v. Nichypor*, 419 Mass 209, 218-219, 643 NE2d 452, 458 (1994); *Com. v. Ferreira*, 417 Mass 592, 600, 632 NE2d 392 (1994); *Com. v. Burke*, supra, 414 Mass at 259-260; *Com. v. Benoit*, supra, 410 Mass at 511-513, 574 NE2d at 351-352 (& citations) (defendant's theory at trial was that he did not make the incriminating statement, not that it was involuntary). Compare *Com. v. Sunahara*, 455 Mass 832, 835-836, 920 NE2d 831, 834-835 (2010) (defendant raised the issue of voluntariness before and during trial, including extensive questioning of detective who took his statement).

[14] See *Com. v. Adams*, 416 Mass 55, 60-61, 617 NE2d 594, 597-598 (1993) (error to exclude testimony of defendant's mother and forensic psychiatrist tending to show that defendant was psychologically coerced into confessing).

[15] See *Com. v. Crawford*, 429 Mass 60, 706 NE2d 289 (1999) (expert testimony on battered woman syndrome and post-traumatic stress disorder). Where the defendant

All incriminating statements made by the accused, even those falling short of a confession, are within the protection of the humane practice.[16] "An incriminating response includes any response, inculpatory or exculpatory, which the prosecution might seek to use against the suspect at trial."[17] The doctrine does not apply to private messages sent by defendant to another individual.[18]

§ 12.2 Involuntariness and Due Process: The Totality of the Circumstances Analysis

Since 1936 the Due Process Clause of the Fourteenth Amendment to the United States Constitution has required exclusion of coerced confessions.[1] This is so because, as Justice Frankfurter later explained, "the methods used to extract them offend an underlying principle in the enforcement of our criminal law: that ours is an accusatorial and not an inquisitorial system—a system in which the State must establish guilt by evidence independently and freely secured and may not by coercion prove its charge against an accused out of his own mouth."[2]

The question of voluntariness turns on whether the suspect's free will had been overborne by law enforcement officials, and this requires examination of the circumstances of the interrogation to determine "whether the processes were so unfair or unreasonable as to render a subsequent confession involuntary."[3] A conviction founded in whole or in part on statements that are the product of physical or psychological coercion deprives the defendant of his right to due process of law.[4] The coercion may take many forms, including threats, inducements or

---

places at issue his mental ability to make a voluntary statement, he may be compelled to submit to a psychiatric evaluation by the Commonwealth's expert, who may testify to his conclusions at trial. See *Com. v. Ostrander*, 441 Mass 344, 351-355, 805 NE2d 497, 504-506 (2004).

[16] *Com. v. Tavares*, supra, 385 Mass at 150, 430 NE2d at 1204-1205 (citing Text).

[17] *Com. v. Montgomery*, 52 Mass App 831, 836, 755 NE2d 1288, 1292 (2001).

[18] *Com. v. Oppenheim*, 86 Mass App 359, 368-369, 16 NE3d 502, 510-511 (2014) (incriminating Internet messages).

§ 12.2 [1] *Brown v. Mississippi*, 297 US 278 (1936). Nor may a coerced confession be used to impeach the defendant. See *Com. v. Dwyer*, 448 Mass 122, 132, 859 NE2d 400, 410 (2006) (co-defendant's coerced admission which contextually incriminated defendant should not have been used to impeach defendant at severed trial).

[2] *Rogers v. Richmond*, 365 US 534, 540 (1961).

[3] *Michigan v. Tucker*, 417 US 433, 441 (1974). See also *Com. v. Molina*, 467 Mass 65, 75-76, 3 NE3d 583, 593 (2014); *Com. v. Hilton*, 450 Mass 173, 177, 877 NE2d 545, 550 (2007).

[4] *Com. v. Mahnke*, 368 Mass 662, 679, 335 NE2d 660, 671 (1975).

promises of immunity or favor. Frequently the coercion involves prolonged questioning under adverse circumstances.[5]

There is no "acid test" for voluntariness.[6] The question is determined on a case-by-case basis in light of the "totality of the circumstances."[7] The relevant factors in assessing voluntariness include the time and conditions under which the questioning took place, the content and form of the questions put to the suspect, and the physical and mental condition of the suspect during the period of interrogation.[8] Regarding the suspect, courts look to the defendant's age, education, intelligence, emotional stability, and experience with the criminal justice system.[9] Regarding the interrogation, courts look to such matters as whether the police initiated discussion of a deal or leniency and whether *Miranda* warnings were given.[10]

The focus is on the manner and duration of the interrogation as well as the particular vulnerabilities of the defendant at the time.[11] The process weighs the circumstances of pressure against the suspect's power of resistance.[12] The task is to ascertain whether the defendant's will was overcome by the particular pressures exerted upon him.[13] Defendant's incriminating statements were ordered suppressed (and his conviction reversed), for example, where the police interrogation was "rife" with false threats that unless he cooperated he would lose all

---

[5] See, e.g., *Com. v. Makarewicz*, 333 Mass 575, 585-586, 132 NE2d 294, 299-300 (1956) (& citations). But cf. *Com. v. LeBeau*, 451 Mass 244, 255-256, 884 NE2d 956, 966-967 (2008), *habeas denied*, *LeBeau v. Roden*, 806 F Supp 2d 384 (D Mass 2011) (statement voluntary even though obtained during confinement in state police barracks from midnight until 7:15 am without sleep).

[6] *Com. v. Mahnke*, supra, 368 Mass at 680, 335 NE2d at 671.

[7] See generally *Procunier v. Atchley*, 400 US 446, 453 (1971); *Com. v. Monroe*, 472 Mass 461, 35 NE3d 677 (2015); *Com. v. Molina*, supra, 467 Mass at 75-77, 3 NE3d at 593-594.

[8] *Com. v. Makarewicz*, supra, 333 Mass at 587, 132 NE2d at 301; *Com. v. Hilton*, 450 Mass 173, 177, 877 NE2d 545, 550 (2007). The fact that a defendant was suffering from a serious and painful injury such as a bullet or knife wound or third-degree burns does not necessarily preclude a finding that the statement was voluntary. See *Com. v. Bell*, 473 Mass 131, 141-142, 39 NE3d 1190, 1199 (2015) (& cases cited).

[9] Interrogators are not required to specifically ask the suspect about these matters. *Com. v. Anderson*, 445 Mass 195, 203, 834 NE2d 1159, 1166-1167 (2005).

[10] *Com. v. Mandile*, 397 Mass 410, 413, 492 NE2d 74, 76 (1986); *Com. v. Azar*, 32 Mass App 290, 297-298, 588 NE2d 1352, 1357-1358 (1992).

[11] *Procunier v. Atchley*, supra, 400 US at 453-454.

[12] *Fikes v. Alabama*, 352 US 191, 197-198 (1957).

[13] *Com. v. Harris*, 364 Mass 236, 242, 358 NE2d 982, 986 (1973); *Com. v. Selby*, 420 Mass 656, 662-663, 651 NE2d 843, 848 (1995).

contact with his infant daughter, who would be taken away and raised by strangers, and where the defendant exhibited clear signs of a disturbed emotional state.[14]

As with any balancing test, no one factor is generally determinative. Thus, while prolonged interrogation alone might constitute sufficient coercion to render a confession involuntary, findings to the contrary have been upheld on appeal.[15]

The United States Supreme Court has held that "coercive police activity is a necessary predicate to the finding that a confession is not 'voluntary' within the meaning of the Due Process Clause of the Fourteenth Amendment."[16] No Massachusetts case has yet adopted this explicit requirement for a finding of involuntariness.

In determining voluntariness, the Supreme Judicial Court has become "increasingly sensitive to consideration of the defendant's mental condition."[17] Statements attributable to a debilitated condition such as insanity, drug abuse or withdrawal symptoms, intoxication, or head injury have been suppressed.[18] A statement is inadmissible if it would not have been obtained but for the effects of the confessor's mental disease or defect.[19]

---

[14] *Com. v. Monroe*, 472 Mass 461, 35 NE3d 677 (2015) (extensive discussion).

[15] See, e.g., *Com. v. Makarewicz*, supra, 333 Mass at 584-589, 132 NE2d at 299-302 (interrogation of 15-year-old boy over course of nine hours); *Com. v. Banuchi*, 335 Mass 649, 656-657, 141 NE2d 835, 839-840 (1957) (interrogation over course of two and one-half days); *Com. v. Tolan*, 453 Mass 634, 643, 904 NE2d 397, 407 (2009) (11 hours in the same room, but defendant was permitted several breaks).

[16] *Colorado v. Connelly*, 479 US 157, 164 (1986).

[17] *Com. v. Chung*, 378 Mass 451, 456, 392 NE2d 1015 (1979) (insanity of defendant). See also *Com. v. Cole*, 380 Mass 30, 40-41, 402 NE2d 55, 62 (1980) (evidence of psychosis); *Com. v. Banuchi*, supra, 335 Mass at 654-656, 141 NE2d at 839 (evidence of effect upon defendant of withdrawal from alcohol at time of confession). Suicidal ideation or threats do not necessarily negate the voluntariness of a confession. See *Com. v. Lopes*, 455 Mass 147, 168, 914 NE2d 78, 95 (2009), *habeas denied*, 2013 WL 819330 (D Mass 2012).

[18] See *Com. v. Allen*, 395 Mass 448, 455, 480 NE2d 630, 635-636 (1985) (& citations).

[19] See *Com. v. Libran*, 405 Mass 634, 639, 543 NE2d 5, 8-9 (1989); *Com. v. Cifizzari*, 19 Mass App 981, 474 NE2d 1174, 1175-1176 (1985). But compare *Com. v. Boyarsky*, 452 Mass 700, 714-715, 897 NE2d 574, 585 (2008) (no *per se* rule against admitting confession of defendant diagnosed with panic disorder; trooper contradicted his assertion that he was having a panic attack when he confessed); *Com. v. Simpson*, 434 Mass 570, 579, 750 NE2d 977, 989 (2001) (evidence of defendant's head injury, intoxication, and agitated conduct did not require finding of involuntariness); *Com. v. Clark*, 432 Mass 1, 11-13, 730 NE2d 872, 883-884 (2000) (statement voluntary even though defendant had gunshot wound to head); *Com. v. Perrot*, 407 Mass 539, 543, 554 NE2d 1205, 1208 (1990) (fact that defendant was depressed and on suicide watch at

Several decisions have discounted expert psychological evidence offered on the issue of involuntariness.[20]

Although intoxication alone is insufficient to render a statement involuntary, "special care" must be taken to review the issue of voluntariness where the defendant claims to have been under the influence of drugs or alcohol.[21] A defendant's statement was found involuntary where he was under the influence of alcohol, nervous and upset, and questioned by three officers at a late hour;[22] but many decisions conclude otherwise.[23] The fact that defendant was in a disturbed

---

time of confession does not mandate conclusion that it was involuntary); *Com. v. Libran*, supra, 405 Mass at 638-639, 543 NE2d at 8 (fact that defendant was retarded and suffering from schizophrenic reaction and manic-depressive condition did not render statements involuntary); *Com. v. Davis*, 403 Mass 575, 578-581, 531 NE2d 577, 579-581 (1988) (confession made in third person by defendant with psychiatric history was voluntary where the interrogation bore no evidence that defendant's will had been broken); *Com. v. Allen*, supra, 395 Mass at 457-458, 480 NE2d at 636 (defendant's statements to nurse were voluntary even though he was recovering from self-inflicted gunshot wound to head); *Com. v. Bandy*, 38 Mass App 329, 331, 648 NE2d 440, 442 (1995) (claim of hallucination resulting from physical injury); *Com. v. Cifizzari*, supra, 19 Mass App at 982, 474 NE2d at 1177 (confession was voluntary despite uncontested evidence that defendant suffered from chronic paranoid schizophrenia).

[20] See, e.g., *Com. v. Tolan*, 453 Mass 634, 646-648, 904 NE2d 397, 409-410 (2009) (it was within judge's discretion to preclude testimony on relationship between certain interrogation techniques and false confessions); *Com. v. Beland*, 436 Mass 273, 279-280, 764 NE2d 324, 331 (2002); *Com. v. Nerette*, 432 Mass 534, 735 NE2d 1242 (2000) (testimony of defendant's psychologist that confession was involuntary not admissible where psychologist based opinion almost entirely on information furnished by defendant, who did not testify, conducted no testing, and did not listen to audiotape of defendant's statement); *Com. v. Perry*, 432 Mass 214, 233-234, 733 NE2d 83, 100-101 (2000) (judge credited Commonwealth's expert on inability of psychological test administered by defense expert to accurately reflect defendant's mental state at time he made statement); *Com. v. Jackson*, 432 Mass 82, 87, 731 NE2d 1066, 1071 (2000) (judge found neuropsychologist's testimony that defendant was mentally incapable of freely waiving rights unpersuasive); *Com. v. Soares*, 51 Mass App 273, 280-282, 745 NE2d 362, 368-369 (2001) (judge properly discounted testimony of forensic psychologist who administered Gudjonsson Suggestibility Scale to defendant and concluded he was highly suggestible).

[21] See *Com. v. Howard*, 469 Mass 721, 727-728, 16 NE3d 1054, 1062 (2014); *Com. v. Mello*, 420 Mass 375, 383, 649 NE2d 1106, 1113 (1995).

[22] *Com. v. Scherben*, 28 Mass App 952, 550 NE2d 899 (1990).

[23] *Com. v. Newson*, 471 Mass 222, 27 NE3d 1282, 1287-1290 (2015) (although it was clear to interviewing detective that defendant had been drinking and vomited as a result, statement was voluntary); *Com. v. Brown*, 462 Mass 620, 626-627, 970 NE2d 306, 312-313 (2012) (defendant's statements were voluntary even though he had just used marijuana and pain medication and his speech was sluggish); *Com. v. Ward*, 426 Mass 290, 294-295, 688 NE2d 227, 231 (1997) ("defendant was a tolerant alcoholic who was often intoxicated but nevertheless able to make apparently rational decisions"); *Com. v. Smith*, 426 Mass 76, 81-82, 686 NE2d 983, 988 (1997); *Com. v. Koney*,

emotional state, or even suicidal, does not automatically make the statements involuntary.[24]

Similarly, the fact that a confession was obtained without a warning to the accused of his constitutional rights[25] is a factor to be weighed in determining voluntariness, but does not automatically bar its admission under Massachusetts law.[26] Where the statement is made in a noncustodial setting, and thus warnings are not required, it is within the judge's discretion to exclude testimony concerning failure to give warnings.[27] Evidence bearing on whether *Miranda* warnings were properly given and waived is relevant to the voluntariness determination and may be considered by the jury in that regard, but the judge need not explicitly instruct the jury as such.[28]

The Supreme Judicial Court has declined to impose a requirement that before a statement may be considered voluntary a suspect must be advised of his status as such or that he is charged with a particular crime.[29] The courts have also declined to impose a "minimal warnings" requirement on interviews regarding possible child abuse

---

421 Mass 295, 304-305, 657 NE2d 210, 215-216 (1995) (rational denials made by motor vehicle homicide defendant demonstrated voluntariness of statements despite his intoxication and emotional state); *Com. v. Mello*, supra, 420 Mass at 383, 649 NE2d at 1113 (despite evidence that defendant ingested beer and inhaled heroin night before arrest, suppression not required where defendant spoke coherently, appeared sober, explained preparation and crime in detail, did not complain of illness, signed waiver form, stated he understood his rights, and agreed to talk to police); *Com. v. Simmons*, 417 Mass 60, 65-66, 627 NE2d 917, 921 (1994) (although defendant was intoxicated, statement was voluntary); *Com. v. Liptak*, 80 Mass App 76, 80-81, NE2d 731, 737 (2011) (defendant's statement was voluntary notwithstanding his intoxication and concussion); *Com. v. Ringuette*, 60 Mass App 351, 801 NE2d 813 (2004), *aff'd on other grounds*, 443 Mass 1003, 819 NE2d 941 (2004) (confession voluntary although made while defendant was in cocaine withdrawal).

[24] See *Com. v. Harris*, 468 Mass 429, 436, 11 NE3d 95, 102 (2014).

[25] See § 12.6.1, infra.

[26] *See Com. v. Vao Sok*, 435 Mass 743, 755, 761 NE2d 923, 933 (2002); *Com. v. Tavares*, 385 Mass 140, 153 n.19, 430 NE2d 1198, 1206 n.19 (1982); *Com. v. Chung*, 378 Mass 451, 458-459 n.9, 392 NE2d 1015, 1020 n.9; (1979); *Com. v. Byrd*, 52 Mass App 642, 645-649, 755 NE2d 785, 788-790 (2001) (statement voluntary even though *Miranda* warnings, while not required, were not given, and defendant was intoxicated).

[27] *Com. v. Nadworny*, 396 Mass 342, 369-370, 486 NE2d 675, 691-692 (1985). See also *Com. v. Werner*, 81 Mass App 689, 703, 967 NE2d 159, 170 (2012) (instructing jury during cross-examination of state trooper that *Miranda* warnings were not required during questioning of defendant in coffee shop since she was not in custody was not abuse of discretion).

[28] *Com. v. The Ngoc Tran*, 471 Mass 179, 27 NE3d 1261, 1267 (2015).

[29] *Com. v. Wills*, 398 Mass 768, 776-777, 500 NE2d 1341, 1346-1347 (1986).

conducted by Department of Social Services (DSS) investigators.[30] Evidence that warnings were given may be admitted on the issue of voluntariness.[31]

The failure to inform a suspect of an attorney's attempts to render assistance goes solely to the legal question of whether a *Miranda* waiver is valid (see § 12.6.4, below) and does *not* affect the voluntariness of the statement.[32] While Massachusetts does not require that a suspect be informed of his right to terminate questioning (a so-called fifth *Miranda* warning), if the officer does give the warning but incorrectly links it to the sole purpose of consulting with an attorney, that may affect the voluntariness of the confession.[33]

The police may not use threats or inducements to secure a confession, but not every promise or inducement renders a statement involuntary.[34] As always, voluntariness is determined on the totality of the circumstances. An interrogator may suggest that it would be better for a suspect to tell the truth,[35] may indicate that the suspect's cooperation will be brought to the attention of the prosecutor or judge, and may state that cooperation has been considered favorably by the courts in the past.[36] What is prohibited is an assurance, express or implied, that it will aid the defense or result in a lesser sentence.[37] Minimizing

---

[30] *Com. v. Morais*, 431 Mass 380, 382-383, 727 NE2d 831, 833 (2000). But see *Com. v. Carp*, 47 Mass App 229, 234-235, 712 NE2d 622, 626 (1999) (discussing 110 CMR § 4.27(5), requiring investigator to deliver statement of rights to interviewee).

[31] See *Com. v. Thad T.*, 59 Mass App 497, 503, 796 NE2d 869, 875 (2003). The fact that the defendant invokes his right to counsel immediately after making an inculpatory statement does not render it involuntary. *Com. v. Spray*, 467 Mass 456, 468, 5 NE3d 891, 902 (2014).

[32] See *Com. v. Vao Sok*, 435 Mass 743, 755-756, 761 NE2d 923, 934 (2002).

[33] See § 12.6.1, infra.

[34] *Com. v. Berg*, 37 Mass App 200, 203-204, 638 NE2d 1367, 1370 (1994) (confession not rendered inadmissible because police truthfully explained to defendant that his mother would be charged unless ownership of drugs was established). See also *Com. v. Doe*, 37 Mass App 30, 32-33, 636 NE2d 308, 309-310 (1994) (no showing that officers misled informant into making incriminatory statement).

[35] See, e.g., *Com. v. Cunningham*, 405 Mass 646, 657-658, 543 NE2d 12, 19 (1989) (neither advice of detective and priest that it would be better if defendant told truth, nor detective's comment that defendant had nothing to worry about if he told truth, invalidated waiver).

[36] See, e.g., *Com. v. Quint, Q.*, 84 Mass App 507, 520, 998 NE2d 363, 373 (2013).

[37] *Com. v. Johnson*, 463 Mass 95, 105-106, 972 NE2d 460, 469 (2012) (officer did not improperly imply that confessing would benefit defendant, but merely told him that this was the time to get out in front of the situation); *Com. v. Tolan*, 453 Mass 634, 642-643, 904 NE2d 397, 406 (2009); *Com. v. Leahy*, 445 Mass 481, 486, 838 NE2d 1220, 1226 (2005); *Com. v. O'Brian*, supra, 445 Mass at 725, 840 NE2d at 504; *Com. v.*

the crime by calling it "understandable" or "justifiable" does not in itself render a confession involuntary, but must be considered along with other factors.[38]

A promise of psychiatric help to a suspect is an interviewing technique which may result in a coerced confession, especially if the help is offered as a quid pro quo for the statement. The promise alone, however, will not invalidate a confession. The issue is whether the promise was so manipulative as to overcome the free will of a person with the defendant's characteristics.[39]

Regarding the use of false information or trickery to elicit a statement, the Supreme Judicial Court has cautioned:

> Even though the use of a ruse by the police is insufficient, by itself, to render a confession involuntary, a false statement concerning the strength of the Commonwealth's case, coupled with an implied promise that the defendant will benefit if he makes a confession, may undermine the defendant's ability to make a free choice. The specter of coercion arises in these circumstances from the possibility that an innocent defendant, confronted with apparently irrefutable (but false) evidence of his guilt, might rationally conclude that he was about to be convicted wrongfully and give a false confession in an effort to salvage the situation.[40]

Jordan, 439 Mass 47, 52-53, 785 NE2d 368, 373-374 (2003); *Com. v. Brandwein*, 435 Mass 623, 633-634, 760 NE2d 724, 732 (2002); *Com. v. Souza*, 418 Mass 478, 481-482, 702 NE2d 1167, 1170 (1998).

[38] Compare *Com. v. DiGiambattista*, 442 Mass 423, 437-439, 813 NE2d 516, 526-528 (2004) (trickery combined with multifaceted and repeated minimization invalidated confession) and *Com. v. Baye*, 462 Mass 246, 259, 967 NE2d 1120, 1131 (2012) (minimization combined with assurances of leniency and exaggeration of the evidence invalidated confession) with *Com. v. Harris*, 468 Mass 429, 436-437, 11 NE3d 95, 103 (2014).(minimization tactic here did not render statement involuntary) and *Com. v. O'Brian*, supra, 445 Mass at 727-728, 840 NE2d at 505-506 (minimization was not combined with any false claim concerning strength of Commonwealth's case). See also *Com. v. Durand*, 457 Mass 574, 590, 931 NE2d 950, 965 (2010).

[39] See *Com. v. Felice*, 44 Mass App 709, 712-713, 693 NE2d 713, 716 (1998) (& citations).

[40] *Com. v. Scoggins*, 439 Mass 571, 576, 789 NE2d 1080, 1084 (2003). For extensive discussion of the analysis of voluntariness cases involving false statements or ruses, see *Com. v. Feeney*, 84 Mass App 124, 994 NE2d 803 (2013) (officer's use of ruse to get defendant to sign inventory form linking him to the crime did not invalidate his confession) and *Com. v. DiGiambattista*, supra, 442 Mass at 432-440, 813 NE2d at 523-528. Compare *Com. v. Tewolde*, 88 Mass App 423, 428-429, 38 NE3d 1027, 1033-1034 (2015) (statement suppressed where police got a subpoena to compel defendant to speak with them after he initially refused, leading him to believe he had no choice); *Com. v. Carp*, 47 Mass App 229, 233-234, 712 NE2d 622, 625-626 (1999) (misinformation by DSS investigator, suggesting that there would be no criminal consequences of

By way of example, a combination of the detectives' false statements regarding the investigation and the strength of the case, assurances that the defendant would only help himself by confessing, minimizing of his role in the crime, and representing that this was his "last chance" to tell his story, resulted in the suppression of the 19-year-old's confession.[41]

Alluding to "ongoing research [that] has identified such use of false statements as a significant factor that pressures suspects into waiving their rights and making a confession,"[42] the Supreme Judicial

---

interview, rendered statement involuntary) with *Com. v. Newson*, 471 Mass 222, 27 NE3d 1282, 1289 (2015) (officer's false assurance that defendant was not under arrest did not require suppression of statement); *Com. v. Spray*, 467 Mass 456, 467, 5 NE3d 891, 901 (2014) (although interrogating officers varied their line of questioning to ask why defendant had committed the murder, they did not make any intentional misrepresentation or exaggerate the strength of the evidence against him); *Com. v. Buckman*, 461 Mass 24, 957 NE2d 1089 (2011) (police officer's noncustodial questions were not so improper as to make defendant's answers involuntary even if he lied to defendant about victim's bloodstains on his duct tape); *Com. v. Colby*, 422 Mass 414, 416-417, 663 NE2d 808, 810 (1996) (Virginia police officer's misrepresentations that polygraph test was infallible and results admissible did not render defendant's statement involuntary); *Com. v. Edwards*, 420 Mass 666, 673-674, 651 NE2d 398, 402-403 (1995) (detectives' false statement that defendant's handprint had been recovered at murder scene insufficient to render statement involuntary); *Com. v. Selby*, supra, 420 Mass at 663-664, 651 NE2d at 848-849 (false representation that defendant's handprint placed him in victim's house did not invalidate statement); *Com. v. Correa*, 437 Mass 197, 202-203, 770 NE2d 435, 440 (2002) (police question "Did you shoot him in cold blood or were you afraid" cannot be understood as misinformation or assurance of leniency); *Com. v. Holley*, 79 Mass App 542, 546-548, 947 NE2d 606, 611-612 (2011) (trooper's false suggestion that defendant had been identified by two sources as being near victim's apartment on night of murder did not render confession involuntary); *Com. v. Jones*, 75 Mass App 38, 44-45, 911 NE2d 793, 798-799 (2009) (defendant's statement not rendered involuntary by police officers' display of objects intended to suggest falsely that they possessed inculpatory DNA evidence, where police made no reference to the objects and no suggestion of leniency); *Com. v. Moran*, 75 Mass App 513, 518-519, 915 NE2d 240, 245-246 (2009) (no evidence that police intentionally placed defendant's sister in interrogation room in order to deliberately monitor his statements or break down his capacity to resist their questions). See also *Com. v. Tremblay*, 460 Mass 199, 206-212, 950 NE2d 421, 427-431 (2011) (extensive discussion of the significance of trickery and deception in the determination of voluntariness) (assuring 50-year old businessman that his statements would be "off the record" during noncustodial interview did not render confession involuntary; but telling suspect his statements will be "off the record" should be avoided, and may result in suppression in other circumstances).

[41] *Com. v. Ortiz*, 84 Mass App 258, 995 NE2d 833 (2013).

[42] For a case considering the admissibility of expert testimony on the subject of psychological manipulation and false confessions, see *Com. v. Robinson*, 449 Mass 1, 4-7, 864 NE2d 1186, 1189-1190 (2007) (proffered testimony did not meet reliability standards established by *Lanigan*, but leaving door open to competent scientific evidence on the matter).

Court suppressed a confession that resulted from an "orchestrated, prearranged plan amongst the officers" to falsely convince the suspect of the strength of the evidence against him and to "minimize" the crime in a way to suggest leniency.[43] The Court has also ruled that repeatedly misrepresenting to a suspect that his only opportunity to tell his story was during the interrogation—the "now-or-never" theme—thereby falsely disclaiming his right to testify at trial, taints any confession and requires suppression.[44] Police may not exploit the suspect's concern for a loved one to extract a confession.[45]

Some additional points regarding confessions should be noted. First,

> Although voluntariness is assessed based on the totality of the circumstances surrounding the interrogation, and not on the reliability of the confession itself . . . [s]ignificant discrepancy between the known facts of the crime and the details of a confession is recognized as an indicator that a confession may be false. Indeed, as one technique to guard against use of false confessions, it is recommended that interrogators get the confessor to give his or her own narrative version of the details of the crime, so that they may be compared with details uncovered in the investigation that would not be known to anyone other than the perpetrator.[46]

Second, where the defendant during interrogation makes self-serving statements to the police that are helpful to his case, that may evidence a rational intellect at work and a finding that his will was overborne is less likely.[47]

Third, where voluntariness is a live issue at trial and the humane practice instruction is given, the jury must also be instructed that the absence of a recording of the interview permits, but does not compel

---

[43] *Com. v. DiGiambattista*, supra, 442 Mass at 434, 813 NE2d at 524-525.

[44] See *Com. v. Novo*, 442 Mass 262, 267-269, 812 NE2d 1169, 1174-1175 (2004).

[45] See *Com. v. Scott*, 430 Mass 351, 355, 718 NE2d 1248, 1251 (1999) and *Com. v. Berg*, 37 Mass App Ct. 200, 206, 638 NE2d 1367, 1371 (1994) (but no finding of exploitation in either case).

[46] *Com. v. DiGiambattista*, supra, 442 Mass at 439 n.15, 813 NE2d at 528 n.15.

[47] See *Com. v. Walker*, 466 Mass 268, 277, 994 NE2d 764, 772 (2013); *Com. v. Wolinski*, 431 Mass 228, 232, 726 NE2d 930, 934-935 (2000) (defendant's first account of events was designed to deflect suspicion and revealed rational effort at self-preservation); *Com. v. Pavao*, 46 Mass App 271, 276, 705 NE2d 307, 311 (1999); *Com. v. Fuentes*, 45 Mass App 934, 936, 702 NE2d 814, 817 (1998). A calm demeanor and lucid conversation suggest voluntariness. See *Com. v. Carlson*, 448 Mass 501, 504-505, 862 NE2d 363, 367 (2007).

them, to conclude that the Commonwealth has failed to prove voluntariness beyond a reasonable doubt.[48]

Fourth, where the statements are not the product of police questioning, but initiated and continued spontaneously by the suspect, there will be no suppression.[49]

Fifth, while the determination of voluntariness is multi-factored, the judge is not obligated to instruct the jury on the specific factors.[50]

Sixth, the Supreme Judicial Court has warned that where the police provide precustodial warnings but ignore the suspect's attempts to avail himself of those rights, "the coercive effect of continued interrogation is greatly increased because the subject could believe that the police promises to provide the suspect's constitutional rights were untrustworthy, and that the police would continue to ignore subsequent invocations, rendering such invocations futile."[51]

Although the range of variables is wide, the following is a sampling of cases emphasizing the two major points of reference in the voluntariness analysis:

The mental or physical state of the defendant:

Cases Finding Statement Involuntary: *Mincey v. Arizona*, 437 US 385 (1978) (seriously wounded suspect questioned in hospital while in considerable pain and barely conscious); *Townsend v. Sain*, 372 US 293 (1963) (confession obtained while defendant was under the influence of drug having the effect of a "truth serum"); *Com. v. Magee*, 423 Mass 381, 387-389, 668 NE2d 339, 344-345 (1996) (defendant's debilitated physical and emotional state, and officer's withholding of medical treatment until she gave statement); *Com. v. Meehan*, supra, 377 Mass at 562-568, 387 NE2d at 535-536 (defendant was 18-years-old, with poor educational background, uninformed of his right to reach his family or friends, his judgment impaired through intoxication, and he confessed after being misinformed by police officer that case against him was established and after receiving assurance that confession would assist his defense).

But compare *Colorado v. Connelly*, 479 US 157 (1987) (mental disorder of defendant not determinative on voluntariness issue in

[48] *Com. v. DiGiambattista*, supra, 442 Mass at 447-448, 813 NE2d at 533-534, discussed in § 12.5, infra.

[49] See *Com. v. Scott*, 463 Mass 561, 578-579, 977 NE2d 490, 503-504 (2012); *Com. v. Damielio*, 83 Mass App 32, 36, 979 NE2d 792, 796-797 (2012).

[50] *Com. v. The Ngoc Tran*, 471 Mass 179, 27 NE3d 1261, 1267 (2015).

[51] *Com. v. Libby*, 472 Mass 37, 48, 32 NE3d 890, 901 (2015) (citation omitted).

absence of coercive police conduct); *Com. v. Johnson,* 463 Mass 95, 103-105, 972 NE2d 460, 468 (2012) (scant evidence that defendant was intoxicated or terrified during interrogation); *Com. v. Morales*, 461 Mass 765, 776-777, 965 NE2d 177, 187-188 (2012) (statement was voluntary despite defendant's two brief emotional breakdowns and lack of sleep); *Com. v. Siny Van Tran*, 460 Mass 535, 558-559, 953 NE2d 139, 160-161 (2011) (incriminating statement to police by Vietnamese immigrant with no experience in the criminal justice system, interrogated with Cantonese interpreter after 20-hour flight from Hong Kong, was voluntary); *Com. v. Martinez,* 458 Mass 684, 694, 940 NE2d 422, 432 (2011) (confession voluntary even though defendant was young, from El Salvador, spoke limited English, was alone at the police station, and kept awake through the early morning hours, where he was questioned in Spanish, coherent, and never indicated he wanted to end the interview); *Com. v. Boyarsky*, 452 Mass 700, 711-715, 897 NE2d 574, 583-585 (2008) (testimony of trooper contradicted defendant's assertion that he was having a panic attack when he confessed); *Com. v. Auclair,* 444 Mass 348, 354-355, 828 NE2d 471, 477 (2005) (statements made by defendant with low intelligence in a debilitated mental condition are involuntary only if affected by that condition); *Com. v. Zagrodny*, 443 Mass 93, 99-100, 819 NE2d 565, 572 (2004) (no reason to conclude defendant's mental illness impeded his ability to make a voluntary statement); *Com. v. Garcia*, 443 Mass 824, 833, 824 NE2d 864, 871 (2005); *habeas denied, Garcia v. Russo*, 894 F Supp 2d 187 (D Mass 2011); (that defendant was diabetic and in need of insulin at time of interview did not render admission involuntary); *Com. v. Hilton*, 443 Mass 597, 607-608, 823 NE2d 383, 393-394 (2005), *appeal after remand*, 450 Mass 173, 877 NE2d 545 (2007) (suspect's inability to comprehend *Miranda* warnings because of mental illness would not, by itself, render her statement involuntary); *Com. v. Larkin*, 429 Mass 426, 438, 708 NE2d 674, 682-683 (1999) (no evidence of any disability and defendant was veteran of criminal process); *Com. v. Colon-Cruz*, 408 Mass 533, 539-540, 562 NE2d 797, 803-804 (1990) (no evidence that, defendant's physical condition was so disabling as to render his statement involuntary, or that the interview involved excessive or unfair pressure, or that defendant was unusually susceptible to police pressure); *Com. v. Paszko*, 391 Mass 164, 175, 461 NE2d 222, 232-234 (1984) (no per se rule excluding statements made during drug withdrawal); *Com. v. Vazquez*, 387 Mass 96, 100, 438 NE2d 856, 859 (1982) (no per se rule excluding statements given by individual suffering severe psychotic conditions); *Com. v. Gerhartsreiter,* 82 Mass App 500,

9511-512, 75 NE2d 890, 900-901 (2012) (defendant's videotaped statement voluntary where judge held a voir dire, heard conflicting testimony from experts on his mental condition, and accepted Commonwealth's expert's opinion); *Com. v. Moran*, 75 Mass App 513, 520-521, 915 NE2d 240, 246-247 (2009) (incriminating statements were voluntary even though defendant was native of Guatemala, only 21 years old, spoke very little English, and had no experience with criminal justice system).

The means used to obtain the confession:

Cases Finding Statement Involuntary: *Arizona v. Fulminante*, 499 US 279 (1991) (defendant was motivated to confess by fear of physical violence from other inmates and promise of protection from police informant); *Com. v. Baye*, 462 Mass 246, 967 NE2d 1120 (2012) (troopers employed multiple problematic tactics repeatedly during ten-hour interrogation, including minimization, mischaracterization of the law, implied assurances of leniency, misrepresenting the evidence, and dissuading him from seeking counsel); *Com. v. Lahti*, 398 Mass 829, 831, 501 NE2d 511, 512 (1986) (defendant's statements were induced by detective's promises and threats); *Com. v. Leon*, 52 Mass App 823, 828-830, 756 NE2d 1162, 1167-1169 (2001) (admissions of Spanish-speaking juveniles who had been in the United States for only short time were products of officer's overbearing inquisitorial style).

But compare *Com. v. Mazariego*, 474 Mass 42, 53-55, 47 NE3d 420, 430-431 (2016) (although detective's ploys and interrogation techniques raise concern, they did not overbear the defendant's will); *Com. v. Montoya*, 464 Mass 566, 576-579, 984 NE2d 793, 802-803 (2013) (confession voluntary even though narcotics defendant was handcuffed to wall until interrogation began in small booking room, and officer told defendant he was charged with serious crime and that his Toyota might be damaged during search); *Com. v. McCowen*, 458 Mass 461, 471-472, 939 NE2d 735, 747-748 (2010) (confession was voluntary even though interview was lengthy and defendant was "marginally retarded"); *Com. v. McNulty*, 458 Mass 305, 327-329, 937 NE2d 16, 33-34 (2010) (confession voluntary even though defendant suffered from PTSD and was naked because his clothes were removed for evidentiary reasons); *Com. v. Durand*, 457 Mass 574, 595-598, 931 NE2d 950, 968-969 (2010) (although officers used a variety of improper interrogation techniques—minimization of the crimes, suggestions of leniency, telling defendant this was his only opportunity to explain—defendant's will was not overborne); *Com. v. Clemente*, 452 Mass 295, 328-329, 893 NE2d 19, 47-48 (2008) (confession was voluntary even though detective suggested that relatives of the murder victim might seek revenge against defendant's family if he delayed making a statement); *Com. v. Jackson*, 447 Mass 603, 612, 855 NE2d 1097, 1104 (2006) (while defendant's lengthy confinement at the police station and inability to obtain prescribed medications were troubling in light of his mental history, trial judge's conclusion after viewing videotape of the interrogation, that statement was voluntary, would not be disturbed); *Com. v. Souza*, 418 Mass 478, 702 NE2d 1167 (1998) (confession voluntary even though defendant interrogated in his underwear, handcuffed to wall, and questioned by series of officers over three and one-half hours); *Com. v. Fryar*, 414 Mass 732, 741-743, 610 NE2d 903, 909-910 (1993) (confession voluntary even though defendant, 17-years-old, had been drinking, had been isolated for over four hours without food or sleep, and was falsely told by police that he had been charged with stabbing victim; and when he gave second statement, he had been handcuffed in room for additional four hours, alone and with no food or sleep); *Com. v. DiGiambattista*, 83 Mass App 180, 982 NE2d 45 (2013) (statement was voluntary even if police officer attempted to play on defendant's emotions in encouraging him to confess and suggested his alcohol abuse might have caused him to make a "mistake" regarding indecent assault); *Com. v. Ashley*, 82 Mass App 748, 755-758, 978 NE2d 576, 583-585 (2012) (statement voluntary even though first two interrogators were persistent and unwavering, but not coercive); *Com. v. Burbine*, 74 Mass App 148, 153-154, 904 NE2d 787, 791-792 (2009) (reversing trial judge's finding that defendant's admission to ownership of gun when questioned by one officer in parking lot was involuntary).

It must be emphasized that the voluntariness of a suspect's statement under Due Process analysis and the voluntariness of his waiver of *Miranda* rights (discussed at § 12.6.4, infra) are separate and distinct issues, even though both are determined in light of the totality of the circumstances and share many of the same relevant factors.[52] Once the issue of voluntariness is raised by defendant, the court is required to

---

[52] See *Com. v. Hoose*, 467 Mass 395, 403, 5 NE3d 843, 852 (2014); *Com. v. Walker*, 466 Mass 268, 274, 994 NE2d 764, 770 (2013).

hold a separate inquiry into the voluntariness of defendant's statement apart from the validity of a *Miranda* waiver.[53]

Absent evidence that the statement was the product of police harassment or of police effort to obtain evidence specifically for a probation revocation hearing, the exclusionary rule for involuntary statements is inapplicable in such hearings.[54]

On appellate review of a voluntariness determination, the court must examine the entire record and make an independent determination of the ultimate issue.[55] The judge's subsidiary fact findings will not be disturbed, however, if they are warranted by the evidence[56] and a finding of voluntariness is entitled to substantial deference.[57] The United States Supreme Court has held that harmless error analysis applies to coerced confessions.[58] Where a confession has been erroneously admitted, the prosecution has the burden of demonstrating beyond a reasonable doubt that the admission of the confession did not contribute to the defendant's conviction.

The imprecise nature of the "totality of the circumstances" analysis led the Supreme Court to develop additional doctrines concerning confessions which apply more specific constraints derived from the

---

[53] See *Com. v. Molina*, supra, 467 Mass at 77-78, 3 NE3d at 594-595; *Com. v. Leahy*, 445 Mass 481, 486-487, 838 NE2d 1220, 1226 (2005); *Com. v. Byrd*, 52 Mass App 642, 645-646, 755 NE2d 785, 788 (2001) ("Thus, even in circumstances where *Miranda* warnings are not necessary, the question of the voluntariness of the defendant's statements remains an issue which must be separately considered"). But see *Com. v. St. Peter*, 48 Mass App 517, 520, 722 NE2d 1002, 1006 (2000) (although separate issues, when *Miranda* warnings immediately preceded statement and judge made findings regarding voluntariness of statement, failure of judge to make explicit findings regarding *Miranda* waiver was not fatal).

[54] See *Com. v. Simon*, 57 Mass App 80, 88-90, 781 NE2d 839, 846-847 (2003).

[55] See *Miller v. Fenton*, 474 US 104 (1985) (voluntariness is not a factual but a legal, issue); *Com. v. Tavares*, 385 Mass 140, 144-145, 430 NE2d 1198, 1206 (1982).

[56] *Com. v. O'Brian*, supra, 445 Mass at 726, 840 NE2d at 505 ("We accept a judge's resolution of conflicting testimony [regarding what suspect was told by interrogators]."); *Com. v. Leahy*, supra, 445 Mass at 485, 838 NE2d at 1225.

[57] *Com. v. Fryar*, 414 Mass 732, 742, 610 NE2d 903, 909 (1993); *Com. v. Cunningham*, 405 Mass 646, 655, 543 NE2d 12, 17 (1989); *Com. v. Tavares*, supra, 385 Mass at 144-145, 430 NE2d at 1206. Where the judge's factual findings are based on a videotape of the interview, the appellate court will take an independent view of the confession and make judgments without deference to the fact finder, who is in no better position to evaluate the contents of the interview. *Com. v. Bermudez*, 83 Mass App 46, 51, 980 NE2d 462, 467 (2012).

[58] *Arizona v. Fulminante*, 499 US 279 (1991). The Supreme Judicial Court has not decided whether the Massachusetts Constitution requires a stricter standard of review. See *Com. v. Durand*, 457 Mass 574, 592, 931 NE2d 950, 966 (2010).

Fourth, Fifth, and Sixth Amendments to the United States Constitution, as outlined in the § 12.6-12.9 below. These doctrines, it must be emphasized, supplement but do not supplant the Due Process standard.

§ 12.3 Statements to Private Parties and Non-Law Enforcement Governmental Officials

Under Massachusetts law, statements extracted by private citizens, even absent governmental involvement, are subject to suppression under the involuntariness standard.[1] "A statement obtained through coercion and introduced at trial is every bit as offensive to civilized standards of adjudication when the coercion flows from private hands as when official depredations elicit a confession. Statements extracted by a howling lynch mob or a lawless private pack of vigilantes from a terrorized, pliable suspect are repugnant to due process mandates of fundamental fairness and protection against compulsory self-incrimination."[2]

With regard to admissions to private citizens, involuntariness has been found primarily where there has been actual physical or psychological coercion.[3] Thus "an admission to a private citizen is admissible unless coerced, even if not the result of a meaningful act of volition."[4]

The question of the voluntariness of statements made to private citizens must be raised by the defendant, and he must offer some proof

---

§ 12.3 [1] See *Com. v. Mahnke*, 368 Mass 662, 679-681, 335 NE2d 660, 672 (1975).

[2] *Id.*, 368 Mass at 680-681, 335 NE2d at 672.

[3] Compare *Com. v. Taylor*, 426 Mass 189, 196, 687 NE2d 631, 636 (1997) (defendant's statement to sister not involuntary even though made while handcuffed at police station); *Com. v. Blanchette*, 409 Mass 99, 106-108, 564 NE2d 992, 996 (1991) (defendant's written and oral statements to uncle and visitor at state hospital were product of a rational mind and voluntary); *Com. v. Libran*, 405 Mass 634, 639-640, 543 NE2d 5, 8-9 (1989) (defendant's statements overheard by another prisoner not involuntary because not result of coercion or mental impairment); *Com. v. Watkins*, 33 Mass App 7, 14, 595 NE2d 786, 791 (1992) (no involuntariness in student's statements to university investigator).

[4] See *Com. v. Anderson*, 445 Mass 195, 204-205, 834 NE2d 1159, 1168 (2005) (notwithstanding consumption of marijuana, defendant's statement to civilian witnesses were not product of impairment or coercion). See also *Com. v. Cutts*, 444 Mass 821, 832, 831 NE2d 1279, 1289 (2005) (intoxication alone not sufficient to invalidate statements made to girl friend and cousin); *Com. v. Zagrodny*, 443 Mass 93, 99, 819 NE2d 565, 572 (2004) (defendant's statement to his family was voluntary).

to support his claim.[5] Massachusetts law then requires the same "humane practice" (see § 12.1) as is applied to statements elicited by law enforcement personnel: The judge should conduct a voir dire to determine the voluntariness of the statements. If the judge determines that the statements are voluntary, the issue of voluntariness should be submitted to the jury for consideration. The Commonwealth has the burden of proving to the judge and the jury the voluntariness of the statements beyond a reasonable doubt.[6]

It has been suggested that the "better practice" is to treat statements to private citizens as if they were statements to the police.[7] Statements made to non-law enforcement governmental officials are also subject to the "humane practice" and voluntariness test under Massachusetts law.[8] Conduct by private citizens does not, however, implicate the federal constitutional prohibition against coerced statements.[9]

The humane practice applies only to admissions or confessions made after the crime has been committed. Statements made to private persons *prior to* the crime are not subject to a voluntariness challenge.[10]

---

[5] See *Com. v. Anderson*, supra, 445 Mass at 205, 834 NE2d at 1168; *Com. v. Smith*, 426 Mass 76, 82, 686 NE2d 983, 988 (1997).

[6] *Com. v. Hunter*, 416 Mass 831, 626 NE2d 873 (1994); *Com. v. Blanchette*, supra, 409 Mass at 106, 564 NE2d at 996; *Com. v. Miller*, 68 Mass App 835, 865 NE2d 825 (2007) (in face of evidence concerning the coercive nature of the questioning, judge was required to follow humane practice to determine the voluntariness of defendant's confession to his employer Home Depot's in-store investigators; extensive discussion).

[7] *Com. v. Paszko*, 391 Mass 164, 182-183, 461 NE2d 222, 234 (1984).

[8] See *Com. v. Carp*, 47 Mass App 229, 712 NE2d 622 (1999) (suppressing statements defendant made to DSS investigator working in tandem with police). But compare *Com. v. Morais*, 431 Mass 380, 727 NE2d 831 (2000) (DSS investigator not required to warn defendant that investigator was obligated to report incriminating statements to law enforcement officials, and statements were held to be voluntary) and *Com. v. Ira I.*, 439 Mass 805, 812-813, 791 NE2d 894, 900-901 (2003) (school officials not acting as agents of police are not required to give *Miranda* warnings prior to questioning student in conjunction with school investigation, even if school's policy was to provide information to police).

[9] See *Colorado v. Connelly*, 479 US 157, 166 (1987) ("The most outrageous behavior by a private party seeking to secure evidence against a defendant does not make that evidence inadmissible under the due process clause.").

[10] *Com. v. Brown*, 449 Mass 747, 766, 872 NE2d 711, 726 (2007), *habeas denied*, *Brown v. O'Brien*, 666 F3d 818 (1st Cir 2012) (statements made to private party as part of purchase of murder weapon were not subject to voluntariness challenge); *Com. v. Netto*, 438 Mass 686, 699-700, 783 NE2d 439, 449 (2003) (defendant's expression of hostile state of mind toward victim prior to murder); *Com. v. LaCava*, 438 Mass 708, 720 n.12, 783 NE2d 812, 822 n.12 (2003) (statements to friends and neighbors prior

§ 12.4 Subsequent Statements and Derivative Evidence

A finding that an earlier statement was involuntary does not necessarily require suppression of a later statement by the accused. The issue is whether the taint from the initial illegal interrogation has been eliminated, in which case the later statement may be admitted. The courts follow two lines of analysis in making this determination. In the first, the question is whether there had been a "break in the stream of events" so that the subsequent statement is sufficiently insulated from the coercive circumstances. The second analysis looks at the defendant's state of mind to determine whether the subsequent statement resulted from the erroneous impression that the "cat was already out of the bag."[1]

Where there is a connection between an unlawfully obtained statement and the defendant's later statement, the Commonwealth bears burden of proving that the connection has become so attenuated as to dissipate the taint.[2] For a discussion of the subsequent statement issue in the *Miranda* context, see § 12.6.5.

Physical evidence obtained as a result of an involuntary confession may also be suppressed.[3]

---

to killing regarding efforts to obtain weapon); *Com. v. Boateng*, 438 Mass 498, 503-504, 781 NE2d 1207, 1213-1214 (2003) (statements made to victim and mother during the extended assault).

§ 12.4 [1] See generally *Com. v. Smith*, 412 Mass 823, 830-831, 593 NE2d 1288, 1292 (1992) (& citations). Compare *Com. v. Meehan*, 377 Mass 552, 569-571, 387 NE2d 527, 537 (1979) (there is strong basis for drawing inference that second confession was product of first, and for permitting inference to be overcome only by such insulation as the advice of counsel or lapse of a long period of time), with *Com. v. Pileeki*, 62 Mass App 505, 508-510, 818 NE2d 596, 599-601 (2004) (defendant's statement at police station was not tainted by prior involuntary statement at hospital because there was a sufficient break in the earlier coercive circumstances and no evidence that second statement was motivated by feeling she had already "let the cat out of the bag"). The cat-out-of-the-bag analysis does not apply where defendant's statement follows a statement elicited from a co-defendant. See *Com. v. Gallant*, 381 Mass 465, 469, 410 NE2d 704, 707 (1980).

[2] See *Com. v. Alicea*, 55 Mass App 505, 511-512, 772 NE2d 48, 52-53 (2002).

[3] See *Com. v. Perrot*, 407 Mass 539, 546-548, 544 NE2d 1215, 1209 (1990) (pocketbook from burglary seized as result of statement illegally obtained from defendant suppressed); *Com. v. Meehan*, supra, 377 Mass at 568-569, 387 NE2d at 536 (evidence seized pursuant to search warrant based on involuntary confession was inadmissible); *Com. v. Barros*, 56 Mass 675, 678-679, 779 NE2d 693, 696 (2002) (suppressing physical evidence obtained as direct result of *Miranda* violation). See also *Com. v. Lahti*, 398 Mass 829, 501 NE2d 511 (1986) (suppressing on Fifth Amendment grounds two victims' anticipated testimony as the tainted fruit of defendant's involuntary statements to police).

Where a defendant takes the stand at trial in response to a confession admitted into evidence but subsequently determined to have been coerced, the defendant's testimony may not be introduced at a subsequent trial.[4]

§ 12.5 Electronic Recording of Interrogations

The Supreme Judicial Court has long been concerned that courts "spend an enormous amount of time and effort trying to determine precisely what transpires during custodial interrogations," and has observed that electronic recording of interrogations would therefore be a "helpful tool in evaluating the voluntariness of confessions."[1] Nonetheless, the Court has resisted imposing a mandate requiring such recording under either the common law or the Massachusetts Declaration of Rights.[2]

While declining to adopt a rule suppressing custodial statements unless they had been electronically recorded, the Court warned in *Com. v. Diaz*:

> There is force to a recording requirement particularly if a defendant is being questioned at a police station. The cost of the equipment and its operation is minimal. The machinery is not difficult to use. A recording speaks for itself literally on questions concerning what was said and in what manner. Recording would tend to eliminate certain challenges to the admissibility of defendants' statements and to make easier the resolution of many challenges that are made. Police officials should be alert to the merits of recording custodial interrogations and be warned that

---

[4] See *Com. v. Brusgulis*, 41 Mass App 386, 389-390, 670 NE2d 207, 209-210 (1996). Compare *Com. v. Luna*, 418 Mass 749, 751-752, 641 NE2d 1050, 1052 (1994) (even if defendant's affidavit was involuntary, it did not compel him to testify at trial). For the claim that a Commonwealth witness's testimony was improperly derived from his coerced statements and should thus be excluded, see *Com. v. Burgos*, 462 Mass 53, 65-66, 965 NE2d 854 (2012).

§ 12.5 [1] *Com. v. Fryar*, 414 Mass 732, 742 n.8, 610 NE2d 903, 909 n.8 (1993).

[2] See *Com. v. Groome*, 435 Mass 201, 219 n.26, 755 NE2d 122, 1239 n.26 (2001); *Com. v. Burgess*, 434 Mass 307, 314, 749 NE2d 112, 118-119 (2001); *Com. v. Freeman*, 430 Mass 111, 115, 712 NE2d 1135, 1140 (1999); *Com. v. Pina*, 430 Mass 66, 69-70, 713 NE2d 944, 948 (1999); *Com. v. Ardon*, 428 Mass 496, 498, 702 NE2d 808, 810 (1998); *Com. v. Fernandes*, 427 Mass 90, 98, 692 NE2d 3, 8-9 (1998).

> the time may come when recording in places of detention, at least, will be mandatory if a statement obtained during custodial interrogation is to be admissible.[3]
>
> Moreover, defense counsel are entitled to pursue the failure of the police to record a defendant's statements. Counsel may, for example, inquire of a testifying police officer . . . whether he or she was aware of the availability of recorders to use during the questioning of suspects. Counsel may argue to a jury and to a judge as fact-finder that the failure of the police to record electronically statements made in a place of custody should be considered in deciding the voluntariness of any statement, whether the defendant was properly advised of his rights, and whether any statement attributed to the defendant was made.[4]

In 2004, the Supreme Judicial Court took the next step by ruling in *Com. v. DiGiambattista* that "henceforth, the admission in evidence of any confession or statement of the defendant that is the product of an unrecorded custodial interrogation, or an unrecorded interrogation conducted at a place of detention, will entitle the defendant, on request,[5] to a jury instruction concerning the need to evaluate that alleged statement or confession with particular caution."[6] The instruction should advise

> that the State's highest court has expressed a preference that such interrogations be recorded whenever practicable, and cautioning the jury that, because of the absence of any recording of the interrogation in the case before them, they should weigh evidence of the defendant's alleged statement with great caution and care. Where voluntariness is a live issue and the humane practice instruction is given, the jury should also be advised that the absence of a recording permits (but does not compel) them to conclude that the Commonwealth has failed to prove voluntariness beyond a reasonable doubt.[7]

---

[3] 422 Mass 269, 272-273, 661 NE2d 1326, 1328-1329 (1996). Cf. *Com. v. Baldwin*, 426 Mass 105, 110-113, 686 NE2d 1001, 1005-1007 (1997) (declining to require electronic recording of court-ordered psychiatric evaluation); *Com. v. Stockwell*, 426 Mass 17, 19-20, 686 NE2d 426, 429 (1997) (no abuse of discretion in denying motion to videotape psychiatric interview).

[4] *Com. v. Diaz, supra*, 422 Mass at 273, 661 NE2d at 1329. See, e.g., *Com. v. Larkin*, 429 Mass 426, 438 n.10, 708 NE2d 674, 683 n.10 (1999) (defense counsel cross-examined troopers about access to recorders).

[5] A trial judge need only give the instruction below upon request. *Com. v. Woods*, 466 Mass 707, 721, 1 NE3d 762, 773 (2014).

[6] *Com. v. DiGiambattista*, 442 Mass 423, 425, 440-449, 813 NE2d 516, 518, 528-535 (2004).

[7] 442 Mass at 447-448, 813 NE2d at 533-534. The ruling applies only prospectively to trials occurring after the issuance of the decision, regardless of the date of the

The instruction must be unqualified,[8] and it must convey both that (1) the state's highest court prefers that custodial interrogations be tape recorded whenever practicable, and (2) where there is not at least an audiotape recording of the complete interrogation, the jury should weigh the defendant's statements with great caution and care.[9] The instructions should convey that while the "failure to preserve evidence of the interrogation in a thorough and reliable form can comprise a basis for concluding that voluntariness and a valid waiver have not been established beyond a reasonable doubt,"[10] the absence of a recording is just one factor to be considered in the totality of circumstances regarding voluntariness, but should not be the dominant factor.[11] A defendant who made voluntary statements at the police station before he was considered a suspect is not entitled to the instruction.[12]

---

interrogation. *Com. v. Zanetti*, 454 Mass 449, 469, 910 NE2d 869, 884-885 (2009). See *Com. v. O'Brian*, 445 Mass 720, 728-729, 840 NE2d 500, 506-507 (2006); *Com. v. Zagrodny*, 443 Mass 93, 100 n.5, 819 NE2d 565, 573 n.5 (2004); *Com. v. Dagley*, 442 Mass 713, 721, 816 NE2d 527, 534 (2004), *habeas denied*, 540 F3d 8 (1st Cir 2008). But see *Com. v. Caswell*, 85 Mass App 463, 477, 11 NE3d 136, 147 (2014) (trial court erred in instructing jury that unrecorded interrogation predated *DiGiambattista*, as the Court directed that the instruction be given without regard to the alleged reasons for not recording).

[8] See *Com. v. Drummond*, 76 Mass App 625, 628, 925 NE2d 34, 37 (2010) (judge improperly conditioned instruction on jury's finding that defendant was not advised of right to a recording and did not decline).

[9] *Com. v. Barbosa*, 457 Mass 773, 800-801, 933 NE2d 93, 116-117 (2010). See also *Com. v. Robinson*, 78 Mass App 714, 720-721, 942 NE2d 980, 987-988 (2011) (portion of instruction concerning voluntariness need only be given where voluntariness is a live issue and the humane practice instruction is given; jury may consider whether or not defendant indicated he did not want interrogation recorded).

[10] *Com. v. Spray*, 467 Mass 456, 467, 5 NE3d 891, 901 (2014), supra, 442 Mass at 441, 813 NE2d at 516.

[11] *Com. v. Drummond*, supra, 76 Mass App at 629-630, 925 NE2d at 38 (jury should be advised that the absence of a recording permits, but does not compel, a finding of involuntariness); *Com. v. Trombley*, 72 Mass App 183, 187, 889 NE2d 446, 449 (2008). Judges should be careful in departing significantly from the lines laid out in *DiGiambattista*, and especially by using the term "waiver" with regard to the defendant's decision not to have a recording made. See *Com. v. Rousseau*, 465 Mass 372, 391-393, 990 NE2d 543, 558-560 (2013). See also *Com. v. Boyarsky*, 452 Mass 700, 710-711, 897 NE2d 574, 581-583 (2008) (trooper's testimony that state police did not have a policy requiring recording of interrogation was admissible to rebut suggestion of misconduct); *Com. v. Wolcott*, 77 Mass App 457, 471-473, 931 NE2d 1025, 1036-1038 (2010) (even though motion judge found the troopers' failure to record interview was reckless, the remedy was the jury instruction, not exclusion of the statement).

[12] *Com. v. Issa*, 466 Mass 1, 19-20, 992 NE2d 336, 351-352 (2013).

Where the prosecution offers a defendant's recorded statement, it may do so without also offering a transcript; but if the recorded statement is in a language other than English, it must be accompanied by an English-language transcript.[13]

The Supreme Judicial Court has declined invitations to revisit the question of whether unrecorded statements should be per se inadmissible.[14]

Evidence suggesting that the defendant refused to have a recording made does not vitiate the need for the instruction.[15] Where appropriate, evidence of a refusal to have his statement recorded may be admitted to inform the jury that the police followed proper procedures.[16]

Absence of a recording of any portion of the interview entitles defendant to the *DiGiambattista* instruction, and testimony by the officer concerning the substance of an unrecorded portion of an interview does not cure the failure to preserve the evidence the first place.[17] Nor may the judge forgo the instruction because the one portion of the interrogation that was recorded was suppressed, and the unrecorded portion introduced.[18]

A defendant who was neither in custody nor in a place of detention when the statement was made is not entitled to the instruction.[19] The courts have declined to adopt a requirement that interviews of alleged victims of sexual assault be electronically recorded.[20]

Where a confession is taped, the "better practice" is to leave the recorder on during the entire interview including silences, emotional displays, and casual conversation among the participants so that the judge and jury are better able to assess the totality of the circumstances.[21]

---

[13] *Com. v. Portillo*, 462 Mass 324, 968 NE2d 395 (2012) (extensive discussion and further direction regarding use of foreign language recording).

[14] See, e.g., *Com. v. Garuti*, 454 Mass 48, 52-53, 907 NE2d 221, 226-227 (2009); *Com. v. Pimental*, 454 Mass 475, 479-480, 910 NE2d 366, 372 (2009).

[15] See *Com. v. Tavares*, 81 Mass App 71, 73, 959 NE2d 449, 451 (2011) (the Commonwealth may of course explain to the jury why no recording was made).

[16] *Com. v. DaSilva*, 471 Mass 71, 79-80, 27 NE3d 383, 391-392 (2015).

[17] *Com. v. Vacher*, 469 Mass 425, 443-444, 14 NE3d 264, 280 (2014).

[18] *Com. v. Woodbine*, 461 Mass 720, 739-740, 964 NE2d 956, 971-972 (2012).

[19] *Com. v. Liptak*, 80 Mass App 76, 85, 951 NE2d 731, 740 (2011); *Com. v. Jones*, 75 Mass App 38, 45, 911 NE2d 793, 799 (2009).

[20] See *Com. v. Niels N.*, 73 Mass App 689, 703, 901 NE2d 166, 178 (2009) (& citations).

[21] *Com. v. Fernette*, 398 Mass 658, 665, 500 NE2d 1290, 1295 (1986).

§ 12.6 Confessions Under the Fifth Amendment *Miranda* Doctrine

§ 12.6.1 The Safeguards

Premised upon the Fifth Amendment privilege against self-incrimination,[1] the landmark decision of *Miranda v. Arizona*[2] adopted a prophylactic scheme designed to limit the coercion inherent in custodial interrogation. In the absence of the now-familiar warnings and a valid waiver, any statement obtained as a result of custodial interrogation (whether incriminating or exculpatory)[3] is inadmissible at trial. A person subjected to custodial interrogation is entitled to the benefit of the *Miranda* safeguards regardless of the nature or severity of the offense of which he is suspected or for which he was arrested.[4] Massachusetts has not adopted the *Miranda* scheme as a means of protecting state constitutional rights, but has established certain state law adjuncts to the *Miranda* rules, as discussed below.[5]

Prior to any questioning, the subject must be advised in clear and unequivocal terms of his right to remain silent and his right to consult with an attorney, and that anything he says can be used against him in court and that if he cannot afford an attorney one will be appointed at state expense. The required warnings need not be given in the precise language contained in *Miranda*.[6] Reviewing courts should not examine the words used "as if construing a will or defining the terms of an

---

§ 12.6 [1] The privilege was applied to the states in *Malloy v. Hogan*, 378 US 1 (1964).

[2] 384 US 436 (1966). The Supreme Court reaffirmed *Miranda* in *United States v. Dickerson*, 530 US 428 (2000).

[3] *Miranda v. Arizona*, supra, 384 US at 476-477. Thus, even if the defendant's motivation for making a statement is to clear himself or another, *Miranda* is designed to ensure that he has the requisite information about his rights before he speaks. *Com. v. Rubio*, 27 Mass App 506, 514, 540 NE2d 189, 194 (1989).

[4] *Berkemer v. McCarty*, 468 US 420, 434 (1984) (misdemeanor traffic offense); *Com. v. Brennan*, 386 Mass 772, 438 NE2d 60 (1982) (driving under the influence charge).

[5] *Com. v. Ghee*, 414 Mass 313, 318 n.5, 607 NE2d 1005, 1009 n.5 (1993); *Com. v. Snyder*, 413 Mass 521, 531, 597 NE2d 1363 (1992).

[6] See *Florida v. Powell*, 559 US 50 (2010) (warning that suspect had "the right to talk to a lawyer before answering any of [the officers'] questions," together with other language, reasonably conveyed that right to counsel applied during interrogation); *California v. Prysock*, 453 US 355 (1981) (warnings not defective even though suspect not explicitly advised that he was entitled to the services of a free lawyer prior to questioning); *Duckworth v. Eagan*, 492 US 195 (1989) (warnings not defective even though suspect advised that free lawyer would be appointed "if and when you go to court");

easement," but rather determine whether the suspect's rights were meaningfully conveyed.[7] Minor variations in the police officers' accounts of the exact language used when administering the warnings do not require suppression as long as it is determined that the content of the warnings had been adequately conveyed.[8]

Where the warnings are translated into the subject's native language, the translation need not track the English warnings word for word, as long as they convey the rights in a meaningful way.[9] But subsequent accurate rendition of the warnings in English does not cure defective warnings administered in the suspect's native language.[10]

Com. v. Colon-Cruz, 408 Mass 533, 539, 562 NE2d 797, 803 (1990) (warnings not defective even though Spanish translator used two words not on *Miranda* card); *Com. v. Colby*, 422 Mass 414, 418-419, 663 NE2d 808, 811 (1996) (officer's departure from standard warning, telling defendant "if he could not afford an attorney the Commonwealth would attempt to provide one for him," was harmless); *Com. v. Gaboriault*, 439 Mass 84, 87-88, 785 NE2d 691, 696 (2003) (detective's use of term "formality" in describing warnings did not render them inadequate). But compare *Com. v. Dagraca*, 447 Mass 546, 551-552, 854 NE2d 1249, 1254 (2006) (police officer's failure to warn defendant that anything he said could be used against him rendered warnings inadequate and his subsequent statements inadmissible); *Com. v. Seng*, 436 Mass 537, 542-545, 766 NE2d 492, 497-499 (2002) (warnings in defendant's native Khmer language were deficient); *Com. v. Ghee*, supra, 414 Mass at 317-318 (warning that implied that, although suspect did not have to talk about offenses with which he was charged, he did have to talk about other offenses, was not adequate); *Com. v. Miranda*, 37 Mass App 939, 641 NE2d 139 (1994) (failure to inform defendant of right to presence of attorney during interrogation rendered warnings inadequate). See also *Com. v. Coplin*, 34 Mass App 478, 612 NE2d 1188 (1993) (complete set of warnings at time of arrest could not be deemed to carry over to remedy omission at station house of warning about possible consequences of forgoing privilege to remain silent).

The Supreme Judicial Court has left open the issue of whether the judge is required to submit to the jury the preliminary factual questions regarding compliance with *Miranda*, including questions as to whether the warnings were given. See *Com. v. Garcia*, 379 Mass. 422, 431-432, 399 N.E.2d 460, 474 (1980); *Com. v. Chung*, 378 Mass 451, 458 n.9, 392 NE2d 1015, 1020 n.9 (1979). For cases upholding the trial judge's refusal to credit defendant's testimony that he did not receive proper warnings, see *Com. v. Corriveau*, 396 Mass 319, 329-330, 486 NE2d 29, 36-37 (1985); *Com. v. Day*, 387 Mass 915, 919, 444 NE2d 384, 386 (1983); *Com. v. Williams*, 378 Mass 217, 226, 391 NE2d 1202, 1207-1208 (1979). See also *Com. v. Johnson*, 41 Mass App 81, 88-89, 669 NE2d 212, 217 (1996) (Commonwealth entitled to introduce transcript of tape recording of interview to rebut defendant's testimony that he had not received warnings).

[7] *Florida v. Powell*, 559 US 50, 60 (2010).

[8] *Com. v. Burgess*, 434 Mass 307, 312, 749 NE2d 112, 117 (2001).

[9] *Com. v. The Ngoc Tran*, 471 Mass 179, 27 NE3d 1261, 1269 (2015).

[10] *Com. v. Seng*, supra, 436 Mass at 545-547, 766 NE2d at 499-500. For cases involving translated warnings, see *Com. v. Bins*, 465 Mass 348, 358-359, 989 NE2d 404, 415 (2013) (warnings given on four separate occasions in continental Portuguese to defendant who spoke Brazilian Portuguese were adequate); *Com. v. Perez*, 411 Mass 249, 255, 581 NE2d 1010, 1014-1015 (1991) (rejecting defendant's contention that he was misinformed of his rights because Spanish translations on *Miranda* cards were

More generally, where two sets of warnings are given and one is defective or incomplete and the circumstances are such that the defendant would be confused by the defect, a resulting waiver is not valid.[11]

The Supreme Judicial Court has approved the practice of police reading the *Miranda* warnings to the suspect from a card, and encouraged officers to do so, because "much of the trial time now spent in trying to establish exactly what warning was given to a suspect or defendant could be saved if he were also given a copy of the card to be kept by him. We also approve the practice of admitting a police copy of the card in evidence. No useful purpose is served by testing on the witness stand the officer's ability to recite accurately from memory the *Miranda* warnings he read."[12] While it is good practice for the prosecutor to introduce the *Miranda* cards in evidence, the failure to do so does not undermine a judicial finding that the warnings had been given.[13] *Miranda* waiver cards signed by the defendant acknowledging that the warnings were given are also admissible.[14] There is no requirement that a suspect be given written *Miranda* warnings.[15]

Although *Miranda* warnings, once given, are not to be accorded "unlimited efficacy or perpetuity," they are generally sufficient to keep the suspect apprised of his rights even if there is a significant lapse of time between the warnings and an inculpatory statement.[16] A lapse of six hours was, for example, held not to negate the defendant's waiver.[17] As a general rule, if a valid waiver is obtained from a suspect,

---

incomplete and inaccurate); *Com. v. Siny Van Tran*, 460 Mass 535, 558, 953 NE2d 139, 161 (2011) (Vietnamese defendant found to have understood Cantonese translation of rights).

[11] *Com. v. Seng*, supra, 436 Mass at 547, 766 NE2d at 500.

[12] *Com. v. Lewis*, 374 Mass 203, 204-205, 371 NE2d 775, 776 (1978). See also *Com. v. Woodbine*, 461 Mass 720, 727 n.14, 964 NE2d 956, 963 n.14 (2012).

[13] See *Com. v. Alcala*, 54 Mass App 49, 54 n.7, 763 NE2d 516, 521 n.7 (2002) (& citations).

[14] *Com. v. Santana*, 465 Mass 270, 285, 988 NE2d 825, 837-838 (2013).

[15] See *Com. v. Smith*, 426 Mass 76, 81, 686 NE2d 983, 988 (1997).

[16] See *Com. v. Cruz*, 373 Mass 676, 687, 369 NE2d 996, 1003 (1977).

[17] See *Com. v. Mello*, 420 Mass 375, 385-386, 649 NE2d 1106, 1114 (1995). See also *Com. v. Martinez*, 458 Mass 684, 692-693, 940 NE2d 422, 430-431 (2011) (period of six hours between warning and second statement; no evidence of unfair techniques); *Com. v. Sirois*, 437 Mass 845, 851-852, 777 NE2d 125, 130 (2002) (lapse of 2 to 3 hours not significant, and police confirmed defendant remembered being advised of rights previously); *Com. v. Silanskas*, 433 Mass 678, 687, 746 NE2d 445, 456 (2001) (lapse of 1 to 2 hours did not require renewed warnings); *Com. v. Colby*, 422 Mass 414, 417-418, 663 NE2d 808, 810 (1996) (new warnings not required after defendant failed polygraph); *Com. v. Ghee*, 414 Mass 313, 317, 607 NE2d 1005, 1009 (1993) (rejecting claim that warnings given by trooper at 7:23 A.M. were not sufficient to advise defendant of his rights when other officers began questioning him at 9:00 A.M.); *Com. v.*

the police are not required to re-advise him of his rights or obtain a second waiver absent a break in the interrogation, such as an exercise of the right to remain silent or to counsel, or a significant lapse of time between the waiver and the statement.[18]

If the suspect at any time prior to or during interrogation indicates that he does not wish to respond to questions or wishes to consult with counsel, interrogation must cease.[19] The suspect has the continuing right to cut off questioning and to consult with counsel.[20] There is, however, no requirement that a suspect be specifically advised in a "fifth warning" that he could stop the questioning at any time.[21]

If the suspect wishes to cut off questioning, he must indicate this in some clear and unequivocal manner.[22] "For the rule of *Miranda* regarding the termination of questioning to apply, there must be either

---

Penta, 32 Mass App 36, 44, 586 NE2d 996, 1001 (1992) (police not required to re-advise defendant of his rights during ride in the cruiser after arrest). But compare *Com. v. Harvey*, 390 Mass 203, 454 NE2d 105, 106 (1983) (statement suppressed where defendant was advised of his rights, declined to be questioned, and approximately eight hours later police elicited statement without re-advising him of his rights); *Com. v. Doe*, 37 Mass App 30, 35-36, 636 NE2d 308, 311 (1994) (lapse of weekend rendered warnings ineffective).

[18] *Com. v. Edwards*, 420 Mass 666, 671, 651 NE2d 398, 401 (1995).

[19] *Miranda v. Arizona*, supra, 384 US at 473-474.

[20] *Com. v. Hussey (No. 1)*, 410 Mass 664, 671, 574 NE2d 995, 999 (1991); *Com. v. Bradshaw*, 385 Mass 244, 265, 431 NE2d 880, 893 (1982). Any waiver may thus be contradicted by an invocation at any time. *Com. v. Clarke*, 461 Mass 336, 342, 960 NE2d 306, 314 (2012) (citing *Berghuis v. Thompkins*, 130 S Ct 2250, 2263 (2010)).

[21] See *Com. v. Novo*, 442 Mass 262, 271, 812 NE2d 1169, 1176 (2004); *Com. v. Lewis*, 374 Mass 203, 371 NE2d 775 (1978) (but the better practice is to give the "fifth warning"). If, however, the warning is given in a way that may mislead the ordinary person, such as "You still have the right to stop the questioning at any time *for the purpose of consulting an attorney*," implying that *the only* reason a defendant may terminate is to speak with an attorney, this may affect the voluntariness of a confession. *Com. v. Wadlington*, 467 Mass 192, 198-199, 4 NE3d 296, 302-303 (2014); *Com. v. Novo*, supra, 442 Mass at 271, 812 NE2d at 1176; *Com. v. Ashley*, 82 Mass App 748, 754, 978 NE2d 576, 582 (2012) (fact that "fifth right" was given defendant, and that it potentially conveyed misimpression that the only reason a suspect could stop answering questions was to consult an attorney, did not invalidate waiver). See also § 12.2, supra.

[22] *Miranda v. Arizona*, supra, 384 US at 473. Neither "I believe I've said what I have to say," *Com. v. Almonte*, 444 Mass 511, 518-519, 829 NE2d 1094, 1101 (2005) nor "Not right now, in a minute. I need to figure some things out," *Com. v. Leahy*, 445 Mass 481, 488-489, 838 NE2d 1220, 1127-1228 (2005), were deemed invocation of the right to remain silent. Although the suspect may say something that might be interpreted as a desire to cut off questioning, if he supplements that with additional remarks that do not convey the same sentiment, it may be insufficient to invoke the right to silence. See *Com. v. Libby*, 472 Mass 37, 53-54, 32 NE3d 890, 904-905 (2015); *Com. v. Rodriguez*, 67 Mass App 636, 648, 855 NE2d 1113, 1122 (2006), *aff'd on other grounds*, 450 Mass 302 (2007). But where the suspect says "I'm done talking. I don't

an expressed unwillingness to continue or an affirmative request for an attorney."[23] Refusal to answer only certain questions or on certain topics may not constitute assertion of the right to silence.[24]

---

wanna talk no more," that is an unambiguous assertion of the right to end the interrogation. *Com. v. Smith*, 473 Mass 798, 808, 46 NE3d 984, 992 (2016).

[23] *Com. v. Pennellatore*, 392 Mass 382, 387, 467 NE2d 820, 823 (1984) (defendant's statements "I guess I'll have to have a lawyer for this" and "Can we stop please?" when viewed in context were not meant as assertion of rights). Compare *Com. v. Hearns*, 467 Mass 707, 717-718, 10 NE2d 108, 116 (2014) (defendant's statement, "Well then, I don't want to talk. I haven't got nothing to say," was a clear invocation of his right to remain silent; defendant made the statement mere moments after waiving his *Miranda* protections, indicating an immediate unwillingness to talk.); *Com. v. Boncore*, 412 Mass 1013, 593 NE2d 227 (1992) (defendant's "No comment" and telephone call seeking his brother, an attorney, constituted invocation of right to remain silent), *Com. v Cobb*, 374 Mass 514, 516-520, 373 NE2d 1145, 143 (1978) (defendant's responses "What can I say?" and "I have nothing to say" construed as invocation of right to remain silent), and *Com. v. Chase*, 70 Mass App 826, 831-832, 877 NE2d 945, 951-952 (2007) ("I ain't talking anymore" was unequivocal assertion of right to remain silent) with *Com. v. Dubois*, 451 Mass 20, 24-26, 883 NE2d 276, 281-283 (2008) (murder suspect's statement to police "maybe I better get a lawyer" was not invocation of right to counsel, and taken together with his failure to respond when asked if he wanted a lawyer, did not demonstrate "expressed unwillingness" to continue the interrogation), *Com. v. Scoggins*, 439 Mass 571, 575, 789 NE2d 1080, 1083 (2003) (mere inquiry regarding the need for an attorney does not require cessation of interrogation), *Com. v. Jones*, 439 Mass 249, 258-259, 86 NE2d 1197, 1206 (2003) (defendant's statement that he was "going to need a lawyer sometime" did not constitute affirmative request), *Com. v. Girouard*, 436 Mass 657, 7665-7666, 66 NE2d 873, 879-880 (2002) (defendant's statement "If I am under arrest, I want an attorney" was not unqualified, unambiguous invocation), *Com. v. Obershaw*, 435 Mass 794, 800-801, 762 NE2d 276, 284 (2002), *habeas petition denied in Obershaw v. Lanman*, 453 F3d 56 (1st Cir 2006) (defendant's question whether he could speak to a lawyer before taking police to his brother's body was not affirmative request for counsel under circumstances), *Com. v. Sicari*, 434 Mass 732, 746-747, 752 NE2d 684, 694-695 (2001) (defendant's interval of silence for 30 to 40 minutes during lengthy interview did not constitute assertion of right to cut off questioning; extensive discussion of whether silence alone mandates termination of questioning), *Com. v. Senior*, 433 Mass 453, 463, 744 NE2d 614, 621 (2001) (defendant's silence in response to one specific question did not constitute affirmative indication he was invoking right to silence).

[24] *Com. v. Roberts*, 407 Mass 731, 733-734, 555 NE2d 588, 590 (1990). A subject cannot pick and choose which questions to answer and later seek to suppress those answers, or his refusal to respond to other questions, at trial. See *Com. v. Robidoux*, 450 Mass 144, 160-161, 877 NE2d 232, 246-247 (2007) (defendant's unwillingness to answer questions about his family was not an assertion of his right to cut off interrogation where he continued to talk about other topics); *Com. v. Santos*, 463 Mass 273, 285, 974 NE2d 1, 12 (2012) (suspect's unwillingness to answer questions on a particular topic is not unambiguous invocation of rights). See also *Com. v. Howard*, 469 Mass 721, 729-734, 16 NE3d 1054, 1063-1066 (2014) ("I'll speak to you but there's certain things that might be kind of sensitive" did not constitute invocation; but later when defendant said "I would like to stop at that point," and the officers sought no clarification, that constituted a post-waiver invocation).

The Supreme Judicial Court has held that the Massachusetts Constitution's right against self-incrimination is more protective than the Fifth Amendment in this regard—it does *not* require a suspect who has never waived his right to remain silent to invoke that right "unambiguously" and with "utmost clarity," as is required by federal law (see *Berghuis v. Thompkins*, 560 US 370 (2010)).[25]

Although not mandating it, the Supreme Judicial Court has emphasized that it is good police practice to ask the suspect clarifying questions when there is ambiguity as to whether *Miranda* rights are being invoked.[26] Where the suspect's initial request to invoke the right to remain silent is sufficiently clear such that a reasonable police officer would understand it to be an actual invocation, the police may not create ambiguity by continuing to question him about it.[27]

Invocation of the right to remain silent does not, however, create an impenetrable wall against further questioning. Rather, the police are permitted to resume interrogation as long as the suspect's right to silence has been "scrupulously honored."[28] The police may not wear

---

[25] *Com. v. Clarke*, 461 Mass 336, 960 NE2d 306 (2012) (extensive discussion of difference between pre-waiver and post-waiver context) (found a sufficient invocation where defendant non-verbally shook his head, indicating a negative response to the detective's question "So you don't want to speak?").

[26] See *Com. v. Howard*, supra, 469 Mass at 734-735, 16 NE3d at 1066; *Com. v. Hearns*, 467 Mass 707, 717-718, 10 NE3d 108, 116-117 (2014) (even if police were uncertain whether defendant was invoking his right to remain silent when he said "Well, then, I don't want to talk. I haven't got nothing to say," the proper course was to attempt to clarify); *Com. v. Santos*, supra, 463 Mass at 286, 974 NE2d at 13 (but police may not inquire as to why the suspect is requesting an attorney); *Com. v. Clarke*, supra, 461 Mass at 351-352, 960 NE2d at 321; *Com. v. Morganti*, 455 Mass 388, 398 n.6, 917 NE2d 191, 201 n.6 (2009) (collection of ambiguous statements). There is no obligation to seek clarification where the defendant simply equivocates, never clearly invoking right to counsel before continuing to speak. *Com. v. Melo*, 472 Mass 278, 295, 34 NE3d 289, 305 (2015).

[27] *Com. v. Clarke*, supra, 461 Mass at 352, 960 NE2d at 321; *Com. v. Hoyt*, 461 Mass 143, 152, 958 NE2d 834, 843 (2011) (post-request responses to further interrogation may not be used to cast retrospective doubt on the clarity of the initial request itself).

[28] *Michigan v. Mosley*, 423 US 96 (1975). For the factors used to evaluate whether defendant's rights were "scrupulously honored," see *Com. v. Howard*, supra, 469 Mass at 735-737, 16 NE3d at 1067-1069. Compare *Com. v. Bins*, 465 Mass 348, 361-362, 989 NE2d 404, 417 (2013) (upon defendant's limited invocation, inviting officers to make renewed attempt to question next day, officers ended the interview and only approached him nine hours later) and *Com. v. Woodbine*, 461 Mass 720, 729-730, 964 NE2d 956, 965 (2012) (no violation where police immediately ceased questioning when defendant stated "I don't want to say anything right now," and only returned to the hospital 17 hours later, re-read him his rights, and resumed questioning), with *Com. v. Smith*, 473 Mass 798, 810-811, 46 NE3d 984, 993-994 (2016) (police did not immediately cease questioning, which continued without a pause, and without a fresh

down the resistance of a suspect who had previously cut off questioning[29] or deliberately elicit a statement from a suspect who has invoked his *Miranda* rights.[30]

It has been held that the police may, subsequent to a suspect's invocation of the right to silence, accurately advise him of a change in circumstances (such as an accomplice's confession) so that he can make "a realistic evaluation of his position,"[31] or truthfully advise him regarding the release of a relative if a confession is made.[32]

If the suspect invokes his right to counsel, an additional safeguard applies—interrogation must cease until an attorney is present (or, as discussed below, the suspect himself initiates further communication).[33] As with the right to remain silent, the suspect must make some

---

set of warnings, and the subject matter remained on the victim's death, rendering defendant's statement inadmissible); *Com. v. Santana*, 465 Mass 270, 282-283, 988 NE2d 825, 836 (2013) (defendant's limited invocation—"I can't say any more"—was not scrupulously honored, and all conversation should have ceased), *Com. v. Clarke*, 461 Mass 336, 344-345, 960 NE2d 306, 315-316 (2012) (detectives did not scrupulously honor defendant's right when they began describing what he could expect if he did not respond to questions, there was no pause, and they then continued to question him about the crimes for which he had been arrested) and *Com. v. Callender*, 81 Mass App 153, 157-161, 960 NE2d 910, 913-916 (2012) (defendant's invocation not scrupulously honored where questioning resumed in only 35 minutes, in same booking room, and without fresh warnings).

[29] See *Com. v. Atkins*, 386 Mass 593, 598, 436 NE2d 1203, 1206-1207 (1982); *Com. v. Brant*, 380 Mass 876, 406 NE2d 1021 (1980) (where law enforcement officials acted to overcome defendant's resistance to interrogation immediately after he invoked his right to silence, statement inadmissible); *Com. v. Jackson*, 377 Mass 319, 325-327, 386 NE2d 15, 19 (1979) (police persistence in questioning and use of trickery in obtaining statement despite fact that defendant twice invoked right to silence rendered statement inadmissible).

[30] See *Com. v. Harvey*, 390 Mass 203, 206, 454 NE2d 105, 107 (1983) (statement suppressed where obtained by confronting defendant with confessed accomplice, a meeting designed to elicit an incriminating response); *Com. v. Gallant*, 381 Mass 465, 410 NE2d 704 (1980) (statement obtained by confronting defendant with his brother's inculpatory statement immediately after defendant asserted right to remain silent was inadmissible). But compare *Com. v. Williams*, 388 Mass 846, 854-855, 448 NE2d 1114, 1120-1121 (1983) (detective's questioning of other suspect in defendant's presence could not be characterized as an impermissible attempt to vitiate defendant's exercise of his *Miranda* rights). See also *Michigan v. Mosley*, 423 US 96 (1975) (where different police officer gave renewed warnings after two-hour lapse and questioned defendant about different crime, earlier refusal to answer questions did not bar admission of the statements obtained in second interrogation).

[31] *Com. v. Jackson*, supra, 377 Mass at 327 n.7, 386 NE2d at 20 n.7.

[32] *Com. v. Hunt*, 12 Mass App 841, 844 n.4, 429 NE2d 379, 380-381 n.4 (1981).

[33] *Edwards v. Arizona*, 451 US 477 (1981); *Miranda v. Arizona*, supra, 384 US at 474; *Com. v. Brant*, supra, 380 Mass at 882, 406 NE2d at 1025-1026; *Com. v. Watkins*, 375 Mass 472, 483-484, 379 NE2d 1040, 1047-1048 (1978) (rejecting argument that *Miranda* prohibits *any* interrogation after suspect requests an attorney).

affirmative statement that can reasonably be construed as a request for counsel; an ambiguous or equivocal reference to an attorney does not require cessation of questioning.[34] Merely musing about the possibility of speaking to a lawyer has consistently been held too ambiguous to constitute an unequivocal invocation of the right to counsel.[35]

Merely providing the suspect at that point with an opportunity to consult with counsel outside the interrogation room is not sufficient;

---

[34] *Davis v. United States*, 512 US 452 (1994) (suspect's remark "maybe I should talk to a lawyer" was not request for counsel). Compare *Com. v. Melo*, 472 Mass 278, 295, 34 NE3d 289, 304-305 (2015) ("I would feel more comfortable if I had a lawyer right now talking, but if you want to show me pictures and names, I'll give it to you" was ambiguous and thus not an effective invocation); *Com. v. Morganti*, 455 Mass 388, 396-398, 917 NE2d 191, 199-201 (2009) (defendant's statement to interrogating officer that he was "thinking I might need a lawyer and want to talk with him before talking to you" was ambiguous and equivocal, and not invocation of right to counsel), *Com. v. Auclair*, 444 Mass 348, 356, 828 NE2d 471, 478-479 (2005) ("That's my story. I'll get a lawyer" did not amount to affirmative invocation), *Com. v. Hussey* (No. 1), supra, 410 Mass at 672, 574 NE2d at 999 (defendant did not invoke right to counsel when he unsuccessfully sought to reach his attorney by telephone and then said "I'm not going to wait. All right I'll tell you what happened."), *Com. v. Todd*, 408 Mass 724, 726-727, 563 NE2d 211, 213 (1990) (defendant "wondered aloud about the advisability of having a lawyer" but made no affirmative request), *Com. v. Corriveau*, 396 Mass 319, 331, 486 NE2d 29, 38 (1985) (defendant's statement, "It's beginning to sound like I need a lawyer" did not constitute request for counsel), *Com. v. Molina*, 81 Mass App 855, 865 -868, 969 NE2d 738, 745-747 (2012), *aff'd*, 467 Mass 65, 3 NE2d 583 (2014) (defendant's statement "if I had known that this would be like this, I honestly would have brought an attorney" was not an unequivocal request for counsel), and *Com. v. Epifania*, 80 Mass App 71, 74-75, 951 NE2d 723, 726 (2011) (defendant's post-waiver question during interrogation regarding whether he would be allowed to have an attorney present during any voice-stress test was not an unambiguous invocation of right to counsel) with *Com. v. Hoyt*, 461 Mass 143, 958 NE2d 834 (2011) (defendant's statement that he wanted an attorney present but could not afford one was an unambiguous invocation of right to counsel), *Com. v. Judge*, 420 Mass 433, 450, 650 NE2d 1242, 1252-1253 (1995) (defendant's initial request that his uncle, an attorney, be called was sufficient to invoke right to counsel despite fact that defendant continued to talk to police), *Com. v. Contos*, 435 Mass 19, 28-30, 754 NE2d 647, 655-657 (2001) (defendant's statement "I think I'm going to get a lawyer" was unambiguous invocation of right to counsel), *Com. v. Segovia*, 53 Mass App 184, 190-191, 57 NE2d 752, 758 (2001) (a reasonable police officer would have understood defendant's request to consult with paralegal friend as request for counsel), *Com. v. Barros*, 56 Mass 675, 681, 779 NE2d 693, 698 (2002) ("I don't want to talk to you anymore without a lawyer" was unambiguous invocation), and *Com. v. LeClair*, 55 Mass App 238, 770 NE2d 50 (2002) (defendant's expressed desire for counsel at scene of arrest and during booking constituted invocation). See also *Com. v. Maynard*, 436 Mass 558, 568-569, 767 NE2d 1, 11-12 (2002) (leaving undecided question of whether suspect's question "should I have an attorney" requires cessation of questioning).

[35] *Com. v. Vincent*, 469 Mass 786, 796-797, 17 NE3d 1045, 1053-1054 (2014) (defendant's several comments about getting a lawyer were all followed by his continuing to talk).

the accused is entitled upon request to have counsel present during questioning.[36] The presence of an attorney during police questioning of a suspect, when the suspect also had an opportunity to consult with counsel beforehand, is an adequate substitute for the giving of *Miranda* warnings under both the federal and state constitutions.[37] The right to counsel in connection with custodial interrogation is the right to effective assistance of counsel—to at least minimally competent advice.[38]

Although a suspect who is not "in custody" has no constitutional right to counsel and thus a request for counsel does not require termination of questioning, the Supreme Judicial Court has admonished police against discouraging the suspect from seeking legal advice; such conduct, if sufficiently egregious, will eviscerate the voluntariness of any subsequent statement.[39]

Once the right to counsel is invoked and questioning is thus terminated, interrogation may be resumed in the absence of counsel only if the suspect himself initiates further communication with the police.[40] This constraint upon further interrogation applies even if the resumed questioning concerns an unrelated offense.[41] Fresh warnings and evidence of voluntariness are not sufficient to overcome the presumption that any subsequent waiver in the absence of counsel is invalid.[42] The purpose of this rule is to protect the suspect from being worn down in his effort to obtain the assistance of counsel.[43] Thus, a

---

[36] See *Minnick v. Mississippi*, 498 US 146 (1990).

[37] See *Com. v. Simon*, 456 Mass 280, 923 NE2d 58 (2010).

[38] *Com. v. Celester*, 473 Mass 553, 567-568, 45 NE3d 539, 552-553 (2016) (counsel's advice to defendant to make an inculpatory statement to police without conducting any investigation of the case was constitutionally deficient).

[39] *Com. v. Groome*, 435 Mass 201, 19-20 & n.21, 755 NE2d 1224, 1236-1237 & n.21 (2001). Compare *Com. v. Gaynor*, 443 Mass 245, 256-257, 820 NE2d 233, 244-246 2005) (defendant's spontaneous remarks made to police while not in custody).

[40] *Edwards v. Arizona*, 451 US 477 (1981); *Com. v. Perez*, supra, 411 Mass at 256-259, 581 NE2d at 1015-1017 (general discussion of *Edwards* rule). Compare *Com. v. Jackson*, 447 Mass 603, 613, 855 NE2d 1097, 1104-1105 (2006) (suspect's unsolicited statements to officer guarding him permitted recommencement of questioning) with *Com. v. Santos*, 463 Mass 273, 286, 974 NE2d 1, 13 (2012) (where defendant continued speaking after invocation of right to counsel, police should have ceased interrogation and sought clarification). A request for consent to search after invocation is not considered a resumption of interrogation. See *Com. v. Letkowski*, 83 Mass App 847, 853, 991 NE2d 1106, 1111 (2013).

[41] See *Arizona v. Roberson*, 486 US 675 (1988).

[42] *Edwards v. Arizona*, supra, 451 US at 484-487; *Com. v. Perez*, 411 Mass 249, 257, 581 NE2d 1010, 1015-1016 (1991).

[43] *Minnick v. Mississippi*, supra, 498 US at 150-151; *Com. v. Perez*, supra, 411 Mass at 257-258, 581 NE2d at 1015-1016; *Com. v. Chadwick*, 40 Mass App 425, 429, 664

valid waiver cannot be established merely by showing that defendant responded to further police-initiated interrogation.[44]

The rule indefinitely terminating questioning applies only where there is continuous custody of the suspect. When there is a break in custody, like the release of the subject, exclusion of a subsequent statement even in the absence of counsel is not mandated. The Supreme Court has determined that the *Edwards* rule does not apply to forbid further interrogation where there is a break in custody lasting 14 days or more, thus allowing time for the suspect to shake off the residual coercive effects of his custody.[45] Where custody is continuous, however, even a lapse of six months between termination of the initial interrogation and the subsequent questioning cannot justify resumption in the absence of counsel.[46]

As noted above, interrogation may resume after invocation of the right to counsel where the suspect himself initiates communication. Although questions relating to the routine incidents of custody do not constitute "initiation," a suspect's question "What is going to happen to me now?" was deemed to evidence a desire for further discussion about the investigation, thus permitting interrogation to resume.[47]

NE2d 874, 876 (1996). See, e.g., *Com. v. Thomas*, 469 Mass 531, 541-543, 21 NE3d 901, 911-913 (2014) (detective, in an effort to change her decision, improperly suggested that by "lawyering up," defendant was losing her opportunity to tell her side of the story). *Thomas* declares improper the interrogation technique of telling the suspect who has invoked the right to counsel that this is the last chance to tell your story (reconsidering *Com. v. Novo*, 442 Mass 262, 267, 812 NE2d 1169 (2004)).

[44] *Com. v. Thomas*, supra, 469 Mass at 539, 21 NE3d at 910.

[45] *Maryland v. Shatzer*, 559 US 98 (2010) (prisoner's return to general prison population on unrelated conviction after invocation of right to counsel constituted a break in custody). For application of *Shatzer*, see *Com. v. Thomas*, 469 Mass 531, 545-547, 21 NE3d 901, 915-916 (2014). See also *Com. v. Lopes*, 455 Mass 147, 163-164, 914 NE2d 78, 92 (2009), *habeas denied*, 2013 WL 819330 (D Mass 2012) (since defendant was no longer in custody after his handcuffs were removed and he was told he was not under arrest, police were not obliged to refrain from questioning him even though he had invoked his right to remain silent); *Com. v. Galford*, 413 Mass 364, 370, 597 NE2d 410, 414 (1992).

[46] See *Com. v. Perez*, supra, 411 Mass at 258, 581 NE2d at 1016.

[47] *Oregon v. Bradshaw*, 462 US 1039 (1983). For cases defining "initiation" in this context, see *Com. v. Thomas*, supra, 469 Mass at 548-549, 21 NE3d at 917-918 (defendant's statement "I'm not a bad person" was sufficient to initiate further discussion with police because it could reasonable be interpreted as relating to the investigation); *Com. v. LeClair*, 445 Mass 734, 737-739, 840 NE2d 510, 513-514 (2006) (defendant twice inquired of officer whether he needed counsel and asked whether he was in "big trouble," thus evidencing a desire for more conversation about the killing); *Com. v. Phinney*, 416 Mass 364, 371, 622 NE2d 617, 622 (1993) (suspect initiated further conversation by asking "What's going to happen to me next?"); *Com. v. Richmond*, 379 Mass 557, 560, 399 NE2d 1069, 1072 (1980) (police could resume interrogation after

The Commonwealth has the burden of proving beyond a reasonable doubt that a defendant who has earlier invoked his right to counsel has nonetheless decided independently to confess without an attorney, i.e., a valid waiver.[48]

Neither a request to consult with a probation officer,[49] nor a family member,[50] nor a high school guidance counselor[51] constitutes a request for counsel for purposes of cutting off questioning.[52] There is no constitutional right to have a family member present during custodial interrogation.[53]

The *Miranda* doctrine does not apply to school officials who are not acting as agents of police; they are not required to give *Miranda* warnings prior to questioning a student in conjunction with a school investigation.[54] Nor were warnings required where defendant spoke with a jail snitch who, acting as a government agent, engaged the defendant in a conversation about the crime.[55]

Neither the defendant's invocation of his *Miranda* rights[56] nor his silence following *Miranda* warnings may be used against him at trial.[57]

---

defendant questioned police as to details of crime); *Com. v. Letkowski*, supra, 83 Mass App at 852-853, 991 NE2d at 1111 (defendant said he had changed his mind and wished to give his side of the story). See also *Com. v. Nom*, 426 Mass 152, 156-158, 686 NE2d 1017, 1022 (1997) (officer's asking defendant why he wanted attorney was not re-interrogation, but only request for clarification regarding defendant's initiation of conversation).

[48] *Com. v. Judge*, supra, 420 Mass at 450-451, 650 NE2d at 1253; *Com. v. Thomas*, supra, 469 Mass at 549-550, 21 NE3d at 917-918.

[49] See *Fare v. Michael C.*, 442 US 707 (1979).

[50] See *Com. v. Bradshaw*, 385 Mass 244, 263-264, 431 NE2d 880, 893 (1982) and *Com. v. Carey*, 26 Mass App 339, 343, 526 NE2d 1329, 1332 (1988).

[51] See *Com. v. Denis*, 442 Mass 617, 631-632, 814 NE2d 1080, 1092-1093 (2004).

[52] See also *Com. v. Jackson*, supra, 377 Mass at 322 n.4, 386 NE2d at 17 n.4 (leaving open question whether request to see parole officer constitutes invocation of rights).

[53] *Com. v. Bradshaw*, supra, 385 Mass at 264, 431 NE2d at 893.

[54] *Com. v. Ira I.*, 439 Mass 805, 812-813, 791 NE2d 894, 900-901 (2003).

[55] *Com. v. Burgos*, 470 Mass 133, 145-147, 19 NE3d 843, 853-854 (2014).

[56] *Com. v. Letkowski*, 469 Mass 603, 15 NE3d 207 (2014) (prosecutor improperly referred to defendant's invocation of rights and silence during questioning of two witnesses and in closing); *Com. v. Isabelle*, 444 Mass 416, 419, 828 NE2d 53, 56 (2005), *habeas denied*, 568 F Supp 2d 85 (D Mass 2008); *Com. v. Toolan*, 460 Mass 452, 470-473, 951 NE2d 903, 920-921 (2011) (permissible for the prosecutor, without reference to *Miranda* rights, to introduce testimony and comment on evidence that defendant's actions upon arrest, and his apparent attempt to use the interview with police to acquire information, showed his sanity; but the references to defendant's constitutional rights came "dangerously close to an improper suggestion that the defendant was manipulating his constitutional rights to his own advantage"); *Com. v. Chase*, 70 Mass App 826, 831, 877 NE2d 945, 950-951 (2007). See also § 12.6.8, infra.

[57] See § 12.6.8.

Provision of the warnings carries the implicit assurance that a defendant's exercise of his rights will not penalize him at trial.[58] A prosecutor may not comment on defendant's invocation of his right to remain silent.[59] Even where defendant does not file a pretrial motion to suppress, a reasonable objection at trial places the burden on the Commonwealth to establish that defendant's rights were not violated.[60] Where defendant speaks following administration of the warnings, his statements may be used at trial to point out differences with his testimony or theory of defense.[61]

Upon arrest or detention, a foreign national is entitled under the Vienna Convention of Consular Relations to be notified without delay that he has the right of consular assistance.[62]

§ 12.6.2 Custody

Custodial interrogation, the event that triggers the *Miranda* protections, is defined as "questioning initiated by law enforcement officers after a person has been taken into custody or otherwise deprived of his freedom of action in any significant way."[63] A person is in "custody" if he is under formal arrest or subject to a "restraint on freedom of movement of the degree associated with a formal arrest."[64] Any formal distinction between "arrest" and "detention" becomes immaterial in light of this definition.[65] A defendant seeking to suppress his

---

[58] *Com. v. Robidoux*, 450 Mass 144, 160, 877 NE2d 232, 246 (2007). The warnings carry that assurance whether or not the defendant was under arrest or in custody at the time. *Com. v. Chase*, 70 Mass App 826, 832, 877 NE2d 945, 951 (2007).

[59] *Com. v. Howard*, 469 Mass 721, 743, 16 NE3d 1054, 1073 (2014); *Com. v. Letkowski*, supra, 469 Mass at 616, 15 NE3d at 217 (prosecutor improperly referred to defendant's invocation of rights and silence during closing, claiming that showed calculated behavior and undercut his defense of lack of responsibility).

[60] *Com. v. Ka*, 70 Mass App 137, 140, 873 NE2d 249, 251 (2007).

[61] See *Com. v. Rivera*, 62 Mass App 859, 861-862, 821 NE2d 928, 931 (2005).

[62] *Com. v. Gautreaux*, 458 Mass 741, 941 NE2d 616 (2011).

[63] *Miranda v. Arizona*, 384 US 436, 443 (1966).

[64] *Thompson v. Keohane*, 516 US 99, 112 (1995); *New York v. Quarles*, 467 US 649 (1984).

[65] See, e.g., *Com. v. Damiano*, 422 Mass 10, 660 NE2d 660 (1996) (defendant in custody while handcuffed in back seat of cruiser; fact that police asserted defendant was not under arrest but in protective custody is not controlling where reasonable person would have believed he was not free to leave).

statement bears the burden of proving custody.[66] Absent custody, *Miranda* does not apply.[67]

"There is no specific formulation on which we can rely as an aid in determining whether a person's freedom of action is sufficiently curtailed so as to require the so called *Miranda* warnings."[68] Rather the test is how a reasonable person in the defendant's position would have understood his situation.[69] *Com. v. Bryant* sets forth four indicia of custody:

1. The place of the interrogation.
2. Whether the investigation has begun to focus on the suspect, including whether there is probable cause to arrest the suspect.
3. The nature of the interrogation, including whether the interview was aggressive or, instead, informal and influenced in its contours by the suspect.
4. Whether, at the time the incriminating statement was made, the suspect was free to end the interview by leaving the locus of the interrogation or by asking the interrogator to leave, as evidenced by whether the interview terminated with the defendant's arrest.[70]

---

[66] *Com. v. Girouard*, 436 Mass 657, 665-666, 66 NE2d 873, 880 (2002); *Com. v. Alcala*, 54 Mass App 49, 53, 763 NE2d 516, 520 (2002) (& citations).

[67] See, e.g., *Com. v. Caldwell*, 459 Mass 271, 286, 945 NE2d 313, 327-328 (2011) (defendant not in custody when he engaged in tape-recorded telephone conversations with informant); *Com. v. Nadworny*, 396 Mass 342, 367-369, 486 NE2d 675, 690-691 (1985) (neither statements made to police officer over telephone, nor conversation at defendant's family home, were custodial); *Com. v. Martinez*, 393 Mass 612, 615, 473 NE2d 167, 168-169 (1985) (defendant's statement, overheard by police officer while she was not in custody and not the product of police questioning, was admissible without proof of warnings); *Com. v. Clark C.*, 59 Mass App 542, 544, 797 NE2d 5, 8 (2003) (juvenile not in custody while making statement over telephone).

The Supreme Judicial Court has declined to reach the question of whether police are required to honor a defendant's *precustodial* invocation of *Miranda* rights. *Com. v. Molina*, 467 Mass 65, 75 n.11, 3 NE3d 583, 592 n.11 (2014).

[68] *Com. v. Haas*, 373 Mass 545, 552, 369 NE2d 692, 698 (1977).

[69] *Com. v. A Juvenile*, 402 Mass 275, 277, 521 NE2d 1368, 1370 (1988) (& citations).

[70] 390 Mass 729, 737, 459 NE2d 792, 798 (1984). See also *Com. v. Hilton*, 443 Mass 597, 608-609, 823 NE2d 383, 394-395 (2005), *appeal after remand*, 450 Mass 173, 877 NE2d 545 (2007); *Com. v. LeBeau*, 451 Mass 244, 254 n.11, 884 NE2d 956, 965 n.11 (2008), *habeas denied*, *LeBeau v. Roden*, 806 F Supp 2d 384 (D Mass 2011); *Com. v. Groome*, 435 Mass 201, 211-215, 755 NE2d 1224, 1233-1236 (2001); *Com. v. Vinnie*,

The issue of whether an interrogation has occurred in custodial circumstances "is a vexing one, susceptible to resolution in most instances only by close scrutiny of the particular questioning session."[71] "The difficulties inherent in determining whether a given confrontation between suspect and police is appropriately characterized as custodial derive from the necessity of answering what is essentially a subjective inquiry—whether, from the point of view of the person being questioned, the interrogation took place in a coercive environment—by reference to objective indicia."[72]

The fact that the investigation has begun to focus on the defendant is not, in itself, sufficient to trigger the *Miranda* protections.[73] Nor is the duration of the questioning determinative.[74] Nor does an interrogation become custodial simply because a suspect's voluntary statements give the police probable cause to arrest unless the police do in fact arrest the suspect or the suspect reasonably believes himself to be restrained.[75] The non-arrest of the suspect at the close of the interrogation is indicative of the lack of custodial atmosphere during interrogation.[76]

---

428 Mass 161, 170-171, 698 NE2d 896, 905 (1998); *Com. v. Morse*, 427 Mass 117, 121-122, 691 NE2d 566, 569-570 (1998); *Com. v. Jung*, 420 Mass 675, 688, 651 NE2d 1211, 1220 (1995); *Com. v. Gallati*, 40 Mass App 111, 661 NE2d 948 (1996).

[71] *Com. v. Bryant*, supra, 390 Mass at 736, 459 NE2d at 797.

[72] *Id.*

[73] *Beckwith v. United States*, 425 US 341 (1976); *United States v. Ventura*, 85 F3d 708, 712 (1st Cir 1996); *Com. v. Libby*, 472 Mass 37, 46, 32 NE3d 890, 899 (2015); *Com. v. Vinnie*, supra, 428 Mass at 171, 698 NE2d at 905; *Com. v. Jung*, supra, 420 Mass at 688-689, 651 NE2d at 1219-1220 (although investigation focused solely on defendants, interrogation was noncustodial because not conducted in aggressive manner, suspects went to police station voluntarily, were free to leave at any time, and were not arrested at end of interview); *Com. v. Phinney*, 416 Mass 364, 370, 622 NE2d 617, 621 (1993); *Com. v. Trombley*, 72 Mass App 183, 186, 889 NE2d 446, 449 (2008) (defendant not in custody even though officers told him that he was suspect and interview took place in police station, because he came to station voluntarily, his interrogation was conversational, and he was permitted to leave with his mother at the end). Compare *Com. v. Molina*, supra, 467 Mass at 74-75, 3 NE3d at 592 (fact that officer aggressively peppered defendant with accusations that he was lying changed interrogation into custodial one).

[74] *Com. v. Comolli*, 14 Mass App 607, 610-611, 441 NE2d 536, 539 (1982) (interrogation of defendant at scene of accident not necessarily custodial even though defendant was questioned in police cruiser for over an hour); *Com. v. Doyle*, 12 Mass App 786, 794 n.2, 429 NE2d 346, 351 n.2 (1981) (rejecting a "quantitative approach").

[75] *Com. v. Bryant*, supra, 390 Mass at 738-739, 549 NE2d at 799 (interrogation did not become custodial where, after suspect stated, "I did it, I shot him," officer made non-accusatorial inquiry as to whether the suspect had anything more to say).

[76] *Com. v. Bryant*, supra, 390 Mass at 742 n.15, 459 NE2d at 800 (& citations); *Com. v. Clemente*, 452 Mass 295, 327-328, 903 NE2d 19, 47 (2008).

Since the courts apply an objective standard of "custody"[77] in which the ultimate issue is whether a reasonable person in the position of the subject would not feel free to leave the place of questioning,[78] neither the subjective feelings of the interrogator or the suspect are determinative. The intent of the police officer to restrain the suspect does not enter into the "custody" determination unless it is communicated to the suspect.[79] How the defendant actually felt at the time is not critical, but instead whether there were objective features of the interrogation that would reasonably lead the subject to believe his freedom of action had been curtailed. "To emphasize a defendant's purely subjective feelings about 'custody,' without considering the reasonableness of those feelings, would allow issues to turn not on the objective circumstances of the questioning, but on the personal idiosyncracies that are neither within the control of, nor necessarily observable by, investigating personnel. The law imposes no burden on the police to divine a suspect's subjective impressions."[80]

Even though a reasonable person in defendant's position might believe he is the subject of the investigation, he is not "in custody" if a reasonable person would have concluded that he was free to terminate the interview and ask the police to leave.[81] A reasonable person who knows of an outstanding warrant and is in the company of police officers who also know of the warrant would recognize he is not free to

---

[77] *Com. v. Bryant*, supra, 390 Mass at 739 n.11, 459 NE2d at 799 n.11.

[78] *Com. v. Larkin*, 429 Mass 426, 432, 708 NE2d 674, 679 (1999) (& citations); *Com. v. Morse*, supra, 427 Mass at 124-125, 691 NE2d at 571-572 (& citations) (officer's pointing out inconsistency between defendant's and witness's statements would not suggest to reasonable person that he was not free to leave).

[79] *Stansbury v. California*, 511 US 318, 323 (1994); *Com. v. Bryant*, supra; *Com. v. Garcia*, 443 Mass 824, 832, 824 NE2d 864, 870-871 (2005) *habeas denied*, *Garcia v. Russo*, 844 F Supp 2d 187 (D Mass 2011) (detective did not communicate to defendant that he had become a suspect); *Com. v. Groome*, 435 Mass 201, 212 n.13, 755 NE2d 1224, 1234 n.13 (2001); *Com. v. Burbine*, 74 Mass App 148, 151-152, 904 NE2d 787, 790-791 (2009) (because officer did not communicate his intent to arrest defendant, he was not in custody and officer was not required to give warnings before asking questions in parking lot concerning weapons in bag); *Com. v. Becla*, 74 Mass App 142, 904 NE2d 783 (2009) (because officer did not communicate his intent to arrest motorist, he was not in custody for purposes of few modest questions); *Com. v. Cameron*, 44 Mass App 912, 689 NE2d 1365 (1998) (officer formed opinion that motorist was intoxicated but did not communicate it to him).

[80] *Com. v. Comolli*, supra, 14 Mass App at 611-612, 441 NE2d at 539-540.

[81] *Com. v. Conkey*, 430 Mass 139, 145, 714 NE2d 343, 349 (1999) (interview took place in defendant's residence, was conducted by state trooper he knew, and was not aggressive). See also *Com. v. Baye*, 462 Mass 246, 254, 967 NE2d 1120, 1128 (2012) (a reasonable person may believe that he is a suspect but also that he is free to terminate the interview).

leave, and is thus in custody.[82] In the case of a juvenile, the focus is on how a reasonable person in the juvenile's position would have understood his situation.[83]

A youth's age is relevant in deciding whether he is in custody, provided the age was known to the officer at the time or would have been objectively apparent to a reasonable officer.[84] Individualized factors peculiar to the defendant, such as status as a special needs student, do not bear on the determination.[85]

Custodial interrogation may occur anywhere—one need not be in a police station to be deemed in custody. Custody has been found where the interrogation has been conducted in the defendant's own bedroom[86] or office.[87] Even though questioning in familiar surroundings like one's home is not often construed as oppressive for *Miranda* purposes,[88] the determinative factor is whether a reasonable person

---

[82] *Com. v. Thomas*, 469 Mass 531, 540, 21 NE3d 901, 911 (2014).

[83] See also *Yarborough v. Alvarado*, 124 S Ct 2140 (2004) (federal law does not mandate that state courts weigh juvenile's age in making custody determination).

[84] *J.D.B. v. North Carolina*, 131 S Ct 2394 (2011). See also *Yarborough v. Alvarado*, 541 US 652 (2004) (juvenile's "actual mindset" does not enter into the analysis); *Com. v. Ira I.*, 439 Mass 805, 814, 791 NE2d 894, 902 (2003) (juvenile not in custody when being questioned by assistant principal in his office).

[85] *Com. v. Bermudez*, 83 Mass App 46, 51-54, 980 NE2d 462, 467-469 (2012) (finding no custody in interrogation of 17-year-old special needs student in police station, where he appeared voluntarily accompanied by his mother, interrogation was conversational, and he was told he was free to leave).

[86] See *Orozco v. Texas*, 394 US 324 (1969) (suspect interrogated by four officers in his bedroom); *Com. v. Coleman*, 49 Mass App 150, 727 NE2d 103 (2000) (defendant questioned in accusatory and aggressive fashion in small bedroom by three officers, one of whom blocked the door). Compare *Com. v. Carnes*, 457 Mass 812, 816-819, 933 NE2d 598, 604-606 (2010) (19-year-old defendant was not in custody where he agreed to meet with detectives in a house owned by his family, his father and baby daughter were present, interview was informal and cordial, and lasted only 75 minutes); *Com. v. Mitchell*, 89 Mass App 13, 17-19, 45 NE3d 111, 116-117 (2016) (16-year-old not in custody when interviewed at his kitchen table, with family present, and officers stated they would leave if anyone felt uncomfortable).

[87] *Com. v. Gallati*, 40 Mass App 111, 661 NE2d 948 (1996) (defendant correctional officer in custody even though not under arrest when questioned by superior in his office, investigation had focused on him, and questioning was domineering and relentless).

[88] See, e.g., *Beckwith v. United States*, supra, 425 US 341 (defendant not in custody when questioned at home by special agents of IRS conducting criminal investigation); *Com. v. Kirwan*, 448 Mass 304, 309-313, 860 NE2d 931, 936-939 (2007) (interrogation not custodial where detective was invited into apartment by defendant's father, who was present during non-aggressive questioning by one officer that focused on general fact-finding regarding the crime), *habeas denied, Kirwan v. Spencer*, 631 F3d 582 (1st Cir 2011); *Com. v. Sneed*, 440 Mass 216, 796 NE2d 1284 (2003) (interview of ill elderly larceny suspect in her home was not custodial where there was no evidence of raised

in the circumstances would have found the setting isolating and coercive.[89]

Conversely, the fact that the interrogation occurs in a police station does not in itself establish it as "custodial."[90] A suspect incarcerated on an unrelated charge may not be deemed in custody where he

---

voices on part of interrogators, she freely left room at one point to speak to daughter on telephone, and she was not placed under arrest at end of interview); *Com. v. O'Brien*, 432 Mass 578, 585-586, 736 NE2d 841, 849-850 (2000) (questioning of juvenile at hospital not custodial when he was interviewed as a robbery victim, not suspect in murder case); *Com. v. Morais*, 431 Mass 380, 382, 727 NE2d 831, 833 (2000) (no custody when defendant was interviewed by DSS investigator after voluntarily appearing at department office); *Com. v. Gendraw*, 55 Mass App 677, 682-684, 774 NE2d 167, 173-174 (2002) (defendant not in custody when he invited police into his home and talked in his kitchen); *Com. v. Eagles*, 419 Mass 825, 832-833, 648 NE2d 410, 416 (1995) (defendant not in custody at residence); *Breese v. Com.*, 415 Mass 249, 255-256, 612 NE2d 1170, 1173-1174 (1993) (no custody where defendant was questioned in familiar surroundings of home and workplace); *Com. v. Tart*, supra, 408 Mass at 258, 557 NE2d at 1131 (no custody where defendant was questioned on board his own fishing vessel surrounded by his employees); *Com. v. Bryant*, supra, 390 Mass at 737-738, 459 NE2d at 797-798 (no custodial interrogation where confession occurred during friendly chat in defendant's home with defendant's acquiescence); *Com. v. Zhan Tang Huang*, 87 Mass App 65, 25 NE3d 315 (2015) (defendant was briefly questioned in a public venue, in the presence of his wife, in familiar surroundings, and the questions were designed to elicit basic information). Compare *United States v. Rogers*, 659 F3d 74 (1st Cir 2011) (member of armed forces was in custody when he was ordered home by his commander and found three police officers in control of his house and questioning his wife); *Com. v. Werner*, 81 Mass App 689, 701-704, 967 NE2d 159, 169-171 (2012) (instructing jury during cross-examination of state trooper that *Miranda* warnings were not required during questioning of defendant at coffee shop since she was not in custody).

[89] *Com. v. Sneed*, supra, 440 Mass at 220, 796 NE2d at 1287.

[90] See, e.g., *California v. Beheler*, 463 US 1121 (1983) (suspect, informed he was not under arrest, agreed to accompany police to station for questioning); *Oregon v. Mathiason*, 429 US 492 (1977) (suspect reported to station voluntarily at officer's request, was informed he was not under arrest, and was not restricted in his freedom to depart); *Com. v. Libby*, 472 Mass 37, 45-46, 32 NE3d 890, 899-900 (2015) (suspect voluntarily accompanied police to the station and was expressly told several times he was not under arrest); *Com. v. Molina*, 467 Mass 65, 73-74, 3 NE3d 583, 591-592 (2014) (defendant voluntarily accompanied police to station for questioning, and interview was relaxed and informal in tone); *Com. v. Morales*, 461 Mass 765, 774-776, 965 NE2d 177, 186-187 (2012) (defendant voluntarily went to police station at request of police, questioning was not aggressive, nothing conveyed that he was a suspect, and he was advised he was not under arrest, not obligated to speak with them, and free to leave); *Com. v. Mejia*, 461 Mass 384, 389-391, 961 NE2d 72, 78-79 (2012) (defendant not in custody when he voluntarily accompanied plain clothes detective to hospital conference room, was not initially restrained, and not told police were seeking an arrest warrant); *Com. v. Bly*, 448 Mass 473, 491-493, 862 NE2d 341, 357-358 (2007) (suspect went to police station voluntarily, was interviewed in an opened door office and not an interrogation room, and the investigation was in its nascent stages); *Com. v., Peterson*, 445 Mass 782, 788-789, 840 NE2d 913, 918 (2006) (defendant was informed twice he

would not reasonably feel himself confined beyond the usual constraints of prison life.[91] Pretrial court-ordered psychiatric

---

was not under arrest and thus not required to go to police station); *Com. v. Almonte*, 444 Mass 511, 518, 829 NE2d 1094, 1100 (2005) (defendant not in custody when he appeared voluntarily at police task force base, officer did nothing to convey to defendant that he was a suspect and in fact had no knowledge of the murder until later on); *Com. v. Hilton*, 443 Mass 597, 609-610, 823 NE2d 383, 395 (2005), appeal after remand, 450 Mass 173, 877 NE2d 545 (2007); (defendant voluntarily accompanied police to station where she had been interviewed two days earlier and allowed to leave); *Com. v. Garcia*, 443 Mass 824, 831-832, 824 NE2d 864, 870 (2005), *habeas denied*, *Garcia v. Russo*, 2011 WL 6370693 (D Mass 2011) (defendant volunteered to go to police station, was escorted through visitor's entrance, interviewed for only short period, and agreed to wait while officers conferred); *Com. v. Murphy*, 442 Mass 485, 492-493, 813 NE2d 820, 828 (2004) (defendant voluntarily accompanied police to station and during informal interview was asked to provide background information about victims); *Com. v. Brum*, 438 Mass 103, 111-112, 777 NE2d 1238, 1246-1247 (2002) (even though interrogation occurred in police station, it was arranged by defendant's brother at time and place of defendant's choosing with an officer already known to defendant, not indicating defendant was a particular suspect, and defendant was expressly told he was free to leave); *Com. v. Groome*, 435 Mass 201, 214-215, 755 NE2d 1224, 1236 (2001) (defendant not in custody although in police cruiser and state police barracks); *Com. v. Sparks*, 433 Mass 654, 656-657, 746 NE2d 133, 135-136 (2001) (defendant went voluntarily to police station and was not restrained in any way while questioned, there was no probable cause to arrest him, and he was not focus of investigation); *Com. v. Duguay*, 430 Mass 397, 400-401, 720 NE2d 458, 461-462 (1999) (defendant not in custody while in cruiser after agreeing to accompany officers to police station), *habeas denied, Duguay v. Spencer*, 462 F Supp 2d 115 (D Mass 2006); *Com. v. Sim*, 39 Mass App 212, 220-221, 654 NE2d 340, 345 (1995) (defendant came willingly to police station, was allowed to roam about, and was not told he was required to stay); *Com. v. Wallen*, 35 Mass App 915, 619 NE2d 365 (1993) (no indication defendant's presence at police station to give his version of events was not voluntary); *Com. v. Greenberg*, 34 Mass App 197, 200-201, 609 NE2d 90, 92-93 (1993) (juvenile defendant not in custody when, at police request, he and his father drove to police station and he was questioned, with father present, for one hour, but not arrested until four days later). See also *Minnesota v. Murphy*, supra, 465 US at 430-434 (probationer appearing for required appearance before probation officer not "in custody" for purposes of *Miranda* protections). But compare *Com. v. Cruz*, 373 Mass 676, 682-684, 369 NE2d 996, 1001 (1977) (defendant voluntarily accompanied police to station for questioning, but after one hour of questioning he was no longer free to leave and thus in custody).

[91] *Maryland v. Shatzer*, 130 S Ct 1213 (2010) (state prisoner's return to general prison population constituted a break in custody for *Miranda* purposes); *Com. v. Smith*, 456 Mass 476, 478-480, 924 NE2d 270, 275-276 (2010) (defendant not in custody even though interviewed as murder suspect by police while in prison on unrelated charge, where interview was in open area, defendant's handcuffs were removed, police did not convey that they believed he killed victim, interviews were free of antagonism, and defendant was not charged at end of interview); *Com. v. John*, 442 Mass 329, 335 n.12, 812 NE2d 1218, 1223 n.12 (2004), *habeas petition denied in John v. Russo*, 455 F Supp 2d 1 (D Mass 2006), *aff'd*, 561 F3d 88 (1st Cir 2009); *Com. v. Girouard*, 436 Mass 657, 7665-7666, 66 NE2d 873, 879-880 (2002) (defendant incarcerated on unrelated

examinations are custodial and thus warnings are required before interrogation.[92]

Because of its noncustodial nature, "on the scene questioning" does not generally require warnings.[93] Roadside questioning of a motorist during a routine traffic stop has similarly been viewed as noncustodial (although subsequent events may render the motorist "in custody"),[94] as is preliminary questioning at accident scenes.[95] Roadside sobriety tests have been held noncustodial and thus not subject to *Miranda*.[96] Moreover, since such tests seek physical and not testimonial evidence, they do not trigger the Fifth Amendment privilege

---

parole violation). But compare *Com. v. A Juvenile*, 402 Mass 275, 277-278, 521 NE2d 1368, 1370 (1988) (confession made by juvenile in detention facility to assistant director was custodial).

[92] *Estelle v. Smith*, 451 US 454, 466-469 (1981).

[93] *Miranda v. Arizona*, supra, 384 US at 477; *Com. v. Callahan*, 401 Mass 627, 630, 519 NE2d 245, 247 (1988) (police officer's "What happened?" question at homicide scene); *Com. v. Podlaski*, 377 Mass 339, 342-343, 385 NE2d 1379, 1382-1383 (1979) (preliminary inquiry to defendant aimed at discovering what he knew about the circumstances of the assault).

[94] See *Berkemer v. McCarty*, 468 US 420, 435-442 (1984); *Com. v. Sauer*, 50 Mass App 299, 737 NE2d 10 (2000); *Com. v. Smith*, 35 Mass App 655, 657, 624 NE2d 604, 606 (1993) ("when a police officer makes a motor vehicle pull over, the driver is not free to move away, but it would surely be untoward to require that a police officer approach a stopped vehicle declaiming the *Miranda* warnings"); *Com. v. Cameron*, 44 Mass App 912, 913-914, 689 NE2d 1365, 1367-1368 (1998) (*Miranda* warnings not required during temporary detention, questioning, and field sobriety tests). But see *Com. v. Torres*, 424 Mass 153, 158, 674 NE2d 638, 642 (1997) and *Com. v. Bartlett*, 41 Mass App 468, 671 NE2d 515 (1996) (police inquiry in routine traffic stop must end on production of valid license and registration unless police have reasonable suspicion of crime).

[95] *Com. v. McGrail*, 80 Mass App 339, 346, 952 NE2d 969, 976 (2011) (questioning of defendant at scene of accident and in hospital was general fact-finding); *Com. v. Lavender*, 79 Mass App 501, 947 NE2d 93 (2011) (defendant questioned in house near accident scene which defendant had entered); *Com. v. Lafleur*, 58 Mass App 546, 791 NE2d 380 (2003) (no custody where defendant questioned by police while strapped in stretcher and taken into ambulance); *Com. v. Seymour*, 39 Mass App 672, 679-680, 660 NE2d 679, 683 (1996) (fact that police officer observed that defendant smelled of alcohol made her focal point of investigation, but did not transform encounter into custodial interrogation); *Com. v. Merritt*, 14 Mass App 601, 604-605, 441 NE2d 532, 535 (1982) (because immediate investigative goal is usually to determine whether crime was committed, limited preliminary questioning is not subject to *Miranda*).

[96] *Pennsylvania v. Bruder*, 488 US 9 (1988); *Vanhouten v. Com.*, 424 Mass 327, 331-332, 676 NE2d 460, 463-464 (1997) (recitation of alphabet); *Com. v. Cameron*, supra, 44 Mass App at 913-914, 689 NE2d at 1367-1368; *Com. v. D'Agostino*, 38 Mass App 206, 646 NE2d 767 (1995).

against self-incrimination.[97] When a suspect is asked for a response requiring him to communicate a fact or belief, such as being asked when his sixth birthday is, there is a testimonial dimension to the response which may implicate the privilege.[98] *Miranda* is applicable during a *Terry* investigative stop if the suspect is taken into custody or if the questioning otherwise takes place in a police-dominated or compelling atmosphere.[99]

"Drawing the line between custodial interrogation and general investigative questioning has not been an easy task for the courts."[100] The Supreme Court has provided the following guidance:

> Any interview of one suspected of a crime by a police officer will have coercive aspects to it, simply by virtue of the fact that the police officer is part of a law enforcement system which may ultimately cause the suspect to be charged with a crime. But police officers are not required to administer *Miranda* warnings to everyone whom they question. Nor is the requirement of warnings to be imposed simply because the questioning takes place in the station house, or because the questioned person is one whom the police suspect. *Miranda* warnings are required only where there has been such a restriction on a person's freedom as to render him "in custody." It was that sort of coercive environment to which *Miranda* by its terms was made applicable, and to which it is limited.[101]

As a suspect makes incriminating statements during an interview, a previously noncustodial setting may become custodial because a person who confesses to a crime would reasonably expect he is no longer free to leave. But the interview does not automatically become custodial at that point. The issue is whether the statement resulted in some difference in how the suspect was treated and questioned.[102] While not constitutionally required, it is suggested practice to inform a suspect

---

[97] *Com. v. Cameron*, supra, 44 Mass App at 913, 689 NE2d at 1367. See also § 5.14.2(b), supra.

[98] See *Com. v. Ayre*, 31 Mass App 17, 21 & n.8, 574 NE2d 415, 418 & n.8 (1991) (citing *Pennsylvania v. Muniz*, 496 US 582, 592-600 (1990)).

[99] *Com. v. Gordon*, 47 Mass App 825, 716 NE2d 1036 (1999) (defendant, handcuffed and locked in back of cruiser, attained level of custody associated with formal arrest). But not every *Terry*-type investigative stop results in custodial interrogation. See, e.g., *Com. v. DePeiza*, 449 Mass 367, 375-376, 868 NE2d 90, 98-99 (2007) (*Miranda* warnings were not required between patfrisk and frisk even though encounter was "police-dominated" and officer asked suspect if he had a firearm).

[100] *Com. v. Doyle*, 12 Mass App 786, 792, 429 NE2d 346, 350 (1981).

[101] *Oregon v. Mathiason*, supra, 429 US at 495.

[102] See *Com. v. Hilton*, 443 Mass 597, 612-613, 823 NE2d 383, 397 (2005), *appeal after remand*, 450 Mass 173, 877 NE2d 545 (2007); (interview did not become custodial

explicitly of the change of his condition from noncustodial to custodial.[103] The imparting of *Miranda* warnings does not itself transform a noncustodial situation into a custodial one.[104]

§ 12.6.3 Interrogation

In addition to "custody," there must also be "interrogation" before the *Miranda* doctrine is applicable. Spontaneous, unsolicited statements or confessions do not come within *Miranda* even if the defendant is in custody at the time.[105] Similarly, when an officer merely answers defendant's question in a conversation initiated by defendant, there has been no interrogation.[106]

---

upon defendant's incriminatory remarks, but only after trooper with expertise in arson entered room and began to question her about the particulars of how she had set fire).

[103] *Com. v. Alicea*, 376 Mass 506, 514, 381 NE2d 144, 150 (1978); *Com. v. Lavender*, 79 Mass App 501, 504-505, 947 NE2d 93, 97 (2011). See also *Com. v. Cruz*, 373 Mass 676, 686-687, 369 NE2d 996, 1003 (1977) (rejecting defendant's assertion that he was not aware of the change in his status from noncustodial to custodial).

[104] See *Com. v. Smith*, 456 Mass 476, 479, 924 NE2d 270, 275 (2010); *Com. v. Hilton*, 443 Mass 597, 610 n.7, 823 NE2d 383, 395 n.7 (2005), *appeal after remand*, 450 Mass 173, 877 NE2d 545 (2007); *Com. v. Liptak*, 80 Mass App 76, 86 n.7, 951 NE2d 731, 740 n.7 (2011) *Com. v. Lawrence*, 404 Mass 378, 386, 536 NE2d 571, 577 (1989).

[105] See *Com. v. Loadholt*, 456 Mass 411, 420, 923 NE2d 1037, 1047 (2010) (defendant's statement admitting ownership of firearm was spontaneous, and not the product of the functional equivalent of interrogation); *Com. v. Diaz*, 453 Mass 266, 276, 901 NE2d 670, 680 (2009) (defendant made statement while engaged in small talk with police, prior to warnings, and not in response to interrogation); *Com. v. Koumaris*, 440 Mass 405, 409-410, 799 NE2d 89, 93 (2003) (inmate initiated statement by insisting on talking to corrections officer to get something off his conscience, and officer simply responded, "Go ahead. Tell me what [you've] got to say."); *Com. v. Woods*, 427 Mass 169, 173, 693 NE2d 123, 125 (1998); *Com. v. Clark C.*, 59 Mass App 542, 545, 797 NE2d 5, 8 (2003) (juvenile's statement "[D]id my grandmother turn me in?" after officer awoke him to serve arrest warrant was spontaneous); *Com. v. Figueroa*, 56 Mass App 641, 643-645, 779 NE2d 669, 671-673 (2002) (defendant initiated conversation and volunteered statements during return trip to Massachusetts in police custody); *Com. v. Gittens*, 55 Mass App 148, 149-150, 769 NE2d 777, 780 (2002) (defendant's statements during booking were voluntary and unprovoked by questioning); *Com. v. St. Peter*, 48 Mass App 517, 520, 722 NE2d 1002, 1006 (2000) (defendant made unsolicited spontaneous statement during warnings).

[106] *Com. v. Duguay*, 430 Mass 397, 401, 720 NE2d 458, 462 (1999), *habeas petition denied in Duguay v. Spencer*, 462 F Supp 2d 115 (D Mass 2006) (defendant asked what police wanted to know, and officer responded, "Just tell them what happened"). See also *Com. v. Delrio*, 22 Mass App 712, 717-718, 497 NE2d 1097, 1100 (1986) (where there is a factual dispute as to whether defendant's statement was spontaneous or in response to question by police, judge is required to hold voir dire).

"Interrogation" occurs when law enforcement officers subject a person to either express questioning, or its functional equivalent—*i.e.*, words or actions (other than those normally attendant to arrest and custody) that the police should have known were reasonably likely to elicit an incriminating response from the suspect given their knowledge of his susceptibility to particular forms of persuasion.[107] The police are not expected to be clairvoyant in predicting a defendant's response to their words or conduct.[108]

---

[107] See *Rhode Island v. Innis*, 446 US 291 (1980) (no "interrogation" where police could not reasonably have expected that conversation concerning possibility of handicapped children finding hidden shotgun would elicit incriminating statement). Compare *Com. v. Martin*, 467 Mass 291, 309, 4 NE3d 1236, 1251-1252 (2014) (jail officer's statement to defendant while in holding cell was the functional equivalent of interrogation), *Com. v. Dixon*, 79 Mass App 701, 709, 949 NE2d 437, 444 (2011) (where booking officer posed question to arresting officer in front of arrestee as to whether a weapon was used in the crime, a reasonable person in defendant's position would perceive the question was directed at him, and his response was thus the product of interrogation and inadmissible), *Com. v. Clark C.*, 59 Mass App 542, 545-546, 797 NE2d 5, 8-9 (2003) (officer's statement to juvenile in custody "You said you were going to turn yourself in yesterday" constituted functional equivalent of interrogation because, consciously or not, it attempted to verify voice on previous incriminating phone call), *Com. v. Chadwick*, 40 Mass App 425, 427-429, 664 NE2d 874, 876 (1996) (police officer's unsolicited explanation of rape constituted impermissible interrogation), and *Com. v. Rubio*, 27 Mass App 506, 511-512, 540 NE2d 189, 192-193 (1989) ("Showing the cocaine in the pocketbook to the defendant in this setting was clearly confrontational and had the force of an implicit question: 'Is this yours?'") with *Com. v. Gonzalez*, 465 Mass 672, 675-676, 991 NE2d 1036, 1040-1041 (2013) (police officer's statement to murder defendant that he was there to transport him to detectives who wished to speak to him did not constitute functional equivalent of interrogation); *Com. v. Mejia*, 461 Mass 384, 391, 961 NE2d 72, 79 (2012) (detective's introductory remark about "what happened" was not interrogation), *Com. v. Braley*, 449 Mass 316, 324, 867 NE2d 743, 752-753 (2007) (trooper's engaging in light banter with defendant in airport while awaiting flight was not interrogation and did not prompt defendant's question "how did you get on to me?"), *Com. v. Caputo*, 439 Mass 153, 160-161, 786 NE2d 352, 358 (2003), *habeas petition denied in Caputo v. Nelson*, 455 F3d 45 (1st Cir 2006) (police officer's request to use defendant's telephone not reasonably likely to elicit incriminating response), *Com. v. Rodriguez*, 75 Mass App 235, 238-239, 913 NE2d 880, 884-885 (2009) (detective's question whether suspect had any extra money for his children was not the functional equivalent of interrogation), *Com. v. White*, 74 Mass App 342, 346-347, 906 NE2d 1011, 1015 (2009) (police officer's statement during frisk that "you better tell us if you have anything because we're going to find it" merely advised defendant of the legal truth, and was not the functional equivalent of interrogation) and *Com. v. Harkess*, 35 Mass App 626, 632, 624 NE2d 581, 585 (1993) (defendant's statement not product of questioning where police officer handled gun merely as piece of evidence collected at scene, and not as accusatory police question).

[108] See *Com. v. King*, 17 Mass App 602, 608-609, 460 NE2d 1299, 1304 (1984) (no interrogation where officer, at defendant's request, showed him arrest warrant).

The test for identifying the functional equivalent of interrogation can be stated as follows: if an objective observer (with the same knowledge of the suspect as the police officer) would conclude that the officer's speech or conduct was designed to elicit an incriminating response, interrogation has occurred.[109] Courts evaluate both the perceptions of the suspect as to whether he is being subjected to coercive pressures and the conduct of the police as to the use of compelling influences or psychological ploys.[110] Even though the standard is an objective one, the intent of the officers to elicit an incriminating statement certainly bears on whether the officers should have known that their words and actions would likely evoke an incriminating response.[111] Awareness of the possibility of eliciting an incriminating statement is itself, however, insufficient to establish the functional equivalent of interrogation.[112] Testimony from the officers that they had *not* expected their conversations to elicit incriminating responses is entitled to some weight.[113]

Miranda warnings are not required prior to routine booking questions regarding the arrestee's name, address, and related matters.[114]

---

[109] *Com. v. Rubio*, supra, 27 Mass App at 512, 540 NE2d at 193.

[110] See *Arizona v. Mauro*, 481 US 520, 528 (1987) (no "interrogation" where police permitted defendant and his wife, both suspects in murder of their child, to speak together in presence of officer and tape recorder); *Illinois v. Perkins*, 496 US 292 (1990) (no "interrogation" where suspect made incriminating statements in conversation with undercover agent placed in jail cell).

[111] See *Com. v. Brant*, 380 Mass 876, 883, 406 NE2d 1021, 1026-1027 (1980) (defendant was "interrogated" where officer informed him that confederate had already made statement and allowed defendant to confer with confederate); *Com. v. Harvey*, 390 Mass 203, 206, 454 NE2d 105, 106-107 (1983) (statement suppressed where obtained by confronting defendant with confessed accomplice, designed to elicit incriminating response). Compare *Com. v. Chipman*, 418 Mass 262, 273, 635 NE2d 1204, 1211 (1994) (no indication that police responses to defendant's questions designed to elicit inculpatory comments); *Com. v. D'Entremont*, 36 Mass App 474, 478-480, 632 NE2d 1239 (1994) (detective's statement to defendant that if he changed his mind she would be willing to speak with him did not constitute interrogation).

[112] *Com. v. Torres*, 424 Mass 792, 796-797, 678 NE2d 847, 850-851 (1997).

[113] *Com. v. Messere*, 14 Mass App 1, 8 n.5, 436 NE2d 414, 418 n.5 (1982).

[114] *Pennsylvania v. Muniz*, 496 US 582 (1990); *Com. v. Mahoney*, 400 Mass 524, 528-529, 510 NE2d 759, 762-763 (1987) (videotape recording of defendant made during booking procedure properly admitted despite lack of *Miranda* warnings because questions were normally attendant to arrest and custody); *Com. v. Ramirez*, 55 Mass App 224, 226, 770 NE2d 30, 32-33 (2002) (request for arrestee's name, which elicited a false name); *Com. v. Kacavich*, 28 Mass App 941, 550 NE2d 397 (1990) (& cases collected). See also *Com. v. White*, 422 Mass 487, 501-503, 663 NE2d 834, 844-845 (1996) (defendant's statement of telephone number he wished to call not result of custodial interrogation); *Com. v. Clark*, 432 Mass 1, 15-16, 730 NE2d 872, 888-886 (2000) (defendant's statement that he was left-handed, made after invocation of right

Where, however, an arrestee's employment status may prove incriminatory, the police must give *Miranda* warnings before asking booking questions about employment.[115] That a defendant refused to answer booking questions may not be admitted or referred to at trial.[116]

Nor are warnings required prior to preliminary questions asked by police at the crime scene to determine threshold facts such as identity or what happened[117] or to secure a volatile scene or determine the need for medical care.[118] Interrogation may occur, however, even with regard to an introductory question, when suspicion has already fallen on the subject.[119]

Where the suspect waives his *Miranda* rights (see § 12.6.4, infra) and indicates a willingness to talk to the police, there is no bar to interrogation and it is not improper for the police to attempt, within proper bounds, to elicit a confession from the defendant.[120]

---

to counsel, was not result of interrogation but response to administrative request). Compare *Com. v. Dixon,* 79 Mass App 701, 707-710, 949 NE2d 437, 443-445 (2011) (defendant's statement "the dude hit us" made during booking in response to non-routine question to police officer, and after defendant invoked his right to remain silent, was the product of interrogation and thus inadmissible).

It has been suggested that a broader prohibition might be derived from art. 12 of state constitution for incriminatory evidence obtained by compulsion in response to booking questions. See *Com. v. Acosta,* 416 Mass 279, 283-284, 620 NE2d 780 (1993). See also *Com. v. Sheriff,* 425 Mass 186, 198-199, 680 NE2d 75, 82-83 (1997) (suggesting that questions to ascertain whether defendant is aware of his surroundings may be in same category as booking questions); *Com. v. Dixon,* 79 Mass App 701, 708 n.10, 949 NE2d 437, 444 n.10 (2011) (suggesting that questions relating to weapons be eliminated from the booking litany).

[115] See *Com. v. Woods,* 419 Mass 366, 372-374, 645 NE2d 1153, 1157 (1995); *Com. v. Dayes,* 49 Mass App 419, 421, 730 NE2d 321, 324 (2000) (since warnings were given at time of arrest and there was no significant lapse, no error in failure to readvise before employment question at booking); *Com. v. Guerrero,* 32 Mass App 263, 266-269, 588 NE2d 716, 718-719 (1992).

[116] *Com. v. Gonsalves,* 74 Mass App 910, 911, 907 NE2d 237, 239 (2009). See also § 12.6.8

[117] *Com. v. Gordon,* 47 Mass App 825, 828, 716 NE2d 1036, 1039 (1999); *Com. v. McGrail,* 80 Mass App 339, 346, 952 NE2d 969, 976 (2011) (questioning of defendant at scene of accident and in hospital was general fact-finding).

[118] *Com. v. Foley,* 445 Mass 1001, 1002, 833 NE2d 130, 133 (2005). A police request for consent to search from an individual in custody is not deemed custodial interrogation. See *Com. v. Wallace,* 70 Mass App 757, 761 n.2, 877 NE2d 260, 265 n.2 (2007) (& citations).

[119] *Com. v. Gordon,* supra, 47 Mass App at 828, 716 NE2d at 1038 (captain's question as to what subject was doing in area at 5:15 A.M. elicited incriminatory response).

[120] See *Com. v. MacKenzie,* 413 Mass 498, 512-513, 597 NE2d 1037, 1046 (1992).

Interrogation by a private person acting as an instrument or agent of the police has been held to trigger the *Miranda* protections.[121] The fact that a private party acting on her own had every intention of providing the police with evidence does not, however, make her an agent of the police.[122]

§ 12.6.4 Waiver

a. Standards and Burden of Proof

If a statement is obtained from a suspect during custodial interrogation, it may be admitted at trial only if the prosecution demonstrates that the warnings and procedures required by *Miranda* were "scrupulously observed" and that the suspect "knowingly, intelligently and voluntarily" waived his privilege against self-incrimination and right to counsel.[123] There can be no valid waiver in the absence of adequate warnings.[124]

Because courts purport to indulge every reasonable presumption against waiver of fundamental constitutional rights, the Commonwealth has a "heavy burden" in demonstrating such waiver.[125] As a matter of Massachusetts practice, it must prove a knowing, intelligent, and voluntary waiver beyond a reasonable doubt.[126]

---

[121] See *Com. v. A Juvenile*, 402 Mass 275, 278, 521 NE2d 1368, 1370 (1988) (assistant director at youth detention facility). Compare *Com. v. Snyder*, 413 Mass 521, 530-532, 597 NE2d 1363, 1368-1369 (1992) (*Miranda* inapplicable where school principal, not acting on behalf of law enforcement officials, questioned student in her office); *Com. v. Sanchez*, 405 Mass 369, 378 n.6, 540 NE2d 1316, 1322 (1989) (no *Miranda* waiver required where information obtained by county nurse acting as private citizen conducting routine medical inquiry); *Com. v. Tynes*, 400 Mass 369, 372-374, 510 NE2d 244, 246-247 (1987) (*Miranda* did not apply where un-uniformed, off-duty police officers directed questions to stopped motorist); *Com. v. Rancourt*, 399 Mass 269, 271-275, 503 NE2d 960, 962-965 (1987) (fellow inmate acted as private party and not government agent when he induced defendant to write letter describing the details of crime); *Com. v. Allen*, 395 Mass 448, 453-454, 480 NE2d 630, 635 (1985) (hospital nurse not acting as agent of police when questioning patient even though officer was present and did nothing to stop the questioning).

[122] *Com. v. Snyder*, supra, 413 Mass at 532, 597 NE2d at 1369.

[123] *Com. v. Corriveau*, 396 Mass 319, 330, 486 NE2d 29, 37-38 (1985); *Com. v. Florek*, 48 Mass App 414, 418-419, 722 NE2d 20, 24 (2000).

[124] *Com. v. Adams*, 389 Mass 265, 270, 450 NE2d 149, 152 (1983).

[125] *Miranda v. Arizona*, 384 US 436, 475 (1966); *Com. v. Taylor*, 398 Mass 725, 728, 500 NE2d 799, 801 (1986); *Com. v. Forde*, 392 Mass 453, 454, 466 NE2d 510, 512 (1984).

[126] See *Com. v. Anderson*, 445 Mass 195, 203, 834 NE2d 1159, 1167 (2005); *Com. v. Judge*, 420 Mass 433, 447, 650 NE2d 1242, 1251 (1995). This standard is more favorable to the defendant than the federal constitutional standard. *Sok v. Spencer*, 578 F

The voluntariness of the *Miranda* waiver and the voluntariness of the statement itself on Due Process grounds (see § 12.2, supra) are separate and distinct issues, although they are both determined in light of the totality of circumstances and share many of the same relevant factors.[127]

There is no rule requiring that a waiver be made expressly in writing or orally. Rather a waiver may be found even in the absence of an explicit statement to that effect; it may be inferred from the suspect's words and actions.[128] While mere silence in response to the warnings is not sufficient to establish a waiver, "the defendant's silence, coupled with an understanding of his rights and a course of conduct indicating waiver" may suffice.[129]

The absence of written confirmation does not vitiate a valid oral waiver, although it may make proof of the waiver more difficult.[130] Conversely, written confirmation of a waiver is not dispositive;[131] the court must still analyze the totality of the circumstances to determine

---

Supp 2d 281, 291 n.4 (D Mass 2008) (extensive discussion). Compare *Colorado v. Connelly*, 479 US 157 (1986) (under federal standard, waiver need be proven only by a preponderance of the evidence). Whether a defendant has validly waived his *Miranda* rights is a question of law for the judge. *Com. v. Sunahara*, 455 Mass 832, 838 n.3, 920 NE2d 831, 836 n.3 (2010).

[127] See *Com. v. Beland*, 436 Mass 273, 279, 764 NE2d 324, 330 (2002); *Com. v. Groome*, 435 Mass 201, 217 n.22, 755 NE2d 122, 1237 n.22 (2001). A finding that defendant was unable to make a knowing, voluntary, and intelligent waiver of *Miranda* rights is not enough, standing alone, to support a finding that the statement was involuntary. *Com. v. Hilton*, 450 Mass 173, 178, 877 NE2d 545, 551 (2007).

[128] See *North Carolina v. Butler*, 441 US 369 (1979); *Com. v. Corriveau*, supra, 396 Mass at 330, 486 NE2d at 38 (waiver established where officer, after informing defendant of rights, asked him whether he understood them and defendant, an experienced and well-educated businessman, responded affirmatively). A suspect who answers select questions and refuses to respond to others has waived his privilege against self-incrimination. *Com. v. Johnston*, 467 Mass 674, 687-689, 7 NE3d 424, 436-437 (2014).

[129] *North Carolina v. Butler*, supra, 441 US at 374 (defendant refused to sign waiver form, but agreed to talk about the robbery being investigated). Compare *Com. v. Watkins*, 375 Mass 472, 484-485, 379 NE2d 1040, 1048-1049 (1978) (defendant's spontaneous declaration of desire to make statement constituted implied waiver of previously claimed desire to speak with counsel), with *Com. v. Cain*, 361 Mass 224, 228-229, 279 NE2d 706, 709 (1972) (mere fact that minor defendant made statement after acknowledging rights does not establish waiver).

[130] The fact that defendant refused to sign a *Miranda* form, or to have the interview recorded does not preclude a finding of valid waiver. See, e.g., *Com. v. Womack*, 457 Mass 268, 277, 929 NE2d 943, 952 (2010); *Com. v. Williams*, 456 Mass 857, 864, 926 NE2d 1162, 1169 (2010); *Com. v. Raposa*, 440 Mass 684, 688, 801 NE2d 789, 794 (2004); *Com. v. Groome*, 435 Mass 201, 217-218, 755 NE2d 122, 1238 (2001).

[131] *Com. v. Groome*, supra, 435 Mass at 218 n.23, 755 NE2d at 1238 n.23.

its validity.[132] Nonetheless, a signed waiver form, while not dispositive, constitutes evidence of voluntariness.[133] Whether express or implied, a waiver must be shown to have been "knowing, intelligent and voluntary."

The judge is not required to submit to the jury the question of the validity of a waiver of *Miranda* rights apart from the over-all determination of voluntariness discussed in § 12.2.[134] Compliance with *Miranda* is a prerequisite for admissibility and thus a question of law for the judge.[135]

b. Knowing, Intelligent, and Voluntary

Waiver requires both comprehension of the rights involved and voluntary relinquishment of them.[136] As the Supreme Court has explained:

> First, the relinquishment of the right must have been voluntary in the sense that it was the product of a free and deliberate choice rather than intimidation, coercion, or deception. Second, the waiver must have been made with a full awareness of both the nature of the right being abandoned and the consequences of the decision to abandon it. Only if the "totality of the circumstances surrounding the interrogation" reveal both an uncoerced choice and the requisite level of comprehension may a court properly conclude that the Miranda rights have been waived.[137]

---

[132] See *Com. v. Magee*, 423 Mass 381, 387 n.8, 668 NE2d 339, 344 n.8 (1996) (concluding that waiver was involuntary).

[133] *Com. v. Melo*, 472 Mass 278, 294, 34 NE3d 289, 304 (2015) (defendant signed the notification of rights form, which expressly indicates that he understood the *Miranda* rights and knowingly waived them); *Com. v. Lopes*, 455 Mass 147, 167, 914 NE2d 78, 95 (2009), *habeas denied*, 2013 WL 819330 (D Mass 2012).

[134] *Com. v. Tavares*, 385 Mass 140, 153 n.19, 430 NE2d 1198, 1206 n.19 (1982); *Com. v. Day*, supra, 387 Mass at 923, 444 NE2d at 388.

[135] *Com. v. Tavares*, supra; *Com. v. Todd*, 408 Mass 724, 727, 563 NE2d 211, 213 (1990). But see *Com. v. Chung*, 378 Mass 451, 458-460, 392 NE2d 1015, 1019-1029 (1979) (where there was credible evidence that defendant was insane at time he made confession, judge erred in failing to adequately instruct jury that knowing, intelligent, and voluntary waiver is prerequisite to questioning). See also *Com. v. Cole*, 380 Mass 30, 41-42 & n.14, 402 NE2d 55, 63 & n.14 (1980) (leaving open question whether jury should be given limiting instructions when defendant's responses to *Miranda* warnings are admitted in evidence).

[136] *Com. v. Freeman*, 430 Mass 111, 114, 712 NE2d 1135, 1140 (1999); *Com. v. Dustin*, 373 Mass 612, 615, 368 NE2d 1388, 1391 (1977).

[137] *Moran v. Burbine*, 475 US 412, 421 (1988).

The ultimate question is: "Did the defendant, with a full knowledge of his legal rights, knowingly and intentionally relinquish them?"[138]

Knowing and Intelligent. The first two requirements focus on whether the defendant understood his or her rights and the consequences of relinquishing them.[139] "A confession can be voluntary in the legal sense only if the suspect actually understands the import of each *Miranda* warning."[140] Thus, where the police provided conflicting advice as to when the suspect could have a lawyer appointed and how he could obtain one, it was clear he misunderstood his right to appointed counsel and the waiver was invalid.[141]

It is not necessary for the defendant to fully understand the legal ramifications and tactical consequences of waiving *Miranda* rights; a general understanding of the rights being waived is sufficient.[142] A misrepresentation of the *Miranda* rights, even if innocent, renders suspect a claim that the defendant knowingly waived those rights.[143] The

---

[138] *Com. v. Cruz,* 373 Mass 676, 687, 369 NE2d 996, 1003 (1977).

[139] See *Moran v. Burbine,* supra, 475 US at 421. Compare *Com. v. Woodbine,* 461 Mass 720, 728, 964 NE2d 956, 964 (2012) (although in hospital recovering from a gunshot wound, defendant was oriented, responsive, not confused, and not on medications that would have impaired his ability to think clearly; waiver was thus knowing and intelligent) with *Com. v. Hoyt,* 461 Mass 143, 153-154, 958 NE2d 834, 844-845 (2011) (where defendant's statement that he wanted an attorney present but could not afford one indicated he did not understand one or more of the warnings, his waiver was not knowing and intelligent).

[140] *Com. v. Garcia,* 379 Mass 422, 429, 399 NE2d 460, 466 (1980). But see *Connecticut v. Barrett,* 479 US 523 (1987) (defendant's ambiguous conduct in refusing to make written statement and then giving oral confession did not invalidate waiver on grounds it was not knowing and intelligent).

[141] *Com. v. Libby,* 472 Mass 37, 53-54, 32 NE3d 890, 904-906 (2015). But compare *Com. v. Mazariego,* 474 Mass 42, 47 NE3d 420 (2016) (defendant's initial response to the warning regarding appointment of an attorney—"On whose side is the attorney?"—did not invalidate the waiver, as his subsequent responses to the detective's explanation indicated he understood his rights).

[142] See *Com. v. Hilton,* 443 Mass 597, 606-607, 823 NE2d 383, 393 (2005) (& citations), *appeal after remand,* 450 Mass 173, 877 NE2d 545 (2007).

[143] *Com. v. Dustin,* supra, 373 Mass at 616, 368 NE2d at 1390-1391 (officer implied that defendant's statement could not be used against him). Compare *Com. v. Magee,* 423 Mass 381, 386-387, 668 NE2d 339, 344 (1996) (officer's response to defendant's inquiry about getting attorney was inadequate and weighed against valid waiver) with *Com. v. Grenier,* 415 Mass 680, 682-684, 615 NE2d 922, 923-924 (1993) (police officer's answer to defendant's question about meaning of *Miranda* warning not misleading or false) and *Com. v. Novo,* 442 Mass 262, 271 n.8, 812 NE2d 1169, 1177 n.8 (2004) (officer's misstatements regarding right to terminate questioning did not invalidate waiver).

fact that a suspect selectively asserted rights to certain questions may evidence a knowing and intelligent waiver as to questions that were answered.[144]

The prosecution may not rely on any presumption that the suspect understood the warnings, but must affirmatively demonstrate such understanding—for example, by showing that the suspect answered affirmatively when asked whether he understood the warnings.[145] Understanding of the warnings may, however, be inferred from "the suspect's outward behavior, most notably his indication that he understands his rights, waives them, and wishes to talk."[146] The issue of the suspect's proper understanding has arisen frequently in the cases of non-English speaking defendants.[147]

"In certain limited circumstances [such as intoxication and mental retardation], the police are charged with observing greater caution

---

[144] See *Com. v. Mandeville*, 386 Mass 393, 404, 436 NE2d 912, 920 (1982).

[145] *Tague v. Louisiana*, 444 US 469 (1980).

[146] *Com. v. Garcia*, supra, 379 Mass at 430, 399 NE2d at 465. Compare *Com. v. Cain*, 361 Mass 224, 228, 279 NE2d 706, 709 (1972) (minor defendant's response "Yes, I didn't do anything" to question whether he waived rights did not indicate with sufficient clarity an understanding of rights and an intelligent waiver) and *Com. v. Coplin*, 34 Mass App 478, 482, 612 NE2d 1188, 1190 (1993) (insufficient proof that defendant, handcuffed and lying on floor, understood warnings) with *Com. v. Cook*, 419 Mass 192, 201, 644 NE2d 203, 209 (1994) (evidence supported finding that defendant either signed waiver card or indicated he understood rights) and *Com. v. Williams*, 378 Mass 217, 225-226, 391 NE2d 1202, 1207-1209 (1979) (police attempted to ascertain whether defendant wanted to waive his rights, and he responded affirmatively).

[147] Compare *Com. v. Seng*, 436 Mass 537, 542-545, 766 NE2d 492, 497-499 (2002) (warnings in defendant's native Khmer language were deficient and confusing) with *Com. v. Bins*, 465 Mass 348, 362-363, 989 NE2d 404, 418 (2013) (differing sets of warnings were not so contradictory as to render waiver involuntary), *Com. v. Jules*, 464 Mass 478, 487-488, 984 NE2d 266, 273-274 (2013) (evidence was sufficient to show that defendant, a native speaker of Haitian-Creole, understood the warnings, even though no recording was made of interview; translator had provided services to police on several prior occasions), *Com. v. Iglesias*, 426 Mass 574, 577, 689 NE2d 1315, 1318 (1998) (fact that warnings were given in English without interpreter to native Spanish speaker does not invalidate otherwise valid waiver), *Com. v. Bui*, 419 Mass 392, 396-397, 645 NE2d 689, 692 (1995) (evidence supported finding that defendant understood his rights when they were given to him in both English and Vietnamese), *Com. v. Perez*, 411 Mass 249, 255-256, 581 NE2d 1010, 1014-1015 (1991) (evidence was sufficient to establish that defendant read and understood Spanish translations warnings on *Miranda card*), *Com. v. Colon-Cruz*, 408 Mass 533, 539, 562 NE2d 797, 803 (1990) (judge's determination that Spanish translator succeeded in communicating the warnings to defendant was supported by the record) and *Com. v. Alves*, 35 Mass App 935, 625 NE2d 559 (1993) (rejecting Portuguese-speaking defendant's claims that language differences and errors in written Portuguese *Miranda* card precluded his understanding of rights).

in relying on signs by the accused that he understands and waives his *Miranda* rights."[148] Special attention must be paid to a defendant's cognitive defects and low intelligence. "Circumstances and techniques of custodial interrogation which pass constitutional muster when applied to an adult of normal intelligence may not be constitutionally tolerable when applied to one who is mentally deficient. People with low intelligence can, however, waive their rights."[149]

Although factors such as the youthful age, intoxication,[150] or diminished mental capacity of the defendant do not automatically invalidate a waiver,[151] the mental condition of the defendant is a significant factor to be weighed in determining whether the waiver was knowing and intelligent.[152] It has been suggested that expert testimony be presented to aid in the evaluation of the effect of custodial

---

[148] *Com. v. Garcia*, supra, 379 Mass at 430 n.4, 399 NE2d at 466 n.4 (& cases cited). But see *Com. v. Anderson*, 445 Mass 195, 204, 834 NE2d 1159, 1167 (2005) (police may rely on suspect's outward appearance of sobriety); *Com. v. Lanoue*, 392 Mass 583, 588-589, 467 NE2d 159, 163 (1984) (rejecting contention that police have obligation to ensure valid waiver through administration of sobriety tests; police are ordinarily entitled to rely on a suspect's outward behavior when deciding whether to proceed with an interrogation); *Com. v. Dunn*, 407 Mass 798, 805, 556 NE2d 30, 34-35 (1990) (defendant did not indicate to officers that he was intoxicated or give any outward appearance of intoxication).

[149] *Com. v. Beland*, 436 Mass 273, 281, 764 NE2d 324, 331-332 (2002). See also *Com. v. Ostrander*, 441 Mass 344, 805 NE2d 497 (2004) (valid waiver by defendant with borderline IQ). *Com. v. Dingle*, 73 Mass App 274, 285-286, 898 NE2d 1, 10-11 (2008); *Com. v. Stone*, 70 Mass App 800, 877 NE2d 620 (2007) (IQ in low to mid-seventies).

[150] See *Com. v. Bigley*, 85 Mass App 507, 513-515, 11 NE3d 1086, 1091-1093 (2014) (intoxicated, emotional, and agitated defendant validly waived rights).

[151] See *Com. v. Wanderlick*, 12 Mass App 970, 428 NE2d 328 (1981) (& cases cited).

[152] Compare *Com. v. Hilton*, 443 Mass 597, 605-607, 823 NE2d 383, 392-393 (2005), *appeal after remand*, 450 Mass 173, 877 NE2d 545 (2007) (waiver invalid where defendant was diagnosed with schizophrenia and personality disorder, was mildly retarded, functionally illiterate, delusional, and unable to comprehend matters such as role of judge and jury), *Com. v. Magee*, 423 Mass 381, 386-387, 668 NE2d 339, 344 (1996) (defendant suffering from lack of sleep and emotionally distraught), and *Com. v. White*, 374 Mass 132, 137-138, 371 NE2d 777, 780 (1977) (waiver invalid because defendant intoxicated by drugs or alcohol) with *Com. v. Delacruz*, 463 Mass 504, 515-516, 976 NE2d 788, 797 (2012) (waiver valid despite testimony from defendant's clinical psychologist witness regarding his limited intellectual functioning); *Com. v. McCray*, 457 Mass 544, 553-555, 931 NE2d 443, 451-452 (2010) (waiver valid despite defendant's claims of mental retardation, intoxication, and illiteracy), *Com. v. Druce*, 453 Mass 686, 699-700, 905 NE2d 70, 81-82 (2009) (waiver valid even though defendant was mentally disturbed and emotional), *Com. v. Diaz*, 453 Mass 266, 901 NE2d 670 (2009) (waiver valid despite Spanish-speaking defendant's claims that he had consumed beer, had been awake for 12 to 15 hours, and did not understand the questions), *Com. v. Murphy*, 442 Mass 485, 493-494, 813 NE2d 820, 828-829 (2004) (waiver valid despite defendant's claim that he was under influence of alcohol and drugs),

interrogation on a mentally deficient defendant.[153] Where the defendant places at issue his mental ability to make a valid waiver, he may be compelled to submit to a psychiatric evaluation by the Commonwealth's expert, who may testify to his conclusions at trial.[154]

Despite the requirement that a waiver be knowing and intelligent, a suspect need not be made aware of all the possible subjects or crimes to be covered in the interrogation in order to make his waiver valid.[155]

Com. v. Zagrodny, 443 Mass 93, 100-101, 819 NE2d 565, 573 (2004) (waiver valid despite defendant's bipolar disorder), *Com. v. Rivera*, 441 Mass 358, 364-366, 805 NE2d 942, 948-950 (2004) (waiver valid even though defendant may have been on medication for schizophrenia that caused memory problems, and there was time lapse of more than three hours between warnings and waiver and confession), *Com. v. Silanskas*, 433 Mass 678, 685-687, 746 NE2d 445, 455-456 (2001) (although officer noted defendant was under influence of alcohol while being questioned in kitchen, defendant's answers were responsive, coherent, and self-serving, and thus waiver valid), *Com. v. Wolinski*, 431 Mass 228, 231-233, 726 NE2d 930, 934-935 (2000) (despite finding that defendant had consumed alcohol and heroin at time of arrest, he was not intoxicated to point where his ability to think freely and rationally was impaired), *Com. v. Pina*, 430 Mass 66, 71-72, 713 NE2d 944, 949-950 (1999) (officers testified that although they recognized indications that defendant had consumed alcohol, based on his outward conduct, responses to questions, and prior experiences with him, he was not intoxicated), *Com. v. Mello*, 420 Mass 375, 383, 649 NE2d 1106, 1113 (1995) (despite evidence that defendant ingested beer and inhaled heroin night before arrest, waiver valid where defendant spoke coherently, appeared sober, explained preparation and crime in detail, did not complain of illness, signed waiver form, stated he understood his rights, and agreed to talk to police), *Com. v. Prater*, 420 Mass 569, 578-579, 651 NE2d 833, 839-840 (1995) (waiver valid even though defendant intoxicated and had low IQ where he had been subject to custodial interrogation before and stated on videotape that the effects of alcohol had worn off), *Com. v. Duffy*, 36 Mass App 937, 629 NE2d 1347 (1994) (judge could properly conclude that neither defendant's mental impairments nor consumption of alcohol impeded his ability to waive rights), *Com. v. Matos*, 36 Mass App 958, 963, 634 NE2d 138, 143 (1994) (even if defendant suffered from diminished mental capacity, evidence of totality of circumstances established valid waiver) and *Com. v. Wallen*, 35 Mass App 915, 619 NE2d 365 (1993) (judge could properly conclude that defendant with IQ between 60 and 70 and third or fourth grade reading level validly waived rights).

[153] *Com. v. Cameron*, 385 Mass 660, 666 n.5, 433 NE2d 878, 883 n.5 (& citation). See also *Com. v. Crawford*, 429 Mass 60, 706 NE2d 289 (1999) (defendant entitled to present expert testimony on battered woman syndrome and post-traumatic stress disorder on issue of voluntariness of her confession to police).

[154] See *Com. v. Ostrander*, 441 Mass 344, 351-355, 805 NE2d 497, 504-506 (2004). See, e.g., *Com. v. Hadley*, 78 Mass App 405, 410-411, 939 NE2d 787, 791-792 (2010) (Commonwealth proffered expert testimony from psychiatrist who evaluated defendant and reviewed his records, and concluded that his bipolar disorder did not preclude capacity to make a valid waiver).

[155] See *Colorado v. Spring*, 479 US 564 (1987) (interrogation switched from firearms charge, for which defendant was arrested, to a homicide); *Com. v. Hensley*, 454 Mass 721, 737-738, 913 NE2d 339, 352 (2009) (fact that police did not explain at outset that suspect was being questioned about victim's murder does not negate validity of *Miranda* waiver or voluntariness of his statements). *Com. v. Medeiros*, supra, 395 Mass at

The police are not required to explain all the possible legal ramifications of the defendant's conduct, such as the theory of joint venture.[156] Nor is it necessary that the person being questioned be told that he is a suspect.[157] A defendant's experience with and in the criminal justice system is a factor weighed in determining whether he understood the warnings and validly waived them.[158]

Under federal law articulated in *Moran v. Burbine*,[159] the fact that police failed to inform a suspect that an attorney retained by a relative to represent him was attempting to see him at the police station did not invalidate his *Miranda* waiver. The Supreme Judicial Court ruled otherwise in *Com. v. Mavredakis*,[160] holding the state constitutional privilege against compelled self-incrimination includes the right to be informed of an attorney's efforts to render assistance. Concluding that the duty to so inform a suspect is necessary to "actualize the abstract rights listed in *Miranda*," the Court mandated that when an attorney identifies herself to the police as counsel acting on the suspect's behalf, the police must stop questioning and immediately inform the suspect of the attorney's request.[161] The duty arises whether the attorney telephones or appears in person at the station. Failure to comply renders any waiver of rights inoperative for subsequent admissions.

While the police are not required to convey verbatim the attorney's message to the defendant, instructions not to talk to the police fall within the duty to inform.[162] But an attorney telling the police to

---

345, 479 NE2d at 1377-1378 (police not required to re-advise suspect of rights when questioning changed from theft to murder; but suspect's ignorance of subject of interrogation is factor to be weighed in totality of circumstances analysis).

[156] See *Com. v. Cunningham*, 405 Mass 646, 656-657, 543 NE2d 12, 18-19 (1989).

[157] *Com. v. Raymond*, 424 Mass 382, 392-393, 676 NE2d 824, 832 (1997); *Com. v. Borodine*, 371 Mass 1, 6, 353 NE2d 647, 653 (1976). *See also Com. v. Carnes*, 457 Mass 812, 817, 823, 933 NE2d 598, 604, 608 (2010); *Com. v. Robinson*, 78 Mass App 714, 718, 942 NE2d 980, 985 (2011) (fact that police failed to disclose that they had obtained an arrest warrant for him did not invalidate waiver).

[158] *Com. v. Bishop*, 461 Mass 586, 594-595, 963 NE2d 88, 95 (2012) (defendant had been a public housing police officer so he was familiar with the *Miranda* protocol and the consequences of waiver); *Com. v. Holley*, 79 Mass App 542, 545, 947 NE2d 606, 611 (2011) (defendant's prior involvement in criminal investigations and the prosecution process).

[159] 475 US 412 (1986).

[160] 430 Mass 848, 725 NE2d 169 (2000).

[161] 430 Mass at 860-861, 725 NE2d at 179.

[162] See *Com. v. Morales*, 461 Mass 765, 778-781, 965 NE2d 177, 189-191 (2012) (extensive discussion); *Com. v. McNulty*, 458 Mass 305, 315-318, 937 NE2d 16, 25-28

tell the defendant not to talk to them is *not* the same thing as an attorney telling police not to talk to the defendant; the former is legal advice to the defendant, while the latter is an attempt by the attorney to invoke his client's right to silence. Accordingly, the police have no duty to convey to the defendant the attorney's directive to the police to stop questioning. That directive only requires that they terminate questioning long enough to afford the defendant the opportunity to avail himself of the attorney's advice.[163]

If the suspect accepts the attorney's offer of assistance, questioning must cease until the suspect consults with the attorney. A suspect may of course choose to decline the attorney's offer; and if, after being informed of the availability of counsel, the suspect decides to continue questioning and has otherwise validly waived his *Miranda* rights, the police may resume questioning despite the attorney's direction to the contrary.[164] A defendant may waive his rights after meeting with an attorney and receiving *Miranda* warnings again.[165]

A third party's promise to obtain counsel for defendant is not deemed a "concrete offer of assistance" for purposes of this doctrine.[166]

Where the suspect retained and consulted counsel prior to his arrest, was informed of his right to have counsel present when he waived his *Miranda* rights, and nonetheless submitted to interrogation, the police were not required to inform him that his attorney had previously requested to be present during any interview.[167]

(2010) (because police did not convey adequately to defendant the substance of his attorney's telephone message and advice, defendant's subsequent indication that he would continue to speak to police did not constitute a knowing and intelligent waiver of his *Miranda* rights).

[163] *Com. v. Rivera*, 464 Mass 56, 64-67, 981 NE2d 171, 180-183 (2013). See also *Com. v. Martin*, 467 Mass 291, 305-307, 4 NE3d 1236, 1249-1250 (2014) (interrogating officers were not required during interview to provide defendant with letter his counsel had sent DA's office requesting that his client not be questioned).

[164] *Com. v. Vao Sok*, 435 Mass 743, 751-753, 761 NE2d 923, 930-932 (2002).

[165] *Com. v. Hoose*, 467 Mass 395, 402, 5 NE2d 843, 851 (2014).

[166] See *Com. v. Nelson*, 55 Mass App 911, 774 NE2d 634 (2002).

[167] *Com. v. Collins*, 440 Mass 475, 799 NE2d 1251 (2003) (refusing to suppress statement). See also *Com. v. Cryer*, 426 Mass 562, 568, 689 NE2d 808, 812-813 (1998) (Article 12 would not apply where it was the New Hampshire police who failed to inform defendant and the Massachusetts officers who interrogated him that defendant's attorney on an unrelated matter had left instructions that he not be questioned).

There is no constitutional duty on the part of police to inform a defendant's attorney that he has been arrested or will be interrogated.[168] Nor is there an affirmative duty on the part of defense counsel to call and direct police to halt questioning of a client.[169]

The Court has cautioned: "That a waiver of rights must be knowing and intelligent does not mean that with the hindsight of conviction the defendant would not have chosen to talk to the police. Rather, it means that police procedures must scrupulously respect the suspect's free choices, made with actual knowledge of his rights at the time of interrogation."[170]

Voluntary. The voluntariness of a waiver is tested by examining "the totality of all the surrounding circumstances."[171] The determination involves essentially the same inquiry as the Due Process standard discussed in § 12.2, supra, focusing on the characteristics of the defendant as well as the circumstances of the interrogation.[172] It must be emphasized, however, that the issues of the voluntariness of the waiver and the confession are separate and distinct.[173]

An important factor to be weighed in determining the voluntariness of a waiver is the length of the interrogation, which if excessive may "raise a suspicion that the police were trying to wear down the defendant's inner resources."[174] "Off-hour questioning" such as during the early morning hours is looked upon with disfavor but does not, in itself, constitute coercion.[175] While there is no *per se* rule regarding

---

[168] *Com. v. Collins*, supra, 440 Mass at 478 n.2, 799 NE2d at1254 n.2.

[169] See *Com. v. Beland*, 436 Mass 273, 288, 764 NE2d 324, 336-337 (2002).

[170] *Com. v. Garcia*, 379 Mass 422, 431, 399 NE2d 460, 466 (1980).

[171] *Com. v. Borodine*, supra, 371 Mass at 6, 353 NE2d at 653.

[172] *Com. v. Edwards*, 420 Mass 666, 670, 651 NE2d 398, 401 (1995). For examples of the analysis, see, e.g., *Colorado v. Connelly*, 479 US 157 (1986) (emphasis on police coercion); *Com. v. Jones*, 439 Mass 249, 256-257, 786 NE2d 1197, 1205 (2003); *Com. v. Gaboriault*, 439 Mass 84, 88-89, 785 NE2d 691, 697 (2003); *Com. v. Freeman*, 430 Mass 111, 114-115, 712 NE2d 1135, 1140 (1999); *Com. v. Coplin*, 34 Mass App 478, 482, 612 NE2d 1188, 1190 (1993). See also *Com. v. McCowen*, 458 Mass 461, 469-472, 939 NE2d 735, 746-748 (2010) (waiver valid where defendant wished to speak to the troopers in an attempt to "straighten everything out," and his refusal to be recorded demonstrated that he could say "no" to police when he wished).

[173] See *Com. v. Williams*, 388 Mass 846, 851 n.2, 448 NE2d 1114, 1118 n.2 (1983) (& citations); *Com. v. Wallen*, 35 Mass App 915, 917, 619 NE2d 365, 367 (1993).

[174] *Com. v. Bradshaw*, 385 Mass 244, 268, 431 NE2d 880, 895 (1982).

[175] See *Com. v. Hunter*, 426 Mass 715, 722 n.3, 690 NE2d 815, 822 n.3 (1998) (& citations).

waivers made during drug withdrawal, the prosecution bears a heavy burden to show that the waiver was voluntary.[176]

A waiver that is the result of police threats, trickery, promises, or deliberate misrepresentations is not voluntary.[177] Trickery alone, however, may not invalidate a waiver if there is evidence, in light of other surrounding circumstances, that it was made voluntarily.[178] An officer may suggest that it would be better for a suspect to tell the truth, as long as there is no assurance that a statement will aid the defense.[179] An officer's promise to make known to the district attorney's office and to judge the defendant's cooperation in making a statement does

[176] See *Com. v. Ringuette*, 60 Mass App 351, 354, 801 NE2d 813, 816 (2004), *aff'd on other grounds*, 443 Mass 1003, 819 NE2d 941 (2004).

[177] *Miranda v. Arizona*, supra, 384 US at 476; *Com. v. Medeiros*, supra, 395 Mass at 345, 479 NE2d at 1378. See, e.g., *Com. v. Jackson*, 377 Mass 319, 327-329, 386 NE2d 15, 20-21 (1979) (officer falsely told defendant that his girlfriend had given police incriminatory statement); *Com. v. Meehan*, 377 Mass 552, 563-564, 387 NE2d 527, 537 (1979) (misrepresentations concerning strength of Commonwealth's case and that confession would benefit defendant); *Com. v. Magee*, 423 Mass 381, 387, 668 NE2d 339, 344 (1996) (promise by officers that defendant would receive psychological help she was seeking if she provided information created quid pro quo undermining validity of waiver); *Com. v. Hunt*, 12 Mass App 841, 844, 429 NE2d 379, 381 (1981) (& citations) (implicit threat or promise that defendant's wife would be released if he confessed and did not implicate her). Compare *Com. v. Groome*, 435 Mass 201, 218-219, 755 NE2d 122, 1238-1239 (2001) (while offers of amenities in exchange for waiver may render it involuntary, trooper's highly unusual promise of a walk outside the barracks if defendant signed waiver form occurred after defendant had already told officers he would speak with them, and had already begun to do so).

[178] See *Com. v. Edwards*, 420 Mass 666, 671, 651 NE2d 398, 402 (1995) (waiver not rendered involuntary by detectives' false statement that defendant's handprint had been recovered at murder scene); *Com. v. Selby*, 420 Mass 656, 663-664, 651 NE2d 843, 848-849 (1995) (false representation that defendant's handprint placed him in victim's house did not invalidate waiver); *Com. v. Forde*, supra, 392 Mass at 455-456, 466 NE2d at 511-512 (defendant made valid waiver even though police officer falsely suggested that his fingerprints had been found on victim's body; the fact that the statement was evoked by trickery is "relevant but not conclusive"). See also *Com. v. Corriveau*, 396 Mass 319, 331-332, 486 NE2d 29, 38-39 (1985) (officer's statement to defendant that others had already spoken to police did not make defendant's waiver the product of coercion where defendant had already observed friend talking to police at the stationhouse).

[179] See *Com. v. Carnes*, 457 Mass 812, 822, 933 NE2d 598, 607-608 (2010) (officer's telling defendant "the truth would come out" did not invalidate waiver); *Com. v. Ortiz*, 435 Mass 569, 577, 760 NE2d 282, 288-289 (2002); *Com. v. Burgess*, 434 Mass 307, 314, 749 NE2d 112, 118 (2001); *Com. v. Souza*, 418 Mass 478, 481-482, 702 NE2d 1167, 1170 (1998) (& citations).

not itself invalidate the waiver.[180] Statements to the defendant disparaging the assistance of lawyers (like "Sometimes they give good advice, but you're your own man") should be avoided.[181]

When an accused has invoked his right to silence or to counsel, a valid waiver cannot be established merely by showing that he responded to further police-initiated custodial interrogation even if it is preceded by *Miranda* warnings.[182] "Where a desire to remain silent was made known to the police, it is infrequent that a valid waiver of constitutional rights will be found when only a short interval existed between the time when a defendant asserted his right to terminate questioning and the time when interrogation was subsequently resumed."[183]

The refusal to allow a family member to participate in the interrogation does not undermine the voluntariness of defendant's waiver as long as the officers do not attempt to trick him into talking without the family member or offer him anything in return for doing so.[184]

c. *Waiver by Juvenile: "Interested Adult" Rule*

The Supreme Judicial Court has observed that "circumstances and techniques of custodial interrogation which pass constitutional muster when applied to a normal adult may not be constitutionally tolerable as applied to one who is immature or mentally deficient."[185] Thus, while both juveniles and mentally deficient adults may make effective waivers, "special caution" must be taken in scrutinizing the totality of the circumstances.[186]

---

[180] *Com. v. Williams*, 388 Mass 846, 852, 448 NE2d 1114, 1121 (1983).

[181] *Com. v. Hoose*, 467 Mass 395, 401-402, 5 NE3d 843, 851-852 (2014).

[182] See *Michigan v. Mosley*, 423 US 96 (1975) and *Edwards v. Arizona*, 451 US 477 (1981) (discussed in § 12.6.1, supra.).

[183] *Com. v. Mandeville*, 386 Mass 393, 403, 436 NE2d 912, 919 (1982). But compare *Com. v. Richmond*, 379 Mass 557, 560, 399 NE2d 1069, 1072 (1980) (defendant waived right to counsel shortly after invoking it by questioning police about the details of crime).

[184] See *Com. v. Brum*, 438 Mass 103, 113, 777 NE2d 1238, 1247 (2002).

[185] *Com. v. Daniels*, 366 Mass 601, 606, 321 NE2d 822, 826 (1975) (moderately retarded young man). See also *Com. v. Williams*, 388 Mass 846, 852, 448 NE2d 1114, 1119 (1983) (& citations).

[186] *Com. v. Philip S., a Juvenile*, 414 Mass 804, 808, 611 NE2d 226, 230 (1993); *Com. v. Tavares*, 385 Mass 140, 146, 430 NE2d 1198, 1202 (1982).

Recognizing the unique problems that arise with respect to waiver when the accused is a juvenile, Massachusetts has adopted an "interested adult" rule regarding confessions.[187] In order to demonstrate a knowing and intelligent waiver by a juvenile, the Commonwealth must show that a parent or interested adult was present, understood the warnings, and had the opportunity to explain his rights to the juvenile so that he would understand the significance of waiver.[188] Where the juvenile is under the age of 14, no waiver can be effective without this protection.[189] Where the juvenile has reached the age of 14, a waiver in the absence of such protection is valid only if the circumstances demonstrate a high degree of intelligence, experience, knowledge, or sophistication on the part of the juvenile.[190] The Commonwealth has the burden to make that showing.[191]

In April 2015, the Supreme Judicial Court modified the interested adult rule in conformity with St. 2013, c. 84, which amended an array of statutory provisions to treat 17-year-olds as juveniles, by prospectively extending the rule to include 17-year-old defendants as entitled to an opportunity to consult with an interested adult.[192]

The standards for determining whether a juvenile has been given sufficient opportunity for consultation have a common-law basis and are not constitutionally mandated.[193]

In deciding whether an adult advising a juvenile during interrogation is an "interested adult" for purposes of the rule, the facts must

---

[187] See *Com. v. A Juvenile*, 389 Mass 128, 449 NE2d 654 (1983).

[188] *Id.*, 389 Mass at 134, 449 NE2d at 657, 658.

[189] *Id.*; *Com. v. Mark M.*, 65 Mass App 703, 706, 834 NE2d 680, 683 (2006).

[190] *Com. v. A Juvenile*, supra; *Com. v. Alfonso A.*, 438 Mass 372, 380, 780 NE2d 1244, 1251 (2003); *Com. v. Berry*, 410 Mass 31, 34-35, 570 NE2d 1004, 1006-1007 (1991). The "interested adult" rule does not apply to persons 17 years or older. *Com. v. Trombley*, 72 Mass App 183, 186, 889 NE2d 446, 448 (2008); *Jones v. Maloney*, 74 Mass App 745, 749 n.4, 910 NE2d 412, 415 n.4 (2009). For a case discussing the "interested adult" rule in the context of successive interrogations where the rule is violated during the initial interview, see *Com. v. Mark M.*, supra, 65 Mass App 703, 843 NE2d 680.

[191] *Com. v. Ray*, 467 Mass 115, 132-134, 4 NE3d 221, 235-236 (2014) (defendant, close to age 17, had experience with the criminal justice system and evidenced understanding of the warnings).

[192] *Com. v. Smith*, 471 Mass 161, 28 NE3d 385 (2015).

[193] *Com. v. A Juvenile*, 402 Mass 275, 279, 521 NE2d 1368, 1371 (1988). See, e.g., *Com. v. Quint, Q.*, 84 Mass App 507, 998 NE2d 363 (2013) (fifteen-year-old had meaningful consultation with his mother where she was actively engaged throughout the interrogation, urged the juvenile to tell the truth, and seemed genuinely concerned for his welfare).

be viewed from the perspective of the officials conducting the interview.[194] "If, at the time of the interrogation (as assessed by objective standards), it should have been reasonably apparent to the officials questioning a juvenile that the adult who was present on his or her behalf lacked capacity to appreciate the juvenile's situation and to give advice, or was actually antagonistic toward the juvenile, a finding would be warranted that the juvenile has not been assisted by an interested adult and did not have the opportunity for consultation contemplated by our rule."[195]

The interested adult rule is not violated, however, merely because a parent fails to provide "what, in hindsight and from a legal perspective, might have been optimum advice."[196] Nor does the fact that the adult has a relationship with the victims preclude her from acting as an interested adult.[197] The critical point is that the opportunity to consult must be with "an interested adult who was *informed of*, and *understood*" the constitutional rights.[198] It is assumed the adult would be present at the interrogation area, if not the interrogation itself.[199] The "interested adults" in the decided cases have all been parents or other relatives.[200]

For juveniles at least 14 years old, the "interested adult" rule requires a showing that the juvenile and the adult were provided a "genuine opportunity" to consult; it does not require that an *actual* consultation occur.[201] As long as the juvenile is at least 14 and has had this opportunity for meaningful consultation, the juvenile may make a

---

[194] *Com. v. Philip S., a Juvenile*, supra, 414 Mass at 809, 611 NE2d at 230-231.

[195] *Id.* See generally *Com. v. Escalera*, 70 Mass App 729, 876 NE2d 493 (2007) (foster parents may serve as interested adult as long as they have a relationship with the juvenile and are sufficiently interested in his welfare).

[196] *Com. v. Philip S., a Juvenile*, supra, 414 Mass at 810, 611 NE2d at 23.

[197] See *Com. v. McCra*, 427 Mass 564, 568-569, 694 NE2d 849, 852-853 (1998) (defendant's aunt was sister of one of victims).

[198] See *Com. v. Alfonso*, 53 Mass App 279, 291, 758 NE2d 1070, 1080 (2001) (juvenile's mother was not even informed of her son's interrogation, let alone his constitutional rights; waiver invalid); *Com. v. Leon*, 52 Mass App 823, 756 NE2d 1162 (2001) (juvenile defendants' Spanish-speaking mothers were "interested adults" because officers conducting interview had objective facts indicating that mothers comprehended events and could assist juveniles; but subsequent statements were involuntary).

[199] *Com. v. Alfonso*, supra, 53 Mass App at 292, 758 NE2d at 1080-1081.

[200] *Id.*, 53 Mass App at 293, 758 NE2d at 1081-1082.

[201] *Com. v. McCra*, supra, 427 Mass at 567-568, 694 NE2d at 852; *Com. v. Philip S., a Juvenile*, supra, 414 Mass at 811-813, 611 NE2d at 232; *Com. v. Berry*, supra, 410 Mass at 35 & n.2, 570 NE2d at 1007 & n.2; *Com. v. Guthrie*, 66 Mass App 414, 419, 848 NE2d 787, 792 (2006); *Com. v. Mark M.*, supra, 65 Mass App at 706-707, 834 NE2d at 683 (grandmother and juvenile should have been given opportunity to consult before questioning began).

valid waiver without actual consultation.[202] Juveniles under the age of 14, however, must actually consult with an interested adult in order for their *Miranda* waiver to be valid.[203]

"[T]he ultimate question is whether the juvenile has understood his rights and the potential consequences of waiving them before talking to the police."[204] The Commonwealth must show "that the presence of [his guardian] gave the juvenile a realistic opportunity to get helpful advice if he needed it."[205]

The Supreme Judicial Court has refused to adopt a fixed rule that a minor's opportunity to consult with an interested adult requires that the police expressly inform the minor and the adult that they may confer *in private*. While the police may not properly deny them that right, it is sufficient if the minor and adult are generally advised of their right to confer.[206] Nor are the officials required to expressly inform a juvenile and his parent that they should use their opportunity to confer for a discussion of the juvenile's rights. The better practice, however, is for the investigating officers to explicitly inform the juvenile's parent, or other interested adult that "an opportunity is being furnished for the two to confer about the juvenile's rights."[207]

---

[202] *Com. v. Alfonso A.*, 438 Mass 372, 380-382, 780 NE2d 1244, 1251-1252 (2003) (repeated offers by police to contact juvenile's mother did not afford "genuine opportunity" because she was not actually present and juvenile would have had to interrupt interrogation and await her arrival; extensive discussion of "interested adult" rule).

[203] *Com. v. McCra*, supra, 427 Mass at 568 n.2, 694 NE2d at 852 n.2.

[204] *Com. v. MacNeill*, 399 Mass 71, 79, 502 NE2d 938, 943 (1987). Compare *Com. v. Philip S., a Juvenile*, supra, 414 Mass at 813-814, 611 NE2d at 233 (nothing to show that juvenile was impaired or that investigating officials used threats, promises, or subterfuge to induce him to talk), *Com. v. Tevenal*, 401 Mass 225, 227-228, 515 NE2d 1191, 1192-1193 (1987) (judge was warranted in finding that defendant and his mother understood his *Miranda* rights, that he had an opportunity to consult with his mother, and that he voluntarily waived his rights), and *Com. v. King*, 17 Mass App 602, 609-611, 460 NE2d 1299, 1305-1306 (1984) (although 16-year-old defendant did not have opportunity to consult with his mother before being questioned by police, evidence warranted finding that waiver was valid) with *Com. v. Guyton*, 405 Mass 497, 502-504, 541 NE2d 1006, 1009-1010 (1989) (Commonwealth failed to sustain burden of establishing that 16-year-old defendant, who did not have the opportunity to consult with "interested adult," had capacity of waiving his rights without consultation), *Com. v. A Juvenile*, supra, 402 Mass at 280, 521 NE2d at 1371-1372 (juvenile did not have high degree of intelligence, experience, knowledge, or sophistication to make valid waiver).

[205] *Com. v. Pacheco*, 87 Mass App 286, 28 NE3d 1172, 1177 (2015) (citation omitted).

[206] See *Com. v. Ward*, 412 Mass 395, 397, 590 NE2d 173, 174 (1992); *Com. v. Pacheco*, supra, 87 Mass App at 286, 28 NE3d at 1177.

[207] *Com. v. Philip S., a Juvenile*, supra, 414 Mass at 811 n.5, 611 NE2d at 232 n.5.

Where the juvenile has had the opportunity to consult with an interested adult and waives his rights, he can still cut-off questioning in mid-interrogation by requesting another consultation with the adult, which must be scrupulously honored.[208]

The interested adult rule is subject to the public safety exception discussed at § 12.6.7, infra.[209]

d. *Appellate Review*

A trial judge's finding of waiver of *Miranda* rights is entitled to substantial deference by the appellate court. Subsidiary findings of fact and credibility will not be disturbed where they are warranted by the evidence, but ultimate findings of constitutional dimension are open for review and independent determination.[210] The use at trial of statements elicited from a defendant in violation of *Miranda* is subject to harmless-error analysis.[211]

§ 12.6.5 Subsequent Statements and Derivative Evidence

Under federal constitutional law, a statement obtained from a suspect subsequent to the elicitation of an earlier statement in violation of

---

[208] *Com. v. Pacheco*, supra, 87 Mass App 286, 28 NE3d at 1178-1180 (2015).

[209] See *Com. v. Alan A.*, 47 Mass App 271, 712 NE2d 1157 (1999) (because officers reasonably feared that they and others were in danger unless missing gun was located, they could question juvenile without *Miranda* warnings or giving juvenile opportunity to speak with parents or interested adult).

[210] *Com. v. Hoose*, 467 Mass 395, 399-400, 5 NE3d 843, 849-850 (2014); *Com. v. Clarke*, 461 Mass 336, 340-341, 960 NE2d 306, 313 (2012). See, e.g., *Com. v. Prater*, 431 Mass 86, 90, 725 NE2d 233, 238 (2000) (although defendant testified he had smoked marijuana prior to arrest, motion judge was entitled to credit testimony of officers that defendant was not under influence of drugs); *Com. v. Herbert*, 421 Mass 307, 313, 656 NE2d 899, 902 (1995) (judge's findings that defendant did not request attorney, was not told by any officer that he should tell truth, and was not told that no attorney was available were properly based on rejection of defendant's testimony and on reasonable inferences from police witnesses); *Com. v. Boncore*, 412 Mass 1013, 593 NE2d 227 (1992); *Com. v. Berry*, 410 Mass 31, 34, 570 NE2d 1004, 1006-1007 (1991); *Com. v. Colon*, 408 Mass 419, 426, 558 NE2d 974, 980 (1990) (judge entitled to discredit defendant's testimony concerning circumstances of waiver); *Com. v. Benjamin*, 399 Mass 220, 222-223, 503 NE2d 660, 663 (1987) (judge's rejection of defendant's assertion that he was confused about rights was supported by record).

[211] See *Com. v. Molina*, 467 Mass 65, 78-79, 3 NE3d 583, 595 (2014); *Com. v. Ghee*, 414 Mass 313, 318-319, 607 NE2d 1005, 1009 (1993); *Com. v. Perez*, 411 Mass 249, 259, 581 NE2d 1010, 1017 (1991).

Miranda is not presumptively inadmissible. "[A]bsent deliberately coercive or improper tactics in obtaining the initial statement, the mere fact that a suspect has made an unwarned admission does not warrant a presumption of compulsion. A subsequent administration of *Miranda* warnings to a suspect who has given a voluntary but unwarned statement ordinarily should suffice to remove the conditions that precluded admission of the earlier statement."[212] Where *Miranda* warnings are deliberately withheld as a tactic in order to secure a first statement to be used to persuade the suspect to repeat it in a subsequent warned interrogation, however, the second statement is inadmissible.[213]

Massachusetts law provides "additional protections."[214] As a common-law rule of evidence, where a statement follows an earlier statement obtained in violation of *Miranda* requirements, the second statement is presumed to be tainted by the first, and the prosecution is required to show more than the belated administration of *Miranda* warnings in order to dispel that taint.[215] The presumption may be overcome by showing either: (1) there was a break in the stream of events after the illegally obtained statement that sufficiently insulated the second statement from the taint of the first; or (2) the illegally obtained statement did not incriminate the defendant, so that "the cat was not out of the bag."[216]

---

[212] *Oregon v. Elstad*, 470 US 298, 314 (1985). See also *Michigan v. Tucker*, 417 US 433 (1974); *Com. v. Rubio*, 27 Mass App 506, 515 & n.9, 540 NE2d 189, 194 & n.9 (1989).

[213] *Missouri v. Seibert*, 542 US 600 (2004).

[214] *Com. v. Snyder*, 413 Mass 521, 530, 597 NE2d 1363, 1368 (1992). See generally Katherine E. McMahon, "Cat-Out-of-the-Bag" & "Break-in-the-Stream-of-Events": Massachusetts' Rejection of *Oregon v. Elstad* for Suppression of Warned Statements Made after a Miranda Violation, 20 WN Eng L Rev 173 (1998).

[215] See generally *Com. v. Thomas*, 469 Mass 531, 551-552, 21 NE3d 901, 918-920 (2014); *Com. v. Smith*, 412 Mass 823, 836-837, 593 NE2d 1288, 1295-1296 (1992). See also *Com. v. Mark M.*, 65 Mass App 703, 708, 843 NE2d 680, 684 (2006) (violation of "interested adult" rule in juvenile's first interview tainted statement secured in second).

[216] The "cat out of the bag" analysis requires exclusion of a statement if, in giving it, the defendant was motivated by the belief that in a prior coerced statement he had already disclosed the information and he had nothing to lose by repetition. See *Com. v. Thomas*, supra, 469 Mass at 552, 21 NE3d at 919-920; *Com. v. Diaz*, 451 Mass 266, 276 n.4, 901 NE2d 670, 680 n.4 (2009) (citing *Com. v. Mahnke*, 368 Mass 662, 686, 335 NE2d 660, 686 (1975)). See also *Com. v. Mathews*, 450 Mass 858, 878 n.20, 882 NE2d 833, 848 n.20 (2008); *Com. v. Larkin*, 429 Mass 426, 436-438, 708 NE2d 674, 682 (1999); *Com. v. Nom*, 426 Mass 152, 155-156, 686 NE2d 1017, 1021 (1997); *Com. v. Torres*, 424 Mass 792, 799-800, 678 NE2d 847, 852 (1997); *Com. v. Prater*, 420 Mass

"The focus and ultimate goal of undertaking either or both lines of analysis is a determination of the voluntariness of the later confession. If the defendant's subsequent statements were not a product of coercion, either by coercive external forces or primarily by a sense of futility that he has already incriminated himself with the first statement, then the Fifth Amendment to the United States Constitution does not require suppression of the subsequent statement."[217]

While federal law does not require the suppression of physical evidence derived from a statement (otherwise voluntary) obtained in violation of *Miranda*,[218] Massachusetts law treats such derivative evidence as presumptively excludable.[219] Under Massachusetts law, statements obtained in violation of *Miranda* cannot be considered in determining probable cause to secure a search warrant or to arrest.[220]

569, 579-581, 651 NE2d 833, 840-841 (1995); *Com. v. Osachuk*, 418 Mass 229, 235, 635 NE2d 1192, 1196 (1994); *Com. v. Garner*, 59 Mass App 350, 367, 795 NE2d 1202, 1216 (2003).

[217] *Com. v. Prater*, supra, 420 Mass at 581, 651 NE2d at 841 (defendant's videotaped statement ninety minutes after first statement was sufficiently removed and thus admissible); *Com. v. Harris*, 75 Mass App 696, 699-701, 916 NE2d 396, 399-401 (2009), *review granted*, 455 Mass 1108 (defendant's second statement to police was not tainted by prior statement obtained in violation of *Miranda*). Compare *Com. v. Damiano*, 422 Mass 10, 13, 660 NE2d 660, 662 (1996) (defendant's later statements not free from taint of earlier *Miranda* violation where questioning was continuous and earlier statement was incriminating). See also *Com. v. Osachuk*, supra, 418 Mass at 235-237, 635 NE2d at 1196-1197; *Com. v. Smallwood*, 379 Mass 878, 886 n.2, 401 NE2d 802, 807 n.2 (1980) (& citations).

[218] See *United States v. Patane*, 542 US 630 (2004).

[219] See *Com. v. Martin*, 444 Mass 213, 827 NE2d 198 (2005) (firearm and ammunition seized by police detective, obtained as result of defendant's statement to police detective without first administering *Miranda* warnings, had to be suppressed as "fruit" of detective's unlawful questioning.) See also *Com. v. DiMarzio*, 436 Mass 1012, 767 NE2d 1059 (2002); *Com. v. Barros*, 56 Mass App 675, 678-679, 779 NE2d 693, 696 (2002) (suppressing physical evidence obtained as direct result of *Miranda* violation); *Com. v. Morales*, 461 Mass 765, 779, 965 NE2d 177, 189 (2012). But see *Com. v. Lites*, 67 Mass App 815, 821, 858 NE2d 302, 307-308 (2006) (applying the inevitable discovery exception to drug evidence seized from defendant as result of a *Miranda*-violation statement).

[220] See *Com. v. Haas*, 398 Mass 806, 808 n.2, 501 NE2d 1154, 1156 (1986); *Com. v. White*, 374 Mass 132, 138-139, 371 NE2d 777, 781 (1977). See also *Com. v. Loadholt*, 456 Mass 411, 422-423, 923 NE2d 1037, 1048-1049 (2010) (third-party consent to search was not the fruit of a *Miranda* violation).

§ 12.6.6 Inapplicability of **Miranda** *to Statements Obtained by Private Citizens, to Grand Jury Witnesses, and to Evidence at Parole Revocation Hearings*

Miranda is inapplicable when a statement is obtained by a private citizen not acting in concert with police.[221] The sole inquiry in such cases is whether the statement was voluntarily made, as discussed in § 12.2, supra.

The *Miranda* protections do not apply to grand jury witnesses,[222] but they do have a statutory right "to consult with counsel and to have counsel present at . . . examination before the grand jury."[223] The Supreme Judicial Court has recently exercised its supervisory powers to adopt a rule requiring advisement of rights "where there is a substantial likelihood that the witness may become an accused; that is, where the witness is a 'target' or is reasonably likely to become one." Thus "where, at the time a person appears to testify before a grand jury, the prosecutor has reason to believe that the witness is either a 'target' or is likely to become one, the witness must be advised, before testifying, that (1) he or she may refuse to answer any question if a truthful answer would tend to incriminate the witness, and (2) anything that he or she does say may be used against the witness in a subsequent legal proceeding. The rule we adopt is meant to discourage the Commonwealth from identifying a person as a likely participant in the crime

---

[221] *Com. v. Ira I.*, 439 Mass 805, 812-813, 791 NE2d 894, 900-901 (2003) (school officials not acting as agents of police are not required to give *Miranda* warnings prior to questioning student in conjunction with school investigation; even if school's policy was to provide information to police, that does not transform school officials into police agents); *Com. v. Snyder*, 413 Mass 521, 531-532, 597 NE2d 1363, 1369 (1992) (school principal); *Com. v. Mahnke*, 368 Mass 662, 676-678, 335 NE2d 660, 669-670 (1975) (private citizens abducted and questioned defendant about missing girl). Compare *Com. v. A Juvenile*, 402 Mass 275, 278, 521 NE2d 1368, 1370 (1988) (assistant director of youth detention facility acted as instrument of the police in questioning juvenile).

Statements elicited by non-police persons considered agents of law enforcement authorities, including court officers and DSS investigators, have been suppressed under the Sixth Amendment when violative of defendant's right to counsel. See *Com. v. Hilton*, 443 Mass 597, 823 NE2d 383 (2005), *appeal after remand*, 450 Mass 173, 877 NE2d 545 (2007) and *Com. v. Howard*, 446 Mass 563, 845 NE2d 368 (2006), discussed in § 12.7, infra.

[222] *United States v. Mandujano*, 425 US 564 (1976).

[223] GL 277, § 14A. See also *Com. v. Griffin*, 404 Mass 372, 374, 535 NE2d 594, 595-596 (1989); *Com. v. Gilliard*, 36 Mass App 183, 629 NE2d 349 (1994).

under investigation, compelling his or her appearance and testimony at the grand jury without adequate warnings, and then using that testimony in a criminal trial."[224]

Inculpatory statements obtained in violation of *Miranda* are admissible at probation revocation hearings.[225]

§ 12.6.7 Exceptions to the Miranda *Doctrine—Public Safety and Impeachment*

Miranda does not apply to custodial interrogations concerning matters that pose an immediate danger to public safety, such as the location of a gun.[226] The Supreme Judicial Court has extended the exception to situations where the safety of the police is threatened, as well as where the public is in danger.[227]

The Supreme Judicial Court has ruled that GL 140, § 129C (requiring a person found with a firearm to exhibit his license on demand of a police officer) does not create an exception to the *Miranda* rule.

---

[224] *Com. v. Woods*, 466 Mass 707, 719-720, 1 NE3d 762, 772 (2014).

[225] *Com. v. Vincente*, 405 Mass 278, 540 NE2d 669 (1989) (& citations); *Com. v. Simon*, 57 Mass App 80, 87, 781 NE2d 839, 845 (2003).

[226] See *New York v. Quarles*, 467 US 649 (1984) ("The gun is over there" in response to a police question in a supermarket was admissible despite absence of warnings); *Com. v. Loadholt*, 456 Mass 411, 416-419, 923 NE2d 1037, 1044-1046 (2010) (police officer's demand to know location of firearm prior to *Miranda* warnings came within public safety exception); *Com. v. Clark*, 432 Mass 1, 13-14, 730 NE2d 872, 884-885 (2000) (officer's question whether defendant was alone at scene of shootout with trooper was posed out of concern for safety of civilians); *Com. v. McCollum*, 79 Mass App 239, 255, 945 NE2d 937,952 (2011) (protective sweep uncovered the presence of a firearm holster); *Com. v. Dillon D.*, 448 Mass 793, 863 NE2d 1287 (2007) (juvenile's statements to police regarding gun were admissible notwithstanding failure to give warnings or comply with interested adult rule); *Com. v. White*, 74 Mass App 342, 347, 906 NE2d 1011, 1015 (2009); *Com. v. Guthrie*, 66 Mass App 414, 848 NE2d 787 (2006), *aff'd*, 449 Mass 1028 (2007) (officers had immediate right to question juvenile about gun).

[227] *Com. v. Loadholt*, 456 Mass 411, 418, 923 NE2d 1037, 1045-1046 (2010) (exception applied to defendant's pre-*Miranda* statement to police that a gun was located in the bedroom closet); *Com. v. Alan A.*, 47 Mass App 271, 712 NE2d 1157 (1999) (because officers reasonably feared that they and others were in danger unless missing gun was located, they could question juvenile without *Miranda* warnings or giving him opportunity to speak with parents or interested adult); *Com. v. Kitchings*, 40 Mass App 591, 598, 666 NE2d 511, 516-517 (1996) (trooper not required to give warnings before demanding to know where gun was located in car, because his safety was in jeopardy). See also *Com. v. Bourgeois*, 404 Mass 61, 66, 533 NE2d 638, 642 (1989).

Beyond ordering the subject to produce a license (which does not involve a testimonial communication), questioning (including whether the subject has a license) must be preceded by the warnings.[228]

Statements obtained in violation of the *Miranda* safeguards but otherwise uncoerced, voluntary, and trustworthy, may be used to impeach the defendant if he takes the witness stand.[229] Involuntary statements cannot be used even for the limited purpose of impeachment.[230]

§ 12.6.8 Pre- and Post-Arrest Silence/Evidence of Invocation of Rights/Defendant's Denials

Under Massachusetts common law principles, the post-arrest silence of a defendant (such as his failure to deny an accusation) may not be used as substantive evidence of guilt.[231] Nor can the prosecutor make reference to the defendant's silence after *Miranda* warnings,[232] or use post-warnings silence (like his failure to offer an exculpatory explanation) to impeach his testimony.[233] "The rule that a defendant has a constitutional right to remain silent at his arrest and while in custody is so fundamental as to require little elaboration. Impermissible comment upon a defendant's right to remain silent is so egregious that reversal is the norm, not the exception."[234]

Federal constitutional standards similarly prohibit post-arrest silence to be used substantively or for impeachment,[235] but do permit the defendant's post-arrest silence to be used for impeachment purposes *if the silence preceded Miranda warnings* and the circumstances

---

[228] *Com. v. Haskell*, 438 Mass 790, 795-797, 784 NE2d 625, 629-631 (2003).

[229] See *Oregon v. Hass*, 420 US 714 (1975); *Harris v. New York*, 401 US 222 (1971); *Com. v. Ly*, 454 Mass 223, 228, 908 NE2d 1285, 1289 (2009); *Com. v. Espada*, 450 Mass 687, 702, 880 NE2d 795, 808 (2008).

[230] *Mincey v. Arizona*, 437 US 385, 398 (1978).

[231] *Com. v. Nickerson*, 386 Mass 54, 59 n.5, 434 NE2d 992, 995 n.5 (1982).

[232] *Com. v. Egardo*, 426 Mass 48, 50-52, 686 NE2d 432, 434-435 (1997).

[233] *Com. v. MacKenzie*, 413 Mass 498, 507 n.8, 597 NE2d 1037, 1043 n.8 (1992) ("Defendant's silence came during a custodial interrogation during which he had been advised of his right to remain silent. In such circumstances, a defendant's silence is 'insolubly ambiguous.'").

[234] *Com. v. Ewing*, 67 Mass App 531, 544, 854 NE2d 993, 1003 (2006), *aff'd*, 449 Mass 1035 (reversing conviction because prosecutor cross-examined defendant about, and referred in closing to, his failure to contact police after arrest to explain his side of alleged rape).

[235] *Doyle v. Ohio*, 426 US 610 (1976).

meet the usual requirements for an adoptive admission—*i.e.*, an ordinary person would be expected to contradict the accusation if false (see § 8.6.5, supra).[236] There is substantial doubt, however, that Massachusetts law would permit the use of post-arrest silence to impeach a defendant under *any* circumstances. Such use raises what the Supreme Judicial Court has described as "troublesome questions" under art. 12 of the Declaration of Rights of the Commonwealth.[237] The Court has advised that "[e]vidence of this nature is to be received with caution, especially in criminal cases, due to the fact that the meaning of a defendant's response, or lack thereof, to an accusatory statement is often ambiguous."[238]

Evidence relating to post-arrest silence has been admitted only on rare occasions[239] and rejected on many others.[240] A defendant's

---

[236] See *Fletcher v. Weir*, 455 US 603 (1982).

[237] *Com. v. Nickerson*, supra, 386 Mass at 58, 59 n.5, 434 NE2d at 995 n.5.

[238] See, e.g., *Com. v. MacKenzie*, supra, 413 Mass at 506, 597 NE2d at 1043 (1992) (defendant's response "We never meant to hurt the woman" did not adopt all details of accusatory statements and should not have been admitted as adoptive admission).

[239] See, e.g., *Com. v. Thurber*, 383 Mass 328, 333-335, 418 NE2d 1253, 1258 (1981) (escape defendant's post-arrest silence was properly allowed to impeach assertion that he had told police he had escaped where issue was opened on cross-examination); *Com. v. Halsey*, 41 Mass App 200, 204-205, 669 NE2d 774, 778 (1996) (testimony regarding defendant's demeanor after receiving warnings relevant on issue of voluntariness and not offered for sole purpose of having jurors infer guilt from silence).

[240] See *Com. v. Grenier*, 415 Mass 680, 690-691, 615 NE2d 922, 927 (1993) (jury should not have been permitted to hear that defendant terminated questioning after being asked whether he wanted to give police truthful statement as to involvement in murder); *Com. v. Cobb*, 374 Mass 514, 380 NE2d 142 (1978) (evidence of defendant's post-arrest refusal to respond to questions improperly admitted); *Com. v. Freeman*, 352 Mass 556, 562-563, 227 NE2d 3, 8 (1967) (judge erred in instructing jury on admission by silence where defendant, although not under arrest, was represented by counsel and entitled to leave all talking to attorney); *Com. v. Andujar*, 57 Mass App 529, 533-537, 784 NE2d 646, 649-651 (2003) (reversing conviction because prosecutor's redirect examination of police witness referred to defendant's post-arrest silence to impeach an exculpatory explanation); *Com. v. King*, 34 Mass App 466, 612 NE2d 690 (1993) (error to permit police officer to testify that defendant refused to answer questions during interrogation after receiving *Miranda* warnings); *Com. v. Ferrara*, 31 Mass App 648, 652, 582 NE2d 961, 964 (1991) (no admission by silence may be offered after defendant has been read his *Miranda* rights, placed under arrest, or so significantly deprived of freedom as to be effectively in police custody). See also *Com. v. Waite*, 422 Mass 792, 800-802 (improper for prosecutor in closing to refer to failure to give honest answers when arrested); *Com. v. Amirault*, 404 Mass 221, 236-238, 535 NE2d 193, 203-204 (1989) (prosecutor's comments on defendant's post-arrest silence improper); *Com. v. Egardo*, 42 Mass App 41, 674 NE2d 1088 (1997) (defense counsel's failure to object to prosecutor's comments regarding defendant's post-arrest silence required new trial). But compare *Com. v. Thompson*, 431 Mass 108, 117-118, 725 NE2d 556,

invocation of his right to remain silent may, however, be presented if necessary to avoid juror confusion about why an interview ended abruptly.[241]

Neither evidence of a defendant's post-*Miranda* warnings exercise of rights, nor reluctance to speak with police without an attorney, nor statements reflecting the process of decision-making as to whether to invoke rights, are admissible under state law.[242] Similarly, the prosecution is prohibited from arguing guilt from a defendant's decision to

---

565-566 (2000) (proper for prosecutor to argue in closing that defendant's failure to inquire about condition of wife and daughter during post-*Miranda* interrogation indicated guilt, because defendant did not invoke right to silence but instead gave far-ranging statement, and questions were ones an innocent party would ordinarily ask; thus remark was not comment on defendant's invocation of right to silence). Cf. *Com. v. O'Laughlin*, 446 Mass 188, 206, 843 NE2d 617, 631-632 (2006), *habeas granted*, 568 F2d 287 (1st Cir 2009) (applying same logic to defendant's revoking of consent to search).

[241] See *Com. v. Torres*, 442 Mass 554, 577-578, 813 NE2d 1261, 1280 (2004) (& citations); *Com. v. Waite*, supra, 422 Mass at 798-799, 665 NE2d at 987-988) (when defendant has cut off questioning testimony regarding cessation may be appropriate to prevent jury confusion even though it reveals post-*Miranda* silence); *Com. v. Martinez*, 431 Mass 168, 182-183, 726 NE2d 913, 927 (2000) (testimony that defendant did not want to talk anymore was admissible to prevent jury confusion about abrupt end to interview); *Com. v. Thad T.*, 59 Mass App 497, 500-501, 796 NE2d 869, 873-874 (2003) (evidence of juvenile's father's terminating interview used to explain why it ended abruptly). But compare *Com. v. Santana*, 465 Mass 270, 282-283, 988 NE2d 825, 836 (2013) (unlikely the jury would have thought termination of six-hour interview as abrupt or in need of explanation); *Com. v. Fowler*, supra, 431 Mass at 38-39, 725 NE2d at 206 (no indication of juror confusion about abrupt termination of interview that would justify mention of defendant's invocation of right to silence). See also *Com. v. Brum*, 441 Mass 199, 209, 804 NE2d 902, 909 (2004) (prosecutor merely responded to defense counsel's inference of police impropriety in questioning officer about defendant's refusal to speak after *Miranda* warnings); *Com. v. Caputo*, 439 Mass 153, 166, 786 NE2d 352, 362 (2003) (defense counsel himself raised defendant's invocation of right to silence during cross-examination of police witness in effort to show statements were coerced); *Com. v. Adams*, 434 Mass 805, 811-815, 753 NE2d 105, 111-113 (2001) (no reversal required where defendant's post-arrest silence evidence was initially introduced by defense counsel as part of trial strategy); *Com. v. Hubbard*, 69 Mass App 232, 238-240, 867 NE2d 341, 347-349 (2007) (redirect examination questions to police sergeant were properly admitted in response to defense suggestions that the interview of defendant was flawed); *Com. v. Wei H. Ye*, 52 Mass App 390, 395-397, 754 NE2d 86, 91-92 (2001) (detective's improper reference to defendant's silence not prejudicial where elicited inadvertently in context of inquiry into defendant's ability to speak English).

[242] See *Com. v. Letkowski*, 469 Mass 603, 15 NE3d 207 (2014) (prosecutor improperly referred to defendant's invocation of rights and silence during questioning of two witnesses and in closing); *Com. v. Beneche*, 458 Mass 61, 72-76, 933 NE2d 951, 962-965 (2010) (detective should not have been permitted to testify that after arrest and warnings, defendant remained silent and expressed his desire not to talk about his son's death); *Com. v. Connolly*, 454 Mass 808, 828-829, 913 NE2d 356, 373-374

consult a lawyer, whether in the context of police interrogation or otherwise.[243] A prosecutor may not comment in closing argument upon the defendant's post-arrest silence.[244] Evidence of a defendant's

---

(2009), *habeas denied*, 2013 WL 139702 (D Mass 2013) (detective should not have been permitted to testify that defendant stated he "did not have anything to say at that time" after receiving warnings); *Com. v. Brum*, 438 Mass 103, 120-121, 777 NE2d 1238, 1252-1253 (2002) (improper for police witnesses to refer to defendant's invocation of right to silence after he provided narrative and answered few questions); *Com. v. Fowler*, 431 Mass 30, 39-40, 725 NE2d 199, 207 (2000) (error for police officers to testify that defendant chose to remain silent, and for prosecutor to use defendant's intention to remain silent in closing argument); *Com. v. Gaynor*, 443 Mass 245, 272, 820 NE2d 233, 255 (2005) (police officer's testimony that defendant had consulted an attorney was interrupted by judge, thereby avoiding improper comment on defendant's exercise of right to remain silent); *Com. v. Farley*, 432 Mass 153, 158, 732 NE2d 893, 897 (2000) (prosecutor improperly cross-examined defendant as to why she failed to provide some information to the police after having been advised of her *Miranda* warnings, and defendant responded that she wanted a lawyer); *Com. v. DePace*, 433 Mass 379, 382-384, 742 NE2d 1054, 1058-1059 (2001) (admission of evidence concerning defendant's invocation of right to counsel required reversal); *Com. v. Letkowski*, 83 Mass App 847, 853-857, 991 NE2d 1106, 1112-1114 (2013) (several instances of improper use of defendant's invocation); *Com. v. Gonsalves*, 74 Mass App 910, 911, 907 NE2d 237, 239 (2009) (improper to admit evidence of defendant's refusal to answer booking questions and request for a lawyer); *Com. v. Clarke*, 48 Mass App 482, 722 NE2d 987 (2000), *habeas denied after conviction on remand*, 585 F Supp 2d 196 (D Mass 2008), *aff'd*, 582 F3d 135 (1st Cir 2009) (prosecutor impermissibly used defendant's post-*Miranda* silence against him by arguing that defendant stopped questioning because he realized he had been caught in a lie). Compare *Com. v. Pytou Heang*, 458 Mass 827, 852, 942 NE2d 927, 948 (2011) (both defendant and defense counsel asked that the entire recorded interview be heard by the jury, including the invocation of rights). See also *Com. v. Brown*, 451 Mass 200, 208-209, 884 NE2d 488, 495-496 (2008) (trial judge implicated defendant's right to remain silent by requiring defense counsel to clarify during direct examination whether defendant had given a statement to the police, which he had not).

[243] See *Com. v. Nolin*, 448 Mass 207, 222, 859 NE2d 843, 856 (2007) (prosecutor should not have been permitted to argue from taped phone conversation between defendant in custody and a friend that defendant's summoning of his lawyer suggested guilt). See also *Com. v. Johnston*, 467 Mass 674, 689, 7 NE3d 424, 437 (2014) (references to defendant's request to confer with counsel at medical intake interview and at Bridgewater State Hospital should have been excluded). For improper reference to defendant's invocation of his right to silence and to an attorney in testimony before the grand jury, see *Com. v. Mathews*, 450 Mass 858, 874, 882 NE2d 833, 846 (2008).

[244] *Com. v. Letkowski*, supra, 469 Mass at 616, 15 NE3d at 217 (prosecutor improperly referred to defendant's invocation of rights and silence during closing); *Com. v. Braley*, 449 Mass 316, 327-328, 867 NE2d 743, 755 (2007) (that defendant never told trooper he had the wrong man and did not kill anybody nor asked why he was being taken back to Massachusetts); *Com. v. Ocasio*, 71 Mass App 304, 311-312, 882 NE2d 341, 347 (2008) (prosecutor should not have invited jury to infer guilt from defendant's failure to inquire why he was being arrested). Compare *Com. v. Womack*, 457 Mass 268, 278, 929 NE2d 943, 952 (2010) (prosecutor's argument that defendant did not tell officers about going to gas station after armed robbery because he was setting up his false alibi was not a comment on his exercise of right to remain silent, because

exercise of his *Miranda* rights is also inadmissible to establish his sanity[245] or to rebut a defense of necessity.[246]

All such evidence conveys to the jury the impression that defendant was hiding information and violates the fundamental due process protection that "a defendant, when in the hands of the police, should be able to invoke core constitutional rights without fear of making implied or adoptive admissions."[247]

The wrongful use of post-arrest silence to impeach the defendant at trial does not automatically constitute reversible error;[248] if the judge immediately instructs the jury to disregard the questions, reprimands the prosecutor, and explains why the questions are improper, the error may be found harmless.[249] It has been noted,

---

he waived that right and agreed to speak with police); *Com. v. Leach*, 73 Mass App 758, 765-766, 901 NE2d 708, 715-716 (2009) (prosecutor's comment was not on defendants' failure to assert their innocence in post-arrest conversation with each other while in holding cells, but rather on certain omissions). See also § 13.2, infra.

[245] See *Com. v. Mahdi*, 388 Mass 679, 694-696, 448 NE2d 704, 713-714 (1983). Compare *Com. v. Brown*, 449 Mass 747, 763-764, 872 NE2d 711, 724-725 (2007), *habeas denied*, *Brown v. O'Brien*, 666 F3d 818 (1st Cir 2012) (prosecutor's question to defense expert regarding significance to defendant's insanity defense of defendant's conversation with police regarding his *Miranda* rights was not improper comment on his right to remain silent, but focused on defendant's apparent comprehension of the rights); *Com. v. Toolan*, 460 Mass 452, 472-473, 951 NE2d 903, 921 (2011) (it was permissible for prosecutor, without reference to *Miranda* rights, to introduce and comment on defendant's actions upon arrest, including his apparent attempt to use the interview with police to acquire information, as showing his sanity; but unless defendant opens the door, it is not proper to elicit testimony referring to defendant's deliberations over whether to exercise his *Miranda* rights).

[246] See *Com. v. Thurber*, 383 Mass 328, 333-335, 418 NE2d 1253, 1258 (1981) (but prosecution properly sought to impeach defendant's testimony by showing that after he was captured he made no statement that he had escaped from Concord institution, because defense counsel failed to make timely objection).

[247] *Com. v. Peixoto*, 430 Mass 654, 658-659, 722 NE2d 470, 474. Compare *Com. v. Thad T.*, 59 Mass App 497, 503, 796 NE2d 869, 875 (2003) (evidence of *Miranda* waiver form noting juvenile invoked his rights properly admitted on issue of voluntariness of statement).

[248] See, e.g., *Com. v. Letkowski*, 469 Mass 603, 617-620, 15 NE3d 207, 217-220 (2014) (prosecutor improperly referred to defendant's invocation of rights and silence during questioning of two witnesses and in closing, but without any objection, no substantial risk of miscarriage of justice).

[249] See *Com. v. Isabelle*, 444 Mass 416, 419, 828 NE2d 53, 56-57 (2005), *habeas denied*, 568 F Supp 2d 85 (D Mass 2008); *Com. v. Toolan*, supra, 460 Mass at 470-473, 951 NE2d at 920-921 (only one reference to defendant's request for attorney, she had mentioned consulting with attorney during her cross-examination, and defendant did not request curative instruction); *Com. v. Brum*, 438 Mass 103, 121-122, 777 NE2d 1238, 1253 (2002); *Com. v. Fowler*, supra, 430 Mass at 42-43, 725 NE2d at 208-209; *Com. v. Peixoto*, supra, 430 Mass at 660-661, 722 NE2d at 475; *Com. v. Chase*, 70 Mass

however, that the nature of such an error is so egregious that reversal is the norm.[250]

There is no federal constitutional bar to the use of a defendant's *pre*-arrest silence to impeach his testimony.[251] But *Com. v. Nickerson* cautions that the pre-arrest silence of the defendant should not be admitted where it would not have been natural for the defendant to disclose the information because it would have incriminated him—"his failure to come forward in these circumstances says little about the truth of his trial testimony."[252] The Court observed:

> In general, impeachment of a defendant with the fact of his pre-arrest silence should be approached with caution, and, whenever it is undertaken, it should be prefaced by a proper demonstration that it was "natural" to expect the defendant to speak in the circumstances. A trial judge should feel free to conduct a voir dire on the question of impeachment of a witness (particularly a defendant) by his silence; and, if admitted, the judge should, on request, instruct the jury to consider that silence for the purpose of impeachment only if they find that the witness naturally should have spoken up in the circumstances.[253]

App 826, 833-836, 877 NE2d 945, 952-954 (2007). But see *Morgan v. Hall*, 569 F2d 1161 (1st Cir 1978) (granting habeas writ, concluding that judge's instructions did not cure error).

"[I]n cases where a prosecutor refers to the defendant's post-*Miranda* silence in a question to a witness or a statement to the jury, or elicits testimony about such silence from a witness, and the offending question, statement or testimony is promptly addressed by the court, in an instruction to disregard and/or strike from the record, there may not necessarily be a *Doyle* violation because the government has not been permitted to 'use' the defendant's silence against him. This is a case-by-case determination." *Ellen v. Brady*, 475 F3d 5, 11 (1st Cir 2007).

[250] *Com. v. DePace*, supra, 433 Mass at 385-386, 742 NE2d at 1060-1061; *Com. v. Mahdi*, supra, 388 Mass at 698 (discussing factors to be considered); *Com. v. King*, supra, 34 Mass App at 469.

[251] *Jenkins v. Anderson*, 447 US 231, 239 (1980).

[252] 386 Mass 54, 60-61, 434 NE2d 992, 996 (1982). See, e.g., *Irwin v. Com.*, 465 Mass 834, 853-854, 992 NE2d 275, 289 (2013) (prearrest silence was not inculpatory where subject was homeless, with three prior convictions, and had many reasons for failing to call detective back).

[253] 386 Mass at 62, 434 NE2d at 997. See also *Com. v. Beneche*, 458 Mass 61, 73 n.13, 933 NE2d 951, 963 n.13 (2010) ("Beneche had the right to remain silent in the face of Officer Gosselin's accusation even before receiving his *Miranda* rights, and admission of such silence as evidence of guilt infringes on that right"); *Com. v. Irwin*, 72 Mass App 643, 893 NE2d 414 (2008) (testimony and argument regarding defendant's failure to communicate with police was impermissible comment on his pre-arrest silence, requiring reversal; extensive discussion); *Com. v. Gonzalez*, 68 Mass App 620, 629-631, 863 NE2d 958, 966-967 (2007) (prosecutor should not have been allowed to impeach murder defendant with evidence that after learning he was a suspect he did

A defendant's failure to report information to someone other than the police would be "an appropriate subject for cross-examination where it would have been natural for the defendant to report those facts."[254]

A defendant who chooses to testify at trial subjects himself (as any witness) to impeachment by prior inconsistent statements, including the omission from a pretrial statement where it would have been natural to include the omitted fact.[255] Where the defendant has spoken to police about matters concerning the crime for which he has been arrested, the prosecutor may cross-examine the defendant about, and comment to the jury upon, any inconsistency or omission from his statement (where it would have been natural to include the omitted fact) that is at variance with his trial testimony, as with any prior inconsistent statement (see § 6.13.2, supra).[256] Where defendant's post-warnings statements are at variance with his trial defense, or suggest

---

not contact police; it would not have been natural for him to do so since he had already consulted with his attorney); *Com. v. Chase*, 70 Mass App 826, 832 n.7, 877 NE2d 945, 952 n.7 (2007).

[254] *Com. v. Nickerson*, supra, 386 Mass at 61 n.6, 434 NE2d at 996 n.6. Compare *Com. v. Sosa*, 79 Mass App 106, 109-113, 943 NE2d 970, 974-976 (2011) (proper for prosecutor to elicit from murder defendant asserting self-defense that he failed, prior to his arrest and receiving warnings, to tell his co-workers that the victim had attacked him), *Com. v. Barnoski*, 418 Mass 523, 535, 638 NE2d 9, 16 (1994) (questions concerning defendant's failure to call ambulance for shooting victim were proper) and *Com. v. Lopes*, 34 Mass App 179, 184, 608 NE2d 749, 752 (1993) (because it would have been natural for defendant to discuss incident with brother, cross-examination regarding what defendant told brother was proper) with *Com. v. Martinez*, 34 Mass App 131, 608 NE2d 740 (1993) (improper for prosecutor to suggest inference of guilt from rape defendant's failure to offer to furnish district attorney with physical evidence). See also *Com. v. Thompson*, 431 Mass 108, 116-117, 725 NE2d 556, 564-565 (2000) (evidence that defendant, prior to arrest and *Miranda* warnings, stared silently at floor upon being told of wife's death, should not have been admitted).

[255] *Com. v. McCollum*, 79 Mass App 239, 256, 945 NE2d 937, 952-953 (2011) (it would have been natural for defendant to include in his affidavit accompanying his motion to suppress that an officer threatened to place his daughter into DSS custody if he did not admit to the firearm's ownership).

[256] See *Com. v. Greineder*, 458 Mass 207, 242-244, 936 NE2d 372. 398-399 (2010) (where defendant, while not in custody and not advised of *Miranda* warnings, made several statements to trooper, and then testified in a different fashion at trial, he could be cross-examined on the inconsistencies); *Com. v. Womack*, 457 Mass 268, 276-277, 929 NE2d 943, 951 (2010); *Com. v. Bell*, 455 Mass 408, 421-422, 917 NE2d 740, 752-753 (2009) (prosecutor could challenge defendant's credibility by confronting him on cross-examination with post-arrest statements he failed to mention on direct); *Com. v. Guy*, 441 Mass 96, 106, 803 NE2d 707, 717 (2004); *Com. v. Thompson*, supra, 431 Mass at 117-118, 725 NE2d at 565-566 (comment on defendant's failure to inquire about condition of wife and daughter); *Com. v. Fowler*, supra, 431 Mass at 37 n.10, 725 NE2d at 206 n.10; *Com. v. Rivera*, 425 Mass 633, 639-642, 682 NE2d 636, 641-642 (1997) (& citations); *Com. v. Martino*, 412 Mass 267, 282-284, 588 NE2d 651 (1992); *Com. v. Sosa*, 79 Mass App 106, 112-113, 943 NE2d 970, 975-976 (2011); *Com. v. Flanagan*, 76

consciousness of guilt, appropriate comment may be made on the statements even if defendant does not testify.[257]

Where the defendant himself testifies on direct examination to his statements to police, including his claim of innocence at the time of arrest, and seeks to explain his failure to disclose exculpatory information, the prosecution may cross-examine defendant and comment in closing on the matter.[258]

Neither the prosecution nor the defense can admit a defendant's unequivocal denial of an accusation after warnings.[259] The core of any prejudice in the admission of post-arrest accusations and denials is more likely caused by the accusation.[260] Where a defendant while under arrest makes an equivocal response to an accusation, both the accusation and reply may be admissible as an admission (providing there

---

Mass App 456, 465, 923 NE2d 101, 109 (2010); *Com. v. Hunt*, 50 Mass App 565, 567-568, 739 NE2d 284, 287 (2000). Compare *Com. v. Rivera*, 62 Mass App 859, 861-862, 821 NE2d 928, 931 (2005) (trial court's decision to allow police detective to testify that, during his interview of defendant, defendant did not mention any witnesses to event at issue, was erroneous).

[257] See *Com. v. Donovan*, 58 Mass App 631, 638-640, 792 NE2d 657, 662-663 (2003) (& citations); *Com. v. Richotte*, 59 Mass App 524, 527-530, 796 NE2d 890, 893-895 (2003).

[258] *Cronin v. Commissioner of Probation*, 783 F3d 47, 52 (1st Cir 2015).

[259] See *Com. v. Spencer*, 465 Mass 32, 48-51, 989 NE2d 205, 218-220 (2013); *Com. v. Womack*, 457 Mass 268, 271-272, 929 NE2d 943, 947-948 (2010) (post-*Miranda* accusatory statements made by officer to defendant during interview, which defendant unequivocally denied, could not be offered in Commonwealth's case-in-chief); *Com. v. Diaz*, 453 Mass 266, 273-274, 901 NE2d 670, 678-679 (2009) (defendant's unequivocal denials should not have been admitted, rejecting Commonwealth's argument that they demonstrated consciousness of guilt); *Com. v. Waite*, 422 Mass 792, 800-801, 665 NE2d 982, 989 (1996); *Com. v. Nawn*, 394 Mass 1, 4-5, 474 NE2d 545, 549 (1985) (offered by defense) (citing Text). See also *Com. v. Reed*, 444 Mass 803, 810, 831 NE2d 901, 907 (2005) (accusatory questions followed by unequivocal denials by defendant are inadmissible). But compare *Com. v. Pytou Heang*, 458 Mass 827, 852-853, 942 NE2d 927, 948 (2011) (both defendant and defense counsel asked that the entire recorded interview be heard by the jury, including his repeated denials); *Com. v. Donovan*, supra, 58 Mass App at 641, 792 NE2d at 664 (common-law rule forbidding denials does not apply where defendant waived his right to remain silent and gave a misleading statement that varied with his defense at trial).

The defendant's *prearrest* denials and exchanges with police do not fall within this exclusion. See *Com. v. Mejia*, 463 Mass 243, 251, 973 NE2d 657, 663 (2012).

[260] See *Com. v. Mejia*, 463 Mass 243, 252, 973 NE2d 657, 664 (2012) (quoting *Com. v. Womack*, supra, 457 Mass at 276, 929 NE2d 943). Where the evidence is cumulative, or where the evidence of denials is of value to the defendant's case, reversal is not required. See, e.g., *Com. v. Emeny*, 463 Mass 138, 148-149, 972 NE2d 1003, 1012-1013 (2012).

is no violation of defendant's right to counsel or privilege against self-incrimination).[261] An assertion of a constitutional right (such as the right to counsel) is not deemed an equivocal response within this rule.[262] False statements made by a defendant to exculpate himself may be admissible to show consciousness of guilt.[263]

§ 12.6.9 Relationship of Miranda *and Voluntariness Standard*

If a statement has been obtained in violation of *Miranda* requirements, it is inadmissible even if found to be voluntary under Due Process and common-law standards (see § 12.2, supra).[264] Conversely, a statement obtained in compliance with *Miranda* is nonetheless inadmissible if found to be involuntary. In sum,

> The question of the voluntariness of the waiver of [*Miranda*] rights and that of the voluntariness of the statements which [the suspect] made to the police may be interrelated, but they are separate and distinct questions. The former is whether the *Miranda* requirement of warnings was scrupulously observed and whether [the suspect] knowingly, intelligently and voluntarily waived the rights covered by the warnings. The latter is whether [the suspect's] statements were made freely and voluntarily when considering the 'totality of the circumstances' in which they were made.[265]

---

[261] *Com. v. Bonnett*, 472 Mass 827, 837-839, 37 NE3d 1064, 1074-1075 (2015) (defendant's denials—"I wouldn't be able to vouch for that [being at the crime scene]"—could be construed as self-incriminating and did not meet requisite unequivocal character to render them inadmissible); *Com. v. Grenier*, 415 Mass 680, 688-689, 615 NE2d 922, 926-927 (1993) (& citations); *Com. v. Valliere*, 366 Mass 479, 488, 321 NE2d 625, 632 (1974); *Com. v. Dupont*, 75 Mass App 605, 611-612, 915 NE2d 1078, 1082-1083 (2009) (exclusion does not apply when defendant responds to accusation in an equivocal, evasive, or irresponsive way inconsistent with his innocence); *Com. v. Walker*, 69 Mass App 137, 140-141, 866 NE2d 958, 962-963 (2007) (rape defendant's post-arrest response to his mother's inquiry, "You know how girls are when you break up with them," was admissible); *Com. v. Kruah*, 47 Mass App 341, 344-346, 712 NE2d 1182, 1186-1187 (1999) (equivocal apology to victim); *Com. v. Estep*, 38 Mass App 502, 507 n.1, 649 NE2d 775, 778 n.l (1995).

[262] See *Com. v. Burke*, 339 Mass 521, 532-533, 159 NE2d 856, 863 (1963). But see *Com. v. Cole*, 380 Mass 30, 42, 402 NE2d 55, 63 (1980) (defendant's responses to *Miranda* warnings admitted on issue of sanity).

[263] *Com. v. Mayne*, 38 Mass App 282, 284, 647 NE2d 89, 91 (1995). See also § 4.2.1, supra.

[264] *Michigan v. Mosley*, 423 US 96, 99-100 (1975).

[265] *Com. v. Garcia*, 379 Mass 422, 428, 399 NE2d 460, 464-465 (1980). See also *Com. v. Cruz*, 373 Mass 676, 688, 369 NE2d 996, 1003 (1977).

§ 12.7 Confessions Under the Sixth Amendment *Massiah* Doctrine

The Sixth Amendment *Massiah*[1] doctrine requires the exclusion of incriminatory statements "deliberately elicited" from a defendant by law enforcement officials in the absence of counsel after the right to counsel has attached. In order to make out a violation, the defendant must demonstrate that the police or their agent interrogated him, or took other action designed to elicit the incriminating statements. *Massiah* represents a basis for suppression distinct from the *Miranda* framework.[2] Several Massachusetts cases have recognized and applied the doctrine.[3] Some have even extended the doctrine under art. 12 of the Declaration of Rights.[4]

"Deliberate elicitation" includes not just interrogation but any "knowing exploitation by the State of an opportunity to confront the accused without counsel being present."[5] The doctrine broadly

---

§ 12.7 [1] *Massiah v. United States*, 377 US 201 (1964) (co-defendant Colson at the request of federal agents initiated a conversation with Massiah resulting in admissions surreptitiously recorded by agents and offered into evidence); *Brewer v. Williams*, 430 US 387 (1977) (detective used "Christian burial speech" to elicit incriminating statements about missing girl); *Fellers v. United States*, 540 US 519 2004) (officers violated Sixth Amendment by deliberately eliciting information from defendant during post-indictment visit to his home absent counsel). The Sixth Amendment was made applicable to the states in *Gideon v. Wainwright*, 372 US 335 (1963).

[2] See generally *Com. v. Rainwater*, 425 Mass 540, 542-546, 681 NE2d 1218, 1221-1223 (1997) (extensive discussion of relationship between doctrines).

[3] See *Com. v. Howard*, 446 Mass 563, 845 NE2d 368 (2006) (incriminating statements taken during interview with DSS investigator acting as agent of law enforcement); *Com. v. Hilton*, 443 Mass 597, 823 NE2d (2005), *appeal after remand*, 450 Mass 173, 877 NE2d 545 (2007) (statements elicited by court officer); *Com. v. Reynolds*, 429 Mass 388, 392-395, 708 NE2d 658, 663-664 (1999) (statements elicited by jailhouse informant at instigation of Commonwealth). Compare *Com. v. Cote*, 386 Mass 354, 359-361, 435 NE2d 1047, 1050-1051 (1982) (no deliberate elicitation by delaying arraignment); *Com. v. Williams*, 378 Mass 217, 227 n.10, 391 NE2d 1202, 1209 n.10 (1979) (doctrine inapplicable); *Com. v. Frongillo*, 359 Mass 132, 136-137, 268 NE2d 341, 344 (1971) (*Massiah* did not require suppression of incriminating statement voluntarily made in conversation initiated by defendant in hope of help on disposition).

[4] See *Com. v. Murphy*, 448 Mass 452, 465-468, 862 NE2d 30, 41-43 (2007) (jailhouse informant).

[5] *Com. v. Hilton*, supra, 443 Mass at 614, 823 NE2d at 398. Compare *Fellers v. United States*, supra (where officers went to arrest defendant at his home after indictment on drug charges and told him "they had come to discuss his involvement in" drug distribution, they had deliberately elicited his information) with *Com. v. Torres*, 442 Mass 554, 572-575, 813 NE2d 1261, 1276-1278 (2004) (troopers went to jail where defendant was being held on unrelated charge to serve indictments and warrant and, without troopers initiating conversation, defendant insisted on speaking) and

prohibits the government, its agents, and anyone acting on its behalf[6] (including informants and "jail plants"[7]) from eliciting information from an accused. Deliberate elicitation may occur where a government informant ingratiates himself through his conduct and creates an environment that lures the defendant into a false sense of trust.[8]

Art. 12 of the Declaration of Rights provides more protection than federal law in shielding defendants from "informants at large" who troll the jail for any information. Where the government enters into an articulated agreement with an inmate containing a specific benefit, the jailhouse informant is a government agent for purposes of the Sixth Amendment even if he was not directed to target a particular

---

Com. v. Hilton, supra, 443 Mass at 617-618, 823 NE2d at 400-401 (defendant spontaneously volunteered statement to court officer, who then responded reflexively without a design to elicit an incriminating response; but court officer's subsequent questions about the crime were reasonably likely to elicit an incriminating response).

[6] See *Com. v. Howard*, supra, 446 Mass at 568, 845 NE2d at 372 (DSS investigator); *Com. v. Hilton*, supra, 443 Mass at 613-617, 823 NE2d at 397-400 (court officer). Compare *Com. v. Moniz*, 87 Mass App 532, 537-538, 32 NE3d 355, 360 (2015) (defendant's court-appointed third-party custodian in Alaska was not acting as an agent of Massachusetts prosecutorial authorities); *Com. v. Bandy*, 38 Mass App 329, 334-335, 648 NE2d 440, 443 (1995) (no showing that probation officer's comment was other than inadvertent).

[7] Compare *United States v. Henry*, 447 US 264 (1980) (post-indictment statements obtained from incarcerated defendant by undercover government informant placed in cell constituted "surreptitious interrogation" which violated Sixth Amendment right to counsel) and *Com. v. Reynolds*, supra, 429 Mass at 392-395, 708 NE2d at 663-664 (jailhouse informant was agent of government at time he elicited statements from defendant if he was promised recognition of cooperation) with *Kuhlmann v. Wilson*, 477 US 436 (1986) (because informant was merely passive listener, police had not "deliberately elicited" statements and Sixth Amendment not violated), *Com. v. Fritz*, 472 Mass 341, 348, 34 NE3d 705, 711-712 (2015) (defendant failed to demonstrate the existence of an agency relationship between jailhouse informant and the government); *Com. v. Tevlin*, 433 Mass 305, 319-321, 741 NE2d 827, 839-840 (2001) (inmate not acting as agent of government even though he indicated to trooper a desire to be transferred in return for providing information), *Com. v. Gajka*, 425 Mass 751, 752-753, 682 NE2d 1345, 1347 (1997) (cellmate not agent of government when he initiated questioning of defendant) and *Com. v. Young*, 73 Mass App 479, 481-483, 899 NE2d 838, 841-843 (2009), *habeas denied*, 2012 WL 3638824 (D Mass 2012) (cellmate was not agent of the Commonwealth at time defendant made incriminating statements). See also *Com. v. Hadley*, 78 Mass App 405, 411-412, 939 NE2d 787, 792-793 (2010) (defendant inmate's statements to corrections officer were spontaneous, and not the result of questioning or elicitation).

[8] *Com. v. Murphy*, supra, 448 Mass at 465-468, 862 NE2d at 41-43.

individual.[9] The Sixth Amendment is not violated when a private citizen, unconnected with law enforcement authorities, elicits an incriminating statement.[10]

The doctrine applies only after the initiation of adversary judicial criminal proceedings—*i.e.*, after indictment, information, arraignment, or preliminary hearing—because that is the point at which the right to counsel attaches.[11] The issuance of a complaint and arrest warrant does not constitute the commencement of adversary proceedings in Massachusetts.[12] In this context, it should be noted that there is no federal or state constitutional right to consult with an attorney before deciding whether to submit to a breathalyzer test.[13] The right to counsel applies to post-indictment, court-ordered psychiatric evaluations.[14]

Prior to the commencement of formal proceedings, incriminatory statements deliberately elicited from the defendant in the absence of counsel are not rendered inadmissible by the doctrine. The Sixth Amendment is offense specific, so that even if the right to counsel has

---

[9] *Com. v. Murphy*, supra, 448 Mass at 456-465, 862 NE2d at 35-41 (extensive discussion; declining to follow *United States v. LaBarre*, 191 F3d 60 (1st Cir 1999).

[10] *Com. v. Allen*, 395 Mass 448, 454, 480 NE2d 630, 635 (1985) (hospital nurse).

[11] See *Kirby v. Illinois*, 406 US 682 (1972); *Com. v. Torres*, 442 Mass 554, 570-571, 813 NE2d 1261, 1275 (2004) (Sixth Amendment attached after indictment, even though defendant had not yet been arraigned). Compare *Com. v. Gaynor*, 443 Mass 245, 257, 820 NE2d 233, 245 (2005) (no criminal proceeding had been instituted).

[12] *Com. v. Holliday*, 450 Mass 794, 813, 882 NE2d 309, 325 (2008); *Com. v. Ortiz*, 422 Mass 64, 67 n.1, 661 NE2d 925, 927 n.1 (1996); *Com. v. Smallwood*, 379 Mass 878, 884-885, 401 NE2d 802, 806 (1980). See also *Com. v. Phinney*, 416 Mass 364, 371 n.4, 622 NE2d 617, 622 n.4 (1993) (no right to counsel during interrogation where defendant had not been charged); *Com. v. Mahoney*, 400 Mass 524, 528-529, 510 NE2d 759, 762 (1987) (right to counsel does not apply during booking procedure); *Com. v. Mandeville*, 386 Mass 393, 436 NE2d 912 (1982) (where neither defendant nor attorney asked that attorney's presence be secured at time of arrest, statements obtained on route to police station following arrest did not violate Sixth Amendment even though police knew that defendant was represented by counsel and had been informed by counsel six days prior to arrest that defendant did not wish to speak to police).

[13] See *Com. v. Brazelton*, 404 Mass 783, 537 NE2d 142 (1989).

[14] See *Estelle v. Smith*, 451 US 454 1981) (where defense counsel was not notified psychiatric examination would encompass issue of client's future dangerousness—an issue material to capital sentencing proceeding—examination violated defendant's Sixth Amendment rights). But see *Com. v. Baldwin*, 426 Mass 105, 110, 686 NE2d 1001, 1005 (1997) (decision to undergo psychiatric evaluation is "critical stage," but interview itself is not; thus no right to attendance of counsel at interview); *Com. v. Trapp*, 423 Mass 356, 359, 668 NE2d 327 (1996) (same; but judge has discretion to allow defense counsel to attend *Blaisdell* interview), *habeas petition denied in Trapp v. Spencer*, 479 F3d 53 (1st Cir 2007); *Com. v. Sargent*, 449 Mass 576, 870 NE2d 602 (2007) (no constitutional or statutory right to counsel at interview with qualified examiner).

attached with regard to one offense, this does not preclude interrogation regarding a different, unrelated offense.[15]

The standard for waiver of the right to counsel would appear to be the same as the standard for waiver of *Miranda* rights—knowing, intelligent, and voluntary.[16] Some waivers, however, will pass muster for *Miranda* purposes but not *Massiah*, as for example where the suspect is not informed his attorney is seeking to reach him during questioning.[17] A defendant may waive the Sixth Amendment right to counsel without consulting with or notifying counsel;[18] but in order to demonstrate a knowing and intelligent waiver by a juvenile, the Commonwealth must demonstrate in most cases that a parent or interested adult was present at time of waiver.[19] Once the right to counsel has been invoked, a valid waiver can still be made out.[20]

---

[15] See *Texas v. Cobb*, 532 US 162 (2001) (Sixth Amendment did not bar police from questioning defendant regarding murders at time he was under indictment only for burglary; Court declines to adopt exception for crimes that are "factually related"); *Moulton v. Maine*, 474 US 159, 180 n.16 (1985) (incriminating remarks relating to crimes not then charged not subject to exclusion); *McNeil v. Wisconsin*, 501 US 171 (1991); *Com. v. Rainwater*, supra, 425 Mass at 546-550, 681 NE2d at 1223-1225 (discussion of "inextricably related" crime exception); *Com. v. Shipps*, 399 Mass 820, 827-828, 507 NE2d 671, 677-678 (1987) (even if police aware defendant had been represented on an unrelated charge the year before, no violation by interrogating him on the current charge); *Com. v. St. Peter*, 48 Mass App 517, 522-523, 722 NE2d 1002, 1007-1008 (2000) (police officers not required to notify defendant's attorney, appointed on DUI charge, of their intent to question defendant about unrelated, uncharged murder); *Com. v. Chase*, 42 Mass App 749, 757, 679 NE2d 1012, 1027 (1997).

[16] See *Montejo v. Louisiana*, 556 US 778, 786 (2009); *Patterson v. Illinois*, 487 US 285, 292 (1988); *Com. v. Torres*, 442 Mass 554, 571-572, 813 NE2d 1261, 1275 (2004) (*Miranda* warnings are also sufficient to convey substance of Sixth Amendment rights, and *Miranda* waiver functions for Sixth Amendment as well); *Com. v. Anderson*, 448 Mass 548, 554-558, 862 NE2d 749, 756-759 (2007) (defendant was fully advised of his *Miranda* rights and that a public defender had been assigned to represent him and was advising defendant not to speak to police); *Com. v. Tlasek*, 77 Mass App 298, 302, 930 NE2d 170, 172 (2010) (a valid *Miranda* waiver suffices to waive one's Sixth Amendment right to counsel; not reaching issue whether waiver of Sixth Amendment also waives parallel right under art. 12 of Massachusetts Declaration of Rights).

[17] *Patterson v. Illinois*, supra, 487 US at 297 n.9, distinguishing *Moran v. Burbine*, 475 US 412, 421 (1986), discussed at § 12.6.4, supra; *Com. v. Anderson*, supra, 448 Mass at 556, 862 NE2d at 757-758.

[18] See *Com. v. Cote*, supra, 386 Mass at 360 n.9, 435 NE2d at 1051 n.9.

[19] See *Com. v. A Juvenile* (No. 1), 389 Mass 128, 134, 449 NE2d 654, 657 (1983).

[20] See *Montejo v. Louisiana*, supra, 556 US 778, 789 (applying the *Edwards v. Arizona* rule, discussed in § 12.6.1, supra). See also *Michigan v. Harvey*, 494 US 344 (1990) (statement obtained in violation of *Michigan v. Jackson* may be used to impeach defendant at trial).

The Supreme Judicial Court has declined to adopt the New York rule that a defendant represented by counsel may not waive his right to counsel in the absence of the lawyer.[21]

The right to counsel does not include the right to have family members present at custodial interrogations.[22]

The United States Supreme Court has refused to adopt a "public safety" exception (analogous to *New York v. Quarles,* discussed in § 12.6.7, supra) to the *Massiah* doctrine.[23] The Supreme Court has ruled that a statement elicited in violation of *Massiah* may be used to impeach defendant's inconsistent testimony at trial.[24]

§ 12.8 Confessions Under the Fourth Amendment "Fruit of the Poisonous Tree" Doctrine

The rule excluding evidence seized in violation of the Fourth Amendment[1] applies to admissions or confessions obtained as a result of an illegal search, arrest, or detention.[2] A statement that is the product of police conduct violative of the Fourth Amendment is thereby subject to suppression even if the statement is "voluntary" under the Due Process standard (see § 12.2, supra) and complies with the requirements of *Miranda* (see § 12.6, supra).[3] The critical question under derivative

---

[21] *Com. v. Anderson*, 448 Mass 548, 556-557, 862 NE2d 749, 758 (2007).

[22] *Com. v. Bradshaw*, 385 Mass 244, 431 NE2d 880 (1982).

[23] See *Moulton v. Maine*, supra, 474 US at 180.

[24] *Kansas v. Ventris*, 556 US 586 (2009).

§ 12.8 [1] The exclusionary rule was imposed upon the states in *Mapp v. Ohio*, 367 US 643 (1961).

[2] See *Dunaway v. New York*, 442 US 200 (1979); *Brown v. Illinois*, 422 US 590 (1975); *Wong Sun v. United States*, 371 US 471 (1963); *Com. v. Reyes*, 38 Mass App 483, 649 NE2d 166 (1995); *Com. v. Martinez*, 74 Mass App 240, 250, 905 NE2d 592, 601 (2009) (defendant's post-arrest statements, which were the result of an unjustified stop and frisk, required suppression). Compare *Com. v. Corriveau*, 396 Mass 319, 326-329, 486 NE2d 29, 36-37 (1985) (defendant's statement at police station was not product of unlawful arrest because defendant voluntarily accompanied police); *Com. v. Bookman*, 386 Mass 657, 659-660, 436 NE2d 1228, 1230 (1982) (although officers lacked probable cause to arrest, defendant voluntarily accompanied them to police station for questioning); *Com. v. Chongarlides*, 52 Mass App 366, 372-377, 754 NE2d 707, 712-715 (2001) (illegal entry into defendant's presumed residence did not taint subsequent statements where two hours passed, defendant willingly accompanied police and consented to speak, received *Miranda* warnings and signed waiver).

[3] *Taylor v. Alabama*, 457 US 687 (1982); *Dunaway v. New York*, supra, 442 US at 216-217; *Com. v. Damiano*, 444 Mass 444, 456-457, 828 NE2d 510, 520-521 (2005) (statement following private citizen's illegal interception of cordless telephone call). For a case addressing the issue of a patient's confession following improper disclosure

evidence analysis is whether the statement was obtained by exploitation of the initial illegality (in which case it must be suppressed), or whether the causal connection had become sufficiently attenuated by the intervention of time or circumstances.[4]

Where defendant is arrested in violation of the rule of *Payton v. New York*[5] requiring an arrest warrant for an arrest in the home, but police had probable cause for the arrest, suppression of defendant's post-arrest statements made at the police station is not required.[6] The penalty for an unlawful entry into defendant's home is suppression of any physical evidence seized and any statements obtained at the time of entry; a statement made later at the police station will be suppressed only if there is a connection between it and the previously unlawfully obtained evidence or statement.[7]

---

of confidential information by a health care provider to police, see *Com. v. Brandwein*, 435 Mass 623, 631-633, 760 NE2d 724, 730-732 (2002) (rejecting contention that confession was fruit of poisonous tree because no police misconduct).

[4] *Taylor v. Alabama*, supra, 457 US at 689-690; *Dunaway v. New York*, supra, 442 US at 217-219 (provision of *Miranda* warnings not sufficient to purge taint of illegal arrest); *Brown v. Illinois*, supra, 422 US at 600-604 (same discussing factors to be weighed in attenuation analysis). For Massachusetts cases applying this analysis, see *Com. v. Estabrook*, 472 Mass 852, 859-865, 38 NE3d 231, 238-242 (2015) (suppressing those statements made by defendants in direct response to being confronted with illegally seized cellular site location information (CSLI), but admitting others that were not the result of police exploitation of the search); *Com. v. Melo*, 472 Mass 278, 307-308, 34 NE3d 289, 298 (2015) (because there was no probable cause to arrest defendant, and no purge of the primary taint because he was questioned at the police station shortly after, defendant's statement must be suppressed); *Com. v. Shipps*, 399 Mass 820, 829-830, 507 NE2d 671, 678 (1987) (taint of illegal arrest removed); *Com. v. Bradshaw*, 385 Mass 244, 258-259, 431 NE2d 880, 895 (1982) (confession properly admitted because taint of illegal arrest had been purged); *Com. v. Komnenus*, 87 Mass App 587, 591-592, 32 NE3d 1286, 1291-1293 (2015) (defendant's spontaneous disclosure of the presence of crack cocaine in his apartment was not the result of police exploitation of their initial unlawful entry); *Com. v. Avellar*, 70 Mass App 608, 616-617, 875 NE2d 539, 546-547 (2007) (nothing to show that defendant's statements were the product of any misconduct during protective sweep); *Com. v. Reyes*, 38 Mass App 483, 487-488, 649 NE2d 166, 169 (1995) (given temporal circumstances of illegal search and arrest and defendant's confession, and lack of an intervening event, confession must be suppressed). For a general discussion of the "fruit of the poisonous tree" doctrine and the two exceptions for evidence obtained through an independent source and evidence that would have been inevitably discovered by lawful means, see *Com. v. Fedette*, 396 Mass 455, 458-461, 486 NE2d 1112, 1115-1116 (1985); *Com. v. Benoit*, 382 Mass 210, 415 NE2d 818 (1980).

[5] 445 US 573, 590 (1980).

[6] See *Com. v. Marquez*, 434 Mass 370, 376-379, 749 NE2d 673, 679-681 (2001) (adopting *New York v. Harris*, 495 US 14 (1990)); *Com. v. Gonzalez*, 59 Mass App 622, 626-627, 797 NE2d 449, 453 (2003).

[7] *Com. v. Cruz*, 442 Mass 299, 307-309, 812 NE2d 1178, 1184-1185 (2004).

The discovery of a witness through unconstitutional police conduct does not automatically preclude that witness's testimony. Admissibility turns on whether the witness's decision to testify was voluntary.[8]

§ 12.9 Other Exclusionary Rules

§ 12.9.1 Delayed Arraignment

The *McNabb-Mallory* rule,[1] which excludes in federal proceedings statements (even if voluntary) that are obtained from a defendant during a period of unreasonable delay between arrest and arraignment, has not been applied to the state courts.[2] Unreasonable delay in arraignment is a factor to be weighed in determining the voluntariness of a confession under Due Process concepts (see § 12.2, supra).

Under the Massachusetts counterpart, exclusion of a confession is an appropriate sanction for violation of Mass R Crim P 7(a), requiring prompt presentment of an arrestee before a court, if it is determined that the delay was arranged by the police with the purpose of procuring a statement from the defendant.[3] *Com. v. Rosario*[4] established a

---

[8] See *United States v. Ceccolini*, 435 US 268 (1978) (Fourth Amendment violation); *Michigan v. Tucker*, 417 US 433 (1974) (Fifth Amendment violation); *Com. v. Caso*, 377 Mass 236, 385 NE2d 979 (1979) (witness discovered as result of illegal wiretap).

§ 12.9 [1] See *Mallory v. United States*, 354 US 449 (1957); *McNabb v. United States*, 318 US 332 (1943). Congress modified the rule in 18 USC § 3501. See *Corley v. United States*, 556 US 1558 (2009).

[2] See *Com. v. Cote*, 386 Mass 354, 360, 435 NE2d 1047, 1051 (1982). Compare *County of Riverside v. McLaughlin*, 500 US 44 (1991) (setting 48-hour period for holding of probable cause hearing for persons arrested without warrant).

[3] See *Com. v. Fryar*, 414 Mass 732, 743, 610 NE2d 903, 910 (1993) (police had not intentionally delayed defendant's arraignment for purpose of interrogating him further without assistance of counsel); *Com. v. Hodgkins*, 401 Mass 871, 876-878, 520 NE2d 145, 149 (1988) (evidence did not support defendant's assertion that delay in arraignment was contrived to procure his participation in videotape reenactment of crime); *Com. v. Cote*, supra, 386 Mass at 361, 435 NE2d at 1051. For discussion of the interaction of Rule 7(a) and the bail statute, GL 276, § 58, in the context of suppression of evidence, see *Com. v. Perito*, 417 Mass 674, 679-680, 632 NE2d 1190, 1193-1194 (1994) and *Com. v. Chistolini*, 422 Mass 854, 855-858, 665 NE2d 994, 996-997 (1996). See also *Com. v. Falco*, 43 Mass App 253, 682 NE2d 900 (1997) (no violation of statutory right to prompt bail hearing where motorist who refused blood alcohol test was held for six and one-half hours).

[4] *Com. v. Rosario*, 422 Mass 48, 55-56, 661 NE2d 71, 76-77 (1996). See generally *Com. v. McWilliams*, 473 Mass 606, 612-615, 45 NE3d 94, 103-105 (2016) (extensive

"safe harbor" rule: An otherwise admissible statement may not be excluded on the ground of unreasonable delay in arraignment if the statement is made within six hours of the arrest, or if at any time the defendant made an informed and voluntary written or recorded waiver of his right to be arraigned without unreasonable delay. Volunteered, unsolicited statements made more than six hours after arrest and before presentment do not require suppression.[5]

The rule is designed to eliminate (or at least reduce) debate over the reasonableness of any delay and to bar admission of a statement made after the six-hour period unless there is a waiver of prompt arraignment. The Supreme Judicial Court has recently rejected the Commonwealth's challenge to the bright-line approach arguing for a totality of the circumstance test.[6]

For purposes of applying the "safe harbor" rule, an "arrest" occurs where there is: (1) an actual or constructive seizure or detention of the person (2) performed with the intention to effect an arrest and (3) so understood by the person detained.[7] The safe harbor period is not

---

discussion). See also *Com. v. Powell*, 468 Mass 272, 10 NE3d 628 (2014) (extensive discussion); *Com. v. Fortunato*, 466 Mass 500, 996 NE2d 457 (2013) (extensive discussion); *Com. v. Butler*, 423 Mass 517, 668 NE2d 832 (1996) (extensive discussion; rule not to be applied retroactively); *Com. v. Beland*, 436 Mass 273, 282-283, 764 NE2d 324, 332-333 (2002) (applying pre-*Rosario* analysis); *Com. v. Ortiz*, 422 Mass 64, 661 NE2d 925 (1996) (informed and voluntary waiver of prompt arraignment would excuse delay, but no waiver necessary if questioning occurs within six-hour period); *Com. v. Jackson*, 447 Mass 603, 612, 614, 855 NE2d 1097, 1105 (2006) (defendant waived his right to prompt presentment). For waiver, see *Com. v. Spray*, 467 Mass 456, 468, 5 NE3d 891, 902 (2014).

Waiver for *Rosario* purposes is to be treated as separate and distinct from the question of a *Miranda* waiver. *Com. v. Siny Van Tran*, 460 Mass 535, 561, 953 NE2d 139, 162 (2011) (error for the judge to conflate the two; defendant's waiver was defective because the translation he received was inadequate to impart the substantive meaning of the right).

The safe harbor rule applies only to persons arrested in Massachusetts; it does not apply to persons arrested in other states on warrants issued in Massachusetts, whose arraignment would need to await rendition to Massachusetts. See *Com. v. Santana*, 465 Mass 270, 287, 988 NE2d 825, 839 (2013); *Com. v. Morganti*, 455 Mass 388, 398-400, 917 NE2d 191, 201-202 (2009). In such situations, the courts consider whether the circumstances of the particular interrogation conducted elsewhere "violated the spirit of the rule." *Com. v. Santana*, supra, 465 Mass at 270, 287, 988 NE2d at 825, 839; *Com. v. Delacruz*, 463 Mass 504, 516-517, 976 NE2d 788, 798 (2012) (but defendant executed an informed and voluntary waiver of his right to prompt arraignment).

[5] *Com. v. McWilliams*, supra, 473 Mass at 612-615, 45 NE3d at 103-105.

[6] *Com. v. Powell*, 468 Mass 272, 275-282, 10 NE3d 628, 632-637 (2014).

[7] *Com. v. Obershaw*, 435 Mass 794, 801-802, 62 NE2d 276, 285 (2002), *habeas denied*, 453 F3d 56 (1st Cir 2006). See also *Com. v. Martinez*, 458 Mass 684, 694-697, 940

charge-specific, i.e., it is not extended when the defendant is questioned about another crime of which he not yet been charged or arrested.[8]

Where the six-hour bright-line exclusionary rule does not apply (as in cases pre-dating *Rosario*), courts consider whether the delay was "so egregious as to put [the voluntary nature] of a defendant's statements in doubt" and whether "the police have engaged in misconduct, other than delay, that would justify suppression as a deterrent against similar future conduct."[9]

A statement obtained during the six-hour period is still subject to suppression if the requirements of *Miranda* are not met (see § 12.6, supra), or if the statement is shown to be involuntary (see § 12.2, supra), or if the arrestee's right to use the telephone pursuant to GL 276, § 33A, is violated (see § 12.9.2, infra). Moreover, the six-hour safe harbor period is tolled if the arrestee is incapacitated because of a self-induced disability, such as the consumption of drugs, or if for other reasons not attributable to the police interrogation is not possible or must be suspended.[10] A rarely invoked emergency exception recognizes that in exigent circumstances not attributable to the police, such as a natural disaster, where interrogation during the six-hour period is not possible, the period should be tolled appropriately.[11]

It has been held that the Vienna Convention, which establishes the right to consular notification when a foreign national is arrested, does not create an exclusionary remedy for violations.[12]

NE2d 422, 432-434 (2011) (defendant was not under arrest at the critical time for purposes of the "safe harbor" rule, as a reasonable person would have felt free to leave where he had gone willingly to the police station when asked, was brought into an open conference room, and sat without handcuffs or other restraint). The six-hour safe harbor period applies only when a defendant is arrested, not where he voluntarily goes to the police station for questioning. See *Com. v. Morales*, 461 Mass 765, 778, 965 NE2d 177, 189 (2012).

[8] *Com. v. Powell*, supra, 468 Mass at 275-282, 10 NE3d at 632-637.

[9] *Com. v. Montanez*, 55 Mass App 132, 141-142, 769 NE2d 784, 793 (2002).

[10] *Com. v. Rosario*, supra, 422 Mass at 56-57, 661 NE2d at 77. For the type of exceptional circumstances contemplated in *Rosario* that would justify tolling the safe harbor period, see *Com. v. Siny Van Tran*, 460 Mass 535, 561-563, 953 NE2d 139, 163-164 (2011) (exceptional circumstances not attributable to the police tolled the six-hour period where defendant was arrested at 11 p.m. Friday after an overseas flight, and could not be questioned until later the following morning because of his exhaustion).

[11] *Com. v. Powell*, supra, 468 Mass at 283-285, 10 NE3d at 637-639 (ongoing murder investigation did not constitute emergency, nor did fact court was not in session).

[12] *Com. v. Diemer*, 57 Mass App 677, 785 NE2d 1237 (2003).

§ 12.9.2 Right to Use Telephone

An inculpatory statement obtained as a result of a violation of GL 276, § 33A, providing that a person in custody must be permitted to use the telephone within one hour and to be so informed, is subject to suppression under a judge-made exclusionary rule for intentional violations.[13] Exclusion has not been required where the statutory violation is found to have been unintentional and not designed to gain inculpatory information.[14]

A violation of the statute also factors into the equation of deciding the voluntariness of a confession.[15] A statement that is the fruit of a prior violation of the statute will be suppressed unless sufficient attenuation has been shown.[16]

The telephone rights provided by the statute are triggered by defendant's formal arrest, not by the "custodial" nature of any pre-arrest interrogation.[17] A person already incarcerated on an unrelated matter

---

[13] See *Com. v. Walker*, 466 Mass 268, 278-279, 994 NE2d 764, 772-773 (2013) (defendant bears burden of establishing that violation was intentional, which was undercut by fact that detectives advised him promptly of his other rights); *Com. v. Leahy*, 445 Mass 481, 489, 838 NE2d 1220, 1228 (2005); *Com. v. Alicea*, 428 Mass 711, 716, 705 NE2d 233, 236 (1999). Providing defendant with a cell phone rather than a police station landline satisfies the statute. See *Com. v. Williams*, 456 Mass 857, 865-866, 926 NE2d 1162, 1170-1171 (2010).

[14] See *Com. v. Espada*, 450 Mass 687, 702, 880 NE2d 795, 808 (2008) (suppression not required where defendant, although not informed about his telephone rights within one hour, nevertheless was informed before the inculpatory statement was made); *Com. v. Jackson*, 447 Mass 603, 612, 614-615, 855 NE2d 1097, 1105-1106 (2006) (defendant initiated discussion with police); *Com. v. Johnson*, 422 Mass 420, 429, 663 NE2d 559, 565 (1996) (delay designed to allow other officers to be present, and defendant not questioned during delay); *Com. v. Parker*, 402 Mass 333, 341, 522 NE2d 924, 929 (1988); *Com. v. Ashley*, 82 Mass App 748, 758-759, 978 NE2d 576, 585-586 (2012) (totality of circumstances of arrest and interrogation did not reveal a plan by police to deprive defendant of right to use telephone); *Com. v. Harris*, 75 Mass App 696, 701, 916 NE2d 396, 401 (2009), *review granted*, 455 Mass 1108 (no intentional violation where police informed defendant there was no telephone in interview room, but he later used telephone at booking within the one-hour statutory period); *Com. v. Rodriguez*, 58 Mass App 610, 622, 792 NE2d 131, 140 (2003) (although not notified, defendant knew from prior experience of right to use telephone); *Com. v. Carey*, 26 Mass App 339, 343, 526 NE2d 1329, 1332-1333 (1988) (no violation of statute where defendant required to wait until completion of booking procedure to use phone, but within one hour statutory period, even though inculpatory videotape made during booking).

[15] See *Com. v. Meehan*, 377 Mass 552, 563, 387 NE2d 527, 533 (1979). See § 12.2, supra.

[16] *Com. v. Alicea*, 55 Mass App 505, 772 NE2d 48 (2002).

[17] *Com. v. Melo*, 472 Mass 278, 295-296, 34 NE3d 289, 305 (2015); *Com. v. Dagley*, 442 Mass 713, 719, 816 NE2d 527, 532 (2004), *habeas denied, Dagley v. Russo*, 540

when questioned by police is not "in custody" for purposes of GL 276, § 33A.[18] The Massachusetts statute does not apply in other states, and thus a defendant interrogated outside the Commonwealth may not rely upon § 33A.[19]

Evidence obtained by police from a defendant's telephone call has been held admissible at trial.[20]

§ 12.9.3 Right to Interpreter for Hearing-Impaired Person/No Right to Interpreter for Non-English Speaking Defendant

A deaf or hearing-impaired person under arrest is entitled to the assistance of a qualified interpreter regarding interrogation, warnings, notification of rights, or the taking of a statement.[21] The statute renders inadmissible in evidence any answer, statement, or admission elicited other than through a qualified interpreter, unless there was a knowing, voluntary, and intelligent waiver of the right to an interpreter.[22] There is no requirement that police provide an independent interpreter when questioning a non-English speaking defendant; a police officer may act as interpreter.[23]

F3d 8 (1st Cir 2008); *Com. v. Novo*, 442 Mass 262, 272, 812 NE2d 1169, 1177 (2004); *Com. v. Rivera*, 441 Mass 358, 374-375, 805 NE2d 942 (2004); *Com. v. Pileeki*, 62 Mass App 505, 510-511, 818 NE2d 596, 601 (2004). See also *Com. v. Hampton*, 457 Mass 152, 154-159, 928 NE2d 917, 920-923 (2010) (judge was entitled to reject the time of arrest stated in booking documents and instead credit the testimony of the police officers as to when the arrest actually occurred).

The Supreme Judicial Court has not decided whether the statute requires that an individual not in custody who has arrived at a police station must be advised of his telephone rights within one hour of the time police have probable cause to arrest, or merely within one hour of his formal arrest. See *Com. v. LeBeau*, 451 Mass 244, 257, 884 NE2d 956, 967 (2008), *habeas denied*, *LeBeau v. Roden*, 806 F Supp 2d 384 (D Mass 2011).

[18] See *Com. v. Perry*, 432 Mass 214, 238, 733 NE2d 83, 103-104 (2000).

[19] *Com. v. Scoggins*, 439 Mass 571, 577-578, 789 NE2d 1080, 1085 (2003).

See also *Com. v. Haith*, 452 Mass 409, 413-414, 894 NE2d 1122, 1126 (2008) (leaving open question of whether § 33A applies to suspect held by federal authorities in another state).

[20] See, e.g., *Com. v. White*, 422 Mass 487, 499-500, 663 NE2d 834, 843-844 (1996) (telephone number defendant called during booking). There is no requirement that defendant be permitted a private call, or that the number not be recorded. See *Com. v. Williams*, 456 Mass 857, 865-866, 926 NE2d 1162, 1170-1171 (2010).

[21] GL 221, § 92A.

[22] See generally *Com. v. Kelley*, 404 Mass 459, 461-462, 535 NE2d 1251, 1253-1254 (1989).

[23] *Com. v. Ardon*, 428 Mass 496, 499-500, 702 NE2d 808, 810-811 (1998); *Com. v. Alves*, 35 Mass App 935, 937, 625 NE2d 559, 561 (1993).

§ 12.9.4 *Statement Made by a Defendant during a Court-Ordered Psychiatric Examination*

A statement made by a defendant during a court-ordered psychiatric examination may be rendered inadmissible by GL 233, § 23B, discussed in § 5.5.6, supra.

§ 12.9.5 *Statements Made During Plea Negotiations, in Connection with Assignment of Counsel, and During Pretrial Diversion Assessment*

Massachusetts practice bars the use in evidence of statements made by a defendant during plea negotiations.[24] Information provided in connection with assignment of counsel based on indigency may not be used in any criminal or civil proceeding except a prosecution for perjury committed in providing the information.[25] No statement made by a defendant during the course of assessment for a pretrial diversion program may be disclosed to a prosecutor or other law enforcement officer in connection with the charge or charges pending against defendant.[26]

§ 12.10 Procedure for Challenging Confessions

The proper method for challenging the admissibility of a confession or other statement is a pretrial motion to suppress or for a voir dire.[1] Defendants have, however, been permitted to rely upon an objection at trial.[2] "When an objection is made at trial to the admission of a defendant's incriminating statement on the ground that it was obtained in violation of the *Miranda* case or was involuntary, or both, and no pretrial hearing has been held, the prudent thing for the judge to do is to stop the trial and conduct an appropriate inquiry."[3]

---

[24] See § 4.6, supra.

[25] SJC Rule 3:10, Sec 9.

[26] GL c 276A, § 5.

§ 12.10 [1] Mass R Crim P 13(c)(2); Superior Court Rule 61; *Com. v. Rubio*, 27 Mass App 506, 511, 540 NE2d 189, 192 (1989).

[2] *Com. v. Rubio*, supra; *Com. v. Adams*, 389 Mass 265, 269-270 & n.1, 450 NE2d 149, 152 & n.1 (1983) ("Even if the defendant has not moved to suppress his statements the burden is still on the Commonwealth, upon reasonable objection, to prove affirmatively, prior to the admission of these statements, that the statements were properly obtained and that the defendant waived his rights.").

[3] *Com. v. Rubio*, supra, 27 Mass App at 511, 540 NE2d at 192.

§ 12.11 Corroboration Requirement

Under Massachusetts law, a criminal defendant may not be convicted solely on the basis of his uncorroborated confession.[1] The rule has been extended to admissions as well as confessions.[2] The corroboration required, however, is minimal. There need only be some evidence besides the confession that the criminal act actually occurred, and the corroborating evidence need not point to the accused as the perpetrator.[3] The primary purpose of the corroboration rule is to "guard against conviction for imaginary crimes."[4]

Testimony admitted as a prior inconsistent statement (and not as substantive evidence) cannot constitute corroboration.[5] Nor can one extrajudicial confession be used to corroborate another extrajudicial confession.[6]

---

§ 12.11 [1] *Com. v. Forde*, 392 Mass 453, 457-458, 466 NE2d 510, 513 (1984).

[2] See *Com. v. Leonard*, 401 Mass 470, 517 NE2d 157 (1988).

[3] *Com v. DiGiambattista*, 442 Mass 423, 430-432, 813 NE2d 516, 522-523 (evidence that fire was set in house and that only someone with key could have gained entrance satisfied requirement; rejecting expansion of rule to require corroboration that defendant was actual perpetrator); *Com. v. Jackson*, 428 Mass 455, 467, 702 NE2d 1158, 1166 (1998) (requirement was satisfied by the testimony of witness who said he saw tangible evidence of the robbery); *Com. v. Leonard*, supra, 401 Mass at 473, 517 NE2d at 159; *Com. v. Manning*, 41 Mass App 18, 668 NE2d 850 (1996) (rejecting federal rule that corroborative evidence must implicate the accused; automobile's position sufficiently corroborated defendant's admission to operating under influence). See also *Com. v. Phinney*, 416 Mass 364, 373, 622 NE2d 617, 623 (1993) (Commonwealth not required to offer physical evidence to support confession where it was undisputed that murder had occurred and confession was supplemented by other evidence pointing to defendant). Compare *Com. v. Landenburg*, 41 Mass App 23, 668 NE2d 1306 (1996) (lack of corroborating evidence required reversal of larceny conviction).

[4] *Com. v. Villalta-Duarte*, 55 Mass 821, 825, 774 NE2d 1144, 1147 (2002).

[5] *Com. v. Costello*, 411 Mass 371, 374-375, 582 NE2d 938, 940-941 (1991). See also *Com. v. Boothby*, 64 Mass App 582, 834 NE2d 1202 (2005) (witness's hearsay statement that defendant was driving vehicle was not sufficient corroboration).

[6] *Com. v. Costello*, supra, 411 Mass at 375, 582 NE2d at 940-941 (& citations).

For application of the corroboration rule in child sexual abuse cases, see *Com. v. Villalta-Duarte*, 55 Mass 821, 826-827, 774 NE2d 1144, 1148 (2002), and *Com. v. Rodriguez*, 76 Mass App 59, 63-65, 918 NE2d 865, 869-870 (2009); in conspiracy cases, see *Com. v. Abdul-Kareem*, 56 Mass App 78, 81, 775 NE2d 454, 456-457 (2002); in possession cases, see *Com. v. Hubbard*, 69 Mass App 232, 235-236, 867 NE2d 341, 344-346 (2007) (extensive discussion of the history of the corroboration doctrine).

CHAPTER

13

OPENING STATEMENTS and CLOSING ARGUMENT

In General

Although neither opening statements nor closing arguments constitute evidence, they are an integral part of the trial.[1] This chapter summarizes the law regarding each.

[1] The criminal defendant's right to present closing argument has been held integral to the fundamental right to the assistance of counsel in both jury and jury-waived trials. See *Herring v. New York*, 422 US 853 (1975). See also *Com. v. Cutty*, 47 Mass App 671, 715 NE2d 1040 (1999) (ordering defense counsel not to argue alibi defense in summation, based on noncompliance with notice procedure, was reversible error); *Com. v. Martelli*, 38 Mass App 669, 651 NE2d 414 (1995) (judge's refusal to hear defense counsel's closing argument entitled defendant to new trial); *Com. v. Miranda*, 22 Mass App 10, 490 NE2d 1195 (1986) (trial court's statement denying defendant's constitutional right to present closing arguments was reversible error despite defendant's failure to preserve objection).

§ 13.1 Opening Statement

An opening statement is designed to outline in a general way the nature of the case which counsel expects to prove.[1] It is not an opportunity for argument.[2] A prosecutor is free to articulate a version of the case as long as there is reasonable and good-faith expectancy that the evidence in the case-in-chief will support it.[3] Counsel may refer to facts that would have to be inferred from the evidence as well.[4]

Counsel should not make a promise to the jury about anticipated testimony without a reasonable belief that it will be presented.[5] The fact, however, that evidence fails to materialize at trial,[6] or the judge

---

§ 13.1 [1] *Com. v. Degro*, 432 Mass 319, 322, 733 NE2d 1024, 1031 (2000); *Com. v. Hoilett*, 430 Mass 369, 372, 719 NE2d 488, 491 (1999).

[2] *Com. v. Croken*, 432 Mass 266, 268, 733 NE2d 1005, 1008 (2000). See also *Com. v. Brown*, 462 Mass 620, 631, 970 NE2d 306, 316 (2012) (judge properly asked defense counsel not to argue in anticipation of what prosecutor would argue in closing); *Com. v. Oliveira*, 74 Mass App 49, 55-56, 904 NE2d 442, 448 (2009) (although unnecessarily argumentative, prosecutor's comments were a fair reference to anticipated evidence on the manner of the assault); *Com. v. Holt*, 77 Mass App 716, 722, 33 NE2d 1011, 1015 (2010) (prosecutor improperly argued in opening that witness had no motive to lie; such argument is only proper in closing, in response to impeachment).

[3] See, e.g., *Com. v. Gomes*, 459 Mass 194, 202-203, 944 NE2d 1007, 1014-1015 (2011) (prosecutor reasonably predicted conflicting evidence on defendant's location at time of shooting); *Com. v. Staines*, 441 Mass 521, 535, 806 NE2d 910, 922 (2004); *Com. v. Qualls*, 440 Mass 576, 586, 800 NE2d 299, 307 (2003); *Com. v. Jones*, 439 Mass 249, 260-261, 786 NE2d 1197, 1207 (2003); *Com. v. O'Connell*, 438 Mass 658, 668, 783 NE2d 417, 426 (2003); *Com. v. Smith*, 58 Mass App 166, 175, 788 NE2d 977, 985-986 (2003), *rev'd on other grounds, Smith v. Massachusetts*, 543 US 462 (2005); *Com. v. Williams*, 53 Mass App 719, 723, 761 NE2d 1005, 1009 (2002) (prosecutor could comment on a witness's motive for testifying). Compare *Com. v. Stuckich*, 450 Mass 449, 460, 879 NE2d 105, 115 (2008) (no basis to argue that police had to "track [defendant] down" out of state); *A.C. Vaccaro, Inc. v. Vaccaro*, 80 Mass App 635, 640-641, 955 NE2d 299, 304 (2011) (civil litigant's counsel improperly referred to opposing parties as "criminals" although he knew they had never been prosecuted).

[4] *Com. v. Stegemann*, 68 Mass App 292, 305, 862 NE2d 381, 391 (2007).

[5] *Com. v. Dwyer*, 448 Mass 122, 134, 859 NE2d 400, 411 (2006) (counsel failed to interview witness). See also *Rivera v. Club Caravan, Inc.*, 77 Mass App 17, 21-22, 928 NE2d 348, 3523 (2010) (trial court's curative instruction requiring jury to disregard plaintiff's opening remarks that bar patron had blood alcohol level of 0.20, where there would be no such evidence, was sufficient).

[6] *Com. v. Sylvia*, 456 Mass 182, 188, 921 NE2d 968, 975 (2010) (reference to victim's death resulting from possible drug deal); *Com. v. Rosa*, 73 Mass App 540, 544, 899 NE2d 887, 891-892 (2009); *Com. v. Weeks*, 77 Mass App 1, 12, 927 NE2d 1023, 1032 (2010). See also *Com. v. Jackson*, 78 Mass App 465, 472, 940 NE2d 460, 466 (2010) (defense counsel was not ineffective by referring in opening statement to witnesses whose attendance could not be secured).

ultimately excludes it,[7] does not itself demonstrate that a prosecutor acted in bad faith in referring to it during the opening. Defense counsel should be particularly careful not to suggest that defendant has the burden of proof.[8] An unkept promise by defense counsel in an opening statement may deny defendant the constitutional right to effective assistance of counsel, and the judge may be required to give curative instructions to the jury where important evidence promised by defense counsel has been excluded.[9]

A prosecutor may not inject his or her personal views of the case,[10] nor improperly seek to elicit juror sympathy for the victim,[11] nor vouch for the credibility of a witness.[12] A mistrial may be

---

[7] See *Com. v. Morgan*, 449 Mass 343, 360-362, 868 NE2d 99, 114-115 (2007), *habeas denied*, *Morgan v. Dickhaut*, 677 F3d 39 (1st Cir 2012) (reference to alleged co-conspirator's statements that were later excluded as hearsay); *Com. v. Halstrom*, 84 Mass App 372, 383-384, 996 NE2d 892, 901-902 (2013) (evidence excluded for lack of authenticity foundation).

[8] See, e.g., *Com. v. Parent*, 465 Mass 395, 406-407, 989 NE2d 426, 436 (2013); *Com. v. Taylor*, 463 Mass 857, 868-869, 979 NE2d 722, 730-731 (2012) (defense counsel's opening statement promise that he would "prove" that defendant did not shoot victim and that the camouflage clothing worn by shooter was commonly worn in the African-American community did not deny defendant effective assistance of counsel).

[9] *Com. v. Chambers*, 465 Mass 520, 531-536, 989 NE2d 483, 492-495 (2013).

[10] See *Com. v. Almonte*, 465 Mass 224, 235, 988 NE2d 415, 424 (2013) (prosecutor did not express personal opinion in opening when beginning with "on [date] defendant murdered [victim] in his apartment"); *Com. v. Pillai*, 445 Mass 175, 189-190, 833 NE2d 1160, 1173 (2005) (prosecutor did not impermissibly inject his personal convictions when he argued during opening "I'm telling you right now that I will prove that to you beyond a reasonable doubt"); *Com. v. Deloney*, 59 Mass App 47, 51, 794 NE2d 613, 618 (2003) (prosecutor could use narrative style as long as it is clear it is a prediction of the evidence and prosecutor was not speaking from personal knowledge).

[11] See *Com. v. Simpson*, 434 Mass 570, 583-584, 750 NE2d 977, 991-992 (2001) (prosecutor's characterization of murder victim as "a family man, a man trained and devoted to the protection of others," and of defendant as having "complete disregard for human life," was improper); *Com. v. Williams*, supra, 53 Mass App at 724, 761 NE2d at 1010 (prosecutor's comments were clearly an attempt to garner sympathy for victim and "quite close to the line of impropriety"); *Com. v. Silva*, 455 Mass 503, 513-517, 918 NE2d 65, 79-81 (2009) (improper for prosecutor to begin opening by saying evidence would show victims were shot "in cold blood," and that shooting of unarmed man was "a slaughter"; but same reference was proper in closing argument). Compare *Com. v. Crouse*, 447 Mass 558, 575, 855 NE2d 391, 405 (2006) (prosecutor's statement that defendant "packaged up [the victim] for disposal as if she were garbage" was proper was based on evidence); *Com. v. Boyajian*, 68 Mass App 866, 869, 865 NE2d 1153, 1156 (2007) (prosecutor's "public safety theme" in OUI case was simply a marshaling of the evidence).

[12] *Com. v. Croken*, supra, 432 Mass at 268, 733 NE2d at 1008 (victims acted courageously by testifying); *Com. v. Riberio*, 49 Mass App 7, 725 NE2d 568 (2000) (telling jurors that victim had no reason to lie was impermissible advocacy).

appropriate "where the force of the prosecutor's opening remarks was overwhelmingly prejudicial and likely to leave an indelible imprint on the jurors' minds."[13]

When an opening statement fails to describe the elements of a cause of action, it is appropriate to direct a verdict for the defendant.[14] A defense counsel's concession of guilt regarding a lesser offense during his opening is not tantamount to a guilty plea, thus requiring no colloquy.[15]

Neither opening nor closing statements bind the party to the theories presented.[16]

§ 13.2 Closing Argument

In closing, counsel may argue to the jury the evidence and reasonable inferences that might be drawn from that evidence.[1] Counsel may "attempt to assist the jury in their task of analyzing, evaluating, and applying evidence" including suggestions as to what conclusions the jury

---

[13] *Com. v. Hoilett*, 430 Mass 369, 372, 719 NE2d 488, 491 (1999). For a case vacating a civil jury verdict because of multiple improper, inflammatory, and prejudicial remarks by plaintiff's counsel in opening and closing statements, see *Fyffe v. MBTA*, 86 Mass App 457, 17 NE3d 453 (2014).

[14] *Island Trans. Co. v. Cavanaugh*, 54 Mass App 650, 654, 767 NE2d 609, 612 (2002).

[15] *Com. v. Evelyn*, 470 Mass 765, 26 NE3d 158 (2015).

[16] *Com. v. Silanskas*, 433 Mass 678, 691, 746 NE2d 445, 459 (2001).

§ 13.2 [1] *Com. v. Britt*, 465 Mass 87, 93, 987 NE2d 558, 564 (2013). See, e.g., *Com. v. Roy*, 464 Mass 818, 829-835, 985 NE2d 1164, 1174-1178 (2013) (prosecutor's comments were all fair inferences and characterizations from the evidence); *Com. v. Buckman*, 461 Mass 24, 37-39, 957 NE2d 1089, 1101-1102 (2011) (prosecutor's statement that scratches on defendant's scalp were inflicted by victim was fair argument); *Com. v. Cheremond*, 461 Mass 397, 412-413, 961 NE2d 97, 109 (2012) (prosecutor's comment that strangulation from between four to six minutes caused victim's death was based on fair inference from pathologist's testimony); *Com. v. Jefferson*, 461 Mass 821, 835-836, 965 NE2d 800 (2012) (prosecutor's assertion that handle of firearm broke because it was thrown from vehicle was grounded in common sense, not requiring expert testimony); *Com. v. Wallace*, 460 Mass 118, 125-126, 949 NE2d 908, 915 (2011) (prosecutor's argument that defendant had asked driver of van to "wipe it down" after shooting was fair inference); *Com. v. Silva*, 455 Mass 503, 516, 918 NE2d 65, 80 (2009) (evidence that victim had been shot in the back of the head provided basis for prosecutor's argument that he was shot when he posed no threat to defendant); *Com. v. Shanley*, 455 Mass 752, 772-774, 919 NE2d 1254, 1270-1272 (2010) (prosecutor's equation of repressed memory theory with ordinary forgetting and remembering was properly based on expert testimony); *Com. v. Pimental*, 454 Mass 475, 483-484, 910 NE2d 366, 374-375 (2009) (prosecutor's proposed inference, that in light of defendant's lack of job or money, he saw an opportunity for robbery with a

should draw,[2] and may "fit all the pieces of evidence together so that they form a comprehensive and comprehensible picture for the jury."[3]

Counsel may not go beyond the scope of the evidence, or refer to or exploit matters that have been excluded,[4] or misstate the

---

defenseless victim in the woods, was permissible); *Com. v. Colon*, 449 Mass 207, 223-225, 866 NE2d 412, 427-428 (2007) (prosecutor's comments referring to defendant as a drug dealer was permissible inference from the evidence); *Com. v. Crouse*, 447 Mass 558, 576, 855 NE2d 391, 405 (2006) (prosecutor's comment that defendant set the fire "without any regard for the lives of the fifty or more people whose apartments were in that building . . . and the fire fighters for the city of Malden who responded" was fair inference); *Com. v. Rice*, 441 Mass 291, 299-300, 805 NE2d 26, 35-36 (2004), *habeas denied*, 564 F3d 523 (1st Cir 2009) (prosecutor properly asked jury to infer victim knew assailant from evidence of absence of signs of forced entry); *Com. v. Montanez*, 439 Mass 441, 450-451, 788 NE2d 954, 963 (2003) (prosecutor's suggestion of consciousness of guilt was fair inference from evidence of inability to locate him); *Com. v. Gerthartsreiter*, 82 Mass App 500, 513-515, 975 NE2d 890, 902-903 (2012) (prosecutor's remark characterizing lack of criminal responsibility defense as defendant's latest manipulation was fair comment on the implausibility of defendant's claim); *Com. v. Faust*, 81 Mass App 498, 501-502, 964 NE2d 987, 990-991 (2012) (references to defendant as a liar and thief were supported by the evidence).

[2] *Com. v. Grimshaw*, 412 Mass 505, 510, 590 NE2d 681, 684-685 (1992).

[3] *Com. v. Corriveau*, 396 Mass 319, 336, 486 NE2d 29, 41 (1985). See, e.g., *Com. v. Robinson*, 74 Mass App 752, 763-764, 910 NE2d 911, 919-921 (2009) (prosecutor could properly argue that defendant failed in duty of care by repeatedly referring to indications in the evidence that would warn a reasonable person that child was dangerously ill).

[4] See *Com. v. Scott*, 470 Mass 320, 334, 21 NE3d 954, 966 (2014) (prosecutor exploited the absence of evidence of victim's risky behavior that had been excluded at his request); *Com. v. Bins*, 465 Mass 348, 368, 989 NE2d 404, 421 (2013) (prosecutor misused statements admitted to establish state of mind, not truth); *Com. v. Rivera*, 464 Mass 56, 79-80, 981 NE2d 171, 190-191 (2013) (prosecutor's remark improperly stated facts that had been redacted from co-defendant's statement implicating defendant); *Com. v. Bolling*, 462 Mass 440, 456, 969 NE2d 640, 654 (2012) (prosecutor improperly implied statements in letter could be attributed to defendant, even though letter was not admissible against him); *Com. v. Cheremond*, 461 Mass 397, 413-414, 961 NE2d 97, 110 (2012) (prosecutor improperly misused propensity evidence that had been limited to motive); *Com. v. Holt*, 77 Mass App 716, 720-722, 33 NE2d 1011, 1014-1015 (2010) (prosecutor's statements were improper, as evidence regarding the matter had been excluded at the behest of the prosecutor); *Com. v. Harris*, 443 Mass 714, 729-733, 825 NE2d 58, 70-73 (2005) (prosecutor exploited rape-shield statute prohibition to argue there was no evidence that complaining witness was a prostitute); *Com. v. Baker*, 440 Mass 519, 531 n.12, 800 NE2d 267, 278 n.12 (2003) (prosecutor engaged in forbidden propensity argument); *Com. v. Carroll*, 439 Mass 547, 554-555, 789 NE2d 1062, 1068-1069 (2003) (prosecutor unfairly exploited defendant's failure to offer evidence that had been excluded at his request); *Com. v. Rosa*, 412 Mass 147, 587 NE2d 767 (1992) (improper use of hearsay testimony that had been admitted solely for impeachment). Compare *Com. v. Benoit*, 452 Mass 212, 228-229, 892 NE2d 314, 328 (2008) (prosecutor did not improperly exploit exclusion of *Adjutant* evidence).

evidence[5] or principles of law,[6] or undercut or misstate the judge's instructions.[7]

---

[5] *Com. v. Evans*, 469 Mass 834, 851-853, 17 NE3d 1084, 1099-1100 (2014) (prosecutor's misstated that defendant's DNA matched profile in all four pockets of victim's pants); *Com. v. Woodbine*, 461 Mass 720, 738-739, 964 NE2d 956, 971 (2012) (prosecutor's statement that police officer had memorialized in a written report an entire unrecorded statement that defendant had given was improper and highly misleading); *Com. v. Silva-Santiago*, 453 Mass 782, 805-807, 906 NE2d 299, 317-318 (2009) (prosecutor's comments were not based on any evidence or fair inference that the eyewitnesses had identified the shooter but were too frightened to inform police); *Com. v. Merry*, 453 Mass 653, 904 NE2d 413 (prosecutor improperly argued from facts not in evidence and misstated other evidence when he asserted in negligent vehicular homicide trial that "we know" defendant was sitting up at the time of the accident and "a person having a seizure [as defendant claimed] does not sit up"); *Com. v. Arroyo*, 442 Mass 135, 145-147, 810 NE2d 1201, 1211-1212 (2004) (prosecutor's DNA profile estimate and reference to caliber of murder weapon were not based on evidence admitted); *Com. v. Hrabak*, 440 Mass 650, 801 NE2d 239 (2004) (prosecutor argued in child rape case, without expert testimony, that rectum of child would not have suffered injury from penetration);*Com. v. Dancy*, 75 Mass App 175, 187-188, 912 NE2d 525, 536-537 (2009) (prosecutor's statement that defendant dealt drugs at NA/AA meetings was improper as not based on any evidence); *Com. v. McIntyre*, 430 Mass 529, 542-543, 721 NE2d 911, 921-922 (1999) (prosecutor's invention of fact, as well as two substantive uses of impeachment evidence, were clear error); *Com. v. Caswell*, 85 Mass App 463, 473-475,11 NE3d 136, 145-146 (2014) (prosecutor misled jury by arguing that defendant's third-party culprit had been vetted by the grand jury; *Com. v. Liptak*, 80 Mass App 76, 86-89, 951 NE2d 731, 741-742 (2011) (prosecutor improperly suggested defendant married his girlfriend to prevent her from testifying, and improperly invited the jury to infer that his mother believed him criminally responsible for the motor vehicle accident when she inquired whether he should retain counsel); *Com. v. Gonzalez*, 59 Mass App 622, 629, 797 NE2d 449, 455 (2003) (suggestion that defendant may have possessed weapon at time of arrest had no basis in evidence); *Com. v. Orton*, 58 Mass App 209, 788 NE2d 1009 (2003) (prosecutor misstated police officer's testimony regarding fingerprints and evidence regarding State lab tests). Compare *Com. v. Andrade*, 468 Mass 543, 551-552, 11 NE3d 597, 604-605 (2014) (prosecutor did not misstate medical examiner's testimony concerning sequence of bullet wounds); *Com. v. Berendson*, 73 Mass App 395, 399-400, 897 NE2d 1276, 1280-1281 (2008) (prosecutor could properly argue that rape is a crime of violence and degradation without expert evidence in the record because that is commonly understood).

It has been suggested that argument comes under the rubric of "evidence" for purposes of Mass R Prof C 3.3(a)(4), providing that "a lawyer shall not knowingly . . . offer evidence that the lawyer knows to be false." *Com. v. Beaudry*, 63 Mass App 488, 498-499, 826 NE2d 782, 791 (2005).

[6] *Com. v. Bins*, supra, 465 Mass at 367, 989 NE2d at 421. The trial judge must inform counsel of its proposed action upon requests for jury instructions prior to closing argument. Mass R Civ P 51(b); Mass R Crim P 24(b). Trial court judges have been instructed that charging conferences should be held on the record, and trial counsel have been advised where necessary to remind the judge of this requirement. See *Com. v. Adams*, 34 Mass App 516, 517 n.3, 613 NE2d 118, 120 n.3 (1993).

[7] See *Com. v. Gray*, 465 Mass 330, 341, 990 NE2d 528, 538-539 (2013).

Nor may counsel's summations infringe or denigrate constitutional rights.[8] A prosecutor may not impugn the character of the defendant,[9] nor suggest he has a propensity to commit criminal acts based on past misconduct.[10] Comment on defendant's appearance at trial is permissible as long as the prosecutor does not argue that an inference of guilt should be drawn from it.[11]

"[E]nthusiastic rhetoric, strong advocacy, and excusable hyperbole are not grounds for reversal. The jury is presumed to have a certain measure of sophistication in sorting out excessive claims on both sides."[12] If in accord with reasonable inferences from the evidence,

---

[8] *Com. v. Thomas*, 401 Mass 109, 113, 514 NE2d 1309, 1312 (1987); *Com. v. Smith*, 387 Mass 900, 903, 444 NE2d 374, 377-378 (1983).

[9] See *Com. v. Simmons*, 419 Mass 426, 646 NE2d 97 (1995) (improper references to defendant's service in Army "where he knew how to kill"); *Com. v. Marrero*, 60 Mass App 225, 232-233, 800 NE2d 1048, 1054 (2002) (suggestion that gang members live by the "law of the jungle"); *Com. v. Gaudette*, 56 Mass App 494, 500-502, 778 NE2d 988, 993-995 (2002) (prosecutor's argument that defendant should be ashamed for letting son lie and take blame for assault improperly impugned defendant's character); *Com. v. Thomas*, 44 Mass App 521, 525, 692 NE2d 97, 101 (1997) (reference to defendant's prior convictions was "blow below the belt"); *Com. v. Lewis*, 81 Mass App 119, 124, 960 NE2d 324, 329 (2012), *review granted*, 461 Mass 1110 (improper for prosecutor to repeatedly refer to defendant and his confederates as "street thugs" with guns and drugs); *Com. v. Silva*, 455 Mass 503, 517, 918 NE2d 65, 88 (2009) (impermissible for prosecutor to refer to congested, residential nature of neighborhood in which defendant repeatedly discharged his firearm as evidence of his indifference to victim's suffering); *Com. v. Stewart*, 454 Mass 527, 540, 911 NE2d 161, 173 (2009) (improper to cast defendant in a bad light by stating that "he hadn't even acknowledged his son from birth"); *Com. v. Saunders*, 75 Mass App 505, 511-512, 915 NE2d 229, 234 (2010) (improper to characterize defendant as "swooping down like a vulture" to take advantage of victim); *Com. v. Ragland*, 72 Mass App 815, 835-836, 894 NE2d 1147 (2008) (prosecutor improperly suggested that defendant had placed recanting witness in fear, ominously painting him as a threatening figure).

[10] *Com. v. Lugo*, 89 Mass App 229, 233-234, 47 NE3d 41, 47 (2016).

[11] See *Com. v. Duncan*, 71 Mass App 150, 158, 879 NE2d 1253, 1260 (2008).

[12] *Com. v. Mazariego*, 474 Mass 42, 58, 47 NE3d 420, 434 (2016) ("We doubt that the prosecutor's needless comment [about leaving the victim's body as if she were litter] had the effect of sweeping the jurors beyond a fair and calm consideration of the evidence"); *Com. v. Burgos*, 462 Mass 53, 71, 965 NE2d 854, 870 (2012) (prosecutor's vivid characterizations of gangs and gang life was permissible enthusiastic rhetoric); *Com. v. Siny Van Tran*, 460 Mass 535, 554, 953 NE2d 139, 157-158 (2011) (reference in opening argument to crime as a "mass execution" and "one of the worst and most violent days in the history of Boston" was not improper in prosecution of execution-style shooing of six men); *Com. v. Silva*, 455 Mass 503, 515, 918 NE2d 65, 79-80 (2009) (reference to defendant's gun as a "cannon" not improper).

counsel may present an argument by dramatizing it in imaginary dialogue or with a hypothetical account.[13] Counsel may use analogy, examples, and hypothesis as aids to effective argument.[14] Speculation, however, is improper.[15]

In prosecutions for murder by extreme atrocity or cruelty, calling the jury's attention to the "defendant's awareness of, but indifference to, or pleasure in, the victim's suffering" is proper, as is the details of the "gore and pain."[16]

---

[13] See *Com. v. Good*, 409 Mass 612, 625-626, 568 NE2d 1127, 1135-1136 (1991). See, e.g., *Com. v. Roy*, 464 Mass 818, 830-831, 985 NE2d 1164, 1175 (2013) (prosecutor's hypothetical dialogue between defendant and victim); *Com. v. Smith*, 450 Mass 395, 408, 879 NE2d 87, 98 (2008) (prosecutor's comment represented imaginary thought sequence of defendant based on the evidence); *Com. v. Burgess*, 450 Mass 422, 437, 879 NE2d 63, 77 (2008) (prosecutor's portrayal of defendant pursuing victim into bathroom was reasonable inference from evidence); *Com. v. Moran*, 75 Mass App 513, 521-524, 915 NE2d 240, 248-249 (2009) (prosecutor's imaginary thoughts of murder defendant were based on defendant's own statements and actions); *Com. v. Lucien*, 440 Mass 658, 665-666, 801 NE2d 247, 255 (2004) (prosecutor's dramatization of conversation and speculation as to defendant's possible motives for murder were based on reasonable inferences from evidence); *Com. v. Nol*, 39 Mass App 901, 652 NE2d 898 (1995) (demonstration in which prosecutor showed that handkerchief held over face would not preclude identification of defendant was proper illustration of testimony). But compare *Com. v. Riley*, 467 Mass 799, 819-820, 7 NE3d 1060, 1077-1078 (2014) (prosecutor's speculative question about what victim was thinking as she was dying was excessive and improper); *Com. v. Bolling*, 462 Mass 440, 455, 969 NE2d 640, 653 (2012) (prosecutor's speculation about conversation between defendant and co-defendant was unsupported by the evidence); *Com. v. Bizanowicz*, 459 Mass 400, 420, 945 NE2d 356, 371 (2011) (speculation by prosecutor about what victim and her daughter might have been thinking during commission of crime was improper); *Com. v. Renderos*, 440 Mass 422, 425-427, 799 NE2d 97, 101-102 (2003) (prosecutor should not have speculated as to defendant's thinking or attributed hypothetical conversation to him); *Com. v. Coren*, 437 Mass 723, 727-733, 774 NE2d 623, 627-631 (2003) (reversal required where prosecutor speculated about dialogue between defendant and victim); *Com. v. Obershaw*, 435 Mass 794, 806-807, 762 NE2d 276, 288 (2002) (no evidence to support inference that victim begged for his life), *habeas petition denied in Obershaw v. Lanman*, 453 F3d 56 (1st Cir 2006); *Com. v. Masello*, 428 Mass 446, 452, 702 NE2d 1153, 1157 (1998) (prosecutor's argument about what defendant had been thinking prior to shooting not based on any testimony, nor permissible "enthusiastic rhetoric"). A prosecutor may not argue that defendant would have committed additional offenses had the victim not moved away. *Com. v. Jones*, 471 Mass 138, 28 NE3d 391 399-400 (2015).

[14] *Com. v. Ridge*, 455 Mass 307, 330-331, 916 NE2d 348, 368-369 (2009).

[15] *Com. v. Bell*, 473 Mass 131, 145-146, 39 NE3d 1190, 1202-1203 (2015) (there was no evidence that police planted evidence on defendant, just speculation); *Com. v. Ayoub*, 77 Mass App 563, 569, 933 NE2d 133, 139 (2010) (improper for prosecutor to speculate on other offenses defendant might have committed had police not come along).

[16] *Com. v. Camacho*, 472 Mass 587, 607-608, 36 NE3d 533, 550-551 (2015). See also *Com. v. Young*, 461 Mass 198, 204-205, 959 NE2d 943, 949 (2012) (prosecutor's

"The rules governing prosecutors' closing arguments are clear in principle. [The courts] have never criticized a prosecutor for arguing forcefully for a conviction based on the evidence and on inferences that may reasonably be drawn from the evidence."[17] Although generally the standards are the same for prosecutor and defense counsel,[18] prosecutors have been held "to a stricter standard of conduct than are errant defense counsel."[19] The identity of the speaker (i.e, prosecutor, defense counsel, co-defendant counsel) can make a difference when determining whether a remark during closing argument was erroneous or prejudicial.[20]

"Within the bounds of the evidence and the fair inferences from the evidence, great latitude should be permitted to counsel in argument," and the judge should not invade the province of the jury to decide what inferences to draw from certain evidence.[21] Further, counsel has been permitted to engage in otherwise improper argument to counteract improper argument by their opponent, and leeway is permitted for comments reasonably within "the right of retaliatory reply."[22] But fair response must be supported by inferences from the

---

statement that defendant had sliced up victim "like an animal" was permissible rhetorical tool and dramatic description relevant to the offense of murder by extreme atrocity or cruelty).

[17] *Com. v. Lawrence*, 404 Mass 378, 391-392, 536 NE2d 571, 579-580 (1989). See also *Com. v. Carriere*, 470 Mass 1, 22, 18 NE3d 326, 343 (2014); *Com. v. Reznikow*, 51 Mass App 330, 335, 746 NE2d 539, 543 (2001).

[18] See *Com. v. Murchison*, 418 Mass 58, 59, 634 NE2d 561, 562 (1994); *Com. v. Santos*, 463 Mass 273, 297, 974 NE2d 1, 21 (2012).

[19] *Com. v. Taylor*, 455 Mass 372, 384, 916 NE2d 1000, 1009 (2009); *Com. v. Perez*, 444 Mass 143, 150, 825 NE2d 1040, 1047 (2005).

[20] *Com. v. Akara*, 465 Mass 245, 263, 988 NE2d 430, 445 (2013) (improper comments by prosecutor are more likely to be prejudicial, because of the institutional role, than comments by defense counsel or counsel for codefendant). See also *Com. v. Marrero*, 459 Mass 235, 243-246, 945 NE2d 284, 292-294 (2011) (defense counsel's statements during closing argument that the prosecutor had the members of the jury as his clients, that the jury's decision regarding guilt or innocence might not be the most important decision they ever made, and that the trial was like a poker game, were ill advised but did not constitute ineffective assistance of counsel); *Com. v. McIntosh*, 78 Mass App 37, 42, 934 NE2d 1279, 1283-1284 (2010) (defense counsel's misstatement of witness testimony during closing argument constituted ineffective assistance of counsel).

[21] *Com. v. Gilmore*, 399 Mass 741, 745, 506 NE2d 883, 886 (1987) (judge improperly interrupted defense counsel's argument). See also *Com. v. Murchison*, supra, 418 Mass at 60, 634 NE2d at 562 (trial court's special curative instruction following defense counsel's argument that testifying police officers were lying prejudiced defendant).

[22] See, e.g., *Com. v. Mello*, 420 Mass 375, 380-381, 649 NE2d 1106, 1111 (1995) (& citations); *Com. v. Amirault*, 404 Mass 221, 236-237, 535 NE2d 193, 203 (1989)

evidence.[23] And the preferred response from prosecutors is to seek redress from the trial judge, by way of objection to the defense misstatement, rather than resort to retaliatory reply.[24] With regard to "fighting fire with fire," the Supreme Judicial Court has warned that "[e]motional responses to defense counsel's closing arguments seldom produce a professional result, let alone a good result."[25]

Counsel may properly comment on the trial tactics of the opponent, including pointing out conflicts in the opponent's version of events.[26] A prosecutor may not, however, make disparaging remarks about the qualifications or motivations of defense counsel or lawyers in general.[27] Nor may defense counsel's vigorous cross-examination of a

---

("Defense counsel clearly invited the prosecutor's comments with remarks in his own closing argument."); *Com. v. Miranda*, 458 Mass 100, 114-116, 943 NE2d 222, 233-235 (2010) (prosecutor's hypothetical questions and statements concerning missing "fourth man" were fair response to defense argument about shoddiness of police investigation); *Com. v. Silva*, 455 Mass 503, 516, 918 NE2d 65, 80 (2009) (prosecutor's comment that while victim had audacity to use drugs, the penalty should not be death, was in response to defense counsel's repeated references to the drugs); *Com. v. Dargon*, 457 Mass 387, 401-402, 930 NE2d 707, 721 (2010) (prosecutor's statement that there was no evidence that a DNA analysis on defendant's fingernails could determine what part of victim's body he touched was appropriate response to defense counsel's argument suggesting that police could have conducted such tests); *Com. v. Flint*, 81 Mass App 794, 807, 968 NE2d 928, 939-940 (2012) (prosecutor's rhetorical questions about why victim would make up her accusations were proper response to defense attack on his motives).

[23] *Com. v. Rosa*, 73 Mass App 540, 548, 899 NE2d 887, 894 (2009).

[24] See *Com. v. Grinkley*, 75 Mass App 798, 807-808, 917 NE2d 236, 243 (2009) (& citations).

[25] *Com. v. DaSilva*, 471 Mass 71, 84, 27 NE3d 383, 395 (2015).

[26] See *Com. v. Ortiz*, 463 Mass 402, 415-419, 974 NE2d 1079, 1089-1091 (2012) (prosecutor's closing argument did not unfairly attack defense counsel as "sadistic bully" but was merely "excusable hyperbole" in response to defense cross-examination of female witnesses); *Com. v. Mosher*, 455 Mass 811, 830, 920 NE2d 285, 301-302 (2010) (prosecutor's statements ridiculed defense theory of the murder); *Com. v. Raposa*, 440 Mass 684, 697, 801 NE2d 789, 800 (2004) (characterizing defense counsel as able to "spin gold from straw" and riddling case with smoke screens); *Com. v. Fernandes*, 436 Mass 671, 674, 766 NE2d 1288, 1291 (2002) (prosecutor's comments on manner in which defense counsel marshaled evidence); *Com. v. Seng*, 436 Mass 537, 555-556, 766 NE2d 492, 506 (2002) (prosecutor's comment that defense had "insulted" jury with insanity defense was close to the line, but not improper); *Com. v. Harbin*, 435 Mass 654, 661, 760 NE2d 1216, 1222 (2002) (statement that defense counsel wanted to "dirty up" Commonwealth witness and other disparaging references were permissible rhetorical devices); *Com. v. Roberts*, 433 Mass 45, 55-56, 740 NE2d 176, 184 (2000) (not improper for prosecutor to comment on defense tactic of degrading Commonwealth's witnesses).

[27] See *Com. v. Taylor*, 469 Mass 516, 529,14 NE3d 955, 966 (2014) (prosecutor's reference to defense counsel's theory as a "bald-faced lie," and suggestion that it would violate juror's oath to accept defense theory, were improper); *Com. v. Lewis*, 465

rape victim be compared to the alleged sexual assault itself.[28] A prosecutor may not remark on what defense counsel did not do or failed to contradict at trial in a manner that shifts the burden of proof to the defendant.[29]

As the opportunity to present third-party culprit evidence is of constitutional dimension (see § 4.2.4, supra), the prosecutor may not denigrate defendant's evidence in this regard as irrelevant and unworthy of credence.[30]

A prosecutor should not suggest that defendant improperly concocted his defense with counsel,[31] and should avoid reference to defendant's opportunity to "rehearse" his or other testimony, as that may impinge on defendant's right to prepare for trial.[32] While it is improper to imply that counsel should not prepare witnesses, fair comment on the extraordinary parallels between witnesses testimony is permissible.[33]

Appeals to racial, religious, or ethnic prejudices are especially improper.[34] It has been observed that "even a totally benign reference to

---

Mass 119, 129-130, 987 NE2d 1218, 1227 (2013) (prosecutor's characterization of "the entire defense case" as "a sham. It's choreographed, it's staged" was grossly improper); *Com. v. Scott*, 463 Mass 561, 574, 977 NE2d 490, 501 (2012) (prosecutor's disparaging personal comments about defense counsel went beyond the bounds of proper argument, but were not prejudicial), *habeas denied Scott v. Gelb*, 2014 WL 3735914 (D Mass 2014); *Com. v. Burgos*, 462 Mass 53, 72 n.24, 965 NE2d 854, 871 n.24 (2012) (improper for prosecutor to state that defense counsel "slap[ped] those brave police officers] around" when he cross-examined them); *Com. v. Gentile*, 437 Mass 569, 580-581, 773 NE2d 428, 439 (2002) (characterizing defense strategy of accusing three other people of committing the crime as "despicable" was improper); *Com. v. Stote*, 433 Mass 19, 28-29, 739 NE2d 261, 268 (2000) (prosecutor's argument that there was "ridiculous evidence of self-defense . . . it insults your intelligence" came very close to crossing line of permissible comment); *Com. v. Burts*, 68 Mass App 684, 687-688, 864 NE2d 562, 565 (2007) (improper for prosecutor to urge jury to take defense counsel "to task" because of the way he argued in closing and the expert testimony he presented); *Com. v. Fletcher*, 52 Mass App 166, 173, 752 NE2d 754, 760 (2001) (improper for prosecutor to suggest that defendant's argument concerning reasonable doubt was merely trial trick).

[28] See *Com. v. Lorenzetti*, 48 Mass App 37, 42-43, 716 NE2d 1067, 1072 (1999) (& citations).

[29] *Com. v. Miranda*, 458 Mass 100, 116-117, 943 NE2d 222, 235 (2010); *Com. v. Tu Trinh*, 458 Mass 776, 785-787, 940 NE2d 871, 881-882 (2011); *Com. v. Ayoub*, 77 Mass App 563, 567-568, 933 NE2d 133, 138 (2010). See also § 3.4.1, supra.

[30] *Com. v. Scesny*, 472 Mass 185, 202, 34 NE3d 17, 32 (2015).

[31] *Com. v. Johnston*, 467 Mass 674, 693-695, 7 NE3d 424, 440-441 (2014) (but no insinuation here).

[32] *Com. v. Dodgson*, 80 Mass App 307, 314-315, 952 NE2d 961, 968 (2011).

[33] See *Com. v. Hanino*, 82 Mass App 489, 497-498, 975 NE2d 876, 884 (2012).

[34] See *Com. v. Montez*, 450 Mass 736, 749-750, 881 NE2d 753, 764-765 (2008) (prosecutor should not have used phrase "torment our women" in an interracial case

group membership may awaken or even exacerbate latent biases among some jurors. For this reason, prosecutors would be well advised to steer . . . clear of making such characterizations in future cases to avoid the possibility of needless retrials."[35] References to the cultural norms of a group in order to explain the behavior of (or absence of) witnesses should be avoided.[36]

While the prosecution is permitted leeway to humanize the victim, it may not appeal to the jury to convict on the basis of emotion or sympathy for the victim,[37] or suggest that the jury put themselves in the victim's position or the victim's shoes, or imagine what the victim experienced. "At a minimum, care should be taken that sympathy-inspiring terms are not casually used when they have no meaningful bearing on the guilt or innocence of the accused."[38] Nor should the

---

of sex and murder;); *Com. v. Phoenix*, 409 Mass 408, 424-425, 567 NE2d 193, 202-203 (1991); *Com. v. Mahdi*, 388 Mass 679, 691-693, 448 NE2d 704, 712-713 (1983); *Com. v. Lara*, 39 Mass App 546, 658 NE2d 692 (1995); *Com. v. Kines*, 37 Mass App 540, 640 NE2d 1117 (1994).

[35] *Com. v. West*, 44 Mass App 150, 152, 688 NE2d 1378, 1380 (1998); *Com. v. Berrio*, 43 Mass App 836, 842, 687 NE2d 644, 648 (1997). But compare *Com. v. Dixon*, 425 Mass 223, 230-231, 680 NE2d 84, 89-90 (1997) (no error although prosecutor's extensive reference to defendant and witnesses as "these people" coming from "a whole different planet" with a "whole different moral code" arguably had racial overtones); *Com. v. Hoa Sang Duong*, 52 Mass App 861, 868, 756 NE2d 1169, 1174 (2001) (references to defendants as "gang of four" and as Asians not, in context, improper reference to race). See also *Com. v. Kee*, 449 Mass 550, 559, 870 NE2d 57, 66 (2007) (references to Springfield as a "dangerous" place and to risks to undercover narcotics officers were based on the evidence); *Com. v. Ashley*, 82 Mass App 748, 763-764, 978 NE2d 576, 588 (2012) (prosecutor's references to defendant's use of ethnic expletives regarding Guatemalan victims were proper based on the evidence and relevant to his motive for attack).

[36] *Com. v. Bior*, 88 Mass App 150, 158-159, 37 NE3d 31, 38-39 (2015).

[37] See, e.g., *Com. v. Tavares*, 471 Mass 430, 443, 30 NE3d 91, 103-104 (2015) (placing unnecessary emphasis on the losses suffered by the victims' families was improper); *Com. v. Cole*, 473 Mass 317, 331-332, 41 NE3d 1073 (2015) (even though murder occurred on Christmas eve, prosecutor's remarks about "peace on earth" and "good will towards men" would have been better left unsaid in murder prosecution); *Com. v. Carney*, 472 Mass 252, 33 NE3d 1234 (2015) (imaginary thought process of victim immediately before killing was improper appeal to jury's sympathy and emotion); *Com. v. Rollins*, 470 Mass 66, 81-82, 18 NE3d 670, 683-684 (2014) (prosecutor's selective reading of legislative findings regarding child pornography law invited the jury to gloss over the photographs that formed the basis for the charges and convict based on their sympathy for those harmed by each viewing).

[38] *Com. v. Poggi*, 53 Mass App 685, 695, 761 NE2d 983, 991 (2002). See, e.g., *Com. v. Alcequiecz*, 465 Mass 557, 567, 989 NE2d 473, 482 (2013) (improper to ask jurors to picture what it was like for victim to be struck in head with object); *Com. v. Mejia*, 463 Mass 243, 253-254, 973 NE2d 657, 664-665 (2012) (prosecutor unduly emphasized the loss suffered by victim's family, and the brutality of the murder scene); *Com. v. Bizanowicz*, 459 Mass 400, 420, 945 NE2d 356, 371 (2011) (improper for prosecutor

prosecution attempt to generate sympathy for the victim by the presence, behavior, or demeanor of others in the courtroom.[39]

It is improper for the prosecutor to suggest that the jury would have to answer to the victim for their verdict, or that they have a duty

---

to urge jury to place themselves in victim's shoes); *Com. v. Gentile*, 437 Mass 569, 580, 773 NE2d 428, 438-439 (2002) (victim "didn't deserve to die this way"); *Com. v. Torres*, 437 Mass 460, 465, 772 NE2d 1046, 1051 (2002) (murder victims "had a right to sleep in their bed without this man coming in there"); *Com. v. Simpson*, 434 Mass 570, 583-584, 750 NE2d 977, 991-992 (2001) (prosecutor's statement that it was "sad" that off-duty police officer murder victim was supposed to be out of danger at time of murder and relaxing with family); *Com. v. Kent*, 427 Mass 754, 759-762, 696 NE2d 511, 515-517 (1998) (repeated statement that victim was nine years old and shot on birthday); *Com. v. Santiago*, 425 Mass 491, 494-495, 681 NE2d 1205, 1209-1210 (1997) (reversal required where prosecutor impermissibly appealed to jury's sympathy for victim by repeatedly referring to her age, pregnancy, and fact she was shot on day before her 18th birthday); *Com. v. Sanchez*, 405 Mass 369, 375-376, 377, 540 NE2d 1316, 1320-1321 (1989) (improper for prosecutor to urge jury to convict defendant in order to end the victim's nightmares); *Com. v. Olmande*, 84 Mass App 231, 234, 995 NE2d 797, 801 (2013) (improper to invite jury into victim's position to arouse sympathy); *Com. v. Grinkley*, 75 Mass App 798, 808-810, 917 NE2d 236, 244-245 (2009) (overwrought and inflammatory appeals to sympathy in child rape case, by asking jury to consider how difficult it was for victims to testify, asking jury to think what it must have been like for victims at time of assault, asking jury to imagine victims undergoing rape examination at hospital, and dwelling on the pain of the rape exam); *Com. v. Saunders*, 75 Mass App 505, 511-512, 915 NE2d 229, 234 (2010) (asking jury to put themselves in child rape victim's place). But compare *Com. v. Harris*, 464 Mass 425, 431-432, 983 NE2d 695, 701-702 (2013) (prosecutor did not improperly attempt to invoke jury's sympathy by playing 911 call during closing); *Com. v. Dumas*, 83 Mass App 536, 540, 986 NE2d 878, 881-882 (2013) (prosecutor's statement that victim feared for her life as result of defendant's threats was "excusable hyperbole"); *Com. v. Young*, 461 Mass 198, 204-205, 959 NE2d 943, 949 (2012) (prosecutor's statement that defendant had sliced up victim "like an animal" was not an improper appeal, but a permissible rhetorical tool relevant to the offense of murder by extreme atrocity or cruelty); *Com. v. Felder*, 455 Mass 359, 916 NE2d 990 (2009) (prosecutor's statement that "I have the burden of proof and there are two young men dead" was not improper appeal to jury sympathy); *Com. v. Gaynor*, 443 Mass 245, 273-274, 820 NE2d 233, 256 (2005) (prosecutor's references to twelve dollars defendant received from pawning victim's earrings, to the "killing zone," and to a "time of terror" in Springfield were not, in context, improper appeals to sympathy); *Com. v. DelValle*, 443 Mass 782, 795-796, 824 NE2d 830, 841-842 (2005) (prosecutor did not impermissibly argue victim had right to live but spoke generally about type of life she led and how she was not prepared for such brutal death); *Com. v. Ruiz*, 442 Mass 826, 836, 817 NE2d 771, 780 (2004) (prosecutor's remarks that victim chose to "meet her fate" trying to protect her children and that victim experienced prolonged suffering were pertinent to charge of murder with extreme atrocity and cruelty). See also *Com. v. Matthews*, 45 Mass App 444, 446-447, 699 NE2d 347, 349-350 (1998) (judge's comments that jurors put themselves in place of victim was balanced by suggestion they place themselves in position of defendant).

[39] See *Com. v. Harris*, 409 Mass 461, 469-471, 567 NE2d 899, 905 (1991) (victim advocate); *Com. v. Woods*, supra, 414 Mass at 358 (victim's parents).

to convict, or are "the conscience of the community,"[40] or equate a guilty verdict with justice.[41] The "conscience of the community" argument has, however, been upheld where the issue is whether the defendant committed murder by extreme atrocity or cruelty.[42] It is not improper for a prosecutor to argue simply that a defendant should be held accountable for his actions.[43]

A prosecutor may not suggest that jurors would have to explain their verdict to anyone, such as family members or friends,[44] nor inflame the jury with references to the potential consequences of a verdict of not guilty.[45] Nor may the prosecutor address the issue of

---

[40] See *Com. v. Miller*, 457 Mass 69, 929 NE2d 999 (2010) (improper to suggest jury had duty to convict); *Com. v. Francis*, 450 Mass 132, 140-141, 876 NE2d 862, 870-871 (2007) (improper for prosecutor to use phrase "justice delayed is justice denied" in 30-year old murder case as it equated guilty verdict with justice); *Com. v. Lewis*, 81 Mass App 119, 124-125, 960 NE2d 324, 329 (2012), *review granted*, 461 Mass 1110 (prosecutor's argument that "the street thugs aren't deciding this case. You [the jury] are" was improper because it implied the jury had duty to convict); *Com. v. Lassiter*, 80 Mass App 125, 131-132, 951 NE2d 961, 966-967 (2011) (improper to suggest that jury should convict OUI defendant because he failed to take responsibility for his actions, appealing to jury's sense of retribution); *Com. v. Baran*, 74 Mass App 256, 282-283, 905 NE2d 1122, 1144-1145 (2009) (improper for prosecutor to exhort jury to return guilty verdict in trial of multiple counts of child rape "in the name of justice and decency," and to suggest they would have to answer to the public should they return a not guilty verdict); *Com. v. Roberts*, 433 Mass 45, 54, 740 NE2d 176, 183 (2000) (improper to ask jury to convict to maintain orderly society, or to ask jury to hold defendant accountable for taking law into his own hands); *Com. v. Andrade*, 422 Mass 236, 661 NE2d 1308 (1996) (suggestion that evidence in murder trial "cried out for justice"); *Com. v. Walker*, 421 Mass 90, 103-104, 653 NE2d 1080, 1087-1088 (1995) (suggestion that jury had duty to vindicate victim's faith in the system).

[41] *Com. v. Carriere*, 470 Mass 1, 20, 18 NE3d 326, 342 (2014).

[42] See, e.g., *Com. v. Torres*, 437 Mass 460, 465, 772 NE2d 1046, 1050 (2002); *Com. v. Fitzmeyer*, 414 Mass 540, 547, 609 NE2d 81, 85 (1993); *Com. v. Lawrence*, 404 Mass 378, 393, 536 NE2d 571 (1989).

[43] The decisions are somewhat split on the use of this language. Compare *Com. v. Tavares*, 471 Mass 430, 444, 30 NE3d 91, 105 (2015) (comments were proper as connected to specific acts that were in evidence), *Com. v. Freeman*, 430 Mass 111, 120, 712 NE2d 1135, 1143 (1999) (prosecutor's remarks concerning defendant's accountability for his actions were appropriate because criminal responsibility was at issue), and *Com. v. Mejia*, 463 Mass 243, 255, 973 NE2d 657, 666 (2012) (prosecutor's comment "In every man's life, in every person's life, there comes a time to be held accountable. And for [defendant] that time is now" was permissible rhetoric), with *Com. v. Jenkins*, 458 Mass 791, 796-797, 941 NE2d 56, 65 (2011) (improper to argue that defendant should be "held accountable").

[44] See *Com. v. Quinn*, 61 Mass App 332, 334-335, 810 NE2d 819, 821-822 (2004).

[45] *Com. v. Thomas*, 401 Mass 109, 117, 514 NE2d 1309, 1314 (1987) (& citations); *Com. v. Smith Com. v. Smith*, 387 Mass 900, 910-911, 444 NE2d 374, 381-382 (1983) (improper for prosecutor to argue that person like defendant should not be let loose on society). But compare *Com. v. Westerman*, 414 Mass 688, 701, 611 NE2d 215, 224 (1993) (prosecutor's statements regarding effect of defendant's actions on the

punishment or make the jury aware of sentencing consequences in closing argument.[46]

An appeal that enlists the jurors on the side of the government as "members of the community" to protect innocent victims from violent crime "has no place in trial advocacy."[47] Nor may a prosecutor seek to align himself with the jury by repeated use of the pronoun "we," or use the pronoun to suggest his own opinion about the credibility of witnesses.[48] A prosecutor may not characterize the trial as a dispute between the victim and defendant, and exhort the jury to dispense justice between them.[49]

Counsel may not inject their own credibility or personal beliefs into closing argument, or suggest they have personal knowledge of the matters,[50] or allude to their own life experiences in their

---

community were not unfairly prejudicial in light of evidence of his involvement with organized crime); *Com. v. Sinai*, 47 Mass App 544, 549-550, 714 NE2d 830, 834-835 (1999) (prosecutor's overzealous comments about adherence to rules to prevent chaos, in prosecution for being disorderly person, were not prejudicial in context); *Com. v. Davis*, 38 Mass App 932, 636 NE2d 1093 (1995) (remark that "the only thing it takes for evil to triumph is for a few good men and good women to do nothing" did not, standing alone, require reversal).

[46] See *Com. v. Duguay*, 430 Mass 397, 404, 720 NE2d 458, 464 (1999), *habeas petition denied in Duguay v. Spencer*, 462 F Supp 2d 115 (D Mass 2006).

[47] *Com. v. Awad*, 47 Mass App 139, 145-146, 712 NE2d 601, 606 (1999).

[48] See *Com. v. Burts*, 68 Mass App 684, 688, 864 NE2d 562, 565 (2007); *Com. v. Dodgson*, 80 Mass App 307, 314, 952 NE2d 961, 968 (2011).

[49] *Com. v. Niemic*, 472 Mass 665, 676, 674, 37 NE3d 577, 586 (2015). See also *Com. v. Scesny*, 472 Mass 185, 200, 34 NE3d 17, 31 (2015) (improper for prosecutor to suggest that he was representing the jurors-as-citizens against the defendant).

[50] See *Com. v. Sylvia*, 456 Mass 182, 193-194, 921 NE2d 968, 979 (2010) (improper for prosecutor to comment on defendant's appearance by stating "I know that he doesn't quite look the same today."); *Com. v. Semedo*, 456 Mass 1, 14, 921 NE2d 57, 69 (2010) (prosecutor's statement that he had no knowledge whether defendant knew of victim's daily routine was mere rhetorical device; but prosecutor should not have later equated what he knew with the question of what the evidence showed); *Com. v. Gaudette*, 441 Mass 762, 770, 808 NE2d 798, 805 (2004) (improper for prosecutor to imply he knew contents of police report not in evidence); *Com. v. Torres*, 437 Mass 460, 465, 772 NE2d 1046, 1051 (2002) (prosecutor's statement "He's guilty as charged" was improper statement of personal belief); *Com. v. Santiago*, 425 Mass 491, 498, 681 NE2d 1205, 1212 (1997) (prosecutor's statement "I suggest to you I overwhelmingly proved who fired that fatal shot" was improper subjective assessment of evidence); *Com. v. Rosa*, 73 Mass App 540, 546-548, 899 NE2d 887, 893-894 (2009) (prosecutor's argument could have been understood by jury to indicate he had knowledge about the relative difficulty of two methods of photographic identification, without any such evidence in the record). But compare *Com. v. Jenkins*, 458 Mass 791, 797-798, 941 NE2d 56, 66 (2011) (prosecutor's use of phrase "mountain of evidence" did not amount to improper expression of personal belief); *Com. v. Johnson*, 412 Mass 318, 326, 588 NE2d 684, 689 (1992) (although prosecutor's restating of witness's prior statements to him came "perilously close to injecting his own personal knowledge and integrity

argument.[51] "To permit counsel to express his personal belief in the testimony (even if not phrased so as to suggest knowledge of additional evidence not known to the jury), would afford him a privilege not even accorded to witnesses under oath and subject to cross-examination. Worse, it creates the false issue of the reliability and credibility of counsel. This is peculiarly unfortunate if one of them has the advantage of official backing."[52] Thus, where the prosecutor recounted in closing argument his own car trip re-tracing the route described by a key prosecution witness to confirm his version of events, that amounted to unsworn testimony and vouching, requiring a new trial.[53]

A prosecutor is free to provide the jury with reasons to find a witness's testimony to be accurate, but she cannot tell the jury that the witness speaks the truth.[54] A prosecutor may, however, express his view of the strength of the evidence.[55] The mere use of a first person pronoun does not interject personal belief into an argument.[56]

---

into his closing argument," no error because witness had agreed she had made the statements); *Com. v. Cohen*, 412 Mass 375, 386, 589 NE2d 289, 297 (1992) (prosecutor's use of term "obvious" in arguing defendant's guilt did not interject his own belief); *Com. v. Cabral*, 69 Mass App 68, 76, 866 NE2d 429, 435-436 (2007) (prosecutor's interjections of her own personal assessment of defendant's guilt should have been omitted, but did not imply private knowledge); *Com. v. North*, 52 Mass App 603, 611, 755 NE2d 312, 319 (2001) (unfortunate hyperbole that "there are very few cases that a prosecutor presents to a jury in which you really get the feeling that you are representing the Commonwealth" carried aroma of personal belief, but not prejudicial in context); *Com. v. Springer*, 49 Mass App 469, 475, 730 NE2d 349, 356 (2000) (prosecutor's statement, "I ask you not to free a guilty man," did not constitute improper expression of personal opinion on guilt).

[51] See, e.g., *Santos v. Chrysler Corp.*, 430 Mass 198, 214, 715 NE2d 47, 59 (1999) (& citations) (counsel's references to his own children in wrongful death action for death of plaintiff's children).

[52] *Com. v. Thomas*, supra, 401 Mass at 115-116, 514 NE2d at 1313-1314).

[53] See *Com. v. Williams*, 450 Mass 894, 902-905, 882 NE2d 850, 857-860 (2008).

[54] *Com. v. Penn*, 472 Mass 610, 627, 36 NE3d 552, 567 (2015).

[55] *Com. v. Grimshaw*, 412 Mass 505, 508, 590 NE2d 681, 683 (1992). *Com. v. Smith*, 387 Mass 900, 906-907, 444 NE2d 374, 380 (1983).

[56] See *Com. v. Young*, 461 Mass 198, 205-206, 959 NE2d 943, 950 (2012) ("To be honest with you, I don't care how [the defendant] was holding the knife" was in response to defendant' testimony, and was used to mean "it doesn't matter"); *Com. v. Espada*, 450 Mass 687, 699, 880 NE2d 795, 806-807 (2008) (prosecutor was merely arguing what average person would do under circumstances); *Com. v. Jenkins*, 458 Mass 791, 797, 941 NE2d 56, 65-66 (2011). *Com. v. LaFontaine*, 32 Mass App 529, 537, 591 NE2d 1103, 1107-1108 (1992) (prosecutor's use of "I submit" was rhetorical device and not assertion of personal belief).

A prosecutor's nonverbal conduct during argument may give rise to a claim of prejudice.[57]

Counsel may not comment (either positively—i.e., vouch for—or negatively) from personal knowledge on the credibility of a witness.[58]

---

[57] See *Com. v. Mercado*, 456 Mass 198, 210, 922 NE2d 140, 150-151 (2010) (but rejecting assertion that prosecutor smirked or otherwise belittled defendant and his family).

[58] See *Com. v. Brown*, 462 Mass 620, 632-633, 970 NE2d 306, 317 (2012) (judge properly admonished defense counsel for asserting in closing "we all know that [other possible culprit] had a gun because [witness] told us he did," as it bordered on inappropriate vouching); *Com. v. Lawton*, 82 Mass App 528, 541-542, 976 NE2d 160, 171-172 (2012) (prosecutor's remark that victim's testimony was guided by the truth edged too close to vouching, but was in response to defense counsel's attack on credibility); *Com. v. Hardy*, 431 Mass 387, 396-397, 727 NE2d 836, 843-844 (2000) (prosecutor improperly personalized process by which witness was granted immunity and attempted to use authority of court to vouch for credibility) *postconviction relief denied* 646 Mass 660, 984 NE2d 727 (2012); *Com. v. Freeman*, 430 Mass 111, 118-120, 712 NE2d 1135, 1142-1143 (1999) (prosecutor's reference to expert witness as "the best there is" was improperly based on personal beliefs); *Com. v. Raymond*, 424 Mass 382, 391-392, 676 NE2d 824, 831 (1997) (discouraging use by prosecutors of ambiguous statements which jury could interpret as vouching for credibility of witness); *Com. v. Baran*, 74 Mass App 256, 282, 905 NE2d 1122, 1144 (2009) (prosecutor improperly bolstered credibility of government's witnesses by expressing his view that the parents, who had endured a "terrible nightmare," would never have permitted their traumatized children to testify to these "horrible bloodcurdling things" unless the allegations were true); *Com. v. McCoy*, 59 Mass App 284, 294-296, 795 NE2d 1183, 1191-1192 (2003) (prosecutor improperly vouched for police witnesses when he argued that if jury believed defense, they'd be calling police officers liars); *Com. v. Dumais*, 60 Mass App 70, 73-74, 799 NE2d 125, 128 (2003) (prosecutor's comments that it was "painfully obvious how truthful [police witness] was" was improper); *Com. v. Omonira*, 59 Mass App 200, 205-206, 794 NE2d 1248, 1252-1253 (2003) (prosecutor's comment that witness was the most "laid back" police officer he had ever seen and was "completely honest" was improper vouching and assertion of personal opinion on credibility); *Com. v. Fredette*, 56 Mass App 253, 262-263, 776 NE2d 464, 472-473 (2002) (as prosecutor's proposition that sexual abuse victims commonly delay disclosure had not been subject of testimony, argument constituted improper vouching for victim's credibility); *Com. v. Bradford*, 52 Mass App 220, 223, 752 NE2d 773, 776 (2001) (when prosecutor sat in witness chair and supported credibility of witness that crossed line and constituted improper vouching); *Com. v. Lindsey*, 48 Mass App 641, 724 NE2d 327 (2000) (prosecutor promised truthful testimony by cooperating witness and suggested that witness knew "the truth"); *Com. v. Meuse*, 38 Mass App 772, 653 NE2d 186 (1995) (prosecutor's references to credibility of witness testifying pursuant to plea agreement, suggested government had verified testimony and thus required reversal). Compare *Com. v. Lessieur*, 472 Mass 317, 330, 34 NE3d 321, 332-333 (2015) (no improper vouching where prosecutor argued that the district attorney "gets involved in" determining the truth of key witness's version of events); *Com. v. Webb*, 468 Mass 26, 35-36, 8 NE3d 270, 277 (2014) (no improper vouching where prosecutor argued regarding two witnesses testifying under grants of immunity that there was no evidence of motivation to lie, and that the incentive was to tell the truth); *Com. v. Rosario*, 460 Mass 181, 190-191, 950 NE2d 407, 416-417 (2011), *habeas denied*, *Rosario v. Roden*, 2014 WL

Otherwise, the credibility of witnesses is a proper subject of comment.[59] "With a basis in the record and expressed as a conclusion to be drawn from the evidence and not as a personal opinion, counsel may properly argue not only that a witness is mistaken but also that a witness is lying."[60]

A prosecutor may, based on the evidence, permissibly argue that defense witnesses including the defendant are not credible or plausible.[61] Similarly defense counsel, with a basis in the record and expressed as a conclusion and not as a personal opinion, may properly

---

7409584 (D Mass 2014) (prosecutor's comments about the credibility of two Commonwealth witnesses willingly putting themselves into the crime scene did not come close to explicit vouching); *Com. v. Tu Trinh*, 458 Mass 776, 785-787, 940 NE2d 871, 880-881 (2011) (prosecutor's reference to witness as honest was not improper vouching, and judge instructed jury that prosecutor did not know whether witness was telling the truth or not); *Com. v. Sanders*, 451 Mass 290, 297, 885 NE2d 105, 113-114 (2008) (prosecutor was entitled to respond to challenge to witness's credibility as he did not ally himself or his office behind her or suggest he had extra-record information); *Com. v. Alisha*, 56 Mass App 311, 315, 777 NE2d 191, 195 (2002) (no improper vouching where prosecutor used rhetorical terms like "I suggest," rather than personal belief, when urging jury to evaluate credibility); *Com. v. Sullivan*, 435 Mass 722, 727, 761 NE2d 509, 514 (2002) (Commonwealth entitled to argue immunity could be considered by jury as indication that witness was telling truth; but colloquial translations of what immunity means are best left unsaid).

[59] *Santos v. Chrysler Corp.*, supra 430 Mass at 212-213, 715 NE2d at 59 (although counsel should have tempered his language, it was permissible to argue that testimony by defendant's witness was a lie so long as supported by evidence and fair inferences). But compare *Com. v. Daley*, 439 Mass 558, 565-567, 789 NE2d 1070, 1076-1077 (2003) (improper to suggest that defendant's "character" as drug dealer and thief should be used to assess his credibility).

[60] *Com. v. Murchison*, 418 Mass 58, 60, 634 NE2d 561, 563 (1994).

[61] *Com. v. Espada*, 450 Mass 687, 699, 880 NE2d 795, 807 (2008) (prosecutor permitted to characterize defendant's story as "ridiculous"); *Com. v. Williams*, 450 Mass 879, 888-889, 883 NE2d 249, 257 (2008) (prosecutor permitted to characterize defendant's story as "hiding behind the convenient veil of self-defense"); *Com. v. Ayoub*, 77 Mass App 563, 567-568, 933 NE2d 133, 138 (2010) (prosecutor permissibly argued that defendant told a "very wild unbelievable story about what happened"); *Com. v. Brum*, 438 Mass 103, 118-119, 777 NE2d 1238, 1251-1252 (2002) (prosecutor permissibly resorted to sarcasm to point out absurdity of defendant's testimony); *Com. v. Obershaw*, 435 Mass 794, 807, 762 NE2d 276, 288 (2002) (prosecutor's reference to defendant as "liar" was fair comment based on contradictions and implausibility of his story); *Com. v. Oliveira*, 431 Mass 609, 613, 728 NE2d 320, 324 (2000) (prosecutor's reference to defendant's "bold-faced lie" had basis in evidence and was not personal comment on credibility); *Com. v. Ormonde*, 55 Mass App 231, 235-236, 770 NE2d 36, 39-40 (2002) (prosecutor's argument that jurors should not "let the smoke fool you," that they should "throw [defendant's testimony] out the window, because it's all baloney," and that defendant tailored his testimony to fit the evidence was permissible challenge to credibility); *Com. v. Youngworth*, 55 Mass App 30, 39-40, 769 NE2d 299, 307-308 (2002) (permissible for prosecutor to argue "don't be fooled by this man" because he's "trying to pull the wool over your eyes" and make a "mockery of this justice

argue that a prosecution witness (including a police officer) was lying.[62] Counsel have been cautioned, however, to avoid prejudicial name calling.[63] Thus, the fact that an expert witness was retained and paid by an opposing party is a proper subject for argument, but use of the term "hired gun" is disfavored.[64] A prosecutor may not go beyond pointing out defendant's obvious bias in his testimony to suggest that it is so incredible as to not qualify as evidence,[65] or disparage defendant's account as "crap, pure and simple."[66]

A prosecutor may argue in support of the credibility of the Commonwealth's witnesses based on their demeanor, motive, and the consistency of their stories, especially in response to defense attacks.[67]

---

system"); *Com. v. Deloney*, 59 Mass App 47, 51-52, 794 NE2d 613, 618-619 (2003) (prosecutor's characterization of defendant as "cocky" and statement that he "thinks he can walk into this courtroom and tell his preposterous story" and "lie to you and that you'll buy it" were proper comments regarding his demeanor and credibility). Compare *Com. v. Waite*, 422 Mass 792, 800-801, 665 NE2d 982, 989 (1996) (clear error for prosecutor to make bald assertion that defendant, who never took the stand, was "a liar"); *Com. v. Rivera*, 62 Mass App 859, 863-864, 821 NE2d 928, 932 (2005) (improper for prosecutor to argue defense witness's testimony should be discounted because she did not call police at time of confrontation where there was no evidence on whether she did call, and no foundation as to whether failure to call would support inference of recent fabrication); *Com. v. Smith*, 40 Mass App 770, 775-776, 667 NE2d 1160, 1163 (1996) (sloganeering manner in which prosecutor admonished jury not to be "conned by the cons," referring to defense witnesses, should have been avoided).

[62] *Com. v. Tu Trinh*, 458 Mass 776, 788-789, 940 NE2d 871, 882 (2011) (improper for prosecutor to criticize defense counsel for "pointing a finger" at the Boston Police Department's investigative failures); *Com. v. Murchison*, supra, 418 Mass at 60, 634 NE2d at 563; *Com. v. Grandison*, 433 Mass 135, 143, 741 NE2d 25, 33 (2001) (improper for prosecutor to argue to jury that it was wrong for defense counsel to question veracity of police officers).

[63] See *Com. v. Martin*, 57 Mass App 272, 782 NE2d 547 (2003) (prosecutor's repeated reference to defendant's alias); *Com. v. Daley*, 55 Mass App 88, 91-92, 769 NE2d 322, 325-326 (2002) (prosecutor asked jury to consider defendant's bad character and repeatedly referred to him as "crack dealer," drug and alcohol user, thief, and probationer); *Com. v. Rivera*, 52 Mass App 321, 328, 753 NE2d 823, 829 (2001) (& citations).

[64] *Com. v. Bishop*, 461 Mass 586, 597-599, 963 NE2d 88, 97-98 (2012) (prosecutor improperly disparaged defense expert witness by referring to his billing rate and suggesting he was "bought"); *Com. v. Cruz*, 424 Mass 207, 212, 675 NE2d 764, 767-768 (1997) (improper for prosecutor to refer to defense psychologist witness as "charlatan"); *Com. v. Benson*, 419 Mass 114, 119-120, 642 NE2d 1035, 1038-1039 (1994).

[65] *Com. v. Niemic*, 472 Mass 665, 674, 37 NE3d 577, 585 (2015)

[66] *Com. v. Cadet*, 473 Mass 173, 188, 40 NE3d 1015, 1028 (2015).

[67] See *Com. v. Caldwell*, 459 Mass 271, 280-281, 945 NE2d 313, 323-324 (2011) (prosecutor's argument that if cooperating witness was "caught in a lie, he'd be facing all of those years" in prison was in response to defense challenge to witness's credibility and not improper vouching); *Com. v. Sylvia*, 456 Mass 182, 194-195, 921 NE2d 968, 979-980 (2010) (although prosecutor should not have made remark about defense

Rhetorical questions like "what reason would this witness have to lie?" are a proper response as well.[68]

A prosecutor may not, however, argue that a victim or any government witness is inherently reliable merely because she subjected herself to the rigors of appearing in court.[69] A prosecutor may not

---

counsel seeking to "convict the police," he was entitled to respond to argument that police planted evidence on defendant); *Com. v. Silva*, 455 Mass 503, 515, 918 NE2d 65, 80 (2009) (prosecutor could respond to defense counsel's attack on Commonwealth's witnesses with age-old expression that "when you prosecute a case in hell, you don't have angels for witnesses"); *Com. v. Payne*, 426 Mass 692, 695-696, 690 NE2d 443, 447 (1998) (prosecutor could ask jury to consider witnesses' fearful demeanor in assessing credibility); *Com. v. Dixon*, 425 Mass 223, 232-234, 680 NE2d 84, 90-91 (1997) (no improper vouching where prosecutor mentioned that witness would be subjecting himself to prosecution for perjury if he lied on stand); *Com. v. Helberg*, 73 Mass App 175, 896 NE2d 651 (2008) (prosecutor's argument that victims had no motive to lie was proper response to defense attack); *Com. v. Ragland*, 72 Mass App 815, 836 n.17, 894 NE2d 1147, 1163 n.17 (2008) (proper for prosecutor to respond to attack on police witnesses); *Com. v. Oppenheim*, 86 Mass App 359, 370, 16 NE3d 502, 512 (2014) (prosecutor's argument referring to multiple academic and professional achievements of five Commonwealth witnesses was fair response to defense attacks); *Com. v. Dancy*, 75 Mass App 175, 188-189, 912 NE2d 525, 537 (2009) (prosecutor's argument that police witnesses were "very believable" was not improper vouching); *Com. v. Raposa*, 440 Mass 684, 694-697, 801 NE2d 789, 798-800 (2004) (prosecutor's comments that under defendant's theory all prosecution witnesses were lying did not improperly suggest only explanation was either truthful testimony or conspiracy; and stating that witness was "one of the nicest people" and "about as forthright" was proper reference to her demeanor); *Com. v. Deloney*, 59 Mass App 47, 52-53, 794 NE2d 613, 619 (2003) (no impermissible vouching where prosecutor suggested child witnesses had no motive to lie; argument did not have the dogmatic "take it from me" quality that is not permitted); *Com. v. Rivera*, 52 Mass App 321, 325, 753 NE2d 823, 827 (2001) (prosecutor's comment that sexual abuse victim "didn't have to subject herself to the humiliation of talking to countless strangers about horribly embarrassing personal experiences in her young life" was not improper vouching).

[68] *Com. v. Mitchell*, 89 Mass App 13, 28, 89 Mass App 111, 124 (2016); *Com. v. Halstrom*, 84 Mass App 372, 385, 996 NE2d 892, 903 (2013).

[69] *Com. v. Beaudry*, 445 Mass 577, 587, 839 NE2d 298, 306 (2005); *Com. v. Ramos*, 73 Mass App 824, 902 NE2d 948 (2009) (prosecutor improperly vouched for witness by conjecturing the embarrassment she would experience in coming before a group of strangers to describe the sexual assault, including her menstruation and use of sanitary pad); *Com. v. Helberg*, 73 Mass App 175, 179-180, 896 NE2d 651, 654-655 (2008). Compare *Com. v. Polk*, 462 Mass 23, 39-40, 965 NE2d 815 (2012) (prosecutor's question to jury during closing argument asking what motive alleged victim had to lie was not improper where defense counsel had challenged her credibility); *Com. v. Shanley*, 455 Mass 752, 774-778, 919 NE2d 1254, 1272-1274 (2010) (prosecutor could comment on voluntary nature of victim's appearance to testify in sexual abuse prosecution as fair response to defense strategy of challenging victim's credibility by suggesting he had a motive to fabricate abuse allegations because of a civil suit he pursued); *Com. v. Morales*, 453 Mass 40, 52-53, 899 NE2d 96, 105-106 (2009) (not improper for prosecutor to state that each witness came forward and subjected himself to cross-examination).

suggest, inferentially or otherwise, that jurors should trust the police witnesses solely because they are police.[70]

A prosecutor in closing argument may restate the government's plea or immunity agreement with a witness and may argue reasonable inferences from the agreement's requirement of truthful testimony, but may not, implicitly or explicitly, vouch for the truth of that testimony to the jury.[71]

The failure of the defendant to take the stand is not a proper subject for comment. See § 5.14.8, supra.[72] Nor may a prosecutor argue (without specific evidentiary basis) that a defendant who "sat through" the Commonwealth's case was thereby able to tailor his testimony accordingly,[73] or that because defendant was not sequestered like

---

[70] *Com. v. Burts*, 68 Mass App 684, 688, 864 NE2d 562, 565 (2007). Compare *Com. v. Ahart*, 464 Mass 437, 444-445, 983 NE2d 1203, 1209 (2013) (prosecutor properly argued that detective should be believed because of his long experience with state police); *Com. v. Smith*, 460 Mass 385, 398-399, 951 NE2d 674, 686 (2011) (prosecutor properly argued that police witnesses should be believed because of the consistency of their testimony and the corroborating evidence). Where the prosecutor intends to offer evidence of an officer's specialized training to bolster his credibility, advance warning should be given to the defendant and the trial judge. See *Com. v. Johnson*, 463 Mass 95, 109-111, 972 NE2d 460, 472-473 (2012) (prosecutor improperly overstated witness's specialized training in eyewitness identification).

[71] Compare *Com. v. Watkins*, 473 Mass 222, 237, 41 NE3d 10, 25 (2015) (prosecutor may argue that plea agreement witness's testimony was truthful) with *Com. v. Marrero*, 436 Mass 488, 501-502, 766 NE2d 461, 471-472 (2002) (although prosecutor could encourage jury to read immunity agreement, he should not have stated that the witness "tells the truth, at least that's as far as [he] could follow it"); *Com. v. Rivera*, 430 Mass 91, 98-99, 712 NE2d 1127, 1133 (1999) (& citations); *Com. v. Lindsey*, 48 Mass App 641, 724 NE2d 327 (2000) (prosecutor promised truthful testimony by cooperating witness, suggested that witness knew "the truth," referred to subculture of drug dealers inhabited by defendants, and appealed for conviction for sake of police officers who risked their lives in war on drugs). Regarding immunity agreements and credibility, see also § 6.15, supra.

[72] Counsel for one defendant at a joint trial may emphasize his own client's decision to testify so long as he does not make direct reference to a codefendant's failure to testify. *Com. v. Akara*, 465 Mass 245, 264, 988 NE2d 430, 446 (2013).

[73] *Com. v. Person*, 400 Mass 136, 139-143, 508 NE2d 88, 90-92 (1987). See also *Com. v. Elberry*, 38 Mass App 912, 645 NE2d 41 (1995) (statement that defendant was only witness with opportunity to hear all evidence and accordingly tailor his testimony was improper); *Com. v. Jones*, 45 Mass App 254, 697 NE2d 140 (1998) (prosecutor's comments that defendant had had pretrial access to Commonwealth's evidence and had remained silent prior to testifying to fabricate version of events). But compare *Com. v. Bolling*, 462 Mass 440, 455-456, 969 NE2d 640, 653 (2012) (prosecutor's argument that defendants "concocted" their story of self-defense after reviewing discovery materials was merely a comment on prior statements that conflicted with the defense); *Com. v. Greineder*, 458 Mass 207, 244, 936 NE2d 372, 399-400 (2010) (prosecutor's argument that defendant had time to think about the case and hear the testimony of the Commonwealth's witnesses before testifying himself was proper and grounded in the record).

the other witnesses he had the opportunity to lie by tailoring his testimony.[74]

A prosecutor should avoid reference to defendant's opportunity to "rehearse" his or other testimony, as that may impinge on defendant's right to prepare for trial.[75]

The Commonwealth may not comment on defendant's failure to produce evidence, or refer to certain facts as "unrefuted" when the defendant is the only one who can contradict the evidence.[76] Prosecutors are admonished to scrupulously avoid any statement or rhetorical

---

[74] *Com. v. Alphonse*, 87 Mass App 336, 29 NE3d 849 (2015) (reversing conviction). Under federal law, a prosecutor's statement to this effect does not offend defendant's right to confront witnesses or testify in his own behalf, or his right to due process. See *Portuondo v. Agard*, 529 US 61 (2000).

[75] *Com. v. Dodgson*, 80 Mass App 307, 314-315, 952 NE2d 961, 968 (2011).

[76] See *Com. v. Silva*, 471 Mass 610, 622-623, 31 NE3d 1092, 1102 (2015) (prosecutor's argument that "there is not a scintilla of evidence to support [the defense theory that his companion killed the victim]" was proper response to the defense argument and a proper comment on the evidence); *Com. v. Silanskas*, 433 Mass 678, 700-701, 746 NE2d 445, 465-466 (2001); *Com. v. Cyr*, 433 Mass 617, 625-627, 744 NE2d 1082, 1088-1089 (2001) (prosecutor's misstatement of certain evidence as "uncontroverted" was error). Compare *Com. v. Garvin*, 456 Mass 778, 798-799, 926 NE2d 169, 185-186 (2010) (prosecutor's argument that "there was no credible evidence presented in this case that it was anyone other than [the defendant]" was comment on the strength of the Commonwealth's case, not an impermissible comment of defendant's failure to testify or produce evidence); *Com. v. Pena*, 455 Mass 1, 17-20, 913 NE2d 815, 828-830 (2009) (even if prosecutor's comment that defendant was only person who knew why he killed victim was reasonably susceptible to being interpreted as comment on defendant's failure to testify, judge's prompt instructions negated any possible prejudice); *Com. v. Stewart*, 454 Mass 527, 540, 911 NE2d 161, 173 (2009) (prosecutor's statement that, while there was no trace evidence to place defendant at scene, there was nothing to exclude him, came close to the line, but was permissible in context); *Com. v. Morales*, 453 Mass 40, 53, 899 NE2d 96, 106 (2009) (prosecutor's response to suggestion that prosecution witnesses had conspired to accuse defendant falsely was not comment on defendant's failure to offer alibi evidence); *Com. v. Francis*, 450 Mass 132, 141-142, 876 NE2d 862, 871 (2007) (prosecutor's assertion that there was no real evidence of defendant's mental illness was merely comment on the evidence presented, not on the failure to produce evidence); *Com. v. Drummond*, 76 Mass App 625, 630-631, 925 NE2d 34, 39 (2010) (Commonwealth's closing argument that there was no evidence that defendant's confession was involuntary did not constitute impermissible comment on his failure to testify); *Com. v. Montez*, 450 Mass 736, 747, 881 NE2d 753, 763 (2008) (prosecutor's statement that defense counsel never addressed the prior bad act evidence was not a comment on defendant's failure to present evidence and did not shift the burden of proof); *Com. v. Francis*, 450 Mass 132, 141-142, 876 NE2d 862, 871 (2007) (prosecutor's assertion that there was no real evidence of defendant's mental illness was merely comment on the evidence presented, not on the failure to produce evidence); *Com. v. Reid*, 73 Mass App 423, 431-433, 898 NE2d 520, 528-529 (2008) (prosecutor's comment that certain evidence was "undisputed" were directed at general weakness of defendant's case, and defendant was not the only one who could contradict the evidence); *Com. v. Boyajian*, 68 Mass App 866,

question that suggests the defendant has any burden to produce evidence.[77] It is improper for a prosecutor to make a missing witness argument without first obtaining judicial approval.[78] Nor may a prosecutor argue that the jury could conclude that the Commonwealth's case was strong based on the fact that defendant chose to put on witnesses even though he has no obligation to do so, as that suggests an adverse inference from the fundamental right to present defense.[79]

A prosecutor is entitled to emphasize the strong points of the Commonwealth's case and the weaknesses of the defense, even

---

870-871, 865 NE2d 1153, 1157 (2007) (prosecutor's remarks that defendant produced no evidence of conditions which may have impaired his driving was in response to defense closing); *Com. v. Boyajian*, 68 Mass App 866, 870-871, 865 NE2d 1153, 1157 (2007) (prosecutor's remarks that defendant produced no evidence of conditions which may have impaired his driving was in response to defense closing).

[77] See *Com. v. Johnson*, 463 Mass 95, 111-113, 972 NE2d 460, 473-474 (2012) (prosecutor's rhetorical question "How is [defense counsel] going to deal with [the stubborn facts]" improperly suggested defendant had a positive responsibility of proof); *Com. v. Degro*, 432 Mass 319, 328, 733 NE2d 1024, 1035-1036 (2000) (although inartful, prosecutor's statement that presumption of innocence "only lasts until evidence is presented to you that a person is guilty of a crime" did not shift burden of proof); *Com. v. Bregoli*, 431 Mass 265, 279, 727 NE2d 59, 71 (2000) (rhetorical questions should not be used if they could be perceived as shifting burden of proof to defendant); *Com. v. Hubbard*, 69 Mass App 232, 241, 867 NE2d 341, 349 (2007) (prosecutor improperly argued "if you look for [reasonable] doubt, you will find doubt"); *Com. v. Hiotes*, 58 Mass App 255, 259-260, 789 NE2d 179, 182 (2003) (improper for prosecutor to suggest rape defendant had burden to produce psychiatric evidence to challenge victim's mental condition); *Com. v. Pagano*, 47 Mass App 55, 61-63, 710 NE2d 1034, 1038-1039 (1999) (prosecutor's statement that "cloak of innocence" comes off at end of trial suggested that defendant had burden to prove innocence, and reference to himself as 13th juror vouched for his version of evidence), *habeas granted by Pagano v. Allard*, 218 F Supp 2d 26 (D Mass 2002) (prosecutor's argument undermined presumption of innocence); Compare *Com. v. Johnson*, 470 Mass 300, 318, 21 NE3d 937, 952 (2014) (prosecutor's comment asking how defendants could "explain to you" a certain fact was not improper comment on defendants' failure to testify); *Com. v. Cook*, 419 Mass 192, 203, 644 NE2d 203, 210 (1994) (statement that jury "should not be intimidated by phrase 'reasonable doubt' " was not improper in context of closing argument). See also § 3.4.1, supra.

[78] *Com. v. Niemic*, 472 Mass 665, 674, 37 NE3d 577, 584-585 (2015).

[79] See *Com. v. Cassidy*, 470 Mass 201, 226, 21 NE3d 127, 149 (2014) (prosecutor's remarks were proper reflection on the weakness of the defendant's case); *Com. v. Bresilla*, 470 Mass 422, 438-439, 23 NE3d 75, 88-89 (2015) (prosecutor did not comment on defendant's failure to contradict evidence, but properly argued in response to defense attack on the police investigation that officers unsuccessfully attempted to contact defendant's alibi witnesses); *Com. v. Hughes*, 82 Mass App 21, 29-31, 969 NE2d 1149, 1155-1156 (2012). See also *Com. v. Carriere*, 470 Mass 1, 19-20, 18 NE3d 326, 341-342 (2014) (prosecutor's comment that it was the jury's job to decide which version to believe did not shift burden to defendant).

though it "may, in so doing, prompt some collateral or passing reflection on the fact that the defendant declined to testify."[80] Comments that suggest a shift of the burden of proof to the defendant are of course improper.[81]

Additional matters:

- A prosecutor may not suggest that the existence of an indictment is evidence of guilt.[82]
- A prosecutor should not attempt to quantify the concept of proof beyond a reasonable doubt, or the accuracy of eyewitness identification, in probabilistic terms in closing argument.[83]
- Prosecutors should proceed with caution when asserting fundamentally inconsistent theories in separate trial involving the same crime.[84]
- Counsel may not encourage the jury to conduct experiments or obtain outside information on their own.[85]
- During closing argument, counsel may read to the jury verbatim portions of a witness's testimony (so long as a copy is provided by opposing counsel).[86]
- With specific reference to sexual assault cases, a prosecutor who seeks to argue that age-inappropriate sexual knowledge exhibited by a child was necessarily derived from the sexual acts charged against defendant must have a firm evidentiary basis for the argument, i.e., some record evidence that the knowledge was not derived from another source.[87]
- For the propriety of comment on a missing witness, see § 3.6.2, supra.

---

[80] *Com. v. Nelson*, 468 Mass 1, 12, 7 NE3d 1084, 1093 (2014).

[81] *Com. v. Lugo*, 89 Mass App 229, 235, 47 NE3d 41, 48 (2016).

[82] *Com. v. Akara*, 465 Mass 245, 261-262, 988 NE2d 430, 444-445 (2013).

[83] See *Com. v. Ferreira*, 460 Mass 781, 955 NE2d 898 (2011) (prosecutor's closing argument that there was a 98 percent probability that the victim's identification of defendant was accurate was fundamentally flawed). See also § 4.2.2.

[84] *Com. v. Keo*, 467 Mass 25, 36-46, 3 NE2d 55, 64-71 (2014) (raising question of admissibility of transcript of conflicting closing argument).

[85] See *Com. v. Beauchamp*, 424 Mass 682, 691, 677 NE2d 1135, 1140 (1997).

[86] *Com. v. Delacruz*, 443 Mass 692, 694-696, 824 NE2d 34, 37-38 (2005).

[87] See *Com. v. Beaudry*, 445 Mass 577, 579-583, 839 NE2d 298, 301-304 (2005) (conviction reversed where there was no evidence of the sexual knowledge of an average child nor anything to indicate victim was a typical child of that age).

- For the impropriety of comment on pre- or post-arrest silence of the defendant or his invocation of rights, see § 12.6.8.

For an extensive discussion of the limits of prosecutorial argument, see *Com. v. Kozec*, 399 Mass 514, 516-521, 505 NE2d 519, 520-523 (1987) and *Com. v. Fitzgerald*, 376 Mass 402, 416-417, 381 NE2d 123, 134 (1978). The First Circuit Court of Appeals aptly captured the constraints:

> Too often a lawyer loses sight of his primary responsibility as an officer of the court. While he must provide "zealous advocacy" for his client's cause, we encourage this only as a means of achieving the court's ultimate goal, which is finding the truth. Deceptions, misrepresentations, or falsities can only frustrate that goal and will not be tolerated within our judicial system.[88]

In order to ascertain whether improper statements during argument require reversal, the court will view the particular statements in the context of the entire argument, the judge's instructions, and the evidence at trial.[89] "[T]he prejudicial impact of the prosecutor's charge should be assessed by looking at the combined effect of all his errors."[90] A single misstatement in a closing argument will likely not

---

[88] *Polansky v. CNA Ins. Co.*, 852 F2d 626, 632 (1st Cir 1988) (quoted in *Fyffe v. MBTA*, 86 Mass App 457, 475, 17 NE3d 453, 466 (2014)).

[89] See *Com. v. Gonzalez*, 465 Mass 672, 680, 991 NE2d 1036, 1044 (2013); *Com. v. Issa*, 466 Mass 1, 21-22, 992 NE2d 336, 353 (2013). See, e.g., *Com. v. Morales*, 461 Mass 765, 783-784, 965 NE2d 177, 192-193 (2012) (prosecutor's misstatement of the law of murder was isolated and comprised only a small portion of his argument); *Com. v. Burgos*, 462 Mass 53, 72, 965 NE2d 854 (2012) (prosecutor's improper statement that members of rival gang knew that victim had been killed by defendant's gang, lacking evidentiary support, was nonetheless a relatively brief point in his argument); *Com. v. Siny Van Tran*, 460 Mass 535, 554, 953 NE2d 139, 157-158 (2011) (if prosecutor bolstered the credibility of a police witness by suggesting that defendant must have been able to speak English when he allegedly made an inculpatory statement to the witness, it was remedied by judge's instructions).

[90] *Com. v. Nelson*, 468 Mass 1, 10, 7 NE3d 1084, 1091 (2014); *Com. v. Borodine*, 371 Mass 1, 11, 353 NE2d 649, 656 (1976). For cases reversing convictions because of improper argument, see *Com. v. Niemic*, 472 Mass 665, 673-677, 37 NE3d 577, 584-587 (2015); *Com. v. Williams*, 450 Mass 894, 902-908, 882 NE2d 850, 857-861 (2008); *Com. v. Clary*, 388 Mass 583, 589-594, 447 NE2d 1217, 1221-1223 (1983) (cumulative effect of prosecutor's improper closing argument in which he referred to matters not in evidence, misstated evidence, and hypothesized an unproved lesbian relationship between defendant and a female companion as the motive for attack); *Com. v. Smith*, supra, 387 Mass at 906-912, 444 NE2d at 379-383 (prosecutor commented on defendant's failure to testify, made inflammatory appeals to jury's sympathy, and remarked

create a substantial risk of miscarriage of justice, especially if it is cumulative.[91]

The courts attribute a "certain sophistication to the jury as aided by the cautionary remarks of the judge. The jury [can] be expected to take [closing] arguments with a grain of salt."[92] Thus the consequences of prosecutorial error depend on a number of factors, such as: Did the

---

on consequences of their decision); *Com. v. Vazquez*, 65 Mass App 305, 311-312, 839 NE2d 343, 349 (2005) (prosecutor overstepped bounds by referring to Church sex-abuse scandal and offering unsupported rationale for victims' late disclosures); *Com. v. Thomas*, 52 Mass App 286, 752 NE2d 835 (2001) (prosecutor's closing argument improperly urged conviction based on guilt by association, unsupported by evidence of actual guilt); *Com. v. Clarke*, 48 Mass App 482, 487-488, 722 NE2d 987, 992 (2000) (prosecutor improperly used defendant's post-*Miranda* silence against him by arguing that defendant had stopped interview in order to change his story), *habeas denied after conviction on remand*, 585 F Supp 2d 196 (D Mass 2008), *aff'd*, 582 F3d 135 (1st Cir 2009); *Com. v. Griffith*, 45 Mass App 784, 785, 702 NE2d 17, 18 (1998) (multiple instances of misconduct, when aggregated, deprived defendant of fair trial); *Com. v. West*, 44 Mass App 150, 688 NE2d 1378 (1998) (prosecutor asserted personal opinion that certain evidence was hearsay and should not have been admitted, distorted defendant's theory of defense, made unsupported assertions that defendant had placed witnesses in fear, and made irrelevant reference to race of defense witness).

For cases finding error, but not reversible, see *Com. v. Miller*, 457 Mass 69, 76-79, 929 NE2d 999, 1005-1007 (2010) (prosecutor's remark regarding previous sexual assaults against the defendant was not based on evidence admitted substantively, but had minimal effect on the jury); *Com. v. McCravy*, 430 Mass 758, 723 NE2d 517 (2000) (prosecutor's assertion that it was "a fact" that reckless-driving defendant killed victim because he drove drunk, appeal to jury that "the world became a worse place because [the victim] was killed," and characterization of the "whole defense" as a "sham" were all improper, but not prejudicial in narrow circumstances of case); *Com. v. Benson*, 419 Mass 114, 642 NE2d 1035 (1994) (reference to nursery rhyme about spider luring victim fly and excessive attack on credibility of defense expert was improper, but not prejudicial); *Com. v. Cohen, Cohen*, 412 Mass 375, 388, 589 NE2d 289, 298 (1992) (although it is "hard to imagine a more potentially prejudicial analogy for the role of the jury and the status of the accused than that of a 'hunter' and a 'hunted' prey," no substantial likelihood of a miscarriage of justice); *Com. v. Carter*, 38 Mass App 952, 649 NE2d 782 (1995) (no reversal required even though prosecutor improperly suggested defendant had intimidated witness without hint of evidence in record to support suggestion).

[91] See, e.g., *Com. v. Wood*, 469 Mass 266, 285-286, 14 NE3d 140, 158-150 (2014) (a single misstatement in the course of a lengthy closing argument, addressed by the judge's specific curative instruction); *Com. v. Almonte*, 465 Mass 224, 239-240, 988 NE2d 415, 427 (2013); *Com. v. Franklin*, 465 Mass 895, 915, 992 NE2d 319, 334 (2013).

[92] *Com. v. Wallace*, 417 Mass 126, 134, 627 NE2d 935 (1994). See also *Com. v. Bibby*, 35 Mass App 938, 941, 624 NE2d 624, 627 (1993) ("Kept in perspective, the prosecutor's remark was not of a sort which would inflame the passion of a jury with normal ignition temperatures. We may assume a certain amount of common sense capacity by jurors to filter out overstatement.").

defendant reasonably object to the argument? Was the prosecutor's error limited to collateral issues or did it go to the heart of the case? What did the judge tell the jury, generally or specifically, that may have mitigated the prosecutor's mistake, and generally did the error in the circumstances possibly make a difference in the jury's conclusions?[93]

"Extraevidentiary remarks in closing arguments are normally neutralized by a timely curative instruction and a general reminder that arguments of counsel are not evidence."[94] Similarly, misstatements of law may be deemed corrected by the judge's final instructions and admonitions that the jury apply the law as the judge defined it.[95] Even egregious transgressions have been treated as ameliorated by aggressive corrective instructions.[96] Not with standing the

---

[93] *Com. v. Taylor*, 469 Mass 516, 529-530, 14 NE3d 955, 966 (2014); *Com. v. Kelly*, 417 Mass 266, 271, 629 NE2d 999, 1002 (1994); *Fyffe v. MBTA*, 86 Mass App 457, 472, 17 NE3d 453, 464 (2014). See also *Com. v. Arroyo*, 442 Mass 135, 147-148, 810 NE2d 1201, 1212-1213 (2004) (applying factors, prosecutor's references to matters not in evidence did not make difference in jury's verdict); *Com. v. Wilson*, 443 Mass 122, 130-134, 819 NE2d 919, 927-930 (2004) (prosecutor's misstatement that witness "didn't get any deal" did not likely influence jury's verdict).

[94] *Com. v. Giguere*, 420 Mass 226, 234, 648 NE2d 1279, 1284 (1995) (& citations). See, e.g., *Com. v. Lally*, 473 Mass 693, 708, 46 NE3d 41, 55 (2016) (judge's instructions mitigated prosecutor's misstatements about DNA evidence); *Com. v. Celester*, 473 Mass 553, 577, 45 NE3d 539, 559 (2016); *Com. v. Walters*, 472 Mass 680, 703-704, 37 NE3d 980, 1001 (2015) (prosecutor's misstatement about police officer's testimony was mitigated by judge's instruction that arguments of counsel are not evidence); *Com. v. Auclair*, 444 Mass 348, 359-360, 828 NE2d 471, 480-481 (2005) (misstatement that all of Commonwealth's medical experts concluded victim was murdered was cured by specific instruction to the contrary); *Com. v. Correia*, 65 Mass App 27, 36, 836 NE2d 517, 525 (2005) (judge's "impeccable" instructions negated any prejudice). But compare *Com. v. Griffith*, supra, 45 Mass App at 789, 702 NE2d at 20 (multiple instances of prosecutorial misconduct suffusing entire trial not cured by general reminder).

[95] See, e.g., *Com. v. Dagley*, 442 Mass 713, 722-725, 816 NE2d 527, 534-536 (2004), *habeas denied*, 540 F3d 8 (1st Cir 2008); (prosecutor's misstatement of definition of manslaughter).

[96] See, e.g., *Com. v. Hardy*, 431 Mass 387, 397-398, 727 NE2d 836, 844-845 (2000) *postconviction relief denied*, 646 Mass 660, 984 NE2d 727 (2012); *Com. v. Rosario*, 430 Mass 505, 515-516, 721 NE2d 903, 910-911 (1999) (prosecutor's argument referring to victim's telephone call as a "call out for help," reference to defendant as a "monster," and throwing of photograph and teeth impressions on table in front of defendant were unprofessional and improper, but mitigated by judge's prompt instructions); *Com. v. Fructman*, 418 Mass 8, 633 NE2d 369 (1994) (misstatements and improper appeal to sympathy remedied by judge's instructions); *Com. v. Olszewski*, 416 Mass 707, 725-727, 625 NE2d 529, 541-542 (1993), *habeas petition denied in Olszewski v. Spencer*, 466 F3d 47 (1st Cir 2006); (improprieties in prosecutor's argument including reference to evidence that had been excluded and to defendant's lack of remorse were promptly remedied by judge's instructions); *Com. v. Taylor*, 455 Mass 372, 381-385,

affirmances of convictions in many of these cases, prosecutors have been repeatedly admonished not to "sail unnecessarily close to the wind" in their closings.[97]

Reversals have not been required where the inappropriate remarks of opposing counsel neutralize each other.[98] While a prosecutor may not "fight fire with fire," an improper argument from the defense may undermine the claim that the prosecutor's improper response requires reversal.[99]

Objection at the conclusion of the opponent's closing argument is sufficient to preserve appellate rights.[100] Failure to object to the prosecutor's closing argument will limit appellate review to the question of whether there is a substantial likelihood of a miscarriage of justice.[101] Moreover, the absence of any objection is important because it indicates that trial counsel "did not consider the tone, manner, and substance of the prosecutor's statement when it was made to be harmful,"[102] that the argument "did not land a hard, foul blow."[103]

When a specific objection is made and rejected by the judge without curative instructions, error in closing argument must be treated as prejudicial and requiring a new trial unless the appellate court can conclude with confidence that the error was not likely to influence the jury's verdict.[104]

---

916 NE2d 1000, 1007-1010 (2009) (although prosecutor's misstatement about witness's testimony went to the key issue at trial, the identity of the murderer, reversal not required).

[97] See *Com. v. Correia*, 65 Mass App 27, 38 n.11, 836 NE2d 517, 526 n.11 (2005). See also *Com. v. Grinkley*, 75 Mass App 798, 813, 917 NE2d 236, 247 (2009) (Berry, J., dissenting) "Where improper arguments presenting 'prosecutorial errors' are offered in case after case, it is my thought that this court should in the future stand more ready to reverse the judgments in such cases, particularly when it appears that the simple precautions suggested herein have not been invoked.").

[98] See *Com. v. Mello*, 420 Mass 375, 380-381, 649 NE2d 1106, 1111 (1995); *Com. v. Cohen*, supra, 412 Mass at 388, 589 NE2d at 298 (& citations).

[99] See *Com. v. Pearce*, 427 Mass 642, 646, 695 NE2d 1059, 1063 (1998).

[100] *Com. v. Person*, 400 Mass 136, 139, 508 NE2d 88, 90 (1987) (& citations). But see *Com. v. Richardson*, 38 Mass App 384, 392, 648 NE2d 445, 450 (1995) (objection not preserved where defense counsel, told by judge to defer objections until conclusion of charge, failed to make any further objection). For more on the timeliness of an objection to argument, see § 1.3.2, supra.

[101] *Com. v. Marquetty*, 416 Mass 445, 450, 622 NE2d 632, 636 (1993). See § 1.3.1, supra.

[102] *Com. v. Talbot*, 35 Mass App 766, 779, 625 NE2d 1374, 1382 (1994). See also *Com. v. Maynard*, 436 Mass 558, 570, 767 NE2d 1, 13 (2002).

[103] *Com. v. Johnston*, 467 Mass 674, 695, 7 NE3d 424, 441 (2014).

[104] *Com. v. Loguidice*, 420 Mass 453, 455-456, 650 NE2d 1254, 1256 (1995).

In civil cases there have been only rare instances in which a new trial was granted because of an overreaching closing argument.[105]

Mass R Crim P 24(a)(1) requires the defendant to present closing argument first, and defendant has no constitutional right to require the Commonwealth to present first in order to have the last word.[106]

Reasonable time limits may be imposed on counsel during closing argument as long as adequate time is allowed to address the pertinent aspects of the case.[107] Judges who intend to enforce a time limit on closing argument are urged to make that clear to counsel in advance, as well as the possibility that the judge will interrupt to warn them of the time remaining.[108]

---

[105] See *Rolanti v. Boston Edison Corp.*, 33 Mass App 516, 529-530, 603 NE2d 211, 220-221 (1992) (& cases collected). See also *Harlow v. Chin*, 405 Mass 697, 704, 545 NE2d 602, 606-607 (1989) (plaintiff's counsel's references to large verdicts in other cases and to salaries of professional athletes improper, but reversal not required). *Gath v. M/A-Com, Inc.*, 440 Mass 482, 493, 802 NE2d 521, 530 (2003) (plaintiff's counsel crossed line with hypothetical references to airline crashes and baseball players' salaries, but judge's instructions cured problem); *Santos v. Chrysler Corp.*, 430 Mass 198, 214, 715 NE2d 47, 59 (1999); *Kirby v. Morales*, 50 Mass App 786, 741 NE2d 855 (2001) (prejudicial comments during opening statement were sufficiently counteracted by judge).

[106] *Com. v. Rocheteau*, 74 Mass App 17, 22, 903 NE2d 598, 603 (2009).

[107] See *Com. v. Johnson*, 42 Mass App 948, 951, 679 NE2d 261, 263-264 (1997) (& citations).

[108] See *Com. v. Brown*, 462 Mass 620, 633 n.11, 970 NE2d 306, 317 n.11 (2012).

CHAPTER

14

EVIDENCE in ADMINISTRATIVE PROCEEDINGS

§ 14.1 Evidentiary Matters: GL 30A, § 11

The State Administrative Procedure Act, GL 30A, which applies to almost all state administrative agencies, departments, boards, and commissions,[1] provides in § 11 the following with regard to evidentiary and related matters:

> (2) Unless otherwise provided by any law, agencies need not observe the rules of evidence observed by courts, but shall observe the rules of privilege recognized by law. Evidence may be admitted and

§ 14.1 [1] See GL 30A, § 1(2) for exceptions including the parole board, the division of dispute resolution of the department of industrial accidents, the personnel administrator, the civil service commission, and the appellate tax board.

given probative effect only if it is the kind of evidence on which reasonable persons are accustomed to rely in the conduct of serious affairs. Agencies may exclude unduly repetitious evidence, whether offered on direct examination or cross-examination of witnesses.

(3) Every party shall have the right to call and examine witnesses, to introduce exhibits, to cross-examine witnesses who testify, and to submit rebuttal evidence.

(4) All evidence, including any records, investigation reports, and documents in the possession of the agency of which it desires to avail itself as evidence in making a decision, shall be offered and made a part of the record in the proceeding, and no other factual information or evidence shall be considered, except as provided in paragraph (5) of this section. Documentary evidence may be received in evidence in the form of copies or excerpts, or by incorporation by reference.

(5) Agencies may take notice of any fact which may be judicially noticed by the courts, and in addition, may take notice of general, technical or scientific facts within their specialized knowledge. Parties shall be notified of the material so noticed, and they shall be afforded an opportunity to contest the facts so noticed. Agencies may utilize their experience, technical competence, and specialized knowledge in the evaluation of the evidence presented to them.

(6) Agencies shall make available an official record, which shall include testimony and exhibits, and which may be in narrative form, but the agency need not arrange to transcribe shorthand notes or sound recordings unless otherwise requested by a party. If so requested, the agency may, unless otherwise provided by any law, require the party to pay the reasonable costs of the transcript before the agency makes the transcript available to the party.

(7) If a majority of the officials of the agency who are to render the final decision have neither heard nor read the evidence, such decision, if adverse to any party other than the agency, shall be made only after (a) a tentative or proposed decision is delivered or mailed to the parties containing a statement of reasons and including determination of each issue of fact or law necessary to the tentative or proposed decision; and (b) an opportunity is afforded each party adversely affected to file objections and to present argument, either orally or in writing as the agency may order, to a majority of the officials who are to render the final decision. The agency may by regulation provide that, unless parties make written request in advance for the tentative or proposed decision, the agency shall not be bound to comply with the procedures of this paragraph.

(8) Every agency decision shall be in writing or stated in the record. The decision shall be accompanied by a statement of reasons for the decision, including determination of each issue of fact or law necessary to the decision, unless the General Laws provide that the agency need not

> prepare such statement in the absence of a timely request to do so. Parties to the proceeding shall be notified in person or by mail of the decision; of their rights to review or appeal the decision within the agency or before the courts, as the case may be; and of the time limits on their rights to review or appeal. A copy of the decision and of the statement of reasons, if prepared, shall be delivered or mailed upon request to each party and to his attorney of record.

It should be noted that § 11 makes no evidence inadmissible except that which is privileged.[2] An agency has wide discretion in ruling on evidence,[3] including admitting hearsay.[4] Notwithstanding GL 30A, some agencies including the Department of Industrial Accidents and the Commission on Judicial Conduct, bind themselves to abide by some or all of the usual rules of evidence.[5] Apart from any statutory or agency rules, the courts impose minimum requirements to ensure that the hearing is fair.[6]

---

[2] See also *Morris v. Board of Registration in Medicine*, 405 Mass 103, 107-108, 539 NE2d 50, 52-53 (1989).

[3] *Massachusetts Automobile Rating & Accident Prevention Bureau v. Commissioner of Ins.*, 401 Mass 282, 285-286, 516 NE2d 1132, 1134-1135 (1987); *Planning Board of Braintree v. Department of Public Utility*, 420 Mass 22, 30-31, 647 NE2d 1186, 1192 (1984); *Northeast Metropolitan Regional Vocational School District School Committee v. Massachusetts Commission Against Discrimination*, 31 Mass App 84, 88, 575 NE2d 77 (1991) (hearing commissioner has discretion to admit evidence, even if it would be inadmissible under rules of evidence, if it bears indicia of reliability).

[4] See *Town of Brookline v. Commissioner of Department of Environmental Quality Engineering*, 387 Mass 372, 389, 439 NE2d 792, 805 (1982) (& citations). See also *Doe v. Sex Offender Registry Board*, 70 Mass App 309, 873 NE2d 1194 (2007) (hearing officer could consider as substantive evidence victim's hearsay statements contained in police report). See also § 1.2, supra.

[5] See Department of Industrial Accidents Rule 1.11(5) (adopting rules of evidence applicable in courts for workers compensation proceedings); GL 211C, § 7(3) (at hearing before Commission on Judicial Conduct, "the rules of evidence applicable to civil proceedings shall apply"), construed in *Matter of King*, 409 Mass 590, 600, 568 NE2d 588, 593 (1991).

[6] See *Ingalls v. Board of Registration in Medicine*, 445 Mass 291, 296, 837 NE2d 232, 236-237 (2005) (due process rights are implicated in administrative proceedings that may affect the right to practice a profession); *Boott Mills v. Board of Conciliation & Arbitration*, 311 Mass 223, 227, 40 NE2d 870, 871 (1942) (each of the parties was entitled to a full hearing, to present all the evidence in his possession that was pertinent to the questions submitted, to learn and meet the claims of the opposing party, and to be heard upon the evidence adduced); *Higgins Case*, 460 Mass 50, 948 NE2d 1228 (2011) (claimant in workers' compensation proceedings is entitled to discovery of medical reports procured by the employer, and to use them in cross-examination of the impartial physician regardless of whether it has been admitted in evidence). For the matter of standing to challenge an administrative decision, see *Reynolds v. Zoning Board of Appeals of Stow*, 88 Mass App 339, 345-346, 37 NE3d 656, 661-662 (2015).

§ 14.2 Burden of Proof

In the absence of a statutory provision to the contrary, proof by a preponderance of the evidence is the standard generally applicable to administrative and quasi-judicial proceedings.[1]

§ 14.3 Subpoenas: GL 30A, § 12

GL 30A, § 12, provides:

> In conducting adjudicatory proceedings, agencies shall issue, vacate, modify and enforce subpoenas in accordance with the following provisions:
>
> (1) Agencies shall have the power to issue subpoenas requiring the attendance and testimony of witnesses and the production of any evidence, including books, records, correspondence or documents, relating to any matter in question in the proceeding. Agencies may administer oaths and affirmations, examine witnesses, and receive evidence. The power to issue subpoenas may be exercised by any member of the agency or by any person or persons designated by the agency for such purpose.
>
> (2) The agency may prescribe the form of subpoena, but it shall adhere, in so far as practicable, to the form used in civil cases before the courts, unless another manner is provided by any law. Witnesses summoned shall be paid the same fees for attendance and travel as in civil cases before the courts, unless otherwise provided by any law.[1]

---

§ 14.2 [1] *Medical Malpractice Joint Underwriting Association of Massachusetts v. Commissioner of Ins.*, 395 Mass 43, 46-47, 478 NE2d 936, 939 (1985); *City of Gloucester v. Civil Service Commission*, 408 Mass 292, 297, 557 NE2d 1141, 1144 (1990). For the burdens in bar disciplinary proceedings, see *In re Murray*, 455 Mass 872, 920 NE2d 862 (2010) (once bar counsel has proved that attorney received cash that belonged to client, did not deposit it in client trust account, and could not account for portion of it, rebuttable presumption arises that attorney commingled funds and client was permanently deprived of them). For the shifting burdens arising from prima facie evidence in workers compensation proceedings, see *Carpenter's Case*, 456 Mass 436, 923 NE2d 1026 (2010).

§ 14.3 [1] See also *Matter of Tobin*, 417 Mass 92, 102-103, 628 NE2d 1273, 1279 (1994) (hearing committee's refusal to issue subpoenas requested by attorney was appropriate because information sought not relevant to proceeding). For a discussion of the procedures for issuing and revoking subpoenas, see *Box Pond Ass'n v. Energy Facilities Siting Board*, 435 Mass 408, 416-417, 758 NE2d 604, 611-612 (2001). For the authority of the State Ethics Commission to summon the subject of a preliminary inquiry to testify under oath, see *Doe v. State Ethics Commission*, 444 Mass 269, 827 NE2d 694 (2005).

§ 14.4 Findings

The provisions of GL 30A, § 11(8) (quoted above in § 14.1) require that an agency make subsidiary findings of fact on all issues relevant and material to the ultimate issue to be decided, and specify the manner in which it reasoned from the subsidiary facts so found to the ultimate decision reached.[1] The agency has a duty to make such findings, including subsidiary findings as to each issue of fact or law, so that the appellate court may exercise its function of appellate review.[2] The agency need not make findings on every controverted issue of fact or law so long as findings indicate the "over-all basis" of the decision and permit effective appellate review.[3]

§ 14.5 Judicial Review: "Substantial Evidence"

GL 30A, § 14(7)(e) provides that the finding of an agency must be supported by "substantial evidence" in order to withstand judicial review. "Substantial evidence" is defined as "such evidence as a reasonable mind might accept as adequate to support a conclusion,"[1] a test which takes into account the entire record, both the evidence supporting the agency's conclusion and whatever in the record fairly detracts from the weight of that evidence.[2] The standard is more stringent than abuse of discretion, but less than preponderance of the evidence; "an agency's

---

§ 14.4 [1] See *Malone-Campagna v. Director of Division of Employment Security*, 391 Mass 399, 402, 461 NE2d 818, 820 (1984) (absent a finding on a critical factual issue, the agency's decision cannot stand even if supported by substantial evidence).

[2] *NSTAR Electric Co. v. Department of Public Utilities*, 462 Mass 381, 390, 968 NE2d 895, 902-903 (2012) (remanding because DPU's order did not contain sufficient subsidiary findings to allow meaningful judicial review); *Rivas v. Chelsea Housing Authority*, 464 Mass 329, 343-344, 982 NE2d 1147, 1158-1159 (2013) (remanding for insufficiency of grievance panel's findings); *Massachusetts Automobile Rating & Accident Prevention Bureau v. Commissioner of Ins.*, 401 Mass 282, 287-288, 516 NE2d 1132, 1135-1136 (1987) (agency should not leave counsel and the courts without the "guidance of proper findings . . . to determine from a voluminous record . . . whether [its] conclusions can be sustained on the evidence"); *Retirement Board of Somerville v. Contributory Retirement Appeal Board*, 38 Mass App 673, 651 NE2d 1241 (1995) (appeal board's decision was arbitrary and would be reversed, even though substantial evidence supported decision, where final adjudication contradicted earlier interim determination made on same record and no reason was given explaining or supporting change).

[3] *Aetna Casualty & Surety Co. v. Commissioner of Ins.*, 408 Mass 363, 374, 558 NE2d 941, 948 (1990); *Massachusetts Automobile Rating & Accident Prevention Bureau v. Commissioner of Ins.*, supra, 401 Mass at 289 n.3, 292, 516 NE2d at 1137 n.2, 1138.

§ 14.5 [1] GL 30A, § 1(6). See also *Schussel v. Commissioner of Revenue*, 472 Mass 83, 86, 32 NE3d 1239, 1243 (2015).

[2] See *Massachusetts Electric Co. v. Department of Public Utilities*, 469 Mass 553, 563, 15 NE3d 176, 186 (2014); *Murphy v. Contributory Retirement Appeal Board*, 463 Mass

conclusion will fail judicial scrutiny if the evidence points to no felt or appreciable probability of the conclusion or points to an overwhelming probability of the contrary."[3]

Substantial evidence has been held to be the appropriate standard in administrative proceedings notwithstanding the fact that the alleged violation underlying the proceeding involves a criminal statute.[4] The substantial evidence standard is also generally applied to agencies not subject to the Administrative Procedure Act.[5]

The evidence necessary to support the agency's decision must be found in the record.[6] Nonacceptance of testimony or evidence by the agency does not create substantial evidence to the contrary.[7] A finding based on incomplete evidence will not stand.[8]

The agency may not use its own expertise or rely on undisclosed evidence unless it takes official notice thereof as a matter of record in

---

333, 344, 974 NE2d 46, 56 (2012); *Chadwick v. Board of Registration in Dentistry*, 461 Mass 77, 96, 958 NE2d 500, 515-516 (2011); *Ingalls v. Board of Registration in Medicine*, 445 Mass 291, 300, 837 NE2d 232, 239 (2005); *Covell v. Department of Social Services*, 439 Mass 766, 783, 791 NE2d 877, 890 (2003). For further discussion and application of the substantial evidence test, see *Tennessee Gas Pipeline Co. v. Board of Assessors of Agawam*, 428 Mass 261, 262, 700 NE2d 818, 819 (1998); *New Boston Garden Corp. v. Board of Assessors of Boston*, 383 Mass 456, 420 NE2d 298 (1981); *Benmosche v. Board of Registration in Medicine*, 412 Mass 82, 86, 588 NE2d 621, 623 (1992); *Zachs v. Department of Public Utilities*, 406 Mass 217, 221-222, 547 NE2d 28, 30-31 (1989) (substantial evidence standard in context of nonadjudicative, policy-making judgments rather than party-specific fact finding); *U.S. Gypsum Co. v. Executive Office of Environmental Affairs*, 69 Mass App 243, 254 n.24, 867 NE2d 764, 774 n.24 (2007). For comparison with a federal judicial review standard, see *School Committee of Brookline v. Bureau of Special Education Appeals*, 389 Mass 705, 715-716, 452 NE2d 476, 483 (1983).

[3] *Police Department of Boston v. Kavaleski*, 463 Mass 680, 692, 978 NE2d 55, 65 (2012); *Duggan v. Board of Registration in Nursing*, 456 Mass 666, 674, 925 NE2d 812, 820 (2010); *Dotson v. Commissioner of Revenue*, 82 Mass App 378, 385, 974 NE2d 69, 75 (2012).

[4] See *Goldstein v. Board of Registration of Chiropractors*, 426 Mass 606, 612 n.5, 689 NE2d 1320, 1325 n.5 (1998) (& citations).

[5] See *The Black Rose, Inc. v. City of Boston*, 433 Mass 501, 744 NE2d 640 (2001) (entertainment license suspension); *Boston Gas Co. v. Board of Assessors of Boston*, 402 Mass 346, 348-349 n.1, 522 NE2d 921, 922 n.1 (1988); *Towle v. Commissioner of Revenue*, 397 Mass 599, 601-602, 492 NE2d 739, 741 (1986)); *Murphy v. Superintendent, Massachusetts Correctional Institution*, 396 Mass 830, 833, 489 NE2d 661, 663 (1986) (prison disciplinary proceedings).

[6] *D'Amour v. Board of Registration in Dentistry*, 409 Mass 572, 585, 567 NE2d 1226, 1233-1234 (1991).

[7] *Salisbury Water Supply Co. v. Department of Public Utilities*, 344 Mass 716, 721, 184 NE2d 44, 47-48 (1962).

[8] *Holyoke Street Railway Co. v. Department of Public Utilities*, 347 Mass 440, 450-451, 198 NE2d 413, 420 (1964).

compliance with GL 30A, § 11(5).[9] While the agency may put its expertise to use in evaluating the complexities of technical evidence, it may not use its expertise as a substitute for evidence in the record.[10] The agency cannot use the computations and opinions of its staff unless they are introduced in evidence.[11]

An agency or board may not sit as a "silent witness" where expert testimony is required to establish an evidentiary basis for its conclusions, but it is free to evaluate evidence in light of its own technical expertise.[12] On judicial review, inquiry into the mental processes of the administrative decision makers is not appropriate.[13]

Hearsay evidence may constitute substantial evidence if it contains sufficient indicia of reliability and probative value.[14]

§ 14.6 Deference to Agency's Findings

In reviewing an agency decision, the court is required by GL 30A, § 14(7) to give "due weight to the experience, technical competence, and specialized knowledge of the agency, as well as to the discretionary

---

[9] *D'Amour v. Board of Registration in Dentistry*, supra, 409 Mass at 584-585, 567 NE2d at 1233; *Salisbury Water Supply Co. v. Department of Public Utilities*, supra, 344 Mass at 721, 184 NE2d at 47-48.

[10] *D'Amour v. Board of Registration in Dentistry*, supra, 409 Mass at 585, 567 NE2d at 1233-1234; *Salisbury Water Supply Co. v. Department of Public Utilities*, supra, 344 Mass at 721, 184 NE2d at 47-48.

[11] *New England Telephone & Telegraph Co. v. Department of Public Utilities*, 372 Mass 678, 684, 363 NE2d 519, 524 (1977).

[12] *Langlitz v. Board of Registration of Chiropractors*, 396 Mass 374, 381, 486 NE2d 48, 53 (1985).

[13] See *Lewis v. Committee for Public Counsel Services*, 50 Mass App 319, 324, 739 NE2d 706, 711 (2000).

[14] *Covell v. Department of Social Services*, supra, 439 Mass at, 785-786, 791 NE2d at 892 (transcript of testimony from prior criminal trial); *School Committee of Brockton v. Massachusetts Against Discrimination*, 423 Mass 7, 15, 666 NE2d 468, 474 (1996) (physicians' letters); *Embers of Salisbury v. Alcoholic Beverages Control Commission*, 401 Mass 526, 530, 517 NE2d 830, 832 (1988) (transcript of testimony by defendant at her criminal trial, corroborated in certain particulars by stipulated testimony of other persons); *Murphy v. Superintendent, Massachusetts Correctional Institution*, supra, 396 Mass at 834, 489 NE2d at 663 (informants' statements); *Doe v. Sex Offender Registry Board*, 70 Mass App 309, 312-313, 873 NE2d 1194, 1196-1197 (2007) (victim's statement in police report was plausible, consistent, highly detailed, and corroborated); *Doe v. Sex Offender Registry Board*, 88 Mass App 73, 78, 35 NE3d 788, 793 (2015) (while generally a non-eyewitness police report, standing alone, cannot constitute substantial evidence, narratives therein may be admissible depending on plausibility and consistency of the victim's story).

authority conferred upon it."[1] This standard of review is highly deferential to the agency on questions of fact and reasonable inferences drawn therefrom, unless they are clearly erroneous.[2] The reviewing court accords an agency's interpretation of its own regulations considerable deference unless it is arbitrary, unreasonable, or inconsistent with the plain terms of the regulations themselves.[3]

The agency's conclusion will stand if it "*could* have been made by reference to the logic of experience."[4] Questions of statutory interpretation are reviewed de novo, but with substantial deference to a reasonable interpretation by the administrative agency charged with its enforcement.[5] Such deference disappears if the statute unambiguously bars the agency's approach, or the agency has failed to adhere to its own regulatory framework or made a decision without sufficient evidentiary support.[6]

---

§ 14.6 [1] See, e.g., *Sy v. Massachusetts Commission Against Discrimination*, 79 Mass App 760, 767, 950 NE2d 75, 81 (2011) (MCAD's interpretation of "availability" of an apartment for rental was entitled to deference due to its specialized knowledge of the housing market).

[2] *Grady v. Zoning Board of Appeals of Peabody*, 465 Mass 725, 728-729, 991 NE2d 1060, 1063 (2013); *Flint v. Commissioner of Public Welfare*, 412 Mass 416, 420, 589 NE2d 1224, 1227 (1992) (& citations). See also *Koch v. Commissioner of Revenue*, 416 Mass 540, 555, 624 NE2d 91, 99 (1993) (in reviewing mixed questions of fact and law, Appellate Tax Board's expertise must be recognized); *Alsabti v. Board of Registration in Medicine*, 404 Mass 547, 549, 536 NE2d 357, 358 (1989); *Stone-Ashe v. Department of Environmental Protection*, 86 Mass App 16, 23, 12 NE3d 1011, 1017 (2014); *Ducharme v. Commissioner of Dept. of Employment & Training*, 49 Mass App 206, 208, 728 NE2d 331, 333 (2000) (mixed law/fact question of whether employer acted reasonably).

[3] *Doe v. Sex Offender Registry Board*, 466 Mass 594, 602, 999 NE2d 478, 484-485 (2013). "The principle if deference, not abdication." *Beverly Port Marina, Inc. v. Commissioner of Department of Environmental Protection*, 84 Mass App 612, 620, 999 NE2d 492, 498 (2013).

[4] *Benmosche v. Board of Registration in Medicine*, 412 Mass 82, 86, 588 NE2d 621, 623 (1992) (emphasis in original) (citations omitted).

[5] *Alliance to Protect Nantucket Sound, Inc. v. Department of Public Utilities*, 461 Mass 166, 171, 959 NE2d 413, 420 (2011); *Fitchburg Gas & Electric Light Co. v. Department of Public Utilities*, 460 Mass 800, 811-812, 956 NE2d 213, 222 (2011); *Attorney General v. Commissioner of Ins.*, 450 Mass 311, 319, 878 NE2d 554, 560 (2008); *Town of Middleborough v. Housing Appeals Committee*, 449 Mass 514, 523, 870 NE2d 67, 76 (2007); *Gauthier v. Director of the Office of Medicaid*, 80 Mass App 777, 783, 956 NE2d 1236, 1241-1242 (2011).

[6] See *U.S. Gypsum Co. v. Executive Office of Environmental Affairs*, 69 Mass App 243, 249, 867 NE2d 764, 770-771 (2007). See also *Franklin Office Park Realty Corp. v. Commissioner of Department of Environmental Protection*, 466 Mass 454, 460-461, 995 NE2d 785, 791 (2013); *Upton's Case*, 84 Mass App 411, 418-419, 997 NE2d 126, 132 (2013) (Industrial Accident Reviewing Board's interpretation contradicted Legislature's restriction on compensation for emotional injury).

A court cannot disturb an agency's decision unless it is based upon an error of law, unsupported by substantial evidence, arbitrary or capricious, an abuse of discretion, or otherwise not in accordance with law.[7] If there is substantial evidence to support the findings of the agency, the court will not substitute its own view of the facts.[8] Judicial review requires a reexamination of an agency's actions, and not a de novo consideration of the merits of the parties' positions.[9]

§ 14.7 Assessing Witness Credibility/Experts

The task of assessing the credibility of witnesses is one uniquely within an agency's discretion.[1] The reviewing court may, however, modify or set aside findings and conclusions on credibility that are arbitrary or unsupported by substantial evidence.[2] A reviewing court

---

[7] GL 30A, § 14(7). See also *M & T Charters, Inc. v. Commissioner of Revenue*, 404 Mass 137, 140, 533 NE2d 1359, 1361 (1989) (court will set aside board's findings only if evidence points to "no appreciable probability of the conclusion or points to an overwhelming probability of the contrary"); *Sugrue v. Contributory Retirement Appeal Board*, 45 Mass App 1, 5 n.5, 694 NE2d 391, 394 n.5 (1998).

[8] *Doherty v. Retirement Board of Medford*, 425 Mass 130, 141, 680 NE2d 45, 52 (1997); *D'Amour v. Board of Registration in Dentistry*, 409 Mass 572, 581, 567 NE2d 1226, 1232 (1991).

[9] *Care and Protection of Isaac*, 419 Mass 602, 610, 646 NE2d 1034, 1039 (1995). For review of an administrative decision after review by the Superior Court, see *Scheffler v. Board of Appeal on Motor Vehicle Liability Policies and Bonds*, 84 Mass App 904, 995 NE2d 816 (2013). For review of the validity of an administrative agency's properly promulgated regulation, see *Massachusetts Teachers' Retirement System v. Contributory Retirement Appeal Board*, 466 Mass 292, 994 NE2d 355 (2013).

§ 14.7 [1] *McGuinesss v. Department of Correction*, 465 Mass 660, 668-669, 991 NE2d 176, 182 (2013); *Ingalls v. Board of Registration in Medicine*, 445 Mass 291, 301, 837 NE2d 232, 240 (2005); *Matter of Tobin*, 417 Mass 92, 99, 628 NE2d 1273, 1277 (1994) (attorney disciplinary proceeding); *Brommage's Case*, 75 Mass App 825, 827-828, 917 NE2d 256, 259 (2009) (findings of fact, assessments of credibility, and determinations of the weight to be given the evidence are the exclusive function of the administrative judge in a workers' compensation case; ALJ was not required to adopt conclusions of IME report where there are deficiencies in its reasoning or findings).

[2] *Herridge v. Board of Registration in Medicine*, 420 Mass 154, 163-166, 648 NE2d 745, 750-751 (1995) (*Herridge I*) (board required to make credibility determination regarding patient's testimony; board could not choose to rely on portions of testimony and reject other portions without explaining its reasons for doing so); *Herridge v. Board of Registration in Medicine*, 424 Mass 201, 675 NE2d 386 (1997) (*Herridge II*); *Bettencourt v. Board of Registration in Medicine*, 408 Mass 221, 227, 558 NE2d 928, 930 (1990) (in deciding whether to believe patient or doctor, board improperly disregarded relevant evidence tending to show that doctor would not have engaged in alleged misconduct; proceeding remanded to board for further consideration of credibility issue). Compare *Friedman v. Board of Registration in Medicine*, 408 Mass 474, 476-477, 561

may vacate an agency's decision as unsupported by substantial evidence if the decision provides no means of analyzing the agency's assessment of credibility.[3]

It is an agency's prerogative to determine the probative value of expert evidence in proceedings before it, but there must be a basis in the record for rejecting uncontradicted expert opinions.[4] An agency may reasonably reject an expert's opinion where there are flaws in his/her methodology or assumptions, or where the opinion is based on conjecture.[5]

§ 14.8 Additional Evidence: GL 30A, § 14

Under GL 30A, § 14(6), a reviewing court may order that additional evidence be taken before the agency, but only upon a showing that it is "material" and that there was "good reason" for the failure to present it in the original agency proceeding.[1]

NE2d 859, 860-861 (1990) (board's decision "thoroughly and logically analyzed the evidence and explained why the board believed the patient's testimony . . . and why the board disbelieved the doctor's explanation. We should not, and do not, consider Friedman's various arguments on matters of credibility. They were for the board to resolve, and it did so."). See also *Zachs v. Department of Public Utilities*, 406 Mass 217, 224-225, 547 NE2d 28, 32 (1989) (deference to agency's credibility determinations); *Morris v. Board of Registration in Medicine*, 405 Mass 103, 106-114, 539 NE2d 50, 51-56 (1989) (board owed substantial deference to credibility findings made by administrative magistrate who heard witnesses).

[3] *Fisch v. Board of Registration in Medicine*, 437 Mass 128, 138, 769 NE2d 1221, 1229 (2002) (but magistrate's decision indicating reasons for crediting some witnesses and not others were adequate); *City of Salem v. Massachusetts Commission Against Discrimination*, 404 Mass 170, 534 NE2d 283 (1989) (remand for new hearing required where credibility of witnesses could not be evaluated on basis of record of hearing held before commissioner who died before rendering decision).

[4] *Chadwick v. Board of Registration in Dentistry*, 461 Mass 77, 99, 958 NE2d 500, 517 (2011); *Pollard v. Conservation Commission of Norfolk*, 73 Mass App 340, 349-351, 897 NE2d 1242, 1248-1250 (2008). The opinion of an expert testifying on behalf of a sex offender, however, need not be accepted by the Registry hearing examiner even where the board does not present any contrary expert testimony. *Doe v. Sex Offender Registry Board*, 459 Mass 603, 637, 947 NE2d 9, 37 (2011). See also *Police Dep't of Boston v. Kavaleski*, 463 Mass 680, 694, 978 NE2d 55, 66 (2012) (Civil Service Commission was entitled to reject expert assessment of police candidate even though there was no contrary expert testimony in record).

[5] *Stone-Ashe v. Department of Environmental Protection*, 86 Mass App 16, 24, 12 NE3d 1011, 1018 (2014).

§ 14.8 [1] See *Benmosche v. Board of Registration in Medicine*, supra, 412 Mass at 88, 588 NE2d at 624; *Com. v. Roxbury Charter High Public School*, 69 Mass App 49, 53-54, 865 NE2d 1183, 1187-1188 (2007) (Superior Court's order granting school's motion to expand record was abuse of discretion as evidence was not material).

§ 14.9 Occupational and Business Licenses

In regard to certain adjudicatory proceedings involving the issuance or revocation of occupational or business licenses, the right to a hearing and procedural due process has been held to be constitutionally required.[1]

---

§ 14.9 [1] See *Langlitz v. Board of Registration of Chiropractors*, 396 Mass 374, 376, 486 NE2d 48, 50-51 (1985); *LaPointe v. License Board of Worcester*, 389 Mass 454, 457-459, 451 NE2d 112, 115-116 (1983); *Konstantopoulos v. Whately*, 384 Mass 123, 132-136, 424 NE2d 210, 217-219 (1981) (extensive review of cases of minimum requirements of due process). Compare *Kearney v. Board of Registration in Pharmacy*, 4 Mass App 25, 340 NE2d 515 (1975) and *Palmer v. Rent Control Board of Brookline*, 7 Mass App 110, 386 NE2d 1047 (1979) (hearing required) with *Lotto v. Com.*, 369 Mass 775, 343 NE2d 855 (1976) (no hearing required to revoke concessionaire's license granted by Department of Natural Resources). See also *Matter of Tobin*, 417 Mass 92, 101-102, 628 NE2d 1273, 1278-1279 (1994) (bar counsel's reliance on documentary evidence did not violate due process on ground attorney was unable to confront witnesses); *Friedman v. Board of Registration in Medicine*, 408 Mass 474, 478-479, 561 NE2d 859, 861-862 (1990) (due process does not require a post-decision evidentiary hearing); *Aetna Casualty & Surety Co. v. Commissioner of Ins.*, 408 Mass 363, 373, 558 NE2d 941, 947-948 (1990) (commissioner's adoption of findings made in prior decision not impermissible where parties were afforded adequate opportunity to present evidence and arguments); *Embers of Salisbury v. Alcoholic Beverages Control Commission*, 401 Mass 526, 531, 517 NE2d 830, 833 (1988) (admission in evidence before commission of transcript of testimony at trial on criminal charges did not deprive licensees of constitutional rights to confront witnesses where licensees did not invoke their right to call the witness); *Massachusetts Outdoor Advertising Council v. Outdoor Advertising Board*, 9 Mass App 775, 405 NE2d 151 (1980) (review of authorities as to when administrative summary judgment procedures may be utilized).

For a discussion of the right to an impartial hearing officer, see *D'Amour v. Board of Registration in Dentistry*, supra, 409 Mass at 579-581, 567 NE2d at 1231; *Civil Service Commission v. Boston Municipal Court Dep't*, 27 Mass App 343, 347-349, 538 NE2d 49, 52 (1989).

Table of Cases

References are to sections.

Table of Statutes

References are to sections.

Massachusetts General Laws

Massachusetts Constitution Part 1, Declaration of Rights

United States Code and United States Code Annotated

Internal Revenue Code

United States Constitution

Table of Rules of Court

References are to sections.

Massachusetts Rules of Civil Procedure

Massachusetts Rules of Criminal Procedure

Massachusetts Rules of Domestic Relations Procedure

Rules of the Supreme Judicial Court of Massachusetts

Rules of the Superior Court of Massachusetts

Massachusetts District and Municipal Courts Rules of Civil Procedure

Proposed Massachusetts Rules of Evidence

Table of Rules

Federal Rules of Civil Procedure

Federal Rules of Criminal Procedure

Federal Rules of Evidence

Index

References are to sections.